DATE DUE

			PRINTED IN U.S.A.

Poetry Criticism

Guide to Gale Literary Criticism Series

For criticism on	Consult these Gale series
Authors now living or who died after December 31, 1959	*CONTEMPORARY LITERARY CRITICISM (CLC)*
Authors who died between 1900 and 1959	*TWENTIETH-CENTURY LITERARY CRITICISM (TCLC)*
Authors who died between 1800 and 1899	*NINETEENTH-CENTURY LITERATURE CRITICISM (NCLC)*
Authors who died between 1400 and 1799	*LITERATURE CRITICISM FROM 1400 TO 1800 (LC)* *SHAKESPEAREAN CRITICISM (SC)*
Authors who died before 1400	*CLASSICAL AND MEDIEVAL LITERATURE CRITICISM (CMLC)*
Black writers of the past two hundred years	*BLACK LITERATURE CRITICISM (BLC)*
Authors of books for children and young adults	*CHILDREN'S LITERATURE REVIEW (CLR)*
Dramatists	*DRAMA CRITICISM (DC)*
Hispanic writers of the late nineteenth and twentieth centuries	*HISPANIC LITERATURE CRITICISM (HLC)*
Native North American writers and orators of the eighteenth, nineteenth, and twentieth centuries	*NATIVE NORTH AMERICAN LITERATURE (NNAL)*
Poets	*POETRY CRITICISM (PC)*
Short story writers	*SHORT STORY CRITICISM (SSC)*
Major authors from the Renaissance to the present	*WORLD LITERATURE CRITICISM, 1500 TO THE PRESENT (WLC)*

ISSN 1052-4851

Poetry Criticism

Excerpts from Criticism of the Works of the Most Significant and Widely Studied Poets of World Literature

VOLUME 18

Carol T. Gaffke
Editor

GALE

DETROIT · NEW YORK · TORONTO · LONDON

STAFF

Carol T. Gaffke *Editor*

Jennifer Daniels, Kathy Darrow, Lynn Koch, Amy Kumm, Marie Napierkowski,
Damon Z. Percy, Susan Salas, Andrew Spongberg, Larry Trudeau,
Contributing Editors

Susan Trosky, *Permissions Manager*
Margaret Chamberlain, Maria Franklin, Kimberly F. Smilay, *Permissions Specialist*

Sarah Chesney, Edna Hedblad, Michele Lonoconus,
Shalice Shah,
Permissions Associates

Steve Cusack, Kelly Quin, Andrea Rigby, Jessica Ulrich,
Permissions Assistants

Victoria B. Cariappa, *Research Manager*

Julie C. Daniel, Tamara C. Nott, Michele P. Pica,
Tracie Richardson, Cheryl L. Warnock, *Research Associates*

Mary Beth Trimper, *Production Director*
Deborah Milliken, *Production Assistant*

Sherrell Hobbs, *Macintosh Artist*
Randy Bassett, *Image Database Supervisor*
Robert Duncan, *Scanner Operator*
Pamela Hayes, *Photography Coordinator*

Library of Congress Catalog Card Number 91-118494
ISBN 0-7876-0958-7
ISSN 1052-4851

Printed in the United States of America
Published simultaneously in the United Kingdom
by Gale Research International Limited
(An affiliated company of Gale Research Inc.)
10 9 8 7 6 5 4 3 2 1

Contents

Preface vii

Acknowledgments xi

Preface

A Comprehensive Information Source on World Poetry

*P*oetry Criticism (PC) provides substantial critical excerpts and biographical information on poets throughout the world who are most frequently studied in high school and undergraduate college courses. Each *PC* entry is supplemented by biographical and bibliographical material to help guide the user to a fuller understanding of the genre and its creators. Although major poets and literary movements are covered in such Gale Literary Criticism Series as *Contemporary Literary Criticism (CLC), Twentieth-Century Literary Criticism (TCLC), Nineteenth-Century Literature Criticism (NCLC), Literature Criticism from 1400 to 1800 (LC)*, and *Classical and Medieval Literature Criticism (CMLC)*, *PC* offers more focused attention on poetry than is possible in the broader, survey-oriented entries on writers in these Gale series. Students, teachers, librarians, and researchers will find that the generous excerpts and supplementary material provided by *PC* supply them with the vital information needed to write a term paper on poetic technique, to examine a poet's most prominent themes, or to lead a poetry discussion group.

Coverage

In order to reflect the influence of tradition as well as innovation, poets of various nationalities, eras, and movements are represented in every volume of *PC*. Each author entry presents a historical survey of the critical response to that author's work; the length of an entry reflects the amount of critical attention that the author has received from critics writing in English and from foreign critics in translation. Since many poets have inspired a prodigious amount of critical explication, *PC* is necessarily selective, and the editors have chosen the most significant published criticism to aid readers and students in their research. In order to provide these important critical pieces, the editors will sometimes reprint essays that have appeared in previous volumes of Gale's Literary Criticism Series. Such duplication, however, never exceeds fifteen percent of a *PC* volume.

Organization

Each *PC* author entry consists of the following components:

- **Author Heading:** the name under which the author wrote appears at the beginning of the entry, followed by birth and death dates. If the author wrote consistently under a pseudonym, the pseudonym will be listed in the author heading and his or her legal name given in parentheses in the lines immediately preceding the Introduction. Uncertainty as to birth or death dates is indicated by question marks.

- **Introduction:** a biographical and critical essay introduces readers to the author and the critical discussions surrounding his or her work.

- **Author Portrait:** a photograph or illustration of the author is included when available.

- **Principal Works:** the author's most important works are identified in a list ordered chronologically by first publication dates. The first section comprises poetry collections and book-length poems. The second section gives information on other major works by the author. For foreign authors, original foreign-language publication information is provided, as well as the best and most complete English-language editions of their works.

- **Criticism:** critical excerpts chronologically arranged in each author entry provide perspective on changes in critical evaluation over the years. All individual titles of poems and poetry collections by the author featured in the entry are printed in boldface type to enable a reader to ascertain without difficulty the works under discussion. For purposes of easy identification, the critic's name and the publication date of the essay are given at the beginning of each piece of criticism. Unsigned criticism is preceded by the title of the journal in which it originally appeared. Publication information (such as publisher names and book prices) and parenthetical numerical references (such as footnotes or page and line references to specific editions of a work) have been deleted at the editor's discretion to enable smoother reading of the text.

- **Explanatory Notes:** introductory comments preface each critical excerpt, providing several types of useful information, including: the reputation of a critic, the importance of a work of criticism, and the specific type of criticism (biographical, psychoanalytic, historical, etc.).

- **Author Commentary:** insightful comments from the authors themselves and excerpts from author interviews are included when available.

- **Bibliographical Citations:** information preceding each piece of criticism guides the interested reader to the original essay or book.

- **Further Reading:** bibliographic references accompanied by descriptive notes at the end of each entry suggest additional materials for study of the author. Boxed material following the Further Reading provides references to other biographical and critical series published by Gale.

Other Features

Cumulative Author Index: comprises all authors who have appeared in Gale's Literary Criticism Series, along with cross-references to such Gale biographical series as *Contemporary Authors* and *Dictionary of Literary Biography*. This cumulated index enables the user to locate an author within the various series.

Cumulative Nationality Index: includes all authors featured in *PC,* arranged alphabetically under their respective nationalities.

Cumulative Title Index: lists in alphabetical order all individual poems, book-length poems, and collection titles contained in the *PC* series. Titles of poetry collections and separately published poems are printed in italics, while titles of individual poems are printed in roman type with quotation marks. Each title is followed by the author's name and the volume and page number corresponding to the location of commentary on specific works. English-language translations of original foreign-language titles are cross-referenced to the foreign titles so that all references to discussion of a work are combined in one listing.

Citing *Poetry Criticism*

When writing papers, students who quote directly from any volume in the Literary Criticism Series may use the following general formats to footnote reprinted criticism. The first example pertains to material drawn from periodicals, the second to material reprinted from books:

[1]David Daiches, "W. H. Auden: The Search for a Public," *Poetry* LIV (June 1939), 148-56; excerpted and reprinted in *Poetry Criticism*, Vol. 1, ed. Robyn V. Young (Detroit: Gale Research, 1990), pp. 7-9.

[2]Pamela J. Annas, *A Disturbance in Mirrors: The Poetry of Sylvia Plath* (Greenwood Press, 1988);

excerpted and reprinted in *Poetry Criticism*, Vol. 1, ed. Robyn V. Young (Detroit: Gale Research, 1990), pp. 410-14.

Comments Are Welcome

Readers who wish to suggest authors to appear in future volumes, or who have other suggestions, are cordially invited to contact the editors.

Acknowledgments

The editors wish to thank the copyright holders of the excerpted criticism included in this volume and the permissions managers of many book and magazine publishing companies for assisting us in securing reproduction rights. We are also grateful to the staffs of the Detroit Public Library, the Library of Congress, the University of Detroit Mercy Library, Wayne State University Purdy/Kresge Library Complex, and the University of Michigan Libraries for making their resources available to us. Following is a list of the copyright holders who have granted us permission to reproduce material in this volume of *PC*. Every effort has been made to trace copyright, but if omissions have been made, please let us know.

COPYRIGHTED EXCERPTS IN *PC*, VOLUME 18, WERE REPRODUCED FROM THE FOLLOWING PERIODICALS:

Agenda, v. 33, Autumn-Winter, 1996 for "'Seeing Things' in a Jungian Perspective: Archetypal Elements in Seamus Heaney's Recent Poetry" by J. R. Atfield.—*The American Book Review*, V. 4, July-August, 1982. (c) 1982 by *The American Book Review*. Reproduced by permission.—*American Poetry Review*, v. 22. March-April, 1993 for "Wang Wei and Saigyo: Two Buddhist Mountain Poets" by Sam Hamill. Copyright (c) 1993 by World Poetry, Inc. Reprinted by permission of the author.—*Arizona Quarterly*, v. 49, Autumn, 1993 for "The Nature of War in Emerson's 'Boston Hymn'" by Eduardo Cadava. Copyright (c) 1993 by *Arizona Quarterly*. Reproduced by permission of the publisher and the author.—*Australian Journal of French Studies*, v. XVI, September-December, 1978 for "Inspiration & Aspiration: Gautier's 'La Diva' and Musset's 'Une Soirée perdue'" by Monica J. Nurnberg. Copyright (c) 1978 by *Australian Journal of French Studies*. Reproduced by permission of the publisher and the author.—*Bulletin de la Société Théophile Gautier*, n. 3, 1981. Reproduced by permission.—*Chicago Review*, v. 36, 1989. Copyright (c) 1989 by *Chicago Review*. Reproduced by permission.—*Chinese Culture*, v. XXX, March, 1989. Reproduced by permission.—*The Dilman Review*, v. XVIII, January, 1970.—*The Dublin Magazine*, v. 10, Autumn-Winter, 1973-74. Reproduced by permission.—*Dutch Quarterly Review*, v. IX, 1979. Reproduced by permission.—*English Journal*, v. 56, October, 1967 for "O Frabjous Day!: Introducing Poetry" by Raymond J. Rundus. Copyright (c) 1967 by the National Council of Teachers of English. Reproduced by permission of the publisher and the author.—*English Language Notes*, v. 20, December, 1982. Reproduced by permission.—*Explicator*, v. 46, Fall, 1987. Copy right (c) 1987 Helen Dwight Reid Educational Foundation. Reprinted with permission of the Helen Dwight Reid Educational Foundation, published by Heldref Publications, 1319 18th Street, NW, Washington, DC 20036-1802.—*French Forum*, v. 7, May, 1982. Copyright (c) 1982 by *French Forum*, Publishers, Inc. Reproduced by permission.—*French Literature Series*, v. XVII, 1990. Copyright 1990 University of South Carolina. Reproduced by permission.—*Harvard Journal of Asiatic Studies*, v. 42, June, 1982. Reproduced by permission.—*Journal of the Association of Teachers of Japanese*, v. 11, January, 1976. Reproduced by permission.—*Kenyon Review*, v. XXIX, January, 1967. Copyright 1967 by Kenyon College. All rights reserved. Reproduced by permission.—*The Literary Review*, v. XXIX, Winter, 1986 for an interview with Seamus Heaney by June Beisch. Reproduced by permission of June Beisch.—*Literature East & West*, v. XVII, June-December, 1973. Reproduced by permission.—*London Magazine*, v. 14, December, 1974. Reproduced by permission.—*The New Republic*, v. 181, December 22, 1979. (c) 1979 The New Republic, Inc. Reprinted by permission of *The New Republic*.—*The New York Review of Books*, v. 23, September, 1976; v. 35, April, 1988. Copyright (c) 1976, 1988 Nyrev, Inc. Both reprinted with permission from *The New York Review of Books*.—*The New Yorker*, v. LXI, September, 1985. (c) 1985 by Helen Vendler. Reproduced by permission.—*Nineteenth-Century French Studies*, v. 20, Fall-Winter, 1991-92; v. 70, Spring-Summer, 1992. (c) 1991, 1992 by *Nineteenth-Century French Studies*. Both reproduced by permission.—*Nottingham French Studies*, v. 16, May, 1977. Reproduced by permission.—*Parnassus: Poetry in Review*, v. XI, Spring-Summer, 1984 for "Crossed Pieties" by Alan Shapiro, v. XX, 1995 for "Stein is Nice" by Wayne Koestenbaum. Both reproduced by permission of the author.—*PMLA*, v. 87, March, 1972; v. 101, May, 1986. Copyright (c) 1972, 1986 by the Modern Language Association of America. Both reproduced by permission of the Modern Language Association of America.—*Poetry Flash*, n. 238, January, 1993 for "Bukowski Unbound" by Stephen Kessler. Reproduced by permission of the author.—*Poetry Review*, v. XXII, July-August, 1931 for "Emerson's Theory of Poetry" by Jean Gorley.—*Poetry*, v. XC, July 1957 for "The Impossible" by John Ashbery. (c) 1957, renewed

COPYRIGHTED EXCERPTS IN *PC*, VOLUME 18, WERE REPRODUCED FROM THE FOLLOWING BOOKS:

PHOTOGRAPHS AND ILLUSTRATIONS APPEARING IN *PC*, VOLUME 18, WERE RECEIVED FROM THE FOLLOWING SOURCES:

Charles Bukowski
1920-1994

(Full name Henry Charles Bukowski, Jr.) American poet, novelist, and essayist

INTRODUCTION

Charles Bukowski was one of the most individual poets of the post-modern age. Influenced by Ernest Hemingway and Ezra Pound, his poetry reflected both the despair of the 1950s' Beat movement and the rebelliousness of the protesters of the 1960s. Although Bukowski lived most of his life in California, he did not belong to or associate with any of the literary circles of Los Angeles or San Francisco, such as the Beats or the Bay Area school. He was a lifelong outsider who mocked the pretensions of the literary elite and developed his own freewheeling, raw, and belligerent style as a means of expressing his dissatisfaction with traditional, middle-class morals and values. His main character-type (which is considered to be a self-portrait), the hard-drinking, womanizing, tough-talking man who associated with the "little people" in bars, race tracks and cheap hotels, came to represent the "Bukowski image" of the isolated individual at odds with society. Such "shock" poetry made Bukowski a seminal figure in underground literature. Within the scholarly community, however, little attention has been given to his poetry and prose.

Biographical Information

Born in Andernach, Germany in 1920, Henry Charles Bukowski, Jr. was the only child of an American soldier and a German mother. The family immigrated to Los Angeles in 1922, and settled in a middle-class neighborhood, where Bukowski was teased by the other children because of his German heritage, making him feel as though he did not belong. Bukowski's father dominated his early life, controlling the household by way of unbreakable rules, reinforced with a strap or a ruler, that were imposed to maintain the façade of middle-class respectability. Bukowski hated his father and all that he represented: the economic and emotional success supposedly offered in return for hard work and patriotism: the American dream. Bukowski's disdain for his father and the lifestyle he embodied is prevalent in all of his poetry and fiction, as well as in his subsequent anti-authoritarian lifestyle. The beginning of the Depression coincided with Bukowski's entering high school, intensifying his father's abusive and tyrannical nature, and driving the young Bukowski to retreat into alcohol abuse. Bukowski attended Los Angeles City College from 1939 to 1941, but dropped out and spent a decade working at menial jobs while struggling with alcoholism. After being hospitalized with a bleeding ulcer in 1955, he curbed his alcoholism and turned to writing poetry.

From the late 1950s onward, Bukowski developed his distinctive montage style and published several long prose pieces in underground literary magazines. These experiments resulted in the irregular, disjointed, and fragmented form seen in *Notes of a Dirty Old Man*, and helped Bukowski to define his literary position as an arrogant, anarchistic, and defiant anti-hero aligned against the literary elite. The late 1960s and the early 1970s was a very productive and creative time for Bukowski, and much of the work produced during this time formed the basis for subsequent books, including *Confessions of a Man Insane Enough to Live with Beasts*; *Erections, Ejaculations, and General Tales of Ordinary Madness*; and *South of No North*. The 70s saw a tremendous increase in his readership and a growing reputation. Focusing on longer fiction, Bukowski produced a number of novels and memoirs in a type of transmogrified autobiographical narrative similar to Kerouac's. In 1987, his novel, *Barfly*, was made into a movie starring Mickey Rourke and Faye Dunaway, for which he wrote the screenplay. He later based a novel, *Hollywood,* on his experiences. Bukowski continued to write prolifically: his 1992 poetry collection *The Last Night of the Earth Poems* is over four hundred pages long. Bukowski died of leukemia in 1994.

Major Works

Despite the number of Bukowski's early chapbooks, it was not until the collections *It Catches My Heart in Its Hands* (1963) and *Crucifix in a Deathhand* (1965) were published in the early 1960s that his poetry attracted critical attention. In his preface to *Crucifix in a Deathhand*, critic John William Corrington characterizes Bukowski's poetry as "the spoken voice nailed to paper." Bukowski's reputation grew as his essays and short fiction were collected and published in *Notes of a Dirty Old Man* (1969). His first novel, *Post Office* (1971), became a counter-cultural classic and helped to establish the "Bukowski image". The transformation of his novel *Barfly* from a novel into a successful film helped bring Bukowski to the attention of the younger "MTV" generation and again expanded his readership. Bukowski wrote prolifically throughout his life, and published poetry, short stories, and novels in underground journals and small presses. With the publication of *Septuagenarian Stew* (1990) and *The Last Night of the Earth Poems* (1992) came grudging acknowledgement by mainstream critics that Bukowski had earned a place in the literary canon. At the close of his life, then, Bukowski was perceived by the bourgeois critics he opposed as the patriarch and appointed spokesman of the newest generation of anti-establishment writers.

Critical Reception

While small presses, literary magazines, and underground journals have published and reviewed Bukowski's work since the 1950s, academic critics and anthologists have largely ignored him. This is due in part to his producing a large number of small chapbooks, often containing only one longer work or a few short poems, rather than full-length books. Other factors influencing the critical neglect of his work include his subject matter and his language, both portraying drunks, bums, and down-and-outs who are street wise and trashy. It is precisely these qualities that has earned Bukowski his large following that cuts across generation lines and includes predominantly non-academic readers with eclectic and anti-establishment tastes. While his work has attracted such a diverse readership and a generation of imitators, acceptance and praise from the literary or academic establishments has been slow in coming, as Bukowski is seen as a writer of quantity not quality. His death in 1994 at the age of 74 has brought about the re-issuing of many of his books as well as a reappraisal of his position within the framework of mid-to-late-twentieth century American poetry.

PRINCIPAL WORKS

Poetry

Flower, Fist and Bestial Wail 1960
Longshot Pomes for Broke Players 1962
Run with the Hunted 1962
Poems and Drawings 1962
It Catches My Heart in its Hands: New and Selected Poems, 1955-1963 1963
Grip the Walls 1964
Cold Dogs in the Courtyard 1965
Crucifix in a Deathhand: New Poems, 1963-1965 1965
Confessions of a Man Insane Enough to Live with Beasts 1965
The Genius of the Crowd 1966
True Story 1966
On Going Out to Get the Mail 1966
To Kiss the Worms Goodnight 1966
The Girls 1966
All the Assholes in the World and Mine 1966
The Flower Lover 1966
Night's Work 1966
2 by Bukowski 1967
The Curtains are Waving 1967
At Terror Street and Agony Way 1968
Poems Written before Jumping out of an 8-Story Window 1968
If We Take.... 1969
The Days Run Away Like Wild Horses over the Hills 1969
Another Academy 1970
Fire Station 1970
Mockingbird Wish Me Luck 1972
Me and Your Sometimes Love Poems 1973
While the Music Played 1973
Love Poems to Marina 1973
Burning in Water, Drowning in Flame: Selected Poems 1955-1973 1974
Africa, Paris, Greece 1975
Weather Report 1975
Winter 1975
Tough Company 1976
Scarlet 1976
Maybe Tomorrow 1977
Love Is a Dog from Hell: Poems 1974-1977 1977
Art 1977
What They Want 1977
We'll Take Them 1978
Legs, Hips, and Behind 1979
Play the Piano Drunk Like a Percussion Instrument until the Fingers Begin to Bleed a Bit 1979
A Love Poem 1979
Dangling in the Tournefortia 1981
The Last Generation 1982
Sparks 1983
One for the Old Boy 1984
War All the Time: Poems 1981-1984 1984
Under the Influence 1984
Alone in a Time of Armies 1985
You Get So Alone at Times That It Just Makes Sense 1986
Gold in Your Eye 1986
The Day in Snowed in L.A. 1986
Luck 1987
The Movie Critics 1988
Beauti-ful & Other Long Poems 1988
The Rooming House Madrigals: Early Selected Poems 1946-1966 1988

Septuagenarian Stew   1990
In the Morning and At Night and In Between   1991
In the Shadow of the Rose   1991
The Last Night of the Earth Poems 1992
Run with the Hunted: A Charles Bukowski Reader   1993
Confession of a Coward   1995
Betting on the Muse: Poems & Stories   1996

Other Major Works

"Aftermath of a Lengthy Rejection Slip"   (short story)
   1944
A Bukowski Sampler   (short stories, poetry, essays)   1969
Notes of a Dirty Old Man   (short stories)   1969
Post Office   (novel)   1971
*Erections, Ejaculations, Exhibitions, and General Tales
   of Ordinary Madness*   (short stories)   1972
2 Letters from Charles Bukowski   (letters)   1972
South of No North: Stories of the Buried Life   (short stories)
   1973
Life and Death in the Charity Ward   (short stories)   1974
Factorum   (novel)   1975
Women   (novel)   1978
You Kissed Lilly   (short stories)   1978
Ham on Rye   (novel)   1982
Horsemeat   (novel)   1982
Bring Me Your Love   (short stories)   1983
Hot Water Music   (short stories)   1983
*The Bukowski/Purdy Letters: A Decade of Dialogue 1964-
   1974*   [with Al Purdy]   (letters)   1983
Barfly   (novel)   1984
There's No Business   (short stories)   1984
The Movie "BarFly"   (screenplay)   1987
Hollywood   (novel)   1989
Screams from the Balcony: Selected Letters 1960's-1970's
   (letters)   1993
Pulp   1994
*Living on Luck: Selected Letters 1960's-1970's, Volume
   2*   (letters)   1995

CRITICISM

Thomas McGrath   (essay date 1962)

SOURCE: "Variety in Verse," in *National Guardian*, May
21, 1962, p. 12.

[*In the following review of* Longshot Pomes for Broke
Players, *critic and poet McGrath finds Bukowski's wry
humor admirable, despite his reservations about the poet's
style.*]

Here's Charles Bukowski's **Longshot Pomes for Broke
Players**. The misspelling in the title will probably cause
one set of potential readers to shy off. But there is nothing
arch about the book. It is an example of what the Beat

was before it fell into holiness and hysteria. While much
Beat poetry has gone dead or "commercial," it had in it
once something of value which we can see clearly in
Bukowski's work. Here is part of **"The State of World
Affairs from a Third Floor Window"** offered as proof.

> I am watching a girl dressed in a / light green sweater
> . . . / as her dirty white dog sniffs the grass /. . . . I
> am upstairs in my underwear, / 3 day beard. pouring
> a beer and waiting / for something literary or
> symphonic to happen; / . . . and a thin old man / in his
> last Winter rolls by pushed by a girl / in a Catholic
> school dress; / somewhere there are Alps, and ships /
> are now crossing the sea; / there are piles and piles of
> H-and-A-bombs. / . . . and the Hollywood Hills stand
> there, stand there / full of drunks and insane people
> and / much kissing in automobiles / . . . well, from the
> looks of things relax; / the bombs will never go off.

What Bukowski finds in his unlikely view from the third
floor is the value of the quotidian, a kind of spiritual
resistance which people put up even when they are not
aware of it—as if it were almost a function of that un-
awareness. This is not far from Sandburg's *The People,
Yes* point of view, but Bukowski is rarely sentimental and
sees his people with a tough-tenderness. This may somewhat limit the point of view, but it sharpens the individual
poem.

This third-floor view is the view of a man who sees
through the deceptions of our society, who protests against
a world where "death wants more death" at the same time
that he is capable of accepting human follies with a wry
smile—as, in fact, he accepts himself. The protest may be
largely negative, but that, in certain things, can be a value.
He dramatizes a world not far from that of the lumpen-
proletariat.

Weaknesses? Mainly language. The loose free-verse is
generally apt to the kind of story-poem Bukowski writes,
but it has a tendency to amplify the anecdotal elements,
to oppose condensation, to keep the poems flatter than
they might have been. Some dead-opposed to the method
would say that it offers the raw material of poems that are
never worked out. The poems have to risk such a judgment, which would make it impossible to look at the work
seriously, since Bukowski's method is primarily anti-lyrical.

R. R. Cuscaden   (essay date 1963)

SOURCE: "Charles Bukowski: Poet in a Ruined Landscape," in *The Outsider*, Vol. 1, No. 3, Spring, 1963, pp.
62-5.

[*In the following review of Bukowski's first three collections, Cuscaden discusses how the poet attempts to overcome despair through his verse.*]

All of Bukowski's major interests and themes are in evidence in his first book, *Flower, Fist and Bestial Wail:*
indeed, they are defined in the volume's title. These early

poems are not equally successful; too much reliance is placed upon a dated surrealistic technique and in neglecting the use of the first person singular Bukowski fails to employ a strength which gives unity to his later work. Nevertheless, everything is here: the obsession with music (his three books mention Bach, Hugo Wolf, Borodin, Brahms, Chopin, Berlioz, Beethoven) and art (Carot, Daumier, Orozco, Van Gogh), and, most importantly, the sense of a desolate, abandoned world.

In his poem in the first volume entitled **"I Cannot Stand Tears,"** the poet, always the non-participant, watches "several hundred fools / around the goose who broke his leg / trying to decide / what to do." A guard walks up, "pulled out his cannon / and the issue was finished." The details here are interesting. The crowd is composed of "fools", the goose implies the golden egg (poetry?), the (perhaps inevitable) guard has not merely a gun but a "cannon." And the issue is especially finished for the poet: "I folded my canvas / and went further down the road. / and bastards had ruined / my landscape. . . ."

A key poem in this first book is **"The Paper on the Floor."** The poet meditates on the enforced soap-opera quality of most lives: "The explanation usually comes in the morning / over the breakfast table," and the overwhelming "nothing nothing nothing nothing" of it all "pushes at the back of my eyes / and pulls my nerves taut-thin from toe to hair-line."

Can life grant only bogus emotions, manufactured experiences? "Very well," Bukowski says in **"The Twins"** (a moving poem about his father's death), but, if so: "grant us this moment: standing before a mirror / in my dead father's suit / waiting also / to die." Grant us, in other words, even occasional moments of meaning. Grant us, at least, the compensatory joy of being ignored. . . .

His second volume, *Longshot Pomes for Broke Players,* presents a more specific vision and definition of our curious world, as in the poem **"Where the Hell Would Chopin Be":** "indented most severely in my mind: the working secret / of a universe shot with flares and rockets, / monkeys jammed / with meteoritic registers of love in space." This is, of course, a kind of protest poetry, but Bukowski's protest is hardly political in the way that much of the poetry of Spender and Auden was during the thirties. Nor is it anti-political as much as it is non-political. This, it seems to me, is because Bukowski visualizes the political approach as impotent, as he indicates in **"Poem for Personnel Managers":** "the world rocks down against us / and we / throw out arms / and we / throw out our legs / like the death kiss of the centipede: / / but they kindly snap our backs / and call our poison 'politics'."

There is a good deal of Jeffers-like pessimism in these poems and Bukowski himself admits this indebtedness: "If I have a god it is Robinson Jeffers, although I realize that I don't write as he does. . . ."

Bukowski rarely gives in completely to utter, hopeless despair, and this, not the variance in style and technique,

marks the essential difference between him and Jeffers. The despair of Bukowski exists just because he continually hopes; Jeffers' despair is the result of no hope at all. "I want trumpets and crowing, . . . I want the whir and tang of a simple living orange / in a simple living tree" Bukowski writes in **"Bring Down the Beams."** But, as he makes clear in the same poem, art—especially the Wednesday sonnet and the Sunday painting—is no substitute for life: ". . . we sit and piddle with charcoal / and talk about Picasso / and make collages: we are getting ready / to do nothing unusual, / and I alone am hungry / as I think about the sun clanging against the earth / and all the bones moving / but ours."

Too often, he feels, the world of art and letters is little more than a morass of gossip and back-biting, as in **"Letter from the North":** "my friend writes of rejection and editors / and how he has visited K. or R. or W. / . . . write me, he says, / I got the blues. / / write you? about what, my friend? / I'm only interested in / poetry."

Run with the Hunted, his most recently published volume of poems (the title, with its compassionate avowal of siding with those on the "wrong," or Algren side of the street, is significant), finds Bukowski far more mellow, far more mature, than in his first two books. It is not too much, even, to term these poems "late". In any case, his awareness of the world's patently obvious absurdities is here stated without what was previously a sort of surprise; he here looks around at a world grown familiar, and comments thereupon in an almost bemused fashion. There is an enlarged and personal vision of subtle horrors in **"The Priest and the Matador"**. . . , in which as always there is the awareness of estrangement, the concern with the failure of response. Although he has not given up hope that response might exist we read in **"Wrong Number":** "carefully, I call voices on the phone, / measuring their sounds for humanity and laughter, / somewhere I am cut off, contact fails."

Without ceasing to fight, his course of action is now less direct; at times, perhaps, a bit more resigned. In **"Sundays Kill More Men than Bombs,"** a narrative of his divorce, he writes: "but that morning when she left / about 8 o'clock she looked / the same as ever, maybe even better. / I didn't even bother to shave, / I called in sick and went down / to the corner bar."

Bukowski is a poet of the permanent opposition. He opposes "the ruin" on a basis of personal anarchy which must attempt the impossible and create its own order. There is nothing about him of the "dumb ox" and he is certainly not a man without art. . . . In the best of his work may be found that quality of courage which, as Michael Roberts wrote, occurs "beyond the inhuman pattern" and persists in "men / broken, ephemeral, undismayed."

Joseph Swastek (essay date 1963)

SOURCE: A review of *Poems and Drawings,* in *Polish American Studies,* Vol. XX, No. 1, January-June, 1963, pp. 55-6.

[*In the essay below, Swastek finds Bukowski's poetry eccentric but honest and authentic.*]

Polish-American poetry, written in English, has had a variety of male and female voices pitched in different keys. The masculine contingent includes Uriel Joseph Piduch (*Autumn Leaves,* 1920), Raymond Kresensky (*Emmaus,* 1931), Edmond Kowalewski (*Deaf Walls,* 1933), Alan Edward Symanski (*Against Death in Spring,* 1934), John H. Drechney (*Nature Smiles,* 1947), Joseph Cherwinski (*No Blue Tomorrow,* 1952), Zygmunt Kurowski (*A Collection of Thoughts,* 1953), and Conrad Lancucki (*The House by the Sea,* 1958)—to mention only the more notable writers and their earliest published collections of poems and verses.

Recently a new voice has joined this male poetic chorus, and it sings not only in a different pitch but also a melody distinctively its own. It is the voice of Charles Bukowski, poem-maker, convention-breaker, and presently the only Polish-American literary beatnik.

If this sounds wild, listen to what's coming. Bukowski was born August 16, 1920, in Andornach, Germany, but was brought to the United States at the age of two. His family had lived in Germany for some time back, but was originally Polish. In any event, Bukowski speaks neither German nor Polish, but has no objection to being classified as a Polish-American: "I am not ashamed of Poland. It is a small nation caught between big nations and this, in history, makes it a loser. The people cannot help this, must only bear it while Paris, London, Berlin, Moscow, Washington, D. C. look good. Poland has poets and Poland has heroes, and, if you want to count me on your side, good."

Bukowski, who began writing at thirty-five, has thus far published three collections of poetry: *Flower, First and Bestial Wail, Longshot Pomes for Brave Players*, and *Run with the Hunted*. The volume under review [*Poems and Drawings*] is his fourth book of poems. A fifth collection is in preparation by *The Outsider*, a poetry magazine.

[The present] collection of Bukowski's work, a "one-man show", contains three ink drawings and fourteen poems. The poems are unlike anything so far written by Polish-Americans. The titles only faintly suggest the distinctive character of the poems they head: **"With Vengeance Like a Tiger Crawls," "The Kings are Gone," "I Have Lived in England," "Goldfish," "On Going Back to the Street after Viewing an Art Show," "Suicide," "Rose, Rose," "Bull," "Where They So Fondly Go," "Spite," "Love & Fame & Death," "The Gift," "A Word on the Quick and Modern Poem-Makers,"** and **"The Miracle."**

When you open this volume, you enter a new dimension of Polish-American poetry, not a twilight zone of make-believe or poetic fantasy, but a hard, concrete corner of contemporary reality—a corner which at times appears to be on the brink of things, of conventions, of traditions, of belief, of everything—just way out, man! Bukowski is no stranger to Shakespeare (whose grandeur does not come

through to him), or to Milton (on whom he is wasted), or Frost ("licking the boots of politicians, / telling the pretty lies / of an addled mind"), or to Ernie ("tagging himself when the time was ready"). He knows "Brahms / stole his First from Beethoven's / 9th"; "Rabelais out of his wits / chasing a rabbit / through the Brahms of my mind"; "Greco / or even a watersnake"; and that "the bull burned within me / my candle of / Jesus."

Bukowski feels contempt for the classics (which he has read) and for conventions (both literary and societary). He applies the mechanics of rhetoric with the abandon and eccentricity of e. e. cummings. His free-wheeling use of invective and profanity almost equals his personalized approach to metric and poesy, to punctuation and capitalization.

Yet some of these poems, which Bukowski has "pulled out of his head", have the authentic ring of reality, not so much because their language is racy and their imagery modern and flip, but because basically they reflect "an honesty of self born. . . . that will not allow me to pretend to be something which I am quite not." One thing for sure, Bukowski is "not cluttering up the exits" of Polish-American poetry, as he sits in his Los Angeles "apt. no. 303", disecting life and literature with his poetic scalpel, sometimes glumly, sometimes gleefully.

John William Corrington (essay date 1963)

SOURCE: "Charles Bukowski and the Savage Surfaces," in *Northwest Review*, Vol. 6, No.4, Fall, 1963, pp. 123-29.

[*In the review below of* It Catches My Heart in Its Hands, *Corrington characterizes Bukowski as a "surface" poet who "is capable of producing a poetry of pure emotion in which idea, information, the narrative or anecdote, is held to a minimum."*]

The recent publication of Charles Bukowski's selected poems [*It Catches My Heart in Its Hands*] marks a kind of watershed in the career of one of the West Coast's most striking poets. . . .

As those who know his poetry will testify, Bukowski's poems go well enough one by one. But there is no substitute for reading a man's work in bulk. . . .

Faced with several score of Bukowski's best poems, the illusion of ignorance or perverse and directionless crudity dissolves like a tar-doll in August sun. Individual poems merge to form together a body of work unrivalled in kind and very nearly unequalled in quality by Bukowski's contemporaries.

Perhaps the most crucial failure of Bukowski's critics is their general blindness to the sort of thing represented by his poetry. It is a vain error to damn oranges because they do not taste like apples—and it is equally profitless to decry what I call a "poetry of surfaces" because it fails to investigate and recreate the depths of human experience.

The phrase "poetry of surface" is not mine. So far as I know, Eliot coined it in an early discussion of Jonson's poetry. It distinguishes between the sort of "vertical" poetry—like *The Waste Land*—which probes the psychological, moral, religious and sociological center of man, and a "horizontal" poetry which concerns itself rather with delineating man in terms of his more visible, more immediate, more physical surroundings. This "horizontal" poetry makes little use of metaphysics. Rather than attempting an X-ray of man's moral skeleton, his spiritual viscera, this kind of poetry contents itself with the flesh, the surface of the human condition. . . .

Now in Bukowski's poetry, this concern for surface—for the color, texture and rhythm of modern life—reveals itself both in what he writes and in what he does not write. On the positive side, it underlies his attention to detail, his consistent presentation of physical minutia of seeming inconsequence:

> . . . and the cat kept looking at me
> and crawling in the pantry
> amongst the clanking dishes
> with flowers and vines painted on them . . .
> **("Love Is a Piece of Paper Torn to Bits")**

The cat and dishes alone would suffice, but Bukowski adds flowers and vines as much from a kind of fidelity to the physical verities as because of the implications carried by flowers and vines in a poem about a collapsing marriage.

Again, in a long poem describing himself and others as the human refuse thrown up by depression and industrial society, **"Poem for Personnel Managers,"** this concern with surface is manifested not by what Bukowski chooses to add to his portrait of hopeless men, but by his pointed avoidance of what might be called the "social implications" of the situation:

> we are shot through with carrot tops
> and poppy seed and tilted grammar;
> we waste days like mad blackbirds
> and pray for alcoholic nights.
> our silk-sick human smiles wrap around
> us like somebody else's confetti:
> we do not even belong to the Party. . . .

"We smoke, dead as fog," Bukowski writes. And his vision of suffering is not adulterated with the academic jargon that, in the face of human agony, seems itself a part of the brutal instrumentality it describes. There is no withdrawal in Bukowski's work. All his poems have the memorable and terrible immediacy of the news broadcast from the scene of the *Hindenberg* crash. There is nothing of the sublimated social-worker or psychiatrist in him, and the endless gabble of the professional injustice-collector is totally absent from his work. In remaining on the surface—staying with sure and certain phenomena, a series of significant acts, events, actors and victims, Bukowski avoids the pitfalls of "motivation" and "meaning." He remains in control of the indisputable, the unquestionable—and leaves the jungle of social and political and moral purpose and counter-purpose to those who find such abstract projections more significant than life itself.

> **All Bukowski's poems have the memorable and terrible immediacy of the news broadcast of the *Hindenberg* crash.**
>
> *—John William Corrigan*

A few weeks ago, Bukowski's work came up in the course of a conversation in Houston. A young woman shivered at the mention of his name. "Bukowski? He's a savage," she said vehemently. "Nothing but a savage." The word "savage" properly applied to Bukowski's poetry may help solve the puzzle of his sensibility and the academic resistance to it.

With the growth of the pseudo-civilized as contemporary norm, "savage"—like "barbarian"—has become a pejorative rather than simply a term descriptive of certain attitudes, convictions, and responses. . . . But pejoration aside, Bukowski stands nearer the world-view, say, of Chief Joseph of the Nez Perce than that of Henry Adams or Bernard Berenson. Bukowski's world, scored and grooved by the impersonal instruments of civilized industrial society, by 20th-century knowledge and experience, remains essentially a world in which meditation and analysis have little part. There is act and observation. . . . That middle stage between act and art, the stage at which one presumes a kind of intellectual gathering and synthesis antecedent to the shaping of image and metaphor, simply does not exist in Bukowski's poetry. Act moves into image directly; feeling is articulated as figure and intellection is minimal. As the savage projects his world in terms of myth, with sight, sound—the natural order of phenomena—as its keystones, so Bukowski remains focused upon the concrete. If there is symbolic value in the work, the reader is spared a kind of burdensome awareness of that symbolism on the part of the writer. Thus, for example, in **"The Tragedy of the Leaves,"**

> I awakened to dryness and the ferns were dead,
> the potted plants yellow as corn;
> my woman was gone
> and the empty bottles like bled corpses
> surrounded me with their uselessness;
> the sun was still good, though,
> and my landlady's note cracked in fine and
> undemanding yellowness; what was needed now
> was a good comedian, ancient style, a jester
> with jokes upon absurd pain; pain is absurd
> because it exists, nothing more;
> I shaved carefully with an old razor
> the man who had once been young and
> said to have genius; but

that's the tragedy of the leaves,
the dead ferns, the dead plants;
and I walked into the dark hall
where the landlady stood
execrating and final,
sending me to hell,
waving her fat sweaty arms
and screaming
screaming for rent
because the world had failed us
both.

It would be folly to try to read such a poem as simple description. But it would be equally foolish to suggest that the poem's surface is, as it were, simply an excuse for its symbolic significance. Symbol rises from event; a kind of 20th-century mythos stands like shadow over and above the specifics of Bukowski's dark hallway. Bukowski's poem is symbolic as all great work is symbolic: the verity of its surface is so nearly absolute that the situation it specifies produces the overtones of a world much vaster than that of the landlady's dark hall.

There is a kind of poetry in which one finds what may be called a resident ideational content. The greater bulk of Wallace Stevens' poetry is of this kind. However opaque the surface of "Disillusionment of Ten O'Clock," a careful reading and a comparison with section VI of "Six Significant Landscapes," quickly shows that Stevens has an idea, a theory in mind, and that, despite the difficulties, he is attempting to transmit that theory through the agency of his verse. Such work presents, as it were, a series of problems to be solved, issues to be clarified, metaphoric complexes to be explicated. This kind of poetry is the proper subject of criticism.

But there is another sort of poetry which, rather than containing ideas, projects a kind of structured emotional and imaginative form. In combination with the sensibility of a reader, this kind of poetry produces ideas not resident in it. An individual poem of this kind serves as a kind of trigger: it sets off a wave of responses in a given reader, and the resultant idea-emotion complex is, in Wordsworth's phrase, "half-created" by the reader—not simply dredged out of the poem's verbalization. Some of Bukowski's poems are of this sort. What, precisely, in terms of idea, are we to make from this:

the blossoms shake
sudden water
down my sleeve,
sudden water
cool and clean
as snow—
as the stem-sharp
swords
go in
against your breast
and the sweet wild
rocks
leap over

and lock us in.
("I Taste the Ashes of Your Death")

A poem of this kind, I think, is ample proof that however little thought Bukowski may give to his writing, he has mastered the literary lessons of the past century. In the tradition of Mallarmé and Lorca, he is capable of producing a poetry of pure emotion in which idea, information, the narrative or anecdotal, is held to a minimum. "The Ultimate Poem," Wallace Stevens has stated in one of his titles, "Is Abstract."

I have not meant to suggest that Charles Bukowski's poetry represents something new or even something basically superior in modern American poetry. Nor have I intended to intimate that sublimation of the intellectual is a value in itself. What I do wish to suggest is that Bukowski's work represents a renewal of interest in the poet as something other than thinker and civilized representative of the University Establishment. It is worth recalling that those poets who have most endured have rarely written the kind of geometric thing we find in contemporary "academic verse." Whatever uses we may find for poetry, the honing of the mind is not properly among them. Thus, in a sense, poetry remains—or should remain—the savage child of the arts. That poetry which fails to stir, which loses its appeal as a sensuous activity, fails, it seems to me, as poetry. Bukowski, standing in a mixed tradition of Whitman and Mallarmé, Jeffers and Lorca, brings back this evocative quality to modern verse. Compared to the work of most of his contemporaries, his poetry relies on the image and its emotional connotations much more than on the idea and its rational concomitants. . . .

It is precisely Bukowski's refusal to become trapped in the cerebral that marks the savage quality, the surface dynamism of his poetry. Whether one chooses to see all this as a reaction to the closely-reasoned and imaginatively sterile work of the academics, or—in a larger and less pointed context—as a predictable and timely revitalization of modern American poetry, Bukowski's work remains a significant force offsetting a recognized and widely lamented atrophy that has, for much of this century, rendered poetry a "sullen art," a series of super-conundrums, a game of the mind or a cultural ritual performed alone. Bukowski's increasing popularity seems to indicate that possibly it is not that people have abandoned poetry, but that poetry has tended to lose its audience by eschewing that savage vitality, that splendid surface that so long distinguished it from fiction or history or philosophy. Lacking imaginative and emotional immediacy, poetry cannot compete. But those poets who have worked more nearly as warlocks than as logicians still find a considerable readership: Dylan Thomas, e. e. cummings, and others. Bukowski, I believe, belongs in this company.

If it is argued that Bukowski lacks depth, one might do well to paraphrase Aristotle: "There is a degree of profundity suitable to every discipline. The wise man does not ask of an art-form that which is not proper to it." If depth is the ultimate criterion of literary value, then Shakespeare fades before Descartes; Coleridge before Kant. But if emotional and imaginative excitement is an acceptable purpose, the poetry of Charles Bukowski is unusually successful, and his surfaces are as valuable in their savage way as are the civilized depths of T. S. Eliot.

The relationship between Bukowski's poetry and his life:

Bukowski a poet? he's 100% poet who writes the way he lives, the way he thinks, *not* in the washed-out tradition established by poets who believe that the mere stating of a word is enuf to communicate & that by trailing together a few words in accordance with our conventional education with a dash of soul creates Beauty & Meaning & Everlasting Truth.

Bukowski is the unnameable, the undefinable, the illimitable—a man filtering in & out of *Everything* in existence. a man who does not state theory or espouse philosophy but acts it out in deed—his poetry displays the totalness of his personality, his commitment, which, in turn, unveils his philosophy. his methods illustrate his mind. he says much about man not by getting lost in generalizations but by unconsciously using himself as an example, as an apologue, thus creating a sense of immediacy & involvement.

Bukowski talks face-to-face with his typewriter. he has not read other poets in order to learn how to write, how to voice himself. he writes the only way possible for himself: the fire finally burning thru the skull onto the page. his scream-of-consciousness poems are relatively simple but this simplicity is underwritten by a most confounding understanding, comprehension & feeling of the tons of complexity of life cascading around us.

A review of Cold Dogs in the Courtyard, *in* Ole,
No. 4, May, 1966.

Charles Bukowski with Robert Wennerstein (interview date 1974)

SOURCE: "Paying for Horses," in *London Magazine,* Vol. 14, No. 5, December, 1974, pp. 35-54.

[*In the conversation below, Bukowski discusses his literary influences, the critical response to his work, and the "Bukowski image."*]

[Wennersten]: *What were your parents and your childhood like?*

[Bukowski]: Oh, God. Well, my parents were of German extraction. My mother was born there; and my father's people were German, although he came out of Pasadena.

My father liked to whip me with a razor strop. My mother backed him. A sad story. Very good discipline all the way

through, but very little love going either direction. Good training for the world, though, they made me ready. Today, watching other children, I'd say one thing they taught me was not to weep too much when something goes wrong. In other words, they hardened me to what I was going to go through: the bum, the road, all the bad jobs and the adversity. Since my early life hadn't been soft, the rest didn't come as such a shock.

We lived at 2122 Longwood Avenue. That's a little bit west and a little bit south of here. When I first started shacking with women, I lived near downtown; and it seems like through the years each move I make is further west and further north. I felt myself going towards Beverly Hills at one time. I'm in this place now, because I got booted out of the house where I lived with this lady. We had a minor split, so all of a sudden I came back south a bit. I got thrown off course. I guess I'm not going to make Beverly Hills.

What changes have you seen in Los Angeles during the years you've lived here?

Nothing astounding. It's gotten bigger, dumber, more violent and greedier. It's developed along the same lines as the rest of civilization.

But there's a part of LA—you take it away from Hollywood, Disneyland and the ocean, which are places I stay away from, except the beaches in wintertime when there's no one around—where there's a good, easy feeling. People here have a way of minding their own damned business. You can get isolation here, or you can have a party. I can get on that phone and in a hour have a dozen people over drinking and laughing. And that's not because I'm a writer who's getting known a little. This has always been, even before I had any luck. But they won't come unless I phone them, unless I want them. You can have isolation, or you can have the crowd. I tend to mix the two, with a preference for isolation.

One of your short stories has this line in it: 'LA is the cruelest city in the world.' Do you believe it is?

I don't think LA is the cruelest city. It's one of the least cruel. If you're on the bum and know a few people, you can get a buck here and there, float around and always find a place to lay up overnight. People will tolerate you for a night. Then you go to the next pad. I put people up overnight. I say, 'Look, I can only stand you for one night. You've got to go.' But I put them up. It's a thing people in LA do. Maybe they do it elsewhere, and I just haven't seen it.

I don't get the feeling of cruelty here that I get from New York City. Philadelphia has nice rays, too; it has a good feeling. So does New Orleans. San Francisco isn't all they say it is. If I had to rate cities, I'd put LA right up on top: LA, Philadelphia, New Orleans. Those are places where somebody can *live.*

I've left LA many times, but I always come back. You live in a town all of your life, and you get to know every street corner. You've got the layout of the whole land. You have this picture of where you are. When I hit a strange town, I seldom got out of the neighbourhood. I'd settle within an area of two or three blocks: the bar, the room I lived in and the streets around them. That's all I knew about a town, so I always felt lost; I was never located, never quite knew where I was. Since I was raised in LA, I've always had the geographical and spiritual feeling of being here. I've had time to learn this city. I can't see any other place than LA.

Do you still travel a lot?

I've done my travelling. I've travelled so damn much, mostly via buses or some other cheap mode, that I've gotten tired of it. At one time I had this idea that one could live on a bus forever: travelling, eating, getting off, shitting, getting back on that bus. (I don't know where the income was supposed to come from.) I had the strange idea that one could stay in motion forever. There was something fascinating about constant motion, because you're not tied down. Well, it was fascinating for a while; and then I got un-fascinated, or non-fascinated. Now I hardly travel; I hate going to the drugstore. . . .

Did you do much writing while you were on the road?

I got some writing done in New York. In Philadelphia, St Louis and New Orleans, too, in my early days. St Louis was very lucky for me. I was there when I got rid of my first short story—to *Story* mag, which was quite a mag in its day. (They discovered William Saroyan and reprinted top-class writers.) I don't remember if I wrote the story in St Louis, because I was moving pretty fast then; but I was there when it got accepted.

You've got to have a good city to write in, and you've got to have a certain place to live in to write. This apartment is not right for me; but I had to move right away, and I got tired of looking around. This place isn't rugged enough. The neighbours don't like any noise at all. It's very constrictive, but I'm not here most of the time. I'm usually over at Linda's big house. I write there and lay around. This place is for when things go wrong with her. Then I come running back here. I call it my office. You see, my typewriter isn't even here; it's over there. I used to pay rent over there. Then we had a split. Now I still live there, but I don't pay rent. That was a smart move.

How did you end up, at one point in your life, on the bum?

It just occurred. Probably through the drinking and disgust and having to hold a mundane job. I couldn't face working for somebody, that eight-to-five thing. So I got hold of a bottle and drank and tried to make it without working. Working was frankly distasteful to me. Starving and being on the bum seemed to have more glory.

There was this bar I went to in Philly. I had the same barstool—I forget where it was now; I think it was on the end—reserved for me. I'd open the bar early in the morning

and close it at night. I was a fixture. I ran errands for sandwiches, hustled a little. I picked up a dime, a dollar here and there. Nothing crooked, but it wasn't eight to five; it was 5 a.m. to 2 a.m. I guess there were good moments, but I was pretty much out of it. It was kind of a dream state.

What poets do you like reading at the moment?

Auden was pretty good. When I was young and I read, I liked a lot of Auden. I was in a liking mood. I liked that whole gang: Auden, MacLeish, Eliot. I liked them at the time; but when I come back on them now, they don't strike me the same way. Not loose enough. They don't gamble. Too careful. They say good things, and they write it well; but they're too careful for me now.

And there's Stephen Spender. Once I was lying in bed, and I opened this book up. You know what happens when a poem hits you. I was thinking of that one with the touch of corn about the poets who have 'left the air signed with their honour'. That was pretty good. Spender got them off. I can't remember them all, but I know that he set me off three, four, five, six times. The more modern poets don't seem to do this to me.

It could be that I was more spiritually available to be turned on at that time and that I wasn't as much into the game. To be sitting in the stands as a spectator and see a guy hit a home run: Holy God, that ball goes flying over the fence, and it's a miracle. When you get down there and play with them and hit a few over yourself, you say, 'That wasn't so hard. I just seemed to tap that ball, and it went over the wall.' When you finally get into the game, miracles aren't as big as when you're looking on from the sidelines. That has something to do with my lack of appreciation now.

Then you meet the writers finally, and that's not a very good experience. Usually, when they're not on the poem, they're rather bitchy, frightened, antagonistic little chipmunks. When they get turned on, art is their field; but when they get out of their field, they're despicable creatures. I'd much rather talk to a plumber over a bottle of beer than a poet. You can say something to a plumber, and he can talk back. The conversation can go both ways. A poet, though, or a creative person, is generally pushing. There's something I don't like about them. Hell, I'm probably the same way, but I'm not as aware of it as when it comes from another person.

Do the classical poets—say, Shakespeare—do anything for you?

Hardly. No, Shakespeare didn't work at all for me, except given lines. There was a lot of good advice in there, but he didn't pick me up. These kings running around, these ghosts, that upper-crust shit bored me. I couldn't relate to it. It had nothing to do with me. Here I am lying in a room starving to death—I've got a candy bar and half a bottle of wine—and this guy is talking about the agony of a king. It didn't help.

I think of Conrad Aiken as classical. He's hardly Shakespeare's time, but his style is classical. I feel it was influenced by the older poets way back. He is one of the few poets who turns me on with classical lines. I admire Conrad Aiken very much. But most of the—what shall I call them, purists?—don't pick me up.

There was one at the reading the other night. William Stafford. When he started turning on those lines, I couldn't listen. I have an instinctive radar, and it shut me off. I saw the mouth move, I heard sounds; but I couldn't listen. I don't want to take castor oil.

What do you look for in a good poem?

The hard, clean line that says it. And it's got to have some blood; it's got to have some humour; it's got to have that un-namable thing which you know is there the minute you start reading.

As I said, modern poets don't have it for some reason. Like Ginsberg. He writes a lot of good lines. You take the lines separately, read one and say, 'Hey, that's a good line.' Then you read the next one and say, 'Well, that's a fair line'; but you're still thinking of the first line. You get down to the third, and there's a different twist. Pretty soon you're lost in this flotsam and jetsam of words that are words themselves, bouncing around. The totality, the total feel, is gone. That's what happens a lot. They throw in a good line—maybe at the end, maybe in the middle or a third of the way down—but the totality and the simplicity are not there. Not for me, anyway. They may be there, but I can't find them. I wish they were there; I'd have better reading material. That's why I'm not doing all the reading I should, or like people say you should.

How much reading should you do? I've always thought that writers who don't read are like people who always talk and never listen.

I don't listen very well, either. I think it's a protective mechanism. In other words, I fear the grind-down of doing something that's supposed to have an effect on me. Instinctively, I know ahead of time that the effect won't be there. That's my radar again. I don't have to arrive there myself to know that there's not going to be anything there.

I hit the library pretty hard in my early days. I did try the reading. Suddenly I glanced around, and I was out of material. I'd been through all the standard literature, philosophy, the whole lot. So I branched out; I wandered around. I went into geology. I even made a study of the operation on the mesacolon. That operation was damned interesting. You know, the type of knives, what you do: shut this off, cut this vein. I said, 'This isn't bad. Much more interesting than Chekhov.' When you get into other areas, out of pure literature, you sometimes really get picked up. It's not the same old shit.

Anymore, I don't like to read. It bores me. I read four or five pages, and I feel like closing my eyes and going to sleep. That's the way it is. There are exceptions: J. D.

Salinger; early Hemingway; Sherwood Anderson, when he was good, like, *Winesburg, Ohio* and a couple of other things. But they all got bad. We all do. I'm bad most of the time; but when I'm good, I'm damned good.

At one point in your life, you stopped writing for ten years. Why was that?

It started around 1945. I simply gave up. It wasn't because I thought I was a bad writer. I just thought there was no way of crashing through. I put writing down with a sense of disgust. Drinking and shacking with women became my art form. I didn't crash through there with any feeling of glory, but I got a lot of experience which later I could use—especially in short stories. But I wasn't gathering that experience to write it, because I had put the typewriter down.

I don't know. You start drinking; you meet a woman; she wants another bottle; you get into the drinking thing. Everything else vanishes.

What brought it to an end?

Nearly dying. I ended up in County General Hospital with blood roaring out of my mouth and my ass. I was supposed to die, and I didn't. Took lots of glucose and ten or twelve pints of blood. They pumped it straight into me without stop.

When I walked out of that place, I felt very strange. I felt much calmer than before. I felt—to use a trite term—easygoing. I walked along the sidewalk, and I looked at the sunshine and said, 'Hey, something has happened.' You know, I'd lost a lot of blood. Maybe there was some brain damage. That was my thought, because I had a really different feeling. I had this calm feeling. I talk so slowly now. I wasn't always this way. I was kind of hectic before; I was more going, doing, shooting my mouth off. When I came out of that hospital, I was strangely relaxed.

So I got hold of a typewriter, and I got a job driving a truck. I started drinking huge quantities of beer each night after work and typing out all these poems. (I told you that I didn't know what a poem is, but I was writing *something* in a poem form.) I hadn't written many before, two or three, but I sat down and was writing poems all of a sudden. So I was writing again and had all these poems on my hands. I started mailing them out, and it began all over. I was luckier this time, and I think my work had improved. Maybe the editors were readier, had moved into a different area of thinking. Probably all three things helped make it click. I went on writing.

That's how I met the millionairess. I didn't know what to do with these poems, so I went down a list of magazines and put my finger on one. I said, 'All right. Might as well insult this one. She's probably an old woman in this little Texas town. I'll make her unahppy.' She wasn't an old woman. She was a young one with lots of money. A beautiful one. We ended up married. I was married to a millionairess for two and a half years. I blew it, but I kept writing.

What happened to the marriage?

I didn't love her. A woman can only tolerate that so long unless she's getting some other type of benefit out of it, either fame or money from you. She got nothing out of our marriage, neither fame nor money. I offered her nothing. Well, we went to bed together. I offered her that, but that's hardly enough to hold a marriage together unless you're a real expert. I wasn't at the time. I was just some guy dressed in clothes who was walking across the room, eating an egg and reading a paper. I was tied up with myself, with my writing. I didn't give her anything at all, so I had it coming. I don't blame her, but she didn't give me much either.

She was arty and turned on to artistic types. She painted badly and liked to go to art classes. She had a vocabulary and was always reading fancy books. Being rich, she was spoiled in that special way rich people are spoiled without knowing it. She had this air that the rich have. They have a superior air that they never quite let go of. I don't think that money makes much difference between people. It might in what they wear, where they live, what they eat, what they drive; but I don't think it makes *that* much difference between people. Yet, somehow, the rich have this separation value. When they have money and you don't, something unexplainable rises up between you. Now, if she'd given me half of her money so that I could have had half of her feeling, we might have made it. She didn't. She gave me a new car, and that was it; and she gave that to me *after* we split, not before.

In a short story you made a sort of self-pitying remark that went something like this: 'Here I am, a poet known to Genet and Henry Miller, washing dishes.'

Yes, that's self-pity. That's straight self-pity, but sometimes self-pity feels good. A little howl, when it has some humour mixed with it, is almost forgivable. Self-pity alone. . . . We all fail at times. I didn't do so well there.

I didn't do so well as a dish washer, either. I got fired. They said, 'This man doesn't know how to wash dishes.' I was drunk. I didn't know how to wash dishes, and I ate all their roast beef. They had a big leg of roast beef back there. I'd been on a drunk, and I hadn't eaten for a week. I kept slicing this goddamned leg. I ate about half of it. I failed as a dish washer, but I got a good feed.

Another time, though, you said you enjoyed anonymity, that you liked the idea of people not knowing who you are. That seems like a contradiction.

There's a difference between being known by another writer and being known by the crowd. A good workman— if we can call it that—like, a carpenter—wants to be known as a good carpenter by other carpenters. The crowd is something else; but to be known by another good writer . . . I don't find that detestable.

Do the critics' opinions of your work ever bother you?

When they say I'm very, very good, it doesn't affect me anymore than when they say I'm very, very bad. I feel good when they say nice things; I feel good when they say unnice things, especially when they say them with great vehemence. Critics usually go overboard one way or the other, and one excites me as much as the other.

I want reactions to my work, whether they be good or bad; but I like an ad-mixture. I don't want to be totally revered or looked upon as a holy man or a miracle worker. I want a certain amount of attack, because it makes it more human, more like where I've been living all my life. I've always been attacked in one fashion or another, and it's grown on me. A little rejection is good for the soul; but total attack, total rejection is utterly destructive. So I want a good balance: praise, attack, the whole stewpot full of everything.

Critics amuse me. I like them. They're nice to have around, but I don't know what their proper function is. Maybe to beat their wives.

In Post Office *there's an episode about the flack you got from the government because of your writing. Did they actually give you a lot of trouble?*

My God, yes. The whole scene underground: one dim light, the handshake, sitting down at the end of a long table, two guys asking me little trap questions. I just told them the truth. Everything they asked, I told the truth. (It's only when you lie that you get your ass in the wringer. I guess the big boys have found that out now.) I thought, Is this America? Sure, I'll back it all the way as really happening. I wrote a short story about it, too.

You've been published a lot in the underground press. Those newspapers, now, seem to have lost their original vigour. What happened to them?

They've turned into a business, and the real revolutionaries were never there. The underground press was just lonely people who wanted to get around and talk to each other while putting out a newspaper. They went left wing and liberal, because it was the young and proper thing to do; but they weren't really interested in it. Those newspapers were kind of a lark. They were a sign to carry around, like wearing a certain type of clothing. I can't think of one underground newspaper that meant anything, shook anybody.

You mentioned your problems with women. Didn't one of your girl friends recently try to kill you?

She found me on my way to another lady's house. I had already been there and gone and was coming back with two six-packs and a pint of whiskey. I was quite high at the time. Her car was parked out in front, so I said, 'Oh, jolly. I'll take her up and introduce her to the other one, and we'll all be friends and have drinks.' No chance. She rushed me. She got those bottles out and started smashing them all up and down the boulevard—including the pint of whiskey. She disappeared. I'm out sweeping the glass up, and I hear this sound. I looked up just in time. She's got her car up on the sidewalk, rushing it towards me. I leaped aside, and she was gone. She missed.

Many of your stories read as if they're written off the top of your head. Do you write that way, or do you rewrite a great deal?

I seldom revise or correct a story. In the old days, I used to just sit down and write it and leave it. I don't quite do that anymore. Lately I've started dripping out what I think are bad or unnecessary lines that take away from a story. I'll subtract maybe four or five lines, but I hardly ever add anything.

And I can't write except off a typewriter. The typewriter keeps it strict and confined. It keeps it right there. I've tried to write longhand; it doesn't work. A pencil or a pen . . . it's too intellectual, too soft, too dull. No machine-gun sounds, you know. No action.

Can you write and drink at the same time?

It's hard to write prose when you're drinking, because prose is too much work. It doesn't work for me. It's too unromantic to write prose when you're drinking.

Poetry is something else. You have this feeling in mind that you want to lay down the line that startles. You get a bit dramatic when you're drunk, a bit corny. It feels good. The symphony music is on, and you're smoking a cigar. You lift the beer, and you're going to tap out these five or six or fifteen or thirty great lines. You start drinking and write poems all night. You find them on the floor in the morning. You take out all the bad lines, and you have poems. About sixty per cent of the lines are bad; but it seems like the remaining lines, when you drop them together, make a poem.

I don't always write drunk. I write sober, drunk, feeling good, feeling bad. There's no special way for me to be.

Gore Vidal said once that, with only one or two exceptions, all American writers were drunkards. Was he right?

Several people have said that. James Dickey said that the two things that go along with poetry are alcoholism and suicide. I know a lot of writers, and as far as I know they all drink but one. Most of them with any bit of talent are drunkards, now that I think about it. It's true.

Drinking is an emotional thing. It joggles you out of the standardism of everyday life, out of everything being the same. It yanks you out of your body and your mind and throws you up against the wall. I have the feeling that drinking is a form of suicide where you're allowed to return to life and begin all over the next day. It's like killing yourself, and then you're reborn. I guess I've lived about ten or fifteen thousand lives now.

Just a minute ago you mentioned classical music, and you make remarks about it in lots of your stories. Are you seriously interested in it?

Not as a conscious thing. In other words, I have a radio—no records—and I turn that classical music station on and hope it brings me something that I can align with while I'm writing. I don't listen deliberately. Some people object to this in me. A couple of girl friends I've had have objected that I don't sit down and *listen*. I don't. I use it like the modern person uses a television set: they turn it on and walk around and kind of ignore it, but it's there. It's a fireplace full of coals that does something for them. Let's say it's something in the room with you that helps you, especially when you're living alone.

Say you work in a factory all day. When you come home, somehow that factory is still hanging to your bones: all the conversation, all the wasted hours. You try to recover from those eight, ten hours they've taken from you and use what juice you have left to do what you really want to do. First, I used to take a good, hot bath. Then I turned on the radio, got some classical music, lit a big cigar, opened a bottle of beer and sat down at the typewriter. All these became habitual, and often I couldn't write unless they were happening. I'm not so much that way now, but at the time I did need those props to escape the factory syndrome.

I like a certain amount of interruption when I'm writing. I do a lot of writing over at Linda's. She has two kids, and once in a while I like to have them run in. I like interruptions, as long as they're natural and aren't total and continuous. When I lived in a court, I put my typewriter right by the window. I'd be writing, and I'd see people walking by. Somehow that always worked into what I was doing at the moment. Children, people walking by and classical music are all the same that way. Instead of a hindrance, they're an aid. That's why I like classical music. It's there, but it's not there. It doesn't engulf the work, but it's there.

There's a certain Bukowski image that's been created: drunkard, lecher, bum. Do you ever catch yourself deliberately trying to live up to that image?

Sometimes, especially, say, at poetry readings where I have a bottle of beer by my hand. Well, I don't need that beer, but I can feel the audience relating when I lift that beer and drink it. I laugh and make remarks. I don't know if I'm playing the game or they're playing the game. Anyway, I'm conscious of some image that I've built up or that they've built, and it's dangerous. You notice that I'm not drinking today. I fooled you. Blew the image.

If I drink two or three days in a row, I get pretty bad. Like I said, I've been in the hospital: My liver is not in great shape, and probably neither are several other organs. I heat up very much; my skin gets red-hot. There are a lot of danger signs. I like drinking, but it should be alternated; so I take a few days off now and then, instead of running a string of drinking days and nights together like I used to. I'm fifty-three now; I want to stay in the game a while longer, so I can piss a lot of people off. If I live to be eighty, I'll really piss them off.

Are poetry readings as bad an experience as you make them out to be in a couple of your short stories?

They are torture, but I've got to pay for the horses. I guess I read for horses instead of people.

How much time do you spend at the track?

Too much, too much, and now I've got my girl friend hooked. I never mention the track to her, you know. We'll be lying down, and morning will come around. Or we'll be writing. (She writes in one corner of the room, and I write in another. We do pretty well that way.) We've been at the track all week, and I'll say, 'We'll get some goddamned writing done today at last.' All of a sudden, she says something about the race track. It could be just a word or two. I'll say, 'All right, let's go. You said it.' That always happens. If she'd keep her mouth shut, we'd never go. Between the two of us, we've got to solve that problem of one wanting to go and the other not.

Races are a drag-down. There are thirty minutes between races, which is a real murder of time; and if you lose your money on top of it, it's no good. But what happens is that you come home and think, 'I've got it now. I know what they are doing out there.' You get up a whole new system. When you go back, either they changed it a little or you don't follow your nose: you get off the system, and the horse comes in. Horses teach you whether you have character or not.

Sometimes we go to the thoroughbreds in the daytime, then we jump over and play the harness at night. That's eighteen races. When you do that, you've had it. You're so tired. It's no good. Between her and me, we've had a rough week; but track season closes in a few days, so my worries will be over. Race tracks are horrible places. If I had my way, I'd have them all burned down, destroyed. Don't ask me why I go, because I don't know; but I have gotten some material out of all that torture.

Horse racing does something to you. It's like drinking: it joggles you out of the ordinary concept of things. Like Hemingway used the bullfights, I use the race track. Of course, when you go to the track every day, that's no damned joggle: it's a definite bring-down. . . .

One last question: Why do you put yourself down so much in your stories?

It's partly a kind of joke. The rest is because I feel that I'm an ass a lot of the time. If I'm an ass, I should say so. If I don't, somebody else will. If I say it first, that disarms them.

You know, I'm *really* an ass when I'm about half smashed. Then I look for trouble. I've never grown up. I'm a cheap drunk. Get a few drinks in me, and I can whip the world . . . and I want to.

Stuart Newton (essay date 1976)

SOURCE: A review of *Poems Written Before Jumping Out of an 8 Story Window,* in *West Coast Review,* Vol. 10, No. 3, February, 1976, p. 41.

[*In the excerpt below, Newton notes Bukowski's equation of individualism with isolation.*]

Poems written before jumping out of an 8 story window is not Bukowski's best book; it is too hurried. But it does contain all his familiar subjects: his drinking, writing, and sex; he haunts dirty bars, cheap hotel rooms, and the night streets of Los Angeles. The classic Bukowski characters are the whores, bums, and the solid bartenders. All this occurs at the brink of modern society: Los Angeles. In fact, Los Angeles is very important in his poems, because the poet who takes this bewildering location as his home will almost surely confront the modern complexity in his poems. Bukowski presents everyone as modern man who has come to know everything, yet at the same time he is so very ugly. Bukowski is certainly ugly. He is even miserable enough to believe that, just as every place is becoming like Los Angeles, everyone is becoming worldly and ugly like him. In **"The Millionaire"** just such a change takes place:

> Look at him
> a withered man
>
> they say he was worth millions

Another of Bukowski's theories is the notion of individualism which seems to mean isolation, and another is that sex is forever entangled with demented love.

"Big Bastard with a Sword" is the best passage in the book. In this poem Bukowski succeeds in sustaining his special view of the world, with the best of his terse style:

> I went to get a haircut,
>
> I found a magazine . . . I turned the page
> . . . there was this big bastard with a
> sword . . . and more photos of beheadings
>
> and then the barber said
> next!
> and I walked over to the chair and my head was
> still on
> and his head said to my head,
> how do you want it?
> and I said, medium.
> but I still kept thinking about the heads.
> My day was spoiled, it would take a night's
> sleep anyway, to get rid of the heads. It
> was terrible to be a human being: there was
> so much going on.
>
> I saw my head in a plateglass window
> I saw the reflection
> and my head had a cigarette in it
> my head looked tired and sad
> it was not smiling with its new
> haircut.

Gerald Locklin   (essay date 1982)

SOURCE: A review of *Dangling in the Tournefortia*, in *The American Book Review*, Vol. 4, No. 5, July-August, 1982, p. 6.

[*In the following essay, Locklin praises Bukowski's work and declares that he is "undeniably a chronicler of politically significant phenomena."*]

Let me at once admit my bias: I think Bukowski is a writer of at least the stature of a Henry Miller. I also think he has been mistreated—or treated to a conspiracy of silence—by the American literary establishment and by factions outside the establishment as well. But he hasn't gone away. To the contrary, he and his American and European publishers have prospered. Films of his work are beginning to appear in Europe, where he seems to have become one of the best known, if not *the* best known, of contemporary American writers. A best-selling underground (or dirty old) man—talk about your oxymorons! Those who despised him as a drunken bum, now despise him as a drunken *rich* bum.

I am not a Bukowski idolater. Even Bukowski (maybe Bukowski most of all) knows that his work is uneven. His defense is that it's his job to write and the job of others to edit and evaluate.

Those who enjoy Bukowski do not have to be persuaded to read everything of his that appears, but I would not have recommended to the uninitiated a couple of his most recent collections because a reader could hit a run of second-rate offerings before encountering vintage Bukowski. I would have recommended *The Days Run Away Like Wild Horses Over the Hills*, for poetry, and his novel *Post Office* or one of the City Lights collection of stories. Or one might find a library with back issues of the *Wormwood Review* and follow his development in its pages over the past twenty years. I wouldn't hesitate to recommend to neophyte or jade this present volume though. I was sixty or seventy pages into it before I realized I hadn't read a poem that was not outstanding. I put the book down happy for Bukowski and happy for all of us who love books that live and will continue to live.

Of course, I've never understood why anyone finds Bukowski depressing. I've always found him a survival story. If he's come through, why can't the rest of us? George Orwell called Henry Miller the proletarian given a voice, and I'd say the remark is even truer of Bukowski. I like him best when he is being funny and dirty and conveying life at the infrared base of the socioeconomic spectrum. He's one of our few naturalists to possess a sense of style and a sense of humor. I like him least when he's waxing pseudopoetic or pseudophilosophical or stacking the deck to favor himself. What seems to bother people most about him, his *attitude* or *attitudes,* doesn't bother me. As just about everyone knows, Bukowski drinks a bit, and he can be unfair, in person and in print, at certain levels of the bottle, but there is also a purity in his unsparing view of humanity.

It's difficult to illustrate Bukowski's craft with excerpts because his poems tend to reach a certain length and the best are often the longest. While others debated how best to restore narrative and dramatic structures to verse, Bukowski just sat down and did it. He has the sense of timing and construction (and the voice) of a W.C. Fields, which is one reason why his infrequent readings, no matter what his state of inebriation, continue to draw throngs. To quote a line here and there makes as much sense as to tell a punch line without the build-up. In what is perhaps my favorite poem in this collection, the seriocomic **"yeah, man?"** the white protagonist pulls a knife on a Latin whose car is blocking his. Later the white returns to find his apartment in a shambles. His walls are spray-painted. His radio, television and electric clock are gone, as are his pillows and sheets. His mattress has been slashed; his faucets are running. His kitchen floor has been pissed on; eggs have been broken on it; garbage is dumped there. Missing are his knives, forks and spoons, the salt and pepper, the bread and coffee, everything in the refrigerator. The toilet paper is gone, and the mirror is broken, and the cabinet has been emptied of razor, shaving cream, Band-Aids, aspirins:

> and then he looked
> in the toilet
> and down in the bowl
> was a freshly-cut
> cat's tail
> furry and still
> bleeding
> in the water
> Larry hit the lever
> to flush it away
> and got an
> empty click
> lifted the lid
> looked inside
> and all the toilet parts
> were gone.

After a couple hits of the beer he has brought back with him, Larry decides

> that it was about time
> he moved
> further west.

This is not simply a nightmare tale of one man's misguided race relations; it is the demographic and demonological saga of white flight. Bukowski may or may not be characterized as a revolutionary, but he is undeniably a chronicler of politically significant phenomena.

His language is the product of a movement towards the spoken idiom that is at least as old as Wordsworth's preface to the second edition of the *Lyrical Ballads* and that weaves its way through, among others, Whitman, Robinson, Frost, Masters, Lindsay, Williams, Oppen, Reznikoff, Rakosi and Edward Field to become one of the dominant modes among young poets today, probably *the* dominant mode in Southern California. A special and striking influence upon the young Bukowski was the recently rediscovered Southern California fiction writer, John Fante, to whom this volume is dedicated and whose works are being re-issued by Black Sparrow.

So why is Bukowski only now beginning to receive his due in his own country? One can only speculate, but he seems to have been perceived for a time, incorrectly I think, as an enemy of women and gays. Actually he is simply an abhorrer of orthodoxies. He has not given people used to respect—professors, for instance—the respect that they are used to. He is sparing in his praise of other writers. He not only knows that the literary world is rife with charlatanism, self-promotion, and mutual back-scratching, but he hasn't hesitated to say so. He proclaims his literary superiority. Frankly, a lot of people seem just plain jealous of him. And he has been his own worst enemy at times, especially when the elixir has elicited his Doppelganger. But it must be admitted that Bukowski seldom initiates a relationship.

Bukowski has just finished his fourth novel, based on his childhood, a book that should go a long way towards making it obvious why he is the way he is and maybe even why we should be glad he is.

Gerald Locklin (essay date 1985)

SOURCE: A review of *War All the Time* and *Horses Don't Bet on People & Neither Do I*, in *The Review of Contemporary Fiction*, Vol. V, No. 3, Fall, 1985, pp. 34-6.

[*Here, Locklin claims that, in his mid-sixties, Bukowski is reaching his prime, composing narratives comparable to those of Ernest Hemingway.*]

I felt that Bukowski returned to top form as a poet in *Dangling in the Tournefortia* (1981). . . . . These two recent collections [*War All the Time* and *Horses Don't Bet on People & Neither Do I*] do not represent a falling off; on the contrary they present numerous examples of Bukowski at work in what has always been his strongest mode: the scenic or dramatic narrative (or more simply, the story poem with lots of setting and dialogue), but added to his achievements of the past is a diversity that should confound those who would parody the "typical" Bukowski poem of booze, horses, and sex.

In *War All the Time* there are poems of the working class, poems of the aspiring writer, poems of the aging writer, antiwar poems, antinuke poems, poems that move in and out of the bourgeois world, sports poems, television poems, European poems, and elegies for a cat and for the Los Angeles writer, John Fante. Of course there are still track poems, but why shouldn't there be? It's a world Bukowski knows intimately, one he can treat as a micro-cosm, one where stories offer themselves—it is a world of inherent narrative tensions. And of course there are still poems about women, but they range from the aroused to the satiric and culminate in a moving remembrance of

a loved woman dead twenty-eight years. There are still poems of intoxication and withdrawal, but even here there is something new in the investigation of the current cocaine epidemic.

It is not that Bukowski is trying to placate any critics in these poems. It is, I think, that his affluence and fame of recent years have widened the world about which he can write firsthand. He may still prefer Hollywood Park to Hollywood premieres but he has been to the latter now as well. While this book contains some withering attacks on turncoat friends and lovers, his greater security also allows him to laugh at himself and to let bygones be bygones. Many if not most poets do their best work young (e. e. cummings is a case in point), but it may be that Bukowski, in his mid-sixties, is indeed, as he keeps insisting, just reaching his prime.

I'll draw examples from *Horses Don't Bet on People* of the narratives that abound in both volumes. Anyone who has ever owned a home can identify with **"Locks,"** a five-page saga of the tribulations of getting the house locks changed. In **"Fight"** the narrator tries to convince his woman that he was made late by stopping to watch a vicious street fight. Those who would insist that there are not significant differences between men and women, or that there shouldn't be, may not like **"Fight"** or a good deal of Bukowski. But a poem's not catering to a current ideology does not by itself mark it as a bad poem in the long run, or even now. **"Independence Day"** provides an object lesson in dealing with juvenile delinquents. The **"Token Drunk"** negotiates a media party in Marina del Rey.

"There Are So Many Houses and Dark Streets without Help" is unfortunate title for an otherwise likable poem psychoanalyzing the poet's penchant for getting wildly lost in his car. All his women have the same explanation: "You're just a fool." The title character of **"A Boor"** wins no laurels from waitresses.

Just to make sure no one is left with the impression that Bukowski has gone soft, the final poem, about the predictable advice given by a talk-show psychologist to a cuckolded husband, is entitled **"In My Day We Used to Call It Pussy-Whipped."**

It is, however, the penultimate poem in the volume, **"Kenyon Review, After the Sandstorm,"** that quietly assesses Bukowski's place in, and importance to, contemporary American poetry:

> coming off that park bench after that all night
> sandstorm in El Paso
> and walking into the library
> I felt fairly safe even though I had less than
> two dollars
> was alone in the world
> and was 40 pounds underweight.
> it still felt normal and almost pleasant to
> open that copy of the *Kenyon Review*
> 1940

and marvel at the most brilliant way those
professors used the language to criticize each
other for the way they criticized literature.
I even felt that they were humorous about it,
but not quite: the bitterness was rancid and
red steel hot, but at the same time I felt the
leisurely and safe places that language had
evolved from: places and cultures centuries
soft and institutionalized.
I knew I would never be able to write
in that manner, yet I almost wanted to be
one of them or any of them: being guarded,
fierce and witty, having fun
in that way.

I put the magazine back and walked outside,
looked south north east west.

each direction was wrong.
I started to walk along

what I did know was that overeffusive language
properly used
could be bright and beautiful.

I also sensed that there might be
something else.

The astounding thing about this revelatory poem is that
Bukowski demonstrates a more objective, fair, and sensitive
appraisal of his place in relation to the literary establishment
than the rest of us, with our supposed aesthetic distance,
have been able to articulate on his behalf. Of course poetry
today, as then, abounds with the bright and beautiful, but
what is Bukowski's "something else"? It is to an extent a
matter of the vernacular (as Professor Julian Smith of
Hull, England, is elaborating in a dissertation-in-progress),
and it has a lot to do with his freedom, but it is perhaps
primarily a matter of his having gone ahead and told stories
in free verse while the "serious" poets continued their
decades-long debates upon the best ways of returning the
narrative and dramatic modes to poetry.

Readers are still surprised to find Bukowski employing
the same stories in poems, short stories, and novels.
They seem to feel there is a law against this, and maybe
such a prohibition is taught in some creative writing
classes, but I have yet to see it written down. And
those readers who do not really like Bukowski's work,
but who bend over backwards to appreciate him, go on
praising his occasional attempts to be bright and beautiful, which generally result in his most parodied efforts.
It is interesting that there are few such poems in these
two volumes: Bukowski has always said that he has no
quarrel with critics of his work, that those who have
bothered to write about him at all have generally written sympathetically. He seems now to have heeded a
valuable message from his parodists and unsuccessful
imitators. Or else, since he has written me that these
poems represent only about a sixth of his poems composed during this time period, the credit may be due to
his editors, John Martin and Marvin Malone. (I can

attest to the acuity of Malone's editing in relation to my
own work.)

Even the poem quoted above, while not an obvious narrative in the manner of the classic **Fire Station** or so
many of the poems of horses, violence, and women, is
certainly a story reminiscent of the most icebergian of
Hemingway's. In less than forty lines we find scene,
characterization, conflict, irony, meditation, resolution,
retrospective. It is a short story of a young writer, down
and out, who reads a literary magazine and experiences a
quiet epiphany of what he will never be and who he *will*
be as a writer in the postmodern world. There is emotional complexity and emotional change. Why is it, although
it has but a single character, no dialogue or waiters, and
the setting is not a café, that this story/poem reminds me
of "A Clean Well-Lighted Place"?

The answer might begin with the observation that not a
word is wrong or wasted or misplaced, and that an entire
lifetime, world, and literary career are left to our inferring.

Hugh Fox on the two sides of Bukowski's poetry:

[A] kind of duality goes on in his poetry. I hate to say that
the "real" Bukowski is a Bretonish surrealist, although
there is *a* Bukowski who gets surrealistic and writes about
the day it rained at the L.A. country museum, about the
Nor'wester that "ripped the sheets like toe-nails," about
an "Alkaseltzer Mass." The other Bukowski is all 300
pound whores (or any variety of whore), rundown bars,
rundown apartments, beer, the D.T.'s, jail, slugging it out,
screwing . . . this is the Great American Myth Bukowski,
a latter-day Hemingway-Henry Miller-Mark Twain (the
irreverent Mark Twain) all rolled up into one, and it's this
Bukowski that the young poet studs have hooked on to.
The other Bukowski, a little scholarly, a little erudite, very
"playful" with reality, has been put in the closet.

Hugh Fox, in a profile of Charles Bukowski in The
North American Review, *Vol. 254, No. 3, Fall,
1969.*

Stephen Kessler   (essay date 1985)

SOURCE: "Notes on a Dirty Old Man," in *The Review of
Contemporary Fiction*, Vol. 5, No. 3, Fall, 1985, pp. 60-
3.

[*In the essay below, Kessler defends Bukowski's writing
from attacks by the literary establishment, arguing that
his work displays "an increasingly persuasive truthfulness, a sense of honest simplicity which makes his books
easy to read, offensive to some, sad and funny—in short,
lifelike."*]

My first direct encounter with Bukowski occurred in 1974,
in a Santa Cruz restaurant in the basement of a building
that used to be the county courthouse but was converted

to a little shopping complex with lots of nice shops for the tourists. The famous writer was in town to read at a poetry festival that evening, had drunk his free meal with the literary hustlers and was looking vaguely bored and pre-obnoxious as zero hour approached. I arrived late as the party was preparing to leave the restaurant, and my first impression of the distinguished guest (to whom I was perfunctorily introduced) was of a man profoundly indifferent to the surrounding bullshit but not really a nasty fellow. He seemed to be someone doing his job, stoically meeting professional obligations, keeping a crusty demeanor on for the sake of self-defense from the admiring vampires, not friendly but coolly tolerant of the attention. In that smallish group, which included Allen Ginsberg and Gary Snyder and a number of lesser literati, Bukowski struck me as being for real in a way that could be trusted.

Later that evening, after a marathon reading at the Civic Auditorium where Bukowski enraged the feminists and delighted the subliterary slobs by being himself on stage, reading in that unshakably murderous monotone for his allotted time punctuated by slurps off his quart of screwdriver, then heckling his colleagues from the audience ("Read ten more!" he yelled at Snyder as the hour approached midnight and the crowd hushed reverently to receive some of Gary's Zen/environmentalist wisdom)— later, after the reading, there was a party to which the bards and their followers were invited. As one of the younger local poets, I had read that night and was honored to be among such illustrious company. At the same time I had a skeptical or even cynical feeling about the whole affair, a sour reaction to the sycophantic frenzy that often surrounds celebrities. Standing off to the side of the room moodily observing the goings-on, I found myself next to Bukowski, who muttered to me in a tone that seemed a mixture of distaste and weary understanding (and maybe even sympathy for my unease), "I guess we have to entertain these people, don't we?"

I think I just shrugged, not wanting to provoke one of the legendary brawls for which the man was famous, but in retrospect there was a gentle sincerity in his voice which was anything but hostile or aggressive. Listening to the undertone of his work before and since—seeing through the stylistic toughness of his poetry and prose—one can detect that kind of compassionate tenderness, an acceptance which softens and absorbs brutality and gives the rawness of Bukowski's voice a deep and humane resonance.

With age, this compassionate quality, which was always present but masked with irony or tough-guy posturing, has risen closer to the surface of his writing and become its informing substance. The key, I believe, to understanding Bukowski's power is in the 1982 novel *Ham on Rye*, where he reveals the origins of his attitude toward life and in an incredibly generous way forgives his cruel and pathetic father for all the abuse the writer withstood as a child. One can begin to comprehend how, in the relentless account of his more-sordid-than-average days and nights prolifically typed and published over the past two or three decades, the act of writing has literally saved his

life. This is what makes Bukowski such an inspiration to the readers who have grown to trust him: if this guy can make it through so much misery, anybody can. His works are a reservoir of earned courage.

If he is a model for other writers, it has less to do with his style—which unfortunately has been imitated to death by a multitude of second-, third- and fourth-rate poets— than with his ability, day after day, to sit down at the machine facing a blank page and to patiently put one word after another. This patience and perseverance in composition has not only tightened and clarified his language over the years, it has cultivated an increasingly persuasive truthfulness, a sense of honest simplicity which makes his books easy to read, offensive to some, sad and funny—in short, lifelike. His writing is proletarian without ever attempting to be politically uplifting; if anything, its rejection of political solutions for human plight and its embrace of such simple consolations as classical music on the radio, playing the horses, drinking and whoring around is what give it its illusionless appeal. Socially, his world is a comic wasteland where stupid jerks redeem their lives only through small acts of unheroic attention.

I write this knowing that there are people who will always see Bukowski as a pig, and that the professors will want some evidence to back up my assertions of his importance. But these are notes, not a doctoral thesis (though I guarantee that the PhD's will descend one day, if they haven't already, to document meticulously the artistic achievement of this barbaric figure), and I want to be sure my subjective reading is not mistaken for scholarship. If the literary establishment has rejected Bukowski's work as beneath any decent New Yorker's dignity, it's partly because his writing resists any form of text-worship or cocktail-party appropriation, partly because he's published by a small press on the West Coast (and has found his audience all along through funky little independent magazines and papers), and partly because—the horror, the horror!—he's from Los Angeles. His presence in that city has, through no intent of his own, been instrumental in helping to generate a large and vital wave of excellent work in poetry and prose by younger writers who learned from his example that one doesn't need New York's approval to become an author under one's own power.

Despite the fact that he's been widely translated and is extremely popular in Europe, Bukowski remains a local writer in the best sense of the term, rooted in his native turf and endlessly unearthing its indigenous reality without ever pretending to speak for the region as a public voice. More subtly and consistently than any other writer I know, Bukowski has mapped the nervous energy of LA's streets, its car culture, its architectural pathos, the truly mundane and unglamorous side of its Hollywood facade. In the novel *Women* especially, which I believe to be his masterpiece, one gets the sense of frenetic desperation that permeates the City of the Angels. But because he was raised in Los Angeles and knows its people—its real people, not the mosquitoes buzzing into the beams of its klieg lights—his portrayal of the city and its inhabitants lacks the bitterness and contempt so often found in the writings of outsiders taking a jaundiced peek into the dream factory. LA was never a dream for Bukowski, nor even very much of a nightmare; it was and is simply a given, a landscape whose reality was never in doubt. I'm convinced that Bukowski's books will be read in the future as maps of Los Angeles in much the same way that Joyce's work is seen as a guide to Dublin.

Within the context of American literature, Bukowski is sometimes compared to Henry Miller. In their radical rejection of mainstream social values, their survival-oriented individualism, the buffoonery of their sexual obsessions, the unabashedly autobiographical/personal orientation of their texts and the sheer productivity of their typewriters, Miller and Bukowski clearly share some territory. But while both are enemies of hypocrisy, Miller is deeply moralistic, often preaching to the reader or arguing for some philosophical position as if it made an important spiritual difference, where Bukowski is below good and evil, literally grounded in his own experience. It's not that he has no imagination, he's just not the metaphysician that Miller is. Bukowski *is* a poet, however, or an antipoet, who achieves a surprising lyricism in the midst of the most talky, typewriterly utterances. And perhaps what the two have most in common is that they're totally unafraid to make fools of themselves.

Bukowski's willingness to write badly without embarrassment, to do the same thing over and over again in poems or in stories, is one of the exasperating and endearing things about him. Exasperating because we've heard it before, endearing because it's *him,* it is the pattern out of which he has always worked, for better and worse. He has mined deeply a relatively modest area of experience: he has not sought exotic adventures or inventions because he recognizes the mundane's amazing capacity for revelation. Besides, he's lazy. He likes to be not too far from a liquor store at any time. He'd rather, like most good-for-nothings, go to the race track than to the wilderness (not to mention work!). He does not set himself up as a model for anything, nor does he presume to be a bad example. In Bukowski's world, there's nothing even to rebel against. Life is the way it is—painful, absurd and scary—and so what.

And what about alcohol? the temperate will ask. Doesn't he glorify and celebrate the dubious pleasures of alcoholism? Hardly. Alcohol for Bukowski is a vice to which he admits, a crutch, a shield, a wall, a last line of defense against a world that refuses to cooperate. He no more advocates its use than he advocates driving on the freeway, but he presents it as one more presence in his milieu, like any other character, however unsavory.

The sexism of which he is sometimes accused is also a bogus charge. The women in most of his poems and stories are real people, they come across as quirky, complete beings, eccentrically individual, not just anonymous genitals on which the writer exercises his fantasies—although there's surely plenty of close-to-the-crotch activity. But fucking, even fucking violently, and eating and drinking and shitting are things that people actually do, and

Bukowski faces these facts because they constitute life as he knows it. In his recent work he seems to be sweetening into a kindly old recluse (some of the poems in *War All the Time* show the emergence of a warmer, softer Bukowski than some readers might have anticipated), but he has earned this more kindly outlook, he didn't decide to be nice.

Like all great writers, Bukowski is a warrior of the spirit, even in his rejection of any form of conventional heroism. He testifies to the fact that even under the worst of circumstances people can remain undefeated. My respect for his work is a personal matter, although it has nothing to do with his personality; that night we met in Santa Cruz was the only time we've spoken face to face. One thing about him that astonishes me is that his work continues to improve, or at least maintain a level of strength that shows he is still creating, not just going through the motions. With each new book I find myself recharged with an interest in the everyday, reminded that the life of every person counts.

Stephen Kessler (essay date 1993)

SOURCE: "Bukowski Unbound," in *Poetry Flash*, No. 238, January, 1993, pp. 1, 6-7, 9.

[*In the following essay, Kessler offers a broad survey of Bukowski's work and describes the poet as "a human being of extraordinary character, an indomitable personality who has grown in stature with every document he produces."*]

The photo in back of Charles Bukowski's latest collection of poems [*The Last Night of the Earth Poems*]—a four hundred page tome turned out as the author was approaching and passing seventy—shows a face seasoned by pain and suffering into an expression of tough equanimity, of weary compassion for the human dilemma. It is a face facing up to its own mortality: wise, gentle, kind. As anyone who's read his recent work is aware, Bukowski has lately lost his edge of angst; his comic meanness has sweetened into a humbly ironic gratitude for survival. The voice of the vicious drunk, while still vulgar in its raw frankness, has taken on a far more philosophical tone, an attitude of acceptance if not quite understanding. Despite the spiky white whiskers grizzling his chin in the picture, his shirt collar is crisply pressed, his fingernails look immaculate: the once disreputable poet/bum as clean old man.

Comfortably ensconced as a homeowner in middle-class San Pedro, chatting across the backyard fence with his neighbors, driving his BMW on the freeways, using his credit cards to cash in on his international success, Bukowski has come a long way from the squalid urban landscape of his formative years in Los Angeles. Readers who dismissed his earlier writing as crude and monotonous are unlikely to find much to admire in the mellower, more prosaic lines of his latest work. And those who loved the wildly anti-literary beast desperately flailing at life's cruelties with flights of salty imagination may be disappointed to find the irascible bard gone soft. But those who have watched in wonder as he has brought forth book after book in an unstoppable flow of personal testimony since the early sixties will find in this new volume further evidence not only of the man's astounding perseverance but something approaching greatness.

It's not just that Bukowski's best poetry and prose—in books like *The Days Run Away Like Wild Horses Over the Hills* (1969), *Mockingbird Wish Me Luck* (1972), *Love Is a Dog From Hell* (1977), *War All the Time* (1984), and the novels *Women* (1978) and *Ham on Rye* (1982)—have such a distinctive clarity, music and courage in their transformation of terrible experience; it is the cumulative proof the writer has provided that even the most apparently hopeless life can be converted to something useful, not only to the self but to others, through the effort of art.

The poems in *The Last Night of the Earth Poems* tend to be typically straight-ahead narratives, little stories both sad and funny, extended meditations laced with aphoristic kickers, accounts of mundane events that in the telling take on a certain matter-of-fact resonance, philosophical reflections on a past that won't go away. While the present may afford him the material luxuries of drinking expensive wine and working on a new computer, the old days at pointless jobs and nights in flophouses continue to bear the fruit of fresh perspectives. The life is a teeming reservoir of material: anything—a traffic jam, a day at the track, a trip to the doctor's office—can be a source of inspiration. This will to excavate one's autobiography in the most direct and 'unpoetic' style is the Bukowski legacy in all its mixed fallout over the last twenty-five years in American poetry: from lesser typists who think that copping an attitude and spilling their guts is all it takes, to original voices liberated to trust themselves in natural modes they might not have discovered without the master's barbaric example. That evident ease of expression, though, is earned. The short or long lines, the talky rhythms, the swiftness with which his utterances unfold, all the signature stylistic touches have been refined over thousands of hours at the typewriter—not in search of the single perfect phrase but in the repeated exercise of spontaneous composition.

Like some character out of Beckett, Bukowski's transparent, persona in its despair, resignation and resolve-to-carry-on-in-spite-of-everything achieves a certain undeniable dignity. Boredom, illness, writer's block become occasions for writing. Even when the results are less than edifying—which is true about three-quarters of the time—there's something poignantly impressive in the struggle to give voice to what others might consider unspeakable or otherwise unworthy of poetry. Rather than discard the weaker poems, Bukowski includes them as part of the public record, the big picture of a work, a life, in progress. His lowbrow eloquence, such as it is, is an antidote to estheticism.

That's why you won't find Bukowski teaching, or being taught, in Master of Fine Arts programs. As he recounts

in the new book, in a poem called **"creative writing class"**:

> I noticed that the professor's advice
> on what to do
> and what not to do
> to become a writer was
> very pale and standard stuff
> that would lead to
> nowhere.

Not that even a singular path like his own leads anywhere, really: "the uselessness of the word is / evident," he writes in another poem.

> this incompleteness is all
> we have:
> we write the same things
> over and over
> again.
> we are fools,
> driven.

Such a bedrock existential admission, echoing the wisdom of Ecclesiastes ("Vanity of vanities . . . all is vanity"), is as much a self-critique as it is a philosophical truism. Preempting those who would bother to take him seriously enough to criticize his shortcomings, Bukowski is profoundly aware of his limitations as a writer. In his own primitively postmodern manner he incorporates this self-awareness into an ongoing commentary on the act of creation. His 'narrative', especially in this latest collection, deconstructs itself almost every step of the way.

In his own primitively postmodern manner Bukowski incorporates self-awareness into an ongoing commentary on the act of creation.

—Stephen Kessler

At the same time he's utterly unapologetic for doing what has kept him alive through an often hellish existence. At one point, "after 50 years in the game," he kisses his typewriter as a way of saying thank you. He is grateful for the occasional fire lighting up his lines, for the mysterious friendliness of his cats, for the taste of decent food after decades of chronic hunger, for the patience of his wife in putting up with him, for the pleasure of feeling the night air on his balcony. Throughout *The Last Night of the Earth Poems*—beyond or within the fear of dying, the pathetic sense of the futility of it all, the sadness of an aging body's failing and an imagination's waning—there is a pervasive feeling of affirmation, of saying yes to life, even as he rejects Sandburgian sentimentality.

> the people survive to come up with flat fists full
> of nothing.

I remember Carl Sandburg's poem, "The
People, Yes."
nice thought but completely inaccurate:
the people did not survive through a noble
strength but through lie, compromise and
guile.
I lived with these people, I am not so sure
what people Sandburg lived
with.
but his poem always pissed me off.
it was a poem that lied.
it is "The People, No."
then and now.
and it doesn't take a misanthrope to
say this.

Elsewhere he expands on this observation:

people are strange: they are constantly angered by
trivial things,
but on a major matter
like
totalling wasting their lives,
they hardly seem to
notice . . .

Bukowski notices, and salvages what truth and comfort
he can by recording the trivial things.

Recording in his case means more than taking note of
what happens from day to day; it also means remembering
everything: a feeling of contentment while eating in some
greasy spoon, a moment of peace in the library stacks as
a miserable young man, the "clean, gentle" satisfaction of
a job unloading boxcars. It is striking how often the word
clean appears in these poems, as if writing about the grimy
past were an act of purification. It's also an act of recovery in every sense of the term. As time runs out on the
life, the mind works harder to resurrect what was, to sa-
vor the fading evidence, to find in what may have seemed
meaningless at the time not a lesson or a moral but an
essence of lived reality and fix it on the page in the plain-
est language. There is no illusion that the words are anything like the actual thing, the experience itself, but the
written record can hint, can suggest, can solace, can
inspire.

I always resented all the years, the hours, the
minutes I gave them as a working stiff, it
actually hurt my head, my insides, it made me
dizzy and a bit crazy—I couldn't understand the
murdering of my years
yet my fellow workers gave no signs of
agony, many of them even seemed satisfied, and
seeing them that way drove me almost as crazy as
the dull and senseless work. . . .

I knew that I was dying.
something in me said, go ahead, die, sleep, become
    as
them, accept.

then something else in me said, no, save the tiniest
bit.
it needn't be much, just a spark.
a spark can set a whole forest on
fire.
just a spark.
save it.

I think I did.
I'm glad I did.
what a lucky god damned
thing.

                                        ("spark")

Bukowski's tendency toward solipsism is corrected by his
regular attention to the world around him, both here-and-
now and then-and-there. Though W.C. Williams is one
precursor he seldom if ever invokes, Bukowski resembles
him not only in his ear for ordinary speech but in the
grounding of ideas in things. Language is not an end in
itself, nor some opaque screen through which to question
itself, but a tool for touching the facts of life, however
unremarkable those facts may seem.

Does this mean that anybody can write a 'Bukowski poem?
Well, yes and no. While he has spawned countless imitators,
especially in the L.A. area, few of these mini-bukowskis
have anything like the naked desperation that gave rise to
the original, and so no matter how well they may mimic
the old man's mannerisms they can't approach the power
of his expression. That's because the nonconformity of
his early daring is what gave those defiant writings their
sense of risk. Here was someone doing the poem his own
way and fuck you if you didn't like it. To model oneself
on such an individual is to miss the point of his distinctive
nerve, the lonely creation of a radically different voice. That
there should now be an unofficial 'school of Bukowski'
may be a tribute to his funky genius, but it makes no
sense in light of his own accomplishment. The fact that
the later Bukowski is a far gentler and in some ways more
refined writer than he was at first does nothing to negate
the integrity of his journey or to contradict its essential
continuity. However many imitators he may have, he remains fundamentally inimitable.

What writers can learn from Bukowski, as from any author
with heart enough to break out of the safety of convention, is to listen for one's own deepest, most authentic
music, no matter how discordant it may sound, and let it
rip. The bottles of booze, the filthy ashtrays, the puke-
stained undershirts, the scummy one-nighters and other
unsavory images so often associated with the Bukowski
legend—even the seemingly ragged yet sneakily crafty
style of his verse—are of little consequence beside the
relentless determination he has demonstrated to carry on
regardless of the revulsion or adulation his work evokes.
Indeed, he seems to have as much contempt for his admirers
as for his critics—maybe more. At least the critics offer
a stimulating opposition analogous to the challenges the
rest of his life has provided: he thrives on resistance. The
fawners, the fellow outlaw-geniuses, the ass-kissers asking
for favors are, to judge from his documentation of their

behavior, a pain in the ass. Though Bukowski has in fact been known to be kind to his fans, from a distance at least—answering their letters, responding to solicitations from unknown editors of upstart magazines—his aloofness from the literary fray, proceeding with his project at whatever cost, is exemplary.

Like an aging boxer losing his speed or a tired slugger whose "batting average has dropped to / .231" (recurrent tropes in the *Last Night* poems for his fate as an ancient veteran), Bukowski sees retirement coming inexorably in the only way that can take him out of the game. Death, a favorite theme for many years, is ever present in this book, a punchline for the ultimate joke at his own expense. We see the poet stoically enduring tuberculosis, cancer, all the indignities of decrepitude, yet somehow resisting destruction by writing it all down in meticulous detail. His tone is less pugnacious than elegaic as he tries out variations on the dirge that will finally honor his own demise.

Given the unlikelihood of his having lived this long, for all we know he may go on to crank out a thousand more pages of reportage, adding a few last-ditch volumes to his already awesome output before the cosmic powers call his number. Either way, even a selective reading of his forty-five books to date reveals a human being of extraordinary character, an indomitable personality who has grown in stature with every document he produces. Whether any individual piece has the requisite artistry or grace or truth to hold up over time remains to be seen—for my money there are many. But odds are that in terms of a life's work there are few contemporaries who can claim to have made a more substantial, accessible, entertaining and enduring contribution.

Robert Peters   (essay date 1994)

SOURCE: "Gab Poetry, or Duck vs. Nightingale Music: Charles Bukowski," in *Where the Bee Sucks: Workers, Drones, and Queens in Contemporary American Poetry*, Asylum Arts, 1994, pp. 56-66.

[*In the essay below, Peters detects a "deterioration" in Bukowski's poetry, but nevertheless celebrates his originality and earthiness.*]

I once witnessed a Charles Bukowski *first:* the debut of the great raunchy poet as actor. The vehicle, "The Tenant," was a two character drama written by Linda King. Bukowski contributed lines of his own, better developing his own image in the play. This line was his addition, as delivered by Miss King: "You may be the greatest poet of the century, but you sure can't fuck." In a lively way "The Tenant" turns upon the problem of whether a super-poet should move in with his girlfriend, who would then, one would suppose, buy him his beer, give him bj's, and let him abuse her. The event was choice. An actor scheduled to read the Bukowski role was unable to show, so Buk took over.

There were twenty people in the well of the Pasadena Museum—sad, alas, because of the significance of the event. Bukowski, script in hand, trod the boards. The props were a telephone—used with nearly as much frequency as Barbara Stanwyck's in "Sorry, Wrong Number"; a mattress upon which King and Bukowski, scripts in hand, fell to enact their erotic comings after dismal separations. The performance, pixie-ish, included a tender moment where Bukowski acted as W.C. Fields towards a child who had a brief moment of stage glory. Needless to say, the small audience chuckled, particularly over Bukowski's Bogart-like delivery. Ms. King, with various stunning Bridget Bardot-esqueries nicely foiled the poet.

"The Tenant" gave Bukowski a chance, under the guise of art and aesthetic distance, to extol his stature as a poet. Buk has never been known for his reticence, and his being utterly ignored hitherto by the literary establishment hasn't affected him in the least.

I remember how zapped I was when I first read him: I was teaching at the University of California at Riverside and had been given *Crucifix in a Deathhand*. I carried the book to a string quartet concert, began reading it before the concert, experienced chills, elevations, charismatic flashes, barber pole exaltations, and fevers in the groin. I had not read such poems since discovering Dylan Thomas in the fifties. Here was something awe-thentic at last! I nudged my companion who thought I was crazy. Bukowski was unafraid of life's terror meat-slabs, and he made the angels sing.

I began to ask others if they had heard of Bukowski. Yes, he was living in a Hollywood dump, they said, dismissing him as a charlatan steeped in booze, flop-gutted, and rancid-breathed. I gave up trying to explain his impact on me. Moreover, I didn't care whether he rolled in his own puke, or swallowed pints of maiden juice. He was a super poet. His example loosened my own writing. Lowell, Snodgrass, Wilbur, Ashbery, and Olson were dilettantes.

One afternoon, carrying a six-pack of Coors, I beat my way to Buk's door, four or five days before Christmas. He and his daughter were trimming a tree. There weren't many ornaments—half a dozen on the low branches. Bukowski asked me in. I found a man of charm—nothing of the horrible-retchable I had been led to expect. I have been a fan ever since. He, though, remembers the visit otherwise, and wrote about it in his collection *Beneath the Fortinaria*.

The appearance of *Burning in Water Drowning in Flame: Selected Poems 1955-1973* invites me to describe what I found so telling in his work and to point up what I find are unfortunate recent drifts. My remarks should dissolve some of the celebrity aura threatening his reputation. *It Catches My Heart in Its Hands* (1963) and *Crucifix in a Deathhand* (1965), two Loujon Press books, are among the dozen most beautifully printed and designed books of poetry ever. Since they are out of print, and rare, it is great to have those reprinted.

"The tragedy of the leaves" propels us into Bukowski's world: hangover, desertion by his woman, the screaming landlady, and a world that's failed him utterly. Set up for the big blubbery whine of self-pity? No! He transmutes all raunchy conditions through unusual images: "I awakened to dryness and the ferns were dead, / the potted plants yellow as corn. . . ." How well *dryness* echoes *awakened;* the latter implies a grappling with the world, moving toward insight. Compression follows:

> my woman was gone
> and the empty bottles like bled corpses
> surrounded me with their uselessness. . . .

The long vowel sounds are well-spaced, and Bukowski, sensing the positive, remarks on the sunlight brightening the landlady's note in its "fine and undemanding yellowness." The occasion, he observes, demands "a good comedian, ancient style, a jester / with jokes upon absurd pain." There's wisdom here: "pain is absurd / because it exists, nothing more." He believes that as a poet he is stagnant: "that's the tragedy of the dead plants." In this concluding passage note the effective slant rhymes *more* and *razor,* and the repeated *dead, dead, dark,* and *stood* accompanying some monosyllabic tough nouns, *Execrating, waving,* and *screaming,* mesh, as *hall, final, hell,* and *failed* weave subtle echoes. Here he manages to be tender towards a harsh landlady:

> and I walked into a dark hall
> where the landlady stood
> execrating and final,
> sending me to hell,
> waving her fat, sweaty arms
> and screaming
> screaming for rent
> because the world had failed us
> both.

Empathy is present in other poems. **"For marilyn m."** avoids sentimentality through a diction suited to the fey person Monroe was:

> . . . and we will forget you, somewhat
> and it is not kind
> but real bodies are nearer
> and as the worms pant for your bones,
> I would so like to tell you
> that this happens to bears and elephants
> to tyrants and heroes and ants
> and frogs,
> still, you brought us something,
> some type of small victory,
> and for this I say: good
> and let us grieve no more. . . .

"The life of Borodin," grandly empathetic, is effective reportage on the miserable composer's life. Wife-hounded, he slept by placing a dark cloth over his eyes. His wife lined cat boxes and covered jars of sour milk with his compositions. Nothing is overstated in this taut free-verse poem. The parallels between Bukowski's life and Borodin's are implicit.

"The twins" evokes another tremulous situation, one that a lesser poet might easily have wrecked. Here Bukowski confronts his hatred of his father, immediately after the father's death: "A father is always your master even when he's gone." To cope, the poet moves through the house stunned, then proceeds outside where he picks an orange and peels it. Common day noises of dogs and neighbors bespeak sanity. Back inside, the poet dons one of his father's suits:

> I try on a light blue suit
> much better than anything I have ever worn
> and I flap the arms like a scarecrow in the wind
> but it's no good;
> I can't keep him alive
> no matter how much we hated each other.
>
> we looked exactly alike, we could have been twins
> the old man and I: that's what they
> said. he had his bulbs on the screen
> ready for planting
> while I was lying with a whore from 3rd street.
>
> very well. grant us this moment: standing before a
>   mirror
> in my dead father's suit
> waiting also
> to die.

The event is stark. To wear another person's clothes is, in a sense, to become that person. Bukowski's mimicry of death as scarecrow is macabre. Despite the hate, the survivor can't bring the dead man back to life.

"Old poet" treats Bukowski's distaste for aging (forty-two at the time) without a public to love his work. Finding his sexual energies diminished, he's reduced to pawing dirty pictures. He's had too much beer and has heard too much Shostakovitch. He swats "a razzing fly" and "ho, I fall heavy as thunder . . ." The downstairs tenants will assume "he's either drunk or dying." Despite his depression, every morning he packs off envelopes of poems, hoping to place them in magazines. Rejection slips annoy him briefly; but soon he's back at his typewriter:

> the editors wish to thank you for
> submitting but
> regret . . .
> down
>   down
>   down
>   the dark hall
> into a womanless hall
> to peel a last egg
> and sit down to the keys:
> click click a click,
> over the television sounds
> over the sounds of springs,
> click click a clack:
> another old poet
> going off.

"View from the screen" might easily have dissolved into narcissism; it has all the accoutrements. It shouldn't work, but it does. The death-whispers of the heron and the bone-thoughts of sea creatures dominate his universe as the poet crosses the room:

> to the last wall
> the last window
> the last pink sun
> with its arms around the world
> with its arms around me. . . .

The sun is benign. Its pinkness produces the pig-image, an unusual trope and one that eschews turning maudlin. The Platonic cave motif is obvious:

> I hear the death-whisper of the heron
> the bone-thoughts of sea-things
> that are almost rock;
> this screen caved like a soul
> and scrawled with flies,
> my tensions and damnations
> are those of a pig,
> pink sun pink sun
> I hate your holiness
> crawling your gilded cross of life
> as my fingers and feet and face
> come down to this. . . .

Writing, for Bukowski, is for getting "feelings down." Now, that may sound like warmed-over Shelley. Bukowski's urge to write, prompted by a mix of sardonicism and angst, is as natural as defecation. An image allows him to translate pain into a testimony for his spirit, one fraught with "madness and terror" along "agony way." There's a time-bomb inside his chest, and if it doesn't go off as a poem it will explode in drunkenness, despair, vomiting, or rage. As long as he writes he leashes terror. **"Beans with garlic"** is about this. A terrific idea—beans as lovers! Beans as your words! Stirring them is like writing poems:

> but now
> there's a ticking under your shirt
> and you whirl the beans with a spoon,
> one love dead, one love departed
> another love . . .
> ah! as many loves as beans
> yes, count them now
> sad, sad
> your feelings boiling over flame,
> get this down.

"A nice day" deals with a knife the speaker carries inside him. Bukowski can't feel doom, so he goes outside "to absolutely nothing / a square round of orange zero." A woman says good morning, thereby twisting the knife:

> I do notice though the sun is shining
> that the flowers are pulled up on
> their strings
> and I on mine:
> belly, bellybutton, buttocks, bukowski
> waving walking
> teeth of ice with the taste of tar

> tear ducts propagandized
> shoes acting like shoes
> I arrive on time
> in the blazing midday
> of mourning.

The concluding pun is effective, and the lines are original. Bukowski produces (invents) his rhetoric, and this sometimes betrays him. Often, his latest voice, in the gabbarfly manner, sounds like imitation Bukowski. His best poems discharge energy. We are touched by a vital creative mind prizing the creative act. Nothing, not even bad booze, can diminish it. Call this *originality;* for, to paraphrase T. S. Eliot on Tennyson, Bukowski has originality in abundance.

In *At Terror Street and Agony Way* (1968) there is evidence of deterioration. Bukowski's paranoia intensifies. He's nastier than he's hitherto been. His sympathies are with outrageous, destructive folks: the guy who emasculates himself with a tin can; "the nice guy" who cuts up a woman and sends the parts to people. Bukowski senses that a sycophantic public expects outrageous cartwheels and titillations, and he obliges. There is a discernible drifting off from the earlier tender humanity. And there is a troublesome loquaciousness; the honed work of the early manner is usurped by rambling, grotty passages of prose masquerading (chopped into lengths) as poetry. And he is vicious to other poets, as he is in a parody of Michael McClure and in a tasteless piece on Jack Hirschman as narcissist Victor Vania.

"Sunday before noon," though it concludes with a funny piece of hysteria, reflects Bukowski's current narcissism:

> going down
> are the clocks cocks roosters?
> the roosters stand on the fence
> the roosters are peanutbutter crowing,
> the FLAME will be high, the flame will be big,
> kiss kiss kiss
> everything away,
> I hope it rains today, I hope
> the jets die, I hope
> the kitten finds a mouse, I hope
> I don't see it, I hope
> it rains, I hope
> anything away from here,
> I hope a bridge, a fish, a cactus somewhere
> strutting whiskers to the noon,
> I dream flowers and horses
> the branches break the birds fall the buildings
> burn, my whore walks across the room and
> smiles at me.

There's evidence of the old originality here in the juxtaposition of peanut butter and roosters, and in the branches and birds, and in the buildings that open the poem and close it. But the stance, the narcissism of "going down," the wish to be wiped out, and to wipe out, is dull. There isn't much in life now (petulance) worth grappling for. There's a nagging tone as Bukowski slips towards the next binge:

and I got out of bed and yawned and scratched my
  belly
and knew that soon very soon I would have to
  get
very drunk again.

Isolating *soon* and *again* with extra spaces emphasizes
the sterility of the writing. Ditto for the repetition of *very*.

Bukowski now cracks wise with editors who reject his
poems. He becomes a rhino-skinned poet s. o. b.:

> when a chicken
> catches its worm
> the chicken gets through
> and when the worm
> catches you
> (dead or alive)
> I'd have to say,
> . . . that it enjoys
> it.
>
> it's like when you
> send this poem
> back
> I'll figure
> it just didn't get
> through.
>
> either there were
> fatter worms or the chicken
> couldn't see.
>
> the next time
> I break an egg
> I'll think of
> you.
> scramble with
> fork
>
> and then turn up
> the flame
> if I
> have
> one.

This poem has an attractive petulance, and the motif of
chicken, worm, egg, is original. Also the minimalist lines
work well. Yet, Bukowski drifts into cuteness; the starch in
the initial images is smothered under narcissism.

Particularly off-putting is Bukowski's obsession with fame.
In "The difference between a bad poet and a good one is
luck," he regales us with his life in Philadelphia when he
was broke, trying to write, and waiting for the ultimate
handout to enable him to sit around "drinking wine on
credit and watching the hot pigeons suffer and fuck." He
hops a train to Texas, and busted for vagrancy, is dumped
off in the next town where he meets a woman who gives
him so many teeth marks he thinks he'll get cancer. In
prime macho fashion, he greets a bunch of his mistress'
cowboy friends:

> I had on a pair of old bluejeans, and they said
> oh, you're a writer, eh?
> and I said: well, some think so.
> and some still think so . . .
> others, of course, haven't wised up yet.
> two weeks later they
> ran me out
> of town.

He seems wistfully amused that trash men busy about
their work don't know that he, Great Poet, is alive—a
thought held, I would guess, by all great men who snicker
in their martinis: "Oh, if they only knew how near to greatness they are banging those trash cans down there . . ." In
"Lost" Bukowski waxes philosophical in the manner of a
hip-Merwin. The Big Conclusion? "We can't win it."
Who's surprised? "Just for awhile," folks, "we thought
we could." This Life Significance Statement serves up
duck-music as distinct from nightingale music. The loquaciousness is typical of his recent poetry. I call it *gab poetry*.
The gab poem is related to Chaucer's fabliaux. Obscenities
are sexual: a husband shoves a hot iron rod up his wife's
lover's anus whilst the lover is taking a crap out her
boudoir window; an old husband's young wife is being
swyved in a tree just out of eyeshot of the old fart, standing
amidst the flowers.

"Hot" is a good example of *gab poetry*. The speaker's been
working at the post office, see, on a night pickup run. He
knows Miriam the delicious whore is at home waiting for
him, deadline 8 p. m. At the last pickup the truck stalls.
Miriam is waiting. Speaker arrives late to find Miriam
gone. She's left a note propped against his pillow, addressed to "son of bitch." The note is held in place by a
purple teddy bear. Speaker gives the bear (heh heh) a
drink and has one himself, the poem is prose cut up into
boozy breath-groups. Nothing much poetically catches the
ear—this is in a sense a one-shot (as in bourbon) piece.

Some poems, like **"Burn and burn and burn,"** set in
bars, exude an easy cynicism. Petulance accompanies the
"vomiting into plugged toilets / in rented rooms full of
roaches and mice":

> well, I suppose the days were made
> to be wasted
> the years and the loves were made
> to be wasted

Instead of the Victorian Ernest Dowson's roses and lilies
of rapture (and vice), vomit and plugged toilets cram Buk's
wasted days.

Perhaps, if we persist, we'll find the secret of life tucked
inside a plastic envelope inside a box of Bukowski Creepy-
Crawly, Vomit, Crunch Cereal. Jesus Christ, says Buk,
"should have laughed on the cross." There's a secret here
somewhere. When Bukowski equates himself with Christ,
he's maudlin:

> out of the arms of one love
> and into the arms of another

I have been saved from dying on the cross
by a lady who smokes pot
writes songs and stories.
and is much kinder than the last,
much much kinder,
and the sex is just as good or better.
it isn't pleasant to be put on the cross and left
there,
it is much more pleasant to forget a love which
didn't
work
as all love
finally
doesn't work. . . .

Beautiful people, says Bukowski, "don't make it . . . they die in flame . . . they commit suicide . . ." They "are found at the edge of a room / crumpled into spiders and needles and silence." They "die young / and leave the ugly to their ugly lives . . ."

One superb new poem, **"the catch,"** is as good as any Bukowski has written. Guesses are that a strange fish is a Hollow-Back June whale, a Billow-Wind sandgroper, or a Fandango Espadrille with stripes. Folks don't agree. They examine the creature; it's "grey and covered with hair / and fat." It stinks like "old socks." Joyously, the creature promenades along the pier chomping hot dogs, riding the merry-go-round, and hopping a pony. It falls into the dust. "Grop, grop," it goes. Followed by a crowd, it returns to the pier where it falls backwards and thrashes about. Somebody pours beer over its head. "Grop, grop." It dies, and people roll it into the ocean and argue further over its name.

Charles Bukowski is an easy poet to love, fear, and hate. He develops personal legends as dude, boozer, and woman-izer. And he can be winsome, almost childlike. By stress-ing his personality I perhaps short change his poetry. It shouldn't matter that he vomits a lot, gets laid less often than he'd like, that seventy-seven new poems appeared in little magazines this year, or that he's Black Sparrow's leading commodity. Many readers prefer his fiction to his verse. The latter, I think, even with the flaws, remains a more durable art than his prose.

FURTHER READING

Bibliography

Dorbin, Sanford. *A Bibliography of Charles Bukowski.* Los Angeles: Black Sparrow Press, 1969, 93 p.
    Partially annotated primary and secondary bibliography through 1968.

Fox, Hugh. *Charles Bukowski: A Critical and Bibliographical Study.* Sommerville, MA: Abyss Publications, 1969, 121 p.
    Fox offers a comprehensive study of Bukowski's work

through 1968, and a comprehensive study of all published work and reviews from 1944 through 1969.

Biography

Cherkovski, Neeli. *Hank: The Life of Charles Bukowski.* New York: Random House, 1991, 335 p.
    Cherkovski presents a detailed biography of Bukowski.

Criticism

Byrne, Jack. "Bukowski's Chinaski: Playing Post Office." *The Review of Contemporary Fiction* 5, No. 3. (Fall 1985): 43-51.
    Surveys critical reaction to Bukowski's work, addressing the thin division between the author and his character Chinaski in *Post Office*.

Review of *Crucifix in a Deathhand: New Poems, 1963-1965*, by Charles Bukowski. *The Carleton Miscellany* VI, No. 4 (Fall 1965): 92-3.
    Praises Bukowski's "absolute lack of self-pity" and "almost terrifying honesty."

Carruth, Hayden. "Images." *Bookletter* (March 31, 1975): 4.
    Poet and critic Carruth praises Bukowski's honest use of language but finds fault with his stock subject matter.

Creeley, Robert. "Think What's Got Away..." *Poetry* Vol; CII, No. 1 (1963): 42-8.
    Review of *Run With the Hunted* praises Bukowski's straightforward language.

Conroy, Jack. "A Skidrow Poet." *The American Book Collector* 16:6 (February 1966): 5.
    Conroy offers praise for Bukowski's collections *Crucifix in a Deathhand* and *Cold Dogs in the Courtyard*.

Evanier, David. "Madman Incarnate." *The New Leader* 56:8 (April 16, 1973): p 19-20.
    Evanier criticizes Bukowski as being self-destructive and erratic, yet values his originality.

Harrison, Russell T. "An Analysis of Charles Bukowski's 'Fire Station'." *Concerning Poetry* 18:1 & 2 (1985): 67-83.
    Harrison illustrates two recurrent conflicts in Bukowski's work, that between men and women and between the individual and the society.

Kessler, Stephen. "Notes On A Dirty Old Man." *The Review of Contemporary Fiction* 5:3 (Fall 1985): 60-3.
    Kessler compares Bukowski's novels to those of Henry Miller, praising him as a warrior of the spirit.

Nolan, James E. and L. John Cieslinski. "Prime Bukowski." *The Small Press Review* Vol. 19, No. 2 (February 1987): 12.
    Review of *Relentless as the Tarantula* asserts that Bukowski's unique style and strong narratives keep his poetry fresh and vital.

Ostriker, Alicia. "Other Times, Other Voices." *Partisan Review* Vol. XXXVIII, No. 2 (1971): 218-26.

Review of *At Terror Street and Agony Way* in which noted critic Ostriker comments favorably on Bukowski's style and his personal as a "likeable male chauvinist."

Sherman, Jory. *Bukowski: Friendship, Fame and Bestial Myth.* Augusta, Ga: Blue Horse Publications, 1981, 38 p.
  Sherman offers reminiscences of Bukowski in his early days, as well as letters from 1960 through 1973.

Smith, Jules. "A singular self." *TLS* No. 4562 (September 7, 1990): 956.
  Review of *Septuagenarian Stew: Stories and Poems* criticizes Bukowski's poetry as overly self-centered and repetitive.

Swastek, Joseph. Review of *Poems and Drawings* by Charles Bukowski. *Polish American Studies* 20:1 (January-June 1963): p. 55-6.
  Swastek praises work for its "hard, concrete corner of contemporary reality."

Interviews

Bukowski, Charles with Marc Chénetier. "An Interview." *Northwest Review* Vol. 16, No. 3 (1977): 5-25.
  Bukowski discusses his aesthetic, his composition method, and his disassociation with prevalent literary movements.

Additional coverage of Bukowski's life and career is contained in the following sources published by Gale Research: *Contemporary Literary Criticism*, Vols. 2, 5, 9, 41, 82; *DISCovering Authors: Novelists Module*; *DISCovering Authors: Poets Module*; *Contemporary Authors*, Vols. 17-20R, 144; *Contemporary Authors New Revision Series*, Vol. 40; *Dictionary of Literary Biography*, Vol. 5, 130; and *Major Twentieth-Century Writers.*

Lewis Carroll
1832-1898

(Pseudonym of Charles Lutwidge Dodgson) English novelist, poet, satirist, and essayist.

INTRODUCTION

Lewis Carroll was the author of the critically acclaimed "children's" stories *Alice's Adventures in Wonderland* and *Through the Looking Glass, and What Alice Found There.* Fascinating both children and adults, the Alice books and the verse contained within them have gained increasing critical interest in recent years. Today, Carroll is best remembered for his vivid imagination, the masterful parody of his nonsense poetry, and his depiction of Victorian attitudes toward children.

Biographical Information

The son of a country pastor, Carroll passed a quiet childhood, showing a precocity in mathematics and poetry. As a child, he and his sisters entertained themselves by writing and performing plays, and even created a literary magazine, where an early incarnation of what would later become "Jabberwocky" was first published. Carroll went to Oxford at age 18, and was made a fellow of Christ Church two and a half years later. He was to remain there for the rest of his life, lecturing in mathematics and writing the occasional satirical poem lampooning a local political matter. It was at Christ Church that Carroll met Alice Liddell, the daughter of the college's dean, for whom he composed the tale of Alice in Wonderland. The normally reserved Carroll lost his shyness and found his voice in the presence of children, and he was able to captivate them for hours with fanciful tales of inquisitive little girls and anthropomorphic animals. Throughout his life, Carroll exhibited this peculiar blend of personalities: on one hand was the reserved and conventional mathematics professor, and on the other was the witty and imaginative author. The story that Carroll made up to amuse his young friend Alice Liddell in 1862 was published in 1865 (after much persuasion on the part of his friends), as *Alice's Adventures in Wonderland,* and his literary reputation was immediately established. Its sequel, *Through the Looking Glass, and What Alice Found There* was published in 1872. While both these books were enormously successful and are the most memorable of Carroll's work, he continued to write poetry and prose. Apart from the Alice books, his most popular works were nonsense poetry, the most famous of which was *The Hunting of the Snark: An Agony, in Eight Fits* (1876). Following his death in 1898, his family was forced to quickly dispose of his possessions which included most of his letters, sketches, photographs, and

games, which were sold at auction. Most of these are now considered permanently destroyed or lost.

Major Works

Carroll's *Alice's Adventures in Wonderland* (1865) has been considered a children's classic as well as an essential book in the English literary canon. It has been criticized as a savage parody of Victorian attitudes toward children, and as a testimony of Freudian analytical theories. Additional interpretations analyze the tale as one which demonstrates both the imagination and the disturbance of its author. The poem, "Jabberwocky," in *Through the Looking Glass* (1872) has been seen as a predecessor of James Joyce's *Finnegans Wake,* as well as surrealist art, and modernist literary concepts. *The Hunting of the Snark: An Agony, in Eight Fits* (1876) is noted for its parody, punning, and mastery of nonsense poetry, a form of poetry arguably part of the historical development of English poetry. Although Carroll's later work is thought to be critically lacking, Carroll's language skills and games have drawn increasing interest and are often additionally seen to be the predecessors of postmodernist theories and poetry.

Critical Reception

Carroll's first published work was actually an uninspired mathematical treatise, *A Syllabus of Plane Algebraical Geometry,* under his real name, Charles Lutwidge Dodgson, in 1860. Carroll was encouraged by friends to publish his tale, *Alice's Adventures in Wonderland,* which he eventually did, enlisting John Tenniel, the popular political cartoonist, to illustrate it. The book was an immediate and an enormous success. First recognized as a children's book, it later came to be of increasing interest to adults as well, and critics have gradually come to include the book in the literary canon. *Through the Looking Glass,* its sequel, contained the nonsense poem, "Jabberwocky," which demonstrated a skillful parody of both poetic form and heroic language. Critics have come to recognize this poem's influence on Joyce's *Finnegans Wake,* and its importance to modernist theories of art and language. Most critics feel that Carroll's later works lack the consummate artistry of the *Alice* books, with the possible exception of *The Hunting of the Snark: An Agony, in Eight Fits.*

PRINCIPAL WORKS

Poetry

Phantasmagoria and Other Poems 1869
The Hunting of the Snark: An Agony, in Eight Fits 1876
Rhyme? and Reason? 1883
Three Sunsets and Other Poems 1898
Collected Verse 1929

Other Major Works

A Syllabus of Plane Algebraical Geometry (essay) 1860
Alice's Adventures in Wonderland (novel) 1865
The Dynamics of a Particle (satire) 1865
The New Belfry (satire) 1872
Through the Looking Glass, and What Alice Found There (novel) 1872
Euclid and His Modern Rivals (essay) 1879
Curiosa Mathematica, Part I: A New Theory of Parallels (essay) 1888
Sylvie and Bruno (novel) 1889
Curiosa Mathematica, Part II: Pillow Problems Thought Out during Wakeful Hours (essay) 1893
Sylvie and Bruno Concluded (novel) 1893
Complete Works (novels, poetry, essays, satires, letters, and rules to games) 1939

CRITICISM

Edmund Wilson   (essay date 1952)

SOURCE: "C. L. Dodgson: The Poet Logician," in *The Shores of Light,* Farrar, Straus and Young, Inc., 1952, pp. 540-50.

[*In the following excerpt, Wilson argues for a serious critical approach to Carroll's work.*]

. . . If Dodgson and his work were shown as an organic whole, his "nonsense" would not seem the anomaly which it is usually represented as being. It is true that on one of his sides he was a pompous and priggish don. He used to write letters to friends the next morning after he had been having dinner with them and beg them never again in his presence to speak so irreverently of Our Lord as they had the evening before, because it gave him infinite pain; and he wrote to the papers in a tone of indignation worthy of Mr. Podsnap protesting against the impiety of W. S. Gilbert in being whimsical about curates on the stage. But even this side of Dodgson should not be kept out of the picture: the *Alice in Wonderland* side has an intimate relation with it. Under the crust of the pious professor was a mind both rebellious and skeptical. The mathematician who invented Alice was one of those semi-monastic types—like Walter Pater, and A. E. Housman—that the English universities breed: vowed to an academic discipline but cherishing an intense originality, painfully repressed and incomplete but in the narrow field of their art somehow both sound and bold. A good deal of the piquancy of the Alice books is due to their merciless irreverence: in Alice's dreaming mind, the bottoms dismayingly drop out of the didactic little poems by Dr. Watts and Jane Taylor which Victorian children were made to learn, and their simple and trite images are replaced by grotesque and silly ones, which have rushed in like goblins to take possession. And in the White Knight's song about the aged man a-sitting on a gate, a parody of Wordsworth's *"Leech-Gatherer,"* Lewis Carroll, in his subterranean fashion, ridiculed the stuffed-shirt side of Wordsworth as savagely as Byron had ever done. Wordsworth was a great admiration of Dodgson's; yet as soon as he enters his world of dreams, Lewis Carroll is moved to stick pins in him. This poem in its original form, before it had been rewritten to adapt it to Alice's dream, had been even more subversive of Victorian conventions:

> I met an aged, aged man
> Upon the lonely moor:
> I knew I was a gentleman,
> And he was but a boor.
> So I stopped and roughly questioned him,
> "Come, tell me how you live!"
> But his word impressed my ear no more
> Than if it were a sieve.

It is curious what ordination as a clergyman of the Church of England can do to an original mind. The case of Dodgson is somewhat similar to those of Donne and Swift—though Dodgson was shy and stammered and never took priest's orders; and he was closer, perhaps, to Swift and Donne than to the merely whimsical writer like Barrie or A. A. Milne, for Dodgson had a first-rate mind of a very unusual sort: he was a logician who was also a poet.

The poetry and the logic in Dodgson were closely bound up together. It has often been pointed out that only a mind primarily logical could have invented the jokes of the Alice books, of which the author is always conscious that they are examples of faulty syllogisms. But it also worked the other way: his eccentric imagination invaded his scholarly work. His *Symbolic Logic* (which had nothing to do with the subject called by the same name of which A. N. Whitehead and Bertrand Russell laid the foundation in their *Principia Mathematica*) contains syllogisms with terms as absurd as any in the Alice books:

> A prudent man shuns hyenas;
> No banker is imprudent.
> No banker fails to shun hyenas.

Dodgson's *Euclid and His Modern Rivals* had nothing to do with non-Euclidean geometry, but in the section called *A New Theory of Parallels* of his *Curiosa Mathematica* he grazed one of the conceptions of relativist theory; and is there not a touch of Einstein in the scenes in which the Red Queen has to keep running in order to remain in the same place and in which the White Queen gives a scream of pain before she has pricked her finger?

In literature, Lewis Carroll went deeper than his contemporaries realized and than he usually gets credit for even today. As studies in dream psychology, the Alice books are most remarkable: they do not suffer by comparison with the best serious performances in this field—with Strindberg or Joyce or Flaubert's *Tentation de Saint Antoine*. One of Alice's recent editors says that the heroine's personality is kept simple in order to throw into relief the eccentrics and monsters she meets. But the creatures that she meets, the whole dream, *are* Alice's personality and her waking life. They are the world of teachers, family and pets, as it appears to a little girl, and also the little girl who is looking at this world. The creatures are always snapping at her and chiding her, saying brusque and rude and blighting things (as if their creator himself were snapping back at the authorities and pieties he served); and she in turn has a child's primitive cruelty: she cannot help mentioning cats when she is swimming around with the mouse, and later on, with the birds all around her, she comes out, as if naïvely, with, "Dinah's our cat. And she's such a capital one for catching mice, you can't think! And oh, I wish you could see her after the birds! Why, she'll eat a little bird as soon as look at it!" But though Alice is sometimes brutal, she is always well-bred; and, though she wanders in a world full of mysteries and of sometimes disagreeable surprises, she is always a sensible and self-possessed little upper-class English girl, who never fails in the last resort to face down the outlandish creatures that plague her: she can always bring the dream to an end by telling the King and Queen and the Court that

they're nothing but a pack of cards or by picking up the Red Queen and shaking her. She can also be sympathetic and sometimes—for example, with the White Knight—exhibits a maternal instinct, but always in a sensible and practical way. Lewis Carroll is never sentimental about Alice, though he is later on to become so, in the messiest Victorian way, in the Sylvie and Bruno books. Yet *Sylvie and Bruno,* too, has considerable psychological interest, with its alternations of dream and reality and the elusive relationships between them. The opening railway journey, in which the narrator is dozing and mixes with the images of his dream his awareness of the lady sitting opposite him, is of an almost Joycean complexity and quite inappropriate for reading to children.

I do not, however, agree with Mr. Herrick, in the case of the Alice books, that the Alice that grown-ups read is really a different work from the Alice that is read by children. The grown-ups understand it better, but the prime source of the interest is the same. Why is it that very young children listen so attentively to Alice, remember it all so well and ask to hear it again, when many other stories seem to leave little impression? It is surely the psychological truth of these books that lays its hold on us all. Lewis Carroll is in touch with the real mind of childhood and hence with the more primitive elements of the mind of maturity, too—unlike certain other writers who merely exploit for grown-ups an artificial child-mind of convention which is in reality neither child-like nor adult. The shiftings and the transformations, the mishaps and the triumphs of Alice's dream, the mysteries and the riddles, the gibberish that conveys unmistakable meanings, are all based upon relationships that contradict the assumptions of our conscious lives but that are lurking not far behind them. . . . I believe that [The *Alice* books] are likely to survive when a good deal of the more monumental work of that world—the productions of the Carlyles and the Ruskins, the Spencers and the George Eliots—shall have sunk with the middle-class ideals of which they were the champions as well as the critics. Charles Dodgson who, in morals and religion, in his attitude toward social institutions, was professedly and as he himself believed, more conventional than any of these, had over them the curious advantage of working at once with the abstract materials of mathematical and logical conceptions and with the irrationalities of dreams. His art has a purity that is almost unique in a period so cluttered and cumbered, in which even the preachers of doom to the reign of materialism bore the stamp and the stain of the industrial system in the hard insistence of their sentences and in the turbidity of their belchings of rhetoric. They have shrunk now, but Alice still stands.

Elizabeth Sewell   (essay date 1961)

SOURCE: "Law-Courts and Dreams," in *The Logic of Personal Knowledge,* The Free Press, 1961, pp. 179-88.

[*In the following excerpt, Sewell argues that the "real world" can be found in nonsense literature, particularly in the Barrister's dream in* The Hunting of the Snark.]

. . . Alongside this law-court of dream [in Shakespeare's "Sonnet 87"] I want now to set another: that which is described in the Barrister's Dream, Fit the Sixth of Lewis Carroll's *The Hunting of the Snark*. Nonsense literature is, I believe, as valid and as closely knit with our ways of thought as any literary genre we have, so this juxtaposition need not, I hope, seem shocking. Its purpose is not to jolt but to help in this investigation, for which these verses provide interesting evidence. Actually, as I have suggested elsewhere, this particular narrative is not pure Nonsense. It admits too much of the real world, which is why it is less successful as Nonsense and highly relevant here and now. Fit the Sixth, like the rest, wavers between flashes of poetry—as in 'There was silence like night' which has a touch of Milton or of Mallarmé, *'Et l'avare Silence et la massive Nuit'*—and an occasional hint of authentic nightmare, 'And the Judge kept explaining the state of the law, in a soft undercurrent of sound.' These are details, however. It is with the Barrister's Dream as a whole that we are concerned, for he dreams, professionally enough, a trial 'in a shadowy Court' where the Snark who is, you may remember, an extremely shadowy entity itself, is Counsel for the Defence on behalf of a pig accused of deserting its sty. The case as it proceeds becomes more and more vague, muddled and self-contradictory. What is interesting is the way in which the various functionaries of the Court abdicate one by one from their functions; the Judge declines to sum up, the Jury refuse to reach a verdict, the Judge cannot pronounce sentence, and little by little the Snark takes on one function after another, returns a verdict of 'Guilty' (although acting supposedly for the defence), and pronounces sentence, 'Transportation for life . . . And *then* to be fined forty pound.' Only at the last is it discovered that the pig had in fact been dead for some years before the case began.

This is not the only law-court in Carroll's dream-writings. *Alice's Adventures in Wonderland,* which is a dream from start to finish, contains two trials, each resembling the more developed law-court in *The Hunting of the Snark* in a number of ways. The trial of the Knave of Hearts at the end of Alice's story proceeds in a no less vague, muddled, topsy-turvy fashion. The jury, lizards, mice and birds as they are, are luckless and incompetent. Witnesses are threatened. The King, sitting as Judge, has no idea of procedure, and due process is subverted—'Sentence first, verdict afterwards.' The second trial in this book occurs earlier and has the look of gratuitous interpolation. This is the Mouse's Long Tale, which runs typographically tail-wise down the page in ever-diminishing print, ending in a whisper as it were: 'I'll be judge, I'll be jury,' said cunning old Fury: 'I'll try the whole cause and condemn you to death.' So ends the trial proposed as a pastime by Fury, the dog, to his mouse-victim. What is interesting is that here, too, Fury, who begins as prosecuting counsel and apparently in fun, absorbs as did the Snark the other functions in the Court, and the trial ends lamentably for the accused.

This gathering up of various judicial roles into one person who then 'embodies the Law' is significant. . . . this dream fusion of legal personnel in Carroll's law-courts is interest-

ing in two other ways. It is, first, an example of those tendencies towards synthesis in dream which Freud wrote of in his great work *The Interpretation of Dreams*, 1900, a process which he called the 'work of condensation'. Second, such a synthesis is no longer a mere matter of the imagination, but has become, within living memory, cold and recurring fact. What were noted or invented as dream phenomena have become actual practice in certain Courts. The metaphor has come true.

On absurdity in Carroll's verse:

Lewis Carroll is one of the greatest writers for children. That he is as deeply ironic as he is absurd is left for the mature mind to discover. He understands perfectly just what a child sees in the looking-glass of his unshadowed and free imagination. He knows, for example, that although the grotesque is, for the adult, often symbolic, it is for the child merely funny: no double meanings occur to the child reading of Jack the Giant-killer, no horror of a mechanized world in the story of the crocodile within whose belly is a clock. The frequently very tragic and awesome plots of fairy tales are quite endurable to children; their faith that all will end well sustains them. Therefore the world of Lewis Carroll is frequently a world of oblique, distorted images, but these images behave perfectly rationally. Carroll realizes that nonsense must be very necessary nonsense. His verse-parody, as his commentator Francis McDermott points out, is based on logic and his favorite device is the *reductio ad absurdum*. Now a child will accept any hypothesis if, once he had done so, he is allowed to follow a reasonable argument to a consequent proof. Given a world where anything absurd may happen and where absurdities function according to logic—and this is the world which Carroll presents—the child has both an entire liberty of imagination and a familiar pattern of events. No mature-mindedness limits his invention, nor is his sense of an orderly universe violated. Lewis Carroll alone of all writers of nonsense verse has just this happy blend of the utterly absurd and the perfectly logical.

Eda Lou Walton, "Verse for Children," in The Nation, *vol. 129, No. 3359, November 20, 1929, p. 594.*

Elizabeth Sewell (essay date 1962)

SOURCE: "Lewis Carroll and T.S. Eliot as Nonsense Poets," in *T.S. Eliot: A Collection of Critical Essays,* Prentice-Hall, Inc., 1962, pp. 65-72.

[*In the following excerpt, Sewell argues the importance of Carroll's nonsense poetry, particularly as an influence on T.S. Eliot's "The Waste Land" and "Four Quartets."*]

> He thought he saw a Banker's Clerk
> Descending from a bus:

He looked again, and found it was
  A Hippopotamus.

(Sylvie and Bruno)

I saw the 'potamus take wing.

("The Hippopotamus")

It was Chesterton, that man of marvellous perception and often perverse practice, who announced in 1904 that Nonsense was the literature of the future. It was a brilliant guess. Even now, however, when it is clear that he was right, when the trials in *Wonderland* and the **Snark** have become prototypes of real trials from Reichstag to McCarthy, and much of our literature—poetry and criticism—and most of our philosophy is shaped on Nonsense principles, people are slow to recognize its importance, or that of Lewis Carroll. Carroll is no *lusus naturae* but a central figure, as important for England, and in the same way, as Mallarmé is for France. Nonsense is how the English choose to take their Pure Poetry, their *langage mathématique* or *romances sans paroles:* their struggle to convert language into symbolic logic or music. It is a serious struggle, but taken this way it need not appear so. Nonsense? A mere game, of course. This is characteristic of us. We like, you might say, to play possum in these matters.

The genre or game of Nonsense has strict rules. The aim is to construct with words a logical universe of discourse meticulously selected and controlled; within this playground the mind can then manipulate its material, consisting largely of names of things and numbers. The process is directed always towards analysing and separating the material into a collection of discrete counters, with which the detached intellect can make, observe and enjoy a series of abstract, detailed, artificial patterns of words and images (you may be reminded of the New Criticism), which have their own significance in themselves. All tendencies towards synthesis are taboo: in the mind, imagination and dream; in language, the poetic and metaphorical elements; in subject matter, everything to do with beauty, fertility and all forms of love, sacred or profane. Whatever is unitive is the great enemy of Nonsense, to be excluded at all costs.

The pure practice of Nonsense demands a high degree of asceticism, since its very existence in the mind depends on limitation and infertility. Nonsense is by nature logical and anti-poetic. The Nonsense poet, therefore, faces a constant paradox of self-denial. Something of the effects of this can be seen in the work of . . . Carroll. . . . With Carroll we move from pure Nonsense in the *Alices* through **The Hunting of the Snark** to *Sylvie and Bruno,* . . . Carroll is the best interpreter we have for Mr. Eliot, and *Old Possum's Book of Practical Cats,* Mr. Eliot's overt Nonsense work, is not a chance production, the master in a lighter mood. It is integral to the whole body of his work, and a key to his poetry and his problem.

Mr. Eliot couches his own autobiography in Nonsense terms, but at one remove, for he parodies Lear's *Autobiography* into "How unpleasant to meet Mr. Eliot!" He is an extensive parodist as Carroll was, and in each case this is a device for handling what might otherwise be dangerous for Nonsense. It is a matter of affirming and denying, and in his autobiography Mr. Eliot affirms and denies Nonsense in its relation to himself. He has told us that he drew from *Alice in Wonderland* that rose-garden with which the first of the *Four Quartets* opens, leading into the image of the rose which pervades and closes the last of them. In his 1929 essay on the Dante he so greatly reveres he says that we have "to pass through the looking-glass into a world which is just as reasonable as our own. When we have done that we begin to wonder whether the world of Dante is not both larger and more solid than our own." Nonsense goes deep in Mr. Eliot. One does not describe one's life, even ironically, construct an image system in serious poetry, nor interpret an honored poet in terms of something one considers trivial. It is we who would be at fault in seeing Nonsense so. What Mr. Eliot is doing here is working at the dilemma of his vocation as a Nonsense poet. The *Four Quartets* epitomize the problem. They are religious poems; yet one of their main images comes from classical Nonsense, the Wonderland rose which becomes the *Paradiso* rose drawn in its turn from a poet to understand whom, according to Mr. Eliot, we have to go through the looking-glass. And Nonsense as a pure systematic art form of mind and language excludes both poetry and religion.

Lewis Carroll, much less of a poet than Mr. Eliot but no less devoted a churchman, faces the same problem. He had, however, two advantages: first, he had an official status in the matter; second, he was luckier in his period. He had a triple identity, as the Reverend Charles Dodgson, as a professional mathematician and symbolic logician, and as a Nonsense writer. The last two, closely allied as they are, were allowed to meet; the first was sealed off, at least up till the *Sylvie and Bruno* period. And the age in which he lived, a pre-Freudian era in which more modern meanings of "repressions" or "integration" were unknown, made possible such a separation and that which resulted from it—the perfection of the *Alices*. (The **Snark** is already much more ambiguous.) It is a pattern that Mr. Eliot might almost envy, if only for its true Nonsense quality. He, in his Nonsense autobiography, describes his own features as being "of clerical cut," and it is remarkable how character after character in the plays is impelled towards Holy Orders. Mr. Eliot's difficulty is that nowadays religion and other such vital subjects cannot conveniently be affirmed and then closed off. One has to be Nonsense man, poet, and churchman all at once. Carroll's hippopotamus, secure in its Nonsense bounds, can remain of the earth, earthy; but Mr. Eliot's has got into the poetry and has somehow to be got into heaven. Yet despite the superficial differences between them, to us readers it is a great help to have one such quadruped by which to measure a second, and Carroll is the best point of reference we have for understanding Mr. Eliot.

Anyone interested in drawing minor parallels between earlier Eliot poems and the *Alices* will find material ready to hand: the reminiscence of the Frog Footman in "Portrait of a Lady" ("I shall sit here . . ."); the executioner who haunts *Sweeney Agonistes* among the playing cards as he does the Queen's croquet game; the echo, also in *Sweeney,* of the riddle of the Red King's dream ("If he was alive then the milkman wasn't"); the reversals or full stops of time in the two writers; the endless tea party, interminable as the Hatter's, in "Prufrock," "Portrait of a Lady," "Mr. Apollinax," "Hysteria," "A Cooking Egg," *The Waste Land* where the typist comes home at tea time, the first scene of *Family Reunion,* Skimbleshanks in *Old Possum,* till only the tea leaves are left in "The Dry Salvages"; and so on. These are not uninteresting, but they are very minor affairs. It is in the major poems, as it should be, that Carroll and Nonsense begin to be really helpful.

The Waste Land is comparable to the *Alices* and to them alone, as Mr. Eliot's nearest approach to pure Nonsense practice. He admits certain elements into his subject matter—myth, love, the poetry and beauty of the past— which are dangerous, but he employs classic Nonsense techniques to control them. Thus the fragmentation in the poem is not to be regarded, in this light, as a lament on our modern condition. It is the Nonsense poet's way of analyzing his subject matter into discrete parts, "one and one and one" as the Red Queen says, to make it workable in Nonsense terms. The same is true of the sterility the poem deals with. This, too, is the Nonsense poet carefully setting up the conditions necessary for the exercise of his special art. To hold the whole poem together, the two classic Carroll frameworks are employed, playing cards and chess, the digits and moves of a game substituted for those dangerous and un-Nonsense entities, human relationships. The Nonsense rules procure the necessary working conditions—detachment of mind from subject matter, analysis of material, manipulation of patterns of unfused images. Into this careful systematics, highly intellectual as Nonsense is, even potentially subversive material can be fitted and held, and the result is probably Mr. Eliot's masterpiece.

With the *Four Quartets,* the situation is made more difficult by what is now the poet's increasing emphasis upon unitive subjects, particularly love and religion. We need here, as points of reference, the *Alices* and the *Snark,* with a glance forward to *Sylvie and Bruno.* The over-all Nonsense control of *The Waste Land* has gone; in its place we have Nonsense procedures still operating, but used now as defenses against particular dangers. We will consider four of these: poetry, words in their nonlogical functions, and the two central images, roses and dancing.

Traditional forms of poetry are admitted into the *Quartets* from time to time, with their complement of metaphor and nonlogical speech so antithetical to Nonsense. When they appear, however, they tend, as in the *Alices,* to be pounced on and immediately subjected to critical analysis. See Part II of "East Coker," for instance, where the passage "What is the late November doing" is followed at once by

> That was a way of putting it—not very satisfactory.
> A periphrastic study in a worn-out poetical fashion.

So Alice says to the Caterpillar after repeating some verses, "Not quite right, I'm afraid. . . . Some of the words have got altered," and receives the reply, "It is wrong from beginning to end." Poetry is dangerous to Nonsense, even if unsatisfactory, even if parodied, and it is as well to reduce it to criticism at once. No one interested in the present hypertrophied condition of literary criticism should overlook the importance of the Caterpillar and Humpty Dumpty as spiritual ancestors of this development. . . .

A rose is about as dangerous an image for Nonsense as could be imagined. It implies an immense range of living company—beauty, growth, the body, sex, love. Roses in Nonsense will need special treatment, and Carroll begins to operate on his immediately, with pots of paint wielded by playing-card people or animated numbers. Mr. Eliot adopts a different but no less effective technique, sterilizing his rose in his turn, at the beginning and end of "Little Gidding," with ice and fire which cancel one another out and wipe away with them the living notion of the rose, leaving only a counter or cipher, suitable for Nonsense, behind.

Lastly, there is the dance, a dangerously living and bodily image, too. Carroll's attitude to it is always insecure. The cavorting Mock Turtle and Gryphon are clumsy and tread on Alice's feet; three times round the mulberry bush is enough for Tweedledum and Tweedledee. Carroll's most revealing dance occurs in one of his letters, where he compares his own dancing to a rhinoceros and hippopotamus executing a minuet together. Carroll is the reluctant dancing hippo. Mr. Eliot is a reluctant dancer also in the *Quartets,* even though dancing is the way to heaven. The dance is constrained: "At the still point, there the dance is," restricted as the circling round the Mad Hatter's table or the crocodile walking up his own forehead in *Sylvie and Bruno.* The best comment on this inhibition of free movement comes in the *Snark.* "In my beginning is my end or say that the end precedes the beginning"; it runs in "East Coker" and "Burnt Norton," and the Bellman, familiar with this condition, describes it as being "snarked," a state when "the bowsprit got mixed with the rudder sometimes." Movement in Nonsense is admitted only to be annulled, if the control and pattern are to be preserved.

Where then can we go now? It seems only towards *Sylvie and Bruno, The Cocktail Party, The Confidential Clerk.* There is already a surprising similarity between Part II of "The Dry Salvages,"

> Where is there an end of it, the soundless wailing,
> The silent withering of autumn flowers

and so on, and the prose poem with which *Sylvie and Bruno* ends, with its chilly mists and wailing gusts over the ocean, its withered leaves of a blighted hope, and the injunction, to the hero sailing for India, "Look Eastward!" as the Eliot poem bears us on to Krishna and Arjuna. Yet this is not Mr. Eliot's last word as Nonsense poet. He will talk about love and God and heaven in the later *Quartets* and plays, as Carroll does in *Sylvie and Bruno Concluded,* but this is not the answer, nor the way in which the hippopotamus can enter heaven. Mr. Eliot's answer is more direct and much more surprising; one hesitates, with any writer calling his book *Old Possum,* to suggest that it seems also largely unconscious. He implies that the way for a Nonsense poet to reach heaven is by Nonsense itself; and so we have *Old Possum's Book of Practical Cats.*

Phyllis Greenacre, M.D.   (essay 1966)

SOURCE: "On Nonsense," in *Psychoanalysis—A General Psychology.* International Universities Press, Inc., 1966, pp. 655-77.

[*In the following excerpt, Greenacre discusses nonsense and aggression as they are manifested in the works of Lewis Carroll and Edward Lear.*]

This paper will deal with nonsense and its relation to aggression and anxiety. It draws largely on the study of the nonsense of Lewis Carroll's Wonderland and Looking Glass countries, and somewhat less on that of the nonsense rhymes of Edward Lear. But before discussing the nonsense of these two authors we must first approach the question of what we mean by nonsense anyway. Very many definitions of nonsense have been given by the various critics of this field of literature. Of these only a few will be mentioned.

Emile Caemmerts (1925) points out that the general opinion of nonsense is that it consists of anything which displeases you or any statement with which you emphatically disagree, and that there are as many different nonsenses as there are individual opinions, so that it would be a hopeless task to distinguish between them, or to attempt to draw up a list of them. He argues further that what is nonsense for one person is very often sense for another—similar to the situation of one man's meat being another man's poison. Someone else has remarked in regard to science fiction and scientific theory that yesterday's scientific nonsense becomes today's scientific sense. . . .

Caemmerts then proceeds to give his own version of poetical nonsense, seeing it as arising from the same matrix as nursery rhymes, viz., the "innocent exuberance of childhood." He believes that writers of nonsense, referring especially to Lear, Carroll, and Kipling . . . wrote their nonsense out of memory of this joyously restless state of childhood and to please child friends of later life. This point of view would certainly oppose the theory that many of the Mother Goose rhymes originated as slyly disguised political satires which only later were incorporated into the lore of childhood. . . . Carroll's friendly relationship to children, almost exclusively to little girls—for he had an open aversion to little boys—was an exceedingly complex one. "Stuff and Nonsense," or "Fiddlesticks," has a considerable excluding aggression in it, like Mrs. Preemby's declaration of nonsense. It is an attitude which may become playfully elaborated when it has gone through another stage of development, achieving some degree of emotional detachment. But Mrs. Preemby could never achieve this and so was always stuck with an argument.

Another writer, Elizabeth Sewall, an English philosopher dealing with the *Field of Nonsense* (1952), goes to considerable length to show that nonsense is an intellectual game with its own rules, and is really a manifestation of the mind's force toward order, and the establishment of order over a counterpull to disorder. Having a stance just the opposite of Mrs. Preemby's, she seems to take nonsense entirely away from any emotional connections. She sees in the extraordinary meticulousness of both Lear and Carroll only an indication of their spontaneous pleasure in "being that way," since they were not compelled by *external* events to behave in this fashion. She seems to see mental health and balance in terms of derangement or no derangement, and scouts the idea that there was emotional disturbance of any importance in either man, ignoring the painfully disturbing symptoms associated with Lear's severe epilepsy during his adult life, and his constant anxiety about money. The fact that neither man married or was known to have a sexual interest in any adult woman appears to her insignificant. The nonsense of these men, she says, represents their sanity and reason. I shall return to look at this from a little different angle later.

Max Eastman (1936), looking at nonsense more from the angle of the effect of the finished product than from that of the process, says that nonsense is only effective if it pretends to make sense, i.e., if in some way it gives the illusion of being sensible. It appears, then, that part of its effectiveness has an element of the practical joke in it; one laughs at oneself for reaching for something that isn't there. Koestler (1964), who quotes Eastman and himself writes only briefly of nonsense, turns his attention at once then to tickling; and it seems possible that there is a connecting link between the two: both are threats that were only play after all.

This discussion will deal chiefly with the nonsense of Carroll in the *Alice* books, but will rely also on the ***Hunting of the Snark*** and the Songs of the Mad Gardener in *Sylvie and Bruno.* No one can talk about nonsense in any serious, sensible way, however, without considering the nonsense rhymes in the *Book of Nonsense* and *More Nonsense* by that master, Edward Lear. These two, Lear and Carroll, are certainly the outstanding professors and practitioners of nonsense. But here may we add the name of another literary man whose work would not generally be considered nonsensical at all, but only gruesome, eerie, and nightmarish. Yet his writings, especially *Metamorphosis, Amerika,* and *The Trial,* contain many of the ingredients of nonsense, without the detachment which permits comical effectiveness. I refer to Franz Kafka.

What do *we* mean by nonsense? Obviously, the word means no sense, i.e., without sense. This would seem to be clear enough. But *sense* is not so clear-cut in meaning as one might at first think. *Sense* at once suggests the intellect and reason, and nonsense would then consist in words or actions which convey an absurd meaning or no meaning at all. But sense also refers to the ability to receive and to respond to stimuli. The senses considered as a total bodily function are distinguished from intellect and movement. Thus the word *senseless* may mean unconscious, or it may refer to something unreasonable, foolish, and apparently meaningless in content. My scrutiny of the nonsense of Lear and Carroll will encompass both meanings of the word *sense,* for it seems to me that the intellect and reason emerge developmentally from the hinterland of the bodily senses, and that the separation of the two areas of functioning is never complete. This becomes more obvious with the examination of the content of the nonsense productions which critics like the philosophically minded Sewall would rule out of the field altogether.

It is an interesting fact that the term nonsense, except when said in a very emphatic tone of voice, is rarely applied to a production without some qualifying adjective. There is "just nonsense," "mere nonsense," "utter nonsense," "sheer nonsense," or, in the extreme, "absolute nonsense." These qualifying adjectives convey the subjective judgment of the spectator or listener, and go all the way from a relatively mild feeling: "I don't understand what you are talking about (or doing). It does not seem reasonable to me," to the extreme judgment of "absolute nonsense," implying: "What you are saying is so unheard of, so generally incomprehensible, that it disturbs me unbearably unless I think that no one can be expected to understand it." Now, absolute nonsense, with the meaning of a complete elimination of any kind of coherence or even cohesiveness of content, and associated with an inability to receive or respond to stimuli from others—the elimination of any degree of relationship whatsoever would mean such a state of disorganization and psychophysical disintegration as to be scarcely compatible with life itself. Like its extreme opposite, absolute perfection, it then becomes static, isolated, and approaches lifelessness. When Lear speaks of his rhymes as "absolute and pure nonsense"—as he does in the introduction to the book *More Nonsense* (1872)—he is using the phrase not to indicate the degree of nonsensical quality, but rather to indicate that his nonsense does not contain any hidden attack on any specific individuals or any sly political satire.

In studying nonsense from the productions of Lear and Carroll, we have to realize further that neither of these men could possibly have come very close to absolute nonsense, not only because of the practical inaccessibility of that chaotic, disorganized, anarchic state except for a babbling idiot incapable of writing or of definite language formation; but because both Lear and Carroll were gifted men, perhaps men of genius. This in itself gives an obligatory inner organization with some extra capacity for rhythm and patterning both in awareness and in execution. Absolute nonsense is incapable of representing itself.

The garden variety of judgment of nonsense may represent the frame of mind of the spectator or listener rather than having much to do with the product itself. Thus, as in Mrs. Preemby's case, it may show rather the antipathy of prejudice with an *accompanying* aggressive wish to rid oneself of the disquieting intrusion. The aggression then may be largely on the part of the spectator, although it is felt by him as a justified reaction to the aggressively nonsensical intruder who must be banished. But with Lear

and Carroll, the object of the nonsense and the subjective audience are essentially the same person—the author of it. The public is only taken in by accident, as it were.

Lear was a painter of considerable ability, and Carroll was a mathematician and an Oxford don, although trained to be a clergyman. Neither made the writing of nonsense his primary profession, and both were puzzled or even annoyed at winning fame more through their nonsense than through their serious professions. Charles L. Dodgson, the Oxford don, was so annoyed, in fact, that at one time he disclaimed knowledge of Lewis Carroll and refused to receive mail directed to Carroll at his, Mr. Dodgson's, address. Carroll's nonsense works have been translated into some thirty to forty different languages, and it is reported that in English-speaking countries the *Alice* books rank next to the Bible in the frequency with which they are quoted. Almost the whole world knows some, at least, of Lear's rhymes, though relatively few know anything of his painting. . . .

In each of the *Alice* stories there is a central theme, though it is almost lost sight of in the nonsensical meanderings of its pursuits. According to Carroll, Alice is a little girl of 7½, though she talks and acts more like a prepuberty child of 9. The aim of Alice's adventures in the first book is to find a secret subterranean garden, toward which she has been led by her curiosity in following a white rabbit, dressed as a gentleman, whom she sees as he disappears into a hole in the ground. In the pursuit of this goal she wanders through a wonderland confused and bewildered. She is never quite sure who she is and time itself is quite mixed up and runs one way and another. In fact, nothing, not even ideas and knowledge, remains reliable. She thinks of bats in connection with rats and mice and then finds herself in a confused doubting "Do rats eat bats? Do bats eat cats?" and a little later she is wondering whether she is herself or Ada who has ringlets or Mabel who is rather stupid. She is constantly growing up or shrinking down and is fearful that she may go out like the flame of a candle, but what is the flame like after it is out? She encounters animals who behave like human beings and human beings who behave like savages. Her hands and feet grow so large and distant that they seem to have identities separate from her own, and she considers sending a letter in order to communicate with her right foot, but realizes that she is talking nonsense. Her voice is so strangely hoarse that it too hardly belongs to her. There are many tears in Wonderland, and once the diminutive Alice nearly drowns in a pool of tears wept by Alice the Great. In general, however, she maintains a somewhat addled philosophical poise through all the faultfinding, bickering, and threats of open savagery. Decapitation is the favorite threat of those in power.

No one laughs much. But the Cheshire cat grins in his superior fashion since he can withstand decapitation by allowing his own body to disappear leaving his grinning head, which in turn fades with the grin, the last part to go. The story begins by Alice being bored at the book her sister is reading to her until she drops to sleep, and dropping to sleep with boredom, even in the thick of an argument, remains one of the retreats of minor character in the tale. At one point, when with a spurt of growth Alice finds herself so large that the room will no longer contain her and she is pressed against all its sides, she considers that when she is (really) grown up she will write a book about herself describing all this. This evidently is the task undertaken then by Lewis Carroll, even though Alice herself could not decide whether it was better to risk growing up to old womanhood or remaining young and doing other people's bidding, even that of cats and rabbits. Then again in a diminished phase when she is very small indeed, she gets into an argument with a caterpillar who, seated on a toadstool smoking a hookah, defends the idea that metamorphous changes need not be upsetting. He admonishes her to curb her temper and directs her to recite that erotically suggestive rhyme about Father William. Soon she is growing so big again that a wandering pigeon mistakes her elongated neck for a serpent.

In her protest that she is only a little girl (and she has jiggled herself small again) she continues to look for the secret garden, and then comes to a diminutive house in the wood. Here she encounters a grotesque version of maternity, in a ferocious duchess who is impatiently nursing her baby while she sings "Speak roughly to your little boy . . ." as she is anxious to be off to a croquet game with the Queen. Complete pandemonium soon reigns. The baby's nose is cut off by a flying saucepan hurled by an enraged cook. The baby himself is thrown into Alice's arms, but quickly turns into a pig and runs off into the woods. The Cheshire cat appears or disappears, as the case may be, and directs Alice to the Mad Hatter, who quickly lands her in the Mad Tea Party, all of whose members are male. She is no better off here, for all her remarks are turned around and used against her until she doesn't know the meaning of anything she has said. The Hatter's remarks seemed to have no sort of meaning at all and yet certainly were in English. (Here Alice certainly seems to agree with Max Eastman's views about effective nonsense.) Confusion is piled on confusion. Time and size are mixed up individually and together. Alice is accused of having beaten Time in her music lessons, and the Hatter is threatened with decapitation for having murdered Time. But in the end Alice does find the door to the secret garden and enters.

This, the royal garden, is as chaotically angry a place as the Duchess's kitchen had been. A rampageous croquet game is in progress. All humans, regardless of sex, age, or rank, look exactly alike from the rear, as they are really animated playing cards. The balls and the mallets, however, are animals who contribute to the general anarchy by doing whatever they please while the Queen threatens decapitation to anyone who displeases her. The Cheshire cat materializes out of his grin and escapes execution, though the King argues that anything that has a head can be beheaded, and the Queen threatens to execute everyone unless a way can be found to execute the cat. The game ends with everyone, even the wickets, being taken into custody, leaving Alice alone with the King and Queen while the King whispers a pardon to all whom the Queen has executed or imprisoned. Alice is taken in charge by

the Gryphon, a hideous composite of lion, eagle, and dragon, who explains to her that the executions are only the Queen's fancy. "They never execute anybody you know." After an interlude of a satirical and whimsically nonsensical discussion of education with the Gryphon and the Mock Turtle (who suffers from sorrow which is only fancy since he is only a *mock* turtle and the source of Mock turtle soup), the messily confused day ends in a trial. The King with the Queen by his side is an uneasy judge fearful lest his own crown may fall off. The Knave of Hearts is being tried for stealing tarts. But execution is threatened to nervous witnesses and then for good measure to nonnervous ones as well. A general atmosphere of execution prevails.

Alice feels herself suddenly growing up, getting too big for all this nonsense. When she at last is called as a witness she has so far outgrown any trepidation that she tips over the jury box with the edge of her skirt and has to pick up the spilled jurors and return them to the box for the trial to go on. Alice's testimony that she knew nothing whatsoever about the business is considered important or unimportant, as the case may be, until an argument arises about it, and Alice herself is ordered out of the court as being too high and mighty. But before she leaves, an incriminating bit of evidence against the knave is discovered in an unsigned set of verses not in the knave's handwriting which prove beyond the shadow of a doubt that the knave is a dishonest man. For why else would he have not signed his name and further gone to the trouble of imitating someone else's handwriting! Alice declares that the verses have not one atom of meaning in them, but the Queen demands the sentence first and the evidence later, while the King thinks that he detects some meaning somewhere. Alice, now full size, declares the whole thing stuff and nonsense, while the Queen shrieks, "Off with her head," and Alice retorts, "Who cares for you, you are nothing but a pack of cards!" Whereupon they all rise up in the air and come flying down at her. She wakes to find her sister brushing away dead leaves that have fluttered into her face. And in the epilogue, when Alice tells her sister the dream, she herself begins to dream Alice's dream and then, half awake, muses that this little sister of hers will soon be a grown woman with children of her own.

I shall not go to as much length in describing *Alice Through the Looking Glass*. It is a less spontaneous production and seems more consciously contrived than *Wonderland,* almost as though Alice herself had become a little more settled. It too is played against the background of a game involving a royal family, the game of chess in which the characters are now three- rather than two-dimensional, and the sexes can be distinguished even from the rear. Alice's aim in this game is to become a queen. There is not quite as much riotous confusion as in *Wonderland,* but the bipolarity of constant doubt is paramount. Many experiences appear in opposites, and many characters are in pairs: Alice and her mirror image, the black kitten and the white one, the Red King and Queen, and the White King and Queen, Tweedledum and Tweedledee, Haigha and Hatta, etc. Alice's size does not change so much as was true in *Wonderland,* but the creatures around her are often outsized, especially the insects; and space and time have a way of extending and contracting themselves that is bewildering.

In the end Alice does find a crown on her head, but her maturity is at once challenged by the Red and White Queens, who then succumb to the fatigue of their own arguments and fall asleep on her shoulder. In the last scene, a coronation banquet is given for Alice who arrives late and is scolded like a bad child. Nothing can be eaten, however, as the food is all animated, and the various dishes behave like guests as soon as they are introduced to Alice. The whole party ends in a riot with the White Queen disappearing into the soup tureen, while the mutton sits in a chair. Alice and all the plates and the candles fly up in the air while the guests lie down in the remaining dishes. Alice completes the destruction by pulling the tablecloth off and dumping everything left onto the floor. She again awoke to find it all a dream.

The Red Queen whom she thought she was scolding for having instigated the mischief turned out to be the Black Kitten whom she had been admonishing for tangling up the yarn at the time she had gone to sleep. In talking to the Black Kitten (alias the Red Queen) Alice gives a valuable clue to the meaning of all this nonsense, when she says, "Let us consider, who it was dreamed it all. You see Kitty, it must have been either me or the Red King. He was part of my dream—but then I was part of his dream too. *Was* it the Red King, Kitty? You were his wife, my dear, so you ought to know—*do* help to settle it!" It may be worth noting, too, that in *Wonderland*, Dinah (Alice's cat) does not actually appear unless we are to consider her reincarnated as the Cheshire cat—and there is no mention of kittens. In the *Looking Glass* world, it is Alice's play with the kittens that initiates her adventurous exploration. Perhaps we may guess that the kittens or the thoughts of kittens have arrived in Alice's life between *Wonderland* and *Looking Glass*. But I shall have more to say of content later.

Carroll's nonsense rhymes are quite different from Lear's in form. They are generally interspersed through his stories, and many among them are parodies. He did not use the *aabba* rhyme form; and his single-verse rhymes, appearing mostly as the Songs of the Mad Gardener in *Sylvie and Bruno*, achieve a comical effect largely through the utter incongruity of the fused pictures and ideas presented.

Thus the rhymes:

> He thought he saw an Elephant
> 　That practiced on a fife.
> He looked again and found it was
> 　A letter from his wife.
> 'At length, I realize,' he said
> 　'The bitterness of Life!'

or:

> He thought he saw an Argument
> 　That proved he was the Pope:

He looked again and found it was
　A bar of Mottled Soap.
'A fact so dread,' he faintly said
　'Extinguishes all hope!'

　　　　　　　　　　　　　(from *Sylvie and Bruno*)

These rhymes spoof the dilemma, critical though it may be, by making it ridiculous, and the rhythm and utter absurdity of the solution have a stimulating, almost staccato effect. This is different from the returning monotony of Lear's last lines in his limericks and is also in contrast to the word distortions and creations of new words which reach their height in the **"Jabberwocky."** This is not only written backward in mirror writing, but it contains twenty-six newly coined words in its five stanzas.

What are the ingredients in the picture of nonsense? The feeling of nonsense materialized by Lear and Carroll has a general background of confusion against which a central bewildered explorer struggles with the problems of life. One aspect of the main problem is that of maintaining a sense of his own identity. With this in jeopardy, there can be no definite decision about which course to take, what road to pursue, or even whether to move forward, go backward, or attempt to stay where he is. This uncertainty of the identity is felt variously not only concerning the self and the own body, but also about all the elements (animate and inanimate) of the environment, which are generally anthropomorphized as well. Activity is the order of every situation, as is shown endlessly in Lear's drawings and in Carroll's prose. This multiplies the confusion since no one—whether Alice or the animals she meets or the path she travels—seems able to keep straight who or what he is; is supposed to be doing; or how it can be done. Even the words get out of hand and cannot be relied upon. A variety of verbal switches are utilized with punning based on klang associations, alliterations, spoonerisms, malapropisms, portmanteau condensations, neologisms, etc. Humpty-Dumpty tries to master words by making them mean whatever he wants them to, but very often, in the struggle, the words themselves win out and seem to go their own way. In other words, even words lose their identity in losing their uniqueness of form and meaning, and seem to run off in various directions. Sometimes the word self-consciously maintains two opposite meanings (as indeed may be the case even with well-behaved words), but in the *Looking Glass* especially, opposites seem like nearly identical twins who are bound in an eternal wrangle as in the case of Tweedledum and Tweedledee.

The portmanteau word is a descriptive phrase originating with Carroll, who applies it to a combination of a number of words in one single one which contains at least the remnants of them all. Thus just as the *snark* is a monstrous combination of animals, so the word itself, like a composite photograph, contains snake, shark, snail, and probably many others. **"Jabberwocky,"** too, is such a portmanteau word, designating a terrifying animal composed of several others. There is one word play used by both Carroll and Lear which has never been given a special name. It consists in the snapping off the end of one word and adding it to the word next to it. Thus in **"Jabberwocky,"** the "slithy toves did gyre and gimble in the wabe." As it is explained later, *wabe* comes from "*way-be*fore" and "*way-be*hind" the sundial in the garden. Lear spoke of a "sill kankerchief," "a nempty stomach," etc. But he was in any case an inveterate tamperer with words, combining phonetic spelling with colloquialism in a way which may make sense to the ear but is grotesquely unfamiliar, when printed, to greet the eye.

A certain compulsiveness appears in Lear's punning, for his journals and letters are heavy with it. To me, at least, it becomes tiresome in its monotonous cuteness, as though it were a repetitive plea not to be taken seriously, and not to be held responsible. In *Looking Glass* in which accusation and trial seem always in the air (and the trial has actually taken place in *Wonderland*) the compulsive nature of the punning is clearly indicated. While Alice finds herself riding in a railroad carriage over the chessboard of life with a variety of animals dressed as humans, as fellow travelers, she hears a hoarse voice down the car a way and thinks to herself that it sounds like a horse. At the same time a very small voice close to her ear says, "You might make a joke of that—something about 'horse' and 'hoarse' you know." When presently she wishes that she could go back to the wood she has just left, the same little voice echoed, "You might make a joke on *that,* something about 'you would if you could, you know.'" It was a gnat that had lodged in her ear and was directing her travels punwise. And just as a bee she had seen only a while ago had become an elephant diving into enormous flowers with his great proboscis, so the gnat flew into a tree and became the size of a chicken.

Tampered-with words resulting in distortions of their form and meaning are obviously closely bound up with problems of their identity, whether these have to do with flora, fauna, or the human species, and involve in turn changes in size and apparent distortions of part or all of the body. Gross changes in size overtake Alice and many of the animals whom she encounters. But since these change individually rather than in an epidemic wave, there are many discrepancies and incongruities. In Lear's rhymes and stories there are more distortions of body shape with accentuation or a practical loss of some body part than changes which involve the entire body. There is not the same fluidity of form as occurs in Carroll's productions. In Lear indeed the body distortions are much more apparent in the drawings than in the rhymes.

The basic sexual identity of the characters is maintained at least in outline by both nonsense writers. Alice does not change into a boy, nor does she behave like a boy; and there is no frank change from one sex to the other. . . . But there is a thinly disguised set of sexual problems in Alice's quest for the secret garden and for queenship. Her dilemma is rather: "What does it mean to grow up, be a woman and have children? How do the two sexes really get together? Is it after all an enviable state to be grown up?" At times it is as though she were saying, "What is happening to my body anyway? It is getting out of hand in its demands on me, and I can't stop it, or can I?" Older people whether men or women are, on the whole, unappe-

tizing and as unpredictable as children in Alice's worlds. But one must remember that Carroll was next to the oldest of eleven children, and a crowded parsonage may well have been tempestuous. . . .

Lear much more openly than Carroll indicated his feeling of inadequacy as a man. Carroll seemed to side-step masculine goals in many ways and identify with the pre-puberty girl who was doubtful but inquisitive about growing up.

A last major ingredient of the nonsense picture, and one which is also part of the identity complex, has to do with the loss of body parts, either in actual fact or threatened as accident or punishment. In Lear's rhymes this is a less frequent occurrence than it is in Carroll's writings. Lear describes the Old Man of the Nile who loses his thumbs as the result of sharpening his nails with a file, and another old man who just escapes catastrophe when he is offered a hatchet with which to kill a flea that is biting him sorely. Then there is the famous Pobble that has no toes, as well as one young person who loses her head by its being fanned off by a too-attentive uncle. Lear also works this theme of loss in reverse in his accentuation or enlargement of body parts and members. It is perhaps most dramatic in his nonsense song of the Dong who fell in love with a Jumbly girl and so grieved when she sailed away and left him that what little sense he had in his head also left him. Consequently, as he wandered disconsolately over the world hunting her, to light his way at night he made an artificial nose with a luminous light on its end, which served as a beacon. He became celebrated then as the Dong with the Luminous Nose.

Lear's "nonsense" pictures of body multilations and compensatory exaggerations are readily recognizable by anyone familiar with the psychology of the unconscious as expressions of severe castration fear which is being expressed directly or in an extreme form of denial.

In the *Alice* books, this is presented differently. Decapitation and extinction by fading out are more frequent threats than those of damage to or loss of a body part. To be sure the baby does lose its nose, sliced off by a flying pan; and the extinction of the Cheshire cat proceeds bit by bit rather than through a massive fading. Decapitation in a less corporeal form is suggested too by Alice's recurrent fear of loss of memory even of her own name and whereabouts, so that she is frequently testing her own mental functioning.

. . . . The thread of the stories in the *Alice* books shows quite clearly the major crises of growing up, with attempts to solve the problems of sexual identity and identification. But the fears of castration and annihilation are so vivid and repetitive as to suggest chronic anxiety of panic proportions. All this is in the general setting of oedipal guilt; but is complicated by the persistence of infantile rage in the case of Carroll, and by real epileptic attacks in Lear. What is striking, however, is that the situations which might produce panic are presented in so exaggerated and confused a way as to appear ridiculous. The panic is quickly muted. The beheading is anticipated on the scale of the French Revolution or worse, only actually "They never behead anyone," and it is all in the Queen's mind anyway. Certainly the sadistic aggression, which is a component of all anxiety and especially of that arising in anticipation of cruelty, is then compounded and directed against the self in guilt—the conscience is on a veritable rampage, until the voice of reason steps in and says, "This is all mental, a dream, a game." In this sense Sewall is right—that with the ability to get some distance, the force of reason prevails over the destructive forces. This control by the rarified counteraggression of reason—the superiority of the mind over primitive instincts—is personified by the Cheshire cat sitting aloft, grinning a superior (rather than a merry) grin, which is the last to go.

But there may be another determinant in the fear of beheadment, to be found in the nature of extreme rage. The enraged person then "loses his head"—he loses his sense of direction and becomes disorganized. He acts, we say, like a chicken with its head cut off. Some think indeed that the epileptic convulsion is intrinsically related to and represents repressed rage. This is a state very close to absolute nonsense. But the ability to write, or to paint, or to reproduce this in a communicable form saves the person . . . from being devastated by it. It is my suspicion that communicating nonsense always requires considerable talent. This is a way of saying that talent provides ways of leaving the purely individual personal experiences, pains, and pressures of life; and through channels of empathic association not open to the less gifted, talent permits the maintenance of a distance from which to hear the collective or even the cosmic beat or see the outlines of organization and feel relationships in that which would otherwise be personally devastating. Communicated nonsense is a defense against destructive forces. But it may be more than a defense in that its very ability to maintain an equilibrium against such odds contains a constructive force offering, at the very least, continuity of existence rather than complete annihilation or disintegration. One might liken it to the expectation of rebirth which sometimes accompanies the intention of suicide. . . .

While the typical fetishist has always to have an object which will be a phallic representative for him if he is to function sexually at all, there is no evidence that Carroll had any sexual interest in any woman, except his lost mother. But just as the fetishist must have his fetish not only for sexual adequacy but for the narcissistic completion of his body image, so Carroll, I suspect, in his voyeurism and intensive interest in prepuberty girls was repetitively confirming his identification with them, thus denying his need for masculine genital adequacy. But this very denial could not help but contribute to a sense of unreality and alienation from his actual body and from the pursuits of family life which constitute so much of the emotional foundation for most of us. It permitted, however, the development of a defensive critical distance in which a sense of nonsense could develop and flourish.

Raymond J. Rundus   (essay date 1967)

SOURCE: "O Frabjous Day!: Introducing Poetry," in *English Journal,* Vol. 56, No. 7, October 1967, pp. 958-63.

[*In the following excerpt, Rundus argues that Carroll's "Jabberwocky" has poetic virtues within the traditional context of the English poetic canon.*]

> Take care of the sense and the sounds will take care of themselves.
>
> —*Alice's Adventures in Wonderland*

> "Contrariwise," continued Tweedledee, "if it was so, it might be; and if it were so, it would be; but as it isn't, it ain't. That's logic."
>
> —*Alice Through the Looking-Glass*

> "But 'glory' doesn't mean 'a nice knock-down argument,'" Alice objected.

> "When *I* use a word," Humpty Dumpty said, in rather a scornful tone, "it means just what I choose it to mean—neither more nor less."

> "The question is," said Alice, "whether you *can* make words mean so many different things."

> "The question is," said Humpty Dumpty, "which is to be master—that's all."
>
> —*Alice Through the Looking-Glass*

To the linguist, to the semanticist, and to the folklorist, Lewis Carroll's **"Jabberwocky,"** from *Alice's Adventures in Wonderland,* has an inescapable attractiveness. (The poem is reprinted here for those who may have forgotten it or who may be unfamiliar with it—God forbid!)

In the first stanza of this piece of "nonsense verse," the linguist finds a unique capsule illustration of syntactic structure and a typical pattern of phonemic/morphemic signals ("nonsense" words italicized):

> 'Twas *brillig,* and the *slithy toves*
>   Did *gyre* and *gimble* in the *wabe;*
> All *mimsy* were the *borogoves,*
>   And the *mome raths outgrabe.*

The linguist can readily point out that here Carroll has retained the function words of the English language (determiners, prepositions, expletives, conjunctions, auxiliary verbs) while filling the remaining slots with "nonsense" words whose grammatical function is signalled syntactically and/or by inflection. Thus "gyre" and "gimble" are both clearly parts of a compound predicate because of their position following the common English auxiliary "did" and their being linked by the coordinate "and." Syntactically, "toves" must be a noun because it follows both the determiner "the" and "slithy," which is given adjectival force because of its "-y" suffix, and also because "toves" precedes and clearly governs the compound predicate. Additionally, the linguist can remark that this same word has the inflection /z/, one of the three most common noun plural markers in English (the others being /s/ and /əz/).

The semanticist (or semiotist) also finds much in the first stanza upon which to wax philosophical. He can reflect upon the portmanteau weight of many of the words ("slithy"="slither"+"slimy"? Perhaps also "lithe"? An entire catalogue of sl- words can be discussed) and suggest that "brillig" indicates the kind of day it is, and not a dismal, gray one, because "brillig" suggests "brilliant" and "bright." And after all the toves would not be gyring and gimbling ("gambolling"?) on an unpleasant day, would they?

Finally, the folklorist can see in **"Jabberwocky"** either a seminal fairy tale or the structure of a "quest" motif. Or perhaps both. Clearly, a father-figure of some sort is giving a warning to the hero (doubtless the youngest of three sons) in the second stanza:

> Beware the Jabberwock, my son,
> The jaws that bite, the claws, that
>   catch!
> Beware the Jubjub bird, and shun
> The frumious Bandersnatch!

But the youngest son, being strong, brave, and not overly impelled by his rather small ration of common sense, sets off anyway; and, in spite of all obstacles, he returns in triumph, even "galumphing," suggesting that if he lacks horse sense, he at least has sense enough to *use* a horse (or perhaps only behave like one, which would not be quite so admirable).

Or perhaps Carroll is giving us a sketch of a chivalric quest. Then the figure speaking in the second stanza is not the father but a feudal knight, an Arthur-figure, advising the bachelor knight of the dangers involved in the world beyond the castle. Then the Jabberwock, who has "eyes of flame," who comes "whiffling through the tulgey wood," is equivalent in status as an opponent to a fire-breathing dragon. (Since it "burbled as it came," we can well assume *some* sort of conflagration in its innards.) If we accept this convention, then we are involved in a mystical and magical world somewhat removed from the fairy-tale world, but one equally as fascinating.

But I seem to have digressed somewhat from my main concern. What, one may ask, does **"Jabberwocky"** have to do with the introducing of poetry, with which, as my title suggests, this paper ought to be concerned?

If the poem does offer such a wealth of material to the linguist, the semanticist, and the folklorist, is there anything left for the teacher seeking an effective way to introduce a poetry course, or a section of poetry in a grab-bag literature course? Here I violate mathematical principles to stress a point: the sum is more than the total of its parts.

Because the teacher of literature should *always* be a linguist and a semanticist and often even a folklorist, **"Jabberwocky"** offers a particularly unique and valuable experience to the student as he is being led into the treasure-house of poetry, the Taj Mahal of literature.

First, although the teacher of poetry is not likely to be a trained linguist, he is, in a different way, nearly as much concerned with sounds as the linguist. And he must also be a semanticist, aware of the richness of connotation and able to point it out to his students. He differs in one important respect: he is a linguist and a semanticist *simultaneously*. He is concerned with the *fusion* of sound and sense and must not here make the mistake of compartmentalizing, and so destroying the fusion that is there. He must recognize that he is approaching an entity on the printed page as static in form as Michelangelo's *Pietà*. If a dynamic experience is to be the result, it will result from the subtle interaction of poet, poem, and audience; the task of the teacher is to make that experience as dynamically charged for his students as possible. . . .

Writing now more pragmatically, I can demonstrate that **"Jabberwocky"** has specific values which qualify it as a touchstone in a poetry course.

For one, the poem can be shown to illustrate all three of the common modes of poetic discourse: lyric (descriptive), dramatic, and narrative. The first stanza (repeated as the last) is clearly lyric, describing a scene and establishing a mood or atmosphere for the subsequent story. The second and sixth stanzas are dramatic: the father-figure (or King Arthur-figure) is addressing the young hero in both stanzas, first warningly and then, upon the hero's return, joyously. The middle three stanzas are narrative, recounting the successful venture of the hero, culminating with the decapitation of the Jabberwock and the bringing of the grisly trophy home, much in the same manner that Beowulf brings the head of Grendel from his dam's lair to Heorot. Thus the poem can be classified, if so desired, as primarily narrative, but with lyric and dramatic elements.

Also as a touchstone poem to introduce poetry, **"Jabberwocky"** offers several characteristics that place it in the mainstream of much of the great body of English and American verse. (1) It is written in four-line stanzas, certainly the most common stanza length. (2) The prevailing rhythm is iambic, by far the dominant rhythm of both English and American poetry. (3) Alternating rhyme is used in most of the stanzas, and all of the rhyme used is masculine. (4) Tetrameter, along with pentameter the most common length of the English-language poetic line, is used throughout. (5) One may also point out that the form of stanzas three, five, and six, except for the lack of alternating trimeter, is identical to that of the prevailing early ballad stanza, still a popular stanza form.

Among other poetic devices that may be pointed out to students are alliteration, assonance, internal rhyme, figurative language, and onomatopoeia. Alliteration, for example, is evident in line two (*gyre* and *gimble*), line eleven (*Tum-*

tum tree), and line twenty-two (*beamish boy*). Assonance is especially remarkable in the repeated stanza through the sounds /i/ (br*i*ll*i*g, sl*i*thy, g*i*mble, m*i*msy) and /o/ (t*o*ves, b*o*r*o*goves, m*o*me) as, to even greater extent, is consonance, with /b/ (*b*rilling, gim*b*le, wa*b*e, *b*orogoves, out-gra*b*e), /g/ (brilli*g*, *g*yre, *g*imble, boro*g*oves, out*g*rabe), and /m/ (gi*m*ble, *m*i*m*sy, *m*ome). Internal rhyme is used in lines eleven (*he, tree*), seventeen (*two, through*), nineteen (*dead, head*), and twenty-three (*day, Callay*). And though it is difficult to distinguish figurative language in "nonsense verse," "eyes of flame" in line fourteen is probably metaphoric. The poem is especially rich in onomatopoetic technique, with such words as "whiffling," "burbled," "snicker-snack," "galumphing," "Callooh! Callay!" and "chortled" as prime examples.

Perhaps by now I have clearly established what value **"Jabberwocky"** has as a poem especially fit to introduce the student to the great depth and breadth of the poetry which has been composed in the English language.

Michael Holquist   (essay date 1969)

SOURCE: "What is a Boojum? Nonsense and Modernism," in *Yale French Studies,* Vol. 43, 1969, pp. 145-64.

[*In the following excerpt, Holquist argues that Carroll's work is essential to Modern Literature Studies and that it it exhibits all the tenets of modernism.*]

Because the question "What is a Boojum," may appear strange or whimsical, I would like to begin by giving some reasons for posing it. Like many other readers, I have been intrigued and perplexed by a body of literature often called modern or post-modern, but which is probably most efficiently expressed in a list of authors: Joyce, Kafka, Beckett, Nabokov, Borges, Genet, Robbe-Grillet— the list could be extended, but these names will probably suffice to suggest, if very roughly, the tradition I have in mind. The works of these men are all very dissimilar to each other. However, they seem to have something in common when compared not to themselves as a class, but to past literature. In casting about for specific terms which might define this vaguely felt sense of what was distinctive and yet shared in these works, two things constantly inhibited any progress. The first was one's sense of the ridiculous: aware of other attempts to define the modern, one knew that it was difficult to do so without becoming shrill or unduly chileastic. There is a group of critics, of whom Ihab Hassan and Nathan Scott might be considered representative, who insist on an absolute cut-off between all of previous history and the modern experience. They have in their characteristically humorless way taken seriously Virginia Woolf's remark that "on or about December, 1910 human nature changed." The work of these critics is easily recognized in the apocalyptic rhetoric which distinguishes their writing, and in the irresponsible application they make of terms derived from modern German philosophy. So one thing which made it difficult to get at distinctive features in

recent literature was the sense that it was very different from previous literature; and at the same time to recognize that it was not the end of history.

Another stumbling block, much less serious, was the constant recurrence of a phrase, which continually passed through my mind as I would read new works. I would read that Gregor Samsa woke up one morning to discover that he was an *Ungeziefer,* and immediately a ghostly refrain would be heard in my inner ear: "Aha, for the Snark *was* a Boojum, you see!" The same thing would happen when in *Lolita,* one discovered that all those strange men following Humbert were Quilty; or when reading in Gombrowicz that there was nothing to identity but the grimace [g ba]; and so on and on—one kept hearing "The Snark *was* a Boojum, you see." Pausing to reflect on this, the association of Lewis Carroll with modern literature seemed natural enough: his name figures in the first Surrealist manifesto (1924); Louis Aragon and André Breton write essays on Carroll; the former attempts a translation of *The Snark* (1929), the latter includes selections from Carroll in his *Anthologie de l'humour noir* (1939). Henri Parisot publishes a study of Carroll in 1952, in a series called, significantly, *Poetes d'aujourd hui;* Antonin Artaud tried to translate the Jabberwocky song; Joyce's use of portmanteau words, without which there would be no *Finnegans Wake,* is only one index of his high regard for Carroll; Borges admires Carroll, and Nabakov translates all of *Alice in Wonderland* into Russian. . . . But such obvious associations of Carroll with modern authors were not, it turned out, the reason why the *Boojum* kept raising its head as I read these men.

Finally, I picked up again, after many years, *The Hunting of the Snark*, and it soon became apparent why its final line kept popping up in connection with modern literature: Lewis Carroll's "agony in eight fits" was not only among the first to exemplify what is perhaps the most distinctive feature of modern literature, it did so more openly, more paradigmatically than almost any other text one knew. That is, it best dramatized the attempt of an author to insure through the structure of his work that the work could be perceived only as what it was, and not some other thing; the attempt to create an immaculate fiction, a fiction that resists the attempts of readers, and especially those readers who write criticism, to turn it into an allegory, a system equatable with already existing systems in thenon-fictive world. In what follows, I propose to outline this pattern of resistances in some detail as it exists in *The Hunting of the Snark*, and then, in a short conclusion to suggest the significance the pattern may have for readers of experimental modern fiction. But before looking at the poem itself, it might prove helpful to have some background information.

Lewis Carroll is, of course, a pseudonym. Characteristically for its bearer, it is an acrostic, based on an inversion of the re-Latinized forms of his two Christian names, Charles Lutwidge. Charles Lutwidge Dodgson is a fascinating object of study in himself, but in what follows I propose to mention only those aspects of his career which bear directly on the significance of the *Snark* poem.

Dodgson's whole career can best be understood as a quest for order, in some ways not unlike that of the White Knight in *Through the Looking Glass*. . . . It should be clear that Dodgson's life, in the large outline of his whole career and in the smallest details of his everyday existence, was dominated by the quest for a more perfect order. I will return to the significance of this point in a moment. But one further aspect of Dodgson/Carroll's existence should first be mentioned. It concerns the necessity of the slash or hyphen which one must use when referring to this author. That is, he is both Charles Lutwidge Dodgson, student (or Fellow) of Christ Church, and Lewis Carroll, author of books of nonsense.

. . . . Much has been made of this dichotomy between Mr. Carroll and Mr. Dodgson, and psychoanalytical studies, such as Phyllis Greenacre's *Swift and Carroll* (New York, 1955), suggest that the man was simply a schizophrenic who found a unique means of adjustment.

A more balanced view has been provided in what are probably the two best studies of Carroll: Elizabeth Sewell's *The Field of Nonsense* (London, 1952) and Alfred Liede's *Dichtung als Spiel* (Berlin, 1963, 2 vols.). These two critics have suggested that the split between Dodgson and Carroll is only an apparent dichotomy, quickly resolved if one sees that there is a common pursuit at the heart of each avatar, a *Drang nach Ordnung* which Dodgson/Carroll sought in mathematics and logic, in the strictly ordered life of an Oxford scholar, in the severely proper existence of a Victorian gentleman—and last but not least, in nonsense. In fact it was in nonsense that Dodgson's compulsion toward order found its most perfect expression. . . . I would further add that the most nonsensical nonsense which Carroll created is *The Hunting of the Snark*. There is an ascending progression toward the apex it represents in 1876, from the first Alice book (1865) through the second (1872); and all the work after the *Snark* was a decline, a falling away which is painful in the last books, (1889) and (1893).

The *Snark* is the most perfect nonsense which Carroll created in that it best exemplifies what all his career and all his books sought to do: achieve pure order. For nonsense, in the writings of Lewis Carroll, at any rate, does not mean gibberish; it is not chaos, but the opposite of chaos. It is a closed field of language in which the meaning of any single unit is dependent on its relationship to the system of the other constituents. . . . As has recently been said, "what we have learned from Saussure is that, taken singly, signs do not signify anything, and that each one of them does not so much express a meaning as mark a divergence of meaning between itself and other signs . . . The prior whole which Saussure is talking about cannot be the explicit and articulated whole of a complete language as it is recorded in grammars and dictionaries . . . the unity he is talking about is a unity of coexistence, like that of the sections of an arch which shoulder one another. In a unified whole of this kind, the learned parts of a language have an immediate value as a whole, and progress is made less by addition and juxtaposition than by the internal articulation of a function which in its own way is

already complete" [Merleau-Ponty, 1964]. My argument here is that *The Hunting of the Snark* constitutes such a whole; it is its own system of signs which gain their meaning by constantly dramatizing their differences from signs in other systems. The poem is, in a small way, its own language. This is difficult to grasp because its elements are bound up so closely with the syntax, morphology, and, fleetingly, the semantics of the English language.

. . . . Nonsense is a system in which, at its purest, words mean only one thing, and they get that meaning through divergence from the system of the nonsense itself, as well as through divergence from an existing language system. This raises, of course, the question of how one understands nonsense. It is a point to which I will return later; for the moment suffice it to say that if meaning in nonsense is dependent on the field it constructs, then the difference between nonsense and gibberish is that nonsense is a system which can be learned, as languages are learned. Thus the elements of the system can be perceived relationally, and therefore meaningfully, within it. Gibberish, on the other hand, is unsystematic.

What this suggests is that nonsense, among other things, is highly abstract. It is very much like the pure relations which obtain in mathematics, where ten remains ten, whether ten apples, ten horses, ten men, or ten Bandersnarks. This is an important point, and helps to define one relationship of nonsense to modernism. For it suggests a crucial difference between nonsense and the absurd. The absurd points to a discrepancy between purely human values and purely logical values. When a computer announces that the best cure for brain cancer is to amputate the patient's head, it is, according its system, being logical. But such a conclusion is unsettling to the patient and absurd to less involved observers. The absurd is a contrast between systems of human belief, which may lack all logic, and the extremes of a logic unfettered by human disorder. Thus the absurd is basically play with order and disorder. Nonsense is play with order only. It achieves its effects not from contrasting order and confusion, but rather by contrasting one system of order against another system of order, each of which is logical in itself, but which cannot find a place in the other. This distinction may help to account for the two dominant modes of depersonalization in recent literature. The absurd operates in the theater, where the contrast of human/non-human serves to exploit the presence of living actors on the stage. Nonsense, understood as defined above, dominates in prose fictions, where the book may become its own hermetic world, its own laboratory for systematic play, without the anthropomorphizing presence of actors. Thus the difference between, say, Beckett's *Waiting for Godot,* and the same author's *Comment c'est.*

Lewis Carroll is one of the most important figures in the movement Ortega y Gasset has called the "dehumanization of art." Kafka was not the first to reduce his hero to an integer; his K has an earlier analogue in one of the many essays Dodgson wrote on Oxford university issues. In 1865 the Regius chair in Greek fell vacant, and Dodgson used the occasion as an inspiration for a little paper called *A New Method of Evaluation of ð:* "Let U=the university, G=Greek, and P=professor. Then GP=Greek Professor; let this be reduced to its lowest terms and call the result I. Also let W=the work done, T=the times, p=giving payment, ð=the payment according to T, and S=the sum required; so that ð=S. The problem is to obtain a value for ð which shall be commensurate with W . . ."

"Let this be reduced to its lowest terms . . ." What Dodgson has expressed here in satire is a fundamental principle of his nonsense. For to reduce a word to one meaning is surely to reduce language to its lowest terms. The effect is to create a condition of what the Russian critic Viktor Shklovsky has called *ostranenie,* or "making it strange." But, again like so much modern literature, the effect in the **Snark** is not just to estrange a character or an event, but to estrange language itself. The technique is usually employed to render some familiar action unfamiliar by describing it naively, as if perceived for the first time. And this is what nonsense does to language. But it has a purpose for doing so, one which Merleau-Ponty has hinted at in another context: "If we want to understand language as an originating operation, we must pretend never to have spoken, submit language to a reduction without which it would once more escape us by referring us to what it signifies for us, [we must] *look* at [language] as deaf people look at those who are speaking." Or, it should be added, *look* at language as children or Lewis Carroll *look* at language.

In order to understand "language as an originating operation" we must, in other words, see it as a process, as a system in itself. By so doing, one becomes aware of its capacity to present us with something new. But in order to achieve this state of radical linguistic innocence it is necessary to put aside all expectations which arise from the habit of creating meaning through systems other than language. Perception has recently been defined as being "primarily the modification of an anticipation." The unfamiliar is always understood in terms of the familiar. This may seem a bit opaque, but it is really quite simple, and an operation we engage in and see performed every day around us. The most common example of it in literary criticism is found in the work of critics who bring to bear on any given text a procrustean system, the sort of thing T.S. Eliot had in mind when he referred to the "lemon-squeezer school" of criticism. A rigidly Freudian critic will never perceive a dark, wet setting as anything but a womb symbol, or an object which is slender and vertical as anything but a phallic symbol, regardless of the fact that, in the system of the text he is treating, the former is a bower in a forest, say, or the latter a cane or spear. This critic has not seen bowers or spears in the one system because his expectations are a function of another system. In order to see a new thing we must be able to recognize it as such, and this is done by the willed inhibition of systems we have learnt before coming upon the novel object, an act performed in the service of learning new systems. If this is not done in literary criticism, all texts become allegories. . . .

Critics of Lewis Carroll have possibly developed this allegorical urge to its ultimate limits. Phyllis Greenacre, a practicing psychiatrist, cannot forget that Dodgson loved to photograph little girls in the nude, with results for her interpretation of the Alice books which are as predictable as they are unfortunate. Louis Aragon, in a 1931 article in *Le Surréalisme au service de la révolution* does a Marxian interpretation of the Alice books, notable for such insights as: "in those shameful days of massacre in Ireland . . . human liberty lay wholly in the frail hands of Alice . . ." William Empson has combined Freudian and Marxian techniques in his reading, "The Child as Swain." Alice experiences birth trauma, and her tears become amniotic fluid; commenting on the famous scene at the end of *Through the Looking Glass* where Alice pulls off the tablecloth, sending plates, dishes, and guests hurtling to the floor, Empson remarks, "It is the High Table of Christ Church we must think of here . . ." A. L. Taylor makes the Alice books into that easiest to find of all allegories, the Christian. I have argued that the Alice books are less perfect nonsense than **The Hunting of the Snark**; therefore they are less hermetic, less systematic in their own right, and thus more porous to other systems.

But even the **Snark** has not excaped the allegorist. Alexander Taylor sees it as an anti-vivisectionist tract and Martin Gardner, in his otherwise fine annotated version, suggests a crude existentialist reading, full of *Angst's,* and in which the Boojum somehow becomes the atomic bomb [Gardner, 1962]. A former dean of the Harvard Business School has argued that the poem is "a satire on business in general, the Boojum a symbol of a business slump, and the whole thing a tragedy about the business cycle." I will not go into F. C. S. Schiller's theory, which states that the **Snark** is a satire on Hegelian philosophy, because Schiller presents his theory as a send-up. But even W. H. Auden has said that the **Snark** is a "pure example" of the way in which, "if thought of as isolated in the midst of the ocean, a ship can stand for mankind and human society moving through time and struggling with its destiny" [*The Enchafèd Flood*, 1967].

Now there is something remarkably wrong about all this. Dodgson himself would be astounded. We have his word that "I can guarantee that the books have no religious teaching whatever in them—in fact they do not teach anything at all." It may be that, knowing how drearily and relentlessly didactic Victorian children's books were, readers have not been able to accept that the most famous representative of the class is without uplift of one sort or another. However a quick comparison of *Alice* or the **Snark** with Charles Kingsley's *The Water Babies* (1863) should be enough to convince any unprejudiced reader of the fact. Kingsley's book, it will be remembered, ends with Tom, the erstwhile fairy, "now a great man of science [who] can plan railroads and steam engines, and electric telegraphs and rifled guns, and so forth." Not content with this, the author adds, to his little readers in the attached "Moral," ". . . do you learn your lessons, and thank God that you have plenty of cold water to wash in; and wash in it, too, like a true Englishman."

Lewis Carroll does not cloy in this way because he had a very sophisticated image of his audience. One may be highly specific about what the word child meant to Charles Lutwidge Dodgson. It meant first of all a girl; further, a girl between the ages of ten and thirteen, who belonged to an upper-middle class family; was beautiful; intelligent; well dressed and well behaved. Anything else was not a child. Now it is obvious that such a restricted view of children cannot be the same one which animates Lewis Carroll the author. Rather, this audience is conceived not in terms of chronology, but as a state of perceptual innocence and honesty. Children are the proper audience of nonsense only to the degree that they let strange things remain strange; to the degree they resist forcing old systems on new, and insist on differences rather than similarities. The allegorists who have written about the **Snark** without having *seen* it are obviously long past such a state of open potentiality.

The best argument against the **Snark**'s allegorization remains, of course, the poem itself. The interpretation which follows is based not only on the poem itself, but on the various ways in which it *is* itself. That is, the poem is best understood as a structure of resistances to other structures of meaning which might be brought to it. The meaning of the poem consists in the several strategies which hedge it off as itself, which insure its hermetic nature against the hermeneutic impulse. Below are six of the many ways by which the poem gains coherence through inherence.

1. The dedication poem to Gertrude Chataway appears at first glance to be simply another of those treacly Victorian set pieces Dodgson would compose when he abandoned nonsense for what he sometimes thought was serious literature. But a second reading reveals that the poem contains an acrostic: the first letter of each line spells out Gertrude Chataway; a third reading will show that the initial word in the first line of each of the four quatrains constitute another acrostic, Girt, Rude, Chat, Away. This is the first indication in the poem that the words in it exist less for what they denote in the system of English than they do for the system Carroll will erect. That is, the initial four words of each stanza are there less to indicate the four meanings present in them before they were deployed by Carroll they at first convey (clothed, wild, speak, begone) than they are to articulate a purely idiosyncratic pattern of Carroll's own devising.

2. Another index of the systematic arbitrariness of the poem is found in the second quatrain of the first Fit: "Just the place for a Snark! I have said it twice: / That alone should encourage the crew. / Just the place for a Snark! I have said it thrice: / What I tell you three times is true." The rule of three operates in two ways. First of all it is a system for determining a truth that is absolutely unique to this poem. When in Fit 5 the Butcher wishes to prove that the scream he has heard belongs to a Jubjub bird, he succeeds in doing so by repeating three times, "Tis the voice of the Jubjub!" Now, there will be those who say that there is no such thing as a Jubjub bird. But in fact, in the system of the Snark poem, there is—and his existence is definitively confirmed through the proof which that system *itself* provides in the rule of 3. In the game of nonsense that rule, and only that rule, works. The system itself provides the assurance that only it can give meaning to itself.

The rule of three also operates as a marker, indicating that the intrinsic logic of the poem is *not* that of extrinsic logic which operates in systems outside the construct of the poem. In other words, it is a parody of the three components of that core element in traditional logic, the syllogism. As an example of this, take an exercise from Dodgson's own book, *Symbolic Logic* (1896): "No one has read the letter but John; No one, who has *not* read it, knows what it is about." The answer is, of course, "No one but *John* knows what the letter is about." The third repetition "Tis the voice of the Jubjub," has the same effect in nonsense that the third part of the syllogistic progression has in logic. The *Oxford Universal Dictionary* defines a syllogism as a major and a minor premise, "with a third proposition called the conclusion, *resulting necessarily from the other two*." If you begin with nonsense, and its conclusion, like the syllogism, results necessarily from the beginning, you also end with nonsense. The progression is closed to other systems. It is not, incidentally, without significance for Carroll's play with words that the etymology of syllogism is a portmanteau from the Greek *syllogizesthai* (to reckon together) and *logizesthai* (to reason) which has its root, *logos*.

3. The same effect of an arbitrariness whose sense can be gleaned only from the poem itself is to be found in the various names of the crew members: Bellman, Boots, Bonnet-maker, Barrister, Broker, Billiard-marker, Banker, Beaver, Baker, and Butcher. They all begin with a B. And much ink has been spilled in trying to explain (from the point of view of the allegory a given critic has tried to read into the **Snark**) why this should be so. The obvious answer, if one resists the impulse to substitute something else for the text, is that they all begin with B *because they all begin with B*. The fact that they all have the same initial sound is a parallel that draws attention to itself because it is a parallel. But it is only a parallel at the level where all the crew members on this voyage will be referred to by nouns which have an initial voiced bilabial plosive. In other words, it is a parallel that is rigidly observed, which dramatizes itself, but only as a dynamic *process* of parallelism, and nothing else.

4. Another way in which the poem sets up resistances which frustrate allegory is to be found in the fifth Fit. The butcher sets out to prove that two can be added to one. "Taking three as the subject to reason about—/ A convenient number to state—/ We add seven and ten, and then multiply out / By one thousand diminished by eight.

The result we proceed to divide, as you see, / By nine hundred and ninety and two: / Then subtract seventeen, and the answer must be / Exactly and perfectly true."

And in fact the answer is perfectly true—but it is also what you begin with. The equation begins with 3—the number the Butcher is trying to establish—and it ends with 3. The math of the equation looks like this: $(X+7+10)(1000-8)/992-17 = X$; which simplifies to x, or a pure integer. The equation is a process which begins with no content and ends with no content. It is a pure process which has no end other than itself. It is thus perhaps the best paradigm of the process of the whole poem: it does what it is about. It is pure surface, but as Oscar Wilde once observed, "there is nothing more profound than surface."

5. A fifth way in which the poem maintains its structural integrity is found in the many coinages it contains, words which Humpty Dumpty defines as portmanteau words, two meanings packed into one word like a portmanteau; words which Giles Deleuze, in the most comprehensive study of Carroll's significance for language, *Logique du Sens,* has so charmingly translated as "les mots-valises." Carroll, in the introduction to the *Snark* writes, ". . . take the two words 'fuming' and 'furious.' Make up your mind that you will say both words, but have it unsettled which you will say first. Now open your mouth and speak. If your thoughts incline ever so little towards 'fuming' you will say 'fuming-furious;' if they turn by even a hair's breadth towards 'furious,' you will say 'furious-fuming;' but if you have that rarest of gifts, a perfectly balanced mind, you will say 'frumious.'"

"If you have that rarest of gifts, a balanced mind . . . ," in other words, you will find just the right word, and not some approximation. In the seventh Fit, when the Banker is attacked by the Bandersnatch, the bird is described as having "frumious jaws." And the Banker, utterly shaken, chants "in mimsiest tones," a combination of miserable and flimsy. For a bird which exists only in the system of nonsense, adjectives used to describe objects in other systems will not do; they are not precise enough, and so the system itself provides its own adjective for its own substantive. Since only the Banker has ever been attacked by a Bandersnatch, it is necessary to find a unique adjective adequate to this unique experience: thus "mimsiest." This attempt to find just the right word, and no other, resulting finally in coinages, is another way in which Carroll's search for precision, order, relates him to language as an innovative process in modern literature. Carroll speaks of "that rarest of gifts, a balanced mind" as the source of his experiment. In our own century it was a man remarkable for *not* possessing that gift who has best expressed the pathos of its absence in the face of language. In one of his fragments Antonin Artaud says "there's no correlation for me between *words* and the exact states of my being . . . I'm the man who's best felt the astounding disorder of his language in its relation to his thought." Carroll's portmanteau words are revealing not only for the way they participate in the self-insuring autonomy of the poem. They also provide an illustration of how Carroll's nonsense is grounded in a logic of surface. The portmanteau word is not only a combination of two definitions, it is a combination of two systems, language and logic. Mention was made earlier of Saussure's insight into the way language *means* through *divergence.* The portmanteau word creates a new meaning by phonologically exploiting the divergence between two old meanings. It thus provides

one of the most economical proofs of Saussure's insight into language. But the portmanteau word is also the third element of a three part progression, from one, furious, to two, fuming, to three, frumious. Like the rule of three it results in a new "truth," and like the rule of three it is a unique kind of syllogism. In order to get a logical conclusion to the syllogism, it must grow out of a divergence between two prior parallel statements.

This is an important point if one is to see the logic which determines that Carroll's system is a *language* and not gibberish. In logic, not all pairs of apparent concrete propositions can result in a meaningful conclusion. Two examples, again taken from our poet's own textbook of *Symbolic Logic* will make the point. The two statements, "No riddles interest me if they can be solved"; and "All *these* riddles are insoluable," cannot lead to a conclusion due to the fallacy of like eliminads not asserted to exist. "Some of these shops are not crowded; no crowded shops are comfortable" cannot lead to a conclusion due to the fallacy of *un*like eliminads with an entity-premise. These and other possibilities for false syllogisms are generally subsumed under the fallacy of "post hoc, ergo propter hoc." That is, the invalidity of the conclusion is a result of incorrect premises. And the criterion for determining whether the primary and secondary propositions are *valid* or not is provided by the rules of logic itself. These rules make up one system. But if one were to create *another* system, which would state that the original premises were correct according to *its* rules, then the same conclusion which the system of logic would call invalid would, perceived as a result obtained according to the new rules, be correct. By extrapolation a true syllogism has been created out of what was in another set false.

The point this arcane diversion into eliminads and entity-premises seeks to make is that the system of Carroll's nonsense is just such an extrapolation, it is the transcendence of the post hoc, ergo propter hoc principle into an aesthetic. Carroll's portmanteaux are *words* and not gibberish because they operate according to the rule which says that all coinages in the poem will grow out of the collapse of two known words into a new one. Carroll can deploy words he invents and still communicate, because he does so according to rules. Whereas an expression of gibberish would be a sound pattern whose meaning could not be gleaned from its *use* according to rules: an expression of gibberish would be a sound pattern whose meaning could not be gleaned either from the syntactic or morphological principles provided by its use, or which would be deducible according to such principles in a known language system. Nonsense, like gibberish, is a violence practiced on semantics. But since it is systematic, the sense of nonsense can be learned. And that is the value of it: it calls attention to language. Carroll's nonsense keeps us honest; through the process of disorientation and learning which reading him entails, we are made aware again that language is not something we know, but something alive, in process—something to be discovered.

6. The final structure of resistance I'd like to mention is contained in perhaps the most obvious feature of the poem,

its rhyme. William K. Wimsatt, in a well-known essay, makes the point that in a poem the rhyme imposes "upon the logical pattern of expressed argument a kind of fixative counterpattern of alogical implication" [*The Verbal Icon* (New York, 1962)]. He goes on to say that "rhyme is commonly recognized as a binder in verse structure. But where there is need for binding there must be some difference or separation between the things to be bound. If they are already close together, it is supererogatory to emphasize this by the maneuver of rhyme. So we may say that the greater the difference in meaning between rhyme words the more marked and the more appropriate will be the binding effect." This important insight into verse is contained in a piece entitled "One Relation of Rhyme to Reason." Now, Lewis Carroll wrote a book entitled *Rhyme? and Reason?* (1883), and I suggest that the distinctive role which rhyme plays in the *Snark* is best caught by means of a titular portmanteau here. That is, it is precisely that one relation of rhyme to reason which Professor Wimsatt evokes in *his* title, which is put into question marks not only by *Carroll's* title of 1883, but which is also put into question in the function rhyme serves in *The Hunting of the Snark.*

Professor Wimsatt suggests that "the words of a rhyme, with their curious harmony of sound and distinction of sense, are an amalgam of the sensory and the logical, or an arrest and precipitation of the logical in sensory form; they are the icon in which the idea is caught." I read this to mean that two words which are disparate in meaning result, when bound by rhyme, in a new meaning which was not contained in either of them alone. In other words, you get a kind of rule of three at work. Like the syllogism, two disparate but related elements originate a third. Thus understood, the rhyme of traditional verse has the effect of meaningful surprise; two rhymes will constitute a syllogism resulting in a new association.

But this is not true of nonsense verse. "They sought it with thimbles, they sought it with care; / They pursued it with forks and hope; / They threatened its life with a railway-share; / They charmed it with smiles and soap." This stanza begins each of the last four Fits, and may stand as an example for what rhyme does throughout the poem. The rhyme words, "care, railway-share," and "hope, soap" would be very different from each other in traditional verse, and binding effects of the sort Professor Wimsatt has demonstrated in Pope or Byron would be possible. Because the language of most verse is simply a more efficiently organized means of making sense of the sort that language *outside* verse provides. Thus, while very different, some kind of meaningful association could be made of them capable of catching an idea.

But "care," "railway share," "hope" and "soap" in this quatrain have as their ambiance *not* the semantic field of the English language, but the field of Carroll's nonsense. In traditional verse "rhyme words . . . can scarcely appear in a context without showing some difference of meaning." But if the whole context of a poem is *without* meaning, its separate parts will also lack it. There can be no differences in meaning between words because they are all equally meaningless in this context. So the reader who attempts to relate rhyme to meaning in Carroll's poem will be frustrated. The syllogism of rhyme, which in other verse has a new meaning as its conclusion, ends, in Carroll's verse, where it began. Instead of aiding meaning, it is another strategy to defeat it. Language in nonsense is thus a seamless garment, a pure cover, absolute surface.

But if *The Hunting of the Snark* is an absolute metaphor, if it means only itself, why read it? There are several answers, but the one I have chosen to give here is that it may help us to understand other, more complex attempts to do the same thing in modern literature. It is easy to laugh at the various casuistries by which readers have sought to make an allegory, something else, out of the *Snark.* But the same sort of thing is being done every day to Kafka or Nabokov. Possibly the example of Lewis Carroll may suggest how far we must go, how much we must forget, how much we must learn in order to see fiction as fiction.

For the moral of the *Snark* is that it has no moral. It is a fiction, a thing which does not seek to be "real" or "true." The nineteenth-century was a great age of system building and myth makers. We are the heirs of Marx and Freud, and many other prophets as well, all of whom seek to explain *everything,* to make sense out of *everything* in terms of one system or another. In the homogenized world which resulted, it could be seen that art was nothing more than another—and not necessarily privileged—way for economic or psychological forces to express themselves. As Robbe-Grillet says, "Cultural fringes (bits of psychology, ethics, metaphysics, etc.) are all the time being attached to things and making them seem less strange, more comprehensible, more reassuring" [*The French Novel Since the War* (London, 1967)].

Aware of this danger, authors have fought back, experimenting with new ways to insure the inviolability of their own systems, to invite abrasion, insist on strangeness, create fictions. Lewis Carroll is in some small degree a forerunner of this saving effort. To see his nonsense as a logic is thus far from being an exercise in bloodless formalism. That logic insures the fictionality of his art, and as human beings we need fictions. As is so often the case, Nietzsche said it best: "we have art in order not to die of the truth."

After having stressed at such length that everything in the *Snark* means what it means according to its own system, it is no doubt unneccessary, but in conclusion I would like to answer the question with which we began. What is a Boojum? A Boojum is a Boojum.

J.S. Bratton   (essay date 1975)

SOURCE: "Comic Ballads in the Drawing Room," in *The Victorian Popular Ballad,* Rowman and Littlefield, 1975, pp. 203-50.

[In the following excerpt, Bratton argues that Carroll's work has origins in the Victorian Popular Ballad form.]

. . . . By the middle of the [nineteenth] century the comic ballad world was . . . established as the domain of the writers who served the middle-class end of the popular audience, and it was adaptable to cater for their tastes and needs in a variety of ways. Two writers then emerged as supreme in whose work, in very different ways, this promise was fulfilled. There was on the one hand Lewis Carroll, who published his first book of comic verse *Phantasmagoria* in 1869 and *The Hunting of the Snark* in 1876, whose work took the comic ballad into the realm of fantasy and escapism, developing it into an art as abstract and devoid of direct relevance as it could well be; and on the other W. S. Gilbert, who collected the *Bab Ballads* into volume form in 1867, and who fulfilled a function parallel to that of Sims in affirming the social and personal identity and solidarity of a class aware of social threats and problems which gave an edge of horror to his comic flirtation with harsh realities.

Dodgson, in his first volume of verse published under the name of Lewis Carroll, approached the comic ballad along conventional paths. In the *Phantasmagoria* volume is a variety of unexceptional comic ballads and songs which includes some conventional popular jokes and subjects, such as the misery of being a fat man with a thin friend and rival (in **"Size and Tears"**) and the horrors of the seaside, including a conventionally indirect reference to fleas (in **"Sea Dirge"**). Besides the popular conventionality of the jokes, the forms used in the telling of them are derived from the expected source of comic verse, the parody: Tennyson (in **"Echoes"**), Longfellow (in **"Hiawatha's Photographing"**), and Swinburne (in **"Atlanta in Camden Town"**) are the most obvious contributors. The mock-Scottish ballad tale of **"The Lang Coortin"** is no more distinguished than these, and is less vividly effective than the traditional ballad parody of some of his predecessors, such as W. E. Aytoun. It has felicitous touches of humour based upon incongruous juxtaposition of ancient form and modern meaning, and of romanticism and practicality:

'And didna ye get the letter, Ladye,
Tied wi' a silken string,
Whilk I sent to thee frae the far countrie,
A message of love to bring?'

'It cam' to me frae the far countrie
Wi' its silken string and a';
But it wasna pre-paid,' said that high-born maid,
'Sae I gar'd them tak' it awa".

The joke, however, is scarcely strong enough to sustain its thirty-seven stanzas, and the incidental humour arising from the ballad common-places used of a modern domestic situation is scattered rather than cumulative in its effect. In the title poem of the volume, however, the elements of parody, incongruity, and the figures of the comic ballad world are worked together into a coherent whole which takes off spectacularly into Carroll's peculiarly potent fantasy world.

The poem is divided into seven cantos, titled medievally from "The Trysting" to "Sad Souvenaunce," and represents the apotheosis of comic medievalism. It takes the domestication of the other-worldly to such an extreme that it becomes once more potent and strange, and the domestic is felt to share the qualities of the supernatural, instead of the other way round. It displays a self-sufficiency and completeness within its own assumptions which renders the ghostly once more extraordinary. The domestic setting is tangibly realistic, beginning with comfortable matter-of-factness in the first stanza:

One wintry night, at half-past nine,
Cold, tired, and cross, and muddy,
I had come home, too late to dine,
And supper, with cigars and wine,
Was waiting in the study.

The cosiness of this picture is later qualified by incidental revelations that the domestic situation described is actually less than perfect: the Villa he calls home is rather small, his study is not as opulent as he tries to suggest—

'Your room's an inconvenient size;
It's neither snug nor spacious.

'That narrow window, I expect,
Serves but to let the dusk in—'
I cried, 'But please to recollect
'T was fashion'd by an architect
Who pinned his faith on Ruskin!'

It is moreover afflicted with loose doors and draughty wainscotting; while his supper is prepared by a cook who uses old peas and sends the toasted cheese up cold; the cigars and wine are indifferent. Into this picture of ordinariness, and indeed so thoroughly involved with it as to be the voice which utters the criticisms just quoted, comes a Thing, soon particularised as a Phantom; and the inversion of the natural order begins. To start with, the Thing, rather than the human narrator, is afraid; and their relationship, developed in the course of conversation to something like affection, consistently flouts every expectation. The Phantom's attitude changes from the timid to the self-justifying, and then to the informative:

Through driving mists I seemed to see
A form of sheet and bone—
And found that he was telling me
The whole of his biography
In a familiar tone.

He becomes critical, and his human host retreats from curiosity to attempting to score debating points and catch him out; they bicker, and conduct a meaningless argument about punning,

Commencing every single phrase
With 'therefore' or 'because'
I blindly reeled, a hundred ways,
About the syllogistic maze,
Unconscious where I was.

Finally they discover that the Phantom is in the wrong house anyway, and he leaves, with a casual farewell which haunts the narrator for a year:

> Yet still they echo in my head,
> Those parting words, so kindly said,
> 'Old Turnip-top, good-night!'

The effect of this reversal of expectations, the narrator's calm acceptance of the ghost and his human relationship with him, is less to tame and make acceptable the ghost as a funny idea than to undermine the reader's convictions about the difference between reality and fantasy. If this very ordinary man, bad at arguments and living in a poky new house with a presumptuous cook and cheap cigars, finds absolutely nothing extraordinary about the visit of a Phantom, perhaps one's own dismissive, amused attitude to the idea is in some way mistaken. The ghost's speeches, which make up the main body of the verse, are both funny and as disturbing as the setting. They take to its final extreme the *Ingoldsby Legends* technique of using strict adherence to verbal logic to set up a parallel world inhabited by supernatural beings subject to a parody of natural law. Carroll reveals the spirit world as a version of the ordinary one, with all its conventional attributes linked with or explained in human terms. The Phantom reveals to the startled narrator that he is as dependent on material considerations as the least spiritual human being, and indeed his self-pitying narrative suggests that his lot is most uncomfortable. Not only is he as liable to physical discomfort and as often hungry and thirsty as Barham's devils, but he is also enmeshed in a restrictive class system, looked down on by Spectres, deprived of preferment by intimidation at elections, and rejected by the snobbish Haunted-House Committee; he is even kept from what a mortal might have thought of as his natural rights by lack of capital. He cannot afford to fly; and when he first set up in business, he says, he

> . . . often spent ten pounds on stuff,
> In dressing as a Double,
> But, though it answers as a puff,
> It never has effect enough
> To make it worth the trouble.

> Long bills soon quenched the little thirst
> I had for being funny—
> The setting-up is always worst:
> Such heaps of things you want at first,
> One must be made of money!

> For instance, take a haunted tower,
> With skull, cross-bones, and sheet;

> Blue lights to burn (say) two an hour,
> Condensing lens of extra power,
> And set of chains, complete . . .

> And then, for all you have to do,
> One pound a week they offer you,
> And find yourself in Bogies!

The humour of this fantasy arises partly from its unexpectedness, the sense of a completely new way of looking at things which is not without consistency and logic, indeed is strictly rational in appearance, but presents notions previously completely unimaginable as if they were prosaic realities. The use of factual reference, which is so disturbingly realistic, to the real world, does not actually mean that the ballad is related to reality at all. As in the case of its predecessors, its relation is to words, concepts and literature detached from the relevance they originally had to fact and physical existence. Carroll creates an imaginary world out of pieces detached from reality by means of the abuse of verbal and conceptual patterns normally used to order and discuss it.

Exactly the same procedure is used in *The Hunting of the Snark*. Out of fragments of factual reality, and by means of literary reference and the manipulation of words freed from their meanings in the ordinary world, Carroll created a dream world ordered by its own purely verbal logic. The detachment of that world from all others is illustrated by the difficulties Henry Holiday, the original illustrator, had with the pictures for it. One, his drawing of the Snark, was rejected by Carroll because 'All his descriptions of the Boojum were quite unimaginable'— they were only verbal, and not even intended to convey a picture to the imagination. They were indeed quite detached from anything but the words they were expressed in, as can be perceived from the synaesthetic statement of the first of the 'Five unmistakable marks' of the snark. It is quite impossible to translate the stanza from words to impressions:

> Let us take them in order. The first is the taste,
> Which is meagre and hollow, but crisp:
> Like a coat that is rather too tight in the waist,
> With a flavour of Will-o'-the-wisp.

The picturing of such a creature is clearly not to be done, and most of the important descriptions and events of the poem have the same quality. Holiday's other problem, however, highlights a quality of the whole which would not appear very readily compatible with this singularity: he said that 'In our correspondence about the illustrations, the coherence and consistency of the nonsense on its own nonsensical understanding often became prominent.' This consistency of the poem is often, as in all Carroll's fantasy writing, called 'dream logic', things having the kind of connections which they have in the suggestive, symbolic, loosely articulated flow of a dream. It is, I feel, better to think of it as something which is much more artistically and consciously created, a logic of verbal connection and suggestion disciplined by reference to the organisational principles and conventions of the ballad tradition. It is as if elements thrown up by free association, and by verbal games (like the party game in which each player in turn has to produce a word connected by some chosen principle, such as its first letter or occurance in a literary quotation, to the last) were organised into a story by literary principles used without reference to likelihood, relevance or possibility, but quite logical and viable in themselves. In such a process of composition a gap yawns between the poem and reality across which are verbal connections which only serve to mislead. W. S. Gilbert's fantasy ballads rely completely upon the connection they have with reality for their humour and their point; but Carroll has taken off into a purely cerebral game of words and literary associations. The poem is not about anything at all, beyond the words of which it is made up.

His reliance upon quite ordinary literary processes of organisation to provide the basis for the fantasy, giving an identifiable and acceptable groundwork for the reader's grasp of the ballad, is the most easily demonstrated aspect of this. He is using a ballad stanza common to many comic verses and versifiers from Hood onwards, a regular four-line stanza enlivened with occasional internal rhymes and double or triple rhyming words, extended lines and frequent use of extra, unstressed syllables to give a conversational, colloquial flow. The language is calculated to provide a deliberately casual, prosaic background against which the nonsense words and ideas will show up the more incongruously and appear the more mind-bendingly peculiar. The urbane relaxation of Carroll's use of words gives the surface a polish which is often itself highly amusing, and might perhaps be said to be descended from the Byronic style:

> The loss of his clothes hardly mattered, because
> He had seven coats on when he came,
> With three pair of boots—but the worst of it was,
> He had wholly forgotten his name . . .
>
> But the valley grew narrow and narrower still,
> And the evening got darker and colder,
> Till (merely from nervousness, not from good will)
> They marched along shoulder to shoulder.

The donnish dryness of 'hardly' and 'wholly', the neatness of the parenthesis, and the easy manipulation of the rhyme, are all delightful.

On a larger scale, the continuity of the story, such as it is, depends on a version of ballad technique. The title is of course suggested by 'The Hunting of the Cheviot,' and the poem is divided, somewhat arbitrarily, into fits (with a pun upon the word—it is 'an agony in eight fits'). More than this, the only continuity throughout is the use of a kind of ballad repetition: the story leaps from incident to incident, but all is held together by a recurring stanza. It is introduced to recall the minds of readers, and, one feels, participants, to the fact that they are nominally hunting the Snark, and coming in abruptly in a variety of contexts it is just as well that it is, like some ballad refrains, quite devoid of sensible meaning, although redolent of poetic suggestiveness:

> They sought it with thimbles, they sought it with
>   care;
> They pursued it with forks and hope;
> They threatened its life with a railway share;
> They charmed it with smiles and soap.

The repetition within the stanza is also of course a common ballad construction, which occurs again, parodying the commonplace which runs

> They had not sailed a week, a week,
> A week but barely ane [or 'A week but two or
>   three']

in the Bellman's speech in the second fit:

> We have sailed many months, we have sailed many
>   weeks
> (Four weeks to the month you may mark),
> But never as yet ('tis your Captain who speaks)
> Have we caught the least glimpse of a Snark!
>
> We have sailed many weeks, we have sailed many
>   days
> (Seven days to the week I allow)
> But a Snark, on the which we might lovingly gaze,
> We have never beheld till now!

A reference to this emphatic repetition is surely also behind the same character's opening words, and his statement that 'What I tell you three times is true.'

Within the framework established by these ballad techniques there is a huge amount of echoing and verbal reference, not only to literature, but to all the set phrases and composite units of meaning which make up ordinary conversation. Common verbal intercourse is not actually a matter of pronouncing and attending to each individual word as it is freshly related to each other word, but rather the emission and reception of expected, pre-set patterns of meaning which approximate to the new, or the old idea we wish to communicate. Carroll's technique is partly the breaking up of these units by totally unexpected juxtapositions—

> There was also a beaver, who paced on the deck,
> Or would sit making lace in the bow.

and also partly, because he was so aware of them, a utilisation of the set phrases and verbal patterns in odd contexts so that the reader is pleased and amused by his own recognition of them. The technique was used much more crudely in the punning and parodying of the minor pieces in *Phantasmagoria,* and appears throughout *The Hunting of the Snark*. One of the more obvious examples is the Baker's life-story in the third fit, which he attempts to tell as a popular tale of tragedy, beginning 'My father and mother were honest, though poor—' which the Bellman will not tolerate. Another phrase from popular use is allowed to pass without comment in the first fit, when the Baker is described as having been 'engaged at enormous expense'.

Even the nonsense words, coinages and transpositions of meaning, are made intelligible—or partly so—if a reader recognises their source and the reference involved. 'Uffish', 'beamish', 'galumphing' and 'outgrabe', all of which occur at some point in the history of the Snark, are taken from Carroll's own work, appearing in **"Jabberwocky"** in the first chapter of *Through the Looking Glass,* and they are in some cases explained there: Humpty Dumpty defined 'outgribing' as 'something between bellowing and whistling', while 'galumphing' is a portmanteau word from 'triumphant' and 'galloping'. The point and effect of all this is not, however, to convey in a veiled and indirect way some sensible everyday meaning, and recognition of references is pleasing for its own sake without adding anything to the objective comprehension of the context in which they occur. Objective sense is not the intention in the employment of these or any of the words of the piece; they are all employed as units of speech detached from their usual meanings and used to make up a new language in a new world, where different rules apply. What is said is intelligible to us because those rules are a version of the patterns of literature, particularly popular literature.

A good example of the detachment of words from their usual sense is the naming of the crew. Carroll would seem to have begun with the captain, the Bellman. The office of bellman was not simply, as Martin Gardner suggests in *The Annotated Snark*, 'another word for a town crier'; in Scotland the 'skellat bellman' of Glasgow, for example, was certainly appointed as town crier, but he had other functions which were a residue of the role of the minstrel or poet of the community. One particularly famous holder of the office, of whom Carroll may well have known, was Dougal Graham, born in 1724, writer and publisher of a series of chapbooks of Scottish tales and jokes. In London, on the other hand, the bellman was rather a night watchman, whose office survived from the fifteenth century until the improvement of the police force in the early nineteenth century, and who traditionally had printed and sold at Christmas a broadside sheet of verses addressed to the householders of his round soliciting their future support and present payment of a seasonal bonus. Carroll was clearly thinking of a ballad story-teller when he used the name, and Holiday would seem to have been thinking of one particular public poet, Alfred Tennyson, when he drew the pictures. The reference is complex—but probably irrelevant. The bellman in the poem, although he makes speeches and is sensitive to the use of literary clichés by others, is a sea captain and a hunter; his literary qualifications do perhaps serve to suggest the verbal, rather than actual, field through which the hunt is conducted.

Having therefore begun with a captain who is a bellman, Carroll proceeded to name the rest of the crew on a purely phonetic principle, with a series of professions beginning with the letter B. Only one, the Butcher (who is not really a butcher, and has moreover forgotten his own name), shows much interest in or preoccupation with his trade. All the others are simply interesting and sonorously appropriate words. The use of the name 'Baker', for instance, adds an extra dimension to the character's actions and fate, but the changing of it, say to 'Boxer' or 'Bagman', or even the substitution of a nonsense word, would not destroy other aspects of the character and its humour. Thus Carroll can make use of words quite arbitrarily selected, and indeed can occasionally change the meaning of a word to suit himself, not only cutting off its old sense but forcing us to assign it another, as in 'in an antediluvian tone' to heighten and intensify the humour of his other world. Gilbert was tied to the contrast with reality for his meaning, and so had to maintain a superficial semblance of possibility and precise meaning for his effects. *The Snark* floats free of relevance and reference. Its connection with reality, if it has one at all, is perhaps philosophic, and many critics have earnestly sought its transcendental meaning, the most recent being Martin Gardner, whose theory is that 'The *Snark* is a poem about being and non-being, an existential poem, a poem of existential agony.' Without agreeing or disagreeing with this sombre pronouncement, one might see in it a possible link between Carroll and Gilbert, for Gilbert is concerned with the 'dimension of anxiety', 'the agony of anticipating one's loss of being', in a much more concrete, and I would suggest conscious, way, in the context of his own class in Victorian society.

On Carroll's parodies:

. . . Carroll was a wretched poet when he tried to be serious: he became mawkish or sentimental. But Carroll was a masterly poet when he parodied—either a particular poem like Wordsworth's "Resolution and Independence" or a type of poem like the ballad. The celebrated **"Jabberwocky"** is a parody of Anglo-Saxon poetry, as Carroll originally printed its first stanza as being—Old English poetry as it would appear to a modern reader. It was probably also a fun-making at the expense of antiquarian scholars who made so much of the archaic poetry which was not to the taste of Carroll: he was very much of a modern and a Tennyson-worshipper.

Generations of scholars have worked at the identification of the poems Carroll parodied: the results of these inquiries are accumulated on the margins of Gardner's *Annotated Alice*. **"You are old, Father William"** is a comic reversal of Southey's "The Old Man's Comforts," and **"Soup of the evening, beautiful Soup"** parodies a music-hall song, "Star of the Evening," which Carroll had heard the Liddell girls sing. Sometimes Carroll was poking fun at a didactic poem like Isaac Watts's "The Sluggard"; but like all good parodists he was capable too of parodying poems and poets he admired (as, in our own time, Henry Reed's "Chard Whitlock" can be a brilliant parody of "Burnt Norton" without implying any denigration of T. S. Eliot). Parody is a highly ambivalent art, capable of praising out of one side of its mouth—for it is a critical act to select a poem as important enough to ridicule—and fun-making out of the other. No single straightforward unequivocal judgment is intended.

Austin Warren, "Carroll and His Alice Books," in
The Sewanee Review, *Vol. LXXXVIII, No. 3,*
Summer, 1980, pp. 331-53.

Beverly Lyon Clark   (essay date 1982)

SOURCE: "Carroll's Well-Versed Narrative: *Through the Looking-Glass*," in *English Language Notes*, Vol. 20, No. 2, December 1982, pp. 65-76.

[*In the following excerpt, Clark discusses Carroll's verse parodies in* Through the Looking Glass *and* Alice's Adventures in Wonderland.]

You say that I'm "to write a verse"—
    O Maggie, put it quite
The other way, and kindly say
    That I'm "averse to write"!

In writing to his child-friends Lewis Carroll was not averse to verse, however he might tease. Nor was he averse in his fiction—for it comprises one of the most memorable features of his *Alice* books. It contributes to the humor and nonsense and absurdity of the books, through its play with "real"-world forms and its parody, and through its concreteness and its interaction with the surrounding prose.

Carroll played with "real"-world forms sometimes by making things more orderly and sometimes by making them less. But of course order and disorder are all a matter of perspective. When Humpty Dumpty defines glory as "a nice knock-down argument" he disorders our real-world semantic order, from one perspective, but the simple act of defining the word, of associating it with a meaning and not leaving it in the limbo of meaningless noises, is itself an act of order. Humpty Dumpty's new order may be unfamiliar, but it is not entirely chaotic. Or take **"Jabberwocky."** Does it disorder our orderly universe? Yes, in part, for "brillig" and "slithy" have no familiar meaning. Yet, as students of language are fond of pointing out, the grammatical structure of the poem is orderly, making it possible for us to decipher, for instance, the parts of speech to which the nonsense words belong. And the words themselves combine consonants and vowels the way English words do (unlike, say, the Wonderland Gryphon's "Hjckrrh!"). Further, Humpty Dumpty's explication provides an ordering of the meaning as well. When he expounds, "*'Brillig'* means four o'clock in the afternoon— the time when you begin *broiling* things for dinner," he describes a world with a modicum of order, one that can be envisioned as in, say, Tenniel's drawing.

Another way of describing Carroll's play with "real"-world forms is in terms of open and closed fields. Susan Stewart, in her recent study *Nonsense,* catalogues nonsense transformations and finds some within the closed fields described by Elizabeth Sewell in her early *Field of Nonsense,* closing what is traditionally open, while others do the inverse, opening what is closed. Yet whatever we call the two transformations—whether we use this broad definition or else associate nonsense only with the first kind of transformation and associate the second with the absurd— Carroll uses both kinds. He sometimes opens what is traditionally closed (making a mirror into a door) and sometimes closes what is traditionally open and on-going (making time stand still at six o'clock). And often what Carroll does is a complex amalgam of both opening and closing. In his parodies, for instance, some of the wordplay focuses attention on the words, fencing them off from reality, making them a closed world: rhyme and alliteration draw attention to the words and distract us from whatever it is the words are meant to refer to. The parodies also close themselves off as separate worlds to the extent that they do not refer to recognizable reality: how does one balance anything as slippery and floppy as an eel on the end of one's nose? On the other hand, the

references to artifacts outside the poems—to other poems—opens the form, and the parodies would also seem to shatter the closed universes of the pietistic poems they mock. The parodies operate in both closed and open fields—they both order and disorder—and part of their effect derives from the confrontation between the two. We can call them nonsense, or something else, but the parodies draw upon both kinds of transformation.

It has become convenient to refer offhand to most of the verse in the *Alice* books as parodies. But again we run into a problem of definition. This time I want to define the term more narrowly, for the very general way in which we use "parody" sometimes blinds us to important distinctions. Sometimes we call something a parody if it reminds us of a previous work, whether or not any satire is intended. But I'd like to reserve parody for something that satirizes. Dwight Macdonald, for instance, situates Carroll's works closer to what he calls burlesque than to parody: "he simply injected an absurd content into the original form with no intention of literary criticism." Macdonald is right for some of Carroll's verse, but I would disagree with his contention that Carroll never intended literary criticism, for sometimes Carroll does intend literary, if not moral, criticism [MacDonald, 1960].

Sometimes, if not always. For only in *Alice's Adventures in Wonderland* is the verse truly parodic. *How doth the little crocodile,* for instance, undermines the pious preaching of Isaac Watts's "How doth the little busy bee," which admonishes children to keep busy and avoid mischief: the crocodile presented for our emulation, far from skillfully building a cell or neatly spreading wax, "cheerfully" and "neatly" and "gently"—snares fishes. Much of the other pious verse that Carroll parodies in *Wonderland* is similarly subverted. While Carroll does not entirely disagree with the sentiments of the poems he parodies—especially in later life, when he wanted to outbowdlerize Bowdler— and thus does not mock that which is preached, he does mock the preaching. Carroll may not be criticizing the content (he surely is not inciting children to be slothful), but he does criticize the literary purpose of didactic verse, the way in which it tried to control children. In part Carroll may simply be entering into the child's perspective, adopting the child's responses to pietistic verse, for he shows considerable sympathy for the child's point of view. And perhaps Carroll's satire of the didacticism of previous children's literature clears a niche for the new kind of children's literature he wanted to write. Much as Alice tries to define herself by attempting to recite familiar verse, Carroll seems, intentionally or not, to be defining his fiction through Alice's failure to define herself, through her mangling of her recitations.

In *Through the Looking-Glass* however, it is as if Carroll's success with his first children's book freed him from the need to comment on what previous writers had done for, or to, children. The verse is less parodic. Although some of it plays with pre-existing poems, it is harder to label such playing parody, harder to convict it of literary criticism. Carroll's "parodies" in the two books might be placed on a continuum, from the true parodies like that of

Watts to reflections of the original that are not necessarily satires (what Macdonald describes), to mere echoes that may not actually be related to a so-called original. The drinking song begot of Scott, sung at the Looking-glass banquet, mimics some lines of the original but probably without any intent to satirize. And still farther from parody is **"The Walrus and the Carpenter,"** which shares its meter and rhyme scheme with Thomas Hood's "The Dream of Eugene Aram" and also the discovery of an unexpected murderer, but which is not otherwise tied to the so-called original. Carroll himself wrote in a letter to his uncle, "I had no particular poem in mind. The metre is a common one, and I don't think 'Eugene Aram' suggested it more than the many other poems I have read in the same metre" (*Letters*).

Looking-Glass verse tends toward this latter end of the continuum. Carroll here does not demolish children's verse. For the most part, he either uses fantastical nursery rhymes, which do not need to be demolished, or else he plays with adult poetry, which can perhaps be poked and prodded at but need not be so utterly crushed as the sugar-coated moralizing intended for children.

I will demonstrate how Carroll uses pre-existing verse in *Looking-Glass* by examining the changes he rings on Wordsworth's "Resolution and Independence." The White Knight's poem includes echoes of other poems—Wordsworth's "The Thorn" and Thomas Moore's "My Heart and Lute"—but I'll concentrate on "Resolution and Independence." Carroll had written an early version of his poem by 1856, and this version describes a situation fairly close to that in Wordsworth's poem: in both the narrator encounters an extremely old man upon the moor, asks his occupation, and is comforted by the exchange—although Wordsworth's narrator is comforted by the man's cheer and steadfastness, while Carroll's is comforted by the man's "kind intent / To drink my health in beer." The closest verbal echoes are in the closing lines. Wordsworth ends with "I'll think of the Leech-gatherer on the lonely moor!" ["The Prelude" edited by Carlos Baker (1954)], and Carroll ends with "I think of that strange wanderer / Upon the lonely moor."

This echoing of concluding lines is emblematic of the relationship between the two poems. While the Watts parody starts off proclaiming the poem it twists, repeating the opening "How doth the little," as well as "Improve" and "shining" in the second line, the Wordsworth derivative waits till the conclusion for a close verbal echo. Furthermore, Carroll entirely omits all reference to the meditative early verses of Wordsworth's poem, and even changes the meter and rhyme scheme. "Upon the Lonely Moor" is simply not very close to "Resolution and Independence." And it is not that Wordsworth's lines utterly forbid parody. Surely, if he had wanted to, Carroll could have embellished "Such seemed this Man, not all alive nor dead, / Nor all asleep" by adding something like (but better than) "Nor scrubbing scones nor eating flies / Nor starting in to weep." He apparently wanted to use Wordsworth's dramatic situation as a scaffolding more than he wanted to use Wordsworth's poem as a source for parody.

The later version of Carroll's poem, the one that appears in *Looking-Glass,* is even farther from Wordsworth. The echo in the last two lines has entirely disappeared, and so has all reference to moors. Instead of situating his aged man on a romantic and evocative moor Carroll sits him on a gate. Compared to the earlier version, the nonsense is better, the parody less.

Nevertheless, Carroll himself did call the poem a parody, in a letter to his uncle—but he went on to modify his use of the term: "'Sitting on a Gate' *is* a parody, though not as to style or metre—but its plot is borrowed from Wordsworth's 'Resolution and Independence' . . ." (*Letters*). Carroll uses the term "parody" for lack of a better word, to describe his borrowing of the plot, or dramatic situation, his use of the poem as a scaffolding. He goes on to indicate what in Wordsworth's poem he might well like to satirize, for it is "a poem that has always amused me a good deal (though it is by no means a comic poem) by the absurd way in which the poet goes on questioning the poor old leech-gatherer, making him tell his history over and over again, and never attending to what he says. Wordsworth ends with a moral—an example I have *not* followed." Carroll uses Wordsworth's dramatic situation here, but doing so, though it may poke fun at the narrator's greater interest in his own thoughts than in human interaction, does not undermine Wordsworth's sentiments, his praise of resolution, nor his communing with nature, nor his introspection. And the final version of the poem has strayed far enough from the original that Carroll needs to stress to his uncle that it *is* a parody.

We may be too eager to find satiric comment on Wordsworth in Carroll's poem, since the convenient label for the poem is parody and that is what parody is supposed to do. But while Carroll might not mind tweaking Wordsworth's nose when he starts platitudinizing, Carroll less clearly satirizes Wordsworth than he does Watts in the crocodile poem. And in other derived poems in *Looking-Glass,* such as that sired by Scott, the original neither pedantic nor moralistic, it is even harder to find what Carroll could be satirizing. The complexity of the relationship between Carroll's and Wordsworth's poems, or Carroll's and Scott's, a relationship not easily defined by our usual interpretation of "parody," complements the complexity of Carroll's nonsense and absurdity, which both reveres and defies, both orders and disorders, both closes and opens.

Another way in which Carroll's verse is humorous and nonsensical, in addition to parodying and playing with forms from the "real" world, is through what Elizabeth Sewell calls "a careful addiction to the concrete," [*The Field of Nonsense* (London, 1952)]. Instead of evoking a twinkling star and comparing it to a diamond, Carroll makes a bat twinkle like a tea-tray. Or he unites shoes, ships and sealing wax, or cabbages and kings. Yet not all of Carroll's verse is humorous in precisely this way. Some of it is less concrete and complete in itself, and part of its humor lies in how it integrates with the surrounding narrative. And since little or no attention has been paid to this other source of humor, I am going to concentrate on it at the expense of "careful concreteness." Again, as with the parodic playing with form, the humor derives from a varying tension, or confrontation, between opening and closing the verse: the concreteness and completeness tend to close it, while the integration with the narrative opens it. In *Wonderland* the King of Hearts attempts to integrate verse into the story when he uses the lines beginning *"They told me you had been to her"* as evidence of the Knave's guilt. Yet the ambiguous pronoun references in the lines invite all interpretations—and substantiate none. And the King's attempt to use this verse as evidence ironically substantiates its inadmissibility and hence underscores the disjunction between verse and story. Much of the humor of the verse derives from the use the King makes of it.

Looking-Glass verse tends to be even more integrated with the narrative. Both form and content are integrated, the latter in four ways. I will first discuss the integration of the content, and then turn to the form.

Overall, the content integrates with the prose thematically. Alice finally says, with only slight exaggeration, that the poetry was "all about fishes." (And in the context of playing with kittens, and frequently thinking about eating, it is not amiss to dream about fishes.) In addition, some of the verse relates directly to the action: the Red Queen sings a lullaby when the White Queen wants to nap; and the creatures sing toasts at the closing banquet. Some of the verse is interpreted by the characters, who thereby attempt, as it were, to accommodate the verse to the narrative: Humpty Dumpty interprets **"Jabberwocky"**; and even the Tweedles offer some interpretations of **"The Walrus and the Carpenter."** Finally, some of the verse is enacted in the story: notably, the nursery rhymes come to life.

In providing sources for Looking-glass characters, the nursery rhymes strengthen the integration of verse and story. Much as Wonderland creatures sprout from metaphoric proverbs (except for the Queen of Hearts and company, derived in part from a nursery rhyme but also from playing cards), such Looking-glass creatures as Humpty Dumpty and the Tweedles derive from nursery rhymes. As Roger Henkle notes, the careers of the nursery-rhyme creatures "are predetermined by the nursery rhymes about them" ["The Mad Hatter's World," in *Virginia Quarterly Review*, 49, 1973]—they derive, in other words, from entire verse-stories, not from mere phrases. Or, even if the creatures are ignorant of their predetermining verses, Alice and the reader are not, and we see how the verse does indeed determine actions, how highly integrated verse and narrative are. In *Wonderland*, on the other hand, while the King acts as if the previous behavior of the Knave of Hearts has been described by a nursery rhyme, Alice and the reader are not convinced. The nursery rhyme does not have determining force there—it is merely posited—while nursery rhymes do affect Looking-glass world, the verse does affect the narrative: Humpty Dumpty does come crashing down.

The appearance of nursery-rhyme characters in *Looking-Glass* also makes the book self-conscious because Alice knows about the characters in the story of her adventures through knowing other stories—she is "in the ambiguous position of being a reader in a story where she meets fictitious characters and so knows all about them" [Barbara Hardy, "Fantasy and Dream" in *Tellers and Listeners,* London, 1975]. This self-consciousness is somewhat different from self-consciousness in *Wonderland*. There Alice may comment that the Mouse has reached the fifth bend of his concrete poem, self-consciously commenting on the poem; but it is only the poem that she views as a literary artifact, not the creatures she encounters. Her comments underline the differences between the poem and the narrative rather than merge them. In *Looking-Glass,* though, she is self-conscious about both poems and narrative, and she even wonders if she herself is part of the Red King's dream. Although Alice may simply be playing another version of "Let's pretend" at the end, when she asks Kitty which dreamed it, her question does hint at a serious issue. And the poem that concludes *Looking-Glass,* ending as it does with *"Life, what is it but a dream?"*, continues the impetus of self-consciousness. Such self-consciousness can at first remind the reader of the boundaries between fiction and reality, since the fiction proclaims its fictionality. Hence it would close the work off from reality. Yet, as Borges queries of the work within a work: "Why does it disquiet us to know that Don Quixote is a reader of the *Quixote,* and Hamlet is a spectator of *Hamlet?* I believe I have found the answer: those inversions suggest that if the characters in a story can be readers or spectators, then we, their readers or spectators, can be fictitious" ["Partial Enchantments of the Quixote" in *Other Inquisitions, 1937-1952,* Austin, 1964]. The self-consciousness in *Looking-Glass* likewise hints that what appears tangible may be only a dream, that presumed realities are really fantasies, that reality is subjective. *Looking-Glass* may not be a fully self-conscious novel, one that, in Robert Alter's words, "systematically flaunts its own condition of artifice and . . . by so doing probes into the problematic relationship between real-seeming artifice and reality" [Alter, 1975], but it does tend somewhat in that direction, to confound reality and fiction. Once again, though indirectly, the *Looking-Glass* verse occasions integration, integration here of the larger realms of fiction and reality. And once again, *Looking-Glass* balances closure and self-containment with openness and permeation.

Enough of metaphysics and back to the verse again: not only is the content integrated with the narrative but so is the form. Not only is there thematic continuity between verse and prose, via fishes, and not only is one sometimes an adumbration of the other—as with the Tweedles, Humpty Dumpty, and the Lion and the Unicorn—but the physical integration of the two has also increased in *Looking-Glass.* Of course, this verse, like the verse in *Wonderland,* is set off from the rest of the text by being in verse form. Yet in *Looking-Glass* the segregation of verse and prose falters. Perhaps even the railway passengers' refrain, "———is worth a thousand———a———," is a verse more completely integrated with narrative, a verse not typographically segregated: Alice considers the refrain "like the chorus of a song."

Once more I would like to amplify the argument by examining specific examples. First I will look at the White Knight's verse and then Humpty Dumpty's, both of which merge with the surrounding narrative.

After droning on *"mumblingly and low"* with his *"so"/ "know"/"slow"* rhymes, the White Knight abruptly ends his poem with *"A-sitting on a gate."* The last line provides the rhyme for "weight" so long held in abeyance, until the record needle finally came unstuck, and hence provides some closure. Yet the poem shows a tendency to continue into, merge with, the ensuing narrative. For the interminable o-rhymes, essentially paratactic, could go on forever, comic invention willing. And they make the abrupt concluding line seem tacked on, anticlimactic. This anticlimax is humorous, as Carroll wants it to be, but it also, as Barbara Herrnstein Smith might note, leaves the reader "with residual expectations." [Smith, 1968] These residual expectations make the reader receptive to the possibility of an additional line or lines. And, in fact, the next words the White Knight speaks are "You've only a few yards to go"—consistent with the poem's meter and rhyme. The poem pushes beyond its physical boundaries.

Humpty Dumpty's verse likewise shows a tendency to continue into the narrative, a merging anticipated by Alice's frequent interruptions during the recitation. Some of the stanzas are as follows:

> The little fishes' answer was
> 'We cannot do it, Sir, because————'
>
> . . . . .
>
> And he was very proud and stiff:
> He said 'I'd go and wake them, if————'
>
> . . . . .
>
> And when I found the door was shut,
> I tried to turn the handle, but————

Alice's comment shortly after hearing the poem, as she leaves Humpty Dumpty, is "of all the unsatisfactory people I *ever* met————." Because of forces working against closure in the poem, her comment would seem to be a reprise of the unfinished sentences in the above stanzas.

Now it is not that there are no forces working to close the poem. The line that Alice speaks and that could continue the poem is not spoken immediately after Humpty Dumpty's recitation, nor is it spoken by the character reciting the poem, nor is it a complete couplet, nor is it metrically consistent with the poem. Then, too, we may resolve some of the poem's lack of closure by declaring it humorous, labeling its dissonance and making it acceptable, so that we need not continue to seek closure. Yet the forces working against closure are stronger.

In the first place, the verse purports to tell a narrative, but its story is truncated. The narrator tells of the need to wake the little fishes and of going to the locked door and

trying to get through. We expect some kind of resolution: perhaps the narrator breaks through the door, perhaps the door proves sentient and assaults the narrator, perhaps the narrator wastes away to a hummingbird egg as the continually pounds and kicks and knocks. Yet the action is not resolved but interrupted. Similarly, we expect resolution of other hints in the plot: what nefarious deed, requiring the presence of the fishes, does the narrator intend to perpetrate with his kettle of water?

Instead of resolving the plot the poem simply stops, defying closure. And Alice, puzzled, acts out the reader's discomfort over the poem's abrupt completion. Alice is particularly puzzled by the concluding stanza, the one in which the narrator tries to turn the handle of the door: she pauses, she asks if the poem is over, she finds Humpty Dumpty's dismissal—of the poem and of her—rather sudden. Humpty Dumpty's abrupt good-bye at the end of the poem reinforces the abrupt stopping of the poem itself.

Not only is the narrative action truncated but so too is the sentence begun in the final stanza, as in the other stanzas quoted above. In both the overall plot and also the sentence, the meaning is lefthanging: both are semantically incomplete. And the sentence is syntactically incomplete as well.

I can elucidate the syntactic and semantic open-endedness of this verse by comparing it to a rather different open-endedness in verse from *Wonderland*. The verse about the Owl and the Panther concludes thus (in some versions of the poem):

> When the pie was all finished, the Owl, as a boon,
> Was kindly permitted to pocket the spoon:
> While the Panther received knife and fork with a
>   growl,
> And concluded the banquet by————

The final line is incomplete, but—guided by meter and rhyme, by our knowledge of panthers, by our knowledge that "by" wants here to be followed by a verb ending in "ing"—we can readily complete the line with "eating the Owl." Even the narrative plot of the verse reaches resolution with this ending, thus reinforcing the implicit closure. With our complicity the verse silently reaches syntactic, semantic, and narrative closure. The *Looking-Glass* verse, Humpty Dumpty's open-ended verse, is rather different. The lines are metrically complete, with appropriate end-rhymes, but semantically incomplete. And the narrative plot is incomplete too. Rather like the later riddle poem, *"'First, the fish must be caught,'"* whose riddle is never solved for us, and perhaps a bit like the riddle posed in his own nursery rhyme, Humpty Dumpty's poem reaches no resolution. Although the stanza reaches prosodic closure, thanks to the tidy end rhyme, the meaning stretches beyond the verse form, eluding closure, eluding the tidy solipsizing of the verse.

Much of the humor of Humpty Dumpty's verse derives from its integration with the narrative, its interruptions, its incompleteness. Some critics find this the least satisfactory of Carroll's verse, and while it is certainly not the best it does become better if we look at it not in isolation but in context. At times the proper unit of analysis is not the poem by itself but the entire dialogue, of which the poem is just part.

Like Humpty Dumpty's poem, if not always to the same degree, the *Looking-Glass* poems are surprisingly integrated into the story, thematically and even physically. Of course, they remain typographically distinct from the prose as well—and again there is a tension between opening and closing. Another site for this tension is the overall structure of *Looking-Glass*. In fact, the greater merging of poetry and prose, compared to *Wonderland,* may in part compensate for a more rigid, closed structure in *Looking-Glass*. Where *Wonderland* describes a relatively aimless wandering, *Looking-Glass* describes a prescribed progression toward a goal, as Alice moves across the chessboard. The individual chapters reinforce the structure by corresponding to individual squares. Carroll counteracts the rigidity of this structure in several ways. One is his placement of lines of asterisks: in *Wonderland* these asterisks, signalling Alice's changes in size, can appear at the end of a chapter, coinciding with and reinforcing a narrative boundary; in *Looking-Glass,* though, Carroll seems careful not to place asterisks, here signalling movement to the next square, at the end of a chapter. Thus Carroll dissipates, a little, the clear demarcations of his narrative. Similarly, in *Looking-Glass* Carroll sometimes does not complete a sentence begun in one chapter until the following chapter: again, Carroll is ameliorating the strict division into chapters. It is as if he wanted to attenuate the rigid boundaries imposed by the chessboard structure. The greater integration of the verse may be similarly compensatory. It attenuates the rigidities of the external scaffolding of the book, much as narrative plays against and dissipates the external scaffolding of the Ulysses story in *Ulysses.*

In fact, Carroll's integration of verse and narrative in *Looking-Glass* is one of the many ways in which he anticipates twentieth-century literature. In some ways *Wonderland* seems rather modern—as in its associative, nonsequential plotting—and in some ways *Looking-Glass* anticipates current fiction. One such way is the way Carroll incorporates verse. His *Looking-Glass* parodies are not true parodies but rather they play against the scaffolding of pre-existing poems, like some of Yeats's poetry, which uses materials in his *A Vision,* yet the images in, say, the Byzantium poems do not need to be followed back to their source before we can appreciate them. Carroll's parodies too can stand alone, divorced from their sources. Though not from the narrative. For the relationship between verse and narrative also seems modern. Recent writers like Vladimir Nabokov, Thomas Pynchon, and Robert Coover have incorporated verse in their novels yet subverted strict boundaries. In Nabokov's *Pale Fire,* for instance, the novel's plot grows out of footnotes presumably annotating a poem: the poem is far from a mere set piece that a character happens to recite. These novelists carry further certain hints in Carroll's work, going farther than he in merging verse and narrative, fiction and reality.

The interaction of poem and narrative in *Looking-Glass* may thus be approaching twentieth-century forms of interpenetration. And Carroll's humor derives in part from this integration and in part from the opposing tendency toward concrete completeness. Likewise it derives in part from parody and in part from simply playing with "real"-world forms. The humor and nonsense and absurdity depend on a confrontation between opposites, a confrontation that we cannot quite resolve in "real"-world terms. Defining "glory" as "a nice knock-down argument" disagrees with our usual use of the term. It is hard even to make it agree metaphorically, as we can when glory is described as clouds that we trail as we come from God. Instead, the odd juxtaposition, the unresolved confrontation, makes us laugh, strikes us as absurd. And we resolve the disparity, a little, by calling it nonsense, something that need not overturn our comfortable real world. Yet despite its resolution it still hints at revolution, still hints at a more serious questioning of reality.

William A. Madden   (essay date 1986)

SOURCE: "Framing the Alices," in *PMLA,* Vol. 101, No. 3, May 1986, pp. 362-73.

[*In the following excerpt, Madden argues that the critically-debated framing poems of the* Alice *books serve several nineteenth-century literary purposes.*]

Over the past thirty years Lewis Carroll studies have both altered and generally enhanced the reputation of Carroll's two *Alices.* Yet from early on in this reevaluation process one feature of these famous stories has posed a persistent critical problem. I refer to the three poems, one prefacing each of the *Alice* books and the third concluding *Looking-Glass,* that, together with the prose ending of *Wonderland,* frame the central tales. The problem is raised in acute form by Peter Coveney in his influential study of the figure of the child in nineteenth-century English literature: praising the central *Alice* dream tales as triumphs of "astringent and intelligent art," he detects in this frame material evidence of what he describes as "almost the case-book maladjusted neurotic." Subsequent critics who have mentioned this feature of the *Alices* have for the most part been similarly dismissive, implying, at least, that the *Alice* frames are best ignored in discussions of the masterpieces they enclose.

The issue has important implications. For one thing, the reputed failure of the frame poems, as I will call them, has sometimes been used as evidence that Carroll's genius was psychologically crippled. Given Carroll's eccentricities, biographical speculation postulating a pathological Dodgson/Carroll personality split may seem a plausible explanation for the apparent erratic working of his acknowledged genius. But the entanglement of an essentially literary question in a nonliterary preoccupation with Carroll's private habits and mental health confuses an issue that needs to be dealt with on literary grounds. While several modern critics have praised the *Alice* frame poems, no one has advanced an extended analysis to support either a favorable or an unfavorable reading, and until the poems' literary status is clarified our estimate of the aesthetic integrity of the *Alices* and our understanding of the books must remain in doubt.

It will be useful at the outset to call attention to a feature of the *Alice* frame poems that helps explain the negative response of modern readers. The three poems are devoid of qualities that the educated reader has come to expect in lyric poetry, qualities summarized by one literary historian as "colloquialism of style and rhythm, realistic particularity, toughness of sensibility, the complex and often dissonant expression of tension and conflict, the resources of irony, ambiguity, paradox, and wit" [Bush, 1963]. The alteration in taste that has led us to value such characteristics was already evident in the work of Carroll's contemporaries Browning and Hopkins, indeed in Carroll's own parodic verses in the *Alices,* but not at all in the frame poems, where these qualities are conspicuous by their absence.

These poems are characterized, rather, by the conventional diction, metrics, and syntax of the main English poetic tradition—revitalized early in the century by Wordsworth—which still shaped the poetic style of those Victorians whose poetry Carroll most admired: Keble, Tennyson, and the Rossettis. . . . Generically, too, the *Alice* frame poems conform to conventions established early in the century. The prefatory poem to *Wonderland,* for example, with its localized setting, feelings originating in a specific event, and a presupposed listener, has affinities with a poem like *Tintern Abbey* and, in its evocation of a dream mood, with the Coleridgean "mystery" poem, whereby "the spell-bound reader sees visions and hears music which float in from a magic realm" [Harper, 1928]. Compared with such prototypes, or with most twentieth-century English or American lyrics, the *Alice* frame poems seem bland indeed—competent minor poems at best and, at worst, symptoms of an exhausted tradition self-indulgently exploited.

It is necessary to concede the surface tameness of the poems in order to avoid defending them on the wrong grounds. I propose an alternative reading that I believe vindicates Carroll's inclusion of them as an integral part of the *Alices* It is not mere paradox to assert that their conventionality provides an interpretive clue. Modern readers who respond negatively do so, I would argue, because they either fail to recognize the conventions at work in the poems or, recognizing them, mistake Carroll's purpose in adopting them. Writing in a late Victorian climate for a special audience, Carroll adopted a form and idiom familiar to that audience, through parody in the dream tales but directly in the frame poems. While the parodies have been increasingly admired, his direct use of conventions in the frame material has been met in recent years with either indifference or dismay. Since we know that Carroll was a knowledgeable and careful craftsman, it is not unreasonable to assume that he employed a familiar lyric form and idiom for a particular purpose.

He chose the "Tennysonian" idiom, I would suggest, because his age regarded it as proper to "serious" poetry,

and he thereby signaled to his audience the serious purpose underlying his books of "nonsense." His choice of a familiar form of the Romantic lyric likewise had a specific purpose: not to create self-standing lyrics but to frame a substantial narrative. In this respect the relevant prototype for the *Alice* frame poems would be the lyric frame in a poem like "The Eve of St. Agnes" or, to cite a more nearly contemporary prose analogue, the narrative frame provided by Lockwood's dreams in *Wuthering Heights* which transform the reader's sense of reality at the outset and color the reader's response to everything that follows. On the one hand, the *Alice* frame poems record an experience of lyric transformation that induces the dream tales that follow, the tales from this perspective serving as sustained extensions of an initial lyric moment. On the other hand, since the dream tales articulate and define the meaning of this initiating lyric experience, the poems remain incomplete, indeed virtually contentless, apart from the tales. It is the mutual interdependence of the frame poems and the dream tales that needs to be recognized if we are to understand why Carroll attached such importance to these poems, never allowing the *Alices* to appear without them and never allowing the frame poems themselves to appear separately.

I

. . . . The apparent anomaly of *Wonderland* ending with a prose narrative and *Looking-Glass* with a lyric poem disappears when we recognize that the *Wonderland* prose ending forms part of the outer-frame structure of which the three frame poems are complementary components. The schema also calls attention to the fact that both books contain inner as well as outer frames, each of which presents a waking Alice in a prose narrative of a kind we might find in a realistic novel. The structure of each book encompasses shifts in the narrative mode, allowing the narrative voice to move into and back out of the central dream tales by modulating from lyric, to realistic fiction, to dream vision, back through realistic fiction, to a final lyric statement.

This organizing structure is similar to that of "The Eve of St. Agnes," and what has been observed of Keats's poem—that "it is the way we are taken into the world of the poem, what happens to us there, and the way we are let out again that matters" [Sperry, 1973]—exactly fits our experience of the *Alices,* indicating the importance of all three phases of the complex experience that is built into the books' structure. The major difference is that the *Alice* frame structure initiates a double rhythm of entry into and withdrawal from the central experience. The reader undergoes at the outset a lyric transformation that anticipates the similar transformation that Alice experiences. A series of transitions—from the reader's ordinary reality to the reality of the restless boat children, through the everyday reality that bores the waking Alice, into the chaotic world of Alice's dream—gradually awakens the reader to a nightmare world that proves to be the reader's ordinary world transformed by a startling perception regarding that reality. Responding to this double rhythm, the reader, too, experiences a "dream within a dream." The central dream tales thus take on their full meaning in relation to this double frame, all three elements together—outer frame, inner frame, and dream tale—embodying in their reciprocal interactions the total vision of the *Alice* books.

I suggest below how the inner frames function within this larger structure. Here, however, I want to stress the answer to the question of why Carroll framed the *Alices* as he did: to establish in the reader a proper orientation toward the central narratives. The lyric effect of the tales themselves is evidenced by the frequent references commentators make to their dream quality. . . . Carroll's skill in adapting the poetic conventions of his day to serve his narrative strategy—to induce and reinforce in the reader a necessary state of "reverie"—emerges clearly from an examination of the frame poems individually and as they vary according to their place and function in the overall structure of the two books.

II

The most complex of the *Alice* frame poems is the prefatory poem to *Wonderland,* which, in occupying the privileged place of inauguration, plays a key role in alerting the reader to the special nature of the Alice experience. Through image, character, and event, the first six stanzas embody the fundamental lyric transaction, the seventh stanza constituting an epilogue to and commentary on what has transpired in the earlier stanzas, including the narrating of the tale that the reader is about to encounter. The opening three stanzas present an idyllic setting ("such an hour . . . such dreamy weather") that is rudely disrupted ("cruel voices") by the three children in the boating party (neutrally designated at this point as Prima, Secunda, and Tertia) demanding that their apparently languid and abstracted companion-attendant entertain them. (It is Secunda who specifically requests "nonsense.") The next three stanzas describe the silence that ensues as the spellbound children are caught up in the storyteller-companion's narrative of a dream child's adventures, interrupting only to demand more whenever the storyteller shows signs of growing weary. This simple plot concludes with the "crew's" merry return home, as the sun is setting, after the tale has been completed to everyone's satisfaction. Imagery of oars, wandering, a journey, and a return home suggests a quest motif, but the "wandering" of the actual boat is aimless, the children's efforts to guide its course futile. Their journey takes on purpose and significance, that is, only with the commencement of the storyteller's narrative. It is thus the imaginative journey on which the narrator's "dream-child" takes the children that carries through the quest motif and sends the children home happy.

What the plot of the poem stresses—once fate, in the guise of the children's request, has issued its command—is the storyteller's initial reluctance and subsequent weariness in attempting to respond to the children's relentless demands. We are made conscious of the speaker of the poem watching his storytelling self, presenting this self as a somewhat feckless, slightly comic figure. The child reader of *Wonderland* can both laugh at and perhaps feel a bit sorry for this imposed-on and seemingly well-intentioned figure but, like the children in the boat, can quickly forget him when the strange adventures of the dream child begin to unfold. Finally, the subdued silence and intense absorption of the original listeners set up in the reader appropriate expectations of excitement and pleasure. That the ending of each story—the dream child's and that of the boat children who hear her adventures—is a happy one can be inferred from the children's merriment as they return home. Exactly what they have heard and why they are "merry" the reader does not yet know, but even the harried storyteller-poet seems content with what has taken place.

These basic elements of plot, imagery, and characterization remain subordinate, however, to the central purpose, which derives from the poem's function as the point of entry into the main story. The lyrical quality and thrust of the poem, the eerie sense of transition the poem both embodies and effects, is essential: the experience is of a transformation that erases the barrier between the "real" and the "unreal." The poem engages us at this deeper level, modifying our approach and hence our response to the dream tale itself. The lyricizing of this originating moment endows a seemingly ordinary boating excursion, involving an inconsequential skirmish between three children and their languid companion, with a visionary quality. The poem achieves this transformation primarily through a subtle variation and interplay of verbal tenses, manifesting the characteristics of what has been aptly named the "lyric present" (Wright). A past event is rendered as though present ("we *glide,*" "little arms *are plied*"). Simple physical gestures, in this case rowing, activate a timeless mental event (the emergence of the dream child). Present-tense verbs portentously carry the reader forward (*"flashes forth,"* "*hopes*") even while the poet is looking to the past ("thus *grew* the tale"). We observe the poet watching himself in the act of creating ("And faintly *strove* that weary one / To put the subject by"). In stanza 6, place and time are finally elevated into a historical present ("and *now* the tale is done, / And home we *steer*"), the scene becoming endlessly renewable as the action resumes each time we read the poem. The crucial event appropriately occurs at the center of the poem, in the pivotal fourth stanza, in which the "dream-child moving through a land / Of wonders" mysteriously appears, leading the boat children (and the reader) across a threshold through a lyric estrangement that transforms the children and the storyteller alike. When the children cry, "It *is* next time," we find ourselves in the alogical and atemporal realm of desire, the realm in which the tale is both told and heard.

The seventh and final stanza of the poem is an epilogue in which the storyteller, who now becomes obliquely identified with the poet, directly addresses "Alice" (so named for the first time) in a more serious tone, gently instructing her regarding the proper disposition of the tale she has just heard. The concluding stanza concentrates the themes and transformations of the previous six stanzas in a single conventional image, the one rhetorical figure that Carroll allows himself in the poem:

> Alice! A childish story take,
>   And, with gentle hand,

> Lay it where Childhood's dreams are twined
>   In Memory's mystic band.
> Like pilgrim's wither'd wreath of flowers
>   Pluck'd in a far-off land.

The opening apostrophe, followed immediately by a shift to the imperative mood, sets off this stanza from the previous six. It is further set off by a slightly weightier cadence and by the relative complexity of the concluding simile. The two main protagonists now emerge: "Alice" as a transformed "Secunda" (the two names are linked by the common epithet *gentle*) and the poet as a transformed storyteller. It was Secunda who had asked for "nonsense," and it is to her, now renamed and thus identified with the dream child (whose name the reader will soon discover), that the poet turns, singling her out to suggest to her the implications of the adventures that had held her and her companions in thrall and sent them home happy. By placing the message in the actual present of the reader about to read the tale, the imperative mood establishes an implicit identity between the reader and the "Alice" addressed. The poet informs "Alice," in effect, that he has given (will give) her something more than the "nonsense" she has asked for (expects); thus he indicates at the outset what the original *Under Ground* ending foreshadowed: the narrator's desire to give Alice Liddell something more than a simple transcription of the original oral tales.

This something more is conveyed through the trope of the pilgrim's wreath, which distills the essence of the lyric action embodied by the poem as a whole and delicately hints at the motive (hitherto hidden) for the narrator's willingness to "hammer out" the story. This image integrates the several dimensions of time evoked in the preceding stanzas, extending backward to the past as a *memorial* of a sacred occasion ("pilgrim's wreath") that gave birth to the tale and forward as an image of the tale itself, a wreath of words woven into artistic form, a circular image of the *promise* of eternity and—in the present—a lover's *gift,* a bouquet ("wreath of flowers"), for all the Alices who will read *Wonderland.* Real time—linear, irreversible, redolent of death—is recognized in the poem: the sun is setting as the boat journey comes to an end, and the wreath itself is already "wither'd" even as the poet presents it. But the linear dimension along which the boating excursion takes place and the spontaneous appearance of the dream child at a particular moment in time are alike arrested in an oneiric timelessness, a vision with roots "twined / In Memory's *mystic* band." Thus the wreath embodies the three dimensions of linear time: a reminder of the meaning and identity that derive from memory's link with the past, a token of love that redeems the present and gives it value, and an emblem of an artwork with the power endlessly to renew a timeless present in which it always *is* next time. Properly understood, the concluding stanza declares, the tale will return the reader to the source ("a far-off land") of wholeness and health and sanity, to the psychic origins of the true human identity of which the dream child is an emblem.

We can now see that Carroll revised the *Wonderland* narrative ending to reinforce the lyric thrust of the prefatory poem. When Alice awakes from her dream, the brief inner frame, basically unchanged from the *Under Ground* version, gives a straight-forward three-sentence account of Alice's report of her dream to her older sister, after which she obediently runs off to tea, the narrator simply concurring in Alice's final feeling that the dream was "wonderful." In what follows, the topical allusions in *Under Ground* to the scene of the boating excursion are gone; the dream events, their violence now emphasized, are recapitulated by the sister; and the description of Alice reporting her dream is expanded to suggest that Alice herself has been brought alive by her dream (Alice now tells the dream instead of, as in *Under Ground,* listening to it being told). Moreover, two substantial added passages make explicit the older sister's acute awareness of how "dull" everyday reality seems, appearing to her in a new and disenchanting light, as "the confused clamour of the busy farm-yard." Her perception has been altered by her exposure to the perspective that informs a dream epitomized by the prefatory poem, in the emphatic rhyme words of its pivotal stanza, as a vision to *pursue,* a vision both *new* and *true.*

Carroll's retention of the *Under Ground* final paragraph virtually unchanged is equally instructive. The older sister instinctively links the motif of retelling the dream story with Alice's "simple and loving heart," clearly implying that the adventures deserve retelling *because* they reveal a simple and loving heart. In thus discerning in the behavior of Alice's dream self an exemplary manifestation of human identity and meaning, the older sister guides the reader in interpreting the dream. In her status as an "elder" she perceives a paradoxical warning that she must keep becoming a child, that a simple and loving heart requires perpetual maintenance in the face of the corrosive pressures of reality, whether these pressures take the form of biological laws of physical survival or, as in the later *Looking-Glass,* of cultural laws of social preferment. The *Wonderland* dream tale becomes, in this context, a reminder to the reader of both the need and the possibility of transcending the debilitating decorums of ordinary existence through a renewal of perception that is the central effect of *Wonderland* itself when the reader fully experiences it.

III

. . . . Turning now to the *Looking-Glass* prefatory poem, we can note first that, while the poem reflects a change in "Alice," its primary function is identical to that of the *Wonderland* frame: to evoke a past communal event by creating from it a lyric present that will guide the reader through the dream tale to follow. Like *Wonderland,* the tale is both a memorial to and a renewal of "happy summer days," a phrase that Carroll incorporates into the *Looking-Glass* poem from the prose ending of *Wonderland.* Since the originating event and its first fruits are already on record, as it were, in *Wonderland,* the poet can now content himself with reinvoking the appropriate mood by referring to the earlier story. The *Looking-Glass* poem is therefore less complex than its *Wonderland* counterpart, the major change deriving from the speaker's more intense time consciousness, rooted in his sense both that the originating event is retreating into the past and that "Alice" is growing away from him. The pressing reality of time is again acknowledged ("though time be fleet"), its emotional effect now overtly expressed ("the shadow of a sigh / May tremble through the story"), and this acute time consciousness makes the speaker's presence more directly felt and the poem's imperatives more urgent than in the *Wonderland* frame material. But if the sense of time irresistibly passing and of absence becoming permanent is strong, so also is the speaker's will to transcend time through a conscious renewal of the original event. Recognizing and accepting the inexorableness of time and change, the poem reasserts the transforming power of the dream child, whose renewable presence the second dream tale is about to enact.

Carroll employs a slightly modified version of the stanza used in the *Wonderland* prefatory poem, so that the *Looking-Glass* prefatory poem's form and language serve as a bridge between the two *Alices*. The poem's structure, unlike the simple plot-cum-epilogue of the *Wonderland* poem, is a series of strophic contrasts, each stanza juxtaposing the temporal and the atemporal, the passing and the enduring. In each stanza the quatrain renders the experience of transience and loss or of anticipated decline or separation; the falling trochaic beats at the end of the second and fourth lines convey a mild feeling of pathos, and each quatrain is balanced by a strong affirmation in the concluding couplet. From the confident invocation of the child muse in the opening lines ("Child of the pure unclouded brow / And dreaming eyes of wonder!") down to the end of the fourth stanza the rhythm oscillates between the sense of time past and passing, on the one hand, and the poet's will to affirm, on the other, with a diminuendo in a "though . . . yet still" movement that reaches a low point in the quiet, almost prosaic statement at the end of stanza 4: "We are but older children, dear, / Who fret to find our bedtime near." For the "melancholy maiden" addressed in these lines there is the early prospect of the "little death" of the marriage bed, and for maiden and poet alike the inevitable grave awaits. But a counterfeeling of hope, rooted in the poet's faith in the power of his visionary gift to redeem the time, emerges with fresh strength in the concluding couplets. The conclusion of stanza 5 invokes the power of the poet's art to protect the maiden against the madness raging outside "childhood's nest of gladness" ("The magic words shall hold thee fast: / Thou shalt not heed the raving blast"), and the terminal couplet of stanza 6 asserts the capacity of the dream tale to render time itself powerless to alter "Alice": "It shall not touch, with breath of bale, / The pleasance of our fairy-tale."

Imagery of frost and fire is related to the deep structure that underpins the stanzaic pattern of strophic oppositions that organize the poem. The natural fire of "summer suns" has departed, but it is replaced by the humanly created fire of a hearth, in the presence of which the poet can retrieve and renew a primordial "now" that is "enough," if the listener will but "hail" his gift and "listen" to what the story has to say. "Come, harken, then" is this poem's imperative. Generative of light and warmth, the fire dispels time's wintry depletions, serving as an emblem of the love that is openly declared in a couplet that simultaneously invites and expresses a hope for an appropriate response: "Thy loving smile will surely hail / The love-gift of a fairy-tale." Against the surrounding night of frost and blinding snow and the temporal prospect of an "unwelcome bed," the poet sets the image of the fire that Alice will find burning on the other side of the mirror in her dream. In offering this second tale as a "love-gift," the poet offers love itself as the only "nonsense" that can effectively confront the surrounding darkness.

The *Looking-Glass* end poem embodies the poet's final statement regarding the Alice experience. The poem functions, at one level, as the equivalent to the prose narrative ending of *Wonderland,* with the reader moved once again out of a nightmare that provokes Alice's violent reaction, through the self-questioning of the inner frame, into final lyric affirmation. It differs from the *Wonderland* ending in that the poet now addresses the reader directly instead of merely reporting the older sister's response, a change prepared for in a closing inner frame significantly more substantial than the *Wonderland* equivalent. This time the response to the dream tale is that of the awakened Alice, who poses a series of questions to herself that lead to a final question: was it she or the Red King who dreamed the dream? The dream, that is, has shaken Alice out of her preoccupation with attaining queenhood into serious reflection about the nature of reality. In the final sentence of the inner frame, the narrator addresses the question directly to the reader—"Which do *you* think it was?"— thereby drawing the reader into the dream and into Alice's radical question, a question that makes all human perspectives relative. In this context the *Looking-Glass* end poem implicitly offers the Alice experience as the answer to this ultimate metaphysical question, a "dream" that contains not only Alice, the Red King, and all the other dream characters but finally the reader and the poet as well.

Structurally, the seven-stanza *Looking-Glass* end poem symmetrically balances the seven-stanza prefatory poem to *Wonderland,* but Carroll now adopts a highly concentrated verse form, a rare trochaic trimeter in triplets, that gives to the end poem a terseness that reinforces the sense of closure. The initial letters of the twenty-one lines of the poem form an acrostic that places "Alice Pleasance Liddell" within the poem, figuratively incorporating Alice Liddell into the books that she inspired and thus assuring her of immortality. While the real Alice Liddell has grown up, the poet rescues and fixes *his* "Alice" by a process that had begun when Alice Liddell became Secunda and Secunda became Alice in the opening *Wonderland* poem, was carried forward in the allusion to pleasance in the middle *Looking-Glass* prefatory poem, and is now brought to completion in her total naming. Whereas the Alice of the *Wonderland* prefatory poem had been near and real and the Alice in the prefatory poem to *Looking-Glass* could still be imaginatively evoked, remaining at least virtually real and present, in the *Looking-Glass* end poem she has been transformed into poetry, the elements of her dismembered name becoming an integral part of the poetic vision that Alice Liddell had inspired long before by awakening the poet's love for her and for what she represented to him.

The opening stanzas go back one last time to the moment of origin, evoking through reverie the benign weather, the boat, and the eager listening children of that long-ago July "evening" (as the poet now autumnally calls it), and for two brief stanzas the scene is again dreamily present. But the third stanza scatters the memory of that moment with shocking finality:

> Long has paled that sunny sky:
> Echoes fade and memories die,
> Autumn frosts have slain July.

Then in the pivotal fourth stanza, in a stunning second reversal, the poet shifts to the lyric present, concentrating the entire Alice experience in a central three-line stanza that is as concise as it is definitive:

> Still she haunts me, phantomwise,
> Alice moving under skies
> Never seen by waking eyes.

The dream Alice is finally apotheosized, fixed in the firmament of the poet's poetic universe, reigning there as an emblem of wholeness and integrity perpetually set over against all that we ordinarily assume to be "real." The fifth stanza, echoing the prose ending of *Wonderland,* anticipates the reembodiment of this lyric vision in works of verbal art capable of making the experience new again and again for "children yet" (both the children to come and those who remain childlike) who listen attentively. As time—that other and more transient dream—moves on, days go by, and other summers die, and we drift down the irreversible stream of time, we can, the concluding stanzas assert, by an act of poetic faith, *linger* in—await, harken to, renew, take hope from—the "golden gleam" embodied in narratives inspired by an extraordinary visionary experience.

IV

In their conventionality and deceptive simplicity the *Alice* frame poems no doubt lend themselves to neglect or misreading. My point is simply that the central tales, however brilliantly achieved, are not the whole story of the *Alices.* The dream tales themselves simply interrogate a reality that is revealed, over and over, as incapable of yielding answers. Their purpose, unlike that of the usual fairy tale, is disenchantment with reality as we normally perceive it, that is, with the reality "grown-ups" accept and seek to exploit out of one or another neurotic impulse. Like certain types of myth, the *Alice* dream tales serve as inverse social charters, subverting our everyday notions of what is important, portraying worlds of potential madness that close in on Alice inexorably, leaving her nowhere to turn. The great danger to which Alice, like every other human being, is exposed (physical extinction is never felt to be an imminent threat in either dream) appears in the pathological behavior that she observes in the dream characters: cowardice in the White Rabbit, furious passion in the Queen of Hearts, calculated aggression in the Red Queen, evasive conformity in the White Queen, melancholy resignation in the Gnat, self-pity in the Mock-Turtle,

insouciance in the Gryphon, arrogance in Humpty Dumpty, madness in the Hare and Hatter, sterile inventiveness in the White Knight, and so forth. The danger that imperils Alice as she grows up is a fatal loss of courage, simplicity, and openness through succumbing to the spiritual death represented in the various dehumanizing forms that she encounters in her dreams, which are ultimately messages from Alice to herself. Her heroism consists in preserving her innate decency against the confusions and dislocations of her dreams through the courtesy and courage that her sister perceives in her dream behavior and that she manifests in her steadfast refusal to submit to absurd or threatening situations.

Carroll's unsentimental view of human nature is pointed up in the realistic inner frames. They show the seeds of spiritual death to be latent even in the innocent Alice: at the opening of *Wonderland* in the form of boredom, self-pity, and an impulse to regressive withdrawal; in *Looking-Glass* in the form of role-playing, manic aggressiveness, and ambition ("Let's pretend we're kings and queens"). Even the child harbors disturbing potentialities ("Nurse! Do let's pretend that I'm a hungry hyaena, and you're a bone!"). The frame poems lead us into, through, and out of this dark central vision, providing the perspective that enables the reader to judge the "mistery of pain," as Joyce glosses the dream world of the *Alices,* and thereby converting the potential nightmare of ordinary existence into a profoundly instructive comedy. It is by their means that we cross the threshold from irreality to reality, from spiritual sleep to intense wakefulness, returning, if we have read the tales attentively, with our vision cleansed. To be awake in the usual sense, the *Alice* books tell us, is to dwell in an absurd kingdom absentmindedly presided over by the Red King sleeping his fatal sleep. To be truly alive we need to dream the Alice dream—to perceive, nurture, and transmit a vision rooted in the heart's deepest desire.

Karen Alkalay-Gut   (essay date 1987)

SOURCE: "Carroll's *Jabberwocky*," in *Explicator,* Vol. 46, No. 1, Fall 1987, pp. 27-31.

[In the following excerpt, Alkalay-Gut analyses "Jabberwocky" and finds it structurally and thematically similar to heroic epics such as Beowulf.*]*

An old professor of mine, warning against the dangers of overinterpretation, would illustrate the extent to which criticism could err by giving an extensive and detailed reading of "Mary Had A Little Lamb" as a religious allegory and "Hickory Dickory Dock" as a paradigm of the existential experience. Perhaps for this reason, I have resisted the temptation to try to understand what has made **"Jabberwocky"** so popular a poem, both with children and adults; but, its continued popularity continues to puzzle. After all, if it is only nonsense, what distinguishes **"Jabberwocky"** from any other nonsense verse, from an obscure modern poem, or from formless gibberish? And if it is purely nonsense, then why is it read? The decision, then, to plumb the depths of **"Jabberwocky"** is based not on a desire to elicit meaning from the poem, but to determine how it manages to communicate despite its defiance of common language.

The first thing to strike the reader about the poem is not its senselessness but its grammatical and structural coherence. **"Jabberwocky"** follows known patterns. Not only can some sense be comprehended concerning the action from the grammatical logic, there is also a structural coherence in the poem, a structure that is made salient by the identity of the first and last verses of the poem. Even if there is no agreed meaning to the words, a sense to the setting and the plot, it is possible to say that whatever happens the poem ends where it begins, with the events in the middle having ultimately altered little.

Were this the only hint of a structural order, the poem would be too short and the words seemingly too insignificant to reach this conclusion. Yet, a glance at the adjacent verses—the second and the second last reveals other parallels:

> "Beware the Jabberwock, my son!
>   The jaws the bite, the claws that catch!
> Beware the Jubjub bird, and shun
>   The frumious Bandersnatch!
> And hast thou slain the Jabberwock?
>   Come to my arms, my beamish boy!
> O frabjous day! Callooh, Callay!
>   He chortled in his joy.

In the former verse, an apparent father-figure speaks, warning the son away from the Jabberwock and the other accompanying monsters. In the latter verse, the same character welcomes the conquering hero on his victorious return. These are clearly equal but antithetical actions. Leaving aside meaning and plot for a moment, the fact that the hero is warned against an action and then praised for the same action by the same elder in itself indicates that in the intervening verses a "turn" has occurred, a "change of fortune."

The third and fifth verse illustrate the same parallelism and the same indication of a "change of fortune" but the implications are more immediate.

> He took his vorpal sword in hand;
>   Long time the manxome foe he sought—
> So rested he by the Tumtum tree
>   And stood awhile in thought.
> One, two! One, two! And through and through
>   The vorpal blade went snicker-snack!
> He left it dead, and with its head
>   He went galumphing back.

Although both verses describe an armed hero, the third verse is concerned with departure, contemplation, and pursuit, and the fifth with action uncomplicated by thought, followed by a return home. The fourth and middle verse, the center of the poem, is the encounter between hero and jabberwock.

It would be easy to conclude from this that Carroll has written a perfectly constructed mock heroic poem, using the structure of the epic, but enveloping it in nonsense in order to prove the ridiculousness of all the heroic tales. But it is also possible to conclude the opposite, that the nonsense takes on special significance in the light of the epic structure and lends it a higher meaning.

When J. R. R. Tolkien was defending *Beowulf* against the charge that the monsters detracted from the dignity of the epic, he noted, "It is not an accident that the tone of the poem is so high and its theme so low. It is the theme in its deadly seriousness that begets the dignity of tone. . . ." Tolkien's contention, that the epic quality of the poem is not diminished because of the seemingly ridiculous subject matter, but that the subject—monsters—becomes elevated to the level of significance because of the seriousness with which it is treated, is also applicable in **"Jabberwocky."**

Tolkien's theory was that the form of the heroic encounter with the forces of evil was a fixed one, that the features of both may change, but the nature and form of their essential conflict remains. The point of **"Jabberwocky"** is that if the form is in place, no amount of nonsense can divert the reader from the essential conflict. On the contrary, by using nonsense words, the poem deflects the reader from transient details and allows him to focus on the eternal human conflict with the forces of evil.

This is the purpose of the first verse, an introduction to a mythical atmosphere where there are no identifiable creatures to orient and fix the reader in a realistic world, where words mean nothing and the only order is grammatical. Animals and atmosphere are interchangeable. The nonsense serves a serious purpose here, to dislodge the reader from the fixed, limited world, and provide the possibility of limitless association. It is precisely the tight structure, parallel verses, and grammatical sense which allow for the freedom of non-sense.

Too often, Carroll's use of nonsense has been considered a secret kind of anagram, a trick, a "portmanteau." Using as great an authority as Humpty Dumpty, the words of **"Jabberwocky"** are dismissed with a "reasonable" explanation. *"Brilling,"* Humpty Dumpty explains in *Through the Looking Glass,* "means four o'clock in the afternoon— the time when you begin *broiling* things for dinner." *"Slithy"* is defined by the same source as "lithe and slimy" "Lithe is the same as active. You see it's like a portmanteau—there are two meanings packed up in one word." *"Mimsy"* by this definition, means "flimsy" and "miserable." But Carroll himself seemed to find the whole search for "portmanteau" meaning a joke on the adult reader, and when the newly formed *Jabberwock* magazine wrote to ask permission to use the word, wrote a preciously pretentious explanation of the word's etymology.

> Mr. Lewis Carroll has much pleasure in giving to the editresses of the proposed magazine permission to use the title they wish for. He finds that the Anglo-Saxon word "wocer" or "Wocor" signifies "offspring" or

"fruit." Taking "jabber" in its ordinary acceptation of "excited and voluble discussion," this would give the meaning of "the result of much excited discussion." Whether his phrase will have any application to the projected periodical, it will be for the future history of american literature to determine. Mr. Carroll wishes all success to the forthcoming magazine.

Concerning this scholarly etymological approach, John Ciardi comments: "Such word-hunting is pleasant enough as a game, and it is clearly founded in the author's own directive. Where, moreover, there is such good reason for believing the poem to be 'nonsense,' little will be served by denying its character as such. But what is 'nonsense'? Is it the same as 'non-sense'? Suppose that Carroll had written not a poem but an orchestral *scherzo,* a simple but brilliant piece of fun-music: Would one be so readily tempted to call such music 'nonsense'? Let the Wocky jabber as it will—and beautiful jabber it is—there is still a second sort of performance to which the appearance of 'non-sense' gives an especially apt flavor. And that second performance involves a great deal of 'sense,' if by 'sense' one means 'meaningful comment upon an identifiable subject.'" Ciardi does not elaborate, but his enjoinder to leave the nonsense as nonsense is an important first step.

The function of nonsense, at least in many of the works of Carroll, is to rid words and events of transient meaning and allow to events their full significance. This is apparently a natural perception for children and corrective measure for the jaded adult. The classical scholar, N. O. Brown, indicated it as a prescription:

> To restore to words their full significance, as in dreams, as in *Finnegans Wake,* is to reduce them to nonsense, to get the nonsense or nothingness back into words, to transcend the antimony of sense and nonsense, silence and speech. It is a destruction of ordinary language, a victory over the reality-principle. . . .

The function of the nonsense is disorientation and reorientation—removing the reader from the world of limited reality and specificity and placing him in a mythical context. Once, for example, we can rid ourselves of the need to define an adjective like "vorpal," we can understand that every hero has *some* weapon that is in some way outstanding, that makes him stronger than the average man, proves that he has been blessed by the gods, and leaves him vulnerable should it be removed from him. It is an acknowledgement that some form of supernatural help is necessary to cope with the magnitude of the human lot. A precise definition of "vorpal" as well as other undefined words, limits the poem, but an acceptance of the nonsense words facilitates the reading.

The first words to follow the scenic introduction are those of warning: "Beware the Jabberwock my son! / . . . / Beware the Jubjub bird, and shun / The frumious Bandersnatch!" This identifies the Jabberwock as the monster, the gratuitous predator with his evil associates. They are evil not by any standards of fluctuating morality—but more basically—because they should be shunned. There-

fore, although we are not told what a "frumious" bandersnatch is, we assume its evil nature because the elder warns against it.

This verse also introduces the basic psychological conflict between generations. For although the "father" (his actual position to the son is rightfuly vague) and son agree on the danger involved, the older generation urges caution, suggesting that problems are eternal and cannot be solved but can only be coped with through avoidance.

The unwillingness of the son to disobey entirely the order of the elders of the uncertainty of his worth for such a ponderous task precipitates a period of meditation. As with the situation of most heroes, the action is not taken precipitously or offensively, but after consideration and under duress. From the Prophets who took on God's task with reluctance to Huck Finn, the major heroes of Western Civilization act only when they must, and then defensively.

Because the hero's greatness is measured by the greatness of his adversary, it is important that the battle scene be described, that there be a furious battle. Since it is only the outcome that is important, the nature of the battle or the means of the return home have no significance, and can be blurred with nonsense. Similarly the exact form of joy taken by the elder is insignificant—what counts is the social acceptance of the heroic act.

The final verse returns the scenes to the past of the introduction—for although much has happened, nothing has changed. Heroes come and go and in an imperfectly understood environment only the danger of evil is clear and eternal. Though the Jabberwock is dead, the monsters of the second verse—the Jubjub bird and the Bandersnatch—remain, and the possibilities are endless.

Carroll was not mocking or parodying the heroic tales, but, like a true mathematician, he was formulating them, bringing them down to their common denominator. This is the denominator at which most children begin to comprehend the great myths of society, and the one that adults, caught in the details of the immediate reality, forget.

FURTHER READING

Bibliography

The Complete Works of Lewis Carroll. Alexander Woollcott, Ed. New York: Vintage Books, 1976, 1295 p.
    Recent compilation of Carroll's complete works.

Kelly, Richard. *Lewis Carroll.* Herbert Sussman, Ed. Boston: Twayne Publishers, 1990, 190 p.
    A biographical study intended for high-school level students. Includes a Chronology and Bibliography.

Biography

Cohen, Morton N. *Lewis Carroll: A Biography*. New York: Alfred A. Knopf, 1995, 565 p.
    A contemporary biography of Lewis Carroll.

Green, Roger Lancelyn. *The Story of Lewis Carroll*. New York: Henry Schuman, 1951, 179 p.
    An early biography of Lewis Carroll.

Hudson, Derek. *Lewis Carroll: An Illustrated Biography*. New York: Clarkson N. Potter, Inc., 1977, 270 p.
    Contains brief, key biographical notes with black and white and color illustrations.

Lennon, Florence Becker. *The Life of Lewis Carroll*. New York: Dover Publications, Inc., 1972, 440 p.
    Biography of Lewis Carroll by a leading scholar.

Woolf, Virginia. "Lewis Carroll." In *Aspects of Alice*. Robert Phillips, Ed. New York: The Vanguard Press, 1971, 47-9.
    An often-cited essay on Carroll.

Criticism

Birns, Margaret Boe. "Solving the Mad Hatter's Riddle." *Massachusetts Review* (Autumn 1984): 457-68.
    Birns traces the imagery of eating and cannibalism in *Alice's Adventures in Wonderland*.

Blake, Kathleen. *Play, Games and Sport: The Literary Works of Lewis Carroll*. Ithaca: Cornell University Press, 1974, 215 p.
    In this book, Blake dissects and explains the games used throughout Lewis Carroll's works.

Cixous, Hélène. Translated by Marie Maclean. "Introduction to Lewis Carroll's *Through the Looking-Glass* and *The Hunting of the Snark*." *New Literary History,* Vol. 13, No. 2 (Winter 1982): 231-51.
    Cixous presents a post-modernist reading of *Through the Looking-Glass* and *The Hunting of the Snark*.

Cohen, Morton N. "The Wonderful Day Gertrude Met the Snark." *London Times,* No. 54, 144 (July 20, 1974): 12.
    Cohen praises Carroll's *The Hunting of the Snark*.

Crews, Judith. "Plain Superficiality." In *Lewis Carroll*. Harold Bloom, Ed. New York: Chelsea House Publishers, 1987, 83-102.
    Crews examines Carroll's games and approaches using the theories of reasoning employed in his books.

de la Mare, Walter. "On the Alice Books." In *Aspects of Alice,* Robert Phillips, Ed. New York: The Vanguard Press, 1971, 57-65.
    A noteworthy and often-cited essay on Carroll's children's novels.

————. *Lewis Carroll*. London: Faber & Faber Limited, 1932, 67 p.
    Discusses the rise of Nonsense poetry in the early nineteenth century, comparing Carroll to Edward Lear and Charles Lamb.

Earnest, Ernest. "'The Walrus and the Carpenter.'" *The CEA Critic,* Vol. XXVI, No. 3 (December 1963): 1, 6-7.
    Earnest suggests that Carroll's work was highly influenced by folklore and myth as much as it was by psychology.

Gardner, Martin. "A review of *The Annotated Snark*." *Times Literary Supplement,* No. 3,175 (February 15, 1963): 111.
    Martin Gardner reviews Carroll's *The Annotated Snark*, doubting that it was Carroll's intent to convey the philosophical issues which literary critics now read into it.

Green, Roger Lancelyn. "You May call it Nonsense: Extract of a talk given to the Society on 6 January 1970." *Jabberwocky,* No. 3 (March 1970): 9-12.
    Green summarizes several views on Carroll's nonsense poetry.

Grotjahn, Martin. "About the symbolization of *Alice's Adventures in Wonderland*." In *Aspects of Alice,* Robert Phillips, Ed. New York: The Vanguard Press, 1971, 308-315.
    Grotjahn discusses the phenomenon of critical analysis of the perceived symbolism in Carroll's classic book.

Haight, M.R. "Nonsense." *The British Journal of Aesthetics,* Vol. 11, No. 3 (Summer 1971): 247-56.
    Haight argues in favor of a serious interpretation of nonsense literature and recaps critical arguments that support his position.

Livingston, Myra Cohn. "But Is It Poetry?" *Horn Book,* Vol. LI, No. 6 (December 1975): 571-80.
    Livingston uses Carroll's parody "Poeta Fit, Non Nascitur" to argue against publishing poetry written by children.

Otten, Terry. "After Innocence: Alice in the Garden." In *Lewis Carroll: A Celebration*. Edward Guiliano, Ed. New York: Clarkson N. Potter, 1982, 51-60.
    A readable essay on psychoanalytic approaches to Alice and the Victorian child.

Parry, Edward Abbot. "The Early Writings of Lewis Carrroll." *The Cornhill Magazine*. Vol. 5 new series, No. 334 new series (April 1924) 455-68.
    Parry praises Carroll's early work, and contradicts a few minor points in Collingwood's biography of Carroll.

Root, E. Merrill. "A review of *The Hunting of the Snark*." *American Opinion,* Vol. IX, No. 4 (April 1966): 73-82.
    Root argues that *The Snark* is a clever attack on collectivism and other socialist principals.

Sibley, Brian. "The Poems to 'Sylvie and Bruno.'" *Jabberwocky,* Vol. 4, No. 3 (Summer 1975): 51-8.
    Sibley discusses the poetic and prose qualities of portions of *Sylvie and Bruno*.

Smith, William Jay. "A review of *The Annotated Snark*." *New York Times Book Review,* Vol. CXII, No. 38, 284 (November 18, 1962): 26.

Smith gives a favorable review of the book.

Sutherland, Robert D. *Language and Lewis Carroll*. Paris: Mouton, 1970, 190 p.

A detailed, complex study of the intricacies of Carroll's language.

Additional coverage of Carroll's life and career is contained in the following sources published by Gale Research: *Nineteenth-Century Literature Criticism,* Vols. 2, 53; *World Literature Criticism, 1500 to the Present*; *Children's Literature Review,* Vols. 2, 18; *Dictionary of Literary Biography,* Vols. 18, 163; *DISCovering Authors*; *DISCovering Authors: British*; *Junior DISCovering Authors*; *Major Authors and Illustrators for Children and Yound Adults*; **and** *Yesterday's Authors of Books for Children.*

Ralph Waldo Emerson
1803-1882

American essayist and poet.

INTRODUCTION

Emerson was one of the most influential American writers of the nineteenth century. He was one of the founders of the Transcendental movement which drew together major New England literary figures who shared beliefs in the divinity of nature and of the individual and asserted that each human must make moral determinations individually, regardless of religious dogma. Emerson's poetry reflects the same optimism, mysticism, and love of nature that his essays expressed. Through his essays and poems, Emerson influenced such acclaimed writers as Walt Whitman, Nathaniel Hawthorne, Henry David Thoreau, Herman Melville, Emily Dickinson, Edwin Arlingtion Robinson, and Robert Frost.

Biographical Information

Emerson was born in Boston on May 25, 1803. His father died when Emerson was eight, and his mother took in borders to meet expenses and keep the family together. Emerson attended Harvard College from 1817 to 1821 and then taught school sporadically from 1821 to 1826. He also attended Harvard Divinity School intermittently from 1825 to 1827. In 1829, Emerson fulfilled the expectations of family members by being ordained, like his father and grandfather before him, as a Unitarian minister. But Emerson brought with him doubts concerning traditional Christian beliefs including the sanctity of the Eucharist, and he resigned from his position as pastor of Boston's Second Church in 1832. His decision to leave the church may also have been kindled in 1831 by the devastating death of his first wife, Ellen, to whom he had been married only a year and a half. After his resignation, Emerson spent the next year traveling in Europe where he met the influential writers William Wordsworth, Samuel Taylor Coleridge, and Thomas Carlyle, and visited the botanical gardens of the Jardin des Plantes in Paris, an experience which inspired his interest in the mystical significance of nature. Returning to America in 1833, Emerson settled in Concord, Massachusetts and began a career of lecturing on the popular lyceum lecture circuit. In 1835, he married his second wife, Lydia Jackson, with whom he had four children, one of whom, his son Waldo, died at the age of six. He anonymously published his essay *Nature* in 1836, admitting to its authorship only after hearing reviewers acclaim it. The same year he also helped establish what became known as the Transcendental Club, a group whose noteworthy members included Henry David Thoreau, Nathaniel Hawthorne, and Margaret

Fuller. Emerson frequently contributed poetry to the *Dial* (1840-1843) the group's journal, and briefly served as its editor. He lived an active life, writing essays, poems and journals, delivering lectures, traveling, and establishing himself as a major American intellectual. He continued to write and lecture into his seventies, coming to be regarded as the "Sage of Concord." His later years, however, were characterized by a gradually advancing senility. He died in Concord in 1882.

Major Works

Emerson's poetry emphasizes nature as a symbol of the divine and focuses on the commonplace and everyday experience. Among his influences are the Romantic British poets Wordsworth and Coleridge, the metaphysical poet George Herbert, and the transcendental Persian poets Hafez and Saadi. The most well known of Emerson's mystical poems influenced by the Persian poets are "The Sphinx," the opening poem of his first volume which establishes Emerson's mysterious, prophetic tone; "Hamatreya," an application of Hindu wisdom to the New England setting; "Bacchus," a celebration of poetic inspiration; "Days," a combination of Puritan values and oriental imagery; and "Brahma," a condensation of Hindu ideas that lead to the association of Nirvana with selflessness. Another of Emerson's major themes was the Romantic tribute to nature. It is represented in such famous poems as "The Snow Storm," a poem in blank verse which depicts a fierce winter storm that transforms the New England landscape, "The Rhodora," a lyrical celebration of the native flower which suggests the presence of a divine force in its creation, along with "The Adirondacs," a blank verse tribute to the mountains and "The Titmouse," a paean to the tiny bird that conquers fear. Another thematic grouping contains poems examining personal issues in Emerson's life, such as "Threnody" about the death of his son, "The Problem" which addresses Emerson's personal dilemma of admiration for church leaders despite his refusal to remain within their ranks and "Terminus," an anticipation of his own death. During his life, Emerson was most noted for his patriotic poems such as the classic, public verses "Concord Hymn: Sung at the Completion of the Battle Monument, July 4, 1837" and "Boston Hymn." His edition *Selected Poems* is a compilation of poems from his first two volumes, rearranged with minor changes. Posthumous publications include *Poems* and the recently published *The Poetry Notebooks of Ralph Waldo Emerson* which makes easily accessible Emerson's rough drafts and comments regarding the composition of his poetry.

Critical Reception

Emerson's poetic skills have always been a matter of debate among critics and approaches to evaluating his poems have been quite varied. The focus on thematic analyses began by questioning Emerson's religious doctrines. The early reviewers of Emerson's first book of poetry challenged Emerson's theological base and judged him lacking in Christian values. As nineteenth-century readers found more liberal statements of faith in the publications of other transcendental poets such as Whitman, critics became less harsh in their judgement of Emerson's poems, shifting their thematic analyses to focus on Emerson's success in writing about nature. By the latter half of the nineteenth century, Emerson's essays had established his reputation as an outstanding American philosopher, and during the remainder of his life, reviewers were generally reluctant to be overly critical of his poems.

Throughout both the nineteenth and twentieth centuries, structural analyses of the poems have acknowledged that they are stylistically imperfect and that Emerson subordinated meter and diction to thematic concerns. Those critics who do not like Emerson's work mark these aesthetic weaknesses as overwhelming flaws in the poetry, while those who enjoy the poems defend Emerson's style as examples of his poetic theory in action, the idea that nineteenth-century American verse needed to be liberated from traditional forms. Albert Gelpi, for example, has asserted that Emerson intended his poems to convey the same moral messages he expounded in his essays and lectures and that he used poetic forms that would best convey these messages as experiences of inspiration. Charles Malloy, an American businessman with a penchant for poetry, was the

first to closely analyze most of Emerson's major poems. During the end of the nineteenth and beginning of the twentieth century he wrote articles for literary journals and delivered lectures in and around Boston explicating and praising individual poems, thus popularizing them. Malloy also founded the Boston Emerson Society, and served as its president for many years. In the 1930s and 1940s studies of Emerson's essay "Persian Poetry" and Emerson's translations of Persian poems resulted in examinations of the degree to which Emerson was influenced by the Persian poets. These studies rekindled interest in Emerson's poems based on analyses of their sources. Regardless of the question of its own merits, Emerson's poetry is often cited as having influenced 'generations of American poets.

PRINCIPAL WORKS

Poetry

Poems 1847
May-Day and Other Pieces 1867
Selected Poems 1876
Poems 1884
The Complete Works of Ralph Waldo Emerson 12 vols. (collection) 1903-4
The Collected Works of Ralph Waldo Emerson 5 vols. to date (essays, poetry, and other writings) 1971-
The Poetry Notebooks of Ralph Waldo Emerson 1986

Other Major Works

Nature (essay) 1836
Essays (essay) 1841; also published as *Essays: First Series*, 1854
Nature; An Essay, and Lectures on the Times (essays) 1844
Orations, Lectures,and Addresses (essays) 1844
Essays: Second Series (essays) 1844
Nature; Addresses, and Lectures (essays) 1849
Representative Men: Seven Lectures (essays) 1850
English Traits (essays) 1856
The Conduct of Life (essays) 1860
Society and Solitude (essays) 1870
Letters and Social Aims (essays) 1876
Natural History of Intellect and Other Papers (essays) 1894
The Journals of Ralph Waldo Emerson. 10 vols. (journals) 1909-14
The Letters of Ralph Waldo Emerson (letters) 1939

CRITICISM

Ralph Waldo Emerson (essay date 1844)

SOURCE: "The Poet," in *American Literary Essays*, edited by Lewis Leary, Thomas Y. Crowell Company, 1960, pp. 161-74.

[*The following is an excerpt from the noted essay, "The Poet," which first appeared as the introductory essay in Emerson's 1844 collection* Essays: Second Series. *In this piece, Emerson describes the poet's intuitive sense and ability to record his perceptions, often with symbols from nature.*]

> A moody child and wildly wise
> Pursued the game with joyful eyes,
> Which chose, like meteors, their way,
> And rived the dark with private ray:
> They overleapt the horizon's edge,
> Searched with Apollo's privilege;
> Through man, and woman, and sea, and
>   star
> Saw the dance of nature forward far;
> Through worlds, and races, and terms,
>   and times
> Saw musical order, and pairing rhymes.
>
> Olympian bards who sung
>   Divine ideas below,
> Which always find us young,
>   And always keep us so.

Those who are esteemed umpires of taste are often persons who have acquired some knowledge of admired pictures or sculptures, and have an inclination for whatever is elegant; but if you inquire whether they are beautiful souls, and whether their own acts are like fair pictures, you learn that they are selfish and sensual. Their cultivation is local, as if you should rub a log of dry wood in one spot to produce fire, all the rest remaining cold. Their knowledge of the fine arts is some study of rules and particulars, or some limited judgment of color or form, which is exercised for amusement or for show. It is a proof of the shallowness of the doctrine of beauty as it lies in the minds of our amateurs, that men seem to have lost the perception of the instant dependence of form upon soul. There is no doctrine of forms in our philosophy. We were put into our bodies, as fire is put into a pan to be carried about; but there is no accurate adjustment between the spirit and the organ, much less is the latter the germination of the former. So in regard to other forms, the intellectual men do not believe in any essential dependence of the material world on thought and volition. Theologians think it a pretty air-castle to talk of the spiritual meaning of a ship or a cloud, of a city or a contract, but they prefer to come again to the solid ground of historical evidence; and even the poets are contented with a civil and conformed manner of living, and to write poems from the fancy, at a safe distance from their own experience. But the highest minds of the world have never ceased to explore the double meaning, or shall I say the quadruple or the centuple or much more manifold meaning, of every sensuous fact; Orpheus, Empedocles, Heraclitus, Plato, Plutarch, Dante, Swedenborg, and the masters of sculpture, picture and poetry. For we are not pans and barrows, nor even porters of the fire and torch-bearers, but children of the fire, made of it, and only the same divinity transmuted and at two or three removes, when we know least about it. And this hidden truth, that the fountains whence all this river of Time and its creatures floweth are intrinsically ideal and beautiful, draws us to the consideration of the nature and functions of the Poet, or the man of Beauty; to the means and materials he uses, and to the general aspect of the art in the present time.

The breadth of the problem is great, for the poet is representative. He stands among partial men for the complete man, and apprises us not of his wealth, but of the common wealth. The young man reveres men of genius, because, to speak truly, they are more himself than he is. They receive of the soul as he also receives, but they more. Nature enhances her beauty, to the eye of loving men, from their belief that the poet is beholding her shows at the same time. He is isolated among his contemporaries by truth and by his art, but with this consolation in his pursuits, that they will draw all men sooner or later. For all men live by truth and stand in need of expression. In love, in art, in avarice, in politics, in labor, in games, we study to utter our painful secret. The man is only half himself, the other half is his expression.

Notwithstanding this necessity to be published, adequate expression is rare. I know not how it is that we need an interpreter, but the great majority of men seem to be minors, who have not yet come into possession of their own, or mutes, who cannot report the conversation they have had with nature. There is no man who does not anticipate a supersensual utility in the sun and stars, earth and water. These stand and wait to render him a peculiar service. But there is some obstruction or some excess of phlegm in our constitution, which does not suffer them to yield the due effect. Too feeble fall the impressions of nature on us to make us artists. Every touch should thrill. Every man should be so much an artist that he could report in conversation what had befallen him. Yet, in our experience, the rays or appulses have sufficient force to arrive at the senses, but not enough to reach the quick and compel the reproduction of themselves in speech. The poet is the person in whom these powers are in balance, the man without impediment, who sees and handles that which others dream of, traverses the whole scale of experience, and is representative of man, in virtue of being the largest power to receive and to impart.

For the Universe has three children, born at one time, which reappear under different names in every system of thought, whether they be called cause, operation and effect; or, more poetically, Jove, Pluto, Neptune; or, theologically, the Father, the Spirit and the Son; but which we will call here the Knower, the Doer and the Sayer. These stand respectively for the love of truth, for the love of good, and for the love of beauty. These three are equal. Each is that which he is, essentially, so that he cannot be surmounted or analyzed, and each of these three has the power of the others latent in him and his own, patent.

The poet is the sayer, the namer, and represents beauty. He is a sovereign, and stands on the centre. For the world is not painted or adorned, but is from the beginning beautiful; and God has not made some beautiful things, but Beauty is the creator of the universe. Therefore the poet is not any permissive potentate, but is emperor in his own right. Criticism is infested with a cant of materialism, which assumes that manual skill and activity is the first merit of all men, and disparages such as say and do not, overlooking the fact that some men, namely poets, are natural sayers, sent into the world to the end of expression, and confounds them with those whose province is action but who quit it to imitate the sayers. But Homer's words are as costly and admirable to Homer as Agamemnon's victories are to Agamemnon. The poet does not wait for the hero or the sage, but, as they act and think primarily, so he writes primarily what will and must be spoken, reckoning the others, though primaries also, yet, in respect to him, secondaries and servants; as sitters or models in the studio of a painter, or as assistants who bring building-materials to an architect.

> **For it is not metres, but a metre-making argument that makes a poem—a thought so passionate and alive that like the spirit of a plant or an animal it has an architecture of its own, and adorns nature with a new thing.**
>
> **—*Ralph Waldo Emerson***

For poetry was all written before time was, and whenever we are so finely organized that we can penetrate into that region where the air is music, we hear those primal warblings and attempt to write them down, but we lose ever and anon a word or a verse and substitute something of our own, and thus miswrite the poem. The men of more delicate ear write down these cadences more faithfully, and these transcripts, though imperfect, become the songs of the nations. For nature is as truly beautiful as it is good, or as it is reasonable, and must as much appear as it must be done, or be known. Words and deeds are quite indifferent modes of the divine energy. Words are also actions, and actions are a kind of words.

The sign and credentials of the poet are that he announces that which no man foretold. He is the true and only doctor; he knows and tells; he is the only teller of news, for he was present and privy to the appearance which he describes. He is a beholder of ideas and an utterer of the necessary and causal. For we do not speak now of men of poetical talents, or of industry and skill in metre, but of the true poet. I took part in a conversation the other day concerning a recent writer of lyrics, a man of subtle mind, whose head appeared to be a music-box of delicate tunes and rhythms, and whose skill and command of language we could not sufficiently praise. But when the question arose whether he was not only a lyrist but a poet, we were obliged to confess that he is plainly a contemporary, not an eternal man. He does not stand out of our low limitations, like a Chimborazo under the line, running up from a torrid base through all the climates of the globe, with belts of the herbage of every latitude on its high and mottled sides; but this genius is the landscape-garden of a modern house, adorned with fountains and statues, with well-bred men and women standing and sitting in the walks and terraces. We hear, through all the varied music, the ground-tone of conventional life. Our poets are men of talents who sing, and not the children of music. The argument is secondary, the finish of the verses is primary.

For it is not metres, but a metre-making argument that makes a poem—a thought so passionate and alive that like the spirit of a plant or an animal it has an architecture of its own, and adorns nature with a new thing. The thought and the form are equal in the order of time, but in the order of genesis the thought is prior to the form. The poet has a new thought; he has a whole new experience to unfold; he will tell us how it was with him, and all men will be the richer in his fortune. For the experience of each new age requires a new confession, and the world seems always waiting for its poet.

. . . . .

[T]hough life is great, and fascinates and absorbs; and though all men are intelligent of the symbols through which it is named; yet they cannot originally use them. We are symbols and inhabit symbols; workmen, work, and tools, words and things, birth and death, all are emblems; but we sympathize with the symbols, and being infatuated with the economical uses of things, we do not know that they are thoughts. The poet, by an ulterior intellectual perception, gives them a power which makes their old use forgotten, and puts eyes and a tongue into every dumb and inanimate object. He perceives the independence of the thought on the symbol, the stability of the thought, the accidency and fugacity of the symbol. As the eyes of Lyncæus were said to see through the earth, so the poet turns the world to glass, and shows us all things in their right series and procession. For through that better perception he stands one step nearer to things, and sees the flowing or metamorphosis; perceives that thought is multiform; that within the form of every creature is a force impelling it to ascend into a higher form; and following with his eyes the life, uses the forms which express that life, and so his speech flows with the flowing of nature. All the facts of the animal economy, sex, nutriment, gestation, birth, growth, are symbols of the passage of the world into the soul of man, to suffer there a change and reappear a new and higher fact. He uses forms according to the life, and not according to the form. This is true science. The poet alone knows astronomy, chemistry, vegetation and animation, for he does not stop at these facts, but employs them as signs. He knows why the plain or meadow of space was strown with these flowers we call suns and moons and stars; why the great deep is adorned with animals, with men, and gods; for in every word he speaks he rides on them as the horses of thought.

By virtue of this science the poet is the Namer or Language-maker, naming things sometimes after their appearance, sometimes after their essence, and giving to every one its own name and not another's, thereby rejoicing the intellect, which delights in detachments or boundary. The poets made all the words, and therefore language is the archives of history, and, if we must say it, a sort of tomb of the muses. For though the origin of most of our words is forgotten, each word was at first a stroke of genius, and obtained currency because for the moment it symbolized the world to the first speaker and to the hearer. The etymologist finds the deadest word to have been once a brilliant picture. Language is fossil poetry. As the limestone of the continent consists of infinite masses of the shells of animalcules, so language is made up of images or tropes, which now, in their secondary use, have long ceased to remind us of their poetic origin. But the poet names the thing because he sees it, or comes one step nearer to it than any other. This expression or naming is not art, but a second nature, grown out of the first, as a leaf out of a tree.

. . . . .

The sublime vision comes to the pure and simple soul in a clean and chaste body. That is not an inspiration, which we owe to narcotics, but some counterfeit excitement and fury. Milton says that the lyric poet may drink wine and live generously, but the epic poet, he who shall sing of the gods and their descent unto men, must drink water out of a wooden bowl. For poetry is not 'Devil's wine,' but God's wine. It is with this as it is with toys. We fill the hands and nurseries of our children with all manner of dolls, drums and horses; withdrawing their eyes from the plain face and suffixing objects of nature, the sun and moon, the animals, the water and stones, which should be their toys. So the poet's habit of living should be set on a key so low that the common influences should delight him. His cheerfulness should be the gift of the sunlight; the air should suffice for his inspiration, and he should be tipsy with water. That spirit which suffices quiet hearts, which seems to come forth to such from every dry knoll of sere grass, from every pine stump and half-imbedded stone on which the dull March sun shines, comes forth to the poor and hungry, and such as are of simple taste. If thou fill thy brain with Boston and New York, with fashion and covetousness, and wilt stimulate thy jaded senses with wine and French coffee, thou shalt find no radiance of wisdom in the lonely waste of the pine woods.

If the imagination intoxicates the poet, it is not inactive in other men. The metamorphosis excites in the beholder an emotion of joy. The use of symbols has a certain power of emancipation and exhilaration for all men. We seem to be touched by a wand which makes us dance and run about happily, like children. We are like persons who come out of a cave or cellar into the open air. This is the effect on us of tropes, fables, oracles and all poetic forms. Poets are thus liberating gods. Men have really got a new sense, and found within their world another world, or nest of worlds; for, the metamorphosis once seen, we divine that it does not stop.

Cyrus A. Bartol (essay date 1847)

SOURCE: "Poetry and Imagination," in *Christian Examiner,* Vol. 42, March, 1847, pp. 250-701.

[In this excerpt from his review of Emerson's Poems, *Bartol offers a theological evaluation determining that Emerson's religious beliefs weaken his poetry.]*

. . . The heart in [Emerson's] poetry is less than the head, and this causes a deficiency for which nothing else can fully atone. Only a transcendent splendor and wealth of intellect could redeem many of his pieces from condemnation and forgetfulness, as being frigid and unfeeling. These are sad flaws in such noble workmanship. Did a fellow-feeling for human nature in all its varieties equal and fill out his other traits, we might think the great poet of America had been born, to bring on our flourishing Augustan age. But, as yet, our hearts acknowledge a more genial and enlivening influence from several of our other native bards. Would that one whom we unfeignedly respect might not only show his power of soaring to the empyrean, but hover with a more wide and loving interest over the lot of his fellow-men! It may be for want of this all-embracing sympathy that his flights are so infrequent, and that he can but seldom continue long on the wing. If he could but kindle his soul with some great conception of human fortunes, and write a generous epic of this our human life, including its great trials and accomplishments, its sublimer aspirations and hopes, we hazard little in predicting that it would be a production to mark the age.

And yet we hardly know how he could have the kind of human sympathy which we most value for the inspiration of such an undertaking, with his present views of religion. There is no recognition in his pages of the Christian faith, according to any, however catholic, idea of it which we are able to form. He seems to have no preference of Jesus over any other great and good man. He either does not accept the evidences authenticating a divine revelation, or they press with but little interest upon his preoccupied mind. But what we must regard as his religious unsoundness strikes still deeper. He does not even appear to own any distinction between man and Deity. He talks of "the gods" as an old Roman would do. One personal Creator is not present to his thought. He does not go for the signs of such a Being into the broad circumference of his works, but confines himself within the little rim of his own individual consciousness. He puts aside Bible and ritual, and all human speech and outward light, for the "super-solar beam." In religion he fills the whole space of thought with that mystic element, which we must perhaps admit, but should confine in a corner. He does not, with a plain trust, examine the world which God has made, but curiously inspects the inverted image of it upon his own mental retina. He does not pay to the instincts of mankind or of society the respect he would render to the peculiar instincts of the animal, the bee or the beaver. And not taking cordially to his heart the Christian doctrines of a Father and a particular Providence, how can he strongly embrace the dependent doctrine of human brotherhood, or feel the unlimited sympathy which this doctrine inspires? We speak here, of course, of his system. We doubt not the kindness of his actual relations with men. We believe a hearty historical faith in Christianity would add greatly to the power of his genius. The views we have alluded to so underlie and run through his writings, as almost to amount to the proposal of a new religious faith,—a presumption which of course astounds us, simple believers in the New Testament on what we deem irrefragable grounds. His ideas carry him wide of the humility of the Gospel,—though they give rise in his own mind not so much to personal pride as to an immense self-respect and an enormous self-reliance. He is willing to trust to or lean upon nothing but himself;—a wonderful state of feeling, when we consider our real condition of dependence in all our powers,—our bodies resting on the attractions of material nature, every vital organ in us doing its part involuntarily, and only a single silvery thread branching into various filaments of the nerves of motion being held by our own will,—our intelligence but the shadowy reflex of Divine wisdom, like the light from distant worlds in the focus of the astronomer's telescope,—and even our moral nature roused not by an internal force of conscience alone, but quickened and kept alive so greatly by instruction and example. We are made to lean, and are stronger when we lean; and, if we do not lean, we fall. Our poet is dragged by his philosophy to a lower, or at least less commanding, height than, with a better understanding on this point, he might well attain.

We ought, however, to say, that the noblest principles of conduct are often asserted in his pages. We rejoice to find instances of a truly grand morality, and surpassing expressions of a pure and beautiful spirit; but are suddenly perplexed, as we proceed, by an optimism confounding all moral distinctions. He seems, in some places, to know no difference between light and darkness, sweet and bitter. Some revelations, hinted at in one of these poems, respecting a moral indifference in all things, are represented as made by **"Uriel,"** and as causing the older deities, who had been in the secret, to blush. Alphonso of Castile, who is said to have thought he could improve upon the world as described in the Ptolemaic system, makes a bold figure, as the *protégé* of our author's pen, entering in heaven's court a general and unqualified complaint about all things under the sun.

There is an undertone of sadness running through these rhymes, sometimes harsh and scornful, and sometimes tender and refined, like angelic melancholy. We fancy this, too, may proceed from the peculiarity of the writer's belief. Seldom do we hear from him the truly cheerful strain which an earnest faith in Christianity would prompt. In that marvelously beautiful **"Threnody,"** near the close of the book, the sorrow at the commencement is out of all proportion to the comfort at the end. It is the song of a stricken and struggling stoicism. The note falls irresistibly into the minor key. The very voice of consolation dies away in a wail. Alas! it is a poor application here made to the heart's wounds. They still bleed into the very ointment and balm. Every stroke of genius seems but to sharpen the regret. We remember in all our reading nothing more cheerless. It is a picture we would not hang in our heart's chambers. Every touch of the pencil draws a tear. As a painting of grief it is unrivaled,—but it is of grief alone. His hand proves false to him, when he undertakes to draw the form of the angel of peace. But that the soul of the poet might be deaf to our entreaty, we would

implore him to turn his eye to those fountains of comfort which God has opened in the Gospel of his Son. For nothing can be more manly than an humble reliance on the means of revival and support, in our distress, which our Father has provided. Let him in lowliness receive these, and then, for the **"Threnody,"** and the **"Dirge"** which precedes it, we should hope to receive lines as highly adorned with the lights of a creative fancy, but gilded from above also by the beams of heaven. There would at least be nothing in them of the "grief whose balsam never grew."

But we must pause. The analysis of Emerson's writings is no short or easy task. We would not pretend to oversee his summit, but only to note our impressions as we stand and contemplate it. His works, on account of their peculiarity, if nothing else, will probably be among the most enduring of the present time. There is much in them to admire and be improved by. And while we must think there is much also that is unsound and must be injurious to any mind imbibing it, we intend no personal commendation in expressing our conviction that he is a true-minded and righteous man, raised above every thing unworthy, and living a blameless life according to the monitions of his own conscience. Our calling is not to speak of the man, but of the author. We think the intellectual states and tendencies which we have noted chill and cripple his genius. He would make better poetry under the sway of views and opinions which he rejects or holds slightly. Were we writing with a different design, we might state other reasons for our regret at some of the sentiments which he expresses. We have now only to say, that they have injured his book, and must restrict the width and impair the quality of its influence. Would he fetch an echo from the universal heart, as it beats in the breasts of men from generation to generation, he must add to his style a faith and fervor as signal as its brilliancy and force.

Orestes A. Brownson (essay date 1847)

SOURCE: "Emerson's Poems," in *Brownson's Quarterly Review*, Vol. 4, April, 1847, pp. 262-76.

[*Brownson, an early Transcendentalist who became an ardent Roman Catholic, edited his own magazine from 1844 to 1875 as a vehicle for his religious beliefs and wrote popular books containing the sensationalized religious tone evident in this excerpt. Here Brownson criticizes Emerson's poetry by describing it as the voice of a depressed and delusional poet under the influence of Satan.*]

. . . Mr. Emerson's poems . . . fail in all the higher requisites of art. They embody a doctrine essentially false, a morality essentially unsound, and at best a beauty which is partial, individual. To be able to regard them as embodying the beautiful, in any worthy sense of the term, one must cease to be what he is, must divest himself of his own individuality, and that not to fall back on our

common humanity, but to become Mr. Emerson, and to
see only after his peculiar manner of seeing. They are
addressed, not to all men, but to a school, a peculiar school,
a very small school, composed of individuals who, by
nature or education, have similar notions, tastes, and id-
iosyncrasies. As artistic productions, then, notwithstanding they indicate, on the part of their author, poetical
genius of the highest order, they can claim no elevated
rank. The author's genius is cramped, confined, and perverted by his false philosophy and morality, and the best
thing we can say of his poems is, that they indicate the
longing of his spirit for a truth, a morality, a freedom, a
peace, a repose, which he feels and laments he has not.

We know Mr. Emerson; we have shared his generous
hospitality, and enjoyed the charms of his conversation;
as a friend and neighbour, in all the ordinary relations of
social and domestic life, he is one it is not easy to help
loving and admiring; and we confess we are loath to say
aught severe against him or his works; but his volume of
poems is the saddest book we ever read. The author tries
to cheer up, tries to smile, but the smile is cold and transitory; it plays an instant round the mouth, but does not
come from the heart, or lighten the eyes. He talks of
music and flowers, and would fain persuade us that he is
weaving garlands of joy; but beneath them is always to be
seen the ghastly and grinning skeleton of death. There is
an appearance of calm, of quiet, of repose, and at first
sight one may half fancy his soul is as placid, as peaceful,
as the unruffled lake sleeping sweetly beneath the summer
moonbeams; but it is the calm, the quiet, the repose of
despair. Down below are the troubled waters. The world
is no joyous world for him. It is void and without form,
and darkness broods over it. True, he bears up against it;
but because he is too proud to complain, and because he
believes his lot is that of all men and inevitable. Why
break thy head against the massive walls of necessity?
Call your darkness light, and it will be as light—to you.
Look the fiend in the face, and he is your friend,—at
least, as much of a friend as you can have. Why complain? Poor brother, thou art nothing, or thou art all.
Crouch and whine, and thou art nothing; stand up erect
on thy own two feet, and scorn to ask for aught beyond
thyself, and thou art all. Yet this stoical pride and resolve
require a violent effort, and bring no peace, no consolation, to the soul. In an evil hour, the author overheard
what the serpent said to Eve, and believed it; and from
that time, it would seem, he became unable to believe
aught else. He loves and wooes nature, for he fancies her
beauty and loveliness emanate from the divinity of his
own being; and he affects to walk the fields and the woods,
as a god surveying his own handiwork. It is he that gives
the rose its fragrance, the rainbow its tints, the golden
sunset its gorgeous hues. But the illusion does not last.
He feels, after all, that he is a man, only a man; and the
enigma of his own being,

> The fate of the man-child,
> The meaning of man,

torments him, and from his inmost soul cries out, and in
no lullaby tones, for a solution. But, alas! no solution

comes; or, if one, it is a solution which solves nothing,
which brings no light, no repose, to the spirit wearied
with its questionings.

. . . . .

There is something weird and mysterious in the thoughts
and feelings which come to us, unbidden, when we leave
faith behind, and fix our gaze intently upon ourselves as
upon some magic mirror. The circle of our vision seems
to be enlarged; darkness is transformed to light; worlds
open upon worlds; we send keen, penetrating glances into
the infinite abyss of being; the elements grow obedient to
us, work with us and for us, and we seem to be strong
with their strength, terrible with their might, and to approach and to become identical with the Source of all
things. God becomes comprehensible and communicable,
and we live an elemental life, and burn with elemental
fire. The universe flows into us and from us. We control
the winds, the waves, the rivers and the tides, the stars
and the seasons. We teach the plant when to germinate, to
blossom, or ripen, the reed when to bend before the blast,
and the lightning when to rive the hoary oak. Alas! we
think not then that this is all delusion, and that we are
under the influence of the Fallen Angel, who would persuade us that darkness is light, that weakness is strength,
that hell is heaven, and himself God. Under a similar
influence and delusion labors the author of these poems.
There are passages in them which recall all too vividly
what we, in our blindness and unbelief, have dreamed,
but rarely ventured to utter. We know these poems; we
understand them. They are not sacred chants; they are
hymns to the devil. Not God, but Satan, do they praise,
and they can be relished only by devil-worshipers.

Yet we do not despair of our poet. He has a large share of
religiosity, and his soul needs to prostrate itself before God
and adore. There is a low, sad music in these poems, deep
and melodious, which escapes the author unbidden, and which
discloses a spirit ill at ease, a heart bewailing its bondage,
and a secret, intense longing to burst its chains, and to soar
aloft to the heaven of divine love and freedom. This music
is the echo of the angel voices still pleading with him, and
entreating him to return from his wanderings, to open his
eyes to the heaven which lies around him, his ears to the
sweet voices which everywhere are chanting the praises of
God. We must hope that ere long he will, through grace,
burst the Satanic cords which now bind him, open his eyes
to the sweet vision of beauty that awaits him, and his ears
to the harmony which floats on every breeze.

Francis Bowen (essay date 1847)

SOURCE: "Nine New Poets," in *The North American
Review,* Vol. LXIV, No. 135, April, 1847, pp. 402-34.

[*In this excerpt, Bowen finds fault with Emerson's meter,
rhyme and "obscure" allusions. Bowen's negative response to the poems represents the general reaction of
early reviewers to Emerson's first book of poetry.*]

. . . [Mr. Emerson's] mystical effusions have been for some years the delight of a large and increasing circle of young people, and the despair of the critics. He is a chartered libertine, who has long exercised his prerogative of writing enigmas both in prose and verse, sometimes with meaning in them, and sometimes without,—more frequently without. Many of his fragments in verse—if *verse* it can be called, which puts at defiance all the laws of rhythm, metre, grammar, and common sense—were originally published in *The Dial, lucus a non lucendo,* a strange periodical work, which is now withdrawn from sunlight into the utter darkness that it always coveted. These fragments, with some new matter, are now first collected in a separate volume, and published, as we believe, with a sly purpose on the part of the author to quiz his own admirers. His prose essays, on their first appearance, were received with about equal admiration and amazement; always enigmatical and frequently absurd in doctrine and sentiment, they also contained flashes of better things. Quaint and pithy apothegms, dry and humorous satire, studied oddities of expression, which made an old thought appear almost as good as a new one, and frequent felicities of poetical and picturesque diction, were the redeeming qualities that compensated the reader for toiling through many pages filled with a mere hubbub and jumble of words. Startling and offensive opinions, drawn mostly from systems of metaphysics that were long ago exploded and forgotten, were either darkly hinted at, or baldly stated without a word of explanation or defence. Poet and mystic, humorist and heretic, the writer seemed, on the one side, to aim at a revival of Heraclitus and Plotinus, and on the other, to be an imitator of Rabelais and Sterne. A few touches of recondite learning, obviously more fantastic than profound, added to the singularity of the compound which he presented to the public. He probably accomplished his first purpose, when his essays simply made people stare,—

> While some pronounced him wondrous wise,
> And some declared him mad.

But it is only in his prose that Mr. Emerson is a poet; this volume of professed poetry contains the most prosaic and unintelligible stuff that it has ever been our fortune to encounter. The book opens, very appropriately, with a piece called **"The Sphinx."** We are no Œdipus, and cannot expound one of the riddles contained in it; but some of our readers may be more successful, and a specimen of it shall therefore be placed before them. It matters not what portion is extracted, for the poem may be read backwards quite as intelligibly as forwards, and no mortal can trace the slightest connection between the verses. . . .

> Uprose the merry Sphinx,
> And crouched no more in stone;
> *She melted into purple cloud,*
> *She silvered in the moon;*
> She spired into a yellow flame;
> She flowered in blossoms red;
> She flowed into a foaming wave;
> She stood Monadnoc's head.

We have not *The Dial* at hand for reference; but if memory serves us aright, in the poem as first published, instead of the lines here printed in Italics, we had the following:—

> She jumped into a barberry bush,
> She jumped into the moon.

This original reading seems to be preferable, as it is more simple and graphic; but the poet probably struck it out, lest he should appear indebted to the highly imaginative lines of Mother Goose,—

> Hey, diddle-diddle, the cat and the fiddle,
> The cow jumped over the moon.

The Sphinx concludes her oracles with this tempting declaration:

> Thorough a thousand voices
> Spoke the universal dame:
> "Who telleth one of my meanings,
> Is master of all I am."

We doubt whether the fulfilment of this promise will ever be claimed by any body; certainly, not by us, for we do not even know what is meant by a "universal" old lady. . . .

Mr. Emerson delights to build a poem on some nearly forgotten anecdote, or myth, or recorded saying of the wise and great, either in ancient times or the Middle Ages. A sort of misty reference to this theme appears here and there in the verses, and if the reader is lucky enough to remember the anecdote, he may flatter himself that he can see a glimpse of meaning in them. But if unlearned or forgetful, no reference, no direct statement, no charitable foot-note, gives him the least hint of the writer's purpose; all is dark as Erebus. Sometimes, an uncouth Sanscrit, Greek, or German compound word stands as the title of a few verses, and answers the poet's object to puzzle his readers quite delightfully. The contrivance is ingenious, and shows how highly obscurity is prized, and that a book of poetry may almost attain the dignity of a child's book of riddles.

Thus, some lines headed **"Alphonso of Castile"** seem to be founded on the saying recorded of this king, ironically surnamed "The Wise," that if the Almighty had consulted him at the creation, he would have made a much better universe. A few lines may be quoted from this poem, as a specimen of Mr. Emerson's more familiar style. It begins in this original manner:—

> I, Alphonso, live and learn,
> Seeing Nature go astern.
> Things deteriorate in kind;
> Lemons run to leaves and rind;
> Meagre crop of figs and limes;
> Shorter days and harder times.

After enumerating many other evils and imperfections, equally important in character, the king proceeds to give his advice to the gods in the following choice expressions:—

> Hear you, then, celestial fellows!
> Fits not to be overzealous;
> Steads not to work on the clean jump,
> Nor wine nor brains perpetual pump.
> Men and gods are *too extense*;
> Could you slacken and condense?
> Your rank overgrowths reduce
> Till your kinds abound with juice?

The poet probably meant to be satirical, referring to the pragmatical and conceited tone of many foolish busybodies in the affairs of this world. The purpose was well enough; we can only call attention to the neatness and elegance of the machinery contrived for this object, and to the poignancy of his wit.

Another string of rhymes, entitled **"Mithridates,"** seems to be founded on the old myth respecting that monarch, that having discovered a sure antidote, he was able to subsist entirely on the most active poisons. After babbling for a time about dogwood, hemlock, "the prussic juice," and upas boughs, the poet breaks out into the following witty and coherent apostrophe:—

> O doleful ghosts, and goblins merry!
> O all you virtues, methods, mights,
> Means, appliances, delights,
> Reputed wrongs and braggart rights,
> Smug routine, and things allowed,
> Minorities, things under cloud!
> Hither! take me, use me, fill me,
> Vein and artery, though ye kill me!
> *God! I will not be an owl,*
> But sun me in the Capitol.

We commend Mr. Emerson's intention not to be an owl, though when he utters such dismal screeches as these, one may doubt whether the transformation has not already been effected. We never before felt the whole force of Horace's exclamation, *aut insanit homo, aut versus facit.* Is the man sane who can deliberately commit to print this fantastic nonsense? . . .

We mean to be fair with the poet. Having read attentively—*horresco referens!*—the whole book, we affirm that the specimens now laid before our readers fairly represent far the larger portion of it. Here and there, a gleam of light intrudes, and we find brief but striking indications of the talent and feeling which Mr. Emerson unquestionably possesses. But the effect is almost instantly marred by some mystical nonsense, some silly pedantry, an intolerable hitch in rhythm or grammar, or an incredible flatness and meanness of expression. In one of the longer poems, **"Monadnoc,"** one may cull a few single lines, and occasionally a couplet, or a quatrain, of great poetic beauty. But these are like a few costly spices flung into a tub full of dirty and greasy water; they are polluted by the medium in which they float, and one cannot pick them out without soiling his fingers. Here is a couplet containing one of the best, and one of the worst, lines in the piece. The poet, addressing the mountain, exclaims with inimitable bathos,—

> Ages are thy days,
> *Thou grand expresser of the present tense!*

The greater part of the poem is made up of such senseless jingle as this:—

> For the world was built in order,
> And the atoms march in tune;
> Rhyme the pipe, and Time the warder,
> *Cannot forget the sun, the moon.*
> Orb and atom forth they prance,
> When they hear from far the rune;
> None so backward in the troop,
> When the music and the dance
> *Reach his* place and *circumstance,*
> But knows the *sun-creating sound,*
> And, though a *pyramid, will bound.*

We can find no nominative to "cannot forget," there is no word to rhyme with "troop," and, in the last four lines, subject and object are mingled in inextricable confusion. . . .

The publication of a volume of such poetry at the present day is a strange phenomenon; but a stranger, still, is the eagerness with which it is received by quite a large circle of neophytes, who look down with pitying contempt on all those who cannot share their admiration of its contents. It is stereotyped, and we hear that one or two thousand copies of it have been sold. How far the taste may be perverted by fashion, prejudice, or the influences of a *clique* or [the Transcendentalists] school, it is impossible to say; but there must be limits to all corruptions of it which come short of insanity. It is possible to profess admiration which one does not feel; or for the faculties to be so impaired by disease as to become insensible to their appropriate gratifications. The ear may lose its perception of the finest harmonies, the olfactory nerve may no longer be gratified by the most delicious perfumes; these would be mere defects, a loss of the sources of great enjoyment. But we cannot conceive of enjoyments being created of an opposite character. The ear cannot be trained to receive pleasure from discords, nor the sense of smell to enjoy a stench. As with the pleasures of sense, so is it with intellectual gratifications. We may never have acquired a relish for them, or we may lose it by neglect. But one cannot change the nature of things, and derive positive pleasure from that which is distasteful and odious by its original constitution. Incoherency of thought and studied obscurity of expression, an unmeaning jumble of words and a heap of vulgar and incongruous images, cannot, as such, be agreeable objects to contemplate. If praised by a sect, it must be because each one relies on the opinion of his fellows, so that there is not one independent judgment among them. If the hierophant of the sect be a shrewd humorist, it is most likely that he is mocking the weakness of his admirers.

Harvard Magazine (essay date 1855)

SOURCE: "Emerson as a Poet," in *Harvard Magazine,* Volume 1, October, 1855, pp. 422-33.

[*In this excerpt from an article appearing in the magazine associated with Emerson's alma mater, Harvard University, the anonymous critic commends Emerson as an intellectual poet whose original verse derives its inspiration from both American nature and Eastern religions. Written eight years after Emerson first published* Poems, *the critic's positive response reflects the changing attitude toward poetic styles during the 1850s.*]

The venerable and historic town of Concord (not Concord, New Hampshire, famous for its small-beer school of politicians) is likely, in addition to its Revolutionary renown as the spot where

> once the embattled farmers stood,
> And fired the shot heard round the world,

to be famous hereafter as the residence of the essayist, poet, popular lecturer, and transcendental philosopher, Emerson, who, whatever may be thought of him by his contemporaries hereabouts, is certainly destined to a permanent and world-wide reputation,—to become a fixed star in that luminous cluster of original thinkers who from their high places exercise a steady and never-waning influence on the intellectual growth of mankind. Concord, Massachusetts, therefore, as the scene of one of the events which inaugurated the American Revolution, and as the home of one of the first intellectual men of the age, is in no particular danger, in the long run, of being eclipsed by its namesake in New Hampshire, though that be the capital of a small State and the home of a small President. However this may be, one thing is certain, that there are few places better adapted to study and the cultivation of letters. Through its meadows and shady intervale lands winds a slow stream, synonymous with the town itself, a stream like the English Ouse or Avon, or the smooth gliding Mincius of classic song, not rapid or turbulent, but with just such a clear and languid current as poets have loved to prose upon from time immemorial. . . .

As a lecturer and prose essayist, Mr. Emerson is even *popularly* known, that is, to the mass of his countrymen; but as a poet he has found a smaller audience, though a fit one. His verses can never become popular. He cannot therefore cry out with Horace, *"profanum vulgus et arceo,"* for the mob of people that read with ease (to alter slightly Pope's lines for the sake of adapting it to the times) will never defile his poetry with their vulgar admiration. It will never fly through the mouths of men like Pope's pithy couplets, or Gray's "Elegy," or Longfellow's "Psalm of Life," but it has already secured for itself a select circle of admirers among the highly cultivated and intellectual, and such a circle it will always retain. It is even now frequently quoted by the ablest writers in the leading reviews and periodicals of England and this country. Indeed, we venture to assert that there are few writers of eminence, either in America or Great Britain, who are not perfectly familiar with the products of the Emersonian Muse, with the strange, weird, abstruse notes of the Emersonian lyre. Like the Theban poet Pindar, Emerson, when he wraps his singing robes about him, addresses himself only to the wise. He has many musical shafts in his quiver, but their music is only audible and intelligible *"ôoî óoöoî ."* His poems are as utterly devoid of anything like sentiment or passion as the versified apothegms of the old Greek philosophers and didactic bards. In fact, sentiment and passion, which are ordinarily supposed to be the very soul and essential principle of poetry, he utterly ignores. His best passages have "the sparkle of the spar," but none of the warmth of flesh and blood. They appeal not to the heart, but to pure intellect. He is not of the romantic school of poets. He is entirely free from "dark imaginings" of the Byronic stamp, and from maudlin, lovesick, moon-nursed fantasies. His Muse traffics not in these woes. She haunts "an intellectual bower." Some of his poetical pieces are pearl-like strings of glittering *sententiæ,* of brilliant and grand thoughts set in a most transparent and crystalline diction. Emerson's poetry, like his prose, is all permeated with emanations from one great central ideal. His peculiar philosophical system, call it by what name you choose, Spinozism, Pantheism, or Transcendentalism, is the master chord of his lyre, as it is the keynote of all his writings, whether in verse or prose. Around this central idea his poetry winds in luxuriant wreaths and festoons, like the leaves and flowers of some gorgeous parasite about a massy trunk. What Emerson's system of philosophy is exactly, it is no easy task to determine. . . . Whatever it is, Mr. Emerson seems to entertain the most sublime confidence in its entire correctness. He evidently looks upon it as the master-key which unlocks the secrets of the universe and the most hidden recesses and profoundest Domdaniel caverns of Nature. Beyond a doubt, Mr. Emerson has the highest qualifications for a poet. Even his prose itself has in passages the golden *rythmus* of the most exquisitely modulated versification. He is profoundly learned, not only in printed books, but also in the book of Nature. All the lore of the East and the West is his. He is as familiar with Hafiz and Firdusi, as he is with Homer and Shakespeare; with the sages and philosophers of India, China, Persia, and Arabia, as he is with those of Greece, Rome, Germany, England, and France. He is deeply versed in the lore of plants, stones, and stars. He has looked on Nature with a lover's eye, and pursued her through all her most intricate windings, and learned to interpret her most mysterious symbols. Mr. Emerson is happy in his choice of language, which in his hands is perfectly plastic and flexible. His words are culled and marshalled with the most exquisite taste. Many of his periods are rounded and enamelled to absolute perfection. It used to be fashionable to speak of Emerson as an imitator of the rough, craggy Carlyle. This idea was without doubt engendered by the fact that several of Carlyle's works were published in this country under the supervision of Emerson, and the editor was naturally confounded with his author. Emerson, in fact, is the very opposite of Carlyle both in style of thought and composition. They no more resemble each other as writers than would an Ithuriel and a Caliban in form and feature if matched together.

But there are great inequalities in Emerson's poetry. While he has passages, indeed whole pieces, which are as fault-less, flawless, and beautiful as some costly gem, he has others which, to the understanding of the uninitiated reader at least, appear to be mere unmeaning strings of words, vague, hyper-metaphysical formulas, and pure balderdash. They are hard sayings, too hard indeed for the compre-hension of any human being except a *Dial*ist. In nearly all Mr. Emerson's poems, it is evident that more is meant than meets the ear and eye. He has an Oriental love of the allegoric and mystical. But above all its other merits his poetry is *sui generis,* original and his own. It is not the product of any second-hand inspiration, awakened by the works of this or that great poet beyond the water, as is the case with the bulk of American poetry. It is not this or that English or German bard diluted and sophisticated, but genuine, unadulterated Emerson, with an unmistak-able smack of the soil of his fatherland about it; for if he has occasion to apostrophize a mountain or river in his verse, he gives a decided preference to Monadnock or the Alleghanies over Olympus and the Alps,—to the beauti-ful rivers of his native New England, with their wild In-dian names, hitherto "unmarried to immortal verse," over the most vaunted streams of the Old World. This is as it should be. But for the most part it is with our poetry as with the wines which we use; both are mere imitations and not natural products, the latter generally consisting of ingenious chemical mixtures, whose rich vinous *hue* and *bouquet* and flavor were not imparted by the glowing sun and genial soil of Burgundy, Champagne, and the African Islands, but by artificial perfumes and dye-stuffs. But we have one American vintage, at least, which does not smell of the apothecary-shop, but of the American soil, of the banks of the Ohio. In like manner we have a few poets who do not derive their inspiration from Tennyson or Wordsworth or Browning, or any other European bard, living or dead, but directly from Nature herself. Mr. Emerson's published poems are all included within the limits of a single small volume; but that volume is infi-nitely suggestive, and contains matter enough, if wire-drawn and reduced, to fill many tomes. In it all the Emersonian prose essays are presented in brief, fused, intensified, and hardened, as it were, into crystals. Virgil himself could not originate a system of philosophy in more honeyed verse. With three or four exceptions, each poem is a chip from a different side of the same block, a variation of the same key-note, a new illustration of one master idea, for there is but one string to Emerson's lyre; but he draws from that solitary chord as many variations as ever did a Paganini. Four, at least, of his poems have become popular, and have been reprinted a thousand times in newspapers, reviews, and specimens of American verse. We allude to the pieces entitled **"Good-Bye," "Rhodora," "The Humble-Bee,"** and **"The Problem."** These are pure ambrosia. The Good-Bye to the world is worthy of the age of Elizabeth, and might have been penned by a Wotton or Raleigh after they had "sounded all the depths and shoals of honor"; indeed, it reminds one of verses which those great statesmen and scholars actually did write after they had become satiated with the world. The lines to the **"Humble-Bee,"** have been compared to the Allegro and Penseroso of Milton. It seems to breathe the very spirit of the delicious months of May and June. It might have been written upon a bank of violets, fanned by the sweet South, such as the impassioned Duke Orsino speaks of. It is enough in itself to give its author a permanent place in English literature. Anacreon has an ode, and Mr. Leigh Hunt has a sonnet, addressed to the grasshopper, both exquisite in their way, but neither comparable to Emerson's lines on the "yellow-breeched" American insect, the tiny and erratic

> Sailor of the atmosphere;
> Swimmer through the waves of air;
> Voyager of light and noon;
> Epicurean of June.
>
> . . . . .
>
> When the south wind, in May days,
> With a net of shining haze
> Silvers the horizon wall,
> And, with softness touching all,
> Tints the human countenance
> With a color of romance,
> And, infusing subtle heats,
> Turns the sod to violets,
> Thou in sunny solitudes,
> Rover of the underwoods,
> The green silence dost displace,
> With thy mellow, breezy bass.
>
> Hot midsummer's petted crone,
> Sweet to me thy drowsy tone
> Tells of countless sunny hours,
> Long days, and solid banks of flowers;
> Of gulfs of sweetness without bound
> In Indian wildernesses found;
> Of Syrian peace, immortal leisure,
> Firmest cheer, and bird-like pleasure.

The very genius of dreamy May and voluptuous June seems to brood over the above lines. A few such passages would be enough to redeem the character of the American Muse from the charge of barrenness and want of originality. Mr. Emerson looks on nature and the visible universe with the eye of a poet and a man of science both. He is a Wordsworth and Linnæus combined. New-England scenery is almost as much indebted to him as the lakes and mountain regions of Northern England are to Wordsworth, Coleridge, and De Quincey. Mount Monadnock, since it has been embalmed in Emerson's verse, need not fear to lift its head beside the most vaunted hill visible from Rydal Mount, where not long since lived the great English high-priest of nature. Emer-son's **"Monadnock"** is one of the richest, most suggestive, and picturesque pieces in the language. What Wordsworth called "the power of hills" must have been on him when he wrote it. The tall form of Monadnock towers in his verse with as much majesty as it does in its native heavens, and henceforth is entitled to be ranked with those immemorial mountains of the Old World, renowned in song.

> Cheshire's haughty hill

has its poet, too, as well as the giant Swiss mountain, whose shadow glides over the valley of Chamouni. A voice, perhaps of the Genius of Monadnock, summons the poet:

> Up!—If thou know'st who calls
> To twilight parks of beech and pine,
> High over the river intervals,
> Above the ploughman's highest line,
> Over the owner's farthest walls!

. . . . .

Mr. Emerson's poetry concerns itself but little with human joys or sorrows. His Muse oftenest affects the "heights of abstract contemplation." His religion (for it is on this subject that his Muse chiefly delights to dwell) appears to be borrowed from Plato and the dreamy mystics of the Ganges. The visible universe, with its myriad forms of animal, vegetable, mineral, and impalpable aerial existences, is in his view simply a masquerade of the World-Soul or Godhead, an infinite variation of the eternal unit, a *monad* which underlies and constitutes everything. God is a vast impersonal, unimpassioned energy merely, a *"vivida vis,"* or creative potency. Man himself, though the highest manifestation of Deity, is, so far as his identity and individual being are concerned, a mere foambell, which arises for a moment on the rushing tides of existence, and is quickly reabsorbed into the oceanic essence of Deity. . . .

Above all its other merits [Emerson's] poetry is *sui generis,* original and his own. It is not the product of any second-hand inspiration, awakened by the works of this or that great poet beyond the water, as is the case with the bulk of American poetry. It is not this or that English or German bard diluted and sophisticated, but genuine, unadulterated Emerson.

—*Harvard Magazine*

It seems to us, in our ignorance, not a little singular that Emerson, with his keen intellect, piercing as a Damascus blade, and his upright moral character, could deliberately turn away from what he himself calls

> The riches of sweet Mary's son,
> Boy-Rabbi, Israel's paragon,

to the altars of a vague, defied abstraction, like the Platonic *Zeus* or the Oriental *Brahma,* for such, as near as we can gather, is the God of his idolatry.

But to attempt anything like a careful examination of Emerson's poems within the compass of a short essay would be impossible, for each would furnish matter sufficient for an article. Suffice it to say, that these poems

are among the most remarkable contributions to the literature of the present age, and as such they will undoubtedly be regarded by posterity.

Charles Eliot Norton   (essay date 1867)

SOURCE: A review of *May-Day and Other Pieces,* in *North American Review,* Vol. CCXVI, July, 1867, pp. 325-27.

[*Norton, an editor of leading journals during the 1860s and a professor at Harvard University for twenty-five years, wrote internationally reknowned literary and social criticism and historical essays that produced a wide cultural influence. In this excerpt, he praises Emerson's second book of poetry by expressing a willingness to accept Emerson's uneven poetic style as a minor flaw in light of the greater contribution made by Emerson's moral and spiritual themes.*]

In the exquisite poem in this volume [*May-Day and Other Pieces*] called **"Terminus"** Mr. Emerson speaks of himself as one who

> Obeys the voice at eve obeyed at prime.

He has, indeed, unquestioned right thus to speak of himself, for he has been true, as few men ever were, to the voice of his own genius, and his obedience has been to him both inspiration and power. Many years ago he said of the poet: "He is isolated among his contemporaries, by truth and by his art, but with this consolation in his pursuits, that they will draw all men sooner or later." And in his own experience he has had proof of this assertion. He has had the happiness of living long enough to see his contemporaries, those at least of the younger generation, drawing to him, and acknowledging him as one of those

> Olympian bards who sung
>   Divine ideas below,
> Which always find us young,
>   And always keep us so.

His first volume of poems and his last, with twenty-one years' interval between them, are in the same key of harmony, and are expressions of the same voice. The first has some tones of youth, some fervors of imagination which are not found in the last, but their place is supplied by the clearer accents and composed strength of mature life. They are both alike the sincere utterances of a strongly marked and individual genius, and both in striking contrast to the popular poetry of the day.

The character of Mr. Emerson's genius is such that its expressions are not, and are not likely to become, in a strict sense, popular. He addresses a select audience, composed of those who like himself hold to their ideals, and have faith in the worth and efficacy of ideas. He speaks to the few, but those few are the masters of the world. As a poet he belongs to the small band of moral poets, of those whose power lies not in imagination as applied to the affairs and interests of men, not in fertility of fancy or in range of conception, but in the perception of the moral and spiritual relations of man to the nature which encompasses him, of the moral and spiritual laws which are symbolized by that nature, and of the universal truths which underlie the forms of existence, and co-ordinate the varieties of human experience. There is little passion in his poetry; passion is in its nature selfish; the emotions which his verses express are seldom personal. The events of life are as nothing to the poet as compared to the ideas which possess his soul. Very few of his poems have a lyrical quality; not one of them is truly dramatic. Men are little to him; man and nature, everything.

Idealist as he is, it is not strange that at times he shows himself the mystic. It is by inspiration, and not by reason, that he is guided, and he has no test of the quality of his inspiration. It may be a revelation of light; it may be an apocalypse of darkness. But poetry and mysticism have nothing properly in common. True poetry is neither a riddle, nor an illusion, and true inspiration is always rational. The inconceivable is as much beyond the reach of intuition as of reason. The vein of mysticism in Mr. Emerson's genius is doubtless the more conspicuous from the comparative subordination in his nature of the artistic to the speculative element. The essence of art lies in definiteness of conception. The artist is he who can perfectly exhibit his idea in form; and excellence of form—whether in line, color, rhythm, or harmony—gives universality and permanence to the work of art. Perfect form is abstract, imperishable, archetypal; and he is the greatest artist who clothes ideas in the most nearly perfect form. Mr. Emerson, idealist as he is, too often pays little regard to this ideal form, and puts his thought into inharmonious verse. His poems are for the most part more fitted to invigorate the moral sense, than to delight the artistic. At times, indeed, he is singularly felicitous in expression, and some of his verses both charm and elevate the soul. These rarer verses will live in the memories of men. No poet is surer of immortality than Mr. Emerson, but the greater part of his poetry will be read, not so much for its artistic as for its moral worth.

The poem which gives its title to the new volume, "**May-Day,**" is a poem of spring,—a collection of beautiful praises and descriptions of our New England May, written by a lover of Nature, to whom she has told many of her secrets, and whom she has cheered with her smile. It is full of the new wine of the year; of the gladness, the comfort, and the purity of the gay season of youth and love. The next poem, "**The Adirondacks,**" is of a different sort, save in its familiarity with nature, and reads like an American episode out of the best part of Wordsworth's "Prelude." Among the Occasional and Miscellaneous Poems which make up the rest of the volume are many already known to the lovers of the best poetry, and which, now collected, will be among the choicest flowers of the most select anthology. We need but name "**Voluntaries,**" "**Days,**" "**My Garden,**" "**Sea-shore,**" "**Two Rivers,**" "**Terminus,**" "**The Past,**" to show what rare treasures this little volume holds.

William Dean Howells (essay date 1867)

SOURCE: A review of *May-Day and Other Pieces*, in *Atlantic Monthly*, Vol. 20, September, 1867, pp. 376-78.

[*Howells, one of the most popular novelists of the late nineteenth century, was an editor of* Atlantic Monthly *for fifteen years. In this excerpt Howells praises selections from Emerson's second book of poetry and states that Emerson's poetry, while challenging, offers great intellectual rewards.*]

We wonder whether those who take up Mr. Emerson's poem now, amid the glories of the fading summer, are not giving the poet a fairer audience than those who hurried to hear his song in the presence of the May he celebrates. As long as spring was here, he had a rival in every reader; for then we all felt ourselves finer poets than ever sang of the season, and did not know that our virtue was but an effect of Spring herself,—an impression, not an expression of her loveliness, which must pass with her. Now, when the early autumn is in every sense, and those days when the year first awoke to consciousness have grown so far away, we must perceive that no one has yet been allowed to speak so well for the spring of our New World as this poet. The very irregularity of Mr. Emerson's poem seems to be part of its verisimilitude, and it appears as if all the pauses and impulses and mysterious caprices of the season—which fill the trees with birds before blossoms, and create the soul of sweetness and beauty in the May-flowers under the dead leaves of the woodlands, while the meadows are still bare and brown—had so entered into this song, that it could not emulate the deliberation and consequence of art. The "**May-Day**" is to the critical faculty a succession of odes on Spring, celebrating now one aspect and now another, and united only by their title; yet since an entire idea of spring is evolved from them, and they awaken the same emotions that the youth of the year stirs in us, we must accept the result as something undeniably great and good. Of course, we can complain of the way in which it is brought about, just as we can upbraid the New England climate, though its uncertain and desultory April and May give us at last the most beautiful June weather in the world.

The poem is not one that invites analysis, though it would be easy enough to instance striking merits and defects. Mr. Emerson, perhaps, more than any other modern poet, gives the notion of inspiration; so that one doubts, in reading him, how much to praise or blame. The most exquisite effects seem not to have been invited, but to have sought production from his unconsciousness; graces alike of thought and of touch seem the unsolicited gifts of the gods. Even the doubtful quality of occasional lines confirms this impression of unconsciousness. One cannot believe that the poet would wittingly write,

> Boils the world in tepid lakes,

for this statement has, for all that the reader can see to the contrary, the same value with him as that preceding verse, telling how the waxing heat

Lends the reed and lily length,
wherein the very spirit of summer seems to sway
and droop.

Yet it is probable that no utterance is more considered than this poet's, and that no one is more immediately responsible than he. We must attribute to the most subtile and profound consciousness the power that can trace with such tenderness and beauty the alliance he has shown between earth and humanity in the exultation of spring, and which can make matter of intellectual perception the mute sympathies that seemed to perish with childhood . . .

Among the other poems in this volume, it appears to us that **"The Romany Girl," "Voluntaries,"** and **"The Boston Hymn"** are in their widely different ways the best. The last expresses, with a sublime colloquiality in which the commonest words of every-day parlance seem cut anew, and are made to shine with a fresh and novel lustre the idea and destiny of America. In **"Voluntaries"** our former great peril and delusion—the mortal Union which lived by slavery—is at first the theme, with the strong pulse of prophecy, however, in the mournful music. Few motions of rhyme so win and touch as those opening lines,—

Low and mournful be the strain,
Haughty thought be far from me;
Tones of penitence and pain,
Moanings of the tropic sea,—

in which the poet, with a hardly articulate sorrow, regards the past . . . .

It is, of course, a somewhat Emersonian Gypsy that speaks in **"The Romany Girl,"** but still she speaks with the passionate, sudden energy of a woman, and flashes upon the mind with intense vividness the conception of a wild nature's gleeful consciousness of freedom, and exultant scorn of restraint and convention. All sense of sylvan health and beauty is uttered when this Gypsy says,—

The wild air bloweth in our lungs,
The keen stars twinkle in our eyes,
The birds gave us our wily tongues,
The panther in our dances flies.

"Terminus" has a wonderful didactic charm, and must be valued as one of the noblest introspective poems in the language. The poet touches his reader by his acceptance of fate and age, and his serene trust of the future, and yet is not moved by his own pathos.

We do not regard the poem **"The Adirondacks"** as of great absolute or relative value. It is one of the prosiest in the book, and for a professedly out-of-doors poem has too much of the study in it. Let us confess also that we have not yet found pleasure in **"The Elements,"** and that we do not expect to live long enough to enjoy some of them. **"Quatrains"** have much the same forbidding qualities, and have chiefly interested us in the comparison they suggest with the translations from the Persian: it is curious to find cold Concord and warm Ispahan in the same latitude. Others of the briefer poems have delighted us. **"Rubies,"** for instance, is full of exquisite lights and hues, thoughts and feelings; and **"The Test"** is from the heart of the severe wisdom without which art is not. Everywhere the poet's felicity of expression appears; a fortunate touch transfuses some dark enigma with color; the riddles are made to shine when most impenetrable; the puzzles are all constructed of gold and ivory and precious stones.

Mr. Emerson's intellectual characteristics and methods are so known that it is scarcely necessary to hint that this is not a book for instant absorption into any reader's mind. It shall happen with many, we fancy, that they find themselves ready for only two or three things in it, and that they must come to it in widely varying moods for all it has to give. No greater wrong could be done to the poet than to go through his book running, and he would be apt to revenge himself upon the impatient reader by leaving him all the labor involved in such a course, and no reward at the end for his pains.

But the case is not a probable one. People either read Mr. Emerson patiently and earnestly, or they do not read him at all. In this earnest nation he enjoys a far greater popularity than criticism would have augured for one so unflattering to the impulses that have heretofore and elsewhere made readers of poetry; and it is not hard to believe, if we believe in ourselves for the future, that he is destined to an ever-growing regard and fame. He makes appeal, however mystically, only to what is fine and deep and true and noble in men, and no doubt those who have always loved his poetry have reason to be proud of their pleasure in it. Let us of the present be wise enough to accept thankfully what genius gives us in its double character of bard and prophet, saying, when we enjoy the song, "Ah, this is the poet that now sings!" and when the meaning is dark, "Now we have the seer again!"

Oliver Wendell Holmes (essay date 1899)

SOURCE: "Emerson's Poems," in *Ralph Waldo Emerson/John Lothrop Motley: Two Memoirs,* Houghton, Mifflin and Company, 1899, pp. 239-64.

[*Holmes, a contemporary of Emerson's, was a famous medical doctor and fellow writer. In the following excerpt, Holmes discusses Emerson's poetry by comparing Emerson to the great writers throughout history, ranking Emerson highly for the moral statements he makes in symbolic terms but also criticizing him slightly for the unevenness of his poetic rhythm.*]

. . . The difference between Emerson's poetry and that of the contemporaries with whom he would naturally be compared is that of algebra and arithmetic. He deals largely in general symbols, abstractions, and infinite series. He is always seeing the universal in the particular. The great multitude of mankind care more for two and two, something definite, a fixed quantity, than for $a + b$'s and x^2's,— symbols used for undetermined amounts and indefinite possibilities. Emerson is a citizen of the universe who has taken up his residence for a few days and nights in this travelling caravansary between the two inns that hang out the signs of Venus and Mars. This little planet could not provincialize such a man. The multiplication-table is for the every-day use of every-day earth-people, but the symbols he deals with are too vast, sometimes, we must own, too vague, for the unilluminated terrestrial and arithmetical intelligence. One cannot help feeling that he might have dropped in upon us from some remote centre of spiritual life, where, instead of addition and subtraction, children were taught quaternions, and where the fourth dimension of space was as familiarly known to everybody as a foot-measure or a yard-stick is to us. Not that he himself dealt in the higher or the lower mathematics, but he saw the hidden spiritual meaning of things as Professor Cayley or Professor Sylvester see the meaning of their mysterious formulæ. Without using the Rosetta-stone of Swedenborg, Emerson finds in every phenomenon of nature a hieroglyphic. Others measure and describe the monuments,—he reads the sacred inscriptions. How alive he makes Monadnoc! Dinocrates undertook to "hew Mount Athos to the shape of man" in the likeness of Alexander the Great. Without the help of tools or workmen Emerson makes "Cheshire's haughty hill" stand before us an impersonation of kingly humanity, and talk with us as a god from Olympus might have talked. This is the fascination of Emerson's poetry; it moves in a world of universal symbolism. The sense of the infinite fills it with its majestic presence. It shows, also, that he has a keen delight in the every-day aspects of nature. But he looks always with the eye of a poet, never with that of the man of science. The law of association of ideas is wholly different in the two. The scientific man connects objects in sequences and series, and in so doing is guided by their collective resemblances. His aim is to classify and index all that he sees and contemplates so as to show the relations which unite, and learn the laws that govern, the subjects of his study. The poet links the most remote objects together by the slender filament of wit, the flowery chain of fancy, or the living, pulsating cord of imagination, always guided by his instinct for the beautiful. The man of science clings to his object, as the marsupial embryo to its teat, until he has filled himself as full as he can hold; the poet takes a sip of his dew-drop, throws his head up like a chick, rolls his eyes around in contemplation of the heavens above him and the universe in general, and never thinks of asking a Linnæan question as to the flower that furnished him his dew-drop. The poetical and scientific natures rarely coexist; Haller and Goethe are examples which show that such a union may occur, but as a rule the poet is contented with the colors of the rainbow and leaves the study of Fraunhofer's lines to the man of science.

Though far from being a man of science, Emerson was a realist in the best sense of that word. But his realities reached to the highest heavens; like Milton,

He passed the flaming bounds of place and time;
The living throne, the sapphire blaze

Where angels tremble while they gaze,
HE SAW.

Everywhere his poetry abounds in celestial imagery. If Galileo had been a poet as well as an astronomer, he would hardly have sowed his verse thicker with stars than we find them in the poems of Emerson.

Not less did Emerson clothe the common aspects of life with the colors of his imagination. He was ready to see beauty everywhere:—

Thou canst not wave thy staff in air,
Or dip thy paddle in the lake,
But it carves the bow of beauty there,
And the ripples in rhyme the oar forsake.

He called upon the poet to

Tell men what they knew before;
Paint the prospect from their door.

And his practice was like his counsel. He saw our plain New England life with as honest New England eyes as ever looked at a huckleberry-bush or into a milking-pail.

This noble quality of his had its dangerous side. In one of his exalted moods he would have us

Give to barrows, trays and pans
Grace and glimmer of romance.

But in his lecture on Poetry and Imagination, he says:—

What we once admired as poetry has long since come
to be a sound of tin pans; and many of our later books
we have outgrown. Perhaps Homer and Milton will be
tin pans yet.

The "grace and glimmer of romance" which were to invest the tin pan are forgotten, and he uses it as a belittling object for comparison. He himself was not often betrayed into the mistake of confounding the prosaic with the poetical, but his followers, so far as the "realists" have taken their hint from him, have done it most thoroughly. Mr. Whitman enumerates all the objects he happens to be looking at as if they were equally suggestive to the poetical mind, furnishing his reader a large assortment on which he may exercise the fullest freedom of selection. It is only giving him the same liberty that Lord Timothy Dexter allowed his readers in the matter of punctuation, by leaving all stops out of his sentences, and printing at the end of his book a page of commas, semicolons, colons, periods, notes of interrogation and exclamation, with which the reader was expected to "pepper" the pages as he might see fit.

French realism does not stop at the tin pan, but must deal with the slop-pail and the wash-tub as if it were literally true that

In the mud and scum of things
There alway, alway something sings.

Happy were it for the world if M. Zola and his tribe would stop even there; but when they cross the borders of science into its infected districts, leaving behind them the reserve and delicacy which the genuine scientific observer never forgets to carry with him, they disgust even those to whom the worst scenes they describe are too wretchedly familiar. The true realist is such a man as Parent du Chatelet; exploring all that most tries the senses and the sentiments, and reporting all truthfully, but soberly, chastely, without needless circumstance, or picturesque embellishment, for a useful end, and not for a mere sensational effect.

What a range of subjects from **"The Problem"** and **"Uriel"** and **"Forerunners"** to **"The Humble-Bee"** and **"The Titmouse"**! Nor let the reader who thinks the poet must go far to find a fitting theme fail to read the singularly impressive home-poem, **"Hamatreya,"** beginning with the names of the successive owners of a piece of land in Concord,—probably the same he owned after the last of them,—

Bulkeley, Hunt, Willard, Hosmer, Meriam, Flint,

and ending with the austere and solemn **"Earth-Song."**

Full of poetical feeling, and with a strong desire for poetical expression, Emerson experienced a difficulty in the mechanical part of metrical composition. His muse picked her way as his speech did in conversation and in lecturing. He made desperate work now and then with rhyme and rhythm, showing that though a born poet he was not a born singer. Think of making "feeble" rhyme with "people," "abroad" with "Lord," and contemplate the following couplet which one cannot make rhyme without actual verbicide:—

Where feeds the moose, and walks the surly bear,
And up the tall mast runs the woodpeck

And how could prose go on all-fours more unmetrically than this?

In Adirondac lakes
At morn or noon the guide rows bare-headed.

It was surely not difficult to say—

At morn or, noon bare-headed rows the guide.

And yet while we note these blemishes, many of us will confess that we like his uncombed verse better, oftentimes, than if it were trimmed more neatly and disposed more nicely. When he is at his best, his lines flow with careless ease, as a mountain stream tumbles, sometimes rough and sometimes smooth, but all the more interesting for the rocks it runs against and the grating of the pebbles it rolls over.

There is one trick of verse which Emerson occasionally, not very often, indulges in. This is the crowding of a redundant syllable into a line. It is a liberty which is not to be abused by the poet. Shakespeare, the supreme artist, and Milton, the "mighty-mouth'd inventor of harmonies,"

knew how to use it effectively. Shelley employed it freely. Bryant indulged in it occasionally, and wrote an article in an early number of *The North American Review* in defence of its use. Willis was fond of it. As a relief to monotony it may be now and then allowed,—may even have an agreeable effect in breaking the monotony of too formal verse. But it may easily become a deformity and a cause of aversion. A humpback may add picturesqueness to a procession, but if there are too many humpbacks in line we turn away from the sight of them. Can any ear reconcile itself to the last of these three lines of Emerson's?

Oh, what is Heaven but the fellowship
Of minds that each can stand against the world
By its own meek and incorruptible will?

These lines that lift their backs up in the middle—spanworm lines, we may call them—are not to be commended for common use because some great poets have now and then admitted them. They have invaded some of our recent poetry as the canker-worms gather on our elms in June. Emerson has one or two of them here and there, but they never swarm on his leaves so as to frighten us away from their neighborhood.

As for the violently artificial rhythms and rhymes which have reappeared of late in English and American literature, Emerson would as soon have tried to ride three horses at once in a circus as to shut himself up in triolets, or attempt any cat's-cradle tricks of rhyming sleight of hand. . . .

It would be a pleasant and not a difficult task to trace the resemblances between Emerson's poetry and that of other poets. . . .

In his contemplative study of Nature he reminds us of Wordsworth, at least in certain brief passages, but he has not the staying power of that long-breathed, not to say long-winded, lover of landscapes. Both are on the most intimate terms with Nature, but Emerson contemplates himself as belonging to her, while Wordsworth feels as if she belonged to him.

Good-bye, proud world,

recalls Spenser and Raleigh. **"The Humble-Bee"** is strongly marked by the manner and thought of Marvell. Marvell's

Annihilating all that's made
To a green thought in a green shade

may well have suggested Emerson's

The green silence dost displace
With thy mellow, breezy bass.

"The Snow-Storm" naturally enough brings to mind the descriptions of Thomson and of Cowper, and fragment as it is, it will not suffer by comparison with either.

"Woodnotes," one of his best poems, has passages that might have been found in Milton's "Comus;" this, for instance:—

All constellations of the sky
Shed their virtue through his eye.
Him Nature giveth for defence
His formidable innocence.

Of course his Persian and Indian models betray themselves in many of his poems, some of which, called translations, sound as if they were original.

So we follow him from page to page and find him passing through many moods, but with one pervading spirit:—

Melting matter into dreams,
Panoramas which I saw,
And whatever glows or seems
Into substance, into Law.

We think in reading his "Poems" of these words of Sainte-Beuve:—

The greatest poet is not he who had done the best; it is he who suggests the most; he, not all of whose meaning is at first obvious, and who leaves you much to desire, to explain, to study; much to complete in your turn.

Just what he shows himself in his prose, Emerson shows himself in his verse. Only when he gets into rhythm and rhyme he lets us see more of his personality, he ventures upon more audacious imagery, his flight is higher and swifter, his brief crystalline sentences have dissolved and pour in continuous streams. Where they came from, or whither they flow to empty themselves, we cannot always say,—it is enough to enjoy them as they flow by us.

Incompleteness—want of beginning, middle, and end—is their too common fault. His pages are too much like those artists' studios all hung round with sketches and "bits" of scenery. **"The Snow-Storm"** and **"Sea-Shore"** are "bits" out of a landscape that was never painted, admirable, so far as they go, but forcing us to ask, "Where is the painting for which these scraps are studies?" or "Out of what great picture have these pieces been cut?"

We do not want his fragments to be made wholes,—if we did, what hand could be found equal to the task? We do not want his rhythms and rhymes smoothed and made more melodious. They areas honest as Chaucer's, and we like them as they are, not modernized or manipulated by any versifying drill-sergeant,—if we wanted them reshaped whom could we trust to meddle with them?

His poetry is elemental; it has the rock beneath it in the eternal laws on which it rests; the roll of deep waters in its grander harmonies; its air is full of Æolian strains that waken and die away as the breeze wanders over them; and through it shines the white starlight, and from time to time flashes a meteor that startles us with its sudden brilliancy.

After all our criticisms, our selections, our analyses, our comparisons, we have to recognize that there is a charm in Emerson's poems which cannot be defined any more than the fragrance of a rose or a hyacinth,—any more than the tone of a voice which we should know from all others if all mankind were to pass before us, and each of its articulating representatives should call us by name.

All our crucibles and alembics leave unaccounted for the great mystery of *style*. "The style is of [a part of] the man himself," said Buffon, and this saying has passed into the stronger phrase, "The style is the man."

The "personal equation" which differentiates two observers is not confined to the tower of the astronomer. Every human being is individualized by a new arrangement of elements. His mind is a safe with a lock to which only certain letters are the key. His ideas follow in an order of their own. His words group themselves together in special sequences, in peculiar rhythms, in unlooked-for combinations, the total effect of which is to stamp all that he says or writes with his individuality. We may not be able to assign the reason of the fascination the poet we have been considering exercises over us. But this we can say, that he lives in the highest atmosphere of thought; that he is always in the presence of the infinite, and ennobles the accidents of human existence so that they partake of the absolute and eternal while he is looking at them; that he unites a royal dignity of manner with the simplicity of primitive nature; that his words and phrases arrange themselves, as if by an elective affinity of their own, with a *curiosa felicitas* which captivates and enthrals the reader who comes fully under its influence, and that through all he sings as in all he says for us we recognize the same serene, high, pure intelligence and moral nature, infinitely precious to us, not only in themselves, but as a promise of what the transplanted life, the air and soil and breeding of this western world may yet educe from their potential virtues, shaping themselves, at length, in a literature, as much its own as the Rocky Mountains and the Mississippi.

Elisabeth Luther Cary (essay date 1904)

SOURCE: "Poems," in *Emerson: Poet and Thinker*, G. P. Putman's Sons, 1904, pp. 205-20.

[*In this excerpt Cary, a professional journalist-biographer, praises Emerson's poetry, finding it equal to William Wordsworth's in its "moral purpose." To Cary, Emerson epitomizes America's mid-nineteenth century call for poets to fulfill an organic ideal of verse.*]

Emerson delayed until 1847 the first edition of his poems, "uncertain always," he wrote to his brother, whether he had "one true spark of that fire which burns in verse." It is not probable that to-day any critic of importance could be found to share his doubt. Whatever may be said of his prose there is one thing that must be said by all men of his poetry, that it is the expression of a poet. We may search for lines that do not scan, for endings that do not rhyme, for a metre that does not flow or march or sing, for dialect and colloquialism, intricacy of diction, and grammatical inversion. We may find any or all of these and we shall not have disturbed by a hair's breadth our inner knowledge that we have been pecking and quibbling over the loveliest product of our national life. "It is his greatest glory as a poet," Dr. Garnett wrote in his account of Emerson, "to have been the harbinger of distinctively American poetry to America." Possibly: but it is not our least glory as a nation that thus early in our literature one poet could make our wilderness blossom like the rose, and we may hope that somewhere the blessed seed lies waiting for his successor, not yet within the field of vision.

We may well enough doubt, however, if Emerson's poetry is ever to be popular poetry. The American people would have fulfilled a high ideal of democracy indeed were that to come about. Every poem is charged with thought and thinking is not popular. But every poem also is an example of Emerson's own theory that poetry is "the perpetual endeavour to express the spirit of the thing," and it is the presence of the spirit, penetrating and informing the thought, that makes Emerson's poetry permanently buoyant. The intellectual element strong as it is in it is borne upward in the flight of powerful sentiment. At one time his essays, so pellucid in their crystallised illustrations, were considered recondite and abstruse, and at the same time his poetry was said to be filled with unintelligible expressions. The day of "popular science" has since arrived, and the popularisation of subjects formerly reserved for the learned is now so extended that one may go far to encounter readers in difficulty over Emerson's erudite allusions. One of his early public was heard not long ago to complain that the **"Threnody,"** beautiful though it was, contained passages of mysticism too complicated for his understanding. But one rereading discovered the fact that while the noble and tender emotion retained its power to fill the eyes with tears, the darkness had become light and not a line of obscurity interrupted the mood of exalted resignation induced by the poet's acquiescence in the harmony of natural laws.

It is then easily conceivable that to the larger number of educated men and women who read poetry, that of Emerson will be continually satisfying. It is inspired by the conviction that in no other way can truth be spoken, a conviction always potent to move sincere minds. And it is raised infinitely above prose by its delicate sensitiveness to suggestion in place of dogma. "God himself does not speak prose, but communicates with us by hints, omens, inference, and dark resemblances in objects lying all around us." Moreover it is essentially the voice of the age and country to which it belongs in its brevity and concentration. "Poetry teaches the enormous force of a few words, and in proportion to the inspiration checks loquacity." There indeed spoke the American, the man of all men to whom ennui is terrible, and diffuse sentiment ridiculous. If the soul is to be revealed there must be no long preamble to the overwhelming vision, and if we are not stirred beyond the possibility of expansive comment we have not seen. This terseness of description has, of course, its defect. It seldom conveys the sense of sweet leisure and the quiet influence of natural objects. In this stanza

from **"Saadi"** its least fortunate aspect is shown, the abruptness of the images having no special fitness to the subject:

> Trees in groves,
> Kine in droves,
> In ocean sport the scaly herds,
> Wedge-like cleave the air the birds,
> To northern lakes fly wind-borne ducks,
> Browse the mountain sheep in flocks,
> Men consort in camp and town,
> But the poet dwells alone.

There is, too, a certain harshness of measure in many of his poems to which our generation responds more readily than the previous one, no doubt, but which is too suggestive of conscious revolution against the insipid melody of much of the poetry of his own day.

> The kingly bard
> Must smite the chords rudely and hard,
> As with hammer or with mace,

he announces in **"Merlin,"** and his intention to make "each word a poem," to fill each word with significance, has sometimes given his vocabulary an excess of substance which it takes all the free strong movement of his thought to carry. And it is true that he seldom used any but the simplest pattern in his constructions. Octosyllabic and decasyllabic lines satisfied his idea of "fit quantity of syllables" for the most part, and metrical intricacy had no charm for him. But to consider him therefore monotonous or unskilled in producing the effects of art is to judge him superficially. Many are his devices, when the ear is at the point of missing the prick of novelty, to seize its attention and renew its interest. Note, for example, how delightfully the slightly irregular jog-trot of the first stanza of the **"Ode to Beauty"** breaks in the second stanza into a pacing measure conveying the very essence of blithe emotion that maketh the heart glad without reason:

> I drank at thy fountain
> False waters of thirst;
> Thou intimate stranger,
> Thou latest and first!
> Thy dangerous glances
> Make women of men
> New-born, we are melting
> Into nature again.
>
> Lavish, lavish promiser,
> Nigh persuading gods to err!
> Guest of million painted forms
> Which in turn thy glory warms!
> The frailest leaf, the mossy bark,
> The acorn's cup, the rainbow's arc,
> The swinging spider's silver line
> The ruby of the drop of wine.

But it would be a difficult matter to analyse Emerson's prosody. He has at least the happy skill to dispose the stress in his lines where it will emphasise the meaning and he does this without regard to arbitrary rules. The result is sometimes rocky syllables that forbid the climbing voice its progress. . . .

Certain mannerisms occur in his poems sometimes as irritating defects, sometimes as quaint ornament suited to the individual style; and grammatical eccentricities are not lacking.

In the lines so often quoted by dismayed critics,—

> The fiend that man harries
> Is love of the best;

it is certainly open to the reader to place the accusative where he will, but these lines can hardly be called representative. Even where equally forced inversion occurs elsewhere the meaning is seldom obscured by it. Another peculiarity which gives an air of mediævalism disliked by exacting critics is the division into two syllables of the ending "ion" and similar endings. But there is nothing really fixed or formal in the poems to give the dialectic mind its opportunity. The description in **"Merlin"** of the true poet takes the precise outline of Emerson's muse:

> Great is the art,
> Great be the manners of the bard.
> He shall not his brain encumber
> With the coil of rhythm and number,
> But, leaving rule and pale forethought,
> He shall aye climb
> For his rhyme.
> "Pass in, pass in," the angels say,
> "In to the upper doors,
> Nor count compartments of the floors,
> But mount to paradise
> By the stairway of surprise."

Surprise is a characteristic element in the larger number of the poems. It piques the imagination and startles the indolent mind, suggesting old truths by fresh figures of speech and furnishing new points of view for poetic thinkers. This perhaps is to be expected in the work of a writer bent upon discarding outworn formulas and the conventions of prosy civilisations. What is remarkable is the extreme beauty of metaphor, paradox, and symbol. It is comparatively easy to be unexpected and nothing is cheaper than the effect when gained merely by the use of unconventional material in language or thought. But beauty, as Emerson knew well, demands an integral idea beneath individual phrases, it demands the curve and balance of interior harmony, a structural expression pervading and accounting for all seeming eccentricity. This first essential was never out of his mind. All his varied rhetoric is chosen to emphasise the unity of man with God and with Nature. Against this noble background his most brilliant colours melt into harmony, his crudest forms appear majestic or at least organic. . . .

Emerson's care to preserve the key-note of joy in being led him frequently to choose epithets with the special aim of suggesting mirth and glee, riotous rejoicing on the part of tree, hill, or planet. The "sportive sun," the World-Soul with cheeks that "mantle with mirth," and Nature "game-

some and good," "merry and manifold," laugh through his poems; "The throbbing sea, the quaking earth, Yield sympathy and signs of mirth," the river is cheerful, the rills are gay, the mystic seasons dance, Love "laughs and on a lion rides," the Spring is merry, the rainbow smiles in showers, and the poet is "Blameless master of the games, King of sport that never shames." Seldom has any such body of verse been so gaily grave, so full at once of dignity and spontaneous joyousness, so eloquent of the spirit which he finds in his forests—

> . . . sober on a fund of joy
> The woods at heart are glad.

It is, no doubt, as the outcome of this rich delight in the healthy aspects of nature, that he so often personifies natural objects and brings them into his poetry as living, warm companions, speaking his familiar language, but, instead of sharing his mood, imposing their own mood, a quite different matter from the "pathetic fallacy." Nature herself frequently appears as a beautiful caressing goddess, shedding smiles and friendliness as she walks the earth among her children. What a free charm is in this careless couplet of that chapter in the *Poems* headed by her name:

> But Nature whistled with all her winds,
> Did as she pleased and went her way!

. . . Emerson's lighter poems not seldom reveal a childlike eagerness to learn the pleasant minor lessons of the outdoor world, and he is not his least poetic self when he is apostrophising the "burly dozing humble bee" or the blackberries of his pasture, "Ethiops sweet," but it is when he is making pictures or thinking in music that he rises to heights of poetic style. Nothing that he wrote combines excellent form with high feeling and beautiful imagery more satisfyingly than the austere and vivid lines on **"Days"** beginning:

> Daughters of Time, the hypocritic Days,
> Muffled and dumb like barefoot dervishes,
> And marching single in an endless file,
> Bring diadems and fagots in their hands.

This stanza of eleven lines is of an exquisite and noble loveliness which has hardly been surpassed in English verse, never in the verse of Emerson's immediate contemporaries and successors. Its mate in pictorial words, delicate reserve, and imaginative power is **"The Rhodora"** in which the simplicity of Emerson's deepest thought similes frankly in our faces from his blossoming New England solitudes. These two poems are types of his truest inspiration, embodying as they do his fervent sense of moral responsibility and his bright freedom from didactic moralising. It was while he strolled musing near the haunts of his fair Rhodora that he attained the curious spiritual passion or ecstasy to which at certain moments Nature inspired him; the upspringing of these central fires of feeling which he thanks the God Pan for keeping in control:

> Haply else we could not live,
> Life would be too wild an ode.

At these moments his pure-minded Bacchus pours "the remembering wine" and fulfils his prayer that he

> Refresh the faded tints,
> Recut the aged prints,
> And write my old adventures with the pen
> Which on the first day drew
> Upon the tablets blue,
> The dancing Pleiads and eternal men.

At these moments he is more the poet of energy, to adopt Matthew Arnold's phraseology, than Wordsworth in his most soaring flight, than Arnold himself at any instant. Mr. Brownell, Arnold's most discerning critic, has said of the latter that he is the poet *par excellence* of feeling that is legitimated by the tribunal of reason, and he finds his poetry "admirably representative of the combined thought and feeling of the era." "But," he adds of his genius, "it is a reflective and philosophic genius, and accordingly its sincerest poetical expression savours a little of statement rather than of song." It is the opposite of this quality in Emerson's most rapturous poems that presses home the conviction of his essentially poetic genius despite flaw and limitation. Reason is not to him a faculty by which imagination is restrained or crippled; it is the ether in which float all consoling and radiant thoughts, flowing into the human mind from the region of perfect bliss. . . .

Arnold found Wordsworth's superiority in the fact that he dealt with more of life than Burns or Keats or Heine, and dealt with life as a whole more powerfully. If this is true of Wordsworth, as indisputably it is, it is true of Emerson who equally with Wordsworth pursued one object, to "attain inward freedom, serenity, happiness, contentment." Those who have found his poetry fragmentary can hardly have felt in it this moral unity. Already he has his expositors, from whom we learn that his **"Brahma"** for example, sums up the burden of the Bhagavad's philosophy, and that his reference to the wheel "on which all beings ride" has its origin in the Rig Veda of the Hindoos, and that "the starred eternal worm" may be identified with the stupendous serpent-god of the Hindoos, and we are told how much of his philosophy he has drawn from the East and how much his poetry is steeped in Eastern feeling, but all this seems very far aside from his real poetic achievement. His real poetic achievement lies outside of his borrowings from Eastern religions although this borrowing was characteristically the outcome of his truly poetic desire to unite the deep thought of the world. His real poetic achievement has its source in his power to penetrate the shows of things and reveal their essence. We cannot ignore his poetry because like that of Wordsworth it deals with reality, with the most real of all realities, the indestructible soul of man. If "how to live" is indeed, as Arnold has said, the important teaching of the greatest poets, and if no more than this is needed, we may class Emerson among them without fear, for if we do not learn from his poetry so far as may be learned from any exterior teaching, how to maintain within ourselves the strength of hope and serene intelligent trust and indomitable moral purpose, we are incapable of feeling the "balm of thoughtful words."

Henry Van Dyke (essay date 1922)

SOURCE: "A Puritan Plus Poetry," in *Companionable Books,* Charles Scribner's Sons, 1922, pp. 335-55.

[*In the following excerpt, Van Dyke emphasizes Emerson's ability to describe the beauty of nature and to spark the reader's imagination.*]

. . . [Emerson's] prose is better known and more admired than his verse, for several reasons: first, because he took more pains to make the form of it as perfect as he could; second, because it has a wider range and an easier utterance; third, because it has more touches of wit and of familiarity with the daily doings of men; and finally, because the majority of readers probably prefer prose for silent reading, since the full charm of good verse is revealed only in reading aloud.

But for all that, with Emerson, (as with a writer so different as Matthew Arnold,) I find something in the poems which is not in the essays,—a more pure and subtle essence of what is deepest in the man. Poetry has a power of compression which is beyond prose. It says less and suggests more.

Emerson wrote to the girl whom he afterwards married: "I am born a poet,—of a low class without doubt, but a poet. . . . My singing, to be sure, is very husky and is for the most part in prose. Still I am a poet in the sense of a perceiver and dear lover of the harmonies that are in the soul and in matter, and specially of the correspondence between them." This is penetrating self-criticism. That he was "of a low class" as poet is more than doubtful,—an error of modesty. But that his singing was often "husky" cannot be denied. He never troubled himself to learn the art of song. The music of verse, in which Longfellow gained such mastery, and Lowell and Whittier had such native gifts, is not often found in Emerson's poetry. His measures rarely flow with freedom and harmony. They are alternately stiff and spasmodic, and the rhymes are sometimes threadbare, sometimes eccentric. Many of his poems are so condensed, so tight-packed with thought and information that they seem to labour along like an overladen boat in a choppy sea. For example, this:

> The journeying atoms,
>   Primordial wholes,
> Firmly draw, firmly drive,
>   By their animate poles.

Or this:

> Puny man and scentless rose
> Tormenting Pan to double the dose.

But for these defects of form Emerson as poet makes ample amends by the richness and accuracy of his observation of nature, by the vigorous flight of his imagination, by the depth and at times the passionate controlled intensity of his feeling. Of love-poetry he has none, except the philosophical. Of narrative poetry he has practically none, unless you count such brief, vivid touches as,—

> By the rude bridge that arched the flood,
>   Their flag to April's breeze unfurled,
> Here once the embattled farmers stood,
>   And fired the shot heard round the world.

But his descriptive pieces are of a rare beauty and charm, truthful in broad outline and delicate detail, every flower and every bird in its right colour and place. Walking with him you see and breathe New England in the light of early morn, with the dew sparkling on the grass and all the cosmic forces working underneath it. His reflective and symbolic poems, like **"Each and All,"** **"The Problem,"** **"Forerunners,"** **"Days,"** **"The Sphinx,"** are full of a searching and daring imaginative power. . . .

His **"Threnody,"** written after the early death of his first-born son, has always seemed to me one of the most moving elegies in the English tongue. His patriotic poems, especially the **"Concord Ode,"** are unsurpassed as brief, lyrical utterances of the spirit of America. In certain moods, when the mind is in vigour and the windows of far vision open at a touch, Emerson's small volume of *Poems* is a most companionable book.

Alfred Noyes   (essay date 1924)

SOURCE: "The Poetry of Emerson," in *Some Aspects of Modern Poetry*, Hodder and Stoughton, N.D. pp. 55-68.

[*Noyes was a prolific, twentieth-century, British poet and the author of books about Tennyson and Voltaire. In the following excerpt, Noyes compares Emerson to Henry Wadsworth Longfellow and Edgar Allan Poe with a focus on the poems, "Humble-Bee," "Give All to Love," and "Bacchus." He also presents Emerson as a creative force in the development of modern poetry linking Emerson to Robert Louis Stevenson and Rudyard Kipling.*]

Twelve years ago, during a first visit to America, I was surprised to find that the man whom I had always believed to be the greatest poet of that country, both in the depth of his thought and in the subtlety of his music, was hardly recognized as a poet at all. He was counted among the first of their prose-writers, very much as Matthew Arnold in England was once held to be primarily a critic. But this American poet at that time was hardly ever mentioned among the poets of his country. They spoke of Edgar Allan Poe, Longfellow, Whitman, Lanier, Bryant, Lowell, and Whittier; but seldom of the man who, as I believed, stood head and shoulders above all these— Emerson. Oliver Wendell Holmes, it is true, with the quick insight of a poet, had long ago said of the **"Threnody"** that it had "the dignity of *Lycidas* without its refrigerating classicism," and that it had also all the tenderness of Cowper's lines on his mother's picture. But the comparisons that he made were not apt, and the general import

of the verdict seemed to have been forgotten. It was the same in England, of course; but there were additional reasons for it here, both in the far greater disproportion of the circulation of Emerson's essays to the almost negligible circulation of his poems, and also in the tone set for criticism by Matthew Arnold, whose essay on Emerson, in many ways, was as mistaken as that on Shelley. Exquisite poet and far-sighted critic as he was, Matthew Arnold did make two or three serious mistakes—one on French poetry, one on Shelley, and one on Emerson.

In his essay on Emerson he seems suddenly to have forgotten some of his own wisest and deepest sayings on the subject of poetry and its world of ideas, and to be asking for a "concreteness," a faith in the fact, that certainly in one example that he gives—"The Bridge" of Longfellow—has failed us. There is, of course, an undiscovered poet in Longfellow, who wrote infinitely better poems than "The Bridge," or indeed any of those verses by which he is usually represented in the anthologies for schools. His "Keramos" is as exquisite as it is unknown. His introductory sonnets to Dante are of a very high order; but "The Bridge," "concrete" as it may be, is neither a good poem nor to be compared for a moment with the best work of Emerson. Moreover, of the right kind of "concreteness" there is more than enough in the poetry of Emerson to refute any suspicion that he too was "an ineffectual angel beating in the void his luminous wings in vain." A poem like **"The Humble-Bee"** is in itself a full answer to that, and also to the suggestion that he is lacking in warmth and colour.

If it be compared with "L'Allegro," as its measure suggests, it will be seen to be richer in colour, more sensuous, and even in music to be a worthy rival of its great forerunner. It is a poem in which you can see and touch and smell the summer meadows, and there is a deliciously fantastic moralizing vein in it which should surely be enough to answer Arnold's demand, even in this subject, for "a criticism of life."

> Thou, in sunny solitudes,
> Rover of the underwoods,
> *The green silence dost displace*
> *With thy mellow breezy bass.* . . .
>
> *Hot midsummer's petted crone,*
> Sweet to me thy drowsy tone,
> Tells of countless sunny hours,
> Long days and solid banks of flowers;
> Gulfs of sweetness without bound
> In Indian wildernesses found;
> Syrian peace, immortal leisure,
> Firmest cheer, and bird-like pleasure. . . .
>
> Wiser far than human seer,
> Yellow-breeched philosopher. . . .

Some of the phrases in those lines have the real magic. "Crone," in the fifth line quoted, is an extraordinary example of the apt use of a word that at first sight would seem to be quite remote from the subject; an extraordinary example of the secondary meanings and associations that can be awakened in such a word by its use at exactly the right moment. In some mysterious way it suggests,by its likeness to another word, the crooning sound of the bee. It suggests, partly by its own meaning perhaps, and partly by the associations of the two opening consonants, the crooked legs and somewhat decrepit appearance of a tipsy bee blundering into a flower. But nothing is forced upon the reader. It merely suggests vividly, by being the right word in the right context.

[James Russell] Lowell said that Emerson had no "ear," and he tells in his letters that Emerson confessed to him that he did not understand "accent" in verse. There is one line in his **"Humble-Bee"** where the accent is misplaced, but it was not misplaced through the lack of an ear for the subtler harmonies of verse. It was misplaced because Emerson pronounced it so. His confession to Lowell has its ironical side, for no comparison is possible between the extreme delicacy of the music that appealed to the ear of Emerson and the carefully measured verses that Lowell wrote. There is a music in the freely moving lines of Emerson's **"Give all to Love"** for which his own generation was not prepared. In fact, many of his readers missed it altogether, and really imagined—some of them imagine still—that those apparently irregular lines were left in that poem because Emerson could not improve them into the slack and regular stanzas of "The Bridge." Yet, if ears had been attuned to hear them, what could be more firm, more precise, more finely balanced, in the right way of the Muses than this:

> Though thou loved her as thyself,
> As a self of purer clay,
> Though her parting dims the day,
> Stealing grace from all alive;
> Heartily know,
> When half-gods go,
> The gods arrive.

> ["Give all to Love"]

We know at once, by the way in which the words, when rightly heard, strike into the mind and endure in the memory, that here the poet is among the immortals and saying immortal things to us. . . .

In Emerson's **"Bacchus"** there is a subtler music yet. It is a marvellous poem, composed surely when the poet had fed on that honey-dew and drunk that milk of Paradise of which Coleridge wrote in "Kubla Khan." This is not the conventional view; but, before the conventional unconventionalist dismisses it, he may be asked to read Emerson's **"Bacchus"** again with care. It is a poem for philosophers; it is one of the very finest of such poems, brimming over with intellectual ecstasy. . . .

There is an intellectual ecstasy in this poem which is hardly to be paralleled elsewhere. The beauty of the best work of Poe is undeniable; but it is the beauty of a cloud catching from a distance the light of a supernal region in which this less familiar poet seems to be carousing with the gods themselves, on the other side of the processes of nature. It is surely necessary, moreover, that one of the accepted verdicts of the past should be revised with regard to the comparative merits of Emerson and Edgar Allan Poe. Emerson may have "confessed" to Lowell that he had "no ear"; but he also confessed to the world that he thought Poe a "jingle-man"; and with the music of his **"Bacchus"** in our own ears, a new and free and subtle music that could hardly be appreciated rightly in his own generation, his thought seems almost to be justifiable. There are occasions when it is right to be a "jingle-man." It was right in "The Bells." Poe had his own great merits; but it is only a very insensitive ear that could think the ethereal cadences of Emerson's **"Bacchus"** inferior to the tawdry rhyming and meretricious mysticism of "Ulalume" [by Poe]. . . .

Emerson was the first writer in American literature to begin that great work of the future—the finding and maintaining of that central position which has been temporarily lost in an age of specialists, that central position from which we shall again see "all things in one," as Thomas à Kempis could see them.

In his essay on *The Poet* he gives one of the most beautiful and profound expositions of the art of poetry that have ever been written. In the fragments of verse that preface it he opens two windows in his central turret, from one of which he sees the rhythmic aspect of the universe, and its relation to the poet's craft, while from the other he surveys once more those divine ideas which are the substance of all poetry.

> Overleapt the horizon's edge,
> Searched with Apollo's privilege;
> Through man and woman and sea and star,
> Saw the dance of nature forward far;
> Through worlds and races and terms and times,
> Saw musical order and pairing rhymes.

He shows, too, how the most "concrete" forms of modern life and activity may find their way into art. He was among the first to suggest the method, the only true method, by which the steamship and the railroad may be touched with the light of poetry. He shows how they can be related to central and permanent ideas; revealing, for instance, the poetry of the great Atlantic liner arriving at her destination with the "punctuality of a planet." With that last phrase alone he founded something like a school—and its influence is to be traced in the work of Stevenson, and even in the *Rhythm of Life* of Alice Meynell.

In fact, the influence of Emerson upon some of the most distinctively modern writers of our day is as remarkable as it is unrecognized. He has undoubtedly, for instance, influenced Kipling—not only in such obvious instances as the poem on the American Spirit (which is of course based on Emerson's **"Brahma"**), but also in what may be called the jungle-poetry. If the four following lines are quoted to the average reader of both authors, he would be uncertain for a moment which of the two had written them:

> Cast the bantling on the rocks,
> Suckle him with the she-wolf's teat.

> Wintered with the hawk and fox,
>   Power and speed be hands and feet.

It is pure Mowgli; but the lines were written by Emerson. Another interesting trace of Emerson's influence on the same writer may be observed by any one who compares the opening lines of **"The World-Soul"** with the later "Native-born."

But Emerson's great value to our own day and to the future is that from his central position he maintained that hope which—oddly enough—even the most negative of his critics, Matthew Arnold, declared to be essential to the greatest art. Arnold declared that Emerson was not among the great writers; yet he quoted as an example of his deepest insight these words: "We judge of a man's wisdom by his hope, knowing that the perception of the inexhaustibleness of Nature is an immortal youth."

Such hope as this has nothing in common with the easy optimism that averts its face from reality. It is at the opposite pole from that superficial kind, though the superficial pessimist will always confuse them. It means simply that neither life nor death may be permitted to utter the last word of denial in this infinite universe. Matthew Arnold contradicted himself curiously on this matter, for he does at last say of Emerson, "Never had man such a sense of the inexhaustibleness of Nature and such hope." If this be true, and if we judge of a man's wisdom by his hope (as Arnold agreed), it is difficult to see how he could avoid the logical conclusion that Emerson must at least have been among the wisest of men.

His abiding word for us, the word by which he still speaks to us, a word that seems to be the inspiration, both in style and thought, of all that was best in the prose of Stevenson, and of at least one of the finest poems of Browning, is this:

"That which befits us, embosomed in beauty and wonder as we are, is cheerfulness and courage, and the endeavour to realize our aspirations. *Shall not the heart, which has received so much, trust the Power by which it lives?*"

Matthew Arnold's personal withdrawal from this unconquerable hope, in his essay on Emerson, seems to be a contradiction of what he says elsewhere, and of what he expresses (though faintly) in the finest of his own poems:

> Whence was it? For it was not mine!

He withdrew from it, hesitatingly, in those moments when he was waiting for the spark from heaven; but when the spark had fallen and kindled the spirit within him his vision was at one with that of Emerson:

> So near is grandeur to our dust,
>   So nigh is God to man.

The hope of Emerson was founded on the only element of which, in the last analysis, we know anything at all, that personality, that soul (it matters very little what we call

it), that individuality through which alone we can approach the universal soul: for it is not true to say that we, who are part of reality, can only know fleeting appearances of the world. We have our own private wicket-gate in ourselves, through which we can pass at will into the eternal world.

We cannot transcend our limited spheres of action in the flesh. We are like travellers on a ship who have freedom to walk east, west, north, or south on its deck, while the ship pursues her own course, bearing us to an end of which we know nothing, except that the ship is being steered by great laws. Occasionally we overhear the orders that are being made around us, even if we do not understand them. We hear commands given in the night. And this we do know—that if the meaning goes out of everything, if the good, the true, the beautiful become a mockery by our abandonment of our belief in their eternal significance, or by the assumption that the voyage has no aim and the ship no steersman, then it is the duty of our own souls, and the part of our human reason, to make the opposite assumption (act of faith though it may be) and to say to our fellow-travellers: Hope. For a meaning is the one thing needful, the one thing that even our limited reason cannot forgo. We cannot accept—the reason revolts from accepting—the suggestion that the universe is a gigantic game of bubbles blown by an imbecile and unweeting Power. It is the failure of our own vision of the universe that makes such a suggestion possible—though again and again in modern literature, a literature moving along narrow lines of specialized thought, this suggestion is logically implied. Even in the depths of our agnosticism, and God knows they are deep enough, there are certain things that we ourselves do know. We know a little of human love. We know that it is a better thing than the dust, and that, by every law of thought, the greater can never be originated from the less or subjected to it.

The value of Emerson to the present day is that he was able to keep open the gates of that knowledge within the soul. In the **"Threnody,"** perhaps the most beautiful and profound poem in American literature, a poem whose music is wrought to the heights of prophetic inspiration, he utters his own hope over the grave of his own child. It is a poem that lends the wings of a Shelley to the weight and thought of a Browning; and if he had written nothing else, it would eventually confirm his right to a place among the master-singers. It is cosmic in its range, and it contains all philosophies. It is human in its grief, and divine in its hope.

Robert M. Gay (essay date 1928)

SOURCE: "Poetry, England, and the War," in *Emerson: A Study of the Poet as Seer,* Doubleday, Doran and Company, 1928, pp. 192-228.

[*Gay edited a collection of verse for college students. In the following excerpt, he criticizes Emerson's poetry for its lack of "smoothness" and links this poetic flaw to what he perceives as Emerson's theory of poetry with its emphasis on the poem as a philosophical statement rather than an aesthetically stylized work of art.*]

In September, 1844, Emerson purchased, on the shore of Walden Pond, a plot of eleven acres, to which, on the advice of friends, he added three or four more of pine woods adjoining. No purchase of his life gave him more pleasure than this. He nicknamed the plot his Garden, visited it almost daily, and composed many of his poems there. In the preceding year he first procured a copy of Saadi's *Gulistan* and was pleased to find that it agreed with the conception of the poem **"Saadi"** written the year before. The attraction of the Persian poets grew with the years, and his references to them or quotations from them in his later books are numerous. His general reading became more and more abstract: the Chinese classics, the *Vishnu Sarna,* Plotinus, Iamblichus, Proclus, Calvin, Behmen, Spinoza, Berkeley, are most often quoted during the years 1843-45, and the references to poetry are much less numerous than formerly. Science still interests him, and a growing interest in history and public affairs is evident. In 1846 he collected his poems.

It is a commonplace of criticism that his poetry lacks art. His chief failing in composition in general, prose and verse, was a lack of sustention, of coherence, of architecture. His verse, like much of his prose, is spasmodic, and it contains, moreover, elementary faults of technique that Macaulay's boy of fourteen could have patched and mended—forced rhymes, arbitrary inversions, lapses of taste; at its worst a certain fuzziness of thought. It is, to use a candy-maker's term, cooked only to the granulated stage, and seldom reaches the smoothness of either the "soft ball" or the "hard ball." It is gritty.

When we seek the cause for these generally recognized defects, we are forced to conclude that they were the result partly of a habit of mind and partly of a theory of poetry. We have seen that his boyhood verse was all too facile, but as he grew older he came less and less to value smoothness and correctness in himself, though he did not cease to admire them in others. He criticized Channing's verses because of their carelessness and of the presence in them of inept lines, and yet we early find Thoreau pleading with him to be more careful of his own, marred as they were by the same faults. In his Journal he records his conviction that logic, coherence, and architectonics in a long poem are evidences of the master and, though a little grudgingly, he praises the beauty and music of Tennyson's earlier poetry. In the same passage, relating to Tennyson, however, we find the clue to his theory, for he condemns much of the English poet's work on the ground that in it the manner is superior to the matter.

There can be no doubt that a theory—many will think an unlucky theory—of poetry reinforced his tendency to think in isolated phrases, and it is possible that his habit of jotting down ideas as they occurred, without carrying on their suggestions or development at the time, was responsible in its turn for the tendency. Of course, thinking in

granules, so to speak, has its strength as well as its weakness. It makes the granules memorable and penetrating, even though it sacrifices the virtues of continuity. It is easy, also, to exaggerate the discontinuity of his verse, for often it is more apparent than real. It is a discontinuity of phrasing, rather than of thought.

It is still true, nevertheless, that his theory of poetry tended to encourage and condone his technical faults. He held the same view of art as Ruskin, that the subject of a work is of the first importance and its expression always a secondary consideration. He was not, however, so careful as Ruskin to explain what he meant by subject, with the result that one cannot be sure. Nowadays we are told that not the subject, but the poet, makes a poem. I think Emerson, when he speaks of "subject," means matter or ideas, rather than the topic or pretext. At any rate, he had little tolerance for what is sometimes called pure poetry. The poet as maker moved him much less than the poet as seer.

With his insistence upon the intellectual content of poetry, it is small wonder if his own verse lacks both passion and music. Its affinities are more with the "metaphysical school" of the Seventeenth Century than with the romantic schools of the Nineteenth. One constantly comes upon snatches that might well have been written by Jonson, Donne, Herbert, or Marvell, and we know that these were favourites of his, as is shown by his quotation from them in the Journal and by his inclusion of their poems in his anthology, *Parnassus.* He was also greatly drawn to the cryptic verse of the old Celtic bards, and, from the date of **"Woodnotes"** onward, liked to write in a "sort of runic rhyme," which reads more like the *Elder Edda* than like any poetry of a less barbaric age. Occasionally he strings couplets together after the manner of Blake in "Auguries of Innocence," and again loads and cramps his verse with all the tortuous obscurity of Meredith in "The Woods of Westermain."

Perhaps the worst that can be said of his poetry is that it begins with an idea instead of an emotion. But to deny that it is poetry at all, as some have done, would be possible only by limiting our definition of poetry so as to exclude a great deal of verse besides his. He is no more abstract than Shelley and no more intellectual than Donne. Critics have brought against him Milton's remark that "poetry is simple, sensuous, and passionate," forgetting that a good deal of Milton's own poetry will hardly bear the test. When all is said, it remains true, I think, that his faults are very largely faults of art or technique. He has hardly a poem that is perfect. But he also has hardly a poem that is uninteresting.

Perhaps the very impulse that militates against his success as a singer is the chief source of his success as a seer. He seems incessantly to have aimed at originality. The great lyric poems have usually been the perfect embodiment of ultimate truisms, rather than statements of a new revelation. There is little else in the most-quoted passages of Shakespeare. It is not really the man who says a thing first, but he who says it best who wins the bays. And yet there is a kind of poet, of whom Blake,

Herbert, and Meredith may be considered widely differing examples, who are stimulating to thought, rather than
to emotion, and whose work is always fresh and fascinating because of the originality or, possibly, the oddity, of
the mind that conceived it. Emerson's verse is largely of
this kind, and is therefore for most readers a cultivated
taste. . . .

Along with the oracular, he possessed so true a lyric note
that one deeply regrets that he did not more often achieve
it. In **"Give All to Love," "Earth Song,"** the Ellen poems,
passages of **"Woodnotes,"** and **"May-Day,"** and here and
there in **"My Garden," "Waldeinsamkeit,"** the **"Concord Ode," "Two Rivers,"** his verse reaches the kindling
point; and in the stately reflective lyric, like **"The Snow-
Storm," "Days," "The Day's Ration," "Musketaquid,"**
he attains a classic calm and quiet.

Certain of his longer poems have considerable autobiographical interest. **"Uriel"** was inspired by the Divinity
School incident; the **"Ode to Channing,"** by the abolition movement; **"Voluntaries,"** in part by the death of
Robert Gould Shaw; **"My Garden,"** by the tract of ground
on Walden Pond. Eminently characteristic, also, and among
his best are such riddle poems as **"Uriel," "The Sphinx,"
"Brahma,"** and **"The Song of Nature."** A group, of which
"Merlin" and **"Saadi"** and the fragments of **"The Poet"**
are representative, have value as expressing his conceptions of poetry. And in almost all of his poems, but especially in the longest, **"May-Day,"** are fresh and lively
images drawn from a landscape indubitably New England. Perhaps his most earthy will always have the
widest appeal.

He can hardly by any definition be called a great poet,
but he will always have his lovers. His future reputation
is likely to be that of his admired Seventeenth Century
men—to be read by a discriminating few, who like what
Rossetti called "fundamental gray-matter" in their poetry.
His influence upon American poetry, though not clearly
traceable, has probably been strong in persuading poets to
turn from English larks and daisies to American chicka-
dees and sumach. Emily Dickinson would have gladly
called him Master. Robert Frost is Emersonian in philosophy and diction, but shows little of his influence in his
subjects or his verse.

Jean Gorely   (essay date 1931)

SOURCE: "Emerson's Theory of Poetry," in *Poetry,* Vol.
XXII, July-August, 1931, pp. 263-73.

[*In the following excerpt, Gorely explores Emerson's
method of poetic composition by referring to his journals
and his essay, "The Poet." She discusses the value that
Emerson places on inspiration and truth as forces that
guide the poet in rhythmical expression.*]

In the first essay of the series of 1844, [*The Poet*] Emerson considers the nature and function of the true poet. He
begins his discussion with these words: "The breadth of
the problem is great, for the poet is representative. He
stands among partial men for the complete man, and
apprises us not of his wealth, but of the common wealth."
The significance of this thought can only be understood
after a study of Emerson's theory of man. That is fundamental. Therefore, very briefly, the main lines of the
doctrine must be indicated, especially man's relation to
the rest of the world, his nature, and his problem.

Emerson believes in the oneness of the world. God, or the
Oversoul, is the life or essence in all things "swallowing
up all relations, parts, and times within itself." This life is
transcendent. It is the source of thought, the starting point
of action. Emerson writes that "the sovereignty of this
nature whereof we speak, is made known by its inde-
pendency of those limitations which circumscribe us on
every hand." Moreover, it is immanent, pervasive. "God
is, and all things are but shadows of him." The closing
lines of **"Woodnotes"** say:

> Thou metest him by centuries,
> And lo! he passes like the breeze;
> Thou seek'st in globe and galaxy,
> He hides in pure transparency;
> Thou askest in fountains and in fires,
> He is the essence that inquires.
> He is the axis of the star;
> He is the sparkle of the spar;
> He is the heart of every creature;
> He is the meaning of each feature;
> And his mind is the sky,
> Than all it holds more deep, more high.

Thus man, with nature, is a part of this great whole. Both
are revelations or manifestations of the Oversoul with the
distinction that nature is its expression in the unconscious
and man in the conscious.

There is a certain infinitude in man. Over and above his
own life or spirit he has this greater life, within which he
is contained, to draw upon.

> It is a secret which every intellectual man quickly learns,
> that beyond the energy of his possessed and conscious
> intellect he is capable of a new energy, . . . by
> abandonment to the nature of things; that beside his
> privacy of power as an individual man, there is a great
> public power on which he can draw, by unlocking, at all
> risks, his human doors, and suffering the ethereal tides to
> roll and circulate through him; then he is caught up into
> the life of the Universe, his speech is thunder, his thought
> is law, and his words are universally intelligible.

Man is also unique. Each is different from every other.
Each is given a particular work to do in the world and
each must carry it out alone. Upon its realization, the
success of the world depends.

Man has a means of communication with the Oversoul.
He is aware of his relation by intuition or inspiration.
What this experience is is not explained. All we know is
that "this sense of being which in calm hours rises, we

know not how, in the soul, is not diverse from space, from light, from time, from man, but one with them, and proceedeth obviously from the same source whence their life and being also proceedeth." It is miraculous only in so far as all life is miraculous. It is a positive universal fact. All tools, inventions, books, and laws came out of the invisible world through the brains of men. When this state, Emerson says, is attributed to one or two persons and denied to all the rest, the doctrine of inspiration is lost.

"God is the all-fair." "Truth, goodness and beauty are but different faces of the same all." Man, then, by virtue of intuition has access to truth, goodness, and beauty. But it is not sufficient to know these. Man must give them expression. This is the problem of man, namely, to listen, to hear and to report. Truth comes

> to the end that it may be uttered and acted. The more profound the thought, the more burdensome. Always in proportion to the depth of its sense does it knock importunely at the gates of the soul, to be spoken, to be done.

These powers, however, are seldom found in perfect equipoise. Rarely is the expression adequate to the thought. "I know not how it is," Emerson says, "that we need an interpreter, but the great majority of men seem to be minors, who have not yet come into possession of their own, or mutes, who cannot report the conversation they have had with nature."

It is the poet who solves the problem. For this reason, he is the representative man. Because of deep insight and a corresponding power of expression "he stands among partial men for the complete man." He is nearest to the centre of the Universe and sees all things in their relation to the Infinite and to each other. "The factory-village and railway fall within the great Order not less than the bee-hive, or the spider's geometrical web." He

> perceives that thought is multiform; that within the form of every creature is a force impelling it to ascend into a higher form; and, following with his eyes the life, uses the forms which express that life, and so his speech flows with the flowing of nature.

The life may be likened to a light with its rays shining in all men. Ordinarily, it is not tended and burns but dimly. Then men must resort to reason. But the poet frees it from all obstruction. It has a brighter flame and things appear in their true relations. His report or expression is poetry. According to Emerson, it is oracular, the report of one who retires into himself to listen, one who is passive, who trusts to instinct and demands no authority but instinct.

> For poetry was all written before time was, and whenever we are so finely organized that we can penetrate into that region where the air is music, we hear those primal warblings and attempt to write them down, but we lose ever and anon a word or a verse and substitute something of our own, and thus miswrite the poem. The men of more delicate ear write down

these cadences more faithfully, and these transcripts, though imperfect, become the songs of the nations.

Fundamentally, Emerson's theory of poetry can be divided into two parts. The first of these is concerned with genesis; the second, with the finished work. In the order of genesis, thought precedes form. Therefore, we shall consider first, the getting of the idea, and, second, the execution or elaboration.

The æsthetic critic, like Pater, analyzes a poem, finding and noting the virtue or virtues by which it produces its effect. But, given all these virtues, he could not create or recreate the poem any more than the scientist can put together the parts of a flower and have a flower. The power comes from without oneself.

It was Emerson's belief that thought comes from the "inner mind," the "mind of the mind," and brings with it the power of expression. At the time of its reception the poet is inspired. In this, as we have seen, he is not different from ordinary men. It is a universal experience and has certain more or less definite characteristics. Inspiration is inconsecutive. There is a flash, a "point of view," a "glimpse," a "mood" and no more. Nor can it be controlled in any way. It comes spontaneously. "When we discern truth, we do nothing of ourselves, but allow a passage to its beams." The poet can neither incite nor prolong it, but he can clear away obstruction.

Moreover, it is unconscious. The worker is often as much surprised at his work as we. Emerson, for example, could never recall having written the poem **"Days."** He says in the *Journal* of 1852:

> I find one state of mind does not remember or conceive of another state. Thus I have written within a twelvemonth verses (**"Days"**) which I do not remember the composition or correction of, and could not write the like to-day, and have only, for proof of their being mine, various external evidences, as the MS. in which I find them, and the circumstance that I have sent copies of them to friends, etc., etc.

But the unconsciousness is merely in relation to us.

> We speak, we act, from we know not what higher principle, and we describe its circumambient quality by confessing the subjection of our perception to it, we cannot overtop it, . . . nor see at all its channel into us. But in saying this we predicate nothing of its consciousness or unconsciousness in relation to itself. We see at once we have no language subtle enough for distinctions in that inaccessible region.

Finally, inspiration is advancing in its nature. The inspired man sees something new, something that nobody else has seen. He does not revert to the past or look to the future, but "lives now and absorbs past and future into the present hour." "Inspiration will have advance," Emerson writes, "affirmation, the forward foot, the ascending state; it will be an opener of doors; it will invent its own methods."

Enthusiasm usually accompanies the state in varying degrees. It may exhibit itself in frenzy or ecstasy, but more often in a warm glow, a thrill of awe and delight.

Although inspiration cannot be brought about at will, there are certain favouring conditions. We all have heard of the ways in which great composers and artists have worked. How Haydn had to be very carefully dressed. How Mozart did best while riding in a comfortable carriage, or lying awake in the silence of the night. In Emerson's *Journal* of 1852 there are these lines:

> Poppy leaves are strewn when a generalization is made,
> for I can never remember the circumstances to which
> I owe it, so as to repeat the experiment, or put myself
> in the conditions.

Emerson does, however, give a list of conditions drawn partly from literary biography and partly from his own experience.

Health, first of all, is indispensable for good work and it can only be maintained by sleep and exercise and a simple life. Wine, narcotics, opium, and sandlewood fumes are not for the poet. They are procurers of animal exhilaration. "The poet's habit of living should be set on a key so low that the common influences should delight him. His cheerfulness should be the gift of the sunlight; the air should suffice for his inspiration." Besides daily rest, rest after years of service renews the faculties.

Human intercourse with its letter-writing, its travel, its conversation, and its reading is of value. Emerson found letter-writing a good companion, or a book very helpful.

A third condition, in contrast to the last named, is retirement into self or "solitude of habit." The poet should go to some place remote from the sounds and work of the house, where he can sit alone and think. Emerson put up at a country inn in summer, or a city hotel in winter when he had a difficult piece of work to do. There, no cares of the farm could disturb him. This need of solitude is organic.

> To the culture of the world an Archimedes, a Newton,
> is indispensable. If these had been good fellows fond
> of dancing, port and clubs, we should have had no
> 'Theory of the Spheres' and no 'Principia.' They had
> that necessity of isolation which genius feels.

Allied to this solitude of habit, is solitary converse with nature. As nature is the "projection of God in the unconscious," it is a revelation to the poet of the life of which he is a part. In it there is perfect order, for all things are regulated by the laws of the Infinite. Thus, if the poet comes close to nature, he can see truth everywhere. This thought is crystallized in **"The Poet"**:

> The gods talk in the breath of the woods,
>   They talk in the shaken pine,
> And fill the long reach of the old seashore
>   With dialogue divine;
> And the poet who overhears
>   Some random word they say

> Is the fated man of men
>   Whom the ages must obey.

The idea of the work, then, comes in inspiration. The poet submits himself to the Universal Mind and is shown things in their right relations. The cares and fears of the day, income tax returns and wireless, sunshine and shadow, have each their place in the order of the world. To us they appear as parts out of place, detached from the whole.

The carrying out of the final work does not receive a very full treatment in Emerson. The poet does not so much create as report. The words he seems to speak are but spoken through him. So the idea takes its own form. The words come naturally and the intensity of the thought makes the language rhythmical. This is the difference between true poetry and the work of a versifier. In the one, sense dictates the rhythm; in the other, sense is adapted to the rhythm. As we have seen, there was no memory of the execution of the poem called **"Days."** In most cases, however, Emerson revised his work. Here is the record of the effect of the sea as it is found in the *Journal* of 1856:

> 'Tis a noble, friendly power, and seemed to say to me,
> why so late and slow to come to me? Am I not here
> always, thy proper summer home? Is not my voice thy
> needful music; my breath thy healthful climate in the
> heats; my touch thy cure?

> Was ever building like my terraces? Was ever couch so
> magnificent as mine? Lie down on my warm ledges and
> learn that a very little hut is all you need. I have made
> this architecture superfluous, and it is paltry beside mine.
> Here are twenty Romes and Ninevehs and Karnacs in
> ruins together, obelisk and pyramid and Giant's
> Causeway; here they all are prostrate or half-piled.

> And behold the sea, the opaline, the plentiful and
> strong, yet beautiful as the rose or the rainbow, full of
> food, nourisher of men, purger of the world, creating
> a sweet climate and in its unchangeable ebb and flow,
> and in its beauty at a few furlongs, giving a hint of
> that which changes not and is perfect.

It reads like blank verse. With very few changes it forms the first twenty-seven lines of the **"Seashore."** How closely they compare:

> I heard or seemed to hear the chiding sea
> Say, Pilgrim, why so late and slow to come?
> Am I not always here, thy summer home?
> Is not my voice thy music, morn and eve?
> My breath thy healthful climate in the heats,
> My touch thy antidote, my bay thy bath?

The history of **"Two Rivers"** was very similar. I give it as he wrote it sitting by the river one April day in 1856 and as it appeared when published:

> Thy voice is sweet Musketaquid, and repeats the music
> of the rain, but sweeter is the silent stream which flows
> even through thee, as thou through the land.

Thou art pent in thy banks, but the stream I love flows in thy water, and flows through rocks and through the air and through rays of light as well, and through darkness, and through men and women.

I hear and see the inundation and the eternal spending of the stream in winter and in summer, and in men and animals, in passions and thought. Happy are they who hear it.

Here are the first three stanzas of the poem:

Thy summer voice, Musketaquit,
  Repeats the music of the rain;
But sweeter rivers pulsing flit
  Through thee, as thou through Concord plain.

Thou in thy narrow banks are pent:
  The stream I love unbounded goes
Through flood and sea and firmament,
  Through light, through life, it forward flows.

I see the inundation sweet,
  I hear the spending of the stream
Through years, through man, through nature fleet,
  Through love and thought, through power and
    dream.

These examples suffice to show how the thought finds its proper wording, rhythm, and melody. There was careful revision. An adjective or a superlative was omitted. Words were changed. Yet there is no loss in the spontaneity. These first expressions, like the blocked-out sketches of an artist, are in complete analogy with the finished work.

And the finished work is organically beautiful. The materials that went into its making—the thought, the melody, the phrasing, the imagery—were all only means to an end. This end in Emerson's doctrine is called Beauty. Although there is no definition of beauty, its conception is deep. It involves not only qualities of sound and colour and excellence of structure, but something deeper. Only through knowledge of the true, can one attain the beautiful.

Wherever snow falls, or water flows, or birds fly, wherever day and night meet in twilight, wherever the blue heaven is hung by clouds, or sown with stars, wherever are forms with transparent boundaries, wherever are outlets into celestial space, wherever is danger and awe and love, there is Beauty, plenteous as rain, shed for thee, and though thou should'st walk the world over, thou shalt not be able to find a condition inopportune or ignoble.

Poetry shows nature and humanity not fancifully, not fictitiously, but more truly as they are by reason of the poet's central position. Truth to the true requires that it have its proper melody and phrasing though often the odds are immense against finding it. Then, each word, and image, and rhyme answer their ends exactly, just as in Amiens Cathedral the covering of enclosed spaces, the forms of the supports, the arches, the tracery and decorative detail have each a constructive reason. Intangible, evanescent,

beauty is something to which the whole of man's nature responds. It brings about harmony between all his powers. Reason acting upon the work finds it true in the proportions and the relations of its parts. The melodious language, the imagery appeal to the senses and the feelings, while the spirit finds radiating from it something "immeasurable and divine."

"Threnody," "Musketaquid," "The Seashore"—any of these might illustrate this. **"Days"** is short and more suited to quotation:

Daughters of Time, the hypocritic Days,
Muffled and dumb like barefoot dervishes,
And marching single in an endless file,
Bring diadems and fagots in their hands.
To each they offer gifts after his will,
Bread, kingdom, stars, and sky that holds them all.
I in my pleached garden, watched the pomp,
Forgot my morning wishes, hastily
Took a few herbs and apples, and the Day
Turned and departed silent. I, too late,
Under her solemn fillet saw the scorn.

Finally, the measure of greatness in poetry is the "cosmical quality, or power to suggest relation to the whole world."

One unfamiliar with Emerson, who reads his work only cursorily says that he lacks method; that his idea of poetry is too vague, too much of a theory. Emerson, himself, acknowledged that he lacked method. "I need hardly say to anyone acquainted with my thoughts that I have no system," and again, "my method is purely expectant. . . . I confine my ambition to true reporting, though I only get one new fact in a year." The theory, however, is a noble one, one that could only be conceived by a man of great intuitive and speculative power. It deals with poetry at its highest. Theorists in this field generally belong to one of two schools. Either they believe that poetry should have no contact with ethics or science but be the expression of emotion in beautiful phrase, image, and melody; or that it should be concerned with truth and human values in life alone. Emerson's theory includes both of these views. Poetry is not poetry if it cloys with the lusciousness of its melody and imagery. Poetry is based on truth and truth requires a consideration of the meanings of things. Moreover, the true isbeautiful and its expression will be beautiful in its symbols, its rhythm, and its form. The stress on inspiration and the intimate relation with the life of the spirit makes the theory something almost religious.

Besides stimulating to thought about poetry and the life of the spirit, Emerson's theory gives a standard for criticism or comparison. It is an aid in distinguishing the good from the bad in what we read. Our personal standards are changeable. Now one type of poetry seems to satisfy them, now another. If we measure by such a standard as this of Emerson's, however, we can have results which are more lasting than our own hastily formed impressions. How this works out in English poetry can be shown almost diagramatically by a series of circles concentric with the ideal of the theory. Very near the centre would be Shakespeare. On the next circle, might come Chaucer and Spenser; farther out, Marlowe, Ben Jonson, Keats, Byron, and Wordsworth. With these the expression is usually outweighed by some deficiency in the thought. Wordsworth is peculiarly a poet of nature. There is too much of the personal element in Byron. "What has Lord Byron at the bottom of his poetry," says Emerson in his *Journal* of 1839, "but 'I am Byron, the noble poet, who am very clever, but not popular in London?'" Next to these would be writers who, in rare moments of greatness, are able to seize the inner meaning of a scene or a life and body it forth. Then would come most of us. "Deep in the heart of man a poet sings." We are capable of poetic thought, but we lack the power of expression. Last of all, on the outer circles, would be the versifiers who care only for form and effect.

Emerson, then, believed that poetry is mystical; that it comes into being as the result of inspiration. In that moment the poet sees the very essence of things. But vision is beyond his will. It comes to him unawares. Moreover, it is sudden and inconsecutive. It is advancing. Health, rest, human intercourse, solitude of habit, and a life in the open are all favouring circumstances. The poet makes the unseen visible by means of language. But he is not here the conscious creator. Vision, also, shows him the symbols and the thought takes its own form in language that is rhythmical. Because of this, there is a certain indwelling beauty in poetry and we measure its greatness by its cosmical quality. In such a theory, *poetry is spiritual and forms a link between the visible and invisible worlds.*

Seymour L. Gross (essay date 1955)

SOURCE: "Emerson and Poetry," in *South Atlantic Quarterly,* Vol. LIV, No. 1, January, 1955, pp. 82-94.

[*Gross is an American-Literature scholar whose area of specialization is Nathaniel Hawthorne with an additional focus on African-American Literature and Emerson criticism. In the following excerpt, Gross examines contradictory aspects of Emerson's theories of poetry and rates Emerson's poetry unfavorably. The critic points out specific flaws in the poems "Each and All" and "The Rhodora" but presents "Days" as Emerson's finest poem.*]

In view of the multitude of learned articles and books on the subject of Emerson's theory and practice of poetry, there is perhaps some need of justifying another treatment of the subject. For the most part scholars and critics have been content to describe Emerson's theory by ample quotation from his writings and have then gone on to cite various poems by way of illustration. On the whole, far too little attention has been paid to the theory's aesthetic validity: that is, whether such a theory as Emerson subscribed to, or at least theoretically advocated, is capable of producing successful poetry, or even poetry at all.

Two extremely opposite positions on Emerson's theory can be seen in the treatments of it by F. O. Matthiessen

and Miss Jean Gorely. After carefully but uncritically delineating Emerson's theory, Miss Gorely concludes her article ["Emerson's Theory of Poetry," *Poetry Review,* July-August, 1931] with this assertion: "In such a theory, *poetry is spiritual and forms a link between the visible and invisible worlds.*" The italics, which are Miss Gorely's, and the romantic cast of the statement, indicate an implicit belief in the validity of Emerson's theory. Matthiessen, on the other hand, in his discussion of Emerson's theory of art, says in part, "We can hardly assess Emerson's work in the light of his theory of language and art, since there is such disproportion between his theory and any practise of it." Somewhat later he goes on to say, "Indeed, the wonder of such views is that any art at all resulted from them" [F. O. Matthiessen, "In the Optative Mood: The Flowing," *American Renaissance: Art and Expression in the Age of Emerson and Whitman,* 1941].

But neither of the above views seems to be wholly correct. First of all, Emerson's theory, which has been termed "organic," if taken without important qualifications, is aesthetically impossible; and, secondly, Emerson in his poetry does seem to be conscious of his theoretic dicta, which, paradoxically enough, cause his poetry to be "inorganic." Emerson's theory of art, like almost everything he wrote, was conditioned by a passionate desire to affirm order in the universe. Once he was metaphysically certain of the basic unity of all experience, each aspect of it with which he dealt had in order to be "true" to be related to the basic nature of the world as he understood it. But unfortunately this compulsion was all too often sheer emotionalism: his feelings rather than his rational faculties determined his statements. But since "feelings" are almost by definition vacillating, it follows that the statements which stem from these feelings can have no more stability than that which motivates them: hence the multitude of contradictions that one finds in Emerson's works. Furthermore, there is the ambivalence of the man himself. He constantly struggled to lift himself from the thrilling apperception of the thing itself (which he did not trust) to a mystical awareness of its spirit. The English metaphysical poets managed to achieve this movement repeatedly, but Emerson could not. Herbert and Donne, unlike Emerson, are rationalists in their poetry and give the semblance of inductive discovery within the poem; Emerson begins with the discovery and is heedless of the process by which discovery is reached. Thus Donne and Herbert give us the density of real experience, while Emerson gives us only the conclusions.

Emerson's ambivalence shows itself in the many statements he makes about art. He seemed to be torn between a belief that art was illusion and that art was the highest possible human activity. In the opening section of *Nature* he relegates art to an almost oriental nothingness. In speaking of the artist he says, "But his operations taken together are so insignificant, a little chipping, baking, patching, and washing, that in an impression so grand as that of the world on the human mind, they do not vary the result." This belittlement of the artist is the perverted result of Emerson's belief that the world is better and more wonderful than anything that can be done with it. To concede that the artist could "vary the result" would have been for Emerson a tacit admission that the world was not the perfect creation he so zealously but naïvely believed it to be.

But in "The American Scholar" of the following year Emerson shifts his ground. He seems to realize that experience is, at least in its superficial aspect, formless; that it is the artist who must find and impart the meaning of life, which for most other men has been obfuscated by the egocentric business of living. "The theory of books is noble. The scholar of the first age received into him the world around; brooded thereupon; gave it the new arrangement of his own mind, and uttered it again. It came into him life; it went out from him truth. . . . It came to him business; it went from him poetry." Here, then, the artist is placed in a new perspective: experience is an endless mass of variety, which, when passed through the alembic of the artist, emerges as truth.

But how precisely was this to be accomplished? Once again Emerson wavers. Selection, the technical foundation of art, recommends itself to Emerson, but when he does accept it, it is with decided misgivings. In his essay *Art* he writes: "The virtue of art lies in detachment, in sequestering one object from the embarrassing variety. Until one thing comes out from the connection of things, there can be enjoyment, contemplation, but no thought." But several pages later Emerson seems to be wondering whether this detachment is not after all a violation of the "Whole." "All works of art should not be detached, but extempore performances." If one may guess at the thought process which caused these two contradictory statements, it might go something like this: The artist in order to convert life into truth must wrench an object out of its experiential context; but the very act of wrenching is apparently artificial, unreal, and consequently a lie. This paradox Emerson solved for himself by means of the symbol. "Every natural fact is a symbol of some spiritual fact. Every appearance in nature corresponds to some state of mind, and that state of mind can only be described by presenting that natural appearance as its picture."

Although Emerson quite correctly realizes that abstractions can be expressed only in terms of concrete images, he makes the crucial mistake of assuming that these natural facts have this power intrinsically: "This power is in the image because this power is in Nature." But this is obviously begging an important question. It is the poet who, after comprehending the experience with which he deals, makes the symbol serve as the vehicle of description and definition. It is, for example, Donne's technical mastery and, of course, his unified sensibility, not the symbol's inherent power, that enables him to use a pair of dividers in "A Valediction Forbidding Mourning" as the means of defining a man's love for a woman. To believe that the compass "so effects, because it so is," is to avoid the fact, as Emerson so often does, that technical mastery is necessary before the symbol is able to achieve the desired effect. The symbols in Emerson's poems **"The Sphinx"** and **"The Humble-Bee,"** because of this theory, are casually relied on to carry their own burden of meaning without any effort at control; consequently these poems

are irrevocably damaged: **"The Sphinx"** by obscurity, **"The Humble-Bee"** by waywardness.

But for Emerson the organic roots of the symbol go deeper than the fact that natural objects symbolize spiritual truths. "Parts of speech are metaphors, because the whole of nature is a metaphor of the human mind." But, for all his faith in the power of the symbol to express the fact and its spiritual counterpart concurrently, he was constantly leaving the symbol behind for the superficial solidity of direct statement. In a real sense he did not trust the symbol, and his distrust arose from his technical inability to manipulate a basically unified metaphor. It is one thing to say that there is no fact in nature which does not carry the whole sense of nature, but it is something quite different to make it work in a poem. This technical inadequacy, which his theory sanctions, causes him to introduce a symbol into his verse, drop it, and go darting after another with irritating abandon. Matthiessen is very much to the point when he says, "though he talked about the unexampled resources of metaphor and symbol, his staple device was analogy." Certainly, Emerson's belief in the symbol's innate power to convey the "whole sense of nature" points more to the use of analogy than symbol. In reading Emerson's poetry one receives the feeling of momentary illustration more than that of the permanent awareness of a symbol fully conceived and exploited. Further, as the poems of Donne and Crashaw abundantly show, the symbol is capable of defining states of feeling, while analogy, with its brief dazzle, is too feeble to catch the density of attitude. To be convinced one need only compare Emerson's **"Initial Love"** with Donne's "Lover's Infiniteness."

The relationship between beauty and art Emerson discusses many times, but perhaps nowhere so poignantly as in *Nature*.

> Nature is a sea of forms radically alike and even unique. . . . What is common to them all,—that perfectness and harmony, is beauty. . . . Nothing is quite beautiful alone; nothing but is beautiful in the whole. A single object is only so far beautiful as it suggests this universal grace. The poet . . . seek[s] to concentrate this radiance of the world on one point. . . . Thus in art does Nature work through the will of man filled with the beauty of her first works.

In short, the artist is filled with the beauty of nature, which fullness causes him to express its beauty in microcosm, which in turn suggests its beauty in macrocosm.

But this beauty signified to Emerson the moral as well as the aesthetic, or rather the single identity of both. He says in the same essay, "Beauty is the mark God sets upon virtue," and again, "Truth, and goodness, and beauty are but different faces of the same All." Emerson wanted desperately to believe this naïve, romantic concept, but even on the very same page he says, "No reason can be asked or given why the soul seeks beauty." This, of course, poses a problem. For if it is incomprehensible why the soul seeks beauty, and beauty is truth, then it is equally incomprehensible why the soul seeks truth; thus man becomes a subrational creature unable to understand why he strives to attain that which will presumably make him free. Certainly Emerson would be aghast at the implications of his own statements. That Emerson could not quite accept (as indeed could no man who has looked around at life) this single identity of truth and beauty is seen in his criticism of Swedenborg's language in *Representative Men.* "In his profuse and accurate imagery is no pleasure, for there is no beauty." In other words, Swedenborg's true imagery is not *ipso facto* beautiful. Emerson, whether he would or not, was sensitive to the beauty of things irrespective of their "spiritual suggestion"; but once having placed his philosophic faith in the romantic creed, he is tossed ambivalently from the sturdy wall of what he felt to the nebulous wall of what he wished to feel. This ambivalence damages the structure of **"Each and All"** and **"The Rhodora,"** as will be seen when we come to an analysis of these two poems.

The perfectness of nature also led Emerson to the criterion by which poetic excellence is to be judged. "For poetry was all written before time was, and whenever we are so finely organized that we can penetrate into that region where the air is all music, we hear those primal warblings and attempt to write them down, but we lose ever and anon a word or a verse and substitute something of our own, and thus miswrite the poem." Nature, then, is to be the eternal standard by which art isto be judged. But how is nature to be ascertained? Emerson's prescription is as terrifying as is any prescription which raises man's instincts above his rational capacities: "The lover of nature is he whose inward and outward senses are still truly adjusted to each other; who has retained the spirit of infancy even unto the era of manhood." This Wordsworthian faith Emerson carries to even more grotesque extremes in his essay *History:* "The idiot, the Indian, the child and unschooled farmer's boy stand nearer to the light by which nature is to be read, than the dissecter or the antiquary." This is faith in the self-reliance of the dog, not the man. How or why the idiot and the ignorant boy are able to pierce the density of experience, when the rational dissecter cannot, is beyond comprehension; in fact it is demonstrably false. This is not to say that the dissecter can solve the riddle of nature, but rather that if that part of us which distinguishes us from beasts cannot arrive at truth, certainly that part of us which we have in common with them cannot.

Emerson's doctrine of inspiration is but the other side of his belief that the simple mind can best read nature. The poet has just such a simple mind in the Emerson scheme. The poet in some way which is undiscoverable becomes intoxicated with inspiration, and "That is the best part of each writer which has nothing private in it; that which he does not know." That is, the poet is presumably able to describe and delineate an experience which he himself does not understand. Strange as it may seem, this is precisely what Emerson believes: "The universal nature, too strong for the petty nature of the bard, sits on his neck and writes through his hand; so that when he seems to vent a mere caprice and wild romance, the issue is an exact allegory." The poet, then, is a mystified middleman, who, through God's gift, is able to pass on the truths of nature to those less gifted. Not only is poetry not a rational process, as we understand the term, it is the product of a divine madness. "The poet knows that he speaks adequately then only when he speaks somewhat wildly. . . . not with the intellect used as an organ, but with the intellect released from all service. . . . with the intellect inebriated by nectar." How such emotionalism is able to reshape experience into coherent, communicable form is difficult to conceive.

Perhaps Emerson's reaction to his intellectual heritage with its Puritanical and, to a lesser extent, Unitarian rigidity of thought drove him to the outrageous belief that "our spontaneous action is always best." This idea is carried over to his literary theory. "The moment our discourse rises above the ground line of facts and is inflamed with passion or exalted thought, it clothes itself in images. . . . This imagery is spontaneous." The poetic process is thus further removed from the realm of the rational: not only is the source of the creative process outside the poet's understanding, but so is the very process itself. It is difficult to imagine how Emerson found "spontaneity" in the wrenched, exciting imagery of the metaphysical poets whom he so admired. Indeed, the use of radical imagery in such a poem of his as **"Spiritual Laws"** betokens more a self-conscious, though unsuccessful, drawing together of incongruous elements and a balancing of antithetical images than any spontaneous emission.

Although Emerson was drawn to the image because he felt that only it could hold language at once to the senses and the intellect, he was decidedly uncomfortable with only the ontological reality: "The details, the prose of nature he [the poet] should omit and give us only the spirit and the splendor." Since for Emerson the primary use of the fact is low, he recklessly leaves it behind in his attempts to grasp the nebulae of spirit; consequently the movement of his verse is fuzzy and unmotivated. His leaps for "the constant fact of life" often rip up the realistic foundations of his image, and we are left in a blurry transcendental haze without knowing how or why we got there.

Perhaps nowhere in Emerson's theory of poetry does his compulsion to relate everything to an organic whole manifest itself so ludicrously as in his theory of meters. He did not see that meter is essentially a tool with which the poet shapes and controls his material, that its superficial artificiality serves the higher function of form. But, since Emerson's philosophical edifice had no readily available niche into which such artificiality could be made to fit, he invented one. "Meter begins with the pulse beat, and the length of lines in poems and songs is determined by the inhalation and exhalation of the lungs."

On first glance, it seems one of the most perplexing of paradoxes that such an enthusiastic devotee of the organic principle in art could so seldom write a poem that holds together. But when we consider the chaotic implications of his theory, we are surprised that one or two of his poems are successful. One Emersonian scholar has excused Emerson by saying that while serving the high cause of spiritual truth he is willing to sacrifice without a qualm the infirm reader's desire for form and transition. But form makes communication possible. If the reader's desire to apprehend logical relationships is "infirm" and unreasonable, poetry is as useless as the average person will have us believe. Perhaps Emerson, sensing this fault in his verse, rationalized it when he said, "The adventitious beauty of poetry may be felt in the greater delight a verse gives in happy quotation than in the poem."

"Each and All," a much admired poem among Emersonians, suffers from such lack of form and transition. The poem opens with a number of particularized examples of the usually unperceived interlocking nature of experience: a scarecrow in the field does not know that you are looking at it; a heifer lows, uncaring and unknowing that its lowing charms a human ear; a sexton does not know that the music of his bells has made Napoleon stop to listen; nor does man know how the example of his life has helped his neighbor's creed. But suddenly there is inserted in lines eleven and twelve the abrupt generalized statement; "All are needed by each one; / Nothing is fair or good alone." These lines, coming without any transition from the particularized suggestiveness of the previous lines, startle us. The symbolic construct of the specific examples is swept away in the clipped meter of the expositional aphorism. The pattern of the first ten lines, that of ascending movement from inanimate to animal to man to spirit, is forced into the direct statement, and the poignancy of concrete awareness is thoroughly effaced.

We are then introduced to the poet, who, as direct participant, is to carry forward the theme that all are needed by each one. But, at this point, the poem, really begins anew. We are able to carry to it only the abstract, generalized statement, which acts with no more force than a sort of thesis sentence.

> I thought the sparrow's note from heaven,
> Singing at dawn on the alder bough.
> I brought him home, in his nest, at even;
> He sings the song, but it cheers not now,
> For I did not bring home the river and the sky;—
> He sang to my ear,—they sang to my eye.

The meaning is clear. The poet found beauty in the sparrow's note only when the bird was part of its natural surroundings; when brought to the poet's home it still sings, but it no longer pleases: it has lost its relationship to totality. Beauty, then, is in the thing connected, not in the thing isolated. Symbols are seemingly set up for this dichotomy: the ear or sound for isolation, the eye or sight for connection. But in the next section of the poem these symbols are jumbled.

> The delicate shells lay on the shore;
> The bubbles of the latest wave
> Fresh pearls to their enamel gave,
> And the bellowing of the savage sea
> Greeted their safe escape to me.
> I wiped away the weeds and foam,
> I fetched my sea-born treasures home;
> But the poor, unsightly, noisome things

> Had left their beauty on the shore
> With the sun and the sand and the wild uproar.

In this section sound is represented as part of the totality: "the sun and the sand and the wild uproar" sing both to the eye and the ear. This hasty dropping of the symbols indicates a certain confusion in the poet's mind, even more clearly seen in the next section.

To this point we are to see that beauty is real only in its natural totality. In the following lines the poet deals with something quite different, unintentionally changing the emphasis:

> The lover watched his graceful maid,
> As 'mid the virgin train she strayed,
> Nor knew her beauty's best attire
> Was woven still by the snow-white choir.
> At last she came to his hermitage,
> Like the birds from the woodlands to the cage;—
> The gay enchantment was undone,
> A gentle wife but fairy none.

This is almost ridiculous. The young woman's natural totality is arbitrary, lacking the "necessity" that the river and the sky have for the sparrow or the sun, sand, and ocean for the seashell. The virgin train is proper to her only while she is a snow-white virgin. To feel cheated that she is no fairy, but only a gentle wife, is to equate peevishly the fluctuating contexts of human beings with the fixed contexts of natural objects; the maid is not isolated, as were the shell and sparrow; for she has exchanged one perfectly natural state for another, virginity for marriage. Therefore, the disillusionment of this section is motivated by an unreasonably romantic turn of mind, the previous two by moral awareness. What is significant is that all three are presented as if identically motivated.

To this point the poem has dealt unsuccessfully with the necessity of totality to beauty. But Emerson's belief that poetry must ascend to the most spiritual of heights, no matter how, causes his poem to carom off into a direction completely unprepared for.

> Then I said, 'I covet truth;
> Beauty is unripe childhood's cheat;
> I leave it behind with the games of youth:'—
> As I spoke, beneath my feet
> The ground-pine curled its pretty wreath,
> Running over the club-moss burrs;
> I inhaled the violet's breath;
> Around me stood the oaks and firs;
> Pine-cones and acorns lay on the ground;
> Over me soared the eternal sky,
> Full of light and of deity;
> Again I say, again I heard,
> The rolling river, the morning bird;—
> Beauty through my senses stole;
> I yielded myself to the perfect whole.

The poet now rejects beauty and chooses truth. But this is not clear. The "truth" of the poem the poet has already apprehended: nothing is beautiful alone. What truth is he then choosing? Unfortunately, this remains an obscure, abstract choice, meaningless and undefined. But the rejection is but momentary: the poet becomes reaware of the beauty of nature, further realizes that this beauty is truth as well ("full of light and of deity"), and succumbs to the total perfection. The poem has ill prepared us for this "discovery." Until this last section it has been solely concerned with the nature of beauty as beauty; therefore, the ideational leap to this "spiritual truth" is effected without logic, force, or conviction.

"The Rhodora" illustrates another aspect of Emerson's difficulty in achieving form. **"Each and All"** suffers from a lack of ideational continuity; this poem lacks what may be termed an emotional continuity. Mark Van Doren, a perceptive critic, has singled out this poem as among the few by Emerson that are even in their excellence, but it seems to have a serious flaw.

The poem breaks sharply into two parts. The first eight lines are a description of the flower itself; the concluding eight are a philosophical generalization, presumably incited by the description.

> In May, when sea-winds pierced our solitudes,
> I found the fresh Rhodora in the woods,
> Spreading its leafless blooms in a damp nook,
> To please the desert and the sluggish brook.
> The purple petals, fallen in the pool,
> Made the black water with their beauty gay;
> Here might the red-bird come his plumes to cool,
> And court the flower that cheapens his array.
> Rhodora! if the sages ask thee why
> This charm is wasted on the earth and sky,
> Tell them, dear, that if eyes were made for seeing,
> Then beauty is its own excuse for being:
> Why thou wert there, O rival of the rose!
> I never thought to ask, I never knew:
> But in my simple ignorance, suppose
> The self-same Power that brought me there brought
>   you.

Although the description in the first eight lines comes dangerously close to being stilted, there is, nevertheless, a quiet charm in them. The rhythm delicately accentuates a gentleness in the descriptive images. We are made to feel the calm emotional undertow of peace and contentment which the poet has found in the wood in contradistinction to the "sea winds which pierced our solitudes." Suddenly, we are torn away from the scene, and the emotion erupts into the frantic "Rhodora!" Nothing in the preceding lines implies this outburst; in fact, they imply quite the contrary. It may be said that the poet has changed his attitude for reasons outside the poem or that he has license to change his attitude as he pleases. If this is so, if the poet does not have to prepare us for the change in attitude, if he does not have to ground his emotional switch in a recognizable conflict, he is not claiming the license of sanity, but of insanity.

The general fault of this poem, aside from such particular faults as awkward grammatical constructions and the almost

unbearable stickiness of "dear" in line eleven, is that no consistent motivation informs both halves of the poem. In his desire "to pass the brute body and search the life and reason which causes it to exist," Emerson has neglected to show us how or why he passed from the "body" to the "reason." In fact, he has given us less than the human situation: effect without cause. For this reason the poem remains irrevocably severed; the leap from the warm, concrete quietude of the first half to the bald, abstract assertions of the second is unreal in the truest sense of the word.

"Days" is probably Emerson's finest poetic achievement. If a successful poem is an indication of moral awareness, he must have understood the terrifying paradox of human choice: that in choosing one thing over another we lose forever the good in what we have rejected.

> Daughters of Time, the hypocritic Days,
> Muffled and dumb like barefoot dervishes,
> And marching single in an endless file,
> Bring diadems and fagots in their hands.
> To each they offer gifts after his will,
> Bread, kingdoms, stars, and sky that holds them all.
> I, in my pleached garden, watched the pomp,
> Forgot my morning wishes, hastily
> Took a few herbs and apples, and the Day
> Turned and departed silent. I, too late,
> Under her solemn fillet saw the scorn.

The Days bring gifts which range from brilliant glory (diadems) to those of humble utility (fagots); but the Days can give no indication of relative worth; they are muffled and dumb. Man's free will chooses from amongst the ascending hierarchy of bread, kingdoms, stars, and sky. The poet's morning wishes for stars and sky are forgotten as he watches the pomp, and he innocently chooses the modest growth of his garden. But he has not really forgotten, for his were wishes, not resolutions. This is significant. A resolution presupposes a vice, but a wish presupposes a yearning. The herbs and apples which the poet chooses are not intrinsically evil symbols, but the measure of excellence of a pleached garden. The poet realizes that he has not chosen evil over good, but rather one good over another, though of a lower order. He yearns for the capacity of higher choice while recognizing his fallible humanity. He has but two hands: to clutch for the stars and sky is to drop the herbs and apples. Yet he realizes that in an absolute sense he has chosen wrong, and the perplexity of his innocent guilt, subtly pointed up by the halting rhythm of, "I, too late, / Under her solemn fillet saw the scorn," touches the pain of the paradox. True, the Days do scorn the poet's choice, but it is the scorn that must come to most human beings for being human.

This poem, unlike almost everything else Emerson wrote, is firmly rooted in what he was able to understand. It does not vaporize into a vague, transcendental ether of intuitive feeling. It is above all intensely human. When Emerson left behind him the frantic leaps for superhuman truth and dealt rationally with experience, he managed to achieve such poetic excellence as **"Days."** But only then.

Emerson as figurist:

. . . As a poet [Emerson] is not an imagist, not a symbolist, but specifically a figurist. That is, he accepts image and symbol as vital, from the natural world; and then his contribution as poet is to show them in new relation. "He knows why the plain or meadow of space was strown with these flowers we call suns and moons and stars . . ." ["The Poet"]. There is the metaphoric way of speaking. He names now by appearances, now by essences, delighting in the intellect's sense of boundaries, and then in the ascension of things to higher kinds, that is, in both being and becoming, the inebriation of thought moving to fact— even in algebra and definitions, the freedom of trope.

Josephine Miles, "Ralph Waldo Emerson," in Six Classic American Writers: An Introduction, *University of Minnesota Press, 1970.*

R. A. Yoder (essay date 1972)

SOURCE: "Toward the 'Titmouse Dimension': The Development of Emerson's Poetic Style," in *PMLA,* Vol. 87, No. 2, March, 1972, pp. 255-70.

[*In this excerpt, Yoder presents a chronological study of Emerson's poems to reveal the development of Emerson's poetic style. Yoder finds that Emerson's use of poetic techniques, his themes, and his poetic structures follow a progression that coincides with his changing concept of the "poet's identity."*]

. . . The task of defining Emerson's poetry is difficult because, unlike Whitman and Emily Dickinson, the acknowledged giants of nineteenth-century American poetry, Emerson has no distinctive, original, easily defined style. It has been customary to borrow Emerson's own favorite organic metaphor and condemn him on just this ground, that his poetry never ripened and blossomed into unique, distinctive expression; in other words, that he never found himself as a poet. The charge carries some truth; Emerson was, after all, a diffident, often dissatisfied experimenter, as he himself wrote:

Our moods do not believe in each other. To-day I am full of thoughts and can write what I please. I see no reason why I should not have the same thought, the same power of expression, to-morrow. What I write, whilst I write it, seems the most natural thing in the world; but yesterday I saw a dreary vacuity in this direction in which I now see so much; and a month hence, I doubt not, I shall wonder who he was that wrote so many continuous pages. . . . But lest I should mislead any when I have my own head and obey my whims, let me remind the reader that I am only an experimenter. Do not set the least value on what I do, or the least discredit on what I do not, as if I pretended to settle any thing as true or false. I unsettle all things. No facts are to me sacred; none are profane; I simply experiment, an endless seeker with no Past at my back. ["Circles"]

And this is perhaps most evident in his poetry.

Given an avowed experimenter, one would plausibly approach his work chronologically, charting the course of successive experiments and thus elucidating at least the pattern, if not an end product, called "Emerson's style." Such an approach neatly parallels the current view of Emerson that looks to the "man thinking" rather than to "Emerson's philosophy," and the emphasis placed, since the study by Stephen Whicher, on the inner process of Emerson's life. Unfortunately for this method relatively few of Emerson's poems can be dated with certainty, and many were composed over a period of years, sometimes ten or more. Nevertheless, I think, some sense can be made of the larger pattern of Emerson's poetic development, based on the approximate dates that we have. Ultimately it is not the exact chronological order that matters so much—there are, in the whole body of his poetry, numerous instances that bear out the passages from "Circles" just quoted, that show us what he writes today may not suit yesterday or tomorrow. And yet, I shall argue, in the whole context these particular inconsistencies will be "rounded by the law of his being, as the inequalities of Andes and Himmaleh are insignificant in the curve of the sphere" ["Emerson, Self-Reliance"]. Thus, from a roughly chronological viewpoint, we can see a pattern in Emerson's poetry that takes its shape from the essential changes in his thought and especially from the fundamental shift in emphasis that must have occurred about 1840, a change that has come to mark the distinction between the "early" and the "later" Emerson.

An exhaustive study would show how Emerson moved from an undergraduate's imitation of Augustan couplets to a variety of less polished and less constraining verse forms—ballads, epigrammatic quatrains, Wordsworthian blank verse in 1827, and the extraordinary if ungainly **"Gnothi Seauton"** of 1831, lines that are as unorthodox in form as they are in doctrine, and that prefigure Emerson's settled practices of a decade later. Emerson was not, however, consciously preparing himself for a poetic career. The role of his journal poetry is unquestionably self-expression, dialogue with oneself—moving away from the style of performance toward a means of formulating one's private convictions, or, as Leslie Fiedler has suggested [in *Waiting for the End,* 1964], toward "the speech of a man urging himself on, rather than appealing to a crowd." To summarize these early experiments we may say that Emerson sought a mode of expression appropriate to the essentially meditative aim of this writing. Not surprisingly, he turned finally to Wordsworth, whose star was just rising on this side of the Atlantic in the late 1820s, and to the Metaphysical tradition of meditative verse, especially to the poetry of George Herbert.

"The River," dated June 1827 in the Centenary Edition [of *The Complete Works of RWE,* 1903-04], and the following lines from Emerson's journal are unmistakably Wordsworthian in setting and cadence:

He is a man who tho' he told it not
Mourned in the hour of manhood, while he saw

The rich imagination that had tinged
Each earthly thing with hues from paradise
/Abandoning/ /Forsake/ forever his instructed eye.

. . . . .

But he was poor & proud & solitary
He would walk forth at moonlight, for the moon
And quick eyed stars do sympathize with all
Who suffer . . .
             When thy soul
Is filled with a just image fear not thou
Lest halting rhymes or unharmonious verse
Cripple the fair Conception. Leave the heart
Alone to find its language. In all tongues
It hath a sovereign instinct that doth teach
An eloquence which rules can never give.
   [*Journals and Miscellaneous Notebooks of RWE*,
   1960]

Associated with Wordsworth's rural solitary is a language sincere and unpretentious, that comes spontaneously from the heart. Emerson's admiration for Herbert over a period of at least seven years culminates in the 1835 lectures, where Herbert is placed foremost among English poets: "I should cite Herbert as a striking example of the power of exalted thought to melt and bend language to its fit expression." Undoubtedly in Herbert—in the "Jordan" poems, for example—Emerson also found an ideal of simple, heartfelt poetry. Herbert's contribution is larger, however, for Herbert provided a model, not merely for simplicity of speech and imagery, but for combining that simplicity with architectonic skill, with the concentrated and integrated organization that distinguishes the seventeenth-century meditative style, just as it distinguishes Emerson's poetry of 1834 from the prosaic, discursive blank verse and free verse that dots his journals between 1827 and 1832. **"Each and All,"** **"The Rhodora,"** and **"The Snow-Storm"** are among the most admired of Emerson's poems. What they owe to Herbert is not explicit, but the debt is clear enough in another poem probably written about this time and later taken for Herbert's own work.

"Grace"

How much, preventing God, how much I owe
To the defences thou hast round me set;
Example, custom, fear, occasion slow,—
These scorned bondmen were my parapet.
I dare not peep over this parapet
To gauge with glance the roaring gulf below,
The depths of sin to which I had descended,
Had not these me against myself defended.

Here, as John Broderick has shown, is a direct parallel with the first line of Herbert's "Sinne," "Lord! with what care hast thou begirt us round." Moreover, the retard effected by the naming or cataloging device in the third line is characteristic of Herbert and may also have been taken over from the catalog somewhat more extended in "Sinne" (though cataloging is a common enough technique among seventeenth-century poets, and Emerson may have found

precedents in Milton, Herrick, or even the American William Bradford). [As discussed by Louis Martz in *The Poetry of Meditation,* 1962] personification of the defenses as "scorned bondmen" calls to mind Herbert's specific recommendation [in his work *Country Parson*] that "things of ordinary use" ought to illustrate "Heavenly Truths." This advice Emerson never forgot; the bondmen of **"Grace"** reappear constantly in his poetry, importing truths well above their station. The "drudge in dusty frock" who appears in **"Art"** has been compared to Herbert's servant in "The Elixir," a poem that Emerson especially admired, and the stooped crones who sweep and scour the poet's cottage in **"Saadi"** are suddenly transformed into gods. Thus there is no doubt about Herbert's influence. More generally—and here I think we can include the poems of 1834 as having the same qualities—Emerson learned from Herbert, and perhaps from some of his contemporaries, the art of "neatness": the way to structure a poem on a single metaphor or situation, the way **"Grace"** is based on the figure of a fortress; the smoothness of tone and rhythm, conversational but always melodic, never jagged but sufficiently pointed and varied to gain the quality of speech, as in the catalog or in the stressed pronouns ("these me") which give the last line of **"Grace"** a peak before it falls off to the diminished feminine ending.

"The Rhodora," one of the 1834 poems, displays the same neat structure and rhythm as **"Grace,"** again modulated by a feminine rhyme that sets off the gnomic couplet, and by the deliberateness of the last line with its hyphenated adjective, monosyllabic parallelism, and pointed pronouns. **"The Rhodora"** conveys, too, the humility and intense dedication that Emerson and Herbert shared. One might go further to argue that Emerson's poem deploys the formal structure of seventeenth-century meditation, beginning with the composition or focusing upon a concrete situation and proposing of the spiritual problem therein dramatized; following with an analysis of the problem; and ending in the colloquy, an intimate conversation and union between the poet and the object of his spiritual exercise. But here I think the essential difference between Emerson and the Metaphysicals is evident: whereas the meditative formula is triadic, the structure of **"The Rhodora"** is clearly binary, two sets of eight lines each. In the first, the situation is posed and the question implied (actually stated already in the subtitle of the poem); in the second, an answer is given immediately, without any deliberation, and the answer itself eschews analysis:

Rhodora! if the sages ask thee why
This charm is wasted on the earth and sky,
Tell them, dear, that if eyes were made for seeing,
Then Beauty is its own excuse for being:
Why thou wert there, O rival of the rose!
I never thought to ask, I never knew:
But, in my simple ignorance, suppose
The self-same Power that brought me there brought
   you.

The rhodora needs no reasoned argument, no "excuse" for its existence. In terms of the meditative formula, we have only "composition" and "colloquy," two parts subtly intertwined. The first part of the poem portrays the rhodora as a humble, self-sacrificing flower which, though equal to the celebrated rose, prefers obscure service to worldy fame. Sacrifice and service are implied, almost to the point of martyrdom, in the fallen petals. In the last eight lines the poet identifies himself with the same Christian virtues: his "simple ignorance" is faith, if not in Providence, certainly in a wise and sensitive Creator; the worshipful humility which the poet and the flower share explains their intimate rapport. The philosophical sages, on the other hand, are shut out; as the flower leans toward Christian sacrifice, the sages are associated with self-seeking, utilitarian interests, perhaps even cavalier interests, who see the flower's charm as "wasted." Thus a dramatic undercurrent—the subtle alliance of poet and flower against the sages—helps to create a mood of religious dedication that excludes the inquiring, analytical mind, and at the same time militates against a narrowly esthetic, "beauty for beauty's sake" interpretation of the poem.

In a number of ways **"The Rhodora"** is consonant with Emerson's achievement in *Nature* (1836). Both works illustrate the attention to structure, the eye for neatness and symmetry, that Emerson cultivated during these years. Herbert, probably Emerson's chief model for the poetry of 1834, is also one of the inspiring spirits of *Nature,* where a large portion of "Man" is quoted. There is a well-known passage concluding the section of *Nature* on "Beauty" that bears out the message of **"The Rhodora"**: "This element [Beauty] I call an ultimate end. No reason can be asked or given why the soul seeks beauty. Beauty, in its largest and profoundest sense, is one expression for the universe. God is the all-fair." Finally, the binary structure of the poem reflects, in its omission of any extended analysis, Emerson's attack on the Understanding in *Nature. . . .*

In the years between 1836 and 1839 Emerson attempted to work out his theory of nature, mainly in lectures that formed the basis for his later published essays. As far as we know, he wrote little poetry (of his major poems, only **"The Humble-Bee"** is traditionally assigned to 1837) and did not publish what he had already written. Suddenly in 1839 he decided to publish some of his early poems, including **"The Rhodora"** and **"Each and All,"** which he sent to James Freeman Clarke's *Western Messenger;* and for the first time Emerson thought of himself as a poet, not merely as a writer of private, meditative verses. Why he had to become a poet, in the broadest sense, is explained in a significant journal passage from 1839:

> As the musician avails himself of the concert, so the philosopher avails himself of the drama, the epic, the novel, and becomes a poet; for these complex forms allow of the utterance of his knowledge of life by *indirections* as well as in the didactic way, and can therefore express the fluxional quantities and values which the thesis or dissertation could never give. [*Journals of RWE,*1909-14]

By 1840 the Heraclitean notion of flux, the fluidity of all real substance which is eternally becoming, had washed away a considerable portion of correspondence, and Emerson had entered upon his skeptical mood. In *Nature* the settled "order of things" had been grounded in the belief that "every appearance in nature corresponds to some state of the mind" and "there is nothing lucky or capricious in these analogies." In contrast to this rather fixed Swedenborgian correspondence, the flux of words as well as things is paramount in Emerson's journal of 1841:

> The metamorphosis of Nature shows itself in nothing more than this, that there is no word in our language that cannot become typical to us of Nature by giving it emphasis. The world is a Dancer; it is a Rosary; it is a Torrent; it is a Boat; a Mist; a Spider's Snare; it is what you will; and the metaphor will hold, and it will give the imagination keen pleasure. Swifter than light the world converts itself into that thing you name, and all things find their right place under this new and capricious classification. There is nothing small or mean to the soul. It derives as grand a joy from symbolizing the Godhead or his universe under the form of a moth or a gnat as of a Lord of Hosts. Must I call the heaven and the earth a maypole and country fair with booths, or an anthill, or an old coat, in order to give you the shock of pleasure which the imagination loves and the sense of spiritual greatness? Call it a blossom, a rod, a wreath of parsley, a tamarisk-crown, a cock, a sparrow, the ear instantly hears and the spirit leaps to the trope. [*Journals of RWE,* 1909-14]

The analogy that was in 1836 neither "lucky or capricious" is now exactly that; the symbol held up earlier as knowledge of a discrete world is now offered for its "shock of pleasure," the surprising kaleidoscopic insights it gives. Symbolic language is still a kind of knowledge—indeed, perhaps the only kind of knowledge—but valuable now because things are free rather than fixed, and because no one set of correspondences is adequate to express Nature—"the slippery Proteus is not so easily caught" [Emerson, "Swedenborg; or the Mystic"].

The doctrine of flux, with its corollary that all inquiry is essentially poetic or metaphorical, liberated Emerson even further from traditional analogies and accepted forms. His most rhapsodic language, in prose or verse, belongs to this moment of enthusiasm and newly sensed freedom. "Poets are thus liberating gods," he repeats in his dithyrambic essay "The Poet," and the kind of verse he expected to issue from this concept of poetry is implied in the well-known journal passage of 1839 calling for "grand Pindaric strokes, as firm as the tread of a horse" or "the stroke of a cannon ball"—"I wish to write such rhymes as shall not suggest a restraint, but contrariwise the wildest freedom." This is the poetic program Emerson attempted to carry out in such poems as **"Woodnotes"** (especially the second part), **"Merlin,"** and **"Bacchus,"** and it is the essential link between Emerson and Whitman.

What becomes apparent, in the full context of Emerson's poetic development, is how brief this enthusiastic moment was, and that alone it cannot serve as the basis for a definition of Emerson's poetic style. The exhilaration of the moment was undermined by Emerson's growing skepticism, that other side of the doctrine of flux that implies an endless, wandering circularity; and his buoyant mood was abruptly cut off by the death of his son Waldo in

1842. The poetic program of 1839-41 clearly displaced Herbert, or even Wordsworth, as a model. Emerson looked then to other sources that corroborated his ideas about poetic freedom, mainly to older traditions, the poetry of Saadi and Hafiz, the Vedas, and the ancient British bards. The last, in particular, offer an important source for explicit ideas about poetic technique. In Sharon Turner's *History of the Anglo-Saxons* Emerson learned that abrupt transitions, clipped syntax, periphrasis, and repeated epithets were all characteristic of the ancient bards, and that they used no rules for meter, "consulting only the natural love of melody." Very likely he also read Longfellow's anthology *The Poets and Poetry of Europe*, published in 1845. In an essay introducing his own translations of Anglo-Saxon lyrics, Longfellow noted especially

> the short exclamatory lines, whose rhythm depends on alliteration in the emphatic syllables, and to which the general omission of particles gives great energy and vivacity. Though alliteration predominates in all Anglo-Saxon poetry, rhyme is not wholly wanting. . . . [Rhyme and alliteration] brought so near together in the short, emphatic lines, produce a singular effect upon the ear. They ring like blows of hammers on an anvil.

Much that Turner and Longfellow describe appears frequently in Emerson's published poems, yet the best evidence that he imitated the metrical half-line, periphrasis, and alliteration of the Anglo-Saxons is in a manuscript trial beginning "Poet of poets / Is Time, the distiller, / Chemist, refiner"

> All through the countryside
> Rush locomotives:
> Prosperous grocers
> Posing in newspapers
> Over their shopfires
> Settle the State.
> But, for the Poet,—
> Seldom in centuries
> Comes the well-tempered
> Musical Man. . . .
> Free of the city,
> Free of the [field] [meadow] forest
> Knight of each order,
> Sworn of each guild
> Fellow of monarchs,
> And, what is better
> [Fellow] Mate of all men.
> [Brackets indicate words crossed out.]

The corrections show that Emerson consciously sought alliteration, and the general mood and descriptive effects of this passage are reminiscent of the Old English lyric. It is a heroic style to fit Emerson's heroic program—and if the passage were written as full four-stress lines (instead of half-lines) and given rhyme, which Emerson thought an essential and primitive quality of poetry, the result would be similar to the staccato tetrameters that are so common in the *Poems* of 1846. . . .

Here, then, is the full movement of Emerson's thinking about what a poem should be: it crystallizes, somewhere between 1834 and 1836, in the idea of a precisely organized, meditative poem modeled after Herbert; it shifts, just before 1840, to an enthusiastic vision of wild, bardic freedom; and it subsides quickly in the 1840's toward a concept of poetry more restrained in tone though not necessarily in form, more serene and detached, and more oblique in its announcements of universal truth.

Inevitably, given the man he was, Emerson's aeolian verses obeyed the winds of thought, so that any discussion of his poetry during its major phase (roughly from 1839 to 1847) must consider the development of his ideas that I have just traced. Generally, the function of his poetry can still be described as meditative, and for a great many of these poems the binary question-and-answer form remains the structural framework on which he built. But there are important differences: appropriately, for expression that is free and spontaneous, Emerson moves toward a much looser form of meditation than that of the 1834 poems. He favors shorter, compressed units of thought, reflected in the choice of meters and the often cryptic or elliptical syntax; his rhythms and language are easy and informal; and the arguments are less explicit, often depending more on imagery than on direct and logical statement. Sometimes it seems, in fact, that Emerson is trying to bring his poetry closer to the actual processes of thought, to create what we today might see as a rudimentary "stream of consciousness" technique.

Such a change can be illustrated by comparing two well-known poems, **"Each and All,"** one of the poems of 1834, and **"The Problem,"** probably written in 1839. Few of Emerson's works are as highly structured as **"Each and All,"** which is carefully divided into parts and then subdivided into instances or images. One can, with some justice, claim that the poem exemplifies the characteristic binary form of the poet's encounter with nature, given over first to his doubts or problem (here the need for proof of Nature's wise aphorism "All are needed by each one; / Nothing is fair or good alone") and then to nature's answer (the last ten lines in which the poet sees the truth without having it proved in any discursive way); and so conceived it shows, as **"The Rhodora"** did, the fundamental distinction between Emerson and the Metaphysicals: for Emerson, analysis is not a means to revelation. The long middle of the poem, which might be taken as an "analysis" of the type appropriate to the seventeenth-century meditative structure, does not lead to the resolution, but curiously to a point where the poet would have discarded beauty in favor of truth. Only in the end, when the poet is taken by surprise, does he realize that truth, beauty, and goodness are not isolated elements but aspects of a "perfect whole." Though rare, this experience is not unknown, for the poet exclaims, "Again I saw, again I heard," recalling lines from another visionary poet whose moments of insight counteract the light of common day. Like Wordsworth's in the "Immortality Ode," Emerson's vision in **"Each and All"** counteracts the common experiences enumerated in the middle of the poem from which the poet infers that beauty is a cheat. The poet's inference is wrong, of course, but it is a legitimate inference given the facts at hand, and his making it dramatizes the weakness and dangers inherent in the analytic method: inference or induction, that is, generalizing from a series of instances, is the way of the Understanding; only direct and intuitive experience "through my senses" brings the positive truth home.

In the style of 1834 and like the poems of Herbert, **"Each and All"** is precisely worked out, an arrangement of discrete parts in a deliberate pattern. Admirable as it is, this formal coherence does have its price—a felt loss in vitality, perhaps, and the friction of such deliberateness in method rubbing against the spontaneity finally endorsed by the poem. As obviously as **"Each and All"** is composed, **"The Problem"** is a casual arrangement, its parts more like beads loosely connected on a string than pieces neatly fitted together. It is a poem of meditation on a matter of great personal concern to Emerson, contrasting again with **"Each and All"** where the theme is more philosophical and objective. From its beginning **"The Problem"** strikes a note of sincerity and simplicity, of the direct rendering of personal feeling:

> I like a church; I like a cowl;
> I love a prophet of the soul;
> And on my heart monastic aisles
> Fall like sweet strains, or pensive smiles:
> Yet not for all his faith can see
> Would I that cowled churchman be.

So brief and straightforward a statement is underlined by the simple, balanced tetrameter and the easy rhymes, and the impression of unreserved candor is always enhanced when one admits liking what one cannot approve. Set beside these the first lines of **"Each and All,"** the relative contrivance of the latter is evident: "Little thinks, in the field, yon red-cloaked clown / Of thee from the hill-top looking down"—despite the rhyme the movement here is of studied blank verse, complicated by inversions and enjambment. Development in **"The Problem"** strengthens the impression that the poem is working out an explanation, not dramatizing one already made. Questions help to break up the pattern of assertion, the arguments are cumulative rather than logical, and the conclusion falls off instead of rising, an abrupt repetition of the opening lines that seems to say, "Even if the explanation has been incomplete or logically unsatisfactory, my conviction remains unchanged." Again, by comparison, the conclusion of **"Each and All"** is staged, more theatrical than dramatic.

Both poems touch upon the relation of beauty to truth. **"Each and All"** reflects Emerson's early faith in a "perfect whole" that unites beauty with truth and goodness; it suggests the same predilection for abstract or philosophical symmetry that we observed in the doctrine of correspondence and in *Nature*. **"The Problem,"** like the 1839 journal passage in which the philosopher becomes a poet shifts from philosophical to esthetic, from transcendent to natural standards. Revelation, according to the argument summarized in the couplet "One accent of the Holy Ghost / The heedless world hath never lost," is available at all times and to all creeds; it is in this sense natural rather than sectarian, identified with passionate acts of creation rather than with statements of belief or dogma. The point of accumulating examples in the body of the poem is to grant "an equal date," that is, equal authority, to both pagan and Christian forms in every era. The assertion that revelation is equally available throws new light on the question Emerson asks himself: why must he insist, in the poem, upon his difference from the bishop, or why, in actual life, did he resign from the church if the way of the priest and the way of the seer are just different paths to the same truth? The answer is that Emerson's touchstone here is beauty, not truth; religion is appealing because it creates beauty—he likes the rhythm of church aisles and Taylor's words "are music in my ear." The revelation available to Phidias, the Delphic oracle, and Michelangelo, as well as to divines, is really artistic inspiration drawn from natural forms. Emerson might still have squared with the bishop if he had introduced the analogy between man's art and God's divine artistry in creating the natural world. But in Emerson's view, art does not create nature, rather nature creates works of art:

> These temples grew as grows the grass;
> Art might obey, but not surpass.
> The passive Master lent his hand
> To the vast soul that o'er him planned;
> And the same power that reared the shrine
> Bestrode the tribes that knelt within.

The "passive Master" fills the role of Emerson's artist, not the orthodox theologian's conception of Jesus or God the Creator. Art and the artist must find their place within the order of nature, and that order, illustrated on all levels in the poem, is development from inside outward and from below upward. "Up from the burning core below" all things are "outbuilt." The individualist and evolutionary implications of such an order are difficult to reconcile with episcopal office, and this imagery of direction or thrust justifies Emerson's making his churchman specifically a bishop.

The structural and conceptual changes illustrated by **"The Problem"** reflect, in part, Emerson's enthusiastic poetic program of 1839, and although one would hardly call the protagonist of that poem "bardic," many of the same principles are applied in the poems that best represent the bardic program. A second important development in Emerson's major phase is the way he modifies the situation and tone in his central encounter between the poet and nature. This, I think, reflects not only his enthusiasm of 1839, but more significantly the doctrine of flux and Emerson's growing skepticism in the years after 1841.

The personality of the poet was a matter of long and serious concern which Emerson tried to resolve in poems, essays, and even in bits of fiction scattered through the journals. Much of the character of the emerging poet-figure is clearly autobiographical and an attempt to state his own concept of the poet's role. But gradually Emerson loosened the identification between himself and the character he created, so that in his later essays, as Whicher pointed out, there are a number of dramatic characters or alter egos who speak for different, often opposite, sets of ideas. And often Emerson was able to heighten the dramatic situation instead of the philosophical resolution in his poems, such as in **"Hamatreya"** and **"Days."**

In the earlier poems the poet-figure is an active and relentless seeker of truth. Whatever frustrations he encounters, there is nevertheless an air of certainty that he is on the right track in verse like the "Dull uncertain brain, / But gifted yet to know" fragment. In "The Poet" he is the bard who will pierce through to central truth, and like the poet-figure of the *Ion* and Coleridge's "Kubla Khan" is set apart from other men. . . . Plagued by having heard only a "random word" and not the whole truth, this poet suffers prolonged periods of despair (the poem's original title was "The Discontented Poet, A Masque"). He complains, in effect, that the law of the spirit is not kept as faithfully as the law that regulates nature. The Chorus of Spirits answer, first, that they and he are brothers by nature and no one can violate his own nature; second, that no one serves the spirit out of physical compulsion or simply to be rewarded, but out of penury and love:

> Serve thou it not for daily bread,—
> Serve it for pain and fear and need.
> Love it, though it hide its light;
> By love behold the sun at night.
> If the Law should thee forget,
> More enamoured serve it yet . . .

Emerson took great pains with this poem and worked on it for some ten years, but he could never finish it. The reason may well be that the poem moves insistently toward a final resolution, but Emerson was never satisfied by any of the answers he could write for the Chorus of Spirits. The second answer given above is already tinged with the doubts of 1842. Emerson stressed the message, in earlier poems with a binary framework, by putting straightforward answers into Nature's mouth. In the **"Dirge"** for his brothers Edward and Charles, which Emerson completed in 1838, the resolution is a "tale divine" told in the song of a bird, more consolatory than philosophical, but explaining why the poet cannot tell others of his deep grief. The same can be said of **"Threnody,"** Emerson's elegy for his son Waldo. A poem written during the later skeptical years (between 1842 and 1845), **"Threnody"** nevertheless posed questions so painful that only a full resolution in the manner of 1834-36 could console the grieving father. Thus **"Threnody"** is a perfect example of the binary form illustrated in **"The Rhodora"**: the first part is the poet's lament, the second—possibly modeled after God's answer to Job—rebukes analysis and offers the consolation of unquestioning faith. **"To Rhea"** and **"Woodnotes,"** whose second part concludes with the most explicit statement Nature gives in any of the poems, belong to the same classification.

Most frequently after 1840, however, Nature is anything but explicit. The poem **"Nature"** (not published until 1867) reveals the relationship between art and nature that is implicit in **"The Problem."** In it Nature is witty and baffling; her chief tools are "Casualty and Surprise," and she is "all things to all men," deceiving them with the illusion of freedom while they inevitably do her bidding. She takes on a secretive and moody aspect, and deliberately taunts men for their ignorance of her mysteries. . . .

. . . In most of the later poems it is no longer so easy for Emerson to identify with the bard piercing through to truth; rather, he is like a spectator who knows where to look but waits for someone more heroic than himself to do the job. **"Monadnoc,"** completed sometime between 1845 and its publication in the volume of 1846, should be compared with an earlier poem of similar design, **"Woodnotes,"** published in two parts in *The Dial,* 1840-41. Both are essentially of the question-and-answer type, encounters between a poet-figure and Nature represented by the mountain or the pine tree. The long monologue of the pine in the second part of **"Woodnotes"** directly answers the forester-hero, and while the concept of nature as flux is invoked, the poem resolves on the theme of unity ordained by "conscious Law," a law personified as "God" the creator and the "eternal Pan." There is no hint of an observer apart from the forester, who is Emerson's primitive poet, "philosopher," "minstrel," "forest seer"; and nothing is equivocal or complex about the pine tree's role as Nature's spokesman. In **"Monadnoc,"** however, as in **"The Sphinx,"** the "I" of the poem (with whom Emerson identifies) is separate: the protagonist of Monadnoc stands as an observer midway between the "spruce clerk" type of the urban tourists who daily climb the mountain in summer and the heroic "bard and sage" whom the mountain awaits. The claims of the mountain are significantly more cautious than those of the pine: the order it hints of is the flux behind solid-seeming things, which is only the first stage of reality in "Woodnotes II." Monadnoc itself belongs to this order; it obeys the law expressed by the gnomic paradox "Adamant is soft to wit," and therefore it will dissolve when the apocalyptic hero comes to solve the riddle of its being:

> And when the greater comes again
> With my secret in his brain,
> I shall pass as glides my shadow
> Daily over hill and meadow.

The secret of the mountain is essentially a scientific account of its nature and origin. Common sense and simple observation see only a solid pyramid, but the mind probes deeper into this mass and "in large thoughts, like fair pearl-seed, / Shall string Monadnoc like a bead." Emerson's repeated image for the ordering of matter is a string of beads:

> . . . these gray crags
> Not on crags are hung,
> But beads are of a rosary
> On prayer and music strung.

The basis for this image is explicated in "Poetry and Imagination"—

> Thin or solid, everything is in flight. I believe this conviction makes the charm of chemistry,—that we have the same avoirdupois matter in an alembic, without a vestige of the old form; and in animal transformation not less, as in grub and fly, in egg and

bird, in embryo and man; everything undressing and stealing away from its old into new form, and nothing fast but those invisible cords which we call laws, on which all is strung.

The beads represent bits of matter, impermanent cohesions and not things-in-themselves; the material world is not built stone upon stone, it is hung upon a string, an organizing principle that corresponds to the divine Idea or Law and gives to the whole image the religious efficacy of a rosary. The string is also a fitting emblem for the concept of rhyme that Emerson defined in the wider sense of any rhythmic pattern. The material universe is really an intellectual dance for which "Rhyme [is] the pipe, and Time the warder." All things begin and end in motion, the mountain itself having begun as "chemic eddies," finally rising "with inward fires and pain" like "a bubble from the plain," all according to the geological theory of upheavals that Emerson had set forth in his early lectures. At its end, the mountain "shall throb," and metaphorically it becomes a monster slain not by the sword but by the song of a "troubadour" who will "string" up the carcass on his rhyme. Then, Monadnoc prophesies, like a whale or volcano,

> . . . I shall shed
> From this wellspring in my head,
> Fountain-drop of spicier worth
> Than all vintage of the earth.

Then the sacramental liquid, what in **"Bacchus"** is called the true wine of remembering, will be reclaimed by man.

The curious thing about **"Monadnoc"** is that the poet-observer who concludes the poem disregards what the mountain has prophesied. This may be because he is not the heroic bard of the future and has been, from the start, concerned with the practical and immediate effect of Monadnoc upon the people who live there, hoping that the mountain would be "their life's ornament, / And mix itself with each event." For him the mountain already dislimns by "Pouring many a cheerful river," which in turn offer practical gifts to the inhabitants. In the final apostrophe to Monadnoc the protagonist is still concerned with the immediately practical, what he calls "pure use." The epithet, surely paradoxical to the Romantic mind, is appropriate because what the poet is trying to define is the fruit or harvest of the "barren cone," the mountain's top above the timberline. The passage then floods in paradoxes—stones that flower, the "sumptuous indigence" of man, the "plenties" of the "barren mound," and the mountain described as an "opaker star" and finally as a "Mute orator." The point made by the poet-observer is that, notwithstanding the mountain's own prediction that it will someday disintegrate, Monadnoc's rocky summit is for men a "type of permanence." It is, too, a religious temple to comfort men's "insect miseries," and no less a "complement" of the erect human form with mind at its summit. Indeed, the triangular shape leading to an apex is a symbol of all progress toward unity, hence of the One or the Good which is now introduced in terms similar to those of **"Woodnotes II":**

> Thou . . . imagest the stable good
> For which we all our lifetime grope,
> In shifting form the formless mind,
> And though the substance us elude,
> We in thee the shadow find.

This statement is, however, much more limited: the substance or reality of the Good, which is formless, we can never know; but it is shadowed forth in all the changing forms of nature, most clearly in the large, stable objects which seem to us to change least. The use of the mountain, then, is purely symbolical, but in a world where motion is ever faster and more frivolous this symbolic role, recalling us in wayside moments and making us sane, is actually more practical than all its physical bounties. This is the thematic paradox at the center of a number of paradoxes evoked in the last section of the poem.

Thus **"Monadnoc"** is a more complicated poem than **"Woodnotes,"** and more suited to Emerson's later thought. It is resolved by the poet-observer distinct from the heroic bard and as concerned about everyday life as about apocalyptic revelation. While the pine tree, a surrogate for Nature, was merely a spokesman for the doctrine of the poem, the mountain wholly displaces doctrine as a center of interest, and the poet-observer recognizes it as a complex symbol of something that cannot be expressed by any other means. Again, to use Emerson's own formula, philosophy becomes poetry, the fluid symbolism of art replaces the more rigid symbolism of correspondence, in the transition from the earlier to the later poem.

As the poet-hero matures into the poet-observer, the ecstatic joy that Emerson expected poetry to release subsides into the tamer qualities of cheerfulness and serenity. The poet's quest and assault, which would have explained all of nature in 1836, turns into a strategy of wit, oblique counterpunching, and finally into appreciative acceptance. Uriel is a truth-seeker, to be sure, but he is a young, mischievous rebel, whereas the protagonist of "The Poet" is ageless and solemn. Uriel's sentiments are gnomic hints whose purpose in the poem is to shatter old decrees and formulas, not to create new ones, and thus Emerson is not pressed for the kind of ultimate answer that he felt obliged to provide in **"Woodnotes"** or **"Threnody."** The same qualities are found in the main speaker of Emerson's short **"Fable,"** a poem based on the question-and-answer form but almost entirely given over to the squirrel's retort to the bullying mountain. The squirrel is spry in word and deed, and he turns the tables on the mountain with Emerson's doctrine of compensation disguised as New England wisecracking:

> Talents differ; all is well and wisely put;
> If I cannot carry forests on my back,
> Neither can you crack a nut.

This smaller voice, full of Yankee cadences and concealing its power in understatement and shafts of oblique wit, is heard frequently in the later quatrains and in poems like **"Berrying," "Hamatreya,"** and **"The Titmouse."**

Merlin is a heroic bard drawn from the legendary past, and the Merlin poems are perhaps the best verse explanations of Emerson's theory of "wildest freedom" in poetry; yet Merlin is not preoccupied with the search for truth or for any answers Nature might give to his questions. His business is primarily social rather than intellectual, a "blameless master of the games" and "king of sport" who dispenses joy and peace to men. Apparently he is not bothered, as the Poet was, by "unhappy times" when inspiration is lax. Hence truth seeks him ("the God's will sallies free") and in the moment of revelation at the end of "Merlin I" finds him effortless and "unawares." **"Saadi,"** although an earlier poem than **"Merlin,"** goes even further in making its protagonist a passive figure, so that Saadi may well stand as the exemplary version of Emerson's later poetic personality. Saadi is the bard and sage mellowed by experience. He sits alone, self-reliant in his complete inactivity—

> Many may come,
> But one shall sing;
> Two touch the string,
> The harp is dumb.
> Though there come a million,
> Wise Saadi dwells alone.

But, like Merlin, he is socially concerned, ever gentle and cheerful to his fellowmen, especially to the "simple maids and noble youth" who need him most. The doctrine of the "sad-eyed Fakirs," a melange of sin and gloom echoing Marvell, the graveyard school, and Byron, is quickly countered by Saadi's effortless optimism: "For Saadi sat in the sun, / And thanks was his contrition." Like Emerson's other poems, **"Saadi"** rises to a peak of intense, momentary vision. But characteristic of the later Emerson, Saadi's truth lies within, not beyond his natural world, in the rule of moderation and the common proverbs of the marketplace: "Nor scour the seas, nor sift mankind," his Thoreauvian Muse advises him. As in "Merlin I" the opening of doors symbolizes a revelation of heavenly truth. But the Muse bluntly tells Saadi, "Those doors are men," and suddenly, for the poet who has not lifted a finger, men are transformed into gods—

> While thou sittest at thy door
> On the desert's yellow floor,
> Listening to the gray-haired crones,
> Foolish gossips, ancient drones,
> Saadi, see! they rise in stature
> To the height of mighty Nature,
> And the secret stands revealed
> Fraudulent Time in vain concealed,—
> That blessed gods in servile masks
> Plied for thee thy household tasks.

Not stars or a Chorus of Spirits, not the eternal ideas or sublime objects of nature, but ordinary life redeems the poet. . . .

. . . In a less touted achievement of these years, **"The Titmouse"** (written and published in 1862), Nature gives no explicit philosophy or lesson except the bird's example of cheerful stoicism in the face of great odds. The little titmouse echoes Saadi and the squirrel of **"Fable,"** and in keeping with the symbolist view of the world as flux, the "antidote of fear" is a matter of playing on words—of leaping to the great conceit that ends the poem, where the bird's song *"Chic-a-dee-dee"* is recast as Caesar's *"Veni, vidi, vici."* The essential transformation or metamorphosis in life is poetic, and we can make it if only we heed the moral of the poem:

> I think no virtue goes with size;
> The reason of all cowardice
> Is, that men are overgrown,
> And, to be valiant, must come down
> To the titmouse dimension.

Reduce! Simplify! Concentrate one's awareness—Thoreau was on Emerson's mind in the early spring of 1862—and thus accommodate the eye to the ordinary world. Were we to judge by **"The Titmouse"** alone, we might conclude that Emerson in later years had solved the problem of the "double consciousness" by trading in his "flash-of-lighting faith" on the continuous, if less spectacular, light of common day. For the great spiritual analogies of Correspondence, bequeathed by Nature in flashes of insight, have no place in this brief tale of wintry courage.

If the poems treated in this essay do represent his poetry as a whole, then clearly the pattern of Emerson's poetry corresponds to the more general development of his thought, moving away from a neat, formal organization toward a loosely connected, casual arrangement. Moreover, his major phase as a poet coincides with a period of growing doubt and detachment, so that these poems, in form as well as substance, show increasing signs of man's limitations, his perplexity in the face of incomprehensible nature, and, at best, his serenity despite his inability to comprehend. This is perhaps why Emerson's poetry appealed so much to Robert Frost—indeed, much of **"Hamatreya"** and a poem like **"The Titmouse"** are the essence of Frost—and why it is increasingly meaningful to the young and the nonspecialists who are often put off by his prose. Often the rhetoric of Emerson's essays is too assured, too conscious of the audience it manipulates, and Emerson seems to look down at us from his podium, himself a genteel Sphinx. His poetry was not this kind of performance, and here he is more commonly on our side, a less pretentious yet representative man, trying with us to sort out the terrible mysteries of this world.

If a single epithet can capture the special quality of Emerson's style, or the direction in which he moved, that one adjective might be "compressed": his tendency was toward compression in both form and consciousness, to concentrate on the small and common experience and relax the grander claims of the formulating intellect—in Emerson's phrase, to "come down to the titmouse dimension." It seems to me therefore that, granting the importance of an apocalyptic imagination and motif for some of Emerson's poems and most of his essays, nevertheless the poetry as a whole points away from that high Romantic vision. I suggest, too, that despite the established link between their ideas, Emerson and Whitman are very dissimilar poets, Whitman's cosmic consciousness and expansive verse standing almost at the extreme from Emerson's. Thus, Emerson's place in our tradition is not, with Whitman, at the head of the "Dionysian strain of American poetry" [Albert Gelpi, *Emily Dickinson: The Mind of the Poet*, 1965] for, as both [H. H.] Waggoner and [Leslie] Fiedler have observed, his poetry must register a very different influence from Whitman's, and in fact did, upon poets like Emily Dickinson, Stephen Crane, Robinson, and Frost, who are his direct descendants [Waggoner, *American Poets from the Puritans to the Present*, 1968, and Fielder, *Waiting for the End*, 1964]. Much as he contributed to Whitman's bardism, Emerson's more important legacy is his compressed style and the dramatic encounter between his small protagonist and unknowable Nature.

Donald Yannella (essay date 1982)

SOURCE: "Artful Thunder," in *Ralph Waldo Emerson*, Twayne Publishers, 1982, pp. 69-96.

[*Donald Yannella is an American educator and a scholar of nineteenth-century American Literature. In this excerpt he shows that while "not all are great" Emerson's poems are "technically accomplished works" worthy of a distinguished rank in American poetry. Yannella begins by interpreting Emerson's poetic theory as stated in "The Poet," and proceeds to explicate a selection of Emerson's poems grouped together thematically.*]

Emerson was forty-three years old when the first of his three volumes of poetry was issued on Christmas Day 1846. (It bears the publication date 1847.) Before any reader addresses himself to the verse, however, it is helpful to have some understanding of Emerson's theory of poetry and his views about the poet's purposes and functions. Properly understood, the poet and his art are central in the Transcendental fabric Emerson wove.

His interest in the subject began early—when he was a schoolboy, in fact—and grew with the years. He read widely and analytically, and was sensitive, discriminating, and articulate on the subject, as is evident from the great amount of space he devoted to aesthetic theory, poets, and poetry in his journals, letters, and lectures. In addition to these numerous references during the 1830s and early 1840s, as well as later, he offered one entire presentation, "The Poet," in the lecture series on "The Times" which he gave in 1841-42. But he made his most comprehensive and lasting utterance on the matter in the opening piece in *Essays: Second Series* (1844), also titled "The Poet." Here he presented the major portion of his mature thought on the role of the poet, as well as his theory of poetry.

In the essay Emerson states that the poet shares the Universe with two other children, the "Knower" and the "Doer," lovers of truth and goodness, respectively. The triumvirate is completed by the poet, the lover of beauty, the "Sayer," or "Namer." Emerson repeats the essential proposition of the Transcendental movement, that nature is symbolic, the universe emblematic; at the same time he reiterates the limitations of the Understanding, the path followed by the sensual man such as the scientist. And he concludes that although "The people fancy they hate poetry," they are, in fact, "all poets and mystics!"

This true poet, this arch-Transcendentalist, however, is discovered only infrequently. Not a mere "thinker," a "man of talent," he is "Man Thinking." His is the genius which will eradicate the ugly as he reintegrates those things which are dislocated and detached from God by perceiving their essential unity with nature and the Whole; the poet grasps the spiritual significance even of the factory-village, the railroad, and, of course, what is ordinarily comprehended as the natural world. By means of his superior insight the poet can induce a sort of transcendence, leading his reader to a vision similar to that described in the transparent eye-ball passage in *Nature*, among other places. Emerson confides that he himself experiences this kind of soaring when he reads a poem which he trusts as an inspiration: "And now my chains are to be broken; I shall mount above these clouds and opaque airs in which I live . . . and from the heaven of truth I shall see and comprehend my relations. . . . This day shall be better than my birthday: then I became an animal; now I am invited into the science of the real." In guiding us through nature, through experience, the poet "unlocks our chains and admits us to a new scene," leads us across the chasm to life and truth, and rescues us from the ironic fate of the "poor shepherd, who, blinded and lost in the snow-storm, perishes in a drift within a few feet of his cottage door." The ultimate, successful Transcendentalist, "the poet turns the world to glass, and shows us all things in their right series and procession." Poets are "liberating gods." Capable of that which all would rightly desire, they stand "among partial men for the complete man. . . . the man without impediment, who . . . traverses the whole scale of experience, and is representative of man, in virtue of being the largest power to receive and to impart." Representing beauty, the poet "is a sovereign, and stands on the centre." He is not merely an arranger, a compiler or composer of meters but a "diviner," a "prophetic speaker," whether in verse or prose, in the vatic tradition. For his conception Emerson was actually reaching back to the ancient notion of the bard, echoing conventional Romantic notions of the poet.

Emerson's poetic theory is intimately related to this conception of the poet. Perhaps the clearest and most widely known public statement he made on the theory of poetry was in the eighth paragraph of the essay "The Poet" where he announced that "it is not metres, but a metre-making argument that makes a poem,—a thought so passionate and alive that . . . it has an architecture of its own, and adorns nature with a new thing. The thought and the form are equal in the order of time, but in the order of genesis the thought is prior to the form." This precept that form is secondary probably helped inspire Whitman, for example, to be hospitable to the freedoms and new disciplines of *vers libre*. But the reader of Emerson's own poetry must be taken aback by his generally close adherence to his period's formal requirements, its conventions of verse. With few exceptions his poems scan easily and offer discernible rhyme schemes and regular line lengths.

His views on the technical requirements of verse are germane. In "Poetry and Imagination"—published in 1875, though portions were composed as early as the 1840s—for example, where he considers matters such as rhyme and meter, it is evident that he was in command of his materials and willing to insist on the conventions of English prosody because he understood their value, not because he accepted them blindly. He defends "the charm of rhyme to the ear" for the relief it offers from monotony and for the symmetry its very repetition provides. He also argues that the poet should allow poetry to "pass . . . into music and rhyme. . . . [which] is the transparent frame that allows almost the pure architecture of thought to become visible to the mental eye. Substance is much, but so are mode and form much." In a similar fashion he insists on the naturalness of meter by suggesting that "Metre begins with pulse-beat, and the length of lines in songs and poems is determined by the inhalation and exhalation of the lungs. If you hum or whistle the rhythm of the common English metres . . . you can easily believe these metres to be organic, derived from the human pulse, and to be therefore not proper to one nation, but to mankind." Since Emerson understood the conventions he observed in his own verse to be "organic," it seems unfair to criticize him for not realizing in his own poetry the innovations Whitman achieved.

My purpose in this [essay] is to discuss most of those poems which seem likely in my judgment to endure in the canon of American poetry. Certainly, not all are great. Many are of middling quality, some are uneven, and a few merely possess eminently quotable lines. What they do collectively, however, is demonstrate a more than respectable achievement in poetry by one of America's principal literary men.

To facilitate matters, particularly for those who are coming to Emerson's poetry for the first time, the poems are discussed within thematic groupings, the most important of which are the role of the poet, Man's relationship to nature, the public issues such as slavery which led to the Civil War, and personal subjects such as love and death. Although this arrangement seems preferable to a discussion of the development of Emerson's poetry in chronological order, my attempt to offer a coherent framework for sensible discussion should not—indeed, must not—preclude a reader's approaching any poem by a different avenue. My framework is a matter of convenience, not an attempt to fix Emerson's rich work in a set of categories.

"Merlin," one of the finest poems in the first collection, reveals Emerson's conception of the poet and his role, and also illustrates his reliance on the "renaissance tradition of paradoxy" [so called by Rosalie L. Colie in Paradoxical Epidemica: The Renaissance Tradition of Paradox, 1966]. The speaker opens "Merlin I" with a tight assertion of what is and is not the "artful thunder" of bardic poetry: "Its chords should ring as blows the breeze, / Free, peremptory, clear" in order to "make the wild blood start / In its mystic springs." Having told us in no uncertain terms in the first eight lines that form and style, however pleasing, do not constitute the poem, he proceeds

to describe the poet and his verse. Not merely a skilled and pleasing musician—a man of talent—this speaker's "kingly bard," Merlin, "Must smite the chords rudely and hard" in order to render organic poetry, the

> Artful thunder, which conveys
> Secrets of the solar track,
> Sparks of the supersolar blaze.

This bard, unencumbered "With the coil of rhythm and number," shall in his transcendence "'mount to paradise / By the stairway of surprise / /.'" Anticipating the theme of opposites to be explored at the start of "Merlin II," Emerson further defines the centrality of paradox to the workings of the bard. Beguiled by Sybarites—the wild dancers of the rituals of classical mythology—Merlin with his "mighty line / Extremes of nature reconciled."

The second poem commences by amplifying this pairing, the balancing and compensating Emerson dwells upon in both series of Essays: "Balance-loving Nature / Made all things in pairs." It is little wonder that Emerson should dismiss the verse of those he judged to be merely talented, jingle-men such as Poe. What he sought, as he stated it succinctly in "Poetry and Imagination," was "The original force, the direct smell of the earth or the sea" as he found them in ancient poetry: the Sagas, English and Scottish balladry, bardic poetry, and, to the point, "Gawain's parley with Merlin" in Morte d'Arthur, which he quotes at length.

He concludes "Merlin II" with an oblique yet incisive description of the price, the "ruin rife," the poet must pay for the genuine bardic experience—the paradox of Merlin, "music-drunken," surrendering his liberty and control to the Fates in order to achieve a more organic relationship with the universe and, therefore, the insight to prophecy. When we consider this paradox, we should recognize the happy balance Emerson strikes in the form of "Merlin." He comes quite close to his own ideal of "metre-making argument" by achieving a successful mixture of the accepted conventions of nineteenth-century verse: the Common Meter of the initial four lines of "Merlin I" and the traditional rhyme schemes and regular line lengths of most of both poems are set off opposite the skillful "irregularly rhymed 'free verse'" of the second stanza of "Merlin I."

Another of his most successful efforts to explore the poet and his art is "Bacchus" (1847). The speaker here seeks the same "wildest freedom" and ecstatic abandon suggested in the "Merlin" poems. Indeed, striving to cast off the restraints of the Understanding, mere common-sense perceptions of experience, the poet courts transcendence, a merging of his Self with creation "Which on the first day drew . . . The dancing Pleiads and eternal men." The importance of this god to Emerson's thinking is perhaps suggested by his reference more than a quarter-century later when he discussed transcendence near the end of "Poetry and Imagination": "O celestial Bacchus! drive them mad, this multitude of vagabonds, hungry for eloquence, hungry for poetry, starving for symbols, perishing for want of electricity." In the transcendent experience described in "Bacchus" and elsewhere there is a suggestion of what has been termed [by James E. Miller, Jr. in *A Critical Guide to Leaves of Grass* as] the "inverted mysticism" of Whitman's poetry: the achievement of merger and vision not through asceticism but by means of bathing in sensual experience. This aspect of Emerson is beautifully articulated in the colloquial and pithy **"Berrying"** (1847), one of his better short poems, in which he uses Calvinist theology to assert the hedonism of the speaker. The irony of the speaker's discovering "dreams thus beautiful" and "wisdom" in the "Ethiops sweet" drives home with singular force his rejection of his Puritan forebears' conception of earth as "a howling wilderness" [as noted by Carl F. Strauch in "Emerson and the Doctrine of sympathy," *Studies in Romanticism* 6 (1967):158].

But the exhilaration, or even ecstasy, enjoyed by the genuine poet requires that he suffer detachment from other men. **"Saadi"** (1842), Emerson's tribute to the Persian author he so admired, is one of his clearest poetic expressions of the loneliness and promise of the poet. Writing for the most part in octosyllabic couplets, Emerson commences the poem in rather breathless, short lines and immediately justifies the bard's aloofness by tracing it back to God's charge that the poet "'Sit aloof.'" Saadi, who "dwells alone," nevertheless loves Mankind. With the integrity of the scholar Emerson had described in his Phi Beta Kappa address, the poet ignores the din of life, reads his runes rightly, minds only his rhyme and listens solely to the whisper of the Muse: "Heed not what the brawlers say, / Heed thou only Saadi's lay." Detachment and commitment are, of course, prerequisites for the conventional Romantic sort of insight and inspiration, but they assure that the poet's words will reveal "Terror and beauty" as well as "Nature veritable." The upshot, the Muse promises, will be the opening of "innumerable doors" from which truth and goodness will flow, and so the poet will be admitted to the "perfect Mind." The promise and the poem conclude with a suggestion that the ultimates sought by the poet reside in the commonplace, the "crones," "gossips," "drones" who "rise in stature / To the height of mighty Nature" to reveal the secret "Fraudulent Time in vain concealed": "That blessed gods in servile masks / Plied for thee thy household tasks." If **"Saadi"** is not one of Emerson's more memorable poetic statements, it is one of his more forthright expressions on the subject, purpose, and means available to the poet. . . .

It is clear that the Transcendental experience in its widest definition is the subject of most of Emerson's poetry. Some of his best recounts the substance of the poet's nonrational encounter with the "Not-Me," as he phrased the world beyond Self in *Nature,* and others explore the dangers and pain of the role itself. Many more, also successful and enduring, focus on nature, including Man's connections to it. Some celebrate Man's right relation to nature while others criticize the materialism of modern culture which distorts life by precluding our having healthy links to the natural world. Two of the more enduring among the earlier nature poems are **"Each and All"** (1839) and **"The Snow-Storm"** (1841).

Judged [by Carl F. Strauch in "The Year of Emerson's Poetic Maturity: 1834," *Philological Quarterly*, No. 34,

1955] to be Emerson's "first unquestionably great poem," **"The Snow-Storm"** was written during the winter of 1834-35. The first of its two stanzas of blank verse offers a general description of the arriving snow as it "veils the farm-house at the garden's end"; notes a foundered sled and the traveler it carries; and, finally, locates the speaker and the reader in the cozy warmth of a classic country homestead inhabited by people seated about "the radiant fireplace, enclosed / In a tumultuous privacy of storm." What Emerson presents here is the conventional setting for the traditional event celebrated in so much New England poetry, the snow-storm. The nineteen lines which comprise the second stanza are among the most vivid and artistically wrought performances in poetic imagery in Emerson's canon. The artist of the passage, the north wind, "Curves his white bastions with projected roof / Round every windward stake, or tree, or door." Then "Mockingly, / On coop or kennel he hangs Parian wreaths; / A swan-like form invests the hidden thorn." The familiar world is enhanced and mystified not randomly or by chance but consciously by art; with dazzling simplicity Emerson conjures up the classic and gleaming white statuary of ancient Greece by referring to the famed marbles of the island of Paros, which is similar to the snowed-in farm not only in its statues but in its pristine artifacts. The stormy, wild, creative period finished, the northwind

> Leaves, when the sun appears, astonished Art
> To mimic in slow structures, stone by stone,
> Built in an age, the mad wind's night-work,
> The frolic architecture of the snow.

As the poem challenges materialism it celebrates the nourishment provided Man by sympathetic communion with nature.

"Each and All," another of the poems composed in 1834—the year which probably was a turning-point in Emerson's poetic development—is another of the finest products of his early career. Composed of only fifty-one lines, it signals a major advance in his perception of Man's relation to nature; by using Reason rather than Understanding the poet perceives unity amid the diversity of the world. Emerson has moved beyond the awe which the natural world inspired among contemporaries who merely observed and classified, and has come to sense a profound if unspoken resonance in nature.

The poem is traditional and conventional in its meters, its logical tripartite structure, and its virtually unrelieved rhymed, occasionally closed, couplets; only three lines are without mates and only the eight lines which commence the final section slip into an *ababcded* pattern. Emerson wisely balances the formality of the technique, however, with the commonplace and simple—but nevertheless evocative—inhabitants of nature. Following his observation that "All are needed by each one; / Nothing is fair or good alone"—a principle which emerges from his observation that nature's creatures, including Man, indeed affect each other—he proceeds to test the proposition by nothing the discordance, even the ugliness, of the sparrow, the seashell, and the bride when they are wrenched from their natural settings. This is one facet of the truth he covets in line 37, the beginning of the third and final part of the poem; penetrating the wood more deeply—encountering on a sensual level the ground-pine, club-moss burrs, violets, oaks, and acorns, as well as the sky, the river, and the morning bird—he reports that "Beauty through my senses stole; / I yielded myself to the perfect whole." In this celebratory and rising couplet we hear a suggestion of the same sort of Transcendental sympathy, even merging, he was to detail so often. If the psychological and spiritual significances and nuances are not uttered here, as they so frequently are in his later writings, it is probably because the experience is novel. But, of course, Emerson was never able or even desirous to reduce the Transcendental experience to the terms of the Understanding; such an attempt, even if conceivable, would necessarily have been frustrated. This reluctance is central in his poetry and should be borne in mind. Emerson frequently prefers to suggest rather than state. . . .

[Emerson's] hero was neither bumpkin nor slicker, but the reconciler of the pastoral and urban, the cosmopolitan who by carrying the lesson of nature to the cities would alter the patterns of life they were developing.

—*Donald Yannella*

One issue which every serious reader must at some time confront is the degree to which Emerson's pastoralism turned him against the developments of urban industrialism in nineteenth-century America. Of course, his dilemma has been shared by intellectuals and artists, including serious writers, since the advent of the industrial revolution. Emerson, as we have seen, has generally been viewed as a figure in the agrarian tradition. His Romantic bias, with its implicit rejection of materialism, has been interpreted as an attempt by him and his fellow Transcendentalists to recapture a sense of awe in the face of nature, a sense of wonder which materialistic urban industrialism had stolen from them. The question can also be explored from a different stance that questions this judgment that Emerson was categorically hostile to the city, an arch-symbol of life in the nineteenth century. The suggestion is that Emerson's observation of the dichotomy between the city and nature was not a conclusion but a point of departure for his hope that the city would become more organically related to nature. His hero was neither bumpkin nor slicker, but the reconciler of the pastoral and urban, the cosmopolitan who by carrying the lesson of nature to the cities would alter the patterns of life they were developing. In short, Emerson was no Huck Finn turning his back on the facts of modern life and lighting out for the territory. He was a realist who confronted the facts of nineteenth-century life but whose vision sprang from the high expectations of an optimistic Romantic. He was as open to the possibilities of the proper development of the

city as he was to the potentials of machine power and even the factory system. In neither case, though, would Emerson tolerate the materialism which resulted in the absurdity of the machine riding humanity, or the city defining life. Which brings us to a few other pieces in which Emerson celebrates Man's right relations with nature. . . .

"Woodnotes" (1840-41) has been judged [by Joseph Warren Beach in *The Concept of Nature in Nineteenth-Century English Poetry*, 1936] to be Emerson's "great comprehensive nature-poem." It is a work of some 460 lines in two parts and relies almost exclusively on octosyllabic couplets. Perfectly traditional in its prosody, it is essentially—at least in the form which Emerson arrived at by the 1876 edition—a celebration of Man's proper relation to Nature. His affirmations are enhanced by the contrasts supplied by several passages in which Man's being out of tune with the cosmos is described. For example, the fifth stanza of "Woodnotes II" commences with an invitation in the voice of the poet to learn with him "the fatal song / Which knits the world in music strong." He sustains the appropriate music metaphor—which he repeatedly sounds when handling Man's relations with the rest of creation—to the point that "Nature beats in perfect tune." This is the reality. But at the same time Man is admonished— "The wood is wiser far than thou." Man, the "poor child! unbound, unrhymed," has somehow in the evolutionary process been "divorced, deceived and left"; he remains undernourished, sickly,

An exile from the wilderness,—
The hills where health with health agrees,
And the wise soul expels disease.

In a word—the one Emerson employs in the first line of the sixth stanza—Man suffers from "bankruptcy" moral, spiritual, emotional, and intellectual. The condition is clearly due to ills such as the "city's poisoning spleen" which had been cited near the beginning of stanza 2 of this second section.

But "Woodnotes," both parts, is largely a celebration of Man's right relation to nature, an exploration of the processes—the surrenders—necessary for him to establish communion and a description of the rewards he will enjoy if he does. Slow-paced and, frankly, prolix and belabored at times, the poem is a Transcendentalist's celebration. Like the titmouse, the pine tree which serves as the subject of the first line of "Woodnotes I" and predominates in "Woodnotes II" serves as a unifying symbol and is key in the illumination which takes place. In short, the lesson offered by the small, commonplace pine—by its very existence and through its hints and bold statements— is crucial to the enlightenment of the consciousness which engages it. In "Woodnotes" as in other poems the poet is not a shaper of nature but rather a seer looking into her.

There is no equivocation in Emerson's establishing the poet at home in the forest. His engagement is simple, physical, and, indeed, Romantic; a "Lover of all things alive," he is a "Wonderer at all he meets, / Wonderer chiefly at himself." At this point the communing poet is cast in the image of Rousseau's awe-struck child during his first encounter with the natural world. Section 2 of **"Woodnotes I"** further describes the vital connections enjoyed by this "forest seer." Sensitive to and knowledgeable about virtually all facets of nature, he is privy to its secrets as well as its revelations, its common and too frequently overlooked phenomena and occurences. Further, the enchanted, even magical, dimensions of this primal engagement are suggested. It is, "As if by secret sight he knew / Where, in far fields, the orchis grew." The phallic suggestion implicit in "orchis" reinforces the vital, vigorous, nonrational dimensions of the experience. This man is no mere naturalist seeking to classify, no slave to the Understanding. He is the "pilgrim wise," the "philosopher" who receives the secrets of the partridge, woodcock, thrush, and hawk—creatures who are only dimly perceived at a distance by ordinary people.

Prosodically, section 3 of the first part stands unique in the poem. Setting aside the octosyllabic couplets he relies on for virtually the entire poem, Emerson moves into chanting pentameters. In tracing the steps of the forest seer he presents the range and poignancy of his experience in the direct fashion of the catalogue: the Maine wilderness, the forest inhabited by the moose, bear, woodpecker, pine. The seer witnesses the lumberman's felling the noble tree, but unlike the exploiters of the wood (plunderers such as the rapacious tribe of Aaron Thousandacres in Cooper's *Chainbearer* and the lumber interests which laid bare the land Faulkner's Isaac McCaslin had known) Emerson's "wise man is at home, / His hearth the earth." In nature he is as much in tune and as reverent as Thoreau, Natty Bumppo, and most of Romanticism's heroes, especially the Americans. His "clear spirit" is "By God's own light illumined and foreshadowed."

Section 4, in which Emerson returns to his ballad measure, climaxes the celebration of Man's harmony in nature. The simple, "musing peasant" who is at the "heart of all the scene" testifies to his utter surrender to the forest and to the spirit which inhabits it. Even in death Mother Nature will embrace, enfold this child as he returns to her arms.

Crucial to the entire poem is the quatrain which introduces **"Woodnotes II"**:

> *As sunbeams stream through liberal space*
> *And nothing jostle or displace,*
> *So waved the pine-tree through my thought*
> *And fanned the dreams it never brought.*
> (Emerson's italics)

The illumination of the receptive consciousness by this humble and commonplace representative of nature, the pine tree, is strikingly captured by means of the sunbeam reference. The pine beckons and enlightens the man, nourishes and sustains him as the sun's rays warm the world. This earth-rooted creature announces the democracy so central to Emerson's thought: "The rough and bearded forester / Is better than the lord." Further, in the evolution of humanity and spirit—creation in general—"The lord is the peasant that was, / The peasant the lord that shall be."

But vitality, youth, vigor are, at least for the time being, the peasant's. In the second stanza the tree announces the services it offers to him who will exist in harmony with it. More important, of course, is the moral and spiritual sustenance it promises the person who eschews the distorting and corrupting influences of the civilized world which his race has created, and embraces the pristine and virtuous natural world: "Into that forester shall pass . . . power and grace." The Mother will protect the "formidable innocence" of her child.

The ecstasy of the wood-god's song intensifies in the third stanza as it offers the "mystic song / Chanted when the sphere was young." Time and space are suspended as the "paean," the song of thanksgiving, rises, "swells." And we are brought back to the "genesis," "The rushing metamorphosis" when fixed nature dissolves and "Melts things that be to things that seem, / And solid nature to a dream." The "chorus of the ancient Causes," however, may not be heard by ordinary mortals whose ears are of stone. Only the pure—the surrendering, transcending seers—may hear it.

The song nears its crescendo as we are invited to compose with the pine a "nobler rhyme." Despite the nationalistic note Emerson injects near the beginning of stanza 4—"Only thy Americans / Can read thy line, can meet thy glance"—the condition the pine has celebrated knows no national boundaries.

In stanza 5, after describing in scorning terms the plight, the tragedy of most people, who are out of tune with the cosmos, Emerson chants the virtues and advantages of the person who will fall into harmony with it and "outsee seers, and outwit sages." The external truth is that "A divine improvisation, / From the heart of God proceeds." Forever evolving, the "eternal Pan" reincarnates itself in "new forms." In describing the Deity in this last and longest stanza of the poem, Emerson reaches for a variety of metaphors: He is the pourer of the precious, nourishing beverage; He is the life-bearing bee, the wide-ranging sheep. Finally, at the end of the pine's increasingly mystical chant, Emerson slips into the abstractions, metaphors, and paradoxes traditional to the explanations of mystics, theologians, and poets:

> Thou metest him by centuries,
> And lo! he passes like the breeze;
> Thou seek'st in globe and galaxy,
> He hides in pure transparency;
> Thou askest in fountains and in fires,
> He is the essence that inquires.
> He is the axis of the star;
> He is the sparkle of the spar;
> He is the heart of every creature;
> He is the meaning of each feature;
> And his mind is the sky.
> Than all it holds more deep, more high.

The nonrational dimension which Emerson has delved into here is impossible to reduce to rational terms. The Transcendental experience he attempts to verbalize plummets to earth the moment it is penetrated and collapsed to ordinary, comprehensible terms. Riddling is evident from the questions posed throughout the poem. How often does wisdom reside in the poignant and penetrating, if unanswerable, question? How frequently is the wise answer in fact a puzzle? Which brings us to the riddle of **"The Sphinx."**

Emerson's regard for **"The Sphinx"** (1841) was probably best expressed by his using it as the lead poem in his first collection. Certainly one of his most enduring poems, and probably one of his greatest, **"The Sphinx"** should be viewed as an expression of the poet's conception of himself as riddler—a revealer of whatever truth he perceives and reports by means of paradox—and as an exploration of the "disjunction between man and nature."

First published in 1841, the poem is more mystical and baffling than most of Emerson's more difficult verse. The sense of eternity and timelessness which emerges near the end of **"Woodnotes II"** is apparent from the first stanza of **"The Sphinx."** From time immemorial, while the ages have "slumbered and slept," the drowsy Sphinx has awaited the seer who will reveal her secret to her. The eternal questions are posed: "'The fate of the man-child, / The meaning of man.'" Man is the culminating and most apparent creature, the fruit or upshot of the "unknown"— the force, spirit, motive—at the center of the cosmos. And the scheme or plan which has produced him is Daedalian, one of cunning artifice. The life cycle is called forth in the second quatrain of the stanza: "Out of sleeping a waking"—nonentity and being are not appropriate substitutes for these metaphors, from the Transcendental point of view—and then back to sleep; death, at least physical death, overtakes life, which is itself another layer of mystery, or "deep," beneath the first.

Beginning with stanza 3, Emerson rehearses the harmony of creation. The palm, elephant, thrush, waves, breezes, atoms exist in mutual and perfect unity, inspirited by the universal being "By one music enchanted, / One deity stirred." The human dimension emerges in stanza 6. The babe appears; the Rousseauistic child of conventional Romanticism, even of Platonism, is "bathèd in joy" and "Without cloud, in its eyes." Naturally, it functions and flourishes on a harmonious, integrated, and nonrational level, basking in an essential and all-too-often ignored sustainer of life itself, such as the sun.

But in the next stanza Man out of tune with the cosmos appears; he "crouches and blushes, / Absconds and conceals"—"An oaf, an accomplice, / He poisons the ground." In stanza 8 the sphinx asks who is responsible for Man's fallen state, the "sadness and madness" from which her boy suffers. The analysis—if it might be called such—of the poet commences in stanza 9. First he blames the "Lethe of Nature": While Man's soul might see or sense perfection and long for a harmonious sharing with the universal spirit which inhabits the rest of creation, animate and inanimate, he nevertheless cannot effect his natural desire: "his eyes seek in vain." Perhaps, the poet suggests, the perfection he instinctively seeks is out of reach; life is in fact a series of plateaus, spires, ever-evolving circles,

the attainment of one inevitably leading him to desire the next "vision profounder" which once found he will spurn in his desire for "new heavens." In his attempt to explain, or at least understand, this poet admits that he himself suffers from the condition and wishes, for example, that his lover were more noble than to settle on him as the object of affection, attraction, aspiration. The flux, the flow, the unceasing evolution of the cosmos are expressed succinctly with "Eterne alternation." The reassurance of Transcendental faith, however, is offered: "Love works at the centre, / Heart-heaving alway."

The ultimate meaning of the poem does not lie in the all-too-facile explanations of this poet. Rather, it resides in the concluding four stanzas in which the poet—who is not to be identified with Emerson—concludes his answer to the sphinx; she in turn responds; and the narrator-poet—who is close to Emerson if not him—forms what conclusion he can from what he reports as having transpired.

There is clearly an underlying superciliousness and an almost comic self-confidence in the reductive simplicity in the answer of the poet—who is not to be confused with the narrator-poet. It is captured tersely in his conclusion, where he addresses her as "Dull Sphinx" and observes that her "sight is growing blear"—recall the babe's clarity of vision, noted above. He even presumes to prescribe the remedy "Her muddy eyes to clear!" The sphinx, the eternal symbol of silent wisdom, rebukes the insolent, even arrogant fellow who would reduce mystery to logical explanation. The point is that what she reveals is not at all clear. Her statement does not unequivocally answer or attempt to correct the poet's explanation. What insight revealed by Reason can ever be so expressed? Rather the sphinx turns the question on him: You yourself, poet, are the "unanswered question" and if you are capable of seeing that, keep asking it, even though you will know beforehand that each successive answer will in fact be a lie. The signs of wisdom are awe in the face of the mystery, appropriate humility and respect.

If the merry poet is not capable of recognizing the justice of the sphinx's good-humored assault on his explanation, the narrator—presumably Emerson—is more than able. For him the sphinx soars into symbol; she and her message inspirit, illuminate, and in fact merge with the representatives of physical actuality—some startling, some commonplace, but all finally wondrous by virtue of her: stone, cloud, moon, flame, blossom, wave, and mountain. She herself becomes the poet and offers hope to Mankind: "'Who telleth one of my meanings / Is master of all I am'" and the telling simply cannot be on the common-sense level of the Understanding. Rationalism, the curse of modern Man, is the cause of his being out of harmony with the cosmos. Reason, the nonrational, is the way to wisdom. This is the secret shared by the sphinx and the genuine poet—the poet as distinct from the verse-maker. As *Dichter, vates,* the inspired and wise speaker of riddles, the poet offers truth—reality—and also secures to the degree possible a right relation to the baffling mysteries of the universe and existence.

The variety of Emerson's response to the natural world would not be appreciated were the reader to ignore the joyful lightness of the colloquial, homespun narrative of **"The Adirondacs"** (1867), a work which reflects his later mellowness and stands in contrast to his Transcendental madness. On its most elementary level the poem records the pleasure experienced by Emerson and his fellows in the Adirondack Club during the 1850s. In recounting the holiday of 1858, he celebrates in a fashion almost cliché the beauty and serenity of the wilderness and the group's shared sense of relief from everyday, insubstantial cares. This is the voice of homespun, laced with a keen sense of the comic:

> Hard fare, hard bed and comic misery,—
> The midge, the blue-fly and the mosquito
> Painted our necks, hands, ankles, with red bands.

Reading even on this level, however, one has to wince at the incongruity, even fatuousness of the joy with which the Transcendentalist reports the vacationers' response to the news that the transatlantic cable has finally been laid. The importance of whether the Princess Adelaide has the whooping cough, the poignant and pointed question raised by Thoreau earlier in the decade, seems of no concern to our speaker in stanzas 17 and 18. Rather, there is a certain resignation—one has to strain too hard to capture an ironic tone—as he accepts his own and his fellows' limited horizons, their apparent inability or lack of desire to engage nature with other than the Understanding. The crowd included the naturalist Louis Agassiz and the comparative anatomist Jeffries Wyman. Stanza 19 commences:

> We flee away from cities, but we bring
> The best of cities with us, these learned classifiers,
> Men knowing what they seek, armed eyes of
>   experts.

The holidays end and civilization intrudes as it simply could not upon the genuine Transcendental experiences he had recorded a decade or two earlier:

> And Nature, the inscrutable and mute,
> Permitted on her infinite repose
> Almost a smile to steal to cheer her sons,
> As if one riddle of the Sphinx were guessed.

It is not unfair to suggest that the sense of mystery held forth by the Sphinx of the earlier poem is at best tolerantly alluded to here; it seems no longer to be really desired. As in poems such as **"Monadnoc"** (1847), **"Musketaquid"** (1847), **"Waldeinsamkeit"** (1858), and **"May-Day"** (1867), the sense of mystery and awe is absent, the bardic chants have been abandoned. In this poem a mellower, warmer Emerson, now fifty-five, offers us a Romantic tenderfoot's sensual experience; absent is the burning need for Reason to command and transcendence to occur. The lesson of the guides, the wilderness men of stanzas 7 and 8, is less a model of engagement with nature and of pristine virtue than a homespun alternative to the perfectly acceptable ways of life of the "polished gentlemen," the "Ten scholars" in whose company Emerson enjoys his

recreation. In short, the civilized and the wilderness seem to have been reconciled in the glow of late middle age.

Not all of Emerson's poetry concerns Man's relations with nature or the art of the poet. Among what promise to be the more enduring works, there are several which contemplate and speak to the issues which gave rise to the Civil War, and several others which articulate deeply felt personal experiences, notably the death of his son Waldo. In addition there is a small gathering of poems for public occasions, the best of which is the **"Concord Hymn."**

The work Emerson placed last in his first collection, **"Concord Hymn"** was first sung at the celebration marking the completion of the Revolutionary War battle monument on which it is carved. A public, patriotic utterance, first delivered on July 4, 1837, the poem stands—and rightly so—as one of the most memorable of its genre. Composed of four quatrains in octosyllabics, it begins with an inspiring tribute to the "embattled farmers" who "fired the shot heard round the world"—one of Emerson's better remembered lines. The second stanza notes the passage of time and the attending change which has been wrought; the third focuses on the events of the commemoration; and the final quatrain sings the message which is the principal purpose of the poem: "Bid Time and Nature gently spare / The shaft we raise." The most remarkable quality of this dignified public poem is its restraint, its controlled emotion and skillful avoidance of mawkish patriotism.

Slavery is one of the thematic groupings in which we find some excellent poems as well as some of moderate success. The **"Ode: Inscribed to W. H. Channing"** (1847) has as its primary concern the materialism which informed the political arena inhabited by Daniel Webster. The poem employs tight, emotionally charged dimeters and trimeters and what is best described as erratic rhyming, both of which communicate the intensity of Emerson's feelings on the subject. The first two stanzas in effect apologize for or justify the distance Emerson chose to keep from the political fray. Neither the "priest's cant" nor the "statesman's rant" will force him to abandon his "honied thought." Indeed, if he leaves his study "The angry Muse / Puts confusion in [his] brain." Emerson will simply not raise the specter of compromise, which would open the possibility of his wavering from a position of principle.

Following this self-justification, the voice launches into an angry, actually sneering, attack on Webster. It commences with a rhetorical question regarding the master politician's empty and foolish lip service to "the culture of mankind, / Of better arts and life?" This is unconscionable prating at a time the expansionist government in its hunger for territory is "Harrying Mexico." More malign than the shortsighted and foolish men of **"Guy"** and **"Hamatreya,"** these materialists are cut from the same cloth as the "jackals" who hold slaves, "little men" before whom "Virtue palters; Right is hence; / Freedom praised, but hid." Reptilian imagery, carrying reference to the betrayal in the Eden myth, winds throughout the poem: "blindworm," "snake," even "stolen fruit." But the climax of Emerson's moral censure and contempt comes in stanzas 6 and 7, which conclude with two of his most memorable lines: "Things are in the saddle, / And ride mankind." The upshot of this gross and callous materialism is that man is unkinged, the "law for thing[s] . . . runs wild." Expansion, commerce, development, and exploitation have become ends in and of themselves. The tone of the last two stanzas is more restrained, prophetic. Emerson is not calling upon the "wrinkled shopman" to commune with nature, nor is he asking the powerful senator to "Ask votes of thrushes in the solitudes." Rather, with the calm assurance of the reflecting and principled Transcendentalist, he is predicting that Freedom will carry the war if not the battle. Flux, change, balance, compensation will right the wrongs. Ultimately, the affairs of the nation will be in the hands of leaders and followers who will be better than the "little men" with whom "The God who made New Hampshire [has] / Taunted the lofty land. . . ."

A few poems which should continue to stand the test of time are autobiographical and reveal the deep stress to which Emerson was subjected during his great creative period in the 1830s and 1840s.

"Threnody" (1847), one of his most personal utterances, is an elegy which bares the emotional pain he suffered when his five-year-old son, Waldo, died early in 1842; it is also a remarkable illustration of the fervor and depth of the poet's Transcendentalism. A fine example of the binary form he favored, the first part sounds the poet's lament and the second expresses what reconciliation, if not consolation, the "deep Heart" offers to assuage the singer's wound. Neither the poem nor the philosophical acceptance of the child's death which it chants was hastily or easily won, as is evident from the slow and difficult development of its sentiments in the journals and letters of the period.

The poem, which is for the most part composed in Emerson's favorite octosyllabic couplets, begins by announcing without irony that, in effect, April is indeed the cruellest month. There is literally no distinction between Emerson and a persona as he reports that the South-wind cannot alter the passing of Waldo, "The darling who shall not return." The poet's anguish is expressed in the commonplace realities—the "empty house"—and vital recollections—Waldo's "silver warble wild"—with which he is left. Most effective in the second stage, and pertinent to the entire poem, is the language of the pulsing, dazzling life which he uses to describe the "wondrous child," the "hyacinthine boy." Stanza 3 asks, among other questions, where the boy is and recalls the enchanting effect he had on the lives he touched, and the next two stanzas are even more specific as Emerson recollects the lad's activities and confronts the emblems of him which remain: the "painted sled," "gathered sticks," "The ominous hole he dug in the sand." And then he offers what becomes an intense and bewildered account of the uninterrupted natural process, which leads him into the transitional passage in which he questions whether there might have been a "watcher," an "angel," in the universe which "Could stoop to heal that only child, / Nature's sweet marvel undefiled." There follows a long section of introspection and a search for philosophical and psychological distinction in which the mourner wonders if, indeed, "Perchance not he but Nature ailed, / The world and not the infant failed." Perhaps the world "was not ripe yet to sustain / A genius of so fine a strain." The eighth stanza, which concludes the first part of the poem, reveals a despairing, confused, and bitter speaker, a man "too much bereft" who can only chant:

> O truth's and nature's costly lie!
> O trusted broken prophecy!
> O richest fortune sourly crossed!

The next two stanzas present the answer of the "deep Heart" which begins with a stern though not scolding response to the anguish of the grieving parent. There is no reason to question Emerson's sincerity in describing the wisdom which sustains him during this period of terrible loss, although readers who seem more emotional than philosophical might wonder at the toughness of the reconciliation. It was a reconciliation, however, won after great difficulty and should even be viewed as an ultimate test of the bereaved father's Transcendental faith. (He addressed the problem in the essay "Experience," which explains some of the thinking necessary to understand the poem.) Beneath his stoicism lies the foundation of compensation and the many other supports of the philosophical system—if it may be labeled such—Emerson had constructed. The wisdom born of speculation and experience was not only hard won but genuine. In a moment of severest test, the death of a loved one—one of the several losses he had endured—the underpinnings he had placed served him well. He did not collapse.

The statement of the "Heart" in **"Threnody"** is conventionally Emersonian. It asks, "But thou, my votary, weepest thou? / I gave thee sight—where is it now?" There is a reason, although it is beyond Man's ability to grasp it. The tone of the Heart softens, however, in the final stanza as it calls the mourner's attention to the larger process, the inevitable flux, of nature and then asks two poignant, rhetorical questions, positive answers to which would be absurd:

> Wilt thou freeze love's tidal flow,
> Whose streams through Nature circling go?
> Nail the wild star to its track
> On the half-climbed zodiac?

Change is at the center of the evolving universe, change from which nothing can escape. Emerson relies on a group of organic metaphors to define this evolution born of flux: "bending reeds, / Flowering grass and scented weeds." If this cannot be reduced to rational terms, to the context of Understanding, so much the better. It is in fact a matter of Reason, of faith; the poet is admonished to "Revere the Maker," who rushes silently "Through ruined systems still restored." Appropriately enough, the paradox of the last line—"Lost in God, in Godhead found"—is introduced by the images of death and larger vision which are joined in the two preceding lines of the poem: "Apples of Eden ripe to-morrow. / House and tenant go to ground"

The stoicism and organicism of **"Threnody"** offer one avenue to the appreciation of **"Give All to Love"** (1847). One senses the same depth of feeling here as in the lament for the dead Waldo. After describing in rather abstract terms the intensity of the emotion and the rightness of surrender, Emerson cautions, "Yet, hear me, yet." Anticipate, prepare for her fleeing by accepting it and recognizing that despite the immediate and apparent pain which the beloved's departure causes, her leaving is natural, even inevitable. Rightly understood, it is even an occasion for rejoicing for new insight: "When half-gods go"— that is, earthly love departs—"The gods arrive" with their wisdom born of Reason. Stoic perhaps even to the point of coldness, the sentiment is from the same Transcendental fabric as that of **"Threnody."**

There is no more fitting work than "Terminus" with which to end this discussion of Emerson's poetry. Although it was collected in *May-Day and Other Pieces* in 1867, it probably was composed in the 1850s, shortly after the burst of poetic activity which preceded the publication of the first collection of poems. **"Terminus"** is a weary and gentle poem, movingly honest and, it seems, overly modest in its assessment of Emerson's own gifts and accomplishments. The fires which had ignited his imagination are at least banked. The poem commences with a lamentation that "It is time to be old, / To take in sail," and he announces that what power has inspired him, "The god of bounds," has ordered him

> No more!
> No farther shoot
> Thy broad ambitious branches, and thy root

The organic metaphor is appropriate; the sense of limit and failing potential is scarcely redeemed by the suggestion that the poet will "Mature the unfallen fruit," perhaps such poems as **"The Adirondacs"** and **"The Titmouse."** More touching and disturbing is the sense of failure which concludes the first stanza. Of course, Emerson is referring to his lineage here, but more important he is describing his own ambivalence, his suspension, which caused his lack of success "Amid the gladiators" of the world of action as well as "Amid the Muses" who left him "deaf and dumb." This is not merely false modesty, a clever if transparent bid for contradiction by the reader, but it might betray a disturbing lack of comprehension of his achievement, or it might even suggest that the piece was composed during a period of deep depression. The bleakness of the poem is scarcely redeemed by the resignation one hears in the last stanza—"I trim myself to the storm of time"—or by the stoic fortitude recommended by the words of the god which conclude the poem:

> Lowly faithful, banish fear,
> Right onward drive unharmed;
> The port, well worth the cruise, is near,
> And every wave is charmed.

The number of Emerson's poems which have endured, and those which might continue to, may be modest. But then, aside from the giants of English poetry who reign as strongly today as they have in the past centuries—Chaucer, Shakespeare, Milton certainly—is Emerson's achievement significantly less than that of others in the second and third tiers of the English poetic tradition? Probably not. Although one early critic [W.T. Harris] undoubtedly overstated the case when he suggested that Emerson's poetry would probably outlast his prose, among American poets Emerson does deserve, by virtue of those remarkably intense and technically accomplished works discussed in this chapter, to hold a place equal to that of our dozen most important poets. At least, to cite a cliché among students of American Romanticism, if Emerson is "not our greatest writer," he is "our only inescapable one. . . . Denied or scorned, he turns up again in every opponent, however orthodox, classical, conservative or even just Southern" [Harold Bloom in *The Ringers in the Tower*, 1971]. True as this less than faint praise may be—and it is perhaps a strategy of defense which the reader should hear with irony—the fact remains that Emerson at his best gave us some of our finest poems.

Eduardo Cadava   (essay date 1993)

SOURCE: "The Nature of War in Emerson's 'Boston Hymn,'" in *Arizona Quarterly*, Vol. 49, No. 3, Autumn, 1993, pp. 21-58.

[*In this excerpt Cadava discusses the relation between historical events and Emerson's poem, "The Boston Hymn," focusing on Emerson's response to the Emancipation Proclamation, abolition, and the moral necessity for the Civil War as factors in the poem's creation. Cadava also links Emerson's presentation of God and use of natural imagery to Puritan concepts.*]

Less than five years before the outbreak of the Civil War, Emerson announces a crisis in the structures of political and linguistic representation. "Language has lost its meaning in the universal cant," he writes, "*Representative Government* is misrepresentative; *Union* is a conspiracy against the Northern States which the Northern States are to have the privilege of paying for; the *adding of Cuba and Central America* to the slave marts is *enlarging the area of Freedom. Manifest Destiny, Democracy, Freedom*, fine names for a ugly thing." He makes this statement within the context of the controversy over the Kansas-Nebraska Act. This Act had repealed the Missouri Compromise and legislated that the question of slavery be determined by individual state constitutions rather than by a national policy of exclusion. For Emerson, that slavery is to be preserved and extended signals a contradiction in the meaning of America, a contradiction that is dissimulated within a rhetoric of representation, democracy, and freedom. Declaring the rhetorical and historical basis of the virtues upon which America was to be founded, Emerson here predicts the crisis of representation that would define the issues over which the coming war would be fought. These issues included debates over who could claim the right to representation and over the relations of power existing between state and federal governments within the system of representation. The crisis to which Emerson refers is therefore a crisis written into the history of America, insofar as America was itself conceived in various efforts to rethink and define the nature and concept of representation.

As Emerson suggests, however, this crisis in political representation is inseparable from the acts of representation that would soon render, and sometimes justify, the suffering and death brought on by the war. What interests him are the various rhetorical means whereby the war or its ideological implications are legitimated. Throughout the war, his lectures, essays, poems, and journal entries persistently challenge the tendencies of contemporary representations of the war either to justify the effects of its violence or to have them disappear in the name of the ideological discourses that helped both the North and the South negotiate the meaning of the war even before it had ended. We should not be surprised if, within this arena of representation, Emerson's attention focuses upon the recourse to a rhetoric of nature. Both Union and Confederate soldiers and civilians enlisted nature in the service of legitimating their respective causes as well as the war's violence. Moreover, the rhetoric of nature was central to the constitution of a nationalist ideology in the antebellum period. Insofar as this rhetoric attempts to dissimulate the violence that has been effected in its name, the historical issues and questions that have led to the civil crisis, or the death and violence of the war, Emerson positions himself against it.

Nevertheless, amidst the brutality and terror of the Civil War, Emerson's own appeal to the virtues of liberty and justice converges with an appeal to a rhetoric of nature. Aroused by the dangers of the war, by the danger that the ethical dimension of the war might be attenuated by the colossal carnage and suffering that define the struggle's most visible effects, he consistently mobilizes his efforts in the direction of stirring up enthusiasm for the war and its moral benefits. Nothing characterizes these efforts more than his use of natural imagery. Men and women need to be moved to act, he argues. They need to be persuaded to make sacrifices in the name of justice and freedom. And nothing moves or persuades people better than the evocation of nature. The idiom of nature is in fact everywhere in Emerson. If he seems to use the same rhetoric used by others to justify the war, though, he uses it in order to trace its operations within the many efforts to define the meaning of the war: he uses this rhetoric in order to mobilize it in another direction. Only in this way, he says, may we take a step in the direction of justice.

The war itself is of course such a step, but Emerson suggests at least two more such steps in his poetry written during this time, each in their own way a turning point for the war—Lincoln's Emancipation Proclamation and the recruitment of black soldiers into the Union Army. In his **"Boston Hymn"** he celebrates the occasion and significance of the Proclamation and in **"Voluntaries"** he eulogizes the heroism of the Massachusetts 54th regiment, perhaps the most renowned black regiment of the war. In both poems, Emerson names the revolutionary forces of emancipation with natural metaphors. In the first, he turns to the natural phenomena of snow to figure the gathering momentum of the Northern drive toward freedom. In the second, he joins this same climatic metaphor to a meteorological one, the aurora borealis, in order to emphasize the moral center around which the North, having welcomed black soldiers into its army, is now magnetized. In the process, the metaphors of snow and the aurora take on specific historical, political, theological, and literary connotations that require us to turn to the relationship between these domains and questions of language. Always in Emerson, the urgency that we align ourselves with the laws of nature corresponds to the necessity that we be attentive to the rhetorical dimension of our historical and political existence. In what follows, I wish to trace the link between nature and politics as it manifests itself in his **"Boston Hymn."** If the political agenda of this poem sometimes seems to support Unionism, it at the same time works to criticize the political and rhetorical assumptions that might ground such support. This work of criticism can often be read more easily in the actual practice of Emerson's writing, that is to say, in its staging and treatment of the rhetoric of slavery and war, than in any explicit and straightforward arguments. This is why much of what follows will involve tracking the history sealed within the language of Emerson's poem. In the long run, this approach hopes to contribute to the recent reevaluations of Emerson's relation to this same history.

Emerson delivered his **"Boston Hymn"** on January 1, 1863, the effective date of the Emancipation Proclamation, at a "Jubilee Concert" in the Boston Music Hall. He praises the Proclamation for having inaugurated the dawning of a new day in the meaning of America and challenges his audience to meet the responsibilities this new day and meaning entail. For him, the Proclamation revises America's legacy and thereby renews the legacy's power and promise. It declares a promise that is also a rethinking of the promise of America's settlement, its revolution and future. This is to say, however, that the Proclamation draws its social and political force from the history it wishes to overcome. If the Proclamation is not to repeat the sins of this history, if it is to realize its promise of political and social change, it must convey the promise of its own truth to all peoples. But this can only happen if the declaration at the same time encourages people to take responsibility for their own history. Men and women must risk thinking the history that has made this declaration necessary. Only in this way may they be prepared to respond to the demands of emancipation. What is at stake for Emerson as he writes his poem is the possibility of translating the truth of the Proclamation into the minds and hearts of his audience. The hymn rehearses the history of the proclamation, of its terms and conditions—in its present form as well as in its Puritan form—and encourages the audience to commit itself to realizing the proclamation within history. Such commitment is necessary because the mere declaration of a promise may never be its realization. The revolutionary emancipation of the slave can only begin with this act and can only take place if it is continually renewed by every individual who receives the force of its truth.

"Every revolution," he explains in his essay "History," is "first a thought in one man's mind, and when the same thought occurs to another man, it is the key to that era." The Proclamation itself attests to this necessity. From the beginning of the war, abolitionists had individually and collectively called for emancipation as a war policy. As the conflict grew in intensity, the exigencies of war began to convince more and more Northerners that emancipation was the only means to victory. Coming as a powerful means of persuasion, the war itself declared what was necessary.

The task of abolitionists and anti-slavery Republicans was, in a fundamental and essential way, a rhetorical one: the North had to be convinced that slavery was the issue of the war. "The negro is the key of the situation," Douglass pronounced in September of 1861, "the pivot upon which the whole rebellion turns. . . . To fight against slaveholders, without fighting against slavery, is but a half-hearted business, and paralyzes the hands engaged in it." Emancipation was presented as a "military necessity." This phrase became the watchword for abolitionists in subsequent months and was eventually cited by Lincoln as the primary reason for his Proclamation. Despite opposition to emancipation within the administration, there was a dramatic increase of emancipationist sentiment in the weeks following the North's defeat at Bull Run. Even the *New York Tribune* and the *New York Times* revised their earlier stances and began to hint at emancipation. Still discouraged by Lincoln's reluctance to forward a resolution for emancipation and by conservative hostility toward their cause, however, abolitionists began a broad program of popular education aimed at moving public opinion toward the abolition of slavery. This new organization, tentatively called the Boston Emancipation League, was to distribute articles and editorials by prominent abolitionists to newspapers all over the North. The campaign was to be kept temporarily under cover because of the prevailing prejudice against abolitionists. This battle of words was supplemented by well-advertised speeches by Charles Sumner, William Garrison, Wendell Phillips and others during the months of October through November. The campaign was successful and on December 16, because of the growing support of emancipation and the consequent increase in the prestige of abolitionists, the Emancipation League brought their organization into the open. In the winter and spring of 1861-62 the number of emancipation organizations and lecture associations grew rapidly. Pressured by the continued defeats of the North and the growing forces of the abolitionist movement, Lincoln finally issued a preliminary Emancipation Proclamation on September 22, 1862.

Although the terms of the proclamation still provoked disappointment and suspicion amongst the abolitionists, most believed that the deliberateness with which Lincoln had finally announced his decision indicated that the President had every intention of putting his promise into effect. Garrison and Phillips encouraged abolitionists to use their forces to influence public opinion in favor of emancipation rather than to denounce the weakness of the administration's announcement. Garrison [in *The Libera-*

tor, Sept. 26, 1862], for example, after having expressed his concern that the emancipation would not be immediate, that it was only confined to the rebelling states, and that once again it was coupled with Lincoln's favorite scheme of gradual, compensated emancipation, publicly rejoiced in the Proclamation as "an important step in the right direction, and an act of immense historic consequence." Within a few days, abolitionists arranged a rally in Boston at which Emerson was asked to speak. Emerson's speech is traversed by the political and rhetorical exigencies of the moment. Linking the Proclamation to such acts as "the plantation of America . . . the Declaration of Independence in 1776, and the British emancipation of slaves in the West Indies," he calls the act "poetic" and encourages his audience to recognize its "great scope." In his famous opening sentences, he writes:

> In so many arid forms which states encrust themselves with, once in a century, if so often, a poetic act and record occur. These are the jets of thought into affairs, when, roused by danger or inspired by genius, the political leaders of the day break the else insurmountable routine of class and local legislation, and take a step forward in the direction of catholic and universal interests. Every step in the history of political liberty is a sally of the human mind into the untried Future. . . . This act makes a victory of our defeats. Our hurts are healed; the health of the nation is repaired. With a victory like this, we can stand many disasters. . . . We have recovered ourselves from our false position, and planted ourselves on a law of Nature.

Emphasizing the poetic and moral force of an act of thought that follows the laws of Nature, Emerson points to the revolutionary character of the Proclamation. The Proclamation is in fact revolutionary because it aligns itself with the forces of Nature, the forces of transformation. The very act of its declaration propels the country beyond the prejudice and legislation that until now had so forcefully determined national sentiment against emancipation. But now "the cause of disunion and war has been reached and begun to be removed." Lincoln's edict reveals its force, its transformative power, by committing the country to justice. In doing so, it promises political and social changes that call forth "a new public . . . to greet the new event." Clearing the way for an "untried Future," the proclamation recalls the American people to their founding in Nature. Both a promise and a memory, it indicates the nation's health. "In the light of this event," Emerson says, "the public distress begins to be removed." Whatever we might have thought of as Lincoln's shortcomings, "every mistake, every delay," may now be called "endurance, wisdom, magnanimity." "Liberty is a slow fruit," Emerson explains, "It comes, like religion, for short periods, and in rare conditions. . . . We are beginning to think that we have underestimated the capacity and virtue which the Divine Providence has made an instrument of benefit so vast."

Emerson's invocation of organic and religious imagery is far more than a spontaneous response to an act whose moral aspect seems unquestionable. In joining an act of great political and national significance with the movement of religious history, Emerson's rhetoric exploits the pervasive sense among many Northerners that God's hand could be recognized in Lincoln's edict. In this edict, religious and political mission are brought together through the promise of their ultimate realization. January 1, 1863, marks a new era in the history of America—an era in which injustice and oppression would be forced to flee before the divine principles of justice and righteousness. The Proclamation itself bears witness to the sacred cause of the war. The justice of the Northern cause turns the Civil War from a crisis of national legitimacy into a conflict with eschatological significance.

For Emerson, the Emancipation Proclamation plays a decisive role within the history of this transformation. It is precisely this role and this history that are the subjects of his **"Boston Hymn."** Written for the specific purpose of celebrating the moral and historical importance of the Proclamation, the poem opened the festivities at the Music Hall. It was read to a wildly enthusiastic audience that included many former slaves. In the poem, Emerson dramatizes the importance of the pronouncement by inscribing it within the form of a jeremiad that presents in small the history of America as "the great charity of God to the human race." Choosing to frame his poem within the jeremiad form in fact enables him to respond to the heterogeneity of his audience. The jeremiad had frequently been adapted by abolitionist and black political writing in order both to reproach a country that had been unfaithful to its sacred beginnings and to recall the promise upon which American was founded. Providing a lesson in national genealogy, Emerson's sermon sets out the sacred history of the New World and describes the typology of the American mission. By situating the significance of the Proclamation within a history that claims to reveal the nation's divine mission, Emerson emphasizes the historical significance of the Proclamation and the political and cultural significance of this Puritan history. He also entwines this history with the motifs of black emancipation and national regeneration at work within antebellum black rhetoric. This joining of the history of recent events with the history of the meaning of America requires that we read every line of the poem according to a double register. For Emerson, whatever significance we may attribute to the force of Lincoln's pronouncement, this significance can only be read through the history of similar pronouncements, each of which, in their own way, have worked to link the destinies of America's peoples.

Still, within the movement of the poem, the particular pronouncement to which Lincoln's is compared is that of God to his chosen people. In both cases, the pronouncement takes the form of a promise, the promise of freedom. If the Emancipation Proclamation has the force of God's edict, it is because it is the promised realization of God's will. What is most striking about this particular jeremiad, however, is that both it, and by implication, the Proclamation, are spoken by God himself. It is God who laments the tyranny and the selfishness of the Old World and who reveals the terms of his promise to his listeners— the Pilgrims mentioned in the poem certainly, but also their descendants, including all Americans of the year 1863:

The word of the Lord by night
To the watching Pilgrims came,
As they sat by the seaside,
And filled their hearts with flame.

God said, I am tired of kings,
I suffer them no more;
Up to my ear the morning brings
The outrage of the poor.

Think ye I made this ball
A field of havoc and war,
Where tyrants great and tyrants small
Might harry the weak and poor?

My angel,—his name is Freedom,—
Choose him to be your king;
He shall cut pathways east and west
And fend you with his wing.

Lo! I uncover the land
Which I hid of old time in the West
As the sculptor uncovers the statue
When he has wrought his best.

Emerson's sources for this emergent allegory of the history of America are the writings of the early colonists. These opening stanzas identify what was perhaps the single most important element in the formation of the colonists' collective identity: their typological reading of history, a reading that both presumes and accounts for their strong identification with the covenanted people of Israel. As Philip Gura has suggested [in *A Glimpse of Sion's Glory: Puritan Radicalism in New England, 1620-1660,* 1984], the New England Puritans defined their community "not so much through its political or territorial integrity as through a common ideology: specifically, their incessant rhetorical justification of what they regarded as their divinely ordained purpose." For the Puritans, the typological relationship that existed between the New Testament and the Old linked the progressive unfolding of history to the possibility of redemption in this world. At the same time, since the New Testament speaks of things still to be realized, when events in England transformed the New England Puritans' relation to their homeland, they came to believe that they alone were left to fulfill Biblical prophecy. It is no accident, then, that the model for the Great Migration to which Emerson alludes here is the Biblical exodus. Guided by the hand of Providence, the pilgrims, like the Hebrews, abandon an oppressive monarchy for a new promised land. The Puritan God delivers the Pilgrims from the rod of tyranny and oppression and leads them to America. Although this country is the latest found, it is also the earliest. Both the New Canaan and the New Jerusalem, this Columbia "Of clouds and the boreal fleece" is integral to God's sacred design. In giving the pilgrims a new opportunity, He calls upon His people to renew their covenant with Him.

The poem's next six stanzas outline the conditions of the covenant, the rules for this alliance between God and his chosen people. He promises to divide his goods. He promises expansion and growth for all of humanity. He offers to all, without distinction of color or creed, the infinite variety of America's natural resources. In return, he asks that the people build schools and churches in his name, govern the land and sea with just laws, not give way to selfish or proud rulers, refuse to swerve away from what is right, and, most of all, never bind another man or woman into their service. For Emerson, the measure of the degree to which the Puritans and their descendants have lived up to their end of the promise, have followed the laws of the covenant, is nothing less than the entire history of America—from the settlement of New England up to the pronouncement he now celebrates. Emerson's judgment here is decisive. Rather than suggest in any explicit fashion what this history has been, he brings his audience to the moment within which they are listening to him deliver his poem:

> Lo, now! if these poor men
> Can govern the land and sea
> And make just laws below the sun,
> As planets faithful be.
>
> And ye shall succor men;
> 'T is nobleness to serve;
> Help them who cannot help again:
> Beware from right to swerve.
>
> I break your bonds and masterships,
> And I unchain the slave:
> Free be his heart and hand henceforth
> As wind and wandering wave.

Fusing the legacy of the Puritan founders with the present—according to a law of reading that recalls the law that governs the pilgrims' reading of their own special place within history—Emerson implies a typological relationship between the promise of the Puritan settlement of America and its fulfillment in the enactment of the Emancipation Proclamation. If the first half of his poem evokes the "birth" of this legacy, the second half will serve to call upon his audience, or rather to have God call upon his audience, to recognize that it is within its support of the Proclamation that the renewal of His promise will take place. But if God's "Lo, now!" calls attention to the present, it at the same time expresses a kind of surprise at what God sees, almost as though He had, in growing even wearier than before in the face of continued disappointment, come to wonder whether or not men could ever "govern the land and sea" with justice. Nevertheless, the Proclamation is presented as a profound indication that "these poor men" can "make just laws."

The directness with which both Emerson and God turn to this act as the fulfillment of the alliance between God and the pilgrims, however, makes it difficult not to notice their silence upon the years that intervene between these two "events." This silence is hardly an omission. Rather it is a quiet condemnation of everything that, within the history of America, has betrayed or breached this special alliance. It is especially an indictment of those transgressions that occurred in the name of this promise, that justified themselves within the rhetoric and claim of God's

grace. If Emerson begins his poem by having God give voice to the terms and conditions of the covenant, he does so not only to draw a link between the covenant and its realization in Lincoln's edict, but also to draw attention to the very rhetoric with which the Puritan founders attempted to conquer and transform the New World in God's name. In giving voice to the story of the covenant, God tells the story of the Puritans as well. That is to say, he tells to the Puritans their own story, the story that they themselves told in order to rationalize the often violent means whereby they settled their new home. The America whose history goes unspoken in Emerson's poem has also been "A field of havoc and war," a place where "tyrants great and small" have consistently oppressed "the weak and poor." The Puritan understanding of the nation's eschatological significance installed an understanding of the sanctity of the national union that in turn enabled the pilgrims to justify westward expansion, slavery, the extermination of the native population, the marginalization of cultural diversity in general, and the idea of manifest destiny. In carrying the notion of America as God's chosen westward, the Puritans and their descendants felt obliged to subdue, transform, and overcome nature. The strong sense of their place within this sacred history gave them license to "cut down trees in the forest / And trim the straightest boughs." The settlement of America, while it may have at one time promised a beneficent reunion with Nature, now revealed the more selfish and material impulses that the vision of a "free" and "prosperous" land proffered.

For Emerson, the Puritan capacity to appropriate anything before them within the rhetoric of the covenant indicates the power of this rhetoric as well as the Puritan will to authority. The legitimacy accorded to their rhetoric, for example, enabled them to determine in advance what belonged to the chosen community and what did not. This rhetoric in fact demanded the marginalization or assimilation of immigrants and other groups who did not fit into their conception of American nationality. In addition to the exclusion of other cultures, this nationalistic dimension of Puritan thought worked to bring the wide range of theological opinion in the colonies within the boundaries of what Gura has called "the internal development of Puritan doctrine." Although there was no unified community of Puritan thought, the unity of purpose and mission claimed by the New England Puritans was not only essential to their social and political organization, but also defended by recourse to the covenant. This unity was then used to require submission to the authority of the founding fathers and their laws, conformity to convention, and reverence for the sacred moral purpose of whatever this community might deem necessary to further its special mission—even if such purpose might in truth go against every one of the terms of the covenant. For Emerson, such respect, conformity, and reverence works against the virtue of independence in the name of which the New World was founded. If Emerson and God turn from the terms and conditions of the covenant directly to the effective date of the Emancipation Proclamation, it is in part because each wishes to suggest that, until this day, the rhetoric of God's promise has been used primarily to promote interests that betray the letter of this same promise. That is to say: since the plantation of America there have been no truly just laws. There have been no laws which protect the divine rights of all men. Only with this Proclamation does America redeem itself; only with this act does it meet the conditions of God's promise. This act works to purify the covenant as it has been passed down from generation to generation, to recover the promise of an America without slavery. Within the terms of Emerson's poem, the emancipation of the slaves will revise older concepts of manifest destiny, concepts which, emerging from the Puritan rhetoric of mission and errand, took their currency, at least implicitly, from the expansion of the southern slaveholding system. . . .

. . . Emerson does not speak for God; he speaks as God. The force of Emerson's rhetoric lies in its assumption of divinity. Emerson's thought is "ejaculated as Logos, or Word." Whenever God says "I," Emerson says "I." Whenever God speaks, He quotes Emerson. Emerson's God is an emanation of Emerson's own rhetoric, a figure for Emerson's ambitions as a powerful political orator. Moreover, in having God speak within his language, Emerson sets up a typological relationship between the revolutionary promise of his earlier writings and the Proclamation as the fulfillment of this promise. In a certain sense, God's voice makes the potentiality within Emerson's language real. If God's rhetoric depends upon Emerson's, Emerson's is in turn enhanced through its being spoken by God. Emerson subsumes his own voice, his own rhetoric, within the voice of God in order to lend it more authority, in order to better persuade his audience of the virtue of the Proclamation as well as the necessity to constantly renew one's commitment to its promise of justice. In the passage from which God derives the sentence He speaks in stanza 13, Emerson claims that "God is God because he is the servant of all." God has served the Puritan founders. Now, in this poem, God serves Emerson as a figure of persuasion. We can only imagine the impact that Emerson's rhetoric would have had upon his audience. Having been recalled to their present moment by the "Lo, now!" of the twelfth stanza, his listeners could not have overlooked the powerful fusion of God's "I" with Emerson's.

We will never know the tone or force with which Emerson read this poem—a poem whose themes had been his for over thirty years—but anyone familiar with Emerson's writings would have certainly heard his voice within the following four stanzas:

> I cause from every creature
> His proper good to flow:
> As much as he is and doeth,
> So much he shall bestow.

> But, laying hands on another
> To coin his labor and sweat,
> He goes in pawn to his victim
> For eternal years in debt.

> To-day unbind the captive,
> So only are ye unbound;

> Lift up a people from the dust,
> Trump of their rescue, sound!

> Pay ransom to the owner
> And fill the bag to the brim.
> Who is the owner? The slave is owner,
> And ever was. Pay him.

God speaks here in the voice of the Emersonian Poet whose task it is to liberate all men. Like the Poet, God breaks the chains that prevent men from recognizing and realizing their divine potential—that "proper good" which determines who man is and what he does. He takes on the Poet's "office of announcement and affirming" and declares the necessity and rectitude of emancipation. Relying on the language of Emerson's essay "American Civilization," He explains that the moment a man lays his hands upon another person and tries to transform this person's "labor and sweat" into "coin," into money, he reverses the "natural sentiments of mankind." In the opening paragraph to this essay, Emerson had already argued that, in accordance with the laws of nature, "man coins himself into his labor; turns his day, his strength, his thought, his affection into some product which remains as the visible sign of his power." To secure this labor for the laborer, this should be "the object of all government." Insofar as the slaveholder presumes that "the well-being of a man" consists "in eating the fruit of other men's labor," however, he not only prevents the establishment of a just government, but he also goes against Nature. Betraying nature, he betrays himself. In exploiting the slave's labor he becomes eternally indebted to him, eternally subjected to the institution of slavery. Emerson had delineated this argument almost twenty years earlier in his address on the "Emancipation of the British West Indies," suggesting that it had in fact played an important role in the history and events that contributed to that emancipation. "It was shown to the planters," he explains, "that they, as well as the negroes, were slaves. . . . The oppression of the slave recoiled on them. . . . Many planters have said, since the emancipation, that, before that day, they were the greatest slaves on the estates." This argument both follows and anticipates those made by Phillips and Sumner as they tried to persuade both the North and the South of the insidiousness of slavery. Slaveholding, they argued, especially corrupted the manners and morals of white Southerners, since it presented their children with examples of brutal violence and despotism. Phillips, in his speech on the "Right of Petition" (1837), had already emphasized national complicity in the issue of slavery. "Our fate is bound up with that of the South," he said, "so that they cannot be corrupt and we sound; they cannot fail and we stand." In his own speech, Emerson hints at the planters' exaggeration of their own suffering in relation to that of the slave and then links Phillips' point to an older, more philosophical issue: "The civility of no race can be perfect whilst another race is degraded. It is a doctrine alike of the oldest and of the newest philosophy, that man is one, and that you cannot injure any member, without a sympathetic injury to all the members. America is not civil, whilst Africa is barbarous." Since "Every man is an inlet to the same and to all of the same," no man can commit a violence upon another without committing a similar violence upon himself. If any man is a slave every man is a slave. For Emerson, this consideration leaves no choice for the country's conscience. In the name of respect, for both ourselves and others, we must rid ourselves of slavery. As he states in his 1851 address on the Fugitive Slave Act, "Everything invites emancipation."

Emerson's God invites emancipation as well. But if His invitation is made in Emerson's language, this language takes a turn in stanza 18 against Emerson's earlier statements—in his addresses on the West Indies, the Fugitive Slave Law, and especially his 1855 speech on "American Slavery"—on the necessity of compensating slaveholders for their losses upon emancipation. Following the example of the British emancipation of the West Indies, Emerson argues in these speeches that Southern slaveholders ought to be paid a kind of "ransom" for their slaves. In his 1851 address against the Fugitive Slave Law, for example, he proclaims: "Why not end this dangerous dispute on some ground of fair compensation on one side, and satisfaction on the other to the conscience of the free states? It is really the great task fit for this country to accomplish, to buy that property of the planters, as the British nation bought the West Indian slaves. I say buy,— never conceding the right of the planter to own, but that we may acknowledge the calamity of his position, and bear a countryman's share in relieving him; and because it is the only practicable course, and is innocent." Such claims were prevalent in the North in the late 1840s and 1850s and were generally made either in the name of preserving the Union or in the name of admitting some shared responsibility in the matter. If Emerson argues for disunion after the passing of the Fugitive Slave Act, we may still question his willingness to risk reinforcing the claim that slaves were property owned by the slaveholders. Indeed, many abolitionists were hostile to compensation for just this reason. Nevertheless, after the outbreak of the war, while Lincoln and others were still making similar arguments in the interest of effecting some kind of wartime compromise, Emerson claimed that such a suggestion was no longer either "practicable" or "innocent." His **"Boston Hymn"** records this turn of mind. If stanza 18 begins by referring to Emerson's earlier appeals to his countrymen to "Pay ransom to the owner / And fill the bag to the brim," it ends by questioning the appeal's assumption that the slave could be considered as property. "Who is the owner?" God asks. "The slave is owner, / And ever was," comes the answer, "Pay him." These lines implicate an earlier Emerson in the outrages the Proclamation wishes to overcome. The poem is at this point a confession of Emerson's shared guilt, a renunciation of his earlier position, and a passionately challenging exhortation that no one ever forget again that the slave has always owned his or her own labor. . . .

The importance of the rhetorical dimension of the poem is highlighted in a striking and unmistakable fashion in its final sentence, as Emerson's God announces the irresistible force of His rhetoric: "My will fulfilled shall be, / For, in daylight or in dark, / My thunderbolt has eyes to see / His way home to the mark." God's unerring flash of lightning recalls the Puritan use of thunder and lightning as signals of God's voice. This topos is pervasive within Biblical literature and commentary and is quite common in Massachusetts literature from the seventeenth-century on. In Michael Wigglesworth's *God's Controversy with New England,* for example, thunder is the voice of God reprimanding the sins of the Puritan pilgrims: "The Air became tempestuous, / The wilderness gan quake: / And from above with awfull voice / Th' Almighty thundring spake." The image also recurs in sermons such as Cotton Mather's "Brontologia Sacra," included in the *Magnalia Christi Americana,* and Jonathan Edwards's *Personal Narrative.* As Mitchell Breitweiser reminds us [in *Cotton Mather and Benjamin Franklin*], Mather's sermon was in fact given "extemporaneously upon the occasion of a thunderstorm in September 1694." "The omnipotent God in the thunder," Mather explained to his audience, "speaks to those hardy Typhons, that are found fighting against him." In Edwards's narrative, the association between thunder and God's voice is made within a discussion of his present understanding of the thunder's significance. "Before," he writes [in *Magnalia Christi Americana*], "I used to be uncommonly terrified with thunder, and to be struck with terror when I saw a thunder storm rising; but now, on the contrary, it rejoiced me. I felt God, so to speak, at the first appearance of a thunder storm; and used to take the opportunity to . . . hear the majestic and awful voice of God's thunder." God's claim for the inevitable power of His rhetoric in the poem's last sentence should be read against the background of this Puritan rhetoric. This is to say that the poem ends where it began—by recalling the rhetoric of the Puritan God. It is framed by the burning words of the God that had earlier filled the Pilgrim's hearts with flame and that now wishes to enflame men and women of all races toward the difficult but necessary work of emancipation.

But the apocalyptic language of the God of 1863 takes a different form than that of the God of the early seventeenth century. The meaning of His covenant has been altered to meet the challenges of the Civil War and of the slave's emancipation. Now the voice of the Puritan God merges with the voice of Emerson's God and together their target is at least fourfold. The primary target is of course emancipation for the slave, but this emancipation can only occur through the cooperation of the audience listening to Emerson and God within the walls of the Music Hall, the men and women called together in stanza 21 to fulfill the terms of God's covenant, and finally the slave himself—although we might say that this last target is implied in each of the other three. That the slave is a mark internal to the others is made clear in the end rhyme of lines two and four in the poem's last stanza—in the rhyme, that is, between "dark" and "mark." The slave is the "dark mark" of God's word. God's word shall reach the ears of the black man and pronounce his freedom. As in stanza 20, God encourages the slave to take part in his own emancipation. In this instance, however, He at the same time condemns the interpretations of the Biblical curse of Canaan and of the exile of Cain sometimes used to justify the black man's color and enslavement. He distinguishes the dark mark to which His voice is now directed from the "dark mark" which, according to these interpretations, His voice had earlier condemned. In the Biblical account, when the drunken Noah realizes that his son, Ham, has been staring at his naked body, he curses Ham's son, Canaan. He condemns Canaan to servitude and, according to Talmudic and Midrashic sources, tells Ham that his seed will from then on "be ugly and darkskinned." As David Brion Davis suggests, [in *Slavery and Human Progress,* 1984], these explanations for the black man's enslavement were most likely intensified by religious cosmologies that "envisioned spiritual progress as the triumph of the children of light over the pagan or infidel children of darkness." For Emerson, however, the difficulty that the issue of slavery poses for people who understand America's mission as furthering the cause of divine truth and enlightenment is precisely that of distinguishing between the forces of light and those of darkness. The rhetoric of this mission has too often been used to reinforce rather than to undo patterns of enslavement among both blacks and whites for such a distinction to be clear. The conditions of genuine emancipation ought to include a reconsideration of the implications of this difficulty. As Emerson declares in his speech on the "Emancipation of the British West Indies," at the moment of emancipation, all "disqualifications and distinctions of color" cease and "men of all colors have equal rights in law. . . . If you have man, black or white is an insignificance."

Rather than curse the black man for any original sin, God prophesies his redemption and emancipation from the sins committed against him in the name of a justice determined by color. If the black man is still marked, he is now marked for freedom rather than punishment. He is marked for inclusion within the family of man. Like the snowflake—whose angles "are invariable" but whose forms exhibit "the greatest variety and beauty" [Early Lectures of Ralph Waldo Emerson, edited by Stephen E. Whicher et. al., 1961]—the black man has a share in what is universal in man's nature, even as he maintains the singularity of his history and existence. God's rhetoric displays its force by re-marking the marks of Cain and Canaan in the direction of a more just understanding of the divinity that the black man shares with all men. In this, God also questions the rhetoric within which both the North and the South described the Civil War as a fratricidal conflict. Each tried to mark the other with the brand of Cain. Each claimed that it was the righteous brother—trying to defend the legacy bequeathed to the nation by the Founding Fathers. Within the context of the poem's last sentence, such branding coincides with the rhetoric and logic of exclusion that has justified and thereby maintained the institution of slavery. If God's thunderbolt does indeed see its way home to the mark, it does so by striking against any rhetoric and logic that would privilege any mark over another. . . .

. . . Emerson writes the **"Boston Hymn"** in order to proclaim the conditions for realizing the promise of emancipation, to signal the divinity that defines our potential for freedom. Like the voice of God that calls forth men and women to realize His will as snowflakes, the poem creates the audience that is to hear it by speaking to it as if it could already hear. The thunderbolt that it is sees its way home to the mark insofar as it brings forth the possibility of a future. This future lies in the hands of the races who, coming like snowflakes, commit themselves to its chances. The **"Hymn"** celebrates an emancipation that does not yet exist but is already occurring in the form of a promise—a promise that has always magnetized American desire.

Rather than distance itself aesthetically from the war, Emerson's **"Boston Hymn"** registers the traces that the Civil War has left upon it. The concern that it expresses over its own status as an act of representation is one and the same with its analysis of the varied cultural and political attempts to invent and enforce particular image of America. Linking its language to the events of its time, evoking their various contexts and enacting the way in which history informs its own movement, the poem also suggests the way in which texts inform the practices of history. If the poem—with its figures, emblems, and symbols—is linked to America's capacity to institute, within a general network of representation, the political experience of its citizens, Emerson wishes it to reflect critically on efforts to evade the historical issues that had led to the civil crisis and to legitimate the war and its violence by recourse to the rhetoric against which the war is being fought. In recalling these issues and this history, in evoking the genealogy of the rhetorics within which his listeners thought about their place within this same history, the poem works to encourage a rethinking of our relation to the meaning of America, to an America that realizes its promise of emancipation.

FURTHER READING

Bibliography

Burkholder, Robert E. and Myerson, Joel. *Emerson: An Annotated Bibliography.* Westport: Greenwood Press, 1994, 234 p.

   Annotated bibliography of writings on Emerson, arranged chronologically between 1980 and 1991.

Burkholder, Robert E. and Myerson, Joel. *Emerson: An Annotated Secondary Bibliography.* Pittsburgh: University of Pittsburgh Press, 1985, 842 p.

   Annotated bibliography of writings on Emerson, arranged chronologically between 1816 and 1979.

Myerson, Joel. *Ralph Waldo Emerson: A Descriptive Bibliography.* Pittsburgh: University of Pittsburgh Press, 1982, 802 p.

   Lists and describes works written or edited by Emerson, arranged chronologically.

Biography

Allen, Gay Wilson. *Waldo Emerson: A Biography.* New York: Viking Press, 1981, 751 p.

Critically acclaimed biography focusing on Emerson's intellectual sources.

Cabot, Eliot. *A Memoir of Ralph Waldo Emerson*, 2 vols. Boston: Houghton Mifflin, 1889, 809 p.

Written by Emerson's friend, literary executor and authorized biographer, it contains material from Emerson's private papers, journals and correspondence providing the standard source for biographical information through the mid-twentieth century.

Conway, Daniel Moncure. *Emerson at Home and Abroad*. 1882; rpt. Boston: James R. Osgood, 1968, 383 p.

An entertaining collection of incidents in Emerson's life set forth from private reminiscences and literary sources.

McAleer, John. *Ralph Waldo Emerson: Days of Encounter*. Boston: Little, Brown and Co., 1984, 748 p.

Focuses on Emerson's interaction with family and friends.

Miles, Josephine. *Ralph Waldo Emerson*. University of Minnesota Pamphlets on American Writers, edited by William Van O'Connor, Allen Tate, Leonard Ungar, and Robert Penn Warren, No. 41. Minneapolis: University of Minnesota Press, 1964, 48 p.

A cogent biographical and critical introduction to Emerson.

Pommer, Henry F. *Emerson's First Marriage*. Carbondale: Southern Illinois University Press, 1967, 126 p.

Provides a sensitive portrait of Ellen Tucker and Emerson's relationship with her.

Richardson, Robert D., Jr. *Emerson, The Mind on Fire*. Berkeley: University of California Press, 1995, 671 p.

A definitive biography, presenting an intellectual, personal and social portrait.

Rusk, Ralph L. *The Life of Ralph Waldo Emerson*. New York: Scribners, 1949, 592 p.

A seminal biography, it provides an abundance of facts gleaned from Emerson's original manuscripts as well as prior critical and biographical sources.

Criticism

Anderson, John Q. *The Liberating Gods, Emerson on Poets and Poetry*. Coral Gables: University of Miami Press, 1971, 128 p.

Discusses Emerson's views on poetry and other poets through a study of his essays, journals, letters and poems.

Arnold, Matthew. "Emerson." In *Discourses in America*, pp. 138-208. 1884; rpt. New York: Macmillan Company, 1924.

Faults Emerson's poetry stating that it lacks concrete imagery, energy, passion, and grace.

Blasing, Mutlu Konuk. "Ralph Waldo Emerson: Essaying the Poet." In *American Poetry: The Rhetoric of Its Forms*, pp. 67-83. New Haven: Yale University Press, 1987.

Provides an overview of Emerson's poetry and essays "in terms of their different yet complementary intentions."

Brittin, Norman A. "Emerson and the Metaphysical Poets." *American Literature* 8 (March 1936): 1-21.

Reviews Emerson's poetry as exemplifying the metaphysical style of poets such as George Herbert.

Cameron, Kenneth. *Transcendentalists in Tradition: Popularization of Emerson, Thoreau and the Concord School of Philosophy*. Hartford: Transcendental Books, 1980, 263 p.

Reveals the roles of Charles Malloy and Franklin Benjamin Sanborn in popularizing Emerson's poems.

Carpenter, Frederic Ives. "The Wisdom of the Brahmins." In *Emerson and Asia*, pp. 103-60. Cambridge, Mass.: Harvard University Press, 1930.

Applies Hindu philosophy to the poems "Hamatreya" and "Brahma."

Eberhart, Richard. "Emerson and Wallace Stevens." In *Of Poetry and Poets*, pp. 153-71. Urbana: University of Illinois Press, 1979.

Compares the characteristics of Emerson's and Stevens's poetry.

Francis, Richard L. "Archangel in the Pleached Garden: Emerson's Poetry." *Journal of English Literary History* 33 (December 1966): 461-72.

Reviews Emerson's mythological and ontological poems that express the "Order" of the universe.

Garrod, H. W. "Emerson." In *Poetry and the Criticism of Life: The Charles Eliot Norton Lectures for 1929-1930*, pp. 85-107. 1931; rpt. New York: Russell and Russell, 1963.

Considers Emerson's poetry to be epigrammatic but, nonetheless, deserving of more praise than it had formerly received.

Gelpi, Albert. "Emerson: The Paradox of Organic Form." In *Emerson: Prophecy, Metamorphosis, and Influence*, edited by David Levin, pp. 149-70. New York: Columbia University Press, 1975.

Examines Emerson's theory of poetics, focusing on the relationship between inspiration and poetic form.

Gilman, Owen W., Jr. "*Merlin*: E. A. Robinson's Debt to Emerson." *Colby Library Quarterly* 21 (September 1985): 134-41.

Reveals similarities between Robinson's poem and Emerson's two "Merlin" poems.

Hakutani, Yohinobu. "Emerson, Whitman and Zen Buddhism." *Midwest Quarterly* XXXI, No.4 (Summer 1990): 433-48.

Discusses Zen concepts evident in Emerson's poems.

Hubbell, George S. *A Concordance to the Poems of Ralph Waldo Emerson*. New York: H.W. Wilson, 1932, 303 p.

Provides a useful concordance as a means to tracing imagery and interpreting symbolism in Emerson's poetry.

Kennedy, William Sloane. "Clews to Emerson's Mystic Verse." *American Transcendental Quarterly*, No. 29 (Winter 1976): 2-20.

Reprints an essay originally published in 1903 explicating mythological, mystical, and occult elements in Emerson's poetry.

Kreymborg, Alfred. "The Intoxicated Emerson." In *Our Singing Strength: An Outline of American poetry (1620-1939)*, pp. 67-83. New York: Coward-McCann, 1929.
Discusses Emerson's poetry emphasizing his occasionally robust tone.

Malloy, Charles. *A Study of Emerson's Major Poems*, edited by Kenneth Walter Cameron, Hartford: Transcendental Books, 1973, 123 p.
Reprints Malloy's explications originally published in literary magazines during the end of the nineteenth and beginning of the twentieth centuries.

Masters, Edgar Lee. "Presenting Emerson." In *The Living Thoughts of Emerson*, pp. 1-41. New York, Toronto: Longmans, Green and Co., 1940.
A laudatory presentation of Emerson's philosophy as found in his essays and poetry.

McEuen, Kathryn A. "Emerson's Rhymes." *American Literature* 20 (March 1948): 31-42.
Defends Emerson's often imperfect rhymes as evidence of his breaking from tradition rather than examples of stylistic incompetence.

Myerson, Joel, ed. *Emerson and Thoreau, The Contemporary Reviews*. Cambridge, England: Cambridge University Press, 1992, 450 p.
Reprints criticism that appeared within a year of the publication of Emerson's works.

Orth, Ralph H.; von Frank, Albert J.; Allardt, Linda; and Hill, David W.; ed. *The Poetry Notebooks of Ralph Waldo Emerson*. Columbia: University of Missouri Press, 1986, 990 p.
Provides Emerson's poetry journals containing previously unpublished verse and details on the composition and publication histories of the poems.

Santayana, George. "Emerson." In *Interpretations of Poetry and Religion*, pp. 131-40. 1900; rpt. Cambridge, Mass.: Massachusetts Institute of Technology Press, 1989.
Praises the beauty and originality of Emerson's poetic style.

Strauch, Carl. "The Year of Emerson's Poetic Maturity: 1834." *Philological Quarterly* 34 (1955): 353-77.
Discusses "Xenophanes," "Each and All," "The Rhodora," and "The Snow Storm" and the influence on Emerson of works by Coleridge, Goethe, and Wordsworth.

————. "The Mind's Voice: Emerson's Poetic Styles." *Emerson Society Quarterly* 60 (1970): 43-59.
Discusses Romantic, Old English, Bardic and Neo-Platonic influences on Emerson's poetic style and defends the poetry as experimental in meter and rhyme, arguing for its effectiveness.

Sudol, Ronald A. "'The Adirondacs' and Technology." In *Emerson Centenary Essays*, edited by Joel Myerson, pp. 173-9. Carbondale: Southern Illinois University Press, 1982.
Provides background and analysis of Emerson's 342-line poem, "The Adirondacs."

Thompson, Frank T. "Emerson's Theory and Practice of Poetry." *PMLA* XLIII, No. 4 (December 1928): 1170-84.
Traces the influence of Wordsworth and Coleridge on Emerson's poetry.

Winters, Yvor. "Jones Very and R.W. Emerson: Aspects of New England Mysticism." In *Maule's Curse: Seven Studies in the History of American Obscurantism*, pp. 125-46. Norfolk, Conn.: New Directions Press, 1938.
Condemns Emerson's poetry as expressing immoral, "pernicious" views.

Yoder, R. A. *Emerson and the Orphic Poet in America*. Berkeley: University of California Press, 1978, 240 p.
Regards Emerson's views on poetry and the role of the poet as adapting and redirecting the convictions of European Romanticism.

Yohannan, J. D. "Emerson's Translations of Persian Poetry From German Sources." *American Literature* 14 (January 1943): 407-20.
Examines and lists the translations of and essays about Persian poetry read by Emerson written by German literary historians.

————. "The influence of Persian Poetry on Emerson's Work." *American Literature* 15 (March 1943): 25-41.
Examines Emerson's references to Persian poetry.

Additional coverage of Emerson's life and career is contained in the following sources published by Gale Research: *Nineteenth-Century Literature Criticism*, Vols. 1, 38; *DISCovering Authors*; *DISCovering Authors: Most-Studied Authors Module*; *DISCovering Authors: Poets Module*; *World Literature Criticism, 1500 to the Present*; *Concise Dictionary of American Literary Biography 1640-1865*; and *Dictionary of Literary Biography*, Vols. 1, 59, 73.

Théophile Gautier
1811-1872

(Full name Pierre Jules Théophile Gautier) French poet, novelist, novella writer, short story writer, critic, travel writer, and dramatist.

INTRODUCTION

Gautier, or *"le bon Théo"* ("the good Théo"), as he was often called, is regarded as one of the most popular literary figures of nineteenth-century France. His poetic work is noteworthy both for its complete engagement with important artistic revolutions of its age--shifting from passionate Romanticism to urbane aestheticsm to Parnassian formalism--and for its singular devotion to the themes and techniques of literary decadence, including the intimate connection of death and the erotic, exoticism, self-conscious narration, and allusiveness. Opposed to philistinism and utilitarianism, all of Gautier's work displays a love for material beauty and extravagance, a love of art not for the sake of any use, but a love of, as Gautier noted, *"l'art pour l'art,"* "art for art's sake."

Biographical Information

Born in Tarbes, a city in the Pyrenees of southwest France, Gautier soon after moved with his family to Paris, where he would live—except for occasional travels—for the rest of his life. At age eleven, Gautier began attending the Lycée Charlemagne, where he met and befriended Gerard Labrunie, who would later become the writer known as Gerard de Nerval. During this time, Gautier studied painting and began writing poems. Although, in 1829, Gautier gave up painting and embraced the literary life after being introduced to Victor Hugo by Nerval, his passions for visual beauty and for visual description in writing—especially the *"transposition d'art"* ("transposition of art"), the depiction in writing of a painting or a sculpture—would become hallmarks of his literary works. As an advocate of Romanticism, Gautier—long-haired and dressed in his signature, flamboyant, *"rouge gilet"* ("red waistcoat")—led efforts to oppose classicists and to promote Romantic drama in the "Battle of *Hernani*." In 1831, with Nerval and other artist/bohemians, Gautier formed the "Petit Cenacle," and later "Groupe du Doyenne," groups dedicated to Romanticism and to unsettling the sedentary bourgeoisie with eccentric behavior. Eventually, however, Gautier realized a need for steady income and employment. In 1835, he began his career as a journalist, and was employed as an art and drama critic for various Parisian newspapers for the rest of his life. Although his reviews were held in high regard, Gautier viewed his journalism as an impediment that kept him from literature, which he believed to be his life's true work. The monotony of work

was occasionally broken by travel, including trips to Spain, Italy, Russia, and the Middle East, and was assuaged by romantic liasons and a passionate, though unrequited, love for the ballerina Carlotta Grisi. Although not actively engaged in politics, Gautier's health was adversely affected by the Prussian siege of Paris in 1870 and the turmoil which followed. Gautier died of heart disease in 1872.

Major Works

Released during the July Revolution in 1830, the publication of Gautier's *Poésies* (1830; *Poems*), a collection of standard themes in standard verse, went virtually unnoticed. His next collection, *Albertus ou l'ame et le péché* (1833; *Albertus, or the Soul and the Sin*), included work from *Poésies,* new poems in the same mode, and a long, narrative poem, "Albertus," which parodied the satanism then fashionable in literature. Though self-referential and often humorous, "Albertus" introduces the themes of the prominence of art and the spectacle of death which would guide Gautier's writing through *La comédie de la Mort* (1838; *The Comedy of Death*) and *España* (1845; *Spain*), a collection of poems inspired by a five-month trip through

Spain. In his last—and what many consider his most important—collection, *Emaux et camées* (1852; translated as *Enamels and Cameos and Other Poems*, 1903), Gautier's poetry changes profoundly, becoming compact and chiselled, treating, as Gautier said, "tiny subjects in a severely formal way."

Critical Reception

Although Charles Baudelaire dedicated his *Les fleurs du mal* to "the impeccable poet, the gentle enchanter of French letters . . . Théophile Gautier," and although at the time of his death eighty fellow writers composed poems in honor of him, Gautier's position as one of the major poets of nineteenth-century France is currently considered questionable. While many critics note the influence of Gautier's impersonal, formal ideals on Parnassians, Acmeists, and Modernists, including T.S. Eliot and Ezra Pound, most believe either that Gautier's poetry simply lacks the profound intensity and spirit—as found in the work of Baudelaire—which is necessary to make poetry great, or that the poetry actively suffers from being mere stylism and escapism. Influenced by deconstructivist theory, some more recent criticism has attempted to excavate the seductive elements of Gautier's self-aware, ironic, and distanced poetry.

PRINCIPAL WORKS

Poetry

Poésies [*Poems*] 1830
*Albertus ou l'Ame et le péché [*Albertus, or the Soul and the Sin*] 1833
La comédie de la mort [*The Comedy of Death*] 1838
España [*Spain*] 1845
Emaux et camées [*Enamels and Cameos*] 1852; enlarged edition (1872) [*Enamels and Cameos and Other Poems,* 1903]
Poésies complètes. 3 vols. [*Complete Poems*] 1932
Gentle Enchanter: Thirty-Four Poems by Théophile Gautier 1961

Other Major Works

Les Jeunes-France, romans goguenards (satire) 1833
Mademoiselle de Maupin (novel) 1835-36 [*Mademoiselle de Maupin,* 1890]
L'eldorado (novella) 1837; also published as *Fortunio,* 1838 [*Fortunio,* 1915]
**Une larme du diable (short story) 1839
Giselle ou les Wilis [with Vernoy Saint-Georges] (ballet scenario) 1841
Tra los montes (travel essay) 1843; also published as *Voyage in Espagne* 1845 [*Wanderings in Spain,* 1853]
Les grotesques (criticism) 1844
Nouvelles (novellas) 1845
Zigzags (travel essays) 1845; also published as *Caprices and Zigzags* (enlarged edition) 1852

Jean et Jeanette (novel) 1850; also published in *Un trio de romans* 1852
Italia (travel essay) 1852; also published as *Voyage en Italie* (enlarged edition) 1875 [*Journeys in Italy* 1902]
Constantinople (travel essay) 1853 [*Constantinople of Today,* 1854]
Les beaux-arts en Europe (criticism) 1855
Théâtre de poche (drama) 1855; also published as *Théâtre* (enlarged edition) 1872
Avatar (novel) 1857
Jettatura (novel) 1857 [*Jettatura,* 1888]
Romans and contes (novels and short stories) 1857
Le roman de la momie (novel) 1858 [*The Romance of a Mummy,* 1882]
Histoire de l'art dramatique en France depuis vingt-cinq ans. 6 vols. (criticism) 1858-59
Le Capitane Fracasse (novel) 1863 [*Captain Fracasse* 1880]
Spirite (novel) 1866
Voyage en Russie (travel essay) 1867 [*A Winter in Russia,* 1874]
Histoire du romantisme (unfinished critical essay) 1872 [*A History of Romanticism,* 1900]
The Works of Théophile Gautier. 24 vols. (novels, short stories, travel essays, criticism, drama, novellas, and poetry) 1900-03
The Romantic Ballet (criticism) 1932
Contes fantastiques (short stories) 1962

*This volume includes material in *Poésies.*
**This volume also includes "Une nuit de Cleopatre," "Omphale," and "La morte amoureuse."

CRITICISM

John Van Eerde (essay date 1963)

SOURCE: "'La Symphonie en blanc majeur': An Interpretation," in *L'Esprit Créateur.* Vol. III, NO. 1, Spring, 1963, pp. 26-33.

[*In the following essay, Van Eerde explores the meaning of the inclusion of the color red at the end of Gautier's otherwise all-white poem and finds that the color communicates emotional need.*]

Marie-Antoinette Chaix, in *La Correspondance des arts dans la poésie contemporaine* (Paris, 1919), considers Théophile Gautier's poem, **"La Symphonie en blanc majeur"** (1849), a literary exercise. H. Van Der Tuin, in *L'Evolution psychologique, esthétique et littéraire de Théophile Gautier* (Paris, 1933), calls it decorative art. Joanna Richardson describes it as a linguistic "tour de force" in *Théophile Gautier, His Life And Times* (New York, 1959). This article would address itself to the matter of Gautier's introduction in the last strophe of pink into an otherwise all-white tableau and its significance for an interpretation of the poem. Whiteness will predominate from the first quatrain. Not until the last strophe does pink intrude:

Sous la glace où calme il repose
Oh! qui pourra fondre ce cœur
Oh! qui pourra mettre un ton rose
Dans cette implacable blancheur.

The preceding seventeen strophes have regaled the reader with a series of images that establish in bold relief the incomparable whiteness of one of the Rhenish swan-maidens. Gautier's static scene echoes his advice in **"L'Art,"** where he writes "Sculpte, lime, cisèle." His swan-maiden enters motionless: "Blanche comme le clair de lune/Sur les glaciers dans les cieux froids." The act of swimming, evoked in the opening lines, is lost in the dazzling white; there is not even a splash.

White marble stillness is to be seen in many of the poems of the *Emaux et Camées*. White imagery is often applied but not limited to a Nature context.

The swan-maiden of Gautier's **"Symphonie"** exemplifies the sculptor's supreme statuary, woman. In **"Le Poème de la femme: Marbre de Paros"** (1849), written under the inspiration of Ingres, the female form is the subject. The poet yearns to protect the whiteness of this form. In **"Rondalla"** (1847) he would shield his beloved's "pieds blancs" from a dirty stream. This whiteness gleams with undiminished beauty through transparent film. So says the poem, **"Caerulei Oculi"** (1852), as a siren disports "sa blancheur bleue" beneath the green enamel of a wave, l. 39. Similarly a silk-stockinged leg "Prend des lueurs de marbre blanc" in **"A la Petra Camara"** (1852), l. 55. Such whiteness is especially poetic in a woman's hand:

Sous le baiser neigeux saisie
Comme un lis par l'aube argenté,
Comme une blanche poésie
S'épanouissait sa beauté.
    "Imperia" (1851), ll. 5-8.

We have referred to Gautier as a sculptor-poet. As is generally recognized, the term might accurately be enlarged to include the word "painter." He wrote of his generation of romantics in *Histoire du Romantisme:* [in ed. Librairie de Bibliophiles] "Quant à nous, comme nous l'avons dit, placé à l'y du carrefour, nous hesitions entre les deux routes, c'est-à-dire entre la poésie et la peinture, également abominables aux familles. Cependant, sans avoir franchi le Rubicon, nous commencions à faire plus de vers que de croquis, et peindre avec des mots nous paraissait plus commode que de peindre avec des couleurs." Red and its variations had a special appeal to this colorist group. Gautier himself felt the appeal, and it was to supplement his attraction to white: "Mais nous avions en outre un goût particulier, l'amour du rouge; nous aimions cette noble couleur, déshonorée maintenant par les fureurs politiques, qui est la pourpre, le sang, la vie, la lumière, la chaleur, et qui se marie si bien à l'or et au marbre. . . ." Gautier shared this taste: "Je connais tous les tons de la gamme du rose," he writes in **"Le Rose"** (1867), l. 1. Recalling the ideal accoutrement for the dashing romantic, he finds the memorable touch to be a "Pourpoint de satin rose," so he tells us in **"Château du souvenir"** (1861), l. 157. Indeed he writes of his famous red waistcoat worn at the opening of *Hernani:* "Nos poésies, nos livres, nos articles, nos voyages seront oubliés; mais l'on se souviendra de notre gilet rouge" (*Histoire du Romantisme*).

But this mania for red (and its nuances, especially pink) is not just an eccentricity in Gautier; it is an artistic necessity. Hence the presence of these tones in his poetry. Venice is pink, and its renowned pigeons are represented by "Deux ramiers blancs aux pieds rosés" in "Madrigal panthéiste" (1849), l. 11. And elsewhere, he invites our attention "Devant une facade rose/Sur le marbre de l'escalier," these lines 23-24 of "Sur les lagunes" (1849) having symbolized Venice for Wilde's Dorian Gray. The rose tone decorates both exteriors and interiors. For example, a pink lamp-shade beckons the poet to stay home on a rainy evening in "La Bonne Soirée" (1868), l. 13. Pink and white, singly or together, are prominent not only in Gautier's description of the sensible universe, but often in his world of abstractions. This is not to exclude other colors. As Louise Bulkley Dillingham says, "Even in Gautier's earliest writing a preoccupation with color is noticeable."

Van Der Tuin sees Gautier subject to a feverish need to find emotional relief in cold, hard stone: "L'apaisement, il le trouvait d'abord dans ces pierreries, dans ces marbres froids, dispersés dans sa poésie et sa prose" (*L'Evolution*). More important for this article than the question of the validity of Van Der Tuin's statement is the fact that Gautier apparently becomes shocked at the cold, uniform white of his own creations. Pink comes naturally to his assistance where the subject is Woman. A coquette, expressing the wish to wear in her coffin the white dress admired by her beloved, adds the desire that her cheeks be rouged, so that she may "Comme le soir de son aveu/Rester éternellement rose" (**"Coquetterie posthume,"** 1851, ll. 6-7). At a masquerade ball, the poet recognizes the marked lady of his choice by her mouth "rose et fraîche" (**"Carnaval,"** 1849, l. 29). Gautier rejoices in Woman as a being of pink and white in the poem, **"A Une Robe rose"** (1850), depicting his beloved in a pink dress: "Et l'étoffe à la chair renvoie/Ses éclairs roses reflétés," ll. 11-12. This poem emphasizes the blending of white and pink in a corporeal context:

D'où te vient cette robe étrange
Qui semble faite de ta chair,
Trame vivante qui mélange
Avec ta peau son rose clair?
    ll. 13-16.

Pink is Nature's dress for Woman's body. Thus Venice, the Venus of the Adriatic, "Sort de l'eau son corps rose et blanc" in **"Sur les lagunes,"** l. 16. This fusion of pink and white proclaims the glory of the female form in **"La Nue"** (1866):

On voit onder en molles poses
Son torse au contour incertain,
Et l'aurore répand des roses
Sur son épaule de satin.
Ses blancheurs de marbre et de neige

Se fondent amoureusement
Comme, au clair-obscur de Corrége
Le corps d'Antiope dormant.
    ll. 9-16.

Gautier quite naturally passes to thoughts of painting and Correggio after blending white and pink in his poem. What he is doing is indicated by the terms he employs to express admiration for Delacroix in *Histoire du Romantisme:* "Sur ces sujets, réduits jusque-là à l'immobilité du bas relief, il répandit les magies de la couleur et fit remonter la pourpre de la vie dans les veines pâles du marbre." Unquestionably Gautier, who once wrote "Si j'étais peintre (et j'ai toujours regretté de ne pas l'être. . .)," injects pink into his scenes as a painter. One thinks here of Edmond de Goncourt's comment [*Journal des Goncourt* (Paris, 1891), V, 111.] on Degas' laundresses and dancers: "En effet, c'est la rose de la chair, dans le blanc du linge, dans le brouillard laiteux de la gaze: Le charmant prétexte aux colorations blondes et tendres."

It is plain that Gautier's emphasis on white and pink in his poetry is an aesthetic device. René Jasinski, in *Les Années romantiques de Théophile Gautier* (Paris, 1929), includes ". . . . La jeune fille au front pur, aux joues roses . . ." among the typical themes of the day to be found in Gautier's *Poésies* (1830). The poet, who called himself a person "for whom the visible world exists," communicates frequently in images that strike the eye. White, for instance, is time and again used for artistic effect. One would not write of Gautier as Dr. Chaix does of Hugo (*La Correspondence*): "Le blanc est réservé à la bonté, à la grandeur, à la noblesse." With respect to his use of pink, it can not be claimed that Gautier is reflecting the widely recognized psychological phenomenon represented by the expression "Il voit la vie tout en rose." Nevertheless, why does a poet who consistently introduces color into his marble, statuesque imagery, ask at the end of the **"Symphonie"** "Oh! qui pourra mettre un ton rose/Dans cette implacable blancheur"? The opinion that the poem is an artistic exercise or "tour de force" is perhaps too influenced by Gautier's role in the development of the *L'art pour l'art* theory.

The great paradox of Gautier's career is that despite his growing dedication to the famous, objective principle of artistic creation, subjectivity remains a strong characteristic of his work as a whole. Dr. Dillingham has something pertinent to say about this:

> Another point to be considered in regard to the form chosen by Gautier for his work is the attitude of the author thereto: shall his production be personal or impersonal. With Gautier the general form is a personal one, for his production plainly expresses his sentiments, his own reactions to existence. It must be noted, however, that the most important of these sentiments are of their nature objectified: it is exterior, visible beauty which Gautier desires to create, something outside himself and removed from personal considerations, which yet represents his inner aspirations (*The Creative Imagination*).

Professor Jasinski, to be sure, often partial to the biographical explanation of literature, calls the Gautier of 1827 "Observateur méticuleux et lucide, il tendit au dessin; imagination sentimentale et rêveuse, déjà mûr pour le romantisme, il aspirait à la poésie . . . Par la suite l'opposition s'atténuera; réalisme et idéalisme se concilieront en lui, créeront pour s'exprimer des transpositions d'art favorables. Mais rien ne détruira ce dualisme fondamental . . ." (*Les Années romantiques*). Joanna Richardson, partial only to Gautier, also finds the poet's life and works to be closely connected. Jasinski identifies the Maria of the poem **"Maria"** as a certain Hélène who used to come to Maupertuis but died: ". . . Théophile connut par elle son premier désespoir." Of the *Albertus* poems Jasinski writes: "L'amour, c'est son idylle timide avec Eugénie," the Eugénie by whom Gautier had a child in November, 1836. Miss Richardson in *Théophile Gautier* uses phrases regarding his attachment to Eugénie, "Perhaps he continued to wait . . . for some impossible Romantic ideal," and to Carlotta Grisi, ". . . the unattainable Carlotta Grisi," that can well apply to some of his poetry. Gautier's life was, as Miss Richardson has shown, one of unfulfilled personal relationships matched by a frustrated professional career. He had a more or less amorous relationship with Alice Ozy who ". . . remained of comparative insignificance in Gautier's life." Despite his admiration of Julia Grisi and adoration of her sister, Carlotta, it was their sister, Ernesta, who was to "dominate his daily existence for twenty years." In the same year in which **"La Symphonie"** was published, Gautier in London met Marie Mattei, of whom Miss Richardson writes: "She alone, Marie, `l'Italienne': she alone, of all the women Gautier had known, gave him the passionate, unfailing, dramatic love he needed." Even this short-lived idyll confirms the central fact of Gautier's emotional life: he was unable to give wholly and permanently of himself. Thus Miss Richardson can write of ". . . his incurable selfishness." Speaking of his long disillusionment within a few years of his death, she says "What he wanted—what he had wanted since the days of *Mademoiselle de Maupin*—was some unattainable Utopia."

In his life were cruelty and tragedy. These are terms that Van Der Tuin applies to **"La Symphonie."** The question "qui pourra mettre un ton rose" is one which introduces into the poem an essential ambiguity, that of the artist and of the man. The full meaning of the question can best be grasped by examining Gautier's novel, *Mademoiselle de Maupin* (1835). This is the work of which Adolphe Boschot has written, "Ce livre qui est Gautier lui-même," and part of which he has called "Une confession lyrique et psychologique." Bearing on the subject of this article is the way white and pink are used in this novel, whose poignant pages express an aesthetic as well as emotional quest, the quest of Woman.

The work vacillates between the real and the imaginary in depicting woman, who pervades the waking world and the dream world with the whiteness of her charms. The ideal mistress of the hero D'Albert's imagination is "blonde" and "blanche comme une blonde." Writing of the nightingale's song that once held the promise of his love-dream's imminent realization, he says: "Il me semblait voir à travers les trilles de son chant et sous la pluie de notes s'étendre vers moi, dans un rayon de lune, les bras blancs de ma bien-aimée" (Paris, 1892). The harem of his imagination is graced by "antiques déesses, qui dressez votre blanc fantôme sous les ombrages du jardin."

In the world of reality where the poet sees every virgin as "Une chaste fleur qui ne déploie sa blanche robe que pour vous seule," woman's whiteness remains as dazzling as in the realm of the imagination. Even the fleeting female figure causing a shudder of excitement as she passes an open doorway is a "chère et blanche apparition."

If occasionally smoothness seems an added attribute in such expressions as "Son beau front d'ivoire" and "L'ivoire poli de ses flancs," whiteness alone is overpowering in the novel. Thus in a complimentary mood D'Albert speaks to his beloved of the "blancheur de ce dos charmant." On another occasion she is "Une goutte de lait, une rose blanche." White permeates the *Maupin*'s ample anatomical inventory, but it is nowhere more effective than in the hand. A pleasant boating-trip remains in memory "Une main blanche qui trempe dans l'eau." The hero exclaims "Comme elle est d'une blancheur vivace." How overpowering the whiteness of a hand can be: "La pensée de cette main me rend fou, et fait frémir et brûler mes lèvres.—Je ferme les yeux pour ne plus la voir; mais du bout de ses doigts délicats elle me prend les cils et m'ouvre les paupières, fait passer devant moi mille visions d'ivoire et de neige—Ah! sans doute, c'est la griffe de Satan qui s'est gantée de cette peau de satin."

White being an important attribute of Woman, it is logical that love, the emotion she inspires, should be associated with it. For example, comparing a new love to the one it has replaced, Gautier writes, "Une illusion plus blonde et plus rosée voltige avec ses blanches ailes sur le tombeau, à peine fermé, de sa sœur qui vient de mourir." As the hero of the novel searches for his ideal woman, the eyes feast continually on her whiteness. Her smooth marble-like texture stands in sharp contrast to the frenzied fever of his pursuit.

Gautier, through his novel's hero, appears as a sated connoisseur of feminine beauty. However, the capital fact is the hero's failure to find the ideal Woman. His quest is preeminently an aesthetic one. Pitifully he declares, "Je ne demande que la beauté, il est vrai; mais il me la faut si parfaite, que je ne la rencontrerai probablement jamais." It is not just the artist's tools that are lacking here. "C'est à l'amour à polir ce marbre et à l'achever, c'est dire assez que ce ne sera pas moi qui le finirai." This is the unending suffering that transcends the novel, so evident to Professor Jasinski, writing "La souffrance, diffuse dans *Albertus* et dans les *romans goguenards*, saigne à vif dans *Mademoiselle de Maupin*" (*Les Années*).

It is this suffering that emerges from the plea for pink in the **"Symphonie."** The poem's basic ambiguity rests in the combination of the biographical elements with the exigencies of the artist's eye. The *Maupin* proves that

Gautier's need of pink is not solely that of the artist. White and varieties of red are an integral part of the previously mentioned quest. The voluptuary imagination of Gautier arrays the beautiful courtesans of the past "sur des lits semés de rose." The ideal of his reveries, brought to life by the nightingale's song, appears thus: "Elle s'élevait lentement avec le parfum du cœur d'une large rose à cent feuilles"; no doubt a pink rose.

The hero calls the lady who fills the pages of the novel Rosette ". . . en mémoire de la couleur de la robe avec laquelle je l'ai vue pour la première fois." Through her we may arrive at a complete understanding of Gautier's addition of pink to his white imagery in **"La Symphonie."** We have but to look at Rosette with the eyes of her lover, whom she awakens one morning: ". . . une belle et jeune femme tout en blanc, dont la chair rosait délicatement la robe transparente aux endroits où elle la touchait . . ."

This is perhaps the appraisal of an artist, but the conclusion drawn from the scene bears directly on the ambigous quest in the *Maupin:* "On a beau faire; le bonheur est blanc et rose; on ne peut guère le représenter autrement."

Of course, the tragic thing in the Rosette relationship is that it proves happiness to be beyond the hero's reach. The reason for this is stated by D'Albert: "Tout le mérite qu'a Rosette est en elle, je nelui ai rien prêté. Je n'ai pas jeté sur sa beauté ce voile de perfection dont l'amour enveloppe la personne aimée." He would give anything to find the woman whom he could so envelop: "Mais cette femme n'existe pas.—Si elle existe;—Je n'en suis peut-être séparé que d'une cloison.—Je l'ai peut-être coudoyée hier ou aujourd'hui. Que manque-t-il à Rosette pour être cette femme-là? Il lui manque que je le croie." This is the deep-lying inability to satisfy what Van der Tuin has called "Le besoin de sortir de son moi" (*L'Evolution*). That is why we have heard Gautier lament, "C'est à l'amour à polir ce marbre et à l'achever, c'est dire assez que ce ne sera pas moi qui le finirai." Here in fact is the mournful message of "Oh! qui pourra mettre un ton rose" in the **"Symphonie."**

Pink in Gautier's works is more than the daub of the painter's brush, although it is this, too. It expresses the deepest need of a writer to whom emotional requirements were inseparable from aesthetic requirements. D'Albert's tragedy is Gautier's: "J'ai pour les femmes le regard d'un sculpteur et non celui d'un amant." D'Albert, abandoned by Madeleine (Mlle. de Maupin), whom he has looked at as flesh and blood only *after* seeing her as a Greek statue, remains essentially alone. He is left with Rosette, to whom he is incapable of giving "Ce voile de perfection dont l'amour enveloppe la personne aimée."

Gautier is admitting the same sort of defeat in **"La Symphonie."** The poem thus is a central one, perhaps *the* central one in the *Emaux et Camées* poems. It was these poems of which Gautier's friend Maxime du Camp wrote in *Théophile Gautier* (Paris, 1895): "Elles ont cela de particulier dans l'œuvre de Théophile Gautier, qu'elles ont été, pour la plupart, inspirées par les incidents mêmes de sa vie. Il en est peu sur lesquelles on ne pourrait mettre un nom." The swan-maiden, effusing light in a seeming artistic triumph, is in the end seen wanting, as her creator must envisage the need of someone else to "mettre un ton rose sur cette implacable blancheur." The artist's incapacity to realize fulfillment is apparent in the course of seeking unattainable perfection. "J'ai si présente l'idée de la perfection, que le dégoût de mon œuvre me prend tout d'abord, et m'empêche de continuer" (*Mademoiselle de Maupin*).

Barbara W. Alsip (essay date 1974)

SOURCE: "Jewel and Metallic Imagery in the Poetry of Théophile de Viau and Théophile Gautier," in *Romance Notes*, Vol. XVI, No. 1, Autumn, 1974, pp. 38-45.

[*In the following essay, Alsip compares the poetic imagery of Théophile de Viau and Gautier, concluding that while Gautier may have been influenced by the earlier poet's imagery, he was not an imitator for he developed different, subtler uses for his imagery.*]

In *Metaphysical, Baroque and Précieux Poetry*, Odette de Mourgues comments ". . . Théophile Gautier, who rediscovered these poets (Théophile, Saint-Amant, and Tristan) and appreciated their art so much that he contrived at times to rival them, found it difficult to achieve their successful blend of light transparence and jewelled richness." Might a comparison of jewel and metallic imagery in the *œuvres poétiques* of Théophile de Viau and Gautier's *Émaux et camées* indeed reveal Gautier to be a conscious imitator of this aspect of Théophile's art?

Gautier knew Théophile's work. His essay explaining his affinity for the seventeenth-century poet and his work is clear in *Les Grotesques* (1835), written nearly twenty years before the first edition of *Émaux et camées* in 1852.

> Avant d'avoir lu un seul de ses vers je lui portais déjà un tendre intérêt à cause de son nom de Théophile . . . je vous avoue que tout le mal que l'on disait de Théophile de Viau me semblait adressé à moi Théophile Gautier . . . il ne me paraissait pas croyable qu'un homme portant mon nom fût aussi mauvais poète qu'on prétendait.

> Il était nécessaire, pour mon repos, de me confirmer dans la supposition tout à fait gratuite que j'avais faite, que Théophile de Viau était effectivement aussi bon poète que moi, Théophile Gautier.

In *Les Grotesques,* a series of biographical studies, Gautier describes Théophile as a lover of beautiful things and as being particularly receptive to the sensual. In short, ". . . c'est une âme facile et pleine de sympathies, prête à se passioner à propos de tout et de rien, un vrai cristal à mille facettes, réfléchissant dans chacune de ses nuances un tableau différent, avivé et nuancé de tous les feux de l'Iris . . ."

Although Théophile never wrote an *art poétique*, a stanza from "Solitude" expresses his ideas on poetic creation.

> Qui voudrait faire une peinture
> Qui peust ses traits representer,
> Il faudroit bien mieux inventer,
> Qe ne fera jamais nature.
>
> ("Ode")

Like the sentiments expressed in Gautier's renowned manifesto, **"L'Art,"** Théophile too seems to maintain that poetry is created through the conscious manipulation and intepretation of natural materials.

Generally speaking, gold images in Théophile's poetry are restricted to equating gold with good fortune or a benevolent attitude—images that were already clichés before he wrote. In one of his poems, gold is not the supreme value; love is. Yet, this comparing a woman to the sun and finding her greater than the treasures of Apollo ("Les Princes de Cypre") is by no means original. It belongs to the *belle matineuse* theme already used by such sixteenth-century poets as Du Bellay. Théophile's most fanciful gold image occurs in a poem describing the grounds at Chantilly.

> Les rayons du jour esgarez
> Parmi des ombres incertaines
> Esparpillant les feux dorez
> Dessus l'azur de ces fontaines.
> Son or dedans l'eau confondu
> Avecques ce cristal fondu
> Mesle son teint et sa nature . . .
>
> ("Ode")

Here molten metal swirls in liquid crystal, as the sunset reflected in a fountain becomes the dazzling colors in an alchemist's vessel.

Gautier makes very little use of the reflection device, although he does compare tops of chestnut trees (**"La Fleur qui fait le printemps"**) to golden crowns. His range is wider and more original. For example, following the method explained in **"L'Art,"** Gautier makes of March a master craftsman who, like an adroit couturier, creates spring flowers.

> Pour les petites pâquerettes
> Sournoisement lorsque tout dort
> Il repasse des collerettes
> Et cisèle des boutons d'or.
> **("Premier sourire du printemps")**

Yellow centers of the daisies metamorphose into golden buttons surrounded by a stiffly starched, fringed collar.

Yet Gautier can inspire horror as well as delight. In his poem on the study of hands, he relates a chilling sight—the mummified hand of the guillotined assassin and minor poet, Lacenaire.

> Un prurit d'or et de chair vive
> Semblait titiller de ses doigts

L'immobilité convulsive
Et les torde comme autrefois.

("Etude de mains")

The sickly, golden color of putrid flesh and the terror which grips the reader marks this passage as one of the mannered Decadent tradition.

Silver occurs infrequently in the poetry of Théophile. One poem ["La Maison de Silvie"] makes mention of two silvery brooks, but this particular image must be considered common even in the early seventeenth century. Théophile generally sees water in terms of crystal and Gautier usually connects moisture with pearls.

More commonly, silver evokes flowers to Gautier. For example: "Le lis à la pulpe argentée" and "le vif-argent aux fleurs fantasques" (**"Symphonie en blanc majeur"**). Even more often, it reminds him of ice or snow, as the mountain tops ". . . coiffés d'argent . . ." (in **"La Fleur qui fait le printemps"**). By far the most delicately wrought cameo involving nature occurs in a picture of winter:

Et les arbres, comme aux féeries
Sont en filligraine d'argent.

("Fantaisies d'hiver")

There is magic at work here, as the ice changes the trees into a glittering, fantastic landscape of bare branches festooned with delicate lace. Gautier's apt choice of the precise word conjures up a winter fairyland.

Gautier sometimes employs silver imagery in his "portraits" of women.

Entre ses lèvres d'écarlate
Scintille un éclair argenté
Et sa beauté splendide éclate
Comme une grenade en été.

("Le Château du souvenir")

The adjective *argenté* connotes something flashing and corresponds precisely with other words in the quatrain: *scintille, éclair, éclat,* and *grenade* (although Gautier means "pomegranate" here, the bursting implication remains). Even *écarlate* may be related, since it is a brilliant, eye-catching color. The vivacity of the passage is all the more surprising when one realizes that Gautier here describes a woman long dead—one whom he recreates from memory alone.

A poem about a pink dress produces sensual images. Gautier heightens the tactile sensation by using such words as *épiderme, glissent, frissons,* and *chair.* The predominance of fricatives, notably "s" and "f," complement the appeal to the sense of touch.

De l'épiderme sur la soie
Glissent des frissons argentés
Et l'étoffe à la chair renvoie
Ses éclairs reflétés.

("A une robe rose.")

As mentioned above, crystal symbolizes water for Théophile de Viau, particularly fountains and pools. This may be a lingering effect of Ronsard's influence. The imagery itself is not all that original: ". . . sa demeure de cristal . . ." and ". . . le cristal de ce ruisseau . . ." ("Ode"); ". . . beau cristal de nos fontaines . . ." ("Ode IX"); and ". . . le cristal des roches et des bois . . ." ("Élégie"). Crystal imagery does not occur in Gautier's collection.

The marble imagery in Théophile's poetry is also confined to the commonplace. The one exception may be waves in winter: "Alors que tous les flots sont transformez en marbres" ("Élégie").

On the contrary, marble summons up visions of a woman's flesh for Gautier. For example, in **"Symphonie en blanc majeur"** one finds the metaphors: "paros au grain éblouissant" and "Le marbre blanc, chair froide et pâle / Où vivent les divinités . . ." Previously, in **"Le Poème de la femme"** the woman's nude body is likened unto "marbre de chair." In **"La Nue"** Gautier fantasizes about a cloud shaped like a woman and sees that "Ses blancheurs de marbre et de neige / Se fondent amoureusement." Perhaps the finest of the images is the following:

Plus loin une beauté robuste,
Aux bras forts cerclés d'anneaux lourds,
Sertit le marbre de son buste
Dans les perles et le velours.

("Le Château du souvenir")

The insistence on flesh and jewels and the voluptuous sentiments they arouse in the poet prefigure, in a sense, Baudelaire's "Les Bijoux." Although not as "colorful" as the images in Baudelaire's poem, the sensuality is there.

Ivory reminds Théophile of a woman's flesh: "doits d'yvoire" and "bras d'yvoire": ("Ode," I, pp. 21-22). Gautier uses ivory in this context: "les bustes d'ivoire" (**"Les Néréides"**).

Precious jewels (diamonds, rubies, sapphires) are infrequently used by the poets. In Théophile's works, most of these images describe colorful points of light reflected by sunshine. One exception exists:

L'Aurore qui dedans mes vers
Voit apprendre à tout l'Univers
Que vostre beauté la surmonte,
Arrachant de ses beaux habits
Et les perles et les rubis,
Elle pleure et rougit de honte.

("Ode")

Here the *belle matineuse* theme, which will be utilized later in the seventeenth century by Voiture and Manville, is again brought into play (see remarks concerning "Les Princes de Cypre," *supra*).

Gautier uses diamonds in a figurative sense when he compares: "Le diamant dans sa lumière / Voici la beauté dans l'amour." (**"Le Poème de la femme"**). More artistically composed and typical of the miniature so often found in *Émaux et camées* is a passage from **"Diamant du cœur."**

> Mais je garde, empreinte adorée
> Une larme sur un papier:
>
> . . . . .
>
> Et pour moi, cette obscure tache
> Reluit comme un écrin d'Ophyr
> Et du vélin bleu se détache
> Diamant éclos d'un sapphir.

The diamond-like tear which has fallen on blue vellum metamorphoses into a diamond and sapphire brooch.

Only one semi-precious jewel has that opaque, iridescent quality which appealed to Gautier—the opal. A single example exists in the collection, not surprisingly in Gautier's most extensive paean to woman, the **"Symphonie en blanc majeur."** It foreshadows the whole world of images later evoked by his pearl and mother-of-pearl poetry. The stanza reads:

> La marbre blanc, chair froid et pâle
> Où vivent les divinités
> L'argent mat, la laiteuse opale
> Qu'irrisent de vagues clartés . . .

Pearls always bring to mind tears or droplets of water for Gautier: "Chaque perle est une larme" (**"Le Poème de la femme"**) and "Sur une gamme chromatique / Le sein de perles ruisselant . . ." (**"Variations sur le carnaval de Venise"**). The most carefully wrought of these images might be:

> De grosses perles de Venise
> Roulaient au lieu de gouttes d'eau
> Grains laiteux qu'un rayon irise,
> Sur le frais satin de sa peau.
>   (**"Le Poème de la femme"**)

Gautier uses a monochromatic color scheme—white on white. In part, at least, visual eroticism is composed not of different colors, but of different textures and nuances of the same color. Although this affinity for white may follow the Parnassian school in tone, it is totally sensual in intensity. That white is an erotic color for Gautier may be reinforced by the following stanza concerning mother-of-pearl:

> Convivant la vue enivrée
> De sa boréale fraicheur
> A des regals de chair nacrée
> A des débauches de blancheur!
>   (**"Symphonie en blanc majeur"**)

No parallel imagery exists in Théophile's work.

In conclusion, it may be said that Gautier was not an imitator of Théophile in regard to jewel and metallic imagery. There are too many dissimilarities in the way these images are used. The question of influences remains. Generally speaking, the themes of both poets center around two topics, nature and women. Yet these are themes timelessly and universally employed by poets of any given epoch.

Both poets do dwell on details: Théophile's melting colors in a fountain, a woman's ivory fingers, frozen marble waves. Gautier, true to the title of his collection, uses the cameo device constantly: daisies, a mummified hand, droplets of water, a tear on blue vellum.

Was Gautier influenced by Théophile de Viau? One cannot be absolutely sure. Perusing the poetry of Théophile, Gautier may have, like a wanderer in the woods, stumbled across these scattered and unexpected metallic and jewel images often half hidden in long and mournful elegies and odes. Being the keen critic of literature that he was, he may well have decided to "chisel, polish and perfect" in his own work that sparkling world of images first perceived by "l'autre Théophile."

David Graham Burnett (essay date 1977)

SOURCE: "The Thematic Function of Sexual Identity in Théophile Gautier's *Comédie De La Mort*," in *Nottingham French Studies*, Vol. 16, No. 1, May, 1977, pp. 38-50.

[*In the following essay, Burnett interprets Gautier's* Comédie *as a heroic confrontation with mortality and a struggle for sexual self-knowledge and artistic wholeness.*]

The decade of the 1830's in France was marked by a lively interest in questions of sexual identity. The clear delineation of masculine and feminine impulses characteristic of the neo-classical perspective yielded to more ambivalent views of sexuality during the era introduced by the "bataille d'Hernani".

This change originated through a combination of social and æsthetic considerations. Gender stereotypes were flaunted by feminist "lionnes" such as George Sand and by the revellers who favoured transvestite costumes for the frequent masked balls of the period. The remarkably numerous followers of Ganneau, the self-styled Mapah (mother/father) of the Evadanist (Eve/Adam) sect, attest to the appeal of a religious dogma which emphasized the equality, if not the indivisibility, of the sexes. As well as serving the social causes espoused by Sand, Ganneau, and others, the attacks on sexual stereotypes also suited the coterie of Romantic artists intent upon shocking the popular imagination. No flight of idealistic speculation was too far-fetched for these revolutionaries, for such exercises served to liberate the artistic imagination from pragmatic concerns. The theme of androgyny was particularly well-suited to this purpose, for it introduced a vision of sexuality which was both disturbing and highly idealized. de LaTouche (*Fragoletta*, 1829), Balzac (*Sarrasine*, 1832, *Valentin et Valentine*, n.d., *Séraphîtus/Séraphîta*, 1835), and Gautier (*Mademoiselle de Maupin,* 1835) each contributed stories in which sexual identity was not based on traditional physical and psychological indices.

Théophile Gautier's attachment to this theme is worthy of particular attention because it is closely linked to his personal life and to his æsthetic philosophy. Critics such as van de Tuin have speculated on Gautier's maternal attachments and his intense need for security, impulses which were difficult for the young artist to reconcile with his desire to lead an æsthetic revolution. Of equal significance is Gautier's concern with the role of the artist in society. When he asserted in the preface to *Mademoiselle de Maupin* that Beauty was the sole concern of artistic endeavour, he failed to resolve the more personal problems which beset him. Was the source of this ideal to be found within the imagination of the artist, or must the artist search out and interpret the "natural" beauty in the world around him? In short, was the role of the artist a passive or an active one?

These psychological and æsthetic questions are set forth and analyzed in one of the most revealing compositions of Gautier's formative years, **"La Comédie de la mort."** First published in its entirety in 1838. **"La Comédie"** was composed over an extended period of time. The first part, entitled **"La Vie dans la mort,"** was written during the years 1831-4 and the second part. **"La Mort dans la vie,"** was not completed until 1837. The long narrative poem is minimally about life and death. Physical death functions in the narrative as a metaphor for all forces and events in life which are beyond the control of the individual. The author is particularly interested in the impact on the individual of the knowledge that such forces exist. This impact, however, is presented as a function of sexual identity, with the relative dependence or independence of individual figures dependent upon gender distinctions. In Part One, the masculine and feminine images are polarized, and the pessimistic tone of this part is as much a product of conflict between masculine and feminine aspirations as it is of death's omnipresence. The introspective second part explores not only the author's responses to death, but also to the recognition of "masculine" and "feminine" needs within himself. The ultimate unification of these impulses in the denouement of Part Two substantiates Gautier's choice of titles for the composition, for the conclusion marks the resolution of this tension and suggests an optimistic future for the poet.

Part One of **"La Comédie"** describes the problems which plague the author. It is a strident, polemical description of the fate of the naïve idealist in a world of corruption and death. The narrator recounts two dreams in which a masculine and a feminine figure watch helplessly through the prism of consciousness after death as their hopes for Love and Glory are shattered by the infidelity, egotism, and materialism of the living. Both are portrayed as helpless pawns in a game of death-decomposition-rebirth conducted by natural forces indifferent to the feelings of the individual.

"La Vie dans la mort" is introduced by the narrator's conscious musings about the desirability of consciousness after death. He thinks naturally of the masculine responses to the inevitable disillusionments which would result from knowledge of the living. The hypothetical responses are of two types, a *far-niente* attitude, and an aggressive reaction. The male who values physical comfort and contemplative joys would wish to return to the peaceful security of the domestic foyer:

> S'en revenir chez soi, dans la maison, théâtre
> De sa première vie, et frileux, près de l'âtre,
>
> S'asseoir dans son fauteuil,
>
> Feuilleter ses bouquins et fouiller son pupitre
> Jusqu'au moment où l'aube, illuminant la vitre,
>
> Vous renvoie au cercueil!

A man of action, on the other hand, would be provoked to seek revenge against an unfaithful mistress, wishing to escape the grave in order to confront the offender:

> "Femme, vous m'avez fait des promesses sans
>   nombre;
> Si vous oubliez, vous, dans ma demeure sombre,
>
> Moi, je me ressouviens.
>
> Vous avez dit, à l'heure où la mort me vint
>   prendre,
> Que vous me suivriez bientôt; lassé d'attendre,
>
> Pour vous chercher je viens!"

In the dreams which follow these conscious reflections, the hypothetical active and passive responses are dramatized in elaborate hallucinations. The passive response is associated with a feminine figure, the nameless virgin whose unhappy fate is the subject of section II. Like many of Gautier's feminine figures in the years before the composition of *Maupin,* she is young, naive, and sensual. Her idealism is predicated on the assumption that others hold the key to her happiness, and she awaits the arrival of her husband on their wedding night confident that he will fulfil her every need:

> Voici l'heure où l'époux, jeune et parfumé, cueille
> La beauté de l'épouse, et sur son front effeuille
>
> L'oranger virginal.
>
> Mon bien-aimé, viens donc! l'heure est déjà passée.
> Oh! tiens-moi sur ton cœur, entre tes bras pressée.
>
> J'ai bien peur, j'ai bien froid.

It is not a young, perfumed husband who arrives to consummate the union, however, but Nature's phallic agent of decomposition, the worm. He admires her physical beauty, but warns that it must inevitably be yielded to him. He offers consolation with a reminder that this loss will ultimately contribute to the production of other examples of natural beauty. The virgin's beauty, and her dependent idealism, are thus subject to forces beyond her control, and she can respond to these disillusioning lessons only with vain pleas for familial protection:

> Quelle torture! O Dieu, quelle angoisse cruelle!
> Mais que faites-vous donc lorsque je vous appelle,
> O ma mère ô ma soeur?

The predicament of the activist is illustrated by the experience of Raphael, the solitary figure in the second dream (section III of the narrative). The *cinquecento* artist-architect has sought to avoid the condition of dependency on natural forces by creating immutable works of art. He is aggressive and individualistic, claiming for himself a "génie" (III, 15) which has permitted him to render his experiences of love and faith in unique paintings. He is incensed that he should be measured as a mere mortal by the materialistic "scientists" of the present age. When his painted figures do not strike down those who fail to recognize his individuality, he concludes with the grandiose prediction that the end of civilization is at hand. Having sought independence through the active pursuit of his own ideal, Raphael must defend his own standards at all cost. Complete isolation and a strong desire for revenge follow naturally from this attitude when his values are rejected by those who remain alive.

In **"La Vie dans la mort,"** the masculine and feminine idealists share a common fate over which they have no control. This fate encompasses more than death, however, for they also share an inability to cope with such variables as the infidelity of loved ones and the flux of social values. The masculine and feminine responses to the failure of idealism reveal the conflicting impulses of the active and passive idealists. When the dream figures are compared to the masculine responses outlined in section I, the male idealist appears as the victim of polarized internal desires. The only common ground between the ignorant and parasitic virgin and the self-centred, pompous Raphael is self-pity, a state of mind which accurately reflects the narrator's fragmented self-image at the end of Part One.

When Gautier returns to **"La Comédie"** following the completion of *Mademoiselle de Maupin,* he explores the personal implications of the condition described in **"La Vie dans la mort."** This exploration takes the form of a voyage through the "pays des phantômes", in which the narrator reviews the failure of his past idealistic aspirations. The immediacy of the dream hallucinations gives way to journalistic reportage as he interviews Faust, Don Juan, and LUI (Napoleon) in an effort to document the errors of his past. This guise of objectivity is made possible by the removal of the prism of death through which the narrative of Part One was refracted. Physical death is acknowledged at the outset of the journey, permitting the narrator to concentrate, as the title indicates, on the problem of living.

Death's omnipresence is acknowledged through the angel of death which accompanies the narrator throughout his peregrinations. Like the other figures in **"La Comédie,"** the angel's importance is revealed by her sexual identity.

The masculine narrator conceives of death in feminine terms, and the portrait of the angel suggests a conception of femininity which is infinitely more complex than the stereotyped virgin of Part One.

The angel is at once sinister and charming hideous and beautiful, demonstrating that such judgments depend on the attitude of the observer rather than on external standards. Her embrace holds the promise of forgetfulness and release from the responsibilities of life, and the erotic appeal of her naked "taille délicate", ivory skin, and ebony hair is undeniable. Yet she is sterile and threatens the male procreator with impotence:

> L'ardent baiser s'éteint sur sa lèvre fatale,
> Et personne n'a pu cueillir la rose pâle
> De sa virginité

She is also demanding and possessive, intolerant of other feminine figures:

> C'est elle qui s'en va se coucher, la jalouse,
> Entre les deux amants, et qui veut qu'on l'épouse
> A son tour elle aussi.

The death angel is the feminine presence in the narrator's mind throughout his introspective voyage. Her portait reflects not only his ambivalent attitude toward the inevitability of death, but also the fear and desire which characterize his attitude toward the feminine dimension of his own personality.

The narrator's past concern with active and passive idealism is explored in the encounters with Faust and Don Juan. The narrator casts the problem in sexual terms by inquiring of Faust if he has found his "maîtresse idéale." The mistress in question is Scientia, whom Faust has wooed in hopes of understanding the mysteries of life. The basis for Faust's cerebral idealism is also the cause of his failure as a lover. He is preoccupied by a need for security and seeks contemplative happiness as his pursuit of rational understanding and unambiguous problem solutions demonstrates. In the encounter with the narrator, these needs appear to inhibit the development of virility. Faust's attempts to court his ideal mistress are characterized by timidity and inexplicable fears. When he assumes the role of active pursuer, Faust lacks the physical prowess to complete his "dives", and his life becomes a series of unconsummated affairs:

> La seiche horrible à voir, le polype difforme,
> Tendaient leurs mille bras; le requin, l'orque énorme
> Roulaient leurs gros yeux verts;
> Mais je suis remonté, car je manquais d'haleine;
> C'est un manteau bien lourd pour une épaule humaine
> Que le manteau des mers!

While Faust's cerebral needs are associated with masculine passivity, Don Juan's sensuality has led him to pursue a life of unrelenting activity. His single-minded concern with physical needs ("volupté") has left him no time to consider the cerebral dimensions of the ideal love relationship he seeks. He has predicated his masculine identity on the physical conquest of women, indiscriminately bedding young innocents and debauched courtesans in his search for his ideal mistress. His physical attachment to women has led to a search for the ideal through human contacts in contrast with Faust's solitary encounters with the world of nature. As failure has followed upon failure, Don Juan has become a living illusion of the physical beauty he seeks, disguising his wasted body under layers of wigs, costumes, and make-up:

> Malgré le fard épais dont elle était plâtrée,
> Comme un marbre couvert d'une gaze pourprée
> Sa pâleur transperçait;
> A travers le carmin qui colorait sa lèvre,
> Sous son rire d'emprunt on voyait que la fièvre
> Chaque nuit le baisait.

Faust and Don Juan reflect the polarized sensual and cerebral aspirations of the youthful narrator. The nature of the feminine ideal which will respond to these diverse impulses is eloquently expressed by Don Juan after the failure of his sensual quest:

> J'avais un idéal frais comme la rosée,
> Une vision d'or, une opale irisée
> Par le regard de Dieu:
> Femme comme jamais sculpteur n'en a pétrie,
> Type réunissant Cléopâtre et Marie,
> Grâce, pudeur, beauté;
> Une rose mystique où nul ver ne se cache;
> Le ardeurs du volcan et la neige sans tache
> De la virginité!

The idealized mother/mistress figure implies the existence of bivalent masculine needs as did the narrator's conscious reflections at the beginning of Part One. The maternal dimension responds not only to the infantile need for security and tranquillity, but also to the inclination, expressed by Faust, to treat the feminine ideal with respectful admiration. While thus fulfilling the contemplative wish for purity of form, the figure is also a potentially responsive mistress, a passionate partner of the virile lover and procreator.

Neither Faust, nor Don Juan, nor the narrator during this phase of his life, has been successful in attaining union with such a figure. The rigid association of masculine identity with the single-minded pursuit of an ideal has necessitated a choice on the part of these masculine figures. The choice has been restrictive, forcing the male to suppress certain compelling needs. Faust and Don Juan are prisoners of this mentality. Having chosen a direction at the "Y" of Pythagoras, and failed, they now compulsively conclude that the narrator should follow the path taken by the other, an irony which relates this moment in the voyage to the narrator's fragmented self-image described in Part One.

As the narrator leaves these compulsive searchers, he encounters Napoleon, whose titles in the narrative suggest his mythical stature as the archetypal male. The narrator

refers to him simply as LUI, and Napoleon himself reveals his awareness of the role he has fulfilled in the public imagination:

> Pourtant l'on me nommait par excellence
>   L'HOMME:
> L'on portait devant moi l'aigle et les faisceaux
>   comme
> Aux vieux Césars romains;

In reviewing the elements of his life, Napoleon documents, by implication, the factors which constitute the popular image of masculine identity. He has been a man of perpetual action, assaulting a variety of enemies, and establishing the illusion that he had taken Destiny into his own hands:

> Pourtant j'avais dix pour me tenir ma robe,
> J'étais un Charlemagne emprisonnant le globe
>
> Dans une de mes mains.

This image has earned him the servile admiration of the masses and no personal satisfaction:

> Je promenais partout ma peine vagabonde,
> J'avais rêvé l'empire et la boule du monde
>
> Dans ma main sonnait creux.

Napoleon concludes his monologue with an expression of his intention to espouse a bucolic mode of existence in the future. He envisages an idyllic life in which his actions will be based on personal desires rather than on the fulfilment of a public image. This response differs radically from the alternatives to failure proposed by Faust and Don Juan. Napoleon rejects the continued pursuit of an ideal mistress and in so doing rejects the association of masculine identity with the active quest. Unlike Faust and Don Juan, Napoleon does not cling to an abstracted idealized mistress in order to find a reason to go on after the failure of his initial plan. He refers instead to his childhood, nostalgically recalling the sweet name of his mother, Laetitia. This evocation of childhood happiness suggests that Napoleon is no longer afraid to acknowledge his less virile sentiments, and the portrait of pastoral life which he draws implies the coexistence of virile and infantile impulses in the masculine personality.

Napoleon is intent upon avoiding the unhappy fate of the compulsive searchers such as Oedipus, whose actions are predicated on a search for meaning in life:

> Le seul qui devina cette énigme funeste
> Tua Laïus son père, et commit un inceste:
>
> Triste prix du vainqueur!

The sexual tension which dominates the Oedipus myth will be absent in the pastoral setting which will be free of sexual stereotypes. Napoleon contemplates a life in which active and passive, sensual and intellectual inclinations are no longer associated with gender:

> Une peau de mouton couvrira mes épaules,
> Galatée en riant s'enfuira sous les saules,
> Et je l'y poursuivrai:
> Mes vers seront plus doux que la douce ambroisie,
> Et Daphnis deviendra pâle de jalousie
> Aux airs que je jouerai.

Napoleon's words mark the termination of the voyage through the "pays des phantômes." In the final section of **"La Comédie,"** the narrator applies the self-knowledge he has gained in this introspective experience to his own future as an artist. The first step in this process is the establishment of a new attitude toward the inevitability of death. This attitude is revealed in a prayer, addressed to the death angel and to Mother Nature, the mistress and mother on whom the poet must depend for life itself. While acknowledging the power of these figures, he shows none of the fear which has previously characterized his attitude toward femininity. The death angel is treated as Don Juan might treat a reluctant mistress. She is cajoled with gallant flattery, promises of continued loyalty, and reminded of her debt to her suitor for his past devotion:

> Vierge aux beaux seins d'albâtre, épargne ton poète,
> Souviens-toi que c'est moi qui le premier t'ai faite
> Plus belle que le jour;
> J'ai changé ton teint vert en pâleur diaphane,
> Sous de beaux cheveux noirs, j'ai caché ton vieux
>   crâne,
> Et je t'ai fait la cour.

The maternal figure is likewise reminded of her nurturant and protective responsibilities toward the infant/poet who makes no attempt to conceal his infantile dependency:

> Ne m'abandonne pas, ô ma mère, ô Nature,
> Tu dois une jeunesse à toute créature,
> A toute âme un amour;

The new attitude is thus marked by confidence that he will receive benign treatment from these feminine figures, because he has acknowledged for the first time his dependency on the forces they represent.

The concluding section of the prayer contains the reason why this acknowledgement is now possible. The poet no longer considers that this admission of dependency is a threat to his own masculine identity. Up to this point, the feminine images in the narrative have reflected the narrator's ambivalent feelings about his dependent state. He has alternated between fear, marked by fatalistic passivity, and desire, marked by an aggressive effort to pursue and conquer the abstracted image of his dependency. In his new life, the feminine image is an integral part of the poet's identity, an ideal mother/mistress which is a dimension of the artist's imagination:

> Avril, pour m'y coucher, m'a fait un tapis d'herbe:
> Le lilas sur mon front s'épanouit en gerbe,

> Nous sommes au printemps.
> Prenez-moi dans vos bras, doux rêves du poète,
> Entre vos seins polis posez ma pauvre tête
>
> Et bercez-moi longtemps.

The feminine *alter ego* emerges in response to this plea in the form of Théone, the personal muse from whom his existence is now inseparable:

> Hâtons-nous, hâtons-nous! Notre vie, ô Théone,
> Est un cheval ailé que le Temps éperonne,
>
> Hâtons-nous d'en user.

The muse Théone displaces the death angel as the feminine dimension of the narrator's imagination. Like the death angel, Théone is a protean figure whose appearance depends on the mood of the poet. But unlike the angel, she combines purity and passion in a manner which suggests-fertility rather than sterility:

> Ta gorge est plus lascive et plus souple que l'onde;
> Le lait n'est pas si pure et la pomme est moins
>   ronde.
>
> Allons, un beau baiser!

When the artist's dependent condition, his need for security and maternal succour, is recognized as being of equal importance to his virile, aggressive impulses, the appeal of the death angel disappears. The poet is no longer obliged to disguise her parasitic qualities, and she appears as the antithesis of the life-oriented Théone:

> Chantons Io, Péan! . . . Mais quelle est cette femme
> Si pâle sous son voile? Ah! c'est toi, vieille infâme!
> Je vois ton crâne ras;
> Je vois tes grands yeux creux, prostituée immonde,
> Courtisane éternelle environnant le monde
> Avec tes maigres bras!

The femininity of Théone, on the other hand, is responsive to the changing needs of the poet/narrator. It is a function of the artistic imagination now symbolized by the androgynous couple Théone/Thé(o)phile. Linked by the common element, "È ó", suggesting the divine or idealized nature of the poet/muse relationship, the names reveal the wisdom or intuition (íó ù) and the love (ëëÐ) which will characterize the unified artistic imagination.

The symbiotic nature of the masculine/feminine rapport is also implied by the mythological origins of the feminine *alter ego*. In the tale recounted by Hygenius, Théone, a daughter of King Thestor, is kidnapped by pirates to Caria. Her sister, Leucippe, is advised by the oracle at Delphi to disguise herself as a priest of Apollo, and to go in search of Théone. Théone falls in love with her disguised sister and orders Leucippe's death when her advances are rejected. The story ends with the recognition of his daughters by Thestor, who is the slave brought in to execute Théone's orders. That Théone can love a "man," whose femininity is also real, strongly suggests a harmonious relationship between the poet and his muse.

"La Comédie de la mort," viewed in this light, resembles a tale of heroism. The narrator is reborn following his descent into the "pays des phantômes". The barriers to his heroism, the conflicting impulses which must be overcome in order for the hero to attain his new life, are surmounted when the virile and infantile needs are reconciled.

In the case of Théophile Gautier, the new life is a modest, but meaningful attainment. He ceased to alternate between masochistic inventories of the world's imperfections and idealized portraits of fantasized perfection. He discovered ambient reality as a source of æsthetic pleasure, and confessed that he had been wrong to criticize as artificial the paintings of the Renaissance masters (in **"Melancholia,"** 1834):

> Non, vous n'avez pas fait un rêve de beauté.
> C'est la vie elle-même, et la réalité.
>
> ("**La Diva**," 1838)

The psychological well-being achieved by Gautier through the introspective experience of **"La Comédie de la mort"** is reflected in his long and productive career in which he drew upon the most diverse sources for the celebration of beauty. While Baudelaire recognized this special ability when he dedicated his masterpiece to Gautier, it is doubtful that the author of "Les Fleurs du mal" could have shared Théophile's sense of self-confidence expressed when he finished **"La Comédie"**:

> Ces désespoirs mortels suivis d'espoirs charmants,
> C'est l'amour, c'est ainsi que vivent les amants.
> Cette existence-là, c'est la mienne, la nôtre;
> Telle qu'elle est, pourtant, je n'en voudrais pas
>   d'autre.
>
> ("**Elégie**," 1838)

Monica J. Nurnberg (essay date 1978)

SOURCE: "Inspiration and Aspiration: Gautier's `La Diva'" and Musset's `Une Soirée perdue'," in *Australian Journal of French Studies,* Vol. XVI, No. 5, September-December, 1978, pp. 229-42.

[*In the following essay, Nurnberg contrasts poems by Gautier and Alfred de Musset with similar subject matter—the recounting of a bittersweet, chance encounter with idealized beauty—in order to highlight and define Gautier's visual aesthetic*]

In 1838, Théophile Gautier published a poem entitled **"La Diva,"** in which he recounts a visit to the Théâtre-Italien. The opera is Rossini's *Mosé*, but Gautier is soon distracted from the stage by the sight of a beautiful woman, Julia Grisi, in a box. Henceforth oblivious of the musical performance, Gautier devotes himself to detailing the physical perfections of Julia, and ends his poem regretting having given up painting in favour of poetry: only painting, he says, can hope to capture the essence of physical beauty. On 14th July, 1840, Alfred de Musset visited the Comédie-Française for a performance of *Le Misanthrope*. He too describes his evening in verse. The play gives him cause for reflection on the moral degeneracy of his own time, and the need for a contemporary Molière to denounce it—Musset himself, perhaps, he muses wistfully. At the same time, his attention is drawn by a girl seated in front of him, and later, when the play is over, he realizes that he has followed her to her front door. His literary reflections and aspirations have given way to the pursuit of physical beauty, which he can no more attain than he can succeed as a satirist; hence the title of the resulting poem: "Une Soirée perdue."

Both works are 'occasional' pieces, inspired by a particular evening, and are not intended first and foremost to be *professions de foi*. Yet in each case a woman, seen unexpectedly in the audience and thereby providing an experience other than that for which our poets went to the theatre that night, serves to crystallize their æsthetics, their aspirations and their regrets. While both poets find themselves hankering after a different career—Gautier as a painter, Musset as a satirist—they nevertheless justify their present occupation by producing lyric verse. Both poems have a bitter-sweet atmosphere: joy at the privilege of witnessing an ideal of beauty, and sorrow at being unable to capture it.

It is possible that Musset knew Gautier's poem from one or other of its appearances in the press or in book-form before 1840. There seem to be, however, no conscious echoes of **"La Diva"** in Musset's piece. It is likely that the similarities in the two poems, striking as they are, are no more than coincidental. Both reveal a manner of theatre-going very different from that which prevails today and which permits the poet to be easily distracted from the stage by a member of the audience. The development of both poems depends on this, although Musset is more involved in the performance of *Le Misanthrope* than Gautier is in that of *Mosé*. The aim of this article is to examine how events with fundamental common factors inspired two poets to produce pieces of verse in which they are led, perhaps to their own surprise, to develop their views on beauty, art and their own vocation. We shall be concerned with showing how, in spite of the obvious parallels which can be drawn, each work reflects the distinct personality and attitudes of its creator.

The outcome of our poets' meditations is foreshadowed from the beginning, in the evening's entertainment chosen by each. For Musset literary mastery is both his inspiration and his objective. He does not seek to forget the art which he practices by attending the opera, or by day-dreams of being a painter. On the contrary, he welcomes the close involvement with the shade of Molière which an almost empty theatre seems to foist upon him; even during the performance, he feels that the role of passive spectator is not sufficient for him:

> Et je me demandais: 'Est-ce assez d'admirer?
> Est-ce assez de venir, un soir, par aventure,

D'entendre au fond de l'âme un cri de la nature,
D'essuyer une larme, et de partir ainsi,
Quoi qu'on fasse d'ailleurs, sans en prendre souci?'
("Une Soirée perdue")

How different is the reaction of Gautier at the Salle Favart! Quite apart from his indifference to opera as a genre ("Aimant peu l'opéra, c'est hasard si j'y vais"), he cannot possibly feel that Rossini is speaking directly and particularly to him:

> . . . la salle,
> Quand on l'eût élargie et faite colossale,
> Grande comme Saint-Charle ou comme la Scala,
> N'aurait pu contenir son public ce soir-là.
>
> **("La Diva")**

> Toutes les voix criaient, toutes les mains frappaient,
> A force d'applaudir les gants blancs se rompaient.
>
> **("La Diva")**

Thus, although Gautier is very moved by what he hears on this occasion, he will feel no compulsion to continue listening, and will soon abandon the aural experience in favour of a visual one.

It is at this point that the inspirational mechanism of each poet's thoughts (and hence of the poems themselves) is seen to function quite differently. Gautier turns away from music as an æsthetic experience, concentrating *instead* on the sight of Julia Grisi; this leads him to consider painting alone as capable of capturing her beauty, superior in this to poetry, which can give but a feeble representation of the visual. On reading "Une Soirée perdue," one might at first think that Musset too will reject one æsthetic experience (literary and theatrical) in favour of another (visual). For he is drawn out of his reflections inspired by the play:

> Enfoncé que j'étais dans cette rêverie,
> Çà et là, toutefois, lorgnant la galerie,
> Je vis que, devant moi, se balançait gaîment
> Sous une tresse noire un cou svelte et charmant.
>
> **("Une Soirée perdue")**

There follow ten lines portraying Musset's reaction to the young girl in front of him, a reaction intimately linked with literary experience. His description of her physical attributes is minimal, namely, the lines quoted above, and the rather banal image in the line which follows them and which adds little: "cet ébène enchâssé dans l'ivoire." However, the girl's appearance reminds Musset of two lines from a fragment by [André] Chénier describing doves, and he uses these to evoke her:

> 'Sous votre aimable tête, un cou blanc, délicat,
> Se plie, et de la neige effacerait l'éclat'.
>
> **("Une Soirée perdue")**

So literature is by no means rejected once Musset catches sight of the girl; nor does he forget the play which is being performed meanwhile. Chénier and Molière can co-exist in his imagination; he dares recall the lines from Chénier,

même devant Molière;
Sa grande ombre, à coup sûr, ne s'en offensa pas.
("Une Soirée perdue")

Indeed he soon returns to his reflections inspired by *Le Misanthrope* and the girl appears to have gone out of his mind completely. The central section of the poem takes up Musset's earlier question on his own role as a writer, on the need for a contemporary Molière to show up the cynicism and depravity of the society in which he lives. At least we must suppose that Musset considers these the vices of his day, for, despite his mounting indignation, the object of his attack remains vague:

> S'il [Alceste] rentrait aujourd'hui dans Paris la
> grand'ville,
> Il y trouverait mieux pour émouvoir sa bile
> Qu'une méchante femme et qu'un méchant sonnet;
> Nous avons autre chose à mettre au cabinet.
>
> **("Une Soirée perdue")**

Thus roused by the performance which he is watching, Musset begs Molière to teach him how to turn his talent towards satire, an aim which he will soon admit to be no more than a fantasy. As an aspiring successor to Molière, his tone seems unduly bitter. Not even the darkest interpretation of *Le Misanthrope* can alone account for Musset's wish to dress "l'homme aux rubans verts" in black, to reveal the shameful truth about the society of his day, described with such derision in lines 37-52. Musset has moved far from the biting, yet humorous irony of his attack on contemporary drama in the opening lines of his poem. More than the play itself, the sparsity of the audience seems responsible for Musset's mood of disillusion:

> Que c'était une triste et honteuse misère
> Que cette solitude à l'entour de Molière.
>
> **("Une Soirée perdue")**

And is it not possible to see the spirit of Chénier hovering over this section of the poem? The lines of his which came into Musset's mind earlier are lyrical, not satiric, but once having invoked Chénier, Musset may well be remembering, if only subconsciously, the combative tone of the *Iambes* and the late odes. Chénier was, after all, for Musset's generation, the last great French satirist, and the poetic tradition which Musset aspires to uphold in "Une Soirée perdue" comes more directly and more recently from Chénier than from Molière. There may be no direct borrowings, but there are echoes of the *Iambes*, particularly of "Comme un dernier rayon," first published in full by Sainte-Beuve in 1839:

> Car à quoi comparer cette scène embourbée,
> Et l'effroyable honte où la muse est tombée?
> La lâcheté nous bride, . . .
>
> **("Une Soirée perdue")**

> J'oserais ramasser le fouet de la satire.
>
> **("Une Soirée perdue")**

Apprends-moi de quel ton, dans ta bouche hardie,
Parlait la vérité, ta seule passion.

("Une Soirée perdue")

However, Musset is not to be a satirist. Not that he objects to portraying and criticizing contemporary *mores* for, as P. van Tieghem points out: [in Musset, *L'homme et l'œuvre*, 1994] "Sile poète doit rester à l'écart de toute agitation politique et sociale . . . il n'en faudrait pas conclure qu'il doive rester étranger à son temps. Musset, au contraire, a maintes fois insisté sur ce fait que le poète doit se faire l'interprète de l'âme de son temps". It is rather that Musset is prevented by a trait of character which features in varied guises throughout his work and which here appears as indecisiveness and lack of will-power. Musset is not single-minded enough to consecrate himself to satire; for even as he prays for inspiration, his attention is drawn back to the young girl, and he follows her unknowingly to her door. She is physical beauty, and Musset, in spite of his spiritual aspirations, is magnetized by her, as Gautier is by Julia Grisi:

Pendant que mon esprit cherchait sa volonté,
Mon corps avait la sienne et suivait la beauté.

("Une Soirée perdue")

Musset's pursuit of beauty is no more successful than that of truth, his other "folle chimère"; the girl disappears into her house, and Musset is left in the street. This is his moment of self-awareness and regret. He cries out:

Hélas! mon cher ami, c'est là toute ma vie.

("Une Soirée perdue")

as Gautier exclaims with similar pathos on realizing that he cannot capture *his* vision of beauty:

Pourquoi, lassé trop tôt dans une heure de doute,
Peinture bien-aimée, ai-je quitté ta route?

("La Diva")

In this final section of the poem, where matter wins over mind, Musset's body bearing him away from the realms of satire towards physical beauty, literary inspiration remains a potent force. The subconscious echo of the late Chénier in the central portion gives way to a recapitulation of the lyrical lines quoted earlier. At first the assimilation is but partial; Musset's own:

Sous une tresse noire un cou svelte et charmant

("Une Soirée perdue")

is modified to admit the quality of whiteness, which is so important an element of Chénier's lines and to which Musset has hitherto alluded metaphorically:

. . . le cou svelte et blanc
Sous les longs cheveux noirs se berçait mollement.

("Une Soirée perdue")

The 'dying fall' of *mollement,* so characteristic of Chénier himself, is a delightful tribute to the earlier master. And the poem ends with a repetition of Chénier's lines in the guise of a refrain; Musset appears to have failed in both his objectives, has woken from his dreams, but the power of words remains to warm his heart:

Et quand je m'éveillai de cette rêverie,
Il ne m'en restait plus que l'image chérie:
"Sous votre aimable tête, un cou blanc, délicat,
Se plie, et de la neige effacerait l'éclat".

("Une Soirée perdue")

.　.　.　.　.

Gautier's mental voyage during the performance of Rossini's *Mosé* ends very differently, with what appears to be a repudiation of poetry:

Que peuvent tous nos vers pour rendre la beauté,
Que peuvent de vains mots sans dessin arrêté,
Et l'épithète creuse et la rime incolore?

("La Diva")

This conclusion is not altogether untypical of the young Gautier, in whose artistic hierarchy painting and sculpture are placed above literature, with music in a much inferior position; in **"La Diva"** music is, of course, rejected near the beginning, when Gautier literally turns his back on the stage. We shall return to Gautier's view of the relative capabilities of the arts shortly. However, before examining Gautier's ideas in **"La Diva,"** it is worth considering two points which might affect how seriously we are to take Gautier's expression of his æsthetic attitudes on this occasion. In the first place, the poem seems to have been conceived primarily as a eulogy of Julia Grisi, for whose appearance Gautier had expressed admiration some three years earlier, in the preface to *Mademoiselle de Maupin*. This intention is confirmed by the main title under which the poem first appeared, namely: "Galerie des belles actrices." It is likely that Gautier's apparent philosophizing in the second half of the poem is much less an attempt to clarify his ideas on the representation of beauty through art than a means of presenting Julia as an ideal of female beauty. The second point is that the existence of **"La Diva"** seems to contradict its main argument: Gautier states firmly that poetry, unlike painting, cannot hope to portray visual beauty successfully, but he does take the trouble to compose over one hundred lines on this very subject. The quality of the verse may seem to us on the whole mediocre, but would Gautier have published the poem had he been so profoundly dissatisfied with the medium and with his own attempt?

With these reservations in mind, what can we learn from **"La Diva"** about Gautier's views on inspiration and on the function and aspirations of the artist? And what is the process by which he is himself inspired to write his poem? Gautier goes to the Théâtre-Italien in search of a new experience:

Moi, plus heureux que tous, j'avais tout à connaître,
Et la voix des chanteurs et l'ouvrage du maître.

("La Diva")

During the first act he is transported by what he hears:

> J'étais là, les deux bras en croix sur la poitrine,
> Pour contenir mon cœur plein d'extase divine;
> Mes artères chantant avec un sourd frisson,
> Mon oreille tendue et buvant chaque son.
>
> ("La Diva")

Yet once he catches sight of Julia, the opera is forgotten; in fact, he scarcely mentions it again, and then only as a negative experience:

> Mon âme tout entière à cet aspect magique
> Ne se souvenait plus d'écouter la musique.
>
> ("La Diva")

> Moins épris des beaux sons qu'épris des beaux
>   contours,
> Même au *parlar spiegar,* je regardais toujours.
>
> ("La Diva")

One may well ask, therefore, why Gautier should have chosen to use the setting of an opera-house. The simplest explanation is the factual one: we have no reason to doubt that Gautier saw Julia Grisi in a box at the Théâtre-Italien during a performance of *Mosé.* Gautier may be doing no more than recording his reactions as they occurred: total involvement in the opera for the duration of one act, followed by equally total neglect of it. Yet there are significant links between his attitude towards the music and his portrayal of Julia. Firstly, Julia Grisi was herself a famous soprano, so it is appropriate that Gautier should use the opera-house as the frame of his picture. It would not however have suited his purpose to depict Julia on the stage, for his vision of beauty is essentially immobile:

> Votre Madone est là; dans sa loge elle pose,
> Près d'elle vainement l'on bourdonne et l'on cause;
> Elle reste immobile et sous le même jour,
> Gardant comme un trésor l'harmonieux contour.
>
> ("La Diva")

The second link between the music and Gautier's presentation of Julia is, curiously, a linguistic one. Near the beginning of **"La Diva"** Gautier restates the long-standing argument for the superiority of the Italian language over the French as a medium for opera:

> Car notre idiome, à nous, rauque et sans prosodie,
> Fausse toute musique.
>
> ("La Diva")

This is a strange admission indeed from a poet, but less so when seen in the context of the poem as a whole. For one of Gautier's main points will be that Italian women are incomparably more beautiful than French ones, which has allowed the Italian masters to depict them as they are, without over-idealization. In other words, Italian women present material that is innately suitable for art. Gautier's contrast between the musicality of the Italian language and the harshness of French prepares the ground for this assertion, which is controversial if taken simply as an artistic principle, but less so when tempered by Gautier's primary concern on this occasion, to flatter Julia Grisi.

The performance of *Mosé* thus serves its purpose in Gautier's celebration of the *prima donna,* but it is soon abandoned, since, in Gautier's view, music cannot express the highest form of beauty. In an article on the composer Niedermeyer, Gautier has this to say of music:

> La musique, et c'est là sa beauté, commence où finit
> la parole; elle rend tout ce qu'il y a dans l'âme de
> vaguement sonore, d'onduleux, d'infini, d'inexplicable,
> tout ce que le verbe n'a pas pu formuler.

From some writers, this would be the highest praise. Yet the adjectives employed by Gautier represent precisely that which is to be avoided in the other arts. We may recall, for instance, the fundamental thesis of *Emaux et Camées* (1852) and in particular of the piece **"L'Art"** (added to the collection in 1858), and, at the earlier end of Gautier's career, the vigorous affirmations of d'Albert in *Mademoiselle de Maupin:*

> Trois choses me plaisent: l'or, le marbre et la pourpre,
> éclat, solidité, couleur. Mes rêves sont faits de cela, et
> tous les palais que je bâtis à mes chimères sont
> construits de ces matériaux . . . Jamais ni brouillard ni
> vapeur, jamais rien d'incertain et de flottant. Mon ciel
> n'a pas de nuage, ou, s'il en a, ce sont des nuages
> solides et taillés au ciseau . . .

By its very nature, and judged by these criteria, music cannot fail to hold the lowest place in Gautier's hierarchy of the arts, as L. Dillingham has pointed out. Nor can visual art which attempts to depict that which is vague, shifting or colourless hope to succeed. The French painter is doomed if he uses native models, for if he is to represent them truthfully, he must portray these very characteristics, as Gautier has found to his cost:

> Jusqu'à ce jour j'avais en vain cherché le beau;
> Ces formes sans puissance et cette fade peau
> Sous laquelle le sang ne court que par la fièvre
> Et que jamais soleil ne mordit de sa lèvre;
> Ce dessin lâche et mou, ce coloris blafard,
> M'avaient fait blasphémer la sainteté de l'art.
>
> ("La Diva")

For art must represent reality. It may be appropriate here to recall Gautier's well-known remark to Sainte-Beuve:

> "On m'appelle souvent un *fantaisiste,* me disait-il un
> jour, et pourtant, toute ma vie, je n'ai fait que
> m'appliquer à bien voir, à bien regarder la nature, à la
> dessiner, à la rendre, à la peindre, si je pouvais, telle
> que je l'ai vue."

His critique of the French female figure in **"La Diva"** reminds one also of his reaction on seeing his first artist's model, in Rioult's studio: a grave disappointment for him, "tant l'art ajoute à la nature la plus parfaite," so that "d'après cette impression j'ai toujours préféré la statue à la femme et le marbre à la chair."

However, the sensual side of Gautier's nature is quite evidently aroused by Julia Grisi, and he is able to rationalize his admiration on this occasion by presenting her as a model of beauty in plastic terms. This allows him to pursue his avowed objective of depicting reality, while enabling him at the same time to retain, rather precariously, his general belief in the superiority of marble to flesh—with the exception of Julia and certain other Italian models. For in their case idealization is unnecessary, and the art which they inspire is "true":

> J'avais dit: L'art est faux, les rois de la peinture
> D'un habit idéal revêtent la nature.
> Ces tons harmonieux, ces beaux linéaments,
> N'ont jamais existé qu'aux cerveaux des amants;
> J'avais dit, n'ayant vu que la laideur française:
> Raphaël a menti comme Paul Véronèse!
> Vous n'avez pas menti, non, maîtres; voilà bien
> Le marbre grec doré par l'ambre italien,
> L'œil de flamme, le teint passionnément pâle,
> Blond comme le soleil sous son voile de hâle . . .
>
>   **("La Diva")**

and so on for another ten lines. Raphael and Veronese are thus supreme artists, directing their genius towards the exact imitation of exceptional beauty:

> Artistes souverains, en copistes fidèles,
> Vous avez reproduit vos superbes modèles!
>
>   **("La Diva")**

These are the theories of artistic creation which Gautier selects to suit his purpose in the poem. But what do we learn of Gautier as a practising artist in **"La Diva"**? By what means does he apply the maxims which he preaches? He has the right model, of course, in Julia Grisi and, although working in words, he will attempt, as he does so frequently elsewhere, to bring his portrayal as close as possible to painting. This is achieved in various ways. The evocation of Julia is contained in lines 33-66 and is resumed, with a certain amount of repetition of earlier material, in line 81; this is the beginning of the last section of the poem, which Gautier may well have written later than the rest.

In the first place, Gautier gives his picture an independent existence by framing it with the surround of the box in which Julia is sitting. This separation of the 'sitter' from the auditorium will serve to put into relief her simple, unadorned beauty, against the background of sparkling diamonds and gold necklaces worn by the other women. The illusion of a *tableau* is strengthened by Gautier's specific reference to two painters, a method of comparison of which he frequently made use:

> Il me sembla d'abord,
> La loge lui formant un cadre de son bord,
> Que c'était un tableau de Titien ou Giorgione,
> Moins la fumée antique et moins le vernis jaune.
>
>   **("La Diva")**

Thereafter Gautier concentrates on three of the essential aspects of pictorial art, namely, immobility, line, and colour and light. Julia's stillness is indicated in line 37 and again in line 93; her occasional change of posture merely serves to create a new *tableau* (a device which reappears in the later **"Poème de la femme"**):

> Au bout de quelque temps, la belle créature,
> Se lassant d'être ainsi, prit une autre posture,
> Le col un peu penché, le menton sur la main,
> De façon à montrer son beau profil romain.
>
>   **("La Diva")**

The emphasis on line occurs frequently, in the description of Julia's hair, her profile, and her head, neck and arm:

> J'admirais à part moi la gracieuse ligne
> Du col se repliant comme le col d'un cygne,
> L'ovale de la tête et la forme du front,
> La main pure et correcte, avec le beau bras rond.
>
>   **("La Diva")**

Gautier later adds to this description a reference to her "nez sévère et droit" and leaves the reader with a final image of her "harmonieux contour." As for his references to colour and light, it is noticeable that Gautier makes deliberate use of the concepts and terminology of painting:

> Son épaule et son dos aux *tons chauds* et vivaces,
> Où l'ombre avec le clair flottaient par larges masses.
>
>   **("La Diva")**

> Elle reste immobile et *sous le même jour.*
>
>   **("La Diva")**

In his *Portraits et souvenirs littéraires* [1875] Gautier remarked that "par suite d'une première éducation et d'un sens particulier, nous sommes plus plastique que littéraire." Nonetheless, his portrait of Julia Grisi owes as much to his literary as to his visual imagination. A particularly interesting example of his combination of literary and painterly allusions occurs in the following lines:

> Tant cette morbidezze et ce laisser-aller
> Était chose charmante et douce à contempler.
>
>   **("La Diva")**

Morbidezze is a term of painting indicating suppleness and delicacy in the representation of flesh; it also carries undertones of its less specialized meaning in Italian of languor and softness. Already used by Montaigne, it soon became *morbidesse,* and as such is found in a variety of seventeenth-century authors. Indeed, the Italian form seems to have disappeared from French quite early on. In the nineteenth century, the French form was the accepted one, and Gautier himself makes use of it in his *Portraits contemporains.* What we have here, therefore, is not simply the introduction of a professional art term to suggest the illusion of painting, but the creation of *verbal* local colour by the re-borrowing of a clearly foreign word. Gautier was of course, like Stendhal, in the forefront of those writers who exploited the possibilities of Italianisms in the 1830s.

Other procedures employed by Gautier to evoke Julia belong firmly to literature and supplement the depiction of external reality. Such are the metaphors:

> Et comme un livre ouvert son front se laissant lire.
> ("**La Diva**")

and the rather more original:

> . . . ce pâle jasmin transplanté d'Italie.
> ("**La Diva**")

Gautier's most striking deviation from the pure *transposition d'art* lies however in his enumeration of the characteristics which his model does *not* possess; this portrayal by negation is possible in literature alone:

> Ni plumes, ni rubans, ni gaze, ni dentelle;
> Pour parure et bijoux, sa grâce naturelle.
> ("**La Diva**")

> Pas d'œillade hautaine ou de grand air vainqueur,
> Rien que le repos d'âme et la bonté de cœur.
> ("**La Diva**")

So Gautier pieces together his picture, with numerous touches of vivid detail and employing the diverse resources of poet and painter. Yet his aspirations remain unfulfilled; words cannot portray physical beauty, he exclaims. His sentiments are paradoxical, for they contradict the very existence of the poem, and they are ironic when contrasted with the feelings of Musset in "Une Soirée perdue". Gautier succeeds in creating a portrait with words and then denounces literature, whereas Musset, retaining his faith in poetry, manages only the briefest sketch of the young girl, relying on Chénier to complete and crystallize his evocation.

It is thus difficult to take Gautier's remarks on the inefficacy of words at their face value; but we cannot ignore the poignancy with which he expresses his regrets in the last fourteen lines of his poem. Forgetting the real reasons which led him to give up painting—short-sightedness and lack of talent—he rails against his own earlier laziness and feeling of inferiority, thereby pathetically revealing his fundamental dissatisfaction:

> Pourquoi, découragé par vos divins tableaux,
> Ai-je, enfant paresseux, jeté là mes pinceaux,
> Et pris pour vous fixer le crayon du poëte,
> Beaux rêves, obsesseurs de mon âme inquiète,
> Doux fantômes bercés dans les bras du désir,
> Formes que la parole en vain cherche à saisir?
> ("**La Diva**")

And in a final homage to his model, Gautier reveals, with the same mingling of joy and sorrow as Musset, the ambivalence of the artist privileged to witness beauty, but unable to capture it:

> Ah! combien je regrette et comme je déplore
> De ne plus être peintre, en te voyant ainsi

> A *Mosé,* dans ta loge, ô Julia Grisi!
> ("**La Diva**")

David Graham Burnett (essay date 1981)

SOURCE: "The Destruction of the Artist in Gautier's Early Poetry," in *Bulletin de la Société Théophile Gautier,* No. 3, 1981, pp. 49-58.

[*In the following essay, Burnett describes the pattern of artistic self-destruction—creation of an ideal, desire for that ideal, and subsequent destruction—prevalent in many of Gautier's early poems.*]

In the concluding stanza of "Albertus" (1832), Théophile Gautier challenges the reader to decipher the "allégorie admirable et profonde" of his "légende théologique". This 1400 line compendium of romantic clichés recounts the saga of the witch, Véronique, who transforms herself into a seductive young woman. By chance, she sees a "fashionable", young, poet/painter, Albertus, and falls in love with him. She arranges to have him brought to her and seduces him after extracting a promise that he will sell his soul to have her. In the midst of their lovemaking, she and her surroundings are changed back to their original, hideous form. Albertus and Véronique fly together to a "sabbat" which ends as follows:

> Le Diable éternua. - Pour un nez fashionable
> L'odeur de l'assemblée était insoutenable.
> - Dieu vous bénisse, dit Albertus poliment.
> - A peine eut-il lâché le saint nom que fantômes,
> Sorcières et sorciers, monstres, follets et gnomes,
> Tout disparut en l'air comme un enchantement.
> - Il sentit plein d'effroi des griffes acérées,
> Des dents qui se plongeaient dans ses chairs
>   lacérées;
> Il cria; mais son cri ne fut point entendu . . .
> Et des contadini le matin, près de Rome,
> Sur la voie Appia trouvèrent un corps d'homme,
> Les reins cassés, le col tordu.

The obvious question that must be answered if the allegory is to be deciphered is, 'who or what kills Albertus'? If the entire ensemble has disappeared and no one is present, to whom or to what belong the teeth and claws that mutilate the poet/painter/hero?

The text of stanza XX furnishes a number of clues to the resolution of this problem. The manner in which Albertus is killed is reminiscent of his orgy with Véronique. While she seduces him by posing as a demure virgin, her aroused physical desire betrays a different dimension of her existence:

> Comme ceux d'une orfraie ou d'un hibou dans
>   l'ombre,
> Les yeux de Véronique un instant d'un feu sombre
> Brillèrent;. . . . . (XCIV).
>   . . . . . Je t'aime!
> Dit-elle bondissant comme un tigre en fureur.
>   (XCVI)

In addition to the capacity to inflict injury through claw-ing, as implied by these images, Véronique's ability to grasp and twist becomes evident as their love-making continues. Albertus becomes the victim of a crab-like crea-ture:

> Le prisme était brisé. = Ce n'était plus la femme
> Que tout Leyde adorait, mais une vieille infâme,
> Sous d'épais sourcils gris roulant de gros yeux
>   verts,
> Et pour saisir sa proie, en manière de pinces,
> De toute leur longueur ouvrant deux grands bras
>   minces. (CV)

As she manifests the ability to inflict the injuries that lead to Albertus' death, Véronique joins a menagerie of fem-inine figures in Gautier's poetry who are portrayed as part animal. The angel of death in **"La Comédie de la mort,"** **"La naïade," "La chimère," "Le Sphinx," "L'ondine,"** and **"Les néréides"** are each presented as embodiments of the dual feminine nature. Foremost among the attributes of these figures is a beautifully formed upper body. The male is consistently attracted by the sight of their exposed breasts. Albertus, for instance, dwells on the aesthetic qualities of Véroniquès transformed body, stressing the perfection of its form and color:

> Cette mamelle flasque, ...
>
> . . . . .
> Se gonfle et s'arrondit; - le nuage de hâle
> Se dissipe; on dirait une boule d'opale
> Coupée en deux, à voir sa forme et sa blancheur.-
> Le sang en fils d'azur y court, la vie y brille
> De manière à pouvoir, même avec une fille
> De quinze ans, lutter de fraîcheur. (XX)

Other suitors in Gautier's early verses, however, seem more attracted to the promise of nourishment and maternal proc-tection offered by the naked breasts;

> Elle pousse en avant deux mamelles pointues
> Dont le marbre veiné semble gonflé de lait.
> 　　　　　　　　　**"Le Sphinx"**
>
> Connaissez-vous dans le parc de Versailles,
> Une Naïade, œil vert et sein gonflé?
> 　　　　　　　　　**"Rocaille"**

What ever their motivations, the male figures become involved with these creatures in spite of the dangers they present to life and limb. Potential lovers of the sphinx are aware that it has claws and that they risk its vampire-like appetites

> Le Sphinx est sans pitié pour quiconque se trompe;
> Imprudent, tu veux qu'il t'égorge et te pompe
> Le pur sang de ton cœur?
> 　　　　　　　**"La Comédie de la mort"**

The fisherman who pursues the undine in her water king-dom is similarly victimized. In general, lovers seeking com-merce with these fabulous figures overlook the unattrac-

tive and dangerous animal dimension, intent as they are on the non-genital aspect of their ideals:

> Mais qui regarde la nageoire
> Et les reins aux squameux replis
> En voyant les bustes d'ivoire
> Par le baiser des mers polis?
> 　　　　　　　**"Les Néréides,"**

Albertus hesitates momentarily before his encounter with the witch. He is clearly aware of the ultimate fate that awaits him when he accepts her invitation to a secret rendez-vous:

> Albertus suivait Juan silencieux et morne;
> Certe, il n'avait ni l'air ni le pas d'un galant.
> —Un larron qu'un prévot conduit à la potence.—
> 　　. . . . .
> Ne marche pas d'un pied plus lent. (LXXXV)

The figure of the hanging man is virtually inseparable from Albertus once he makes the commitment to the tryste with Véronique. Such a figure still attached to the scaf-folding accompanies the "lovers" on their broomstick ride to the witches sabbath and the mountain-top orgy is peo-pled with grotesquely mutilated visions:

> Pendus tirant la langue et faisant des grimaces:
> Guillotinés blafards, un ruban rouge au col. (CXII)

It is possible, then, that Albertus' fate, i. e. death from a twisted, broken neck and a crushed body, has resulted from his sexual encounter with the witch. Clearly her animal nature has the potential to inflict such injury and these precise types of damage are characteristic of involvement with the castrating vampire/woman.

The male figure is not, however, always a passive victim in Gautier's poetry. Albertus himself is a piquant amal-gam of paradoxical qualities:

> Cet ensemble faisait l'effet le plus étrange;
> C'était comme un démon se tordant sous un ange,
> Un enfer sous un ciel. Quoiqu'il eût de beaux yeux
> De longs sourcils d'ébène effilés vers la tempe,
> Se glissant sur la peau comme un serpent qui
>   rampe,
> Une frange de cils palpitants et soyeux,
> Son regard de lion et la fauve étincelle
> Qui jaillissait parfois du fond de sa prunelle
> Vous faisaient frissonner et pâlir malgré vous. (LXI)

Albertus' animalism is buried under layers of repressive mechanisms. In addition to his basic "purity" (Son âme, qu'il niait, cependant était pure. LXXIV) Albertus has developed an elaborate mask of ironic indifference. Strong stimulation is necessary, in the form of Rhine wine and Véronique's advances, in order to disrupt his placid ve-neer. Once aroused, however, he apparently acquits him-self of his duty with considerable enthusiasm.

On occasion, Gautier's male figures acknowledge the re-pressed beast within directly. Using the heavy-handed idiom that characterizes these adolescent verses, the narrator of **"Le Lion du cirque"** speaks to his own desire:

> Le temps n'est pas venu de te démuseler.
> En attendant le jour de revoir la lumière,
> Silencieusement, à l'angle d'une pierre,
> Ou contre les barreaux de ton noir souterrain,
> Aiguise le tranchant de tes ongles d'airain.

Male desire, then, is characterized by the same physical accoutrements as female animal behavior. The artist who successfully mounts the female figure in **"La Chimère"** masters the female through the use of his legs to squeeze her flanks and his hands like claws to grasp her mane. Like the male victims of female desire, the chimera is ultimately unable to sustain her flight and to satisfy the rider. She weakens, leaving the male without support on his flight of passion.

A significant pattern emerges from these brief reviews of sexual interaction between male and female figures each with split personalities. While the roles of aggressor and victim in such relations are interchangeable and do not follow gender distinctions, the role of victim is characterized by a loss of "purity" and physical decomposition. Should the female dominate, the male is violated by vampire-like demands and ultimately disfigured. Should the male be sufficiently aroused to consumate the affair, the youthful virginal aspect of the female decomposes instantaneously, leaving the male in the embrace of the animalized female on the verge of his own destruction. It becomes ultimately impossible to distinguish between victim and aggressor once these instincts are liberated. The potential for self-destruction inherent in active/passive, angelic/demonic, purity/passion dichotomies is realized when the barriers of *far-niente* are broken down.

Albertus' adventure is a systematic exercise in self-destruction. From the moment he reluctantly agrees to follow Don Juan through the underground passage, past the guard dogs, and to drug himself on wine, he becomes the agent of his own demise. The veneer of indifference crumbles (in fact he sees double as if to witness his former self disappear), culminating in his vicarious participation in the mountain-top orgy presided over by a devil/dandy who is a carbon copy of Albertus himself. This devil figure does not apparently disappear as do the other creatures when Albertus utters "God bless you." The autoscopic vision, it seems, is the diabolical agent of the poet/painter's self-destruction.

This interpretation of the Albertus legend offers a useful thematic structure for the analysis of several adolescent poems by Gautier. These works are often presented as dream narratives, but their imagery reveals that they are variants of the artist's self-destruction motif. In **"Le Cavalier poursuivi,"** the male poet/dreamer rides a "horse" that is reminiscent of the chimera figure. The creature has wings on its feet, gleaming eyes, and a "folle crinière" that the rider grasps until his mount looses strength and is overtaken by the vampire, "ennui". Unable to reach a higher level once his agressive instincts are aroused, the rider self-destructs in the familiar manner:

> C'en est fait,—le voilà, mes prières sont vaines;—
> Il m'éteint les regards et m'entr'ouvre les veines
> De ses ongles de fer,
>
> (st. 14)

Another poem rendered more comprehensible, and less gratuitous by the application of the self-destruction motif is **"Cauchemar,"** the semi-parody made famous by Gautier's self-citation in *Les Jeune France*. The final lines of the poem are offered as evidence of Daniel Jouvard's conversion to romanticism:

> J'aperçois bientôt, non loin d'un vieux manoir,
> A l'angle d'un taillis, surgir un gibet noir
> Soutenant un pendu; d'effroyables sorcières
> Dansent autour, et moi de fureurs carnassières
> Agité, je ressens un immense désir
> De broyer sous mes dents sa chair, et de saisir,
> Avec quelque lambeau de sa peau bleue et verte,
> Son cœur demi-pourri dans sa poitrine ouverte.

This vision follows a turbulent flight from a severed hand, armed with nails of steel. The dreamer is ultimately overcome by crows, dogs, snakes, and crabs that pick, claw, and squeeze him. Like Albertus, however, his ordeal does not end at this point. He also flies off to the orgy outlined in the final lines, separated, as he puts it, from his former self. In the concluding vision, the unarticulated wish that   has provoked the anxiety-filled nightmare reaches some measure of symbolic articulation. To take part in the orgy is to cannibalize oneself.

The most subtle and complex manifestation of this self-destructive tendency is found in the poem entitled **"Ballade."** The first fifteen stanzas recount, in a single sentence, the poet's description of the ultimate `far-niente' expérience. As in another poem entitled **"Far Niente,"** the state of mind is linked to passivity and indifference. The time of year is autumn, when the animals peacefully pursue the quest for winter provisions, and the earth is dry and windless. As in **"Albertus"** (LXXIII), floating particles of dust here symbolize the detached consciousness of the idle poet.

In the warm sun, however, the poet begins to dream and the "real" countryside is systematically replaced in his mind with a "new world" of his own creation. It is filled with chateaux, vast panoramas, and monumental cities and the season subtly changes from autumn to spring. The dreamer's attention comes to focus on a "vieux manoir" inhabited by a chatelaine, a dwarf, and surrounded by a hunting party of men and women, servants, horses, and a pack of dogs. While based on the lesson of **"Cauchemar"** one might expect a scaffold nearby, instead the castle is guarded by crows that sit on each turret. The castle itself is described as having enormous drawbridges and gigantic portals.

Abruptly the narrative flow is interrupted by the hunting call, as a stag appears from nowhere. In three rapid stanzas, the beast is pursued, worn down, cornered by the dogs, downed and killed. In fact, its limbs are even cold fifteen lines after the sighting. In the concluding two stanzas, the poet explains that this dream is neverending, but that when he tires of it, he goes to sleep in the shade of dark shadows.

The dream of the stag that has come too close to the guarded female symbol is reminiscent of the story of Diana (Artemis) and Acteon. The transformation of Acteon into a stag is recounted by Ovid (Book IV of *The Metamorphoses*) and recalled by Gautier in "Parfois une Vénus . . ." *(Dernières Poésies)*. As in Ovid's tale, the stag in "Ballade" also sheds a tear that goes unnoticed by the dogs and men who kill it.

The Ovidian story furnishes a model for the dream of selfdestruction. The female (goddess) is responsible for the transformation of the innocent male into an animal, just as Véronique transforms Albertus from stony indifference to impassioned diabolism, but the resulting destruction is a product of the male's own animals. In **"Ballade,"** the dreamer's physical desire, implicit in his creation of springtime, castles, and fountains, supercedes his "farniente" passivity. Once desire is aroused, his potential for self-destruction is animated as well. The orgiastic aspects of the stag's death are clear:

> Il chancelle, il s'abat.
> Pauvre cerf, son corps saigne,
> La sueur á flots baigne
> Son flanc meurtri qui bat;
>
> (Stanza 16)

There is nothing more for the dreamer to do, but go to "sleep", a sleep presumably deeper and more permanent than the "sleep" during which he has been dreaming.

The impulse to self-destruction in these early works of Gautier is clearly related to the process of artistic creation. In virtually all cases, the female figure or its representation is the product of the artist/dreamer's imagination. It is never simply a product of "nature" encountered by chance. This form of creativity produces an incestuous structure through which the artist seeks commerce with his own creations, thus bypassing any "natural" or uncontrollable interactions. The pattern requires the supression of the male artist's undisciplined impulses as well, however, and this necessity leads him to an obligatory pose of blasé indifference. If the (self)-stimulus of the imaginary feminine figure overcomes this defense, the artist becomes the victim of his own destructive tendencies.

This pattern of artistic incest offers a useful approach to other authors as well. Additional research will indicate, I believe, that such compositions as Beaudelaire's "Le Vampire," "L'Héautontimorouménos," and "Duellum" are in part inspired by Gautier's treatment of this theme. So too are "Au Lecteur" and "Métamorphoses d'une vampire" which bear a remarkable similarity to **"Albertus"** and **"Le Cavalier poursuivi."**

David Graham Burnett (essay date 1982)

SOURCE: "The Architecture of Meaning: Gautier and Romantic Architectural Visions," in *French Forum*, Vol. 7, No. 2, May, 1982, pp. 109-116.

[*In the following essay, Burnett discusses the evolving role of the poem-as-architecture in Gautier's* La comédie de la mort.]

In 1838 Théophile Gautier published a collection of poetry entitled **La Comédie de la mort**. The volume opens with the poem **"Portail"** and closes with **"Le Sommet de la tour."** In both works the poet casts himself in the role of architect, laboriously erecting a gothic cathedral from crypt to pinnacles. His verses are the building blocks to which he gives the charge:

> En funèbres caveaux creusez-vous, ô mes vers!
> . . . . .
> Puis montez hardiment comme les cathédrales,
> Allongez-vous en tours, tordez-vous en spirales.

While these sometimes tortuous metaphorical efforts occasionally make tedious reading, they do reveal the problematics of poetry as architecture. The poet's verses have both function and form, as do their architectural counterparts. Gautier's verses function as tombs for his dead illusions:

> Mes vers sont des tombeaux tout brodés de
>   sculptures;
> . . . . .
> Chacun est le cercueil d'une illusion morte.
>
> (**"Portail"**)

The form of the construction is flaming gothic: the wedding-cake school of design in which one more "feston" or "dentelle" can only enhance the gay fantasy effect:

> Ce ne sont que festons, dentelles et couronnes,
> Trèfles et pendentifs et groupes de colonnes
> Où rit la fantaisie en toute liberté.
>
> (**"Portail"**)

The relationship of form to function in these verses is thus paradoxical, if unoriginal. The somber funereal function contrasts sharply with the purposefully self-indulgent form.

The poet's concern with decoration, with embroidering his construction, is so great that he calls the very notion of function into question. The notion of verses as containers for dead illusions is essentially ambiguous to begin with. Dead illusions, presumably "killed" in confrontations with reality, are no longer illusions at all, but memories, wishes, or fantasies. Thus both the nature of the contents and the very function as tomb are highly elusive. Gautier implicitly acknowledges this ambivalence by inviting the reader/viewer of his construction to create function through the perceptual process:

> Aussi bien qu'un tombeau, c'est un lit de parade,
> C'est un trône, un autel, un buffet, une estrade;
> C'est tout ce que l'on veut selon ce qu'on y voit.
>
> (**"Portail"**)

The elaborately decorated, illusory tomb for illusions is presented to the reader as a *repository* for meaning. Definition and purpose reside not in construct, but with the perceiver. As if to underline the role of the poetic cathedral as fantasy-generating void to be filled, Gautier closes **"Portail"** with a question, wondering how and whether his edifice will be occupied: "L'église est toute prête; y viendrez-vous mon Dieu?"

The architectural/verbal construct as a fantasy-generating device appears in a poem from *La Comédie* entitled **"Notre-Dame,"** written in 1832 when Gautier was 21 years old. The poem, subtitled **"Ode à Victor Hugo,"** narrates the young poet's ritual visit to Notre-Dame de Paris at sunset. This visit is prompted, Gautier tells us in the first stanza, by his desire to escape the claustrophobic effects of his daily life. The reader can anticipate, then, that the cathedral will serve, or at least Gautier hopes that it will, as a stimulus to his own stifled imagination. That is, it will serve him in the same way as his poetry is intended to serve the reader.

The development of the poet's perceptual fantasies is, of course, aided by the magical, multicolored effects of the sunset. Even before the narrator sights the church he spots cloud cathedrals in the evening sky. This vision, in turn, is reflected in the mirror-like surface of the nearby Seine. In one brief stanza, however, the evening breeze dissolves the image in the sky and distorts its reflection by rippling the surface of the river:

> Cathédrales de brume aux arches fantastiques,
> Montagnes de vapeurs, colonnades, portiques,
> Par la glace de l'eau doublés;
> La brise qui s'en joue et déchire leurs franges
> Imprime, en les roulant, mille formes étranges
> Aux nuages échevelés.

The double deformation of the anticipatory vision introduces the notion of instability into the perceptual process even before the church is sighted. The convenient binary categories of up/down, inside/outside are destabilized.

When, in stanza five, the cathedral does come into view, it triggers in the narrator's perception a flood of highly mobile images. From a distance, it appears as a praying figure opening its eyes, a giant crab with moving pincers, an enormous spider spinning a web, and, as the poet approaches, a raucous conglomeration of monsters, gargoyles, crows, and angels alternating with conspicuous voids above the gaping portals. There is no mention throughout these verses of the religious function of the building. While it is beyond the scope of this discussion to explore the significance of each of these sometimes conflicting personal fantasies, it is worth while to point out the highly personal nature of the crab vision. This obsessive image dominates Gautier's work of the period and occurs in at least three other poems composed between 1830 and 1832; the crab is usually in pursuit of the poet. Here the sunset vision of the cathedral provokes a reappearance of this private, threatening demon that is very much a part not of the cathedral, but of the poet's own imagination.

In Section II of **"Notre-Dame,"** the notion of instrumental perception continues to dominate the narrative. Mounting the tower, the poet uses the building to reach a "new perspective," suspended in the void half way between the heavens above and the chaos below. His position, atop the undulating spire, is characterized by the reflected void—"le vide par-dessus et par-dessous l'abîme." His vision, in turn, is as undifferentiated as the space in which he finds himself. He is bathed in a sense of total unity, in an embryonic state of consciousness of endless murmurs amid "ce grand tout."

Even as the poet is able to distinguish specific details of the panorama that surrounds him, he remains entranced by the grandeur and beauty of the "prodigieux amas." The moving tower and surrounding sea of roofs combine with the setting sun on the Seine below to produce an impression not of chaos or warring significance, but of all-encompassing unity.

Section III of the narrative takes up the rebirth of the poet at street level and his subsequent efforts to preserve the stability of the quasi-divine unified vision. Faced with the loss of the unifying perspective provided by the lofty spire, the poet clings to the church as a symbol of maternal consolation and purity:

> On dirait à te voir, Notre-Dame chrétienne,
> Une matrone chaste au milieu de catins!

The *function* of the cathedral reasserts itself. The hollow structure, previously a means to mobile fantasy and to oceanic consciousness, now has an essence: **"Le Seigneur habite en toi."** Meaning, once apparently extrinsic to the construct, is now intrinsic. The role of the narrator, the former generator of meaning, is converted to that of explicator. He finds that the form of the building *exemplifies* its function as a "maison de Dieu."

The characteristics of the Mother Church, its authority, dignity, piety and chastity, are directly represented in the immensity, regal splendor, and apparent immortality of Notre-Dame, the cathedral. As the bearer of meaning, the container for the body of Christ (Gautier calls it "un immense ostensoir," an immense monstrance, the church focuses the mind of the viewer on itself, rather than provoking the creation of fantasies. Gautier's reading of the architectural text is no longer instrumental, but explanatory.

This divine stature of Notre-Dame creates a privileged position for the cathedral with respect to more mortal architectural efforts. If gothic architecture is exemplary of Christian meaning, then all constructions of pagan inspiration are necessarily heretical. And, in fact, Soufflot's difficulties in the construction of the Panthéon are taken to exemplify the shortcomings of "atheistic" architecture:

> Qui pourrait préférer, dans son goût pédantesque,
> Aux plis graves et droits de ta robe dantesque
> Ces pauvres ordres grecs qui se meurent de froid,
> Ces Panthéons bâtards, décalqués dans l'école,
> Antique friperie empruntée à Vignole,
> Et dont aucun dehors ne sait se tenir droit?

If Notre-Dame is a chaste matron, the Parthenon can only be a whore.

The problem for the reader of Gautier, of course, is to understand this remarkable transformation of Notre-Dame de Paris from unstable existence to unified essence following the narrator's provisional suspension in the void midway between human chaos and divine unity. In this task two important intertexts prove very valuable.

First, the biblical engravings of John Martin, the English painter who, having received a medal from Charles X in 1829, had the foresight or poor taste to dedicate his "Fall of Ninevah" to the last of the Bourbons the following year. Although Gautier did not write in detail about Martin until 1837, the latter's work, especially "Balthazaar's Feast" and "The Fall of Babylon," had been discussed by Sainte-Beuve as early as 1829. Gautier himself mentions Martin in the Preface to *Maupin*. All of Martin's work that attracted the attention of the French Romantics dramatized what Sainte-Beuve called the "épouvante biblique," that is, the human reaction of awe and terror in the face of divine intervention. The elements of Martin's conception are repeated in many of his works: an immense edifice that dwarfs the human figures present while symbolizing their self-centered accomplishments is displaced and "overshadowed" in the composition by the manifestation of Jehovah. This presence, generally conveyed by a light source of surpassing brilliance, is so concentrated that it reduces the human construct and its inhabitants to a poorly defined, decentered mass that trails off into surrounding darkness.

Gautier was not enamored of Martin the painter, but he was full of praise for the latter's engravings. Of particular interest is the terminology he adopted to praise "Balthazaar's Feast" in his 1837 article. Gautier wrote: "an architectural ode filled with lyricism," that is, a work in which a formal, public form of expression (here the fanciful oriental/Greek/Byzantine architecture of Martin's palaces and cities) is put to the service of a private vision. In Martin's case the private vision is one in which Divine Order confronts the impressive, but ultimately feeble and monotonous, regularity of human constructions. The viewer of Martin's engravings observes this confrontation, and the dialated space in which it takes place, from a unique perspective, an intermediate position half way between the human chaos below and the divine presence above. It is as though the composition has been assembled from a position atop a tower or by an observer suspended in space.

This perspective, of course, duplicates that of the narrator of **"Notre-Dame"** atop the tower in Section II of the poem. Looking out over Paris, what Hugo called "la reine de nos Babylones et de nos Tyrs," the poet senses the ordering power of this quasi-divine perspective. While recognizing that the beauty of the unified vision depends on the privileged position at the top of the tower, the poet carries the wish for this essential harmony back down to street level. He anticipates a concrete manifestation of the Divine, a Martin-like miracle with Notre-Dame as the sign of this presence:

A regarder d'en bas ce sublime spectacle,
On croit qu'entre tes tours par un soudain miracle
Dans le triangle saint Dieu va se faire voir.

But if Gautier's **"Notre-Dame"** owes its interpretation of the perspective atop the tower to Martin's biblical engravings, it owes its self-consciousness as poetry to the Prefaces of Victor Hugo written in the 1820s. As gothic architecture (in its grandeur and dignity) tempts the poet to "see" God, so the poetic ode offers Gautier a public, formal structure for his own construct. In the progressively more polemical prefaces to his *Odes* (eventually *Odes et ballades*), Hugo had made the appropriation of this public form of expression for individual purposes a major project of the Romantic movement. Specifically, Hugo had counselled two approaches that shape Gautier's **"Notre-Dame"**: (1) the ode was to exploit Christian, rather than Classical, imagery [*Odes*, 1823]; and (2) Classical confidence in notions of mathematical symmetry and regularity to produce harmony and beauty was to be replaced by confidence in the unifying, if idiosyncratic, vision of the individual consciousness [*Odes*, 1826].

In light of these tenets of Hugo's Romanticism, Gautier's **"Notre-Dame"** can be read as a kind of set-piece illustrating contemporary poetic dogma. The final section, with its very orthodox Christian imagery, disdains all classical references. The Neo-classical materialists, with their rulers and compasses, come in for substantial abuse as petty and uninspired builders who mistake "regularity" for "Order," to use Hugo's words from the Preface of 1826.

It is more interesting, however, to consider Gautier's **"Notre-Dame"** in its broader context, as a personal statement that appropriates public forms, the Church and the ode. Recalling the introductory poem of *La Comédie de la mort*, **"Portail,"** it is clear that **"Notre-Dame"** is a building block in a larger verbal construct that Gautier is erecting. Moreover, in typically Romantic fashion, Gautier is both the contractor and the occupant, the subject and the object, of the compositional task. He is, in fact, composing a multifaceted narrative of his own interactions with the building, Notre-Dame de Paris, as a source of mobile fantasy, as a staircase to a quasi-divine perspective, and as an exemplum of an intuited divine presence on earth. As he constructs his own verbal gothic cathedral (the image effectively conveys the idiosyncratic nature of the task), each of these "illusions mortes" is fixed in verse, making the church a self-generated structure. In using the ode, another collective or public form is reshaped to express the widest range of individual sentiments.

It is necessary to go beyond this level of interpretation, however, for one must ask what are the implications for poetry itself of the poet as architect. Will the poetic edifice be a fantasy-generating void as is Notre-Dame in Section I of Gautier's poem, or an exemplum of the poet's divine mission? Gautier's poetry struggles implicitly with these questions. **"Portail"** defines poetry as primarily decorative. Its function, to contain dead illusions, is itself illusory, for dead illusions are not illusions at all. The reader's instrumental perception creates the meaning of these hollow verses ("c'est tout ce que l'on veut selon ce qu'on y voit") designed to inspire the reader's fantasy.

The poem **"Notre-Dame"** explicitly conveys another definition of poetry. The church in Section III is "un monde de poésie en ce monde de prose," that is to say, poetry is discontinuous from reality, a privileged world of language containing meaning to be discovered by the reader. The role of the poet is thus quasi-divine, that of a Moses-like conveyer of essential truths or laws. Section III of **"Notre-Dame"** would seem to foreshadow a shift from preciousness to dogmatism in Gautier's poetry, if the dramatic redefinition of architectural/poetic purpose found there is indeed permanent.

There is certainly evidence, in *La Comédie de la mort* and in later works, to suggest that Gautier sought meaning in formal dogmatic structures. Well-known poems such as **"Thébaïde"** document his struggles to espouse the orthodox Christian tenets that shape Section III of **"Notre-Dame."** But there are generally few examples in which the poet puts his poetry at the service of a particular ideology. More typical are works such as the final poem of *La Comédie,* **"Le Sommet de la tour,"** which recognize a problematic poetics stopping well short of essentialistic claims. The title of the poem is particularly revealing in this respect, for it recalls the intermediate position attained by the poet-narrator in **"Notre-Dame."** Suspended in the void, "le vide par-dessus et par-dessous l'abîme," the narrator enjoys a privileged view of human chaos just as the engravings of Martin offer the viewer a privileged perspective on human insignificance. Yet these unified visions are neither permanent nor divine. Gautier's perspective from the top of Notre-Dame quickly diversifies, obliging him to attempt a nostalgic preservation of unity through his essentialistic interpretation of gothic architecture. His own poetic cathedral, he confesses in **"Le Sommet,"** is not unified, but idiosyncratic. The images to which he reverts to characterize his edifice are not religious or technical or literary, but organic:

> Patient architecte, avec mes mains pensives
> Sur mes piliers trapus inclinant mes ogives,
> Je fouillais sous l'église un temple souterrain.
> Puis l'église elle-même, avec ses colonnettes,
> Qui semble, tant elle a d'aiguilles et d'arêtes,
> Un madrépore immense, un polypier marin;
>
> ("**Le Sommet**")

There is no unity based on eternal verities, only a cumulative organic unity based on a single consciousness. Like **"Portail," "Le Sommet"** ends with a question that betrays uncertainty about ultimate meaning:

> Du haut de cette tour, à grand'peine achevée,
> Pourrais-je t'entrevoir, perspective rêvée,
> Terre de Chanaan où tendait mon effort?
>
> ("**Le Sommet**")

That Gautier, like his mentor Hugo, aspired to the role of a poetic Moses is clear enough. But Gautier, for one, was never sure that he had enticed a god to inhabit the cathedrals he built. Meaning, like his visions of ideal beauty, remained elusive, fleetingly encountered in privileged moments on the margins between chaos and order.

Lloyd Bishop (essay date 1989)

SOURCE: "The Earnest but Skeptical Questor: Gautier's *Albertus* and *Mademoiselle de Maupin*," in *Romantic Irony in French Literature from Diderot to Beckett*, Vanderbuilt, 1989, pp. 83-95.

[*In the following essay, Bishop discusses the use of a complex, romantic irony which Gautier employed for humorous effect and for the fuller treatment of serious themes.*]

No French author has better epitomized the romantic dilemma than Théophile Gautier. His lifelong yearning for the ideal was accompanied by a career-long pessimism that told him his frantic search was futile. He suffered the agonizing dual awareness that, on the one hand, the human condition was intolerable and, on the other, transcendence was impossible. One tries to spread one's wings, says the heroine of *Mademoiselle de Maupin,* but they are weighed down by slime, the corrupt body anchors the soul to earth. Critics have spoken of Gautier's Gnostic and Manichaean dualism, of his view of the universe as a battleground upon which the forces of good and evil fight for dominance. But for this unbeliever, orthodox Christianity—especially its analysis of man's dualism—provided the central text, and Gautier found it eloquently expressed in Hugo's preface to *Cromwell,* which "shone in our eyes," says Gautier of himself and his fellow romantics of 1827, "like the Tables of the Law on Sinai."

Gautier's aesthetic was likewise dualistic. He never fully abandoned his romantic belief in the relativity of taste and the importance of the artist's private vision, his individual genius, imagination, and inspiration, but even during the days of the Petit Cénacle he also thought of art in terms of craftsmanship, hard work, and the universality of the classical ideal. Even as late as *Emaux et camées* (first published in 1852) Gautier combines impassive and impersonal texts inspired by the doctrine of art for art's sake with other texts expressing an intense personal lyricism.

Johanna Richardson (*Théophile Gautier*) and James Smith ("Gautier") have shown that Gautier's belief that everything useful is ugly, that only those things having no purpose can be beautiful, had to cohabit with a conflicting doctrine: that art and artists must be *practical.* "Nowadays," says Gautier, "Benvenuto Cellini would not refuse to make tops for . . . canes and paperweights." Gautier was capable both of railing against the railroads and against the ugliness of industrial progress in general and of praising with genuine enthusiasm the inauguration of new railway lines.

Gautier's aesthetic was indeed elastic enough to include objectivity and subjectivity, discipline and caprice. Caprice could even take the extreme form of preciosity: "The most exquisite preciosity pushes right and left its capricious tendrils and its bizarre flowers with their intoxicating perfumes—preciosity, that beautiful French flower." And his conception of the well-wrought artifact does not preclude what Friedrich von Schlegel had boldly touted: buffoonery and the baroque arabesque.

> Beyond the compositions that can be called classical
> . . . there exists a genre for which the name "arabesque"
> would be appropriate, in which, without great concern
> for linear purity, the pencil engages in a thousand
> baroque fantasies.

> We believe that one can admit these comic caprices
> into poetry just as one admits arabesques into painting.

Two of Gautier's major themes are the impermanence of life and of love and the uncertainty of "reality." Short stories like "Une Nuit de Cléopâtre" (1883) and "Le roman de la momie" (1857) treat of impossible love while Gautier's report on his extensive travels in Spain speaks of the inevitable decay and destruction even of great civilizations and religions. Georges Poulet has noted (*Etudes*) that Gautier's visual power made him more painfully aware than other writers of the perishable nature of things:

> The object appears simultaneously as beautiful—and
> beauty seems invested with eternity or atemporality—
> and as already corroded by time. Nothing must have
> seemed more intolerable to Gautier than this
> *simultaneous* apperception of "eternal beauty" and of
> the eternal work of dissolution that accompanies its
> presence. The sensible object was seen, *simultaneously,
> at the very same time,* as eternal and ephemeral, as
> unalterable *and* deteriorating. (Emphasis added)To take
> a single example:

> Marble, pearl, rose, dove,
> Everything is dissolved, everything is destroyed;
> The pearl melts, the marble falls,
> The flower fades and the bird flies away.
> **("Affinités secrètes" in *Poésies Complètes*)**

The futility of everything is the major theme of Gautier's ironic romance, *Le Capitaine Fracasse* (1861), and the uncertainty of everything underlies the plot of *La Morte amoureuse* (1836). In the latter work ontological uncertainty is joined with moral ambiguity. As Richard Grant (*Gautier*) sums up: "It is not only hard to know who one is but also who one ought to be."

Gautier was an admirer of E. T. A. Hoffmann, and Hoffmann's direct influence can be seen in works like *Onuphrius Wphly* (1832) and *Deux acteurs pour un rôle* (1841). The *fantastique,* of whichGautier was not only a great admirer but a prolific producer, has been related by critics such as Hubert Juin, Roger Caillois, and Tzvetan Todorov to what can be called an uncertainty principle. Caillois, for instance, defines the fantastic as "a break in the recognizable order of things, the eruption of the unacceptable in the midst of the unchanging daily legality."

The main source of terror in the fantastic, says Richard Grant (*Gautier*), is the sudden discovery that what was thought to be an orderly, rational world breaks down, "one can no longer be certain of the rules of the game." Gautier, the visual poet for whom the external world exists, is also a poet possessed by a "feeling for the invisible world" (*Italia*). Michael Riffaterre ("Rêve et réalité") has shown that even in Gautier's most objective and realistic descriptions, as in the *récit de voyage,* there are sudden eruptions of the supernatural or the fantastic.

> Mobility is conferred on that which in real life is
> immobile, animation on that which is inert: movement
> surrealizes, so to speak, the real.

> Solids dissolve, lines are displaced, landmarks change,
> in short, every certainty of the real is called into
> question once again.

Gautier only half-believed many of his most cherished convictions. Even his belief in the divinity of art was tempered at times by the gnawing thought that art is an illusory good. Beginning his career as one of the most excessively ardent romantics, as his history of romanticism vividly tells us, he soon became an ardent critic of romantic excesses, including his own. He and Musset were among the first romantics to criticize romanticism in general as well as *their own romanticism,* that is, to indulge in self-irony and self-parody. The key texts for Gautier in this regard are **Albertus** (1832), *Les Jeunes-France* (1833), and the vaudeville, *Un voyage en Espagne* (1843), first published under the title of *Tra los montes.* Even as late as *Spirite* (1865) we witness an author who warns his readers to beware of unreliable authors and their narrators and who deliberately deflates a theme—the problem of reality versus ideality—that he obviously takes seriously. It is not surprising, then, to find Gautier indulging in parabasis and the destruction of artistic illusion in a play like *Une Larme du diable* (1839) in which the author appears as one of the characters and speaks directly to the audience about the inadequacy of the play's structure. In a somewhat similar vein the hero of *Le Capitaine Fracasse,* who has joined a wandering theatrical troupe, varies the tone of his voice within the same scene and wears only a half-mask so that the audience can see both the actor and the real man.

. . . . .

Albertus and d'Albert, both of whom are autobiographical figures, tell us much of the author's most intimate feelings during his early, romantic period. The entire first section (chapters 1-5) of *Mademoiselle de Maupin* is devoted not to the heroine but to the hero, who gives us a lyrical confession in the *enfant du siècle* mode, although the *siècle* is displaced for the sake of historical accuracy to the turn of the eighteenth century. The main components of d'Albert's psyche are ones we would expect to find in a romantic hero: boredom, melancholy, misanthropy, cynicism, solitude, and the vague *élans sans but,* yearnings prompted by no precise object. Such yearnings are also felt by the heroine, who is an alter ego of d'Albert and the author as well as the incarnation of their ideal (i.e., perfection symbolized by the heroine's bisexuality and by her obsession with hermaphroditism,which represents completeness and perfection through the [impossible] harmony of opposites).

Mademoiselle de Maupin begins exactly like Senancour's *Obermann*, with the hero writing to a friend not of the events of his life, since there aren't any, but of his ideas and feelings. The language is identical: "But, since you insist that I write to you, then I must tell you what I think and what I feel, and I must tell you the story of my ideas, for lack of events and actions." A passive hero, he spends his life, like Obermann, "waiting." For what? He does not know. He is tormented by the same vague desires and passions as René; like René's, one of the objects of these desires is an ideal woman; but another component is latent homosexuality.

Like Benjamin Constant's *Adolphe*, d'Albert is supremely indifferent to everything around him and, like him, enjoys a lukewarm affection for a mistress he soon wants to be rid of. The hero's indecisiveness in this regard is finely analyzed and is worthy of the pen of Constant: "I am almost angry at her for the very sincerity of her passion, which is one more shackle, and which makes a breaking of our relations more difficult or less excusable." Like Adolphe, d'Albert speaks to his mistress of love for fear of speaking of its disappearance.

When he describes for us his heroic otherness, d'Albert gives us an almost direct translation from *Manfred:* "My heart beats for none of the things that make most men's heart beat.—My sorrows and my joys are not those of my fellow beings." Manfred had proclaimed,

> From my youth upwards
> My spirit walked not with the souls of men,
> Nor looked upon the earth with human eyes;
> The thirst of their ambitions was not mine,
> The aim of their existence was not mine;
> My joys, my griefs, my passions, and my powers
> Made me a stranger. Although I wore the form,
> I had no sympathy with breathing flesh.

At times d'Albert is a stranger even to himself: "The meaning of my existence escapes me completely. The sound of my own voice surprises me to an unimaginable degree, and I would be tempted at times to take it for the voice of another"—a disconcerting sensation that will be retold by Malraux in *La Condition humaine.*

The hero describes himself as a romantic *puer senex.*

> Is it not strange that I, who am still in the blondest months of adolescence, I have reached that degree of satiety as to be no longer tickled by anything except by the bizarre or the difficult . . . ?

> I am stricken by that malady that attacks whole populations and powerful men in their old age:—the impossible.

He is explicitly called by Rosette a *beau ténébreux,* a hero wrapped in Byronic gloom, and he calls himself a marked man, a fated and fatal hero: "Everyone is born with a black or white seal. Apparently mine is black."

However, we are not allowed to take d'Albert's problems, which are real and grave, with tragic seriousness. The novel is frequently interrupted by allusions to the fact that this *is* a novel, a "glorious novel," an "illustrious novel," a "truly French novel," and so on. The author tells us that it is boring to write a novel and even more boring to read one. In one place the author will apologize for an awkward simile; in another the narrator will bemoan the inordinate length of a really fine and sincere burst of lyricism: "Ouf! there's a tirade of interminable length, almost straight out of the epistolary style.—What a long-winded passage!" And at another point the author tells us that he cannot go on with his story; his idea of perfection makes him feel nothing but disgust for this inferior novel he is writing.

The story proper is framed with ironic detachment. Here is the beginning:

> At this point in the story, if the debonair reader is willing to allow us, we are going for a time to leave to his reveries the worthy character who up to now has occupied stage center all by himself and speaks for himself, and return to the ordinary form of the novel, without however forbidding ourselves to assume later on the dramatic form, if the need arises, and reserving for ourselves the right to dip again into that kind of epistolary confession that the aforesaid young man was addressing to his friend, persuaded as we are that, however penetrating and sagacious we may be, we surely ought to know less about these things than he himself.

And here is the ending, the moment when d'Albert finally receives Madeleine's nocturnal visit, which is both the climax of the "plot" and the beginning of the dénouement: "Who was surprised?" says the narrator to the reader. "It's neither you nor I, for you and I have been prepared for this visit for quite a while now." Thus, d'Albert's great moment is deflated more cruelly than Stendhal would ever have done to Julien. The reader is not allowed to share the hero's excitement vicariously: "He uttered a little cry of surprise midway between oh! and ah! However I have every reason to believe that it was closer to ah! than oh!" The novel's sad ending is punctured by a final ironic intervention:

> At the end of the week, the unhappy, disappointed lover received a letter from Théodore [Madeleine], which we are going to transcribe. I do fear that it may not satisfy either my male or my female readers; but, in all truth, the letter was such and not otherwise, and this glorious novel will have no other conclusion.

>   . . . . .

Not only is Gautier's Albertus still another incarnation of the romantic hero, but the author seems to go to some pains to ensure that he is a stereotypical one. A number of critics have condemned the lack of originality in the poem, but I don't believe that the presentation of a unique hero is really one of the author's or, better, the work's intentions. At any rate Albertus is indeed a stereotype of the romantic hero. He has, for instance, the *regard de lion* of the Hugoesque hero—

> His lion's stare and the wild spark
> That leaped at times from his eyes
> Made you shiver and pale despite yourself.

—a reminiscence, too, of the Byronic hero whose cold stare dazzles but also "chills" the vulgar heart. Albertus's lip is "severe" and forms the mocking smile of the Giaour. But his principal expression, the narrator tells us, is a "great disdain" for everything and everyone. He is a sad, bored, solitary misanthrope; "his door is closed to all." He is, inevitably, a *puer senex:*

> —Having always inquired, ever since his birth,
> About the why and wherefore, he was pessimistic
> As is a man grown old.
>
> —A great knowledge is a great scourge;
> It turns a child into an old man. . . .
> . . . . .
> As soon as the cause is seen, one already knows
>   the effect.
> Existence weighs down upon you and everything
>   seems insipid.
> . . . . .
> Love is now but a spasm, and glory an empty
>   word,
> Like a squeezed lemon the heart becomes arid.
> —Don Juan arrives after Werther.

Driven by a Faustian urge to obtain divine omniscience and omnipotence, he learns all of human knowledge that one can learn and, possessing that, promptly wants to die. Only fear deters his suicidal hand. But at twenty he is already ripe for death.

Like Musset's Hassan, Albertus does not believe in true love and settles for a quantitative ethic in which repeated superficial pleasures serve as opiate to his anguish.

> . . . What does it matter, after all, if the cause
> Be sad, provided the effect produced be sweet?
> —Let's enjoy ourselves, let's make for ourselves a
>   superficial bliss;
> A beautiful mask is better than an ugly face.

Although good-hearted at bottom, he believes in neither worldly nor otherworldly values and proposes for his life no lofty goals: "He let his life go at random."

In a second Faustian impulse, he sells his soul to the Devil in exchange for a brief moment of love with the beautiful witch, Véronique. Although he knows perfectly well that the love won't last, he is still greatly shocked when the beautiful maiden at midnight (the conventional hour should warn us not to take with excessive gravity the conventionality of the hero) turns into the old hag once again, and the Devil, after an orgy in which all the inhabitants of hell participate, comes to claim him for his own.

A sad career indeed, but the tale is not told, of course, in the lugubrious tone that my résumé suggests. We are advised in the Preface that the tale is only "semi-diabolique"; it is also "semi-fashionable"; the latter, significantly, is the most prominent adjective in the poem and tells us at once that the clichés and plagiarisms are meant to be ironically transparent and the hero something less than heroic. The poem is half-serious and half-ironic, the mixture producing romantic irony since the ironic does not simply cohabit with the serious, it invades it. We need not linger over the devices used to produce this irony; we have seen them before: authorial intrusions, some of which disparage the very poem in progress, digressions (i.e., structural irony), asides to the reader, and especially a constant short-circuiting of the narrative in favor of allusions to the *composition* of the narrative. In stanza 59, to take a single example, the poet tells us that it is "now time to get back to the subject" of this rambling and disconnected tale; then, instead of simply introducing us to the hero, he tells us that "before going further, it might be a good idea to sketch his physical portrait." The portrait itself is done with a certain playfulness and *désinvolture.*

> —His hair, thrown into disorder by his fingers,
> Fell around a brow that Gall, in ecstasy,
> Would have examined for six months and used as
>   source
> For a dozen treatises.

Gautier, then, uses most of the basic strategies of the romantic ironist. Rather than give a detailed rehearsal of them, it would seem more profitable at this point to explore the serious implications of the irony in both works, especially since this is still largely unexplored territory. As late as 1975 a critic [Tennant] can wonder whether *Albertus* can be interpreted at all, and another critic considers the poem unsuccessful because "the style continually distracts from the subject" [Richardson]. Similarly, *Maupin* has been condemned by a good number of critics for its incoherent structure. In my view the style of the poem and the novel, especially their romantic irony, is both the foundation of their subject matter and the key to their interpretation. I also believe that Gautier, as much as any other French or German writer, gives us many insights into the mainsprings of romantic irony.

Consider first the concluding stanza of *Albertus*.

> —This heroic and unequaled poem
> Offers an admirable and profound allegory;
> But, in order to suck the marrow, one must break
>   the bone,
> . . . . .
> —I could have clearly explained every detail,
> Nailed a learned commentary to every word.—
> I believe, dear reader, that you are intelligent
>   enough

To understand me.—So, goodnight.—Close the door,
Give me a kiss goodnight, and tell them to bring
    me
A volume of Pantagruel.

Despite the cavalier, tongue-in-cheek tonality, there is a half-serious Rabelaisian invitation to find the "substantific marrow" within the bone, to find serious subject matter despite the playful treatment. The invitation is convincingly reinforced by the fact that roughly 50 percent of *Albertus* and 95 percent of *Maupin* are dead serious.

A serious theme running throughout the poem that can be considered its chief one is the instability of human sentiments. In one of his digressions the narrator tells us about his own love life, which was an ecstatic but evanescent affair.

All that happiness is no more. Who would have
    thought it?
We are as strangers to one another; all men
Are thus;—their "forever" does not last six months.

Their "forever" *does not last six months*—this antithesis catches one of the moods behind romantic irony. A philosopher-critic who has captured the mood well is Vladimir Jankélévitch.

Our feelings are ephemeral and our beliefs unstable . . . . the passion will end, despite all our pledges; we swear to heaven that the loved person is irreplaceable and, when we have replaced her, we envisage, not without a smile, that disappointing absolute which is always eternal during the occurrence and provisional afterwards. Attrition or conversion—a feeling is eternal only until further notice! A definitive vow is definitive only until Easter! What creature here below can say Forever?

Even the witch Véronique recognizes this sad truth:

Man loves as he lives: one day.

The romantic ironist presents us with sudden shifts of tone or mood that are playful on the surface, but if one looks beneath this surface, one sees the dangerous undertow. In *Mademoiselle de Maupin,* for instance, the author shows us how the romantic *vague des passions* can lead to cynicism, then to emotional aridity, and finally to self-irony. For lack of the right nourishment the passions *feed on each other* and become internecine:

All my unoccupied passions are quietly snarling in my heart, and devour each other for lack of any other nourishment.

Tossing and turning within me are vague desires that fuse together and give birth to others which then devour them.

Nothing is so tiring as those motiveless whirlwinds of desire and those yearnings without an object. . . . I laugh in my own face.

Even when a man's heart is not filled with vague passions, it is filled with "absurdities," irreconcilable "contradictions" that prevent him from ever being more than "half-happy" or half-sad, half-moral or half-immoral, half-serious or half-ironic. Romantic irony is the science of the half rather than the whole. Not only do human sentiments keep changing, they change with such alarming rapidity that one's actions cannot keep up with them.

Whenever I write a sentence, the thought that it renders is already as far from me as if a century had passed instead of a second, and *I often mix with it, in spite of myself, something of the thought that has replaced it in my mind.*

That is why I would never be able to discover how to live,—either as a poet or as a lover.—I cannot render the ideas that I no longer have;—I possess women only when I have forgotten them and when I am in love with others; . . . how could I express my will, since, no matter how much I hasten, I no longer have the feeling that corresponds to what I am doing. (emphasis added)

How, then, can one measure the moral worth of others or even of oneself at any particular moment? "There are moments when I recognize only God above me, and other moments when I judge myself to be the equal of the bug under the rock or the mollusc on its sandbank." Romantic irony expresses a moral agnosticism ("I have completely lost the knowledge of good and evil") based partly on the fact that human sentiments are contradictory and fleeting and also on the conviction that there are no absolute standards. The heroic mode, under these conditions, seems "silly"; the mock-heroic is the best defense against disillusion; self-mockery is a protection against self-deception. All this can be read on Albertus's face:

The imperial brow of the artist and poet
Occupying all by itself *half* of his head,
Broad and full, bending under the inspiration,
Which hides in each premature wrinkle
A superhuman hope, a great thought,
And bears written these words:—Strength and
    conviction.—
The rest of the face corresponded to this grandiose
Brow.—However it had something
Unpleasant about it and, although faultless,
One would have wished it different.—Irony
And sarcasm shone there more than genius.
    The lower part seemed to mock the upper.

The peculiar tension produced by romantic irony also reflects the unbridgeable gap between reality and ideality. In *Albertus* we catch a fleeting view of the gap in the following lines:

Benevolent reader, this is my entire story
Faithfully told, as well as my memory,
A disorganized register, has been able to remind me
Of those nothings that were everything, of which
Love is composed and of which later one makes
    fun.

—Excuse this pause: The bubble I enjoyed
Blowing and which floated in the air, multicolored,
Has suddenly collapsed into a drop of water;
It broke on the corner of a pointed roof.
—Because it knocked against the Real, my pleasant
Chimera broke. . . .

And in *Maupin* we have a vivid image of this romantic dilemma:

I can neither walk nor fly; the sky attracts me when I am on the ground, the earth when I am in the sky; above, the North wind pulls off my feathers; below, the pebbles offend my feet. The soles of my feet are too tender to walk on the broken glass of reality; my wingspread too narrow to soar above things.

Romantic heroes, even those not treated with romantic irony, all share this predicament. In each one the idealist is restrained by the cynical realist, and the latter is restrained by the *idéaliste malgré lui*. Since he has a home in neither world, he yearns for the one while immersed in the other, or when presented from the viewpoint of romantic irony, he shuttles—playfully *and* painfully—between the two.

In *Maupin* the hero describes his life in terms of this shuttle but also as "an absurd treadmill." And when the narrator of *Albertus* speaks of "this silly story," both the general and the immediate context make the epithet polyvalent: it applies simultaneously to the poem in progress, to the hero's entire career, and to life in general. It is an intimation of the Absurd.

Before the romantic period, with the notable exceptions of Sterne and Diderot, the narrator's attitude toward his hero or his story, or the hero's attitude toward himself in first-person narratives, was usually unequivocal: it was either positive or negative. Or if it was ambivalent, the ambivalence was clearly stated and explained; or if it was ironic, the irony was transparent, since it was almost always a form of antiphrasis, the narrator obviously blaming the person or thing he was pretending to praise, or vice versa. With the romantic period the narrative point of view begins to become more and more problematic; we cannot measure the exact dosage of antipathy or sympathy, of authorial identification or alienation in works informed by romantic irony. We can only feel the tensions, observe the shuttlings and oscillations, admire the complexities and, finally, puzzle at the paradoxes.

Constance Gosselin Schick (essay date 1990)

SOURCE: "*Albertus:* Narrating Poetic Allegory," in *French Literature Series,* Vol. XVII, 1990, pp. 60-68.

[*In the following essay, Schick explores the ironic and seductive effects of* Albertus's *intratextual weaving.*]

Theophile Gautier's talent as a storyteller is much more readily appreciated today than his talent as a poet. Para-doxically, the recognition of his narrative abilities generally focuses on the poeticity of his prose fictions, a poeticity itself attributed in large measure to the fantastic thematics of his narratives, their self-conscious *écriture,* the plasticity of this writing, and their expansive, gratuitous delight in verbal pyrotechnics—all factors which, when applied to his poems, usually serve to diminish *their* "poeticity."

Interestingly, Gautier's first narrative was a poem. Composed in 1831-1832, **"Albertus"** is made up of 122 stanzas, each one consisting of eleven alexandrines and one concluding octosyllabic verse. It is generally categorized as a "long narrative poem" although, in fact, the narrative of **"Albertus"** is embedded within the self-referential meta-poem of its writing and its reading. The penultimate stanza proclaims:"-Joyeux comme un enfant à la fin de son thème, / Me voici donc au bout de ce morale poème! / En êtes-vous aussi content que moi, lecteur?"; and the final verses of the poem conclude:

—J'aurais pu clairement expliquer chaque chose,
Clouer à chaque mot une savante glose.—
Je vous crois, cher lecteur, assez spirituel
Pour me comprendre.—Ainsi, bonsoir.—Fermez la
  porte,
Donnez-moi la pincette, et dites qu'on m'apporte
Un tome de Pantagruel.

The poem therefore does not so much constitute a narrative as the narrative serves to make up the poem.

Gautier himself seems to confuse the distinction between narrative and surrounding or enveloping poetry in his titles. *Albertus ou l'âme et le péché, légende théologique* is the title given to the entire collection of poems published in 1832, a collection which includes a preface and twenty poems preceding the closing **"Albertus"** poem. Gautier explains the titular synecdoche of his collection rather simply in its preface: ". . . l'on aboutit à la légende semi-diabolique, semi-fashionable, qui a nom **"Albertus,"** et qui donne le titre au volume, comme la pièce la plus importante et la plus actuelle du recueil" (84). The poem's own title and subtitle, **"Albertus, poème,"** interestingly omits the allegorical reference *ou l'âme et le péché,* as well as the generically narrative specification, "légende théologique" and substitutes the generic attribution, "poème."

What both sets of titles do maintain is the accompanying epigraph (with error) taken from *Hamlet:* "You shall see anon, 'tis a knavith / Piece of work." What I propose is that, like *Hamlet's* play-within-the-play, Gautier's first narrative should be read as a *mise-enabyme:* the story of Albertus is an ironic or "knavish" narrative allegorizing the ironic or "knavish" allegory that is poetry. The Albertian fabula of illusion constitutes and mirrors the narrative illusion which in turn constitutes and mirrors the illusion of poetic textuality which in turn lays bare and deconstructs all illusions. By indirection can directions be discovered, directions which are themselves indirection.

The poem begins with that for which Gautier, both as poet and as prose writer, is perhaps most famous / infamous: a description which quickly assumes the allusions and the illusion of a *transposition d'art*. The poem thus begins with that old and well-known poetic chestnut: *ut pictura poesis*. Most readers ignore the opening three descriptive stanzas of the poem, presumably reading them according to the conventional schema in which description is subservient to narrative, a kind of *mise-en-scène* which "gets lost" as message to the extent that it is successfully consumed in and by the narrative illusion. As such, the initiating description can be seen to participate, ironically and allegorically, in the narrative of **"Albertus"** as an example or as a victim of textual violence and seduction. Inasmuch as it is the representation of a 17th-18th Century Dutch genre-painting, the epitome of bourgeois "realism": "Confort et far-niente!-toute une poésie / De calme et de bien-être, à donner fantaisie / De s'en aller là-bas être Flamand," the *transposition d'art* offers little motivation or referentiality for the ensuing gothic supernaturalism of the fabula other than that of a common locale, the unnamed village which serves as home to Véronique. Even this geographical link is most tenuous however, for the primary setting of the narrative events which take place is not this village but Leyden; furthermore, the fabula concludes, mysteriously, on the Appian Way near Rome. Just as Albertus succumbs to the magical / diabolical make-over of Véronique and forsakes the memory and his painterly representations of his dead Venitian mistress, the reader is seduced into forsaking the purely poetic or aesthetic delight of the *pictura/poesis* and succumbs to the fiction of a narrative, which fictionality is clearly signified by the stock pretense of authenticity, "dit la chronique."

Furthermore, this descriptive poem-within-the-poem itself effects a seduction of the reader by the writer into its own illusion or fiction. Shrewdly (knavishly) calling attention to the *texte de plaisir* that is his description, "-Vous reconnaissez-vous?-Tenez, voilà le saule, / De ses cheveux blafards inondant son épaule / Comme une fille au bain . . . ," the poet-narrator expands and converts the entirely recognizable and therefore culturally comfortable and pleasurable world of the Dutch painter Teniers, (a world which however does resonate with the blissful dangers of the *profond* of its canals, the *aigus* of its roofs, the *blafards* of its willows, and the "cabarets bruyants qui regorgent d'ivrognes") first to the drunken enchantment *à la* Brawer, then to the warm ease *à l'*Ostade and finally to the tenebrous fantasies of a Goethe and a Rembrandt. From the comfort and *farniente* of an aesthetic illusion, "Il ne manque vraiment au tableau que le cadre / Avec le clou pour l'accrocher," the reader / spectator is enticed into the fantasy of the description's "reality," into the fantasy of becoming one of Brawer's drinkers and one of Ostade's inhabitants:

> Près du poêle qui siffle et qui détonne, au centre
> D'un brouillard de tabac, les deux mains sur le
>   ventre,
> Suivre une idée en l'air, dormir ou digérer,
> Chanter un vieux refrain, porter quelque rasade,

and finally into the fantasy or "reality" of being himself a poet, of being himself a painter . . . and therefore both an alter-narrator and an alter-Albertus. The direct address of stanza III confirms the seduction or the appropriation of the reader by the poet-narrator, by and into the illusion of his poetic description, and eventually by and into the fiction of the narrative: "—A vous faire oublier, à vous, peintre et poète, / Ce pays enchanté", which is the same enchanted *topos* that Albertus will abandon in his seduction by Véronique. Like Albertus (and of course like Gautier), the reader, now become poet / painter, forsakes the world of sun-filled images, Venitian blue, marble palaces, and soft serenades, to enter the world of Faustian "murs verts de mousses" and "ténèbres rousses," of chronicles and devilry. Jean-Luc Steinmetz remarked insightfully: "La transformation de Véronique, l'épouvantable sibylle, en jeune femme est plus qu'une trouvaille narrative s'insérant dans les données du genre; elle s'y révèle un symbole d'écriture." The narrative of **"Albertus"** is the allegory of the seduction that is poetic writing and of the seduction that has already been and is being effected by the poem.

The transformation of Véronique's world occurs textually before the story recounts the metamorphosis. In the midst of his virtuoso deployment of romantic motifs and his *tour-de-force* display of vocabulary and technical skill, the poet-narrator admits the obvious: "Pourtant cet enfer est un ciel pour l'artiste." Véronique's hometown, which, as we mentioned earlier, is the one tenuous referential link between opening description and fabula, is scratched out as reality in its very realization, that is in its writing and reading. Its grotesqueness is metamorphosized into the literary sublime, and becomes home to a whole list of types, motifs and characters. "Je lejurerais presque, / Celui qui fit l'hymen du sublime au grotesque, / Créa Bug, Han, Cromwell, Notre-Dame, Hernani, / Dans cette hutte même a ciselé ces masques!" The magical / diabolical kingdom of textuality can expand and convert ugly huts into Notre-Dame's, Flanders into Scotland, a *matou* into a "philosophical Murr" or into a *confidence personnelle*:

> Mon pauvre Childebrand à l'amitié si franche,
> Le meilleur coeur de chat et l'âme la plus blanche
> Qui se puissent trouver sous des poils aussi noirs,
> Cet ami dont la mort m'a causé tant de peine,
> Que depuis ce temps-là j'ai pris la vie en haine.

Just as Albertus gives himself up completely to Véronique's power, the poet-narrator immerses himself in the delight of the narration and participates in the narrative illusion. Both seducer and seduced (and therefore both Véronique and Albertus), he becomes the most unreliable of narrators: the omniscient, manipulative, ironic narrator-as-author, the commenting, interpreting narrator-as-reader, and the empathizing narrator whose focalization is that of at times one at times the other of the protagonists. Véronique's unrequited love for Albertus occasions no less than twelve stanzas of authorial reflection and confession on the illusions of love and art (XLVII-LIX); before her soon-to-be-exposed nudity, the narrator voices his "fears" of disillusionment ("Hélas! car bien souvent avec le voile tombe / L'illusion et le désir.") and at the unveiling of her nudity, he extols the superiority of natural beauty and divine creation over artistic dreams and creations!

Yet from all this dissembling, "truths" and revelations seem to emerge: "Car la foi seule peut nous faire voir le ciel / Dans l'exil de la vie, et ce désert du monde / Où la félicité sur le néant se fonde" (138) and again "—Jouissons, faisons-nous un bonheur de surface; / Un beau masque vaut mieux qu'une vilaine face"—"truths" which have been attributed to Gautier ever since they were written for the chameleonic narrator of **"Albertus."** From behind the staged curtains of love-making, play-acting and text-writing, when, as the narrative tells us, "Les rideaux sont tombés," epiphanies do occur as *plaisir* gives way to *jouissance* and the surface cracks to reveal its edges and its void:

> La lampe grésilla.—Dans le fond de l'alcove
> Passa, comme l'éclair, un jour sanglant et fauve;
> Ce ne fut qu'un instant, mais Albertus put voir
> Véronique, la peau d'ardents sillons marbrée,
> Pâle comme une morte et si défigurée
> Que le frisson le prit;—puis tout redevint noir.—

So persuasive / seductive are these moments of "negative revelation" within the narration that the narrative does *appear* to be allegorical in the sense that it does *seem* to offer some kind of figurative significance, some marrow for which it is worth breaking the bone, as the poet invites his reader to do in the last stanza. P.E. Tennant is one reader, for example, who finds it "fascinating to follow the poet's attempts to resolve the conflicts in his own nature under cover of Albertus' fictional case." Jasinski too concurs that in **"Albertus:"** "Surtout se heurtent des tendances contraires . . . tous les tumultes d'une époque trouble et d'une âme tourmentée éveillent ainsi des résonances profondes." Gautier's admission that "le surnom d'Albertus me resta et l'on ne m'appelait guère autrement" suggests that his contemporaries also read the poem as having some kind of confessional significance.

Yet the illusion and the seduction in **"Albertus"** is never deception. As Richard Grant states, it is "impossible for the reader to suspend disbelief willingly, to be caught up in the spell that such a story could cast." By means of every kind of digression, of authorial intrusion, of literary reminiscence and painterly comparison, the poem "is presented with tongue in cheek" and clearly signified as "artifice" and as "spoof." Parabasis, pastiche and parody, including self-parody, are so ubiquitously present in the narration (as well as in the metapoem) that both narrative and poeticity are constantly being unveiled as specious and as play. Albertus "n'était pas un homme à se laisser surprendre / Aux lacs que Véronique essayait de lui tendre" the narrator informs us. He too has perceived the winks and nods revelatory of illusion ("le vit-il ou bien crût-il le voir?" the narrator queries in a *mise-en-abyme* reference to the simultaneous ambiguity and expressivity of illusion). If, upon seeing Véronique, Albertus "crut voir sa Vénitienne," it was only "un instant" and Véronique's

posturing "à faire illusion" did not pretend to delude but was a deliberate *tape-à-l'oeil:* "—Connaissant Albertus et son humeur fantasque, / La sorcière avait cru devoir prendre ce masque / Pour contenter sa passion." Similarly, the narrative illusion is a matter of *tape-à-l'oeil* virtuosity which seduces by means of its "humeur fantasque" rather than by deception.

It is paradoxically but precisely as disillusioned illusion that allegory acts. In Paul De Man's important study of "The Rhetoric of Temporality," allegory is shown to be the language which knowingly establishes itself in the void of a difference, the language which necessarily contains the negative moment of the loss of self in death or in error. Purely textual, allegory knows itself to be displacement; its ideality is separate from any "real" experience; its meaning an illusion created by the repetition of arbitrary and / or conventional signs. It therefore has the schizophrenia for which Albertus can be seen to be the personification:

> Un front impérial d'artiste et de poète, . . .
> Qui *cache en chaque ride* avant l'âge creusée
> Un espoir surhumain, une grande pensée,
> Et porte *écrit* ces mots:—Force et conviction.—
> Le reste du visage à ce front grandiose
> Répondait.—Cependant il avait quelque chose
> Qui déplaisait à voir, et, quoique sans défaut,
> On l'aurait souhaité différent.—L'ironie,
> Le sarcasme y brillait plutôt que le génie;
> Le bas semblait railler le haut. (emphasis mine)

The "grande pensée" is held and hidden in the creases (an *entre* which is perhaps a prefiguration of the Mallarmean *pli* or hymen). Allegory consists of a paradox which faithfully includes the perfection and the noble mien of its written words yet simultaneously and ironically wishes itself other. **"Albertus"** constant parabasis reflects this paradox as it delights in its textual ideality / illusion but prevents reader and author from "forgetting" the essential negativity of the fiction (De Man).

To *illusionner* and *désillusionner* what is already illusion and disillusionment; that is, to narrate poetic allegory, is no easy, nor logical, matter. From the very beginning, Albertus is already a "cadavre sans illusions." Before his fall to the "fatal attraction" of Véronique, he is already that fatal attraction, already Véronique before ever being her seduced victim: "Son regard de lion et la fauve étincelle / . . . Vous faisaient frissonner et pâlir malgré vous. / . . . Devant cet oeil Méduse à vous changer en pierre, / Qu'il s'efforçait de rendre doux" (157). The narrative of **"Albertus"** therefore must develop sequentially the essentially repetitive and / or *abimée* nature of allegory. According to a chiastic and deconstructive economy, the poem narrates the disillusionment of illusion to the extent that it effects an illusion from its own disillusionment, that is from its own literariness. Gautier's narrative operates in the "milieu, pur, de la fiction" where, as Derrida says in "La Double séance," anything and everything can happen because nothing ever happens (239); the milieu where "ce qui a lieu n'a jamais lieu."

Thus, the world of Gautier's narrative(s) is a world of the most obvious fantasy, the most obvious arbitrariness, the most obvious cultural or conventional commonplaces, the most obvious textual playfulness.

Of course, there is a difficulty in bringing such a narrative to a close. It "lives," after all, on the very textuality that makes it dead. The narrator-poet of **"Albertus"** admits his difficulty to dispose of his hero and his narrative.

> En vain depuis deux mois, pour clore ce volume,
> Mes doigts faisaient grincer et galoper la plume;
> Le sujet paresseux marchait avec lenteur.
>   . . . . .
> . . . . . et moi, perdant courage,Je me disais
>   toujours:—Demain!

The hero's renunciation of his soul, Véronique's midnight demetamorphosis, the gallop into the clutches of the devil's cohorts, all serve to extend the life and pleasure of this textual fantasy. It is finally by means of a pun, a verbal *faux-pas* that the protagonist is killed and that the narrative ends. "Que Dieu vous bénisse," Albertus says to a sneezing Lucifer. "A peine eût-il laché le saint nom que . . . / Tout disparut en l'air comme un enchantement." Like Derrida's Mallarmean Pierrot-Mime, Albertus, protagonist and **"Albertus,"** allegorical figuration, narrative and poem, die from laughing and laugh from dying—"Joyeux comme un enfant à la fin de son thème." That allegory is only a play on and with words will always kill the illusion and there is nothing like the evocation of a "transcendent" referent (*Dieu*) to reveal the malapropism (difference) of its enchantment.

The closure, however, allows the opening of another book, of another allegory in this endless series of repetitive, intertextual signs. "Mais pour sucer la moëlle il faut qu'on brise l'os." The bone that is being picked, broken and sucked is not only a Rabelaisean opening; is not only Albertus' broken ribs and twisted neck; it is the exposed bone of Gautier's poetic writing. In the **"Préface,"** Gautier describes (or gives a pre-face to) the collection's poetry as beginning with "depetits paysages à la manière des Flamands . . ." but "A mesure que l'on avance, le dessin devient plus ferme, les méplats se font sentir, les os prennent de la saillie, et l'on aboutit à la légende . . . qui a nom 'Albertus'". . . In **"Albertus,"** Gautier uses the narrative to break open poetic allegory by spreading out (disfiguring) its simultaneous ambi- and poly-valences onto successive moments and different characters; for example the life-death of its existence as text, the ideality and the irony of its supplementation, the seductiveness and the lucidity of its illusion, etc. The narrative does serve, therefore, as Barbara Johnson has shown in the case of Baudelaire's *Petits poèmes en prose*, to reveal the limits of poetry. However, what **"Albertus"** also reveals is that poetry extends the limits of the narrative. Any one of *its* moments is also subject to textual dis-memberment, spreading out its own network of allegorical-narrative possibilities, endless *mise-en-abymes* or prefigurations of the primary narrative (which is already itself a secondary or embedded narrative within the metadiscourse of poetic

literariness). Thus, the *matou* brought forth the story of Childebrand; the Venitian mistress was "Un roman entier que cette histoire-là"; and Albertus' death ushers in Pantagruel. For all its "Revenons au sujet," the narrative is allegorical and therefore always pointing elsewhere than itself.

In terms of Gautier's poetics, the importance of **"Albertus"** is attested to by the fact that Gautier placed it at the head of the 1845 edition of his *Poésies complètes,* an edition to which, according to Jasinski, Théophile gave much attention, and kept it in that position for all the reeditions which appeared in his lifetime. Its importance in terms of Gautier's fictional *oeuvre* is evident not only because it is his first fiction, but also because it offers the matrix of all his subsequent fiction: the *gageure* of Gautier's narratives will always be to seduce by means of the blatantly textual and intertextual; to seduce by means of and despite allegory.

Eric J. Lien (essay date 1991)

SOURCE: "The Prefatory Poetics of Théophile Gautier," in *Romance Notes,* Vol. XXXII, No. 1, Fall, 1991, pp. 47-54.

[*In the following essay, Lien examines the role of the prefatory poem in reconciling Gautier's aesthetic of emotional detachment with an impulse toward sentiment in* La comédie de la mort, Espñna, *and* Emaux et camees.]

Although his position as precursor of the Parnassian movement remains undisputed, readers and critics alike tend to relegate Gautier the poet to the status of reformed Romantic whose **Emaux et camées** illustrate his doctríne of "l'art pour l'art." His earlier poetry and the development of his personal poetics remain shrouded in the anthology formula of descriptive poet with a limited emotional range. As is so often the case in the nineteenth century, these "idées reçues" are the by-product of the author's own prefatory discourse, most notably the preface to **Albertus** (1832) in which Gautier distances himself from both the emotional grandiloquence of the early Romantics and the socio-political concerns that pervaded the literary circles during the 1830s. Indeed, Gautier must have seemed a curious figure with his call for artistic expression the utility of which resided in its beauty alone.

One must remember, however, in spite of the burgeoning stylistic virtuosity that one already finds in this collection, that Gautier possessed, as Baudelaire pointed out long ago, "cette fameuse qualité que les badauds de la critique s'obstinent à lui refuser: le sentiment." In spite of the somewhat misleading emphasis on the formal aspects of his work found in his prefaces, a complementary reading of the poems reveals that Gautier's poetry combines affective impulses with a well-crafted form in order to create works of enduring art. I propose then to examine, through an exploration of his prefatory poems, Gautier's struggle to reconcile these two traditional facets of poetry.

In order to prepare readers for his treatment of death in the long title poem of his next "recueil," *La Comédie de la Mort* (1838), Gautier makes use of a prefatory poem rather than the more didactic prose preface. His prologue's very title, **"Portail,"** immediately sets up the metaphoric equivalence between collection and monument; and like the portal of a Gothic cathedral, it not only serves as means of entry into the volume but provides a descriptive presentation of the ideas and events that inspired its construction. The poem opens with a direct address to the readers:

> Ne trouve pas étrange, homme du monde, artiste,
> Qui que tu sois, de voir par un portail si triste
> S'ouvrir fatalement ce volume nouveau.
>
> Hélas! tout monument qui dresse au ciel son faîte,
> Enfonce autant les pieds qu'il élève la tête.

Expanding upon this concept of the necessarily dual movement of the monument, the following stanzas accumulate details contrasting that which one sees at the top of the cathedral with that which is found below. A single example will suffice as a paradigmatic illustration of the connotations associated with each:

> En bas, l'oiseau de nuit, l'ombre humide des
>   tombes;
> En haut, l'or du soleil, la neige des colombes . . .

Only after this descriptive passage is the implied comparison between monument and poetry overtly acknowledged:

> Mon œuvre est ainsi faite, et sa première assise
> N'est qu'une dalle étroite et d'une teinte grise
> Avec des mots sculptés que la mousse remplit.
>
> Dieu fasse qu'en passant sur cette pauvre pierre,
> Les pieds des pèlerins n'effacent pas entière
> Cette humble inscription et ce nom qu'on y lit.

These stanzas substantiate the reader's intuition that for Gautier the poem can, by the sculpted quality of the verses with which the poet creates his work, attain the durability of architecture. This explanation, however, hardly seems to justify such a development of the dual nature of the monument, whether poetry or cathedral; and a perusal of the rest of the work indicates that Gautier is not simply indulging in superfluous pictorial detail here. The "clef de voûte" of his poetic construction, clearly indicated by the titles of the two main sections of the poem, **"La Vie dans la Mort"** and **"La Mort dans la Vie,"** is the constant interpenetration of life and death. The poem's emphasis on the necessarily connected nature of these two spaces then subtly foreshadows the work's thematic development.

On another level, the juxtaposition of these two spaces, which one could define as the exposed outer surface of the monument and its hidden inner space, also serves to underscore the figurative nature of poetry as a metaphor of the work's metaphors. Gautier's remark on the exterior reality of his "cathedral" shows his awareness that readers' perceptions of his work will vary: "C'est tout ce que l'on veut selon ce qu'on y voit." This same comment, implies that there may well be more than meets the eye in Gautier's poetry: the metaphor's "vehicle" points to another referent, implicit and unseen by the inattentive reader, its "tenor." The accumulation of descriptive details in Gautier's poetry then serves as a means of objectifying his psychical reactions to certain situations. In **"La Comédie de la Mort,"** hidden beneath the exterior beauty of the sculpted words, one inevitably finds the rotting corpse that provoked the artistic response:

> Toujours vous trouveriez, sous cette architecture,
> Au milieu de la fange et de la pourriture,
> Dans le suaire usé le cadavre tout droit

If such a reminder of the polysemantic nature of poetry is hardly needed here for the reader to become aware that this entire work has "le teint pâle des morts," it nonetheless serves to underscore the inevitably dual nature of Gautier's entire *œuvre*, whose descriptive facade has often led critics to ignore its human, and even emotional, qualities. Might one not view the following verses as applicable to the majority of his work?

> Mes vers sont les tombeaux tout brodés de
>   sculptures;
> Ils cachent un cadavre, et sous leurs fioritures
> Ils pleurent bien souvent en paraissant chanter.
>
> Chacun est le cercueil d'une illusion morte;
> J'enterre là les corps que la houle m'apporte
> Quand un de mes vaisseaux a sombré dans la mer;
>
> Beaux rêves avortés, ambitions déçues,
> Souterraines ardeurs, passions sans issues,
> Tout ce que l'existence a d'intime et d'amer.

Gautier's next collection, *España* (1845), which one critic has termed "l'adieu aux thèmes romantiques et le salut timide au Parnasse," also begins with an aptly titled opening poem: **"Départ."** This poem creates an image of the poet that comes to light as the reader is presented with a prefatory explanation of the reasons behind the voyage, i.e., the text, that the poet has undertaken. The poem begins with the poet's rationalisation of his voyage:

> Avant d'abandonner à tout jamais ce globe,
>   . . . . .
> J'ai voulu visiter les cités et les hommes
> Et connaître l'aspect de ce monde où nous sommes.

Immediately afterwards, however, he indicates another reason for his departure that is perhaps more revealing of the poet's veritable attitude: "J'étouffais à l'étroit dans ce vaste Paris." Indeed, the poet seems tortured by an almost Baudelairian *ennui*.

The readers must then reconcile this posited identity of the poet with their perception of the apparently objective transcription of reality found in so much of this work. This is quite easily done since the purely representational value of the numerous references to the countryside, customs, art and people of Spain is constantly undermined by the fact that each is "visualised through the deforming prism" [P. E. Tenant, *Théophile Gautier*] of the poet's overriding personality. The preceding discussion of the poem **"Portail"** indicated what Riffaterre's exemplary reading of one of this collection's poems, **"In Deserto,"** forcefully confirms: "However verifiable the text's mimetic accuracy . . . it also consistently distorts the facts or at least shows a bias in favor of details able to converge metonymically on a single concept." By identifying the poetic persona whose vision informs the entire work, Gautier's prefatory poem pushes the reader toward an interpretation that goes beyond the mere "meaning" of the referential detail in favor of a more global understanding of the various poems' "significance."

The voyage upon which we embark is at once a geographical displacement and an itinerant exploration of the poet's psyche as seen in the attendant themes of death, violence, love, forgetfulness and the passing of time. The poet's imagination then transforms his description of the voyage in such a way that the presented exterior world materializes his various states of mind; yet these attitudes must in turn be transformed to fit into the poem's thematic and structural framework. Reality, be it exterior or interior, necessarily undergoes transfiguration in the process of poetic creation:

> Poète, tu sais bien que la réalité
> A besoin, pour couvrir sa triste nudité,
> Du manteau que lui file à son rouet d'ivoire
> L'imagination, menteuse qu'il faut croire.

Up to this point, Gautier endowed his prefatory poems with titles implicitly marking their status as prologue, subtly transforming them into a "mode d'emploi" of the text that follows. With *Emaux et camées,* the very title of the opening poem forces the reader to consider its value as preface. Not paratext, but simply text that one must read at once as both poem and preface, this poem subverts the reader's conventional generic expectations in order to force a close reading of it. At first glance, **"Préface"** simply informs readers of the circumstance under which the collection was composed:

> Pendant les guerres de l'empire,
> Goethe, au bruit du canon brutal,
> Fit *le Divan occidental.*
> Fraîche oasis où l'art respire.
>
> Pour Nisami quittant Shakespeare,
> Il se parfuma de çantal,
> Et sur un mètre oriental
> Nota le chant qu'Hudhud soupire.
>
> Comme Goethe sur son divan
> A Weimar s'isolait des choses
> Et d'Hafiz effeuillait les roses,
>
> Sans pendre garde à l'ouragan
> Qui fouettait mes vitres fermées,

> Moi, j'ai fait
> *Emaux et Camées.*

The two quatrains present an image of Goethe, removed from the fracas of wartime events and devoting his energy to artistic creation. This image serves, of course, as point of comparison for the poet's own attitude: the metaphoric "vitres fermées" convey his refusal to participate in the raucus antics of recent political events, "l'ouragan." Complementary to this apolitical stance, the poem develops the theme of the artist's dedication to his art: with its obligatory formal constraints, the use of a sonnet here reflects the necessity of technical proficiency on the part of the poet.

Gautier ends his poem by reiterating the collection's title in order to underscore its importance. Moving from monument to miniature, the title's reference to these two "arts mineurs" suggests the restriction of subject. One finds few themes that require extensive philosophical or emotional development, and the concision of the octosyllabic line reinforces this tendency. The definitions of these art forms indicate that their value resides above all in their delicately crafted form: Littré defines a "camée" as a "pierre ou coquille qui, composée de différentes couches, est sculptée en relief," and "émaux" as "décorations de peintures appliquées sur métal." Gautier's identification of the poet as craftsman, which receives a more overt treatment in the closing poem, **"L'Art,"** is thus immediately implied. Metaphorically, these definitions point to the poet's intricate use of language, and so to the reader's task of deciphering the text. If cameos are composed of "différentes couches," the enameling process consists of mixing metal oxides with the enamel in order to "colorer le fondant [l'émail], tout en lui laissant sa translucidité." Both make use of a technique that produces a multi-layered work of art, just as poetry's inherently figurative nature leads to the textual density created by the poet's combinations of tropes that transform description into significance, and which the reader can only discover by becoming aware of the poem's multiple levels of articulation.

The following poem, **"Affinités secrètes,"** which by its position informs the rest of the collection, expands upon this idea of transformation. One could even view this poem as the work's prologue, and indeed, it carries the same thematic thrust as Gautier's earlier prologues: the inevitable interdependence between various aspects of reality in his works. The poem seems at first a typically Romantic reflection on the transitory nature of things; this dissolution, however, leads to revival, for the various objects are soon reincarnated in other forms. The poet's seemingly wistful attitude thus gives way to the insight that:

> Par de lentes métamorphoses,
> Les marbres blancs en blanches chairs,
> Les fleurs roses en lèvres roses
> Se refont dans les corps divers.

Such metamorphoses are, of course, the product of the poet's imagination, and the analogies found between seemingly exclusive realities form the basis of Gautier's poetic creation. For example, references to both plastic and literary works of art abound here as points of reference, but transformed by the poet's creative process; thus, we find the image of woman idealized into a series of sculptural poses in **"Le Poëme de la femme."** As the preceding prologues already made clear, such metamorphoses are not limited to external reality, artistic or otherwise, and in **"Le Château du souvenir,"** the poet transforms his own memories into a veritable museum.

The restricted universe of the poet posited in the preface can then be defined as the textual space in which the integration of objective reality and subjective emotion takes place. As Benesch correctly argues, it is from this "confrontation de son monde intérieur avec le monde extérieur que va naître son œuvre." Like dreams, which acquire their disturbing quality by combining psychic impulses with events and objects from the external world, Gautier's poetry creates an ambiguous atmosphere that may be either haunting or whimsical. Indeed, the reader can perhaps best define Gautier's poetry by its "hermaphroditic" mix of external and internal realities that is complemented by the analogous "bizarre mélange" (**"Contralto"**) of passion and impassibility found in Gautier's poetic persona.

It then remains for the poet to indicate the manner in which this combinatory creation can itself take on life. This of course is the subject of the well-known poem, **"L'Art,"** which Gautier insisted close the collection "dont elle résume la pensée," and which one might well consider the collection's postface. The only means by which the poet's dreams may take on a certain reality can be by fitting them into an appropriate form; a form that, through the poet's solid craftsmanship, may turn the poem into a thing of beauty. The final stanza's well-known enjoinder to sculpt, file, or chisel away in order to attain that synthesis of dream and reality, which for Gautier constitutes poetry, may then be seen as the conclusion to his incessant quest—the stages of which are marked by the prefatory poems that accompany his works—for poetic purity:

> Sculpte, lime, cisèle;
> Que ton rêve flottant
> > Se scelle
> Dans le bloc résistant!

Constance Gosselin Schick (essay date 1991)

SOURCE: "Théophile Gautier's Poetry as *Coquetterie Posthume*," in *Nineteenth-Century French Studies*, Vol. 20, No. 1 & 2, Fall-Winter, 1991-92, pp. 74-81.

[*In the following essay, Schick explores the poem, "Coquetterie posthume," and discusses how its seemingly paradoxical conjunction of seduction and death can illuminate other aspects of Gautier's poetics.*]

Ever since Georges Poulet's seminal work [*Etudes sur la temps humain,* 1950] on time in Gautier, it is generally acknowledged that Gautier's obsession with death is a matrix not only for his choice of themes but also for his esthetics and poetics. "Tout passe.—L'art robuste / Seul a l'éternité." and "Les dieux euxmêmes meurent. / Mais les vers souverains / Demeurent / Plus forts que les airains" (**"L'Art"**) are verses that most popularly identify Gautier's place in the 19th Century canon. Recently, the poet Jacques Lardoux offers the poem **"Coquetterie posthume"** as evidence that Gautier's "pierres précieuses" are "un défi, en dernière instance, lancé au temps et à la mort par les plus petits objets, les plus petits poèmes."

"Coquetterie postume"

> Quand je mourrai, que l'on me mette,
> Avant de clouer mon cercueil,
> Un peu de rouge à la pommette,
> Un peu de noir au bord de l'oeil.
>
> Car je veux, dans ma bière close,
> Comme le soir de son aveu,
> Rester éternellement rose
> Avec du kh'ol sous mon oeil bleu.
>
> Pas de suaire en toile fine,
> Mais drapez-moi dans les plis blancs
> De ma robe de mousseline,
> De ma robe à treize volants.
>
> C'est ma parure préférée;
> Je la portais quand je lui plus.
> Son premier regard l'a sacrée,
> Et depuis je ne la mis plus.
>
> Posez-moi, sans jaune immortelle,
> Sans coussin de larmes brodé,
> Sur mon oreiller de dentelle
> De ma chevelure inondé.
>
> Cet oreiller, dans les nuits folles,
> A vu dormir nos fronts unis,
> Et sous le drap noir des gondoles
> Compté nos baisers infinis.
>
> Entre mes mains de cire pâle,
> Que la prière réunit,
> Tournez ce chapelet d'opale,
> Par le pape à Rome bénit:
>
> Je l'égrènerai dans la couche
> D'où nul encor ne s'est levé;
> Sa bouche en a dit sur ma bouche
> Chaque *Pater* et chaque *Ave.*

"Coquetterie posthume" is usually read in terms of a biographical reference. Madeleine Cottin states that the source of this poem is Marie Mattei; that it "est né de [ses] confidences," and "Il y aurait tout un roman à écrire sur l'inspiratrice de ce poème." She anecdotally adds that the original manuscript reveals a tear stain on the 6th stanza of the poem, which tear drop is itself the inspiration for the following poem of the collection, **"Diamant du**

coeur.'' René Jasinski's brief comments on the poem also exclusively deal with Marie Mattei, although he demurs as to the teardrop: "Cet autographe . . . porte plusieurs taches dont il est malaisé de déterminer la nature, et la strophe 6 ne nous paraît guère avoir été `noyée' par l'une d'elles.''

While the correspondence between Mattei and Gautier does testify to her very real fear of death and to her tortured feelings of passion, guilt, and religious exaltation; and while I do not mean to deny that this poem, like all the so-called Mattei poems, was probably written in response to her concerns as well as to Gautier's own emotional involvement with both her and with time and death, the poem's charming gallantry and badinage do appear to be quite distant, quite displaced from any serious consideration of issues such as death, afterlife, and remembrance of time past. If read referentially, that is in terms of separation from a beloved and in terms of death, **"Coquetterie posthume"** supports the all too familiar view of Gautier as the poet who escapes from harsh realities and finds superficial refuge in "les belles apparences.'' "La poésie de Gautier est . . . uné poésie d'oubli dans *le charme de l'apparence*" [Gabriel Brunet].

I propose to read the poem according to its allegorical rhetoric; a reading that, as I will show, provides some very interesting insights into Gautier's poetics as a prescription for the paradoxical juxtaposition of seductive charm and of death, of *la coquetterie* and of *le posthume.* The vanity of coquetry, its utter futility within the state of posthumousness, and the impossibility of any corpse, however well embalmed/dressed/made-up, to say her rosary, are all ungrammaticalities or catachreses that discourage an exclusively referential reading of the poem. Functioning within an allegorical code, the poem's feminine protagonist can be read as the personification of the titular abstraction, *coquetterie posthume,* which conversely is the metonymy of the poem's own desire to be a reiterating, exquisite corpse. From an indirect general exhortation, "que l'on me mette," to a direct address, "drapez-moi, posez-moi, tournez . . . ,'' the poem's voice apostrophizes the reader to effectuate the appropriate ritual dressing by which it will become, if not a living, at least a gesturing ("je l'égrènerai") simulacrum of a former reality. Accepting the notion that rhetoric calls attention to itself; that, as Paul de Man has demonstrated of allegory and Jonathan Culler of apostrophe, tropes serve to signify the speaking voice, the now of lyrical discourse rather than any exterior reference, I propose that what the poem thus affirms is its own desire for an esthetics, that is the desire to transform inadequate being into beautiful, seductive semblance; and its own desire for an *écriture,* that is the desire to reiterate and to repeat tropological signifiers: the "égrenage" of gem-like beads (a variant of **Enamels and Cameos**), substitutes for the *Paters* and the *Aves,* themselves substitutes for "infinite kisses." What seems spurious and even nonsensical in terms of a mimetic referentiality, that is in terms of Marie Mattei's absent lover and future dead body, becomes significant in terms of poetic self-reflexivity.

"Coquetterie posthume" therefore signifies the Ronsardian afterlife of verse (itself a repetition of Petrarchian *écri-*

ture): "Vous vivrez, croyez-moi, comme Laure en grandeur, / Au moins tant que vivront les plumes et le livre" (*Sonnets pour Hélène II,* ii). It is an afterlife that knows and reveals itself to be allegory, that is a dead and coquettish figure existing only as rhetoric, living only as text-being-read. Charles Cros, writing for the *Tombeau de Théophile Gautier* pays a fittingly coy tribute to this coquettish afterlife of Gautier's poetry:

> La splendeur de ta vie et tes vers scintillants
> Te défendent, ainsi que les treize volants
> Gardent rose, dans leurs froufrous, ta Moribonde.
> Elle et toi, jeunes, beaux, pour ceux qui t'auront lu
> Vous vivrez. C'est le prix de quiconque a voulu
> Avec son corps, avec son âme orner le monde.
>
> ("Morale")

Germain Nouveau too, in his own poetic testament, adorns himself lightheartedly and repetitively in the textual afterlife that is **"Coquetterie posthume":** "Pas de suaire en toile bise . . . / Tiens! c'est presque un vers de Gautier" ("Dernier madrigal")

The poem was first published with two other allegorical poems dealing with the life-death and the reality-simulacrum dialectics of art and poetry, **"Etude de mains"** and **"Nostalgies d'obélisques".** It proposes a variant of "la morte qui parle," a theme that Léon Cellier has shown to be analogous to the power of the poetic voice in the work of Gautier as well as of Hugo, Baudelaire, and Mallarmé. What distinguishes the development of "la morte qui parle" in **"Coquetterie posthume"** is that she is made up according to the (supposedly) banal code of coquetry rather than according to the more poetic or sensational codes of "mémoire d'outre-tombe," "voix d'ombre," rotting Baudelairian carrion, or "sépulcre solide où gît tout ce qui nuit." The poem weaves its textual shroud as an intertwining of the two codes, "sacred" embalmment and coquettish toilette, both self-referentially signifying the poem's own prosodic ritual. Rime, assonance, octosyllabic meter, word play, and poetic *lieux communs* ritualistically and coquettishly make up the poem-as-allegory, like the rouge and kohl make up the cadaver. "Un peu de rouge à la pommette" evokes the pink of "le soir de son aveu" and the desire to "Rester éternellement rose"; the "un peu de noir au bord de l'oeil" is poeticized by means of the linguistic exoticism *kh'ol,* which serves as the contrasting dark underlining for the clairvoyant synecdoche "oeil bleu"; the muslin dress, consecrated by the "regard amoureux" and garnished with the ravishing and flight-provoking semes of both the magical number thirteen and the *vol* of *volants,* is, linguistically, a most worthy life-evoking shroud, yet remains at the same time only a fashionably ruffled dress. Finally, the rosary, required sacramental for all Catholic entombments and anointed vehicle/medium for the *morte's* prayer, is also endowed with coquettish qualities, namely its bejeweled, opal beads and its plosively alliterative verse: "Par le pape à Rome bénit."

This mingling of the poetic and the vain, the trifling and the esthetic, the idyllic and the parodic is very characteristic of Gautier, and has been very susceptible to unappreciative criticism. "On ne tarde pas à s'apercevoir que le procédé de l'auteur ne se conforme pas toujours au sujet, n'est pas . . . proportionné à l'idée ou au sentiment . . ." Sainte-Beuve wrote in 1838. David Kelley interpreted the "superficialité voulue" of *Emaux et camées* as an ironic technique by which Gautier attempts to be faithful at once to time and to an ideal, which attempt Kelley likens to Baudelaire's innovations in the *Petits Poèmes en prose.*

> Il cherche à se servir du 'joli', du sentimental et du badin pour créer un poème à résonances éternelles et universelles sans toutefois être infidèle à la trivialité qui permet à ces manifestations du mauvais goût de résumer l'ambiance affective, la vie même, du siècle.

I would add that this catachresis that juxtaposes the coquettish and the poetic not only serves to express the ambiguity of time within art—the necessity for both a "beauté transitoire" and a "beauté éternelle" as Baudelaire was to make clear after Gautier—but also expresses the polyvalence inherent to the textuality of the poem. Sacred in its ritualistic evocation/recollection of a realm in which fusion occurs at the sacrifice of life, it is also an illusory vanity, a sham, an ostentation that is only a dressed up corpse. The fusion of past, present and an eternal future, the fusion of lovers, occurs only as and by means of allegory.

Gautier's poetry does not only poetize the banal; it seriously and lucidly trivializes the poetic; that is, it reveals its limits as rhetorical artifice. All its lovely prosody, all its lovely signifiers of life-in-death admit to being mortuary cosmetic and ritual; admit to being allegory, to being that which "designates primarily a distance in relation to its own origin, and, renouncing the nostalgia and the desire to coincide, . . . establishes its language in the void of this temporal difference" (De Man, "Rhetoric") Baudelaire saw Gautier as an author who "à une époque pleine de duperies, . . . s'installait en pleine ironie et prouvait qu'il n'était pas dupe." Gautier's perceived superficiality, his stylism, in short the *coquetterie* of his poetry, can therefore be read as the lucid acceptance of textuality.

While Gautier's irony thus deconstructs his signifiers of life-in-death and reveals them for what they are, posthumous coquetry, his poetics nevertheless acknowledges that these are the simulacra necessary to seduce and to please, one might say to charm into the necessary "suspension of disbelief" or acceptance of illusion. The thirteen *volants* and the opal beads that are to be placed on the corpse by the addressed *vous* are the signifiers that are to effect the "sorcellerie évocatoire," as Baudelaire will say, by which the dead can, if not really speak, at least signify signifiers. Roland Barthes agrees [in *Le Plaisir de texte,* 1973] that this ability to charm is necessary for any *plaisir de texte.* Textual eroticism occurs, Barthes explains, not in nudity but in the gape of a dress. "L'endroit le plus érotique d'un corps n'est-il pas là où le vêtement baîlle?" Consequently, texts have to be dressed up, given that comfortable, euphoric, likable and reassuring cultural cover so as to entice the reader to its edge, to the gape where (s)he can be

lost in the void/the dead. Barthes' textual pleasure is thus the product of a *coquetterie posthume*. "[S]'ils veulent être lus," Barthes insists, even the most terrible texts must have within them a neurosis by which they are *"tout de même des textes coquets."* Typical of much of Gautier's poetry, **"Coquetterie posthume"** simply reverses this modern duplicity or neurosis: it is a "texte coquet" that is *tout de même* a "texte terrible."

In fact, the poem addresses itself most fittingly to being the Derridean *pharmakon,* that is, writing that "n'est pas la répétition vivante du vivant."

> La magie de l'écriture et de la peinture est donc celle du fard qui dissimule le mort sous l'apparence du vif. Le *pharmakon* introduit et abrite la mort. Il donne bonne figure au cadavre, le masque et le farde. Le parfume de son essence. . . . Il transforme l'ordre en parure, le cosmos en cosmétique. La mort, le masque, le fard, c'est la fête qui subvertit l'ordre de la cité . . . (Derrida.)

Paul De Man has noted "the latent threat that inhabits prosopopoeia, namely that by making the dead speak, the symmetrical structure of the trope implies, by the same token, that the living are struck dumb, frozen in their own death" ("Autobiography") Gautier's substitution of one set of signs: the shroud, the yellow *immortelles,* and the tear-embroidered cushion, each implied to be too deadly, by the supposedly more living, evocative and charming simulacra, the dress and the lace pillow, ironically effects an equivalence between the signifiers of life and the signifiers of death, and in fact between time-laden living experience and dead rememoration. **"Coquetterie posthume"** reveals its "living things" to be commodities as dead and deadly as is the shroud. They are *la mort-dans-la-vie,* the inevitable analogue to *la vie-dans-la-mort,* a relationship that Gautier made explicit in ***La Comédie de la Mort.*** The loving look that consecrated the dress ("Son premier regard l'a sacrée") and the dress' power of seduction are identified with the null and void as the past definite form of *plaire* rimes not only richly but homophonically with the negative [*ne*] . . . *plus.* The loving privileged moment of the lovers' union existed "sous le drap noir des gondoles," already a figuration of dead existence just as is its projected recollection under the folds of the white shroud in the tomb. The lace pillow's "life" is meaningful only because of the tropes—metaphor and personification—that make this anorganic prop a witness: "Cet oreiller . . . / A vu dormir nos fronts unis,/ Et . . . / Compté nos baisers infinis." A mise-en-abyme of the entire allegory that is the poem, the seductive, pretty and therefore coquettish "oreiller de dentelle" is the rhetorical recorder of *infinite* kisses (an infinity deconstructed by the narrative fact that the moment is gone/dead and therefore revealed to be mere cliché, at once banal and poetic), just as the pretty corpse/allegorical poem is the sayer of prayerful/decorative beads.

What has therefore been misunderstood or unappreciated in Gautier's poetics is that it honestly makes evident the phantasm and the essential deadliness of the *pharmakon* that is art, writing, and beauty; yet still faithfully uses this *pharmakon* to subvert the phantasm and the essential deadliness that is the bourgeois "order of the city" as well as the order of time and death. Walter Benjamin writes that "Being moved by beauty is an *ad plures ire*." In voicing this desire to be esthetically "among the dead," **"Coquetterie posthume"** expresses the void that necessitates the semblance/supplement that makes it desirable; while still revealing this simulacrum to be superfluous ostentation, the appearance of an absence. Georges Poulet has noted the devitalizing process of Gautier's writing. The more he succeeds in giving a linguistic realization to his dream/ideal, "le moins elle appartient au monde de la vie. Elle devient cette morte vivante, ce personnage de tableau jamais entièrement détaché de son cadre; que sont toutes les créatures de Gautier" (*Trois essais*) Gautier's poetry is true to the essential otherness of art and beauty. It affirms the esthetic desire to idealize the real and realize the dream while at the same time revealing the deadliness and the vanity of this Pygmalion fantasy. It admits that beauty is allegory, that art is substitution, and that "substituer = subsister + tuer" as Barbara Johnson has coyly-coquettishly stated in her study of Baudelaire.

La vie-dans-la-mort therefore not only expresses the poetic power that Cellier studied (88), but also expresses poetic impotence. Paul Bénichou writes that Gautier "est à l'origine de ce qu'on pourrait appeler, chez les poètes de la seconde moitié du XIXe siècle, le sacerdoce du Dépit, en prenant ce mot dans son sens le plus grave: âcre désappointement de l'Esprit, qui voit sans crédit réel les valeurs qu'il prétend porter en lui . . ." The *sacre de l'écrivain* turns against itself and in the ensuing "religion poétique négative . . . il y a, et il y aura longtemps, une marque d'impuissance, un signe et une tentation de vide" (Bénichou) For the many readers who, like Bénichou, regret Gautier's tendency "à se réfugier dans une futilité provocante," there are other readers, like Baudelaire and Mallarmé, who admire the humor, the fidelity and the serenity with which he *poetically* pursued the beautiful, that is with which he sought to manifest the triumph of the nothingness that is beauty and poetry while concomitantly revealing its vanity. There is no escapism in the poetics of a **"Coquetterie posthume."** It reveals a literariness that *is* unreal, that *is* gratuitous, that *is* repetitive, and that *is* both mortally seductive and seductively deadly.

"Coquetterie posthume" allegorically prescribes the poetry that Baudelaire saw in "Ténèbres": "ce chapelet de redoutables concetti sur la mort et le néant . . ." (*Histoires*) In it, the figure of "la morte qui parle" distances itself from its supernatural origins to assume its modern poetic significance: a self-referential signifier of poetic potency and of poetic impotence, demystifying both the symbolic pretensions of the former and the tragic failures of the latter. It pursues self-consciously its ritual, funereal, and coquettish task of esthetic substitution, transfering from dead hands to pale wax to prayerful rosary beads to charming opals: "Entre mes mains de cire pâle, / Que la prière réunit, / Tournez ce chapelet d'opale,/ Par le pape à Rome bénit"; yet, in the process, actualizing and paradoxically juxtaposing each variant's own meaning and interpretant. Knowing itself to be allegorical, that is fundamentally

separate from and consequently impotent in relation to its "real" referent, Gautier's poetry is faithfully and playfully the posthumous coquetry that repeats previous signs; it is Jacques Lardoux's precious stone thrown as a *pharmakon* against "the order of the city," against the order of time and death.

James M. Vest (essay date 1992)

SOURCE: "Théophile Gautier's `Albertus' and the Thematics of Nailing," in *Nineteenth Century French Studies*, Vol. 20, No. 3 & 4, Spring-Summer, 1992, pp. 317-28.

[*In the following essay, Vest explores Gautier's use of images of nailing in "Albertus."*]

To dismiss **"Albertus"** as a gratuitous, puerile fantasy or as a frenetic exercise in poetic license is to deny Gautier his due. Although the young writer's penchant for *l'emphase* and for heterogeneous subjects and styles is evident in **"Albertus,"** yet it is also true that this poem was carefully reworked prior to publication in 1832 and that, for all its posturing and rambling, it exhibits considerable thematic and organizational coherence. Contributing to that cohesiveness is Gautier's insistence on images of nailing, images that directly counter its apparent predilection for chaotic movement. It is no accident that **"Albertus"** begins and ends with references to *clous* and that allusions to nailing recur at important points in this and others of Gautier's writings. The present study will not attempt to reassess the psychosexual implications of the *clou,* but will instead concentrate on the intellectual and symbolic importance of this recurrent image that constitutes a unifying metaphor in **"Albertus"** and that provides a useful reference point for understanding Gautier's outlook on literature and on life.

The first stanza of **"Albertus"** offers what seems to be one of the "transpositions d'art" for which Gautier is justly famous, a painterly verbal *tableau* that in this case ends with a disconcerting reference to a nail. The landscape is carefully drawn in six 12-syllable lines:

> Sur le bord d'un canal profond dont les eaux vertes
> Dorment, de nénuphars et de bateaux couvertes,
> Avec ses toits aigus, ses immenses greniers,
> Ses tours au front d'ardoise où nichent les cigognes,
> Ses cabarets bruyants qui regorgent d'ivrognes,
> Est un vieux bourg flamand tel que le peint Teniers.

But Gautier does not content himself with word-painting, sinuously wrought. After presenting additional details of the romantic *paysage* and an aside to the assumed reader, the second half of his first stanza, another six-line unit, concludes:

> —Il ne manque vraiment au tableau que le cadre
> Avec le clou pour l'accrocher—

These trimmings effectively delimit the scene, framing it, cutting it off, thus purposefully distancing the actual reader from its contents and thereby leading that reader to consider it as a creation, as a work of art. Yet, although the detail of the "clou" completes the image of landscape *qua* objet, the authorial comment in which it occurs interjects a potentially unsettling element of subjectivity and judgment, while the curt octosyllabic line by which it is conveyed suggests incompleteness. In fact, like the frame, the nail is, and remains, lacking. This initial reference to nailing—or, more accurately, to not nailing—establishes the keen sense of incongruity that will be essential to Gautier's ironic goals throughout **"Albertus,"** where to nail or not to nail ultimately becomes a question of life and death.

In this first stanza the comment about missing frame and nail establishes a perspective of critical distance while laying the groundwork for the conflict between fixity and metamorphosis that will characterize this poem. The theme of mutability is evident at every stage in the narrative, as a sorceress named Véronique magically turns herself into a lovely temptress who seduces Albertus and gives him over to Satan. Still the vigorous activities of this poem's main scenes—physical transformations, temptation and seduction episodes, witches' sabbath—are all counter-balanced by concrete details that tend to immobilize the action until, in the end, Albertus lands with a thud, a broken mass, motionless on the Appian Way. These details have often been dismissed as romantic bric-a-brac. Yet they have the effect of sealing in time the scenes of frenetic movement that they describe. They serve like the frozen frames in a film to fix a scene in the viewer's mind. Nail-like, they pin the action down, make it stick.

The image of the nail also suggests finality. If the picture is ready to hang it should be complete. Similarly the decorative "clous d'acier" covering the "coffre" mentioned in stanza LXXXVIII indicate that it is, artistically speaking, a finished, polished product. The received idea that Gautier frequently had trouble completing his poems is based in part on a candid assertion by the autobiographical narrator of this poem, who heaves a gargantuan sigh of relief when his tale is finally done (stanza CXXI). The picture of the first stanza, ready to frame and hang, and the nail-studded box are recalled by the narrator's admission at the end of **"Albertus"** that conclusions are hard to come by and should be appreciated when found. Thus, in the context of hyperactive, digressive storytelling, the nail comes to represent not only fixity, but also that hard, definitive finishing touch of the artisan that attests the completeness and, by extension, the permanence that, throughout his life, intrigued the author of *Emaux et camées.*

The interplay between disintegration and permanence is a *leitmotif* in Gautier's work. The vital struggle against decomposition informs his poems, stories, and plays. The absorbing quest for permanence amid mutability gives meaning to the detail of the frame and nail that would finish off the picture at the beginning of **"Albertus"** and of the "coffre à clous d'acier" that resembles a coffin in Véronique's boudoir. That association with death is reinforced by Gautier's use of the verb *clouer* in stanza LXXI, where the sense of finality is directly linked to thoughts of mortality, and in stanza CXXII, where hints of extinction

extend to communication and to creation itself. Motifs of deathlike immobilization, as evident in these images of nailing as they are in the lava imprint of *Arria Marcella* or in a mummy's foot, are reflections of Gautier's life-long struggle with the idea of death.

The interplay of life and death, of freedom and judgment, of nailing and of refraining from nailing, is highly pertinent to Gautier's ironic stance in **"Albertus"** where a syncopated verse form supports the ideas of playfulness and freedom within a narrative structure that is primarily associational rather than logical. Hence the importance of the teasing banter in the first stanza where, from the outset, the assumed reader is addressed and manipulated, with humor based on deflation of expected norms:

> —Vous reconnaissez-vous?—Tenez, voilà le saule,
> De ses cheveux blafards inondant son épaule
> Comme une fille au bain, l'église et son clocher,
> L'étang où des canards se pavane l'escadre.

The aside to the assumed reader sets the tone for subsequent familiarity and for caustic, occasionally cynical comments addressed to that reader in which deflation or demystification is the goal. Similarly the inverted syntax of lines 8 and 10 creates a setting where the actual reader's linguistic and semantic expectations are brought into question, crossed, diverted. The trenchant, unsettling irony that Gautier had encountered and admired in the works of Scarron and Rabelais recurs throughout **"Albertus,"** focused by poetic devices such as chiasmus (e.g., stanzas XCIII and CXXII) and reinforced by the alternating *rime plate* and *rime embrassée* as well as by the short, pithy final line in each stanza. Nail-like, that irony functions both to pique curiosity and to puncture it.

Right through its final image of the missing, affixing nail, the opening stanza of **"Albertus"** sets the ironic tone of "what you see is *not* what you get" that pervades the entirety of this work. Here as elsewhere, Gautier was preoccupied with questions of hiddenness and mutability, to which nailing may be seen as a definitive response. It is in this larger thematic context that the initial comment about frame and nail as well as the detail of the "coffre à clous d'acier" take on emblematic significance, particularly as we look back at them, as is prudent when considering a work whose internal development is largely associational, from the all-inclusive perspective of the end.

The concept of mystification lies at the heart of the concluding stanzas of **"Albertus,"** which in their rollicking way summarize all that has gone before. In a sardonic epilogue (stanzas CXXI-CXXII) Gautier's narrator, swept away by the *furor poeticus,* judges his job masterfully done. Declaring his work "sans égal au monde," he claims that it is an "allégorie admirable et profonde." This "allégorie" has a quintessentially Rabelaisian character that gives Gautier's poem its final ironic series of connecting punches, each efficacious, each evocative of earlier jabs and hooks. **"Albertus"** ends with a reference to Pantagruel preceded by an allusion to bone marrow recalling Rabelais's "substantifique moelle."

. . . pour sucer la moelle il faut qu'on brise l'os,
Pour savourer l'odeur il faut ouvrir le vase,
Du tableau que l'on cache il faut tirer la gaze,
Lever, le bal fini, le masque aux dominos.
—J'aurais pu clairement expliquer chaque chose,
Clouer à chaque mot une savante glose.—
Je vous crois, cher lecteur, assez spirituel
Pour me comprendre.—Ainsi, bonsoir.—Fermez la
   porte,
Donnez-moi la pincette, et dites qu'on m'apporte
Un tome de Pantagruel.

The narrator's concluding remarks are coupled with a reference to a "tableau" reminiscent of that which began the poem and culminate, like that initial reference, in an allusion to nailing, or rather to the absence of nailing. The resounding "J'aurais pu . . . clouer" is heralded by a reiterative sequence of paired images—marrow/bone, odor/container, painting/cover, masqueraders/mask—that are all variations on a single antiphonal theme: things are not always as they appear and active undoing is required to reveal the truth. While dramatically setting up the poem's final statement on nailing, these "il faut" assertions also recapitulate earlier references in **"Albertus"** related to the theme of hiddenness, including this poem's most frequently cited passage:

> —Jouissons, faisons-nous un bonheur de surface:
> Un beau masque vaut mieux qu'une villaine face.
> —Pourquoi l'arracher, pauvres fous?

The truth is masked, and properly so. Before Ibsen, Gautier advanced the idea of a life-lie, a cover-up that allows one to continue living: "déception sublime, admirable imposture." A similar meaning is suggested by the covered "tableau," recalling that of the first stanza, which at the poem's end is shown in its true hiddenness. Its mystery, like that of the Rabelaisian "moelle," can be savored only if one can "tirer la gaze" or break into a bone or release odors from a closed container. Yet, as Albertus learns the hard way, such disclosing may prove fatal.

The conjunction between mask, bone, "tableau," and "gaze," made explicit in the vivid revelations of the seduction scene is recalled here, mixed with the odor of death. Attractive smells are conspicuously lacking from Gautier's description of Véronique. Instead the odor emanating from the vase at the end of **"Albertus"** calls to mind one of the most memorable and grotesque details of Véronique's hovel: the smell of rotting fetuses in bottles (stanza IX, 1: 131). Urn-like vase and bottle both evoke death. For Gautier, enclosed, hidden, sealed spaces betoken the tomb. Thus the "coffre à clous d'acier" in the seductress's chamber is a coffin-like chest complete with nails that recalls the casket mentioned in a pivotal stanza describing the *Weltschmerz* of "notre héros" Albertus (stanza LXXI), where the verb *clouer* designates the ultimate seal of death:

> —A vingt ans l'on pouvait le clouer dans sa bière,
> Cadavre sans illusions.

This statement, from an author recently turned twenty, leads directly to the reflections on masks in stanza LXXII,

quoted above. That striking use of *clouer* reverberates in the reader's mind as **"Albertus"** draws to a close with its final reference to nailing, reminding the wary reader that nailing can be deadly.

In his concluding remarks (stanza CXXII), just after the interconnected references to marrow, vase, picture, and mask, Gautier makes a leap to the back of one of his favorite hobbyhorses, thereby connecting two ranges of meaning associated with nailing. The phrase "savante glose" recalls Gautier's numerous invectives against Boileau and other seventeenth century "grammarians" who, he claimed (particularly in *Les Grotesques* and in *Daniel Jovard, ou la conversion d'un classique*), effectively retarded the course of French poetry for two centuries. The idea of affixing a specific interpretation to each word recalls not only Gautier's railings against the academicians (cf. "messieurs les rigoristes," 1: 176) but also his impatience with the *romans à clef* of the "soi-disant grand siècle" in his essay on Scudéry and elsewhere. Such an action would limit the freedom of the word, immobilize it, imprison it, bury it.

Thus for Gautier the phrase "clouer à chaque mot une savante glose" evokes a Rabelaisian reaction to the idea of pinning down words by limiting them to specific meanings while it connects through Gautier's own expansive usage of *clou* and *clouer* to the idea of imprisonment and entombment. Connotations associated with nailing in **"Albertus"**—suggestions of limiting, restraining, finishing off—also underlie Gautier's descriptions of the unfortunate imprisonments of Villon and Viau in *Les Grotesques*. His resentment against that sort of immobilizing sequestration is clear. To him, the judgment that produced those incarcerations seems profoundly unjust. A Rabelaisian love of linguistic and personal freedom energizes Gautier's artistic expression. Verbal fixity and artistic restraint are linked for him with a troubling sense of injustice.

The ideas of the unfairness of judgment and the inappropriateness of imprisonment are inextricably linked in Gautier's *œuvre* with a notion of sin and retribution. Young Théophile Gautier heard the judgment passed against his "homonyme" Théophile de Viau as if it were meant for him personally:

> *Maudit sois-tu Théophile!* [italics Gautier's] Maudit soit l'esprit qui t'a dicté tes pensées, maudite soit la main qui les a écrites, malheureux le libraire qui les a imprimées. . . . (*Les Grotesques*)

"Le bon Théo" could never forget the irony implicit in his Christian name, just as he could never forgive God for allowing death. René Jasinski insists that the subtitles associated with **"Albertus"**—**"L'Ame et le péché"** and **"Légende théologique"**—are not entirely facetious. He points out that Albertus resists Véronique's temptation better than other mortals and concludes that Albertus yields "par lassitude et apathie plus que par désir, et il ne succombe que dans l'ivresse" (*Années,* [1929] 116). What might be considered a peccadillo in another context here leads to death. That seems harsh punishment indeed, especially since the character named Albertus is described as being very much like the narrator (stanzas L - LVIII and LXVIII) who in turn resembles the author whose nickname in the Petit Cénacle was Albert or Albertus.

. . . . .

In addition to its immediate applications within the story and structure of **"Albertus,"** the nail has broad implications for Gautier's work as a whole, because of its peculiar association, for him, with death and decomposition. It is a truism that Gautier was preoccupied with death. That subject informs much of his poetry as well as his prose and theater. When the noun *clou* or the verb *clouer* is involved, the result is often an image of entombment in a claustrophobic, impotent world, an inescapable "gouffre" not unlike the horrid pit of Poe's premature burials. That connection is the subject of another of Gautier's poems from the mid-1830s:

> Ce fer que le mineur cherche au fond de la terre
> Aux brumeuses clartés de son pâle fanal,
> Hélas! le forgeron quelque jour en doit faire
> Le clou qui fermera le couvercle fatal!
> A cette même place où mille fois peut être
> J'allai m'asseoir, le cœur plein de rêves charmants,
> S'entr'ouvrira le gouffre où je dois disparaître,
> Pour descendre au séjour des épouvantements!
>
> ("Stances")

Comparable images appear elsewhere in Gautier's poetry, occasionally in humorous contexts (e.g., **"Coquetterie posthume"**). Although often ironic, these images are, in general, deadly serious. In one striking example from *Emaux et camées* a prison cell is substituted for the tomb and the nail becomes the prisoner-writer's stylus:

> Ainsi dans les puits de Venise,
> Un prisonnier à demi fou,
> Pendant sa nuit qui s'éternise,
> Grave des mots avec un clou.
>
> ("L'Aveugle")

The phrase "à demi fou" recalls the "pauvres fous" of the most celebrated lines from **"Albertus"** (stanza LXXII; quoted above). When one is "fou" or "à demi fou," nothing is as it appears. Even the fixity and stability symbolized by a nail are suspect. The nail-bedecked "coffre" in **"Albertus"** is openable. Its mysterious contents may be revealed. A picture can be taken down. A mask can be lifted, a curtain parted.

Imprisonment, writing, words, cells represent so many "coffres," so many masks, so many calls for revelation and transformation. In **"Albertus"** Véronique's disguise is, like the "coffre à clous d'acier," representative of humanity's penchant for concealing and masking. That idea is developed in **"Nostalgies d'obélisques,"** where Gautier avers that beneath the most attractive civilized exterior lurks a skeleton:

> Oh! dans cent ans quels laids squelettes
> Fera ce peuple impie et fou,
> Qui se couche sans bandelettes
> Dans des cercueils que ferme un clou . . . !

Here "clou" is again rhymingly connected to "fou" in a statement, poetically attributed to an Egyptian obelisk, which comes close to unveiling the mystery of Gautier's fascination with nails. The subject is interment, as opposed to mummification. Burial, particularly Christian burial, is intimately linked in Gautier's mind with a profound fear of death—and nailing.

Gautier's condemnation of the Christian attitude toward death and burial is thematically connected, through the verb *clouer,* to the crucifixion of Jesus. This connection becomes clearer in the title poem from the collection *La Comédie de la mort* where a crucifix in the narrator's dimly-lit, sepulcher-like room is presented in the context of both *cadre* and *clou:*

> Dans son cadre terni, le pâle Christ d'ivoire,
> Cloué les bras en croix sur son étoffe noire,
> Redoublait de pâleur.
>
> ("La Comédie de la mort")

Here, presented in relief, nailed limbs constitute an arresting part of the artistic vision, which, although "finished," still retains the power to communicate life-sapping pallor.

The image of "le Christ cloué" is recast in an even more personalized way in a series of reflections on a painting in a poem called **"Magdalena"**:

> Je regardais le Christ sur son infâme bois,
> Pour embrasser le monde ouvrant les bras en croix.
> Ses pieds meurtris et bleus et ses deux mains
>   clouées
> Ses chairs par les bourreaux à coups de fouet
>   trouées.
>
> ("Magdalena")

In **"Magdalena"** the crucifixion event itself becomes increasingly internalized as the motif of the penetrating and rending of flesh is developed and prompts an extended meditation that merits quoting in full:

> Et je me dis: "O Christ! tes douleurs sont trop
>   vives;
> Après ton agonie au jardin des Olives,
> Il fallait remonter près de ton Père, au ciel,
> Et nous laisser, à nous, l'éponge avec le fiel;
> Les clous percent ta chair, et les fleurons d'épines
> Entrent profondément dans tes tempes divines.
> Tu vas mourir, toi, Dieu! comme un homme. La
>   mort
> Recule épouvantée à ce sublime effort;
> Elle a peur de sa proie, elle hésite à la prendre,
> Sachant qu'après trois jours il la lui faudra rendre,
> Et qu'un ange viendra, qui radieux et beau
> Lèvera de ses mains la pierre du tombeau;
> Mais tu n'en as pas moins souffert ton agonie,
> Adorable victime entre toutes bénie;
> Mais tu n'en as pas moins, avec les deux voleurs,
> Etendu tes deux bras sur l'arbre de douleurs.
>
> ("Magdalena")

Here is the shocking, immobilizing, deflating experience *par excellence*. This nailing transcends one life. It transcends life itself, as it transcends time. For Gautier it has profound negative overtones, which are echoed in many of his works. In *Arria Marcella,* for example, the crucifixion is linked to that cosmic dislocation of time that dethroned the old gods and made sensual love sinful. The entire complex of Gautier's anger and guilt is wrapped up, and pinned, in this symbol.

It remained a symbol to Gautier, a mystery that he recognized with great personal pain and that he tried to accommodate through the sculptural, impassive art of *Emaux et camées,* but never completely understood: "Les dieux eux-mêmes meurent . . ." ("L'Art"). The mystery of mortality and the concomitant question of afterlife remained for Gautier a covered "tableau," a nail-studded "coffre," a mask scented with haunting perfume suggestive of love and death.

. . . . .

Perpetually confronted by the piquant irony of decomposition, as well as composition, the inventive poet's only recourse was humor. Here was a hard bone to crack, and one solution was to fight irony with irony. Thus Gautier resorted in "Albertus" to Rabelaisian language and tactics. Just before his caustic epilogue, there is a passage which recalls the riveting scene of the crucifixion. It is the denouement of Albertus's story, which has perplexed commentators. Most critics state simply that Albertus dies after his ordeal with Satan. Jasinski notes, more accurately, that Albertus lies broken ("brisé") on the Appian Way (*Années* 102). Gautier put it this way:

> Et les contadini le matin, près de Rome,
> Sur la voie Appia trouvèrent un corps d'homme
> Les reins cassés, le col tordu.

The significant details of the "reins cassés" and the "col tordu" are reminiscent of Villon's double-edged reflections on love-making, drinking, aging, hanging, and decomposing, which Gautier echoed in his early poetry (e.g., "Cauchemar," "Frisson," "Débauche") and to which he would return in *Les Grotesques.* The precipitous ending of Albertus's story recalls that of Scarron's *Roman comique,* which inspired both the last essay in *Les Grotesques* and Gautier's novel *Le Capitaine Fracasse.*

Even in the truncated denouement of "Albertus" there is room to evoke certain aspects of the gnawing problem of *thanatos.* Thrown down like Lucifer, Albertus crashes on a site associated with both Christianity and pagan antiquity. Associations with damnation and diabolical destruction are clear. But is there not also in this description something of a perverted image of Christ on the cross? Albertus's last memory is of hard, pointed objects—claws and teeth—tearing at his flesh. "Ses chairs lacérées" (stanza CXX) echo the imagery of crucifixion in "Magdalena." Albertus expires with a cry like that of Vigny's Christ in the garden: "Il cria; mais son cri ne fut point entendu . . ." (stanza CXX, ellipsis Gautier's).

Gautier's resentment of death finds expression both in the imagery and in the organization of "Albertus." From beginning to end, images of nailing suggest attempts at solidity or fixity, limitation or finality in a work whose structure, tone, and thrust tend toward experimentation and freedom. In the context of the author's preoccupation with life characterized by movement and mutability, nailing represents an unwarranted act of pinning down, deflating, incarcerating, or entombing. Immobility betokens brokenness, or worse. Applied to words, thoughts, and creativity, nailing signals death. It is the death suggested by academic labels, by frames and closures, by coffins and crucifixes: death associated with the finality of judgment. Poets or poetry judged to be "finished," words authoritatively "glossed," and traditional notions of sin and religion all represent for the author of "Albertus" forms of imprisonment to be resisted. The incongruity fostered by traditional appeals for permanence and completeness in a disintegrating world where a finishing touch seems unwelcome if not impossible helps create the dramatic tension at the heart of this poem about creativity and culpability, about the limitations of living and communicating.

Like the prisoner with only a nail for a stylus, the writer carves and scratches with a nail-like pen. In "Albertus" it is an implement for joining and for splitting that at once unites and sunders on diverse planes. Through his references to ill-fated nailing, Gautier satirizes all that is mutable, including his readers and himself, as well as all human attempts at immutability. Like love, freedom and creativity are forever fleeting, changing, transient:

> Toujours! songes-y bien, d'un éternel amour
> Il n'est dans l'univers qu'un seul être capable,
> Et cet être, c'est Dieu,—car il est immuable;
> L'homme d'un jour n'aime qu'un jour.

In this eternal paradox Gautier sees the essential irony of human existence.

That vital incongruity renders attempts to pin down what "Albertus" means particularly difficult, and that difficulty is part of Gautier's plan. In the text itself the issue of the poem's meaning is purposefully sidestepped by the narrator's tongue-in-cheek invitation in the final stanza to continue looking for clues. Nor was that to be the disingenuous enchanter's final word on the subject. Albertus was revived many times in other works in which Gautier attempted to pursue the meaning of his story—as Albert in *Celle-ci et celle-là* and in *Le Bol de punch,* as d'Albert in *Mademoiselle de Maupin,* as Duke Albert in *Giselle,* and in the other masks through which Gautier projected his fragile psyche and which, as he maintained, make us true.

FURTHER READING

Biography

Richardson, Joanna. *Théophile Gautier: His Life and Times.* London: Max Reingardt, 1958, 335 p.
   The definitive English-language critical biography.

Criticism

Bristol, Evelyn. "The Acmeists and the Parnassian Heritage." In *American Contributions to the Tenth International Congress of Slavists,* edited by Jane Gary Harris, pp. 71-81. Columbus, Ohio: Slavica, 1988.

> Explains the effects Gautier's emotional and materialistic poetry and poetics had on the Acmeists, especially Nikolai Gumilev.

Dillingham, Louise Bulkley. *The Creative Imagination of Théophile Gautier.* Princeton, N.J. and Albany, N.Y.: Psychological Review Co., 1927, 356 p.

> Psychological investigation into Gautier's motivations and techniques, tracing his artistic evolution from Romanticism to Realism and finding him to be, overall, more prosaic than poetic.

Grant, Richard. *Théophile Gautier.* Boston: Twayne, 1975, 179 p.

> Overview of Gautier's life and work, inluding commentary on his poetry.

Haxell, Nichola A. "Hugo, Gautier and the Obelisk of Luxor (Place de la Concorde) During the Second Republic." *Nineteenth-Century French Studies* 18, No. 1 & 2 (Fall/Winter 1989-90): 65-75.

> Contrasts Victor Hugo's political and Gautier's historical/mythical treatments of the subject of the obelisk.

Killick, Rachel. "Gautier and the Sonnet." *Essays in French Literature* No. 16 (November 1979): 1-16.

> Examination Gautier's use of the sonnet form which claims that Gautier's sonnets, though mostly derivative, at times indicate new possibilities for visual description in poetry.

Riffaterre, Michael. "The Poem's Significance." In his *Semiotics of Poetry,* pp. 1-22. Bloomington: Indiana University, 1978.

> Argues that Gautier's "In Deserto" is properly understood not as a descriptive poem but as a set of shifting, semiotic codes.

Scott, Clive. "The Octosyllable, Rhythmicity and Syllabic Position: Gautier's *Emaux et camees.*" In his *A Question of Syllables: Essays in Nineteenth Century French Verse,* pp. 31-60. New York: Cambridge University Press, 1986.

> Explores the scintillating effects of the octosyllabic line on the meaning of the poems.

Temple, Ruth Zabriskie. "Algernon Charles Swinburne: Notes of an Important Poet on Important Poets." In her *The Critic's Alchemy: A Study of the Introduction of French Symbolism into England,* pp. 77-92. New York: Twayne, 1953.

> Describes the influence of Gautier's poetry, poetics, and criticism on Swinburne's work.

Tennant, P.E. *Théophile Gautier.* London: Athlone, 1975, 149p.

> Overview of Gautier's theories and works, including a substantial treatment of Gautier's poetry.

Additional coverage of Gautier's life and career is contained in the following sources published by Gale Research: *Short Story Criticism,* Vol. 20 and *Dictionary of Literary Biography,* Vol. 119

Hagiwara Sakutarō
1886-1942

Japanese poet, critic, and essayist.

INTRODUCTION

Hagiwara is considered by many critics to be the father of modern Japanese poetry. He was among the first poets to break away from the traditional, strictly metered forms of Japanese poetry as practiced in the writing of tanka and haiku. He also established a new aesthetic in Japanese poetry in which he attained a sustained poetic lyricism by using colloquial Japanese speech in free-verse poems. Hagiwara was deeply influenced by European nihilistic philosophies, and his poems, which often center on existential anxiety, are pervaded by melancholy and nostalgia.

Biographical Information

Hagiwara was born into a middle-class family in the provincial town of Maebashi, where his father was a successful physician. While in middle school he took a keen interest in literature and began submitting traditional tanka poems to the literary magazine *Bunko.* He later withdrew from school due to poor health, and he made sporadic attempts to earn his high school degree into his twenties. At home Hagiwara devoted himself to poetry and the study of Japanese and European literature. He also had an aptitude for music and became accomplished on mandolin and guitar. By 1910 Hagiwara had become a regular contributor to several poetry journals. He spent several years living a somewhat bohemian life, drifting between his hometown and Tokyo. During this time he explored his interest in Western philosophy and literature, and for a brief period he attended Christian churches. His lifestyle drew criticism from the Maebashi bourgeoisie, and his poetry includes many spiteful remarks about his native community. In 1916 he cofounded the magazine *Kanjo* with Muro Saisei, an author whose poems he greatly admired. The magazine featured a new style of modern Japanese poetry that was distinct from the highly intellectual poems that other magazines of the day were publishing. The following year Hagiwara published his first poetry collection, *Tsuki ni hoeru* (*Howling at the Moon*). The collection, which introduced Hagiwara's extraordinary talent for using colloquial speech in a free-verse style, gained wide critical acclaim and established his reputation as a significant new voice in Japanese poetry. He followed this success with several more volumes of poetry, criticism, and literary theory. Despite his high standing in the world of Japanese letters, Hagiwara relied on his family for financial support throughout his life. In 1919 he married Uedo Ineko, with whom he had two daughters. The marriage ended in divorce in 1929. His second marriage, to Oya Mitsuko in 1938, lasted only eighteen months. Much of Hagiwara's poetry conveys the isolation and loneliness that he felt, and his later works, particularly the poems in his 1934 collection *Hyoto,* are characterized by an increasingly despondent and nostalgic tone. He taught at the University of Meiji in Tokyo from 1934 until his death in 1942.

Major Works

Hagiwara's first poetry collection, *Howling at the Moon,* had a wide and immediate impact on the Japanese literary community. Although the collection contains some traditional tanka, many of the poems use colloquial language and are written in a loose, unmetered form. Hagiwara's success at elevating common Japanese speech to a poetic form was unprecedented. In this volume, commentators noted, Hagiwara essentially created a new aesthetic in modern Japanese poetry. In the preface to the work Hagiwara wrote: "Before this collection not a single poem had been written in colloquial language of this style, and before this collection the animation in the poetry one senses today did not exist." Critics also note that the poems in *Howling at the Moon* were among the first in modern Japanese poetry to address questions of existential anxiety. In the title piece Hagiwara likened the desperate psychological state of humanity to a lonely dog plaintively wailing at the moon. Throughout the collection Hagiwara created characters who are ridden with despair. Hagiwara's second collection of poems, *Aoneko,* achieved even greater critical acclaim than his first. The poems in this volume reveal Hagiwara's personal interest in the nihilistic philosophy of Arthur Schopenhauer and the pessimistic ideology of Buddhism. The collection centers on abstract, metaphysical themes in which characters are nostalgic for times and places that they have never experienced. Hagiwara published a second "definitive" edition of this volume in 1936, in which he included the poem "The Corpse of a Blue Cat." The piece is a sad and nostalgic love poem in which time and memory are displaced. In it, the speaker says, "We have no past, no future, / And have faded away from the things of reality." Hagiwara's last major collection of poetry, *Hyoto* (1934), received mixed critical reviews. In this volume, Hagiwara abandoned his innovative use of colloquial Japanese and returned to writing in a more formal language in metered verse. The poems in the volume are set in a more realistic context, and they convey an over-whelming sense of despair and bitterness. In the autobiographical poem "Returning to My Parents' Home," for example, Hagiwara recounted the anger and rejection that he felt after his first wife left him. In addition to his poetry, Hagiwara was widely respected for his volumes on poetic theory. His most noted theoretical work, *Shi no genri* (1928), laid out his conception of what he contended should be the principal aims of poetry. In aphoristic statements Hagiwara asserted that poetry should strive to convey transcendental themes and be critical of reality.

Critical Reception

Critics agree that Hagiwara's poetry profoundly changed the face of modern Japanese poetry. His use of vernacular Japanese demonstrated that the language of the people could also be a poetic language, full of artistic depth and resonance. While other poets had attempted to write in the vernacular, the effect had always been that of everyday speech. It took Hagiwara's skillful use of words to prove that vernacular Japanese could in fact be used artistically in verse. His first collection, *Tsuki ni hoeru* (*Howling at the Moon*), met with enthusiastic critical acclaim and was recognized as a thoroughly modern expression of fear, a fear that Hagiwara described as a "physiological fear" that threatens man's mental well-being. Another important contribution to modern Japanese poetry was his successful creation of a body of poetry motivated by the existential angst of a modern individual. Greatly influenced by Schopenhauer and Nietzsche, Hagiwara embodied the Western attitude of pessimism and despair. The bleak poetry of *Howling at the Moon* and *Aoneko* represented the first instance of Japanese poetry imitating modern Western philosophical ideas. His interest in free verse and colloquial language represented a watershed in modern Japanese poetry, and irrevocably brought the Japanese poetic tradition closer stylistically and philosophically to that of Western literature.

PRINCIPAL WORKS

Poetry

Tsuki ni hoeru [*Howling at the Moon*] 1917
Aoneko [*The Blue Cat*] 1923
Chō yumemu [*Dreaming of Butterflies*] 1924
Junjo shokyoku shu [*Collection of Short Songs on Innocent Love*] 1925
Hyōtō [*The Iceland*] 1934
Shikumei [*Destiny*] *1939*
Face at the Bottom of the World, and Other Poems 1969

Other Major Works

Shi no genri (criticism) 1928
Nekomachi [*Cat Town*] (short story) 1935
Kyoshu no shijin Yosa Buson (criticism) 1936

CRITICISM

Donald K. Shults (essay date 1973)

SOURCE: "Hagiwara Sakutarō's Fitzgerald," in *Prairie Schooner*, Vol. 47, No. 2, Summer, 1973, pp. 174-77.

[*In the following essay, Shults reviews Graeme Wilson's translation of Hagiwara's poetry in* The Face at the Bottom of the World, and Other Poems.]

To most of us the dark vault of Asian literature would remain forever locked without the work of such men as the aviation expert, diplomat, scholar Graeme Wilson, one of that small band of occidentals literate in Japanese, a language that is often difficult even to those whose native tongue it is.

"Perhaps our greatest modern poet," said one Japanese scholar when asked about Sakutarō's work, "but difficult." *Difficult* is the word that best describes Hagiwara Sakutarō the man as well as the poet. A photograph, reproduced in the book, shows a thin haggard face, lank black hair, long nose, mouth with a trace of petulence, and head thrown back—an arrogant face. Wilson, in a long and informative introduction, traces the outline of Sakutarō's career. He was a sickly *botchan* (mother's darling) to the end of his days, unsuccessful as student, musician, and husband, financially dependent upon his father, an alcoholic, yet he did produce a considerable body of work before his death from pneumonia in 1942.

After an apprenticeship in the traditional *tanka* form, "suddenly in 1913, he began writing those astonishing and essentially modern poems on which his real and lasting reputation rests." Using *kōgatai* (the spoken colloquial language), he wrote "poems in all manner of irregular and typically *modern* forms . . . the first Japanese poet to successfully exploit the innovations of form derived from western examples for the expression of traditional Japanese lyricism." In many of the poems, Hagiwara does achieve a sustained flight of lyric intensity; the very length—unusual in Japanese poetry—lending movement to what had become a static form. But his wings are those of the night-moth, finding only destruction in warmth and light. According to Wilson, "Hagiwara, for all his brilliance, seems somehow to switch on darkness, to radiate black luminance." The subjects are dark and cold: **"Death of an Alcoholic," "Enchanted Graveyard"** (*sic*), **"Rotten Clam."** The colors, too, are cold ones: blue, silver, black, and over and over, green.

In **"Airen,"** the first poem of the collection of forty, there is the "ooze from blue bruised grasses," and even the passion of the sexual act begrudged: "Hard as I hug your breasts, your body/ Hard-presses mine that we/ May squeeze from this abandoned place/ Our snaking ecstasy." In **"Duel"** the color changes to Sakutarō's favorite green; the lines jingle rather than flow: "Both earth and sky are greennesses,/ Greens that explode and expand:/ Shoes flash like fish as I tread the seas,/ And hang like fish when I stand."

At the heart of the poems is "A cold, an absolute/ Quintessence of distress," being hurt and demanding to be hurt again until we "To death's menagerie/ Stagger away." He continues to demand answers: Who am I? Why am I here? These are certainly not original observations and questions; nevertheless, they are the things that man will continue to scream into the void until the world's end. These and Sakutarō's imagery, his brilliant figurative language, the intensity of his despair make his narrow vein flow through a universal body—"a living synthesis of alien elements . . . successful integration of the Japanese and western poetic traditions."

What then of the translations? Mr. Wilson acknowledges that his are "translations only in the sense that Fitzgerald's *Rubaiyat* is a translation of the work of Omar Khayyam. I have not regarded the literal words in Hagiwara's texts as of prime or even secondary importance. Instead, I have sought to convey the feel and intent of his work." Several Japanese scholars who have read these *translations* have remarked that they are not Japanese at all, and Wilson is ready to accept the blame: "If these versions of Hagiwara's poetry can in any way foster a reappraisal or a wider recognition of his work, I gladly risk that complete oblivion which is a traitor's fittest doom."

In the Japanese language there are connotations that are lost in translation. Along with literal fidelity, Mr. Wilson has chosen to sacrifice many of these delights, and perhaps for his avowed purpose of making Sakutarō known to the world it is the wise choice. Without Fitzgerald, who today would know Omar? Wilson has followed a dictum of the late Sir Thomas Beecham, who once told his orchestra that he would allow the composer the "virgin notes on the stave," with which he would proceed to do exactly as he wished.

All very well so long as it is done with taste, but at times Wilson has added too many ornaments to a simple eloquent cry, as in the following:

"Kanashi Tsukio"

Nosuto-inu mega,
Kusata hatoba-no tsuki-ni hoeteiru.
Tamashi-ga mimi-o sumasuto,
Inkikusai koeoeshite;
Kiroi musumetachi-ga gashōshiteru,
Gashōshiteru,
Hatobano kurai ishigaki-de.

Itsumo,
Naze ore-wa kōnanda,
Inuyo.
Aojiroi fushiawase-no inuyo.

"Sorrowful Moonlit Night"

The thief dog!
Barking at the moon on the rotten pier
When the soul listens attentively,
With a melancholy voice;
Yellow daughters chorus,
Chorus,
On the dark stone wall of the pier.

Always,
Why thus? (Why am I thus?)
Dog!
Pale unlucky dog!

Mr. Wilson's version:

"Sad Moonlit Night"

On the rotting wharf that pilfering cur,
Pale yapping waif of a wharfinger,
Barks at the moon:
The lonelier at the lonelier.

O listen hard. By the wharf's stone wall
Where in the dark the water curls
To lap at land's ramshackledom,
There gloomy voices rise and fall,
Gloomy voices of yellow girls
Singing, singing of kingdom's come.

Why must I hear such singing; why
Must I be so ware of the world gone wry;
And why, pale dog,
Unhappy dog, am I always I?

The original contains only eleven short lines devoid of such encrustations as "Pale yapping waif of a wharfinger" or "ramshackledom," and sings no songs of "Kingdom's come." The expression *kiroi musume tachi* (yellow *daughters,* not *girls*) is apt and sad, a poignant note of reproach. And why, one asks, did the translator destroy the simple piercing quality of the final cry?

The good translator needs to be a poet, too, and when he is good Mr. Wilson is very good, as in **"Winter," "The Person Who Loved Love," "Moonlight and Jellyfish," "Night Train," "Death of a Frog,"** and the quatrain **"Eggs"**; this last one reminds the reader of Wallace Stevens. . . .

How much is Wilson and how much is Sakutarō? I suppose the answer is not too important to the general reader. Of real importance is the fact that Graeme Wilson has, in introducing the "Japanese Baudelaire" to Western readers, performed a valuable service. Sakutarō's poetry, cold and green, glittering with terror, is now available to us, another tiny compartment unlocked in a vast dark vault.

Reiko Tsukimura   (essay date 1976)

SOURCE: "Hagiwara Sakutarō and the Japanese Lyric Tradition," in *Journal of the Association of Teachers of Japanese,* Vol 11, No. 1, January, 1976, pp. 47-63.

[*In the following essay, Tsukimura provides an analysis of Hagiwara's poetic techniques.*]

Hagiwara Sakutarō had published over 200 tanka before he began his career as a poet writing in the free modern style at the age of twenty-seven. His earliest published compositions are five poems in the tanka form which appeared in 1902 under the general title **"One Night's Bond"** (**"Hitoyo enishi"**) in the alumni magazine of the Maebashi Middle School where he was then a third-year student. In them, the young Hagiwara expressed his feelings for the beauty of Kyoto in spring:

nagarekite
Kamogawa samuki
haru no yoi
Kyo no obashima
hito utsukushiki

As I drift along to
the Kamo River, it flows cold
this spring evening,
lovely are the Kyotoans
by the railing.

and:

akebono no
hana ni yorikoshi
sozoromichi
sozoro au hito
mina utsukushiki

Seeking the flower of
spring morning
I have wandered out onto this
roadway,
where everyone who passes me by
is beautiful.

The second poem echoes Yosano Akiko's:

Kiyomizu e
Gion o yogiru
sakurasukiyo
koyoi au hito
mina utsukushiki

This moonlit night of
cherry-viewing,
as I cross from Gion to
Kiyomizu,
everyone who passes me by
is beautiful.

Hagiwara created his poem obviously under the influence of Akiko's *Midaregami* (*Dishevelled Hair,* 1901), in which the poem just quoted appears. Using the technique of *honkadori,* a traditional poetic device of "allusive variation," Hagiwara borrowed Akiko's words *au hito/mina utsukushiki* and her topic, cherry-viewing. He chose in contrast morning as opposed to night. In addition, another clear distinction exists between the two poems: Akiko presents a vivid picture of the scene of cherry-viewing, and the cadence of Hagiwara's words suggests a young cherry-viewer's leisurely walk. The soft sounds of the first line, *akebono no,* set the tone of Hagiwara's poem. The term *akebono* refers to a morning in spring, while the first word of the second line, *hana,* is also a symbol of spring. And the warmth and happiness of youth are felt in the rich use of the vowels *a* and *o.*

The first of the five-poem group, **"One Night's Bond,"** also indicates that Hagiwara was not merely a simple imitator, but that he had his own distinctive voice:

ochitsubaki
fumite wa hito no
koishikute
harubi nanuka o
unjinuru sato

Longing sharpens
as I tread on fallen camellias;
I have grown weary of the
village,
where seven days of spring
have passed.

The excitement the young poet feels in the old capital is juxtaposed to his boredom with life in the country. His sense of ennui and his unhappy awareness of the contrast between country and capital were to become recurring themes. This sense of boredom is conveyed by both the descriptive image of the fallen camellias and the sound of the word, *unjinuru,* "grown weary."

The descriptive and symbolic are fused in the next:

matsuochiba
fumitsutsu yukeba
sato chikashi
asamoya michi ni
usureyuku

Stepping on
the fallen needles of pine
I have come near the village.
Along the road
morning mist fades out.

The fading of the mist might be suggested by the irregularly short final line.

Hagiwara made an ambitious attempt at fanciful images in the last of the five poems:

asa yuki ni
hitome suzushiki
hama ya hama
ogutsu tamagutsu
sazanami no ato

In early morning
I have come to the beach,
clear and fresh to the eye
with small and jewelled
footprints of ripples.

None of the five poems reminds us of the quivering nerve symbolized by the images of roots and thin blades of grass in **Barking at the Moon** (**Tsuki ni hoeru,** 1917), his first anthology, which both confirmed his originality and marked a new epoch in modern Japanese poetry. Rather, the five poems are closely linked to *The Blue Cat* (*Aone-ko,* 1923) in their rhythmic quality and in the languid atmosphere already dominating the life of the sixteen-year old Hagiwara. These poems also show his ability to evoke lyric emotion through a harmonious flow of words in which the mental state of the speaker and the scene of the poem are smoothly united.

These features of Hagiwara's earliest compositions later found their way into his critical and theoretical writings. He maintained throughout his life that a good poem has its own rhythm which is the true voice of the poet. This emphasis on rhythm led him to compile a unique anthology of representative poems from the *Man'yōshū* and the *Eight Imperial Anthologies.* He called his anthology *Ren'aimeikashū* (*A Collection of Celebrated Love Poems*), as he selected mainly poems dealing with the theme of love, an essential quality of lyric poetry. In May, 1931, the anthology was published with lengthy analytical commentaries on the poems. Two months later an essay, "Waka no inritsu ni tsuite" ("On the Prosody of the Waka"), appeared as a summary of his analysis made in *Ren'aimeikashū.*

In the essay he compares *ritsu* (the syllable pattern) and *in* (rhyme) to "beat" and "note" in music, respectively. Recognizing the ineffectiveness of as well as the possible adverse results of rhyme in Japanese poetry, Hagiwara attempts to exemplify rhyming devices used traditionally in tanka by carefully analyzing the poems he selected for the anthology. The most often used rhyming techniques, he reports, are *tōin* (alliteration), *kyakuin* (end-rhyme), *tsuiin* (parallel-rhyme), and *juin* (assonance). Although he attempts to discover general rules for rhyming, or correspondences of sounds, in the poems, it was not his intention to establish rigid versification as a modern standard. On the contrary, he emphasizes the flexibility, spontaneity and freedom from the mechanical in the rhyming devices he found. The spontaneous nature of this rhyming is what he calls "the rhythm of a poem," without which the poem cannot speak to the reader.

The following examples will show that Hagiwara used the word *in* (rhyme) in a broad sense in order to include all possible correspondences of sounds. He points out in the poem

> *wari naku mo*
> *netemo sametemo*
> *koishiki ka*
> *kokoro o izuchi*
> *yaraba wasuremu*

> I do not know
> why love seizes me
> whether asleep or awake.
> Where could I discard this heart
> to forget my love?

the rhyme *wari naku mo, netemo,* and *sametemo.* The effect of the rhyme is explained as follows:

[By the rhyme] the anxiety of love is expressed so that one can feel the poet's sorrow. This poem well exemplifies a successful rhyme attained spontaneously.

By quoting

> *kaze o itami*
> *iwa utsu nami no*
> *onore nomi*
> *kudakete mono o*
> *omou koro kana*

> Buffeted waves crash
> against the rock.
> Broken, I alone
> fall into melancholy.

he shows two parallel rhymes. The rhythmic effect of this poem depends on the tonal parallelism found in the repetition of the consonant *k* in the words *kaze* and *kudakete* at the beginning of the two major units, and in the sound of *mi* triplicated by the words *itami, nami,* and *nomi.* This analysis shows that the rhymes create the illusion of one's actually hearing the sound of the waves and that they cause us to make an unconscious association between these waves and the restless heart of the poet.

Hagiwara finds the best example of *jūin* (assonance) in the famous tanka by Izumi Shikibu:

> *arazaramu*
> *kono yo no hoka no*
> *omoide ni*
> *ima hitotabi no*
> *aukoto mo gana*

> Soon I will be no more
> For a keepsake,
> I long to take with me
> one last meeting
> beyond this world.

In the first five syllables of this poem the vowel *a* is repeated; in the next seven and five syllable lines *o* dominates; in the seven-syllabled fourth line *a* and *i* alternate; and in the final seven syllables *a* and *o* are repeated as if echoing the vowels of the first two lines. Moreover, Hagiwara points out a sharp YinYang (positive and negative) contrast between *a,* the first vowel of the poem, and *i* at the beginning of the fourth line, or the second half.

The device of *jo* (introductory lines) also attracted Hagiwara's attention. On the renowned poem of the *Kokinshū:*

> *hototogisu*
> *naku ya satsuki no*
> *ayamegusa*
> *ayame mo shiranu*
> *koi mo suru kana*

> Cuckoo cry
> and iris bloom

in the breeze of May;
I am trapped
within the maze of love.

Hagiwara wrote:

> Stylistically speaking the first three lines form a *jo*,
> introducing the latter half of the poem. This *jo* does
> not remain simply a technical form but provides an
> objective picture of the season and of nature which is
> inseparably and organically related to the subjective
> mental state. The poem also has a unified musical tone
> which induces the dreamy atmosphere of the season.

He had already discussed this *Kokinshū* poem in one of
his early notebooks dating from around 1914. He had
also expressed in the notebook his view of another important convention of classical Japanese poetry, the *kakeko-
toba* (pivot word). He considers this traditional poetic
device more than simple word-play: it serves to create a
rhythmic flow of words and to evoke a mood symbolically.

In December, 1913, Hagiwara published in the *Jōmō shim-
bun,* a local newspaper, ten tanka under the general title,
"Kokinshinchū." The title suggests imitation of the *Eight
Imperial Anthologies;* and in his prefatory note to the
poems he refers to the *Shinkokinshū* and its compiler,
Fujiwara Teika, with warm admiration. But these poems
must not be labeled simply imitation; they are, after all,
poetic exercises in which Hagiwara has tried to express
himself by adapting verses of several famous classical
tanka poets. A good example of his mixing of old and
new expressions is found in the following imaginative
and nostalgic poem:

> *Enechiya no*
> *gondora bito mo*
> *shizukokoro*
> *nakute ya yanagi*
> *chiri suginikeri*

> Are the *gondoliers* of Venice
> restless too?
> Drifting by,
> The scattered willow leaves
> pass.

The phrase *shizukokoro nakute* and the image of falling
leaves or petals recall the famous *Kokinshū* poem:

> *hisakata no*
> *hikari nodokeki*
> *haru no hi ni*
> *shizukokoro naku*
> *hana no chiru ran*

> On this day in spring
> When the lambent air suffuses
> Soft tranquility,
> Why should cherry petals flutter
> With unsettled heart to earth?

> (tr. by Brower and Miner)

When we arrange Hagiwara's poem into five lines, the
cadence of the third and fourth lines seems forced: he
changed the model *shizukokoro naku* into *shizukokoro
nakute ya* and divided the words into two lines in order
to match the number of syllables required by convention.
But is this change simply observance of traditional versification? Elsewhere he disagrees with the custom of writing tanka in five lines:

> Never does a five-line *uta* (or tanka) exist: all syllable-
> units in every *uta* are inseparable, as they have a close
> and organic linkage somewhere in the five or seven
> syllable groups.

If we read the poem aloud, or as Hagiwara suggests, write
it out in one line, we can feel the smooth musical flow
enhanced by the words *shizukokoro nakute ya.* The structural bridge they provide between the nostalgic beginning
and the descriptive ending creates an emotional fusion.

A modern adaptation of the poetic device, the *kakekoto-
ba,* is found in one of forty poems written down in his
notebook during April, 1913:

> *ito shigeku*
> *koishisa masari*
> *shinoburedomo*
> *nao amaririsu*
> *hana sakinikeri*

> My hopeless longing
> deepens to burst forth,
> though I try to suppress it.
> Amaryllis has come to bloom.

This poem echoes another famous tanka:

> *asajuu no*
> *ono no shinohara*
> *shinoburedo*
> *amarite nado ka*
> *hito no koishiki*

> In the field of short reeds
> *shino* grass grows.
> Why does my hopeless longing
> burst forth, though
> I try to suppress it?

Hagiwara's interest in this tanka by Minamoto no Hitoshi
of the mid-tenth century developed into an analysis of its
effective use of the sounds *no* and *shi.* Hagiwara points
out that the repetition of these sounds in the first three
lines serves to establish a link between the introductory
lines (*jo*) and the third. This link tonally conveys the irrepressible longing which is the theme of the poem.

The young Hagiwara seems to have imitated this repetition by using the sound of *shi* once in each of the first
three lines of his poem. It is interesting to note, however,
that the vowels *i* and *o* appear eleven and six times respectively in Hagiwara's poems while the frequency of

these vowels are exactly reversed in the model. The dominance of *i* in his poem partially derives from his borrowing of the key words: *koishi* in *koishiki* (line 5) and *shinoburedo*, the entire third line. The sound of *i* is also repeated seven more times in his own words: *shigeku* "deep, dense" (line 1); *masari* "increasing" (line 2); *amaririsu* "amaryllis" (line 4) and *sakinikeri* "has come to bloom" (line 5). But these words are not present merely for the sake of their sounds. Three of the four are connected to the botanical images, *asajuu* "short reeds," and *shino*, "*shino* grass or small bamboo," in the first two lines of the old tanka.

One does wonder why Hagiwara adds an extra syllable to the third line by changing *shinoburedo* into *shinoburedomo*. Obviously the addition of a single *o* in *mo* is not sufficient to alter the comparative scarcity of this vowel. He seems rather to have aimed at linking the third and fourth lines with this vowel (*shinoburedomo* / *nao*) and at creating a similar tonal effect, though not as rich, as in the first and second lines of the model *asajuu no* / *ono no shinohara*. At the same time this *jiamari* (excess syllable) has a thematic function, suggesting the overflow of irrepressible longing. Hagiwara places the syllable before the words *nao amari* "still too much," in the fourth line, *nao amaririsu*. The phrase *nao amari* is a clever shuffling of the original fourth line, *amarite nado ka*. As in the original *shinoburedo* / *amarite*, Hagiwara's third line, *shinoburedomo*, "though I try to endure," syntactically leads to *nao amari*, "still too much," in the fourth line. But *amari*, a part of the word *amaririsu*, "amaryllis," is used as a pivot word.

In contrast to the desolation in the *Gosenshū* poem, Hagiwara's amaryllis that "has come to bloom" gives color to his tanka. Phonetically, the term helps to produce the prevalence of the clear sound *i*. The *jo* in the poem by Minamoto no Hitoshi which he borrowed from a tanka in the *Kokinshū* serves to evoke the desolate atmosphere. But Hagiwara discards this conventionally-used *jo* and creates a modern pivot word which suggests the restless state of mind of the young poet.

Comparison of the poems by Minamoto no Hitoshi and Hagiwara Sakutarō indicates that Hagiwara composed his tanka by using the traditional technique of adaptation (*honkadori*), as he did in 1902 when he modeled his poem on Yosano Akiko's tanka of cherry-viewing in Kyoto. Our analysis shows that Hagiwara by 1913 had gained considerable sophistication in the use of this technique.

The preceding poems by Hagiwara are only a few samples of his experimental compositions. While not first-rate works, they are valuable for understanding the style of his later poems even though these early poetic exercises suggest that by 1914 he had not yet found his style. It was also around this time that, influenced by Ishikawa Takuboku, he wrote three-line tanka. More importantly, he had come to realize that he could no longer express his feelings using the traditional tanka form. In a notebook attributed to the year 1914 he wrote:

> When we are unable to utter spontaneously deeply felt emotions, *uta* [the thirty-one syllable poem] declines; when we cease to have sentiments, *shi* [modern poetry] disappears; when we lose truth, all forms of literary art die. . . . Unable to give spontaneous utterance to emotion, one is no longer qualified to write *uta;* and he naturally moves to *shi.*

He says further that *uta* is nothing other than the utterance of deep emotion, which found culmination in the superb *Man'yōshū.*

Later, in the **Ren'aimeikashū** (1931), he expressed a similar view about the unequaled power and naturalness of lyric expression exemplified in the *Man'yōshū*. By 1914, he seems already to have sensed his inability to recapture the qualities admirable in the ancient poets of Japan. Thus, having become keenly aware of himself as a modern poet, he started to write poems in the modern form of *shi*, revealing the influence of the other contemporary poets, particularly that of Kitahara Hakushū. Through the hard struggle to establish his own mode of expression, he reached out for that nervous, imagistic style which characterizes **Barking at the Moon**. To be sure, the poems of this anthology are not all imagistic, nor are they written in a purely colloquial style. Some of them even show that Hagiwara used rhymes to achieve rhythmic effect. Yet the musical aspect of his poetic creation was to be fully revived in his second anthology, **The Blue Cat**, where he exhibited remarkably original assimilation of the Japanese lyric tradition into an accomplished colloquial style.

In an essay entitled "Aoneko sutairu no yōi ni tsuite" (The Intent of the Style Used in **The Blue Cat**), Hagiwara explains why and how he used the word, *yōni*, "like," in many of these poems. He begins his explanation by establishing a distinction between comparison and symbolization. The distinction is shown by the two phrases: *sumi no y ni ankoku no yoru*, "night dark as black ink," and *hakaana no yōni ankoku no yoru*, "a night dark as the inside of a tomb." The former phrase offers an adjectival use of the word *yōni*, while the latter evokes a mysterious sense of fear through the image of a tomb closely associated with night. The one is limited, the other extended.

We may argue here that this explanation is not so much concerned about the word *yōni* itself, as with symbolic use of the image of a tomb. Hagiwara anticipates this argument and adds that the phrase *hakaana no yōni ankoku no yoru* can be simply reduced to the three words *hakaana*, "tomb," *ankoku*, "darkness," and *yoru*, "night" with intervening commas, and without the word *yōni*, if one wants to convey merely the content. Then, he continues:

> Yet, poetry transmits the delicate sentiments of the poet not simply by nouns but by the conjunctive particles, *te ni o ha*, and through the tonal relationships of words. The true complexity of meaning and emotion of a poem can be conveyed only in this manner. Therefore, if words are listed disjointedly, the poem cannot be complete.

After this introductory discussion on the difference between comparison and symbolization, Hagiwara enters into an exegesis of his own poetry. He first chooses the following lines from **"A Song Untitled"**:

Like the sunburned naked women of the South Seas a mysterious, red-rusted steamship appears far from the harbor where summer grass is thriving.

He warns us not to establish the grammatical relationship wherein the first line, "Like the sunburned naked women of the South Seas," modifies "rusty ship" of the second line, because:

. . . the line about the "naked women of the South Seas" can stand as independent, projecting the scene of an island in the South Seas. Thus, the meaning would not be changed even were we to rewrite the first two lines as follows: There are sunburned, naked women on an island in the South Seas. / And a mysterious, red-rusted steamship appears / far from the harbor where summer grass is thriving.

But further on he says:

This version makes a clear cut between the two lines, such that the first line gives the impression of its being an independent line, and, by so doing, disrupts the rich poetic link between the two lines [of the first version]. More importantly, with this change the first line is turned into a mere description of nature and of the scene. However, the poem must carry some subjective expression of indistinct, atmospheric feeling in addition to the description of the island. Therefore, the first line is not satisfactory if it remains a mere description of scenery. Rather it must suggest the scene, while a subjective emotive rhythm is conveyed. When the two lines are linked by the vague word *yōni* ["like"], rather than by *sōshite* ["and"], the first line, serving as a description of the scene, evokes a weakened picture; but exactly because of this softening effect the picture then shades off into subjective emotion. The poem succeeds in creating a subtle fusion of its descriptive and emotive, or objective and subjective, elements.

He continues by saying that when a poem aims at the evocation of some soft, mysterious sentiment the word *yōni* is effective. *The Blue Cat* is one example.

A statistical study of the diction of Hagiwara's poetry indicates that the term *yōni* was used the most frequently in *The Blue Cat*. The word appears sixty-two times in *The Blue Cat* period, while in that of *Barking at the Moon* we find only twenty-nine instances. Other colloquial words with similar resonance such as *konna*, "like this," *nantoiu*, "how, what," and *sōshite*, "and then" appear most often in the poems of *The Blue Cat* period.

Hagiwara's view of the rhythmic fusion between objective description and subjective emotion in poetry reflects his early statement about the effective use of *jo* in classical tanka. The *jo* works at once as a description of the scene and as a rhythmic link between the *jo* and the rest of the poem, suggesting its emotion. Therefore, lines in Hagiwara's poems joined by the word *yōni* can be regarded as his original assimilation of the traditional poetic device *jo* into the modern colloquial poetry of Japan.

He must have been conscious of a fundamental spiritual affinity between *The Blue Cat* and the *Shinkokinshū* when he defined in his **Ren'aimeikashū** the salient features of the celebrated Imperial anthology as follows:

To say it in a word, the poems of *Shinkokinshū* are at once bright and doleful, technically excellent and deeply moving, devoted to beauty and darkened with pessimism. They represent the art of decadence, smelling something like a decorated corpse.

These words can describe the characteristics of *The Blue Cat* itself. The *Eight Imperial Anthologies,* particularly the *Shinkokinshū,* must have been his model, but he could no longer imitate them as he had done when he was young and wrote in the traditional form.

As a final note, I should like to add that Edgar Allan Poe's "Philosophy of Composition" may have been a strong impetus for Hagiwara in developing his analysis of the sound pattern of classical Japanese poetry. Hagiwara not only read Poe's work carefully, but used it as a model for his poem, **"Cockerel,"** which I have discussed elsewhere. As Pablo Picasso frankly admitted to being an earnest assimilator, so too was Hagiwara a tireless and great assimilator of both native and foreign heritages.

Hiroaki Sato (essay date 1978)

SOURCE: Introduction to *Howling at the Moon: Poems of Hagiwara Sakutarō,* pp. xi-xxvi. Tokyo: University of Tokyo, 1978.

[*In the following essay, Sato offers an overview of Hagiwara's development as a poet.*]

Hagiwara Sakutarō was born the first son of a prosperous physician in Maebashi, Gumma. Toward the end of his life Sakutarō described his birthplace as a "sanguinary, barbarous blank-paper zone utterly devoid of any cultural tradition," but to be fairer to reality, it was a place close enough to Tokyo for him to go there as he liked, yet far enough for him to yearn for "the city" until he finally moved there to live. Traditionally, the first son enjoys most of the family's attention, but in the case of Sakutarō the pampering was extreme. Once, when Sakutarō stubbornly clutched his friend's music box, someone was immediately dispatched to Yokohama to buy one of these rare and expensive imports for him. In bad weather, he was taken to school in his father's jinrikisha. His father's comfortable income supported this indulgence, but the real source was Sakutarō's mother, Kei. Her influence remained so strong that various elements throughout Sakutarō's life and his work cannot be considered without Kei: the equation of "mother" and "lover" in the poem

"Rooster"; the sermons to women throughout his writings; the disintegration of his two mariages, his first wife eloping with another man and his second separating within a year; and his pronouncement that a married couple can enjoy sex more under the mean, watchful eye of the husband's mother. Although he seems to have maintained surly defiance to the father whose money supported him until his death, Sakutarō remained submissive to his mother while at the same time fearful of her.

Sakutarō began by writing tanka; his earliest published pieces are a set of five tanka that saw print in a school magazine when he was sixteen. He wrote in this traditional form for more than ten years before switching to *shi*— "poems" as distinct from tanka, haiku, and *kanshi* (verse written by Japanese in Chinese)—and was even the tanka editor for a local newspaper. Yet most of his tanka are undistinguished, strongly reminiscent of Yosano Akiko (1878-1942) and Ishikawa Takuboku (1886-1912). Although he stopped writing tanka in the early 1910s, he continued a lively interest in the form. After his reputation as a poet was established, he frequently challenged tanka poets to debate, and they responded. He often analyzed tanka in discussing Japanese prosody, and in 1931 he published an anthology of classical tanka on love. His involvement with haiku, though it did not occur until much later, resulted in his 1936 book on Yosa Buson (1716-83), which, along with his 1935 commentary on the twelfth-century tanka poet Princess Shikishi (died 1201), deserves the critical esteem Sakutarō has won. Toward the end of his life he apparently regarded tanka as the supreme embodiment of poetry.

During his tanka writing period Sakutarō moved from his native Maebashi to Kumamoto, then to Okayama, and finally to Tokyo, showing an increasing inability to complete school. Feeble and prone to illness, he once considered suicide rather than face the prospect of continuing academic failures. Still, his father's wealth was sufficient to permit him to live in Tokyo without any definite goal for nearly three years. Sakutarō, then in his mid-twenties, was quick to make use of his opportunities. Of the many concerts and stage productions he attended, such as one of *A Doll's House,* he reported his impressions to his sister Yuki in lengthy letters. In Tokyo, Sakutarō, who later founded a musicians' club when he returned to his home town, learned to play the mandolin and the guitar.

In early 1913 he read some poems of Muroo Saisei (1889-1962) in *Zamuboa* and was moved to write poems. In May that magazine, edited by Kitahara Hakushū (1885-1942), published five poems that Sakutarō wrote. Although he had written and published poems (distinct from tanka and other forms of poetry) before then, the publication in *Zamuboa* meant recognition by a distinguished magazine and its editor-poet. It also marked the beginning of the most intense, productive, and inspired period in Sakutarō's life as a poet.

On reading Saisei's poems he wrote to the poet and at once became his close friend. Sakutarō's admiration for Hakushū, in the meantime, turned into a series of pas-

sionate "love letters," in one calling him "mother far more than my blood relation [mother]." Over the years, the intensity of his feeling for Hakushū may have lessened, but not his love of his work, in particular, *Omoide (Memories)*, a collection of poems on his childhood, published in 1911, and *Kiri no ha (Paulownia Leaves)*, a selection of tanka published in 1913. Early in 1914 Sakutarō became acquainted with such poets as Takamura Kōtarō (1883-1956), Ōte Takuji (1887-1934), and Yamamura Bochō (1884-1924). In June, he, along with Saisei and Bochō, set up *Ningyo Shisha* ("Mermaid Poetry Society") to study poetry, religion, and music. In September he became a contributing editor of Hakushū's new magazine, *Chijō junrei (Pilgrimage on Earth)* and a contributing member of another, begun by Oyama Tokujirō (1889-1963), *Itan (Heresy)*. Throughout the year—the year, one may note, when World War I began—Sakutarō wrote many poems which were published in noted magazines.

In March 1915 the *Ningyo Shisha* issued a monthly called *Takujō funsui (Table-top Fountain)*. During this period many literary magazines, somewhat noisily launched, disappeared as quietly after a brief spell. *Takujō funsui* was no exception. Of its scant three issues, however, a few things should be mentioned. According to Saisei, one of its three editors, Sakutarō wanted a Reuter dispatch printed verbatim on the first page of the second issue—a dispatch saying that because of the war Kaiser Wilhelm II's hair grayed precipitously and he looked emaciated. Such an idea was novel enough to discomfit Saisei then and give the magazine an "advanced" touch. The magazine also printed poems of Kambara Ariake (1875-1952), an established symbolist poet whom Sakutarō admired, Maeda Yūgure (1883-1951), a tanka poet who helped Sakutarō publish his first book of poems two years later, and Hinatsu Kōnosuke (born 1890), who was to make a memorable observation, "Hagiwara is illiterate, that's the fellow's strength more than anything else." Of course, Sakutarō printed his own poems in *Takujō funsui*, too, but published many more in other magazines, and all in all, during the first six months of 1915 he wrote and published as many poems as he had throughout the previous year.

Then, around mid-1915, he abruptly stopped writing poems, announcing to Hakushū, "Let the one called Hagiwara Sakutarō be a poet who will never make poems again." The announcement obviously disturbed Hakushū, but Sakutarō did not clarify the reason for his decision. From a series of delirious letters written to Hakushū, however, it is evident that Sakutarō's poetically productive period, which lasted about two years, corresponded to a period of severe mental disorder that peaked in the spring of 1915. The day after sending Hakushū the card reproduced below, he sent him another, saying: "Yesterday, I nearly breathed my last, it was a painful day indeed, because I went on a binge the day before yesterday the usual disease (of the nervous system) surfaced, my this disease is exactly the same as Garshin the writer of *Red Flower* was afflicted with, I clearly see and hear with indescribable terrible memories the lips of a faintly white woman who laughed after copulation and my abominable act and language that I uttered while drunk, each time I have the terrible pain that seems to tear up my nerves, because I dashed my head against the column many times yesterday it still hurts this morning, I even thought I was going mad."

This was followed by a year of silence, at the end of which he thought he "discovered" his own god. Yet, as he soon began exchanging lengthy letters with a fellow poet in Maebashi to discuss Christianity, Dostoevski, and Tolstoi, Sakutarō admitted, "I am after all exactly what I was, far from being saved I am in a much more painful hell." Sakutarō was, in fact, never free of various forms of mental affliction until his death; but few episodes were as intense or as conducive to poetry as those during the two years from 1913 to 1915.

In February 1917 Sakutarō published his first book of poems, *Tsuki ni hoeru* (*Howling at the Moon*). It was an immediate success. Not only most of the well-known poets but the reviewers for major newspapers acclaimed it, so that less than two months after the publication Sakutarō thought of a second printing. An unusual arrangement of publishing Hakushū's extravagant preface in a leading newspaper one month before the book actually came out doubtless contributed to its success; so too probably did the news that two poems were deleted on order of the Ministry of the Interior for "disturbing the social customs." But what counted was the book, and two aspects of it struck the contemporary reader: language and imagery. The language was such that Sakutarō was not exaggerating when five years later he called the book "epoch-making." A collection of poems written at a time when literary diction was being replaced by everyday language, it deliberately blended the two and the effect was unsettling enough to make the words themselves appear poetic. But the language would have had little force without the imagery. Of this Sakutarō was well aware. Instead of putting his more romantic pieces first, he ingeniously opened the book with a cluster of poems powerful in imagery, beginning with **"Sickly Face at the Bottom of the Ground"**:

> At the bottom of the ground a face emerging,
> a lonely invalid's face emerging.
>
> In the dark at the bottom of the ground,
> soft vernal grass-stalks beginning to flare,
> rats' nest beginning to flare,
> and entangled with the nest,
> innumerable hairs beginning to tremble,
> time the winter solstice,
> from the lonely sickly ground,
> roots of thin blue bamboo beginning to grow,
> beginning to grow,
> and that, looking truly pathetic,
> looking blurred,
> looking truly, truly, pathetic.
>
> In the dark at the bottom of the ground,
> a lonely invalid's face emerging.

This set the tone. Though the book had some abstract pieces and some descriptive of homely things, what was striking was the unadorned projection of images contemplated by an "invalid fearful of diseases." Kambara Ariake, for example, distinctly remembered a quarter century afterward the "effect of taut nerves" that the book had on him. The best poems in it have continued to surprise readers with their power to suggest without hinting at anything definite. Recognizing this quality, Mori ōgai (1862-1922) incisively described *Tsuki ni hoeru* as a collection of "true symbolist poetry written in Japanese for the first time."

Through this year until early 1918 Sakutarō continued to publish. Then, for about forty months, he virtually stopped publishing poetry. Instead, he turned to prose and wrote two types of it: one consisted of discussions of poetry, and the other of pieces on a great variety of subjects. His poetry criticism was initially planned as a book soon after *Tsuki ni hoeru,* but it had to wait ten years to take its final form and see publication under the title *Shi no genri* (*The Poetic Principle*). Sakutarō chose to call the second type of prose aphorisms, and *Atarashiki yokujō* (*New Desire*), published in 1922, was the first collection of them. This period spelled a turning point in his literary career; for, though he noted in his preface to *Atarashiki yokujō* that if his "lyrics" represented him as a poet, the aphorisms represented him as a thinker, and though he continued to believe that poet and critic were "synonyms," his creative period as poet would end shortly, with the publication in January 1923 of his second book of poems, *Aoneko* (*Blue Cat*). After this, Sakutarō the prose writer became increasingly productive, and Sakutarō the poet had to be content mainly talking about poetry, not writing it.

The reason that he was unable to steadily keep up his poetry writing is explained in his own preface to *Tsuki ni hoeru*: "Poetry is the intellect's product in one second. A certain type of sentiment that one ordinarily has touches something like electricity and for the first time discovers a rhythm. This electricity is, for the poet, a miracle. Poetry is not something anticipated and made." And he explained how he wrote poems in a letter to a friend: "Toward my own poems, at the time of creating them I am nearly blind and myself don't even know what sort of thing I am singing of. What thought, what sentiment I myself have, what sort of thing I myself am attempting to write, I am utterly carried away. I am merely catching a kind of rhythm that flows at the bottom of my heart and unconsciously pursuing the rhythm, therefore at the time of creation my own self is merely something like a half unconscious automatic machine." Sakutarō was strictly an "inspirational" poet. And he did not try to open his way out of it, either. The poetic theory he developed tended to narrow his scope, not expand it. He insisted that lack of lyricism was "fatal" to the poet, that the lyric was the only "poem." He had followed the "main road of lyric poetry," he said to a young poet in 1936, but he had no other road, and his had reached a dead end a long time before.

If *Aoneko* meant a virtual end to Sakutarō's creative period as a poet, it also meant the publishing world's recognition of him as an established poet. The book was put out by Shinchōsha, a commercial house, and the more than twenty books that followed were published by similar houses. Financially, this may have meant little to Sakutarō, who, with his independent income, would probably have done much of what he wanted to without commercial support. But, artistically, it meant a progressive drain on his time, energy, and, eventually, on his intellect. Aside from the inevitable redundancy, many of his frequent calls for "a return to things Japanese"—his last three collections of essays were entitled *Nippon e no kaiki* (*Turning Back to Japan*), *Kikyōsha* (*The Man Who Came Home*), and *Atai* (*Idiot*)—may not have had to be written had it not been for the continuous demand for filler that is the curse of all established authors of Japan.

[Of Sakutarō's six books of poetry, the first two, *Tsuki ni hoeru* and *Aoneko,*] were written at the height of his power. . . . The third, *Chō o yumemu* (*Dreaming of Butterflies*), published half a year after *Aoneko*, is a book of poems uncollected in his first two books plus eight reprints from them. *Junjō shōkyoku shū* (*Collection of Short Songs on Innocent Love*), published in 1925, consists of eighteen poems mostly written before those collected in *Tsuki ni hoeru* and ten others written in 1924 and 1925. The ten latter poems are composed in literary language—a "humiliating retreat," to use Sakutarō's phrase describing the same diction employed throughout his fifth book, *Hyōtō* (*The Ice Land*), published in 1934. *Shukumei* (*Destiny*), published in 1939, is a collection of "prose-poems" written over twenty years. Sakutarō had some hesitation in using the term "prose poem," and these short pieces may well be grouped with his aphorisms as they originally were.

Sakutarō's poetic achievement is firm, but not entirely undisputed. The common put-down that his poetry is for sexually frustrated adolescents may be dismissed, but his scope is certainly narrow. He seldom steps out of his mind. Even when he chooses to talk about laborers in **"A Sad Distant View,"** he ends up astringing them into a "shriveled heart." Here is his **"Pale Horse"**:

> Under the frozen weather of winter's cloudy sky
> in so melancholy a nature
> wordlessly eating roadside grass
> it's a miserable, forlorn, destiny's, cause-and-
>   effect's, pale
>   horse's shadow
> I move in the shadow's direction
> and the horse's shadow seems to be watching me.
>
> Ah move fast and leave the place
> from my life's movie screen
> quickly, quickly drag yourself away, turn off an
>   illusion
>   like this
> I want to believe in my Will. Horse!
> From cause-and-effect's, destiny's, fixed law's
> dry plate of a landscape on which despair has
>   frozen
> run away the pale shadow.

Compare it with "Tattered Ostrich" of Takamura Kōtarō, which Sakutarō described as "nihilistic" but having a "ray of hope":

> What fun is there in keeping an ostrich?
> Don't you see how in the twenty square yard mire
>   of the
>   zoo
> its legs make too great strides?
> How its neck is too long?
> How for a country with snowfall its feathers are too
>   tattered?
> It gets hungry, so it eats hardtack, sure,
> but don't you see how the ostrich's eyes are
>   looking only
>   into the distance?
> How they aren't all there, burning?
> How they're waiting for an emerald wind to blow
>   at any
>   moment?
> How its small innocent head is swirling with
>   boundless
>   dreams?
> How it no longer is an ostrich?
> Come on, people,
> stop it, stop this sort of thing.

Or with a poem of Miyazawa Kenji (1896-1933) dealing with the same animal, "The Horse":

> After working one whole day among mugwort,
> the horse, rotting like a potato,
> feeling the juice of the bright sun pouring
> on his rumpled head crusted with salt,
> crunched, crunched, crunched on bamboo grass
> at the edge of the field.
> When the blue night came at last,
> he returned to his stable
> where, as if a high voltage wire caught him,
> suddenly he went wild, a mute struggle.
> Next day he was cold.
> They all got together, made a huge hole
> at the back of the pine woods,
> bent his four legs,
> and slowly put him down into it.
> They sprinkled clods of earth
> over the lolling head.
> They shed clods of tears.

Unlike Kōtarō's ostrich or Kenji's horse, Sakutarō's horse is not a real animal but a "shadow," and whereas Kōtarō and Kenji treat their animals as entities independent of their beings, Sakutarō depicts his only as it affects his inner self. But it is precisely this shadow as it affects his mind that concerns him, and the relentless pursuit of that shadow on paper is what makes him a unique, modern poet. If he had remained content to write under the influence of Hakushū and Saisei, he would still be a good, though dated, singer of urbane sensuality and youthful suffering, as may be seen from *Junjō shōkyoku shū*. But it did not take him long to become dissatisfied with Saisei's poems, such as "Rain over the Dune," which he had initially admired so much:

Over the dune the sound of rain fades
The grass is hushed
The sea is hushed
Delicate memories of summer
Are faint in me
I touch the grass and the grass is blue
I touch the rain and the rain is blue
Am I to leave your name buried in the dune
Or memories of summer that passed in vain
The clump of beach grass is a nest of melancholy
A gull's egg, unhatched
Has rotted in bright light

Instead, he was attracted to Bochō's approach, as in "Great Imperial Edict":

Headhair wire
joining platinum hands
separating from the platinum hands
a smouldering cigarette.
From the eye of a silverfish on the table
aiming at a woman's navel
spouting fountain
oh no one knows
shining in heaven a nosetip
silverfish eye
making a red cup dance.

Bochō's method probably gave Sakutarō the courage to project images as he saw them in his mind. But he soon found Bochō unsatisfactory, calling him "pretentious," because, while Bochō's were no more than images formed through a "prism"—his book with the poem cited above was published in 1915 under the title *Sacred Prism*—Sakutarō's images were rooted in his psyche. Sakutarō's effectiveness as poet lasted only while the shadow lay on his psyche, for about ten years and intermittently. During that time he was completely himself, utterly unaffected by all that astonishing variety of movements that poured into Japan then: neo-romanticism, dadaism, expressionism, symbolism, mysticism, nihilism, neo-classicism, futurism, cubism, realism, and so forth. The way Sakutarō lost his poetry as the shadow faded is evident in the poems he grouped as "after *Aoneko*." There, inquiry after things lost or even non-existent becomes more and more insistent. Given Sakutarō's elusive psyche and his manner of pursuing this psyche in poetic form, to discuss his inability to externalize his subject is important, if intended to point to his strength; otherwise it would be merely asking for something that isn't there.

There is a presumption made upon approaching Sakutarō's poetry that it is musical. The main source for this seems to be Saisei's famous encomium to Sakutarō which was placed as the afterword in the first edition of *Tsuki ni hoeru*:

There has been no one, as far as I know, who gave as much attention to the *shades* and *depths* of the Japanese language as you [Sakutarō] did. . . . Aside from the fact that you were a musician yourself, you were one of the most advanced poets who turned the Japanese syllabaries into [piano] keys.

Saisei, in so praising his friend and fellow poet, called attention to the "shades" and "depths" of language essential to any poet. His unfortunate equation of music and Sakutarō's language should, however, be considered in contrast to an earlier essay in which Sakutarō, complimenting Saisei's poetry, had warned against the "common folly" of confusing melodious verse with music:

Through the free verse form the poet has been able to freely reveal the perfect *rhythm* of his ego for the first time. When it broke every unreasonable constraint and escaped from the bondage of music, poetry for the first time was able to discover its legitimate route and construct the "music of words" in the true sense.

What is "rhythm"? It meant two things to Sakutarō. In the functional sense, rhythm in free verse was something as "natural" as that in daily conversation. In the philosophical sense, rhythm was the same as poetry, which in turn he defined as any noticeable "sentiment." Since Sakutarō felt that a sentiment came as an image, the poet's task was to express his subjective image as accurately as possible. Poetry was a "direct expression of music" only when the poet succeeded in projecting his "inner rhythm," namely, his "vision."

Sakutarō's poems are in fact never as "musical" as, for example, Hakushū's—a fact of which he was aware rather early. Instead, they are studded with a variety of verbal infelicities that ought to be attributed largely to his effort to be true to his vision. The most conspicuous throughout *Tsuki ni hoeru* and *Aoneko* is the admixture of two dictions, literary and everyday, in individual poems. "**A Case of Murder,**" for instance, is all written in everyday diction except for the third line from the end and the single word that follows: "haya hitori tantei wa urehi o kanzu. / miyo." That the sudden shift is not made for mellifluous reading may be known by replacing "urehi o kanzu" with "urehinu." No less conspicuous is that peculiar locution known as *hon'yaku-chō* or translation style, which is a euphemism for the kind of writings that read like clumsy translations from Western languages. Sakutarō exclusively employs this "style" in "Two Long Poems," but his use of it is more prevalent than may be expected.

If these practices may be termed distortions, at least six other types of distortions exist in Sakutarō's poetry. One is misuse of verbs. To give a few examples, in the last part of "**Pale Horse,**" which is quoted above in translation, "kamban kara/ aozameta kage o tōsō shiro" is syntactically impossible; so is "haha ni mo chichi ni mo shiranai" in "**Lonely Personality.**" In "shita bero o . . . moeizuru" in "**Rotten Clam,**" the verb is intransitive when it should be transitive. A second type is mixture of past and present tenses, as in "**Looking Up at the Top of a Blue Tree**" and "**Odious Scenery**"; this occurs more frequently in *Aoneko* than in *Tsuki ni hoeru*. A third type of distortion is mix-up of the subject; in "**Climbing a Mountain,**" what starts with a description of at least two persons' activities ends up as a description of the speaker's alone. A fourth type is unconventional application of words and phrases; one example is "birabira" in the last line of **"Alcoholic's Death,"** which usually modifies "yureru" ("waver, flap") or some such verb, not "warau" ("laugh, smile"). A fifth is the switch in tone in the middle of the poem, as in **"Daybreak,"** where the poetically heightened description is ended with a flatly conversational phrase, "da yo." A sixth type is coinage; though in Sakutarō's case it is difficult to draw a line between plain misuse and deliberate coinage, "touen" in **"Black Harmonium"** and "shimmen" in **"The World of Fantasy the Buddha Saw"** may be given as his genuine inventions.

Such verbal infelicities and oddities cannot, of course, be reproduced well in another language, and in that sense Sakutarō is a difficult poet to translate. Nevertheless, to smooth them out in the name of "music" would do injustice to what Sakutarō tried to do. On the contrary, by staying close to his original wording, much of his poetry comes through translation, I believe, because it is realized through singular and precise images.

Donald Keene (essay date 1984)

SOURCE: "The Taisho Period (1912-1926)," in *Dawn to the West, Japanese Literature of the Modern Era: Poetry, Drama, Criticism*, Vol. 25, Holt, Rinehart and Winston, 1984, pp. 255-91.

[*In the following excerpt, Keene discusses the emotional characteristics of Hagiwara's poetry and his innovative use of colloquial language.*]

Hagiwara is by common consent the chief figure of modern Japanese poetry. He is not an easy poet, and the exact interpretations of many works elude the exegesis of even his most devoted admirers, but his work both commands the respect of other poets and critics and is popular with the general public. The novelist and poet Fukunaga Takehiko gave a representative evaluation: "Hagiwara Sakutarō is the outstanding writer of Japanese modern poetry; it is a recognized fact that his works constitute the most beautiful crystallizations of the Japanese language."

Hagiwara was born in Maebashi, an unremarkable city famous chiefly for its gusty winds. He is known as a poet of nostalgia, and a number of moving poems are recollections of Maebashi; but these are essentially references to his own past, rather than affectionate descriptions of buildings or landscapes. Although imposing mountains are visible from Maebashi, and the nearby countryside was still beautiful in Hagiwara's youth, he frequently expressed his lack of interest in the country and his love of the crowds and excitement of a big city. Eventually he moved to Tokyo, but his early collections were composed in Maebashi, where he lived in comfortable circumstances as the chief literary light of a provincial town.

Hagiwara first began to submit his poetry to *Myōjō, Bunko,* and other Tokyo magazines while he was still in middle school. Poetry absorbed him so completely that he neglected his studies; he did not graduate from middle school until he was twenty and kept up his spasmodic attempts to finish high school until he was twenty-five; he was apparently under no pressure from his family to earn a living. Hagiwara also studied the mandolin and the guitar, even intending at one time to become a professional musician. So far little suggested he would develop into the great Japanese poet of the twentieth century.

In 1913 Hagiwara published some tanka in the magazine *Zamboa (Pomelo),* then being edited by Kitahara Hakushū. An infatuation with Hakushū's poetry colored his early work, and this association with *Zamboa* marked the beginning of his serious work as a poet. Twenty-seven was unusually late for a start; most Meiji poets produced all of their important work before they were thirty. But Hagiwara seems to have been in no hurry to impress the literary world. In 1914, having reconciled himself to living in Maebashi, he built a study in the corner of his parents' garden, furnished entirely in Western style. There he drank black tea, still an exotic beverage in Maebashi, played the mandolin, and read European literature. He began to attend Christian churches and visit the houses of foreign missionaries, enjoying this approximation of life abroad. It was about this time that he wrote the poem **"Ryojō"** (**"Going Away"**). It begins:

> I think I would like to go to France,
> But France is so very far away;
> At least I will try to take a trip of my own choosing,
> Wearing a new suit of clothes.

In June 1914 he and the two poets Murō Saisei and Yamamura Bochō formed the *Ningyo Shisha* (Mermaid Poetry Society), which had as its avowed purpose the study of poetry, religion, and music. Hagiwara's interest in Christianity lingered on a few years longer. One night in April 1916 he experienced a kind of religious ecstasy, the source no doubt of the distinctly religious tone in part of his first collection, **Tsuki ni hoeru** (**Howling at the Moon**), published in February 1917. Words like *tsumi* (sin), *inoru* (to pray) and *zange* (confession) dot the first half of the collection, as in the well-known poem **"Tenjō Ishi"** (**"A Hanging in Heaven,"** 1914):

> Tōyo ni hikaru matsu no ha ni,
> Zange no namida shitatarite,
> Tōyo no sora ni shimo shiroki,
> Tenjō no matsu ni kubi wo kake.
> Tenjō no matsu wo kouru yori,
> Inoreru sama ni tsurusarenu.

> Onto pine-needles glittering in the distant night
> Drip the tears of his confession;
> White in the sky of the distant night
> The pine of heaven where he hangs.
> For having loved the pine of heaven
> He has been strung up in a posture of prayer.

This difficult poem has been analyzed [by Tanazawa Eichi in *Taishōki no Bungei Hyōron*] in these terms: "What is meant by the 'pine of heaven' where a man is hung?

Obviously it does not refer to a tree. The 'pine of heaven' stands for the sacred, for God, for purity, and so on. It is a place of confession, designated in visionary terms. When the poet speaks of being 'strung up in the posture of prayer,' this metaphor expresses the intensity of his confession; while in this posture his confession is completed by death." Hagiwara wrote on a picture of the Crucifixion he owned at the time the words **"A Hanging in Heaven."**

The poem is certainly not typical of Hagiwara's early poetry as a whole, but it displays one important characteristic: apart from its religiosity, it is striking because of the obscurity of expression, which arouses not a sense of bewilderment or irritation but of mystery and depth, similar to the effect of yūgen in the classical tradition. Although Hagiwara is celebrated as the first master of the free-verse, colloquial poem, this work (like many others in *Howling at the Moon*) was in the classical language and in regular meter, each line consisting of seven plus five syllables.

A few months later Hagiwara wrote the short poem **"Kaeru no Shi"** (**"Death of a Frog,"** 1914), also included in *Howling at the Moon*:

Kaeru ga korosareta,
Kodomo ga maruku natte te wo ageta,
Minna issho ni,
Kawayurashii,
Chidarake no te wo ageta,
Tsuki ga deta,
Oka no ue ni hito ga tatte iru.
B shi no shita ni kao ga aru.

A frog was killed.
The children, forming a circle, raised their
  hands;
All together
They raised their adorable,
Blood-smeared hands.
The moon came out.
Someone is standing on the hill.
Under his hat is a face.

This poem is in the colloquial, and the meter is free, confirming Hagiwara's self-assertive claim: "Before this collection not a single poem had been written in colloquial language of this style, and before this collection the animation in the world of poetry one senses today did not exist. All the new styles of poetry sprang from this source. All the rhythms of the lyric poetry of our time were engendered here. In other words, because of this collection a new epoch was created."

The fact that the language of this poem is simple—common words drawn from daily speech—does not mean that the meaning is obvious. The last line startles not by unusual imagery but by the flat statement of a seemingly irrelevant fact: of course there was a face under the man's hat, but why mention it? Is this the face of an adult watching the children at their cruel sport? Or of the poet himself, as a child detachedly observing his companions? The ambiguity compounds the basic unreality: Did the children really lift their blood-smeared little hands in the moonlight? The poem is an enigma that somehow strikes the heart, fulfilling the definition of poetic expression Hagiwara gave in the preface to the collection:

> The object of poetic expression is not merely to evoke an atmosphere for its own sake. Nor is it to describe illusions for their sake. Nor, for that matter, is it to propagandize or make deductions about any particular variety of thought. The true function of poetry is, rather, to scrutinize the essential nature of the emotions vibrating in a man's heart and to disclose these emotions to the full through poetic expression. Poetry is a capturing of the nerves of the emotions. It is a living, functioning psychology.

Later in the preface he wrote:

> What I hope for from readers of my poetry is that they will perceive through their senses not the ideas expressed on the surface nor the "circumstances," but the feelings that are the internal core itself. I have expressed my "grief," "joy," "loneliness," "fear," and other complicated and particular emotions difficult to express in words or sentences through the rhythm of my poetry. But rhythm is not an explanation; it is a communion of mind with mind. Only with the man who can without words sense that rhythm can I converse, taking his hand in mine.

Despite the difficulties involved in interpreting Hagiwara's poems, the reader never receives an impression of willful obscurity. His disciple Miyoshi Tatsuji, contrasting Hagiwara's ambiguities with those of Kitahara Hakushū, claimed that Hagiwara rejected the "mystification" of the late Symbolist poets, and treated by preference events and emotions associated with ordinary life. Miyoshi went so far as to suggest that Hagiwara, despite his reiterated dislike of the Naturalists, was actually influenced by their manner of expression; certainly some of his most affecting poems are direct to the point of Naturalism. **"Yogisha"** (**"Night Train,"** 1913), Hagiwara's first important poem, describes the break of day in the oppressive atmosphere of a night train, where the poet and another man's wife share passion and despair. But the more typical poems in *Howling at the Moon* go beyond direct personal experience to the realm of the vision, as in **"Take"** (**"Bamboo,"** 1915):

On the shining ground bamboo grows,
Green bamboo grows;
Below the surface bamboo roots grow.
Roots gradually tapering,
From the root ends fine hair grows,
Faintly smoldering fine hair grows.
It faintly trembles.

On the hard ground bamboo grows,
On the ground, sharply, bamboo grows,
Precipitously bamboo grows;
The frozen knots piercingly cold,
Under the blue sky bamboo grows,
Bamboo, bamboo, bamboo grows.

The rhythm of the poem creates its atmosphere; obviously Hagiwara did not intend it as a realistic description of growing bamboo. The season is early spring, when the bamboo breaks the hard ground; but the poet's thoughts turn to the invisible roots extending fine hairs into the darkness of the soil. It has been suggested that these images are related to the poet's psychological state. A few years earlier he had written of "always stretching his hands toward the light" but of "falling instead, increasingly, into a dark abyss." The morbid sensitivity of his poetry is suggested by the fine hairs extending into subterranean depths. The poem not only expresses Hagiwara's feeling for bamboo but his own psychology.

Hagiwara's first poem in the colloquial, **"Satsujin Jiken"** (**"A Case of Murder,"** 1914), was of crucial importance in his development as a poet. Kawaji Ryūkō (1888-1959) had published some graphically realistic poems in the colloquial a few years earlier, and Kitahara Hakushū had also experimented with the colloquial, but Hagiwara was essentially correct when he boasted of being the first to employ this medium successfully. **"A Case of Murder"** opens with these lines:

> Tōi sora de pisutoru ga naru.
> Mata pisutoru ga naru.
> Aa watakushi no tantei wa hari no ishō wo kite,
> Koibito no mado kara shinobikomu,
> Yuka wa shōgyoku,
> Yubi to yubi no aida kara,
> Massao no chi ga nagarete iru,
> Kanashii onna no shitai no ue de,
> Tsumetai kirigirisu ga naite iru.

> In the distant sky a pistol resounds.
> Again the pistol resounds.
> And my detective, in his clothes of glass,
> Slips in through the lady's window.
> The floor is of crystal.
> From between her fingers
> Deathly pale blood flows,
> And on the unhappy woman's corpse
> A chilly grasshopper sings.

The colloquial is used to superb effect, its casual tone making the unbelievable "facts" related seem all the more extraordinary. The cold, glassy surface of the poem and the atmosphere of fantasy share much with other poems in the collection, but it also has the faintly humorous overtones of a silent film.

When *Howling at the Moon* was first published it fell under the ban of the censors because it contained two poems adjudged to be harmful to public morals. These poems, **"Airen"** (**"Love"**) and **"Koi wo koi suru Hito"** (**"A Man Who Loves Love"**), are without question sensual, but hardly a danger to morals. **"Love"** concludes:

> Ah, I hug your breasts tightly to me;
> And you press with all your strength against my
>   body.
> In this manner, in the middle of this deserted

> field,
> Let us play as snakes play.
> I will treat you with piercing tenderness, in my
>   fashion,
> And smear your beautiful skin with juice from
>   green leaves of
>   grass.

In some poems Hagiwara experimented with the musical values of the colloquial and of onomatopoeia. In **"Kaeru yo"** (**"You, Frog!"**) he twice gives the line:

> Gyo, gyo, gyo, gyo, to naku kaeru.

> "Gyo, gyo, gyo, gyo," cries the frog.

These sounds, to at least one Japanese commentator, conveyed an impression of "blank loneliness." Other examples of Hagiwara's use of onomatopoeia included dogs barking in the distance (*no-oaaru, to-oaary, yawaa*), and roosters crowing *to-otekuu, to-orumou, to-orumou*. Hagiwara explained the latter:

> I have represented cockcrows heard in the distance from my bed at daybreak with the sounds *too-ru-mor, too-te-kur,* and have employed these sounds as the principal idea-words of the poem. Properly speaking, the crying of animals, the noise of turning machinery and the like are purely auditory; unlike words, they have no meaning of their own to put forth; they can therefore be interpreted as expressing anything one pleases, according to the subjective feelings of the listener. As a consequence, such sounds make excellent materials that provide a maximum freedom of use in the expression of poems centered around musical effects.

Years later (in 1933) Hagiwara recalled:

> Among the poems I wrote years ago there is one called **"Niwatori"** (**"Rooster"**). To tell the truth, this was an adaptation of Poe, and my representation of the rooster's crowing as *totekuu, mouruto* and so on was an attempt to produce a poetic effect similar on the whole to Poe's "Raven" by means of similar techniques of expression.

He analyzed "The Raven" in these terms:

> The expressive effect of Poe's unrhymed (*sic*) poem "The Raven" results from the repeated echoes of the gloomy, eerie sounds of such words as *nevermore* and *Leonore,* which sound like the wind blowing from some lonely, distant graveyard. Poe intentionally repeated these words, and made the feelings produced by their periodic repetition serve as the motifs of the entire poem. If these sounds were removed from "The Raven," nothing would remain; the poem would be no more than a meaningless arrangement of letters. Could any translator, no matter how gifted, transfer this effect to Japanese? This example makes it evident how impossible it is to translate poetry.

Hagiwara's fascination with Poe and his use of sound suggests his connection with Baudelaire, another great admirer of Poe.

Whether or not dogs barking in the distance actually sounded like *no-aaru, to-oaaru, yawaa* to Hagiwara, he used the transcription to superb effect in a poem suggesting a child's terror at hearing strange noises at night; *no-oaaru to-oaaru, yawaa* evoke the mystery of the dark far better than a mere *woof-woof*. Onomatopoeia is also at the heart of the short poem **"Neko" ("Cats")**:

Makkuroke no neko ga nihiki,
Nayamashii yoru no yane no ue de,
Pin to tateta shippo no saki kara,
Ito no yō na mikazuki ga kasunde iru.
"Owaa, komban wa"
"Owaa, komban wa"
"Owaaa, koko no ie no shujin wa byōki desu"

Two jet-black cats
On a melancholy night roof:
From the tips of their taut tails
A threadlike crescent moon hangs hazily.
"Owaa, good evening."
"Owaa, good evening."
"Owaaa, the master of this house is sick."

Hagiwara's interest in sound was not restricted to animal noises. Many poems deliberately employ repetitions of words and phrases in the interests of rhythm. **"Shun'ya" ("Spring Night,"** 1915) opens:

Asari no yō na mono,
Hamaguri no yō na mono,
Mijinko no yō na
   mono. . . .

Something like a mussel,
Something like a clam,
Something like a water-flea. . . .

Later in the poem these lines occur:

Soyo soyo to shiomizu nagare,
Ikimono no ue ni mizu nagare. . . .

Soyo-soyo the salt water flows,
Over living creatures the water flows. . . .

Such uses of sound create a peculiarly dreamlike atmosphere, evocative of a spring night. The words go beyond their conventional meanings to approach the realm of pure sound.

The insistence on sound, as opposed to verbal meaning, should not, of course, suggest that Hagiwara intended his poetry to be read as pure melody, nor that the poet is absent from his creations. The portrait of the poet dimly visible behind the early poems is of an acutely sensitive man with a masochistic sense of guilt. Although Hagiwara lost his interest in Christianity, he retained an awareness of original sin that continued to torment him. His long poem **"Sabishii Jinkaku" ("A Lonely Character,"** 1917), written while under the influence of Dostoevski, has been interpreted as a release from his guilt and inferi-

ority complexes. Dostoevski certainly figured prominently in his thoughts. In the preface to *Howling at the Moon* he wrote:

People, individually, are always, eternally, perpetually in terrible solitude. . . . Our faces, our skins are all different, one from the other, but as a matter of fact each human being shares traits with all the others. When this commonality is discovered among fellow human beings, "morality" and "love" among humankind are born. When this commonality is discovered between human beings and plants, "morality" and "love" in nature are born. And then we are never lonely again.

This was the "salvation through love" Hagiwara found through Dostoevski. He also explained his opposition to the "sensual mysticism of the school of Mallarmé and to the Symbolist poetry of that school" as a result of his contact with "the philosophy of Dostoevski."

Hagiwara's second collection, *Aoneko* (*The Blue Cat*, 1923), was greeted with even greater enthusiasm than *Howling at the Moon*. In 1934, when he published the "definitive edition" of *The Blue Cat*, he explained in the preface the circumstances of composition and the meaning of the title:

Mr. Hinatsu Kōnosuke, in the second volume of his *History of Poetry in the Meiji and Taish Eras,* has stated that my *Blue Cat* is merely an extension of *Howling at the Moon* and contains no changes or development, but as far as I am concerned, this collection was a *poésie* that sprang from totally different and separate origins. My maiden collection *Howling at the Moon* had a purely imagistic vision for its poetic domain, and its basic quality was a physiological terror, but *The Blue Cat* is quite different; the basic nature of its *poésie* arises entirely from pathos. There are no tears or pathos in *Howling at the Moon. . . .*

There is no collection of my poetry I think of with such nostalgia and sadness as *The Blue Cat*. The images and the vision in its poems are magic-lantern pictures reflected on a retina of tears; though I wipe them away, these representations of grief keep returning again and again, like mist on a windowpane on a rainy day. *The Blue Cat* is not an Imagist collection. Together with my recently published *The Iceland,* it is for me a collection that sings of pure feelings. . . .

I have frequently been asked about the meaning of the title of the book, *The Blue Cat*. I intended by the word "blue" the English word: that is, I used it to embrace the meanings of "hopeless," "melancholy," and so on. . . . The meaning of the title is, in other words, "a melancholy-looking cat." Another meaning, also found in the title-poem **"The Blue Cat,"** was the result of imagining that the bluish-white sparks from electric lines reflected on the sky over a big city were a huge blue cat. This meaning conveyed the intense yearning I felt for the city while writing these poems in the country. In addition, I was infatuated with Schopenhauer when I compiled the collection, and a world-weary, passive ennui based on his philosophy of the negation of the will, together with the Hinayana Buddhistic pessimism of bliss through annihilation, inevitably lurked beneath the sentiments in the poems.

Fukunaga Takehiko characterized the differences between *Howling at the Moon* and *The Blue Cat* in other terms: "In *Howling at the Moon* he believed in what he could see with his eyes. The sick man's world really existed. But here he believed in what he could not see, and attempted to see conceptual objects beyond his life, to fix his fugitive emotions."

The Blue Cat is marked by the frequent use of the word *yūutsu* (melancholy or depression), and the collection has been termed "a confession of failure in life." The title poem is especially important. The first half describes his longing for the metropolis, its excitement, tall buildings, and beautiful women; the second half, in a more characteristic vein, suggests more elusively the nature of his fascination with Tokyo:

> Ah, the only thing that can sleep at night in this
> huge city
> Is the shadow of one blue cat,
> The shadow of a cat that tells the sad history of
> mankind,
> The blue shadow of the happiness we are ever
> seeking.
> That must be why, in quest of such a shadow,
> I have longed for Tokyo even on days of sleet;
> But huddled with cold against a back-street wall,
> This beggar who resembles a man—what is *he*
> dreaming of?

The last lines indicate the poet's awareness of the misery crouching in the streets of the city he longs for so passionately; but because the beggar is treated with irony rather than compassion, Hagiwara's lack of concern with social issues shocked the critics; even his disciple Miyoshi Tatsuji compared these lines to Bashō's equally "unfeeling" verse on seeing an abandoned child at Fuji River. Hagiwara was interested only in his inner feelings; the beggar was not so much a fellow human being in distress as a projection of his own uncertainties.

The Blue Cat contains poems that represent Hagiwara's most successful experiments with the modern Japanese language. **"Kuroi Fōkin" ("Black Harmonium,"** 1918) opens:

> Orugan wo o-hiki nasai onna no hito yo

> Play the organ, please, good woman!

Not only is there alliteration on words beginning with *o*, but this vowel occurs seven times out of the sixteen in the line. Of the twenty-eight lines in the entire poem, eleven begin with *o* and nine with *a*, the vowel with which *o* is associated in the quoted line. Apart from these effects of repetition, the distinctively colloquial rhythms produce effects that would have been impossible in classical Japanese. Hagiwara's use of alliteration and related conso-

nants suggests at least indirect influence from the French Symbolists like Gustave Kahn, who in 1885 wrote, "Free verse, instead of being, as in old verse, lines of prose cut up into regular rimes, must be held together by the alliterations of vowels and related consonants."

When the "definitive edition" of *The Blue Cat* was published, Hagiwara added various poems composed after the original compilation in 1923. **"Neko no Shigai" ("The Corpse of a Cat")** was among these additional poems. It has been described as being "the apogee of the love poetry composed after the early works in *The Blue Cat*." It concludes:

> We have no past, no future,
> And have faded away from the things of reality.
> Ula!
> Here, in this weird landscape
> Bury the corpse of the drowned cat!

In his notes to the poem Hagiwara wrote:

> This Ula is not a real woman, but a ghostwoman dressed in vaporous garments who breathes amid the images of a love poem. She is a lovable, melancholy woman smeared with the fresh blood of passion. This nostalgically remembered woman always reminds me of music. It is a music connected sadly and inconsolably to the past, present, and future, that breathes painfully in a calendar of eternal time.

> That is why the central theme of the poem is concentrated on the sound *Ula*. If the reader can sense the musicality of Ula by pronouncing the name, he can probably grasp quite clearly the main thought of the poem; if he fails to sense it, he probably will be unable to understand the meaning of the poem as a whole. To put it in different terms: *Ula* serves the same function with respect to the formal structure of the composition as *Nevermore* or *Leonore* to Poe's "Raven."

Hagiwara elsewhere compared the world evoked by this poem, which reflects his own life at the time of composition, to "The Fall of the House of Usher":

> My family life in every way resembled "The Fall of the House of Usher." There was no past, no future, and the portentous, accursed, empty present—a present appropriate to the House of Usher—had faded away from the "things of reality." This ominous, squalid situation was symbolized by the muddy corpse of the cat. Ula! Don't touch it! I was always, instinctively afraid. I shuddered, weeping in my dreams.

The poem has also been interpreted as Hagiwara's farewell to the poetic world he created in *The Blue Cat:* this is the corpse he intends to bury.

In 1925 Hagiwara moved definitively to Tokyo. In the same year he published the collection *Junjō Shōkyoku Shū (Short Songs of Pure Feelings)*. The first half of this book consists of early poems antedating even *Howling at the Moon,* the second half of ten poems composed in 1924 describing scenes at Maebashi. The early poems include such famous works as **"Night Train,"** the later ones some of Hagiwara's masterpieces. Although, as we have seen, Hagiwara had a special place in his heart for *The Blue Cat,* there is something morbid about these poems, and the reader may turn with relief to the "pure feelings" of the later collection. A period of ten years separates the composition of the first and second halves of the book, but Hagiwara himself felt that unity was provided by their both being in the same style, poems written in plangent literary language.

Hagiwara did not state his reasons for returning to the classical language after ten years of brilliant colloquial poems. Undoubtedly the choice was dictated by the materials he used, remembered scenes more easily described in the classical language, with its own distant associations, than the aggressively contemporary modern language. When he published his last collection of poetry, *Hyōtō* (the cover bears the English title *The Iceland*), in 1934 he stated that his use of the literary language was a "retreat" after years spent opposing it and perfecting free verse in the colloquial. "But," he went on, "when I wrote the poems in *The Iceland,* the literary language was for me an absolutely necessary poetic diction. In other words, it was impossible to express the emotions in that collection in any other language but the literary one." No doubt much the same reasons impelled Hagiwara to choose the literary language for his "poems of pure feeling." A well-known work in this series was the short **"Koide Shindō"** (**"New Koide Road,"** 1925):

> The new road opened here
> Goes no doubt straight to the city.
> I stand at a crossway of this new road,
> Uncertain of the lonely horizon around me.
> Dark, melancholy day.
> The sun is low over the roofs of the row of houses.
> The trees in the wood have been sparsely felled.
> How, how to change my thoughts?
> On this road I rebel against and will not travel
> The new trees have all been felled.

Compared to the poems in *The Blue Cat,* the meaning is clarity itself, though commentators have emphasized the obscurities. But even if fine points can be debated, there is no mistaking the poet's sense of desolation over the road that now rips through the forest he had loved.

Other poems in the sequence are dominated by the same mood, and sometimes the same turns of phrase recur. The finest poem, **"Ōwatari-bashi"** (**"Ōwatari Bridge"**), was praised by Miyoshi Tatsuji in these terms: "It is not only the jewel among Hagiwara Sakutarō's poems, but a masterpiece that occupies a prominent place among the countless poems written since shintaishi became free verse."

> The long bridge they've erected here
> No doubt goes from lonely Sōsha Village
>   straight to Maebashi
>   town.

> Crossing the bridge I sense desolation pass
>   through me.
> Carts go by loaded with goods, men leading the
>   horses.
> And restless, nagging bicycles.
> When I cross this long bridge
> Twilight hunger stabs me.

> Ahh—to be in your native place and not go
>   home!
> I've suffered to the full griefs that sting like salt.
> I grow old in solitude.
> How to describe the fierce anger today over bit-
>   ter memories?
> I will tear up my miserable writings
> And throw every scrap into the onrushing Tone
>   River.
> I am famished as a wolf.
> Again and again I clutch at the railing, grind my
>   teeth,
> But it does no good: something like tears spills
>   out,
> Flows down my cheeks, unstanched.
> Ahh—how contemptible I have been all along!
> Past me go carts loaded with goods, men leading
>   the horses.
> This day, when everything is cold, the sky dark-
>   ens over the plain.

The self-hatred and nihilism that mark this poem reached even greater extremes of expression in Hagiwara's last collection of poetry, *The Iceland,* which consisted of poems composed between 1916 and 1933. These poems are not only in the classical language but have (for Hagiwara) an exceptionally high proportion of words of Chinese origin. Hagiwara characterized the poetry in *The Iceland* as "screams" (*zekkyō*) of anger, hatred, loneliness, denial, doubt, and all the other strong emotions he felt. Words of Chinese origin, with their sharper contours, were better suited to such expression than the softer Japanese words. The poems are otherwise marked by the strong influence of Nietzsche. The best-known work in the collection, **"Hyōhakusha no Uta"** (**"The Wanderer's Song"**), especially reveals the influence of *Also Sprach Zarathustra*. The poet sees himself as a lonely wanderer:

> You, wanderer!
> You come from the past and go by the future,
> Pursuing your eternal nostalgia.

The poem concludes:

> Ah, man of loneliness,
> You climb the slope of the sad sunset
> And wander over the precipice of will-lessness,
> But you will not find a home anywhere.
> Your home surely does not exist!

The value of this poem and, indeed, of the entire collection *The Iceland* has been much debated by Japanese poets and scholars. Hagiwara's outstanding disciple, Miyoshi

Tatsuji, labeled the collection the work of a jejune and decadent period in Hagiwara's life. He found that it consisted of "odd repetitions and distasteful retrogressions" and that, for a collection by Hagiwara, the workmanship was extremely poor. His strictures were echoed by Naka Tarō, who believed that Hagiwara, having realized that the springs of his creative imagination had dried up, was forced to describe a commonplace world of which he himself probably felt ashamed. But *The Iceland* has also had its defenders, some because they welcomed the light it sheds on a particularly unhappy period of Hagiwara's life, others because they are convinced that this collection was the crowning masterpiece of his career.

The poems in *The Iceland* are almost without exception gloomy in tone, with frequent repetitions of such words as *sabishiki* (lonely), *yūshū* (melancholy), *kyomu* (nothingness), *kodoku* (solitude), and *uree* (grief). It is easy to imagine why certain critics have read these poems mainly as autobiographical documents describing Hagiwara's lonely life after separating from his wife. But they are certainly more than items of historical interest; the poems have a lean, stark beauty that is not the product of an exhausted mind but of a ripe and austere one.

During the years between the publication of *The Iceland* in 1934 and his death in 1942 Hagiwara composed almost no poetry. He wrote numerous works of poetical criticism including a famous essay on Buson, aphorisms, and brief studies of the nature of Japanese culture. The great esteem he enjoyed during his lifetime has never wavered since.

FURTHER READING

Ueda, Makoto. "Hagiwara Sakutarō." In his *Modern Japanese Poets and the Nature of Literature*, pp. 137-83. Stanford: Stanford University Press, 1983.

> Examines the concept of poetry that Hagiwara advanced in his theoretical writings and analyzes his works within this critical framework.

Wilson, Graeme. Introduction to *Face at the Bottom of the World, and Other Poems* by Hagiwara Sakutarō, pp. 11-32. Rutland, VT: Charles E. Tuttle Co., 1969.

> Discusses Hagiwara's contributions to modern Japanese poetry, noting the influences of European philosophy on his works and his success at integrating western and Japanese poetic styles.

——. "Some Longer Poems of Hagiwara Sakutarō." In *Japan Quarterly* 19, No. 2 (1972): 170-81.

> Assesses critical studies of Hagiwara's works.

Additional coverage of Hagiwara's life and career is contained in the following source published by Gale Research: *Twentieth-Century Literary Criticism*, Vol. 60.

Seamus Heaney
1939-

(Full name Seamus Justin Heaney) Irish poet, critic, essayist, editor, and translator.

INTRODUCTION

Heaney is widely considered Ireland's most accomplished contemporary poet and has often been called the greatest Irish poet since William Butler Yeats. In his works, Heaney often focuses on the proper roles and responsibilities of a poet in society, exploring themes of self-discovery and spiritual growth as well as addressing political and cultural issues related to Irish history. His poetry is characterized by sensuous language, sexual metaphors, and nature imagery. Soon after he won the Nobel Prize for Literature in 1995, commentator Helen Vendler praised Heaney "the Irish poet whose pen has been the conscience of his country."

Biographical Information

The eldest of nine children, Heaney was raised a Roman Catholic in Mossbawn, County Derry, a rural community in Protestant Northern Ireland. At age eleven he received a scholarship to Saint Columb's College in Londonderry, Northern Ireland, and left his father's farm. At Queen's University in Belfast, he was introduced to Irish, American, and English literature and exposed to artists such as Ted Hughes, Patrick Kavanaugh, and Robert Frost. While at university, Heaney contributed several poems to literary magazines under the pen name Incertus. After graduating with honors in 1961, he taught secondary school, later returning to Queen's University as a lecturer. During this time he also established himself as a prominent literary figure with the publication of *Death of a Naturalist* in 1966, his first volume of poetry. In 1969, when fighting broke out between Catholics and Protestants in Belfast, Heaney began to address the unrest's causes and effects in his poetry. He and his family moved to a cottage outside Dublin in 1972, where he wrote full-time until he accepted a teaching position at Caryfort College in Dublin in 1975. He has also taught at Harvard and Oxford Universities and has frequently traveled to the United States and England to give poetry readings and lectures. Having already won numerous awards for his poetry and translations, Heaney was awarded the Nobel Prize for Literature in 1995.

Major Works

Heaney's first volume, *Death of a Naturalist* (1966), is imbued with the colors of his Derry childhood; these early works evince sensuous memories associated with nature

and with his childhood on his family's farm. Evoking the care with which his father and ancestors farmed the land, Heaney announces in the first poem in the collection, "Digging," that he will figuratively "dig" with his pen. In his next published volume, *Door into the Dark* (1969), Heaney also incorporates nature and his childhood as prominent themes.

Much of Heaney's poetry addresses the history of social unrest in Northern Ireland and considers the relevance of poetry in the face of violence and political upheaval. In his next collection *Wintering Out,* for example, are a series of "bog poems" that were inspired by the archaeological excavation of Irish peat bogs containing preserved human bodies that had been ritually slaughtered during the Iron Age. Heaney depicts the victims of such ancient pagan rites as symbolic of the bloodshed caused by contemporary violence in Ireland. *North* (1975) develops this historical theme further, using myth to widen its universality. In such poems as "Occan's Love to Ireland" and "Act of Union," Heaney portrays the English colonization of Ireland as an act of violent sexual conquest. *Field Work* (1979) does not depart from Heaney's outrage at the violence in Northern Ireland but shifts to a more personal tone. The collection encompasses a wide range of subjects: love and marriage, mortality, and the regenerative powers of self-determination and the poetic imagination.

Translating *Sweeney Astray* (1984) from the Irish tale *Buile Suibhne* allowed Heaney to work with myth, for he brings to the English-speaking world the warrior-king Sweeney's adventures after a curse has transformed him into a bird. *Station Island* (1984) is also concerned with Irish history and myth. Patterned after Dante's *Divine Comedy* in its tripartite structure, the central section describes a three-day pilgrimage taken by Catholics to the Irish Station Island seeking spiritual renewal. There the narrator encounters the souls of his dead ancestors and Irish literary figures who speak to him, stirring from him a meditation on his life and art.

The Haw Lantern (1987) contains both parables of Irish life and poems such as "From the Republic of Conscience" and "From the Canton of Expectation." This volume also includes a series of poems entitled "Clearances," which chronicles his relationship with his mother. In *Seeing Things* (1991) Heaney diverges from his previous emphasis on politics and civic responsibility, returning to the autobiographical themes of childhood experience and Irish community ritual. Feelings of loss and yearning are prominent motifs in the collection, as many poems evoke celebratory images of Heaney's deceased father, who appears frequently throughout the volume.

Critical Reception

Critics of Heaney's early work were immediately impressed by his freshness of expression and command of detail. He has been praised for his political poems, especially those that depict the violence between Roman Catholics and Protestants in Northern Ireland. In these poems, it has been noted that Heaney also addresses Ireland's cultural tensions and divisions through the linguistic duality of his poetry, which draws upon both Irish and English literary traditions. Critical commentary has traced the thematic development of Heaney's work, contending that as his later poems continue to address the unrest in Northern Ireland, they also incorporate a more personal tone as Heaney depicts the loss of friends and relatives to the violence. As his most recent work diverges from his previous emphasis on politics and civic responsibility, Heaney returns to the autobiographical themes of childhood experience and Irish community ritual. Many critics have lauded these poems for their imaginative qualities and their focus on visionary transcendence experienced through ordinary life events.

Heaney has been commended for his experimentation with form and style, in particular in the volumes *Seeing Things* and *Station Island*. His efforts to integrate meaning and sound often result in vivid descriptions, witty metaphors, and assonant phrasing. By most critics he is acclaimed as one of the foremost poets of his generation and is very favorably compared to such poets as Derek Mahon, Michael Longley, Michael Hartnett, and Ted Hughes.

PRINCIPAL WORKS

Poetry

Death of a Naturalist 1966
Door into the Dark 1969
Wintering Out 1972
North 1975
Field Work 1979
Poems: 1965-1975 1980
Station Island 1984
Sweeney Astray: A Version from the Irish [translator and adapter] (poetry) 1984
The Haw Lantern 1987
Seeing Things 1991
The Spirit Level 1996

Other Major Works

Preoccupations: Selected Prose 1968-1978 (essays) 1980
The Government of the Tongue: Selected Prose, 1978-1987 (essays) 1988
The Cure at Troy: A Version of Sophocles' Philoctetes (drama) 1990
The Redress of Poetry (lectures) 1995

CRITICISM

David Galler (review date 1967)

SOURCE: "Description as Poetry," in *Kenyon Review,* Vol. XXIX, No. 1, January, 1967, pp. 140-46.

[*In the following excerpt, Galler explores the expository nature of Heaney's poems in* Death of a Naturalist.]

Description—the details of what is being observed or performed—is the basis of all writing: epic, narrative, dramatic, or lyric. And this is the case whether the mind works *through* the eye directly or *behind* the eye by the various methods of analogy. But prior to this century poetry was not made of the kind of description that permits the reader no leap whatever to a plane of experience related to but more complete than that which is being observed. What has happened in this century increasingly, and in America especially, is the trend toward description replete with exposition, but lacking complication. . . .

Death of a Naturalist, Seamus Heaney's interesting first book, is made up of description whichremains exposition, with one or two exceptions (notably **"For the Commander of the 'Eliza'"**). Heaney, a young Irishman, has been absurdly compared to Edwin Muir by his publisher and presumably by some reviewers. Both poets grew up on farms, and there the similarity ends. Heaney's characteristic poems describe specific events with which he appears to be more familiar than many of us—as in **"Churning Day"**:

A thick crust, coarse-grained as
    limestone rough-cast,
hardened gradually on top of the
    four crocks
that stood, large pottery bombs,
    in the small pantry.
After the hot brewery of gland,
    cud and udder
cool porous earthenware fermented
    the buttermilk
for churning day, when the hooped
    churn was scoured
with plumping kettles and the busy
    scrubber
echoed daintily on the seasoned
    wood.
It stood then, purified, on the
    flagged kitchen floor. . . .

This poet leaves no doubt as to what he's seeing—and all the doubt in the world as to what he's perceiving. The number of adjectives is daunting; they are huddled close by their nouns, for mutual safety. Then, there are those phrases with mysterious implications: bombs, hot brewery of gland, churning day, busy scrubber, seasoned wood, purified, flagged kitchen floor. But this poem, like most in the book, comes to nothing—or, to put it more fairly, it comes to an accumulation of details. Heaney's work is dense with exposition; if the level of simple metaphor is ever reached, it is all but obscured by a windmill of details. This is a pity, because even the passage quoted shows Heaney to be more than adroit with sounds and rhythms.

Another kind of poem appears in this book, similar to the kind above in trying to make terribly sure that the reader sees exactly what the poet sees, but a little more enterprising because it employs dramatic action. Such a poem is **"An Advancement of Learning."** Here (the subject is the poet's fear of rats), the language is less clogged with detail; the emphasis is on a walk (movement allowing of less detail, probably) over a bridge, the sighting of a rat emerging from water, the poet's fascination (adjectives and nouns are prominent), and the resolution as follows:

This terror, cold, wet-furred,
    small-clawed,
Retreated up a pipe for sewage.
I stared a minute after him.
Then I walked on and crossed the
    bridge.

That is the poem's close; that, presumably, the advancement of learning. Complication, if it can be called that, exists as a rather common reaction and action. It is possible, of course, that Mr. Heaney is overawed—or I am underawed—by certain things as they are. There are two poems in the book which interest me more: **"For the Commander of the 'Eliza,'"** mentioned earlier, and **"The Play Way."** The first—because it takes off from a reported incident, is cast in the dramatic form of a soliloquy by a speaker other than Mr. Heaney, and has as its theme his most established concern, the cruelty of man toward man—

indicates a direction in which this poet might operate more to his profit. It is a direction in which some complication of detail is virtually forced upon him. **"The Play Way"** suggests another facet of Heaney's sensibility which might prove fruitful in the making of poems: a didactic vein played off ironically against the amassed detail. In this connection, Heaney approaches the method of Philip Larkin, the poet by whose example, more than any other's at this point, he might benefit.

Bruce Bidwell (essay date 1973-1974)

SOURCE: "A Soft Grip on the Sick Place: The Bogland Poetry of Seamus Heaney," in *The Dublin Magazine,* Vol. 10, No. 3, Autumn-Winter, 1973-1974, pp. 86-90.

[*In the following essay, Bidwell draws a connection between Heaney's metaphor of the bog and Irish republicanism.*]

In the spring of 1781 Lord Moira, a landlord with vast holdings in County Down, was approached by his rather sheepish estate agent with a story which led to the first documented find of what are now referred to as the bog-people. He presented Lord Moira with a plait of hair which had been found on a human skull—a skull belonging to a woman buried in the bog nearly 1800 years before.

The details of the discovery can be found in Lady Moira's account published in a contemporary London archaeological journal. While cutting turf the previous autumn in a small peat bog on Drumkeragh Mountain, one of Lord Moira's tenants had sliced into the skull of the woman. He had immediately reburied her but not before removing the clothing and ornaments found in the grave. It was only through bribery that Lady Moira was able to get the story in front of her husband and only by offering rewards did she finally recover some of the clothing and gems taken over the winter.

Upon investigation, the skeleton was found lying under a thick bed of peat at the bottom of the bog. A gravel layer provided a base and large stones had been placed at both the head and feet. The woman had been covered with a woolen rug and a veil of light fabric covered her face. She was supposed at the time to be a Danish Viking queen.

The importance of the discovery for archaeologists lies in the preserving quality of her bog grave. Under normal circumstances, any trace of clothing would have long since disintegrated but in this case it was recovered in quite reasonable condition.

The details of this and similar exhumations of the bog-people have now become the unique artistic property of Seamus Heaney the widely-read poet from Belfast.

It was in 1969 that Heaney read *The Bog People*, a study of these discoveries by the Danish archaeologist P. V. Glob, but an examination of his earlier poetry shows that he was well prepared to assimilate the book's influence.

As early as 1967 he was using the turf image as metaphor for the elemental:

> . . . it's like going into a turfstack,
> A core of old dark walled up with stone
> A yard thick. When you're in it alone
> You might have dropped, a reduced creature
> To the heart of the globe.

And in **"Bogland"** written about the same time, he dwells on the preserving quality of the bog:

> They've taken the skeleton
> Of the Great Irish Elk
> Out of the peat, set it up
> An astounding create full of air.
>
> Butter sunk under
> More than a hundred years
> Was recovered salty and white.

In fact so many of his poems deal with "water and ground in their extremity," "alluvial mud, bogwater and tributaries," or "humus and roots," that it can be argued that his art was waiting for a symbol which could somehow contain them all.

His interest can be seen, for instance, in the poem **"Bog Queen,"** published in November, 1972, and based on the County Down find:

> I was barbered
> and stripped
> by a turf-cutter's spade
>
> Who veiled me again
> and packed coomb
> softly between the stone jambs
> at my head and feet.
>
> Till a peer's wife bribed him.
> The plait of my hair,
> A slimy birth-cord
> of bog, had been cut
>
> And I rose from the dark. . . .

In a poem published in his collection, *Wintering Out* (1971), he shows a similar fascination with the Tollund Man, so called because he was discovered by peatcutters in the Tollund Fen in the Bjaeldskov valley of central Denmark. This man, alive during the early Ice Age, was so well-preserved by the bog that we can see exactly what he looked like right down to the gentle expression on his face.

> Some day I will go to Aarhus
> To see his peat-brown head,
> The mild pods of his eyelids,
> His pointed skin cap.

Scientists have been able to examine the contents of his stomach to find that his last meal was a gruel of cultivated and wild winter grains. They have suggested that this meal and his subsequent death may have been part of a ritual sacrifice to some fertility goddess. It is this point that Heaney emphasizes:

> Bridegroom to the goddess,
> She tightened her torc on him
> And opened her fen,
> Those dark juices working
> Him to a saint's kept body. . . .

He goes on in the poem to relate this 2000 year-old death to more recent killings in Northern Ireland and finds his attitude to the foreign parishes of Denmark not unlike his feelings about the North:

> Out there in Jutland
> In the old man-killing parishes
> I will feel lost,
> Unhappy and at home.

More recently he has published the poem **"Bone Dreams"** where he again returns to the Jutland bog-people, this time to explore the women (witches?) found staked and buried in the bogland:

> Now my hands have found that queen
> staked in the bog, and I unpin
> her darkness: out of the black maw
> of the peat, sharpened willow
> withdraws gently.

Certainly Heaney has found rich ground in the bogland metaphor and will draw poetic strength from the images he develops here. There is the suggestion, however, that his interest in the bog-people goes beyond more fascination.

During a programme broadcast on Radio 4 (BBC Belfast) Heaney spoke of his feeling about the Republican movement in the North: "The early Iron Age in Northern Europe is a period that offers very satisfactory imaginative parallels to the history of Ireland at the moment." This is particularly true, he said, of the earlier involvement in vegetation religions, blood letting, and ritual sacrifice. "In many ways the fury of Irish Republicanism is associated with a religion like this, with a female goddess who has appeared in various guises. She appears as Cathleen Ni Houlihan in Yeats's plays; she appears as Mother Ireland. I think that the Republican ethos is a feminine religion, in a way. It seems to me that there are satisfactory imaginative parallels between this religion and time and our own time."

So far his collected poetry has made only indirect reference to the Northern troubles and he has berated himself in one place for deserting his native region. But the image of the bog people "rising from the dark" to reassert their ancient existence is not far from a parable of the drama now being enacted in Ulster.

In 1966 he wrote about the situation in the North and the result he foresaw for the poets of Northern Ireland: "This kind of tension might be expected to have either of two effects on the artistic life of the place. It might induce a sense of claustrophobia and a desire to escape or it might concentrate a man's energies on the immediate dramatic complex of tension and intrigue." Of course, a lot has changed since 1966 and Heaney claims, and rightly so, that he is not a political poet. Yet it is clear that he recognizes his essential affiliation with the North. He put the word on himself in that regard in a poem entitled **"Whatever You Say, Say Nothing":**

> Yet for all this art and sedentary trade
> I am about as capable as fungus
> of breaking my soft grip on the sick place
> or its on me.

Perhaps in his use of the bog-people he has found a way of coming to terms with that grip.

Robert Buttel (essay date 1975)

SOURCE: "Beginnings," in *Seamus Heaney,* Bucknell University Press, 1975, pp. 19-35.

[*In the following excerpt from the full-length study of Heaney's work, Buttel examines the seminal influences on Heaney's early poetry.*]

"A poet begins involved with craft, with aspirations that are chiefly concerned with making," Seamus Heaney has said in a statement about his aims which he wrote two or three years ago to accompany a selection of his poems (*Corgi Poets in Focus 2*). The poet "needs a way of saying and there is a first language he can learn from the voices of other poets, dead and alive." He could have cited **"Turkeys Observed"** as an illustration of part of his own apprenticeship; this poem, which appeared in the *Belfast Telegraph* in 1962 (and later in *Death of a Naturalist*), was his first published one aside from several published before then over the pseudonym Incertus in *Gorgon* and *Q,* Queen's University literary magazines. It is not that one detects specific models; rather, the poem seems an exercise in applying some of the standard practices of modern poetry. The poem is characterized by imagistic exactitude: a dead turkey is "A skin bag plumped with inky putty." And it employs a conceit of the sort favored by the Thirties poets: "I find him ranged with his cold squadrons:/ The fuselage is bare, the proud wings snapped,/ The tail-fan stripped down to a shameful rudder" (with the pathos of these concluding lines sunk by the weight of contrivance). Some of the alliteration may be heavy-handed, as in "*Bl*ue-*br*easted in their indifferent *m*ortuary,/ *B*eached *b*are on the cold *m*arble sla*b*s/ In i*mm*odest under-wear *fr*ills of *f*eather"—the apprentice reveling here in the craft of prosody; and the word "cowers" in "a turkey cowers in death" may be excessive, but the poet has care-fully maintained the elegiac tone, in the modern way, by the "non-poetic" subject matter, by the objectivity of the title, and by the neutrality of the opening line—"One observes them, one expects them." The controlled move-ment of the poem also sustains the tone: within the four-line stanzas the rhythms are fluent but firm, and, since evidently no rhyme scheme arose naturally in the genesis of the poem, none was forcibly imposed. Although the turkeys, in the setting of "bleak Christmas dazzle," are surely emblems of mortality, their symbolic import is not overly insisted upon.

Basically this is a well-made poem, an academic exercise in the modern mode, the voice for the most part anonymous, still to be discovered. Only in the graphic force of the line "A skin bag plumped with inky putty" and in the second stanza, particularly in the oxymoron "smelly majesty" with its earthy adjective and in the energy of the phrase de-scribing the inert beef, "A half-cow slung from a hook," does the poem anticipate the poet's distinctive manner:

> The red sides of beef retain
> Some of the smelly majesty of living:
> A half-cow slung from a hook maintains
> That blood and flesh are not ignored.

A very promising apprentice poem, then. Heaney, again in the *Corgi* statement, refers to this stage of a poet's development as "a mimicry and a posturing that leads to confidence, a voice of his own that he begins to hear, prompting behind lines he has learned."

The poet's confidence was emerging rapidly at this time, for **"Mid-Term Break,"** a *Death of a Naturalist* poem, published in *Kilkenny Magazine* not long after the ap-pearance of **"Turkeys Observed,"** indicates how ably he could now apply his new-found craft to a poetic statement concerning a painful personal experience. Heaney says that the poem, an elegy for a young brother killed in an auto accident, came to him quite spontaneously, that it almost wrote itself without his thinking about craft. Only in the prosodic overdetermination of the first two lines (the speaker "sat all morning in the *college* s*ick* bay/ Counting *bell*s *k*nel*l*ing *classes* to a *close*") is there an intrusion of the craftsman at work. The rest reads as a straight recital of the literal details; a litany of trite com-forting words becomes part of the quiet testimony of grief: "Big Jim Evans saying it was a hard blow," "And I was embarrassed/ By old men standing up to shake my hand/ And tell me they were 'sorry for my trouble,'" "as my mother held my hand/ In hers and coughed out angry tearless sighs." The lament is undramatized, controlled, simply reported:

> Next morning I went up into the room. Snowdrops
> And candles soothed the bedside; I saw him
> For the first time in six weeks. Paler now,
>
> Wearing a poppy bruise on his left temple,
> He lay in the four foot box as in his cot.
> No gaudy scars, the bumper knocked him clear.
> A four foot box, a foot for every year.

The ritual effect of the snowdrops and candles occurs because it was part of the ritual scene; "poppy bruise" is poetically shocking because descriptively accurate; the laconic explanation, "the bumper knocked him clear," and the cruel mathematics of the one-line coda accentuate the understated bitter sadness. The directness, openness, and apparent matter-of-factness in this poem, on a difficult subject for poetry, have become recurrent characteristics of Heaney's voice.

"An Advancement of Learning," however, published in the *Irish Times* following the two previous poems and later in *Death of a Naturalist*, begins to project much more clearly the poet's individual voice. "Here," to quote once again from the *Corgi* statement, "craft passes into technique which is the ability to send the voice in pursuit of the self," and in this poem we follow this very process. If, as Heaney continues, "Technique is dynamic, active, restless, an ever provisional stance of the imagination towards experience," we see here imagination and technique rising to a greater degree of individuality; the poem is definitely in the poet's own idiom though it does exhibit a residue of "mimicry and posturing." The *Times Literary Supplement* reviewer of *Death of a Naturalist*, although finding the volume substantial and impressive, complained that "the most obvious surface fault is the rather glib or incongruous imagery stuck on in what seems to be an attempt to hit the required sophistication," quoting as illustration the first two stanzas of the poem, which concerns an encounter with a rat:

> I took the embankment path
> (As always, deferring
> The bridge). The river nosed past,
> Pliable, oil-skinned, wearing
>
> A transfer of gables and sky.
> Hunched over the railing,
> Well away from the road now, I
> Considered the dirty-keeled swans.

For the reviewer "'nosed' and 'pliable' are surely doubtful; 'oil-skinned' is clever, but introduces an extraneous association; 'transfer' is somehow uncomfortably neat and final." I would quibble some with this assessment: "Transfer" is clever, all right, but it does indicate the observer's indulgence in idle romantic musings, seeing a pretty picture on the river surface despite the pollution, and it is not final since the pictorial image is picked up in the following stanza in the word "smudging," when the observer's reverie is intruded upon by the obscene reality of a rat which "slobbered curtly, close,/ Smudging the silence."

But more important than the question of limitations is the fact that in this early poem Heaney seized upon an area of subject matter and knowledge congenial to the discovery of his authentic voice. The vividness of physical detail in "back bunched and glistening,/ Ears plastered down on his knobbed skull" and the energy of word and speech in "But God, another was nimbling/ Up the far bank" and "A rat/ Slimed out of the water"—with adjective and noun here metamorphosing into disturbing active verbs: these are typical qualities in the first volume. One notes too the physical accuracy of the response in "My throat sickened so quickly that/ I turned down the path in cold sweat," with the repetition of sound in "sickened" and "quickly"

an aural counterpart of actual constrictions in the throat. The effect comes naturally, denying thoughts of either craft or technique; here imagination is in full accord with the experience, and the experience occurs with a psychological rightness, moving from sickening shock to "thrilled care" and observation to a control of the situation; yet at the end a subtle balance of ambiguous reactions is struck, with both distaste and sympathy for the creature bound together with a recognition of man's pollution of nature— "This terror, cold, wet-furred, small-clawed,/Retreated up a pipe for sewage." The discoveries in this poem prepared for the thoroughly distinctive and successful title poem of the collection, *Death of a Naturalist*, which I will discuss later.

Heaney's literary and linguistic background was not unusual for a boy brought up on a Country Derry farm. Like other children at that time in the environs of Mossbawn, between Castledawson and Toome Bridge, along the Bann River just north of where it emerges from Lough Neagh, about thirty miles northwest of Belfast, he was exposed to the remnants of the oral tradition, the local lore and anecdotes, and the stories brought home from or heard at cattle fairs. He tells me that one of his father's cousins, who might be described as one of the surviving hedgerow "schoolmasters," would visit once a week and read and recite to the children in the family. Occasionally as a young boy and as the eldest child in the family he was called upon at a children's party or when friends and relatives visited to recite verses or sing a song, sentimental or patriotic things, Michael Dwyer's "Sullivan Beare," say, or "Me Da" by the Ulster folk poet W. F. Marshall, or a Percy French ballad such as "The Four Farrellys." Like his fellow students he received training in Gaelic, an extension of his linguistic identity and at least an acquaintance with another and yet a native linguistic tradition. As a boy, though, he wrote next to no poetry, unless one were to count the adolescent, roguish Latin verses that he, along with some his schoolmates at St. Columb's, wrote now and then for amusement and passed surreptitiously to one another. Perhaps, however, it is a sign of his future interest in writing poetry that while at St. Columb's he did try his hand at composing some Miltonic verses, though he got no further than three lines. While there he had one particular advantage, a very good English teacher who had his students reading deeply and thoroughly in Shakespeare, Chaucer, Wordsworth, and Keats, and he recalls reading Eliot's "The Hollow Men" at that time.

Heaney is a Catholic poet and fully aware of inner tensions the Catholic is heir to; constantly redeemed and constantly instilled with guilt.

—Robert Buttel

At Queen's University Heaney's interests became more definitely literary. There in the English syllabus he encountered a wider range of literature, other poets in the

English tradition such as Clare and Hardy (as John Press in an article in *The Southern Review* has pointed out) and Hopkins, but also twentieth-century poets. At the same time he was becoming conscious of the Irish tradition, Yeats of course and other poets, both Anglo-Irish and unhyphenated Irish. He remembers reading Patrick Kavanagh's "The Great Hunger" during this period, and its powerful effect on him, for it was a modern poem that suggested possibilities for treating Irish subject matter. Then, while at St. Joseph's College of Education in 1961-62, he discovered and read *Six Irish Poets,* edited by Robin Skelton and including Austin Clarke, Richard Kell, Thomas Kinsella, John Montague, Richard Murphy, and Richard Weber. Also he wrote for a course he was taking a long paper on literary magazines in Ulster and learned through this project that a body of poetry could exist outside the classical English canon. Here were Irish poets, what's more Northern Irish poets, who had created a poetry out of their local and native background—W. R. Rodgers and John Hewitt especially. In the latter Heaney found not only a regionalist but one who was also quite urbane. Meanwhile he was continuing to discover other, non-Irish, poets too, R. S. Thomas and Ted Hughes, for example. It was also during this time, while these various influences were contributing to his own interests and urgings and adding to his growing assurance, and while his poems were beginning to be published, that he became one of a group of young writers who met regularly to discuss their work at the home of the English poet Philip Hobsbaum, who had come to teach at Queen's the year Heaney was at St. Joseph's. This was a group, says Heaney, that "generated a literary life" in Belfast; it was in this group that the poet met his friend and fellow poet, Michael Longley. Now he was no longer working in isolation. Here was a "forum" where he received serious criticism which countered the pleasing corroboration he felt when editors began accepting his poems.

The relatively few poems he wrote as an undergraduate dramatize the leap he was to make so shortly afterward. **"Reaping in Heat,"** for example, depends on such poeticisms as "sycamores heaved a sleepless sigh" and "Lark's trills/ Shimmered" and it concludes on a Keatsian-Georgian note:

> . . . Lower
> And deeper and cooler sinks now
> The sycamores' shade, and naked sheaves
> Are whitening on the empty stubble.

"October Thought" shows the impress of Hopkins on the neophyte poet:

> Minute movement millionfold whispers twilight
> Under heaven-hue plum-blue and gorse pricked with
>   gold,
> And through the knuckle-gnarl of branches, poking
>   the night
> Comes the trickling tinkle of bells, well in the fold.

Heaney says that he was captivated by Dylan Thomas's poetry at this time too and published in *Gorgon* or *O* a poem very much in the Welsh poet's manner (though I have been unable to locate this poem and one or two others). **"October Thought"** is typical of what any number of university students might produce, though few of them would develop beyond this point. We can see in hindsight, however, that Heaney's obvious imitation of Hopkins (and I suspect that the same could be said of the Thomas poem) was, in its intricate wordplay, assonance, and alliteration, an initial learning of his craft, a prelude to his transposing of the primitive skills in this poem into his own mature technique and voice. Furthermore, in another poem, **"Lines to Myself,"** we observe the poet goading himself into a more trenchant, forceful style:

> In poetry I wish you would
> Avoid the lilting platitude.
> Give us poems, humped and strong,
> Laced tight with thongs of song.
> Poems that explode in silence
> Without forcing, without violence.
> Whose music is strong and clear and good
> Like a saw zooming in seasoned wood.
> You should attempt concrete compression,
> Half guessing, half expression.

And here both the advice and the style itself anticipate the course Heaney was to follow.

His rapid maturing as a poet who some four years later would publish an impressive first book is not entirely surprising. During this relatively brief period that I have been discussing, a number of literary stimuli seem to have converged for Heaney into a provisional poetics, a poetics for which he required some form of confirmation, of validation. A poetry of fuselages or of sociology was not authentic for him; what was, a poetry concerned with nature, the shocks and discoveries of childhood experience on a farm, the mythos of the locale—in short, a regional poetry—was essentially a counterpoetry, decidedly not fashionable at the time. To write such poetry called for a measure of confidence if not outright defiance. Indeed, Anthony Thwaite in his *New Statesman* review of *Door into the Dark* sees the authenticity of the poems but finds their appeal exotic, adding wryly, "Turbines and pylons for the 1930s: bulls for the 1960s. It's an odd progression." And a number of reviewers misleadingly have linked the poet with the Georgians, who relatively speaking played over the bucolic surface of nature whereas Heaney digs into the archetypal roots and into the psychic roots of his own being as well. As John Press says in his article, regionalism "may lend itself to a kind of universality which escapes the poetry of men whose material is derived from a study of contemporary politics." Put another way, it is what the poet does with his donné that matters. If the result is effective it makes little difference whether the poet begins with bulls or, as in the case of Alan Ginsberg, with supermarkets or other heterogeneous details of American culture.

Two poets in particular, it seems clear, served to release the young poet's latent purposes, to offer the validation he required. Frost was one, certainly a pivotal figure for

Heaney. Benedict Kiely; in his *Hollins Critic* article, "A raid into Dark Corners: the Poetry of Seamus Heaney," reports the poet's saying "that the first poet who ever spoke to him was Robert Frost." "Leaving stains upon the tongue and lust for picking," a line in **"Blackberry-Picking"** (*Death of a Naturalist*) which bears an imprint of Frost's "After Apple Picking," is only one of a number of resemblances showing how well the Irish poet heard the American: both poets excel at rendering physical detail and sense experience. And Heaney must have noticed in Frost a poet who went against the grain of obvious experimentalism in his era and wrote verse in traditional forms— traditional forms but charged with the rhythms of natural speech. He must have noticed other characteristics too: a vision of nature which includes dark forces as we as benign ones; the human pain and tragedy suffered as profoundly by rural inhabitants as by others; the combining of matter of fact with transcendental inclinations; the appreciation of native skills and disciplines which have their correspondences to the art of poetry. (The poet informs me, incidentally, that although he was generally unenthusiastic about farm work and not especially adept—like Frost— the one exception was his skill with a pitchfork, for which he earned some local acclaim.) Heaney, however, did not become a servile imitator even though specific signs of Frost's influence persist, with decreasing frequency, into *Wintering Out,* his most recent volume. He had found a twentieth-century model for the kind of poetry he desired to write, a model more recent than, say, Wordsworth or Clare, and he set about creating work that in theme and style diverges markedly from Frost's.

The other poet is Ted Hughes, whose poetry he came upon around 1962, and who provided a contemporary source of encouragement, a reinforcement of that given by Frost. One can perceive what this English poet meant, and still means, to Heaney when we read him saying in his review of Hughes's *Selected Poems* ("Deep as England" in *Hibernia,* December 1, 1972) that "Hughes brought back into English poetry an unsentimental intimacy with the hidden country. Probably not since John Clare had the outback of hedge and farmyard been viewed so urgently." But that intimacy goes deeper with both poets than hedge and farmyard; Heaney says that in Hughes's poetry "racial memory, animal instinct and poetic inspiration all flow into one another," and he might as well be speaking of his own poetry, a point that should become apparent in the course of this study. With an exception or two—"the last wolf killed in Britain" in Hughes's "February" and "the wolf has died out/ In Ireland" in Heaney's **"Midnight"** (*Wintering Out*)—it is not a matter of direct parallels or borrowings: superficial comparisons are easy enough to find in the rank, brute particulars of nature exploited by both poets. More important are the general affinities as, for example, the attraction of the archetypal and pagan for both. And Heaney's statement about Hughes, "It is not enough to praise his imagery for 'its admirable violence' or its exact sensuousness," could again refer to himself. He says that the chief effect on him was in the matter of diction, and the similarity here is pronounced: in both poets words erupt with kinesthetic and visceral force; a line will turn on a deliberately "unpoetic" word. Heaney

speaks for both when he says, "Into the elegant, iambic and typically standard English intonations of contemporary verse he interjected an energetic, heavily stressed, consciously extravagant and inventive northern voice." Even here, however, it is not a case of direct borrowing; Heaney, as the sudden outpouring of his poems suggested, had his own inner board of language. Hughes was a fortuitous example. As John Press says, it was not so much discipleship: Hughes "saved [him] from making a false start." The important thing is that as he was getting started Heaney felt affinities with a number of poets, from Wordsworth to Hughes, who helped reveal to him his own resources.

Superseding literary influences and affinities in importance are the poet's identification with place and his intense engagement with language. These, I believe, would have enabled him to survive any false start. "Our poesy is as a gum which oozes/ From whence tis nourished": he is fond of this utterance by the poet in *Timon of Athens* and has quoted it more than once, one occasion being in an article he wrote for *The Guardian* in May, 1972, "The Trade of an Irish Poet," a key statement on the origins of his poetry. Press quotes him as saying that "Wordsworth was lucky and . . . I was lucky in having this kind of rich, archetypal subject matter . . . as part of growing up." Whereas Frost vitiated some of his poetry by becoming too often the poseur of his region, Heaney writes out of what is inextricably his birthright. Rural life itself has a rhythm determined by the cycle of the seasons and the round of tasks; it becomes a ritual of the land. Birth and death, immediate events, are parts of that rhythm too. In this setting a child's life has its full quota of drama, real terrors merging into the realm of legend: "the bog was rushy and treacherous," Heaney reports in the *Guardian* article, "no place for children. They said you shouldn't go near the moss-holes because 'there was no bottom in them.'"

And in this setting the landmarks of Irish history and myth project themselves into present consciousness. Benedict Kiely tells us that "Rody McCorley, the patriot boy renowned in balladry, was hanged at the Bridge of Toome in 1798" and he continues,

> To the west of the loughshore are the Sperrin mountains to which O'Neill withdrew between Kinsale and his final flight to Europe. Glanconkyne, where he stayed for a while, has a complicated mythology associated with the autumn festival of Lugh, the father, in the mythologies, of Cuchullain. The mountains are plentifully marked by pre-Celtic standing stones and stone circles.

Thus it is an area where history, with its battles, heroes, subjections, and famines, flows back into prehistory, legend, and myth. In this rich primal material not only does the past inform the present but fable and land are conjoined, and it is against this background that one takes on a clear but complicated identity.

Looking back now, Heaney can see that he grew up in a center that did hold. Despite the history of discord and the recent eruption of conflict and violence that has so horribly blighted life in Northern Ireland, he did as a boy experience comparative stability. Catholics, the majority in his area, lived in relative harmony with the Protestants, a sharp awareness of differences notwithstanding. (George Evans, a Protestant neighbor, on one occasion brought rosary beads back from Rome and presented them to the Heaneys: "I stole them from the Pope's dresser," he said.) The differences were inescapable, however. Heaney says, again in the *Guardian* article, that in Mossbawn, between Castledawson and Toome, he was "symbolically placed between the marks of English influence and the lure of the native experience, between 'the demesne' [Moyola Park, now occupied by Lord Moyola, formerly Major James Chicester-Clark, ex-Unionist Prime Minister] and the 'bog' . . . The demesne was walled, wooded, beyond our ken."

This symbolic split has meant that the poet writes out of a dual perspective, and it has had special import for the language of his poetry. "The seeds," he has told me, "were in language, words." Even when a youth, before he was struck by any overt urge to write poems, individual words were compelling, to be mulled over in the mind. With more self-awareness now he can analyze the twinsources of his language, the literary words and the words of place, of origins or, put another way, the English and the native. Is Mossbawn, he wonders in the *Guardian* essay, a Scots-English word meaning the planter's house on the bog, or since "we pronounced it Moss Bann, and ban is the Gaelic word for white," might it not mean "the white moss, the moss of bog cotton? In the syllables of my home I see a metaphor of the split culture of Ulster." The names of the nearby townlands of Broagh and Anahorish "are forgotten Gaelic music in the throat, *bruach* and *anach fhior uisce,* the riverbank and the place of clear water," and they made their way into two of the poems in **Wintering Out** for which they serve as subject and title. Two other names in the immediate area, Grove Hill and Back Park, "insist that this familiar locale is a version of pastoral"; "Grove is a word that I associate with translations of the classics." His auditory imagination prefers another name, "The Dirraghs, from *doire* as in Derry," but nonetheless Spenser and Sir John Davies, who played their parts in the crushing of the indigenous culture, are also as poets figures who command his attention, contributing to the complex education one receives in this "split culture." The article concludes with this paragraph:

> Certainly the secret of being a poet, Irish or otherwise, lies in the summoning and meshing of the subconscious and semantic energies of words. But my quest for precision and definition, while it may lead backward, is conducted in the living speech of a landscape that I was born with. If you like, I began as a poet when my roots were crossed with my reading. I think of the personal and Irish pieties as vowels, and the literary awareness nourished on English as consonants. My hope is that the poems will be vocables adequate to my whole experience.

Although he wants his idiom to adhere closely to the speech he was born with this does not mean that the effort should be methodical and deliberate, an effort to apply rigidly the view, "formulated most coherently by Thomas McDonagh," the scholar-activist slain in the 1916 uprising, that "the distinctive note of Irish poetry is struck when the rhythms and assonances of Gaelic poetry insinuate themselves into the texture of English verse." Sympathetic to the attempts of Austin Clarke and others to apply Gaelic techniques systematically, he finds "the whole enterprise a bit programmatic." It is better, he implies, to trust to one's roots and let the language of the poems arise naturally. This is what he has done, to singular advantage.

He is conscious of other divisions as well. Press quotes him as having experienced an "exile from a way of life which I was brought up to . . . from a farming community to an academic . . . exile in time . . . from childhood." This exile has resulted in an acute search into his cultural roots, accentuated by his moving in the conflicting worlds of Mossbawn-Belfast, Ulster-Ireland-England, Ireland-America. The search has been inward too, into the sources of self, which are also, ultimately, the sources of poetry. Further, he is a Catholic poet and fully aware of inner tensions the Catholic is heir to; constantly redeemed and constantly instilled with guilt. Benedict Kiely reports his saying, "Penance indeed was a sacrament that rinsed and renewed . . . but although it did give a momentary release from guilt, it kept this sense of sin as inseparable from one's life as one's shadows." But if some of his poems can be said to depend on a Catholic imagination, he has not been content to rest there; he has probed into the unconscious. As he asserts in *The Listener* (February 5, 1970), "circumstances have changed and writing is usually born today out of the dark active centre of the imagination . . . I think this notion of the dark centre, the blurred and irrational storehouse of insight and instincts, the hidden core of the self—this notion is the foundation of what viewpoint I might articulate for myself as a poet."

Richard Murphy (review date 1976)

SOURCE: "Poetry and Terror," in *The New York Review of Books,* Vol. 23, No. 15, September 30, 1976, pp. 38-40.

[*In the following laudatory review of* North, *Murphy discusses the defining characteristics of Heaney's poetry.*]

Visitors to Ireland have often remarked that we seem to live in the past. They note our strong attachment to beliefs which were held in the Dark Ages and our inability to end a conflict which goes back to the religious wars of the seventeenth century. Our moist green landscape charms them, where it remains unpolluted by modern industry. They see fields full of cattle, which have been a source of wealth since the mythical wars of Cuchulain and Maeve. The oceanic island atmosphere takes away their sense of time, and gives them instead an illusion that the past is retrievable, perhaps even happening today. Clergy strengthen this illusion by teaching in churches and schools that the dead will be resurrected. Our earth itself, with those vast wet bogs in the center of the island, seems to absorb the present and preserve the past. Here funerals draw much larger crowds than weddings. Ruins and buried remains are so plentiful that archaeologists have an endless future digging back through time. In this climate poetry flourishes, and the poet who has shown the finest art in presenting a coherent vision of Ireland, past and present, is Seamus Heaney.

He was born on a farm in a townland called Mossbawn, near Lough Neagh between Belfast and Derry, thirty-seven years ago, the eldest of nine children in a Catholic family. After six years at St. Columb's College, run by the Diocesan priests, in Londonderry, he studied English language and literature at Queen's University in Belfast, where he began to write poetry under the spell of Gerard Manley Hopkins. His first volume, *Death of a Naturalist,* was published ten years ago in 1966. "Words as bearers of history and mystery began to invite me," he has said about this period in his life. By birth and upbringing he belonged to the ancient world of the Irish countryside and traditional culture, with roots in a pre-Christian legendary past: but his education brought him into the modern world, where he discovered English poetry. The tension you can feel in Ireland between the two cultures, you also feel in his poetry.

He is the antipode of Yeats, who extended English poetry out beyond the demesne walls into the Irish countryside to appropriate its legends. Heaney brings the Irish countryside through his own voice into English poetry.

> Those hobnailed boots from be-
>   yond the mountain
> Were walking, by God, all over the
>   fine
> Lawns of elocution.

The result is a new and exciting sound. Granted he has Irish antecedents—Patrick Kavanagh, for example—and granted he has learned the craft of being true to his own Irish voice from a number of English and American poets, such as Edward Thomas, Robert Frost, and Ted Hughes. His original power, which even the sternest critics bow to with respect, is that he can give you the feeling as you read his poems that you are actually doing what they describe. His words not only mean what they say, they sound like their meaning. Often in his early poems he celebrates hard physical work, such as digging, bulling cows, ditching, ploughing, catching eels: all kinds of activities associated with ancient rural crafts and fertility which he witnessed as a child, a dead life which his poetry resurrects in a living body of words. His work has the potent charm of bringing back an old kind of beauty and a numinous fear, which cruder industrial terrors have all but blotted out: and it celebrates the newly discovered force of the poetic craft itself.

His primary statement about this craft, in the opening lines of his first book, connects poetry with terror.

> Between my finger and my thumb
> The squat pen rests, snug as a gun.

Bullfrogs are compared to "mud grenades," and butter crocks on a pantry shelf to "large pottery bombs." Even allowing for the fashion in the Sixties for overemphasizing the toughness and cruelty of nature, you feel that these images are true. Grenades and bombs kept on some remote Irish farms during his childhood. So aptly in **"The Barn,"**

> The musty dark hoarded an ar-
>   moury
> Of farmyard implements harness
>   plough-socks.

Heaney's second volume, *Door into the Dark*, appeared in 1969, the year when violence in Northern Ireland became world news. For three years he remained in Belfast, living with his wife and two sons in a "Protestant" street near the university where he taught. On the corner of this road a pub and its owner were blown up. Poetry that can digest this kind of horror is rare, though horror of this kind has produced much ill-digested poetry.

In 1972 he published his third collection, *Wintering Out*, which confirmed his gradual inward emigration into a new world of language.

> The tawny guttural water
> spells itself: Moyola
> is its own score and consort,
>
> bedding the locale
> in the utterance,
> reed music, an old chanter
>
> breathing its mists
> through vowels and history.

Four years ago he moved south across the border with his family to live in a cottage on the edge of the Wicklow Mountains; choosing to become "an inner émigré," like the Russian poets Mandelstam, Akhmatova, and Pasternak. Heaney defines this role at the end of *North*, in "Exposure":

> I am neither internee nor informer;
> An inner émigré, grown long-
>   haired
> And thoughtful; a wood-kerne
>
> Escaped from the massacre,
> Taking protective colouring
> From bole and bark, feeling
> Every wind that blows;

"The fear that goes with the writing of verse," says Nadezhda Mandelstam in *Hope Against Hope*, "has nothing in common with the fear one experiences in the presence of the secret police. Our mysterious awe in the face of existence itself is always overridden by the more primitive fear of violence and destruction. M[andelstam] often spoke of how the first kind of fear had disappeared with the Revolution that had shed so much blood before our eyes."

Seamus Heaney brings both kinds of fear together—the creative awe and the destructive horror—connecting the brutal real atrocities we have been shown on television for the past seven years with rituals of human sacrifice in remote antiquity. His poetry traces modern terrorism back to its roots in the early Iron Age, and mysterious awe back to the "bonehouse" of language itself. He looks closely in *North* at our funeral rites and our worship of the past. The whole of northern civilization from Denmark to Donegal is his "locale." We hear of Thor and Gunnar as well as Hercules; the Vikings as well as Sir Walter Raleigh. The central image of this work, a symbol which unifies time, person, and place, is bogland: it contains, preserves, and yields up terror as well as awe.

The nature of peat is to preserve certain things that are buried in it: primeval forests, elks, butter, suicides, strangled victims. In a lecture called "Feeling into Words," addressed to the Royal Society of Literature in London on October 17, 1974, Heaney said: "I began to get an idea of bog as the memory of the landscape, or as a landscape that remembered everything that happened in and to it. In fact, if you go round the National Museum in Dublin, you will realize that a great proportion of the most cherished material heritage of Ireland was 'found in a bog.'" He went on to say that he "had been reading about the frontier and the west as an important myth in the American consciousness, so I set up—or rather, laid down—the bog as an answering Irish myth." This is the conclusion of his poem **"Bogland,"** at the end of *Door into the Dark*:

Our pioneers keep striking
Inwards and downwards,

Every layer they strip
Seems camped on before.
The bogholes might be Atlantic
  seepage.
The wet centre is bottomless.

Heaney's original idea of bogland as a symbol of memory was objectively confirmed and extended by both political event and archaeological discovery. In 1969 the civil-rights marches in the city of Derry, and the counter-marches by the Royal Ulster Constabulary with batons drawn, focused world attention on the Catholics who lived in a low-lying slum called the Bogside. In a short while the word became synonymous for minority resistance to police oppression, and subsequently Irish Catholic resistance to British misrule. Bog itself is one of the few words of Irish origin to have been assimilated into English. Literally it means "soft." In English it acquired, perhaps because of its Irish origin as well as its color, connotations of shame, as in the slang of "bog" meaning "lavatory." Heaney carries the word up the ladder from the foul rag and boneshop to give it a nobler meaning. He was helped by publication in 1969 of *The Bog People* by the Danish archaeologist P. V. Glob What this fascinating book meant to him is best described in Heaney's own words.

It was chiefly concerned with preserved bodies of men and women found in the bogs of Jutland, naked, strangled or with their throats cut, disposed under the peat since early Iron Age times. . . . P. V. Glob argues convincingly that a number of these, and in particular, the Tollund Man, whose head is now preserved near Aarhus in the museum at Silkeborg, were ritual sacrifices to the Mother Goddess, the goddess of the ground who needed new bridegrooms each winter to bed with her in her sacred place, in the bog, to ensure the renewal and fertility of the territory in the spring. Taken in relation to the tradition of Irish political martyrdom for the cause whose icon is Kathleen Ni Houlihan, this is more than an archaic barbarous rite: it is an archetypal pattern. And the unforgettable photographs of these victims blended in my mind with photographs of atrocities, past and present, in the long rites of Irish political and religious struggles.

Heaney first made a connection between these Danish murders of two thousand years ago and modern Irish politics in a powerful poem called **"The Tollund Man"** in *Wintering Out*. Now in *North* he has created a cycle of six or more bog-sacrifice poems, compressing the archaeological information given by Glob into personal imagery. You could call them love poems that resurrect the dead in poetry. The language, like seed, is compact with life, sexual, even necrophiliac.

I reach past
The riverbed's washed
Dream of gold to the bullion
Of her Venus bone.

You can feel the joy as well as the terror of ancient rites, a victim "hung in the scales / with beauty and atrocity," whose spine is "an eel arrested / under a glisten of mud." Sometimes the poet assumes a victim's identity, as in **"Bog Queen,"** who speaks of her burial and resurrection in the first person: "My skull hibernated / in the wet nest of my hair." The short lines, the seminal images, and the vast connections in time or space between fragile details build up in **"Kinship"** (a six-page poem in six movements), which begins with a figure of circles: neck, nest, and a dog's motion before lying down.

Kinned by hieroglyphic
peat on a spreadfield
to the strangled victim,
the love-nest in the bracken,

I step through origins
like a dog turning
its memories of wilderness
on the kitchen mat:

Many dead words are revived. From Old English and Norse he digs up *bonehouse* from *bānhūs* meaning body; *scop* meaning poet; and *holmgang,* a duel to the death. Irish words are slipped in, like foreign coins in a meter: *crannog,* an ancient lake dwelling; *aisling,* a vision; *bawn,* a ringed mound or fort; *slobland,* a marsh. He brings out refined shades of meaning in verbal sounds. "Dublin" is "spined and plosive." Remembering the laid-out corpses of the dead in his childhood, he recalls "their dough-white hands

/ shackled in rosary beads." The dead subject, the dead past, is described in language that's vividly alive: a grim statement in a joyful style. The "swimming tongue" of a Viking longship is "buoyant with hindsight"; and the final message of this tongue to Ireland in the future is:

> Keep your eye clear
> as the bleb of the icicle,
> trust the feel of what nubbed
>   treasure
> your hands have known.

Heaney has said that "the bog bank is a memory bank." How does it store and yield information? The symbol suggests that the past is continuously present under the ground we tread, permanently preserved, static and dead. It also suggests that no improving human change is possible, because all action is absorbed by the soft wet ground forever. Digging up the past, or writing poetry, appears to be the only way of redemption or renewal: a kind of resurrection. The symbol conveys a profound truth about Irish consciousness, and how we keep the past alive. But the bog has *not* "remembered everything that happened in and to it." Most of what happened has been forgotten. A few sacred objects congenial to itself are preserved by its acids: and what the peat yields up when the poet digs down deep enough is a strangled victim or a severed head. The bog does not liberate us with new knowledge of accurate history: it horrifies us with timeless myths perpetuating acts of cruelty based upon errors of judgment.

Heaney is the antipode of Yeats, who extended English poetry out beyond the demesne walls into the Irish countryside to appropriate its legends. Heaney brings the Irish countryside through his own voice into English poetry.

—Richard Murphy

The dreadful power of the symbol is generated by the poetry with fascination amounting to approval. The poems embody the myths. In other poems, such as **"Ocean's Love to Ireland,"** the vision is more historical. In **"Act of Union"** Heaney imagines the relationship between England and Ireland in the past as the rape of a feminine land by a male imperial power. No attempt here to demythologize the past. As in the bog poems—significantly it begins with an image of the bog—it acts like the peat itself, converting history into myth.

Are these images of human sacrifice redemptive in the same sense that tragedy can be? I think this poetry is seriously attempting to purge our land of a terrible blood-guilt, and inwardly acknowledging our enslavement to a sacrificial myth. I think it may go a long way toward freeing us from the myth by portraying it in its true archaic shape and color, not disguising its brutality. Naturally we wonder where Heaney himself stands in relation to the victims and the killers, what he has called "the tail end of a struggle in a province between territorial piety and imperial power." He makes no pretense about his deep uncertainty. *Incertus* was once a pseudonym he used. Some of his poems are "trial pieces," and they follow a thought "like a child's tongue following the toils of his calligraphy."

Heaney looks for companions in literature. He's both resourceful and protean. His ear is always to the ground from which, like Antaeus, he draws his strength. He converses with historical or literary figures, Breughel or Hamlet. Does he approve of Diodorus Siculus in a poem called **"Strange Fruit,"** about a "girl's head like an exhumed gourd"? This puzzled me until I found in my battered ninth edition of the *Encyclopaedia Britannica* that Diodorus Siculus "as a critic . . . seems to have been altogether ignorant of the ethical advantages of history, and shrinks from administering praise or blame to the persons whose history he writes." So too Heaney's detachment could be a necessary element in the purification of our guilt.

Although Heaney commits himself to no belief in the causes that might claim his allegiance, such as the unification of Ireland, he embodies in poetry some of the terrorist actions that he refuses to endorse; as in a frightening poem called **"Punishment,"** about the penalties inflicted in ancient Jutland and modern Belfast on girls who might have misbehaved. There is much sad truth in that evasive word "almost" in this passage:

> My poor scapegoat,
>
> I almost love you
> but would have cast, I know,
> the stones of silence.

At the end of **"Kinship"** he addresses Tacitus, who reported with urbane critical accuracy the custom of human sacrifice among the barbarous Germani, and tells him he has found "a desolate peace." This involves self-lacerating recognition, *almost* rejection, of the goddess, whose victims are in other poems treated as "holy blissful martyrs," their bodies preserved like those of the saints. The repulsion in these lines is far from Yeats's vision of the terrible beauty born in the sacrifice of Easter 1916, and closer to Joyce's:

> Our mother ground
> is sour with the blood
> of her faithful,
>
> they lie gargling
> in her sacred heart
> as the legions stare
> from the ramparts.
>
> Come back to this
> "island of the ocean"
> where nothing will suffice.
> Read the inhumed faces

of casualty and victim;
report us fairly,
how we slaughter
for the common good
and shave the heads
of the notorious,
how the goddess swallows
our love and terror.

To bring together things, feelings, and ideas in words which have never before been connected is imagination of the highest kind; and in this rare quality Seamus Heaney's *North* excels. I read it as a triumph of art over terror. It has the fear of death on almost every page, and brings the terror under artistic control. The book's weakness is confined to a small section at the end, added like a print-room to a gallery of paintings. Here the poems are lower-keyed, more talkative. The verse is looser, the language and imagery are not so inspired.

Terror darkens this book, but the poem which has the last word appears as a frontispiece. Every word in it rings true to the culture, to my memory of Ireland in the past, to its sad beauty. The play of light and shadow in this poem, the spaces filled by sunlight, the woman baking bread, the tick of two clocks work like a revelation as in the art of Vermeer. I'm thinking of the *Officer and Laughing Girl* at the Frick, where a dark moment of time is suspended forever in a ray of light that pours through an open window, crosses a blank wall under a map of Holland, and is caught up by a girl's ecstatic smile. Heaney's poem is called **"Mossbawn: Sunlight,"** after his birthplace.

There was a sunlit absence.
The helmeted pump in the yard
heated its iron,
water honeyed

in the slung bucket
and the sun stood
like a griddle cooling
against the wall

of each long afternoon.
So, her hands scuffled
over the bakeboard,
the reddening stove

sent its plaque of heat
against her where she stood
in a floury apron
by the window.

Now she dusts the board
with a goose's wing,
now sits, broad-lapped,
with whitened nails

and measling shins:
here is a space
again, the scone rising
to the tick of two clocks.

And here is love
like a tinsmith's scoop
sunk past its gleam
in the meal-bin.

Robert Pinsky (review date 1979)

SOURCE: A review of *Field Work,* in *New Republic,* Vol. 181, No. 3389, December 22, 1979, pp. 31-3.

[*In the following essay, Pinsky provides a favorable review of* Field Work.]

The poems of Seamus Heaney give several kinds of pleasure: first of all, he is a talented writer, with a sense of language and rhythm as clean, sweet, and solid as new-worked hardwood. Beyond that, his previous book, *North,* showed inspiringly that his talent had the limberness and pluck needed to take up some of the burden of history—the tangled, pained history of Ireland. Heaney's success in dealing with the murderous racial enmities of past and present, avoiding all the sins of oratory, and keeping his personal sense of balance, seems to me one of the most exhilarating poetic accomplishments in many years.

It is no real dispraise of *Field Work* to observe that it is a less original, less heroically stretched work than *North.* There is a distinct feeling of artistic rightness about the relatively more measured qualities of these new poems: they present a less agonized manner, and a more actual Ireland, seen from closer to ground level.

In *North,* the English language was partly reinvented to emphasize words rooted in the tongues of the remote Scandinavian invaders, a thorny cadence and vocabulary of Germanic and Celtic parts jammed together, with Frenchified or Latinate bits floating in a calculated violent relation to the whole. And while an American reader's first mental picture of Northern Ireland may be (by virtue of television) grimly urban, Heaney's speech in *North* was rooted in farmland and fen. When, in the first sentence of **"Come to the Bower,"** the poet reaches into the peat soil that mummifies the past and sustains the present, the language he uses corresponds to the physical action:

My hands come, touched
By sweetbriar and-the tangled vetch,
Foraging past the burst gizzards
Of coin-hoards

To where the dark-bowered queen,
Whom I unpin,
Is waiting.

The freshness of the idiom seems openly made out of something like archaeological discovery: each word ("forage," "vetch," "gizzards") set to suggest that the flecks of dark, rich mold have just been brushed from it.

In *Field Work,* the characteristic gestures seem less intuitive and sensory, more direct and prosaic. When the poet asks the Sibyl, "What will become of us?" she begins her answer in a suitably grave, prophetic way: "'I think our very form is bound to change./ Dogs in a siege. Saurian relapses. Pismires./ Unless forgiveness finds its nerve and voice.'" This in itself confirms that the title *Field Work* denotes (among other things) an outward, daylit kind of attention; and the Sibyl's conclusion touches an even more prosaic level:

'My people think money
And talk weather. Oil-rigs lull their
 future
On single acquisitive terms. Silence
Has shoaled into the trawlers' echo-
 sounders.

The ground we kept our ear to for so long
Is flayed or calloused, and its entrails
Tented by an impious augury.
Our island is full of comfortless noises.'

Of course, this speech is not in the poet's own voice; and it is one of the most explicitly public and civic passages in this volume. But just the same, the passage exemplifies Heaney's "field" in these poems, some of them elegies for the victims of civil troubles.

In the affecting poem **"Casualty,"** one such victim blunders into a pub that is blown up, on a night he decides to defy an IRA curfew—or rather, to ignore the curfew, because he is stubborn, and likes to drink. In a bar out of his own neighborhood, he is "blown to bits" by the side that is more or less "his": killed more or less by accident, through having needed to be himself, as naturally as a fish.

He had gone miles away
For he drank like a fish
Nightly, naturally
Swimming toward the lure
Of warm lit-up places,
The blurred mesh and murmur
Drifting among glasses.
In the gregarious smoke.

The sad comedy of this picture—the doomed man (who once took the poet fishing) as a fish, the pub as a net— embodies what is best about these poems: Heaney's sense of individual human character as not at all heroic, but somehow glorious, in its persistence.

Heaney's description of the casualty ("I loved his whole manner") perhaps strikes, glancingly, a small note of self-portraiture: "Sure-footed but too sly,/ His deadpan sidling tact,/His fisherman's quick eye/And turned observant back." The tact, the sure-footedness, and most of all the "turned observant back," all suggest the way *Field Work* hails its materials: an agile attention, too reserved for the front-squared gaze of the journalistic.

I have dwelled, somewhat misleadingly, on the role of Northern Ireland in Heaney's work, because national matters seem to provide the most immediately available examples of his accomplishments. Perhaps those matters have impelled him to his accomplishments. But it is a strength of the volume as a whole that not all of its poems are concerned with the stresses of Ireland (though the stresses for an Irish artist born in the North are never distant, in *Field Work*, for long).

There is, for instance, a genial, untamed sensuality in the poems, winningly countered by Heaney's shrewd comic sense. In a pretty, small poem (**"The Guttural Muse"**), the country accents of teenagers leaving a bucolic "disco-theque" rise up to his hotel room: voices and accents "thick and comforting/ As oily bubbles the feeding tench sent up." The slime of the tench, the poem mentions, is said to cure wounds on other fish—and then, there is a girl in a white dress, "being courted out among the cars": "As her voice swarmed and puddled into laughs/I felt like some old pike all badged with sores/Wanting to swim in touch with soft-mouthed life." I enjoy the sense of Heaney's particular, complicated personality here, especially as it grins at itself: the homely, pragmatic grotesqueness of the metaphor; the way an erotic moment comes spinning into his imagination out of a glimpse of white dress and, most characteristically, out of a local form of speech.

Perhaps the center of *Field Work* is the sequence, **"Glanmore Sonnets"**; in one set of terms, these poems are about living in a rural cottage for a time. The poems are pastoral: "The mildest February for twenty years," says the first sonnet: "Now the good life could be to cross a field/And art a paradigm of earth new from the lathe/Of ploughs." But it is a disturbed, in fact a haunted pastoral, as the last lines of the same sonnet acknowledge: "Breasting the mist, in sower's aprons,/My ghosts come striding into their spring stations./The dream grain whirls like freakish Easter snows."

The **"Glanmore Sonnets"** play the dark, pre-Norman sounding diction of *North* ("Old ploughsocks gorge the subsoil of each sense") in a comic way against Latin and French roots, which in self-parody are made to seem mincing and affected. In one sonnet, the poet begins to muse upon a comparison of himself and his companion with William and Dorothy Wordsworth, in *their* country retreat—a comparison briskly dismissed by the woman. On the way to his literary-biographical venture, the poet writes two lines, using such Latinate and/or French diction, that are quite funny in context: about some sundown bird-songs, "It was all crepuscular and iambic"; and about some deer, "Like connoisseurs, inquisitive of air."

This bantering lyricism, like the idea of writing a sequence of actual sonnets, presents a particularly un-American side of Heaney. A prosodist and a humanist, he seems to incorporate a *literary* element into his work without embarrassment, apology, or ostentation. I think that such a sense of other writing—that is, of "literature"—as just one more resource may come less freely to many American poets of Heaney's age (around 40).

Having said that, I will admit that there are times when some of these poems do seem literary in a pejorative sense.

One might use that word for an occasional stale, bardic note ("Everything in me/Wanted to . . ." etc.). And when the "boortree," another name for "elderberry," turns out to be a form of "bowertree," the poem made out of all that word-worrying seems held together too much by will and by learning—not helped by a self-apostrophe as "etymologist of roots and graftings." But these lapses don't matter much in a book of so much grace, generosity, wit, and seriousness.

Field Work ends with a translation, the Ugolino material from the *Inferno*. It's a marvelous job, in idiomatic, but forcefully compressed language, and lines of loose, rhymed pentameter. The story of unquenchable anger ends with Dante's execration on the city of Pisa. In the context of Seamus Heaney's last two books, the passage is also a kind of admonition, a minatory urging of forgiveness as well as a curse. It recalls the Sibyl's prediction of cannibalism ("Dogs in a siege. Saurian relapses. Pismires,") "Unless forgiveness finds its nerve and voice":

> Pisa! Pisa, your sounds are like a hiss
> Sizzling in our country's grassy language.
> And since the neighbor states have been
>   remiss
> In your extermination, let a huge
> Dyke of islands bar the Arno's mouth, let
> Capraia and Gorgona dam and deluge
> You and your population. For the sins
> Of Ugolino, who betrayed your forts,
> Should never have been visited on his
>   sons.
> Your atrocity was Theban. They were
>   young
> And innocent: Hugh and Brigata
> And the other two whose names are in my
>   song.

Historical, and yet concluding with the particularity of individual names; as coolly detached as a "turned back," and yet as intense as their language—these translated lines, and the sure instinct to put them as concluding words, are another measure of Heaney's art.

Rita Zoutenbier (essay date 1979)

SOURCE: "The Matter of Ireland and the Poetry of Seamus Heaney," in *Dutch Quarterly Review*, Vol. IX, No. 1, 1979, pp. 4-23.

[*In the following excerpt, Zoutenbier traces the thematic and stylistic development of Heaney's verse.*]

Seamus Heaney was born in Country Derry, Northern Ireland, in 1939, the oldest of nine children; and spent the first fourteen years of his life at Mossbawn, near Lough Neagh in County Derry, where his father was a farmer and cattle dealer. From the primary school at Anahorish, he moved on to St Columb's, a Catholic boarding school in Derry, and then to Queen's University, Belfast, where he read English and where, after working in a Belfast secondary school and in a teacher training college, he returned to teach. In 1972, he gave up teaching for full-time writing, moving with his family to the Irish Republic, to a cottage that was a gate lodge of Glanmore Castle on the former Synge estate in Wicklow. He has since moved back into Dublin, living with his wife and three children in Sandymount, and teaching at Carysfort College, a Catholic teacher training college, where he is head of the English department. He is a member of the Irish Arts Council, and runs a fortnightly book programme on Irish radio. So far Heaney has published four volumes of poetry, *Death of a Naturalist* (1966), *Door into the Dark* (1969), *Wintering Out* (1972), and *North* (1975); a collection of short autobiographical fragments *Stations* (1975); and a number of critical articles and uncollected poems in different magazines.

Heaney's rural background and the "matter of Ireland" provided him with a subject; his reading of English literature helped to shape his language; or as Heaney has said himself: "I began as a poet when my roots were crossed with my reading". A book by the Danish archeologist, P.V. Glob, *The Bog People,* which Heaney first read in 1969, became important to him, when what he found there merged with his own images of bogland, and helped him towards finding symbols and a myth for his own writing. The reading of the Glob book set off a further interest in archeology, which is apparent in *North*: some of the poems in that volume being inspired by recent excavations in Ireland. And this interest in archeology coincides with Heaney's notion of a poem as an archeological find, dug up from the depths of the memory or imagination.

The fact that Heaney's poetry is so much tied up with a particular locale may seem a limitation, but his feeling for his own territory is a source of emotion for the poet, which infuses his language, and makes it come alive. In a lecture called "The Sense of Place" Heaney has talked about the "vital and enhancing bond that exists between our consciousness and our country", and about a "grounding of the self" and an "earthing of the emotions". In Heaney's later poetry his response to the Irish situation has become increasingly imaginative and visionary as a "country of the mind" has replaced the geographical country, though the former is still rooted in the latter.

One could say that the poetry of Seamus Heaney starts from a sense of displacement, personal and cultural—Heaney moved away from his home area, physically as well as in the mind, and has moved away again from Northern Ireland—which leads to a search for identity and roots through language; or as Heaney has put it himself, to the making of a "myth of identity through language". This search starts with the rediscovery and recreation of Heaney's personal past in *Death of a Naturalist* and *Door into the Dark,* volumes which include among other things reminiscences of a country childhood. Towards the end of *Door into the Dark* and in *Wintering Out* Heaney widens his scope to Irish history, and goes deeper into the origins of his country's culture. The first part of *North* continues this quest, while the second part deals with day-to-day personal and political events.

There is a continuous development of theme and style throughout the four volumes that Heaney has published so far. He has extended his subject matter from personal memories and private experience to history and mythology and the origins of a culture. The landscape, which features throughout the poetry, has become associated with history and with language, changing from the actual physical landscape of Heaney's home area, to a conceptual, cultural landscape embodying the past, or to a visionary landscape which reveals a kind of sacral history.

Heaney has become more certain of his subject as he has got a closer grip on it with his language: one could characterize his poetry as a continuous attempt to get in touch with a subject or a vision, something that is already there in the imagination, but needs to be brought out into the light. Unlike Joyce who uses experience as a starting-point from which his language and his imagination take off, Heaney moves inward to his subject. He goes back to the structures which underlie experience, to a life "deeper and older than himself"; and again unlike Joyce he submits himself to his country's history and culture, finding himself through a sense of community rather than in isolation and exile.

Death of a Naturalist

In **"Digging"**, the opening poem of Heaney's first volume, several items of theme and style that turn out to be characteristic of Heaney's poetry are already evident: the precise observation of physical phenomena (as in the beginning of Joyce's *Portrait* all the five senses play a part); memory which goes back from father to grandfather; a sense of unease and alienation ("But I've no spade to follow men like them"); the search for roots; and the continuation of a tradition (digging with the pen instead of with a spade). The father digging, "nicking and slicing neatly", is the first example of a series of portraits of local craftsmen as a metaphor for the poet: as in **"The Diviner"**, **"The Thatcher"**, and the smith in **"The Forge"**, and others. The "nicking and slicing neatly" corresponds to the craft of the poet shaping his language, while the "going down" and "digging" are another task for the poet, like the plumbing of hidden sources of the diviner. "Making" and "discovering", the "craft" and the "gift" are words which Heaney himself has used several times for these two activities. There are other poems about the writing of poetry in *Death of a Naturalist* and *Door into the Dark*. In **"Personal Helicon"** Heaney states that the writing of poetry is a search for the self:

> Now, to pry into roots, to finger slime,
> To stare big-eyed Narcissus into some spring
> Is beneath all adult dignity. I rhyme
> To see myself, to set the darkness echoing.

In **"The Peninsula"** (*Door into the Dark*) poetry is the re-shaping of past experience in order to create the self, and to get in touch with the outside world.

The poems in *Death of a Naturalist* can be loosely divided into groups according to theme. The largest group are the poems about childhood, which read like a kind of *Bildungsroman* in verse. They move from a child's fear in **"Death of a Naturalist"**, and **"The Barn"** to the conquering of that fear in **"An Advancement of Learning"**, and the shrugging of shoulders at the sight of drowning puppies; **"Follower"** and **"Ancestral Photograph"** are about the son succeeding the father. **"At a Potato Digging"** and **"For the Commander of 'Eliza'"** treat a subject from Irish history, the great famine. **"Docker"** and **"Poor Women in a City Church"** present images of the two cultures in Ireland: the violence of the Belfast docker whose idea of God is "a foreman with certain definite views / Who orders life in shifts of work and leisure"; and the submissive women kneeling in a church: "Golden shrines, altar lace, / Marble columns and cool shadows / Still them." The volume ends with a group of love poems, and a group of poems about art and artists such as Synge and Saint Francis who like Heaney derive their subject from nature.

Death of a Naturalist contains a variety of styles. On the one hand there is a poem like **"Turkeys Observed"**, a description of slaughtered turkeys in a poultry shop, which is among the earliest poems that Heaney wrote, a very neat and accurate exercise, very limited in tone and subject-matter. Contrasting with that there is the group of poems about childhood, where the tone is very personal and open. Most of those poems are written in free verse. They are the most successful in the volume, where the language gets closest to the experience, even though Heaney lays it on rather thick at times, for example in the excessive description in the title-poem **"Death of a Naturalist"**. The influence of Hopkins, whom Heaney read as a student, is noticeable in some of the early poems, in heavily alliterated lines like "the squelch and slap / Of soggy peat, the curt cuts of an edge". In **"At a Potato Digging"** the language imposes a vision on an observed scene, which does not fit. The potato-diggers are seen as enacting a kind of pagan ritual, but the religious sentiment expressed does not belong to them, nor does it belong to Heaney. In a poem like **"Waterfall"**, where a waterfall is compared to "villains dropped screaming to justice", and the poet poses as the self-conscious observer: "My eye rides over and downwards, falls with / Hurtling tons that slabber and spill", the language becomes too fanciful in its metaphors and diverts attention from the object described. Heaney is at his best in this volume when he describes his own personal experience, and he has not much grip yet on a subject that lies outside himself, like history or inanimate nature.

Door into the Dark

The poems in *Door into the Dark* are linked not so much by a theme as by a common mood or metaphor. Darkness in one form or another occurs in most of the poems and embodies different though not unconnected things. In the title-poem it dramatizes the poet's uncertainty: "All I know is a door into the dark". In this volume Heaney is groping about in the dark, trying to get a grasp on his subject. In a poem like **"The Forge"** he is not very successful. The smith, like Kelly's bull in **"The Outlaw"**, retires into the dark, as if he ultimately escaped the poet. In the first three poems of the volume, **"Night-Piece"**, **"Gone"** and **"Dream"**, the subjects seem to come up out of the dark of the imagination, but they remain half-hidden there. In **"The Peninsula"** and in **"In Gallarus Oratory"** the dark is the place where one needs to retire in order to achieve a vision. This vision is not something that lies outside the common order of things, but an illumination or heightening of the ordinary: "things founded clear on their own shapes", "the sea a censer, and the grass a flame", like the renewal of the "smells of ordinariness" in **"Night Drive"**. In the latter poem the movement is the same as in the other two: travelling, immersion in the dark, and coming back with a vision. There are sexual undertones, but they escape analysis. These poems are as much about how to live, as how to write or to make art. For both it is necessary to establish an intimate contact with the outside world. In **"In Gallarus Oratory"** this amounts to the erotic vision of the mystic; but the poem is about that kind of vision or writing, it is not itself an embodiment of it, as are some later poems of Heaney's. **"The Plantation"** is another poem about the problem of living and/or writing. Losing oneself without being lost, "following whim deliberately" (**"The Return"**), to be in control while at the same time surrendering oneself, are necessary conditions. "A line goes out of sight and out of mind / Down to the soft bottom of silt and sand / Past the indifferent skill of the hunting hand" (**"Settings"**), is another metaphor for the writing of poetry. In **"A Lough Neagh Sequence"**, a poem about the life-cycle of eels, the dark has a more explicitly sexual meaning in the life of the eels, as well as cosmic significance. It is a poem full of circular movements, dramatizing this cycle and the "horrid cable" in which both human and animal are caught without distinction. The sequence ends in fear (a more adult version of the fear in *Death of a Naturalist*) of the dark cosmic processes for which there is no resolution.

The latter part of *Door into the Dark* contains a few poems which point forward to further developments. "Relic of Memory" is the first poem about relics in the bog and the attraction they have for the poet. **"Shoreline"** is about the ritual timeless moment which brings the poet into contact with sacral history, which is revealed in the landscape:

> Listen. Is it the Danes,
> A black hawk bent on the sail?
> Or the chinking Normans?
> Or currachs hopping high
>
> On to the sand?

"Bogland", at the end of the volume, is the first poem where the bog becomes a mythical landscape and a symbol for Ireland:

> Melting and opening underfoot,
> Missing its last definition
> By millions of years.
> They'll never dig coal here,

> Only the waterlogged trunks
> Of great firs, soft as pulp.
> Our pioneers keep striking
> Inwards and downwards,
>
> Every layer they strip
> Seems camped on before.
> The bogholes might be Atlantic seepage.
> The wet centre is bottomless.

Wintering Out

In *Door into the Dark* Heaney had already extended his scope beyond the strictly personal; in *Wintering Out* he goes further in this direction, though he approaches his subject-matter in a rather cautious and hesitant manner at first. The five poems with which the volume opens are about the Irish colonial past, but this is only indicated through allusions. The mood in the poems is desolate, there is a sense of starvation and of the shrinking of life, but one does not know why. They are not located specifically in time or place. "These long nights", "those mound-dwellers", "the back end of a bad year", "some outhouse", could be any time and any place. The poet's vision is blurred by fog and rain ("mizzling rain / blurs the far end / of the cart track", "Those mound-dwellers / go waist-deep in mist") and he is hesitant to approach or accept it. He is merely pondering a possibility: "I might tarry / with the moustached / dead", "Perhaps I just make out / Edmund Spenser". The poem **"Bog Oak"** presents a rather sharp contrast between the English and native experience:

> Edmund Spenser,
> dreaming sunlight,
> encroached upon by
>
> geniuses who creep
> "out of every corner
> of the woodes and glennes"
> towards watercress and carrion.

Edmund Spenser's pastoral vision is not for Ireland, but these poems are not entirely desolate. **"The Last Mummer"** ends with hope and the possibility of a new beginning. **"Anahorish"** (meaning "place of clear water") is a version of Gaelic pastoral or the poet's personal Helicon, which first fertilized his imagination. It is the first poem where landscape becomes language: "soft gradient / of consonant, vowel meadow".

"Land," **"Gifts of Rain"** and **"Oracle"** present the poet in a relationship of close intimacy with the land. In **"Gifts of Rain"** he states what this intimacy means to him as a poet:

> I cock my ear
> at an absence—
> in the shared calling of blood
>
> arrives my need
> for antediluvian lore.
> Soft voices of the dead
> are whispering by the shore

that I would question
(and for my children's sake)
about crops rotted, river mud
glazing the baked clay floor.

The function of poetry is no longer private: the shaping of one's own identity. But the poet assigns himself a public role:

a mating call of sound
rises to pleasure me, Dives,
hoarder of common ground.

The next series of poems are about language and landscape and the two cultural and language traditions in Ireland. **"Toome,"** like **"Broagh"** and **"Anahorish"** is a place-name poem (the writing of poems explaining the names of places is an old genre in Irish literature). Here the sound of the Gaelic words "anahorish", "broagh" and "Toome" (all names connected with Heaney's home area), draw the poet back into the past of the land and the language. These poems, like **"A New Song,"** are an attempt to incorporate and combine both the Gaelic and the English tradition. Heaney himself, in an interview with Seamus Deane, has said about these poems: "I had a great sense of release as they were being written, a joy and devil-may-careness, and that convinced me that one could be faithful to the nature of the English language—for in some senses these poems are erotic mouth-music by and out of the anglo-saxon tongue—and, at the same time, be faithful to one's own non-English origin, for me that is County Derry." **"A New Song"** is a rallying poem, written out of impatience with the state of cultural affairs, the separateness of the two cultures:

But now our river tongues must rise
From licking deep in native haunts
To flood, with vowelling embrace,
Demesnes staked out in consonants.
And Castledawson we'll enlist
And Upperlands, each planted bawn—
Like bleaching-greens resumed by grass—
A vocable, as rath and ballaun.

Words like "demesne", "Castledawson", "Upperlands", "bawn", "bleaching-greens" call up the English colonization of Ireland. In **"The Trade of an Irish Poet"** Heaney has said: "I think of the personal and Irish pieties as vowels, and the literary awarenesses nourished on English as consonants. My hope is that the poems will be vocables adequate to my whole experience."

"Linen Town," the poem that precedes the sequence **"A Northern Hoard,"** is about the irreversibility of history. **"A Northern Hoard,"** like the introductory poem of *Wintering Out* about an internment camp, treats the present violent situation in Northern Ireland, in language that refers to the actual situation (words like "gunshot", "siren" and "clucking gas" and "sniper") but also puts it in a mythological perspective. **"Roots,"** the first poem of the sequence is about the "nightmare of history" intruding into people's private lives, and the failure of ordinary human

feelings like love, in that situation. In **"No Man's Land"** there is a sense of guilt at the inadequacy of one's reaction. **"Stump"** is about the failure of poetry: "What do I say if they wheel out their dead? / I'm cauterized, a black stump of home". In **"No Sanctuary"** and **"Tinder"** there is a sense of complicity within a community. In **"Tinder"** "cold beads of history and home", relics of the past, fail to light up the imagination: "What could strike a blaze / From our dead igneous days?" The present violent situation cuts one off from a sense of continuity with the past: "new history, flint and iron / Cast-off, scraps, nail, canine." The poems are full of images of pagan rituals and animal savagery and have an almost surrealist quality:

Leaf membranes lid the window.
In the streetlamp's glow
Your body's moonstruck
To drifted barrow, sunk glacial rock.

And all shifts dreamily as you keen
Far off, turning from the din
Of gunshot, siren and clucking gas
Out there beyond each curtained terrace

Where the fault is opening. The touch of love,
Your warmth heaving to the first move,
Grows helpless in our old Gomorrah.
We petrify or uproot now.

"The Tollund Man" is the first of a series of poems about bog people which Heaney wroteafter reading *The Bog People*. The poems of **"A Northern Hoard"** can be said to be public poems in so far as they deal with communal experience. In **"The Tollund Man"** Heaney goes on a private imaginary pilgrimage to Denmark: "Some day I will go to Aarhus"; but he hesitates to commit himself fully to this pagan religion: "I could risk blasphemy / Consecrate the cauldron bog / Our holy ground". The poem ends in speculation:

Something of his sad freedom
As he rode the tumbril
Should come to me, driving,
Saying the names

Tollund, Grabaulle, Nebelgard,
Watching the pointing hands
Of country people,
Now knowing their tongue.

Out there in Jutland
In the old man-killing parishes
I will feel lost,
Unhappy and at home.

The first section of *Wintering Out* ends with a few poems which recall again scenes from Heaney's home area, but there is a felt distance now:

What can fend us now
Can soothe the hurt eye
Of the sun,

Unpoison great lakes,
Turn back
The rat on the road.

If one takes the introductory poem of *Wintering Out* as the context for the whole volume, then the poems of the second part seem a retreat into a private world of marriage and home, or to stand for the continuity of ordinary human life in the context of violence. Of the marriage poems the best is **"Summer Home,"** about guilt and complicity in a private relationship. The form of the poem is much freer than that of the rest of the poems in the volume: and the breaking off of the lines in the middle of a sentence after a stressed syllable, creates the tension the poem is about.

Apart from the marriage poems there is a group of poems about Irish folk-tales written in a dramatic narrative style reminiscent of Robert Frost—who influenced Heaney to some degree—especially the poem **"Shorewoman."** In **"First Calf"** Heaney projects his own changed sensibility and the pain of existence into a recalled scene, whereas the poem **"May"** presents a picture of original innocence and peace. In the final poem in the volume **"Westering"** Heaney takes his distance from Ireland:

Six thousand miles away,
I imagine untroubled dust,
A loosening gravity,
Christ weighing by his hands.

North

Whereas the introductory poem of *Wintering Out* puts the volume into a context of violence, the two introductory poems of *North* put it in a framework of peacefulness and permanence. **"Sunlight"** is a very clear and tranquil vision of a domestic scene; and in **"The Seedcutters"** a pastoral scene which lies fixed in history outside time, is embodied in a very balanced poem. The poem expresses a desire for permanence:

O calendar customs! Under the broom
Yellowing over them, compose the frieze
With all of us there, our anonymities.

The volume *North* itself is divided into two contrasting sections. Heaney told Seamus Deane "the two halves of the book constitute two different types of utterance, each of which arose out of a necessity to shape and give palpable linguistic form to two kinds of urgency—one symbolic, one explicit." Yeats and Kavanagh represent these two poles in poetry, they "point up the contradictions we have been talking about: the search for myths and sagas, the need for a structure and a sustaining landscape and at the same time the need to be liberated and distanced from it, the need to be open, unpredictably susceptible, lyrically opportunistic."

The first section of *North* begins and ends with two not very successful allegorical poems **"Antaeus"** and **"Hercules and Antaeus."** Antaeus is an image of the instinctive poet who derives his strength from the earth and whose "elevation" or education is his "fall". The application of the allegory in the context of the volume is not very clear.

"Belderg" is a poem about an excavation done in Mayo. The "quernstones out of a bog" connect the imagination with the past:

To lift the lid of the peat
And find this pupil dreaming
Of neolithic wheat!
When he stripped off blanket bog
The soft-piled centuries

Fell open like a glib:
There were the first plough-marks,
The stone-age fields, the tomb
Corbelled, turfed and chambered,
Floored with dry turf-coomb.

A landscape fossilized,
Its stone-wall patternings
Repeated before our eyes
In the stone walls of Mayo.

The discussion about the word "Mossbawn" (the name of Heaney's birth-place), which is seen to contain Irish, Norse and English roots and therefore represents the mixed cultural heritage of Ireland, is resolved by the poet, who passes "through the eye of the quern", in a test of the imagination, and sees "A worldtree of balanced stones, / Querns piled like vertebrae, / The marrow crushed to grounds"—an image of a mixed culture.

"Funeral Rites" is again (like **"A Northern Hoard"**) a poem which combines the actual with the mythological. In the first part the poet sees himself as a member of a culture in which the dead are buried with elaborate ritual. There is a detailed description of the dead, as in the poems about bog corpses, in a volume where Heaney is preoccupied with fossils, bones, skeletons, corpses. In the second and third parts the poet imagines the reinstitution of ritual, which involves the whole country in a gigantic funeral procession, to cope with the present situation in Ireland, in which murder is a frequent occurrence.

In **"North,"** as in the poem **"Shoreline"** in *Door into the Dark*, there is a shift from the secular to the sacral, and the poet is almost overwhelmed by a vision of Viking raids in Ireland, of which the present situation is a continuation ("memory incubating the spilled blood"). But he is told to retain his power of vision and to go on writing:

It said, "Lie down
in the word-hoard, burrow
the coil and the gleam
of your furrowed brain.

Compose in darkness.
Expect aurora borealis
in the long foray
but no cascade of light.

Keep your eye clear
as the bleb of the icicle,
trust the feel of what nubbed treasure
your hands have known."

The poem **"Viking Dublin: Trial Pieces"** is one long
flowing line of associations, starting at the sight of a piece
of incised bone exhibited in the National Museum in
Dublin, and involving history and art and death, in language that implies a gay acceptance:

"Did you ever hear tell,"
said Jimmy Farrell,
"of the skulls they have
in the city of Dublin?

White skulls and black skulls
and yellow skulls, and some
with full teeth, and some
haven't only but one,"

In **"Bone Dreams,"** as in the poem **"Toome"** in *Wintering
Out*, the poet goes back to origins which lie beyond language:

Come back past
philology and kennings,
re-enter memory
where the bone's lair

is a love-nest
in the grass.
I hold my lady's head
like a crystal

and ossify myself
by gazing: I am screes
on her escarpments,
a chalk giant

carved upon her downs.
Soon my hands, on the sunken
fosse of her spine
move towards the passes.

In **"Funeral Rites"** Heaney imagined a community and
a ritual for the community; in the series of poems about
bog corpses he turns to communion with the landscape,
and what is concealed there, in private meditation, in
order to come to terms with the violence in Ireland.
The tone of these poems is much more assured than in
"The Tollund Man" in *Wintering Out*. Heaney has now
found a focus for his imagination, a myth which encompasses past and present. The intimate communing with
these preserved bodies leads to an almost complete identification:

I can feel the tug
of the halter at the nape
of her neck, the wind
on her naked front.

But in the same poem (**"Punishment"**) Heaney admits to
an ambiguity of feeling:

I almost love you
but would have cast, I know,
the stones of silence.
I am the artful voyeur

of your brain's exposed
and darkened combs,
your muscles' webbing
and all your numbered bones:

I who have stood dumb
when your betraying sisters,
cauled in tar,
wept by the railings,

who could connive
in civilized outrage
yet understand the exact
and tribal, intimate revenge.

Though these poems contain references to the present
situation in Ireland, they can also be read as poems about
the universal fate of man:

As if he had been poured
in tar, he lies
on a pillow of turf
and seems to weep

the black river of himself.

The bog is not only a symbol for Ireland as a female
goddess to whom sacrifices are made, but also the "all-
tombing womb" of the earth-mother where the bog corpses
lie buried like embryos awaiting rebirth. These poems
may express an unwillingness on Heaney's part to come
to terms with the situation in Northern Ireland in more
direct terms, but they may equally stem from a private
need to come to terms with universals. The poem **"Kinship"**
is a kind of finale which gathers up the images of the bog
that have occurred in Heaney's poetry. It contains references
to earlier poems, and there is a kind of ritual summing
up:

Earth-pantry, bone-vault,
sun-bank, embalmer
of votive goods
and sabred fugitives.

Insatiable bride.
Sword-swallower,
casket, midden,
floe of history.

Ground that will strip
its dark side,
nesting ground,
outback of my mind.

Walking down the bog the poet walks back in time and stands "at the edge of centuries / facing a goddess"—the earth-goddess of Irish history and of time. In the poem **"Bogland"** in *Door into the Dark* the "wet centre" of the bog was "bottomless". Here the centre has gathered meaning, and "holds and spreads"; it has revealed the congruence between present and past, and given an image of the country's cultural identity. The poet accepts being tied to this ground, which means an acceptance of the culture of which he is a member, and of history and fate:

> I grew out of all this
> like a weeping willow
> inclined to
> the appetites of gravity.

In the second part of *North* Heaney turns from Norse mythology to the actual North of Ireland and a more public kind of poetry:

> I'm writing just after an encounter
> With an English journalist in search of "views
> On the Irish thing".

The style has changed from the heightened to the satiric and the debunking with stanzas rhyming a-b-a-b:

> Yet I live here, I live here too, I sing,
>
> Expertly civil tongued with civil neighbours
> On the high wires of first wireless reports,
> Sucking the fake taste, the stony flavours
> Of those sanctioned, old, elaborate retorts:
>
> "Oh, it's disgraceful, surely, I agree,"
> "Where's it going to end?" "It's getting worse."
> "They're murderers." "Internment, understandably . . ."
>
> The "voice of sanity" is getting hoarse.

"Whatever you say, say nothing" is like **"The Other Side"** in *Wintering Out*, about rituals of co-existence between the two communities, which imply submitting to a code:

> "Religion's never mentioned here," of course.
> "You know them by their eyes," and hold your
>   tongue.
> "One side's as bad as the other," never worse.
> Christ, it's near time that some small leak was
>   sprung
>
> In the great dykes the Dutchman made
> To dam the dangerous tide that followed Seamus.
> Yet for all this art and sedentary trade
> I am incapable. The famous
>
> Northern reticence, the tight gag of place
> And times: yes, yes. Of the "wee six" I sing
> Where to be saved you only must save face
> And whatever you say, you say nothing.

It is also a poem about different kinds of language: the language of codes of the community, the clichés of journalism ("escalate", "backlash", "crack-down") and the language of poetry, all inadequate to cope with the situation:

> (It's tempting here to rhyme on "labour pangs"
> And diagnose a rebirth in our plight
> But that would be to ignore other symptoms.
>
> Last night you didn't need a stethoscope
> To hear the eructation of Orange drums
> Allergic equally to Pearse and Pope.)
>
> On all sides "little platoons" are mustering—
> The phrase is Cruise O'Brien's via that great
> Backlash, Burke—while I sit here with a pestering
> Drouth for words at once both gaff and bait
>
> To lure the tribal shoals to epigram
> An order. I believe any of us
> Could draw the line through bigotry and sham
> Given the right line, *aere perennius*.

"Freedman" is about the poet's emancipation from submission to religion and society, and yet another kind of language ("Memento homo quia pulvis es") to the freedom that poetry has given him. It precedes the sequence **"Singing School"** where Heaney returns to autobiographical material, but in a very different way than in *Death of a Naturalist*. The landscape is now peopled by policemen and Orangemen instead of local characters. The quotation from Wordsworth "Fair seedtime had my soul, and I grew up / Fostered alike by beauty and by fear" gets another poignant meaning in a Northern Irish context, where one's name assigns one to one side of the community and where a representative of the law, or the threatening sound of Orange drums, inspire one with fear. **"Summer 1969"** (a summer in which trouble broke out in Belfast) is again about the need for myth or art to come to terms with present happenings. At a remove from the actual situations, watching television during a holiday in Spain, and hearing the news from home, the poet retreats to the Prado to look at **"Shootings of the Third of May,"** a painting by Goya, which is a more real representation of violence than the impersonal "real thing" on television. According to this poem the only possible commitment is through art, though it also suggests the other possibility:

> "Go back," one said, "try to touch the people."
> Another conjured Lorca from his hill.

In the next poem **"Exposure,"** the last in the volume, neither possibility offers solace. The poet is removed from his people—unlike in the first poem of the second part, **"The Unacknowledged Legislator's Dream,"** where the poet sees himself in a dream at the centre of his community and poetry has also lost its meaning:

> How did I end up like this?
> I often think of my friends'
> Beautiful prismatic counselling
> And the anvil brains of some who hate me

As I sit weighing and weighing
My responsible *tristia*.
For what? For the ear? For the people?
For what is said behind-backs?

Rain comes down through the alders,
Its low conducive voices
Mutter about let-downs and erosions
And yet each drop recalls

The diamond absolutes.
I am neither internee nor informer;
An inner émigré, grown long-haired
And thoughtful; a wood-kerne

Escaped from the massacre,
Taking protective colouring
From bole and bark, feeling
Every wind that blows;

Who, blowing up these sparks
For their meagre heat, have missed
The once-in-a-lifetime portent,
The comet's pulsing rose.

This seems like an ending but more likely points to a different direction in Heaney's development. He has talked about this in an interview with Monie Begley [in *Ramble in Ireland,* 1977]:

> The book ends up in Wicklow in December '73. It's in some ways the book all books were leading to. You end up with nothing but your vocation, with words and your own free choice. Isolated but not dispossessed of what produced you. Having left a context, stepped away, you can't really go back. It ends up with just the responsibility of the artist, whatever that is, and that responsibility has no solutions.

> I would say that I am a product of that isolation we were talking about before. And for me now it's just the usual middle-age coasting toward extinction, but trying to define the self. I'm not interested in my poetry canvassing public events deliberately any more. I would like to write poems of myself at this age. Poems, so far, have been fueled by a world that is gone or a world that is too much with us—public events. Just through accident and all the things we've been talking about, I've ended up with myself, and I have to start there, you know.

Alan Shapiro (essay date 1984)

SOURCE: "Crossed Pieties," in *Parnassus: Poetry in Review,* Vol. XI, No. 2, Spring-Summer, 1984, pp. 336-48.

[*In the following review of Heaney's two volumes of collected poetry and prose, Shapiro relates the stylistic and thematic development of Heaney's poetry to his assertion of personal and national identity.*]

There's an old Gaelic poem which goes, "Who ever heard/ Such a sight unsung/ As a severed head/ With a grafted tongue." This image—of a culture severed from the body of its own traditions and forced to speak another language—indicates the profound dilemma facing every Anglo-Irish poet fated to discover and express in English, the oppressor's tongue, his personal and national identity. One might even say that this identity resides, if anywhere, in the hyphen separating the Anglo from the Irish. Pulled in one direction by the English literary tradition, pulled in another by a social and political tradition which continues its centuries-old antagonism to all things English, the Irish poet finds himself inescapably involved in a bleak and unromantic triangle: if Irish culture is his wife, English is his mistress, and to satisfy one is necessarily to betray the other. And yet it is precisely in the Irish poet's response to this dilemma, in the thematic and stylistic strategies he devises to maintain his own identity in the oppressor's language, that one can find in Anglo-Irish poetry what seems distinctly Irish.

No contemporary Irish poet has struggled with this problem more self-consciously, or more successfully, than Seamus Heaney. In both *Preoccupations,* his recently collected essays and reviews, and in his first four books of poetry now published together under the title, *Poems: 1965-1975,* these tensions and crossed pieties inherent in Irish poetry are what preoccupy him most. In one essay he defines the role of poetry "as divination . . . as revelation of the self to the self, as restoration of the culture to itself." He desires a poetry of place and origins, of connection to the Irish past, and of almost sacramental fidelity to the physical contours of the Irish present. In his first two books, *Death Of A Naturalist* and *Door Into The Dark,* Heaney attempts to satisfy this desire by writing almost exclusively of regional life and work, of hunting, blackberry picking, turfgathering, and of the various ways "living displaces false sentiments" in the rural world. The characters he's drawn to—thatchers, diviners, farmwives, and fishermen—embody continuity with the past, seem to bear or affirm the past in what they do. In one poem, he sees in laborers gathering potatoes ("Heads bow, trunks bend, hands fumble toward the black/ Mother") "centuries of fear and homage to the famine God." In another, he calls the door into a blacksmith's shop "a door into the dark"; and though the dark is actual, it also becomes a figure for an older way of life, as later in the poem the blacksmith, standing in the doorway, "recalls/ A clatter of hoofs where traffic is flashing in rows/ Then, grunts and goes in," turning his back on the present.

Unlike the blacksmith, however, Heaney moves in two ways in these poems, turning, as he says in one essay, outward to the present, "to a clarification of life," as well as inward, "to a ramification of roots and associations." Yet in neither movement does he succeed in articulating an indigenous poetic idiom. And I think we can find the reasons for this failure in **"Digging,"** the opening poem of *Death Of A Naturalist,* and the first poem in which Heaney claims to have gotten his feelings into words, "or, to put it more accurately, where I thought my feeling got into words." **"Digging"** defines the kind of poetry the beginning Irish poet wants to write. Sitting by a window, he hears his father digging turf outside in the same way his grandfather dug turf twenty years earlier, and the two figures, one real, the other recollected, merge into an image of continuity:

> Nicking and slicing neatly, heaving sods
> Over his shoulder, going down and down
> For the good turf. Digging.
>
> The cold smell of potato mould, the squelch and
>   slap
> Of soggy peat, the curt cuts of an edge
> Through living roots awaken in my head.

Yet realizing he has "no spade to follow men like that," he says, "Between my finger and thumb/ The squat pen rests./ I'll dig with it." **"Digging"** bears all the earmarks of a Heaney poem, the qualities for which he's justly admired: an intense regard for metaphor, a dense specificity of detail, and a rich evocation of place. Descriptive language, here and throughout his work, is his most effective way of preserving his own identity and at the same time asserting his regional allegiance.

Yet one feels that Heaney protests too much in **"Digging,"** as though the bold, untroubled confidence—"I'll dig with it"—belies an underlying fear that in writing poetry he'll be departing, rather than continuing, the family (and cultural) tradition. He evades this fear, I think, refraining from making it part of the subject, by the very qualities we admire. Description enables Heaney to sidestep the difficulties inherent in this enterprise. For despite his desire to restore "the culture to itself," the principal influences on his early work are American and English as much as Irish. Along with the Irish poet Patrick Kavanagh, poets such as Wordsworth, Hopkins, Frost, and Ted Hughes (some of whom he writes about at length in *Preoccupations*) stand behind his first two books. Kavanagh may influence what he chooses to articulate, that is, a close, unromantic attention to rural life, but it is the American and English poets who influence the manner of articulation. It is difficult, for instance, not to hear Wyatt's "My Galley Charged With Forgetfulness" in these lines from **"Valediction,"** a poem from *Death Of A Naturalist*:

> . . . In your presence
> Time rode easy, anchored
> On a smile; but absence
> Rocked love's balance, unmoored
> The days . . .
>   Need breaks on my strand;
> You've gone, I am at sea.
> Until you resume command
> Self is in mutiny.

Or Frost's "For Once, Then, Something" in these lines from the personal **"Helicon"**:

> As a child, they could not keep me from wells
> And old pumps with buckets and windlasses.

I loved the dark drop, the trapped sky, the smells
Of waterweed, fungus and dank moss. . . .

> Now, to pry into roots, to finger slime
> To stare, big-eyed Narcissus, into some spring
> Is beneath all adult dignity. I rhyme
> To see myself, to set the darkness echoing.

More than the darkness echoes in this poem. Considering that many poets learn to write by imitating the best poems in the language, and that the best poems in English are not all by Irishmen, it's no wonder that Heaney's early poems, impressive as they are, are mostly apprentice pieces.

In one essay, Heaney distinguishes between craft and technique. "Craft," he says, "is what you can learn from other verse. Craft is the skill of making. . . . Technique," on the other hand, "involves not only a poet's way with words, his management of meter, rhythm and verbal texture, it involves also a definition of his stance toward life, a definition of his own reality." If we associate technique with Heaney's Irish loyalties, his passionate regionalism, and craft with his English literary training, we can say that what characterizes these early poems is a craft at odds with and insufficient for the full expression of a burgeoning technique. This tension between craft and technique accounts for the formal awkwardness of many of these poems, for Heaney's compulsion to swim too hard against the iambic current.

Two blank verse poems, **"For The Commander Of The Eliza"** and **"Death Of A Naturalist,"** illustrate my point. Set in the mid-nineteenth century during the Irish potato famine, **"For The Commander Of The Eliza"** is a dramatic monologue spoken by an English sea captain who comes upon a boatload of starving Irish peasants and refuses to give them aid. Because the speaker is English, Heaney can let him speak a clean blank verse line with little rhythmical variation. Even when the variations do occur, the iambic cadence still rings clear:

> We'd known about the shortage but on board
> They always kept us right with flour and beef
> So understand my feelings, and the men's
> Who had mandate to relieve distress
> Since relief was then available in Westport—
> Though clearly these poor brutes would never make
>   it . . .
>
> Next day, like six bad smells, those living skulls
> Drifted through the dark of bunks and hatches
> And once in port I exorcised my ship
> Reporting all to the Inspector General . . .

In addition to the emphatic meter, the almost complete absence of grammatical pauses within the line increases the sense of regularity and restraint appropriate to the speaker's strained attempt to keep his guilt in check as he clumsily rationalizes his refusal to help the poor.

If **"For The Commander Of The Eliza"** is hyper-metrical, **"Death Of A Naturalist"** isn't metrical enough. The verse is heavily varied because Heaney himself is speaking, not an English persona:

> All year the flax-dam festered in the heart
> Of the townland; green and heavy headed
> Flax had rotted there, weighted down by huge sods.
> Daily it sweltered in the punishing sun.
> Bubbles gargled delicately, bluebottles
> Wove a strong gauze of sound around the smell.
> There were dragon-flies, spotted butterflies,
> But best of all was the warm thick slobber
> Of frogspawn that grew like clotted water
> In the shade of the banks. Here, every spring
> I would fill jampotfuls of the jellied
> Specks to range on window-sills at home,
> On shelves at school, and wait and watch until
> The fattening dots burst into nimble-
> Swimming tadpoles . . .

This is a poem about the loss of innocence and the realization of the presence of evil in the natural world and, by implication, in the self. One day the speaker finds that "the angry frogs" had "invaded" the flax dam:

>   . . . I ducked through hedges
> To a coarse croaking that I had not heard
> Before. The air was thick with a bass chorus.
> Right down the dam gross bellied frogs were
>   cocked
> On sods; their loose necks pulsed like sails. Some
>   hopped.
> The slap and plop were obscene threats. Some sat
> Poised like mud grenades, their blunt heads farting,
> I sickened, turned and ran. The great slime kings
> Were gathered there for vengeance and I knew
> That if I dipped my hand the spawn would clutch
>   it.

In overall design and tone this incident recalls the boat-stealing episode in "The Prelude." "The great slime kings" are Heaney's version of Wordsworth's "huge peak, black and huge." Like Wordsworth, out of a troubled conscience Heaney attributes a sense of retribution to the natural scene. But the blank verse is anything but Wordsworthian. Heaney thickens the pentameter line with heavy syllables to the point of clotting ("Flax had rotted there, weighted down by huge sods"), and dense, figurative language ("Poised like mud grenades, their blunt heads farting"). He remains close enough to the iambic norm to keep it as constant expectation, but one he continually disappoints. He reminds us, in other words, that he's writing blank verse only to dramatize his independence from the tradition that blank verse implicates. The result is that his subject has to fight against the form; that is, the formal properties seldom issue from or respond to what he's trying to say. And this flaw applies, I think, to much of Heaney's accentual-syllabic verse, early and late. It's not that he's incapable of writing a passage of regular blank verse, as the passage from **"For The Commander Of The Eliza"** demonstrates. Rather, Heaney feels compelled by his Irish pieties to break or maim the formal elements, even if it means writing awkwardly, in order to assert his own identity.

In the essay "Belfast," Heaney discusses this divided consciousness; in his terms, poetry emerges from a quarrel with the self, a quarrel that's both national and sexual: "The feminine element for me involves the matter of Ireland, and the masculine strain is drawn from the involvement with English literature. . . . I was symbolically placed between the marks of English influence and the lure of the native experience, between 'the demesne' and 'the bogs.'" With this quotation in mind, it is possible to read two related poems, **"Antaeus"** and **"Hercules and Antaeus"** (from his fourth book, *North*), as acting out this quarrel in his work between the Irish and the English influences, which is to say, between his Irish technique and his English craft. In **"Antaeus,"** written actually in 1966, the year *Death Of A Naturalist* was published, Antaeus describes himself as nursed by "earth's long contour/ her river-veins," "cradled in the dark that wombed me/ and nurtured me in every artery/ like a small hillock." Antaeus represents the native culture, the indigenous experience, whose power depends entirely on contact with the earth or region that nurtured him:

> Let each new hero come
> Seeking the golden apples and Atlas.
> He must wrestle with me before he pass
>   Into the realm of fame
>   Among sky-born and royal:
> He may well throw me and renew my birth
> But let him not plan, lifting me off the earth,
>   My elevation, my fall.

The tone here is as innocently confident as the tone of **"Digging,"** but it's qualified, as the tone of **"Digging"** isn't, by what we know will happen to the giant. If Antaeus is the spirit of native culture, Hercules in **"Hercules and Antaeus"** is a figure for "the masculine strain" within the poet "drawn from involvement with English literature":

> Antaeus, the mould-hugger,
>
> is weaned at last:
> a fall was a renewal
> but now he is raised up—
> the challenger's intelligence
>
> is a spur of light,
> a blue prong grasping him
> out of his element
> into a dream of loss
>
> and origins—the cradling dark,
> the river-veins, the secret gullies
> of his strength,
> the hatching grounds
>
> of cave and souterrain,
> he has bequeathed it all
> to elegists. Balor will die
> and byrthnoth and Sitting Bull.

Just as the English once subdued the Irish, the Herculean poet vanquishes his own experience in writing about it, destroying its terrestrial power "into a dream of loss . . . pap for the dispossessed."

"**Antaeus**" is not as full a treatment of this quarrel as "**Hercules and Antaeus.**" For one thing, the hero does not figure in the poem, and so the giant's faith in his native strength is as yet untested. For another, the poem suffers, as most of Heaney's early work does, from being the product of a literary tradition at odds with his passion for locale and place. In terms of craft, "**Antaeus**" is already vanquished by his anticipated adversary, despite the boast that he can beat all challengers. The enforced variety of rhymes (some hardly rhymes at all) betray how hard the poet has to strain to find them. And the antithesis which closes the poem, "My elevation, my fall," makes Antaeus sound more like an Augustan poet than a regional spirit.

On the other hand, though the giant is defeated in "**Hercules and Antaeus,**" in terms of form and phrasing the poem is itself a kind of triumph. Part of the reason is that Heaney by this time has moved to a short free verse line which allows him more freedom in drawing the syntax through the poem. In "**Antaeus,**" the line breaks are dictated by the form and meter, not by the meaning. Here they dramatize the action and emotion of the poem. And in so doing they realize the two senses of the word 'verse,' which Heaney cites in his essay on Wordsworth's music: "'Verse' comes from the Latin *versus* which could mean a line of poetry but could also mean the turn that a ploughman made at the head of the field as he finished one furrow and faced back into another." In "**Hercules and Antaeus**" the syntax turns expressively from line to line. This is especially true in the break between the third and fourth stanzas ("into a dream of loss/ and origins") which not only emphasizes Hercules' triumph as he lifts Antaeus off the ground, "out of his element," but also acts out the severing from origins that the lines describe.

In "Belfast" (quoted earlier), Heaney says that he thinks of "the personal and Irish pieties as vowels, and the literary awareness nourished on English as consonants." One can hear and see this distinction effectively yet unobstrusively at work in the two names, Hercules and Antaeus, as well as in the way Heaney associates the hard consonants with Hercules ("Snake-chocker, dung heaver"), and the softer vowels and assonances with Antaeus ("the secret gullies/ of his strength,/ the hatching grounds/ of cave and souterrain"). This is further reason for reading "**Hercules and Antaeus**" as an oblique comment on Heaney's practice as a poet, on the English and Irish tensions in his work, as much as a political allegory.

I have gone on at length about these two poems because they illustrate what happens when Heaney changes from traditional form to free verse, a change which first takes place in *Door Into The Dark*, his second book. It is by no means an exclusive change or a conversion, for Heaney continues to write in form; but his best poems, the ones that come closest to perfecting a personal and Irish idiom, are written in the short, dense free verse line. Free verse seems to liberate Heaney from the stylistic self-consciousness that burdens his formal work; it enables him to get free of the compulsion to smudge or crack the English lens, instead of seeing through it. And the reason is, obviously, that free verse does not bear as much traditional connotation and influence as the accentual syllabic line; it becomes, for him, a more pliable instrument, more responsive to his temperament and to his desire to articulate the lore of native life. It's not surprising then that his first fully achieved free verse poem, the last poem in *Door Into The Dark*, "Bogland," is about the bog as a distinctly Irish symbol of geographical memory, bearing and preserving within itself the Irish past:

> We have no prairies
> To slice a big sun at evening—
> Everywhere the eye concedes to
> Encroaching horizon,
>
> Is wooed into the cyclops' eye
> Of a tarn. Our unfenced country
> Is bog that keeps crusting
> Between the sights of the sun.
>
> They've taken the skeleton
> Of the Great Irish Elk
> Out of the peat, set it up
> An astounding crate of air.
>
> Butter sunk under
> More than a hundred years
> Was recovered salty and white.
> The ground itself is kind, black butter
>
> Melting and opening underfoot,
> Missing its last definition
> By millions of years.
> They'll never dig coal here,
>
> Only the waterlogged trunks
> Of great firs, soft as pulp.
> Our pioneers keep striking
> Inwards and downwards,
>
> Every layer they strip
> Seems camped on before.
> The bogholes might be Atlantic seepage.
> The wet centre is bottomless.

In addition to the usual evocative detail, there's much to praise here: the way the rhythm quickens and slows in response to what's described, as light syllables give way to heavy ones ("Melting and opening underfoot" "The waterlogged trunks/ Of great firs, soft as pulp"); the way the line breaks here and there quietly dramatize the sense ("Our pioneers keep striking/ Inwards and downwards/ Every layer they strip/ Seems camped on before"); or the way the last line ends on such lightly stressed syllables that the line produces the very sensation of bottomlessness that it presents.

"**Bogland**" is, I would argue, the decisive poem in Heaney's collection, for the best poems in *Wintering Out* and *North*, his next two books, grow naturally, without awkwardness, out of its implied equation between land-scape and mind. In **Wintering Out** especially, place and language seem almost interchangeable, as language is seen as shaped and nurtured by the soil and weather, inflected by the contours of the land itself. If the river Moyola in **"Gifts of Rain"** is a metaphorical statement about language ("an old chanter/ breathing its mists/ through vowels and history/ . . . hoarder of common ground"), the act of speaking in **"Toome"** becomes the penetration of a landscape ("My mouth/ holds round/ the soft blastings/ *Toome, Toome,/* as under the dislodged slab of the tongue/ I push into souterrain"), just as in **"Anahorish,"** Heaney's "place of clear water" turns into a "soft gradient/ of consonant, vowel-meadow." In almost imagist fashion, language and landscape interanimate each other, so much so that to explore one is inevitably to discover something about the other. It is as if despite a history of dispossession and political oppression, as in Hardy's "In Time of 'The Breaking Of Nations'" the land provides a source of enduring value, is itself the figurative and literal origin of culture (in all senses of the word), transcending yet authenticating the language of the tribe.

Descriptive language, here and throughout his work, is Heaney's most effective way of preserving his own identity and at the same time asserting his regional allegiance.

—Alan Shapiro

Not surprisingly, in **"The Tollund Man,"** Heaney's most compelling exploration into the Irish past and its relation to the Irish present, what symbolizes the Celtic past, its legacy of violence, and its tradition of political martydom still painfully alive today, is the severed head of a man killed and dumped in a Jutland bog as a sacrificial offering to the Mother Goddess. And perhaps it's not too far-fetched to see **"The Tollund Man"** as also symbolizing the plight of the Irish poet. Heaney would pray to this severed head, as to a Saint, "To make germinate/ The scattered, ambushed/ Flesh of labourers,/ Stockinged corpses/ Laid out in the farmyards":

> Something of his sad freedom
> As he rode the tumbril
> Should come to me, driving,
> Saying the names
>
> Tollund, Grauballe, Nebelgard,
> Watching the pointing hands
> Of country people,
> Not knowing their tongues.
>
> Out there in Jutland
> In the old man-killing parishes
> I will feel lost,
> Unhappy and at home.

"The Tollund Man" does for Irish culture what in one essay Heaney claims for Patrick Kavanagh's "Great Hunger": it satisfies "the hunger of the culture for its own image and expression." The image, however, is by no means a consoling one; though Heaney would feel at home standing before it, he would, in essence, feel at home in loss, in "the old man-killing parishes." Yet despite the unflinching acknowledgement of violence and dispossession, there is something genuinely consoling in the articulation itself, in the ability of the intelligence to face up to and define the barbarism that persists within the psyche and the culture, just as it was once preserved within the bog.

In **North**, Heaney continues his free verse investigation into the stratified layers of the Irish past, "Striking inwards and downwards." As in **"The Tollund Man,"** the memories he unearths are never comforting, nor is his relationship or kinship with the past a simple one. If poetry involves the restoration of the culture to itself, what he restores are images of atrocity and sectarian violence predating the English invasion. **"The Grauballe Man,"** for instance, now perfected in Heaney's memory (which like the bog transforms and preserves what it contains) "is hung in the scales/ with beauty and atrocity/ . . . with the actual weight/ of each hooded victim/ slashed and dumped." Though he still regards the bog with an almost sexual love, "the Goddess Mother" is also implicated in the violence she preserves, mingling the erotic and the violent, "the love seat" and "the grave," as though human sexuality and violence were merely the animation of principles at work within the physical world. In one line Heaney can declare, "I love the spring/ off the ground," and in next, "Each bank a gallows drop." In **"Kinship,"** the bog is "insatiable bride./ Sword swallower,/ casket, midden." "Our mother ground," he tells us in another section of the poem, "is sour with the blood/ of her faithful,/ they lie gargling/ in her sacred heart." Here as in many of the poems in **North**, it is difficult to distinguish the tone of bitter disgust from that of reverence.

This ambivalence accounts for the undeniable power of the best poems in the book (**"Punishment," "Hercules and Antaeus,"** and **"Funeral Rites"**—perhaps the best political poem since Yeats's "Easter 1916"). It also accounts for why **North** seems less successful as a whole than **Wintering Out**. Many of these poems are damaged by qualities we might be at first inclined to praise: a dazzling metaphoric ingenuity, a profoundly sensuous regard for language, and a fastidious attention to the physical world. I suggested earlier that this richness of descriptive language is one strategy by which Heaney can assert his personal identity and at the same time remain faithful to his national one. Description, in other words, functions as a kind of safeguard against the English elements of his literary heritage. In **North**, however, description takes on the aura of theatricality, a stage-Irish flaunting of his powers, not a legitimate use of them. It no longer serves to keep in check the English influence; it protects him, rather, from the legacy of violence he finds within his national past (and present). It is almost as if Heaney attempts to resolve his complicated attitude, his fascination and repulsion, stylistically through the dazzle of descriptive language; but the language only sanitizes the violence it appears to articulate so unflinchingly.

Consider, for instance, how the phrase "the mild pods of the eye-lids," from **"The Tollund Man,"** does more than just describe or beautify the subject. Once we recall that the Tollund Man was sacrificed to the Mother Goddess in order to insure the renewal and fertility of spring, we realize that the simile sets up and justifies Heaney's later prayer to him "to make germinate" (within Heaney's imagination) "the scattered, ambushed/ Flesh of labourers." In contrast, these lines from **"The Grauballe Man"**— "As if he had been poured/ in tar, he lies on a pillow of turf/ and seems to weep/ the black river of himself"—or these lines from **"The Bog Queen"**—"My body was braille for the creeping influences"—seem like a mere display, demonstrating what W. S. Di Piero has called "a too exclusive attention to the sheen and noise of language, such that flamboyance and inventiveness, however sincere and in service to however serious a theme, come to displace clarity and integrity of feeling." Even the language/ landscape trope begins to sound a little overdone ("I push back,/ through dictions,/ Elizabethan Canopies./ Norman devices,/ the erotic mayflowers/ of Provence." "This is the vowel of earth/ dreaming its root"). What once had the freshness and excitement of discovery in *Wintering Out* takes on in *North* the stale predictability of mannerism, whose function is to shield Heaney from, by prettifying, the realities it once enabled him to explore.

A harsh judgment. But having made it, I now want to add that only a poet of major talent can err so skillfully. Even when he is not at his best, Heaney remains an engaging and serious poet, capable of working the language with an intensity we would be quick to praise in a lesser poet's work. Part of this capability derives from sheer talent; but perhaps a more important part derives from native talent responding to the pressures of social and political circumstances, to the crossed pieties inherent inthe very language Heaney speaks and writes with. If these pressures sometimes cause Heaney to work the language too intensely until, in the words of the neo-Augustan critic, Archibald Alison, he deserts "the end of the art, for the display of the art itself," they also give his best work an intelligent urgency (and I stress both words here) that no other poet writing in English today can equal. In *Poems: 1965-1975* and *Preoccupations,* as well as in his fifth collection of poetry, *Field Work,* Heaney struggles honestly and often brilliantly to satisfy "the hunger of the culture for its own image and expression." His best poems— **"Bogland," "The Tollund Man," "Funeral Rites," "Punishment"** and **"Casualty"** (from *Field Work*)—satisfy that hunger. And not just for the Irish, but for all of us who look to poetry for a clarification of life.

Helen Vendler (review date 1985)

SOURCE: A review of *Station Island,* in *The New Yorker,* Vol. LXI, No. 31, September 23, 1985, pp. 108, 111-12, 114-16.

[*In the following excerpt, Vendler examines the major themes of Heaney's* Station Island.]

Station Island, also known as St. Patrick's Purgatory, is an island in Lough Derg, in northwest Ireland. It has been a site of pilgrimage for centuries; tradition says that St. Patrick once fasted and prayed there. The island gives its name to Seamus Heaney's purgatorial new collection, containing five years' work—*Station Island.* The book reflects the disquiet of an uprooted life—one of successive dislocations. Heaney's life began in Castledawson, in Northern Ireland; he was educated at St. Columb's College, in Derry, and then at Queen's University, Belfast (where he later taught); he moved in 1972 to the Republic of Ireland, first to Wicklow and later to Dublin, free-lancing and teaching. A stint of teaching at Berkeley, from 1970 to 1971, began his acquaintance with the United States; now he is the Boylston Professor of Rhetoric and Oratory at Harvard, and divides his time between Cambridge and Dublin. Though these dislocations and uprootings have been voluntary, they could not be without effect, and the title poem of the new volume reviews, in a series of memorial encounters, the "stations" of Heaney's life— especially that of his adolescence, hitherto scanted in his work. The poet moves amid a cloud of ghosts, familial, sexual, and professional. Some are admonitory, some reproachful, some encouraging. These spirits appear and disappear after the manner of Dante's purgatorial shades, as the fiction of the poem brings Heaney as one penitent among a crowd of pilgrims to Station Island, where he stays for the obligatory three-day ritual—fasting, sleeping in a dormitory, attending services at the basilica, walking barefoot round the circular stone "beds," or foundations of ruined monastic beehive cells. The difference between Heaney and the other penitents is that he is no longer a believer. One of the shades, a young priest, accuses him:

> "What are you doing here?
>
> . . . All this you were clear of you walked
>   into
> over again. And the god has, as they say,
>   withdrawn.
> What are you doing, going through these
>   motions?
> Unless . . . Unless . . ." Again he was short
>   of breath
> and his whole fevered body yellowed and
>   shook.
>
> "Unless you are here taking the last look."

"The last look"—traditionally taken before dying—is not quite what Heaney is up to in this sequence, but he certainly uses the twelve "cantos" of the poem to look back at many of his dead: Simon Sweeney, an old "Sabbathbreaker" from Heaney's childhood; the Irish writer William Carleton (1794-1869), who after he became a Protestant wrote "The Lough Derg Pilgrim," satirizing Catholic superstition; the twentieth-century poet Patrick Kavanagh, who also wrote a poem about the Lough Derg pilgrimage; an invalid relative who died young; the young priest, dead after a few years in the foreign missions; two schoolmasters; the little girl Heaney first felt love for; a college friend shot in his shop by terrorists; an archeologist friend who died young; a cousin murdered by Protestants; an executed Catholic terrorist; a monk who prescribed as penance a translation from John of the Cross; James Joyce. All these characters (with the exception of the invalid young relative) speak to Heaney, and the poem offers a polyphony of admonitions, ranging from the trite ("When you're on the road/give lifts to people, you'll always learn something") to the eloquent—Joyce's advice to the hesitant poet:

> "That subject people stuff is a cod's game,
> infantile, like your peasant pilgrimage.
>
> You lose more of yourself than you
>   redeem
> doing the decent thing. Keep at a tangent.
> When they make the circle wide, it's time
>   to swim
>
> out on your own and fill the element
> with signatures on your own frequency,
> echo soundings, searches, probes, al-
>   lurements,
> elver-gleams in the dark of the whole sea."

More striking than the attributed voices is Heaney's own self-portrait, full of a Chaucerian irony overpainted with Dantesque earnestness. In *Station Island*, Heaney is sometimes (as with Joyce) the abashed apprentice, sometimes (as with his murdered cousin) the guilty survivor, sometimes the penitent turning on himself with hallucinatory self-laceration:

> All seemed to run to waste
> As down a swirl of mucky, glittering flood
> Strange polyp floated like a huge corrupt
> Magnolia bloom, surreal as a shed breast
> My softly awash and blanching self-
>   disgust.

Though the narrative armature of *Station Island* is almost staidly conventional—borrowed from Dante, even down to his traditional words for the appearance and fading of ghosts—the writing often moves out, as in the passage I have just quoted, to the limits of description. Heaney has always had extraordinary descriptive powers—dangerous ones; conscious of the rich, lulling seductions of his early verse, he experiments here in resourceful and daring ways with both the maximizing and the minimizing of description. The dream passage about the corrupt polyp interrupts lushness with the surgical slash of the shed breast; the same typical self-correction can be seen in a passage where William Carleton plays the surgical role interrupting the dreamy language of the poet:

> "The alders in the hedge," I said
>   "mushrooms,
> dark-clumped grass where cows or horses
>   dunged,

> the cluck when pith-lined chestnut shells
>   split open
>
> in your hand, the melt of shells
>   corrupting,
> old jampots in a drain clogged up with
>   mud—"
> But now Carleton was interrupting:
>
> "All this is like a trout kept in a spring
> or maggots sown in wounds—
> another life that cleans our element.
>
> We are earthworms of the earth, and all
>   that
> has gone through us is what will be our
>   trace."
> He turned on his heel when he was saying
>   this
>
> and headed up the road at the same hard
>   pace.

This small sample will do to show why Heaney's lines are not corrupted by pure linguistic revel—as Dylan Thomas's often were, their simpler phonetic indulgence unchecked by astringency. Heaney works, in Yeats' phrase to "articulate sweet sounds together" in ways not cloying to the ear, often restraining his delight in the unforeseen coincidences of language, sometimes allowing the delight to break loose. Under the influence of Lowell, Heaney pruned his young luxuriance severely in some of the poems of *Field Work* (1979). The rapturous lyricism of the early poetry, though neverlost, adapted itself to a worldlier tone, released in *Station Island* into mordant vignettes of Irish social life. Here Heaney describes the ordination of the young priest and his visits back to the parish from the missions:

> Blurred oval prints of newly ordained
>   faces,
> "Father" pronounced with a fawning
>   relish,
> he sunlit tears of parents being blessed.
>
> I met a young priest, glossy as a blackbird
>
>   . . . his polished shoes
> unexpectedly secular beneath
> a pleated, lace-hemmed alb of linen
>   cloth. . . .
> "I'm older now than you when you went
>   away,"
>
> I ventured, feeling a strange reversal.
> "I never could see you on the foreign
>   missions.
> I could only see you on a bicycle,
>
> a clerical student home for the summer
> doomed to the decent thing. Visiting
>   neighbours.

Drinking tea and praising home-made
bread.

Something in them would be ratified
when they saw you at the door in your
    black suit,
arriving like some sort of holy mascot."

The village round sketched here would be familiar to anyone raised in Ireland. Heaney's satiric phrases—"fawning relish," "holy mascot"—defamiliarize the pieties; the sharpness of his eye is matched in such places by sharpness of tongue. A brave exactness in saying the socially unsayable appears in Heaney's epigrammatic summation of the society of his youth. Though the nostalgia for his "first kingdom"—so evident in his earliest poems—is still present, he has added an adult judgment on the deficiencies of its people:

They were two-faced and accommodating.
And seed, breed and generation still
They are holding on, every bit
as pious and exacting and demeaned.

The five adjectives and the four nouns in this passage hold on to their places in the lines as if they were sentinels guarding a fort. They cannot be budged (as anyone can discover by trying to put "two-faced" in the place of "demeaned," or "generation" in the place of "seed"). The words act out the tenaciousness of the Catholics of Northern Ireland, surviving in spite of being—necessarily—"two-faced and accommodating." When words fit together in this embedded way, they make a harsh poetry far from the softer verse of Heaney's youth. It is a poetry aiming not at liquidity but at the solidity of the mason's courses.

At the same time, Heaney's native tendernesses, beautifully realized, ornament his pages. In a typical passage, Heaney as a boy sits in a beech tree, where "the very ivy/ puzzled its milk-tooth frills and tapers/over the grain." In this short spill of words, there are no obvious beauties of alliteration, assonance, rhyming; instead, there is the pure discovery of language adequate to the combination of ivy and bole. What is the right verb for the way ivy moves over a tree trunk? What is the right word for baby ivy leaves? What are the words for their shape and edges? "Its milk-tooth frills and tapers" becomes the reflexive object of the oddly transitive verb "puzzled" as the ivy instinctively plots out its new route and puts out its young delicate sprays and tendrils at the same time. A poet can find such words only by analogy with his own inner life; he feels what it is like when consciousness or perception leafs itself out along a new puzzling path. When he needs a word for the ivy, it comes from his own kinesthetic awareness of the body. Everywhere, Heaney's inner life gives life to outer life, attaching to it the felt inner coursings of physical and mental existence.

In one *ars poetica,* **"The King of the Ditchbacks,"** Heaney describes this uncertain and tentative effort of the poet to track down his inner stirrings and translate them into words that are at the same time adequate for his perception of the external world. The poet, says Heaney, feels his ghostly other—his phenomenological self, one might say—making a track, an unintelligible code, "a dark morse along the bank;" the poet follows:

If I stop
he stops
like the moon.

He lives in his feet
and ears, weather-eyed,
all pad and listening,
a denless mover.

A prose poem continues the relationship:

He was depending on me as I hung out
on the limb of a translated phrase like a
youngster dared out on to an alder branch
over the whirlpool. . . . I remembered I had
been vested for this calling.

Like a priest being ordained, Heaney is vested for the calling of poet in a mysteriously beautiful poem that attempts to exemplify the paradoxical total naturalness and total social estrangement of the office of the poet. He recounts the day of his "sense of election," when he was camouflaged and taken bird hunting:

When I was taken aside that day
I had the sense of election:

they dressed my head in a fishnet
and plaited leafy twigs through meshes

so my vision was a bird's
at the heart of a thicket

and I spoke as I moved
like a voice from a shaking bush.

That day, the hunters catch no birds, but Heaney is urged to return in the fall, "when the gundogs can hardly retrieve/what's brought down." The poet realizes he will return, but not to hunt; rather, he will return in spirit, as a watcher, a disguised Keatsian icon of the harvest:

And I saw myself
rising to move in that dissimulation,

top-knotted, masked in sheaves, noting
the fall of birds: a rich young man

leaving everything he had
for a migrant solitude.

The echo of the Gospel confirms the depth of the election. The elegiac richness of the language argues the aristocracy of the poet's calling, but the memory of the stealthy self, "a denless mover" living in his senses, argues also for the intimacy of this aristocracy with the biological origins of all social forms.

The allusion to the Gospel recurs in the last poem of *Station Island*—"On the Road"—where Heaney recalls "that track through corn/ where the rich young man/ asked his question—/ *Master, what must I/ do to be saved?*" In raising this ultimate question, Heaney asks what all the self-born must ask: If the gods of the parental hearth, the altars of the local church, the teachers of the native schools do not suffice as guardians and mentors, then where is one to turn? This is the central outcry of Heaney's book, and it leads him first into the affronting encounters with family, school, and church which fill the long title poem. But after that it ushers him into a strange and unpopulated realm, which one can only call the space of writing. The refusal of the social plenum leaves the artist empty, but his kingdom becomes the entire scope of consciousness. The significant word "empty" recurs several times in this volume, notably in **"On the Road"**:

> In my hands
> like a wrested trophy,
> the empty round
> of the steering wheel.

The end of the intellectual, emotional, and aesthetic struggle to discard false gods seems to be a far-stretching empti-ness, but it is one in which the steering wheel is in one's own hands, a prize of victory.

"On the Road," seeking a solution to its sense of bewil-derment and depletion, drives itself, finally, to a rock wall incised with a prehistoric carving. There it halts, observing the first, ancient human testimony to the power and strength of form—a form that takes its own inspiration from the contours of its rock matrix:

> There a drinking deer
> is cut into rock,
> its haunch and neck
> rise with the contours,
>
> the incised outline
> curves to a strained
> expectant muzzle
> and a nostril flared
>
> at a dried-up source.

The poet would "meditate/that stone-faced vigil" of the drinking deer

> until the long dumbfounded
> spirit broke cover
> to raise a dust
> in the font of exhaustion.

"Dumbfounded" is one of the words in this volume (others are "bewildered," "defensive," "evasion," "guilty," "com-plaisant," and "emptied") which convey the many confu-sions and fears undergone by any independent mind in defining and defending its own solitude. Against these self-doubts—arising from the social disobedience so nec-essary for art but so disturbing to the hitherto obedient—

are set various phrases of clarity and self-fortification. Some are sensual—"hands at night/ dreaming the sun in the sunspot of a breast." Others are experiential—"we are earthworms of the earth, and all that/ has gone through us is what will be our trace." Still others are aesthetic. In his tribute to Hardy, **"The Birthplace,"** for example, Heaney remembers how as a boy he found in Hardy a writer describing the life he himself was living on an Irish farm. The shock of that first perceived correspondence between life and art closes Heaney's homage:

> Everywhere being nowhere,
> who can prove
> one place more than another?
>
> We come back emptied . . .
>
> Still, was it thirty years ago
> I read until first light
>
> for the first time, to finish
> *The Return of the Native*?
> The corncrake in the aftergrass
>
> verified himself, and I heard
> roosters and dogs, the very same
> as if he had written them.

Poems like **"The Birthplace"** record, as I have said, private moments of sustenance in the wilderness of middle life. This wilderness necessarily includes for Heaney the state of his country, and there are many direct, and some indirect, references here to Heaney's troubled relation to the insol-uble events in Northern Ireland. The dangers of propa-ganda and of loyalties unmediated by intelligence haunt any writer born into historical crisis. Heaney quotes Czeslaw Milosz's "Native Realm": "I was stretched between con-templation of a motionless point and the command to participate actively in history." The contemplation of a motionless point—as one pole of the artist's duty—is reflected here in Heaney's ascetic translation, in the *Station Island* sequence, of a poem by John of the Cross on the dark night of the soul; the command to participate actively in history is reflected in the terse and committed poem **"Chekhov on Sakhalin,"** based on a fragment of Chek-hov's life. In the poem, Chekhov drains a last glass of Moscow cognac after travelling thousands of miles from Moscow, through Siberia, to the island of Sakhalin, be-tween Russia and Japan; the island is a Russian prison colony, and Chekhov is paying his "debt to medicine" by investigating the penal conditions. He forces himself to watch floggings and then leaves to write about them, "to try for the right tone—not tract, not thesis." Chekhov's predicament is that of any poet trying to write about histor-ical conditions, but the deeper truth of the poem appears in the closing lines, in which Chekhov's own origin ("born, you may say, under the counter") compels him to his present expiatory inquiry, and to a perpetual identifica-tion with the convicts:

> He who thought to squeeze
> His slave's blood out and waken the free

man
    Shadowed a convict guide through
       Sakhalin.

For the last twenty years, each of Heaney's books—from *Death of a Naturalist* (1966) through *Station Island*—has exhibited an experimental advance on its predecessors. Without losing his early sensual depth and sympathy, Heaney has added social and political dimensions to his writing. In assimilating the mythical and organic voice of *Door Into the Dark* (1969) to the compelled social voice of *Wintering Out* (1972), with its epigraph on "the new camp for the internees," Heaney assumed a civic relation to his larger society—a position consolidated in *North* (1975), one of the few unforgettable single volumes published in English since the modernist era. In *Field Work*, the formality of Heaney's earlier prosody relaxed into a deft and unassuming phrasal and conversational line—a stylistic consequence of letting the political and social dimensions of life in Northern Ireland invade his adolescent world of nests, aeries, and immemorial agricultural rituals. "I remember writing a letter to Brian Friel just after *North* was published," Heaney once remarked, "saying I no longer wanted a door into the dark—I want a door into the light. . . . I really wanted to come back to be able to use the first person singular to mean *me* and my lifetime."

It is this completed voice that speaks in *Station Island*. When a poet remakes his voice, everything already said has to be said over, in the new, more adequate tonality and diction. The imagination, as long as it remains alive, never ceases to reconsider and to rewrite the past; its poems are circumscribed by the potential adventures of the voice. If a poetic voice lacks volatility and modulation, it cannot be convincing in dramas of volatility and modulation; if it lacks a public dimension, it cannot enunciate public life; if it is wanting in inwardness, it cannot convey private intensity. To attempt a new complexity of voice is to create future possibilities for one's past; and in this volume Heaney has in effect rescanned his past, using the accomplished and complicated voice of his fifth decade. The earliest voice, the limited one inherited from ancestors, will "have to be unlearned":

    even though from there on everything
    is going to be learning.

    So the twine unwinds and loosely widens
    backward through areas that forwarded
    understandings of all I would undertake

Heaney's present voice benefits from his recent work on *Sweeney Astray* (1984), a translation of a medieval Irish poem, "Buile Suibhne," in which Sweeney, an Irish king, is cursed by the priest Ronan, who turns him into a bird. Sweeney's dour and lively voice from the trees is blended with Heaney's own in the group of poems making up the third part of the *Station Island* volume, a sequence called "**Sweeney Redivivus.**" These poems form a dry and almost peremptory autobiography, stunningly different from the warm-fleshed account given in Heaney's early books.

It is difficult to choose among the Sweeney poems, since they so illuminate each other. For a view of Heaney's current hard poetic, one would have to quote his poem on Cézanne, called simply "**An Artist**":

    I love the thought of his anger.
    His obstinacy against the rock, his
      coercion
    of the substance from green apples.

    The way he was a dog barking
    at the image of himself barking.
    And his hatred of his own embrace
    of working as the only thing that
      worked.

For an impression of Sweeney's tart spite—a tone perhaps impossible for Heaney *in propria persona*—one would have to read Sweeney's hatred for the Cleric who, bringing Christianity to Ireland, robbed him of his native ground:

    If he had stuck to his own
    cramp-jawed abbesses and intoners
    dibbling round the enclosure,

    his Latin and blather of love,
    his parchments and scheming
    in letters shipped over water—

    but no, he overbore
    with his unctions and orders,
    he had to get in on the ground.

If one wanted to see Heaney's first moments as a modern writer, the old rural life left behind, one would quote "**Sweeney Redivivus,**" the ironically dissolving title poem of the sequence:

              Another smell
    was blowing off the river, bitter
    as night airs in a scutch mill.
    The old trees were nowhere,
    the hedges thin as penwork
    and the whole enclosure lost
    under hard paths and sharp-ridged houses.

    And there I was, incredible to myself,
    among people far too eager to believe me
    and my story, even if it happened to be
      true.

The fine-edged precision of naming in these poems—the line of the hedges thin as penwork, the hard paths and sharp-ridged houses—has become for Heaney the ethic under which he works. He has written more than once about the "cool" temperature of early Irish verse, contrasting it with the warmer and rounder tones of English poetry; his current effort seems to be directed toward retaining the spareness and chill of the early Irish tonality while not forgoing altogether what he has called "those somewhat hedonistic impulses towards the satisfactions of aural and formal play out of which poems arise."

The "aural and formal play" in these poems is satisfyingly subtle. In **"The First Gloss,"** for instance—the four-line poem opening the Sweeney sequence—the formal decisions are very modest: the rhymes are slant; the second couplet is composed of lines shorter than those of the first. But these formal moves stand for the two themes of the poem—disobedience and independence. Heaney imagines in this quatrain the first scribe who decided to violate a vellum margin with a thought of his own about the sacred word that he was copying:

> Take hold of the shaft of the pen.
> Subscribe to the first step taken
> from a justified line
> into the margin.

In one of his first poems, **"Digging,"** Heaney had imagined his pen as a spade, and had made the work of writing poetry strictly analogous, in the mental sphere, to the physical work of planting and harvesting. This comforting fiction has been supplanted in **"The First Gloss"** by a recognition of the inherent outlawry and heterodoxy in writing—what it entails in the way of departure from socially justified limits and from the self-sufficient sacred word.

Readers who know Heaney's autobiography in verse from previous books will want to retrace it in this verbally firm and assured but psychologically beset and uncertain mid-life recapitulation. Those interested in the social history of Ireland can find here Heaney's visceral account of how things stand, and will notice especially the horrifying record of killings in the title poem, as well as Sweeney's tragicomic satire on cultural life in Ireland. (The *mots justes* for personal and public life, past and present, seem to come to Heaney with the unforced sureness of instinct.) For me, it is not chiefly the autobiography or the cultural history—though each is accurate with a poet's accuracy—that draws me to this book. Rather, it is a poetic handling of language so variable that almost any word, image, or turn of phrase might appear at any moment. In a typical moment, Sweeney gibes at the monks writing in the scriptorium:

> Under the rumps of lettering
> they herded myopic angers.
> Resentment seeded in the uncurling
> fernheads of their capitals.

Rumps and fernheads, herding and seeding, capitals and angers, resentment and myopia—these words from medicine, ethics, husbandry, botany, chirography, psychology jostle each other for position. (Of course, there would be no pleasure in this if the words did not embody as well the metaphorical animus by which Sweeney turns the intellectual scribes into thick-witted herdsmen, demeans their art to a venomous proliferation.) Heaney's voice, by turns mythological and journalistic, rural and sophisticated, reminiscent and impatient, stern and yielding, curt and expansive, is one of a suppleness almost equal to consciousness itself. The two tones he generally avoids—on principle, I imagine, and by temperament—are the pro-phetic and the denunciatory, those standbye of political poetry. It is arresting to find a poetry so conscious of cultural and social facts which nonetheless remains chiefly a poetry of awareness, observation, and sorrow.

Seamus Heaney with June Beisch (interview date 1986)

SOURCE: An interview with Seamus Heaney, in *The Literary Review*, Vol. XXIX, No. 2, Winter, 1986, pp. 161-69.

[*In the following interview, Heaney discusses his writing habits, the origin of* Sweeney Astray, *and the work of other contemporary poets.*]

Seamus Heaney, the poet from Ireland, has just been granted tenure at Harvard. We can all breathe a sigh of relief, now that we now have an important poet in residence (half-time) in Cambridge who is impeccable in his behavior and projects a dignity that students can respect. As a matter of fact, so popular is Heaney with the students that they speak of him with a near-reverence (in spite of the difficulties they have getting into his "limited-enrollment" workshops). His spring lectures, which are held in the auditorium hall at the Science Center, are always filled with admirers, both students and faculty, and a feeling pervades that these comments on poetry will someday be of historical significance. And, true to form, the talks are beautifully crafted, highly informed appraisals of contemporary poets (and coevals of Heaney himself), full of wit and drawn out of his own deep fund of erudition.

Heaney is a difficult poet to get to know. A good-natured, cheerful man, of a muscular, thewy build, his muted persona contrasts sharply with the flamboyance of Irish poets who came before him—poets like Brendan Behan whose excesses in drink and womanizing added to his legendary status. Next to them, Heaney is soft-spoken, modest, and intensely private. Robert Lowell once called him "the greatest Irish poet since Yeats," but he is hardly a Yeatsian figure, either poetically or temperamentally. (Heaney has confided that Yeats, given the opportunity to marry Maude Gonne, wouldn't have known what to do with her.) He is also a man of great ambivalence and contradictions. While dedicated to his native tongue and the advancement of the Irish heritage, he does not want to become a "curiosity" in America himself (i.e., the "Irish" poet). While concerned about his country's political turmoils, he also feels strongly that the role of the artist is to create art, and not to become embroiled in political issues.

But few poets have achieved as much as Heaney at such a young age. He publishes a new book almost yearly, and his last two books of poetry, *Sweeney Astray* and *Station Island*, have been widely praised by critics, who find a new and growing maturity in his work. Heaney, says Blake Morrisson in his biography *Seamus Heaney* (Methuen), manages to confront in his poetry the "simple-minded belief that poems with rural or archaic images aren't engaging to the modern world," and this is a key to much of Heaney's work. Robert Frost once wrote that poetry "began as a lump in the throat, a lovesickness, a homesickness"; it often seems as though Heaney's poetry thrives on his homesickness. Raised on a working farm in Ireland, in love with his native soil (an element he describes as "black butter/ melting and opening underfoot"), he sees the underlying harmony between land and language. In this respect, he has been compared to the pastoral poets, including Wordsworth, who find hidden meanings in the lush, rural landscapes. But with Heaney, there is a sense that the more modest the expression, the closer to silence, the better. Morrisson writes that for Heaney, "language is almost a kind of a betrayal," and this attitude might have derived from acommunity of terse, hard-working Irish people that comprised Heaney's childhood. To them, any kind of a public life was anathema, so when Heaney began to write poetry, he wrote under an alias (Incertus).

Heaney's themes are manifold. Love, religion, mortality, darkness, all are touched upon in his many volumes. Michael Longley, in his *Time* essay on Ulster poetry (March 19, 1984), found Heaney's poem **"Personal Helicon"** to be both credo and manifesto. "I rhyme/ To see myself, to set the darkness echoing." But the second book includes an opening poem, **"Night Piece,"** that probes another kind of darkness:

> Must you know it again?
> Dull pounding through hay
> The uneasy whinny
>
> A sponge lip drawn off each separate tooth
> Opalescent haunch
> Muscle and hoof
>
> Bundled under the roof.

Heaney's life has become increasingly complicated now that he must spend half the year at Harvard and half back in Ireland with his wife Marie and their three children. Although he deplores these complications, some poems seem to arrive out of the exacerbation of his loneliness. In **"The Guttural Muse,"** he describes watching a young crowd from his hotel window over a car park. "A girl in a white dress/ Was being courted out among the cars/ As her voice swarmed and puddled into laughs/ I felt like some old pike all badged with sores/ Wanting to swim in touch with soft-mouthed life."

In another poem, **"The Otter,"** his images are strong:

> I loved your wet head and smashing crawl

and then, at the end of the poem:

> And suddenly, you're out
> Back again, intent as ever,
> Heavy and frisky in your freshened pelt,
> Printing the stones.

and finally, in his poem, **"Oysters,"** we get a sense of what Heaney is aiming for in his poetry: "clear light, like poetry or freedom."

Eating oysters, Heaney's "tongue was a filling estuary/ My palate hung with starlight/ As I tasted the salty Pleiades/ Orion dipped his foot into the water." But, as Heaney eats, he also consumes his experience of the day: "Deliberately, that its tang/ Might quicken me all into verb, pure verb."

Sweeney Astray, Heaney's translation of a medieval Irish myth, was called "exhilarating" by Brendan Kennelly in *The New York Times Book Review* (May 27, 1984). It was the week following this review that I called on Seamus Heaney at Adams House, his residence at Harvard, to talk about *Sweeney Astray* and about poetry.

. . . . .

[BEISCH]: *How do you feel about being here? Could you see yourself living here permanently?*

[HEANEY]: No, I don't see myself settling here. I mean, my fiction is that I'm not really here. And yet this is my fourth year at Harvard, and my third in a row. My home, my house, my den, nevertheless, is in Ireland. There's a great hospitality and generosity in the American academic world, but I don't feel it's my first milieu. If I came here to live, I would be just an "ethnic curiosity."

Does being in another culture provoke something in the way of material for your poems?

Well, I don't know about that. I kind of relish the charge of energy here, but I think it's very difficult to be a writer in this country.

Why do you say that?

Well, because the expectations of the successful writer are too much. I mean, first of all, he's asked to contribute poems everywhere and unless he or she has a very strong sense of his own pace, productivity becomes a danger. Also, just being celebrated by people. There are a lot of readings and that can drag you away from your work.

Your first day in class, you said that the real test for a poet is his ability to "survive his career." Perhaps this is what you're talking about.

Yes.

How much of your normal life have you had to give up for the sake of the commitments around your poetry?

None. I mean, whatever poetry has entailed has *become* normal. Interviews, then, are part of the normality. Alas.

When do you do your writing?

All the time. I don't have a schedule. I wait for times when I'm in a writing mood, and I tend to be a binge writer. I think a lot of people do too much writing. One of my impatiences is with poetry that's well done but doesn't need to be done. I still cling to my first position that a poem is a gift and that it stirs unexpectedly and can't be summoned by the will and that it has an individual genetic life of its own, almost. And without that initial impulse, I can't sit down.

Does the mood become more frequent as you get older?

It's about the same. I get more pleasure from it, now. I prolong it, I work at it longer now.

Tell me a little about **Sweeney Astray***. How did it all begin?*

Well, it began in 1972 when I resigned my teaching job at Queens University in Belfast. I was embracing a schedule of full-time writing and I wanted to have a task that would keep me in work. The thing about lyric poetry is that you have to wait for it, so I thought I needed something at which I could work day by day. And, I'd always had an interest in Sweeney. I'd never looked at the whole text, but I'd seen little stray pieces here and there and the material attracted me. The other thing that the Sweeney poem was—it was a story about displacement. I mean, Sweeney was a Northerner and I had a little bit of identification going on there. I did a version of it in 1972 or 1973 but it was quite free—did not give much obedience to the original text, and it substituted imagery for declaration in places. It took the sense and embellished it, and so when I finished, it was neither one thing nor the other. It wasn't free enough to stand on its own as a reinvention of the text, yet it was too disobedient to stand as a translation. Three-quarters of it, moreover, was free verse and there were these very strictly rhymed pieces also, so I knew I had to come back to it. So I worked on it and it became more faithful to the original in metrical terms and in terms of the line-by-line sense of the thing.

I see Sweeney coming up again in your new book of poems, **Station Island***, in a section called "Sweeney Redivivus."*

Well, he's a mask for some aspects of myself. Twenty poems in *Sweeney Astray*, some of them in his voice and some using his situation. A sense of displacement. He's a point of view, really.

Do you find a lot of newer poets working in forms again?

I see a number of people writing in traditional forms. I don't know whether it's a reaction to free verse or if it's in imitation of poets like Elizabeth Bishop, who was a formal writer and has had a late flowering. James Merrill has had a flourish of presence in the literary moment and he's writing a lot in forms. There is a kind of natural swing that way but I don't think that traditional form for its own sake is necessarily a good thing or a bad thing. I think it has a lot to do with the temperament and imagination of the writer himself or herself. You can't imagine Whitman or D.H. Lawrence fulfilling his imaginative destiny in metrical verse. I mean, Lawrence's rhyming poems are like seeing a man in the wrong outfit.

For a lot of American writers, the true American form is free form and that is an ideological position, so perhaps there is something ideological also about taking up a traditional form. Writers like Robert Pinsky came out of literary training with Yvor Winters where there was an ideology implicit in the use of traditional forms and also a critical attitude implicit in it.

I think the Americans feel the burden of the past more; the sense that it's difficult to surpass what has already been written. They feel they've been less well-educated and are more self-conscious about traditional forms.

Well, I think you learn to write by reading. Reading will influence your notion of what writing should be. And there is so much self-conscious activity in the search for the American poem. You have Williams and the Black Mountain School. I suppose Pound does a big American experiment. All of those ratify the open forms. On the other hand, you have Stevens who is majestic, traditional, a rhetorician, and you have Frost.

In your own private anthology of contemporaries, whom would you include?

Hass and Pinsky over on the West Coast. I liked Pinsky's last book. Frank Bidart seems to be an original. There's a hell of a lot of talent around.

What about breaking new ground?

Well, in Ireland, there's a poet named Paul Muldoon who's very original, and in England there's a new group who've established a new idiom. How deep a furrow it ploughs is another matter. It's a school of metaphorical writing and very laid-back and clever. Craig Raine and James Fenton have been a part of it and it's been described in England as the "Martian School"—all springing from a poem by Craig Raine called "The Martian Sends a Postcard Home," so it's that kind of displaced look at the world.

I think that the writing for the last twenty years in places like Poland—writers like [Zbigniew] Herbert and [Czeslaw] Milosz—people who are involved in a moment of historical crisis—writing that springs from that kind of pressure of being a witness is exciting. And in that respect, I think Derek Walcott has a kind of founding status as the poet for a new culture, a post-colonial situation. He's doing new work in drama and poetry and he's under the same kind of pressure that all emerging cultures are under. To decide whether to build a kind of ethnic barrier, excluding the modes of the colonial culture or to keep the resources of the old imperial master and use them to new effect. I think Walcott's exemplary in that he doesn't throw away any artistic resource, either English or Caribbean. He's been resolute in distinguishing between the ethnic political resentment and the artistic resources.

Someone said that American poets simply haven't suffered enough to write great poetry. What do you think?

I think there's plenty of suffering in America. The Civil War, for example, and the Vietnam War. But there's an inward existential distress, which is clearly the case here. There are different penalties in different situations. The Americans are at bay in their own freedom.

Do you mean the tyranny of freedom?

There's so much available here and people are driven in on their First Person Singular in a distressed way and, of course, this makes them yearn for the kind of collective identity some other countries have; yearn for conditions of extreme duress, even. Yet, I think it was Joseph Brodsky who was saying that freedom is more important than art. And Brodsky spoke there as a man who has suffered, has been exiled, has been treated as a social parasite.

Go on.

I get impatient with the self-flagellating thing, and the self-indulgent surrealism and the lack of encounter here with the nitty-gritty. The problems of social justice do not seem to concern the intellectual community very much here. The fulfillment of the self seems to be the priority.

One of our playwrights, Sam Shepard, talks about the fact that there are some Americans who simply can't stand "not being a star."

But being a "star" is different from being successful.

It's jargon for the same thing—a star in your own firmament.

Well, you can't become a poet just because you want to be one.

How much support does a young poet need? How important is a mentor?

I've always been a teacher as well as a poet and I don't see any radical difference between teaching graduates or teaching kindergartners. It's important to have class activities for members of a workshop just to let them discover themselves. But I have an ambivalent attitude toward workshops. I would try to keep them as objective as possible—talk about craft, line endings, etc. Yet there's a lot of writing that's highly competent that I'm just not interested in but that I have to work with.

So you can learn to write.

If you have the equipment to begin with.

In one of your poems you say: "How perilous is it to choose not to love the life that you're shown . . ."

That poem is called **"Badgers"** and it's about the night life of the community. The Badgers are a kind of analogue for IRA activity. It's really about the relationship between yourself and the shadow self; the question of political solidarity with a movement becomes an extension of that.

Would you rather your poetry not be politically involved?

It's necessarily involved. Obviously, you would rather live in a society where there was composure rather than discomposure or decomposure.

Look. There's always that tussle between the purely artistic element and the civic element. I think of Lowell or Snyder, Ginsberg or Adrienne Rich. Even Bly. Now, Bly's an interesting example in that his poetry is pure lyric and his engagement with the culture is critical and didactic. And the same is true with someone like Rich or with Levertov, Snyder, or Ginsberg. There's poetry, but, then too, there's the program. With the black writers of the sixties, there was that tension between civic and artistic.

In your book, Preoccupations, *you have a quote from Ted Hughes in which you say that the poetic imagination is finally determined by the state of negotiation between man and his idea of a creator. Do you agree with that?*

I do. I think it's a vague statement, but I think to have been brought up Catholic, as in my case, with some idea of eternity, is to live forever with some sense of the provisional or secondary nature of historical experience. It's to live haunted by some Platonic idea of possibility and with a certain magical notion of language. It does change your notion of poetry. Poetry to me doesn't have to have any message. It can be praise or have the status of hymn or lament and these final postures of the voice which are religious are related to some first notion of the sacred word. It's difficult for poetry to survive in a society that loses its religious dimension. It then becomes a religious act in itself and not a parallel.

So we need our mythology. Stevens thought poetry could replace it.

In the Celtic society, there was an official status for the writer. He wrote satires and kept the history in stanzas to retain it in the memory. That changes the more advanced a society becomes. For a while in America in the sixties or the seventies, there was a great nostalgia for the primitive and everyone wanted to be an Indian again.

So you think language is more poetic the less advanced the society?

Yes. There's something colorful, much more metaphorical, in say, Homer. Something pristine about the figures of speech; but I'm not sure if you'd been living in those societies that you'd have been aware of the poetical nature of your language. There's always the nostalgia factor at work for us.

Henry Hart (essay date 1987)

SOURCE: "Seamus Heaney's Poetry of Meditation: *Door into the Dark*," in *Twentieth Century Literature*, Vol. XXXIII, No. 1, Spring, 1987, pp. 1-17.

[*In the following prize-winning essay, Hart analyzes the opposing, yet interwoven themes of Heaney's poetry, maintaining that the poet finds "precedents in a tradition of Catholic meditation but give to the old forms a new complexity and an attractive, personal finish."*]

Images of dark and light appear so frequently in poetic tradition that, when summoned for contemporary use, they run the risk of being immediately obsolescent. Each poet must dust off the old clichés and glaze them with new varnish. For Seamus Heaney, who is more attached to tradition than most, darkness and light dramatize his most pressing concerns. In his first book, **Death of a Naturalist,** as Dick Davis has pointed out, "Darkness is associated with an uncontrollable fecundity, a pullulation of alien, absorbing life." Darkness is persistently linked to Heaney's adolescent fears of sex and death, and light to their possible transcendence.

Many critics refuse to accept Heaney's second book, **Door into the Dark**, as an "advance on its predecessor," but surely it indicates a significant psychological advance. Rather than run from the dark, Heaney now faces up to it with grim determination, or actively seeks it out. He mines the metaphor of a "door into the dark" so extensively that many of his poems can be read allegorically. Still preoccupied with country matters—with farming, fishing, thatching, forging—he casts his rural personae in roles that dramatize the oppositions dueling in his imagination. Dark and light are now associated with speech and writing, forgetting and remembering, expiration and inspiration, blindness and insight, destruction and creation. The poems are intensely self-reflexive as they investigate their own perplexed making. Although Blake Morrison claims that "**Door into the Dark** is more promise than fulfillment, more hovering on the threshold than a decisive arrival," Heaney's narrators restlessly cross back and forth over thresholds [*Seamus Heaney,* 1982]. Like traditional Christian meditations, their crossings from confusion to revelation, from mute blindness to luminous communion with the divine, are overshadowed by the Cross itself.

For a poet who attended a Catholic school as a young man (St. Colomb's College), the *Spiritual Exercises* of St. Ignatius Loyola, as well as of his compatriots St. Teresa of Avila and St. John of the Cross, must have presented obvious parallels to poetic practices. James Joyce, whose role as a mentor Heaney acknowledges at the end of **"Station Island,"** may have suggested some of these. Stephen Dedalus in *A Portrait of the Artist* finds Loyola's "composition of place" in the hellfire sermon so imaginatively effective that its central dictum "to imagine with the senses of the mind . . . the material character" of all things and events, when filtered through Aquinas, becomes his fundamental aesthetic principle. In *The Poetry of Meditation*, Louis Martz has demonstrated how Renaissance poets often derived narrative models from Loyola's pattern of composition of place, self-analysis, and colloquy, and dwelled on the psychological processes behind them: memory, reason, and will.

While Heaney's meditations focus on scenes of artistic rather than Christian passion, they employ traditional meditational techniques in doing so. Their "compositions" of rustic artificers, who sacrifice financial contentment and bodily vigor in their devotion to outmoded crafts, act as reflectors in which Heaney analyzes his own procedures. His soul-searching is often self-incriminating. Rather than carry on a colloquy with the godhead, normally he bears silent witness to craftsmen of his own ilk. Like Joyce, he finds in the divine author of creation a metaphor for the authorial imagination, praising and accusing it accordingly. Poetry, which for Heaney includes all makings, is a substitute religion, but one which he never wholeheartedly reveres since it too mystifies the word. While his meditating narrators withdraw from the world into a pregnant, darkened silence, he often accuses them of narcissism, of stubbornly denying life. If in the womb of the imagination secular as well as holy words are made flesh, as Dedalus attests, the desire to regress can be infantile and defeating.

Heaney's emblematic "door into the dark" has numerous religious and literary precedents. It may come from the Bible: "I am the door: by me if any man shall enter in, he shall be saved" (John, 10:9), where Christ is promising salvation for all. St. Teresa uses the metaphor in the initial stages of her meditational treatise, *The Interior Castle,* declaring: "the door by which to enter this castle is prayer and meditation." It is implicit in St. John of the Cross's meditation, *The Dark Night,* in which the soul passes through a door in a darkened "house of the senses" to venture into a night infused with divine illumination. St. John explains:

> When this house of the senses was stilled (that is, mortified), its passions quenched, and its appetites calmed and put to sleep through this happy night of the purgation of the senses, the soul went out in order to begin its journey along the road of the spirit, which is that of proficients and which by another terminology is referred to as the illuminative way or the way of infused contemplation. . . .

Poems form the kernels of St. John's meditations, and Heaney translates one of these ("Song of the Soul that Rejoices in Knowing God through Faith") in **"Station Island,"** and compares its theme of the dark night to St. Patrick's Purgatory on Lough Derg. In his second book the "dark night" is a metaphor for the imagination which burns most intensely when darkened to the world.

Heaney's "door" is archetypal rather than specific. It may echo the "spiritual windows and doorways" in *The Cloud of Unknowing,* the anonymous medieval book on mysticism which holds that the doors of worldly perception must be closed so that the meditator can approach God's light. According to Benedict Kiely, Heaney's poetics are based on "the cloud of unknowing [and] . . . what Patrick Kavanagh . . . called the fog, 'the fecund fog of unconsciousness'" [in *The Hollins Critic* VII, No. 4]. Kavanagh said that we have to shut our eyes to see our way to heaven. "What is faith, indeed, but a trust in the fog; who is God but the King of the Dark?" In "A Raid into Dark Corners," Kiely traces Heaney's poetic mysticism to Catholic roots. From what Heaney calls the "negative dark that presides in the Irish Christian consciousness . . . the gloom, the constriction, the sense of guilt, the self-abasement," comes his poetic contention: "I think this notion of the dark centre, the blurred and irrational storehouse of insight and instincts, the hidden core of the self—this notion is the foundation of what viewpoint I might articulate for myself as a poet."

Joseph Conrad's "door of Darkness" and "door opening into a darkness" in *Heart of Darkness,* Robert Frost's poem, "The Door in the Dark," and the illuminating, purgatorial darknesses in Yeats's "Byzantium" and Eliot's *Four Quartets,* perhaps gave further support to Heaney's metaphor. But Heaney stakes out territory that is unmistakably his own even while occupying the eminent domain of others. His emphasis on ascetic withdrawal into the dark, for example, remains free of the mystic's grim desire for mortification. While St. John and St. Teresa relish God's "delicious wounds of love," and Loyola advises the retreatant to end his first week by chastizing "the body by inflicting actual pain on it . . . by wearing hairshirts or cods or iron chains, by scourging or beating," Heaney retreats from temporary distractions and confusions in a less melodramatic way: by walking, driving his car, or, like Kavanagh, by simply shutting his eyes.

Heaney embraces the mystic's sensory deprivation and renewed concentration, but for secular purposes. St. Teresa summed up the contemplative's "rite of passage" in the Fifth Mansion of *The Interior Castle:* "God deprives the soul of all its senses so that He may the better imprint in it true wisdom: it neither sees, hears, nor understands anything while it lasts." For the traditional Christian, the purgative way culminates in unity with God through grace and love. But when Heaney requisitions Catholic spiritual exercises, he does so to focus better on their hallowed assumptions, which now seem hollow, and attacks their methods even as he employs them. If he aims for transcendent clarity, it is to obtain a better view of the ground he is trying, often foolishly, to transcend. If he quests for unity with a mysterious creative source, usually he finds it in a peat bog, his own head, or his wife, rather than in God. Rather than climb a ladder to heaven, Heaney opens his front door and discovers avatars of the Creator in the blacksmiths and thatchers of an ordinary town.

Perhaps the best example of Heaney's meditative style can be found in **"The Forge,"** a sonnet whose first line provides the title of his second book. Unlike Yeats, who celebrated golden smithies of an ancient Byzantine empire, or Joyce, whose smithy was an adolescent aesthete dreaming of forging art but never quite managing to, Heaney fastens on a brawny artisan who, "leather-aproned, hairs in his nose," hammers out horseshoes. Heaney approaches this "maker" or "artist-god" in a traditional meditative way, by entering a dark "cloud of unknowing." He declares, "All I know is a door into the dark." The door is knowable but the dark beyond blinds him to a creative process which is ultimately unknowable. Heaney intimates correspondences between his blacksmith and a god, but then retracts them. The blacksmith may be one

of God's intermediaries, a priest transubstantiating the materials of common experience into holy artifacts, but at the end he is fundamentally a common laborer beating "real iron out."

Profane denotations undercut their sacred connotations. The blacksmith's anvil resembles a mysterious omphalos at the center of space and time. Heaney says, "The anvil must be somewhere in the centre." It is "Horned as a unicorn," a product of fairy tale and legend, as well as an eternal, "Immoveable . . . altar" where the blacksmith "expends himself in shape and music." Against this mythical background, however, he attends to secular makings rather than sacred ones, artifice rather than sacrifice, horseshoes rather than communion wafers. God's spirit in the last lines is no holy wind or breath inspiriting the soul of a communicant, but simply the air pumped from the bellows onto the forge's coals. If the blacksmith is an archetype (a type of Hephaestus) he is also a common man on the verge of obsolescence, sadly at odds with the modern-day world of traffic outside his door. Cars have made horses nearly redundant, yet he continues to recollect better days and bang out shoes with heroic, if not pigheaded, devotion:

> He leans out on the jamb, recalls a clatter
> Of hoofs where traffic is flashing in rows;
> Then grunts and goes in, with a slam and flick
> To beat real iron out, to work the bellows.

While Heaney admires his artificer, he refuses to gaze at him through the mystic's mystifying spectacles. By the end of the poem he has grounded the blacksmith firmly in the social and economic factors which determine and indeed threaten his existence.

Both Heaney and blacksmith follow the meditational paradigm of renunciation and reunion. While Heaney withdraws from the noisy bustle of traffic and the decaying yard of rust outside to glimpse the work inside, the blacksmith leans out the jamb and then returns to his forge. For Heaney, the outside world is governed by a grim, incontrovertible law of entropy and corruption, the inside world by a passionate, irrational will to creation:

> Outside, old axles and iron hoops rusting;
> Inside, the hammered anvil's short-pitched ring,
> The unpredictable fantail of sparks. . . .

Outside things fall apart; inside, "somewhere in the centre," they are held together and hammered into unity.

In **"The Forge"** Heaney illustrates the preliterature, instinctual, unconscious urges and binary oppositions he finds at the center of all creation. His essay, "The Makings of a Music," reveals these oppositions in similar fashion, but now in terms of Wordsworth and Yeats. In Wordsworth's poetry, he writes, "What we are presented with is a version of composition as listening, as a wise passiveness, a surrender to energies that spring within the centre of the mind." Likewise, in **"The Forge,"** Heaney listens passively to the "short-pitched ring" of the anvil "in the centre" of the shop. But he follows Yeats too, for whom "composition was no recollection in tranquility, not a delivery of the dark embryo, but a mastery, a handling, a struggle towards maximum articulation. . . . Thoughts do not ooze out and into one another, they are hammered into unity." "All reality," Yeats notes, "comes to us as the record of labour." Although Heaney's smith recollects the old equestrian days, at the end he repudiates nostalgic musing and hammers "real iron" in a fury of labor.

Blake Morrison contends in his book on Heaney that "What links the various traders, labourers and craftsmen who fill his first two books is that, unlike him, they are lacking in speech" and that Heaney, embarrassed by the linguistic sophistication provided by a university education,

> found himself in the position of valuing silence above speech, of defending the shy and awkward against the confident and accomplished, of feeling language to be a kind of betrayal. . . . But the community Heaney came from, and with which he wanted his poetry to express solidarity, was one on which the pressure of silence weighed heavily.

In Catholic Northern Ireland, speaking your mind can be a dangerous business. For social and political reasons Heaney elevates his mother's dictum, "Whatever you say, say nothing," into a poetic principle. He celebrates silence to underscore solidarity with his Irish Catholic ancestors and peers. But silence is also part of the knowing "ignorance" and self-inflicted "blindness" of meditation. "You must become an ignorant man again," Stevens said in his long meditation, "Notes toward a Supreme Fiction," "And see the sun again with an ignorant eye." In **"The Forge,"** when the smithy ignores the fleeting present and focuses in silence on a radiant, sempiternal source (the forge of blazing coals), Heaney follows suit. Expiration—his figurative dying away from the environment—necessarily entails a repression of speech which, with luck, makes way for linguistic inspiration and the sublimation that is writing. Heaney and his compatriots may keep quiet to avoid sectarian recrimination; they also keep quiet to meditate and write.

Oppositions such as speech and writing, myth and fact, intellect and intuition, work and play, and hierarchies that have valued one over the other, receive a new ordering from Heaney. If a logocentric preference for the spoken has devalued the written in Western thought, as Derrida insists, Heaney tends to celebrate the concrete accomplishment of writing over the evanescence of speech. While traditional Christian meditations culminate in colloquies, "in which the soul speaks intimately with God and expresses its affections, resolutions, thanksgivings, and petitions," Heaney's conclude with speechless, writerly acts. His blacksmith, for example, merely "grunts"—he never speaks. In "deconstructing" the hierarchies foisted by Platonic and Christian tradition, Heaney is also going against an Irish grain. Hugh Kenner points out in *A Colder Eye* that:

> Irish writers have always been naggingly aware that Irishmen do not as a rule buy books, have never

bought them, have even inherited a tradition whereby to write when you might be talking is an unnatural act. . . . And sensing that written words can even be *dangerous,* the Republic employs pretty active censors, who in addition to keeping out *Playboy,* contraceptive advice, and tons of quick-turnover porn, have interfered with some poets and with nearly every major prose writer [*A Colder Eye,* 1983].

Heaney protests the view that writing is "unnatural" as well as Socrates' view that it is a superfluous supplement, a "semblance of truth" causing forgetfulness and deception. He affirms that, like sex, it derives from a natural urge to reproduce life out of life, and that its considered messages may contain more pungent truths than the less premeditated utterances of speech.

In **"The Peninsula"** Heaney specifically addresses the traditional opposition of speech and writing, and casts his investigation in the form of a meditation. The poem recounts a passage into a "dark night" which blinds the poet to an unremarkable present so that, like the blacksmith, he can recall the past in graphic detail. Writing here is not an unnecessary appendage to or a repression of speech; it is a natural complement of speech:

> When you have nothing more to say, just drive
> For a day all round the peninsula.
> The sky is tall as over a runway,
> The land without marks so you will not arrive
>
> But pass through, though always skirting landfall.

At the start, the landscape appears to be a text, but one erased of all "marks" of speech and writing. The emptying is a necessary purgation which, in time, will make space for a new "annunciation," a new influx of words. The "negative way" has its dangers (landfalls, darkness), as the mystics warned, but Heaney's journey ends with renewed inspiration. Reality is eclipsed, but then recalled by the mind as it finds what will suffice for its poem:

> At dusk, horizons drink down sea and hill,
> The ploughed field swallows the whitewashed gable
> And you're in the dark again. Now recall
> The glazed foreshore and silhouetted log,
> That rock where breakers shredded into rags,
> The leggy birds stilted on their own legs,
> Islands riding themselves out into the fog. . . .

The birds and islands are emblems of the poet who is also doubled-back on himself, who meditates on the writerly imagination by means of the imagination. When the meditation concludes, perception is clarified. Things are seen in their *quidditas,* their unique thingness, radiantly and cleanly defined. Previously unfocused, the speechless poet is now prepared to uncode the landscape and translate what he reads into writing. Heaney admonishes:

> drive back home, still with nothing to say
> Except that now you will uncode all landscapes

By this: things founded clean on their own shapes,
Water and ground in their extremity.

Rather than write an imagist poem Heaney writes a poem about how one gets written.

In an intriguing essay on Andrew Marvell's use of the "self-inwoven simile or . . . short-circuited comparison," Christopher Ricks quotes from **"The Peninsula"** to show how Heaney draws on the earlier poet's legacy. "The reflective image," Ricks claims, "simultaneously acknowledges . . . opposing forces and yearns to reconcile them," and may refer to the "art of poetry . . . philosophical problems of perception and imagination" as well as to the raging factions in Marvell's England and Heaney's Northern Ireland [*The Force of Poetry*, 1984]. While Heaney's "self-inwoven" meditations become more overtly political in later books, in *Door into the Dark* they aim primarily at reconciling factions poised in the poetic imagination. The symbolic "birds stilted on their own legs" and "Islands riding themselves out into the fog," while providing images for the self-conscious poet also dramatize the paradox of creation, which is partly controlled and partly uncontrollable. Frost once claimed that a poem evolved through a happy series of accidents like a piece of ice on a hot stove riding on its own melting. Heaney's islands ride the same conscious and unconscious flow.

"The Peninsula," in its "self-inwoven" way, criticizes meditative tradition even as it follows its basic structures. Like Roland Barthes, who complained in his essay on Ignatius Loyola [*Sade, Fournier, Loyola,* translated by Richard Miller, 1976] that too often commentators on *The Spiritual Exercises* succumb to "the old modern myth according to which language is merely the docile and *insignificant* instrument for the serious things that occur in the spirit, the heart or the soul," Heaney deems language all-important and all-encompassing. In *The Spiritual Exercises* themselves, Barthes notes, "there is the awareness of human aphasia: the orator and the exercitant, at the beginning, flounder in the profound deficiency of speech, as though they had nothing to say and that a strenuous effort were necessary to assist them in finding a language." He concludes: "The invention of a language, this then is the object of the *Exercises*." This is the object of **"The Peninsula"** as well, where the silent driver quests for linguistic renewal.

But Heaney's new encoding is stubbornly rooted in the material world. Loyola has a more transcendent goal. He develops a language of prayers that, paradoxically, subvert human language as they prepare the meditator for an otherworldly sign. Loyola strives for "indifference," the opposite of language, which is a system of differences. God the Maker is God the Marker. He signifies the way as the meditator searches for election and vocation:

> The exercitant's role is not to choose, i.e., to mark, but quite the contrary to offer for the divine mark a perfectly equal alternative. The exercitant must strive not to choose; the aim of his discourse is to bring the two terms of the alternative to a homogeneous state. . . .

This paradigmatic equality is the famous Ignatian *indifference* which has so outraged the Jesuit's foes: to will nothing oneself, to be as disposable as a corpse.

Heaney's meditation moves in an opposite direction. He passes through linguisticindifference (the unmarked landscape and his own silence) to a situation where differences are marked, distinct shapes uncoded, and not by God but by himself.

Heaney's parable of reading and writing could have been suggested by Joyce's *Ulysses* where Stephen takes an epistemological stroll along Sandymount strand ("water and ground in their extremity"). Stephen reads in the "signatures of all things," wondering whether the world is an apparition of words in his head or composed of actual objects that might hurt if he knocked his head against them. Both Dedalus and Heaney conclude that the world has a degree of independent existence, but that the writer's duty is to manipulate codes of realism in order to deliver a facsimile of "things founded clean on their own shapes."

If Heaney is prescriptive (he asserts "you *will* uncode all landscapes") he is also diagnostic, analyzing how the mediative mind capitulates to "codes" that mystify as they pretend to mediate reality. Mystics of the *via negativa*, following the example of Dionysus the Areopagite, assert that only signs or signatures of God can be known and that God's book (the created universe) conceals as much as it reveals. Heaney diagnoses this linguistic mystification in the poem, **"In Gallarus Oratory,"** a title combining notions of speech (oratory) and religious withdrawal (an oratory is a small chapel for special prayers). As in **"The Forge"** and **"The Peninsula"** Heaney renounces speech as he enters the sacred dark of the early Christian oratory (in Gallarus on the Dingle peninsula), but his composition of place and self-analysis, rather than bringing him closer to God, brings him closer to those monks in the past whose rapport with God he respects but cannot quite share.

His oratorical poems, so conscious of their rhetoric and fictive status, resemble the oratorical prayers of the monks in their passion but not their goals. While drawn to the old chapel, like Larkin in **"Church-Going,"** he also intimates that the earlier communicants were both literally and figuratively "in the dark." All the images contribute to a sense of claustrophobic oppressiveness. The community's awareness of sin and fallenness is so strong it resembles a gravitational force pulling them down and burying them in a grave or "barrow." Heaney's meditative door opens on "A core of old dark walled up with stone / A yard thick." The monks, not unlike Robert Frost's "old-stone savage" who "moves in darkness . . . / Not of woods only and the shade of trees" ("Mending Wall"), enter a dark night that Heaney records with ambivalence:

> When you're in it alone
> You might have dropped, a reduced creature
> To the heart of the globe.

What for Heaney is a hypothetical situation, however, for the earlier monks was a dire exigency. Their sense of fallenness was irrevocable: "No worshipper / Would leap up to his God off this floor." The "heart" and "core" of this place at first seem radically different from the creative altar "at the centre" of the blacksmith shop.

But as Heaney begins the sextet of his sonnet, he reveals the traditional turn of a meditation from dark trials to uplifting illuminations, from morbid concentration on evil to a vision of God's grace. The dead awaken, as if resurrected from their graves (but, ironically, like pagan Vikings who were once buried in barrows):

> Founded there like heroes in a barrow
> They sought themselves in the eye of their King
> Under the black weight of their own breathing.
> And how he smiled on them as out they came,
> The sea a censer, and the grass a flame.

Although the monks obediently scour their souls, they seem pressured into doing so by the "king." They burrow inward, but have nowhere else to go. When they emerge after systematically deranging their senses, as Rimbaud would say, they uncode all landscapes, but in a sacramental as opposed to a realistic way. For a Catholic from Northern Ireland, "King" is hardly an innocent word. If for the monks it signifies an angry, jealous God, for Heaney it also implies the brutality of an imperialist master.

At the center of the Gallarus chapel is the oratorical scene in which spiritual words are delivered up to God, who in turn in-spirits the communicants with holy Words and with a mystic vision of censers and flames. But in this logocentric arena Heaney does not offer the traditional Catholic response. He does not pray or speak; he observes and writes. He may be recollecting the instructions of Loyola, "Every time I breathe in, I should pray mentally, saying one word of the 'Our Father' . . . so that only one word is uttered between each breath and the next," but he also mocks his heavy-breathers by making them seem uncontrollably narcissistic. The communicants, "Under the black weight of their own breathing," pray in a gothic atmosphere worthy of the stultifying enclosures of Edgar Allan Poe. Their sublime visions of censers and flames may be hallucinations bred out of repression. A nonbeliever, Heaney still expresses empathy for the Gallarus monks. "On a television talk," Benedict Kiely remarks, Heaney explained "how he felt that if all churches were like this one, 'congregations would feel the sense of God much more forcefully.'" That force, however, may be a psychopathological one.

Heaney stakes out territory that is unmistakably his own even while occupying the eminent domain of others.

—Henry Hart

As Heaney dismantles a religious heritage to which he still feels partly enthralled, his poems resemble a workshop littered with old icons and "trial pieces" constructed to replace them. His narratives, which are full of grammatical negatives, usually negate past myths to make way for more realistic alternatives. His meditations, like their classical paradigms, move toward love with increasing frequency, but celebrate its worldly rather than its apocalyptic vestments. In **"Girls Bathing, Galway 1965,"** he begins negatively:

> No milk-limbed Venus ever rose
> Miraculous on this western shore.
> A pirate queen in battle clothes
> Is our sterner myth.

After the first negation, Heaney draws attention to the way his mind doubles back on itself, washing away the dusty images of the past after it casts them up for contemplation: "The breakers pour / Themselves into themselves, the years / Shuttle through space invisibly." In time the apocalyptic sea changes them too, mixing tales of Christian judgments with tales of Irish pirates:

> The queen's clothes melt into the sea
>
> And generations sighing in
> The salt suds where the wave has crashed
> Labour in fear of flesh and sin
> For the time has been accomplished. . . .

Heaney brilliantly invokes expectations of Christian apocalypse only to assert the living reality that such myths deny. Unlike St. John on Patmos, who envisioned a sea offering up the dead for judgment, Heaney imagines the sea offering up ordinary girls in bathing suits:

> As through the shallows in swimsuits,
> Bare-legged, smooth-shouldered and long-backed
> They wade ashore with skips and shouts.
> So Venus comes, matter-of-fact.

While Christian mystics clamor for spiritual marriages with the divine love, and classical mythmakers dream of beautiful women born out of sea foam like Venus, Heaney welcomes a flesh-and-blood beauty, to counter the etherealized women of old.

In tracing the arduous process in which the mind purges its images to create them anew, Heaney's meditations resemble what Mircea Eliade called "the eternal return." They seek to abolish temporal history in order to recover the timeless void out of which new order or "cosmos" burgeons. For cultures that regard action as ritualistic repetitions of archetypes, Eliade claims:

1. Every creation repeats the pre-eminent cosmogonic act, the Creation of the world.

2. Consequently, whatever is founded has its foundation at the center of the world (since, as we know, the Creation itself took place from the center.) [*The Myth of the Eternal Return*]

For Joyce, the artist repeated the cosmogonic act by writing, so that "the mystery of esthetic like that of material creation is accomplished." Heaney's imagination is similarly ritualistic, gravitating toward "centers" in order to repeat profane as well as sacred acts of creation which, he often painfully confesses, are wedded to destructions. In **"The Salmon Fisher to the Salmon,"** a poem reminiscent of Robert Lowell's metaphysical fishing poems, the poet is the Fisher King, both victimized fish and Christ-like, "recreational" fisherman. Heaney, *in imitatione Christi*, follows the fish as it withdraws from the sea toward an interior space, a contemplative center. Here destruction is united with its opposite:

> you flail
> Inland again, your exile in the sea
>
> Unconditionally cancelled by the pull
> Of your home water's gravity.
>
> And I stand in the centre, casting.

At the "centre" a created and captivating "lure" unites fisher and wounded fish.

> I go, like you, by gleam and drag
>
> And will strike when you strike, to kill.
> We're both annihilated on the fly.

If at-one-ment with God's crucified body (Christ's symbol was the fish) is the sacred analogue, Heaney repeats it in the common experience of fishing. As the lure unifies opposed forces, so does the poem, which is a love song to the fish as much as an elegy for its annihilation.

Heaney may have found support for his views on circularity and recurrence in Emerson, who in his essay "Circles" wrote:

> The eye is the first circle; the horizon which it forms is the second; and throughout nature this primary figure is repeated without end. It is the highest emblem in the cipher of the world. St. Augustine described the nature of God as a circle whose centre was everywhere and its circumference nowhere.

Heaney, likewise, finds circles everywhere. In **"The Plantation,"** for example, he maps an eternal cycle of creation and destruction, which at first bewilders him. As he withdraws from the disturbing present—the "hum of the traffic"—his meditation as before strives to locate emblems for its own doubling back, its own circularity. The plantation provides a historical emblem too; the cycle of invasion and domination has recurred so many times in Ireland that Heaney regards it as archetypal. His act of communion invokes master and slave, victim and victimizer English landlord (Munster was divided into hierarchical plantations in the 1580s) and Irish tenant. Heaney dramatizes the combination of psychological and historical antinomies with a familiar but haunting fairy tale:

> You had to come back
> To learn how to lose yourself,
> To be pilot and stray—witch,
> Hansel and Gretel in one.

When he begins his investigations, "Any point in that wood / Was a centre." Now he is lost, traveling in circles, like the "toadstools and stumps / Always repeating" themselves. A meditative darkness ("the black char of a fire") marks his exclusion from society, but reveals those who have made similar journeys before: "Someone had always been there / Though always you were alone." As in **"The Salmon Fisher to the Salmon,"** Heaney finally reveals his dual role as destroyer and creator, which unites him culpably to a process he would rather repudiate. He must play the reclusive witch, sacrificing childlike enthusiasms in order to redeem them in poems.

The last poem in *Door into the Dark* finds a new and startling image for the contemplative mind and its sacrifices in that most common of Irish landscapes: the bog. Rather than to a door in a blacksmith's shop or oratory, here Heaney is drawn to the bottomless "wet centre" of a tarn. His concentration is Emersonian; a "transparent eyeball" focuses in ever-intensifying circles on a mysterious center:

> We have no prairies
> To slice a big sun at evening—
> Everywhere the eye concedes to
> Encroaching horizon
>
> Is wooed into the cyclops' eye
> Of a tarn.

Concealing the sunlit world outside but penetrating the "dark night" inside, Heaney's eye glimpses its own reflection in the tarn, where images are received, broken down, preserved, and exhumed. The ground, like the mystic consciousness "wounded" by love, opens itself to all like

> kind, black butter
> Melting and opening underfoot,
> Missing its last definition
> By millions of years.

Its *caritas* seems ineffable and unknowable, archetypal rather than historical. He concludes:

> Our pioneers keep striking
> Inwards and downwards,
>
> Every layer they strip
> Seems camped on before.
> The bogholes might be Atlantic seepage.
> The wet centre is bottomless.

Common acts in the present again echo sacred ones of the past. His pioneers are turf-diggers who, like spiritual questors, ritually reenact the "eternal return" in their search for a mysterious, cosmogonic source.

The contrast between the expansive prairie and the vertical descent into the bog intimates a conflict in Heaney's mystic stance. If Heaney, like many Irishmen before him, is attracted by the "mystic" democracy of America (the country of prairies and pioneers), whose apotheosis is Walt Whitman's cosmic embrace of all created things, he is also irrevocably European as he plumbs tradition's hoard. He goes outward "to encounter the reality of experience," but also downward like an archaeologist to retrieve its reliquary forms. More like Joyce and Yeats than Whitman and Williams, he struggles to find in central institutions, such as the Catholic Church and its spiritual exercises, rituals and symbols for a faith he has lost but rediscovered in *poesis*. Whitman's apocalyptic rejection of European traditions is tempting, as is the American penchant for leveling hierarchies, decentering central institutions, and questing for democratic ideals in transcendent spaces, but Heaney's sensibility is as inextricably rooted in traditional poetic forms as in the political and religious institutions of Ireland. He wields the iconoclastic ax, but for the sake of revision rather than outright rejection. His emphasis on order and pattern is doggedly formalist, even though he overhauls old forms to make them consistent with contemporary experience.

While critics suspect Heaney's formalism to be part of a larger conservatism, and accuse him of stubbornly refusing to modernize himself, his unsettled attitudes with regard to both past and present seem particularly modern. [In *New York Review of Books,* March 1980] A. Alvarez, for example, chastises Heaney for repudiating Modernism's "literary declaration of Independence" (however antiquated it may be in the 1980s) and claims: "If Heaney really is the best we can do, then the whole troubled, exploratory thrust of modern poetry has been a diversion from the right true way." But Heaney's skepticism of "right true ways" and of the sensibility that tenders such illusions, makes him seem more modern than his detractors. His meditative style *is* troubled and exploratory. If it is not specifically informed by structuralist and post-structuralist debate, as Blake Morrison occasionally worries, it often predicts their major themes. Obsessed with such hierarchical oppositions as writing and speech, forgetting and remembering, blindness and insight, profane and sacred love, marginal and central institutions, Heaney typically reveals a dialectical relation where oppressively one-sided relations were the rule. His doors into the dark open onto a present inextricably wedded, for better or worse, to the past.

In "Literary History and Literary Modernity," an essay in *Blindness and Insight,* Paul de Man points out: "As soon as modernism becomes conscious of its own strategies . . . it discovers itself to be a generative power that not only engenders history, but is part of a generative scheme that extends far back into the past." Heaney's premeditated forgettings and renunciations in *Door into the Dark* aim to purge earlier anxieties and the images that provoked them. "Make it new," for Heaney as for Pound, also means "make it old." De Man writes: "When [writers] assert their own modernity, they are bound to discover their dependence on similar assertions made by their literary predecessors, their claim to being a new beginning turns out to be the repetition of a claim that has always already been made." Heaney's meditations, which scrutinize their own procedures and compare them to all makings, find precedents in a tradition of Catholic meditation but give to the old forms a new complexity and an attractive, personal finish.

Helen Vendler (review date 1988)

SOURCE: "Second Thoughts," in *The New York Review of Books,* Vol. XXXV, No. 7, April 28, 1988, pp. 41-2.

[*In the following favorable review, Vendler explores the defining characteristics of the poems compiled in* The Haw Lantern, *asserting that the volume is an expression of the natural loss of middle-age.*]

Here are thirty-two new poems by Seamus Heaney—the yield since *Station Island* (1985). Heaney is a poet of abundance who is undergoing in middle age the experience of natural loss. As the earth loses for him the mass and gravity of familiar presences—parents and friends taken by death—desiccation and weightlessness threaten the former fullness of the sensual life.

The moment of emptiness can be found in other poets. "Already I take up less emotional space / Than a snowdrop," James Merrill wrote at such a point in his own evolution. Lowell's grim engine, churning powerfully on through the late sonnets, did not quite admit the chill of such a moment until *Day by Day:*

> We are things thrown in the air alive
>   in flight . . .
> our rust the color of the chameleon.

It is very difficult for poets of brick and mortar solidity, like Lowell, or of rooted heaviness, like Heaney, to become light, airy, desiccated. In their new style they cannot abandon their former selves. The struggle to be one's old self and one's new self together is the struggle of poetry itself, which must accumulate new layers rather than discard old ones.

Heaney must thus continue to be a poet rich in tactile language, while expressing emptiness, absence, distance. *The Haw Lantern*, poised between these contradictory imperatives of adult life, is almost penitentially faithful to each, determined to forsake neither. Here is the earlier Heaney writing fifteen years ago about moist clay:

> They loaded on to the bank
> Slabs like the squared-off clots
> Of a blue cream. . . .
>
>   Once, cleaning a drain
> I shovelled up livery slicks
> Till the water gradually ran
> Clear on its old floor.

Under the humus and roots
This smooth weight. I labour
Towards it still. It holds and gluts.

Image and sound both bear witness here to the rich fluidity of the natural world. Now, in *The Haw Lantern*, Heaney finds he must, to be truthful to his past, add manufacture to nature. When he looks with adult eyes at his natal earth, he finds machinery there as well as organic matter; and he writes not with fluidity but with aphoristic brevity:

When I hoked there, I would find
An acorn and a rusted bolt.

If I lifted my eyes, a factory chimney
And a dormant mountain.

If I listened, an engine shunting
And a trotting horse.

. . . . .

My left hand placed the standard
iron weight.
My right tilted a last grain in the
balance.

"Is it any wonder," the poet asks, "when I thought / I would have second thoughts?" (**"Terminus"**).

The Haw Lantern is a book of strict, even stiff, second thoughts. Such analytical poetry cannot permit itself a first careless rapture. No longer (at least, not often) do we follow the delightful slope of narrative: "And then, and then." Instead, we see the mind balancing debits and credits. "I balanced all, brought all to mind," said Yeats, using a scale to weigh years behind and years to come. A poet who began as luxuriously as Heaney could hardly have dreamed he would be called to such an audit. The need for adult reckoning must to some degree be attributed to his peculiar internal exile. Born among the Catholic minority in British Protestant Ulster, he came young to social awareness; now removed to the Catholic Republic of Ireland, he is part of an Ulster-bred minority substantially different in culture and upbringing from the majority.

The poetry of second thoughts has its own potential for literary elaboration. *The Haw Lantern* is full of parables and allegories, satires of Irish religious, social, and political life. The blank verse of these allegories is as far from the opulent rhymed stanzas of Heaney's sensual, Keatsian aspect as from the slender trimeters and dimeters of his "Irish" side. The strangest poem in *The Haw Lantern*, a blank verse piece called **"The Mud Vision,"** arises from Heaney's desire to respect amplitude, even in an analytic poem. I don't find the effort wholly successful, but I see in it the way Heaney is willing to flail at impossibility rather than divide his believing youth from his skeptical middle age.

This religious-political-social poem begins with a bitter satiric portrait of an unnamed country dithering between atavistic superstition and yuppie modernity. The landscape displays a thin layer of industrial modernization over a desolate rural emptiness; in a typical scene, terrorist casualties are carried, in a heliport, past the latest touring rock star:

Statues with exposed hearts and
barbed-wire crowns
Still stood in alcoves, hares flitted
beneath
The dozing bellies of jets, our menu-
writers
And punks with aerosol sprays held
their own
With the best of them. Satellite link-
ups
Wafted over us the blessings of
popes, heliports
Maintained a charmed circle for idols
on tour
And casualties on their stretchers.
We sleepwalked
The line between panic and
formulae, . . .
Watching ourselves at a distance,
advantaged
And airy as a man on a springboard
Who keeps limbering up because the
man cannot dive.

In that last image, Heaney catches the "advantaged and airy" complacency of an impotent nation congratulating itself on political flexibility as a way of concealing indecisiveness. The despair brilliantly hidden in this sketch casts up a compensatory vision. What if a dispossessed country could believe not in its useless statues of the Sacred Heart nor in its modern veneer of restaurants and heliports, but in its own solid earth? In the "mud vision" of the title, a whirling rainbow-wheel of transparent mud appears in the foggy midlands of this unnamed country, and a fine silt of earth spreads from it to touch every cranny. Heaney tries to catch the vision and its effect on those who see it:

And then in the foggy midlands it
appeared,
Our mud vision, as if a rose window
of mud
Had invented itself out of the glittery
damp,
A gossamer wheel, concentric with
its own hub
Of nebulous dirt, sullied yet lucent.
           . . . We were vouchsafed
Original clay, transfigured and
spinning.

The poem runs out of steam trying to imagine how the "mud vision" banishes traditional religion (bulrushes replace lilies on altars, invalids line up for healing under the mud shower, andso on). Eventually, of course, the vision disappears in the "*post factum* jabber" of experts. "We had our chance," says the speaker, "to be mud-men, convinced and estranged," but in hesitation, all opportunity was lost.

"Vision" is meant in the entirely human sense, as we might say Parnell had a vision of a free Ireland, or Gandhi a vision of a free India, but **"The Mud Vision"** puts perhaps a too religious cast on clay. Can a vision of the earthy borrow its language from the conventional "vision" of the heavenly ("a rose window . . . lucent . . . original . . . transfigured")?

"The Mud Vision" puts many of Heaney's qualities on record—his territorial piety, his visual wit, his ambition for a better Ireland, his reflectiveness, and his anger—and attempts somehow to find a style that can absorb them all. However, **"The Mud Vision"** has none of the *sprezzatura* and firm elegance of other poems in *The Haw Lantern*, such as **"Wolfe Tone."** In this posthumous self-portrait, the speaker is the Irish Protestant revolutionary (1763-1798) who attempted a union of Catholics and Protestants against England, and was captured in 1798 after his invading fleet was defeated off Donegal. Tone committed suicide in prison before he could be executed for treason. He symbolizes the reformer estranged by his gifts, his style, and his daring from the very people he attempts to serve:

> Light as a skiff, manoeuvrable
> yet outmanoeuvred,
>
> I affected epaulettes and a cockade,
> wrote a style well-bred and impervious
>
> to the solidarity I angled for . . .
>
> I was the shouldered oar that ended
> up
> far from the brine and whiff of
> venture,
>
> like a scratching post or a crossroads
> flagpole,
> out of my element among small
> farmers.

Though the first two lines of **"Wolfe Tone"** owe something to Lowell's *Day by Day,* the poem has a dryness and reticence all its own. The force of the poem lies in the arid paradox—for reformers—that authentic style is often incompatible with political solidarity with the masses (a paradox on which Socialist Realism foundered). The desolate alienation of the artist/revolutionary is phrased here with the impersonality and obliqueness of Heaney's minimalist style (of which there was a foretaste in *Station Island*'s **"Sweeney Redivivus"**).

I hope I have said enough to suggest where Heaney finds himself morally at this moment, poised between the "iron weight" of analysis and "the last grain" of fertile feeling, between cutting satire and a hopeful vision of possibility. Besides the blank-verse political parables I have mentioned, *The Haw Lantern* contains several notable ele-

gies, among them a sequence of eight sonnets (**"Clearances"**) in memory of Heaney's mother, who died in 1984. To make this hardest of genres new, Heaney moves away from both stateliness and skepticism. Borrowing from Milosz's "The World," a poem in which a luminous past is evoked in the simplest, most childlike terms, Heaney writes a death-sonnet that imagines all Oedipal longings fulfilled:

> It is Number 5, New Row, Land of
> the Dead,
> Where grandfather is rising from his
> place
> With spectacles pushed back on a
> clean bald head
> To welcome a bewildered homing
> daughter
> Before she even knocks. 'What's
> this? What's this?'
> And they sit down in the shining
> room together.

Such felicity brings Milosz's "native" effect fully into our idiom, and displays the self-denying capacity of the son to write about his mother as ultimately her father's daughter.

But **"Clearances"** also touches on the irritability, the comedy, and the dailiness of the bond between sons and mothers. In one of its best sonnets son and mother are folding sheets together; and here I recall Alfred Kazin's recent memoir of his youth in the Thirties, when he wrote for a freshman English class at City College "an oedipal piece about helping my mother carry ice back to our kitchen, each of us holding one end of a towel":

> This was such a familiar and happy experience for me in summer that I was astonished by the young instructor's disgust on reading my paper. He was a vaguely British type, a recent Oxford graduate . . . who openly disliked his predominantly Jewish students. My loving description of carrying ice in partnership with my mother seemed to him, as he tightly put it, "impossible to comprehend."

It is useful to be reminded how recently literature has been open to such experiences. Here is Heaney with his mother folding the sheets:

> The cool that came off sheets just
> off the line
> Made me think the damp must still
> be in them
> But when I took my corners of the
> linen
> And pulled against her, first straight
> down the hem
> And then diagonally, then flapped
> and shook
> The fabric like a sail in a cross-wind,
> They made a dried-out undulating
> thwack.

Petrarch or Milton could hardly have imagined that this might be the octave of a sonnet. Yet the pretty "rhymes" echo tradition, as *line* stretches to *linen* (the clothesline and the sheets), and as *them* shrinks to *hem* (a folded sheet in itself). Frost, Heaney's precursor here, would have recognized the unobtrusive sentence-sounds; the line "Made me think the damp must still be in them" could slip into "Birches" without a hitch. (The "dried-out undulating thwack," though, is pure Heaney; Frost's eye was more on Roman moral epigram than on sensual fact.)

The seven-line "sestet" of the sonnet closes with a muted reference to the writing of the poem (the poet is now inscribing his family romance on a different set of folded sheets), but this literary marker is almost invisible in Heaney's intricately worked plainness:

> So we'd stretch and fold and end up
> 　hand to hand
> For a split second as if nothing had
> 　happened
> For nothing had that had not always
> 　happened
> Beforehand, day by day, just touch
> 　and go, ·
> Coming close again by holding back
> In moves where I was x and she was o
> Inscribed in sheets she'd sewn from
> 　ripped-out flour sacks.

Taut lines and folded sheets connect mother and son, in art as in life.

Like **"Clearances,"** the other elegies in this volume combine the density of living with the bleakness of loss, preserving the young, tender Heaney in the present stricken witness. **"The Stone Verdict"** is an anticipatory elegy for Heaney's father, who has since died; other poems commemorate his young niece Rachel, dead in an accident; his wife's mother (**"The Wishing Tree"**); and his colleague at Harvard, Robert Fitzgerald. Heaney affirms that the space left in life by the absence of the dead takes on a shape so powerful that it becomes a presence in itself. In the elegy for his mother, Heaney's emblem for the shocking absence is a felled chestnut tree that was his "coeval"—planted in a jam jar the year he was born. Cut down, it becomes "utterly a source,"

> Its heft and hush become a bright
> 　nowhere,
> A soul ramifying and forever
> Silent, beyond silence listened for.

Heaney's sharply etched "nowhere" is a correction not only of Christian promises of heaven, but also of Yeats's exuberant purgatorial visions of esoteric afterlifes. It returns Irish elegy to truthfulness.

Heaney has said that because people of any culture share standards and beliefs, the artist's "inner drama goes beyond the personal to become symptomatic and therefore political." To ascribe immense and unforgettable value to the missing human piece, simply because it is missing, is to put the power to ascribe value squarely in the human rather than in the religious sphere. Since institutional ideology everywhere reserves to itself alone the privilege of conferring value, it is all the more important for writers to remind us that control of value lies in individual, as well as in collective, hands.

Heaney directly addresses the question of value in **"The Riddle,"** the poem placed last in this self-questioning book. His governing image here is the ancient one of the sieve that separates wheat from chaff. Such sieves are no longer in use, but the poet has seen one:

> You never saw it used but still can
> 　hear
> The sift and fall of stuff hopped on
> 　the mesh,
> Clods and buds in a little dust-up,
> The dribbled pile accruing under it.
>
> Which would be better, what sticks
> 　or what falls through?
> Or does the choice itself create the
> 　value?

This is the poem of a man who has discovered that much of what he has been told was wheat is chaff, and a good deal that was dismissed as chaff turns out to be what he might want to keep. Coleridge, remembering classical myths of torment, wrote, "Work without hope draws nectar in a sieve"; Heaney, rewriting Coleridge, thinks that the endless labors of rejection and choice might yet be a way to salvation. He asks himself, at the close of **"The Riddle,"** to

> . . . Work out what was happening in
> 　that story
> Of the man who carried water in a
> 　riddle.
>
> Was it culpable ignorance, or was it
> 　rather
> A via negativa through drops and
> 　let-downs?

The great systems of dogma (patriotic, religious, ethical) must be abandoned, Heaney suggests, in favor of a ceaseless psychic sorting. Discarding treasured pieties and formed rules, the poet finds "drops and let-downs," and he refuses to take much joy in the task of sifting, though a middle couplet shows it to be undertaken with good will:

> Legs apart, deft-handed, start a
> 　mime
> To sift the sense of things from
> 　what's imagined.

In Heaney's earlier work, this couplet would have been the end of the poem, breathing resolve and hope. Now he ends the poem asking whether his sifting should be condemned as "culpable ignorance" (the Roman Catholic phrase is taken from the penitentials) or allowed as a *via negativa*. The latter phrase, which is also drawn from Catholicism, is a theological term connected to mysticism, suggesting that we can know God only as he is not.

The elegiac absences and riddles of *The Haw Lantern* are balanced by powerful presences, none more striking than the emblematic winter hawthorn in the title poem. This poem, by dwelling throughout on a single allegorical image, displays a relatively new manner in Heaney's work. In the past, Heaney's imagery has been almost indecently prolific; readers of *North* (1975) will remember, for instance, the Arcimboldo-like composite of the exhumed cadaver called Grauballe Man:

> The grain of his wrists
> is like bog oak,
> the ball of his heel
>
> like a basalt egg.
> His instep has shrunk
> cold as a swan's foot
> or a wet swamp root.
>
> His hips are the ridge
> and purse of a mussel,
> his spine an eel arrested
> under a glisten of mud.

It is hard for a poet so fertile in sliding simile to stay put, to dwell on a single image until it becomes an emblem; it means going deeper rather than rippling on. **"The Haw Lantern,"** doing just this, fixes on the one burning spot in the blank landscape of winter—the red berry, or haw, on the naked hawthorn branch. At first the poet sees the berry as an almost apologetic flame, indirectly suggesting his own quelled hopes as a spokesman. He goes deeper into self-questioning by transforming the haw into the lantern carried by Diogenes, searching for the one just man. The stoic haw, meditation reminds the poet, is both pith and pit, at once fleshy and stony. The birds peck at it, but it continues ripening. In this upside-down almost-sonnet, the stern haw lantern scrutinizes the poet scrutinizing it:

> The wintry haw is burning out of
>   season,
> crab of the thorn, a small light for
>   small people,
> wanting no more from them but that
>   they keep
> the wick of self-respect from dying
>   out,
> not having to blind them with
>   illumination.
> But sometimes when your breath
>   plumes in the frost
> it takes the roaming shape of
>   Diogenes
> with his lantern, seeking one just
>   man;
> so you end up scrutinized from
>   behind the haw

> he holds up at eye-level on its twig,
> and you flinch before its bonded pith
>   and stone,
> its blood-prick that you wish would
>   test and clear you,
> its pecked-at ripeness that scans you,
>   then moves on.

Like other poems in Heaney's new volume, **"The Haw Lantern"** reflects a near despair of country and of self.

Heaney's burning haw can bear comparison with Herbert's emblematic rose, "whose hue, angry and brave, / Bids the rash gazer wipe his eye." Forsaking topical reference, the artist writing in such genres as the emblem-poem (**"The Haw Lantern"**) and allegory (**"The Mud Vision"**) positions himself at a distance from daily events. Such analytic, generalized poetry hopes to gain in intelligence what it loses in immediacy of reference. (The greatest example of such an aesthetic choice is Milton's decision to write the epic of Puritan war, regicide, reform, and defeat by retelling Genesis.)

Heaney has several times quoted Mandelstam's "notion that poetry—and art in general—is addressed to . . . 'The reader in posterity';

> It is not directed exploitatively towards its immediate audience—although of course it does not set out to disdain the immediate audience either. It is directed towards the new perception whichit is its function to create.

The social, historical, and religious perceptions of *The Haw Lantern*, if they should become general in Ireland, would indeed create a new psychic reality there. Such a prospect seems so unlikely now that it is only by believing in "the reader in posterity" that a writer can continue to address Irish issues at all.

I have saved the best of this collection for the last: two excellent poems about the life of writing. The first, **"Alphabets,"** written as the Phi Beta Kappa poem for Harvard, presents a series of joyous scenes that show the child becoming a writer. The alphabets of the title are those learned by the poet as he grew up: English, Latin, Irish, and Greek. They stand for the widening sense of place, time, and culture gained as the infant grows to be a youth, a teacher, and a poet. Against Wordsworth's myth of a childhood radiance lost, the poem sets a countermyth of imaginative power becoming fuller and freer with expanding linguistic and literary power.

With great charm, **"Alphabets"** shows us the child in school mastering his first alphabet:

> First it is 'copying out', and then
>   'English'
> Marked correct with a little leaning
>   hoe.
> Smells of inkwells rise in the class-
>   room hush.

A globe in the window tilts like a
   coloured O.

Learning Irish, with its prosody so different from those of
English and Latin, awakens the boy's Muse:

   Here in her snooded garment and
      bare feet,
   All ringleted in assonance and
      woodnotes,
   The poet's dream stole over him like
      sunlight
   And passed into the tenebrous
      thickets.

The boy becomes a teacher, and the verse makes gentle
fun of his self-conscious and forgivable vanity:

   The globe has spun. He stands in a
      wooden O.
   He alludes to Shakespeare. He
      alludes to Graves.

"Alphabets" closes with a hope for global vision, based
on two exemplary human images. The first is that of a
Renaissance humanist necromancer who hung from his
ceiling "a figure of the world with colours in it," so that
he could always carry it in his mind—

   So that the figure of the universe
   And 'not just single things' would
      meet his sight

   When he walked abroad

The second figure is that of the scientist-astronaut, who
also tries to comprehend the whole globe:

      . . . from his small window
   The astronaut sees all he has sprung
      from,
   The risen, aqueous, singular, lucent O
   Like a magnified and buoyant
      ovum.

Heaney implies that whatever infant alphabet we may start
from, we will go on to others, by which we hope to encompass the world. Ours is the first generation to have a
perceptual (rather than conceptual) grasp of the world as
a single orbiting sphere—"the risen, aqueous, singular,
lucent O"; and the almost inexpressible joy of sensuous
possession lies in that line, a joy Heaney sees in the cultural
and intellectual possession of the world, whether by
humanist or scientist. **"Alphabets"** combines a humorous
tenderness of self-mockery with an undiminished memory
of the vigilant vows of youth, proving that middle age
need not mark a discontinuity in life or writing.

The other brilliant poem here, **"From the Frontier of
Writing,"** offers a *vie de poète* altogether different from
that of **"Alphabets."** Written in an adapted Dantesque
terza rima, **"The Frontier"** retells a narrow escape from
a modern hell. It takes as its emblem the paralyzing experience—familiar even to tourists—of being stopped and
questioned at a military roadblock in Ireland. The writer,
however, has not only to pass through real roadblocks but
to confront as well the invisible roadblocks of consciousness and conscience. In either case, you can lose your
nerve: in life, you can be cowed; in writing, you can be
tempted to dishonesty or evasion. I quote this report from
the frontier in full.

   The tightness and the nilness round
      that space
   when the car stops in the road, the
      troops inspect
   its make and number and, as one
      bends his face

   towards your window, you catch
      sight of more
   on a hill beyond, eyeing with intent
   down cradled guns that hold you
      under cover

   and everything is pure interrogation
   until a rifle motions and you move
   with guarded unconcerned accelera-
      tion—

   a little emptier, a little spent
   as always by that quiver in the self,
   subjugated, yes, and obedient.

   So you drive on to the frontier of
      writing
   where it happens again. The guns on
      tripods;
   the sergeant with his on-off mike
      repeating

   data about you, waiting for the
      squawk
   of clearance; the marksman training
      down
   out of the sun upon you like a hawk.

   And suddenly you're through, ar-
      raigned yet freed,
   as if you'd passed from behind a
      waterfall
   on the black current of a tarmac road

   past armour-plated vehicles, out
      between
   the posted soldiers flowing and
      receding
   like tree shadows into the polished
      windscreen.

This poem is so expressive of the present armed tension
in Ireland that it is political simply by being. It produces
in us an Irish weather—menacing, overcast, electric—so
intense that for a while we live in it. It has the allegorical

solidity of the *déjà vu,* and the formal solidity of its two twelve-line roadblocks.

But formal solidity is not the only manner in which Heaney composes good poems. He has always had a talent and an appetite for the organic (growing and decaying at once), for which he invented the "weeping" stanzas of the bog poems. The elusive short couplets in **"Wolfe Tone"** and **"The Riddle"** suggest a third temper in Heaney, one represented neither by commanding masonry nor by seeping earth but rather by rustling dust, leaves, and feathers. The epigraph to *The Haw Lantern* epitomizes this third manner as the poet waits for a sound beyond silence listened for:

> The riverbed, dried-up, half-full of
>   leaves.
> Us, listening to a river in the trees.

In deprivation, the poet trusts the premonitory whisper from the stock of unfallen leaves. *The Haw Lantern* suggests the trust is not misplaced.

Seamus Heaney with Randy Brandes (interview date 1988)

SOURCE: An interview with Seamus Heaney, in *Salmagundi,* No. 80, Fall, 1988, pp. 4-21.

[*In the following interview, Heaney discusses his poetry, especially the poems in* The Haw Lantern, *as well as American poets that have influenced his work.*]

[BRANDES]: *With your recent birthday (your 49th), you are entering what MacNeice called "the middle stretch." Do you feel you are at a pivotal point in your work?*

[HEANEY]: Ever since I published a book, I have felt at a pivotal point. Publication is rather like pushing the boat out; then the boat/book turns into a melting ice floe and you have to conjure a second boat which again turns into a melting floe under your feet. All the stepping stones that you conjure disappear under the water behind you. So the condition of being on a moving stair that gets you only as far as you are is constant. But like everyone else, I have the sense of two special moments, in your 30s, and then some where later down the line—in your 40s or 50s; in fact, you have to start three times. First, you start to write and that's one initiation, the *sine qua non* of the other two, obviously.

Are you drawing here on the Wordsworthian format you mention in your TLS *piece on Plath?*

No. I hadn't even thought of that. I'm just thinking first of all of the excitement of beginning. Secondly, the redefinition of that—going on from the fundamentally narcissistic experience of the first self-expression. Instead of repeating your first success, your first note, you try to get a second note that does more work. But then there is obviously a third moment, that has to do with the biological

attenuations and dessications, a whole set of conditions that entail a rethink. And once a rethink is forced upon the creature, the art in some way has to be rethought, or reformed. The whole relationship between a writer's spiritual/emotional condition and the kind of wordstuff and form-making that's going on in his work is an interesting one. When I was an undergraduate, there was a glib notion around that there was no reason to suppose a bad man could be a good writer. Part of my gradual education of myself has been to think that there is a deep relationship between the nature of the creature and the worth of the art.

That's the way you end the Plath essay. You argue that the life when you aren't writing is as important as when you are.

That's a trope to resolve what is clearly a puzzle. The very best moments of artistic action, the most exhilarating for the writer and the reader, are gift-things—poems which arrive on their own energy, poems that in Shakespeare's term "slip" from you. So there is almost this sexual release, which is not glandular but which is analogous to the glandular. What is the relationship between pleasure and truth?

Again, thinking about Auden, do you have to choose between those two?

No, of course not, I am setting them up far too strongly in opposition. But you have to worry that bone.

At one point you talk about Auden sacrificing the beauty and strangeness of his poetry for truth and meaning. I'm sure that all poets that make it to the "middle years" must worry about this. How do you perceive this in relationship to your own writing—being too controlled?

All of these things you're talking about are awarenesses shared by anybody who's interested in literature. And a writer is not different from a reader, in that the common ragbag of orthodoxies and assumptions is what a poet has to work with as well. It turns out that motifs in the poems have been a sort-of preparation for the re-think of those MacNeican "middle years." I found—at the end of *Station Island* and through *The Haw Lantern*—that one of the genuinely generative images I had was of the dry place. And throughout *The Haw Lantern* these images were happily assembled but weren't desperately hunted for— images of a definite space which is both empty and full of potential. My favorite instance of it is in the tree at the end of **"Clearances"**. There's also the clearing in **"The Wishing Tree,"** the space at **"From the Frontier of Writing"** and it's in **"The Disappearing Island."** It's a sense of a node that is completely clear where emptiness and potential stream in opposite directions. And I'm delighted to find in one of my favorite earlier poems— **"Mossbawn Sunlight"**—a line (I don't know where it came from): "Here is a space again."

I suppose Mircea Eliade's monograph on sacred and profane space is relevant here. I believe that the condition into which I was born and into which my generation in

Ireland was born involved the moment of transition from sacred to profane. Other people, other cultures, had to go through it earlier—the transition from a condition where your space, the space of the world, had a determined meaning and a sacred possibility, to a condition where space was a neuter geometrical disposition without any emotional or inherited meaning. I watched it happen in Irish homes when I first saw a house built where there was no chimney, and then you'd go into rooms without a grate—so no hearth, which in Latin means no *focus*. So the hearth going away means the house is unfocused. It sounds slightly sentimental to speak like this, it's the kind of tourist-industry sentiment that you want to beware of, and yet at the same time, it represents a reality: the unfocusing of space and thedesacralizing of it.

Then in **The Haw Lantern**, *that space that has potential— your landscapes—aren't soggy anymore, they're hard. Your stone images are very fertile.*

Actually when you mentioned that I thought of **"The Stone Verdict."**

When we were in Dublin, you told me you'd considered titling The Haw Lantern, The Stone Verdict, *but that another author was using a similar title.*

Richard Murphy had a book called *The Price Of Stone* and I thought to bring out a book entitled *The Stone Verdict* would be susceptible to the wrong interpretation.

How did you decide to use **The Haw Lantern**?

I don't know. I went through a lot of uncertainty about what to call the book. "Haw" has always had a strange fascination for me. I like it as a little thing, as one of the little fruits or stones of the earth. Also I liked the phrase in the poem, "a small light for a small people." That's a true middle-years vision of the function of poetry. And yet I shouldn't really say that. The function of poetry is to be more than a "small light for a small people." The function of *poetry* is to have a bigger blaze than that, but *people* should not expect more from themselves than adequacy. They should not confuse the action of poetry, which is at its highest, visionary action, with the actuality of our lives, which at their best are adequate to our smaller size. In **"The Haw Lantern"** poem, there's a sense of being tested and earning the right to proceed.

There seems to be a duality at work in the **The Haw Lantern**. *On the one hand there is the* jouissance, *the bliss beyond speech, on the other hand there is the awareness of being scrutinized and judged.*

Well maybe that is just a natural consequence of my particular experience in Northern Ireland. As a member of the minority, solidarity was expected; and yet you were not just behaving in accordance with expectations, you were behaving naturally along ingrained emotional grain lines. There is actually a phrase in one of those **"Sweeney Redivivus"** poems, about being "split open down the lines of the grain" and that image of the private consciousness

growing like a growth ring in the tree of community is true to what people experience in Northern Ireland. But there is a second command besides the command to solidarity—and that is to individuate yourself, to become self-conscious, to liberate the consciousness from the collective pieties.

In **"A Placeless Heaven"** *you describe the chestnut tree. Do you see an analogy between yourself and what happened to Kavanagh in your re-evaluation of Kavanagh?*

I guess that essay on Kavanagh is really about the way one would like to be able to do it oneself. Kavanagh seemed to me to retain the abundant carelessness of lyric action into his bleaker later life. Whereas a writer like T. S. Eliot, awesome as his later work in the *Four Quartets* is, Eliot seems to have lost it. Writers who kept it, and they are rare enough, are more interesting. Yeats, for example. He kept the well spurting up in the dry place.

As in "Grotus and Coventina"?

Right. The mixture of votive action and pure gift.

Your earlier "touchstones" were Yeats, Wordsworth, Hopkins, and Hughes, to name a few. Are you discovering anyone new now or rediscovering anyone as in the case of Kavanagh?

Well, I suppose I went through a phase of enormous delight and fortification reading Czeslaw Milosz and Zbigniew Herbert and writers like that.

When did you first read these poets?

First, in Penguin anthologies in the 1960's. And then I began again about 8 or 10 years ago.

By the early 80s?

Certainly, by then. What I really like about Milosz is hearing a personal voice in which the poignance and emotional coloring and *coloratura* spring from the inner lining of the self. And yet at the same time, one recognizes that that feeling center is situated within a large, stern intellectual circumference. What Milosz can do is to rhyme, if you like, his personal biography with the history of western civilization. He passed a childhood among the woods of Lithuania in a scene that was fundamentally still medieval—hay wains and orchards, hunts and lakes and church bells. This was all authentic. He has gone through that, the 30s in Poland; he's gone through Warsaw, the Nazi and Soviet devastations; he has gone through himself, intellectually, coming within the sphere of Marxist orthodoxy, detaching himself from that at the cost of great personal solitude and hurt, leaving that milieu in the 1950s, ending up now in his own 60s, 70s, and 80s in California in a kind of free gravity-less modernity. So in a life-time he has moved from Medieval Catholicism, with a deep root back into early Christian time, right up into late twentieth century post-modernism. And he has this gift, as I said, for rhyming autobiography and history. He can be a serf on the road to Mass or he can be a weight-less astronaut walking out there. And I find that authority irresistible, because there is the weight of personal hurt and loss, and the weightlessness of impersonal despair for the humanist venture.

Apparently then you see some parallels between your own experiences and Milosz's? Not direct, but similar.

Well, the parallel that I have not mentioned is a background of Catholicism. I have been speculating recently that the unconscious of the English language is, by now, secular. Therefore, for someone from a marginal society, like Ireland, where the society is more-or-less secularized, but where the common unconscious is still a religious unconscious,—for somebody like that, the reading of poetry in English doesn't satisfy those needinesses which must be satisfied in the biggest poetic experiences. But when I read, even in translation, the poetry of the Poles, I find sub-cultural recognitions in myself which are never called up or extended by English poetry. I just find an experience of fullness and completion which is new and refreshing to me.

What about the politics?

Well, it's the unfinished quality of things in Poland. But of course I'm also responding to the *chicness* of Polish writing just now. I wouldn't be reading this stuff unless it was available and published. We are all subject to the fashions of the market.

Who else are you reading? In your prose we see Mandelstam and you just mentioned Herbert.

Well, Herbert I think is a finished writer, in the good sense. I don't think anybody can learn much from Herbert. Except to be absolutely honest and thorough. His is a kind of writing shared by many language groups, at least from what I see in translation—Rumanian, Czech, Polish and Hungarian—writing in which the poetry is in the plotting, where the poetry doesn't seem to reside in the dwelling upon a privileged moment of insight or joy. The poetry dwells more in the laying bare of patterns in a reality beyond the poet. Like the animated cartoons that come from Middle European countries; they too are both lyrical and politically tough-minded. Vasco Popa, for example, from Yugoslavia has a little series called "Children's Games." And one of the games is "You be the hammer, I'll be the nail." That obviously speaks volumes. It's very merry, and it's very fierce.

Then what you're saying is that in those parables, and fables, it's not the lyrical moment that you're after.

It's the truth-seeking dimension of poetry. It's what Horace called *utile*. And yet, I do think that in poetry just being useful is a bigger sin than just being pleasurable.

Speaking about Eastern European poets, you said—"even in translation." What do you look for in translation? Authenticity? Clarity?

As a reader, I want to lift a book in translation and feel it's like any other book. I want the book to do it for me. We know that there are great poets out there in other languages who haven't *done it* yet in English. For a long time, I think, Rilke was in that situation. I unfortunately cannot read German. And I share the prejudice of my New Critically trained generation against fuzzy language, abstractly swooning language. So translations of Rilke generally didn't come through to me; I opened the book and it didn't do. Until recently, when Stephen Mitchell's translation of Rilke came out. Now I find some of those translations becoming a possession—I love his translation, for example, of the first sonnet to Orpheus. So as I said, at the personal level of opening a book, I want translation to be neither too literary, too cliché, nor too of its age. I mean, there are translations you open and you can see the poet being a poet, flourishing an inventiveness, complacently taking over the clichés, and I tend to resist that. You just want the standards that usually operate; you want a certain decorum, chastity and integrity of language to be maintained.

I believe that there are two good motives for translation and they both sponsor slightly different procedures. One motive, which is the absolutely pure one, is to so love the work in the first language that you're hurt that it isn't shared in the next language. You will do everything that is possible to bring across the unique and beloved features of the original, and this will involve an attempt at all kinds of precisions, equivalents, and honesties. And you keep saying: "Oh no, it's not like that." You hurt until it gets nearly right and then you end up unsatisfied because it never can be the same in the other language. That kind of absolute command which is there if you love the thing in the original and know it deeply, that produces the highest motive and the highest kind of translation and the highest failure. So there are two motives, one of which is that pure one, and another of which is impure. But the impure motive has its own *verité*. You are listening through the wall of the original language as to a conversation in another room in a motel. Dully, you can hear something that is really interesting. And you say: "God, I wish that was in this room." So you forage; you blunder through the wall. You go needily after something. This is what happened in English with the sonnet form when in the sixteenth century the courtly makers heard through the wall of English the Italian melody and the Petrarchan thing. One of the greatest sonnets in English is an abusive translation of Petrarch: Wyatt's "Whoso list to hunt I know where is hind." Wyatt indulges in a kind of Lowellesque bullying of the Petrarchan original and yet his poem is a great gift to the second language. I think that is the Lowell pattern, and it's the Chaucerian, the notion of translation as taking it over: taking it over in two senses—in the slightly imperial sense and in the original etymological sense of carrying a thing across. I had that motive, I suppose, in relation to the Ugolino section that I did from the Dante. It was a very famous purple passage, but it also happened to have an oblique applicability (in its ferocity of emotion and in its narrative about a divided city) to the Northern Irish situation. So one foraged unfairly into the Italian and ripped it untimely from its place. To some extent that was also true of *Sweeney Astray*. Even though I can read Irish, the *Buile Suibhne* wasn't singing in me as a great structure that I previously knew and loved in Irish. In fact, it was in order to get to know it that I wanted to pull it out of Irish. And of course I felt I had the right to it. It wasn't that original linguistic love-right, but it was a cultural, political, historical in-placeness, a "we are all in there together" feeling.

Did you feel the same way about "A Ship of Death"?

I did, yes. That was born out of an opportunity, which I sadly didn't have the stamina to carry through, to translate *Beowulf*. The funeral scenes in it are wonderful, both heartbreaking and stony. They are descriptions of true rituals.

The poem becomes the ship as in Lawrence's "Ship of Death."

One of my favorite poems. "Build me the ship of death."

Let's talk about poets who are obviously important to you; ones who are still in your imagination, but you haven't tackled in individual essays, such as Frost, Hardy, or Eliot. Are they precipitating in your mind?

I found myself having to talk about Eliot a couple of months ago and what emerged was basically an account of my different bewilderments as I read Eliot. I ended up realizing that Eliot is a terrifically pure influence on readers, because the one thing you read in Eliot is what he wrote. There is no ancillary baggage. With Hardy, you can read folk England, you can read landscape, you can read sentiment, you can read nostalgia, you can read thatch and pewter mugs and yokels, a scene that pre-dates Hardy and has a stereotypical stock response built in. The matter of Hardy, the matter which he works upon, could be mistaken for the Hardyness which he turns it into. But, with Eliot, all you have is the Eliotness. The language has become a pure precipitate of sensibility. And the older you get, the more you realize that—that is what it's all about. So your respect for this strange bat-squeak in Eliot, this pure, odd, querulous, but utterly trustworthy note, rises. I can illustrate this simply by two occasions. First, I went in 1968 to East Coker where Eliot is buried. I was surprised to see a deep lane, where you would have to stand in from a lorry. Which is exactly what is described in "East Coker," but somehow I had never credited Eliot's writing with any documentary truth whatsoever. But even more, I felt that when I went to Burnt Norton, the house outside Stratford. The opening sections of the "Burnt Norton" poem, those lines about following a thrush into a garden, first parents moving without pressure on the grass, voices of children—all that's a kind of phantasmagoria. It's eerie, both a landscape and an echo-chamber. Language has become like the pastoral symphony, full of little cries across itself to itself. It is a musical acoustic more than it is a landscape. So then you go to Burnt Norton and you see a dry pool. You see a rose garden. You hear that there were children in the garden and somewhere deep down you are disappointed. Of course, you are delighted too,

but not in the way you are when you go to Yeats's tower and your heart sings because of the reliability and the equivalence there between thing and word. When you go to Burnt Norton your heart sinks a little; you don't quite want the place because you now truly know that Eliot's poetry is still late 19th century symbolist writing. He's not painting the forest but, as Mallarmé says, he's painting the deep thunder of the leaves. I think that Eliot is pure poet in that sense, the life of his art is completely conjured Ariel-life.

Is it an accurate assumption that the poets who appear in your prose are also simultaneously reflected in your poetry? Do you feel that kind of correspondence? How would you describe your critical approach?

Eliot has this lovely, haughty yet frigid term—a practitioner. He speaks of writing the criticism of the practitioner. I would say that's what I do. Nevertheless, a practitioner is a reader when he or she sits down. On the whole the poets who appear in my prose, aside from ones occasionally reviewed, are people who are part of my memory. The only way I can write with any conviction is out of love. Not necessarily from my long immersion in the poet, but the poet's long immersion in me. I suppose my criticism is some form of autobiography. It's a communing with a previously excited self and when I write those essays it's a resuscitation of what has been already settled. Now it can be tossed about and talked about.

How would you describe your feelings toward what you accomplished in Preoccupations *and compare that to what you did in your new collection,* The Government of the Tongue?

In *Preoccupations* I think I was spinning off that entrancement I mentioned earlier as the first stage of writing. Those essays are fundamentally the orchestration of my own surprise that I had begun to write. Like a long exclamation mark. But *Government of the Tongue* is not about the writing process. In *Preoccupations* I looked at Wordsworth or Hopkins . . . The way poems come about, the inner geologies, the underlying artesian energy that gets tapped in the poem. *The Government of the Tongue* is much more about the achieved work. In general, the pieces are about the responsibilities that come with delighted utterance. I think that all of the writers discussed there have conducted themselves well.

What do you mean by "conducted themselves well"?

They were writers who were forced into self-consciousness about what they were doing. And they proceeded, artistically, to deal with that self-consciousness. In some cases—in the case of Auden for example—they allowed the ethical questioner in themselves to slightly dumbfound the lyrical and self-conscious poet. In other cases, as in the case of Robert Lowell, the ethical questioner is overborne by the effrontery of the lyric poet. Mandelstam, again, writes some politically hot couplets and then stops and suffers the consequences forever. But he proceeds to overbear the conditions by lyric utterance. In Mandelstam, lyric utterance becomes radical witness. He speaks of breathing freely. So lyric poetry is his means of resistance. It isn't the language of protest; it is an authentic existential act, a pitting of breath and being against many coercions.

You've written on Plath and Lowell and you mention Frost; are there any other American poets that interest you? These could be either contemporary or modern poets.

As I said, I tend to write about people that have become part of my memory. And my memory was formed before I arrived in the U.S. But if I were going through a complete memory list I would have to add John Crowe Ransom. He is deeply laid down. His is a less ambitious but nonetheless a well-perfected achievement.

What about Wallace Stevens?

Wallace Stevens I am helplessly in awe of but my response is as helpless as it is awed. When I open the door into that great cloudscape of language, I am transported joyfully. And I have got to a stage of reading Stevens where—to mix the metaphor—I can feel the bone under the cloud. I love his oil-on-water, brilliant phantasmagoria. And there is deep mind-current under the water, and a kind of water-muscle mind at work, but I find it difficult to hold that in my own reader's mind. I find it difficult to see a Stevensian gestalt in the way that I can see Frost as a whole. I can see Frost defined against a sky or landscape. Somehow with Stevens, I cannot see the poetry defined. It is conterminous with the horizon. That says a lot for him but it also means he is difficult to think about.

Are there other Americans who fit in that category?

I would have said Ashbery except Ashbery is oddly enough more historical than Stevens. It is obvious that the Stevensian example is stylistically important, that the same beautiful musical waftage is part of Ashbery's gift. Ashbery has a rhythmic amplitude that is almost Swinburnian. I think it was inspired of him to call a book *April Galleons* because there is a sumptuousness, a full-rigged, under-full-sail, galleon-like progress in the word flow of his language; but there is also a paper boat mockery. Yet there is also in Ashbery something much more timey and placey than there is in Stevens. That timiness and placiness is evident in the paraphernalia of the poetry, in the way that the roughage of the contemporary comes into it—the pop culture, the jingles, the language slurry and material detritus that we live with—and that makes him of his time and place. I think that Ashbery's sensibility is symptomatic of the moment. Stevens' was overbearing at the moment, immensely odd and immensely powerful. Ashbery's gift is to be tremendously sympathetic to the usual and to be a barometer. I don't mean that he just writes clichés. He writes *with* clichés against clichés. I understand more, now that I have been in America for 5 or 6 years, his popularity. It's because he registers a bemused, disappointed but untragic response to the evacuation of meaning from most people's lives.

Stylistically, he's almost antithetical to what you're about?

That's always been part of my fascination with American writing, precisely this approach to the antithetical. When I came from Belfast in the early 70s to Berkeley, I came as a writer of thin cross-legged quatrains and narrow little knitting-needle forms into Beatsville, into the big open howl of the Ginsbergian. I was curious about how to listen to poetry such as Snyder's in which I liked the elements but couldn't hear the beat. Even though I knew Carlos Williams, I wanted to know what he was about. So my venture in America was to encounter the other, to put the screws on my own aesthetic. You kept hearing that British poetry and European sensibilities were too constricted, so I did my best in the first Californian quest to come to grips with what was different, like the poems of Charles Olson. I actually liked Olson's book *Call Me Ishmael* best of everything he's done, but I also read the body of his poetry and I have to say I found it a toil much of the time. So after justly opening myself and saying, "Be pervious to this—c'mon, open up," I could see what I ought to feel but I couldn't really feel it. And then there comes a point when honesty to your prejudice is as proper as attempts to overcome it. Fundamentally, what I want from poetry is the preciousness and foundedness of wise feeling become eternally posthumous in perfect cadence. Good poetry reminds you that writing is writing, it's not just expectoration or self-regard or a semaphore for self's sake. You want it to touch you at the melting point below the breastbone and the beginning of the solar plexus. You want something sweetening and at the same time something unexpected, something that has come through constraint into felicity.

You don't find that in American poetry?

Sometimes I think that the thing I want to hear is not even sought after. This is very generalized, but let's say that the American cadence and the American ear tends to run to the edge of the page. It tends to be fluid and spread. Whereas my predisposition and my prejudice is toward poetry that contains and practices force within a confined area. Therefore I suppose I can understand immediately the aims of the poetry of someone like Elizabeth Bishop or James Merrill. I'm not saying Merrill writes like a European; but he operates within a defined enclosure, a writer who has been true to his gift. His gift was always for a kind of figure-skating joy and he never abandoned that figure cutting discipline. The danger of that kind of writing is that it can remain weightless—and the other danger is that a writer with that gift may deliberately seek to import heaviness. Merrill did not groan into heaviness, which would have been an offense against his nevertheless good aesthetic manners. But by remaining true to himself, he accrued weight.

A lot of what you are describing is the Whitmanian inheritance.

But the Whitmanian inheritance must beware of becoming the American equivalent of the English Augustan inheritance. English poetry's danger is in becoming "Anglican," moving from the temperate chastity of an earlier, thoroughly earned poetry like George Herbert's, who is in the good pristine sense Anglican, to the automatic intonation of the balances and comforts which Herbert actually fought for. American poetry is not out of a similar danger, using the robust Whitmanian uplift as a roller-coaster. A collusion is possible between a comfort-dispensing narcotic, drifting Reaganism and a Whitmanian optimism-and-overflow poetry. I am suspicious, I suppose, of the large gestures which are expected of American poets.

You argue in the Yale Review *that American poets use myth and surrealism as a ring of literary defense against life. Is this in the same vein?*

Residence in America has forced me back on what I am myself. There are times when I do not understand what is going on in the poetry. At the beginning I thought I did. Of course, there is a vast, inflationary, reputation-making business and I myself am part of it too. I have received as many amplified, overstated praises as the next. But American poets have to negotiate that language of inflation, in their society and unfortunately also in blurb-speak: there is a disgraceful abdication from truth in the words that are wrapped around books. Within the collective of poets, there are a few people I meet who know that this is generally blather and generally very bad. I have an impulse to flee from it, even while benefitting from it.

Getting back to your most recent volume **The Haw Lantern***, would you agree that what you've done in this volume is certainly more abstract and opaque than* **Station Island***?*

It is abstract in the sense that some of the poems are abstracted versions of what has been fleshed out already in other things, poems of an allegorical sort in which it isn't quite my voice speaking. It's a made-up other voice—a tone rather than a voice. They are like pseudo-translations from some unspecified middle European language.

But you still find these abstractions viable?

They are, I'd like to think, "a game of knowledge"—that's what Auden called poetry. And so are little swift poems like **"The Riddle"** and **"The Milk Factory."** The process is one where childhood sensation gets abstracted into a sense of wonder.

And "Hailstones"?

"Hailstones"—again, it's the palpable, documentary, remembered thing becoming a sensation of its own memory—and that to me is what abstraction is in art.

However, you still draw upon images from your rural childhood in that volume. Is this an endless well? Are those images still useful?

They remain utterly useful to me. I have little else.

Your childhood. I guess that's true.

The difficulty comes when what has happened between the original place and the moment of writing doesn't intervene in the writing itself. I see it as a process of continual going back in to what you have, changing it and coming out changed.

So that's how you would answer someone who argues that your rural childhood images do not speak to the modern urban audience.

I think that's a completely irrelevant objection to any work.

It's one that comes up often in the criticism.

But that's a sociological notion of what a work of art is—that a work of art is something designed to help people by reflecting their contemporary conditions. That's a terrifically deterministic sense of the function of art—to show people back the usualness of their life. That is *one* function of it indeed. But the fact that it's a rural image—the danger there is that people like the poetry because for them it's nostalgic. And the danger for me as a writer is that *I* may like the stuff because it's nostalgic. But that is something that it's possible to be too vigilant about. The audience's response to it as picturesque material is their problem. My problem is to make sure that the return to that enabling source is not simply nostalgic. You have to make it take the strain of adult experience. That's why I feel OK about things like **"Hailstones,"** or **"Alphabets"** or **"The Milk Factory"**—there is a bemused, abstracted distance intervening between the sweetening energy of the original place and the consciousness that's getting back to it, looking for sweetness.

Which poems in **The Haw Lantern** *provided you with the greatest satisfaction in working out technical difficulties?*

The first one, **"Alphabets,"** satisfied me because **"Alphabets"** was commissioned. I had a real problem: Write a poem for the Phi Beta Kappa at Harvard that had to be spoken aloud, and be concerned with learning. And that poem is precisely about the distance that intervenes between the person standing up in Sanders' Theatre, being the donnish orator, and the child, pre-reflective and in its prewriting odd state. I also like **"Mud Vision"** because it's an abstract poem which follows its own inventiveness—and it has a slightly zany logic to it.

So you felt you were taking a risk there?

It began by looking at a work done in Dublin by an English painter called Richard Long. This was in the Guinness Hops Store that is now an art gallery. Long had made a huge "flower face" or rose window type of structure entirely by dipping his hand in mud and placing his handprints so as to begin with four handmarks in the shape of a cross or compass. When you put four more in the northeast, southwest and so on, so you have eight radiating from the center—then you begin to move out from that. So there it was, this immense design made of mud. So that was the original inspiration for the poem. But obviously a whole

Irish Catholic subculture of apparitions and moving statues and such like went into it also.

One would imagine that the "Clearances" sequence was difficult to write, but why did you choose the sonnet form for the elegy? Sonnets are usually made to hold little things in a little room. How do you see that in terms of sonnet sequences?

I didn't choose it really. It accidentally occurred and accrued. The sonnet just turned into a habit. Good or bad? I couldn't say.

Do you still at this time believe that "the end of art is peace"? How do you understand Patmore's statement?

That's a quoted statement. I enjoy the triple take of it because Coventry Patmore said it, Yeats used it and I used Yeats using it. Obviously no matter how turbulent, apocalyptic, vehement or destructive art's subject is or that which is contained with art, no matter how unpeaceful the thing previous to art is—once it has been addressed and brought into a condition called art, it is, if not pacified, brought into equilibrium. For a moment the parallelogram of forces is just held. The minute after art, everything breaks out again. Art is an image. It is not a solution to reality, and to confuse the pacifications and appeasements and peace of art with something that is actually attainable in life is a great error. But to deny your life the suasion of art-peace is also an unnecessary Puritanism. It is an unnecessary extreme.

All the same, I am very attracted to that extreme of denial. In post-Holocaust, and post-nuclear conditions, the seeming smarminess of offering art as peace, the slightly sanctimonious, unearned "Let's go out and enjoy the alibi of art"—the indulgence is a possible affront. But to carry that denial too far, to demean the possibility of art and say that that is all art is capable of is also a great error. The greatest art confronts every destructiveness that experience offers it and in Thomas Kinsella's terms, "digests it." So, when we salute art with joy, we acknowledge that it has managed to overcome all the dice that were loaded against it. Can you write a poem in the post-nuclear age? Can you write a poem that gazes at death, or the western front or Auschwitz—a poem that gives peace and tells horror? It gives true peace only if the horror is satisfactorily rendered. If the eyes are not averted from it. If its overmastering power is acknowledged and unconceded, so the human spirit holds its own against its affront and immensity. To me that's what the "end of art is peace" means and understood in those terms, I still believe in it.

Henry Hart (essay date 1989)

SOURCE: "Seamus Heaney's Anxiety of Trust in *Field Work*," in *Chicago Review,* Vol. XXXVI, No. 3, 1989, pp. 87-108.

[In the following essay, Hart determines the influence of Robert Lowell on the poems of Field Work, *and praises Heaney's willingness to take risks in this volume.]*

Most poetic careers advance like waves disturbed by a central event, each new pulse collapsing only after the tensions impelling it have been exhausted. Heaney's career is no exception. His image of the family's drinking water shaken by the train in **"Glanmore Sonnets IV"** (the "small ripples . . .vanished into where they seemed to start") brilliantly captures this contrapuntal progress. Following Blake's assertion that "Without Contraries is no progression," Heaney has made sure that his surges are always matched by equally powerful counter-surges. His early pastoralism in *Death of a Naturalist*, for example, relied on an opposing "anti-pastoralism" for credibility and contemporaneity. Without the recognition of rural hardship, his enchantment with agrarian ways would have seemed foolishly nostalgic. Similarly, his meditational *via negativas* in *Door into the Dark*, while aimed at recollecting sacred lights (the altar-like anvil wreathed with sparks in the forge, the grass flaming outside the Gallarus Oratory), gained intensity from the "dark night" they struggled to illuminate. In *Wintering Out* scholarly disquisitions on place names in Northern Ireland drew mythic and political force from the Protestant and Catholic conflicts raging beneath their linguistic surfaces. And in *North* the apocalyptic desire to raise the dead for judgment and to invoke history as a guide to a saner future achieved pathos from the "counter-revelation" of Irish history as a dark, tragic mire of bloody feuds and mindless sacrifices.

In this series of oscillating movements, *Field Work* marked a new departure and is crucial to the understanding of the books that come after. Seismic Ireland is still the central event resonating through the poems, but here Heaney writes from the south rather than the north. The move from Belfast to Wicklow in 1972 (and to Dublin four years later), whose political ramifications were declaimed by the press, initiated a stylistic shift as well. The narrow, constricted poems like **"Punishment,"** in which Heaney excoriated his failure to become more actively engaged in the political events of Northern Ireland, modulate here into a more relaxed, melodic verse. In his interview with Frank Kinahan, [in *Critical Inquiry,* Vol. 8, Spring 1982] when asked whether substance determined style, Heaney remarked: "the line and the life are intimately related, and that narrow line, the tight line [in *North*] came out of a time when I was very tight myself." When he began lengthening his lines in *Field Work*, "the constriction went, the tension went." Addressing the severed heads and strangled victims of Iron Age fertility rites and their modern-day equivalents in Northern Ireland, Heaney took on a grim Anglo-Saxon abruptness and ornamental complexity. He believed that the musical grace of the English iambic line was "some kind of affront, that it needed to be wrecked." In Wicklow, in the pastoral landscape of Glanmore surrounded by a Catholic majority rather than a Protestant hegemony, he felt that he had reached a "kind of appeasement." As he wrote Brian Friel, he now wanted to open "a door into the light" rather than "a door into the dark" [from an interview published in *Ploughshares,* 1979].

In one of the most perceptive reviews of *Field Work*, Christopher Ricks pointed out that "the word which matters most is "trust". . . . Heaney's poems matter because their uncomplacent wisdom of trust is felt upon the pulses, his and ours, and they effect this because they themselves constitute a living relationship of trust between him and us." In an "Ireland torn by reasonable and unreasonable distrust and mistrust" the "resilient strength of these poems is in the equanimity even of their surprise at some blessed moment of everyday trust." [*The London Review of Books*, 1979]. At first glance, it would seem that Heaney's new trust arose from his new sense of a "trusting" audience, of the assumed covenant between himself and his new community of predominantly Catholic and Republican citizens in the South. But while his new trust was more artistic than political (it depended more on private impulses than public compulsions), and while he wanted "to bring elements of . . . [his] social self, elements of . . . [his] usual nature" towards center stage in *Field Work*, there are few signs that he trusted his audience any more than he did in the past, and little to prove he trusted his new-found door into the convivial light any more than his door into the primal, uncivilized dark. Although the diction and rhythms of *Field Work* resemble the kind of relaxed, accessible style Robert Lowell popularized in *Life Studies* and later volumes, and although he strives for the collo-quial luminosity of Dante's verse, like his two precursors Heaney gives equal time to the unenlightened darknesses he finds in himself and everywhere around him.

Just as "the light of Tuscany" wavers through the clear pool in **"The Otter,"** Heaney wavers in *Field Work* be-tween trusting and distrusting "transparent" communica-tion with his new, receptive community. His anxiety over trust is nothing new. Early on, Heaney admits, he "had absolutely no confidence as a writer qua writer"; he af-fixed the pen-name, Incertus, to his first poems to acknow-ledge his uncertainty. From Hughes and Kavanagh he learned the "thrill . . . of trusting . . . [his] own back-ground," which was the dark hinterland of bogs, beasts, and rural laborers in Northern Ireland; he claims, "Philip Hobsbaum . . . gave me the trust in what I was doing." But even while writing *North,* his most successful book up to that time, his confidence swayed. If he trusted his predilections, he distrusted those of his audience: "I was expecting *North* to be hammered, actually. I thought it was a very unapproachable book. But I was ready for the reaction, because I trusted those poems." The "wisdom of trust" in *Field Work* is similarly counterpointed. To Frank Kinahan he confessed:

> I suppose, then, that the shift from *North* to *Field Work* is a shift in trust: a learning to trust melody, to trust art as reality, to trust artfulness as an affirmation and not to go into the self-punishment so much. I distrust that attitude too, of course. [*Critical Inquiry,* Spring 1982]

Antaeus, proponent of dark, instinctual beliefs, and Hercules, skeptical light-bringer and demolisher of irrational cre-dences, continue to wrestle in Heaney's mind, just as they did in *North*.

Moving to the Republic for Heaney was both a flight to freedom—away from the burdensome "position of . . . a representative of the Catholic community" in the north—and a return to old responsibilities and anxieties. If he no longer had to agonize over "the political colouring" of his utterances, as he told Robert Druce, now his dreams of political freedom were rebuked by the atrocious situation he couldn't leave behind. His sensuous feast in **"Oysters,"** for example, turns out to be a disturbing meditation on old acts of imperialist aggression and privilege. He recalls Rome but is thinking of England too (as it gluts itself on Ireland):

> Over the Alps, packed deep in snow,
>   the Romans hauled their oysters south to Rome:
> I saw damp panniers disgorge
>   the frond-lipped, brine stung
>   Glut of privilege . . .

Heaney wants to celebrate uncluttered sensuality and the transcendental light beyond politics, but history's under-tow will not let him go. His anger is kindled by the fact that his "trust could not repose/ In the clear light, like poetry or freedom/ Leaning in from the sea." Part of the reason, he explains, lies in the "Irish Catholic . . . distrust of the world" and "distrust of happiness" stamped on his childhood psyche. Among the Irish, as among the Span-ish and Russians, he claims, "There's a more elegiac and tragic view of life; they're less humanist; they're less trust-ing in perfectibility." This mistrust of humanist ideals stimulates Heaney's preoccupation in *Field Work* with bestiality. As in Ted Hughes's poetry, Heaney offers a zoological array of otters, skunks, oysters, dogs, pismires, badgers, cuckoos, corncrakes, and other species. Ascents to humane, civilized orders are everywhere undercut by "saurian relapses." If Heaney consecrated his idea of poetic and political freedom by leaving Belfast, he nevertheless returned obsessively in his poems to witness its bestial ways, and to explain how his former environment was the breeding ground of his distrust.

In his essay "Responsibilities of the Poet" [*Critical Inquiry,* Vol. 13, Spring 1987], Robert Pinsky (who had reviewed *Field Work* in 1979) could be thinking of Heaney when he links "responsibility" to "sponsor" and "spouse," and explains the poet's contradictory need "to feel utterly free, yet answerable" to the community around him. Pinsky declares that the poet doesn't need an audience so much as the compulsion within himself to "respond" to one. He is responsible to the living, to spouse and readerly sponsors, but this bond is always taxed by his responsibility to the dead and unborn: "one of our responsibilities is to mediate between the dead and the unborn: we must feel ready to answer, as if asked by the dead if we have handed on what they gave us or asked by the unborn what we have for them." The poet is responsible for his culture, for witnessing its exemplary and unexemplary acts, and for reinvigorating its language. But this plunges the poet into quandaries. Pinsky explains:

> The poet's first social responsibility, to continue the art, can be filled only through the second, opposed

responsibility to change the terms of the art as given—
and it is given socially, which is to say politically.

These contrary forces form the fundamental tension in
Field Work, where marriage poems speak of tearing responsibilities toward spouse and art, and political poems
speak of similar tearing responsibilities toward poetic freedom and tribal demands. In poems like **"Casualty"** Heaney
honors the dead by elegizing members of his Catholic
community, but also rebukes its terms and ethics by celebrating a man who renounced "tribal" expectations, and
died as a result. His commemorative poems to artistic
"sponsors," whether to Lowell or Ledgwidge, maintain
their freedom from the august dead in order to mock them
as well as praise them. His **"Ugolino"** and other Dantesque poems again demonstrate his responsible willingness to be the beneficiary of a "trust," to accept the riches
of tradition and pass them on, but also his freedom from
tradition, his legitimate insistence on altering the past to
fit his needs and beliefs.

[In *Seamus Heaney,* 1986] Neil Corcoran has argued that
"the major poetic presence in *Field Work* . . . is not
Lowell . . . but Dante," and cites Heaney's serial encounters
with the dead and his "awareness of the intimate relationship between the personal and the political or historical"
as the two most obtrusive resemblances. Heaney himself
has written in "Dante and the Modern Poet" that it was
the way the exiled and embittered Florentine poet "could
place himself in an historical world yet submit that world
to scrutiny from a perspective beyond history, the way he
could accommodate the political and transcendent" that
stimulated his attempts to emulate him. Dante's exploration of political and psychological divisions makes him
seem Heaney's contemporary ally rather than his archaic
master. "The main tension" felt by poets in Ireland, and
felt by Dante in a Florence ripped apart by Guelph and
Ghibelline, Heaney claims, "is between two often contradictory commands: to be faithful to the collective historical experience and to be true to the recognition of the
emerging self." In this case, however, Heaney is referring
to Dante's influence on **"Station Island"** and not *Field
Work*. Although Dante certainly reinforced Heaney's thematic concerns in the earlier volume, the texture of diction and imagery is always closer to the poetry of Robert
Lowell.

The echoes of Lowell are so unmistakable that several
critics have accused Heaney of playing magpie to the
American poet's magisterial song. Lowell's powerful,
burnished rhetoric and his penchant for long chains of
adjectives, reverberate through *Field Work*. Lowell's
example was liberating as well as constraining. His furi-
ously candid self-scrutiny, his guilty dramas of the poet's
conflicting responsibilities to marriage, society, and art,
and his sad confessions of failure to spouses and sponsors, encouraged Heaney to mine a rich new vein.

Heaney's relation to Lowell is perhaps best characterized
not by Harold Bloom's "anxiety of influence," but by his
own perplexed "anxiety of trust." When asked about his
friendship with Lowell, Heaney remarked, "There was a

certain trust and intimacy. He had a great gift for making
you feel close, and he had tremendous grace and insight."
In his review of *Day by Day,* Heaney praised Lowell as
one of the exemplary masters, "obstinate and conservative
in his belief in the creative spirit, yet contrary and disruptive in his fidelity to his personal intuitions and experiences" [*Preoccupations,* 1980]. And in the memorial address delivered after Lowell's death, he specifies what he
trusts most in Lowell's art, and what, in turn, he feels
obligated to entrust to others.

> He was and will remain a pattern for poets in his
> amphibious ability to plunge into the downward
> reptilian welter of the self and yet raise himself with
> whatever knowledge he gained there out on to the
> hard ledges of the historical present, which he then
> apprehended with refreshed insight and intensity, as in
> his majestic poem 'For the Union Dead,' and many
> others, especially in the collection *Near the Ocean.*

It is interesting to note that Heaney originally distrusted
the majesty of "For the Union Dead." In a review published in 1966 [in *Outposts,* Vol. 68, Spring 1966], he
tells of "reading and wondering about the little poem," of
wanting "to feel that it is an achievement as solemn and
overwhelming as it seems to be." In the end he concludes,
"although I find it at once public and personal, dignified
and indignant, I miss the impregnable quality that comes
when a poem is perfectly achieved. The transitions, if not
arbitrary, are not inevitable and the rhythm in the middle
stanzas does not body forth the ominous tone." Heaney's
personal and literary bonds with Lowell obviously grew
closer over the years, yet uncertainty and doubt remained.
"Heaney's trust in other poets is itself part of his art,"
Christopher Ricks claims. It may be more correct to say
that his art is a force field in which trust and distrust exist
in tense proximity.

A "Profile" in *The Observer* divulged some of the reasons
for Heaney's wariness of Lowell. According to the anonymous author, Heaney "has found it hard to live down a
reputation for obligingness," some of

> which goes back to the trick that a mad Robert Lowell
> played, crankily testing him out, when Heaney visited
> him in hospital in 1976. (The previous night Lowell
> had broken out of hospital to award Heaney the Duff
> Cooper Memorial Prize.) 'Would you like some of
> this benedictine?' Lowell invited him. Heaney eyed
> the bottle suspiciously, was reassured that it did indeed
> contain Benedictine, and took a swig of what turned
> out to be after-shave. [*The Observer,* June 21, 1987]

Heaney's elegy to Lowell in *Field Work* is certainly no
gullible obeisance to the American poet. Rather it is a
knowing testimonial which also testifies against Lowell
for his notorious shenanigans. Although Heaney delivers
a responsible avowal of indebtedness, flattering the
"sponsor" by imitating him, he also writes a declaration
of independence which slyly mocks the great artist's great
faults. While Lowell made Heaney drink after-shave,
Heaney imagines Lowell drinking a bitter potion too:

You drank America
like the heart's
iron vodka,

promulgating art's
deliberate, peremptory
love and arrogance.

The metaphorical American "spirits" Lowell drinks are the spirits of the dead (Jonathan Edwards, Cotton Mather, Captain Ahab), whose violent spiritual devotions reflect his own. Lowell, the literary "master," also wields some of the peremptory arrogance of a political taskmaster. His nickname, Cal, after all referred to Caligula, and in "Beyond the Alps" (a poem **"Oysters"** echoes) he identified with the latter imperialistic tyrant, Mussolini, stipulating that "the skirt-mad Mussolini unfurled/ the eagle of Caesar. He was one of us/ only, pure prose." For Heaney, whose poetry from the start has registered the most minute tremors of imperialistic aggrandizement (even in the very consonants and vowels of his words), the Latinate "deliberate" and "peremptory" suggest Lowell's de-liberating, emperor-like ways.

"Elegy," in fact, is as much an allegory of invasion and conquest as Heaney's etymological poems in *Wintering Out* and historical narratives in *North*. In earlier poems such as **"Anahorish," "Toome,"** and **"Broagh,"** which are all place-names in Northern Ireland, Heaney sketched out phonetic allegories in which vowels represented his native Gaelic (and by extension his Catholic and Republican sentiments), consonants represented his Anglo-Saxon heritage (and the Protestant and Unionist faction), and vocables represented their ideal harmony on Irish soul. A poem like **"A New Song"** advocated a deliberate repossession of the linguistic ground dominated for centuries by the English empire and its recalcitrant heirs. Heaney imagines the Irish uprising as a mellifluous Gaelic river (like Joyce's Anna Livia Plurabelle) flooding its banks and then assimilating the consonantal demesnes of foreign Protestant nobles. He declares:

But now our river tongues must rise
From licking deep in native haunts
To flood, with vowelling embrace,
Demesnes staked out in consonants.

The linguistic geography is emphatically political here, as Heaney explains in his biographical reminiscence, "1972":

I was symbolically placed between the marks of English influence and the lure of the native experience, between the 'demesne' and 'the bog'. The demesne was Moyola Park, an estate now occupied by Lord Moyola . . . ex-Unionist Prime Minister of Northern Ireland. The bog was a wide apron of swamp on the west bank of the River Bann.

At the end of **"A New Song"** Heaney promises to invite his traditional enemies to join him in the struggle toward Irish unity. He addresses numerous emblems of British dominance—townlands, plantations, fortified "bawns" and "bleaching greens" used by planters in their flax and linen work—but ultimately offers Irish emblems (the Gaelic hillfort and ritual basin stone in the last line) to signify incorporation:

And Castledawson we'll enlist
And Upperlands, each planted bawn—
Like bleaching-greens resumed by grass—
A vocable, as rath and bullaun.

Heaney will enlist the opposition to form an ecumenical phalanx, just as he will merge Gaelic vowels with Anglo-Saxon consonants to make "poems [that] will be vocables to my whole experience."

In his **"Elegy,"** he similarly plans to enlist Lowell's patriarchal "English" attitudes and then recast them according to his Irish point-of-view. Enthralled by Lowell, he identifies with other Irishmen "enthralled" by imperial conquerors, and distrusts his reverence. In the allegory Lowell and his art appear as a figurative ship mastering the "ungovernable" Irish sea (like Raleigh and Spenser in earlier poems), a sea which Heaney has historical reasons to fear:

As you swayed the talk
and rode on the swaying tiller
of yourself, ribbing me
about my fear of water,

what was not within your empory?

The "master" here is dictating how the conversation flows, but is also swaying with inebriated enthusiasm as his ego cuts ahead like the ship's prow. The "empory," the territory of the emperor, is that ground "possessed" by Lowell that Heaney wants to repossess, just as he so often talks of reclaiming Catholic Ireland once possessed by Protestant England. Heaney settles his differences with Lowell by inscribing them into his tribute. Lowell, after all, was tracing the same route as past empire-builders, sailing from England with his aristocratic wife, Lady Caroline Blackwood, to property they owned in Ireland.

As Heaney fills out his "life study" of Lowell, the older poet emerges as linguistic imperialist "Englishing Russian," curmudgeonly artist "bullying out" sonnets to Harriet and Lizzie, and Roman gladiator (*retiarius*) throwing a net over his victim to hold him down (the sort of event Caligula would applaud with great glee, although Heaney is no doubt referring to Lowell's artistic "fishnet of tarred rope" in "Dolphin"). He is also that uproarious sailing carnival, the "night ferry," that crosses regularly between England and Ireland. In the end, the portrait of Lowell turns out to be an ambivalent response to a heroic artist's tragic flaws. Heaney's line, "Your eyes saw what your hand did," a borrowing of Lowell's confession in "Dolphin," reveals Lowell as the self-interrogatory, self-accusing and self-punishing poet that he was. If he is emperor he is also humbled slave, rendered timorous and pedestrian by his manic conscience. If he is the shielding and shielded patriarch of his early poems, he is also the shieldless victim of his later period. He is the majestic clipper ship and ordinary ferry, conquering seaman and conquered islander, ungovernable plunderer and governed native. Like the other artists memorialized in *Field Work*, he becomes Heaney's double, an ambiguous persona dramatizing his own confusions. Heaney, too, is "imperially male," as he confesses in "Act of Union," and like Lowell he explores a psyche and heritage divided by masterful and servile impulses. In examining Lowell, he strives for empathy, but at the same time submits the other poet's masterful images and authoritarian ways to a vigilant distrust, and attacks himself in the process.

Heaney's other elegies fasten on artists for similar reasons of identification, self-diagnosis, and judgment, and test the risks that trusting others involves. Trusting Lowell was made more difficult because of the different traditions the two poets represented. At the end of **"Elegy"** it is "the fish-dart" of Lowell's eyes "risking, 'I'll pray for you,'" that reminds Heaney of the Anglo-Protestant (turned Catholic and then agnostic) dangerously risking intimacy with the Catholic Irishman (although lapsed), and the long history of sectarian distrust that such a gesture implies. In his elegy to Sean O'Riada, the famous Irish composer who died in 1971, Heaney borrows Lowell's style ("a black stiletto trembling in its mark" is vintage Lowell), but his bond with the other Catholic artist from Ulster is more intimate from the start. O'Riada resembles Heaney's actual father rather than his artistic "father," Lowell. He "herds" the orchestra with his baton, as Patrick Heaney once herded cattle in County Derry.

> He conducted the Ulster Orchestra
> like a drover with an ashplant
> herding them south.
> I watched them from behind,
>
> springy, formally suited,
> a black stiletto trembling in its mark,
> a quill flourishing itself,
> a quickened, whitened head.

The political and religious implications of this gesture are born out at the end: "he was jacobite,/ he was our young pretender." That is, he resembled the defeated Catholic James II and his son rather than William of Orange and his Protestant ascendancy. As in the Lowell elegy Heaney tends to obscure O'Riada with a plethora of metaphors. He, like Lowell, is a boat and fish, but also a drover, knife, quill, head, fisherman—but "more falconer than fisherman"—king, king's son, gannet, minnow, and wader. He invokes this multitudinous bestiary, however, for a definite purpose: to underscore the artist's necessary but problematic trust in feral instinct and his related bestial distrust of too much cerebration. "He had the *sprezzatura*," Heaney declares, the nonchalance and natural skill of an animal, "trusting the gift,/ risking gift's undertow." As Lowell certainly knew, the Muses are often Sirens, dragging the artist down into oceanic depths. But Heaney celebrates O'Riada's courage in courting the Muse through risky submission rather than controlled exertion (he works by lying down "like ballast in the bottom of the boat/

listening to the cuckoo"). Heaney, too, will take his chances. He will risk getting pulled under as he learns to trust the Lowellish melodies of *Field Work*.

Some of the political and religious tergiversation that appeared in the Lowell elegy reappears in the elegy to Francis Ledgwidge, which in some ways is a rewriting of Lowell's "For the Union Dead." Here, rather than the bronze statue of Colonel Shaw and his negro infantry, "The bronze soldier hitches a bronze cape/ That crumples stiffly in imagined wind." The historical monuments for both poets inspire meditations on the vestiges of old divisions in their personalities and nations. For Lowell the American Civil War still trembles through his TV set's news of racial strife in contemporary Boston. His mind is similarly split between despair and a violent, primitive desire to plunge into battle, like Colonel Shaw, and die in the struggle for moral reformation. Lowell suffers a further division because of his affiliation with Southern culture (the Fugitives like Tate and Ransom were his early mentors) and his native New England culture of transcendentalists and abolitionists. For Heaney, Ledgwidge is another Shaw, an emblem of loyalties split between North and South, but in the context of Irish battles between Protestant and Catholic, British unionist and Irish nationalist. As Heaney explains in a review of Alice Curtayne's biography, Ledgwidge was a Catholic from Southern Ireland and a Sinn Fein sympathizer who supported the Easter Rising of 1916. Paradoxically, he also accepted patronage from an Anglo-Irish lord and allowed his first book to be "introduced to the world by a Unionist peer," and finally joined the British army only to die fighting alongside his traditional foes in 1918. As Lowell traces the native haunt of Colonel Shaw on his retrospective walk around Boston, so Heaney walks with his Aunt Mary around Drogheda where Ledgwidge engaged in "genteel trysts with rich farmer's daughters." The abrupt transitions between Heaney's personal memories, his speculations on his aunt's life during the Great War, quotations from Ledgwidge, and his vision of him in a Tommy's uniform in the Dardanelles at Ypres, lacks Lowell's uncanny ability to make disparate elements cohere. At the end, however, Heaney resurrects Ledgwidge as spokesman for his own Catholic and republican pieties, and through him delivers a moving address:

> In you, our dead enigma, all the strains
> Criss-cross in useless equilibrium
> And as the wind tunes through this vigilant bronze
> I hear again the sure confusing drum
>
> You followed from Boyne water to the Balkans
> But miss the twilit note your flute should sound.
> You were not keyed or pitched like these true-blue
>   ones
> Though all of you consort now underground.

Having betrayed his community's trust by following the English army on a massive "Orange Day" march into the First World War, Ledgwidge now consorts with dubious allies and obvious enemies—uselessly, since, as a corpse, he can do nothing to redress the many divisions he was prey to.

Heaney tries to redress his nation's wounds by simply addressing them, although as he witnesses exemplary figures of the past he also announces his own sectarian proclivities. He expresses solidarity with the dead, tracing his vacillations in terms of theirs and, like the dead in Revelation, he awaits a last judgment that will pitch him toward heaven or hell. His eschatological anxiety, as he once said of Lowell, "arises from one felt responsibility clashing against another." In his essay "Current Unstated Assumptions about Poetry," he speaks of Lowell's covenants with different factions, again in terms of trust and judgment. *Life Studies* "trusts that it has an audience" which will empathize with the poet's divisive responsibilities to family, literature, society, and history and understand his inevitable failings. Heaney is speaking of his own ideals when he says of Lowell's:

> we respond to Lowell's implicit trust in poetic art as a vocation. We register and are fortified by the commitment that has made possible the note of command . . . we feel that this writer is forging his covenant with the past and the future."

When Heaney accepted the Bennet Award from *The Hudson Review* in 1982, he seized the occasion to remind himself and his audience "of the responsibilities of the creative life" and then spoke of his own sense of a trusting covenant: "I thank and congratulate the sponsors of this prize for ratifying in such an open-handed way that covenant we all hope for between artist and audience." With so many commitments, it is no wonder the poet often found himself rattling the chains of his own making.

Domestic covenants between father and son, which were collapsing in **"Elegy,"** are mended in **"The Harvest Bow."** Here Heaney's father is a shield for his son, an icon the poet yearns to trust and revere, but the son's image reflected in the shield is the "Lockjawed, mantrapped" one that Heaney delineated in **"An Afterward."** For both father and son the shield represents the hard, silent, repressed mask that conceals but also reveals the violence of their instinctual energies beneath. Heaney's father is both overtly brutal and appealingly mellow. He laps "the spurs on a lifetime of gamecocks" and whacks "the tips off weeds and bushes," yet in "mellowed silence" he weaves the beautiful harvest bows. The poem owes some of its pastoral quiet to Keats's "Ode to a Grecian Urn" and "To Autumn" (Keats was Heaney's original poetic father), but Heaney is hardly as sanguine about art's ability to reconcile opposites as his early "sponsor." Truth and beauty, like the poet's contradictory need for both contemplative quiet and a voice to speak against political atrocities, are at violent odds. The poem is as much a confession as an esthetic treatise, as much a guilty, distrustful exploration of the tangled genealogical roots of Heaney's social quietism as an apology for them.

As Neil Corcoran has pointed out [in his *Seamus Heaney,* 1986], **"Harvest Bow"** can "be considered a revision of **'Digging.'"** In addition, it harks back to **"Boy Driving his Father to Confession,"** an uncollected poem written at about the same time (1965), in which a tender filial relationship is disturbed by the son's growing sense of disillusionment. Heaney recounts: "Four times [I] found chinks in the paternal mail/ To find you lost like me, quite vulnerable." The chinks, in this case, reveal little of the man beneath the armor. So Heaney wonders: "What confession/ Are you preparing? Do you tell sins as I would?/ Does the same hectic rage in our one blood?" By the time he wrote **"The Harvest Bow,"** father and son had been reconciled, paradoxically, by their mutual feelings of "otherness." The bow twisted out of what Keats once called "the alien corn" is an emblem of their alien status, of their social unease and political disenchantment, which amounts to an indifference toward vocal protest against and active participation in current events. Both affirm the silent, peaceful art of making. If Heaney groped "awkwardly to know his father" as a young man in **"Confession,"** now he offers "a knowable corona" which knots them together. To the question "Do you tell sins as I would?" he answers, "I tell and finger . . . [the bow] like braille,/ Gleaning the unsaid off the palpable." His familiarity with his father's silences allows him to forge an understanding that approaches complete trust. His father no longer has to tell his son "what is going on/ Under that thick grey skull," as Heaney rather indecorously put it in the earlier poem. Identifying with his "otherness," Heaney can now "read" his father's mind with all the assurance of a blindman reading braille.

In *Field Work* Heaney often appears to be walking through a mine field of his own design. He knows where the mines are, locates them, defuses them, but as he keeps versing and reversing over the field he continues, almost against his will, to plant new ones.

—*Henry Hart*

Like Stephen Dedalus searching for real, artistic, and mythical fathers in *Ulysses,* what Heaney keeps finding at the end of his quests is himself. His father appears as his artistic shadow, not a cattle dealer worrying about the price of grain and farm equipment so much as an exemplary artistic "father," an O'Riada or Lowell, who trusts the "gift and worked with fine intent" until his masterful "fingers moved somnambulant." From the talismanic harvest bow Heaney conjures up an image that implies that the child is father to the man. If Heaney trusts his paternal "sponsors" like himself, he also submits both self and other to wary scrutiny. The submerged quarrel with his father in **"The Harvest Bow"** is fundamentally a quarrel with himself. Like Yeats, Heaney knows that poetry is born from this inner battle, but he also yearns for a peaceful reconciliation. The poem's motto taken from Yeats, "the end of art is peace," is ironic, because both poets distrust peace as anything but a momentary pause in art's continuing, potentially tragic, yet ultimately fruitful dialectic.

After the father's shaping "intent" is found culpably apolitical and his gift judged a seductive snare, Heaney implies that neither his spirit nor the corn's spirit have been put to peaceful rest. If peace was permanent, art would end permanently too. To rest in peace is a temptation that Heaney, like "the spirit of the corn," has slipped from at the end.

Poetic quarrels with real and artistic fathers have their obvious corollaries in Heaney's political and marital poems. They too recognize the ineluctable conflict that is at the root of creation. They hoist the white flag for peace and then, in a more sober mood, cannot swear allegiance to it. Heaney's marriage poems have been praised for their "unromanticizing exactitude," and yet they seem natural offshoots of what Geoffrey Hill (borrowing a line that Keith Sagar applied to Ted Hughes) has called the "major Romanticism of our time": the struggle to negotiate a productive alliance between the individual mind and everything that is beyond it, [in *The Lords of Limit,* 1984]. Or, as Sagar puts it, to find "a way for reconciling human vision with the energies, powers, presences, of the non-human cosmos." The urge to distrust all peaceful reconciliations is also, as Hill points out, part of the inner dynamic of Romanticism: "Romantic art is thoroughly familiar with the reproaches of life. Accusation, self-accusation, are the very life-blood of its most assured rhetoric." Heaney's marriage poems, which trace separations and reunions, domestic squabbles and partial mendings, fit neatly into this Romantic loop. What is startling and disturbing about them is their tendency to envision women as part of the "non-human cosmos," as animals, trees or, even more unflatteringly, as mud or water. Heaney, though, is not as insouciant as he first appears. Rather than relegate women to a demeaning niche on the phylogenetic scale, his purpose is to break down stuffy views of marriage and squeamish attitudes toward sexual and artistic creation. His vision is androgynous rather than misogynist. His metaphor of marriage on its most primal level involves a trusting at-one-ment between self and other, individual vision and actual fact, and he depicts this bond ecologically, in terms of human interaction with animals, vegetation, and minerals.

The tension that shudders through these poems again arises from the two charged poles of trust and distrust. As Christopher Ricks has said [in *The London Review of Books,* November 8, 1979] of Heaney's Lowellish **"The Skunk,"** a poem about the separation from his wife when he taught in California, it is an "exquisitely comic love-poem, and you have to love your wife most trustingly, and trust in the reciprocity, before you would trust yourself to a comparison of her to a skunk." It is the skunk and not the wife, however, that dominates the poem, although wife and skunk ultimately merge into a figure of otherness, of what Heaney has called in his discussion of another animal poem, **"The Badgers,"** "the night-self, the night part in everybody, the scuttling secret parts of life." The word, "night," in fact, is repeated five times in **"The Skunk."** It has some of the religious connotations of St. John of the Cross's "dark night," just as it does in Lowell's "Skunk Hour," although Lowell's 'otherworld' in which he search-

es for love, divine or profane, is hellishly unfulfilling. Heaney is more contented, and more enthusiastic about the religious alliance of sacred and profane, Christian and pagan, than Lowell. His totemic skunk is first compared to a celebrant wearing ecclesiastical vestments ("the chasuble") at a funeral mass, as if he were about to commune with God. The skunk is a kind of medium, whose purpose is to deliver the shamanistic poet into the spirit world. The word "wife" has a similarly magic power. It transubstantiates what is absent (Heaney's real wife) so that the word's "slender vowel" takes on her bodily form and his wife's presence permeates "the night earth and air/ of California." In **"The Skunk"** the process by which the "otherness" of Heaney's wife is sacramentalized in the California night is complex but lyrically provocative:

> The beautiful, useless
> Tang of eucalyptus spelt your absence.
> The aftermath of a mouthful of wine
> Was like inhaling you off a cold pillow.

In his deft way, Heaney is turning his uxorious skunk and his letter-writing to his wife into a miniature fable of what David Jones (in a book Heaney had read by this time) described as man's "extra-utilist, or sacramentalist" vision:

> The Incarnation and the Eucharist cannot be separated; the one thing being analogous to the other. If one binds us to the animalic the other binds us to artefacture and both bind us to *signa,* for both are a showing forth of the invisible under visible signs.

For Heaney in **"The Skunk"** sacred and profane love intermingle as ordinary objects become signs bodying forth the invisible presence of his wife.

The poem ends, however, with a more candid 'bodying forth.' If wife and skunk have been sacramentalized, "damasked like the chasuble" at mass, now the ornamental garment is stripped off, the "ordinary" body unveiled. Voyant and voyeur comically merge as Heaney watches his wife disrobe before bed. In her ultimate re-veiling, "The black plunge-line nightdress" she puts on recalls the black chasuble in the first stanza, although this ceremony is erotic rather than funereal.

Heaney's journeys into the fecund night often resemble prayers and Catholic meditations, although with a deliberately sexual slant. **"Homecomings,"** in which "love is a nesting trust," as Ricks observes, also articulates a prayer for the self's deliverance. Here a male sandmartin "veering/ breast to breast with himself" is Heaney's symbol for the self-preoccupied artist. His flight is a meditative one, a transport from the diurnal ego toward the desired other. The meditation requires "A glottal stillness," an attentive tuning in to an autochthonous demiurge. His wife once again becomes the "dark lady," both earth mother and muse, sandmartin and sandy bank in which she nests. Heaney prays for the kind of self-occlusion that will lead to luminous revelation:

Mould my shoulders inward to you.
Occlude me.
Be damp clay pouting.
Let me listen under your eaves.

Again the wife is rather unflatteringly anatomized, and again she becomes a projection of the poet's oracular "night self," his creative unconscious. Although Heaney promised to open a door into the light in *Field Work*, he keeps opting for a door into the dark.

The mythic equation between women, nature, and imagination implicit in Heaney's poetry from the start, receives a more candid, pared-down avowal in these later poems. Few early poems, for example, have the passionate brevity of **"Polder,"** where the wife is cast as a stormy sea dyked and transformed by her husband into a fertile land ("polder" is the Dutch word for reclaimed land):

I have reclaimed my polder,
all its salty grass and mud-slick banks;

under fathoms of air, like an old willow
I stir a little on my creel of roots.

As usual, though, Heaney seems hesitant to explore the sexual politics and gender stereotypes that these poems suggest. In **"The Otter,"** an amphibious Heaney (like Ted Hughes in "An Otter" and "The Thought-Fox") enters the animistic "otherworld" to write his poem, and characteristically the otter *is* the other, his wife and muse. She delivers the poem like a gift after the poet's sexual plunge into what he partially fears (the symbolic waters). Risk and trust, for Heaney, is as important to love-making as to poetry-writing. After his wife "swims" on her back, she "gives birth," "printing the stones" like Hughes's "thought fox" printing the page after "It enters the dark hole of the head."

As for Stephen Dedalus, who quests for a father but, in the end, finds a mother, Heaney's ultimate symbol of the unified self he yearns for is a woman. Not to be outdone by Joyce, who mythicized his wife into an archetype of all wives, mothers, and daughters, whether Virgin Mary or pagan fertility goddess, Molly Bloom or Anna Livia Plurabelle, Heaney transforms his own Marie into an emblem of a universal *élan vital*, then launches forth to make her example his own. This is the gist of the title poem, **"Field Work,"** where loosened meters and relaxed diction underscore the journey towards spontaneous fecundity and the trust in his wife which mirrors his trust in himself. The poem commences in separation but concludes, after national and personal boundaries have been crossed and old suppositions negated, with the poet at one with his anointed image. Although Heaney dramatizes his process of "individuation" in terms of multiple crossings, he chooses bodily symbols rather than the Cross to carry his meaning. Still, Christ the wounded, healing God is behind them all.

Trust and faith are obviously more pressing issues when wife and husband are on different sides of the world. In **"Field Work,"** however, Heaney faithfully travels back across the Atlantic to wife and home and, unlike Ahab, persistently seeks an emblem of concord rather than adversity, of contraries crossed in a regenerative unity rather than crucified into oblivion. Ring symbols of moon and coin highlight this "marriage-in-separation":

Our moon was small and far,
was a coin long gazed at

brilliant on the *Pequod's* mast
across Atlantic and Pacific waters.

As the poem progresses, it counters images of destruction, disease and death with those of burgeoning fertility. It traverses a *via negativa* from imaginary, nocturnal unions in California to actual, sexual unions in Ireland. Even though he proposes that his mythic image of woman, his mandala of a unified self, is "Not the mud slick . . . and pock-marked leaves," "Not the cow parsley in winter/ with its old whitened shins," "Not even the tart green shade of summer thick with . . . fungus," but the radiant "sunflower, dreaming umber," his intention is to subsume these negatives rather than pit them against each other.

The ritualistic finale reenacts a strange but touching scene of marital rapprochement. To Yeats's observation "love has pitched his mansion in/ The place of excrement," Heaney adds Lawrentian details: "Catspiss smell,/ the pink bloom open." He presses the flowering currant to his wife's skin for her "veins to be crossed/ criss-cross with leaf-veins," and "anoint[s] the anointed/ leaf-shape" with his thumbprint. The new mark, like a stigmata of the cross, testifies to crucifying trials and exemplary faithfulness. The divisions in the poem between husband and wife, imagination and reality, "perfect" animal existence and "imperfect" human travail, vegetation goddess and actual woman, are fused in the final mark made by the leaf and mould. "You are stained, stained/ to perfection," Heaney declares at the end, thinking of the redemptive ordeals through which both wife and poem have passed.

Freedom and responsibility, trust and doubt, rend the political poems in *Field Work* as well as those dramatizing marital and literary relations. As he bears witness to sectarian killings, Heaney invokes the dead to corroborate his dilemmas. Almost without exception his victims are innocent bystanders (like himself), who for one reason or another refuse to get embroiled in political battles but also refuse to get out of their way. Those who repudiate the Troubles, going about their business as if nothing unusual is happening, usually end up dead. "Too near the ancient troughs of blood/ Innocence is no earthly weapon," Heaney might say with Geoffrey Hill (in "Ovid in the Third Reich"). Like Hill he feels obvious empathy for the unearthly innocents, yet he distrusts their freedom from worldy exigencies as well. In his elegy for Sean Armstrong, for example, he tells how his Queen's University friend who "dropped-out" to pursue the pot-smoking, communal lifestyle of the sixties, only to return to work at childrens' playgrounds in Belfast, was "changed utterly" by an assassin's bullet:

Drop-out on a come-back
Prince of no-man's land
With your head in clouds or sand,
You were the clown
Social worker of the town
Until your candid forehead stopped
A pointblank teatime bullet.

In this Lowellish "life-study," when Heaney observes "Yet something in your voice/ Stayed nearly shut/ . . . It was independent, rattling, non-transcendent/ Ulster," he is also observing his own reluctance to speak out. His portrait of iconoclastic independence, in the end, is a confessional self-portrait which delineates his distrust of political absent-mindedness, especially when it leads to martyrdom.

Louis O'Neil, Heaney's drinking friend who was blown up by the IRA in his father-in-law's pub (the bombing was a reprisal for the Bloody Sunday murders by British paratroopers), is another authorial double—the illiterate, nearly silent, slyly independent self Heaney would like to trust but ultimately distrusts. The poem describes a series of "turnings," in which his friend, having turned his paradoxically "observant back" on straightforward engagements with the Troubles, is partly to blame for their continuing cycle. When Heaney asks, "How culpable was he/ That last night when he broke/ Our tribe's complicity?" he turns the question on himself, since he too seeks to break free from tribal complicity. The futile turning away from sins of commission, however, only perpetrates sins of omission. Like the figures bound to Yeats's gyres and Eliot's stairways, Heaney seems entrapped in purgatorial anxiety. If Heaney's purpose in **"Casualty"** is to bury the dead, he fails. O'Neil's ghost is "revenant" at the end, haunting him with accusations of guilt.

Heaney's attitude toward the IRA is deeply ambivalent and perhaps the fundamental wound behind his many festering political anxieties. In **"Triptych"** he elegizes Christopher Ewart-Briggs, murdered by the IRA in 1976, and again plunges into the familiar dialectic, yearning for freedom and fertility—"a stone house by a pier./ Elbow room. Broad window light," with a down-to-earth vegetation goddess "Carrying a basket full of new potatoes,/ Three tight green cabbages, and carrots"—while painfully aware that his quest for poetic freedom and creativity only makes his sectarian affiliations more agonizing. His psyche is as riven as Ireland itself. His nation's "saurian relapses" and negative sea changes (its "comfortless noises" allude to those in *The Tempest*), in fact, are his own. He hopes "forgiveness finds its nerve and voice," but when he examines his native ground, he finds only a "flayed or calloused" corpse whose voice has been strangled in blood. In the third section his emblems of religious transcendence, like Lowell's statue of the Lady of Walsingham in "The Quaker Graveyard in Nantucket," whose face, "expressionless, expresses God," again rebukes his dream of trust, freedom and deliverance. "On Boa the god-eyed, sex-mouthed stone" is "two-faced, trepanned," a mirror image of Heaney's own ambiguous stance, which echoes the poet's "silence with silence."

As he examines the Christian ruins on the islands in Lough Beg, and the ruins Christian factions have littered across Ireland for centuries, he finally acknowledges his own vestigial Catholicism, since it provides a way to confess to collusion and work toward therapeutic redemption:

Everything in me
Wanted to bow down, to offer up,
To go barefoot, foetal and penitential,

and pray at the water's edge.

Yet he feels impelled "to bow down" partly because "The helicopter shadowing" the march at Newry forces him to, and partly because of his urge for a womb-like withdrawal from all political activities. As Stephen Dedalus was shocked by the word *foetus* carved in the desk at his father's old school (since it suggests his failure to be artistically born), Heaney is shocked by his similar failure to be politically born and to establish a credo he can trust and act on. He wants to return home, as in **"The Toome Road,"** to that "untoppled omphalos" of Mossbawn where political and religious turmoil was eclipsed by pastoral calm and where beliefs were more certain, more stable. He distrusts that nostalgia too, just as he distrusts the peaceful "snare" of the harvest bow. As **"Triptych"** attests, he engages in the protest march, but still can't be convinced that he has done enough.

In *Field Work* Heaney often appears to be walking through a mine field of his own design. He knows where the mines are, locates them, defuses them, but as he keeps versing and reversing over the field he continues, almost against his will, to plant new ones. The things he is most devoted to—his Irish heritage, poetic craft, marriage—exercise his rigorous sense of responsibility to the breaking point. He wants to "respond" to "sponsors" and "spouses," actual and imaginary, literary and familial, but their diverse claims fill him with moral anguish. Freedom from those claims is a transcendence hoped for but renounced. If *Field Work* indicates a partial relaxation of the constrictions Heaney felt in Belfast and scored into the tight stanzas of *North* in Wicklow, it also agonizes over that relaxation. To slip through the harvest bows that promise deceptive peace and to escape the paramilitary groups assuring prolonged violence requires persistent vigilance. Those who relax in *Field Work* often get shot or blown up.

Heaney insists that his art, like his marriage and politics, depends on trust. Nevertheless, as he freely avails himself to that constellation of otherness—audience, wife, spirit, animal, vegetation, the earth itself—he recoils in uncertainty and distrust, as if always fearing bedevilment by the forces that originally succored him. The "others," as the poems show, comprise a "compound ghost," which is really Heaney's multi-faceted mask or shadow. Although many of the poems in *Field Work* resemble "trial-pieces" (similar to but not as accomplished as the **"Trial-Pieces"** in *North*), they are courageous in their willingness to explore new territory, to trust hunches and take risks. While some careers would wilt under the intense self-scrutiny Heaney applies to himself and his art, his career seems to gain force and immediacy because of it. As Heaney said of Lowell, whose influence is noticeable in almost every poem in *Field Work*, he "dared to perceive himself historically, as a representative figure." Heaney also dares to test his poetic accomplishments with unprecedented self-questionings and self-accusations. Although he is aware of the dangers of plunging forward encumbered with responsibilities, his dedication has paid off. As Lowell was once lauded as the representative poet of America, so Heaney is now deemed the exemplary poet of Ireland by a swelling audience of critics and ordinary readers alike.

Sidney Burris (essay date 1990)

SOURCE: "Heaney and the Pastoral Persuasion," in *The Poetry of Resistance: Seamus Heaney and the Pastoral Persuasion,* Ohio University Press, 1990, pp. 1-34.

[*In the following excerpt, Burris places Heaney's poetry within the context of pastoral tradition.*]

Abducted by Hades and spirited away to the underworld, Persephone ate several seeds from a pomegranate, the fruit traditionally associated with marriage and fertility cults. The price of her impudence was her freedom. Ingestion of the fruit sealed the marital alliance, and Demeter, Persephone's mother and one of the oldest, most powerful goddesses of the Greek pantheon, lost her daughter to an infernal son-in-law. With Zeus as her advocate, however, Demeter struck a deal with Hades, and Persephone was allowed to live with her mother for the better part of each year. During this time, the crops flourished. But when Persephone returned to the underworld to spend the remaining months with her husband, the earth became cold and barren. For the Greeks, the seasonal cycle—the pastoral calendar—sprang from a pomegranate seed.

The etymological history of the word "pomegranate" claims an essentially pastoral lineage, one that exemplifies what Puttenham, in *The Arte of English Poesie* (1589), described as the genre's tendency to employ "rude speeches to insinuate and glance at greater matters." Its Latin root "granatus" means, simply, "having many seeds," and the Romans used the substantive "granatum" to denote the same fruit, centuries before them, that the Babylonians had thrown on the floor of the bridal chamber—the fat, ripe pomegranates would burst open, scattering their seeds and, it was hoped, their fertility, on the newly married couple. Later, the French realized that the pomegranate exploded in much the same fashion as one of their own implements of war, and their coinage eventually yielded our "grenade," or "hand grenade," as it is most commonly known. This duplicity of the word "grenade," with its obvious allegiance to the martial tradition but with its informing vision of marital fertility, makes it one of the luminous words in the title poem of Heaney's first book, *Death of a Naturalist* (1966):

Then one hot day when fields were rank
With cowdung in the grass the angry frogs

Invaded the flax-dam; I ducked through hedges
To a coarse croaking that I had not heard
Before. The air was thick with a bass chorus.
Right down the dam gross-bellied frogs were
     cocked
On sods; their loose necks pulsed like snails. Some
     hopped:
The slap and plop were obscene threats. Some sat
Poised like mud grenades, their blunt heads farting.
I sickened, turned, and ran. The great slime kings
Were gathered there for vengeance and I knew
That if I dipped my hand the spawn would clutch
     it.

Puttenham would not have acknowledged **"Death of a Naturalist"** as a work of pastoral art, even though its language is muscularly rude. The glittering pastures that he envisaged lay far from the open countryside, and these "self-same hills," when depicted in "Lycidas" and early Renaissance poetry, arrive with cartographic accuracy from Virgil's "Eclogue 4," an eclogue radiant with the promise of a restored Golden Age. Such promises, however, make exacting demands on the poet. To dream of a Golden Age, to create the illusion of perfection, pastoral writers sparingly deployed the particularizing detail that might suddenly have transported their readers from an Arcadian vale to an English valley. A decision to write pastoral poetry automatically entailed formal requirements, and these forms dictated the predictable conformations of pastoral landscapes. Suited in such constrictive armor, the genre would seem impervious to the obsessive particularity of Heaney's poem. But even the earliest English pastorals are partly shorn of their Grecian garb, incorporating specific details of the English country side while preserving themes and ideas inherited from the classical models. Digression often breeds irrelevancy, but the various registers of the pastoral voice are nowadays as elusive as they once were alluring; Heaney's version of pastoral develops several strategies native to the tradition, and an analysis of these strategies will provide the historical background necessary to assess the exact nature of Heaney's accomplishment.

With its opening invitation, Robert Herrick's "The Wake" (1648) recalls an invitation found in Christopher Marlowe's "The Passionate Shepherd to His Love" (1599), written a half-century earlier. "Come live with me, and be my love," began Marlowe's shepherd, in the land with "Vallies, groves, hills and fields" that have become for many readers the emblematic topography of classical pastoral. But Herrick's speaker, perhaps equally idealistic in his travel plans, exhibits a more English, more localized sense of place than that of his predecessor:

Come, Anthea, let us two
Go to Feast, as others do.
Tarts and Custards, Creams and Cakes,
Are the Junketts still at Wakes:
Unto which the Tribes resort,
Where the business is the sport.
Morris-dancers thou shalt see,
Marian, too, in Pagentrie:

And a Mimick to devise
Many grinning properties.
Players there will be, and those
Base in action as in clothes;
Yet with strutting they will please
The incurious Villages.
Near the dying of the day
There will be a *Cudgell*-Play
Where a *Coxcomb* will be broke,
Ere a good *word* can be spoke:
But the anger ends all here,
Drenched in Ale or drowned in Beere.
Happy Rusticks, best content
With the cheapest Merriment;
And possesse no other feare
Than to want the Wake next Yeare.

The vision here of rural simplicity and abundance is common to pastoral writing from its beginnings in Theocritus and Virgil. If Herrick's seems a somewhat decadent, condescending version—his rustics, after all, are "drowned in Beere"—his affable setting, a Bruegel scene in all its particularity, begins to color the pastoral horizon. In 1629, Herrick became a country clergyman in Devonshire; since 1623, he had been a member of Jonson's literary coterie in London, and the splenetic rural clergyman never forgot the splendid royal courtier. Although employing the generalized, pastoral themes of simplicity and abundance, the poem relies on its subversive particularity—as the tarts and custards yield to ale, beer, and drunkenness—to chart the peot's disgruntlement.

With one eye on the shepherd and the other, for example, on Milton's "Corrupted clergy," pastoral poets have always been walleyed, and this skewed vision accounts for the pastoral's notoriety as a genre susceptible to social and political commentary. In Heaney's case, the concreteness and vivid detail of his writing subsume the several pastoral conventions that still survive to structure his poems. At first glance, his work has little in common with what is habitually labeled pastoral. If **"Death of a Naturalist,"** a poem whose "fields were rank with cowdung," appears perfectly opposed to the "beds of roses" in Marlowe's "The Passionate Shepherd to His Love," such opposing appearances are resolved by Puttenham's suggestion that pastorals employ their rude diction to "insinuate and glance at greater matters." Where grenades are found in Heaney's work, so too are pomegranates, and this subliminal attempt to reconcile the violent particularity of his landscape with some of the generalizing conventions of pastoral poetry aligns him with an important aspect of the genre's tradition.

Displaying these powers of insinuation that Puttenham described, much of Heaney's work remains faithful to its pastoral origins. To speak of contemporary poetry as pastoral in nature is not to speak of its adherence to a set of formal conventions. Swinburne's elegy, "Ave Atque Vale," which appeared in 1868, claims the honor of being the last unquestionably great English elegy to boast of its classical parentage, and by then even that magnificent lamentation seems a step removed from late Victorian verse—the poem excels as much in its nostalgic rarity as in its stunning poetic accomplishments. Heaney would have bewildered Puttenham, as Swinburne would have dismayed him, but he would also have been brought up short by the antipastoral, by Stephen Duck's "The Thresher's Labour" (1736). Although originally from the Wiltshire countryside, he was eventually adopted as a kind of court poet in London, and as a consequence, his verse lost much of its idiosyncratic stamp. Yet Duck's best work insists on the vigorously revisionary impulse that characterizes antipastoral writing and survives to build the foundation for the dissenting voice, the voice of the Northern Irish Catholic heard in Heaney's verse. Here is Duck, in "The Thresher's Labour," protesting and disabusing:

The Shepherd well may tune his Voice to sing
Inspir'd with all the Beauties of the Spring.
No fountains murmur here, no Lambkins play,
No Linnets warble, and no Fields look gay;
'Tis all a gloomy, melancholy Scene,
Fit only to provoke the Muse's Spleen.

But even older, less drastic examples show a similar sensibility. Would Puttenham have recognized the pastures surrounding Penshurst in Jonson's poem of 1616, a time much closer to his own? Though he would have found satyrs lurking and muses lounging and dryads gamboling about the grounds, Puttenham would also have heard a wistful appraisal of feudal harmony at the Penshurst manor, a house whose walls were "rear'd with no man's ruine, no man's grone. . . ." The manor house, once a symbol of power and patronage, of a cooperative understanding between lord and laborer, already appears in the poem bathed in the flattering glow of a distant Golden Age. Because the social order of rural seventeenth-century England relied upon the stabilizing influence and regional authority of the major families, James I had tried to force the English nobility to forsake the indulgent pleasures of London and assume their rightful post as lord and lady of the manor house. Jonson's poem, celebrating Penshurst, the ancestral home of Sidney, presents an enticing vision of Protestant moderation ("Thou art not, Penshurst, built to envious show") and English ascendancy ("Sidney's copse").

But even in the early seventeenth century, some poets were hearing the laborer's groan; some were beginning to claim the hardships of the laborer's life as a subject for poetry and were doing so by deploying their disgruntlements as correctives to pastoral commonplaces. A new realism is afoot and the first two couplets of Francis Quarles's "On the Plough-Man" (1635) succinctly contrasts the traditional pastoral image with the author's qualifying observation, at once generic and political in its objection:

I heare the whistling *Plough-man,* all day long,
Sweetning his labour with a chearefull song:
His Bed's a Pad of *Straw;* His dyet course;
In both, he fares not better then his *Horse.* . . .

As startled as Puttenham would have been to find these poems included in a discussion of pastoral poetry, he would have sympathized in equal measure with the involved arguments that landed them there. Quarles's objection represents an early example of the pastoral's propensity for social and political criticism. Part of Heaney's success in dramatizing the various quandaries faced by the Catholic population of rural Northern Ireland derives from the pastoral's ability to undermine a literary convention with a particularized description. The toppled assumption— whether political or literary—is a less visible result of pastoral writing than of polemical speech making, but the tradition has provided verbal strategies that allow Heaney to depict his own culture in ways that reveal its integrity while gently dispersing the English culture that would disfranchise him. The neat distinctions implied by the terms "pastoral" and "antipastoral" seem to clarify the essential development of a long tradition in English writing: by the late eighteenth and early nineteenth centuries, the laborer's groan was at least as loud as the shepherd's song, and the literature that had once celebrated the harmonies of the countryside now exposed the poverty and hardships suffered by its people.

Yet the story is not so simple. When read closely, the early commentaries reveal a clear awareness of the difference between a plowed field engaged in hawthorne and an emerald pasture rimmed in laurel. Real shepherds, the commentators have always claimed, never enjoyed the carefree ease of the rural life depicted by the classical pastoral. One of the first attempts to develop a systematic exposition of the rudiments and origins of English verse, Puttenham's treatise devotes little space to the pastoral mode or "kind." But his reply to the widely popular notion that the pastoral, because it dealt with an ancient, even prehistoric way of life, represented the oldest form of writing in existence shows that he understood the essential problems confronting all critics who attempt to define the literature:

> Some be of the opinion . . . that the pastoral Poesie . . . should be the first of any other . . . because, they say, the shepheards and haywards assemblies and meetings when they kept their cattell and heards in the common fields and forests was the first familiar conversation, and their babble and talk under bushes and shadie trees, the first disputation and contentious reasoning. . . . And all this may be true, for before there was a shepheard keeper of his owne, or of some other bodies flocke, there was none owner in the world, quick cattell being the first property of any forreine possession. . . . But for all this, I do deny that the *Eclogue* should be the first and most ancient forme of artificiall Poesie, being perswaded that the Poet devised the *Eclogue* long after *drammatick* poems . . . to insinuate and glance at greater matters. . . .

> (book 1, chapter 18)

Puttenham gives full credence to the methodology of an argument that would define a literary genre by locating its origin in the world of daily affairs, of "quick cattell"; when he finally discourages the application of that argument to the "Eclogue," he does so by implying that a realistic representation of the country life was never the intention of pastoral writing. But the charge had been

leveled, and an essential aspect of the pastoral had been recognized: in its attempt to describe theperfected rural society, a society removed from the daily affairs of the city and capable of rendering implicit judgments on those affairs, the best pastoral writing developed rhetorical strategies both to describe the world as it is and to envisage the world as it had been in a past Golden Age. Heaney's earliest verse often depicts the fondest recollections of a childhood passed in the country with an aggressive, even militaristic diction, emphasizing at once the integrity of his culture and the violence that has become a part of its daily ritual. Puttenham is fully aware of the pastoral's natural proclivity for commenting on social or political affairs, for glancing at "greater matters," and he soundly rebuffs the theory that the literature represents the original literary endeavors of the rural society it described.

Puttenham discouraged such notions of authenticity but recognized at the same time that the pastoral's ability to keep one eye trained on the realistic, particularized landscape and one on the idealized vista of a better world represented the genre's most compelling feature. He does not banish the English and European disciples of Virgil to a charmed pleasance; he argues that the countryside, with all of its trappings and accouterments, provides the writer with a vehicle for glancing at matters beyond its immediate purview. Puttenham's elaborate refutations were designed precisely to emphasize the artifice of the genre, to prevent the sixteenth-century reader from viewing the pastoral as a piece of sociological field work. By the eighteenth century, pastoral poets had become so dependent on this same literary artifice only hinted at by Puttenham that critics were once again correcting abuses. When shepherds debate foreign policy, they argued, readers are asked to suspend their disbelief beyond credibility.

The idea of credibility, in one guise or another, has informed both the major critiques and the persuasive examples of pastoral literature from Puttenham's time to the present. One luminous example chosen from the imposing body of critical material demonstrates how thoroughgoing was this corrosive worry over the shepherd's life in the hills and the accuracy of its representation in the work of art. The sophistication of an articulate shepherd has historically been one of the least tolerated sophistications in English writing, and Dr. Johnson's diatribe on "Lycidas," that "easy, vulgar" poem, is one of the most infamous attacks in the critical canon. Continually, the pastoral has confronted the accusations of debunking realists, and the confrontation emphasizes the curiously large degree of social responsibility and realism—the literary device most often associated with social responsibility—expected of the pastoral author. Johnson, though not one of the early commentators, neatly and caustically speaks for the many doubters who preceded him:

> It is therefore improper to give the title of a pastoral to verses in which the speakers, after the slight mention of their flocks, fall to complaints of errors in the church and corruptions in the government, or to lamentations of the death of some illustrious person, whom when once the poet has called a shepherd, he has no longer

any labour upon his hands, but can make the clouds weep, and lilies wither, and the sheep hang their heads, without art or learning, genius, or study.

Nothing is so tiringly conventional as an insignificant pastoral, and even those writers most invigorated by its formal strictures seem wary of the living shepherd who wearily follows his sheep from grazing to grazing. The eighteenth century, remarkable in this context because it was the last era to view the composition of the pastoral as an ordinary poetic enterprise, abounds with theoretical writing on the subject. Pope, for example, cared nothing for tooth and claw, and his comments on the pastoral portray a writer aware of the fact that shepherds named Corydon, wandering through an anglicized Arcadia, do not face the hardships of shepherds named Michael who move stones at Grasmere. That Pope would even respond to such an obvious assertion emphasizes how enduring this concern for authenticity and credibility had become for both critics and poets alike. In his "Discourse on Pastoral Poetry," he states baldly that the work of the pastoral poet lies "in exposing the best side only of a shepherd's life, and in concealing its miseries." Although not all early pastoral writers had been so idealistic—not Spenser, for example, in "January," from *The Shepheardes Calender*—Pope's position represents the purest excrescence of pastoral theory, emphasizing its power to idealize but ignoring its tendency to recognize the quotidian reality and its attendant miseries.

Extremity in religion and literature breeds heresy, and when Pope claimed that two and only two of Virgil's *Eclogues* were truly pastoral works, he showed how exhausted traditions end in denial. Although Johnson, on the other hand, does not suggest that the poet dwell on miseries, he clearly presses for a measure of credibility. This represents a significant shift in emphasis. By attacking several glamorous abuses of pastoral writing, he makes us suspicious of it all. Johnson's strictures, unlike Pope's, are less definitive and more hopeful.

Johnson's witty assessment was prompted by his own famous definition of pastoral earlier in the same piece: a "representation of an action or passion by its effects upon a country life." These actions or passions, then, must not be "inconsistent with a country life." It is difficult—and unfair—to guess how Puttenham would have replied to Johnson; the body of material that concerned Puttenham was smaller and more orderly in spirit than the vast and varied pastorals that Johnson read. As the ranks of the literature swelled, encompassing the lyric, the elegy, the romance, and the drama, so too did the definitions. Whereas the critics of Puttenham's time could quibble over the details of a convention, Johnson's age was attempting to reconcile the inconsistencies of a literary behemoth that had begun to violate, transgress, and redefine its traditional boundaries.

Both Puttenham and Johnson were bothered by the issue of credibility, and to justify their anxiety they discovered a reason for it: the language of pastoral was not the authentic language of the pasture. Literary realism, in nineteenth-century fiction, was most often summoned to correct abuses and reveal hardships, and the pastoral did not escape untainted by this important development. The reformative zeal for authenticity, when it finally evolved as the domineering concern of the poetry, helped to form the characteristic tone of the antipastoral, a relatively modern development of the late eighteenth and early nineteenth centuries. Crabbe's *The Village* (1783), for example, intends to indict social injustice by providing "the real picture of the poor. . . ." But this is a literary revolution in its late stages. The beginnings of a healthy skepticism, the first stirrings of a countermovement against the established conventions of pastoral writing, were evident as early as the sixteenth century. From the beginning, the literature developed tactics of diversion and inference that characterize Heaney's development as he consolidates his savvy political voice.

> **The pastoral, freely admitting allegorical language and implicitly encouraging resistance and deception, allows Heaney to enshrine his culture while fashioning a cogent and subversive response to the problems faced by the Catholic minority in Northern Ireland.**
>
> **—Sidney Burris**

The earliest pastoralists obviously had not seen the stern reprimands handed down by Johnson. Spenser, identified by Puttenham as "that other Gentleman who wrote the late shepheardes Callender," was well aware of the satirical possibilities inherent in one of the most prevalent pastoral conventions, the poet, or in Spenser's version, the knight as shepherd. In book 6, canto 9 of *The Faerie Queene*, Sir Calidore has arrived in Arcadia and fallen in love with Pastorella; when she proves invulnerable to his knightly charms, he changes his "loftie looke" for the authentic look, the "shepheards weed," and quickly wins her love. Lest this seem too blatantly erotic, the story takes yet another turn. What Pastorella had loved in her lowly shepherd was, in fact, his courteous qualities, shining through the warp and woof of his native flannel. Eventually, blood as well as water seeks its own level: Pastorella was of a pedigree higher than had previously been suspected, so their attraction to each other, in both the environmental and hereditary sense, was a natural one.

The masquerade reveals a more serious aspect of pastoral, one in which Calidore assumes the appearance of a shepherd, traditionally connoting honesty, even gullibility, to further his designs on Pastorella. When Calidore strikes out across the fields with Pastorella on his arm, he is using the pastoral mode literally, in Puttenham's terms, to "insinuate and glance" at other women, and the reader witnesses a convincing demonstration of the pastoral's capacity for deception and subterfuge. Today Irish nationalists dressed in English tweeds roam the streets of London, occasionally lionized by the literary community they oppose, so artful has been their opposition. In 1983, Heaney published a response to his inclusion in an anthology of verse entitled *The Penguin Book of Contemporary British Poetry;* his rural and "anxious" muse is "roused on her bed among the furze," and his abdication reveals how successful his ruse has been:

> Yet doubts, admittedly, arise
> When somebody who publishes
> In LRB and TLS,
> > *The Listener*—
> In other words, whose audience is,
> > Via Faber,
> A British one, is characterized
> As British. But don't be surprised
> If I demur, for, be advised
> > My passport's green.
> No glass of ours was ever raised
> > To toast *The Queen.*

This inclination toward subterfuge, which is in turn facilitated by the genre's tendency to cast its characters in deceptively conventional roles, is clearest in Spenser's "Colin Clouts Come Home Again." The poem is organized as a dialogue between Colin Clout, who has just returned from a trip across the sea, and ten shepherds and shepherdesses, who ply him with questions about his traveling partner, his sea voyage, and his visit to the court of Cynthia. The poem details an Irish homecoming, and although Colin's sympathies are not those of a modern Irish nationalist, the poem remains a skillful pastoral rendition of the various skepticisms that historically characterized relations between Ireland and England. Spenser's biography has figured prominently in many interpretations of the work, and commentators have closely examined the various landscapes of the poem, particularly the one portrayed in the myth of Bregog and Mulla (11.104-55). The precise situation of the rivers, the mountain called "Mole . . . /That walls the Northside of Armulla Dale," and "the ragged ruines"—all of these specific geographical details have led critics to believe that the home referred to in the title is indeed Spenser's Cork County estate. And near the end of the poem, when Colin has described the bounties of Cynthia's court, Thestylis wonders why anyone would return from such a happy place "to this barrein soyle/Where cold and care and penury do dwell" (11.656-57). Colin's answer begins the section on the corruption of the court.

Thestylis's dreary depiction of his homeland has led some critics to speculate on Spenser's happiness in Ireland: perhaps these descriptions represent affective portraits of Spenser's thoughts and feelings while living away from England. But the evaluation of the poem is not solely a matter of biography. Spenser's descriptions, most fruitfully read in the tradition of the perfected landscape, the earthly Eden, incorporate varying levels of particularity and biographical reference within familiar pastoral contexts. Several shepherds, more obviously than others, represent important historical figures; some rivulets more clearly than others portray actual streams.

But the idealized landscapes in Spenser's pastoral poems often show traces of the persistent attention to regional detail that will dominate late twentieth-century poetry. Under the aegis of the pastoral, much of this poetry finds its distant and surprising ancestor. In Heaney's work this persistence in meticulous description is carefully marshaled to transcend its particularity, creating that distinctly pastoral tension between the idealized landscape of the past— the Golden Age—and the realistic depiction of Irish geography. In a poem such as **"Anahorish,"** Heaney imagines that the name itself possesses ineffable powers of cultural sovereignty. Irish place-names in the United Kingdom become for Heaney subversive incantations that both glorify his Celtic lineage and establish its integrity in British Northern Ireland. The poem dexterously appropriates a landscape politically British in its legal demarcation but linguistically Irish in its nomenclature:

> My "place of clear water,"
> the first hill in the world
> where springs washed into
> the shiny grass
>
> and darkened cobbles
> in the bed of the lane.
> *Anahorish,* soft gradient
> of consonant, vowel-meadow,
>
> after-image of lamps
> swung through the yards
> on winter evenings.
> With pails and barrows
>
> those mound-dwellers
> go waist-deep in mist
> to break the light ice
> at wells and dunghills.

The genealogy established here between the people of Heaney's childhood and the "mound dwellers"—they are practically coalesced into one ancestor—lies entrenched beyond the reach of English bloodlines, and the poem combines a quiet celebration of an Irish childhood with a strenuous resistance to cultural hegemony. Within the pastoral context, these often contrary concerns are reconciled.

The allegorical quality of pastoral writing has been a stable part of the tradition since Virgil's time. But the literature carefully discriminates between these conventional references to living people and the broader, less conventional attempt to incorporate into the poetry the specific details of character or landscape that might dissipate the gleaming innocence of the pastoral vision. Accordingly, the matter of poetic diction, whether based on the regional pidgin or the royal parlance, became an important issue in pastoral theory. In *The Renewal of Literature,* Richard Poirier argues that the "self-analytical mode" of the modernist text instituted a "form of cultural skepticism," which in varying degrees "is to be found earlier on, as in, say, Spenser's transformations of the allegorical tradition. . . ." Following a rapturous description of Cynthia in "Colin

Clout Comes Home Again," Cuddy chides Colin for his elevated speech:

> *Colin* (said *Cuddy* then) thou has forgot
> Thy selfe, me seemes, too much, to mount so hie:
> Such loftie flight, base shepheard seemeth not,
> From flocks and fields, to Angel and to skie.
>
> (11.616-19)

The pastoral illusion here is qualified, if slightly so. By reminding Colin that shepherds must use a baser English than the one he has been using, Cuddy does not argue for a dialectal purity but ironically insists on one of the genre's conventions: in essence he reminds Colin of Puttenham's notion that pastoral writers must employ "rude speeches." Governed by this irony, Colin's lofty flights become the unconventional element of the passage. But this insight comes at the end of a circuitous path; the rigidity of the pastoral form has begun to loosen a little, revealing glimpses of the world beyond the pasture.

The subject of poetic diction concerns all poets, but Irish authors have addressed the matter with exceptional vigor, emphasizing the political implications of choosing or ignoring various words and figures of speech. Heaney's etymological interests have occasioned several of his finest poems, but only a few have openly addressed the political questions that confront the Irish writer. From **Wintering Out**, the first section of **"Traditions"** states the case succinctly:

> Our guttural muse
> was bulled long ago
> by the alliterative tradition,
> her uvula grows
>
> vestigial, forgotten
> like the coccyx
> or a Brigid's Cross
> yellowing in some outhouse
>
> while custom, that "most
> sovereign mistress,"
> beds us down into
> the British Isles.

The feeling of linguistic displacement in the poem is shared by many Irish writers. Tom Paulin, a poet and critic from Belfast who currently resides in England, has argued passionately for the establishment of an Irish English dictionary, finding an analogy in Noah Webster's dictionary and his *Dissertations,* the treatises that examined the influence of the American language on the country's concepts of nationhood. Such a dictionary in Ireland would have a redemptive effect:

> Many words which now appear simply gnarled, or which "make strange" or seem opaque to most readers, would be released into the shaped flow of a new public language. . . . A confident concept of Irish English would substantially increase the vocabulary and this would invigorate the written language. A language that lives lithely on the tongue ought to be capable of becoming the flexible written instrument of a complete cultural idea.

"A new public language," "a complete cultural idea"— the phrases resonate with a shrewd and subtle republicanism. The dialectal words and rhythms in Heaney's verse, similar to the "rude speeches," those wayward words often labeled "variant" by lexicographers, represent the common inheritance of the Catholic culture of rural Northern Ireland, a culture that from Heaney's standpoint has suffered political displacement. The pastoral, freely admitting allegorical language and implicitly encouraging resistance and deception, allows Heaney to enshrine his culture while fashioning a cogent and subversive response to the problems faced by the Catholic minority in Northern Ireland.

The word "subversive," when used accurately in this context, describes the way in which pastoral writing balances social criticism and aesthetic design. Pastoral poetry had always been used for polemical purposes, and when Milton prefaces "Lycidas" with his announcement that he "by occasion foretells the ruin of our corrupted Clergy," he is working within a well-defined literary tradition of political and religious dissent. Accordingly, the American reader who innocently opens Empson's seminal work on the subject, *Some Versions of Pastoral* (1935), will be surprised to find the first chapter entitled "Proletarian Literature." Empson begins by introducing the subject of "proletarian art" and declares it "important to try and decide what the term might mean. . . ."

His diction alone plays to the political sensibility, a sensibility that will bear fruit when evaluating Heaney's version of pastoral. Aside from several notable examples, academic criticism in America has avoided political engagement, and the shopworn tenets of New Criticism, with their emphasis on poetic form and an ahistorical aesthetic, provide an excellent example. The few critics and poets who undertook the sweeping examinations such engagements required have traditionally earned the unfortunate title "men of letters." Edmund Wilson appears on this role, and, surely, T. S. Eliot.

Yet for the English and Irish critics, raised on the subterfuges of Auden's early poetry, on the volunteer spirit fostered by the Spanish Civil War, and finally on the hardships of a World War fought at home, the political dimension of literature excited a compelling, if sometimes breast-beating, urgency in many of the writers. Empson is always honing his insights into pastoral literature with the gritty observations of a social worker. Although Heaney's verse generally transcends the confinements of the political arena, the confrontations encountered there account for one of the defining strengths of his work and clarify his relation to the pastoral. Here is an example of Empson's method: "Of course there are plenty of skilled workers in England who are proud of their skill, and you can find men of middle age working on farms who say they prefer the country to the town, but anything like what I am trying to call pastoral is a shock to the Englishman who meets it on the Continent." Empson's sociopolitical program always stands as the foil for his brilliance as a literary critic; the work of art, whether *Paradise Lost* or *Alice in Wonderland,* always corners his attention. But not all critics so acrobatically walk the fence between facile sloganeering and felicitous phrasing. Other problems associated with the term "pastoral" must be resolved before Heaney's work assumes its rightful place in the tradition.

In a review of *The Penguin Anthology of Pastoral Poetry,* Heaney summarizes his opinion regarding the modern usage of the word, and if he lacks the accuracy theoreticians might require, he nonetheless reflects a widespread opinion: "'Pastoral' is a term that has been extended by usage until its original meaning has been largely eroded. For example, I have occasionally talked of the countryside where we live in Wicklow as being pastoral rather than rural, trying to impose notions of a beautified landscape on the word, in order to keep 'rural' for the unselfconscious face of raggle-taggle farmland." In most informal writing, the word "idyllic" often substitutes for "pastoral"; a cottage in the country might reasonably be described as both "idyllic" and "pastoral" because either word conjures up a similar range of associations. Yet if Heaney seems perfectly suited to be a pastoral poet, why then does he resist—it is as if he were being sentenced— the title "idyllic poet"? The latter phrase assigns him to the charmed existence of "farmer Allan at the farm abode," as Tennyson has it in "Dora," while the former commands for him the integrity of a literary tradition. The term "pastoral," often undefined and inaccurately deployed, commands a general field of reference that seems to describe much of Heaney's early poetry. But the poet's own definition of the term limits its usage: "beautified" will simply not suffice for the frogs in **"Death of a Naturalist"** with their "blunt heads farting."

Certain themes and literary strategies are native to the pastoral tradition, and their recurrence, with or without the attendant shepherd, shapes the modern pastoral. Perspective, theme, and imagery are the watchwords. In the same review, Heaney continues: "Obviously, we are unlikely to find new poems about shepherds that engage us as fully as 'Lycidas,' but surely the potent dreaming of a Golden Age or the counter-cultural celebration of simpler life-styles or the nostalgic projection of the garden on childhood are still occasionally continuous with the tradition as it is presented here." Heaney's point is clear. Although much of the traditional machinery of the pastoral—the shepherds, the singing contests, the personification of the natural world in its elegiac posture—fell long ago into a benign disrepair, the desires that fueled the machinery, "the potent dreaming of a Golden Age," remain immediate, vivid, and urgent. John Lynen, in his book on Robert Frost's pastoralism, clarifies the relation between literary convention and pastoral myth, a clarification that succinctly explicates an essential feature of the genre's development:

> The conventions are not the true basis of pastoral, but an outgrowth of something deeper and more fundamental. Pastoralism requires an established myth of the rural world, and the conventions gradually

developed through tradition belong to the myth of Arcadia. They are formalized symbols whose function is to evoke an imaginative vision of this world. But Arcadia is not the only version of rural life, and it is possible for a poet to write true pastorals within the context of some other mythic rural world.

The work of each author will have its own unique shape, its own version of pastoral. Such freedoms encourage abuses in the literary critic who finds traces of pastoral in any poem, novel, song, or play remotely concerned with the country life. Open doors can lead to indiscrimination, and prolonged, persistent indiscrimination to fatuity and mental flatulence. Andrew Ettin, one of the most recent critics attempting to distill the essence of pastoral writing, offers this insight:

> Not all nature writing . . . is pastoral. What makes a work pastoral are its attitudes toward the natural world and human experience. In pastoral literature, experiences and emotions are contained within finite limits. Those limits are implied by the patterns revealed within the natural world and within the pastoral way of life, consonant with the patterns of the natural world. The containment is necessitated by the fragility or delicacy of the experiences and emotions, or by tension between pastoral and nonpastoral experience.

Ettin shrewdly embraces what others before him have disparaged. Pastoral experience, fragile and delicate, is contained and circumscribed by nonpastoral experience, and the resulting tension between the two worlds characterizes most pastoral literature. When he uses the word "attitudes," he is tipping his hat to another critic whose helpful insights Ettin acknowledges. In his book, *Pastoral Forms and Attitudes,* Harold Toliver gives us a sound piece of advice for shaping our own attitudes toward the latter-day pastoral. Aside from analyzing the predictable authors such as Spenser, Shakespeare, Marvell, and Milton, he includes chapters on Stevens and Bellow. Of his introductory statements, one is worthy of engraving in stone: "Whether or not the texts examined here need all be considered 'pastorals' is not as important finally as our discovering something in them through this lens that would be less noticeable through another. Much of Heaney's poetry is enlarged and clarified through such a lens. His enlargements and clarifications not only situate him in a literary tradition, they reevaluate the literature of that tradition, echoing, as they do, the old forgotten melodies. . . .

Robert Pinsky (essay date 1992)

SOURCE: A review of *Seeing* Things, in *The Yale Review,* Vol. 80, Nos. 1-2, 1992, pp. 236-54.

[*In the following essay, Pinsky provides a favorable review of Heaney's* Seeing Things.]

Seamus Heaney's poems have earned a host of literary awards and about as much public celebration as is likely for any poet in our time. A native of Northern Ireland, a man of great personal charm, wit, eloquence in speech, and probity, Heaney has attracted the attention of journalists in this country and around the world. His work has been embraced by academic critics, taught in schools and universities, and made the object of Ph.D. dissertations.

Nevertheless, he is a wonderful poet, one of the best writing, as his new book *Seeing Things* demonstrates anew. The book also provides a comparison of poetry's dual presence—immediate and yet of the past, of the earth and of the air, of the voice and of the mind—in the work of these three younger Americans and in poems by a European of Heaney's generation.

The two mighty roots of this volume are familiar to Heaney's readers. One is the talismanic force of objects: the often humble implements and artifacts, pitchfork, settle-bed, coping-stone, biretta, school-bag, made sacramental by their human meaning and by Heaney's luminous seeing of them. "Secure / The bastion of sensation," says a poem early in the extraordinary sequence **"Squarings,"** "Do not water / Into language. Do not waver in it." Related to these often domestic objects is the second root, which is reverent memory, in this book frequently elegiac. There are extremely touching, indelible poems in memory of the poet's father and of several friends.

As he has done before, Heaney frames the volume with translations, a passage from Canto III of the *Inferno* at the end and fifty lines from the *Aeneid* as a prefatory poem. In the *Aeneid* passage, the hero asks the Cumaean Sibyl for passage to the Underworld so that he can look again into the face of his dead father. The Sibyl tells Aeneas that to return living from the realm of death he must pluck the golden bough from the sacred grove—" And when it is plucked," says Heaney's version, "A second one always grows in its place, golden again." And in the closing lines of his preface:

> If fate has called you,
> The bough will come away easily, of its own
> accord.
> Otherwise, no matter how much strength you
> muster, you never will
> Manage to quell it or cut it down with the toughest
> of blades.

These lines invoke the ancient spirit of poetry, straightforwardly and confidently.

Then, in the first poem of the volume proper, the ghost of the poet Larkin—" a nine-to-five man who had seen poetry"—surprises the living poet on a city street, and the shade quotes Dante, a passage where at nightfall when all other creatures rest the poet goes forth to his duty. Though Heaney enjoys the incongruity between the rush-hour buses and Larkin's "Still my old self Ready to knock one back," his connection to the old line of poetry is largely one of congruity. This fact is visible in the distinctive, polished-thorn texture of Heaney's language; it is partly a matter of cultural setting, a setting where poetry's place is less

of an open question than in America, more assuredly a place resembling one that it always had.

It has been Heaney's genius to invoke the heroic perspective for the most immediate and personal kinds of experience. Every mode of narrative or image seems available and readily modulated from one kind of eloquence, one scale, to the next. In the title poem, rendering what could have been a small family anecdote, the closing section begins "Once upon a time my undrowned father / Walked into our yard." The father has had a close call in the river, after a minor disagreement with the child. Heaney in the final passage returns to the note of the opening "once upon a time":

> That afternoon
> I saw him face to face, he came to me
> With his damp footprints out of the river,
> And there was nothing between us there
> That might not still be happily ever after.

This is a remarkably subtle ending, full of strong but understated emotional color: rueful and ironic about the realities between father and son. Because we have read the opening *Aeneid* passage a few pages before, and then an elegy for the father's own father, the moment, when the two look on one another's face is also part of an epic pattern.

Leaving Dante and Virgil aside, consider the many Heaney poems where, just as archaic language overlaps with the language of crafts or farming or region (James Joyce's "feast of the Holy Tundish"), the folklore and figures of his experience overlap with mythology (**"Squarings,"** xviii):

> Like a foul-mouthed god of hemp come down to
> rut,
> The rope-man stumped about and praised new rope
> With talk of how thick it was, or how long and
> strong,
>
> And how you could take it into your own hand
> And feel it. His perfect, tight-bound wares
> Made a circle round him. . . .

In another poem of the sequence,

> Even a solid man,
> A pillar to himself and to his trade
> All yellow boots and stick and soft felt hat,
>
> Can sprout wings at the ankle and grow fleet
> As the god of fair-days, stone posts, roads and
> crossroads,
> Guardians of travellers and psychopomp.
>
> 'Look for a man with an ash plant on the boat,'
> My father told his sister setting out
> For London, 'and stay near him all night
>
> And you'll be safe.' Flow on, flow on,
> The journey of the soul with its soul guide
> And the mysteries of dealing-men with sticks!

Other poems describe the feeling of an eelskin bracelet putting water-wheel strength into your shoulder, or the ritual entering of a new life through a girdle of straw rope on St. Brigid's Day, one sequence for men, one for women:

> The open they came into by these moves
> Stood opener, hoops came off the world,
> They could feel the February air
>
> Still soft above their heads and imagine
> The limp rope fray and flare like wind-borne
>   gleanings
> Or an unhindered goldfinch over ploughland.

This is a world in which the centaur of the past is a few steps closer than for the young Americans, and not only for the colloquial Halliday but for Mitchell as well. The folklore is only one token of a setting in which the contradictions between the art's history and its present are less sharp, less open-ended.

No judgment of value is implied by seeing this difference of kind. Exactly because the scope and power of Heaney's poems are well established, it is worth noting that like other European poets he is in some ways closer to the literature and language of the past, and to the folk beliefs of the past, than many American poets are likely to be.

This idea represents only one strain in Heaney's work, a strain that reminds me of two other poems. One is Czeslaw Milosz's "Bypassing Rue Descartes," in which the poet remembers streaming into Paris as the capital of the world, and of "the universal," in the time between the wars, along with other young people from "Jassy and Kolivar, Wilno and Bucharest, Saigon and Marrakesh." "Soon enough, their peers were seizing power / in order to kill in the name of the universal, beautiful ideas," while the city goes on pursuing its worldly nature. At the end of the poem, Milosz returns to the idea of folk beliefs:

> As to my heavy sins, I remember one most vividly:
> How, one day, walking on a forest path along a
>   stream
> I pushed a rock down onto a water snake coiled in
>   the grass.
>
> And what I have met with in life was the just
>   punishment
> Which reaches, sooner or later, the breaker of a
>   taboo.

The immense force of Milosz's lifework is related to the stretch from his classical education, the beliefs of his province, the great world of his youth, to his experience of the war and its aftermath, the poet clinging to the thread of poetry through that maze of disillusion, catastrophe, and faith. This force is relevant to Heaney's cultural situation, and to the American one as well: the scale of the Milosz poem helps show the difference in the situations.

The other poem I am reminded of is Alan Shapiro's "Mud Dancing," which I have quoted already. Reading Heaney's

masterful deployment of his vocabulary of *rut* and *wares, grow fleet* and *psychopomp, fray* and *flare,* and *unhindered goldfinch,* I thought of the moment when Shapiro, in his poem of the bewildered ghosts of the tortured touching the immovable cast-off garments at Woodstock, giving voice to the dead, reaches for an archaic word:

> Was this some new phase of their affliction?
> The effect of some yet new device?
> To make them go on dreaming, even now,
> some version of themselves so long accustomed
> to their torment that they confused
> torment with exaltation, mud with light?
>
> *Frau History,* they asked, *is this the final
> reaving of what we loved well . . . ?*

Reaving (spelled differently in Faulkner's title): plundering, robbing, tearing apart, or carrying away. It seems an appropriate term for addressing Frau History. The archaism gives the thrown-off clothing more meaning, in a moment that is part of a continuum with the poems of Milosz and Heaney, suggesting that there is a question, a question about the place of memory in the present, that all true poetry, in one way or another, presents to its readers.

William Logan   (review date 1992)

SOURCE: A review of *Seeing Things,* in *Poetry,* (Chicago), Vol. CLX, No. 3, June, 1992, pp. 170-74.

[*In the following mixed review, Logan faults Heaney for writing "poems" instead of poetry, asserting that the poems in* Seeing Things *lack passion and instinct.*]

It is almost impossible to dislike a poet as gifted as Seamus Heaney. His later poetry has been so well mannered and well marveled, so shapely and infused with the dark instinct of life, so full of respect for the ancients of poetry and for the form itself, so little afflicted by the international bonhomie that grates in the poetry of Brodsky and even Walcott, so moodily decent and eloquently anguished that it seems churlish to suggest that much of his new poetry consists of the smile without the Cheshire cat. It seems churlish because *Seeing Things* is a more distinguished book than any of the others under review—indeed, it is a more distinguished book than most books of the past decade. My difficulty with Heaney is not with what he *can* do (with what he can do perfectly easily, as if it meant nothing at all), but with what he no longer thinks it worth his trouble to do.

Admirers of Heaney divide into those (often Irish or British) who prefer the poetry before *Field Work,* the more rugged and costive volumes from *Death of a Naturalist* through *North,* and those (often American) who prefer the more leisurely and open-hearted (if at times similarly bleak and guilt-laden) style of the later poetry. No doubt this division is an argument of national character, though I notice that those who came later to the poetry often prefer the later poetry—Heaney was a phenomenon at home long before he was noticed abroad. The books from *Field Work* to *Seeing Things* now form a second arcana (major or minor according to one's disposition), and the transition from a poetry often aroused by the art of writing in the act of writing to a poetry worried about its place in literature is typified by the translations from the *Inferno* which close those two later volumes. The younger Heaney wrote like a man possessed by demons, even when those demons were very literary demons; the older Heaney seems to wonder, bemusedly, what sort of demon he has become himself.

To make the devil's case, I must argue for the graces. The fluent, homespun style Heaney assumes in *Seeing Things* is a style so easy it hardly seems a style at all. In poetry, the pure assumptions of voice are often highly literary (they usually appear so to later generations), but they create for an age the manner of its speech. Heaney's poetry speaks for his age—this flattering age of prose—in the way that Eliot's, or Auden's, or Lowell's did for theirs: it is not a transcription of expression so much as what we wish our expression were, an implement purely responsive to minor acts and desires. Eliot remarked, in "The Music of Poetry," "No poetry, of course, is ever exactly the same speech that the poet talks and hears: but it has to be in such a relation to the speech of his time that the listener or reader can say 'that is how I should talk if I could talk poetry." And even if one suspects that this is exactly what Heaney says to himself, he has abandoned the more studied art of language to sustain a way of speaking. Such a poet creates his voice by a set of articulating discoveries.

This style is rendered responsible by continuous supplication to, and frequent invocation of, the dead: the shades of Heaney's past, and the literary figures under whose shadows he writes. The volume begins with the *Aeneid* and ends with the *Inferno,* and both scraps of translation mark voyages to the underworld. The translations are pallidly conversational—they do not aspire to something as unmannerly as style (this criticism might be made of classical translation in general, which is why Christopher Logue's gall may be necessary). There is a certain donnish wit in translating these incidents, the humility of translation not quite concealing the esteem that identification with Aeneas and Dante confers on the poet.

It is not without delicate irony, then, that after the prologue from the *Aeneid* the book begins with the shade of Philip Larkin (whose death has occasioned a number of elegies unusual for their deep affection—as a misanthrope Larkin was an utter failure) in **"The Journey Back"**:

'And not a thing had changed, as rush-hour buses

Bore the drained and laden through the city.
I might have been a wise king setting out
Under the Christmas lights—except that

It felt more like the forewarned journey back
Into the heartland of the ordinary.
Still my old self. Ready to knock one back.

A nine-to-five man who had seen poetry.'

A nine-to-five man is of course what Heaney is not (Larkin's orderliness and punctuality of address were just those of a nine-to-five man)—for him the local has permanent access to the mystical. Hallucinations, ghosts, shadings of the past: Heaney has become a poet increasingly at the mercy of seeing things. For a poet of the quotidian, the everyday either embodies the reductive mysteries of the world (as it did for Williams, or Larkin for that matter), or provides the focus of the historical or metaphysical force outside the world. The former ground permits (though it does not entail) the consolation of cynicism; the latter the irritation of faith, or something very like faith. In this Heaney is the proper heir to Yeats.

My difficulty with Heaney is not with what he *can* do (with what he can do perfectly easily, as if it meant nothing at all), but with what he no longer thinks it worth his trouble to do.

—William Logan

But Yeats did not like the quotidian; he liked the other world much better. Heaney is mired again in Ireland, and for him part of the burden of seeing things that are not there is seeing things that are. Like other poets of a withdrawing temperament, he is drawn to narrative, but he cannot shape a story with the rude tempo or inevitability of Frost. Narrative requires a poetry more centrally uneasy than the still lifes he still favors. Many of the poems in *Seeing Things* suffer fatally nervous, finicky hoardings of noun and adjective:

Riveted steel, turned timber, burnish, grain,
Smoothness, straightness, roundness, length and
  sheen.
Sweat-cured, sharpened, balanced, tested, fitted.
The springiness, the clip and dart of it.
                              ["The Pitchfork"]

This is a pitchfork, but it might as well be a carriage wheel or a demonic pencil. Heaney's portraits and objects (a biretta, a settle bed, the pitchfork, a basket of chestnuts) sometimes have a dusty, passive air, like objects in an abandoned shop-front. But this makes them pliant to a transformation out of the demotic into a realm almost demonic, as in **"The Biretta"**:

Now I turn it upside down and it is a boat—
A paper boat, or the one that wafts into
The first lines of the *Purgatorio*
As poetry lifts its eyes and clears its throat.

Or maybe that small boat out of the Bronze Age
Where the oars are needles and the worked gold
  frail
As the intact half of a hatched-out shell,
Refined beyond the dross into sheer image.

But in the end it's as likely to be the one
In Matthew Lawless's painting *The Sick Call,*
Where the scene is out on a river and it's all
Solid, pathetic and Irish Victorian.

In which case, however, his reverence wears a hat.
Undaunting, half-domestic, loved in crises,
He sits listening as each long oar dips and rises,
Sad for his worthy life and fit for it.

Heaney is a master of the dazzling mock-religious transfiguration. For all its seeming indolence, his poetry lacks any weedy excess—it is a meditation that is finally a sort of mediation. Much of *Seeing Things* is unfortunately given over to forms too partial to respond to anything like meditation: a second sequence of Glanmore sonnets, not nearly as owl-eyed or willful as the first sequence in *Field Work,* and a long, peculiar series of twelve-line poems called "Squarings," which takes up the second half of the book.

"Squarings" is composed with a very writerly confidence, but the poems have an irresolute, unfinished air: fragments shored against his ruin, they are not backed up in the immaterial realm. The eight or ten which accrue around a kernel of incident point out the losses of attention elsewhere. Many poets would be pleased by—they would award themselves a Pulitzer for—a handful of poems as sincerely exposed (the best are i, vi, vii, viii, xv, xvii, xxvi, xxxiii, xlii, xliv), but against Heaney's better work they seem offhanded and a little desperate.

Each recent book by Heaney has made the previous book seem better: this means that it is difficult to take proper measure of the new work until it is the work of the past, not that Heaney has gradually been getting worse. Most of Heaney's books have been books of transition, if not transformation: by the time the reader adapts to the angle of vision, the chameleon has moved on. However darkly moral and moderating the later Heaney has been, he is sometimes only a compound ghost of his earlier self. *Seeing Things* includes many achieved and remarkable and individual poems—as would be expected, since Heaney is one of the best poets we have; but the early work, the work before he was writing poems, was better poetry. I'm not sure anyone has been moved by a late Heaney poem—he seems incapable now of writing anything instinctive or marked or passionate.

There comes a moment when a man doesn't *want* to write poetry as much as he wants to write poems (perhaps he can do nothing else *but* write them), and it isn't necessarily a change to be discouraged. Poets this good are natural forces, like avalanches. They cannot be argued with—one can only get out of their way.

J. R. Atfield   (essay date 1996)

SOURCE: "*Seeing Things* in a Jungian Perspective: Archetypal Elements in Seamus Heaney's Recent Poetry,"
in *Agenda,* Vol. 33, Nos. 3-4, Autumn-Winter, 1996, pp. 131-43.

[*In the following essay, Atfield offers a Jungian interpretation of the poetry found in the volume* Seeing Things.]

Seamus Heaney is clearly conversant with Jung's psychology and its relevance to art, specifically literature: in a conversation with Borges [in *The Crane Bag,* Volume 7, 1983], he referred to the "Jungian archetypes" as "valid explanations of what we experience in the subconscious worlds of dreams and fiction," and more recently in *The Government of the Tongue,* he used Jungian terminology quite naturally when he emphasised that poetry and the imaginative arts "verify our singularity, they strike and stake out the ore of self which lies at the base of every individuated life." He has spoken of "The secret between the words, the binding element . . . a psychic force that is elusive, archaic and only half apprehended by maker and audience"; [in *Memories, Dreams, Reflections,* 1963] Jung refers to "The energy underlying conscious psychic life" and the "archetypes, which are pre-existent to consciousness and condition it." Seamus Heaney uses the Jungian concept of mythical archetypes to explore himself, his family and his race; to understand the origins of his own creative energies and the distortion of creativity in the destructiveness of his society.

Through his understanding and use of Jungian perspective Heaney defends himself against the charge that lyric poetry is a luxury that Ireland cannot afford; this does not merely illuminate his poems but constitutes a thesis of the value of poetry itself. In this sense his poems are virtually (though tangentially) concerned with the very issues that superficially they seem to evade.

[In *Archetype: A Natural History of the Self,* 1982] Anthony Stevens has argued that, "Jung knew that people needed myths if they were to remain vitally in touch with the archetypal core of their nature. Myths provide an entire cosmology compatible with a culture's capacity for understanding . . . ." In his poetry Heaney can be seen to reflect the Jungian concept of myth as the human attempt to appreciate and apprehend life, not as a mere existence but as the intercommunication of the whole complexity of body, intellect and psyche. A number of poems in *Seeing Things* reflect the Jungian parallels of conscious and unconscious, and the extension of the ego to fuller realisation of the Self archetype in "the individuation process . . . to integrate the unconscious into consciousness."

In "Casting and Gathering," Heaney presents the conscious and unconscious "voices" through two views of fishing, recognising that he has long been concerned with opposition and tensions, as "Years and years ago, these sounds took sides," yet "I am still standing there, awake and dreamy." The "dreamy" state is an appropriate one in which to listen to the voice of the unconscious, or to be aware of the tension between that and the conscious, as he is also "awake." [In his *Collected Works,* edited by H. Read, M. Fordham, G. Adler, Vol. 9, 1953-78] Jung explained, "Once the unconscious content has been given form and the meaning of the formulation understood . . . The position of the ego must be maintained as being of equal value to the counterposition of the unconscious and vice versa . . ." Later in the same essay he refers to a dialogue which an "other voice" and the poem can be read as a dramatisation of this kind of psychic dialogue:

> One sound is saying, "You're not worth tuppence,
> But neither is anybody. Watch it! Be severe."
> The other says, "Go with it! Give and swerve.
> You are everything you feel beside the river."

In this formulation of the two styles of fishing the alert attention of the ego "voice," "Watch it!" is balanced in counterposition of the affective mode of the unconscious, "everything you feel."

In equilibrium between them Heaney sums up, "I trust contrariness." If the Jungian reading of the poem is continued, the trusting of contrariness could reflect Anthony Stevens' comment on the transcendent function, "when permitted to do so, the psyche transcends reason and the rules of logic, no less than the opposites, for it sees no problem in the simultaneous perception of incompatibilities." If Heaney speaks for his race, which is divided against itself, his poetry must embrace the conflicts but more, the incompatibilities are essential.

In *Seeing Things*, Heaney mythologies his father; his examination of self is powerfully extended through the father archetype, enabling him to confront the archetypal experience of death. Jung's researches revealed that "it not infrequently happens that the archetype appears in the form of a spirit in dreams or fantasy-products, or even comports itself like a ghost . . . it mobilizes philosophical and religious convictions . . ." Heaney's father is embodied in the landscape he dominated; as adult the son is constantly reminded, he finds he "cannot mention keshes or the ford / Without my father's shade appearing to me / On a path towards sunset," the young child

> was inside the house
> And saw him out the window, scatter-eyed
> And daunted, strange without his hat,
> His step unguided, his ghosthood immanent . . .

Heaney's recollection of this incident reflects Jung's comments directly: "I must have been three or four. I wasn't there, but it was as if I saw it all, him falling off, the cart going into the river. I remember him coming back and walking towards me in a dream, and the strangest thing was seeing him without his hat . . ." [*The Independent on Sunday,* May 19, 1991].

Heaney achieves a skilful balance between the material and the spiritual in his reminiscences, establishing his father in terms of the motif of the ashplant, his badge of authority, as the "Wise Old Man" archetype recorded in Jung's psychiatric studies. This frequently repeated image of the ashplant creates a microcosm of the responsibility and respect accorded the cattle dealer:

> "Look for a man with an ashplant on the boat"
> My father told his sister setting out
> For London, "and stay near him all night
>
> And you'll be safe. . . ."

Heaney movingly describes his father's urgent clinging on to this symbol of authority on his death-bed, as if once he has it in his grasp he is himself again, with his powers restored, as his son would have wished equally desperately:

> As his head goes light with light, his wasting hand
> Gropes desperately and finds the phantom limb
> Of an ash plant in his grasp, which steadies him.
> Now he has found his touch he can stand his
> ground . . .

The concept of continuity and tradition linked with the archetypal significance of the character is encompassed in the marvellous economy of haiku form as Heaney describes how he, now head of the family as the eldest son, takes on the authority and self-confidence of his dead father, represented yet again in the ash-plant:

> Dangerous pavements.
> But I face the ice this year
> With my father's stick.

The title of the poem, **"1.1.87,"** in its stark numerals, suggests the bleak isolation of the world bereft of the father, yet also the directness of determination to start a new year and a new phase of life with confidence gained from the father within the son.

It is only at his father's death that he can fully acknowledge his filial debt, in the archetypal experience of death of the self as a child. As Jung explained, "There are as many archetypes as there are typical situations in life. Endless repetition has engraved these experiences into our psychic constitution, not in the form of images filled with content, but at first only as *forms without content*, representing merely the possibility of a certain type of perception and action. When a situation occurs which corresponds to a given archetype, that archetype becomes activated . . ." This seems to be exactly the experience explored in the concise lyricism of the final poem of the **"Squarings"** sequence:

> Strange how things in the offing, once they're
> sensed,
> Convert to things foreknown;
> And how what's come upon is manifest
>
> Only in light of what has been gone through.

The movement, progression in self-development and realisation, after his father's death, is a release celebrated in many moments in the **"Squarings"** sequence of poems, in relation to the creative energy of the poet's gift. As Heaney suggested in *The Government of the Tongue*, ". . . poetry, having to do with feelings and emotions, must not submit to the intellect's eagerness to foreclose . . . art does not trace the given map of a better reality but improvises an inspired sketch of it . . ." In *Seeing Things* there are a number of poems which present the concept of a journey or progression outwards, into the freedom of a wider range of reference than was accessible to the poet in earlier collections. It is the trusting of this level of experience and response which gives the work its depth in relation to archetypal expression, in Jung's terms, "The creative process, so far as we are able to follow it at all, consists of the unconscious activation of an archetypal image and in elaborating and shaping this image into the finished work."

There are uncertainties and hesitancies however, acknowledged in the poems themselves. There is the exciting challenge of "Unroofed scope" in **"Lightenings (i)"** but in the next poem the denial of the freedom glimpsed calls for repressive action in appropriately constrained staccato phrases, "Roof it again. Batten down. Dig in." In the next there is a tentative response to the unknown but it is restricted and fearful, "You squinted out from a skylight of the world." The progression is charted through this sequence, as a bolder reaction is encouraged, when as in so many earlier works, Heaney effectively blends description of the countryside setting with the practice of the poetic art:

> Improvise. Make free
> Like old hay in its afterlife
> High on a windblown hedge.

In Heaney's own words, the freedom of the form is described with a sense of excitement and exuberance, "There's a phrase I use, 'make impulse one with wilfulness': the wilfulness is in the 12 lines, the impulse in the freedom and shimmer and on-the-wingness. Until recently I had no titles or numbers for these poems, as if they were afloat all at once but moving separately, like mosaics."

The idea of the poems having their own power, "unconscious activation of an archetypal image," with order imposed by the poet "shaping this image into the finished work" but initially driven by impulse rather than will, reflects Heaney's protean concept of the "government of the tongue," both governed by the poet and governing the poet. Referring to his chosen title for the T.S. Eliot memorial lectures, he explained, "When I thought of 'the government of the tongue' as a general title . . . what I had in mind was this aspect of poetry as its own vindicating force . . . form is achieved not by dint of the moral and ethical exercise of mind but by the self-validating operations of what we call inspiration . . ." This is very close to the description of creative energy in the poet as Jung depicted it: ". . . he is overwhelmed by a flood of thoughts and images which he never intended to create and which his own will could never have brought into being, yet in spite of himself he is forced to admit that it is his own inner nature revealing itself and uttering things which he would never have entrusted to his tongue."

Heaney's own remarks on Kavanagh can equally well be related to himself when he suggests, "This then is truly creative writing. It does arise from the spontaneous overflow of powerful feelings but the overflow is not a reactive response to some stimulus in the world out there. Instead it is a spurt of abundance from a source within and it spills over to irrigate the world beyond the self." Again, Jung's words complement these, " . . . We would do well, therefore, to think of the creative process as a living thing implanted in the human psyche."

The welcome release of this freedom and self-vindication of poetic power in maturity is presented in **"Fosterling"**:

> Heaviness of being. And poetry
> Sluggish in the doldrums of what happens.
> Me waiting until I was nearly fifty
> To credit marvels. Like the tree-clock of tin cans
> The tinkers made. So long for air to brighten,
> Time to be dazzled and the heart to lighten.

The contrast with the earth-bound quality of earlier poetry in terms of lightness, in opposition to both heaviness and darkness, is developed further in relation to the burden of responsibility to the Northern Irish political situation. As Douglas Dunn has noted [in *The Irish Times,* June 1, 1991], "Poets ask a great deal of themselves these days when they decide to set out in search of an uncompromised route into the detached and disinterested realm of poetry itself and its special truths. More ordinary beginnings need to be explored first, as well as the loyalties attached to them, those local and national pieties which are more insistent than what can be yielded by an imagination in its freedom."

This is Heaney's particular skill, to use the "ordinary beginnings" and in this volume, to have the courage to reach out beyond the ordinary and "credit marvels" yet still retain the connection with "local and national pieties." This is effectively demonstrated in **"The Settle Bed,"** where the physical heaviness of the wooden cot-bed, "standing four-square as an ark," is potently infused through the tactile description with the "local and national pieties" filtered into the poet's consciousness during childhood occupation of the bed, tapping into the "collective unconscious" of the race:

> . . . I hear an old sombre tide awash in the
>   headboard:
>   . . . Anthems of Ulster, unwilling, unbeaten,
>
> Protestant, Catholic, the Bible, the beads . . .

the burden of this "inheritance" is emphasized aptly in terms of the solidity and impenetrable qualities of the wood, "unshiftably planked . . . un-get-roundable weight." These awkward, bulky sounds from a poet so honed in the mellifluous sensuousness of language enforce the sense of "insistence" noted by Dunn, yet later in the poem the resistance claimed by "the imagination in its freedom" is celebrated through the freedom of spaces created by skilful enjambment, a positive response to the "burden" according with Jung's remark, ". . . it is not surprising that when an archetypal situation occurs we feel an extraordinary sense of release, as though transported, or caught up by an overwhelming power. At such moments we are no longer individuals but the race; the voice of all mankind resounds in us . . . ."

Such a voice could in itself become part of the burden; could drown the individual voice; or could be taken up as Heaney does, and turned from constraint to freedom, "It's a poem about turning heavy things into light things, It's saying: you can handle experience."

> . . . to conquer that
> weight,
> Imagine a shower of settle-beds tumbled from
>   heaven
> Like some nonsensical vengeance come on the
>   people,
> Then learn from that harmless barrage that whatever
>   is
> given
>
> Can always be reimagined . . .

Heaney does not escape by ignoring the situation; however, he suggests ways to "handle experience," finds objective correlatives for his own circumstances, as in his poem **"Sounds of Rain"** he identifies with Pasternak in his sense of responsibility:

> "I had the feeling of an immense debt,"
> He said (it is recorded). So many years
> Just writing lyric poetry and translating.
> I felt there was some duty . . . Time was passing.

The psychologically saturating voices of his conscience and the collective unconscious or "national pieties" are powerfully evoked in insistent sibilants:

> The eaves of water-fringe and steady lash
> Of summer downpour: *You are steeped in luck.*
> I heard them say, *Steeped, steeped, steeped in luck.*

The tension between the constraints of responsibility and poetic freedom are further examined in Heaney's essays, ". . . lyric poetry, however responsible, always has an element of the untrammelled about it. There is a certain jubilation and truancy at the heart of an inspiration. There is a sensation of liberation and abundance which is the antithesis of every hampered and deprived condition. And it is for this reason that, psychologically, the lyric poet feels the need for justification in a world that is notably hampered and deprived." He has suggested, ". . . it is tempting to view the whole syndrome in the light of Jung's thesis that an insoluble conflict is overcome by outgrowing it, developing in the process a 'new level of consciousness.'"

Although Heaney used the analogy originally in a lecture in 1984, referring to poets of Northern Ireland in the 1960s and onwards, he has reprinted it in his *Government of the Tongue* collection, and the continuation of the reference to Jungian psychotherapy is still relevant to his work in *Seeing Things*: "This development involves detachment from one's emotions:

One certainly does feel the affect and is tormented by it, yet at the same time one is aware of a higher consciousness looking on which prevents one from becoming identified with the affect, a consciousness which regards the affect as an object, and can say "I know that I suffer. . . ."

"The affect" means a disturbance, a warp in the emotional glass which is in danger of narrowing the mind's range of response to the terms of the disturbance itself. In our case, this affect rose from the particular exacerbations attendant on natives and residents of Northern Ireland at that time."

Heaney's explanation of the affect as "a warp in the emotional glass" is directly taken up in another poem examining the privilege of art in "hampered and deprived" conditions, through memories of sightseeing on his London honeymoon:

> . . . like refections staggered through warped glass,
> They reappear as in a black and white
> Old grainy newsreel, where their pleasure-boat
> Goes back spotlit across sunken bridges
> And they alone are borne downstream unscathed . . .

The sense of responsibility hampers the reminiscence of youthful freedom, given chilling physicality later in the disturbing image of "a silk train being brushed across a leper"; such riches in a time of diseased distortion of creativity mean those so privileged have to shoulder the consequent burden, and risk "narrowing the mind's response to the terms of disturbance itself":

> So let them keep a tally of themselves
> And be accountable when called upon
> For although by every golden mean their lot
> Is fair and due, pleas will be allowed
> Against every right and title vested in them
> (And in a court where mere innocuousness
> Has never gained approval or acquittal.)

Heaney continues his analogy with Jung's terminology, "By the 1960s, in Jung's scenario, 'a higher consciousness' was manifesting itself in the form of poetry itself, an ideal towards which the poets turned in order to survive the stunting conditions." This "higher consciousness" is reached through the mythological dramatisation of the circumstances, as in the last of the "Crossings" poem, depicting the "stunted conditions":

> As danger gathered and the march dispersed . . .
>
> We were like herded shades who had to cross
>
> And did cross, in a panic, to the car
> Parked as we'd left it, that gave when we got in
> Like Charon's boat under the faring poets.

The past tense of this scene is counteracted with the final hopeful encounter at the end of the volume, in which the present tense emphasises Heaney's freedom from the "herded shades," rising to a "higher consciousness" through the acknowledgement that he does not have to accept the world of the dark but can reach out, beyond, into the light. He is encouraged to reject the threat of the Shadow archetype represented by those turned to "shades":

> No good spirits ever pass this way
> And therefore, if Charon objects to you,
> You should understand well what his words imply.

Thus one reason to welcome recent ceasefires is the need of the joy that the political struggles destroy. Heaney keeps alive the belief in and hope for that joy: the life of the spirit as a possibility through poetic imagination, when any kind of war threatens total despair. Through the Jungian interpretation of the mythical archetypes employed in the poems of *Seeing Things*, the reader can identify with Heaney's comment, partly quoted in the opening paragraph of this paper and now in fuller context, confirmation that "Here is the great paradox of poetry and of the imaginative arts in general. Faced with the brutality of the historical onslaught, they are practically useless. Yet they verify our singularity, they strike and stake out the ore of self which lies at the base of every individuated life. In one sense the efficacy of poetry is nil—no lyric has ever stopped a tank. In another sense, it is unlimited."

FURTHER READING

Biography

Buttel, Robert. *Seamus Heaney*. Lewisburg, PA: Bucknell University Press, 88 p.
Biographical and critical study of Heaney.

Corcoran, Neil. *Seamus Heaney*. London: Faber and Faber, 1986, 192 p.
Provides a biographical and critical overview. Corcoran includes a select bibliography.

Quinlan, Kieran. "Tracing Seamus Heaney." *World Literature Today* 69, No. 1 (Winter 1995): 63-8.
Overviews the poet's life and verse, emphasizing the political nature of both.

Criticism

Andrews, Elmer. "The Gift and the Craft: An Approach to the Poetry of Seamus Heaney." *Twentieth Century Literature* XXI, No. 4 (Winter 1985): 368-79.
Determines the influence of Patrick Kavanaugh and William Wordsworth on Heaney's work.

Balakian, Peter. "Seamus Heaney's New Landscapes." *The Literary Review* XXXI, No. 4 (Summer 1988): 501-5.
Praises Heaney's use of sensuous language and of Irish landscape and culture.

Beaver, Harold. "Seamus Heaney: Prospero or Ariel?" *Parnassus* XVI, No. 1 (1990): 104-13.
Juxtaposes the tone and themes of Heaney's poetry against his essays.

Brown, Duncan. "Seamus Heaney's 'Book of Changes': *The Haw Lantern*." *Theoria* LXXIV (October 1989): 79-96.
Marks the volume as a significant development in the poet's career, noting the influence of Mandelstam, Blake, Wilbur, and Zbigniew Herbert on Heaney's style and themes.

Burris, Sidney. *The Poetry of Resistance: Seamus Heaney and the Pastoral Tradition*. Athens: Ohio University Press, 165 p.
Analyzes the pastoral elements of Heaney's work and places his poetry within the context of the pastoral tradition.

Hart, Henry. *Seamus Heaney: Poet of Contrary Progressions*. Syracuse: Syracuse University Press, 1992, 219 p.
Collection of critical essays by Hart, including his prize-winning essays "The Anxiety of Trust," and "Seamus Heaney's Poetry of Meditation: *Door into the Dark*."

Hunter, Jefferson. "The Borderline of Poetry." *Virginia Quarterly Review* 68, No. 4 (Autumn 1992): 801-08.
Positive review of *Seeing Things* and *The Cure at Troy: A Version of Sophocles' Philoctetes,* modernized for the Irish theater in 1990.

Kinzie, Mary. "Deeper than Declared: On Seamus Heaney." *Salmagundi* No. 80 (Fall 1980): 22-57.
Offers a thematic study of *Poems 1965-75,* focusing on the verse written after *North*.

Lloyd, David. "The Two Voices of Seamus Heaney's *North*." *Ariel* X, No. 4 (October 1979): 5-13.
Examines the disparity between the voices of Part I and Part II of *North*.

Longley, Edna. "'Inner Emigré' or 'Artful Voyeur'? Seamus Heaney's *North*." In *Poetry in the Wars,* pp. 140-69. Newcastle upon Tyne, Eng.: Bloodaxe Books, 1986.
Lauds *North* as Heaney's best poetry to date and his most politically significant.

McGuirk, Kevin. "Questions, Apostrophes, and the Politics of Seamus Heaney's *Field Work*." *Ariel* XXV, No. 3 (July 1994): 67-81.
Analyzes *Field Work* in the wake of violence in Belfast in 1969.

McLoughlin, Deborah. "'An Ear to the Line': Modes of Receptivity in Seamus Heaney's 'Glanmore Sonnets'." *Papers on Language and Literature* XXV, No. 2 (Spring 1989): 201-15.
Discusses thematic and stylistic aspects of the sonnets in *Field Work*.

Macrae, Alasdair. "Seamus Heaney's New Voice in *Station Island*." In *Irish Writers and Society at Large,* edited by Masaru Sekine, pp. 122-38. Totowa, N.J.: Barnes & Noble Books, 1985.
Views *Station Island* in light of the relationship of the modern poet to his or her society.

Moldaw, Carol. "A Poetic Conscience." *Partisan Review* LXII, No. 1 (Winter 1995): 144-48.

Reviews *Selected Poems* and *Seeing Things,* noting the "geological shift" which occurs in Heaney's poetry.

Molino, Michael R. "Flying by the Nets of Language and Nationality: Seamus Heaney, the 'English' Language, and Ulster's Troubles." *Modern Philology* 91, No. 2 (November 1993): 180-201.

Explores Heaney's polyphonic, Anglo-Irish voice in *Wintering Out* as the poet speaks of the political events in Northern Ireland.

Owens, Colin. "Heaney's 'Polder.'" *The Explicator* 52, No. 3 (Spring 1994): 183-85.

Interprets Heaney's "Polder" as a love poem.

Sandy, Stephen. "*Seeing Things:* The Visionary Ardor of Seamus Heaney." *Salmagundi* No. 100 (Fall 1993): 207-25.

Perceives *Seeing Things* as the introspective, meditative testimony to Heaney's Northern Irish heritage.

Tapscott, Stephen. "Poetry and Trouble: Seamus Heaney's Irish *Purgatorio*." *Southwest Review* 71, No. 4 (Autumn 1986): 519-35.

Places Heaney and his contemporaries among their Anglo-Irish models, Yeats and Joyce, finding Heaney aligned with the former's historicism and the latter's Catholicism.

Watt, R.J.C. "Seamus Heaney: Voices on Helicon." *Essays in Criticism* XLIV, No. 3 (July 1994): 213-34.

Maintains that Heaney's voice is as divided as his Northern Ireland community.

Additional coverage of Heaney's life and career is contained in the following sources published by Gale Research: *Contemporary Literary Criticism,* Vols. 5, 7, 14, 25, 37, 74, 91; *DISCovering Authors: British; Contemporary Authors,* Vols. 85-88; *Contemporary Authors New Revision Series,* Vols. 25, 48; *Concise Dictionary of British Literary Biography 1960 to Present; DISCovering Authors: Poets Module; Dictionary of Literary Biography,* Vol. 40; *Dictionary of Literary Biography Yearbook,* Vol. 95; **and** *Major Twentieth-Century Writers.*

Mikhail Yuryevich Lermontov
1814-1841

(Also transliterated as Yurevich, Yurievich, Yur'evich; also Lermontoff) Russian poet, novelist, and dramatist.

INTRODUCTION

Lermontov wrote during an important transitional period in Russian literature when the novel began to eclipse poetry as the prevalent mode of literary expression. This movement is reflected in the development of his writings, in which he perfected then exhausted many poetic themes, styles, and forms before experimenting with the novel form. Despite the brevity of his life, Lermontov made extraordinary contributions to Russian letters. His prose works are considered among the finest in Russian literature, especially the innovative novel *Geroi nashego vremeni* (1840; *A Hero of Our Time*), which is regarded as the first Russian psychological novel and a forerunner of the novels of Leo Tolstoy and Fedor Dostoevski. Lermontov also distinguished himself as a writer of richly Romantic poems which have been appreciated by Russians for over a century, ranked second only to those of Alexander Pushkin. Most notable among these narrative poems are *Mtsyri* (1840; *The Novice*) and *Demon* (1856; *The Demon*). Strongly influenced by the romanticism of George Gordon, Lord Byron, Lermontov wrote lyrics, longer narrative poems, and verse dramas on themes ranging from personal freedom and frustrated idealism to revolt and the conflict between the poet and the mob. "The active heroic spirit of his poetry, its lyricism, the depth of thought, subtlety of psychological analysis, the simplicity, combined with a sublime perfection of form and, finally, the amazing melodiousness of his poetry and prose," remarked Irakli Andronikov, "all put Mikhail Lermontov among the world's greatest writers."

Biographical Information

Born October 2, 1814, in Moscow, Lermontov was the son of a poor army officer of Scottish descent and a young woman from a wealthy Russian family. When his mother died in 1817, he was adopted by his maternal grandmother, who tried to alienate the boy from his father but provided an excellent secondary education and trips to the Caucasus region for her grandson's health. Admitted to the Moscow University in 1830, Lermontov distanced himself from other students and began to write poetry in imitation of Byron, and emulated Friedrich Schiller's style in the melodramatic plays *Ispantsy* and *Menschen und Leidenschaften*. In 1832 he entered the elite Guards Cadet Academy at St. Petersburg, where he wrote the scurrilous "Hussar Poems." In both his role as an officer in the Life Guard Hussars and in society circles, Lermontov cultivated

a gloomy, incurably Romantic pose in the manner of a Byronic hero. He became enraged when the narrative poem *Khadzi Abrek* was published without his permission in 1835, the same year he also completed his finest play, *Maskarad (Masquerade)*. After Pushkin was killed in a duel in 1837, Lermontov wrote *Na smert' Pushkina (The Death of Pushkin)*, an angry poem that implicated the government in the poet's death. The poem circulated in thousands of manuscript copies, and eventually government officials arrested and exiled him to the Caucasus. During this period he began the composition and endless revisions of the narrative poems *The Demon* and *The Novice*. Upon his return to St. Petersburg in 1838 he found that *The Death of Pushkin* had made him a celebrity. After receiving a pardon and rejoining the Hussars, Lermontov further enhanced his reputation with the publication of his masterpiece, *A Hero of Our Time,* and *Stikhotvoreninya* (1840), the only collection of his poetry published in his lifetime. Exasperated by fame and bored by literary society, he engaged in a duel with Ernest de Barante, son of a French ambassador, and again was transferred to the Caucasus. Assigned to a front-line regiment, where his life would be at greatest risk, Lermontov instead was cited for bravery twice, but denied offical recognition by Tsar

Nikolas I. He became increasingly irritated with his treatment by the authorities, but he eventually obtained a two-months' furlough at St. Petersburg in early 1841, hoping to retire soon and devote his life to literature. While on leave at the spas of Pyatigorsk the next summer, Lermontov provoked Nikolay Martynov, a former classmate at the Academy and retired major, to a duel on July 15, 1841. Martynov killed Lermontov with his first shot.

Major Works

Lermontov wrote about three hundred lyrics and eighteen narrative poems of varying length, but only one book of poetry and a handful of individual poems were published during his lifetime. Many survive as folk songs in the popular culture of Russia. His early lyrics reflect his feelings of isolation and melancholy that arose from his divisive family situation. Much of his early poetry shows the influence of Pushkin, Schiller, and especially Byron, on whom he modeled his own brooding, rebellious poetic persona. Lermontov mastered Byron's confessional poetic technique, most notably in the lyrics "The Angel" (1831) and "The Confession" (1831), while many of his early narrative poems, particularly *Izmail-Bey* (1832), *Khadzhi Abrek,* and *Bojarin Orsha* (1836) are essentially imitations of Byron's youthful verse. In his later years Lermontov composed more reflective and philosophical lyrics and several longer narrative poems that represent the zenith of Russian Romanticism. The lyrical poems concern themes of freedom, solitude, the depravity of society, and the conflict between the poet and the crowd, yet not all of his later poems are accusatory or pessimistic—some express instead the poet's love of Caucasian folklore and natural beauty. Later narrative poems include *Pesnya pro tsarya Ivan Vasilievicha, molodogo oprichnika i udalogo kuptsa Kalashnikova* (1838; *The Song of Tzar Ivan Vasiljevich, His Young Life-Guardsman, and the Valiant Merchant Kalashnikov*), which is based on a traditional Russian folksong and presents the story of the revenge of the merchant Kalashnikov who murders the tsar's bodyguard for dishonoring the merchant's wife, and *Tambovshaya kaznacheysha* (1838; *The Tambov Treasurer's Wife*), which relates the pursuit of a provincial lady by a dashing officer, who eventually wins his beloved at a card game. *The Novice* and *The Demon,* perhaps the finest of Lermontov's poems, are passionate statements of romantic eloquence. The former depicts the romantic ideal of the fusion of nature and the human ego in a Caucasian orphan who wanders from a Russian monastery, and *The Demon,* which Lermontov revised eight times, recounts the story of a fallen angel's love for a woman set in the Caucasian countryside. Incidentally, the word "demon" entered the Russian vocabulary via the poem's title.

Critical Reception

Even though Lermontov is recognized as a writer of the first order, little has been published about him in English. For much of the twentieth century, critical debate in Russia centered on whether Lermontov moved from Romanticism to Realism or remained a Romantic throughout his life. John Mesereau, Jr., observed that Lermontov's "mature work reveals him as Janus-faced: his poetry and prose embody features typical of Russian romanticism, but they also establish patterns that were to become canonical for Russian realism." Comparative studies traditionally have likened him Pushkin and Byron for similarities in style, tone, and theme, but recent scholarship has found sources of and parallels to Lermontov's works in such disciplines as geography, theology, linguistics, and physiognomy. Although most of the details of Lermontov's life are well known, his poems usually lack a definitive text, particularly in the case of *The Demon.* Nonetheless, most critics have viewed Lermontov's poetry as the quintessence of Russian Romanticism, and in Russia Lermontov's work is considered classic. Even his juvenile "Hussar" poems have enjoyed something of a rehabilitation. Such poets as Aleksandr Blok and Boris Pasternak emulated his innovative use of language and meter. Pasternak called Lermontov "a passionate and personal" poet, commenting that "whereas Pushkin is realistic and exalted in poetic activity, Lermontov is its living personal testimony." In his assessment of Lermontov's life and writings John Garrard concluded: "Perhaps the metaphor of the comet best captures the impression he made upon his contemporaries and on later generations: brilliant but alarming, fleeting but unforgettable."

PRINCIPAL WORKS

Poetry

Khadzi Abrek 1835
Na smert' Pushkina [*"The Death of Pushkin"*] 1837
Pesnya pro tsarya Ivana Vasilievicha, molodogo oprichnika i udalogo kuptsa Kalashnikova [*The Song of Tzar Ivan Vasiljevich, His Young Life-Guardsman, and the Valiant Merchant Kalashnikov*] 1838
Tambovskaya kaznacheysha [*The Tambov Treasurer's Wife*] 1838
Stikhotvoreninya 1840
Skazka dlja detej [*A Fairy Tale for Children*] 1842
Demon [*The Demon*] 1856
Demon. Angelj. Rusalka. Pisnia pro Kalashnikova. Mtsyri. Borodino. Duma. 1874
Poems of Michael Lermontov 1917
The Demon, and Other Poems 1965
A Lermontov Reader 1965
Mikhail Lermontov: Major Poetical Works 1984

Other Major Works

Geroi nashego vremeni [*A Hero of Our Time*] (novel) 1840
Sochineniya. 2 vols. (poetry, prose, and drama) 1847
Vadim [*Vadim*] (novel) 1873
Ionsekia drama M. O. Lermontova (drama) 1880
Maskarad [*The Masquerade*] (drama) 1891
Selected Works (poetry, novel, and drama) 1976

Sobranie sochinenii v chetyrekh tomakh. 4 vols. (poetry, novels, prose, and drama) 1979-81

*This work includes the dramas *Ispantsy, Menschen und Leidenschaften, Strannjichelovekj,* and *Dva brata.*

CRITICISM

B. M. Eikhenbaum (essay date 1924)

SOURCE: An introduction to *Lermontov: A Study in Literary Historical Evaluation,* translated by Ray Parrott and Harry Weber, Ardis, 1981, pp. 9-20.

[*In the following essay—originally published in Germany in 1924—Eikhenbaum analyzes Lermontov's poetry as an expression of his "historical individuality" rather than his "natural (psycho-physical) individuality."*]

To date Lermontov's creative work rarely has been interpreted as a literary historical fact. The traditional history of literature has regarded him only as a "reflection" of social moods, as a "confession of a member of the intelligentsia of the 30s and 40s"; other studies possess the character of impressionistic interpretations of a religio-philosophical or psychological type. Despite his extraordinary popularity, the revival of literary science begun some fifteen years ago in Russia has barely touched Lermontov. Apparently, this is explained by the fact that Lermontov does not stand in the rank of poets whose artistic influence has been clearly felt by the new generation and which once more has attracted the attention of critics and researchers. In the make-up of the literary traditions which formed Russian Symbolism, the name of Lermontov cannot stand alongside the names of Tyutchev and Fet, despite individual poet's attraction to him (especially Blok's).

Lermontov proved useful during the period of fascination with "Nietzscheanism" and "God-seeking" (Merezhkovsky, Zakrzhevsky), but that is all. This period passed and the question of Lermontov ceased to be immediate, although it remained unclear as before. The one-hundredth anniversary of Lermontov's birth, which coincided with the beginning of the European war (1914), did not introduce anything vitally new into the study of his creative work. The Academy edition of his work bypassed this literary historical problem, citing Belinsky's "brilliant appraisal" (as if the problem were a matter of a simple, aesthetic evaluation), and justified the omission by referring to the fact that posterity's conflicting opinions about the character and essence of Lermontov's poetry were "the best indicator of how much there is that is puzzling, unclear, and moot in the poet's multifaceted soul."

Lermontov cannot be studied until the question about him is posed concretely and literarily-historically in the real sense of the word. Religiophilosophical and psychological interpretations of poetic creativity always will be and inevitably must be debatable and contradictory because they characterize not the poet but that historical moment which produced them. Time passes, and nothing remains of them except "debatable and conflicting judgements" prompted by the needs and tendencies of the epoch. One must not confuse a history of the understanding and interpretations of artistic works with the history of art proper. *To study* a poet's creative work does not mean simply to evaluate and interpret it, because in the first instance it is examined historically on the basis of special theoretical principles, and in the second, impressionistically, on the basis of premises of taste and world-outlook.

The real Lermontov is the *historical* Lermontov. To avoid misunderstandings, I must make the reservation that in saying this I do not at all mean Lermontov as an individual event in *time*—an event which simply has to be restored. Time and, by the same token, the concept of the past do not comprise the bases of historical knowledge. Time in history is a fiction, a convention which plays an auxiliary role. We are studying not motion in time, but motion as such: a *dynamic process* which in no way can be fragmented is never interrupted, and precisely for that reason does not possess actual time within itself and cannot be measured by time. Historical study reveals the dynamics of events, the laws of which operate not only within the limits of a conditionally selected epoch, but everywhere and always. In this sense, no matter how paradoxical it sounds, history is a science about the constant, the immutable, the motionless, although it concerns itself with change and motion. It can be a science only to the extent that it succeeds in converting real motion into a schema. Historical lyricism, like being in love with one or another epoch for its own sake, does not constitute a science. To study an event historically does not at all mean to describe it as an isolated instance which has meaning only in the conditions of its own time. This is a naive historicism which renders science sterile. It is not a matter of a simple *projection into the past,* but of understanding the historical *actuality* of an event, of determining its role in the development of historical energy, which, in its very essence, is constant, does not appear and disappear, and therefore operates outside of time. A historically understood fact by the same token is removed from time. Nothing repeats itself in history precisely because nothing vanishes, but only mutates. Therefore, historical analogies are not only possible but even necessary; and the study of historical events outside the historical process as individual, "unrepeatable" self-contained systems is impossible because it contradicts the very nature of these events.

"The historical Lermontov" is Lermontov *understood historically*—as a force entering into the general dynamics of its epoch, and, by the same token, generally into history as well. We study a historical individuality as it is expressed in creative work, and not a natural (psycho-physical) individuality, for which completely different materials must be adduced. The study of a poet's creative work as an immediate emanation of his soul or as a manifestation of his individual, self-contained "verbal consciousness' leads to the destruction of the very concept of individuality as a stable unit. Encountering the variety and changeability or contradictoriness of styles within the limits of individual creativity, investigators are forced to qualify almost all writers as "dual" natures: Pushkin, Gogol, Lermontov, Tyutchev, Turgenev, Tolstoy Dostoevsky, etc., all have passed through this qualification. Together with "demonism" in Lermontov one finds "blueness" (see S. Durylin's article in *Russkaya mysl*, 1914, X), because in his work not only eyes, the sky and the steppes, but even the stars are "blue." On this path of "immanent" interpretations we have reached an impasse, and no compromises on a linguistic or any other basis can help. We must decisively reject these attempts which are dictated by world-view or polemical biases.

. . . . .

The literary epoch to which Lermontov belonged (the 1830s and 40s) had to resolve the struggle between poetry and prose, a struggle which clearly had developed by the mid-20s. It was impossible to proceed further on the basis of those principles which had shaped Russian poetry at the beginning of the 19th century and which had created the verse of Pushkin. It was necessary to find new aesthetic norms and expressive means for verse because nothing other than feeble imitation could appear on the former course. There came a period of a lowering of poetic style, a decline of the high lyrical genres, the victory of prose over verse, the novel over the poem. Poetry had to be given more "content," to be made more programmatic, the verse as such less noticeable; it was necessary to intensify the emotional and ideational motivation of poetic speech in order to justify anew its very existence. As always in history, this process develops not in the form of a single line of facts, but in the complex form of an interweaving and contrasting of diverse traditions and methods; it is the struggle between these elements which shapes the epoch. The supremacy of one method or style arises as the result of this struggle—as a victory—after which a decline invariably follows. Other poets are acting simultaneously with Pushkin, not only those who are associated with him but also those who proceed by different paths unrelated to Pushkin: not only Vyazemsky, Baratynsky, Delvig, Yazykov, etc., but also Zhukovsky, and Tyutchev, and Polezhaev, and Podolinsky, and Myatlev, and Kyukhelbeker, and Glinka, and Odoevsky, and Benediktov, etc. It is the same later also: alongside Nekrasov stands Fet, witnessing by his creative work that Nekrasov alone does not form the epoch and that beside Nekrasov's method there is another one, which it is true, is not fated to become the main, the pre-eminent one within the limits of its own epoch.

The sharp historical break separating the 30s from the 20s is felt already in Pushkin's creative work. People of the 40s, looking back at the recent past of Russian poetry, clearly felt its *historical* sense. Aksakov, who himself had experienced the force of this upheaval, speaks about it very clearly:

> Poetic activity in Russia had to reach the limit of its tension, to develop its apogee. For this the highest

poetic genius was necessary and an entire throng of poetic talents. It may appear strange why the setting down of speech in a particular meter and the binding of it with assonances becomes, for certain persons in a given epoch, an irresistible attraction from childhood on. The history of all the arts gives an answer to this question by analogy. In general, when in the spiritual organism of a people the need arises to manifest some special force, then, in order to serve this force, in some inscrutable way people are born into the world with a single common calling. However, they maintain all the diversity of the human personality, preserving its freedom and all the visible, external, accidental qualities of existence. Poetic creativity in its new (for us) measured speech was fated to arise in Russia at a historical turn: and so, you see, at the appointed hour, literally by a mysterious hand, the seeds of the necessary talent are scattered in the wind. They fall haphazardly, now on the Molchanovka in Moscow, on the head of the son of the Guard Captain-Lieutenant Pushkin, who consequently is born with an apparently unnatural inclination for rhymes, trochees, and iambs; now in the Tambov village of Mara on the head of some Baratynsky, now in the Bryansk backwoods on Tyutchev, whose mother and father never even attempted to delight their son with the sound of Russian poetry. It is evident that in these poets, as well as in others contemporaneous to them, unconsciously even for themselves, verse creation was the fulfillment not only of their personal but also of the historical summons of the epoch. . . . Their verse form breathes with a freshness that does not and could not exist in the verse creations of a later period; the fresh trace of victory gained over the material of the word still lies on their verse form; the exultation and joy of artistic possession is still heard. Their poetry and their very relationship to it is stamped with *sincerity*. Lermontov stands on the threshold of this period of sincerity in our poetry. Through the direct force of talent he is affiliated with this brilliant constellation of poets, though remaining detached. His poetry is set off sharply from theirs by the negative character of its content. We see something similar in Heine (although we are not thinking of comparing them), who completed a cycle of German poets. Only one step separates a negative tendency from that tendentious point at which poetry turns into a means and recedes to the background. It has all but been taken. It seems to us that the imprint of this *historical necessity* and sincerity no longer lies on the verse of our time, because to our mind the very historical mission of verse creation has been concluded.

As we see, Aksakov sensed the movement of Russian poetry precisely as a *historical process* possessing its own dynamics and not conditioned by the psychic attributes of authors. He feels Lermontov's appearance is foreordained a historically necessary fact prepared by the previous movement of poetry.

The creation of new artistic forms is not an act of invention, but one of discovery, because these forms exist latently in the forms of preceding periods. To Lermontov fell the task of discovering that poetic style which had to appear to provide a way out of the poetic impasse created after the 20s and which already existed potentially among some poets of the Pushkin epoch. He had to pass through

a complex period of school work in order to orient himself amidst the material accumulated and the methods
developed to find a historically-actual path. Between the
Pushkin and Nekrasov-Fetepochs a poetry had to be created which, while not breaking with the traditions and
achievements of the previous epoch, at the same time
would be something distinct from the style which had
reigned in the 20s. The time had not yet arrived for a
revolution, but the necessity of reform already was sensed
very clearly. One had to know how to discard what had
become obsolete, and to bring together what was left
that still had not lost its vitality, notwithstanding certain
inner contradictions occasioned by the struggle of various traditions. It was necessary to blend genres, to invest the poetic line with special emotional intensity, to
weight it with thought, to impart to poetry the character
of an eloquent, passionate confession, even if as a result
of this the strictness of style and of composition suffered. An ornamental airiness of form ("silliness" in
Pushkin's words) among the epigones degenerated into
a monotonous pattern which repeated itself mechanically and was therefore no longer sensed. A crowd of poets
appeared but "no one was listening to poetry when everyone started to write it" (Marlinsky, in the article "On
the Novels of N. Polevoy," 1833).

> To Lermontov fell the task of discovering
> that poetic style which had to appear to
> provide a way out of the poetic impasse
> created after the 20s and which already
> existed potentially among some poets of
> the Pushkin epoch.
>
> —*B.M. Eikhenbaum*

Essentially Lermontov's course was not new; the same
traditions remained and the basic principles characteristic
for Russian poetry of the 20s underwent only slight
modification. Lermontov was a direct disciple of this epoch
and did not repudiate it in his creative work, as Nekrasov
later did. He appeared at the moment of its decline, when
the struggle between the various poetic tendencies had
cooled down and a need for reconciliation and summation
of results was felt. The struggle of the archaists with
Pushkin and Zhukovsky, the quarrels about the ode and
the elegy—none of this touched Lermontov. Having skirted
this party struggle, which had developed toward the
mid-20s and had given rise to Tyutchev's poetry along
with Pushkin's, Lermontov weakened those formal problems which disturbed the poets of the older generation
(mainly problems of lexicon and genre). He concentrated
his attention on other things: on intensifying the expressive energy of the verse line, on imparting an emotional-
personal character to poetry, on developing poetic eloquence. Poetry took the form of a lyrical monologue; the
verse line once more was motivated as an expression of
psychic and intellectual ferment, as a natural expressive
means.

The period of high verse culture was ending; poetry had
to gain for itself a new reader, one who would demand
"rich content." Belinsky, who stood at the head of these
new readers, in a contradistinction to other critics (Vyazemsky, Polevoy, Shevyryov) who represented literature, hailed
Lermontov as a poet capable of meeting this demand. For
him it was important that profound "content" had been
introduced into poetry by Lermontov, something which
was not to be found in Pushkin, but at the same time
Pushkin had not been repudiated. "As the creator of Russian
poetry Pushkin eternally will remain the teacher (mae-
stro) of all future poets; but if any one of them, like
Pushkin, should be concerned only with the idea of artistry,
this would be clear proof of a lack of genius or greatness
of talent. . . . Pushkin's pathos lies in the sphere of art
itself; Lermontov's pathos lies in the moral problems of
fate and the rights of the human personality. . . . The
poetic line for Lermontov was only a means for the expression of his ideas, profound and at the same time simple in
their merciless truth, and he did not set too much store by
it." (*Otechestvennye zapiski*, 1843, No. 2). In a letter to
Botkin, Belinsky expresses his view of Lermontov even
more definitely: "Lermontov is much inferior to Pushkin
in artistry and virtuosity, in the musicality, elasticity, and
versatility of his verse line; he yields even to Maykov in
all this; but the content of his verse, drawn from the depths
of a profound and powerful nature, the gigantic sweep,
the demonic flight . . . —all this compels one to think that
in Lermontov we were deprived of a poet who, in terms
of content, would have progressed further than Pushkin."
(*"Pisma" V. G. Belinskogo*, vol. II). While not resolving
to renounce the past and still preserving complete respect
for Pushkin, nevertheless Belinsky already is raising his
hand against the "idea of artistry" and beginning to speak
about "content" as something special and more important
than Pushkin's "artistry." From this it is only one step to
the situation which arose in the 60s when only Nekrasov
was permitted to write poetry, if, after all, he was unable
to express his thoughts in any other way, while Pushkin
was ridiculed and discarded as mere verbiage. Lermontov
stands on the boundary of these two epochs: while himself bringing the Pushkin epoch to a close, at the same
time he is preparing an onslaught against it.

Belinsky's judgment is characteristic for readers of his
time. Belinsky is unable to say anything concrete about
Lermontov's poetry, as well as about other literary phenomena. In these instances, as a typical reader, he speaks
about Lermontov's verse in general phrases and vague
metaphors ("a crack of thunder," "a flash of lightning,"
"the slash of a sword," "the whine of a bullet"). Much
more interesting and valuable as material for a concrete,
literary-historical study of Lermontov are the judgements
of other critics from the writers' camp. Their opinions are
notable for far greater restraint: Lermontov's poetry does
not produce upon them the impression of a new course.
They find "eclecticism" and imitativeness in him; they
reproach him for prolixity and vagueness. Only the critic
for the *Severnaya pchela*, V. Mezhevich, is close to Belinsky's opinion. In his article the decline in interest in
poetry and verse-creation itself is emphasized (speaking
about an 1840 anthology of Lermontov's work): "This is

such a precious gift for our time, which has become almost unaccustomed to truly artistic works that it really is impossible to admire sufficiently this unexpected find. . . . One must possess a great deal of strength, uniqueness, and originality in order to rivet general attention to *poetry* at a time when verse has lost all of its credit and has been abandoned *to the amusement of children*" (*Severnaia pchela,* 1840, Nos. 284-285, signature L. L.). Shevyryov understood Lermontov's creative work differently. As a subtle critic and poet groping after new methods beyond Pushkin and standing on the same path as Tyutchev, his opinion is extremely important, the more so since it is distinguished by its sharp definition and concreteness. Shevyryov notes in Lermontov

> an uncommon Proteanism of talent, truly remarkable, but nonetheless dangerous to original development . . . you hear in turn the sounds of Zhukovsky, Pushkin, Kirsha Danilov, and Benediktov. Even the form of their works is noticeable in everything, and not only in the sounds. Sometimes Baratynsky's and Denis Davydov's phrases flash by; sometimes the manner of foreign poets is evident. And through all this outside influence it is difficult for us to ascertain what properly belongs to the new poet and where he himself stands. . . . Does not the new poet appear to us as some kind of eclectic, who like a bee gathers to himself all the former sweets of the Russian muse in order to create from them new honeycombs? Eclecticism of this kind has occurred in the history of art after its well-known periods: it could also recur among us in accord with the unity of its laws of ubiquitous development. . . . As a poet Lermontov initially appeared as a Proteus with an uncommon talent: his lyre still had not revealed its special pitch; he brings it to the lyres of our best-known poets and with great art is able to tune it to an already well known pitch. . . . We hear the echoes of the lyres already familiar to us and read them as reminiscences of Russian poetry of the last twenty years." (*Moskvitianin,* 1841, pt. II, No. 4).

In Shevyryov's opinion "a certain personality peculiar to the poet" is revealed in some of Lermontov's poems (**"The Gifts of the Terek," "Cossack Cradle Song," "Three Palms," "To the Memory of A.I. O-yi," "A Prayer"**), but "not so much in the poetic form of expression as in the mode of thoughts and in the feelings given to it by life." Such things as **"It is both boring and sad," "The Journalist, Reader and Writer,"** and **"A Meditation"** produce a "distressing impression" upon Shevyryov due not to the shortcomings of the verse or the style, but again because of the thoughts and feelings contained in them: "Poet! If indeed such thoughts visit you, it would be better to keep them to yourself and not entrust them to carping society. . . . It seems to us that faithful fragments from real life accompanied by an apathy of observation are unseemly for Russian poetry, and even less so are dreams of despairing disappointment flowing from nowhere." Shevyryov defends high poetry: "a poetry of inspired insights, a poetry of creative fantasy rising above everything essential." In Shevyryov's last reproaches his party position is revealed, but he correctly sensed the presence of a threat in Lermontov's poetry.

Vyazemsky wrote Shevyryov concerning this article (on the 22nd of September, 1841, that is, already after the death of Lermontov): "Apropos of Lermontov. You were too severe with him. Granted, recollections and borrowed impressions are reflected in his talent; but there was also a great deal that signified a strong and fundamental originality which subsequently would have overcome everything external and borrowed. A wild poet, that is, an ignoramus like Derzhavin, for example, could be original from the outset; but a young poet, educated by any learning, upbringing, and reading whatever, inevitably must make his way along well-trodden paths and through a series of favorites who awakened, evoked, and, so to say, equipped his talent. In poetry, as in painting, there must be schools" (*Russkii arkhiv,* 1885, Book 2). In essence Vyazemsky does not object to Shevyryov's basic thesis, but only softens its severity and this, seemingly, only under the fresh impression of Lermontov's tragic death. Later (in 1847, in the article "A Survey of Our Literature During the Decade after Pushkin's Death"), Vyazemsky expressed himself on Lermontov even more severely and decisively than Shevyryov: "Lermontov had a great gift, but he did not have time to develop himself fully and perhaps couldn't have. To the end Lermontov adhered to the poetic devices for which Pushkin had been celebrated at the beginning of his own career and by which he drew after him the ever impressionable and frivolous crowd. He did not go forward. His lyre did not resound with new strings. His poetic horizon did not expand. An entire, living world is reflected in Pushkin's creations. In Lermontov's works a theatrical world vividly stands out before you with its wings and prompter, who sits in his booth and prompts a speech euphoniously and fascinatingly repeated by a masterly artist" (*Polnoe sobranie sochinenii,* II).

Not to Shevyryov alone belongs the feeling that Lermontov's poetry is eclectic ("recollections of Russian poetry of the last twenty years"), that it had absorbed various, even contradictory, styles and genres struggling against one another. As early as 1824, speaking out against Zhukovsky's poetry (*Mnemozina,* part II) and defending the rights of "high" poetry, Kyukhelbeker expresses himself in the same vein, acknowledging only that the very process of collecting or fusing heterogeneous poetic tendencies is a serious and historically-necessary matter. In his diary for 1844 he notes: "Question: can the talent of an eclectically imitative writer, such as Lermontov is in the greater part of his pieces, rise to the point of originality? The simple or even best imitator of a great or simply gifted poet, of course, would have done better had he never taken pen in hand. But Lermontov is not such a person; he imitates or, rather, one finds in him echoes of Shakespeare, Schiller, Byron, Zhukovsky, and Kyukhelbeker. . . . But in his very imitations there is something of his own, if only the ability to fuse the most heterogeneous verses into a harmonious whole. And this is not a trifle" (*Russkaia starina* 1891, Vol. 72, Book X). Kyukhelbeker, who by this time already had withdrawn from direct participation in the literary struggle, apparently himself tended toward the thought of reconciling the parties and saw in Lermontov the possibility of such a reconciliation. Belinsky, too, expresses this same thought, saying that "we see already the beginning of a genuine (not joking) reconciliation of all tastes and all literary parties in the case of Lermontov's compositions." The special emphasis which Belinsky gives to the words "not joking" indicates that a need for reconciliation was sensed and stated even earlier; Lermontov's unique "eclecticism" arose in fulfillment of this need because it represented not a simple aping of one tendency but something different. Shevyryov turned out to be Lermontov's most severe judge precisely because he continued to occupy a militant position and did not strive for "reconciliation." The struggle of the ode and the elegy had to lead to the disintegration of both these genres and, on the one hand, resulted in the lyrics of Tyutchev where the ode, while preserving its oratorical pathos, was condensed and transformed into a lyrical "fragment" (Tynyanov). On the other hand, this disintegration led to the poetry of Lermontov, where the elegy lost its airy classical features and appeared in the form of a declamatory meditation or "reflection." The admirers of strict lyrical genres, like Shevyryov, most acutely felt the instability and fluidity of this form. Gogol, in whose mouth "finished form" or "definitiveness" were the highest form of praise (see, for example, "The Portrait") also sided with him. He does not see this "finality" of form in Lermontov's creative work and explains this by the absence of love and respect for his own talent: "No one has played so frivolously with his talent, and no one has tried so hard to display an even boastful contempt toward it as Lermontov. Not one poem has gestated full term in him, has been lovingly and thoughtfully fussed over like one's own child, has "settled" and become concentrated in itself; the verse line itself still has not acquired its own firm personality and palely recalls now Zhukovsky's verse and now Pushkin's; everywhere there is excess and prolixity. There is much greater merit in his prose works. Among us no one has written such correct, fragrant prose."

All the judgements cited clearly show that for Lermontov's contemporaries there was nothing unexpected or mysterious in creative work; on the contrary, many of them hailed him precisely because they saw in him the fulfillment of their desires and aspirations. The struggle, of course, had not ended. Belinsky indicates that of all Lermontov's pieces the poem **"It's both boring and sad"** "attracted the special hostility of the old generation." As we have seen, precisely this piece among others produced a "distressing impression" upon Shevyryov, and provoked a long tirade as to what Russian poetry ought to be like. It is not just a matter of generations here. Shevyryov correctly perceived in these poems of Lermontov the beginning of a course leading to a lowering of the high lyric and to the triumph of verse as an emotional "means of expression" over verse as a self-sufficient, ornamental form. As an archaist and fighter for "a poetry of inspired insights," he did not wish to yield first place to a poetry reduced to the level of an album meditation or to the topical publicistic essay. He was obliged to yield, for precisely that kind of poetry was victorious and became predominant for a time. But "high" lyric poetry, of course, not only did not disappear in Lermontov's time, but even in Nekrasov's time— only the interrelation of these styles changed, which exist and more or less bitterly struggle with one another in

every epoch. Nekrasov displaced Fet, but later, in turn, Balmont, Bryusov, and V. Ivanov appeared, and the Nekrasov principle modestly found refuge in "The Satyricon" ("Sasha Chyorny" and others) in order later to blare forth with new strength in the verse of Mayakovsky. A prevailing tendency does not in itself exhaust an epoch and taken in isolation characterizes not so much the state of poetry as readers' sensibilities. In reality the movement of art always is expressed in the form of a struggle for co-existing tendencies. Every literary year accommodates within itself works of various styles. The victory of one of them is a result of this struggle and at the moment of its complete expression is no longer typical for the epoch because behind this victor stand new conspirators whose ideas recently seemed antiquated and worn-out. Every epoch is characterized by a struggle between at least two tendencies or schools (in fact, many more) of which one, gradually triumphing and thereby transforming itself from a revolutionary to a peaceably ruling tendency, becomes encrusted with epigones and begins to degenerate, and another, inspired by a rebirth of old traditions, begins anew to attract attention to itself. At the moment of the disintegration of the first, yet a third tendency usually is formed which attempts to occupy a middle position and, demanding reform, attempts to preserve the main achievements of the victor without condemning itself to an inevitable fall. On the secondary paths, fulfilling temporarily the role of reserves, tendencies remain which do not possess sharply expressed theoretical principles while in practice they develop non-canonized, little-used traditions and, since they are not distinguished by a definiteness of style and genres, work out new literary material.

I return to Lermontov in order to conclude this introductory chapter. **"It's both boring and sad"** must have disturbed Shevyrynov because here the elegy had sunk to the level of a "keepsake" meditation. There is a "low" conversational-melancholic intonation ("Desires! . . . what's the use of eternally and vainly desiring? . . . To love . . . but whom?") and a prosaic phraseology ("it's not worth the effort," "and when you look at life"), which threatened the high lyrical style with such consequences as the poetry of Nadson. On the other hand, it is only one step from **"A Meditation"** and **"The Journalist"** to the poetry of Nekrasov. But all the same Lermontov himself does not take this step, remaining on the boundary of two epochs and not breaking with the traditions which formed the Pushkin epoch. He does not create new genres, but on the other hand unhurriedly moves from one to another, blending and smoothing out their traditional particularities. Lyric verse becomes "prolix" and takes the most diverse forms from album notes to ballads and declamatory "reflections"; the poema, so advanced by Pushkin in descriptive and narrative portions, is shortened, acquiring a conventionally decorative character and developing its monologic portion. The genre becomes unstable, but then emotional formulae acquire an extraordinary strength and keenness, which, as will be seen further on, Lermontov carries over from one piece to another without paying attention to distinctions of styles and genres. While not permitting the publication of verses written earlier than 1836, at the same time he constantly employs ready-made formulae coined as early as the period 1830-31. His attention is directed not toward the creation of new material, but to the fusion of ready-made elements. Put somewhat differently, in Lermontov's poetry there is no genuine, organic *constructiveness* in which the material and the composition, mutually influencing one another, make up the form; this is replaced by a tense lyricism and emotional eloquence which is expressed in fixed verbal formulae. All Lermontovian forms tend equally toward their formation, linking the lyric with the poema, the poema with the story *(povest')*, the story with the drama. This, of course, is not a peculiarity of his soul, of his temperament, or, finally, of his individual "verbal consciousness" but an historical fact characteristic of him as an historical individuality who was fulfilling a specific mission required by history. Therefore, neither here nor elsewhere in this book should my words be understood as a simple aesthetic evaluation. This is not an aesthetic but a literary-historical evaluation, whose basic spirit is an enthusiasm for the assertion of fact.

Henry Lanz   (essay date 1943)

SOURCE: "Demon-Prometheus," in *Slavic Studies,* edited by Alexander Kaun and Ernest J. Simmons, Cornell University Press, 1943, pp. 64-74.

[*In the essay below, Lanz considers the similarities between the classical myth of Prometheus and* The Demon, *noting that "the Demon is the Russian Prometheus."*]

It may seem strange to say that Lermontov, perhaps more than any other Russian poet or novelist, is entitled to a place in world literature. If we agree to understand under the term "world literature" an interrelated system of themes and dramatic situations that influence each other and are in the relation of parents and children with respect to one another; if we think of world literature as a great circle, every point of which is organically connected with every other point by the same central law of evolution—then the Russian contributions, Russian novels and dramas, however great in themselves, too often go off on a tangent. They do not belong to the great circle, even though they may take their origin in it.

But Lermontov does belong to the great circle. By temperament and underlying philosophy he belongs to the great undercurrent of European tradition—that tradition which is paradoxically concerned not with the glorification of the Good, but with the justification of the Evil. This tradition, which is so repugnant to the heart of the orthodox, and so incomprehensible to the Philistine, originates with Aeschylus, and more precisely with his profound treatment of the story of Prometheus. Hence the title of my [essay] which, in the hands of a more ambitious and competent writer, could be profitably expanded into a book on Lermontov and Aeschylus.

In pursuit of my task allow me first of all to remind the reader of the contents and implications of the myth of Prometheus. Prometheus was a Titan, a semi-god (or a demon, if you wish) of the older dynasty conquered by Zeus. In the Christian terminology he would be called a fallen angel, Satan or Lucifer, who once enjoyed the confidence of the Almighty. We hear that "when Zeus had settled accounts with his celestial enemies, he looked about him and saw with disgust the race of men, so suffering and futile, and determined to wipe them out of existence." Prometheus loved men, and resolved to save them. To do so, he stole fire from heaven and gave it to man. And for this transgression against the newly established sovereignty of Zeus, Prometheus, the friend and savior of mankind, was doomed to suffer a severe punishment; he was chained to a cliff in the far-away Scythian mountains of Kaukasos, our Caucasian mountains, "his breast transfixed with a blade of adamant"; a vulture was sent daily to devour his liver which, by the inscrutable justice of the Omnipotent, was to grow again during the night.

Aeschylus has worked out this impressive myth into a beautiful tragedy, probably the greatest tragedy that has ever been written. A minor Athenian demigod, protector of smiths, whose altar was shared by Hephaistos, was elevated to the dignity of a cosmic symbol. In a long chain of subsequent literary imitations and variations, Prometheus leads the revolt of Earth against Heaven. He is the eternal victim of tyranny and injustice, not a mute and inarticulate sufferer of the masses, but a self-conscious and proud individual, a revolutionist rising against oppression, an archangel in revolt and in defeat.

The great philosophical idea that lies at the basis and explains the meaning of the tragedy is the idea of cosmic injustice, which Gilbert Murray has recently written about, and with such characteristic clarity that his words may be quoted with profit: "I think there can be no doubt that the moral sense of civilized man, or of anything that claims the flattering title of *homo sapiens* in whatever stage of development, is at times shocked and bewildered by the behavior of the external world. He is its slave, and it cares nothing for him; its values are not his values; and the more he thinks of the world as alive and acting by conscious quasi-human will, the more profoundly is he shocked. The fires, floods, and famines, the great inevitable miseries of nature, are not things which any good man would think of causing or permitting even against his worst enemies, if he had control over them. The rebellion of certain religions against the Ruler of the World, so far as the ordinary run of events can serve as evidence of his character and intentions, is a rebellion of the moral sense not exactly against facts, but against the claim that because they are facts they must be good" (Gilbert Murray; *Aeschylus, the Creator of Tragedy*). In other words, man, with his admittedly meager and feeble conscience, is morally superior to God and justly becomes His ethical accuser.

In the light of this interpretation the tragedy of Prometheus has become the model of similar stories throughout world literature, in the subsequent history of which we find innumerable variations of this Promethean *Leitmotiv;* in its Christian form, it has penetrated into Western literature probably together with the exiles of the Iconoclastic movement and with the spread of the Manichean heresy which is peculiarly near and congenial to our contemporary mentality. In all these legends, poems, and dramas, *God stands on trial* for the creation of this abominable world in which we are compelled to live. As it is characteristic of Christianity, in the development of this particular theme as in everything else, the ancient Greek tradition joins hands with Hebrew speculations concerning Creation, and thus gradually Prometheus is transformed into Lucifer, or Satan, or Mephisto, or Cain, or whatever other name he may assume. In Byron's definition these names are all

> . . . rebellious
> Souls who dare look the Omnipotent tyrant in
> His everlasting face, and tell him that
> His evil is not good.

For all those "souls," those variations, the problem remains the same: the revolt of a proud and indomitable human will against the unjust government of the universe, a metaphysical wrestling match of human conscience with divine omnipotence. We find it in Milton's *Paradise Lost* and Goethe's *Faust;* we find it in William Blake and Lord Byron.

This revolt is intimately associated with the growth of democracy in Europe. On the Continent this reversal of celestial perspective, by which the attributes of the common "God" were transferred to the Devil or to a Demiurge and *vice versa,* was accomplished by the Manicheans, whose innumerable ramifications represented the seeds of incipient democracy in Europe. The democratic factor inherent in Manichean philosophy grew stronger in the proportion in which Manicheans were in opposition to the official church and, consequently, to the existing social order. In England this peculiarly democratic undercurrent of European tradition has become particularly effective—paradoxically effective in two opposite directions: it is manifested in the democracy of Puritanism, and in the revolutionary democracy of Byronism.

In its Byronic form the myth of Prometheus reached Poland and Russia and found its most powerful expression in Lermontov's **Demon**. What makes this arrival of Prometheus in Russia especially interesting and intriguing from the point of view of world literature is the fact that with this new variation the story *comes back to its geographical origin,* the Caucasian Mountains, and thus completes its circle. The Demon flies and suffers precisely around the place where Prometheus was chained to a cliff.

This is by no means an external coincidence. The fact, of course, that the scene for both tragedies is laid in the Caucasian Mountains is historically an accident. But the spiritual kinship between Prometheus and the Demon is neither an accident nor a matter of subjective analogy. The Demon is the Russian Prometheus. Let us see what are the spiritual traits common to both of them.

First of all, both are celestial revolutionists; one is a fallen angel, the other a defeated god. Both are, so to speak, irreconcilable enemies of the present celestial administration, the foes of God,—not two different foes, but one foe in two different forms. "Behold me," says one, "an outcast god, the foe of Zeus, me who have incurred the enmity of all . . ." "I am nature's foe," says the other, "the world's despair, and heaven's woe. All living things malign and curse me for their doom." One is an outcast god, the other an "exile from paradise." Both are endowed with absolute knowledge. "I know what comes and how," says Prometheus. "I am the lord of understanding," says the Demon. Both find their superior knowledge a burden and difficult to endure. And, what is most important, both are conscious of the injustice in the universe and hate its existing order. True, they hate in two different ways. Aeschylus condemns the world in a determined, rational, and quiet way, as a mature thinker and as a wise old man; condemns it with clear logic and calm mathematical rigor, as a mountain condemns the turbulent lava that is burning beneath its majestic weight. Lermontov hates it with all the passion of youth, with a power of feeling that scarcely has its equal in the whole history of poetry, but dim and vague in proportion to its emotional intensity, as a storm hates the imperturbability of the ocean on the surface of which it rages. But even though their modes of hatred are different in their national color, and in the color of the age, both are inspired by the same ethical pathos of indignation against the cold and cruel way in which the external world tortures men. Both have reached the conception of a Supreme Tyrant, the real metaphysical enemy of understanding and freedom, and, on the other hand, of a champion of truth, standing up against Him. The champion is utterly inferior in strength to God, but he is superior to God in his moral strength and substance. The true source of strength that both, Prometheus and the Demon, have is their immortality and their indomitable will. They both feel, in Milton's words, that

> All is not lost; the unconquerable will,
> And study of revenge, immortal hate,
> And courage never to submit or yield . . .

They are both motivated, nay, swayed by what Nietzsche, another spiritual descendent of Prometheus, has aptly called "holy hatred."

. . . [T]he spiritual kinship between Prometheus and the Demon is neither an accident nor a matter of subjective analogy. The Demon is the Russian Prometheus.

—Henry Lanz

Still another point of contact between Prometheus and the Demon is their loneliness and their essential dependence upon sympathy and human love. Even though the Demon makes men suffer and enjoys it, this wicked disposition is merely on the surface. Down deep in his heart he loves his victims and makes them suffer only as a sort of impotent protest against the stupidities of life. He does evil, but he seeks good,—real good, one that is not contaminated by "divine conventions". He hopes to find it in Tamara's love, which is a faint and feeble echo of another great tradition in world literature,—salvation through love. Aeschylus calls it sympathy.

The Greek όόìðáè íá is a stronger word than our Christian "love." It means "co-suffering," or "co-operation in pain," not merely a sentiment. "One of the most sublime of the Stoic doctrines," writes Gilbert Murray, "was the conception that every joy or pain felt by an individual soul vibrates through the universe, so that with any great martyr or Savior, the whole of life suffers. This idea finds perhaps its earliest expression in one of the songs of the Daughters of Ocean in the *Prometheus;* they suffer with him, the whole world suffers, and the fiercest and wildest of men are heart-sore because of him" (*Aeschylus, the Creator of Tragedy.*) I shall quote the passage in full (in Murray's translation), because the Caucasian Mountains are here directly mentioned by Aeschylus:

> A great cry hath risen from the whole world's
> compassion;
> The peoples of the sunset, they go grieving by the
> sea
> For a beauty long ago, for a greatness of old
> fashion,
> Thine and thy brethren's, in the days when ye were
> free.
> In the Lords of Holy Asia there is wakened a
> strange passion,
> And the lips of them that perish pine for thee.
> And the hordes that wander in fierce places
> At the world's rim, the Scythians of the Mere;
> And hard men, of Araby the flower,
> Where the high crags of Caucasus advance,
> They groan in their mountain-builded tower
> Amid great wrath and flashing of the lance.

>   . . . . .

> The breakers of the sea clash and roar
> Together; and the gulfs thereof are sore
> With longing. There is murmur of hearts aching
> In Hades and the Caverns of the Deep;
> And the torrents of the hills, white breaking,
> For pity of thy pain weep and weep.

The Daughters of Ocean weep for Prometheus. They love him. But they regret to have lost on account of him their innocent existence, when they knew nothing and were undisturbed by uncomfortable thoughts and unanswerable questions:

> It was happiness to live thus for ever,
> Untroubled, without fear of things to be,
> Making joy by the music of the river;
> But I tremble as mine eyes turn to thee,

And I know the long chain of thy torments,
Pain on pain.

In Lermontov's *Demon* this idea of sympathy assumes a more elementary and naïve form. The place of the Daughters of Ocean is here taken by Tamara. Despite his universal knowledge and his Byronic disillusionment, the Demon, like an inexperienced school boy—and not unlike Dr. Faust, for that matter—falls in love with the beautiful eye-lashes and captivating ankles of a Georgian princess. This becomes his real downfall, the aesthetic fall of Lermontov himself. However that maybe, admitting that feminine charms are capable of captivating even the most spiritual of males, let us accept this undignified love affair as a conventional tribute to a great tradition and to the author's youth. In spite of it, Tamara, just like Gretchen in *Faust,* does fulfill a higher purpose. She is a new, personified and dramatized form of the Aeschylean chorus. She is there to pity and to sympathize with the Demon's suffering. And in substance such is the Demon's technique: he wins her heart through pity. Like the Daughters of Ocean, she was content and happy in her ignorance of life, "without fear of things to be," like them "making joy by the music of the river." Thus undisturbed, she lived in a lofty castle that the gray-haired Goudal, her father, built in his youth:

> From morn, across the hillside slope,
> Broad shadows from its high walls were thrown;
> From the tower lead steps of rough hewn stone
> To the stream's transparent water.
> And wrapped in a veil dazzling white
> Would descend Goudal's young daughter,
> Princess Tamara, with footsteps light
> To the river's stream for water.

Thus untroubled, too, flows Tamara's life, "making joy by the music of the river," until Demon-Prometheus comes and "takes away her peace of mind for ever."

This analogy between the Daughters of Ocean and Tamara may seem somewhat strained and, perhaps, far-fetched. I am aware, of course, that Lermontov did not deliberately imitate Prometheus. But he was familiar with the play from the time he was in school. Whether he read it himself, or whether the contents of it were told in class by his teacher in literature, Dubenski, we do not know. But we do know from his letter to his grand-aunt, Mary A. Shan-Guirey, (1829), that he wrote a class report on Prometheus which, he says, the principal of the school, Professor Pavlov, wished to utilize for a prospective school journal. The coincidence is not entirely a matter of accident. That the idea of "sympathy" was introduced by Lermontov in the shape of a Georgian girl, may be regarded as an accident; further, it may be regarded as an accident that the scene of action in *The Demon* is laid in the Caucasian Mountains, the place of Prometheus' punishment and suffering. But the fact that Lermontov's mind was peculiarly susceptible to the kind of tragic philosophy that had been expounded by Aeschylus, was by no means an accident. Once introduced, the theme, with the spiritual help of Byron and Shelley, was bound to grow to its predestined form, just as a seed grows into a beautiful plant.

Let us see what was the characteristic feature that struck such a sympathetic note in Lermontov's mind? Aristotle tells us that "comedy" is a mimesis, or aesthetic imitation of persons "lower than ourselves," whereas tragedy is a representation of persons higher and nobler than ourselves. It is strange that precisely the higher and nobler persons are those who suffer defeats. For the ordinary lot have nothing to offer that could be a subject either for victory or defeat. One fails in the proportion in which one can be significant. If Washington had failed, he would be a notorious criminal in England's colonial history. Only prospective heroes are failures of history. Hence the peculiarly Russian interest, at times almost bordering on adoration, in failures. The whole of Russian literature is a great apology for failures, for all those "rejected and despised" who are crushed and defeated by life. They all, including Oblomov and Akaki Akakievich Bashmachkin, seem to have a touch of tragedy. The first among the Russians of the nineteenth century who conceived life in that peculiarly tragic color was Lermontov with his idea of the individual as a victim burdened with the dullness and petty cruelties of daily life. Hence, again, his spiritual kinship with the fifth-century Greeks. "Most nations," writes Professor Murray, "in contemplating life through the drama, have insisted upon having pleasant stories or at least happy endings. They preferred not to look on the darker sides of life, and thereby for the time could forget them. But the fifth-century Greeks were ready to look straight at its most awful possibilities, to show men terrified by them, overthrown and destroyed by them, so long as by some loftiness in the presentation or some nobility of the characters or perhaps some sheer beauty of inspiration in the poetry, one could feel in the end not defeat, but victory, the victory of the spirit of man over the alien forces among which he has his being." (*Aeschylus, the Creator of Tragedy*.) And that is precisely what one so clearly feels in Lermontov's poetry: a victory in pessimism. In his passionate lamentations one cannot help feeling the strength of a creed, not the weakness of a pessimistic infidel. That is what reconciles us with his, perhaps too ostentatious, self-advertising pessimism; that is what stimulates and invigorates his reader and makes one feel his strength even in his apparent weakness. For it is the weakness of an eagle placed behind iron bars. His pessimism is, like the fatalism of Aeschylus, a sign of protest; it is a challenge to the iron bars of life, by no means a submissive resignation. In this sense it is a victory in defeat, which is the essence of tragedy.

There is a lyric poem in Euripides, as Professor Murray points out, consciously claiming this power for tragedy. Why did the bards of old, asks Euripides, waste their music on festivals and occasions of joy? When men are happy they do not need poetry, and as a matter of fact do not much listen to it:

> But all the darkness and the wrong,
> Quick deaths and dim heart-aching things,
> Would no one ease them with a song
> And music of a thousand strings?

That is what we commonly understand tragedy to be: the song or fiction that does deal with quick deaths and dim heartaching things, and vouchsafes us the revelation—or maybe the illusion—that there are other values accessible to man beyond the obvious pains and miseries of life, that there is for him another world of majestic and mysterious reality whose wealth and strength are but vaguely reflected in the "weary songs of the earth." All Lermontov's poetry is an effort to remember the "original" melody. Such is the idea of one of his most beautiful poems, *The Angel*. It is nothing else but a variation of the Platonic idea of *anamnesis*.

In conclusion, I would like to say a few words about the consistency—or inconsistency, if you wish—of Lermontov's philosophical background. It may be objected that Lermontov's Aeschylean protestations stand in flagrant contradiction to his Platonic Idealism. The latter affirms and even glorifies precisely that metaphysical background which the former so passionately attacks and rejects. The Angel accepts the rule of God which the Demon finds unbearable and despicable. And Lermontov is obviously both, the Demon and the Angel. Is that possible?

Of course, it is possible. We are, all of us, bundles of contradictions. Aeschylus himself, for that matter, suffers from the same contradiction, even more flagrantly expressed, between his revolutionary condemnation of Zeus as the world's tyrant, and his acceptance of his celestial administration as the age of celestial enlightenment. The contradiction is something in the nature of a religious antinomy and can probably never be solved. All that an individual thinker can do is to offer a new version of it. Lermontov's life was very brief. It would be futile to guess what might have been the outcome of his creative activity if he had lived longer. But one may surmise with a high degree of probability that his poetic personality would have developed along the lines of that fundamental contradiction, each phase being a step toward its unattainable solution. Admitting this contradiction, and fully appreciating the value of it, we only regret so much more painfully that Lermontov was not allowed to finish what he had scarcely begun, namely, a reconciliation between Aeschylus and Plato.

Vladimir Nabokov (essay date 1945)

SOURCE: "The Lermontov Mirage," in *Russian Review*, Vol. 1, No. 1, 1945, pp. 31-9.

[*In the following excerpt, Nabokov reviews Lermontov's contributions to Russian poetry.*]

Michael Lermontov was born when Pushkin was a lad of fifteen and he died four years after Pushkin's death, that is, at the quite ridiculous age of twenty-seven. Like Pushkin he was killed in a duel, but his duel was not the inevitable sequel of a tangled tragedy as in Pushkin's case. It belonged rather to that trivial type which in the eighteen-thirties and forties so often turned hot friendship into cold murder—a phenomenon of temperature rather than of ethics.

You *must* imagine him as a sturdy, shortish, rather shabby-looking Russian army officer with a singularly pale and smooth forehead, queer velvety eyes that "seemed to absorb light instead of emitting it," and a jerky manner in his demeanor and speech. Following both a Byronic fashion and his own disposition, he took pleasure in offending people, but there can hardly be any doubt that the bully in him was the shell and not the core, and that in many cases his attitude was that of a morbidly self-conscious, tender-hearted, somewhat childish young man building himself a sentiment-proof defense. He spent the best years of his short life in the Caucasus, taking part in dangerous expeditions against mountain tribes that kept rebelling against imperial domination. Finally, a quarrel with a fellow-officer, whom he had most methodically annoyed, put a stop to his not very happy life.

But all this is neither here *nor* there. What matters is that this very young, arrogant, not overeducated man, mixing with people who did not care a fig for literature, somehow managed, during the short period granted him by the typically perverse destiny which haunts geniuses, to produce verse and prose of such virility, beauty, and tenderness that the following generation placed him higher than Pushkin: the ups of poets are but the seesaw reverses of their downs.

At fourteen he wrote a short lyrical poem **"The Angel"** which Russian critics have, not inadequately, described as coming straight from paradise; indeed, it contains a pure and truly heavenly melody brought unbroken to earth. At twenty-three he reacted to Pushkin's death by writing a poem which branded with its white fire the titled scoundrels who baited the greatest of all poets and kept fanning the flames of his African passions. And at twenty-five he resolutely turned to prose and would have achieved great things in that medium had not a perfectly avoidable bullet pierced his heart.

He was an ardent admirer of Byron, but his best work discloses hardly a trace of this influence. Superficially, this influence is quite clear in his earlier lyrics.

> Farewell! Nevermore shall we meet,
> We shall never touch hands—so farewell!
> Your heart is now free, but in none
> Will it ever be happy to dwell.
>
> . . . . .
>
> One moment together we came:
> Time eternal is nothing to this!
> All senses we suddenly drained,
> Burned all in the flame of one kiss.
>
> Farewell! And be wise, do not grieve:
> Our love was too short for regret,
> And hard as we found it to part
> Harder still would it be if we met.

Women prefer him to Pushkin because of the pathos and loveliness of his personality, singing so urgently through his verse. Radical critics, people who expect poets to express the needs of the nation, have welcomed in Lermontov the first bard of the revolution. Although he did not allude to politics in his works, what they admired in him was his violent pity for the underdog, and one pessimistic critic has suggested that had Lermontov lived he might have used his talent in the 'sixties and 'seventies to write novels with an obvious social message. Here and there, in the sobbing rhythm of some of his lines, I cannot help feeling that the tearful rhymsters of later generations, such as Nadson, who wallowed in civic lamentations, owe something to Lermontov's pathos in singing the death of a soldier or that of his own soul. Children in schools have been greatly tormented by being made to learn by heart yards and yards of Lermontov. He has been put to music by composers. There is a dreadful opera by Rubinstein based on his **Demon**. A great painter treated his **Demon** in quite a different way and in terms of such peacock colors amid diamond-blazing eyes and purple clouds that Lermontov's genius ought to sleep content. Though decidedly patchy, he remains for the true lover of poetry a miraculous being whose development is something of a mystery.

It might be said that what Darwin called "struggle for existence" is really a struggle for perfection, and in that respect Nature's main and most admirable device is optical illusion. Among human beings, poets are the best exponents of the art of deception. Such poets as Coleridge, Baudelaire, and Lermontov have been particularly good at creating a fluid and iridescent medium wherein reality discloses the dreams of which it consists. A geological transverse section of the most prosaic of towns may show the fabulous reptile and the fossil fern fantastically woven into its foundation. Travellers have told us that in the mysterious wastes of Central Asia mirages are sometimes so bright that real trees are mirrored in the sham shimmer of optical lakes. Something of the effect of these manifold reflections is characteristic of Lermontov's poetry, and especially of that most fatamorganic poem of his which might bear the title: A Dream in a Dream of a Dream in a Dream. In this respect the poem is, as far as I know, perfectly unique. But curiously enough, none of Lermontov's contemporaries, least of all the poet himself, ever noticed the remarkable telescopic process of images that it contains. Here is this fourfold dream:

> I dreamt that with a bullet in my side
> In a hot gorge of Daghestan I lay.
> Deep was the wound and steaming, and the tide
> Of my life-blood ebbed drop by drop away.
>
> Alone I lay amid a silent maze
> Of desert sand and bare cliffs rising steep,
> Their tawny summits burning in the blaze
> That burned me too; but lifeless was my sleep.
>
> And in a dream I saw the candle-flame
> Of a gay supper in the land I knew;
> Young women crowned with flowers. . . . And my name
> On their light lips hither and thither flew.

But one of them sat pensively apart,
Not joining in the light-lipped gossiping,
And there alone, God knows what made her heart,
Her young heart dream of such a hidden thing. . . .

For in her dream she saw a gorge, somewhere
In Daghestan, and knew the man who lay
There on the sand, the dead man, unaware
Of steaming wound and blood ebbing away.

Let us call the initial dreamer A^1, which will thus apply to the poetical personality of Lermontov, the live summary of the mirages involved. For simplicity's sake we shall ignore the argument that it was not he who really dreamt, but the poet he imagined dreaming. He dreams of his lifeless body lying among the yellow cliffs, and this second personality we shall call A^2. This A^2 dreams of a young woman in a distant land, and here is the central and deepest point of the whole image complex, which point we shall term A^3. In so far as the imagined existence of the young woman is implied, her dream of A^2 should be called A^4: however, this A^4 is a reversion to A^2, though not quite identical with it, and thus the circle is completed. The dreamer drifts back to the surface, and the full stop at the end of the poem comes with the exactitude of an alarm clock.

Incidentally, the poet got so thoroughly immersed in these dreams within dreams that in the last stanza he committed a solecism (omitted in my translation) which is also unique; for it is the solecism of a solipsist, and solipsism has been defined by Bertrand Russell as the *reductio ad absurdum* of subjective idealism: we dream our own selves. So, even in the methodical approach itself, we observe a quaint mirage of two terms which look almost alike. The solecism in question has been unconsciously retained (and aggravated) in John Pollen's translation of the poem in Leo Weiner's *Anthology of Russian Literature*. The young woman dreams that on that torrid sand "the well-known body lay." Lermontov has "the familiar corpse" ("znako-myi trup"), his intention having been evidently to say as tersely as possible: "the corpse of the young woman's good acquaintance." This "familiar corpse" or "well-known body" was unfortunately produced not merely as a phenomenon of bad grammar, but because in the poem itself the dead and the living got so hopelessly mixed. In a way, perhaps the poem would be less miraculous had not that blunder occurred, but I am afraid that what a Russian reader can skip, will not escape the humor of an Anglo-Saxon, and anyway Pollen's "well-known body" is much too large. And I am reminded, too, of that Chinese poet who dreamt he was a butterfly and then, when he awoke, could not solve the problem whether he was a Chinese poet who had dreamt that entomological dream, or a butterfly dreaming that it was a Chinese poet.

To be a good visionary you must be a good observer. The better you see the earth the finer your perception of heaven will be; and, inversely, the crystal-gazer who is not an artist will turn out to be merely an old bore. Lermontov's long poem **The Demon** devoted to the lurid love-affair between a demon and a Georgian girl is built on a com-

monplace of mysticism. But it is saved by the bright pigments of definite landscapes painted here and there by a magic brush. There is nothing of an Oriental poet's passion for gems and generalizations here; Lermontov is essentially a European traveller, admiring distant lands, as all Russian poets have been, although they might never have left their hearths. The very love for the native countryside is with Lermontov (and others) European, in the sense that it is both irrational and founded on concrete sensual experience. "An unofficial English rose," or "the spires and farms" seen from a hilltop in Shropshire, or the little river at home which a Russian pilgrim, many centuries ago, recalled when he saw the Jordan, or merely those "green fields" a famous fat man babbled about as he died, offer a thrill of indescribable love for one's country that history books and statues in public gardens fail to provoke. But what is quite peculiar to "native land" descriptions in Russian poems is the atmosphere of nostalgia which sharpens the senses but distorts objective relationships. The Russian poet talks of the view from his window as if he were an exile dreaming of his land more vividly than he ever saw it, although at the moment he may be actually surveying the acres he owns. Pushkin longed to travel to Africa not because he was sick of Russian scenery but because he was eager to long for Russia when he would be abroad. Gogol in Rome spoke of the spiritual beauty of physical remoteness; and Lermontov's attitude to the Russian countryside implies a similar emotional paradox.

If I do love my land, strangely I love it:
'Tis something reason cannot cure.
Glories of war I do not covet,
But neither peace proud and secure,
Nor the mysterious past and dim romances
Can spur my soul to pleasant fancies.

And still I love thee—why I hardly know:
I love thy fields so coldly meditative,
Native dark swaying woods and native
Rivers that sea-like foam and flow.

In a clattering cart I love to travel
On country roads: watching the rising star,
Yearning for sheltered sleep, my eyes unravel
The trembling lights of sad hamlets afar.

Also I love the smoke of burning stubble,
Vans huddled in the prairie night;
Corn on a hill crowned with the double
Grace of twin birches gleaming white.

Few are the ones who feel the pleasure
Of seeing barns bursting with grain and hay,
Well-thatched cottage-roofs made to measure
And shutters carved and windows gay.

And when the evening dew is glistening,
Long may I hear the festive sound
Of rustic dancers stamping, whistling
With drunkards clamoring around.

Janko Lavrin (essay date 1954)

SOURCE: "Lermontov," in *Russian Writers, Their Lives and Literature,* D. Van Nostrand Company, 1954, pp. 80-99.

[*In the excerpt below, Lavrin discusses the literary influences in Lermontov's writings, providing an overview of his life and career.*]

The romantic movement, for various reasons, affected Russia less many-sidedly than was the case with other European countries. The influence of Byronism itself was limited only to some of its aspects, and even those were partly conditioned by a regime under the pressure of which the few liberties still left seemed to be going from bad to worse. In Pushkin's day there was at least the atmosphere of the *pléiade,* the members of which firmly believed in literary culture and were able to stimulate one another. The growing vigilance of the Nicholas' police made fellowships on such a scale impossible even in matters of culture, let alone politics. As there was no outlet for any independent initiative and ambition of one's own, a number of gifted young men were bound to turn into "superfluous" Childe Harolds of the peculiar Russian brand, so conspicuous in the literature of that country. But the danger of maladjustment loomed large from another quarter also. There were signs that the patriarchal-feudal system, based on serfdom, would have to yield, before long, to the advent of a capitalist era, demanding an economic as well as psychological change which could not be achieved overnight. A feeling of vacillation and general uncertainty was in the air, and no gendarmes, no political straitjackets were able to eliminate the bewilderment arising in the public mind.

In this respect, too, there was a difference between the generation of Pushkin and that to which his immediate successor, the poet Mikhail Lermontov, belonged. In spite of all personal adversities, Pushkin was still rooted in his age, in his class and in the culture of which the members of the advanced gentry-elite were rightly proud. Even the "Decembrists" who rebelled in 1825, did so because they believed in certain values which they, as the most progressive representatives of their own class, were called upon to uphold. Yet the social and mental atmosphere of the next generation was no longer the same. The leadership on the part of a gentry-elite became impossible, because such an elite as a compact group or body no longer existed. The best representatives of that class suddenly found themselves in a vacuum. Others were absorbed by the bureaucratic system, or else went to seed in their provincial back-waters. Even the slowly emerging intelligentsia—an amalgam of the gentry intellectuals and the educated "commoners"—was of no use to many of those who were unable or else unwilling to adapt themselves to the spirit of the age. And Lermontov, for all his genius, was the least adaptable of men.

This fact alone determined the basic character of his work. If Pushkin introduced the "superfluous man" on a romantic or quasi-romantic plane, Lermontov added two salient features to this phenomenon. First, he deepened the *inner* isolation of such an uprooted individual until he touched upon that metaphysical region which, later on, was disturbingly tackled by Dostoevsky. And secondly, he gave a psychological analysis of a tragic Russian descendant of Childe Harold (via Pushkin's Onegin) so brilliantly as to affect thereby, romantic though he was, quite a few facets of Russian realism. He is still regarded as being the greatest and also the most Byronic romanticist in Russian literature; yet his Byronism was not an imitation but had certain definite traits of its own. He himself said in one of his early poems:

> No, I'm not Byron, I'm different,
> I'm still unknown, a man apart,
> Like Byron by the world rejected,
> Only I have a Russian heart.

In spite of this "Russian heart" on which he insists, or perhaps because of it, Lermontov's *mal du siècle,* with all its ingredients, sprang not only from social but from what might be termed spiritual causes. His nostalgia resembled that of a fallen denizen of a different timeless realm, who still vaguely remembers its enchantment and therefore finds it impossible to fit into any conditions of the actual world, least of all into those of Russia under Nicholas I. When Lermontov was only seventeen, he wrote the following poem, called **"The Angel"**, which may provide a clue to the undercurrents of his romanticism:

> An angel was flying through night's deep blue
> And softly he sang as he flew.
> Moon, stars and clouds in a wondering throng
> Listened rapt by that heavenly song.
>
> He sang of the blest, who live without stain
> In God's garden, a shining train.
> He hymned the Lord's might, and his voice rang
>   clear,
> For he sang without guile and fear.
>
> He bore in his arms a young soul to its birth
> On the dark and sinful earth,
> And the Angel's song remained in the soul
> Without words yet unblemished and whole.
>
> Long after on earth when the soul would tire,
> It felt a strange, aching desire
> For the music of heaven which it sought for in vain
> In earth's songs of sorrow and pain.

The poem could serve as an epigraph to the whole of Lermontov's work. It goes a long way to explain his difference from Byron, the character of his pessimism, and of his protest against the realities he saw around. This again was intertwined with a number of less "transcendental" elements, the nature of which will become clearer if we approach Lermontov through some of his biographical data. For in contrast to Pushkin, Lermontov was the first great poet in Russian literature who deliberately turned his entire work into an inner biography; that is into a personal confession of a poignant and often glowingly passionate kind.

Born in 1814, Lermontov had some Scottish blood in his veins. One of the Learmonths entered the Russian service at the beginning of the 17th century, settled in his adopted country and altered his ancestral name to make it sound Russian. (In some of his early poems, especially in **"The Wish"**, Lermontov alludes to Scotland as his distant homeland.) His father was an impoverished landowner who had married the daughter of a rich, capricious, and overbearing woman and was always treated by his mother-in-law, Mme. Arsenyeva, as a "poor relation." As his wife died after a few years of marriage, Mme. Arsenyeva took her little grandson to her own estate where he was brought up until the age of twelve. Puzzled by the family quarrels, spoiled by his grandmother's adulation, and at the same time deprived of congenial companions, the boy must have felt lonely even in those formative years. Gradually he developed into a self-centered dreamer, anxious to conceal his passionate nature under the mask of aloofness, and his innate idealism behind the pose of callous flippancy. His poetic gift, which remained his only outlet for self-expression, began to develop rather early and was fostered by two circumstances: his visit to the Caucasus at the age of eleven, and his education in a Moscow boarding school (from 1827 onwards) which was not devoid of literary interests. Under the guidance of such teachers as Merzlyakov and Raitch, young Lermontov was initiated into the principal works of Russian literature, as well as into those of Byron, Moore, Goethe, Schiller, and Scott. He was much impressed by Thomas Moore's biography of Byron (he read it in 1830) and, in his early years, his own translations from Byron helped him to work himself into Byronic moods. At the same time he cultivated his own aloofness to such a degree that even on entering, in 1830, Moscow University, he showed but little inclination to mix with his fellow-students and paid hardly any attention to the fact that after the *débâcle* of the "Decembrists" the University of Moscow, with its debating circles, became the actual focus of Russian culture. The Stankevich circle, with the subsequent critic Vissarion Belinsky as one of its members, was exploring all sorts of literary and philosophic problems. The youths gathering round Herzen and the poet Ogaryov showed, however, a keener interest in the social questions of the day, the liberal "Decembrist" spirit still hovering over their debates.

... [I]n contrast to Pushkin, Lermontov was the first great poet in Russian literature who deliberately turned his entire work into an inner biography; that is into a personal confession of a poignant and often glowingly passionate kind.

—*Janko Lavrin*

German philosophy, notably the ideas of Schelling and Hegel, happened to be one of the strong influences among the intellectuals of that period. Another stimulus came from the French Utopian socialists. Their theories were later combined by quite a few firebrands (Belinsky included) with "left" Hegelianism, and the two together helped to shape the radical and revolutionary thought of Russia.

Lermontov did not belong to any of these groups. Besides, in 1832 he suddenly left the University and went to Petersburg where he entered a military school and, after two years of detestable training, obtained a commission in the Guards. In 1837 he was transferred (or, rather, exiled) to a Caucasian regiment on account of his aggressive invective, *The Death of a Poet,* written on the day of Pushkin's death (January 29th). The poem could not be printed [in a footnote Lavrin adds: "It first appeared in print in 1856, in Herzen's *Polar Star,* published in London. Two years later the poem was printed also in Russia."], but as it was read in countless written copies, it made Lermontov's name known from one end of Russia to the other. In the Caucasus, which was fated to be strangely connected with his life, his work, and even with his death, he met another poet, the banished "Decembrist" Alexander Odoevsky—one of the few people he really befriended. Owing to his grandmother's influence, Lermontov was allowed to return at the end of the same year to his old Hussar regiment, and he made a considerable impression in St. Petersburg. By this time he was already regarded as one of the great hopes of Russian poetry and a successor to Pushkin. He was admired, lionized, but in spite of his numerous conquests among the society ladies, he remained as bored and lonely as ever. Mixing a life of dissipation with intensive poetic activities, he did not care to make himself popular either in society or among his own comrades. As for literary men, he knew very few and seemed to avoid them on purpose. After a duel he had in February 1840 with the son of the French ambassador, M. de Barrante, he was arrested and again sent to the Caucasus. He took part in some dangerous expeditions against the mountaineers, in which he displayed reckless courage. One of such engagements—the battle on the river Valerik (on July 11th, 1840)—he described in a most beautiful poem. In the spring of 1841 he made a flying visit to Petersburg in the hope of being allowed to remain there, but without success. On his return to the Caucasus he stopped for a longer period at his favorite spa Pyatigorsk. The place was full of summer guests. Among them there were ubiquitous society people, including some of his old acquaintances. One of them, a certain Major Martynov, whom he tactlessly ridiculed in the presence of a lady, challenged him to a duel. The duel took place outside Pyatigorsk on July 27th, 1841, and the poet was killed on the spot. He died at the age of twenty-seven, i.e. ten years younger than Pushkin.

The best of Lermontov's work is second only to Pushkin's, but with reservations. Pushkin showed even in his early verse great technical skill and finish. In the case of Lermontov, however, it is only the mature work—roughly from 1836 onwards—that really counts. His youthful writings, whether poems or plays, compare with his later products chiefly as a series of experiments. He was perfectly aware of this and even kept returning to some of his themes again and again in order to perfect them during his later and more mature phase, until they received an adequate form. Yet however much he differed from Pushkin in his outlook and temperament, he could not do without Pushkin's influence. Even Byron was at first approached by him mainly through Pushkin. His two immature tales in verse, *The Circassian* and *The Prisoner of the Caucasus* (both written at the age of fifteen) were imitations of Pushkin's Byronic tales with the Caucasus as the exotic "Eastern" background. After a more thorough acquaintance with Byron's work Lermontov wrote his longer Caucasian tales *Ismail Bey* (1832) and *Hadji Abrek,* the latter having been his first longer poem to be printed in a periodical in 1835.

In the meantime Lermontov tried his hand also at plays. They are pretentiously romantic, redolent of Schiller's "storm and stress" period but much more juvenile and with an obvious tendency towards self-dramatization. *Men and Passions* (to which, for some reason, he gave a German title, *Menschen und Leidenschaften,* 1830) and *A Queer Fellow* (1831) must have been written under the impact of the family quarrels between his grandmother and his father. His later drama, *The Masquerade* (1835), overstated though it be, is more impressive in its combination of blind jealousy (the influence of *Othello*) on the one hand, and of a conflict between the self-centered individual and society on the other. Whereas Pushkin the poet could and did rise to that affirmative attitude which made him look sympathetically upon life at large, Lermontov was too often inclined to reduce the whole of life to the moods and demands of his own frustrated ego and to treat it accordingly. He also preferred to Pushkin's visual imagery the more visionary symbols often originating in the realm of the spirit (like his **"Angel"**). The language of many an early poem of his seems rather blurred. At his best, however, he soon developed a matchless pictorial gift. Lermontov the romantic has certain features in common with the other-worldly romanticism of Zhukovsky; yet instead of sharing Zhukovsky's passivity and quietism, he remained a "Byronic" rebel to the end. Like Byron, too, he broke morally with his own class, even if he was unable to do so socially. And as in the case of Byron again (or for that matter of Gogol), the virulence of his romantic indictment taught him to watch and to expose life also by realistic methods. These he kept perfecting with such success as to emulate, in his mature stage, the disciplined realism of Pushkin himself.

Lermontov's unfinished realistic tale *Sashka* (1836) is an offspring mainly of Byron's *Don Juan* and, to some extent, of the first chapter of Pushkin's *Onegin.* It is a scathing and at times obscene satire against the provincial gentry in its process of moral decomposition. The realism of another tale inverse, *A Treasurer's Wife* (1837), written in the Onegin stanza, is modelled on Pushkin's *Count Nulin* and, through the latter, on Byron's *Beppo.* It gives a humorously caustic picture of provincial officials, one of whom gambles away his pretty wife to an army officer. At times Lermontov the realist actually reaches Pushkin's simplicity and detachment. In *Borodino* (1837), for example, he renders to perfection the tone, the manner and

also the grumbling humor of an old veteran who talks to his grandson about Napoleon's first defeat during his invasion of Russia in 1812. And if the realism in some of his poems (such as his famous **"Cossack Cradle Song"**) can be poignantly touching, it acquires a dynamic matter-of-factness in the already mentioned picture of the battle on the Caucasian river Valerik—an anticipation of Tolstoy's battle scenes in *War and Peace.* The pathos of his **"Testament"** again is due to the discrepancy between the tragic situation of a soldier dying of wounds and the almost jokingly casual tone in which he tells his last wishes to a comrade due to go home on leave.

> But if somebody questions you
> About me as they may:
> Just say that a certain bullet flew—
> My chest was in the way;
> Say I died bravely for the Tsar,
> And say what fools our doctors are,
> Tell them I send my duty
> To Russia, home and beauty.
>
> Mother and Dad—surely they still
> Alive can scarce remain.
> At any rate I'd hate to fill
> Those old folks' days with pain.
> But, if one of them lingers yet,
> Just tell that there's no use to fret:
> They've sent us to the fighting,
> And I'm no hand at writing.
> [Translated by V. de Sola Pinto.]

The height of poetic detachment was reached, however, by Lermontov in a great work of a different order: *The Song about Tsar Ivan Vasilyevich, the Young Body-Guard and the Brave Merchant Kalashnikov.* This poem is the finest literary emulation of the historical folk-songs (similar to, and formally like the *byliny*). Here Lermontov came at least as close to the spirit of the people and to folk genius as Pushkin did in his poetic transposition of fairy tales. But this is Lermontov at his best rather than his most typical. Essentially subjective, he succeeded only during the last period of his life in turning his personal moods and attitudes into great poetry, notably so when face to face with nature. This poem, the whole of which consists of one single sentence, can serve as a proof:

> When o'er the yellowing corn a fleeting shadow
>   rushes,
> And fragrant forest glades re-echo in the breeze,
> And in the garden's depths the ripe plum hides its
>   blushes
> Within the luscious shade of brightly verdant trees;
>
> When bathed in scented dew, the silver lily,
> At golden morn or evening shot with red,
> From out behind a leafy bush peeps shyly,
> And nods with friendly mien its dainty head;
>
> When down the shady glen the bubbling streamlet
>   dances,
> And, lulling thought to sleep with its incessant

song,
Lisps me the secrets, with a thousand glances,
Of that still corner where it speeds along;

Then does my troubled soul find solace for a while,
Then vanish for a time the furrows from my brow,
And happiness is mine a moment here below,
And in the skies I see God smile.

Pushkin would not have used so many adjectives and "purple patches" as Lermontov was wont to do, yet this does not mean that all his poems are full of them. Nor is he often as conciliatory as in the quoted lyric. His awareness of the difference between the world to which he was chained, and the timeless realm of the spirit was too painful to make him accept his fate. Besides, like so many romantics, he derived his poetic power principally from protest, rebellion, and that proud isolation which repudiates anything tainted with the stigma of the "human-all-too-human."

Oh gloomy and dreary! and no one to stretch out a
   hand
In hours when the soul nears disaster . . .
Desire! but what use is an empty desire without
   end?
And the years, the best years, but fly faster.

To love! yes, but whom? It is nothing in time's
   little space.
No love has an endless to-morrow!
Just look at yourself: what is past does not leave
   any trace.
They are nothing—both pleasure and sorrow.

What is passion? That sickness so sweet, either
   early or late,
Will vanish at reason's protesting;
And life, if you ever, attentive and cool,
   contemplate,
Is but empty and meaningless jesting.

So the mood of **"The Angel"** keeps recurring in Lermontov's poetry like a permanent refrain to his own life. And since both his pessimism and his rebellion were due to metaphysical nostalgia, they often gave him that well-nigh elemental force of negation and challenge which came out in his two principal works, *The Novice* (1840) and *The Demon* (1841).

These two tales in verse represent the climax of Lermontov's romanticism and poetic genius in one. *The Novice,* in particular, is the most glowing assertion of freedom that ever came from the pen of a Russian poet. Full of unsurpassed pictures of nature, it has nothing of the slow despondent rhythm of his famous **"Meditation,"** beginning with the line, "Sadly do I look upon our generation." The very pace of *The Novice* (he calls it in Georgian—*Mtsyri*) is so manly and bracing that there are no feminine endings in its four-footed iambics. The theme itself goes back to Lermontov's early period. He began to work upon it in 1830. Five years later he embodied it as one of the motifs

in his somewhat confused romantic tale in verse, *The Boyar Orsha,* and completed its final draft in the last year of his life. The tale is in the form of a confession on the part of a young Caucasian mountaineer who as a child had been captured by the Russians and was then left in a Georgian monastery where he became a novice. But the monastery walls did not obliterate the memories of his childhood and his yearning for freedom. Determined to see his native place and to taste of a free life once again, he escapes, wanders amidst the gorgeous Caucasian scenery, but in the end is found dying of exhaustion and starvation not far from the spot where his adventure had started. Having thus completed the vicious circle, he is brought back to the monastery. He knows that his hours are numbered, but his spirit refuses to surrender. In words burning with passion he confesses to an old monk the reasons why he escaped and perseveres in his defiance to the end.

Tragic, but in a different sense, is Lermontov's "Eastern tale," *The Demon*. He had started working at it as far back as 1829 and 1830, took it up again in 1833, then during his stay in the Caucasus in 1837, and completed it (after several previous drafts) in 1841. The demon of this tale is Lermontov's own double, projected into the realm of the spirit. He is a rebellious exiled angel who still remembers his one-time bliss (**"The Angel"** motif again), but is doomed to be imprisoned in his own isolation till the end of time. The theme bears traces of Byron's influence—especially of his *Heaven and Earth,* of Thomas Moore's *The Love of Angels,* of *Eloa* by Alfred de Vigny, but in spite of this it remains Lermontov's most typical and personal creation. For it combines, in an intensified symbolic manner, all the features of his own nature: his feeling of loneliness, his rebellious pride, his secret wish as well as his inability to come to terms with life.

Unhappy Demon, spirit of exile,
Soared high above the sinful world,
And memories of the days of erstwhile
Before him brooding vision whirled,
Of days when in the light of grace
A cherub bright and pure he shone,
When in the swift, unending race
The comet turned its smiling face
To greet him as they fastened on;
When through the everlasting gloaming,
Athirst of knowledge he pursued
The caravans of planets roaming
Through endless space without a goal,
When faith and love imbued his soul,
The happy first-born of creation,
Unknown to fear or pride's inflation,
Nor came to haunt his limpid mind
The threat of endless years of pain . . .
And much, so much he strove to find
Deep in his memory, but in vain.

And since this is an "Eastern tale," the Caucasus—the Russian romantic East—is introduced as the only adequate background for a spirit of such stature. It is the Caucasus Lermontov had known and admired since his boyhood.

Then o'er the high Caucasian maze
The banished angel slowly rose,
Kazbek with glinting lights ablaze,
Stood clad in everlasting snows.
And deep below, an inky track
Like a dark serpent's hiding-crack,
The winding Darial met his gaze.
The Terek like a lion bounding
With shaggy mane upon the peak
Set all the hollow vales resounding;
And beasts upon the mountain bleak
And birds aloft in heaven's light
Both harkened to its thundered word;
And golden clouds in endless flight
Sped with it northward undeterred.

The beauty of Gruzia or Georgia, embedded in that scenery, is

Spread out in glittering, gorgeous views,
Ablaze with morning's rosy dews,
With lofty ruins ivy-decked
And purling brooks that flow unchecked
O'er beds of multi-colored stones.

It is amidst the most beautiful views in the world that the Demon suddenly beholds Tamara—the most beautiful of mortals, and falls in love with her. But Tamara, already betrothed, is expecting the arrival of her bridegroom who, accompanied by a whole caravan, hurries to the wedding. Tamara and her girl-friends while away the time with innocent pleasures.

And on the roof in rich array
The bride sits with her maiden throng,
Filling the hours with play and song
Till o'er the distant hills the day
Warns them that night will not be long.
Their palms in gentle measure clapping,
They sing, and then the young bride takes
Her tambourine, which, gently tapping
Above her head, she gaily shakes
With a lily hand that faintly quakes.
Now lighter than a bird she dashes,
Then, pausing, she will fix her gaze
While two moist eyes are seen to blaze
Beneath their jealous tapering lashes;
Now she will raise her brows with pride,
Now suddenly her form incline,
Then o'er the patterned floor will glide
Her foot so lovely, so divine!
And oft her face will sweetly smile
With gentle mirth devoid of guile.
A beam of moonlight faintly trembling
Upon the ruffled water's face,
Though much her wreathed smile resembling,
Can scarce compare for light or grace.

The Demon sees to it that the caravan of the wedding guests is dispersed, while the bridegroom himself is killed. In despair, Tamara retires to a convent, but here the Demon begins to tempt her in her dreams. He does this with no evil intentions, for Tamara's beauty has made such a profound change in him that he actually hopes his love for her might save him at last from isolation and even reconcile him to God and His world. Invisible, he whispers to her:

The gentle prayer of love unending
I bring to thee with heart aglow,
On earth my spirit's first unbending,
The first tears from my eyes to flow.
O let them not unheeded go!
Heaven knows that one word of thine
Can make my simple soul surrender,
And clad in thy love's light divine
In Paradise again I'd shine
Like a new angel in new splendor.

But this is not granted to him. When, finally, he embraces Tamara, she dies from the kiss of an immortal. Her soul is taken away by a messenger of God, while the Demon is left in the same cosmic loneliness as ever.

Again he roamed in desolation,
The haughty exile of creation,
On whom no hope or love shall gleam.

In spite of its somewhat operatic theme and setting, this poem remains one of the masterpieces of Russian literature. Lermontov expressed in it symbolically the depth of his own uprootedness as only a romantic of his brand could have done. Yet the plane of such poetry was too vague, too far removed from the actualities of the day and the conditions of an entire generation lost as it were in the desert of Russian life under Nicholas I. So he decided to tackle the problem from a different angle and in prose; which he did in his novel, *A Hero of Our Time* (1840). . . .

Frustrated strength, doomed to turn against itself or else to degenerate into the nihilistic "will to power"—such was the inner tragedy of Lermontov's own personality. Through his masterly analysis of this tragedy Lermontov deepened the problem of the "superfluous man" and thus became the creator of the psychological novel in Russian literature. He was among the first to tackle some of those aspects of individual frustration which afterwards were further developed in Dostoevsky's writings.

Even the "demoniac" pride and self-assertiveness of Dostoevsky's complex heroes, such as Raskolnikov and Stavrogin, have some of their roots in Lermontov. Whereas one aspect of Dostoevsky's work goes back to Gogol, the other points to Lermontov, and via Lermontov to Byron—however distant the affinities may be at times.

As a painter of the "superfluous man" Lermontov forms a link between Pushkin on the one hand, and Turgenev and Goncharov on the other. As a psychologist, however, he leads to Dostoevsky. By his frankness and his refusal to indulge in any shams or rosy spectacles, he introduced into Russian literature that psychological and moral honesty which often verged on recklessness. Both as poet and novelist, Lermontov inaugurated the vertical direction in

Russian literature. It was he who made it *conscious* of depth (which is something different from the unconscious depth) at a time when the more horizontal "natural school" was already branching off into a number of those aspects which formed the basis of the subsequent Russian realism.

John Mersereau, Jr. (essay date 1962)

SOURCE: "Artistic Maturity: 1837-1841," in *Mikhail Lermontov*, Southern Illinois University Press, 1962, pp. 63-74.

[*In the essay below, Mersereau treats the themes of Lermontov's mature verse.*]

The choice of the year 1837 as the beginning of Lermontov's last period of creative activity has a certain logic, for that year brought about not only drastic developments in the poet's personal fate but was marked by his arrival at complete artistic maturity. Everything he wrote after that date bears the stamp of perfection, and it is upon these works that his reputation is almost exclusively founded.

In attempting to define the essence of Lermontov's mature art, scholars and commentators have come forth with a number of generalizations, most of which are true in some respects but far from sufficiently comprehensive. He has been called the poet of negation, doubt, despair, solitude, protest, and tendency, and, conversely, the poet of resignation, religiosity, and humility. The last three definitions could be substantiated by references to individual poems, but to posit them as true to the essence of his art is to ignore its dominant tenor and content.

The lyrical poems written after his first exile—there are less than seventy of them—are concerned with a number of themes, but the most recurrent are those of freedom, solitude, and the turpitude of society. These themes appear not only in poems where they are the organizing idea but are alluded to constantly throughout his verse. So many of these poems of the poet's last years reveal a maturity of outlook and a sense of duty not evident in his earlier works. The self-centered youth who once wrote mostly of unrequited love and dark passions now begins to raise his voice not only on his own behalf but in support of truth, freedom, honesty, dignity, and common sense. In the best tradition of Russian authors, he becomes part of the national conscience. Dismayed at the level to which his fellow man has sunk, he cries shame upon him. Contempt and scorn for society pervade such works as *Death of the Poet* (1837), "Meditation" (1838), "Three Palms" (1839), "The First of January" (1840), and "Goodbye, Unwashed Russia" (1841). As a poet he considers himself a prophet, and he knows that not only are prophets without honor but, in his country, often the object of severe reprisals. Nonetheless, he speaks out against the vices of his era in completely unequivocal and condemnatory terms, and he will not be silenced in spite of the obvious consequences. In fact, the accusatory tone becomes increasingly evident and the critical attitude ever more pronounced. A

whole cycle of poems details the conflict between the poet and the crowd, including "The Poet" (1838), "Don't Trust Yourself" (1839), "The Journalist, Reader and Author" (1840), and "The Prophet" (1841).

[Lermontov] has been called the poet of negation, doubt, despair, solitude, protest, and tendency, and, conversely, the poet of resignation, neligiosity, and humility.

—*John Mersereau, Jr.*

Of course, awareness of the constant hostility of society and the impossibility of any *rapprochement* intensify his pessimism, not only about his country's future but about his own. Feelings of estrangement, frustration, and futility are bitterly expressed in "Don't Laugh at my Prophetic Anguish" (1837), "I Look at the Future With Fear" (1839), "It's Dull and Dreary" (1840), "Gratitude" (1840), and "The Oak Leaf" (1841).

Most of these works have a particular rhetorical quality which admirably suits the subject matter. Avoiding the pitfalls of pomposity or bathos, the poet expresses himself with lucidity and conviction. These poems read like prose, but prose charged with emotions of anger or sorrow. They lack intimacy, and by their very style they beg to be declaimed from the forum steps. Yet not all of Lermontov's last works are accusatory or even pessimistic. The consolation that the poet could not find in human associations was provided by nature, and at times it was even able to inspire a mood of reconciliation with life. In "When the Yellowing Fields Billow" (1837), scenes of the seasons lead to a vision of God, and it is the night sky of "Alone I go Along the Road" (1841) which causes pain and troubles to be forgotten in hopes of the peaceful freedom of a sleep-like death. Again it is the nature of his homeland, its rivers, steppes, and forests that bring him to express his "strange love" for Russia in "Motherland" (1841). He also writes on occasion a ballad, such as "Gifts of the Terek" (1839) or "Tamara" (1841), both of which have Caucasian settings and show an abiding appreciation for the lore and the nature of his place of exile. And for sheer mellifluousness nothing can surpass his tender lullaby, "A Cossack Cradle-Song" (1840).

In his final period Lermontov completed five narrative poems and began two others. Three of these continue the well-defined line of the romantic tale in verse which stretches back to the poet's first attempts at this genre, three represent the light, satirical narrative first exemplified by *Mongo,* and one, *The Song of the Merchant Kalashnikov,* is in a class by itself.

The dates of composition of a number of these narrative poems have not been clearly established. Apparently the poet worked on some of them sporadically, at times laying them aside while he turned to other works in poetry or prose. In the opinion of some commentators, *Sasha,* an unfinished satirical poem of some 1700 lines, was begun as early as 1835 and worked on as late as the end of 1839. It is fairly obvious, however, that the major part of it belongs to the period following the poet's exile in 1837.

In this work Lermontov attempted a synthesized portrait of a young man of his times in the style of *Eugene Onegin* and *Beppo.* Owing to the leisurely pace and incessant digressions the plot was barely initiated after the first one hundred and fifty stanzas, but evidently it was to involve the attempt of the cynical young Sasha (diminutive for Alexander) to introduce a prostitute into Petersburg society. With considerable humor and no little ribaldry the author discloses his hero's formative experiences and irregular education, mixing all this with numerous comments on gentry customs and institutions in general.

A similar satirical vein—but of a more printable nature—is represented by *The Tambov Treasurer's Wife* (1837), a tale related in the stanzaic form of *Eugene Onegin.* Lermontov takes the usual situation of a dashing officer in love with a provincial lady and, varying the theme, has the officer win his beloved at cards. The whole mood is light and witty, and even the gibes at provincial society are good-humored.

The last of the satirical narrative poems was *A Fairy-Tale for Children,* an unfinished work probably dating from mid-1839 to mid-1840. The protagonist is a petty demon who recounts his observations on the development of a young girl from the Petersburg gentry with whom he is in love. As the poem terminates before any evident line of intrigue has been established, it is difficult to determine in what way Lermontov intended to treat his theme of a demon's love for a mortal. The extant portion has an obvious satirical inclination, directed at Petersburg society, and there is a measure of self-disparagement in the poet's words concerning his previous handling of the demon theme:

> Upon a time I sang of a different demon:
> That was senseless, passionate, childish raving.

But it would be risky to generalize from these limited indications that, had the work been finished, it would have lacked a romantic essence. It might well have developed a strong satirical-realistic current, but this would not necessarily have been at the expense of the romantic elements. In general Lermontov's realism developed along with his romanticism and to some extent influenced it. One might say that his realism matured his romanticism, which at one time had, indeed, been close to what he calls "childish raving."

In the area of the narrative poem, the mature romanticism of Lermontov is demonstrated by three compositions of this period, *The Fugitive, Mtsyri,* and the final version of *The Demon.* The first of these, written sometime during or after the poet's first Caucasian exile, is a short treatment of a Circassian folksong or tale about a young warrior who flees the battlefield without having avenged the death of his father and brothers. In concise and even verse the poet recounts the coward's futile attempt to find refuge with a friend, his beloved, and finally with his mother. Branded a craven and a slave by all, he commits suicide.

Mtsyri (Georgian for *novice*) is one of Russian literature's finest examples of romantic eloquence. Lofty and impassioned, it is the history of a soul tortured by the physical and spiritual captivity of civilization, a soul which for a brief moment returns to nature and becomes a part of it, an animal among animals, a companion of the birds, a beast of prey and a hunted creature. In the depiction of the romantic ideal of the fusion of nature and the human ego, the work is a real *tour de force.*

The brief introduction relates how the novice had been left at a monastery as a child of six by his Russian captors. Memories of his native tongue, his parents and his homeland become increasingly dimmed by the passage of time, but his innate love of freedom and nature remain as strong as ever. He flees the monastery, and for three days wanders through the beautiful countryside, shunning man, without food or shelter, but free. Attacked by a panther, he becomes an animal himself and destroys his enemy, but not before he is cruelly wounded. Finally he unknowingly circles back to the monastery, and it is the realization that he is fated never to return to the land of his childhood which deprives him of his final strength. Discovered by the monks, he is taken to the cloister, and in his dying "confession"—really a *profession de foi*—he tells the abbot of his adventures while free.

The poem is a wonderfully unified piece, and it defies the destructive analysis of the anti-romantic critic. It must either be accepted or rejected, but it can't be picked to pieces. When the novice exultingly declares that he became friends with the storm and seized lightning with his hands, one doesn't feel that this is too extravagant, because the whole work is extravagant, in its basic concept and in the elevated flight of its verse. One colorful scene replaces another, and the reader is borne along the waves of poetry, delighted by the view and fearful of obstacles, but the pace and emotional tension are maintained until the end.

An achievement of equal brilliance is *The Demon,* some earlier versions of which have already been discussed. In 1838 a sixth variant was completed, which differed markedly from the earlier ones. The previous rather indefinite locale was replaced by a Caucasian setting, and the anonymous nun was recast as the passionate Georgian princess Tamara. The same year the poet again rewrote the work, incorporating other changes which he hoped would make it acceptable to the censors—but in vain. Finally, in 1841, the eighth and final version was prepared. Like *Mtsyri,* this work is the quintessence of romanticism. It is picturesque, visionary, and sensual. It is as extravagant as an ostentatious ruby, but it has a ruby's brilliance and color. If not the poet's best work, it has been one of his most popular and well-known.

The Song of the Merchant Kalashnikov must be defined as a romantic narrative poem, but it has qualities which distinguish it from *Mtsyri* and *The Demon* and put it in a class by itself. First of all, it is a stylization of the traditional historical folk-song, whose rhythm and diction the poet imitated with apparent if not complete accuracy. Exteriorly, it presents the story of the revenge of the merchant Kalashnikov, who deliberately kills an *oprichnik* (bodyguard) of Ivan the Terrible for having dishonored his, the merchant's, wife. The work is full of the color and spirit of the times of Muscovy, and is indisputably the most successful attempt by any author to reproduce the form and style of the popular historical song. Yet many details of the plot and characteristics of the principal figures—the merchant, his wife, and the Tsar's body-guard—suggest strongly that this work was a veiled treatment of the circumstances surrounding Pushkin's duel with d'Anthès. Scattered throughout the poem are a number of hints that the story, despite its sixteenth-century setting, is actually a modern one.

The piece was written in the early months of Lermontov's first exile, and it is quite likely that he planned it as a secret revenge on his persecutors. A straightforward account of Pushkin's death would, of course, never have been passed by the censors, but there was at least some satisfaction for the poet in having an allegorical treatment accepted for publication by the unsuspecting authorities. The work was, in fact, published in 1838 and thus did become, as Lermontov had intended, a sort of poetic Trojan horse.

> **The development of Lermontov's art in its final stage is distinguished . . . not so much by movement towards realism, which would suggest the abandonment of romanticism, but by a broadening of the scope of his art to embrace realism.**
>
> **—*John Mercereau, Jr.***

Like all great authors, Lermontov is unique, and thus it is not easy to impose upon him or his work any ready-made formulas. His is a special combination of outlook, feelings, judgments, methods, and inspiration which make his art original and individual. *Mtsyri* and *The Demon*, representative of Lermontov's most successful ventures in the romantic mood, are proof enough that during his last years the fires of romanticism were far from burning out. But, at the same time, he was more than casually disposed towards realism. The lyric poems *Borodino* and "Valerik," to mention just two, show that on occasion the poet could achieve a high degree of objectivity and convey a graphic impression of reality. Even such a poem as "Meditation" is more logically classified as a work of realism than of romanticism, although it was inspired by romantic indignation at the divergence between reality and the ideal. And the same is true of a number of other poems written during the final period, which, like "Meditation," have the character of editorials in rhymed prose. Obviously the

product of romantic disillusionment, their subject matter and its treatment link them closely with realism.

The development of Lermontov's art in its final stage is distinguished, therefore, not so much by movement towards realism, which would suggest the abandonment of romanticism, but by a broadening of the scope of his art to embrace realism. At the same time, the romantic element in his work was undergoing its own evolution. The arm-waving and teeth-gnashing aspects were being deemphasized in favor of qualities more appealing to the mature intellect. The poet was not less sensitive or moved than he had been earlier, but now he had control of himself and his art.

William H. Hopkins (essay date 1976)

SOURCE: "Lermontov's Hussar Poems," in *Russian Literature Triquarterly*, Vol. 14, Winter, 1976, pp. 36-47.

[*In the following essay, Hopkins challenges a prevalent criticism of Lermontov's "Junker" or "Hussar" poems that dismisses them as juvenile "pornography," citing evidence that they may have influenced both the poet's literary reputation and subsequent writings.*]

Mikhail Lermontov (1814-1841) entered the School of the Ensigns of the Guards and the Cavalry Cadets in 1832 and in 1834 received a commission in the Hussars of the Guards. During the two years in the school he wrote a number of poems containing a genital semantic function, his so-called "Junker" or "Hussar" poems. [In a footnote the critic adds: "The Hussar poems are described as being 'pornographic.' The problem of definition of the term is complex and cannot be dealt with at length here. However, one attribute of the category 'pornography' seems to be sexual content. In a brilliant discussion of 'pornography' Morse Peckham has pointed out that it is impossible to create a tenable definition by discussing pornography as that which has sexual content, because in the post-Freudian era the term 'sex' has been subjected to semantic branching to the extent that anything can be interpreted as 'sexual.' See Morse Peckham, *Art and Pornography* (New York, 1969), 40-43. Nevertheless, reflection indicates that broadly speaking the attribute 'pornography' is most frequently applied to sequences of semiotic verbal behavior which contain cognitive model configurations of genitalia, descriptions of implied or explicit genital behavior, or scatology, through one or more semiotic verbal utterances. All such cognitive model configurations irrespective of their acceptability in a culture are subsumed here under the rubric 'a genital semantic function.' This is a more neutral designation than 'pornographic' elements or 'erotic' elements, for example."] They are frequently dismissed from critical consideration because they are "pornographic." For example, one reads that "Lermontov's Junker poems . . . are pornography . . . having no pertinence to . . . poetry." The Junker poems are excluded from a recent, very complete Soviet collection of Lermontov's works. It is stated that "all of Lermontov's poetic works are included with the exception of his Junker poems which are unsuitable for print." P. Antokolsky says of the poems:

> These "unprintable" lines of Lermontov cannot add anything to his poetic aspect. With childish diligence he pushes into his iamb the most outrageous bad language which can exist in the Russian language. There is no trace of ingenuity, nor humor, nor wit. There is only one thing: the desire to be reputed an experienced Hussar-cynic. The alien element mastered under compulsion monstrously protrudes from his poems. That which to another person comes easy, for Lermontovwas the torture of a Procrustean bed.

Whatever one's moral or esthetic evaluation of these poems, it seems unreasonable to ignore the works completely. It has been observed, for example, that at the school Lermontov's poetry "turned from the magniloquent introspections of his earlier youth to frankly coarse, unprintable cadet poems—which however, are the first germs of his later realism."

The atmosphere in an all-male boarding school was undoubtedly conducive to the kinds of remissive behavior which are encountered and frequently enouraged in such homosocial organizational environments. By the time Lermontov entered the Cadet School he had mastered the craft of writing poems. In his reminiscences of Lermontov, A. M. Merinsky, a school friend, remarks that the students would frequently sing indecent songs, which they especially liked. For the amusement of his comrades Lermontov would rework various songs and introduce a genital semantic function. The contents of these "poems" were so indecent that Merinsky deemed them unfit for print.

The students also published a literary "journal" called *School Dawn (Shkolnaia Zaria)*. Only seven numbers of it came out. Merinsky gives some background about this endeavor.

> In . . . the beginning of 1834 someone among us proposed putting out a magazine . . . in handwritten form. . . . The magazine was supposed to come out once a week on Wednesdays; articles accumulated in the course of seven days. Whoever wrote and wanted to place his composition [in it] put the manuscript in a designated drawer of one of the tables which was located by the beds in our rooms. The author could remain anonymous. On Wednesdays the articles were taken out of the drawer, sewn together, comprising quite a thick notebook, which on that very evening when we were all grouped together was read very loudly. During this the laughter and the jokes never stopped. Several such numbers of the journal accumulated. I do not know what happened to them; but in them many poems of Lermontov were placed, it is true, a large portion of them were not completely decent and are not subject to print as, e.g., *The Ulans' Woman, A Holiday in Peterhof* and others. *The Ulans' Woman* was the Junkers' favorite poem; probably now also in the present school a secret notebook clandestinely passes from hand to hand.

Three of the poems which Lermontov wrote for the magazine under various pseudonyms were published in 1879 in Geneva in an anonymous collection of pornographic Russian poems entitled *Éros russe: Russian Eroticism Not for Women (Éros russe: Russkii Erot ne dlia dam)*. These include: **"The Hospital" ("Goshpital"), "To Tizengauzen" ("Tizengauzenu"),** and **"Ode to the Latrine" ("Oda k nuzhniku").**

Perhaps because of the publication abroad of some of the Junker poems in *Russian Eroticism* an anonymous author wrote an article in 1882 for *Russian Antiquity (Russkaia starina)* which described the content of *School Dawn*. The author says an original journal was preserved by Prince V. S. Vyazemsky, identified as a schoolmate of Lermontov. The writer became acquainted with the magazine in 1879, he says, "thanks to the mediation of V. N. Polivanov," son of N. I. Polivanov, another schoolmate.

Some of the contents of *School Dawn* are briefly described: "the famous joke poem *The Ulans' Woman*, signed with the pseudonym 'Gr. Dyabekir'; *Frontier News (Pogranichnye izvestiia)*, a *pereponiia* (in prose) signed 'Stepanov,' a joke in which Lermontov's comrade Prince Shakovskoi is the hero." The author also quotes extensively from **"Oda . . ." ("Oda [k nuzhniku]"),** which he bowdlerizes. He only mentions a verse epistle **"To Tizengauzen"** and the poem **"The Hospital in Peterhof—A Story."** In this last poem the heroes are identified as Lermontov's schoolmates Prince A. I. Baryatynsky and N. I. Polivanov. A few lines of the poem are quoted and the plot is given, albeit in modest form. The writer concludes the short article with the following observation: "The verses are partially quite sonorous, but the content—by virtue of its scabrousness—just about surpasses the works of the notorious Barkov."

It is not to our purpose to analyze Lermontov to postulate the authorial intent behind these poems. Still it may be useful to keep in mind the general context in which they were written. This was a military school and the majority of the pupils were young aristocrats. According to various reminiscences about him, Lermontov apparently disliked everything "false, stretched or unnatural." In Merinsky's reminiscences Lermontov is portrayed as interested in gaining approval by being a wit, but it is noted that he had something of a penchant for cutting, impromptu epigrams. Some of the boys may not have appreciated being the butt of his acerbic wit. Still he could take jokes about himself as well as make them about others.

Viskovatov suggests that Lermontov also had a hidden life during this period in which he gave himself over to serious literary endeavor. But as can be imagined, these young men were not especially drawn together by intellectual or literary interests. Lermontov could write poems that amused the others, and whether it was for a laugh or to win group acceptance, it is clear he turned out such poems. It would be impossible to establish conclusively whether the episodes depicted in them represent real happenings or the tall-tale, fantasizing common in homosocial organizations. The latter seems more probably the case, for if the antics are true, it is surprising that the culprits would not have been punished. On the other hand the moral latitude permitted the boys was great and in fact may have reached the proportions described in the poems. Probably the poems are a montage of fact and fiction.

Rather than dismiss the poems as pornography we shall describe these rather unknown poems and examine a few aspects of them as they redounded on Lermontov's reputation and his subsequent artistic endeavors. Some critical evaluations of the works will be cited.

In **"The Hospital"** Prince A. I. Baryatinsky and "Lafa," identified as N. I. Polivanov, bet to see which of them can seduce Marisiya, a young servant girl. A drunken Baryatinsky, sexually aroused, sneaks into her quarters in the hospital and in the darkness mistakenly molests an old woman. A man who comes to her aid starts to beat the Prince, who runs into another room. In the next room the man is startled to find "Lafa" and Marisiya engaged in sexual activity. "Lafa" attacks the man, calls Baryatinsky from hiding, and the two go home together. The boys find it easy enough to bribe their way out of punishment for the fiasco. The last stanza is devoted to the figure of Marisiya. She disappears without a trace and is sincerely missed. There is a note of sadness at her absence. The poem begins and ends on such a note of nostalgia for her.

As might be expected in an all-male atmosphere, some of the poems deal with homosexuality. In **"To Tizengauzen"** the narrator admonishes the boy, who was suspected of homosexual behavior, to change his ways. He is warned of Divine retribution and profound regret. The first part of *Ode to the Latrine* is written in an exalted odic form and includes jocular scatological elements. The latrine is praised as a place of privacy. Suddenly the tone changes and there is a description of a nighttime homosexual assignation between two "shadows." The narration suddenly breaks off before the description turns into a "malicious rebuke."

In *Peterhof Holiday,* against the background of a colorful crowd watching holiday fireworks, a Junker clearly identifiable as D. S. Bibikov, a high-stakes gambler who has left his comrades, is seen standing drunk and alone on a bridge. He complains about the discipline of the school. A flirtatious girl attracts his attention. She runs away and he pursues her. When she falls down, he catches her and they have sexual relations. Afterward the girl demands money from him and he is insulted. The deflated Junker returns home, and while cleaning off his pants philosophizes about the fortunate man who is not acquainted with prostitutes.

In *The Ulans' Woman* there is the description of the transfer of the Cavalry Squadron of the Junker School to Peterhof and their nighttime halt in the village of Izhora. The tired, drunken quartermaster is "Lafa," again N. I. Polivanov. When the men have settled down for the night, a drinking bout begins. "Lafa" suggests that everyone go with him to visit a local girl and have sexual relations with her. They rape her, and the men apparently believe the girl

begins to enjoy the gang rape. Suddenly it is morning and the drunken Ulans are departing. Prince "Nose" (I. Shakovskoi), called "Trigger" by the boys because of his big nose, is among the company. One of the final images in the poem is that of the ravaged girl emerging from the granary. Only "Lafa" recognizes her and in parting hollers, "Peace to your ashes, Tanyusha." In the last lines it is remarked, poignantly enough, that many days have passed since that time, but the girl has forever retained the nickname "the Ulans' woman."

Eventually the boys left the school for their various careers and copies of *School Dawn* made their way into the "bachelor circles of the 'golden youth' of . . . the capital, and in such a fashion Lermontov's first poetic fame was the most ambiguous and did him much harm.

In 1835 a friend had Lermontov's tale in verse *Khadzhi-Abrek* published, but his real public literary career began with *On the Death of Pushkin* which circulated in the *proto-samizdat* after 1837. In 1837-38 and especially after 1839 Lermontov's works began to appear in print more frequently.

Against the background of his burgeoning literary success, he sought acceptance in Petersburg society, but for the most part he was rebuffed. This can in part be attributed to the fact that many knew him on the basis of his Junker poems and were indignant that he should "dare to come out in public with his works. There were cases where sisters and wives were forbidden to talk about the fact that they read Lermontov's works; this was considered compromising.

His unsavory reputation, a legacy of the Junker poems, created a jaundiced and prejudicial view of the man and the artist. This feeling began to abate to some degree in St. Petersburg society after the publication of a collection of his poems and the novel *A Hero of Our Time,* however, this was only shortly before his death. Writing in 1891, a full fifty years after Lermontov died, Viskovatov observed that this attitude about Lermontov could still be felt. Many of the author's school comrades outlived him, they attained high rank and died only in the 1870's and 1880's. N. I. Polivanov, "Lafa," apparently continued to view these works with good humor and as the "apotheosis of Hussar recklessness or dissipated 'dashingness.'" Yet not everyone took such an attitude.

The critic Durylin quotes P. A. Viskovatov, who was acquainted with several of Lermontov's school comrades, to the effect that a number of the personages so thinly disguised in these Junker poems subsequently became Lermontov's most vicious enemies. Prince A. I. Baryatinsky (Prince "B" of **"The Hospital"**), who later became a General Field Marshal and subjugated the Caucasus, was particularly malicious, calling the poet a most "immoral person" and a "mediocre imitator of Byron." He was astonished that people would be interested in Lermontov to the point of collecting materials for his biography. Viskovatov remarks that it was only later when the school notebooks came into his hands that he understood the reason for such maliciousness. He goes on to state that "these people even hindered Lermontov in his service career, which they themselves passed through successfully."

Whatever their literary-philosophical starting point, many critics have predictably condemned the genital semantic function in these works. In 1899 the mystical philosopher and critic Vladimir Solovyov wrote that these were "productions infused with the demon of impurity," and he places these works outside of "literature."

Academician P. N. Sakulin, however, in an article entitled "The Earth and the Sky in Lermontov's Poetry" wrote:

> If one forgets about an ethical evaluation of these works, then it is necessary to give them an important significance in the evolution of Lermontov's creation. Like the comical and erotic *povesti* of other poets (e.g., Pushkin) Lermontov's frivolous *poemy* brought into his poetry a stream of simplicity and liveliness, features which were so lacking in the "Romantic" *poemy* of Lermontov and his contemporaries.

The Formalist critic B. M. Eikhenbaum in writing about the Junker poems also reveals a prejudice against the genital semantic function in literature and incidentally offers his notion of the distinction between "erotica" and "pornography." He writes:

> Here the influence of Pushkin's verse (e.g.,—the description of Peterhof) takes shelter, But when Pushkin's erotica did not represent any deviation or contradiction and easily entered the general system of his creation, Lermontov's erotica produces the impression of some kind of temporary drinking bout and has not so much an erotic as a pornographic character. Erotica differs from pornography in that it finds clever allegories and puns for the most frank situations—and this gives it its literary value. Since poetry in general is almost completely the art of speaking allegorically . . . it is completely understandable that an erotic theme, as one which is forbidden and does not have for its expression legitimized poetic stock-phrases, interests a poet as a purely-literary stylistic problem. Such is the nature of Voltaire's *Pucelle* or Pushkin's *Gavriiliada*. In Lermontov there is something completely different: in place of allegories and puns we see in them scabrous terminology, the coarseness of which produces no impression, because it is not an artistic device (when at least in Pushkin the unexpected coarse swearing in the poem "The Wagon of Life" acts comedically, because it is the result of the development of a profound metaphor). . . .
>
> I am inclined to view [these poems] not as literary works, but as a psychological document, which justifies the division of Lermontov's creation into two periods (1829-1832 and 1836-1841).

It is not to our purpose to sort out and refute the unsubstantiated assertions concerning erotica and pornography in this argument. However, this Formalist, who might be expected to take a less prejudiced attitude toward "naughty" words, nevertheless reveals a quaint, pietistic horror (from the point of view of his deity, Art) at the ikonographics of certain words; but he accepts a genital semantic function in the category "Art," if it is conveyed by a pun or "clever" allegory.

Notwithstanding an initial proviso, Durylin makes a statement that ought to help save the Junker poems from the dust bin of critical or other prejudice:

> No matter how negatively one responds to the themes of these works or regrets the loss of the poet's creative strength . . . an important fact remains indisputable: *in the Junker "poemy" Lermontov the writer for the first time turned to the direct reproduction of reality in the form of a realistic story.*

It is obvious that the Junker poems should be very important to any student seriously interested in Lermontov's transition from "Romanticism" to "Realism." On the thematic level there are in some of these poems elements which Lermontov was to develop in his later, respectable works. In Lermontov's novel, *A Hero of Our Time,* there are innumerable themes and motifs (semantic functions). For example, the capers of aristocratic young army officers play an important role, as does the genital semantic function. While there are no overt descriptions of genital behavior in the story, the depiction of Pechorin's relations with Bela, Vera and Princess Mary is ultimately predicated on the assumption of indulgence in genital behavior. Another theme is his cavalier treatment of each of these women for which he suffers no real consequence on any level. This is but one aspect of the work; however, in his other behavior, Pechorin also consistently fails to accept responsibility for his actions and in a similar fashion endures no consequences for them. An American critic [J. Mersereau, Mikhail Lermontov, 1962] has provided a most incisive view of this character:

> Lermontov demonstrates that his hero rejects fatalism in favor of free will, as this is more gratifying to his ego, but he refuses the concommitant burden of responsibility. With the revelation of this moral deficiency, it becomes finally clear why his life is essentially aimless and often destructive. . . . His only imperatives are those dictated to him by his passions.

In many of the Junker poems the aristocratic young officers reveal the same sort of cynicism *vis-a-vis* the anticipated norms of interpersonal behavior. In many of these "heroes" we see a germ of some important themes in *A Hero of Our Time,* for example, the permitted remissive behavior of the military and the lack of responsibility and consequences for one's action. There are no real consequences for any of the "heroes" in the Junker poems; however, through the persona's attitude to the action there is frequently an insinuation of the possibility of consequence or at least a judgmental tone. This aspect deserves a little exploration.

Every society has areas of permitted remissive behavior, and considerations extrinsic to that particular context cannot be allowed to intrude, or the purpose of permitting the remissive behavior is lost. In such areas certain rules are allowed just not to apply. Although everyone acts as if he really does not approve of such remissive behavior, in fact the society needs it for various reasons and it is approved. In the Junker poems a sour note of sorts is introduced into what are supposed to be humorous poems because the narrator allows attitudes to reveal themselves which are inappropriate to areas of permitted remissive behavior. Insinuations of the behavioral norms validated by the macrocosmic culture are juxtaposed to the norms of permitted remissive behavior of the microcosm. It is hard to say whether the judgmental aspects implied in the narrator's world view are intentional or inadvertent, but their very presence seems to obviate the humor of the works. The students apparently found the poems funny in a certain time and setting, however, as we have already seen, even for many of those who participated in the remissive behavior, the works lost their comedic aspects.

> It is obvious that the Junker poems should be very important to any student seriously interested in Lermontov's transition from "Romanticism" to "Realism." On the thematic level there are in some of these poems elements which Lermontov was to develop in his later, respectable works.
>
> *—William H. Hopkins*

It is as impossible to isolate the constitutive elements of the "humorous" as of the "pornographic." Both these categories depend on the perceptions and cognition of the individual. The full ramifications of this are too broad for discussion here. Perhaps we can best state the case of what constitutes the "humorous" and the "pornographic" through the formula: stimulus—>individual cognitive model retrieval—>response. The elements of each of the members of the expression are independent variables. Perhaps this explains why some people can tell a joke, why others cannot; why some people can tell a "dirty" joke, and others cannot, and why auditors respond as they do. Surely it helps understand why responses to sequences of verbal and semiotic verbal behavior are so particular to an individual.

We have cited enough evidence to indicate that some have found the Junker poems "humorous," and some have found them "pornographic." Not all critics have found them lacking in literary worth. All these particular judgments must be left up to individual readers with their peculiar sensibilities. For those aghast at the presence of the genital semantic function (dirty words and descriptions of sexual activity, for example), perhaps the judgmental elements insinuated by the narrator can be equated with "redeeming social value." They spoil the jokes, after all. Whatever the literary value of the Junker poems, if one is interested in Lermontov, it seems indefensible simply to

ascribe negative value to them and dismiss the works as "pornography."

Michael R. Katz   (essay date 1976)

SOURCE: "Lermontov's Literary Ballads," in his *The Literary Ballad in Early Nineteenth-Century Russian Literature,* Oxford University Press, 1976, pp. 166-82.

[*In the following essay, Katz traces the thematic, stylistic, and linguistic sources of Lermontov's literary ballads, highlighting the poet's contributions to the genre.*]

In 1838 Lermontov became acquainted with Zhukovsky in St. Petersburg and the two poets continued to meet until Lermontov's departure for the Caucasus in April 1841. Zhukovsky's influence on his poetry is evident from the very beginning of Lermontov's literary career, both in his experiments in the ballad genre and in his application of balladic techniques in his lyric poetry. As Pushkin had progressed from imitation to parody of Zhukovsky's ballads, so too did Lermontov. From 1830 Lermontov began to parody precisely those elements of Zhukovsky's style which he had previously imitated. But in his ballad cycle of 1832, and particularly in those works written between 1837 and 1841, Lermontov transformed the ballad genre into a form capable of expressing his own deeply personal inspiration.

Lermontov's earliest experiments with the literary ballad were based on German and English sources. Both his choice of models for imitation and the style of these experiments reflect the strong influence of Zhukovsky's ballads. The first of these works, **Ballada ('Nad morem krasavitsa-deva sidit')** (1829), is Lermontov's reworking of Schiller's ballad *Der Taucher,* which Zhukovsky also began translating in 1825 (and published under the title *Kubok* in 1831). In Lermontov's version a mermaid asks a young man to brave the depths of the sea in order to retrieve her necklace and, by so doing, to demonstrate his love for her. The youth accomplishes this task, but when she sends him down again to fetch her some coral, he does not return.

Lermontov's characters and setting are described in language characteristic of Zhukovsky's ballads: the heroine is a *krasavitsadeva;* the hero is referred to as *drug, yunosha,* and *mladoi udalets;* and the sea is variously depicted as *puchina, pennaya bezdna, grot,* and *chernoe dno;* the manuscript variants for the last phrase include the typical Zhukovsky combinations *mrachnoe dno* and *uzhasnoe dno.* The numerous exclamations (*O schast'e! on zhiv*) and the repeated interruptions in the narrative are also characteristic of Zhukovsky's syntax; however, it is in the frequency and range of its epithets that Lermontov's style reveals the most notable influence of Zhukovsky's vocabulary, in expressions such as *no mrachen kak byl* (early variant: *on vykhodit pechalen i mrachen kak byl*); *vlazhnye kudri; pechal'nyi vzor;* and *dusha beznadezhnaya.*

In 1829 Lermontov also translated Schiller's *Der Hands-chuh: Eine Erzählung* as *Perchatka; Zhukovsky* translated it under the same title in 1831. The subject is similar to that of *Ballada,* although its resolution is different: an aristocratic lady allows her glove to fall among the wild beasts in an arena in order to test her knight's affection. He retrieves the glove, but tosses it in her face in protest at her caprice.

The language of Lermontov's version and its emphasis on the theme of Fate paradoxically render it more Zhukovsky-like than Zhukovsky's own, relatively literal, translation. . . .

Lermontov's short fragment **'V starinny gody zhili-byli'** (1830) may possibly be a translation of an unidentified German source. The single stanza which describes two knights who returned from the crusades in Palestine echoes the theme and style of Zhukovsky's translation of Schiller's *Ritter Toggenburg* in 1818, and also resembles his later translations of Uhland's ballads.

The ballad *Gost'* (**'Klarisu yunosha lyubil'**), sub-titled *Byl'* and written in the early 1830s, represents the culmination of the German influence on Lermontov's literary ballads. It describes the love affair between Klarisa and Kalmar, whose marriage plans were disrupted when war broke out; Kalmar, after hearing Klarisa's pledge of eternal faithfulness, goes off to fight. However, when springtime arrives, Klarisa decides to marry someone else. At the wedding feast, a silent guest in military dress at last reveals himself to be none other than the corpse of Kalmar, and there he reclaims his Klarisa.

Basically a reworking of Bürger's *Lenore,* Lermontov's *Gost'* also combines motifs inherited from the Russian ballads of the 1790s (war as the obstacle to love; death of the hero; and subsequent union with the heroine) and from Zhukovsky's literary ballads. Kalmar, *tomim toskoi,* expresses a favourite Zhukovsky theme in unmistakably Zhukovsky language. . . . Even Kalmar's corpse resembles those of Zhukovsky's heroes (*pryam i nedvizhim*), while the atmosphere of *strakh,* created in part by *kakoi-to stran-nyi zvuk,* is also characteristic of Zhukovsky's ballads.

While Schiller and Bürger, both in the German originals and in Zhukovsky's free renditions, served as one source of Lermontov's early ballads, English literary ballads provided the poet with another source of inspiration. In 1829 Lermontov wrote *Dva sokola,* a reworking of *The Twa Corbies,* based either on Pushkin's version of 1828, or on Scott's text.

Lermontov's version was not intended as an imitation of the traditional genre; it is in the form of an extended lyrical dialogue between two misanthropic falcons, each expounding why he has come to hate the world and its inhabitants; the first is disenchanted with rampant hard-heartedness; the second, with common deceitfulness, particularly as embodied in women. . . . Even more than Pushkin, Lermontov emphasizes the theme of infidelity, which is here made explicit in Zhukovsky-type language.

In 1830 Lermontov composed two works based on Byronic subjects. *Chelnok* presents a balladic situation: a small boat, manned by two oarsmen, is buffeted about by a storm; a mysterious *chto-to,* wrapped up in white canvas, lies in the bottom of the boat. This victim of some unexplained crime is described in epithets borrowed from Zhukovsky's ballads. . . . The enigma is left unresolved; instead, there follows a lyrical reflection on the poet's own expectation of happiness in life and the comforting proximity of peace in death.

The second work, *Ballada* (**'Beregis'! Beregis'! . . .**), is an unfinished and inaccurate translation of the ballad inserted between stanzas 40 and 41 of the sixteenth canto of Byron's *Don Juan.* It describes an extraordinary 'black friar' who refused to be driven from the house of a local nobleman when the Moors overran Spain. Once again, Lermontov's style, particularly his choice of epithets, reflects the influence of Zhukovsky's ballads: *chernyi monakh, mrak nochnoi, rodimyi dol,* and *blednaya luna.*

Another ballad entitled *Gost'* (**'Kak proshlets inoplemen-nyi'**) and written in 1830 represents the culmination of the English influence on Lermontov's ballads. It is a reworking of the theme used by Zhukovsky in his ballad *Pustynnik* (1812), which in turn is a translation of Goldsmith's *The Hermit.* Lermontov's guest, a *bednyi monakh,* arrives at an unfamiliar house late one night and is given shelter. He recognizes the lady of the house as his former beloved, and hurls himself at her feet. Then the guest retires to his chamber to sob away the night; in the morning the hosts discover his corpse.

The scene of the lovers' recognition in *Gost'* is almost identical in situation and language to that in Zhukovsky's ballad. . . . Furthermore, one of Zhukovsky's favourite epithets, *pechal'nyi,* is applied both to the features of the monk . . . and to the cloak which covers those same features, now lifeless. . . .

Scott, Ossian, Byron, and Goldsmith—in their original language and in Zhukovsky's versions—provided Lermontov with models of English literary ballads. While under their influence (1830-2) Lermontov also attempted to employ the stylistic devices of the ballad genre in traditional lyric forms, for example in *Pesn' barda, Mogila boitsa* (sub-titled *Duma*), and *Russkaya pesnya* (**'Klokami belyi sneg valitsya'**).

The most interesting of these experiments, *Ballada* (**'Viz-bushke pozdneyu poroyu'**), is in the form of a mother's song addressed to her infant. She recounts her husband's heroism in leading the Russians against the Tartars. Suddenly the husband returns, mortally wounded; he reports the Russians' defeat and expires. The mother urges her child to avenge his father's death in a speech which concludes with a fair measure of bathos. . . . After a period of considerable experimentation with German and English sources and skilful imitation of Zhukovsky's literary ballads, Lermontov wrote a series of parodies on the ballad genre and on its foremost practitioners. The first of these, *Nez-abudka* (1830), sub-titled *Skazka,* is a witty parody of

Schiller's *Der Taucher*, which had previously served as the model for Lermontov's own *Ballada* ('**Nad morem**'). *Nezabudka* begins with a comparison of human affections, past and present, and concludes that formerly love and fidelity were stronger emotions than now. An example follows: two lovers are sitting near a brook; the heroine asks the unsuspecting hero to pick a blue flower for her in order to prove his love. He succeeds, but on his way back the ground gives way under him. As he bids his last farewell to his beloved, he tosses her the flower and begs her not to forget him: hence, the name of the flower— *nezabudka*.

Schiller's tragic subject, the test of affection occasioned by a lady's caprice which results in her lover's death, is here cast in a comic vein. The descriptions of the hero (*rytsar' blagorodnyi; moi milyi*), the heroine (*lyubeznaya; deva*), and the idyllic setting (*Pod ten'yu lipovykh vetvei; Svod nad nami yasnyi*) echo phrases from Zhukovsky's ballads. At the climax Lermontov combines elevated abstract substantives with the most frequent epithets of Zhukovsky's vocabulary in delicious bathos. . . . Other epithets in *Nezabudka* would seem to parody Lermontov's own language in his earlier *Ballada* ('**Nad morem**'): for example, *pechal'nyi vzor* and *dusha beznadezhnaya* of the former work are superseded by *tsvetok pechal'nyi* and *ruka beznadezhnaya* in the parody.

Ballada ('**Iz vorot vyezhayut**'), written in 1832, turns the first two lines of a German folk-song, *Die drei Ritter*, into a parody of Zhukovsky's chivalric ballads. Three knights ride off into battle, leaving their three loves behind; the knights are slain and the women grieve; then three *new* knights come to court them, and the ladies forget their sadness.

Each line of the ballad is followed by the exclamation *uvy!* or *prosti!;* this device, particularly the ironic conclusion, is effectively used to parody the chivalric ideal of true love. . . .

Lermontov's ballad '**On byl v krayu svyatom**' (1832) is a parody of Zhukovsky's *Staryi rytsar'* (1832), which in turn was a translation of Uhland's *Graf Eberhards Weissdorn*. Zhukovsky's knight, having heroically defended the Faith in Palestine, spends his old age dozing tranquilly under an olive-tree which had grown from a branch he had taken from a tree in the Holy Land and planted. Lermontov's knight returns from Palestine bald and battered, having spent his time there pillaging and raping; he finds his wife pregnant and his children unruly. Each stanza of Lermontov's parody begins in earnest and is followed by an ironic twist which deflates its meaning. . . .

The final parody, *Yugel'skii baron* (1837), was a joint effort by Lermontov and V. N. Annenkova, a poetess and close friend of Lermontov's grandmother, to caricature Zhukovsky's translation from Scott, *Zamok Smal'gol'm* (1822). Lermontov's baron summons his page to deliver a letter to the baroness; the page refuses, and finally reveals that she has been unfaithful in the baron's absence. The baron laughs and explains to the page that 'northern women' are *always* faithful to their husbands. . . . The page listens carefully, admits his mistake, and agrees to deliver the baron's message.

Zhukovsky's style is subjected to merciless parody—in Lermontov's excessive use of verbs (*I kusal on, i rval, i pisal, i strochil*), in the interrogative intonation (*Ne devitsa l' ona? . . . i odna li verna?*), and particularly in the choice and use of epithets. On the one hand Lermontov employs precisely those epithets which Zhukovsky used to characterize his heroes: the baron is described as *znamenityi* and *vysokii*, his wife as *odinoka, bledna, milaya, vernaya;* and the page as *molodoi*. On the other hand, Lermontov takes Zhukovsky's unwieldy *topor . . . / Ukreplen dvadtsatifuntovoi*, and replaces it with the splendid *dolgovyazyi lakei / Tridtsatipyatiletnyi durak*.

In much the same way as Pushkin, Lermontov also proceeded from imitation to parody. From *Nezabudka* (1830) to *Yugel'skii baron* (1837) he attempted to overcome Zhukovsky's influence by parodying the themes and style of ballads he had previously imitated. With his ballad cycle of 1832 Lermontov began to use the form in a creative and individual way.

In 1832 Lermontov composed three literary ballads: *Trostnik, Rusalka,* and *Ballada* ('**Kuda tak provorno**'). Similarities in the treatment of emotional experience in the three works and their pervading lyricism enable the critic to consider them together as a ballad cycle.

The first, *Trostnik,* is a nature-magic ballad which is said to have been influenced by Victor Hugo's poetry. A fisherman plucks a reed and blows through it: the reed relates the sad tale of a young girl who was held prisoner in her stepmother's house. When she spurned the amorous advances of the woman's evil son, the girl was mercilessly killed. The reeds which grow above her grave contain her sadness.

Sadness (*pechal'*) is the theme of the ballad; Lermontov emphasizes the intimate connection between human suffering and nature, between the girl's soul and the 'animate' reeds (*budto ozhivlennyi*). . . . In contrast to this sadness, the fisherman, whose presence is used to frame the ballad, is described as *veselyi;* he is incapable of helping the girl or even sharing her experience (*A plakat' ne privyk*).

The girl's monologue is related simply and its language is rich in repetitions (*ostav'; rybak*), internal rhymes (*devitsa, krasavitsa, temnitsa*), and folk elements (*slezy goryuchie; na bereg krutoi; na sini volny*), as well as literary elegiac themes (*ya nekogda tsvela; i rannyuyu mogilu*). Lermontov's fisherman, like the *rybak* in Zhukovsky's ballad, is not in spiritual sympathy with nature; but instead of being seduced by the force of nature-magic, in *Trostnik* the fisherman is merely involuntarily employed to express the girl's *pechal'*.

The second work in the cycle, *Rusalka,* is another nature-magic ballad and probably has as one of its sources an early ballad by Heine, *Die Nixen*. It's narrative element is far less important than is that in *Trostnik. Rusalka* consists entirely of a mermaid's lament: she begins with a description of her luxurious kingdom beneath the sea and then describes the lifeless corpse of a handsome *vityaz'* who will not respond to her amorous advances. As in *Trostnik,* nature is animate: for example, the waves are described as *revnivy.* Motifs from the earlier ballad (such as *trostniki* and *krutoi bereg*) are repeated in *Rusalka;* however, the theme of *pechal'* has become the vaguer *neponyatnaya toska,* although the word *pechal'* occurs in the original manuscript. The manuscript also contains more extensive description of the mermaid herself (including *vlazhnaya; khladnaya; belaya grud'; belaya ruka*)—all of which was rejected in the final version.

The subject and characters of *Rusalka* are relatively unimportant compared to the richness of the visual imagery in the description of the mermaid's underwater realm, where a profusion of colours and materials dazzles the senses: *serebristaya pena, zlatye stada (rybok), khrustal'nye goroda, yarkie peski, shelkovye kudri, sinyaya reka,* and so on. Lermontov returned to this underwater motif in a later ballad, *Morskaya tsarevna* (1841), in which the treatment is more narrative than lyrical.

The last work in the 1832 cycle, *Ballada* (**'Kuda tak provorno'**), is not a nature-magic ballad, although it too is said to have been influenced by Hugo. Here all the emphasis is placed on the action and on the creation of atmosphere. A young Jewess hurries through the streets to warn her Russian lover that their affair has been discovered and that her father has threatened to take revenge on them both. She urges him to flee and swears that she will never reveal his identity. The lover replies by stabbing her and then killing himself. Their corpses are discovered in the morning.

The heroine, an exotic 'alien', is described in the manuscript as having *vlazhnye ochi, volshebnye ochi*—in the final version the only epithet which remains is *bledna* (*Kak mramornyi idol bledna*); the hero, referred to by the Jewess as her *angel prekrasnyi,* remains still and silent in contrast to her movement and agitation: *I mrachen glukhoi byl otvet.* The balladic motifs are numerous: the midnight setting; the father's revenge; the knife (*nozh rokovoi*); and the enigmatic *chto-to,* referring first to the knife (9: 3) and then to the heroine's corpse (10: 1). Whereas in *Trostnik* the theme is *pechal'* and in *Rusalka toska,* in *Ballada* it is the emotion of *strakh* and the heroine's *tainaya nadezhda. . . .* The brevity of each of the three ballads in the 1832 cycle, the lyricism and the imagery of the nature-magic ballads emphasized at the expense of characterization and narrative, and the emotionally charged atmosphere of *Ballada* are an indication of Lermontov's future contributions to the ballad genre.

In 1837-8 Lermontov experimented with certain balladic narrative techniques in his historical poems. The most popular of these, *Borodino* (1837), had been preceded by lyrical work, *Pole Borodina* (1831), in which the account of the battle was presented in fairly conventional language by a participant. In the later, better-known reworking of the theme Lermontov introduced the figure of the young listener, and further characterized the narrator as a simple 'everyman' by means of the alternating *prostorechie* and pathos of his speech and his ironic sense of humour.

Lermontov's next literary ballad, *Tri pal'my* (1839), influenced by Hugo's *Les Orientales,* is a reworking of the theme treated by Pushkin in his *Podrazhanie Koranu IX* (1824). Pushkin's tale, a close rendition of a passage in the Koran, is narrated in the poet's so-called Eastern style, supplemented by humorous details of realistic local colour. In Lermontov's version, three proud palmtrees on a desert oasis complain to God because they seem to serve no useful purpose in the world. Suddenly a caravan appears, and the palm-trees welcome their unexpected guests. That night the travellers chop down the trees and use them for firewood; in the morning the caravan departs, leaving behind only a pile of ashes.

Lermontov preserves Pushkin's Eastern landscape (desert, oasis, and palm-trees), but for Pushkin's one palm, *kladez,* and *putnik* he substitutes three trees, *ruchei,* and *karavan.* He also borrows some of Pushkin's diction with slight modifications; for example, Pushkin rhymes *kholodnyi* with *bezvodnyi* (1:4), which Lermontov repeats in 9:4 with an ironic twist: instead of referring to the spring-water, *kholodnyi* modifies the ash left from the charred palms. Pushkin's first line, *I putnik ustalyi na Boga roptal,* supplies Lermontov with two lines: *No strannik ustalyi iz chuzhdoi zemli* (2:2) and *I stali tri pal'my na Boga roptat'* (3:1). Pushkin's transition, *I mnogie gody nad nim protekli,* becomes Lermontov's *I mnogie gody neslyshno proshli.*

In spite of the similarities in the Eastern colour and in some of the phraseology, Lermontov significantly altered the meaning of Pushkin's work. Pushkin's subject is the punishment of a tired traveller for his *ropot* against God. When he awakes from his long sleep, the traveller realizes that his youth has vanished; he is restored to his former condition only by means of a miracle, and he continues on his way with true faith in God. Lermontov places the palm-trees in the centre of the ballad: it is their *ropot* against God which results in the arrival of the caravan and in the final destruction of the trees. The palms are punished for their sin of pride (*Tri gordye pal'my,* 1:2; *I, gordo kivaya makhrovoi glavoyu,* 7:4) and man is depicted as both the ungrateful despoiler of natural beauty and the involuntary instrument of God's revenge.

Tri pal'my is rich in visual and aural imagery. The oasis setting is described as *zelenyi, goluboi,* and *zolotoi;* the caravan as *uzornyi, chernyi,* and *belyi;* the ash left behind is *sedoi.* The peaceful silence of the desert, broken only by the *zvuchnyi ruchei,* is shattered with the arrival of the caravan; after its departure, the silence which returns is the silence of death: without the shade of the palmtrees, the stream has dried up. There remains only the *sled pechal'nyi*—a totally subjective expression to convey the poet's own emotional reaction to the events. Having borrowed Pushkin's Eastern landscape and some of his vocabulary, Lermontov, with his reinterpretation of the theme and his introduction of rich imagery, transforms the narrative of *Tri pal'my* into an intensely personal statement about his own favourite themes of pride and inhumanity.

Lermontov's next ballad, *Dary Tereka* (1839), is said to have been influenced both by the spirit of popular Cossack songs and tales and by the style of Hugo's Oriental ballads. The River Terek in the Caucasus flows down to the turbulent Caspian Sea, bearing gifts to placate it. First the river offers the body of a Kabardian warrior, but the sea is not appeased; then the Terek offers the body of a young Cossack woman: the Caspian accepts it greedily, *s ropotom lyubvi.*

The river and the sea are both personified: the Terek is depicted as *lukavyi, laskayas', and buinyi;* the Caspian is an indifferent *starik,* until the *kazachka* appears. . . .

The language of *Dary Tereka* combines folk elements— such as the river's ternary address to the sea, various repetitions, and popular expressions—with literary devices, such as the image of the warrior's armour with its inscription from the Koran, and the description of the *kazachka's* corpse. . . . The *kazachka's* wound corresponds to the Cossack's bloodied moustache. . . . Both wounds are unexplained; the resulting enigma and the poet's non-interference in the ballad are in complete contrast to the more personal themes expressed in *Tri pal'my.*

During the year 1840, while under arrest for his duel with the son of the French ambassador, Lermontov once again experimented with balladic techniques in his narrative verse. *Vozdushnyi korabl'* is a historical poem based on J.C.F. von Zedlitz's ballad *Das Geisterschiff.* In it Lermontov returns to the Napoleonic theme which first attracted him in his lyrics of 1829-30. *Vozdushnyi korabl'* emphasizes the themes of Napoleon's personal loneliness and of his deep love for France. *Sosedka* takes the form of an extended lyrical reflection by a prisoner who would waste away were it not for the fact that his *sosedka,* the gaoler's daughter, suffers the same spiritual confinement as he does. In *Plennyi rytsar'* a knight compares his own glorious past with the squalor of his present imprisonment. The lyric *Lyubov' mertvetsa* (1841) is based on motifs borrowed from Bürger's *Lenore.* It was not until 1841 that Lermontov returned to the literary ballad to make what was to be his most original contribution to the genre.

The first of these ballads, *Spor,* is in the form of a debate between two mountains in the Caucasus: the wise Shat and the impetuous Kazbek. Shat warns Kazbek that he too, like his predecessors, will be conquered and exploited by the peoples of the East. Kazbek replies that he does not fear the *dryakhlyi Vostok.* Suddenly the two mountains notice the advance of Russian regiments towards the East; Kazbek tries to count them, but fails and sinks into silence.

This ballad has been interpreted as an expression of Lermontov's sympathy for the Caucasian peoples and of his recognition that Russian annexation of the Caucasus would lead to economic and cultural betterment of the area. In fact this ideological theme is as unimportant as the narrative element. *Spor* consists of three distinct groups of visual and aural images. The first, presented by Shat, describes man's destructive power and its effect on the Caucasus (*dymnye kelii, zheleznaya lopata, strashnyi put'*). The second, presented by Kazbek, is a colourful characterization of the slumbering peoples of the East (*pena sladkikh vin; uzornye shal'vary, tsvetnoi divan, zadumchivyi fontan, raskalennye stupeni*). The third group of images, provided by the narrator, describes the colours and sounds of the advancing army (*strannoe dvizhen'e*), followed by the emotional reaction of Kazbek (*tomim zloveshchei dumoi; polnyi chernykh snov; grustnyi vzor*). As in *Tri pal'my,* Lermontov's theme in *Spor* is man's destruction of natural beauty; the poet's method is the creation of vivid imagery.

Lermontov's most original literary ballad, *Tamara* (1841), is probably based on an old Georgian legend, although no immediate source has been identified. It tells the story of the beautiful princess Tamara whose seductive voice attracts travellers to her castle; there they are treated to a night of amorous delights while strange sounds echo through the forest. In the morning the only sounds are those of the roaring Terek carrying away the bodies of the hopeless victims and the sweet farewells of Tamara.

The tale is related in pure romantic Russian, with few folkloric expressions. The manuscript version in particular shows Lermontov's attempts to overcome the continuing influence of Zhukovsky's style. The setting of *Tamara* is mysterious and foreboding; the tower is described as *starinnaya, vysokaya,* and *tesnaya* (in the manuscript, as *ugryumaya* and *zubchataya*); it stands on a black cliff (*cherneya na chernoi skale*) overlooking a deep ravine. The visual details and the language of the landscape description closely resemble the settings in Zhukovsky's ballads.

The heroine of Lermontov's ballad, however, is unlike Zhukovsky's idealized Svetlanas and Minvanas (*Eolova arfa*). Tamara combines the principles of both good and evil. . . . Her supernatural charms are described as *vsesil'nye* (in the manuscript as *moguchie* and *volshebnye*); her power is *neponyatnaya.* The nights of passionate love are accompanied by *strannye, dikie zvuki,* the explanation for which again emphasizes the heroine's dual nature. . . .

The *mrak i molchanie* of the morning after replaced the original *glukhoe smerti molchan'e,* which is typical of Zhukovsky's style in its explicitness and in its choice of epithet. Similarly the *bezglasnoe telo* was originally described as *ch'e-to bezglasnoe telo,* the vague *ch'e-to* being another favourite Zhukovsky device. Lermontov eliminated the most imitative Zhukovsky-like elements from his final text, and the result is an original literary ballad, haunting and enigmatic. *Tamara* is, in a sense, Lermontov's own interpretation of the nature-magic theme treated by Zhukovsky in *Rybak* and by Pushkin in *Rusalka:* the attraction of the supernatural and the subordination of human will to higher powers. But in Lermontov's version the implicit ambiguity is made explicit in the nature of the heroine (good and evil) and in the consequences for the victims (love and death).

Lermontov's last literary ballad, *Morskaya tsarevna* (1841), treats the same nature-magic theme as *Tamara,* and is, in fact, a reworking of his own *Rusalka* (1832). Whereas in the earlier ballad both the narrative element and the theme are relatively unimportant when compared with the imagery, *Morskaya tsarevna* has both an engaging narrative and a meaningful theme. A young tsarevich, while bathing his horse in the sea, is invited by a mermaid to spend one night with her. The impetuous youth seizes the poor mermaid and pulls her ashore despite her angry protests. When his comrades rally to inspect his catch, instead of a beautiful creature, they discover only a scaly sea-monster muttering incomprehensible reproaches.

Once again Lermontov's theme is the mysterious attraction of supernatural beauty; however, instead of submitting to its power, man attempts to capture that beauty and to bring it back into his own world in order to exert his will over it and to preserve it. This attempt to master the supernatural is doomed to failure; the tsarevich remains *zadumchivyi,* and is left with only an image of the beautiful mermaid in his memory.

The language of the ballad is simple and dynamic; verbs tend to replace epithets as the principal means of description. . . . *Tamara* and *Morskaya tsarevna,* both written between May and July 1841, demonstrate Lermontov's success in overcoming what he perceived as the limitations of Zhukovsky's style.

While Lermontov's most original ballads are similar to Pushkin's inasmuch as they avoid the tendency to 'show off' their 'ancient lore', to 'put wild . . . sentiments in stilted eighteenth-century dialogue', and to 'revel in the . . . pathetic', they are not 'models' in the sense that Pushkin's ballads are, nor do they share the characteristics of the traditional folk genre. For Lermontov, the literary ballad was merely one available lyrical form, not *the* most fashionable genre in Russian poetry. When Belinsky wrote in 1843 that 'the reading of marvellous ballads no longer provides any pleasure, but produces apathy and boredom', his description of the demise of the genre was all too accurate.

John Garrard (essay date 1982)

SOURCE: "Lermontov and Posterity," in *Mikhail Lermontov,* Twayne Publishers, 1982, pp. 145-50.

[*In the essay below, Garrard summarizes Lermontov's literary legacy, his politics, and his contributions to Russian literature.*]

Lermontov's Legacy

Lermontov left a remarkable legacy for one who died so young. Scholars have traced echoes of his poetry in the works of later Russian poets, and such men as Alexander Blok and Boris Pasternak greatly admired him as a poet. He made his greatest impact on Russian literature as a

prose writer, however. Gogol was perceptive when he told his friend Sergey Aksakov that Lermontov would be a greater novelist than a poet. Had Lermontov lived longer, that might easily have been the case.

Tolstoy, Dostoevsky, and Chekhov were all influenced by Lermontov's prose. Tolstoy's descriptions of the Caucasus, his battle scenes, his satire against high society, all go back to Lermontov. Dostoevsky developed Lermontov's antihero and his interest in metaphysical questions. Both Tolstoy and Dostoevsky carried the psychological novel initiated by Lermontov to perfection. For Chekhov Lermontov was the great stylist, the writer of perfect stories.

Vladimir Fisher argues that toward the end of his life Lermontov had worked out his own style, the "best in Russian literature." "In comparison," he says, "Pushkin is archaic, Turgenev prosaic, Tolstoy and Dostoevsky ponderous, and Gogol incorrect" [Poetika Lermontova, 1914].

As Lermontov matured he gained a fuller perception of his own dilemma and that of his generation. Pechorin [in *Hero of Our Time*] was designed to shock the reading public into a recognition of the malady threatening to destroy Russian society.

I believe that Lermontov had completely fathomed the impact of the Byronic hero and its ultimate contradictions by the time he wrote his novel. The later emanations of the Byronic type continued well into the twentieth century, and their power and glamour were not so well understood by later generations. In his study *L'Homme révolté* [The Rebel, 1951], Albert Camus attempts to analyze the causes of state terrorism in Nazi Germany and Stalinist Russia by tracing the development since the eighteenth century of metaphysical rebellion, or what he calls "le crime logique" as opposed to "le crime de passion." Camus sees the history of the last two centuries as "the history of European pride." He traces that history through Milton's Satan, the Marquis de Sade, the Byronic hero (he refers to "the Romantic hero" and "the revolt of the dandies"), nihilism, and Dostoevsky's Ivan Karamazov to twentieth-century dictators who argue that individuals may be killed if need be in order to create a glorious future for all mankind.

It is of some interest that Camus quotes Lermontov rather than Byron, and finds in the Romantic period the beginnings of a fatal confusion between good and evil:

> In order to combat evil, the rebel, because he judges himself innocent, renounces good and creates evil once again. The Romantic hero introduces the profound and, one might say, religious confusion between good and evil.

The hero is outraged by injustice and by his inability to right the wrongs he sees around him: "The romantic hero feels compelled to do evil by his nostalgia for an unrealizable good. His excuse is sorrow." This formulation tells us much both about Lermontov himself and his hero.

Lermontov and Politics

Lermontov had the misfortune to grow up in the reign of Nicholas I. Young men like him belonged to a "lost generation" of the 1830s, a time when the exhilaration created by the French Revolution in Europe and the early liberal years of Alexander I's reign in Russia had been crushed. In fact, there is an interesting parallel between the mood in Russia and the gloom that pervaded French thought and literature after the restoration of the Bourbons in 1815. It is no accident that Byronism and the cult of Napoleon as romanticized liberator were most popular in France and Russia. The sociopolitical atmosphere in both countries was hospitable to the rebellious outsider who despaired of finding a constructive outlet for his talents.

The exact nature of Lermontov's political beliefs, as of his personality in general, has long been a matter of great controversy. During the nineteenth century, conservatives regarded him as a moral outcast: his own behavior and that of his hero Pechorin brought disrepute to the good name of Russia. Soviet scholars, for quite understandable reasons, have sought by and large to demonstrate that Lermontov was really a political liberal, if not a closet revolutionary.

I have tried to show [in my book *Mikhail Lermontov*] that this latter view cannot be sustained by the facts. Lermontov had an aristocrat's distaste for the herd. He was never a joiner, and all his instincts militated against association with such men as Alexander Herzen and other liberals of the time. Even in the 1830s, when he was out of favor with the authorities, Lermontov refused to engage in serious political discussions with the Decembrist exiles he met in the Caucasus. For example, Mikhail Nazimov recalls engaging in wide-ranging conversations with the poet but becoming irritated because he seemingly had no firm beliefs and refused to take reform proposals seriously. When Nazimov upbraided him for his flippancy and asked him for his evaluation of contemporary youth, Lermontov mockingly replied: "We have no direction at all; we just meet, have a good time, make our careers, and chase after women." As often as not their conversations ended with Nazimov upset and Lermontov enjoying his discomfort.

Far from being a political liberal, Lermontov was rather close to the Slavophile outlook, a point well made by V. D. Spasovich and developed in 1914 by N. L. Brodsky, who emphasizes the personal ties between Lermontov and the Slavophiles Vladimir Odoevsky, Aleksey Khomyakov, and Yury Samarin.

Lermontov and Literature

Lermontov's literary views are even more difficult to define. He was not a man of letters and never belonged to any literary groupings. Not much of his correspondence has survived, and what there is of it has little to say about literature. We do not have his library, and we do not know what he read, except for a few references in his poetry and prose. He wrote no literary criticism.

Orthodox Soviet critics have a ready-made framework into which they try to squeeze Lermontov. The literary equivalent of a political liberal or revolutionary is a Realist, so they bend every effort to show that Lermontov is a Realist. Much Soviet criticism on Lermontov is given over to the question of whether he moved from Romanticism to Realism or remained a Romantic to the end. Such a late prose character sketch as "Kavkazets" [The Caucasian], some maintain, marks Lermontov's advance along the "road to Realism." If so, what are we to make of the Romantic "Shtoss," written after "The Caucasian"?

It makes as little sense to term Lermontov a Realist as it is to call Gogol a Realist. For one thing, until the very end of his life, Lermontov continued to write poetry which dealt with the same subjects he had treated at the beginning. The crucial difference was that from 1837 on Lermontov wrote with vastly superior artistry. Both his prose and his poetry continued to be autobiographical, but now he probed more deeply and completely controlled his materials. It is clear also that Lermontov looked back coolly at his earlier Byronic enthusiasms. This new maturity is obvious in *A Hero of Our Time,* and also in his album verses **"Lyubil i ya v bylye gody"** [I Too Loved in Years Gone By], where he says he is now bored with the "noisy storms of nature" and the "secret storms of passions" described in "incoherent and deafening language."

No one can say how Lermontov might have developed as a writer. Like John Keats, who also died very young, Lermontov underwent a relatively long period of apprenticeship and displayed the same astonishing "self-corrective growth" demonstrated by Keats. It comes as a shock to realize that in speaking of Lermontov's mature period we are referring to works he wrote between the ages of twenty-two and twenty-six. If Dostoevsky and Tolstoy had died at the same age as Lermontov, they would scarcely merit a footnote in the history of Russian literature.

Dmitry Merezhkovsky once wrote that "Pushkin is the diurnal luminary and Lermontov the nocturnal luminary of Russian poetry." Halley's Comet flashed across the night sky of St. Petersburg on 13 November 1835, not long before Lermontov began his public career as a writer. Perhaps the metaphor of the comet best captures the impression he made upon his contemporaries and on later generations: brilliant but alarming, fleeting but unforgettable.

Anatoly Lieberman (essay date 1983)

SOURCE: "Lermontov as a Poet," in *Mikhail Lermontov, Major Poetical Works,* University of Minneapolis Press, 1983, pp. 8-22.

[*In the following essay, Lieberman studies Lermontov's poetics, demonstrating that the poet "became the first impressionist in the history of Russian letters."*]

Lermontov was confronted with the most difficult poetic task—to overcome the Pushkin canon (Eikhenbaum).

To be so dependent on Pushkin, so totally, so completely, so slavishly; and to shake off this dependence—this is where Lermontov's genius manifested itself

(Anna Akhmatova, as reported by Lidia Chukovskaya).

The enormous literature on Lermontov falls roughly into six groups.

1) *Biography*. In 1841 Lermontov's readers knew nothing at all about his life. Even several decades later, the political scandal associated with his name sealed many mouths. His letters were destroyed, and his friends kept their recollections to themselves. At the same time his enemies spoke often and readily. Thanks to the toil of scholars, we now know Lermontov's biography rather well (including a lot of details that he would rather not have divulged). However, Lermontov's last duel is partly wrapped in mystery, and the dates of his works often remain unclear. The life of no other Russian author has given such impetus to the detective genre as it flourishes in Lermontov studies. An investigator can read hundreds of pages, race from town to town, peruse voluminous archives, and so on, to learn only that the name of the lady in whose house Lermontov stayed two days is beyond recovery but that both of her daughters seem to have died unmarried.

2) *Textology*. This is a traditional and indispensable area. It plays a very important role in Lermontov's case, for he was indifferent to the fate of his manuscripts, and his poems usually lack a definitive text. Most of **The Demon** scholarship, for instance, consists in attempts to find such a text.

3) *Ideological interpretation*. Probably three-quarters of everything written on Lermontov falls under this rubric. Studies of Lermontov's religious views, moral attitudes, and political creed belong here. Every epoch and trend discovered in Lermontov what it needed, emphasizing in turn his mysticism, his atheism, his Slavophile bias, his dedication to Belinsky's cause and his influence on Belinsky, his melancholy, his militant spirit, his moral degradation, his tenderness and purity, or whatever. As a rule, Lermontov and his lyric hero have been treated as one person.

4) *Comparative literature*. Lermontov was a cultured man: He read poets in three European languages, apart from Russian, and his works are full of borrowings. Some of his predecessors played an outstanding role in his development. For years it was common to search for Lermontov's "sources." In the Soviet Union this practice came to an end with the official position that foreign influences on Russian authors are always questionable; also, Lermontov had been proclaimed a classic and as such was allowed a certain degree of independence. In recent years, sources of and parallels to Lermontov's work have again attracted some attention, and the *Lermontovskaya Èntsiklopediya* (1981) treats this subject with all the seriousness it deserves.

5) *Lermontov's artistic method*. Literary historians are seldom interested in literature itself. In Lermontov's case, they have always preferred to discuss his attitude toward his God, his monarch, and his female friends, rather than analyze his poetics. After reading hundreds of critical essays, one gathers the impression that Lermontov's principal merit is that he was very melancholy or very brave or very profound, that he sympathized with the mountaineers, loved liberty, and described the Caucasus. There are almost no works that question whether Lermontov was a great *poet* and whether his fame is deserved. Lermontov's contemporaries also treated his production in a strictly utilitarian way (for instance called it antipatriotic, immoral, etc.), and Belinsky, Lermontov's greatest supporter, was as utilitarian as any of them, only his approach was "progressive." The *Lermontovskaya Èntsiklopediya* is an important step forward.

6) *Popularization*. Lermontov is regularly studied in Soviet schools, colleges, and universities, and this fact has called forth numerous commentaries, bibliographies for teachers, children's editions, and the like. Here the most popular genre is a semischolarly book of the Great Lives type. A spate of monographs exists called *Lermontov,* but few of them are original.

[Elsewhere] I drew on the observations of various people, regardless of their main sphere of interest, but this article will be devoted entirely to one subject: Lermontov's poetics. Section B is the result of my own research, and the few scholars who are my direct allies have been cited in full. My view of Lermontov's style is the translator's view and differs considerably from what students of Russian literature find in manuals and textbooks.

A. The World of Lermontov's Lyric Hero

Lermontov's lyric hero, "'mid men a wanderer and stranger" and a plaything of fate, is strongly attached to this life and craves the love of women and the friendship of men. But the women of his choice seldom want him. Overweening and smug, or simply indifferent, if not callous, they pass him by. He is haunted by the fear that he will finish his days on a scaffold and is sure that his death will shake the world; then the woman he has loved will be exposed to the mob's wrath—but let her not curse his memory. Although uncertain of himself, he can arouse love, but he is unable to reciprocate the woman's feeling and brings about her sorrow or death. His friends are few. The worthiest of them die young, others forget him the moment he is out of sight. The feast of life is forever going on, and he pretends to be part of it, but he knows that he is a stranger at this feast—an unbidden, bored guest.

All is rootless and volatile around him. Attachments, passions, and people are like clouds in the sky: the wind drives them on, but no one can guess whether or from whence. Nothing in the world leaves a trace. Nor does he; his many travels are useless, because he has no destination. Far, very far away, his true homeland lies in all its beauty. Perhaps long ago he was there; he seems to remember that land, but to return to it he must die. If it were possible to combine life and death: to die and not become dust! Other opposites meet: all things are amusing and sad at the same time; when in love, we are cold, though our blood is afire; the very mineral spring in the Caucasus is boiling ice; but the union of life and death will never come about, for dead men either cannot respond to other people's love, or fail to find the oblivion without which Paradise is worse than hell.

Earthly existence is full of noises: each object gives forth a rasping sound of its own. "The music of heavenly grace" is stronger, but this music can at times be drowned out by the cacophony of life. Everyone the hero meets wears a mask. It is hard to live among puppets, but this masquerade is a blessing in disguise. What would happen if we started exposing our sores to view? The hero is at peace with himself only when his soul merges with nature and becomes part of the universe. Then, tears flow from his eyes, and these tears are like the gentlest, the sweetest strains of music.

Lermontov's hero is doomed to be a poet and a prophet. Although he is solitary and sad, he is ready to tell the world his message; but the rabble will not listen, and his only reward is a wreath of thorns. Sometimes his pent-up passions, his thirst for activity will break through, and then leopards are not stronger than he.

This is not a sketch of Lermontov's own character, but of the inner world of his hero. The most noticeable feature of this hero is that he has almost no points of contact with the world of men. In his dealings with men, repulsion largely prevails over attraction, and he is pushed to the outskirts of life. He retains the sharpness of his vision but is made to look at everything from a distance. Consequently, he always sees the whole better than details. It is my goal to show that, given the estrangement of Lermontov's lyric hero from his fellow men, Lermontov's poetic technique was the best possible.

B. Lermontov's Poetic Technique

At a technical level, half of the history of poetry is the history of the epithet, and nothing is more revealing in Lermontov's authorship than his use of the epithet. His texts are full of qualifying adjectives; in some poems there is one before each noun, but they are seldom informative. The sea in Lermontov's works is always blue, waves are also blue and constantly chase one another; sand is golden (and only golden), Chechens are angry, and horses raven black. Since in most cases Lermontov does not imitate folklore, these words lack the dignity of "fixed" epithets and sound repetitive and trivial. "Eternal" crops up in nearly half of his lyrics. Very many things are called mysterious (tale, saga, sadness, ideas, conversation, etc.), and what is not "mysterious" tends to be *besplódny* ('arid, barren, futile': science, struggle, soil, fields, Russia herself). Some epithets are downright puzzling. A dead girl's shoulders [**"The Terek's Gifts"**] are swarthy and pale at the same time. She has a fair-colored braid, but her head is white as snow. Teheran in **"The Debate"** dreams on a variegated divan before an emerald fountain, and an emerald fountain lulls the youth to sleep in the 1832 **"Wish."** Both times "an emerald fountain" must have been chosen

for the sake of its verbal appeal. In the original of **"Three Palms"** most epithets are redundant: hard humps (about camels), swarthy arms (about women), and the like. In **"The Terek's Gifts"** (discussed a few lines above) we come across such dubious embellishments as "a noble trickle of burning blood" (on the dead Cabardinian's head) and "a crimson trickle of blood" (on the dead Cossack girl). The more one reads Lermontov's lyrics, the clearer it becomes that the poet was often indifferent to the exact meaning of his epithets. They are either too hackneyed to add anything, or too vague. But, indifferent to the epithet, he was extremely sensitive to other elements (see below), so the picture would emerge unexpectedly good. As pointed out in Section A, Lermontov had no other choice than to observe life from the outside, and therefore he saw the whole rather than the many details. He did not care whether each of his strokes was justified, as long as he made the finished canvas tell a convincing tale. If a term is needed, we can say that Lermontov was an impressionist.

From time to time scholars have realized this all-important circumstance, but either because the term impressionist has been applied to Tyutchev, Fet, and Ánnenesky but not to Lermontov, or because it is unusual to find an impressionist so early—in an epoch usually typified by the question, "Romantic or Realist?"—the observations to this effect by several critics have hardly been understood, let alone developed.

In 1924 Eikhenbaum published his innovative book on Lermontov. In later days (until at least 1959, the year of Eikhenbaum's death), it was customary to treat this book with condescension; allegedly, it is full of Formalistic excesses (besides, Eikhenbaum had a low opinion of Belinsky's verbiage), which the distinguished author overcame in his subsequent works. In reality, strangled by a host of mediocre and self-seeking opponents, Eikhenbaum overcame his originality, his insights, and his intuition. Among other things, he said in 1924:

> Lermontov writes in formulas that seem to hypnotize the author himself: he no longer feels semantic shades and details in them, they exist for him as abstract speech blocks, as *alloys* of words and not as concatenations. He is interested in the general emotional effect, as if he presupposed a quick reader who would not stop at details of meaning and syntax but would seek only the impression of the whole. The semantic base of words and word groups begins to dim, but then their declamatory coloring (that of sound and emotion) begins to shine with unprecedented brilliance. This shift in the very nature of the poetic language, the change of the dominant from the effects inherent in sing-song declamational verse, is the main peculiarity, strength, and essence of Lermontov's poetics. Herein lies the cause of his fascination with lyric formulas and his attitude toward them as permanent clichés. And this is the source of some of Lermontov's expressions and phrases, which are hard to notice—so strong is the emotional hypnosis of his speech. [*Lermontov. A Study in Literary. Historical Evaluation*]

Soon after Eikhenbaum P. M. Bitsílli discovered the unusual quality of Lermontov's vision. If Eikhenbaum's book was dismissed as youthful folly, Bitsilli's article published in an emigrant edition remained quite unknown in the Soviet Union (even the 1981 *Lermontovskaya Èntsiklopediya,* which refers to non-Soviet sources in Russian, seems to have missed it). In Western works, too, references to it are incidental and rare. In my general evaluation of Lermontov, as is reflected in the Commentary, I am especially indebted to Bitsilli, whose analysis is deep, subtle, and to the point. Bitsilli's statements quoted below are a compression of several passages from his article.

> In the world open to our feelings he seems lost, as if he could not see and hear well. When he tries to write like everybody else, the result is such: beautiful granite, high breast, white arms, black eyes, heavy storm, tall plane tree, mighty Kazbék; and this is not only in his childish works: the last three examples are from his masterpieces of the mature epoch. But he is at home in the world of echoes, glimmers, shadows, and wraiths created by imagination in the half-light of dawn, in the mist; in his symbolism very important are such expressions as "shadows of traces," "shadows of feelings," "shadows of clouds," "an echo of Paradise"; and the words "mist," "clouds," and so forth turn up all the time. To attract his attention, concrete objects must be grand, dazzling, . . . but then he sees things that nobody seems to have seen before him: he sees waves "singing a lullaby to the shadow of the cliff," he sees "clouds, wrapped in the mist, embrace and, intertwined like a heap of snakes, dream carefree on their rock" and finds connections between properties and things that nobody had ever found before him. . . . What in anyone else would be an expression of weakness, awkwardness, lack of talent, in Lermontov . . . testifies to his strength, genius, the exclusiveness of his poetic nature. . . . Lermontov is like a person looking at the Earth literally from some "interplanetary" point of view. . . . He is able, as it were, to occupy a position exterior to himself. . . . Among us he is like a far-sighted man among myopics: he sees distant objects better than what is near. . . . When it comes to things that surround us, that are close and visible to others, he is *blind.* . . . When he is at a distance from this world, which is too narrow for him, when he flies over it, he sees it all in perspective; changing epochs, historical and cosmic, open up to him . . . ; he sees the way to "the unknown land,". . . . he waits for death in order to watch "a new world" that he has anticipated in his imagination. He treasures things around him, insofar as they are an image and likeness of the other world.

With time Lermontov's artistic method was studied less and less by literary historians. "Formalism" was wiped out and the greatest concern of a whole army of scholars became to show what a brave man Lermontov had been, how he had hated the Tsar and how the Tsar had hated him. As in all Soviet humanistic studies, the main focus was shifted to matters historiographic and pseudo-sociological. An important exception was a long and interesting article by Pumpyansky (who wrote an illuminating essay on Tyutchev in 1928). In places, the article is somewhat rambling, but its idea is worthy of every consideration. According to Pumpyansky, two themes dominate Lermontov's authorship: that of unfulfilled social activity (one might perhaps say "of thirst for action and of social frustration") and that of *naródnost'* relatedness to the people.

> Two different styles and two different patterns of his poetic speech correspond to these two main themes. Of course, there is no clear-cut chronological border; beginning with 1837, the second style becomes more noticeable, but some of the best works of the first style, e.g., "In Memory of Odoevsky," were written just in the very last years. Quite provisionally and with reservations we will define this first style as a style of inexact wording, a style that certainly does not go back to Pushkin; the second style we will call exact, but its relative proximity to Pushkin's stylistic norm is in no way a return to Pushkin, it is a phenomenon peculiar to Lermontov.

Examining the structure of **"Mother of God, I Shall Pray in Humility,"** he went on,

> Everything is insufficient and therefore requires immediate continuation, a hookup, a helping hand, for separate notions to be able to move all together. The unit of style is not the line of verse, and within the line not the word, as with Pushkin, but the movement of speech (though, naturally, this juxtaposition is not absolute; different styles can in general be only relatively different). . . . We can see quite a new, autonomous phenomenon, autonomous in the etymological sense of the word, i.e., conforming to its own Lermontovian law. After B. M. Eikhenbaum's 1924 work it is well known that this law came as a result of a special trend in Russian poetry as far back as the Twenties and is represented by Kozlóv, Podolínsky, and very many others; but this only confirms the fact that this style was historically determined.

It is of course the style of inexact wording, the style in which movement alone defines the poetic effect that can be called impressionistic.

To make our approach to Lermontov's poetic method more convincing, we can use a parallel from the sphere of comic art. Why is Gogol so irresistibly funny? His situations are either trivial (cf. the insignificant anecdotes that gave rise to *The Inspector General* and *Dead Souls*), or sad. The main source of merriment is his style. The stupid dialogue of his personages, the grotesque descriptions, and so on, make everything he wrote funny. Critics have been wondering for years what attracts readers to the seemingly shallow Oscar Wilde. To be sure, Oscar Wilde was not at all shallow, but his magnetism does not depend on his intellectual depth; its secret should be sought in the beauty of his language. Gogol's immortality has nothing to do with his attitude toward bureaucracy; similarly, Lermontov's appeal to many generations of people is not fed by his melancholy or his hatred of Pushkin's murderers, Many cursed bureaucracy and the palace clique, and even more people were solitary and unhappy and put their feelings into versified lines. Nobody remembers them today. Lermontov, as well as Gogol, as well as any author, survives only because he is a great master. Such a conclusion would be self-evident in the history of painting or music, but it usually shocks literary historians.

Impressionism was a perfect medium for a poet with Lermontov's psyche and fate. The difference between him and the French impressionists, for example, Monet and Pissarro, is that the Frenchmen were aware of their method and their rupture with tradition; therefore, they took pride in their innovations. Lermontov's aesthetics, i.e., a system of conscious views on literature, cannot be reconstructed (the few attempts known to me were not worth making), but he must have looked upon himself mainly as Pushkin's follower. He learned from Pushkin and Byron and respected his predecessors. But in spite of his admiration of and indebtedness to Pushkin, he was the very opposite of Pushkin (as Eikhenbaum and Pumpyansky quite correctly pointed out). Pushkin and Lermontov exist side by side in human memory and university syllabi, and, when they are juxtaposed, critics usually contrast them with regard to their temperament. The polarities are expressed in terms of day versus night, sun versus moon, peace versus rebellion, relentless thought versus inner feeling, etc. But the two are not different thinkers, philosophers, or lovers; they are different poets, and the opposition between them rests on their different approach to language.

Pushkin's epithet is varied and amazingly rich in overtones, but it is never ambiguous or imprecise. When Pushkin says in a lyric that a room is suffused with an amber light, he means exactly what he says, but when Lermontov writes that the eyes of his beloved are full of azure light [**"How Very Often at a Fashionable Ball"**], this pronouncement is not a statement of fact. First, "full of azure light" is simply a figure of speech, another way of saying "blue"; secondly, *azure* is one of Lermontov's favorite words, and he endows everybody he loves with azure eyes. Lermontov is a whole stage closer to the Symbolists than Pushkin. He does not yet speak of the "shadows of uncreated creatures" like Bryusov (though remember his "shadows of traces" and "shadows of feelings"!), but, as we have seen, almost everything he describes becomes misty and mysterious. The outlines of the objects he studies are often vague. Russian Symbolists worshiped Pushkin, but, consciously or unconsciously, they owed much more to Lermontov. Blok is the best but not the only example of the link between Lermontov and the Symbolists. Andrey Bely cites admiringly the "azure light" in *The First Encounter* ('Pervoe Svidanie'), and, indeed, in the amber light of Pushkin's poetics he would have felt too exposed and uncomfortable.

Lermontov's impressionism is also evident from his choice of subject-matter and treatment of "plots." He likes landscape and all kinds of descriptions. **"The Debate"** is outwardly a long piece about the conquest of the Caucasus, but the political issue and even the philosophical theme (man versus nature) is little more than a frame: the poem seems to have been written for the sake of the strikingly memorable descriptive passages. Another example is **"My Native Land"**. Again, it starts like a political lyric but after the first six lines becomes a beautiful—though slightly

sentimental—landscape. Even *Borodino* abounds in descriptions and is not quite what it pretends to be, i.e., a ballad of a great battle. A glance at Lermontov's poem addressed to Countess Rostopchina [**"To Countess Rostopchina"**] shows how naturally landscape takes over in his works. **"The Cliff"** (No. 79) is a masterpiece that could have been put to music by Debussy, and the dedication to Vorontsova-Dashkova [**"To a Portrait"**] one of the most elegant poems written in Russian, is a perfect impressionistic portrait (note that it was inspired by a picture that is in no way impressionistic). More than half of Lermontov's lyrics can be analyzed along similar lines.

If we admit that Lermontov was an impressionist, we will be able partly to explain the main riddle of his maturation. The riddle is known to everybody who has read the complete Lermontov. Between 1828 and 1837 he wrote thousands of lines (counting only lyrics, but there were also dramas, long narrative poems, and novels). In this juvenilia one runs against several gems, such as **"The Angel," "The Mermaid"**, and **"The Sail,"** and a half-dozen touching love lyrics, but most of it is stodgy and dull. Then suddenly something happened: he exploded in *The Poet's Death* and after that never produced a bad poem. Moreover, what he wrote was becoming better and better. Nothing is easier than to show that almost every line in Lermontov's mature works derives from some place in or even occurs in his early works, but in doing so we only make the riddle more insoluble: if everything is the same, then why are the early poems bad and the later ones good? I can think of few cases in which art cries louder to be explained in terms of art. Lermontov's miracle is his discovery and conscious use of his own poetic style, "the style of inexact wording." If he had written only *The Poet's Death,* **"Meditation,"** and so forth, he would have been another author like Ryléev, Khomyakóv, or even Odóevsky, though obviously more talented. Lermontov, the great Russian lyric poet (for the moment I am leaving out of discussion his narrative poems, especially *The Demon*), is first and foremost a master of "inexact wording." When he had realized his main strength and become aware of his limitations, that is, learned to avoid doing what he could not do well, he stopped composing bad poetry. Nearly all his best lyrics written before 1837 are impressionistic, and that is why they are good.

There is nothing unique in Lermontov's experience. Hans Christian Andersen produced mediocre novels for years and would never have written a book worth reading if he had not discovered that he could tell a fairy tale. Corot was fond of painting "realistic" portraits of women (which made him famous), and even Levitán tried his hand at portraiture. If both had persisted in their folly, the nineteenth century would have lost two of its greatest landscape painters. Lermontov, in spite of his Romantic apprenticeship, did not know what to do with a love story, and this is another proof of his impressionistic sympathies. By 1837 at the latest Lermontov had realized that he must leave the love genre to others. His avoidance of love lyrics was an important victory at a time when everyone wrote them. Impressionism in poetry is an effective vehicle for the most tender lyrics because it is not encumbered with the ballast of details. One of the peaks of Lermontov's lyricism is his poem **"In Memory of A. I. Odoevsky."** On the face of it, the poem is about a dead friend, but this is almost an illusion. Only the beginning is really about Odoevsky; all the rest is about someone with azure eyes who had a warm and kind heart but was not spared by God or men, who died surrounded by callous fools and whose grave is in a beautiful corner of the earth. Part of it is the same as *The Poet's Death,* part is close to the later **"All Alone Along the Road I Am Walking,"** half is transposed from other poems. **"In Memory of A. I. Odoevsky"** is so good just because it is not a biography of any concrete man. Scholars are apt to apologize for Lermontov's habit of transferring lines and entire passages from poem to poem, but the essence of Lermontov's method was writing in lyric formulas, as Eikhenbaum called them, in huge blocks, and it is no wonder that those formulas (of any length) were transferable.

In a historical perspective, two important questions arise: (1) What makes Lermontov a great author if so many of his lines are traceable to somebody else? (2) How did he survive as a poet when behind him was Pushkin, who eclipsed all his contemporaries, and before him were such giants as Blok, Pasternak, Akhmatova, Mandelshtam? Actually, this is one question split into two. The answer can be given only if we realize the full extent of Lermontov's originality. As mentioned above, he was not a follower of Pushkin: he was a new page in Russian poetry. Anyone who tried "to follow" Pushkin suffered an immediate and dismal defeat, for there was nothing left for such a poet to do after Pushkin (compare Schubert's complaint, "Beethoven has done it all!"). Lermontov says everything in his own way. Even when he repeats somebody's words, it matters little, because the familiar phrase becomes part of a different system and is almost impossible to recognize. It has taken critics more than a hundred years to notice that part of line 33 [in] **"A Branch from Palestine"** is a direct quotation from Pushkin's *Bronze Horseman (prozrachny sumrak)*. Lermontov's lyric poetry is a perfect unity of content and form: his impressionism was ideally suited to his message. Those who imitated him neither felt nor realized this fact: they parroted his formulas without sharing the peculiarities of his vision and invariably looked banal, approximately as a well-meaning professor of botany could if he set out to faithfully copy Monet. In Bitsilli's words, "what in anyone else would be an expression of weakness, awkwardness, lack of talent, in Lermontov testifies to his strength, genius, the exclusiveness of his poetic nature."

Recognizing Lermontov's method is only the first step toward understanding him, because impressionism is too general a term. So far I have spoken of Lermontov's choice of words, specifically of epithets. Equally important are his technical predilections manifested in his syntax and metrics. I will barely touch on this subject, for neither a poet's syntax nor his metrics (let alone rhythm) can be studied in translation. The most important statements have been made by Eikhenbaum and Pumpyansky, both of whom have pointed out that the main unit of Lermontov's style is not the line of verse, and within the verse not the word, but the movement of speech.

Lermontov was very sensitive to the metrical arrangement of his lyrics, as could be expected from a poet who depended to such an extent on the movement of speech. Even in his earliest works he often experimented with unusual meters, but at that time the four-foot iamb remained his main medium. The situation changed after 1837, and one of the most important features of his mature style is great metrical variety. Almost every piece contains some novelty.

Yuly Aikhenval'd once remarked that Lermontov had a perfect ear. This is only partly true. To many things he was surprisingly deaf. Thus, he often did not hear jarring sound combinations in his lines, something like '*vnimál v nemóm* blagogovénii' [**"The Poet"**]; such examples are rather numerous. He was indifferent to rhyme. It is good in his long narrative poems (in which his impressionism all but disappears) and unimaginative in his lyrics, but he took infinite care to organize a convincing and mellifluous whole. He was fond of parallel and symmetrical constructions, of mathematically exact antitheses, and pointed aphorisms at the end and resorted to the subtlest effects. Thus, at the beginning of *Tamara* the castle blackens on a black rock and at the very end something whitens from its window; at the beginning of **"The Mermaid"** the water maiden swims along a lightblue river, and in the finale the river is dark blue (I was unable to render the difference between *golubaya* and *sinyaya* in translation). He used to the full the force of anacrusis, the beauty of trochee and dactyl, the power of an unusual strophe (as in [**"In Memory of A.I.O . . ."**]), the charm of multiple alliterations and recurring vowels. All these things he "heard." His ear was selective, and his goal directed his choices.

One of the traditional questions of Lermontov scholarship is whether he was a Romantic or a Realist. His development was not unlike Pushkin's (from "The Gypsies" to *Evgeny Onegin*) or Byron (from *Childe Harold* to *Don Juan*). Lermontov began with Romantic lyrics and ended up with *A Hero of Our Time* and the confession to Karamzina; but *Mtsyri* (No. 91) and *Tamara* (No. 82) are equally late, and he kept working on his most romantic poem *The Demon* (No. 92) until 1839. At one time it was usual in Soviet criticism to praise Lermontov for his shift to realism, because realism was supposed to be a higher stage of literary evolution than Romanticism (Romanticism, "critical" realism, "socialist" realism). At present it is more customary to recognize the importance of Lermontov's Romanticism, though no conclusion has been reached as to how to classify *A Hero of Our Time*. The debate is scholastic (like all classificatory debates) and is fed by the indeterminacy of the main terms. The worst of them is *realism,* which is made to cover the phantasmagorical images of Gogol, Dickens's freaks, and Dostoevsky's devil, along with the dullest creations of fifth-rate authors, provided they are lifelike; but Romanticism is an equally vague term, and long ago Pushkin wondered what it meant.

For our evaluation of Lermontov's way we can easily do without definitions, but we have to distinguish between

Romanticism as an approach to literature and art (philosophy) and Romanticism as a system of devices (style). Romanticism in its philosophical aspect is a victory of beauty and grandeur over ugliness and filth. It is a longing for the ideal and a superhuman attempt to find it. Romanticism normally accompanies transitional epochs and looks for a golden age—sometimes in the future, sometimes in the past. All religions and social utopias, as long as they offer a picture of Paradise, are children of the Romantic spirit.

Lermontov remained a militant Romantic all his life. As a literary movement, and more precisely, as a nineteenth-century movement, Romanticism had its favorite subjects, imagery, and devices. The devices included specific epithets and similes, recurring references, and so on. All of this is too well known to need recapitulation. This stylistic framework played its role and underwent utter degradation at the hands of epigones. Soon after the triumphs of the great masters it became common property, divorced from the spirit that had given it birth. Few literary movements knew such a speedy and catastrophic rupture between the original content and the hopelessly vulgarized form. No one with any aesthetic sense could have remained faithful to the conventional Romantic style after it had deteriorated into a set of clichés, totally predictable and mechanically reproduced. Romanticism, like many a trend before and after, was killed by the accessibility of its form. Pushkin was aware of it (hence his Lensky). Lermontov was aware of it, too. He was sorry that the style he loved had become ludicrous and renounced pseudo-Romantic phraseology but not Romanticism. His lifelong loyalty to the method that gave the world Byron and Delacroix is not fortuitous, for nineteenth-century Romanticism, with its taste for generalized descriptions in literature and contrasting masses of color in painting, is closer to Symbolism and impressionism than realism in its classic form ever was, and thus served as a good school and a proper source of inspiration for the poet who became the first impressionist in the history of Russian letters.

Nina Diakonova (essay date 1988)

SOURCE: "Byron and the Evolution of Lermontov's Poetry 1814-1841," in *Renaissance and Modern Studies*, Vol. 32, 1988, pp. 80-95.

[*Below, Diakonova shows how Byronism affected Lermontov's artistic development.*]

As an influence in the artistic development of Lermontov, Byron comes second only to Pushkin. This is a point that has been taken for granted by scholars both old (N. Storozhenko, V. Spasovich, A. Veselovskij, E. Djushen, M. Rozanov, S. Shuvalov, N. Dashkevich) and new (B. Ejkhenbaum, V. Zhirmunskij, L. Grosman, N. Brodskij, B. Tomashevskij, A. Fedorov, M. Nol'man, K. Chernyj). The latter have convincingly proved that the Russian poet's Byronism was part of the Byron-worship characteristic of Russian letters and culture in the days of reaction preceding

and following the defeat of the Decembrists' attempt, in 1825, to break down the autocracy of the crown and liberalise its policy.

In the period before the beginning of a wider and more democratic opposition to the rulers of the Russian Empire, Byronism came to be the embodiment both of tragic disappointment with the prospects of immediate liberation and of heroic stoicism—of staunch refusal to submit to official ideology and to accept defeat as final.

It was precisely the blend of 'titanic despair' (Belinskij) with violent protest against oppression and active participation in the world's battles for freedom that attracted progressive Russians to Byron's poetry and all it stood for. Of the many poets of the romantic movement which swept through Europe he alone would not seek solace in religion or any of the ethic and aesthetic utopias the romantics abided by; he scoffed at their high-souled idealism and particularly at their illusions concerning the infallibility of the priest-like functions of art. The conflicting tensions between profound disillusionment and unceasing striving for revolutionary action on whose results Byron did not pin much hope, clearly expressed the divided mentality of the thinking few confronting an unlovely age.

Thus Byronism became an important element in Lermontov's general outlook and aesthetics. But its impact was different in each of the periods of his evolution.

I: The earliest period (1828-1829).

This is the period of first youthful endeavours—he started writing when he was fourteen. By that time he was well-read in Russian poetry. Not only had he devoured Pushkin, Zhukovskij, Griboedov, Baratynskij, Rylejev, but also minor poets, particularly those who translated and imitated Byron. As Lermontov did not know English in his adolescence, his first knowledge of Byron came to him partly through French prose translations but mostly through numerous Russian poetical translations (Zhukovskij's *Prisoner of Chillon*, 1822; Kozlov's *Bride of Abydos*, 1826; Verderevskij's *Parisina*, 1827), as well as through Byron-inspired poems by Kozlov, Podolinskij and others.

The impression made by these poems on the youthful imagination of Lermontov was, however, modified by the tremendous influence of Pushkin, both direct, through his Byronic poems (*Kavkazskij plennik* [*The Prisoner of the Caucasus*] of 1820-1821, *Brat'ja razbojniki* [*The Robber-Brothers*] of 1821-1822, *Bakhchisarajskij fontan* [*The Fountain of Bakhchisaraj*] of 1823 and *Tsygany* [*The Gypsies*] of 1824), and indirect, for he had influenced Lermontov's other models.

The large number of verbal coincidences between the texts of Pushkin's poems (as well as those of his followers) and the texts of Lermontov's youthful works (**"Cherkesy"** [**"The Circassians"**], 1828; **"Kavkazskij plennik,"** 1828; **Korsar"** [**"The Corsair"**], 1828; **"Prestupnik"** [**"The Criminal"**], 1828; **"Dva brata"** [**"The Two Brothers"**], 1828) illustrate the heaviness of his debt to Pushkin's Byronics.

The draft copies of the young poet's early efforts have come down to us and testify to the deliberation and care taken during his apprenticeship: he actually started by copying Pushkin's *The Prisoner of the Caucasus* and Zhukovskij's *The Prisoner of Chillon*. He then rewrote the poems in his own way, generally supplying them with ends even more lugubrious than those of his models: in the former poem, for example, he passed a death sentence not only upon the heroine but also upon the hero.

II: The second period (1830-1835).

In the autumn of 1829 Lermontov started to learn English by reading Byron and was never to be seen without a large volume of his works under his arm. This must have been the one-volume edition published by Thomas Moore (*The complete works of Lord Byron. Including his suppressed poems with others never before published,* Paris, 1830). In fact, this was also the first edition to contain *Stanzas to Augusta* and *Epistle to a Friend.* Lermontov imitated the first and translated the second; neither of these lyrics had appeared in the one-volume editions of 1826-1829.

In the poems of 1830-1831, starting with **"Dzhulio"** [**"Julio"**], **"Litvinka"** (**"The Lithuanian"**) and **"Ispoved"** (**"The Confession"**), the direct influence of Byron can be traced. There is, for instance, an obvious similarity between the description of the hero in the latter's *The Corsair* (I, xi) and the following description in **"Litvinka"** 'Before, he, too, despised men, but then from a madman he became wicked. What else could he be with his keen mind and fiery heart?'

Lermontov's **"Azrail"** and **"Angel smerti"** (**"The Angel of Death"**) of 1831 owe a great deal to Byron's *Cain* and *Heaven and Earth.* Like the characters of the famous Mysteries, Azrail is beautiful, immortal and doomed to solitude. In the first stanza of "Angel smerti" there are also reminiscences of Byron's *The Giaour:* 'Oh, golden East, land of wonder, love and voluptuousness . . . where all is plentiful but happiness . . . and the world retains all the charm of the days when . . . the stamp of evil had not dishonoured the soul of man'. Not a word of this can be said to render Byron literally, but the general tone and the contrast of peaceful nature and wicked man are much the same.

In his poem concerning Adzhi the Avenger (**"Kally,"** 1830-1831), whom injustice turned into an outlaw, Lermontov imitates *The Giaour* and *The Corsair.* In his **"Aul Bastundzhi"** (**"The Mountain Village of Bastundzhi"**), 1833-1844, there is no likeness in the plot to any specific poem by Byron, but the tale of a love that is stronger than death and becomes the cause of death certainly goes back to his Oriental tales.

Of Lermontov's early Byronic poems **"Izmail-Bey"** (1832) is of the greatest interest. Its plot is more original than that of his other poems and the *motif* of vengeance makes a far more integral part of the liberation theme than, say, in Byron's *Lara.* The story of the heroine who, disguised as a man, serves her lover under the name of Selim, repeats the story of Gulnare-Kaled in *The Corsair* and *Lara.* The essentially Byronic nature of Izmail himself and his affinities with the famous characters of the English poet have also been commented on. Thus, Lermontov's references to him as one who had been deceived by the world in which he had trusted too much and one who had come to despise the traitors (III, x) is very close to Byron's characterisation of the Corsair: 'Warped by the world in disappointment's school . . . Doomed by his very virtues for a dupe' (I, xi).

Curiously enough, even in this very early poem Lermontov is not an entirely slavish pupil: his Izmail 'despised the world' while the Corsair only cursed his own 'virtues as the cause of ill'. Lermontov also breaks up the monotonous regularity of Byron's verse; besides, his tale of the *mores* of Caucasian tribes, though very much in the style of Byron's stanzas on the Albanians in *Childe Harold* (II, 65-68), introduces more local colour than his master did.

Besides thematic, psychological and particularly verbal borrowings from Byron (such as, for example, the dramatic end of Izmail: 'Let him finish life as he began it, alone' which is an echo of Manfred's words: "I'll die as I have lived, alone', Act III, Sc. 4), Lermontov imitated the structure of the English poet's Oriental tales: dramatic struggle for love or vengeance as the central motif of the poem, the intensity of the passions agitating the protagonists, their exotic background, the predominance of lyrical subjectivism over merely epic elements, the prevalence of striking and uncommon situations over ordinary ones. All these Byronic structural devices were adopted by Lermontov in **"Izmail-Bey"** and other early poems. He emphasised his closeness to the English poet by attaching epigraphs from the latter's poems to *Kally* [from *The Bride of Abydos*], to **"Izmail-Bey"** [from *The Giaour* and *Lara*], among others.

After 1833 Lermontov wrote fewer Byronic poems. But among them **"Khadzhi Abrek"** (1833) stands out. Like its predecessors, it resembles *The Giaour,* the heroine bearing the name of Byron's Leila; but instead of two dead bodies, Lermontov produces three, including that of the hero. The poem **"Bojarin Orsha"** (**"The Nobleman Orsha"**), 1835-1836, follows *Parisina* in describing a passion that becomes the cause of a fierce conflict with society; Orsha's harsh judgment over his daughter and her lover reminds one of Lambro's on a similar occasion (*Don Juan,* IV, 47-50), and the hero's desertion of his own people is easily associated with the renegade misdeeds of *Alp* (*The Siege of Corinth*).

Whatever Byron's influence on Lermontov's poems of the thirties may have been, the Russian poet was beginning to outgrow his model. In **"Bojarin Orsha,"** the protagonist, as distinct from Byron's, does not deal in crime; his struggle to win love is much more closely linked with his struggle for freedom. The characters are depicted against a more clearly defined historical background. While following Byron in his taste for 'noble robbers', like Selim or Conrad, who make their vengeance part of their liberation, Lermontov leaned even more heavily on the poetry of those Decembrists who had glorified the deeds of heroic leaders of popular uprisings.

Iraklij Andronikov's *Lermontov. Issledovanija i nakhodki* (Moscow, 1977) argues that Lermontov's interest in social anthropology took him beyond Byron's rather abstract Orientalism. In his early historical novel *Vadim* (1833-1834), Lermontov draws mostly upon Walter Scott's and Victor Hugo's works, though reminiscences from Byron's crop up now and again. One example is to be found in the description of Olga, the heroine. Lermontov calls her an angel banished from Paradise for having grieved too much for men. This comes very close to Byron's lines about Aurora who 'looked as if she sat by Eden's door / And grieved for those who could return no more' (*Don Juan*, XV, 45). Note also the likeness between:

Byron

He shouted Allah! And saw Paradise
. . . With prophets, houris, angels,
    saints described
In one voluptuous blaze—and then
    he died
But with a heavenly rapture on his
    face.

            (*Don Juan*, VIII, 115-116).

Lermontov

He smiled when dying and saw, perchance,
    the maid of paradise coming
down to him, waving a rainbow-like crown
            ("Khadzhi-Abrek," 55-59).

The most interesting part of *Vadim* is that which has little in common with Byron: the presentation of the popular uprising that Vadim supports possesses local and historical specificity. There are elements of truth to national character in Lermontov's popular heroes, while Byron's either stand for abstract heroism, like the Maid of Saragossa (*Childe Harold*, I, 54-56), or as embodiments of abstract Rousseauism, like the Chamois Hunter in *Manfred*.

The same tendency to originality is characteristic of Lermontov's lyrical poetry. Byron's influence decreases by the mid-thirties, but remains powerful in the earlier thirties. Under Nicholas I Byronism had become a synonym of sorrowful and rebellious thought. The English poet's protest against political and national oppression, his glorification of any fight for liberation, his contempt for the ruling classes, their prejudices and traditions, his enthusiasm for nature and the world of natural feeling, his disappointment with men and women, with love and friendship, all these features we associate with Byron are characteristic of Lermontov's early lyrics.

The inner world revealed in his poetry is also very close to Byron's. None knew it as well as Lermontov himself: 'Our souls are one; our sufferings are the same' ("K***. **Ne dumaj chtob ja byl dostoin sozhalen'ja"** - "To***. **Do not think I deserve regret,"** 1830). The reason, most obviously, is the similarity of their biographies and their characters: both belonged to old aristocratic families, both were from infancy involved in domestic tragedies, both were lonely as boys, the one unhappy about his lameness, the other about his looks, both suffered from early unrequited love and the subsequent marriages of their respective beloveds, both were exiles for their political poetry, both died far away from home.

Of course, Lermontov never had the opportunity of doing, saying and even writing the things Byron did; he was an officer of junior rank, his life was one of constant repositing, he could easily be disgraced and imprisoned for life, he could not leave his country and could in no way join either the attempted revolution of the Italian Carbonari or the revolt of the Greek insurgents. And yet, his pride, his resolute refusal to conform to received opinions, customs and beliefs, his longing for activity, for feats of courage, for civic and military glory, his continuous endeavours to conceal his real self under the mask of a cynical dandy and daredevil, his capacity for self-analysis, all these are very similar to Byron's.

The two poets were alike in the very inconsistency of the mentality revealed in their writings; in the poetry of both we find an odd assortment of violent passions and coldly rational analysis, of striving for action coupled with a fatalistic sense of doom, of scorn of high life while keenly sensing himself part of it.

Nowhere can the likeness between the two poets be observed more clearly than in their love lyrics where love is presented as an all-powerful emotion conducive to bleakest grief as well as to utter bliss. It is in these lyrics that the stylistic affinity between the poets stands revealed most completely: flights of oratory, taste for hyperboles, antitheses, for absolutes destroying all shades and fine distinctions, for aphoristic sententiousness, no less than such formal characteristics as habitual use of five-feet iambics with male rhymes and three-syllable measures. All these characterise both Lermontov and Byron. As A. Fedorov's *Lermontov i literatura jego vremeni* (Leningrad, 1967) correctly argues, the study of Byron in the original helped the younger poet to rid himself of the clichés of sentimental diction (p. 318).

Lermontov's manner of assimilating his senior's experience can be studied through his numerous attempts to adapt Byron's verse to the Russian language. He started in 1830 with prose versions of Byron's *Darkness (T'ma)*, three fragments of *The Giaour, Napoleon's Farewell* and a few lines from *Beppo*. But it is, naturally, poetic translations which claim the greatest interest. What is of interest here is that they are infinitely closer in spirit to Lermontov's original poetry than any of his translations from other poets.

In 1830 the poet translated Byron's *Farewell! If ever fondest prayer . . .* under the title **"Farewell."** The translation is very close (save the concluding lines of the second stanza to which he found himself unequal). In the same year Lermontov translated the ballad of the *Black*

Friar interpolated between stanzas 40 and 41 in Canto XVI of *Don Juan*. He observed its general style, rhythm and metre, though he considerably shortened it. Finally at about the same time, Lermontov composed **"V Al'bom"** (**"Entry in an Album"**) where he characteristically combined his own original verses (first stanza) and a translation from Byron's *Lines Written in an Album, at Malta:* the simile that opens Byron's first stanza concludes the second in Lermontov's poem. Considerably later, in 1836, he returned to this poem and achieved greater closeness to the original and greater mastery. It was then that he began to produce real masterpieces of the art of translation which, in their turn, became at the same time choice examples of the Russian lyric. These are **"Dusha moja mrachna"** (**"My soul is dark"**), **"Umirajushchij gladiator"** (*The dying gladiator—Childe Harold*, IV, 139-140).

In 1831 Lermontov did not so much translate Byron as imitate him. Two of his poems—**"U nog drugikh ne zabyval"** (**"At the feet of others I did not forget"**) and **"Podrazhanije Bajronu"** (**"Imitation of Byron"**)—are three times shorter than their originals and do not contain a single line that exactly echoes Byron (the model of the first was *Stanzas to a lady on leaving England,* the second was *Epistle to a Friend*). The paradox is that in rendering Byron Lermontov discovered himself as a poet. Altering and re-shaping the English poet's works was his way of studying the art of poetry. He never considered publication of these early efforts and it is sometimes difficult to draw the line between his variations on Byron's themes and his own lyrical experiments.

The philosophic and often abstract nature of Lermontov's lyrical poetry, his reflections on man and God, on the universe and its laws, his religious doubts are all part of a wide European context with Byron playing first fiddle. Lermontov voiced Cain-like questions concerning the wisdom of God: 'If the Creator meant us to live in meek ignorance, he would not fill our souls with unattainable desires' (**"Kogda b v pokornosti neznan'ja"**, 1831) or 'I did not love heaven though I wondered at boundless space and envied its creator' (**"Otryvok—A Fragment,"** 1831). Lermontov's **"Smert'"** (**"Death,"** 1830/1831), **"Noch' I"** and **"Noch' II"** (1830), with their hatred of unavoidable dissolution and of the cruelty of the one who so ordained it, are also inspired by Byron. So are the reflections on those who would wish 'to take the whole of nature in their breast and with their suffering and their proud victory over all that is earthly buy the boundless freedom of the divine soul'(**"Unylyi kolokola zvon"**—**"The Dismal Chimes of Bells,"** 1830-1831).

Having accomplished his independence after the early thirties, Lermontov became less given to scepticism than Byron. He can be said to have belonged to a different, rather more religiously oriented stage of philosophic development, which brought him in touch with Russian philosophical poetry (the *ljubomudry*) and with German idealism.

III: The last period (1836-).

After 1836 Byron's influence upon Lermontov loses its decisive role and, though still to be felt, is accepted in an increasingly critical spirit. The change is manifest in the transformation of Lermontov's epic tales. Byron's rather abstract admiration of lands untouched by European civilisation in the work of the Russian poet grows into an absorbing interest for the Caucasus as a definite historical and ethnographical reality. Something of this attitude, we know, showed in his earlier Caucasian tales, but is much more characteristic of his last works, both in poetry and in prose.

Lermontov's 'Byronic hero' achieves a new stage in *Mtsyri* (1839-1840). The eponymous hero is, as many scholars have pointed out, as much a refutation of the egotistically haughty individualism of Conrad and Lara as a triumph, in the teeth of defeat, of a noble, no longer anti-social love of freedom. Torn from his natural surroundings, from the activities natural to him and the people he belongs to, Mtsyri sacrifices his life in the attempt to join them. That attempt was doomed to failure, for he was a victim of a weakness born in the metaphysical prison that was, in reality, a monastery. Mtsyri thereafter became a romantic symbol of the tragedy of several generations of the Russian intelligentsia who found themselves unable to fight the battle for freedom.

Far more complex than in Lermontov's earlier work was the interrelation of his art with that of Byron in his most famous poem *The Demon* (1829-1839). It was later turned into an opera by Anton Rubinstein and rendered on to canvas by Mikhail Vrubel'. The history of a fallen angel was suggested by other sources: Milton's *Paradise Lost,* Alfred de Vigny's *Eloa,* Thomas Moore's *Love of the Angels*. Nevertheless, Lermontov's treatment of the central character differs from that of his predecessors. His Demon is not so much a spirit of evil as an embodiment of suffering. Of Byron's works it is certainly Cain that is the main source of *The Demon:* a spirit powerful and rebellious, melancholy and haughty, one clearly modelled on Lucifer. His great vow (Part II, 10) was at least partly inspired by the grandiloquent vow-like speeches of Cain himself ('All the stars of heaven,/The deep blue noon of night' . . . , etc.) and Lucifer ('No! by heaven, which He / Holds, and the abyss, and the immensity / Of worlds and life' . . . —Act II, sc. 2)—as well as, one might add, by the final words of the archangel Raphael in *Heaven and Earth:* 'I loved him—beautiful he was: oh heaven! / Save him who made, what beauty and what power / Was ever like to Satan's?' (Part I, sc. 3).

The complex nature of Byron's impact upon *The Demon* is obvious in the fact that literary influence goes together with the huge impression that the popular interpretation of Byron's personality made on Lermontov. This interpretation is eloquently voiced in a poem by Alphonse de Lamartine, a poet whom Lermontov knew very well and often recited. In his *Méditations poétiques,* 1820, the second is devoted to Byron: *L'Homme. À Lord Byron.* The author compares Byron to Satan whose glance has measured the depth of abysses; his domains are in the heart of night and horror; his soul is remote from the light of day and God, he has bidden an eternal farewell to hope and he sings but the god of evil. Such is the lot of man: a fallen

God, he remembers heaven; a slave, he is born for freedom. Lamartine calls upon Byron, the poet of hell, to send his songs to heaven and, like the child of a divine race, like an eclipsed ray of heavenly splendour, like a fallen angel soar on his wings from the depths of eternal shadows.

The concept of the Demon, a fallen angel longing for the lost bliss of Paradise and light, whose soul is equally open for the best and the worst, has something in common with Lamartine's portrait of Byron. Lermontov's presentation of the profound humanity of his Demon has a great deal to do with Lamartine's association of Lucifer with his creator, thus emphasising the satanic features of the poet and the human traits of his character.

The demonic figure to whom Lermontov kept returning all through the thirties clearly shows the poet's development away from an ardent and uncritical admirer of Byron. We see him reformulating his conception to new, independent purposes.

That independence makes itself felt in the way Lermontov made use of *Don Juan* and *Beppo* whose significance he realised only in his later years. Following his own insights, he went beyond his source's romantic poems. Even then he did not entirely free himself from Byron's experience or from Pushkin's transformations of it in *Evgenij Onegin, Domik v Kolomne (A Little house in Kolomne),* but his attitude to it is more detached. Lermontov's fragment of the *Skazka dlja detej (Fairy-story for children,* 1839-1841), the introductory stanzas of the poem *Sashka* (1835-1839) describing the hero's upbringing, the lengthy digressions *à propos de rein* throughout the poem, the reflections on literary subjects, numerous parenthetical remarks, mostly ironical, are all typical of Byron's satirical vein. So, too, are the parody of romantic clichés, the 'low' metaphors and similes, the predilection for details of 'low life' and, correspondingly, low colloquial diction along with conversational syntactic patterns, a comical abuse of archaic turns of speech and quotations. All these features are common both to Lermontov's and Byron's comic poems. In his portrayals of unadorned reality the former even outdoes the latter but hardly ever attempts to compete with him in the universality and historical awareness of his presentation of various aspects of modern civilisation. . . .

It seems safe to conclude that although after 1836 Lermontov did not overcome Byron's influence, he depended on it less. Lermontov's later lyrics are more intimately personal, more confessional, more deeply individualised psychologically, better motivated and more deeply rooted in specific situations than Byron's. They present a peculiar blend of lyrical and political emotion, of protest and suffering. They are also expressed with far greater brevity and simplicity, are more close to the spoken language. Whatever Byron's innovations—in his satires, in romantic epics, in the subjectivity of his lyrics—his verse and his language are within the range of accepted conventions (*Don Juan* being the only exception to that rule). The persona in the greater part of his poetry is invariably himself, 'a man of mystery and doom'; his language is essentially in keeping with the language of classical tradi-

tion (to which he invariably gave his theoretical support even while he departed from it).

For Lermontov classicism is a thing of the past; it has nothing to do with the present. It was the least classical of Byron's works that impressed him most: *Darkness, The Dream,* the Mystery plays. His more progressive philosophy, as distinct from Byron's, indicated a complete break with the Enlightenment; he had none of Byron's belief in the power of reason, his Demon would never repeat with Lucifer: 'Nothing can / Quench the mind, if the mind will be itself / And centre of surrounding things—'tis made / To sway . . . ' (*Cain,* Act I, sc. 1). While sharing Byron's doubts, Lermontov, in accordance with the new spirit of the age in philosophy, tends to seek for answers in religion; this is obvious in his three **"Molitvy" ("Prayers").**

The moral ideas of Lermontov in the last years of his life also differ from Byron's. Though both loathe the cant and hypocrisy of their age and defy public opinion, Byron's views are, to the end, more conventional: he would never make a prostitute the heroine of his poem as Lermontov does in *Sashka.* (It is not without irony that he gives her the name of Thyrza, a name appearing in a number of Byron's most poetic lyrics).

In two of his pieces, two versions of the same subject, (**"Prelestnitse," ["To a lovely woman"],** 1832 **"Dogovor" ["A Contract"],** 1841), Lermontov quietly and coldly speaks of his joyless union with a woman scorned by everybody—and scorns that scorn. Byron describes one whose 'vows are all broken', whose fame is light and shares in her shame (*When we two parted*). For Byron (except for *Don Juan*), despite that lack of any illusion so clearly demonstrated in his comic poems and his prose, the object of his passion and, accordingly, the passion itself are associated with tragedy and poesy; with Lermontov both feelings and the manner of their wording are more simple and prosaic.

One of Byron's last lyrics, often called his last—*On this day I complete my 36th year*—is remarkable for lofty heroics, stilted diction, elevated metaphors, involved syntax and abstractions. It stands in striking contrast to one of Lermontov's last poems **"Vykhozhu odin ja na dorogu" ("I come out alone on to the road,"** 1841) where all is simple, quiet, subdued, sadly resigned and penetrated with religious feeling.

In making his persona a simple soldier (**"Borodino,"** 1837), a lower rank officer (**"Zaveshchanije" ["A Testament"],** 1840) and **"Ja k vam pishu," ["I am writing to you"],** 1840), Lermontov achieves that highest simplicity and objectivity that never were Byron's.

Folklore becomes one of the sources of the radical changes in his poetic language. Popular songs, tales and ballads begin to inspire the deliberate simplicity of his verse and its prosaic intonations; we note also a tendency to express emotion by telling moving stories which totally dispense with poetic imagery. This is characteristic of the speech of such folklore characters as the mother who sings the

"Kazach'ja kolybel'naja pesnja" ("A Cossack Lullaby," 1840) and the speech of those whom Lermontov
admires as fighters for freedom.

Byron, too, felt a life-long interest in folklore and blended folklore motifs with revolutionary ones, but he never
tried, as Lermontov did, to achieve a union between the
lyrical persona and the folklore hero. Byron's emotions
and the diction of his songs are only indirectly connected
with his own emotions and his mode of self-expression.
Lermontov succeeded in connecting the two in the later
thirties, in poems like **"Uznik" (The Prisoner,** 1837),
"Sosedka" ("The Neighbour," 1840). For this reason so
many of his poems became popular songs in later years
(the present writer when living in a village as a child used
to sing a folk song called **"Trostnik" ("The Reed")** only
to learn later that it was a poem by Lermontov written in
1832).

Lermontov's folklore poems are much more national than
Byron's—they are closely bound with Russia's past, as
well as with the Caucasus. Poems like **"Borodino"** and
**"Pesnja . . . pro kuptsa Kalashnikova" ("Song . . .
about the merchant Kalashnikov,"** 1837) make it clear
how much Lermontov, a follower of the Decembrists,
reflected on the past of his country. Byron called himself a citizen of the world and drew his subjects and
motifs from the life and literature of other countries:
Albania, Italy, Greece.

The simplicity, the psychological and social realism of Lermontov's lyrics, their national orientation, their freedom from
classicist tradition and diction, testify to his rupture with
Byron, to his emergence as a national poet. But this did not
cure him from the inveterate habit of recalling lines from
Byron in his poems. I list below some parallels taken from
his later works:

Byron

I love that language, that
soft bastard Latin / That
melts like kisses from a
female mouth

(*Beppo,* 44).

We wither from our youth, we
gasp away—/ Sick—sick . . .

(*Childe Harold,* IV, 124).

I have not loved the world,
nor the world me; / I have
not flattered its rank
breath, nor bow'd / To its
idolatries a patient knee.

(*Childe Harold,* III, 113).

Lermontov

She sings and sounds melt like kisses
on the mouth (1837).

At the beginning of our path we
wither without a struggle

("Duma"—"Meditations," 1838).

But I do not bow my knees before
the idols of the world

("Dogovor"—"The Contract," 1841).

These Byronic echoes are infrequent in Lermontov's last
years as he grew to be a poet of national stature and as
he strove for a synthesis of the lyrical impulse with a
moral purpose and of the pathetic and the comical. Like
Pushkin, Lermontov sought to rise from subjectivity to
objectivity, from heroic individualism to a sane evaluation
of the relation between man and society.

Like Byron and Pushkin before him, Lermontov attached
a particular importance to prose, and no less than Pushkin
succeeded where Byron failed: he created his famous novel
Geroj nashego vremeni (*A Hero of our time,* 1840) that
had its roots in recent tradition (in Pushkin and early
nineteenth-century French novelists) and which, at the
same time, marked a new stage in the development of the
European psychological novel. Students of Lermontov
have repeatedly emphasised his debt to Constant's *Adolphe*
(1810-16) to Châteaubriand's *René* (1802), to Senancour's
Obermann (1814) and to Musset's *Confession d'un enfant du siècle* (1836). What Lermontov scholars have failed
to observe, obvious though it might seem, is that the *Letters
and Journals of Lord Byron with notices of his life* published by Thomas Moore in 1830 came to be the most
vital source for the journal written by the central character, Pechorin. Lermontov's knowledge of the publication
has already been noted. He made three references to it in
his autobiographical notes, as well as in the phrase 'On
reading Moore's Life of Byron' after the heading of the
lyric **"K ***—Ne dumaj chtob ja byl dostoin sozhalen'ja"**
("To ***, 1830).

Byron's correspondence, no less than his diary, reveals a
complex personality whose passions are inseparable from
rational analysis and self-analysis. Such a personality could
not but highly impress Lermontov, fascinated as he was
by Byron's poetry. He endowed his 'Hero of our time'
with the distinctly Byronic features revealed in the *Letters
and Journals.* Pechorin is the author of a journal, entitled
like Byron's a *zhurnal* (journal), not *dnevnik* (diary). The
philosophical tone of Byron's prose writings, the numerous
aphorisms and maxims he introduces, the prosaic details,
the humorous sallies directed against common poetic clichés, the alternation of subjective lyric narration with ironic
and objective comment and scenes from everyday life are
similarly characteristic of Lermontov's prose.

But the difference between them is even more important
than the points of similarity. In Byron's *Letters and Journals* the hero is the author himself, while Pechorin as the
author of his Journal is a character of Lermontov's and a
fictional character at that. His is not just another personal
confession. It is a generalised experience of a whole generation, and he rises to be the hero of a realistic psychological novel. Lermontov deliberately endows Pechorin

with Byronic features and demonstrates their tragic effect both on himself and on those emotionally dependent on him. But Lermontov rises above his hero. Pechorin embodies Byronism as a peculiar phase in the development of thought and feeling, yet he also represents a treatment of character that differs from Byron's. Everything that in the latter's journal was a mood, a personal feeling, in Lermontov's book grows into moral judgments embodied in an elaborately contrived system of stylistic devices, in persistently repeated parallels and contrasts. It was the experience of Pushkin which helped Lermontov to create a character that is at one and the same time infinitely subtle and mobile. It was to make him the centre of a realistic novel in prose which was to inaugurate a new phase in the history of the European novel. But that is another story.

FURTHER READING

Biographies

Garrard, John. *Mikhail Lermontov*. Boston: Twayne Publishers, 1982, 173 p.
> Appraises Lermontov's works in a biographical and cultural context.

Lavrin, Janko. *Lermontov*. London: Bowes & Bowes, 1959, 111 p.
> Bio-critical study of Lermontov's writing career.

Criticism

Bowra, Sir Maurice. "Lermontov." In *Oxford Slavonic Papers,* edited by S. Konovalov, pp. 1-20. Oxford: At the Clarendon Press, 1952.
> Thematic and stylistic study of Lermontov's poetry.

Freeborn, Richard. *"A Hero of Our Time." The Rise of the Russian Novel,* pp. 38-73. Cambridge: Cambridge University Press, 1973.
> Discusses Lermontov's novel in the context of the genre's evolution in nineteenthcentury Russia.

Gascilo, Helena. "Lermontov's Debt to Lavater and Gall." *Slavonic and East European Review* 59, No. 4 (October 1981): 500-15.
> Examines the influence of Lavater's theories about physiognomy and Gall's theories about phrenology on Lermontov's fiction.

Jones, Lawrence G. "Distinctive Features and Sound Tropes in Russian Verse." In *Russian Poetics,* edited by Thomas Eekman and Dean S. Worth, pp. 195-208. Columbus: Slavica, 1983.
> Analyzes common linguistic elements in a poem by Lermontov and one by Pushkin.

Kelly, Laurence. *Lermontov: Tragedy in the Caucasus.* New York: George Braziller, 1978, 259 p.
> Studies the influence of the Caucasus region in Lermontov's writings and life.

Lavrin, Janko. "Some Notes on Lermontov's Romanticism." *Slavonic and East European Review* 36, No. 86 (December 1957): 69-80.
> Assesses stylistic qualities of Lermontov's novels and poetry, claiming the poet exhibited "romanticism in reverse."

MacCarthy, Desmond. "Lermontov." In *Memories,* pp. 121-29. London: MacGibbon & Kee, 1953.
> Critical impressions of Lermontov's work by noted *Sunday Times* (London) literary critic.

Mersereau, John, Jr. "M. Yu. Lermontov's 'The Song of the Merchant Kalashnikov': An Allegorical Interpretation." In *California Slavic Studies,* edited by Nicholas V. Riasanovsky and Gleb Struve, pp. 110-33. Berkeley: University of California Press, 1960.
> Considers parallels between Pushkin's biography and the content of "The Song," a narrative poem written in the tradition of the Russian folk epic and unique in Lermontov's canon.

Paul, Alec. "Russian Landscape in Literature: Lermontov and Turgenev." In *Geography and Literature: A Meeting of the Disciplines,* edited by William E. Mallory and Paul Simpson-Housely, pp. 114-31. Syracuse: Syracuse University Press, 1987.
> Compares Lermontov's representation of the Caucasus and Ivan Turgenev's of the Russian Plain, demonstrating the transition from romanticism to realism in Russian literature.

Reid, Robert. "Lermontov's *Demon:* A Question of Identity." *Slavonic and East European Review* 60, No. 2 (April 1982): 189-210.
> Identifies major critical responses to the question of the Demon's identity, arguing that the Demon is indeed the Devil.

> Additional coverage of Lermontov's life and career is contained in the following sources published by Gale Research: *Nineteenth-Century Literature Criticism,* Vol. 47.

Gertrude Stein
1874-1946

American novelist, poet, essayist, biographer, and playwright.

INTRODUCTION

Stein is regarded as a major figure of literary Modernism and is one of the most influential writers of the twentieth century. Rejecting the conventions of early nineteenth-century literature, she developed an abstract manner of expression that was a counterpart in language to the work of the Post-Impressionists and Cubists in the visual arts. Stein wrote prolifically in many genres, composing novels, poetry, plays, biographies, and opera libretti.

Biographical Information

The youngest daughter of a wealthy Jewish-American family, Stein spent most of her childhood in Oakland, California. In 1893 she enrolled in the all-female Harvard Annex, which later became Radcliffe College. There she attended classes taught by the psychologist William James, who influenced her intellectual development. Intending to become a psychologist, she began medical studies at Johns Hopkins University, but left without completing her degree.

Stein then devoted herself to her writing, starting work on her first novels. However, commercial publishers initially rejected her work, and Stein was forced to subsidize the printing of her first books. In 1903 she and her brother Leo settled in Paris. Their apartment became the gathering place of artists and writers, most notably Pablo Picasso, whose work Stein greatly admired. He and other Cubist painters broke their subjects down to essential geometric forms, then reassembled those forms in ways that offered the viewer startling new perceptions. This revolution in the visual arts encouraged Stein to formulate a literary aesthetic that would similarly violate existing formal conventions in order to allow the reader to experience language and ideas in provocative new ways. In 1909 Stein began living with Alice B. Toklas, a young woman from California, with whom she developed a close relationship that Stein referred to as a marriage. Toklas played a vital part in Stein's literary work, helping her to prepare manuscripts, providing her with much-needed encouragement, and serving as a subject for Stein's poetry. They remained together for the rest of Stein's life. During World War I, Stein won commendation for her volunteer work as a medical supply driver. After the war, Stein became the friend and mentor of a number of American writers gathered in Paris during the 1920s, including Ernest Hemingway, F. Scott Fitzgerald, and Sherwood Anderson. At this time, Stein was as well known for her

many friendships with talented artists and writers and with wealthy and famous persons as for her literary work. Urged by a publisher to write her memoirs, she produced *The Autobiography of Alice B. Toklas,* which became a best-seller and made her an international celebrity. Forced to remain in Nazi-occupied France during World War II, Stein and Toklas, both Jewish, were protected from anti-Semitic persecution by friends and local officials. Stein continued to write prolifically and maintained a very active social life until her death from cancer in 1946.

Major Works

Although she is regarded as an experimentalist, the works for which Stein is best known are written in more conventional forms: *Three Lives* (1909), *The Autobiography of Alice B. Toklas* (1933), *Everybody's Autobiography* (1937), and *Wars I Have Seen* (1945). These works span the three chronological phases into which Stein's literary career is often divided: The first includes her early novels; the second is marked by the 925-page-long *The Making of Americans* (1925); the third offers the popular *Autobiography of Alice B. Toklas* (1933) and other personal memoirs, some of social and political import such as *Brewsie and Willie* (1946), a set of dialogues pertaining to the atomic bomb and World War II.

Throughout all these periods, she wrote poetry. *Tender Buttons* (1914) was the only volume to appear during her life. This book, a presentation of prose poems arranged in three sections, *Objects, Food,* and *Rooms,* has been decoded as a set of romantic praises to Toklas. The poems make playful use of words and purposefully reject the restrictions of form that Stein associated with the poetry of a "patriarchal" tradition. Her other poems were published posthumously in the *Yale Edition of the Unpublished Works of Gertrude Stein.* Among the most critically examined of these are "Patriarchal Poetry" and "Lifting Belly" from *Bee Time Vine and Other Pieces 1913-1927,* "With a Wife" from *Painted Lace and Other Pieces 1914-1937,* "A Birthday Book" from *Alphabets and Birthdays* (1924), and "Stanzas in Meditation," a lengthy introspective work, included in *Stanzas in Meditation and Other Poems* (written between 1929-1933). Critics have found in many of these poems expressions of her relationship with Toklas, using private symbols to obscure their homoerotic theme.

Critical Reception

Stein's work has not lent itself to the thematic textual explications that have dominated critical approaches in the twentieth century. Commentary abounds with marginalizing terms such as "hermetic," "difficult," "experimental," and "inaccessible." Rather than interpret her poetry, critics often simply labeled Stein as a renegade contributing to the innovations of modern poetry through her eccentric style. Reactions to Stein's poetry were frequently characterized by derision and suggestions that the poems were mere nonsense. After Stein's prose received critical acclaim and popular acceptance through her publication of *The Autobiography of Alice B. Toklas* (1933), attempts were made by critics to explain *Tender Buttons,* the only book of Stein's poetry accessible to the public at that time. B.F. Skinner created controversy by asserting that *Tender Buttons* is an experiment in "automatic writing," a topic Stein studied during medical school. Stein responded: "Artists do not experiment." A more direct approach to understanding her style was taken by some critics after the publication of Stein's essay "Poetry and Grammar" in *Lectures in America* (1935), reading her poems in light of her stated theories. In the 1950s, Yale University Press's publication of eight volumes of previously unpublished poems by Stein created a renewed academic interest in decoding her works. Allegra Stewart's studies of Stein, beginning in the late fifties, use Jungian analysis to suggest that Stein's creativity is a form of religious meditation. During the 1960s and 1970s, critical approaches focusing on the structure of the poems frequently compared Stein's fragmented style to that of Cubist paintings. At the same time, the women's movement produced a new interest in Stein's poetry. Feminist critics, notably Marianne DeKoven, examined the works in relation to those of Stein's contemporaries as statements of rebellion against a male-dominated tradition. Since the 1970s, a number of critics, starting with Richard Bridgman, have focused on erotic readings of Stein's work, using biographical information to detect a symbolism that they claim veils Stein's expressions of lesbian love. In the 1980s and 1990s, the emergence of semiotics resulted in criticism that attempted to come to terms with the great diversity, play, resonance, and perception in Stein's work.

PRINCIPAL WORKS

Poetry

Tender Buttons: Objects, Food, Rooms　1914
Before the Flowers of Friendship Faded Friendship Faded: Written on a Poem by Georges Hugnet　1931
Two (Hitherto Unpublished) Poems　1948
Bee Time Vine and Other Pieces 1913-1927, Vol. 3 of *Unpublished Works of Gertrude Stein*　1953
As Fine as Melanctha 1914-1930, Vol. 4 of *Unpublished Works of Gertrude Stein*　1954
Painted Lace and Other Pieces 1914-1937, Vol. 5 of *Unpublished Works of Gertrude Stein*　1955
Stanzas in Meditation and Other Poems, Vol. 6 of *Unpublished Works of Gertrude Stein*　1956
Alphabets and Birthdays (poetry and essays), Vol. 7 of *Unpublished Works of Gertrude Stein*　1957
Lifting Belly (also included in *Bee Time Vine and Other Pieces*)　1989

Other Major Works

Three Lives: Stories of the Good Anna, Melanctha, and the Gentle Lena (novellas)　1909
Geography and Plays (drama and prose)　1922
The Making of Americans: Being a History of a Family's Progress (novel) 1925; also published as *The Making of Americans: The Hersland Family* [abridged edition] 1934
Composition as Explanation (essay)　1926
Lucy Church Amiably (prose)　1930
How to Write (prose)　1931
Operas and Plays (drama)　1932
The Autobiography of Alice B. Toklas (autobiography)　1933
Matisse, Picasso, and Gertrude Stein with Two Shorter Stories (portraits)　1933
Four Saints in Three Acts (libretto)　1934
Lectures in America (lectures) [includes the essay "Poetry and Grammar"]　1935
Narration (lectures)　1935
The Geographical History of America; or, The Relation of Human Nature to the Human Mind (prose)　1936
Everybody's Autobiography (autobiography)　1937
Ida (novel)　1941
Wars I Have Seen (prose)　1945
Brewsie and Willie (prose)　1946
Four in America (prose)　1947
The Mother of Us All (libretto)　1947

Things as They Are (novel) 1950; also published as *Q.E.D.* 1971

The Yale Edition of the Unpublished Works of Gertrude Stein. 8 vols. (novels, poetry, essays, lectures, and novellas) 1951-58

CRITICISM

Donald Sutherland (essay date 1956)

SOURCE: "Preface: The Turning Point," in *Stanzas in Meditation and Other Poems* by Gertrude Stein, Yale University Press, 1956, pp. v-xxiv.

[*In the following excerpt from his introduction to* Stanzas in Meditation and Other Poems, *Sutherland discusses the evolution of Stein's poetics.*]

The works in [*Stanzas in Meditation and Other Poems*] were written between 1929 and 1933, one of the most dramatic periods in Gertrude Stein's long life with literary form. The period was in a way the climax of her heroic experimentation with the essentials of writing; it tired her, and after it came her popular, broader and easier, more charming and personal works, but while the period lasted she carried writing as high and as far in her direction as she could, to a point that is still, over twenty years later, a crucial one for writing in general. Her summit of innovation, this last reach of her dialectic, is not easy of approach, the atmosphere is rare, but even the approaches are exhilarating and it is not difficult at least to map out the region and the way she came, much of it being our own ground at present.

In the preceding period, from 1911 to 1928, she had written about things and people in space—on the analogy of painting or the theatre. She had done so naturally, as that period was great in painting and lively in the theatre, and nearly everybody's writing was controlled by imagery. The spatial existence of anything made it real enough to write about and indeed to sustain the existence of the writing, but then something happened—even before the crash of 1929 and the small and large world events after it—something happened that took the sufficiency out of spatial existence. Painting went literary, even the movies began to talk, and writing abandoned imagery gradually for other kinds of reality, especially discourse. Why this all happened I don't know, but it did, and set up a situation I believe still remains to be resolved, both in theory and in practice. It goes something like this:

The mind—that is, the active, live, and most actual meaning—of a written work manifests itself in the ways it treats three materials: sight, sound, and sense, as Gertrude Stein counted them. They can as well be called the pictorial, musical, and ideal elements, or again, the spatial, temporal, and conceptual, but however roughly they may be distinguished a writer usually feels only one of them

to represent the foremost face of natural reality and make the sharpest challenge to the mind, which means to make what it does at least as real to itself as the natural or given world. This one leading material or dimension assures the adequate reality of the work, while the other two may serve to reinforce, or refresh, or accompany, or arm, the mind in its major action upon the primary element. For some plain examples: In Pope the sense is primary or the authenticating element, while the sight and sound are there for emphasis and ornament, to help what oft was thought be well expressed or dressed; in Swinburne the sound—the whole musicality of rhythm and rhyme—is primary, while the sense and sight are embellishments; and in say Amy Lowell the sight is everything while the sound and sense are as may be. A similar prevalence of one element over others happens within the art of painting, where the validating element will be now line, now color, now volume, etc.; and within music, where it will be now melody, now harmony, now rhythm.

One might, with a preference for stability over excitement, like to place the excellence of a written work in an equal force or balance of sight, sound, and sense at once, but the trouble (or the mercy, if you prefer) is that rarely if ever in any historical period is experience lived equally in terms of space, time, and ideas, though of course they are always together in experience in some proportion or other. If the period is tranquil the sense of time is likely to be less vivid than the sense of objects in space; if the period is violent and changeable the sense of time will dominate. Sometimes the rationality of the universe is convincing enough and sometimes the irrationality of it is more so, so thought as the validating element in writing comes and goes.

Actual periods are of course more complex than that, as many writers work counter to their period in some way or degree, and the spatiality of writing in the period 1911 to 1928 was in part a counter to what was left of the late 19th century sense of time as history or even biology moving vastly on through a universe which was, if not rational, at least scientifically minded. So time and ideas were still interesting, but they had become problematical, indeed an annoyance to not a few, and all sorts of games could be played with them, while space was a given and saving reality, even to Proust and Joyce, as well as to Gertrude Stein.

But in about 1928 the general sense of the authenticity of space weakened. The pictorial element in writing, which had been highly evolved technically, continued of its own inertia, but it continued rather as decoration or illustration or symbol, because at this time writing began to base its reality on thought.

Most of the thought was political or religious or philosophical. T. S. Eliot went that way; so did Pound; Auden and that generation arrived, all bristling with ideas. Some absconse erudition and some Freudian apparatus did still hang on, passing for thought and even sounding like it, but I believe most of the thought was direct, fresh, and contemporary, really rousing at the time. Only, an idea that is exciting to live with rarely stays exciting long when written, supposing it even begins to be exciting enough for writing of such high intensity as poetry: it is awful what quantities of that poetry, written with a content of the most urgent ideas, are now no longer so much as curious, because the ideas were incompletely converted into the subjective continuum of poetry, and the pressing objective context which kept them alive for a time has withdrawn into history and left them stranded. So much of that poetry, being *about* ideas and not instinct with the poetry *of* ideas, has turned out parochial or didactic in the deplorable sense.

Gertrude Stein once said there were no ideas in masterpieces and next to no masterpieces in philosophy, yet at this time she felt, like everybody else, the need of ideas in writing, as experience was composing itself predominantly into issues, not states or events as before. But she knew very well that ideas had to be made intrinsic to poetry, made to exist as poetry, not used as external props, as occasions or justifications of poetry as if philosophy or religion or politics could delegate some of their authority and interest to poetry while remaining themselves and outside it. . . .

In her way Gertrude Stein solved the problem of keeping ideas in their primary life, that is, of making them events in a subjective continuum of writing, of making them completely actual. For one thing, the ideas she uses, in **"Stanzas,"** are about the actual writing before one, sometimes about her previous writing, other people's writing, or the ordinary events of her life at the time of writing. So the writing is, insofar as it is about anything, about ideas about writing, and this reflexive or so to say circular reference of the ideas is one way of making them self-contained and, while moving certainly, absolute. She was interested at this time in composition as something folded upon itself or contained in itself, and here the movement and reference of the ideas make such a thing. By taking as her center of reference the actual writing rather than writing in general, she gains a greater immediacy and completeness than other works on much the same scheme— the *Ars Poetica* of Horace, that of Boileau, that of Verlaine, and so on.

While one can, with the requisite attention, follow the movements of the ideas among or against each other and in relation to the verse, the very tense and elegant behavior of the syntax, she has so thoroughly suppressed the connections between these formal or verbal configurations of the ideas and any practical, theoretical, or historical context from which they have been abstracted that the work is at first bewildering. Often, yes, one can tell what the specific subject or occasion of a passage or stanza was, or make a sufficiently shrewd guess at the subject for the whole body of references to fall into place in history or philosophy, and take on an objective or extrinsic meaning, but this kind of clarity is, if a relief sometimes when it comes, really a temptation and a distraction from the actual aesthetic object. Gertrude Stein meant these lines of verse to be as attenuated and disembodied as the drawing of Francis Picabia—with whom a few of the stanzas are concerned—

and who, she observed in *The Autobiography of Alice B. Toklas,* was in pursuit of "the vibrant line." Whether Picabia often captured it is a question, but a very good example of its capture would be the draughtsmanship of the Greek vase painter Exekias, if he were more familiar. At any rate, in a stanza concerning Picabia she says she told him to forget men and women—meaning that the line should become so intensely its own entity and sustained by an energy or "vibration" now intrinsic to it, that it could disengage itself from the character of the figures it began by bounding or delineating or expressing. Just so, she wanted her own writing—the grammatical sequence, the rhetorical figures, the line of discourse—to disengage itself by virtue of its own intensity of assertion from the concrete or specific situation whose articulation or definition or "bounding" was precisely the genesis of the idea in the form of a statement, a proposition, a sentence, a word, or whatever.

But can the "lyricity" of ideas really be made to fly, to transcend its origins and their references to any such degree, even if drawing sometimes can? Perhaps not, but I think anyone can see that a writer could passionately want it to be done—to go on, so to say, where Pindar and Plato left off, and create a continuum of absolute writing or absolute thought in words as it can be created in numbers. The audacity of the attempt in itself is staggering, and the difficulty was exhausting. Gertrude Stein finally gave it up and turned to writing about historical relations, and even the easier way out that symbolism is, though she indulged in it not very often.

(In **"Stanzas"** she does, if infrequently, use symbolism or a degree of it, metaphor: the first line of the first stanza is "I caught a bird that made a ball"—meaning "I captured a 'lyricity' that constituted a complete and self-contained entity." Such figures are not typical of what the work generally is or does. Her express attitude toward symbolism was to refuse it as such but to allow in theory and sometimes to practice what she called "symbolical literature"—apparently a literature containing symbolical imagery as above, but an imagery created for the sake of its character in the immediate composition, not for the sake of such a meaning as I have deciphered above. Symbolization would then be a method, like abstraction, of transmuting raw material into art, and not meant to "signify" the raw material—which is, like Picabia's "men and women," to be forgotten. This is theoretically all very well, and I admit that symbols provide a richness, a substantive weight, and some color in a perhaps too purely linear style, if they are taken literally as images and not interpreted, but they inevitably tempt one into interpretation, or me they do, and I mistrust them both in theory and in practice. I find them too interesting and not exciting enough. But a reader who can take them as they are meant—literally, as images and nouns—may well find they help to brace and sustain the "vibration" instead of interrupting it. However one feels about symbols, they are not, in this work, many.)

One of her difficulties was the fluidity of English, the invertebrate sequence and blur of overtones it has in normal use. Its Latin element is no longer a structural or linear resource, but mainly color or pedal, and at one point in the stanzas she longs for Italian, wishing "Italian had been wiser," that is, no doubt, that the superb rhetorical buoyancy and sharpness of Italian had not gone flaccid and indiscriminate as it did after Dante—or Tasso at the latest. Shelley could still use the "clear and complete language of Italy" as spoken or sung, for a foil or scale against which to make English even more fluid than it is, but current Italian is not the help it might have been in forcing English, saturated as it is with the indeterminate concreteness of the English mind, to the expression of what Gertrude Stein called with abundant reason the abstractness of the American mind. The clarity and completeness of Italian might help, but its lusciousness, which afflicted even Dante who invented the language, spoils when brought into American severity, rawness, edginess, what you will. Spanish is more promising, and Hemingway tried it, but something goes wrong there too. The only consolation is that translations of Gertrude Stein and imitations of Hemingway make excellent Italian literature. The real problem, of how to get a foreign language like English to express the exact tone and accent and movement of the American mind, still remains, and one may attach considerable importance to this most heroic attempt to solve it.

The above makes it sound like a laboratory and rather a grim go, which it is not. Gertrude Stein sacrificed to the Graces, and in the course of the **"Stanzas"** we have a good deal of comedy, general gayety, and such companionable remarks to the reader as "Thank you for hurrying through" or "I could go on with this." I have not, myself, seen all there is in the **"Stanzas,"** far from it, nor all of what they are, but there is a luxuriance of pleasures waiting for almost any reader who is willing to enter into the **"Stanzas"** and stay a while. They are far more hospitable than they may at first appear.

The frugality of imagery will seem less forbidding if the reader sees that imagery was just what had to be reduced or liquidated at the time, in order to clarify the draughtsmanship of ideas, or if he recalls Dryden and the Metaphysicals when they are operating on the bare articulation of the language and the verse, with a minimum of coloristic or affective flourish. I think we now have to make some such effort, some deliberate tuning or focusing of the attention, since more recent poetry has disinterred if not revived imagery, in the lurider colors of its disintegration.

It may also require effort now to face a long philosophical poem, but the form was, oddly, of the period, as Bridges' *The Testament of Beauty* appeared then, Pound's *Cantos* were being written, and, on a smaller scale, T. S. Eliot's *Four Quartets*. Gertrude Stein's style and purpose have little enough in common with these poems, or with *The Excursion* or with *In Memoriam*, but the **"Stanzas"** do, by their general form, belong both to a fashion and to the tradition of the long, rambling, discursive poem whose interest and energy are primarily in the movement of the poet's mind writing.

A continuum of discourse, or of *sense* on its own, has a *sound,* an intrinsic musicality of its own, not only as Plato called philosophy a kind of music but as the ideas eventuate or evolve and move in the articulated time of the poem, so such poems are naturally called *The Prelude* or *Cantos* or *Four Quartets;* and the continuum has a space of its own, not only the marked "space of time" that a canto or stanza is, or by imagery when there is any, but by the extensions of thought which sentences are. Gertrude Stein kept, from grade school, a passion for the diagramming of sentences, and in most of her styles she wrote sentences as a kind of diagram of thought. Her superb sense of syntax led her to use it as a kind of draughtsmanship, sometimes as the basis of a more flowing calligraphy, but in these Meditations rather as a "vibrant line" on the order of Picabia's or Exekias' or of that in much Byzantine painting. The intellectual space, rarely so reinforced by imagery and symbol as in Pound or Eliot, or by landscape as in Wordsworth, is both a matter of the stanza—as literally a "room"—and of the extent of the sentence, doubled or further articulated by the extent of the line of verse. To be a little clearer about it: She had said that sentences are not emotional, paragraphs are—that is, that a sentence lives by the balance or tension of its internal syntactical structure (not by its words as successive events), but the paragraph lives by the succession and culmination of the sentences in it—and much the same quality and kind of organization hold for the relation of line to stanza. The line, like the sentence, is conceived as primarily structural, or diagrammatic, as it were spatial and all but static, while the succession of the lines making up the stanza is conceived as temporal. Her lines have, usually, the extremely dry and tense syntactical posture of the 18th century line, or, better, of the closed 18th century couplet, but the stanzas have the mounting and sumptuous progress to a fullness of say the Spenserian stanza or the Tasso octave. I think she would have said this is an American kind of composition, not unlike the sequence of units in a comic strip—in any case very unlike the Miltonic or Romantic permeation of lines by the syntax, where the periods are "variously drawn out from one verse into another."

The metric itself, usually a very plain iambic affair with reversed feet ad libitum as is normal in discursive English poetry, does not really move much through the lines but is rather a matter of immediate emphasis, a rhetorical accent rather than a properly temporal element, or musical. It is what one could call an intensive, as against a progressive, metric, and surely the commonest kind in modern poetry. And the words themselves, being preponderantly monosyllables, tend to stay put and not to progress, to stand or arrive intensively—to vibrate—but to contain no succession.

Still, if one likes, there is a syntactical *phrasing* as well as structure, and one could call that a musicality, like the succession of the sentences and lines, but even the phrasing is staccato and in any case both the temporality and the spatiality of the **"Stanzas"** are "ideal"—functions of the sense, of the articulate "thoughts" succeeding each other in a meditation. Though there are exceptions enough,

I think this is true, that as a rule the **"Stanzas"** re-create a temporality and a spatiality out of the single ideal element, rather than taking them as separate and extrinsic elements brought in for the embellishment or reinforcement of the first. Thus they have little to do with real time and space, but are as it were native to the poem, functions of the moving and extending sense, as that sense moves upon or around itself.

It is high time for an example. Here is a relatively simple one, Stanza VIII in Part V:

> I wish now to wish now that it is now
> That I will tell very well
> What I think not now but now
> Oh yes oh yes now.
> What do I think now
> I think very well of what now
> What is it now it is this now
> How do you do how do you do
> And now how do you do now.
> This which I think now is this.

This stanza is more readily glossed than most, and so not a fair example of disembodied sense, but the form is easier to appreciate perhaps against so plain and immediate a meaning. The poem expresses the action of the mind willing and realizing its own presence, in the present, to its own thought. It begins by recognizing that the actual present is the time to tell one's thought, in the very instant of thinking (not, for example, that the present is to be used for preliminaries and plans for expressing the results of one's present or past thinking later on, as is most common with methodical thought). Then there come various exclamations, questions, and greetings to the present, and the resolution of the question and effort in a recognition that what the mind is present to in its act of presence is simply the *thisness* of any object.

The meaning, or so much of it, can be further discoursed and commented upon by the reader, to the effect that, yes, the nowness and thisness of a thought, not its connections with past or future thoughts or with an objective context of thoughts, are the conditions of its life, and of thought generally at its most vibrant. Plato's dialogues, when the thoughts are instantaneous in the conversation (and not, as, alas, they often are, simply exposition disguised as interrupted monologue), and Montaigne's essays, where the thoughts are explicitly just passing events in his Grand Central of a mind or only valid for the passing moment and not even for the next essay, would seem to agree. Contrariwise one can meditate upon the thatness of objective thought, the beyondness of universalizing thought, or the thenness of historical and anthropological thought, as limitations to their interest. Such excursions into the factual and philosophical context from which the **"Stanzas"** were drawn, abstracted and constructed, are a pleasure, and one can be sure that most if not all the ground one is likely to cover came within Gertrude Stein's immense knowledge of such matters; but excursions into the original context, however rich, do desert the intensiveness and immediacy of the abstracted thought as expressed.

One should stay with the text, and yet the excursions do make one realize the amount of accepted material and value that Gertrude Stein sacrificed for the sake of an uncertain result, with an audacity of decision that marks the major poets, philosophers, saints, generals, and financiers.

The resultant and *intensive* meaning of these poems is the movement of the mind within the poem itself, and in this case the movement of thought, which is positive and active at every syllable, and so has a very high frequency and continuous immediacy, is further intensified by the extreme compression of phrase and the irreducible simplicity of vocabulary. This last, which is not unlike that of Plato, or Aristotle, or Seneca—or, better, that of Voltaire of Diderot or Hume—not only provides an elegant singleness of meaning word by word, thus adding to the tenseness and intensity, but also forces the expression to be a matter of syntax and rhetorical figure of a most linear kind, like a drawing done with a very fine stiff pen. With next to no sonority or harmonics the poems operate on sheer melodic shape, phrasing, and rhythm, other supports being only the bracing or balancing of the syntactical units on or over the line, the repetition of words and phrases, and a very spare use of internal rhyme—that much harmonics if you will. But it is all in a quite pure harpsichord manner.

The single lines are sometimes divided: by rhyme (as in "That I will tell very well"), by repetition (as in "How do you do how do you do"), and by question and answer (as in "What is it now it is this now"). Then there is a balancing or drawing taut of the line by repetition with differing emphases—as in "I wish now to wish now that it is now," where each *now* has a different syntactical use as well as emphasis—and by a kind of binding symmetry as in "And now how do you do now" and in "This which I think now is this." The rhetorical emphasis is sometimes thrown to the end of the line as a climax—as in "not now but now" and in "oh yes oh yes now"—or suspended as in the almost parenthetical "now that it is now"—or recovered for a fresh sequence and line by subordination—as in "that I will tell very well / What I think . . ."—or by question and answer, as in "What do I think now / I think . . ." Such variations of emphasis and balance, the changes of speed, the changes from statement to exclamation to question to answer to a question that is not a question but a greeting (how do you do)—all this does, once you have your eye on it, make an extremely eventful and vibrant stanza, culminating in the symmetrical, balanced, triumphant statement and conclusion "This which I think now is this."

I have made this rather minute analysis, which suspends the live continuity of the poem and so is false to the essential, in order to show that the poem, which looks at first childishly simple and unorganized, is in fact a very varied and complex and highly organized expression, out of the simplest elements of language and thought. The "beautiful disorder" *is*, rigorously, "an effect of art." But her staying with such rudiments of thought, word, and figure, making everything of them, living in their sacredness and preciousness, when these are so often profane and despised, is a natural result of that purity and tenderness and all but religiosity of intention toward language which Sherwood Anderson remarked in her long ago—especially toward "the little housekeeping words, the swaggering bullying street-corner words, the honest working, money saving words, and all the other forgotten and neglected citizens of the sacred and half forgotten city [*of words*]." So that when, as she said, she "completely caressed and addressed a noun" in writing "A rose is a rose is a rose is a rose," it was not a passing fancy but from the center of her intention.

With the best will in the world, our sense of language is debauched, as politics, advertising, the newspapers, and even conversation rarely spare it, so it may be difficult to focus on the small essentials of the language or to see a full beauty in them; and yet a reader who is really accustomed to modern poetry or to say Gerard Manley Hopkins may have less trouble. Hopkins deals in a richer musicality and a sumptuous imagery, but as a rhetorician and, intellectually, as an *actualist* to the verge of heresy, he is germane to the manner. His sense of the syllable, the monosyllable and its placing, with its fullest meaning, and his sense of the simplest and minutest grammatical and rhetorical figures, if familiar to the reader at all, may help him with these **"Stanzas,"** if the **"Stanzas"** are unfamiliar.

Few of the **"Stanzas,"** are as easy as the one I quoted, and only the most intrepid reader should try to begin them at the beginning and read through consecutively. If read at random, as one may read the Old Testament or *In Memoriam,* they yield more readily, or so they have to me. Another way of warming to the work or of getting one's attention in focus, is to pick out the one-line stanzas scattered through the work and get the hang of them before trying the longer ones. For the sake of a little more order and method in case of need, I offer this list of relatively simple stanzas, though it should be strayed from:

> Part II, 14, 18; Part III, 2, 10, 12; Part IV, 9, 24; Part V, 5, 13, 25, 29, 33, 41, 48, 51, 59, 60, 61, 63, 75.

No, they are better read at random, because one of the delights of rambling about in them is encountering very fine aphorisms. Here are a few I liked:

"In changing it inside out nobody is stout"—meaning nobody thrives by making the subjective objective. This could lead directly to a dispute about the "objective correlative" as against a subjective correlative, but it is meant to stand and not lead, not even to the thought which succeeds it in the meditation.

"That which they like they knew"—meaning that what people like is what is already familiar. Here, explanation is otiose to the point of fatuity, except that by contrast a paraphrase does point up the solid elegance of Gertrude Stein's expression, the fine ring of her new coinage of an old commonplace.

"There is no hope or use in all." This axiom is as pretty in itself as Euclid's on the straight line, and its applica-tions are many, but in the **"Stanzas"** the natural application is to writing, and there it is true enough, that a complete work or a complete thought is an absolute in itself and contains no future, neither hope nor use, and this may exalt you or horrify you, depending on what you feel a piece of writing should be or do, on whether you like thought as an end or as a means.

"What is strange is this." Or, it is immediate experience, not the remote and imagined, which contains novelty and romance. The sentence could stand as a motto for nearly all of Gertrude Stein's work, or of Hopkins', or indeed for all philosophies of immanence or presence. One may disagree with such an aphorism, as one may not agree that all things flow or that to be is to be perceived, but one cannot resist the shapeliness of its utterance, nor even deny that it covers its immense ground, indeed holds it.

The other long work in this volume, **"Winning His Way,"** is a narrative poem, written in 1931, the year before the **"Stanzas,"** and is less concerned with *sense*. It is based rather on *sound*—on the musical and temporal elements of writing—and on what I have called absolute eventuality. Narrative poetry was not much of an issue in 1931, but eventuality as "narrative" did offer—as did *sense*—an extrication from *sight* then, and I believe it is an even more promising solution now, not so much from *sight* as from the current exasperation of *sense*.

One constant problem of narrative poetry is to keep clear of the versified novel, or short story, or drama, that is, to make the poem so essentially and energetically a poem that it carries the narrative element instead of being carried by it. I know of no great success with such a poem since Pushkin, for the later 19th century swamped the lyricity of its narrative in pictorial and novelistic developments. If there is to be a tradition behind what I am persuaded is the coming narrative poetry, it will have to be pre-Tennysonian and probably, to support a concentration and intensity proper to our times, rely on the medieval *lay* rather than the epic or even the ballad, which has a way of being a series of lyricible situations. I may easily be mistaken about all this, but even if the coming composition is to be more a matter of dispersion than of concentration and onward eventuality, the dispersion will surely be pyrotechnic rather than developmental as in the 19th century or the average epic. In any case, **"Winning His Way"** is interesting as opening possibilities of technique, in this perspective.

It professes to be "a narrative poem of poetry"—as reflexively as the **"Stanzas"** are discursive poems of or on poetry—but it does treat lyrically the bits of scenes, situations, events, and relationships that would make up a regular narrative. The "story," as a structure of consecutive happenings to be followed, has been pretty thoroughly destroyed by its explosion or transsubstantiation into lyricism, and the "narrative" is now almost entirely in the verbal and lyrical events of the poem itself, which moves at an astonishing pace. The movement seems to have surprised Gertrude Stein herself, for she announces quite early in the poem:

And so. Now. A poem.
Is in. Full swing.

And it goes on to a conclusion of Mozartean sweep and dash—and with his perfect saturation of instant by instant eventuality, For example, the device of sentences made of one or two or a few more words is in part a simple brisk staccato but it also breaks down the syntactical *structure* of the thought or statement into a series of disjunct *events*. Where, in the **"Stanzas,"** the line and sentence do not progress but their series does, here progression is induced into the line or sentence itself, making for much greater and quicker movement, and a lyricity sustained in part on the perpetually exclamatory sense. The exclamation is controlled of course by the larger sense running through the sentences, and varied considerably by the number of words to the sentence and the number of sentences to the line. It is certainly a simple device, but the range of effects and the variety of speed and movement Gertrude Stein draws from it are extraordinary. Here is a fair example—with a few bright remains of *sight* for heightening:

> It. Which. Is a suspicion. Of the, Imagination.
> They will part. But. Not partly.
> Because after all it is convincing.
> That he is great. And she is. Right.
> Let her eat. Plums and an apple.
> Let him. Eat. Currants and lettuce.
> Let them eat. Fish and bread.
> And all the other things. That make. Cake.
> Was theirs. Hers. A disturbance.
> He spoke reasonably. And authoritatively.
> And they. Will know. That.

Whether coming narrative poetry uses a consecutive story or whether it uses, like this, fragments and aspects of a story as the occasions for continuous lyrical events, the problem of making the lyrical movement, that is, the specifically poetic movement, dominate and control the inert lapse of regular narrative time will still be an essential problem to narrative poetry, and **"Winning His Way"** is very instructive in this regard, a technician's paradise. Besides which it is one of Gertrude Stein's happiest works, where she is not so much struggling to create the form as possessing it and playing it for all it is worth. If one accepts the terms of the game it makes delightful reading, not very difficult, and much lighter and slighter than the **"Stanzas."**

The remaining poems, the shorter ones, have charms and interests of their own, though I think some of them contain weary or perfunctory passages, like **"A Poem"** of 1933 and **"Poems"** of 1931—and even these have their good moments. But all of them are interesting as versions of or sketches for or relaxations from the two major performances, the **"Stanzas"** and **"Winning His Way."** **"For-Get-Me-Not,"** of 1929, is an early exercise in the staccato style, a series of short lyrics, some of them of great beauty, like **"Advice about Roses,"** but only a beginning toward the larger use of the method in **"Winning His Way"** and *A Wedding Bouquet.* **"A French Rooster,"** **"Abel,"** **"Narrative,"** and **"A Ballad"** are all exercises in poetic

narrative and in the interactive movement and balance of line, sentence, and stanza. Some of these still rely on the pastoral sweetness she had mastered in 1927, in *Lucy Church Amiably,* and on a brilliant, lavish, and tender use of color, but the severer and intenser forms are gradually becoming articulate. **"To Help,"** of 1930, turns these accomplishments to a very gay and simple miniature drama, a predecessor of *A Wedding Bouquet,* **"Short Sentences,"** and a good many other poetic dramas or plays, even operas, as this vein of experiment broadened.

"A Little Love of Life," of 1932, is a loose and lively discursive poem containing such lines as "Eat your apple darling" and no doubt a distraction from the rigors of the **"Stanzas."** So, no doubt, was **"Margite Marguerite and Margherita,"** a discursive description, in much the same verse as the **"Stanzas,"** of three women with not quite the same name and not quite the same character—a pretty elaboration of the fancy she had already exploited in the play "The Five Georges," that people with the same name resemble each other in character.

In 1932, after reaching the terrible attenuation of the **"Stanzas"** at their purest, she suddenly changed and, partly for distraction, wrote *The Autobiography of Alice B. Toklas,* concrete to the point of gossip, and as simple a narrative as anyone could ask, though in some of the purest prose of our time. Though many works were still to come, and many handsome exploits both in her popular style and in more difficult styles, she never, I think, returned to the problem of the **"Stanzas."** The forms she used for philosophical discourse were in many ways richer, with plays and images and parables, with a great variety of intellectual games, but none of them is quite the monumental attempt at absolute thought the **"Stanzas"** are. She left off abruptly but at the same time deliberately and with a curious acquisition of calm, a sort of rocklike wisdom. The poems called rightly enough **"Afterwards"** and **"First Page,"** written in 1933, mark her departure and a new beginning. They are less intense, less vibrant, than the **"Stanzas,"** but they have a very moving tranquillity. In **"First Page"** comes the passage:

This which I say is this. One way of being here to-day.

> I simply wish to tell a story, I have said a great many things but the emotion is deeper when I saw them [*that is, when her writing was largely sight or "painting"*]. And soon there was no emotion at all and now I will always do what I do without any emotion which is just as well as there is not at all anything at all that is better.

Not that she did not return to emotion, for World War II brought out some of her most passionate and eloquent writing, but this lucid tranquillity remained at the heart of it, and gave her courage to face the dangers of the war, and afterwards to die as she chose. But all that belongs to her life, her legend, her writing. It is, as she would say, all there. And I think the **"Stanzas"** and **"Winning His Way"** are, rather, *here,* that it is at the point at which she left them that we come in.

Wallace Fowlie (review date 1956)

SOURCE: "The State of Change," in *Saturday Review*, Vol. 39, No. 51, December 22, 1956, pp. 21-29.

[*In the following review, Fowlie praises* Stanzas in Meditation and Other Poems, *noting the power of Stein's poetic rhythms.*]

The poetry published in Gertrude Stein's volume *Stanzas in Meditation* was written between 1929 and 1933. It is now presented as the sixth volume in the Yale edition of her unpublished writings. Donald Sutherland, biographer of the writer and one of the editors of this edition, describes in his preface the moment in Miss Stein's career when these poems were composed. For several years before 1929 she had written extensively on painting. Then her preoccupation began to center on ideas of a political and philosophical nature. She was well aware of the weakness of poetry which is simply about ideas and of the need to make ideas coexistent with poetry, intrinsic to poetry. (In fact, she once said, in her familiar aphoristic style, that there are no ideas in masterpieces.)

"Stanzas in Meditation" is a long poem filling more than one-half of the present volume. It is a meditation on the ideas which rise up in the poet's mind during the process of writing, or on the ideas which involuntarily form in her mind when she considers the writing or the art of someone else. For the most part this meditation is infinitely difficult to follow. Miss Stein usually suppresses all connections between the idea which is being generated in her mind and the object associated with it and the moment in time when the association is made. In the course of his preface Mr. Sutherland proposes detailed "explications" of one or two passages which will serve as a helpful method to follow in reading this poetry.

Gertrude Stein's manner and style are fully expressed in "Stanzas in Meditation," and in the semi-narrative poem "Winning His Way," which was written a year before the "Stanzas." The poems are about her mind engaged in the process of writing the poems. They form a diagram of ideas evolving and moving. The preponderance of monosyllables, of what Sherwood Anderson called "street-corner words," forces the reader to concentrate on the essentials of speech and on the slow progress of the mind exploring itself. The aphorisms which turn up on almost every page seem to be extended to the reader as rewards for his having accepted the terms of this art and the rules of this game. The monosyllable of everyday speech—"wish," "please," "give," "did," "had"—is so repetitiously employed that a more unusual word when it appears ("acacia," "nightingale," "Picabia") stands out in sudden illumination.

"The Autobiography of Alice B. Toklas" was written the year after these poems were completed. They may be looked upon therefore as stylistic exercises which helped the writer to reach the extreme simplification in language for which she is famous. In these poems, as well as in the later prose, Gertrude Stein has eliminated words of any emotional color. In describing her own method she claims that she was always "possessed by the intellectual passion for exactitude in the description of inner and outer reality." Such an oracular statement finds its justification in *Stanzas in Meditation,* where no analogous "poetic" terms are permitted as substitutes for the simple direct speech which Gertrude Stein considers her utterance of a poet.

She never relinquishes the strictest, most intimate relationship between her words and her thought. I would say that her poetry comes not from her words but from the intimacy of this contract. The experience of the reader is an awareness of this contract which grows until it becomes an obsession. The poems prepare and create, in a strangely powerful way, the reader who is destined to read them. He will find himself involved in a relationship far different from the habitual relationship of reader and poem. For this book is poetry about poetry. It is a poem about the essence of the poem.

The aphoristic style and the conciseness of the formulas express the energy of this writer's consciousness, which appears almost excessive. Her language is affirmed in slow tempo, with a marked degree of solemnity, as it seeks to acquire a certain weight of one-syllable words. It represents finally a summation of things felt, lived with, possessed. It is common language and yet it relates an experience of intimacy which is the least communicable of all experiences. A word used by Gertrude Stein does not designate a thing as much as it designates the way in which the thing is possessed, or the way in which the thing is destroyed, or the way where-by the poet has learned to live with it. The movements of the poem are continuously varied, and yet the same short staccato words keep recurring until the reader accepts the obsession of their nature and welcomes the state of change and development which they celebrate.

John Ashbery (review date 1957)

SOURCE: "The Impossible," in *Poetry*, Vol. XC, No. 4, July, 1957, pp. 250-54.

[*In the following review of* Stanzas in Meditation and Other Poems, *Ashbery describes the difficult, ambitious nature of Stein's experiments with language.*]

[*Stanzas in Meditation*] will probably please readers who are satisfied only by literary extremes, but who have not previously taken to Miss Stein because of a kind of lack of seriousness in her work, characterized by lapses into dull, facile rhyme; by the over-employment of rhythms suggesting a child's incantation against grownups; and by monotony. There is certainly plenty of monotony in the 150-page title poem which forms the first half of this volume, but it is the fertile kind, which generates excitement as water monotonously flowing over a dam generates electrical power. These austere "stanzas" are made up almost entirely of colorless connecting words such as "where," "which," "these," "of," "not," "have," "about," and so on, though now and then Miss Stein throws in an orange, a lilac, or an Albert to remind us that it really is the world, our world, that she has been talking about. The result is like certain monochrome de Kooning paintings in which isolated strokes of color take on a deliciousness they never could have had out of context, or a piece of music by Webern in which a single note on the celesta suddenly irrigates a whole desert of dry, scratchy sounds in the strings.

Perhaps the word that occurs oftenest in the **"Stanzas"** is the word "they", for this is a poem about the world, about "them". (What a pleasant change from the eternal "we" with which so many modern poets automatically begin each sentence, and which gives the impression that the author is sharing his every sensation with some invisible Kim Novak.) Less frequently, "I" enters to assess the activities of "them", to pick up after them, to assert his own altered importance. As we get deeper into the poem, it seems not so much as if we were reading as living a rather long period of our lives with a houseful of people. Like people, Miss Stein's lines are comforting or annoying or brilliant or tedious. Like people, they sometimes make no sense and sometimes make perfect sense; or they stop short in the middle of a sentence and wander away, leaving us alone for awhile in the physical world, that collection of thoughts, flowers, weather, and proper names. And, just as with people, there is no real escape from them: one feels that if one were to close the book one would shortly re-encounter the **"Stanzas"** in life, under another guise. As the author says, "It is easily eaten hot and lukewarm and cold / But not without it."

"Stanzas in Meditation" gives one the feeling of time passing, of things happening, of a "plot", though it would be difficult to say precisely what is going on. Sometimes the story has the logic of a dream:

> She asked could I be taught to be allowed
> And I said yes oh yes I had forgotten him
> And she said does any or do any change
> And if not I said whom could they count.

while at other times it becomes startlingly clear for a moment, as though a change in the wind had suddenly enabled us to hear a conversation that was taking place some distance away:

> He came early in the morning.
> He thought they needed comfort
> Which they did
> And he gave them an assurance
> That it would be all as well
> As indeed were it
> Not to have it needed at any time

But it is usually not events which interest Miss Stein, rather it is their "way of happening", and the story of **"Stanzas in Meditation"** is a general, all-purpose model which each reader can adapt to fit his own set of particulars. The poem is a hymn to possibility; a celebration of the fact that the world exists, that things can happen.

In its profound originality, its original profundity, this poem that is always threatening to become a novel reminds us of the late novels of James, especially *The Golden Bowl* and *The Sacred Fount,* which seem to strain with a superhuman force toward "the condition of music," of poetry. In such a passage as the following, for instance:

> Be not only without in any of their sense
> Careful
> Or should they grow careless with remonstrance
> Or be careful just as easily not at all
> As when they felt.
> They could or would would they grow always
> By which not only as more as they like.
> They cannot please conceal
> Nor need they find they need a wish

we are not far from Charlotte's and the Prince's rationalizations. Both **"Stanzas in Meditation"** and *The Golden Bowl* are ambitious attempts to transmit a completely new picture of reality, of that *real* reality of the poet which Antonin Artaud called *"une réalité dangereuse et typique".* If these works are highly complex and, for some, unreadable, it is not only because of the complicatedness of life, the subject, but also because they actually imitate its rhythm, its way of happening, in an attempt to draw our attention to another aspect of its true nature. Just as life is being constantly altered by each breath one draws, just as each second of life seems to alter the whole of what has gone before, so the endless process of elaboration which gives the work of these two writers a texture of bewildering luxuriance—that of a tropical rain-forest of ideas—seems to obey some rhythmic impulse at the heart of all happening.

In addition, the almost physical pain with which we strive to accompany the evolving thought of one of James's or Gertrude Stein's characters is perhaps a counterpart of the painful continual projection of the individual into life. As in life, perseverance has its rewards—moments when we emerge suddenly on a high plateau with a view of the whole distance we have come. In Miss Stein's work the sudden inrush of clarity is likely to be an aesthetic experience, but (and this seems to be another of her "points") the description of that experience applies also to "real-life" situations, the aesthetic problem being a microcosm of all human problems.

> I should think it makes no difference
> That so few people are me.
> That is to say in each generation there are so few
>   geniuses
> And why should I be one which I am
> This is one way of saying how do you do
> There is this difference
> I forgive you everything and there is nothing to
>   forgive.

It is for moments like this that one perseveres in this difficult poem, moments which would be less beautiful and meaningful if the rest did not exist, for we have fought side by side with the author in her struggle to achieve them.

The poems in the second half of the book are almost all charming, though lacking the profundity of **"Stanzas in Meditation."** Perhaps the most successful is **"Winning His Way,"** again a picture of a human community: "The friendship between Lolo and every one was very strong / And they were careful to do him no wrong." The bright, clean colors and large cast of characters in this poem suggest a comic strip. In fact one might say that Miss Stein discovered a means of communication as well suited to express our age as in their own way, the balloons (with their effect of concentration), light bulbs, asterisks, ringed planets, and exclamation marks which comic-strip characters use to communicate their ideas. In **"Winning His Way,"** for example, she experiments with punctuation by placing periods in the middle of sentences. This results in a strange syncopation which affects the meaning as well as the rhythm of a line. In the couplet

> Herman states.
> That he is very well.

the reader at first imagines that she is talking about a group of states ruled over by a potentate named Herman; when he comes to the second line he is forced to change his idea, but its ghost remains, giving a muted quality to the prose sense of the words.

Donald Sutherland, who has supplied the introduction for this book, has elsewhere quoted Miss Stein as saying, "If it can be done why do it?" **"Stanzas in Meditation"** is no doubt the most successful of her attempts to do what can't be done, to create a counterfeit of reality more real than reality. And if, on laying the book aside, we feel that it is still impossible to accomplish the impossible, we are also left with the conviction that it is the only thing worth trying to do.

James K. Feibleman (essay date 1970)

SOURCE: "The Comedy of Literature: Gertrude Stein," in *In Praise of Comedy: A Study in Its Theory and Practice,* Horizon Press, 1970, pp. 236-41.

[*In the following excerpt, Feibleman describes* Tender Buttons *and* Geography and Plays *as comically meaningless works, of interest only for the connotative value of their nonsensical words.*]

The Stein which is represented by [*Tender Buttons* and *Geography and Plays*] is essentially the comedian. That Gertrude Stein would probably not agree with this estimation is nothing to the point. When we consider artistic accomplishments, we can ignore the intentions of the artist, which may have been in direct contradiction with what was actually accomplished. In all likelihood, Miss Stein began her career as an iconoclast, like so many of her "lost generation." She wrote with her tongue in her cheek and an ambition to *épater le bourgeois*. But whether such was her intention or no, we may assert that it is what her books reveal, and thus it is all we need be occupied with

considering. Fortunately or unfortunately for the artist, works of art once delivered to the public are public property, and there are many who are more equipped to assign them their proper place than the artist himself. Thus we are justified in calling Miss Stein a comedian provided only that we can show wherein the comedy lies. . . .

One joke and one alone underlies the Stein writings, although there are many implications. The juxtaposition of words in sentence form, which tantalizingly sound as though they had a meaning when they have none, in an effort to ridicule meaning itself, is the formula. It is a subtle variety of the comedy of meaninglessness. In one kind of writing it relies upon sheer monotony.

"The same examples are the same and just the same and always the same and the same examples are just the same and are the same and are always the same. The same examples are just the same and they are very sorry for it" [Stein, *Useful Knowledge*]. The monotony becomes unbearable, whereupon we are presented with a bewildering kind of half-truth which we may or may not be expected to take seriously; this is the familiar trick which is employed over and over. It can of course be equally effective if reversed:

"Supposing no one asked a question. What would be the answer.

"Supposing no one hurried four how many would there be if the difference was known" [*Useful Knowledge*]. These passages are characteristic. Fragments of meaning are found, distorted, broken, and utterly simple; but we can make nothing of them. The gamut of meaninglessness is run, all the way from pages of unbearable repetition, such as the following:

"Yes and yes and more and yes and why and yes and yes and why and yes. A new better and best and yes and yes and better and most and yes and yes and better and best and yes and yes and more and best and most and yes and yes" [*Useful Knowledge*]. And so on, to passages of beauty which are almost intelligible poems, such as this, for example:

> If you hear her snore
> It is not before you love her
> You love her so that to be her beau is very lovely
> She is sweetly there and her curly hair is very
>   lovely
> She is sweetly here and I am very near and that is
>   very lovely.
> She is my tender sweet and her little feet are
>   stretching out well
> which is a treat and very lovely
> Her little tender nose is between her little eyes
>   which close and
> are very lovely.
> She is very lovely and mine which is very lovely.
>   [*Useful Knowledge*]

The trick of putting together ideas which do not belong together because they are not on the same level of analysis, used so often by Miss Stein, is an old one but always effective, because it ridicules the commonest error of bad thinking. *Tender Buttons*, *Geography and Plays:* the pointed meaninglessness is so effective that it could hardly have been accidental. The practice of considering together ideas which do not belong together, and of making fun of them thereby, has been noted by other theorists of comedy as well as by other comedians. It is what Freud calls "the comic of speech or of words," [Sigmund Freud, *Wit and Its Relation to the Unconscious*] but it is rather the comedy of erroneous logical analysis. Freud quotes two examples of this kind of comedy: "'With a fork and with effort, his mother pulled him out of the mess,' is only comical, but Heine's verse about the four castes of the population of Göttingen: 'Professors, students, Philistines, and cattle' is exquisitely witty."

Another variety of comedy employed by Stein is the use of platitudes in a way which is capable of restoring their original powerful meaning. We have . . . seen this take superb form at the hands of a master, as when used by Joyce, but Miss Stein's method is slightly different. She falls back more upon meaninglessness of an orthodox nature. The phrase "before the flowers of friendship faded" is so trite and disgustingly sentimental an expression that nobody would think of taking it seriously. Gertrude Stein uses it with her trick of repetition, and it is funny. "Before the flowers of friendship faded friendship faded." Again meaning aggravatingly looks out and we are almost tempted to avail ourselves of a serious reading.

There is an aspect of Stein's writings which leads us to the assumption that she is attempting to work only through the connotation of words, avoiding any real detonation. Her close connection with the magazine, *Transition,* and with its editor, Eugene Jolas' "revolution of the word" would convict her of aiming at the deepest kind of irrationalism. The group of writers in Paris which centred about this periodical flirted with all the Chthonic deities. Various methods of writing, such as Joyce's stream of consciousness, automatic writing, and "the language of night," have doubtless had their effect upon Stein.

Yet, as we have pointed out before, it is not what she may have set out to do but what she did that matters. In poker it is not the betting but the cards which count. Over against the influences we have mentioned it should also be noted that Stein studied under William James, and she has been friendly with Alfred North Whitehead. However, these direct rationalists (we can count James a rationalist in so far as he was a philosopher at all) seem to have exercised no influence upon her. There can be little doubt that Stein considers herself a proponent of irrationalism. Actually, her work itself has little to do with irrationalism or the Chthonic deities. What she may be said to have demonstrated is that irrationalism will not work; that the extreme irrationalist position is untenable. Thus she is a comedian in the deepest sense of the word, and this because she accomplished the opposite of what she set out to do. She really succeeded in defending reason; she has reaffirmed by implication the infinite and necessary relatedness of all things in a certain order, and thus refuted the nominalism with which she started.

Stein's comedy of meaninglessness has been very useful. It has served as an instrument of liberation. She has freed modern literature from the sterile formalism and Victorian smugness and outworn pretence with which it was encumbered when she first appeared upon the contemporary scene. This was a task which very much needed doing. Her books have helped to reacquaint us with the naked sound of our language, hitherto only available to foreigners, and allowed us to examine its connotations in isolation.

It is hard to forgive her, though, simply because she does not know what she does. Her ignorance of her own function is illustrated by the two meaningful autobiographies in which she talks chiefly about herself and in high seriousness. We are at last allowed to see the meaning, we are taken behind the scenes and permitted to hear Miss Stein talk in a normal tone of voice. It is quite an *exposé*, because we learn for the first time, and after much puzzlement, that there is no meaning at all. And we are angry with ourselves for not having guessed as much. Having nothing else to talk about, after years with gibberish, she talks about herself: her own life and her genius. And we long for the gibberish again, for that at least was self-contained. It is like looking inside a balloon after having for some time admired its shining surface, only to learn that there is nothing to it but surface. What a clever trick it was after all, and how amusing. For Miss Stein is a comedian and nothing else, and her words have a meaning only when she is talking nonsense.

Pamela Hadas   (essay date 1978)

SOURCE: "Spreading the Difference: One Way to Read Gertrude Stein's *Tender Buttons,*" in *Twentieth Century Literature,* Vol. 24, No. 1, Spring, 1978, pp. 57-75.

[*In the following essay, Hadas provides a biographical interpretation of* Tender Buttons *which includes explanations of Stein's feelings for her brother, Leo Stein, their mutual interest in the psychological theories of William James, and Stein's relationship with Alice B. Toklas.*]

Whether she is known as the "Mother Goose of Montparnasse," the "mama of dada," the affectionate mother country called "Gert" by G.I.s in Paris, or "Baby," as her companion Alice called her in private, makes little difference to our reading of Gertrude Stein's work. Yet the phenomena of Gertrude Stein's versatile selves—none and all and more than the above—and her perception of the differences between herself and the selves of others do. In *Tender Buttons* these differences are as important as the identifications. At least this is one way to read it, and the one I intend here, although of course there is no one way to read it that can fathom a final difference. The spaces are exceptionally wide between the lines and separate minds here, but there is where differences can begin the work (and play) of bringing them together.

Most readers, at first, do not know what to make of *Tender Buttons* at all—a joke perhaps. One doesn't know whether to call it prose, poetry, philosophy, or nonsense; does it make a difference or doesn't it? If one does not care for language as a lover, is not in a playful frame of mind or curious at heart, then perhaps it does not make a difference. To me it does; it *commits* differences, points them out, makes use of many, solves a few. The section of *Tender Buttons* subtitled *Objects* begins the work and begins by announcing "an arrangement in a system to pointing" where all points rapidly scatter—not unlike, one might say, the matter of the universe itself—"[a]ll this and not ordinary, not unordered in not resembling." The extraordinary suggestiveness, the order that is claimed, and the resemblances that are not are all part of a central preoccupation with differences and change; that is to say, with diffusion of a center (not there) or of many possible centers (all here). This is how and why [t]he difference is spreading" (*Objects*, **"A Carafe, That Is a Blind Glass"**).

"The elementary fact to understand about Gertrude Stein is that she is incomprehensible because there is nothing there to comprehend" [Francis Russell, *Three Studies in Twentieth Century Obscurity*]. Though this statement was made more than two decades ago, this is still a fairly prevalent attitude toward Gertrude Stein. Its less vehement form: "Gertrude Stein? Hmmm. For some reason I never could read Gertrude Stein." Or one might go so far as to admit that it is interesting to psychologize about the weirdest of her writing, convinced that in itself it is more valuable as soporific than stimulant. The work most often directly responsible for these and other generalized negative assessments or simple neglect of Gertrude Stein's work, critically speaking, is *Tender Buttons*. John Malcolm Brinnin, who has great love for the woman herself, blames "a language inscrutable to inquiry on both logical and semantic levels." "Her initial error," as he calls it, is to regard words "as if they were unencumbered plastic entities of such and such texture, weight and resilience," "divorced from thought" [Brinnin, *The Third Rose*]. There is some truth in this statement, but it is not true that thought had no part in the determinations of Stein's composition, and the absence of logic and consequential thought does not signify an absence of meaning. In an interview with Robert Haas in 1946, Stein claims that as she became interested in individual words (as opposed to paragraphs or sentences), "I took individual words and thought about them until I got their weight and volume complete and put them next to another word, and at this same time I found out very soon that there is no such thing as putting them together without sense. It is impossible to put them together without sense. I made innumerable efforts to make words write without sense and found it impossible" [Haas, ed., *A Primer for the Gradual Understanding of Gertrude Stein*]. Impossible?

> A no, a no since, a no since when, a no since when since, a no since when since a no since when since, a no since, a no since when since, a no since, a no, a no since a no since, a no since, a no since. (*Tender Buttons*)

This is the way one item of *Food*, **"Orange In"** (for Arrangin'?), ends: Is there, we might ask, *no since when,*

that is, only fresh and continuous beginnings? Is it lots of *no sense*—nonsense? Is it *a nuisance,* repeated and repeated? Is it music? Is it *no sins,* or *innocence?* Of course if one does not give willing attention to the individual words as sound as well as sense, one misses the sound sense of having so many possibilities—the major enchantment of such a chant. If there is too great a difference between the acts of creator and re-creator, no amount of weight and volume, of gravity—or levity either—will sufficiently bring their acts together.

Approaches to *Tender Buttons* are not easy. Gertrude Stein herself gives one major reason for this in an essay written about the same time, a portrait called "Two: Gertrude Stein and Her Brother" where she admits "protecting herself in exposing what she was approaching." The obscurity that results provides a real problem as well as a real expression of thematic differences. Covers, curtains, tops, shadows, and denials are everywhere—in *Objects*, in *Food*, in *Rooms*—as they separate and hold the work's three parts together. The surrounded and surrounding, the entering and entered, the contained and all sorts of containers—all add up to a house in significant disorder, but it is not impossible to attend its Saturday night *salons*—the echoes of them anyhow—or to be fascinated by its forms of family romance. It is not unrealistic, either, to demand and receive suggestions as to how our own minds might work in response to all this "not unordered in not resembling." In any case, "real is, real is only, only excreate, only excreate a no since." Yes, it demands all the innocence we can creatively excrete—in a sense.

"When I was young," reminisces the not unpretentious Leo Stein [in his *Journey into the Self*], "I was perceptually using the Phrase, 'Keep your eye on the object and let your ideas play about it.'" This is how this connoisseur and patron (a successful one—one of the first to buy works by Matisse and Picasso) "learned to see"; and it is safe to assume that this is one of the things he taught his little sister. Her other early hero, William James, had been teaching that "[a]ssociation, so far as the word stands for an *effect, is between* THINGS THOUGHT OF—*it is* THINGS, *not ideas, which are associated in the mind.* We ought to talk of the association of *objects,* not the association of *ideas*" [James, *Principles of Psychology*]. But, then, he admits that "[t]he 'objects' and the 'ideas' fit into parallel schemes, and may be described in identical language". What matters most—the objects or the thoughts or the self thinking or the relations of all of these? In reading Gertrude Stein's *Objects*, we are liberated from the objects themselves by an atmosphere of play, between them as well as between them and her, which associates and transforms. It is as if she let the "words write" their own meanings, but certainly, certainly not unconsciously.

It is interesting, in a way, to go through *Tender Buttons* as one would a book of riddles trying to guess the "answers"—what aspect of what descriptions really describe what she really saw—and Stein herself encouraged the idea that she was captivated by a desire for super-accuracy in this respect, but this approach (as she surely knew and was amused by) can only lead to overingeniousness on the one hand and frustration on the other. Just "keep your eye on the object and let your ideas play about it"; this strikes me as closer to the method of composition than any self-conscious riddle mongering. As Leo Stein remarks, in a letter written in 1913, "[t]here is very little, if any, difference in the wrinkling of the brow, etc., between looking sharply at a thing and thinking deeply."

While Leo was theorizing about such things, Gertrude, much to his chagrin, was producing them and making the most of all differences, from the one between her and Leo down to those between individual words, letters, and single sounds. Between noise and articulation there is only a custom of the tongue. "This is no dark custom and it even is not acted in any such a way that a restraint is not spread" (*Objects*, **"A Piano"**). Gertrude tells us, in the portrait "Two" that "he had the clamour that was not refusing using laughing and abusing and indicating. He did not like clamour" [*Two: Gertrude Stein and Her Brother, and Other Early Portraits (1908-1912)*] Gertrude's attitude toward Leo is not unequivocal. There is only a letter's difference between amuse and abuse. She discovers him "exactly laughing" and mentions that what she is "expecting" from him "is not destroying actual respiration," which is to say she's not holding her breath, not for his praise, and not for his long-loudly-promised masterpiece. Yet she shows restraint. Sometimes it expresses itself as nonsense, as music, sometimes as a catalogue of eccentric adverbs or a racket of particles. Poor Leo was getting deaf, literally and literarily: "he did not catch what was not showing meaning" ("Two").

Leo's incessant need to lecture understandably got on Gertrude's nerves: "To consider a lecture, to consider it well is so anxious and so much a charity and really supposing there is grain and if a stubble every stubble is urgent, will there not be a chance of legality. The sound is sickened . . . ." (*Rooms*, *Tender Buttons*). Supposing he does possess a grain of truth, it is the postharvest debris that is hard for a sister to take. It is my feeling that if *Tender Buttons* is read in the broad context of the differences sought by and between Gertrude Stein and her brother, of an immanent change in their living arrangements, of a change which includes Alice Toklas, then all the "tender buttons," seeds or buds, of this most resistant of twentieth-century imaginative works will begin to yield some of their happily artificial flowers. "Actually not aching, actually not aching, a stubborn bloom is so artificial and even more than that, it is a spectacle, it is a binding accident, it is animosity and accentuation" (*Objects*, **"A Chair"**).

In the 1946 interview mentioned above Gertrude Stein admits, of *Tender Buttons*, that "[t]his book is interesting as there is as much failure as success in it. When this was printed I did not understand this creation. I can see now, but one cannot understand a thing until it is done . . . ." I am intrigued by the suggestion that there is a "story" connected with the fragments of sensibility called *Tender Buttons*, and the more I have thought about it, the more it does seem to circumscribe or allude to or avoid the telling of a personal story, a story of what we may surmise was Gertrude Stein's inner and outer experience of the period 1910-13, when *Tender Buttons* was incipient or actually being written. It is a story of how one lives with perceptions of change and differences of all sorts, from the unreliable meanings of language to those psychological differences between men and women, past and future, brothers and sisters, and signs of life among them. All these differences are reflected in the unhabitual perceptions that Stein brings to the objects, food, and rooms that constitute her most private life. The broadest questions are implied in the seemingly most inconsequential; one might even say that questioning of all sorts is the theme of the work as importantly as the differences which provoke the questions. All the questions add up: What/ who makes a differences, and how much? How much does it cost?

"The power of conceptual thought and the consequent ability to realize difference and likeness are the grounding of imagination. Time ceases to be of necessity succession and when desired becomes simultaneity." So states Leo Stein in his unfinished treatise on self-analysis and improvement. Leo shared (perhaps even helped to inspire) Gertrude's passionate reverence for William James, who emphasizes the themes of discrimination and identity throughout his *Principles of Psychology*. Given this theme, even the scientist waxes poetic:

> This *consciousness of serial increase of differences* is one of the fundamental facts of our intellectual life. More, *more*, MORE, of the same kind of difference, we say, as we advance from term to term, and realize that the farther on we get the larger grows the breach between the term we are at and the one from which we started. . . . The louder than the loud is louder than the less loud; the farther than the far is farther than the less far; the earlier than the early is earlier than the late; the higher than the high is higher than the low; the bigger than the big is bigger than the small; or, to put it briefly and universally, *the more than the more is more than the less; such is the great synthetic principle of mediate comparison which is involved in the possession of the human mind of the sense of serial increase.*

One item among the *Objects* of *Tender Buttons* is entitled simply **"MORE,"** and comparatives, usually and characteristically incomplete, abound throughout the entire work. For instance:

"DIRT AND NOT COPPER"

Dirt and not copper makes a color darker. It makes the shape so heavy and makes no melody harder.

It makes mercy and relaxation and even a strength to spread a table fuller. There are more places not empty. They see cover.

Darker, harder, fuller, more than what? The kettle that shines? But that is not the point. In any still life, some parts are stiller. Things are connected to things by virtue of their differences; dirt and copper are relatives, or are seeking cover for other relations. Or consider the following: "A transfer, a large transfer, a little transfer, some transfer, clouds and tracks do transfer, a transfer is not neglected" (*Food*, **"Roastbeef"**). Here the differences are between "a," "a large," "a little," and "some"; at the end we are reassured that the indefinite "a transfer" is not to be slighted—any is as good as a particular one. Another difference, despite the sameness of the sound, is that between the word "transfer" used as a noun and used as a verb, with the complication that "some transfer" can be read as both. We may not be able to translate the sentence in any "meaningful" (by ordinary standards) way, but we should, if we are paying attention, come away with the sense of more and more possibilities in verbal texture. It grows; "the difference is spreading."

From sounds alone (the same difference James points out between *"Pas de lieu Rhône que nous"* and "paddle your own canoe") to human perplexities, "what choice is there when there is a difference"? (**"Roastbeef"**). Each thing stands apart as well as in relation. If one knows one's own mind—or at least perceives strong identity there—noticing a difference may be identical with choosing; in a way, one has already chosen. It is only between things perceived as identical that choice is precarious, in danger of being arbitrary and/or meaningless.

"It is so easy to exchange meaning, it is so easy to see the difference. The difference is that a plain resource is not entangled with thickness" (**"Roastbeef"**). Despite her claimed allegiance to the plain and simple, a great deal of Stein's *Tender Buttons* is "entangled with thickness," which makes it difficult to see what choices and why choices are made. Nevertheless, "every time there is a suggestion there is a suggestion and every time there is a silence there is a silence" (**"Roastbeef"**), and to take some of the former to fill some of the latter is not an unrewarding experience, as "[t]he teasing is tender and trying and thoughtful" (*Food*, **"Sugar"**).

Throughout *Tender Buttons* we feel the constant pressure of chaos. It is so easy for sense to fade, despite Stein's insistence that she couldn't make words write without it. Words out of place, grammar ignored, classes of things willfully mismatched, pure self-indulgent sound play; it is a constant effort for the reader to guess where order and goodness lie, and some places they do lie. If we persist, it is in great measure due to a kind of ordering power in the tone of *Tender Buttons* alone; it is really remarkable that this tone preserves such indubitable authority, even or especially when the subject or apparent object is the production of uncertainty. It is certainly this, rather than any independent interest in Stein's peculiar objects, food, and rooms, that leads us on in reading. Any subject—**"Roastbeef,"** for instance—leads not to understanding of its own superficial nature, but to the author's general and firm perception of a general nature. Of time and space and difference:

> The time when there are four choices and there are four choices in a difference, the time when there are

four choices there is a kind and there is a kind. There is a kind. There is a kind. . . . The kindly way to feel separating is to have a space between. This shows a likeness.

The more intrigued we become with the nature of this generalizing authority, the more we want to know and feel the motivations behind the teasing and lecturing, the exact nature of the chaos and what causes it to be felt.

What is the connection, often suggested in *Tender Buttons,* between "kind" (the sort sort) and "kindly"? The former separates related beings; the latter relates separate beings. In both operations the separation is necessary to the relation. Two "kinds" must be in some sense close for separation to mean anything much. When the two are kin, likeness and liking may be at odds, and kindness may make or break all the difference. "Out of kindness comes redness and out of rudeness comes rapid same question out of an eye comes research, out of selection comes painful cattle" (*Objects*, **"A Box"**). Kindness can cause blushing; the blush of anger, however, is not that different and is caused by or can provoke unfriendly rhetorical grilling. The eye here is judging and separating and it is painful. Cattle? Cattle are *kine*, which is not so far from *kin* in Stein's game; more and more, the evidence seems to suggest a family quarrel among the domestic objects, words, and differences in *Tender Buttons*. At least this is one way to read it.

One does not have to read at great length in the letters and memoirs of Leo Stein to see that he is an avid classifier and orderer of all experience, but particularly aesthetic experience. It is well known that he was fond of giving lectures on modern art to any and all who visited 27, rue de Fleurus. It seems to me that when *Tender Buttons* is read in light of Leo's predilection for academic discourse and aesthetic pontification, all the anger, love, mocking, and teasing disorder seem part of one ongoing, close, and precarious relationship of brother and sister. "There was a whole collection made," says the sister, giving a list of disparate items including an (aphrodisiac?) oyster and a (narcissistic?) "single mirror"; "[t]his shows the disorder, it does, it shows more likeness than anything else, it shows the single mind that directs an apple." Moreover, I believe, it *shows him*, the ego behind the Adam's apple, the "little lingering lion" in her *Rooms*. What is nourishment for Eve sticks in her professor's throat, and she is not unamused.

He thought she was silly. She thought he was tiresome. One thing they shared until the end, however, was the Jamesian care for shared space and its necessary arrangements. The problem, as James puts it:

> How do we ARRANGE *these at first chaotically given spaces into one regular and orderly "world of space" which we now know?* . . .

> Spacial order is an abstract term. The concrete perceptions which it covers are figures, directions, positions, magnitudes, and distances. To single out any

one of these things from a total vastness ispartially to introduce order into the vastness. To subdivide the vastness into a multitude of these things is to apprehend it in a completely orderly way.

Leo, unable to bring anything from his inner being to completion, was constantly rearranging the intellectual objects and aesthetic principles he formed outside himself. Gertrude, unable to form hierarchies of values and opinions outside of herself, was constantly bringing her innermost being to artistic completion. All the same, despite these differences, they were both passionately interested in introducing order into the vastness. The question as it interested Gertrude is not simply how to introduce order into chaos, however, but whether you can have *both* order and chaos, introduce order without ordinary sense and meaning, invent an extraordinary order.

The touching thing is that the two of them try to fill the same space. They share its objects, food, rooms. Literally, it is the space of 27, rue de Fleurus; psychologically, it is the space between themselves; more deeply psychologically, one might say that they were both, like everybody, playing with cultural objects in order to fill up the space and time between them and the egoistic utopias of their babyhoods, where there are no separations between one's self and objects, food, and rooms, where it is all one.

Tender Buttons is full of images of cutting, wounding, separating, replacing, exchanging, emptying, and filling. "A hurt mended stick, a hurt mended cup, a hurt mended article of exceptional relaxation and annoyance, a hurt mended, hurt and mended is so necessary that no mistake is intended" (*Food*, **"Breakfast"**). In the *Rooms* of *Tender Buttons* we find the personal, "fifteen years and a separation of regret. . . . This which is mastered has so thin a space to build it all that there is plenty of room and yet is it quarreling, it is not and the insistence is marked. A change is in a current and there is no habitable exercise." In the years immediately before and while *Tender Buttons* was being written there was an important change of "being existing" in the Stein household. Alice B. Toklas had been living there since 1909, and by 1913 Leo had decided to remove himself.

Leo writes to Mabel Weeks (February 7, 1913) that "[o]ne of the greatest changes that has become decisive in recent times is the fairly definite 'disaggregation' of Gertrude and myself." Decisive or fairly decisive, the separation was drawn out and difficult. Gertrude writes, in *Tender Buttons,* "Some increase means a calamity and this is the best preparation for three and more being together" (*Objects*, **"A Substance In A Cushion"**). For Gertrude, however, the permanent relationship with Alice could be seen as restitution for the loss of Leo. In addition, the writing of *Tender Buttons* itself seems intended to fill a real or at least potential vacancy. Thus, "A large box is handily made of what is necessary to replace any substance. . . . A custom which is necessary when a box is used and taken is that a large part of the time there are three which have different connections" (**"A Box"**). And, one might add, for a large part of the space the three are out of their

corners, edgy, ready to fight for a certain symmetry where all three are uncertain.

"The difference is spreading." Spreading to include Alice, spreading into more differences, spreading into pages of curious manuscript describing the surroundings and surrounded. . . . "This was the hope which made the six and seven have no use for any more places and this necessarily spread into nothing. Spread into nothing" (*Objects*, **"A Little Bit of a Tumbler"**). "Rectangular ribbon [surrounding a gift-boxed life?] . . . means that if there is no place to hold there is no place to spread" (**"Roastbeef"**). Space is limited, granted, but its very limitations are what is responsible for its ability to contain meaning; a vacancy represents opportunity at the same time as it may represent loss. Following the passage from **"Roastbeef"** just quoted is a catalogue of rooms with suggested activities, concluding that "all room has no shadow." Mysteries replace mysteries in filling any place, be it that in a family, in a domicile, on a page; and "[t]he pleasure that is spread is not removed when the change is replaced. This was the remainder of there were having been or being any martyr. He was not the object."

Leo might easily have seen himself as a martyr. It was he that chose to live in Paris, and now Gertrude was to stay and he was to go. It was *his* household and now Gertrude was taking over. It was his famous art collection, after all, and he was the genius in the family. Now the paintings were to be divided and Gertrude was claiming to be the genius. It was he who had discovered Picasso, and now the painter was mainly Gertrude's friend. It was he who had all the sense, intellect, artistic destiny, but Gertrude was the one who was producing. He wrote to Mabel Weeks: "Now everything with me seems so changed that there are hardly more than points of resemblance between the conduct of life as it is now and as it was before," Meanwhile, Gertrude was writing, in "Two," ". . . as he was observing there is being existing the changing that is concluding, there is the changing that is commencing and if that is arriving and is resulting from something then something is being existing . . . ." Alice B. Toklas, one something of Gertrude's which was not one of Leo's discoveries originally, was to take his place. Again, from "Two":

> . . . he was ending, and ending sound was sounding and coming out of him. He was not ending, that was what he was doing, waiting not being existing, and he was waiting and waiting he was not listening.

> She was ending and ending she was not telling that she was ending. . . . She was not waiting and not waiting she was listening and listening she was ending.

But, to go back a bit, to the first page of *Two: Gertrude Stein and Her Brother:*

> There are two of them and one is a man and one is a woman. . . .

> There are not two of them. There is one of them, and there is one of them. There are sometimes two of them,

the one and another one. Each one of them has a sound in them. Each one of them has sound coming out of them. . . .

They are alike. . . . they are not alike.

One wonders, as one goes along, slowly, through this memoir of a relationship and its breakdown, why there is so much continued insistence on the separation of the two. The difficulty Gertrude had in seeing herself as a being apart from her brother is impressive. One often has the sense that one is reading, not just a description of two selves, but an exorcism of a part of one self. Sometimes it seems like a kind of prayer.

She was changing. He was changing. They were not changing. . . .

He was one. She was one. He was one. . . . Each one of them is one expressing something of everything being, going to be being, needing to be being, having been being, continuing to be being, completely being, intending to be being existing. . . . They are different. . . . They are very different the one of them from the other one of them. (*Two*)

Leo's method of exorcising Gertrude from his system is naturally the same and different. He likes to compare the two of them in more particular terms as to ability and accomplishment. In Leo's autobiographical fragment, for instance, he notes that geniuses always seem to have excellent memories of their childhoods, as he of course does, and reveals that ". . . Gertrude remembers almost nothing. Was it because her childhood was happy and mine was not? I don't know the answer, but the difference is enormous." *Touché*. But Gertrude is not interested in the past; as she sees it,

He said that he had, as all is all, he had that which was not the same but similar.

He modifying was not strengthening remaining changing. He was allowing that he was remaining changing by arranging modifying regeneration. He was saying all he was saying. (*Two*)

Whereas,

. . . she was aspiring in beginning, she was aspiring in needing changing, she was exalting in sound coming, she was escaping in attacking, she was emphasising in expressing, she was asking in coming, she was coming in changing, she was protected in resting she was keeping in needing, she was accomplishing having had something. (*Two*)

Making art out of real live discomfort and hopefulness is "accomplishing having had"; it makes over and makes for good, a kind of covenant. "Why is the perfect reëstablishment practiced and prized, why is it composed. . . . This is a result. There is no superposition and circumstances, there is hardness and a reason and the rest and remainder.

There is no delight and no mathematics" ("**Roastbeef**"). But only for a single moment. It is as if the components of the situation described by parts of *Tender Buttons* were thrown again and again, like yarrow sticks, falling in different, even contradictory, patterns. Yet there are insights in this randomness, even a certain amount of prophecy, but nothing exact; nothing counts exactly, but it all counts: "One, two and one, two, nine, second and five and that." "It is no use to cause a foolish number" ("**Sugar**" and "**Cake**"). Leo sometimes fancied himself a mathematician. For his sister crazy mathematics may or may not be better than "no mathematics." It is most uncertain.

One thing is certain. Gertrude is ready to have something different; and she has an excuse where "[a]n excuse is not dreariness, a single plate is not butter, a single weight is not excitement, a solitary crumbling is not only martial" ("**Breakfast**"). Small changes, making butter *better,* weight *wait,* and martial *marital,* explain that to be alone, to have to wait alone, would not be an excuse to separate. The deterioration of the relationship Gertrude is concerned with is not unlike a marital battle, where one flesh suddenly divides, or slowly divides, to be two, to spread into more. There is cause to celebrate "the one knowing the two of them was knowing that she was a different one from the other one." The differences are difficult—difficult to see, to maintain, to settle.

We come to Alice. She is, as far as Gertrude is concerned, a welcome treasure, but complicated feelings do not keep her from appearing in *Tender Buttons,* under the rubric "**Cooking**," as *alas:* "Alas, alas the pull alas the bell alas the coach in china, alas the little put in leaf alas the wedding butter meat, alas the receptacle, alas the back shape of mussle, mussel and soda." No matter how hungry one is, one must regret the price. Following "**Cooking**" are four elaborations, all called simply "**Chicken**":

CHICKEN
    Pheasant and chicken, chicken is a peculiar
bird.
CHICKEN
    Alas a dirty word, alas a dirty third alas a
dirty third, alas a
dirty bird.
CHICKEN
    Alas a doubt in case of more go to say what
it is cress. What is it. Mean. Potato. Loaves.
CHICKEN
    Stick stick call then, stick stick sticking,
sticking with a chicken. Sticking in a extra
succession, sticking in.

Make what you will of that. Sound it.

Perhaps Leo and Gertrude would have grown apart and eventually divided their household anyway; there is no doubt, though, that the installment of Alice accelerated the division. The following cryptic descriptions come from the section of *Tender Buttons* subtitled *Food,* "**Breakfast**" (a fast break or a beginning?):

A change, a final change. . . . What language can instruct
any fellow.
A sudden slice [Alice?] changes the whole plate, it does so
suddenly.
Anything that is decent, anything that is present, a calm
and a cook and more singularly still a shelter, all these show the
need of clamor. . . .
What is a loving tongue . . . when tears many tears are
necessary.
. . . A white cup means a wedding. A wet cup means a
vacation. A strong cup means an especial regulation. A single
cup means a capital arrangement. . . .
. . . If the persecution is so outrageous that nothing is
solemn is there any occasion for persuasion.
. . . all the pliable succession of surrendering makes an
ingenious joy.
A breeze in a jar and even then silence, a special anticipation
in a rack . . . does this incline more than the original division
between a tray and a talking arrangement and even then a
calling into another room gently with some chicken in any way.
Take no remedy lightly, take no urging intently, take no
separation leniently. . . .

"A breeze in a jar" is not so violent as a tempest in a teapot, perhaps not even so windy as a lecture by Leo, but it is something moving and incongruous, perhaps a welcome illusion if the atmosphere in the jar has been felt to be too close. The persecutions and persuasions suggested by Gertrude's strange text are not unloving but highly complex with both love and regret. Many arrangements have been considered, apparently, with respect to talking and eating—one with a solitary tray and another with her own chicken in another room, "calling . . . gently."

Part of the "remedy," which is not to be taken lightly, is in the final change itself; made up of "sudden" components (related to the washing and cleaning undercurrents of [*Tender Buttons*] by recurring "suds"?), the final decision is not sudden, or cleansing either; it is, at least some of the time, a dirty and painstaking slow business. "This is a sound and obligingness more obligingness leads to a harmony in hesitation" (*Rooms*). Another part of the remedy, I believe, is in the writing of *Tender Buttons* itself, no less an exorcism than "Two" "[a] work which is a winding a real winding of the cloaking of a relaxing rescue" ("**Breakfast**"). It is a labyrinth of privately colored and coded musings on the subjects of separation and replacement, the objects of anger and love. The "cloaking,"

with any particular chicken in mind, becomes a "clucking," a domestic sound to replace the "[l]ecture, lecture and repeat instruction" (*Food*, "**Mutton**") from which one needs timely rescue. All in all, *Tender Buttons* is "a mixed protection, very mixed with the same actual intentional unstrangeness . . . not more a sign than a minister." A mixed blessing, yet ministering a certain caring, *Tender Buttons*, in describing itself describes the pain as well as pleasure of relationships; it is a real embodiment of differences, "a separation . . . kept well and sectionally" ("**Sugar**").

Some people are naturally more adept or lucky in the resolving of differences than others. Where differences breed more differences, love may not be out of the question, as Gertrude Stein makes clear in "Two":

> . . . he was expressing that he not being loving, love being existing, he was not being loving, love being existing, he was being one not explaining not explaining loving being existing, not expressing being loving. . . . he was expressing explaining beginning, he was expressing explaining not continuing. . . . In being one he was not loving. . . . she was one who was expressing that love being existing she had been loving and being loving she had been being loved and having been being loved she had needed what she had come to be having. (*Two*)

Love and identity not unusually come together, and they make the differences between people all the more clear. It is from the vantage point of these that love is put into relief. As Gertrude expresses a part of this feeling in *Tender Buttons*, "Cuddling comes in continuing a change" ("**Sugar**"). Still, it is not all pleasure that is to be anticipated in the change, but "[t]ender colds, seen eye holders, all work, the best of change, the meaning, the dark red, all this and bitten, really bitten" (*Food*, "**Milk**"). Among the number of things that this "milk" implies—the comfort of a woman's breasts, those whites of eyes that hold eyes, both best and bitter meanings, perhaps the tender buttons bitten by conscience—is the changeable nature of all nourishment. One can receive from so many sources; one must choose from so many meanings. A single tone—monotony—is not possible.

> This which makes monotony careless makes it likely that there is an exchange in principle and more than that, change in organization.

> This cloud does change with the movements of the moon and the narrow the quite narrow suggestion of the building. It does and then when it is settled and no sounds differ then comes the moment when cheerfulness is so assured that there is an occasion. (*Rooms*)

As the organization of the household changes, as the shadows in rooms change according to architecture versus the moving moon, differing parties may eventually reach a changing accord. It is this sort of perception that brings celebration to Gertrude Stein's description of her relationship with her brother in "Two" as well as to the concluding passages of *Tender Buttons*.

There is no change lighter. It was done. And then the spreading . . . and yet the time was not so difficult as they were not all in place. They had no change. . . . that settlement was not condensed. It was spread there. Any change was in the ends of the centre. A heap was heavy. There was no change. (*Rooms*)

The spreading of a difference, of many differences, and the constant nature of inconsistency and change eventually result in "no change." For one who lives in the continuous present, "it means no more than a memory, a choice and a reëstablishment, it means more than any escape from a surrounding extra" (**"Roastbeef"**). "A receptacle and a symbol and no monster were present and no more. This made a piece show and was it a kindness . . . (**"Mutton"**). A receptacle has been found for the loving, and a symbol— literally somethings thrown together as much as those of *Tender Buttons* are—has become, for the present, permanent. There is no "monster"—no showman, no threat—to the receptacle and the text received. The peace that shows at the end is the only showpiece for all the labor of change and its interpretations. So. Was it all of a peace? Was it of kindliness as well as of differing kinds? The answer must be yes.

But the answer is to be

> not always, not particular, tender and changing and external and central and surrounded and singular and simple and the same and the surface and the circle and the shine and the succor and the white and the same and the better and the red and the same and the center and the yellow and the tender and the better, and altogether. (**"Roastbeef"**)

We may question any affirmative conjunction, but for the moment of it, it stays and is an agent of the whole. This is all one can say for the moment, for the moment of anything. Yes. Yes, but . . . each will eventually come to her own difference, a difference that points to identities, a difference that is as difficult to make as a conclusion.

Perhaps all we can hope to do is illuminate what seems light and to darken the outlines of the dark. *Tender Buttons* is written in a very private idiolect. No certain criticism being possible in such a case, all we can do is try to translate into more common language, at least for the moment, a piece here and there (it is so all here and there). The author even seems to ask us to "translate more than translate the authority, show the choice and make no more mistakes than yesterday" (*Rooms*). We can find our own use in strange usage and wonder why one question stands out more than another; for instance, "Why is there so much useless suffering. Why is there" (*Rooms*). And why is here as well, since:

> The author of all that is in there behind the door and that is entering in the morning. Explaining darkening and expecting relating is all of a piece.

> . . . The whole arrangement is established. The end of which is that there is a suggestion. . . .

. . . The reason that nothing is hidden is that there is no suggestion of silence. No song is sad. (*Rooms*)

Tender Buttons is a mysterious opera. We must keep talking about it. Sing if we can.

Neil Schmitz (essay date 1983)

SOURCE: "The Gaiety of Gertrude Stein," in *Of Huck and Alice: Humorous Writing in American Literature,* University of Minnesota Press, 1983, pp. 160-99.

[*In the following excerpt, Schmitz explains some of Stein's puns and identifies humorous references to Alice B. Toklas in* Tender Buttons.]

The speculative play of Gertrude Stein's humor first appears in the carefully wrong discourse of *Tender Buttons*, Here is a carafe, "nothing strange," *definiendum,* and there is a glass, *definiens.* Definition is the work of knowledge. It is the first lesson in Aristotle's primer on analytic thinking, the *Categories,* and Gertrude Stein uses it as her *mise-en-scene.* A carafe is a kind of glass. So Western Thought designates the World of Things, establishes Things in the World, species into genus, and constitutes the proper text. But something happens in Gertrude Stein's definition, the spectacle of an effacement, the spectacle of a metaphor, a split in the statement of the object, and all this changes her text, changes the lesson. *That,* which ought to place the carafe categorically before us, do its simple work of reference in the sentence, instead demonstrates its own importance. It makes a statement about statement, turns the simple object into a complex trope, the blind glass through which we see darkly, and holds these discursive antinomies (identity, difference) in bemused regard. "A carafe, that is a blind glass." Keeping strictly within the rules of grammar and syntax, within the logical structure of the predicating sentence, which is always impeccably written in *Tender Buttons,* Gertrude Stein begins here to write a decentered and alogical discourse that will unerringly provide the right answer to the wrong question. The impersonal pronoun that merely points, the prop and pivot of this sentence, points to her determined alienation from the Name of the Father, *Noema,* Aristotle, *et al.,* and the authority of his proper nouns. We will get nowhere in this curious text if we do not recognize at the start the blank figure of her estrangement, how it is written into the equivocal being of the pronoun, that term which does its silent work in the sentence of transferring meaning, placing objects, conjoining substantives, and is typically excluded from the question about reality. In the discourse Aristotle defines, and hands down to us as the *Organon,* the Instrument, the work of knowledge is with nouns.

So *that* begins the play of *Tender Buttons.* It makes us turn to it, to what it does, the activity of referring, this *that,* which, along with its relatives *this* and *there,* is curiously 'free,' without feature or gender, always naming and never the name. *That* is, to a large extent, the heroic utterance of *Tender Buttons*, the purest sign of Gertrude Stein's escape from the fix of definition, for the proper noun that names her surely did not, and her writing now reflects the composure of her difference. What *are* these strange objects: blind glass, glazed glitter, a substance in a cushion, a box, a piece of coffee? And what is the relation or resemblance of the entry to its titular subject? We commonly look at the world, at the text, through Aristotelian spectacles, and see kinds of everything, kinds of glasses, kinds of writing, the nominal realm of logic and philosophy, the metaphorical realm of rhetoric and poetry, and therein distinguish the carafe from the blind glass. This text, for example, 'looks like' an inventory, a lexicon, an "arrangement in a system to pointing" [*Tender Buttons* in *Gertrude Stein, Writings and Lectures*]. Looks like, but the information, the data, the flow of the discourse, does not specifically fit into the logical system, does not properly respond to the question: what is this, where does it fit, what does it mean? "Nickel, what is nickel," she writes below **"Glazed Glitter"** "it is originally rid of a cover," and the exchange repeats the exchange of the original proposition, deflects the ordinary course of signification into the surprise of metaphor. This posing of her difference, the perfect obscurity of her *that*, is kept constantly before us, and yet *Tender Buttons* has its meanings, is "not unordered in not resembling." The objects, as objects, tell us we are in the presence of Gertrude Stein's immediate reality, the domestic space of her apartment, the particular site of her writing, that they are instances of attention, and the problem of relation, of resemblance, which the pronoun focuses, at once illustrates a major theme in the text and renders the politics of her discourse. In the play of question and answer, of enigmatic statement, as *that* describes and explains, Gertrude Stein appropriates, in her own chosen terms, her sense of this dwelling.

For all its mystery, *Tender Buttons* continually discusses the pleasure of inhabitation. We do not ever leave the inclosure of her apartment, this small world where the eye lovingly remarks the familiar and all reference is privily self-centered, this and that. We move from *Objects* to *Food* into the final section, the amplitude of *Rooms*, and all the while the text is brimming with good humor, with puns, jokes, facetious gaming, cozy talk. The writer is humorously uxorious, contemplates the domestic articles, the domestic activity of cleaning, arrangement, sewing, cooking, and imaginatively reconceives their significance, gives them new meaning. There has been a change in the apartment, in the situation of Gertrude Stein's Writing, and this is the new arrangement that requires a different statement. "The change has come," she declares early in the text, and there is continual reference to it, the terms of the change, the problem of the change, the delight of the change. Her thinking has changed, her writing has changed, and the change is before us in her style. If, as she would later argue in her lecture "Poetry and Grammar," *Tender Buttons* represents an artistic breakthrough, is the single text in which she broke the "rigid form of the noun" ["Poetry and Grammar" in *Gertrude Stein, Writings and Lectures*], turned from belabored prose to beguiling poetry, it is a breakthrough *into* the possession of this particular space, the dwelling.

There is, almost, the feel of the raft in *Tender Buttons*, that feeling of being in a protected place, of being comfortably within, a Huckish exaltation. The writer evokes it through her playful interest in domestic concerns, her description of the gear and the provisions, these routines of explanation, and in her obvious relish of the daily fare, pain (bread) soup, creamed cucumber, and roast beef. "This makes no diversion," she reminds us, "that is to say what can please exaltation, that which is cooking." And *that*, of course, is not just the meal, but also the preparer, the person. A "sister" appears in the text, sharing the ambiguity of the writer's *that*, like and unlike, whose cookery and cleaning, whose intimacy, is woven into the intellectual and imaginative work of the writer. She is addressed: "A table means does it not my dear it means a whole steadiness." She is the sign of the writer's change, the problem of it, and the delight. "The sister was not a mister," we learn in *Rooms*. "Was this a surprise. It was. The conclusion came when there was no arrangement. All the time that there was a question there was a decision. Replacing a casual acquaintance with an ordinary daughter does not make a son." What is the relation of this sister, whose near-names are readily given (aider, aleless, alas), to the particular feeling of this discourse, its humor, and what, in the blind glass of the text, is her likeness? She is for the writer the positive identification of a likeness, a part of *that*, the sister self, the daughter self, a reflection, and in *Tender Buttons* (tend her buttons) she is positively cherished. Here is the connubial vow: to sort out dinner, to remain together, to surprise no sinner, to share everything, and it is tenderly recited:

> To bury a slender chicken, to raise an old feather, to surround a garland and to bake a pole splinter, to suggest a repose and to settle simply, to surrender one another, to succeed saving simpler, to satisfy a singularity and not to be blinder, to sugar nothing darker and to read redder, to have the color better, to sort our dinner, to remain together, to surprise no sinner, to curve nothing sweeter, to continue thinner, to increase in resting recreation to design string not dimmer.

We need look nowhere outside the text to see this much in the text, its place, persons, convivial humor, its principled evasion of specific reference. The inside narrative of *Tender Buttons* is just there, inside. At the end of the entry **"Book,"** in the first section, Gertrude Stein reflects upon the phrase "put a match to the seam," a loaded phrase she considers in its several loadings: hot evidently in its sexuality, cold in its textile reference, and a warning in its textual significance against that literal interpretation which would match imaginative characters and events to historical persons and events, looking into the text for its singular and essential definition. Yet the questioning of resemblance in *Tender Buttons*, which keeps us from matching seems, easily and continually becomes a play on resemblance. It is there surely in the optical motif: the blind glass becomes a "spyglass," later an "eye glass," and the single occasion of the first person pronoun in the text is the line "I spy." Here, provocatively, she gives us just such a 'leading' scene, a clue, the semblance of a picture postcard posing familiar figures, before abruptly retrieving the anonymity of *that*.

> Please a plate, put a match to the seam and really then really then, really then it is a remark that joins many many lead games. It is a sister and sister and a flower and a flower and a dog and a colored sky a sky colored grey and nearly that nearly that let.

That nearly let, let us in past the rigorous objectivity of the text to make an exact resemblance, put a match to the seam, writing sister to sewing sister. If the reader were informed, he might indeed espy, against a certain landscape, Gertrude Stein, Alice B. Toklas, and their dog, Polybe, and yet the play of this partial disclosure is not primarily with the reader, is not *for* any reader. It is the play of the writer with her intention, and if it solicits a reader, that person would be the one who holds the plate, who brings the plate. The inside narrative of **Tender Buttons** remains securely inside the present articulation of Gertrude Stein's writing.

The next entry reinstates the freedom of ambiguity, is sweetly wicked in its innocence. Under *Peeled Pencil, Choke,* she writes "Rub her coke." Children who stick sharpened pencils into their mouths often choke on them, an admonition we have all heard, but the rhyme and the reason of the succeeding line go awry, erase one meaning to show another: a sexual act, masturbation; a sexual object, the dildo. "Put a match to the seam" is a remark that joins "many many lead games." A sister and a flower. The last entry in *Objects* rejoins the play on the name: *This is the Dress, Aider.* An aider is a helper as well as the near-name, Ada, the adorable. If we recognize this name as the one Gertrude Stein had earlier given to Alice B. Toklas in the portrait **"Ada,"** that is all to the good, and useful, but the entry itself simply bespeaks through the pun an endearing interruption: "Aider, why aider why whow, whow stop touch, aider whow, aider stop the muncher, muncher munchers." We are at the end of the first section, of the *mise-en-scène,* and, beyond this munching, a rare meal is to be served. *Food* begins with the prospect of a menu, a sampling of the courses. Here is a partial list: "Roastbeef; Mutton; Breakfast; Sugar; Cranberries; Milk; Eggs; Apple; Tails; Lunch; Cups; Rhubarb; Single Fish; Cake; Custard; Potatoes; Asparagus; Butter; End of Summer." The lexicon is now culinary, but the cuisine is of course literary, the cooking of an allusive meditation, a stirring in of some Shakespeare and Blake, of some "Leaves in grass." And here, too, the singular name is sounded.

"Cooking"

> Alas, alas the pull alas the bell alas the coach in china, alas the little put in leaf alas the wedding butter meat, alas the receptacle, alas the back shape of mussle, mussle and soda."

It is a kind of inscription, this *aider,* this *alas,* a kind of *Ma Jolie. Alas/Alice* is remarked in all these things and activities: little, receptacle, mussle, answering the door,

serving a meal, cooking, and the punned name sounds the wifely complaint, alas. The significance of *Alas,* the playful naming, is the key to the specular politics of **Tender Buttons**. Turned, *sister/aider/alas* takes us through the looking-glass into Alice's other-world, the discourse of the other (wifely chatter), and shows us the mazy nature of Gertrude Stein's reflection. In the blind glass is the double, the other, on whom the writer projects at once her desire for recognition and the question of her identity. And here, of course, is the duality (sister as wife, sister as husband) that requires duplicity, that gives Gertrude Stein her multifarious usage of double-talk. The text resounds with the exchanges of these two figures, lover/beloved, writer/speaker, both of whom mirror each other. Lovetalk is double-talk, *ma jolie,* and the lovetalk of wedded lesbians is doubled double-talk, turned against the espionage of the straight world.

Picasso will publish his *amour* on his canvas, an *amour propre,* with magisterial ease. Here is an account of one of his several *Ma Jolies* aptly recorded in the *Autobiography of Alice B. Toklas.* Picasso has just moved to an atelier in the rue Ravignan. "One day we went to see him there. He was not in and Gertrude Stein as a joke left her visiting card. In a few days we went again and Picasso was at work on a picture on which was written ma jolie and at the lower corner painted in was Gertrude Stein's visiting card. As we went away Gertrude Stein said, Fernande is certainly not ma jolie, I wonder who it is. In a few days we knew. Pablo had gone off with Eve." Gertrude Stein's card goes into Picasso's painting; Picasso's device (the integration of found objects, the jocular reference to his love life) will reappear in **Tender Buttons**. The play on *Alas* as a version of *Ma Jolie* relates **Tender Buttons** to the ongoing direction of Cubist painting, and yet Gertrude Stein's rendering of it distinguishes her conceptually from the Cubists. Before we continue our scrutiny of the texture of **Tender Buttons**, we need to consider that difference, and how, for example, chatter, the usage of the discursive-immediate, enters Gertrude Stein's text.

Like much Cubist painting (Picasso is at work in 1911-12 on *Ma Jolie, Woman with Guitar,* as Gertrude Stein writes **Tender Buttons**), the discourse of **Tender Buttons**, as we have seen, exists in the question of relation and resemblance. *That* relates carafe to blind glass, sister to sister, and *that* is always the question, the hedge, the hinge, between the inscrutable intention of an unseen interiority, a perfect absence, and the pure presence of what is objectively stated in the text. "The author of all that," we are told in *Rooms*, "is in there behind the door and that is entering in the morning." Who steps into the room? We see simply in the busy metaphor, *that,* the copresence of identity and difference, an act of opening and closing, the play of the writer with designation. The geometry of early Cubist painting works similarly on traditional perspective, suggesting a picture only to deconstruct it. Forms and figures are presented, harlequins and nudes, mandolins and fruit dishes, but their ordinary existence in the pictorial frame is displaced, reorganized. The illusion of depth, of volume, of looking in upon a scene as through a window, is dispelled by the interlocking and overlapping of geometrical planes, by a new sense of light and color, all of which retains perception at the flat surface of the painting. Just as we have to read *Tender Buttons* differently, accept *that*, so we must look differently at the composition of *Ma Jolie*, Each work in its own idiom actively prevents us from realizing in it a certain defined or privileged meaning, distracts the presupposing mode of our attention, and substitutes, through the instrumentality of the pronominal feature, *that*, the geometrical factor, a 'cube,' its discrete and separate existence. The nominal character of the author "in there" behind her text, justifying it, is no longer the issue. A carafe is lost and found in the blind glass. Picasso had his *Ma Jolie*, Gertrude Stein had hers. . . .

Chatter enters Gertrude Stein's writing, enters it as a positive value, as a resource, and it places before the writer, who meditates, topics, special terms, feelings. These discourses—**"No, One Sentence"** (1914), **"Possessive Case"** (1915), and **"Lifting Belly"** (1915-17)—are as immediate as line sketches, improvisational, written in short lines, often wonderfully curious, and yet, for all their divergent phrasing, they are invariably situated by the presence of an aider, the seamstress/amanuensis who copies the manuscript, who is told to leave a space between the two requests to sew buttons on gloves. It is indeed a small joke which "Tender" sets in motion since earlier in **"No"** Gertrude Stein had complained: "I should have told you that between pages when there is no intermission and it is on top there's a space" [*As Fine as Melanctha*]. So the written "space" is typed into the copy and there is this little piece of weaving. The integration of the present moment, its bits and pieces, its oddities, into the text gives us the charm of spontaneity, and yet even as this is so, the chatter also expresses at once the intimacy of the sisters and the artistic importance of that intimacy. For it is spoken from an interior, the inside of a shared life, this chatter, this inconsequent and freely moving discourse, the common speech of the household, and it is herein rendered, twisted, twining, as a language sufficient for the uses of poetry. So it goes in **"Possessive Case"**:

> She has nothing to do at a moment's notice.
> Shall I get you your apple now.
> Bring me a new fig.
> Samples are more necessary than ever.
> That is not the way to lament.
> You needn't have everything taken out. You will never tell your sweet sad story better than that.
> Gardens mustn't frighten baby.
> They always are a funny pair

"Reading Gertrude Stein in this period," Richard Bridgman has observed, "is rather like listening to an interminable tape recording made secretly in a household. Amid domestic details, local gossip, references to failed ambition, to sewing, to writing, recriminations, apologies, and expressions of remorse come passages of intimate eroticism, sometimes quite overt in meaning" [Richard Bridgman, *Gertrude Stein in Pieces*]. And this is true, these discourses, which present the chatter of a "funny pair," are

revealing. "With startling audacity," Gertrude Stein writes in **"Possessive Case,"** "he [she] has in many cases called them by their real names." For Bridgman these pieces constitute something of an excursion, an idyllic interlude in which Gertrude Stein allowed the "demon of noon" to caper openly through her work. "Gertrude Stein continued to experiment," he notes, "but her aesthetic advances were overshadowed by autobiographical details." It is a distinction that misconstrues the nature of Gertrude Stein's experiment in this period. The *Ma Jolie* expressed in these writings, directly voiced, is the *Ma Jolie* whose value, whose useful knowledge, helps situate the play of *Tender Buttons*. Chatter, after all, not only discloses a certain reality of the interior life, household life, names "real names," but it is also, in some sense, a discursive skin that fits round, contains closely, is nearest to, the interior-life of consciousness itself. "Oranges are painful," Gertrude Stein writes at the close of **"Possessive Case."** "They are so interior." In its effortless and casual flow, its associative movement, its themes, its commonplaces, chatter is akin to the 'free' language of dreams. It is brought, this 'idle' gossip, this jesting sweet-talk, within the scrutiny, the propriety of writing, and it speaks humorously to the writer:

> Please mention me.
> I am delighted with that.
> You know you mustn't.
> Please mention me

In **"Lifting Belly"** (1915-17), perhaps the most telling of these pieces, Gertrude Stein works a refrain of endearing diminutives into the composition (pussy, baby, honey, hubbie), establishing in her prosy poem the tonal equivalent of Krazy Kat's effusive "'Lil Dahlink." Nearly all the pieces written around *Tender Buttons* are humorous and written in a changed style that recalls, in its byplay, the exchanges present in Huckspeech. It is an assertive and anxious Tom Sawyerish writer who continually says "I said believe me I am praised," and a Huckish voice, somewhat Krazy, that typically responds "Shall I get you your apple now?" Around 1909-10 Alice B. Toklas enters Gertrude Stein's writing in several guises, as *Ma Jolie*, the demoiselle, as wife and sister, as the Maker of the Home, this interior space that becomes the site of Gertrude Stein's text. She is also the amanuensis, directly addressed in the writing, used as a mirroring intelligence. She is effectively the framing language of the domicile, a feminine speech distributed among its traditional concerns—household objects, food, rooms—and therein a response to the question in Gertrude Stein's mind about relation and resemblance. So Alice B. Toklas is in *Tender Buttons*, not as an autobiographical reference, not as a specific character, but as the very space in which the writing (and the question) of *Tender Buttons* takes place, as the tender *and* the button.

Linda Mizejewski (essay date 1986)

SOURCE: "Gertrude Stein: The Pattern Moves, the Woman Behind Shakes It," in *Women's Studies,* Vol. 13, Nos. 1 and 2, 1986, pp. 33-47.

[In the following essay, Mizejewski contrasts Stein's perceptions of self in Tender Buttons *with examples of how feminist writers of her era treated the theme of female self-perception.]*

Since Gertrude Stein's **Tender Buttons** was published in 1914, its colorful chunks of language and imagery have been shaken in the kaleidoscopes of a dozen critical modes to produce a myriad of readings, designs, and explanations. The multitude of critical approaches attests to its brilliance and obscurity at once: readers presented with this wild, semi-verbless appraisal of objects, food, and rooms are justifiably intimidated but also challenged to find the "key" to a work in which "A Piece of Coffee" is "More of a double. A place in no new table," and in which "Red Roses" are "Cool red rose and a pink cut pink, a collapse and a sold hole, a little less hot" [**Tender Buttons**].

Tender Buttons has been described as a series of prose poems, although no traditional genre can do justice to its departures from all traditions, genres, and syntax. Divided into three sections, *Objects, Food,* and *Rooms,* it uses things, occasions, or phrases as the starting points of "descriptions" that do not describe or "definitions" that do not define. Under *Objects* we find word-portraits or meditations on everything from the trivial to the obscure: **"A Substance in a Cushion," "Dirt and Not Copper," "A Shawl," "It Was Black, Black Took."** *Food* begins with a sensual five-page contemplation of **"Roastbeef"** ("There is coagulation in cold and there is none in prudence. Something is preserved and the evening is long and the colder spring has sudden shadows in a sun") and moves on to **"Sugar," "Lunch," "Orange In,"** and so on. *Rooms* is the last and longest piece, describing space as tangentially as any of the previous pieces had "described," and including non-linear, semi-syntactical observations that are alternately rhapsodical and comic: "Alike and a snail, this means Chinamen, it does there is no doubt that to be right is more than perfect there is no doubt and glass is confusing it confuses the substance which was of a color. . . . Startling a starved husband is not disagreeable." As several critics have pointed out, the text is meant to be read aloud and its sense of humor cannot be ignored in the most serious of its readings.

These various readings, and the causes to which **Tender Buttons** has been rallied, include automatic writing, literary Cubism, religious mysticism, linguistic experimentation, perceptual innovation, Jungian "mandala," postmodernist narrative, and conflict with Stein's brother Leo. Without denying the validity of these readings—and crediting the genius of the text for accomodating multiple readings—I would like to propose one more, one that illuminates a relationship between Stein and several women modernist writers. The third party in this nexus is Alfred North Whitehead, whose thinking has been linked to Stein in the past and who was named by Stein, along with herself and Picasso, as one of the three "first class geniuses" of her lifetime [*The Autobiography of Alice B. Toklas*]. For the past decade, feminist philosophers have aligned themselves with Whitehead's process thought as a viable meta-physics for a feminist perspective. Taking this idea into the literary realm, a Whiteheadian perspective clarifies the dilemma of self-identification that occurs in the works of several feminist modernists: Virginia Woolf, Charlotte Perkins Gilman, Katherine Mansfield, and Kate Chopin. By identifying the similarities in Stein's and Whitehead's idea of self, we can understand the problem posed frequently in modernist literature, that of the integrated self caught in the language and philosophy of a dualistic culture.

Such a reading is not a "standard" feminist reading of Stein, as for example Cynthia Secor would give us in her biographical approach to Stein's novel *Ida.* Secor sees Stein's womanhood and lesbianism as the dynamic of her work: a radical re-definition of self and reality in reaction to patriarchal culture. Secor's thesis concentrates on *Ida,* but she refers to **Tender Buttons** briefly as a "celebration of the domestic and sensual aspects of [Stein's] relation with Toklas [Secor, "*Ida,* A Great American Novel" in *Twentieth-Century Literature,* 24 (1978)].

Such a reading, I believe, tends to attach a literalness of narrative to the text which seems to strain too much in the direction of "meaning." As Pamela Hadas notes, "It is interesting, in a way, to go through **Tender Buttons** as one would a book of riddles trying to guess the answers . . . but this approach (as [Stein] surely knew and was amused by) can only lead to overingenuousness on the one hand and frustration on the other" ["Spreading the Difference: One Way to Read Gertrude Stein's **Tender Buttons**, *Twentieth Century Literature,* 24 (1978)]. Seeing life with Alice as the "answer to the riddle" cheats **Tender Buttons** of its linguistic and perceptual answer-in-itself described by Bridgeman, Hoffman, and Weinstein.

My approach to Stein is, on the other hand, feminist in an indirect way. I am connecting Stein with other female modernists through a consciousness that I believe can be accurately described as Whiteheadian. While Secor believes that Stein is reacting *primarily* to patriarchal culture as a woman, I am asserting that she is reacting *primarily* to a problem in language and self-perception that is part of the accoutrement of that patriarchal culture, a problem for men and women alike, but which manifests itself in the writing of women in a particular way. My purpose is not to claim **Tender Buttons** as a feminist text, but to show how Stein might be a link to a Whiteheadian consciousness that is as useful for feminist readers and writers as it has been for feminist philosophers.

The dilemma of self-identification in modernism arises in a tension between delineation and flux, between the need for a room of one's own and the resistance to confinement. Woolf's Mrs. Dalloway, for example, is suspended in this kind of self-perception: "She sliced like a knife through everything; at the same time was outside, looking on" [*Mrs. Dalloway*]. This tension strains between the yearning for knife-like integrity and the knowledge that the self is not a "knife" at all, but a fluid process sunk into multiple processes. This sensibility is complicated in that the values of autonomy and affinity are set into opposition in our culture and related to gender. Valerie C.

Saiving, describing traditional modes of identity, uses the terms "individuality" and "relatedness" to describe sexual stereotypes:

> We are taught that men are . . . *essentially* self-directing, autonomous, and unique individuals whose needs, interests, and activities are valuable in themselves. In contrast, we learn . . . that women are, or should strive to become, beings whose existence is *essentially* constituted by their relationships to others. ["Androgynous Life: A Feminist Appreciation of Process Thought" in *Feminism and Process Thought: Harvard Divinity School/Claremont Christian Center for Process*]

In such a dichotomy, the woman naming the self as separate is considered unnatural; moreover, her definitions and names are those imposed by a male culture, as Mary Daly and others have pointed out.

Resistance to names and boundaries occurs in a number of women writers and their protagonists in the early part of the century when the confining definitions imposed by the Cult of True Womanhood were being defied. Barbara Welter describes the demands of True Womanhood as "piety, purity, submissiveness, and domesticity. Put them all together and they spelled mother, daughter, sister, wife—woman." When Stein wittily gives the non-definition of "Custard" as "Not to be. Not to be narrowly," she could be giving the motto for Kate Chopin's protagonist in *The Awakening,* for Woolf's undefinable Orlando, or for several of the women in Katherine Mansfield's stream-of-consciousness story "Prelude." The women in "Prelude," in fact, give us a paradigm of the dilemma: they are expected to fall into patterns like the domestic ones they arrange: "Everything in the kitchen had become part of a series of patterns" for the arranging grandmother, but her daughter, stultified in the male-defined roles of child-bearer and mate, is happiest when she is left alone, when the patterns of the walls themselves begin to move:

> . . . she traced a poppy on the wallflower. . . In the quiet, and under her tracing finger, the poppy seemed to come alive . . . Things had a habit of coming alive like that. Not only large substantial things like furniture, but curtains and the patterns of stuffs. . . .

Driven much further into madness by her condescending husband and her circumscribed Victorian life, the narrator of Charlotte Perkins Gilman's "The Yellow Wallpaper" hallucinates the trapped woman behind the wallpaper in her room: "The front pattern *does* move—and no wonder!" she discovers excitedly, "The woman behind shakes it!" She has had a long history of having "to be narrowly."

Of all these protagonists, only Orlando, in the fantasy of easy androgyny, is not disturbed, repressed, or mad. Edna Pontellier of *The Awakening* does not survive her journey into selfhood at all; she clearly knows what she does *not* want to be, but in rejecting one set of structures—the True Womanhood precepts—she finds herself in another: the structures and patterns of heterosexual romance. Dis-

appointed in the latter, she feels she has no choices, no delineated self. Only the water seems unstructured enough; swimming is her way of "reaching out for the unlimited in which to lose herself." Her "unlimited" sense of self, however, can be attained only by her self-extinction. Likewise, Gilman's narrator of "The Yellow Wallpaper" pulls herself out of the patterns at the price of her sanity. Finally, the women of "Prelude" float like ghosts in their male world, feeling unconnected to their private "real" selves. The young unmarried Beryl is miserable, sensing that her trained flirtatiousness and defence to men is a "false" self. "She saw the real Beryl—a shadow . . . A shadow. Faint and unsubstantial she shone. What was there of her except the radiance? And for what tiny moments she was really she." The "unsubstantial" self has no mode of being. Like the other women in the house, she ends by dressing and answering for and to men, complying with her society's given definitions because the undefined self remains elusive and inarticulate.

In all cases, the non-delineated self, in a culture that respects clear-cut, autonomous classifications, has no power. Woolf's woman writer, after all, needs a room of her own not simply for practical purposes, but for the self-definition, the self-assertion of having private space. Mrs. Dalloway's habitual retreat to her attic room is a deliberate refusal of her role as wife/mother and an assertion of an earlier, purer self:

> So the room was an attic; the bed narrow; and lying there reading, for she slept badly, she could not dispel a virginity preserved through childbirth which clung to her like a sheet. Lovely in girlhood, suddenly there came a moment . . . when, through some contraction of this cold spirit, she had failed [her husband].

The ambiguous nature of the retreat, however, is revealed in the connotations of death, the retreat from life itself: the narrow bed is a coffin as well as a virginal renewal; the sheet a shroud. The "cold spirit" in its refusal of sexuality is also a refusal of life.

Moreover, Mrs. Dalloway is later confused when her life-expanding empathy, which seems to dissolve walls and rooms, is confronted by the terrible facts of the rooms themselves. She watches the old woman in the next house move as Big Ben strikes, and senses that the woman moves "as if she were attached to that sound, that string. Gigantic as it was, it had something to do with her . . . Clarissa tried to follow her . . . ." Unfortunately, her sense of being connected to the woman, having "something to do with her" like the sound, is elusive, is both true and not: "And the supreme mystery . . . was simply this: here was one room; there another." The self remains in the confines of its walls, retreats to it, and at the same time resists those walls.

Stein's ***Tender Buttons*** resembles, in its methods, this wall-dissolving, pattern-shaking motif. Without ascribing to it a theme or narrative, we can at least see in it a consciousness that is deliberately breaking down categories of perception, time, space, and language. Rebelling against the confinements of definition, Stein liberates our habitual ways of seeing ordinary objects. She turns our eye to what the domestic woman traditionally deals with: household objects, kitchen items, the home. Then she explodes our traditional perceptions, asking us to understand eyeglasses as "A color in shaving," or asparagus as "wet wet weather." Her own categorization into *Objects, Food,* and *Rooms* is deliberately deceptive, for her definitions overlap, the distinctions break down, so that **"Roastbeef"** sounds like a room, "In the inside there is sleeping, in the outside there is reddening," while a room is described as time and action: "The author of all that is in there behind the door and that is entering in the morning. Explaining darkening and expecting relating is all of a piece." Sometimes the object is a series of impressions: **"A Petticoat"** is "A white light, a disgrace, an ink spot, a rosy charm." At other times the object is a process: **"Milk"** is "Climb up in sight climb up in the whole utter needles and a guess a whole guess is hanging." The total effect is a radical shaking of the categorical Victorian world.

Given the linguistic eccentricities of this text, it is not difficult to see why early critics [such as B.F. Skinner] wrote it off as an experiment in "automatic writing," a phenomenon Stein had researched in medical school. Later critics related it to the techniques of Picasso, explaining that Stein's refractions of reality are the literary equivalent of Cubism. Michael Hoffman, who once allied himself with that theory, later qualified, explaining that the use of one medium to describe another is "at best a metaphor." Stein's association with Picasso is not entirely irrelevant, however, for as Hoffman points out, "What she opted for was the same freedom to dislocate the previous forms and concentrations of the literary tradition" [*Gertrude Stein*]. Most critics have concurred in that opinion, and detailed analyses of the poetic and stylistic techniques have begun with the assumption that Stein's purpose is the achievement of a new mode of perception, one that begins with the object but does not remain with it, and one that constructs the moment in an alternate perception of time. Stein herself calls this structure of time "the continuous present," which she says is "a natural composition in the world . . . I knew nothing of a continuous present but it came naturally to me to make one." ["Composition as Explanation" in *Selected Writings of Gertrude Stein*].

Of *Tender Buttons* Stein wrote, "I struggled with the ridding of myself of nouns." She does not quite succeed in doing that, only occasionally discarding syntax altogether: "Aider, why aider why whow whow stop touch" is her description of the last "object" in the first section—actually not an object at all but the statement, "This Is the Dress, Aider." Even an impressionistic **"More"** depends on nouns: "An elegant use of foliage and grace and a little piece of white cloth and oil." Studies of her language are as numerous as studies of her perceptual experimentation. Norman Weinstein explains the syntactical play as an approximation of the attempt of consciousness to articulate experience as it occurs. He calls the gathering of the chaotic multitude of words "the linguistic moment" [*Gertrude Stein and the Literature of Modern Consciousness*]. Like other critics, Weinstein is interested in Stein's part in the creation of a modernist liter-

ature that takes linguistic risks in order more accurately to catch human perception. Critic Neil Schmitz goes further than this, however, seeing in *Tender Buttons* a heralding of the "post-modernist" concerns with narrative and point of view taken up later by Barthes and Barthelme ["Gertrude Stein as Post-Modernist: The Rhetoric of Tender Buttons," 1974]. Stein looms in the venerable position, then, of one of the recognized architects of modern literature, and *Tender Buttons* as its monument. Weinstein calls the work "a child's first guide to the twentieth century," though it is, ironically, considered unreadable by a majority of twentieth-century readers.

The relationship of Stein's alternate modes of perception to the philosophy of Alfred North Whitehead has been frequently cited and accurately qualified by critics who point out that the iconoclastic Stein is no philosopher. Allegra Stewart, however, connects the theory of religion and art shared by Stein and Whitehead, the creative act and the act of meditation, both being acts of "presence, by which the dualism of experience is overcome here and now . . . Knower and known are joined . . ." ["The Quality of Gertrude Stein's Creativity," in *American Literature,* 28 (1957)]. Reading *Tender Buttons* as an act of meditation, Stewart makes the point that it is an attempt to unify the dissociations of experience. She later [in *Gertrude Stein and the Present*] takes this further in an extended Jungian interpretation of Stein, in which *Tender Buttons* is seen as a "mandala," a ritualistic meditative prayer structured to bring the subconscious in contact with the universal subconscious. In general, this, along with Secor's feminist interpretation, is one of the few readings that attempts to see *Tender Buttons* as other than a linguistic, narrative, and perceptual experiment.

With Bridgman, Hoffman, and Weinstein, I agree that interest in the text must center on its method, not its meaning, and that its method is directly concerned with the presentation of an alternate means of perception. While such critics do justice to the *art* of Stein's dealing with the "continuous present," however, I feel the need to extend this approach into its philosophical implications. Placing Stein into the context of Whiteheadian process thought does not tailor her into a philosopher, for she resisted systematic philosophies as much as she resisted categories of identity. Process thought, however, gives us a way of understanding not only a work such as *Tender Buttons*, but the sensibility of a Mrs. Dalloway, an Edna Pontellier, and a Mrs. Ramsay. If feminist philosophers are right, such an understanding might help us in the shifting of attitudes necessary to achieve an androgynous culture.

Such a reading requires that Whiteheadian thought be considered seriously, not just in its general ideas about religion or creativity, but in its metaphysics. While a comprehensive analysis is not possible in this format, a brief summary is necessary. Whiteheadian metaphysics differs from most philosophical systems in that the latter ask us to think of ourselves as rooms in which events (thoughts, experience) occur, while Whitehead [in *Process and Reality: An Essay in Cosmology*] asks us to think of ourselves as events, constantly coming into being through interaction which other events—which include perceptions, actions, other persons, and the immediate and distant past. These multiple "pulsations" of process unite in "concrescence" to constitute a moment of experience. The individual person's "subjective aim" is capable of infinite creativity in the use of past and present moments of process, and the person is in fact made up of a complexity of past and present occasions, always in the moment of creation.

Stein's method of the "continuous present" is congruent with Whitehead's description of how the present moment actually occurs and how the individual consciousness "occurs" *with* the present moment. It is certainly easier to think of the items in *Tender Buttons* as "occurrences" rather than "descriptions." The "experience" of the object is occurring simultaneously with a multitude of other physical and mental experiences—or prehensions. The radical subjectivity of the text, then, prevents an "analysis" not only of the New Critical variety, but of the feminist literary variety, too, for such readings ultimately depend on meaning and relationship to at least a minimally objective reality. On the other hand, philosophical analysis is equally unsuitable as the final "key" to this work. We can only say that Whiteheadian process thought gives us a way to approach it by placing it into a context that Stein would have approved—sanctifying Whitehead's view of reality by enshrining him in that sacred trio with herself and Picasso.

Whitehead is especially concerned about the "mistaken" perception of reality and individuals as "enduring substances." "The simple notion of an enduring substance sustaining persistent qualities . . . expresses a useful abstract for many purposes of life," he writes. "But whenever we try to use it as a fundamental statement of the nature of things, it proves itself mistaken. In *Tender Buttons,* no object, space, or person "endures" in time. **"A Brown,"** for example, is "Not liquid not more so is relaxed and yet there is a change, a news is pressing." In *Rooms* she explains changes in space in this way: "Explaining darkening and expecting relating is all of a piece . . . and yet there comes a change, there comes the time to press more air. This does not mean the same as disappearance." The "change" is clearly not an "event" in the conventional understanding, nor is the color a "thing," nor is the person a delineated entity: **"A Little Called Pauline"** is "A little called anything shows shudders. Come and say what prints all day. A whole few watermelon. There is no pope." We can call this "stream of consciousness," or "the linguistic moment," or "free association," but as a "description" of Pauline it certainly opposes our traditional idea of personhood. The notion of enduring substances, says Whitehead, "arose from a mistake and has never succeeded in any of its applications. But it has had one success: *it has entrenched itself in language,* in Aristotelian logic, and in metaphysics" (italics mine).

The "entrenchment" in language Whitehead refers to here has to do with constructions of Aryan languages which separate person from action. Such a language is fairly incapable of expressing a Whiteheadian (and Steinian) perception of reality—though one might argue that the visual arts are more capable of doing so in phenomena such as Cubism. When Stein tells us that she is attempting to "rid" herself of nouns, she is imagining a process language—one entirely made of verbs—that Whitehead must have admired when he met her a few years later in the "beautiful country" around Paris: "Doctor Whitehead and Gertrude Stein never ceased wandering around in it and talking about all things" [*The Autobiography of Alice B. Toklas*].

Relating Stein's breakdown of language to the breaking down of the categorical modes of perception and identification, critics such as Weinstein have readily connected her to major trends in modernism. If we further link her perspective to a Whiteheadian one, then the sensibility of the modernist writers discussed previously can also be examined in the perspective of process thought. In Woolf, Gilman, Mansfield, and Chopin, characters who vacillate between defined identity and the flux of interrelatedness fear that the latter will result in a loss of "self." Mrs. Dalloway, Edna Pontellier, and the "Prelude" women retreat to rooms and enclosed spaces because they sense that their only means of self-assertion consists in claiming such defined spaces. This retreat is, in fact, the metaphor culture has given them: the self as an "enduring substance" in space, asserted by ownership of space—colonization, conquests of frontiers, capitalism. In such a culture, too, Edna Pontellier's search for self in *The Awakening* instinctively takes her out of her husband's home and into her own "pigeon-house." The move to different space fails, however, and she later understands all her options as pigeonholes too narrow and bound for her liking.

When these protagonists feel they have no options, they are expressing the reality of their language and cultural perception, which divided "self" and "other" categorically and absolutely. In Whiteheadian metaphysics, on the other hand, such a dichotomy is impossible, for the "self" is *constituted* of its interrelations with all other experience. Saiving explains that in process thought, "Not only are individuality and relatedness compatable aspects of every actuality, these two principles require each other. And since they require each other, neither is more 'real,' important, or valuable than the other" [in "Androgynous Life . . ."].

Consequently, the experience of these protagonists as *both* self and other is a more "true" experience than that of the autonomous self. There is no doubt that the "truth" Gilman's tormented narrator of "The Yellow Wallpaper" sees in the shifting wall patterns is more valid than the sane, honeyed, artificial world imposed upon her by her husband: "'Bless her little heart!' said he with a big hug 'she shall be as sick as she pleases! But now let's improve the shining hours by going to sleep . . . .'" Likewise, Edna Pontellier, shaking all the patterns of her previous life, is condescendingly humored by her husband, to whom her new behavior is either sick or mad. Edna's "problem" is her refusal to identify with a single, recognizable "self"; when she "searches" for a new identity, she expects actually to *find* one—unable to understand that her self *is* the process of its changes. Again, the villain is cultural expectation of enduring consciousness. Cartesian philosophy, Whitehead points out, "conceives the thinker as creating the occasional thought. The philosophy of organism inverts the order, and conceives the thought as a constituent in the creation of the occasional thinker."

Is this tension between "self" and "interrelatedness" an intrinsically female problem? Saiver has pointed out that women are traditionally expected to be more "related" to others than men. Penelope Washbourn [in "The Dynamics of Female Experience: Process Models and Human Values"], writing of the female experience and its expression in process thought, notes that the experience of pregnancy and menstrual cycles tend to "erode" in women traditional distinctions between self/other and mind/body. Certainly the dilemmas of the previously discussed protagonists are centered on female sexual experience—on wifehood and motherhood. The sexual experience, then, may trigger the self/other or substance/flux problem in women in a particular way because sexuality more obviously demonstrates to women the metaphysics that Whitehead claims is actually universal. However, the problem is a cultural one, not an inherently female one, and further study would show, I think, that the problem manifests itself in the writings of men in other ways.

Having placed Stein's **Tender Buttons** in these contexts, I believe that this approach accords with that of Anna Gibbs, who uses the feminist criticism of French novelist Hélène Cixous to understand Stein "in terms of the possibilities she opens up for other women writers." Gibbs too avoids a biographical-feminist reading of Stein and allies herself and Cixous with a "third wave" of feminist criticism that centers on writing as self-creation and self-naming. She finds that Stein and Cixous share the dynamics of transformation and repetition that produce "entity writing" instead of "identity writing." Entity writing concentrates on continuous presence, "so that consciousness is forced to become reflexive, and writing becomes a process of concentration, or intensification."

This concept of writing as "intensification," which is repetitious in its exploring of the alternate possibilities of the moment, is very similar to Whitehead's description of the creative process in *Religion in the Making*. While all existence is naturally "creating" in process, the artist "brings together something which is actual and something which, at its entry into the process, is not actual. The novelty must *resemble* the actual, "but it must contrast with it in respect to contrary instances so as to obtain vividness and quality." Donald W. Sherburne has done an extended study of Whiteheadian aesthetics and explains the metaphysics of creativity as a "horizontal" prehension of experience, which is usually prehended "vertically." The creative perception is sensitive to areas of consciousness not explored in commonplace experience; while "vertical" perception involves the integration of microcosmic entities into one macrocosmic prehension, the "horizontal" and creative perception is able to "concentrate macrocosmic entities into *one focal point of experience*" [A Whiteheadian Aesthetic].

Thinking of **Tender Buttons** in relation to Whitehead is, I hope, a "horizontal" perception of several modernist writers and ideas. It involves the belief that feminist criticism must look beyond social context in literature to the philosophical context as a way to pinpoint the dilemmas of self-identity. The result may give us a more "complete" perspective on our experience in the world. Whitehead gives us a complex but viable model for that perspective, while Stein, ultimately iconoclastic, gives us the sound and sense of it: "The care with which there is incredible justice and likeness," she concludes, "all this makes a magnificent asparagus, and also a fountain."

Marianne DeKoven (essay date 1992)

SOURCE: "Breaking the Rigid Form of the Noun: Stein, Pound, Whitman, and Modernist Poetry," in *Critical Essays on American Modernism,* edited by Michael J. Hoffman and Patrick D. Murphy, G. K. Hall and Company, 1992, pp. 225-34.

[*In the following excerpt, DeKoven examines Stein's use of nouns in* Tender Buttons *in the context of Modernist poetry.*]

Poetry, for Gertrude Stein, is painfully erotic. She defines it in "Poetry and Grammar" by means of a series of verbs addressed sexually to what she is pleased to call "the noun": "Poetry is concerned with using with abusing, with losing with wanting, with denying with avoiding with adoring with replacing the noun. . . . Poetry is doing nothing but using losing refusing and pleasing and betraying and caressing nouns. . . . I made poetry and what did I do I caressed completely caressed and addressed a noun ["Poetry and Grammar," in *Lectures in America*]. "The noun" becomes on the next page "the name of anybody one loves." Poetry therefore is "really loving the name of anything," which is a generalization to the level of literary genre of the private erotic act of "calling out the name of anybody one loves." Stein repeats that account of movement from private erotic act to generic definition of poetry in a comic and ambivalent parable that narrates a literary primal scene. She and her brother, presumably Leo, found "as children will the love poems of their very very much older brother." Leo, of course, was the dominating, inhibiting, disapproving presence in Stein's earlier literary life, whose replacement on the domestic front by Alice Toklas catalyzed a profound transformation in her writing. This little story of finding love poems is staged within a multiply constraining patriarchal scene: in the company of the close brother who immediately dominates her, she finds the heterosexual love poetry of a "very very much older brother." Here is her account of the discovery:

> This older brother had just written one and it said that he had often sat and looked at any little square of grass and it had been just a square of grass as grass is, but now he was in love and so the little square of grass was all filled with birds and bees and butterflies, the difference was what love was. The poem was funny we and he knew the poem was funny but he was right, being in love made him make poetry, and poetry made

him feel the things and their names, and so I repeat nouns are poetry.

Poetry is patriarchal; it is written by a "very very much older brother." But Stein can join with both brothers in mocking, leveling laughter: "the poem was funny we and he knew the poem was funny." Furthermore, the poem concerns "a little square of grass." Whitman is a crucially legitimizing poetic precursor for Stein, as she makes clear in this essay. Her very very much older brother might write a ludicrous poem about a little square of grass, but her true literary older brother has written a liberating grass poem expanding to the horizon the boundaries of all little squares.

Stein credits Whitman in this essay with a mode of literary transformation she usually reserves almost exclusively to accounts of her own breakthrough into the modern or American twentieth century out of what she generally calls the English nineteenth century: "Naturally, and one may say that is what made Walt Whitman naturally that made the change in the form of poetry . . . the creating it without naming it, was what broke the rigid form of the noun the simple noun poetry which now was broken." In "How Writing Is Written," a 1935 lecture also delivered "in America," Stein says definitively "And the United States had the first instance of what I call Twentieth Century writing. You see it first in Walt Whitman. He was the beginning of the movement" [Gertrude Stein, "How Writing is Written"].

Stein, like Whitman in *Leaves of Grass,* has broken in *Tender Buttons* the rigid form of the noun. In its rigidity, its decline into automatic, reflexive chains of association, the patriarchal noun has lost the ability to "create it without naming it," to make us "feel the thing anything being existing." The modernist poetics articulated by Ezra Pound, particularly in his imagist and vorticist manifestos, also aims at breaking form in order to create it without naming it and to make us feel the thing anything being existing. In important ways, Stein articulates belatedly in "Poetry and Grammar" a modernist poetic credo. I want to investigate both the similarities and the differences in Stein's and Pound's versions of breaking and remaking poetic form.

Stein's tribute to Whitman in "Poetry and Grammar" is as unambivalent as it can be. Pound's early poetic tribute to Whitman, "A Pact" of 1913, almost contemporaneous with *Tender Buttons*, is highly ambivalent:

> I make a pact with you, Walt Whitman—
> I have detested you long enough.
> I come to you as a grown child
> Who has had a pig-headed father;
> I am old enough now to make friends.
> It was you that broke the new wood,
> Now is a time for carving.
> We have one sap and one root—
> Let there be commerce between us.

(One wonders whether Stein got her figure of breaking, in association with Whitman and poetry, from this poem.)

Where Stein wholly approves of and identifies with Whitman's breaking, considering it the determining act of the new poetry, Pound sees it as only a rough beginning, an artisan's rather than an artist's act. And while Pound's poem ostensibly represents a reconciliation of the newly reasonable adult poet, the "grown child," with the "pig-headed father," the almost deliberately childish formulation "I am old enough now to make friends" calls attention to the "child" in "grown child," still in the relation to the "pig-headed father" of resentful, threatened, overly self-assertive son: four of the poem's nine lines begin with "I," and the poem is charged with anger and contempt. The conciliatory tone of the last four lines actually feeds the poet's assertion of superiority: having established his primacy, he can afford this pact. It will be made on his terms; he will carve where Whitman merely broke new wood; and he closes the poem with a decree in the Creator's voice, which at the same time manages to mock Whitman's American marketplace mundanity and ruefully to acknowledge Pound's own inescapable derivation from it, "Let there be commerce between us."

Pound's ambivalence toward Whitman parallels the ambivalence in his modernist poetics toward breaking the rigid form of the noun. The tone of his imagist and vorticist pronouncements is very much informed by the spirit of breaking, and his "direct treatment of the 'thing,' whether subjective or objective" is very close to, and perhaps one inspiration for, Stein's various formulations for "replac(ing) the noun by the thing in itself" and "creating it without naming it." Similarly, Stein's statement that "Language as a real thing is not imitation either of sounds or colors or emotions it is an intellectual recreation" reminds us of Pound's definition of the image as "that which presents an intellectual and emotional complex in an instant of time" [Ezra Pound, "A Few Don'ts by an Imagiste," in *The Modern Tradition*]. In "Transatlantic Interview," Stein says, criticizing a word choice in one of the *Objects* poems of *Tender Buttons,* **"A Piece of Coffee,"** that "Dirty has an association and is a word that I would not use now. I would not use words that have definite associations" ["A Transatlantic Interview" in *A Primer for the Gradual Understanding of Gertrude Stein,* by Robert Bartlett Haas]. This statement is highly reminiscent of Pound's attack on symbolism: "The symbolists dealt in 'association,' that is, in a sort of allusion, almost of allegory."

It is in relation to the question of rigidity that Stein and Pound most palpably diverge. For Pound, carver of new wood, the rhetoric of the new poetry is very much a rhetoric of domination: "The statements of 'analytics' are 'lords' over fact. They are the thrones and dominations that rule over form and recurrence. And in like manner are great works of art lords over fact, over race-long recurrent moods, and over to-morrow."

Stein describes her method of composition in writing *Tender Buttons* as a complex simultaneity of concentration on external objects and words recreating those objects as they form themselves in her mind: "I used to take objects on a table, like a tumbler or any kind of object and try to get the picture of it clear and separate in my mind and create a word relationship between the word and the things seen." Boundaries between outer and inner, and among objects, images, words, and mind, become fluid, unfixed, finally invisible, irrelevant, wholly permeable. Stein describes explicitly here the action of breaking the rigid form of the noun, language's prime implement of subject-object separation and domination. . . .

To the extent that she participated in the modernist moment of representation, Stein, like Pound, was ambivalent about the twentieth-century revolution of the word both of them did so much to shape and foment. Unlike Pound, Stein did not reinvent the rigidity of the form of the noun, nor did she work toward domination, containment, compression, or abstract conversion of her erotic-poetic impulse. Stein is writing from the position of the woman modernist: her fearful ambivalence toward the unequivocal assertiveness of her program of breaking and remaking emerges in diction of violence and anxiety.

In a vividly erotic passage I have already cited from "Poetry and Grammar," Stein's negative feeling toward her poetic project erupts in a series of predominantly anxious and violent verbs: "Poetry is concerned with using with abusing, with losing with wanting, with denying with avoiding with adoring with replacing the noun. . . . Poetry is doing nothing but using losing refusing and pleasing and betraying and caressing nouns." Similarly, Stein associates the process of making poetry with a painful intensification of erotic feeling: "you can love a name and if you love a name then saying that name any number of times only makes you love it more, more violently more persistently more tormentedly."

The overall tone of *Tender Buttons*, as many critics, including myself, have claimed, is one of joyous lightness and miraculous plenitude. That tone is fulfilled in its last line, a utopian invocation of paratactic gender equality: "all this makes a magnificent asparagus, and also a fountain" [*Tender Buttons*]. But such confident serenity is regularly punctuated by diction with reverberations of a more tormented sort.

"Sugar"—to use a section from *Food* that Stein assesses favorably in "Transatlantic Interview" (she finds "unsuccessful" several other segments of *Tender Buttons*)—begins

> A violent luck and a whole sample and even then quiet. Water is squeezing, water is almost squeezing on lard. Water, water is a mountain and it is selected and it is so practical that there is no use in money. A mind under is exact and so it is necessary to have a mouth and eye glasses.
>
> A question of sudden rises and more time than awfulness is so easy and shady. There is precisely that noise.

Stein particularly likes those opening paragraphs. Their overall tone expresses an excitement tinged with violence, not simply in the opening "violent luck" but in the rep-

etition of "squeezing," counterbalanced by an unexpected "quiet," which reinforces by opposition that violent excitement; also in the slightly disgusting erotic suggestiveness of water squeezing on lard, and in the suggestion of drowning in "a mind under." Again, the energy required for breaking the rigid form of the noun is a threateningly violent force; the erotic charge of that breaking is tinged with disgust.

Unlike the longer sections at the beginning of *Food*, "Sugar" goes on for just another page, but it is still too long to quote in its entirety. The following excerpts, which continue the tone of the opening lines, taken together represent approximately half of the poem:

> A question of sudden rises and more time than awfulness is so easy and shady. . . . Put it in the stew, put it to shame . . . A puzzle a monster puzzle, a heavy choking, a neglected Tuesday. . . . Wet crossing and a likeness, any likeness, a likeness has blisters, it has that and teeth, it has the staggering blindly . . . Cut a gas jet uglier and then pierce pierce in between the next and negligence. . . . A collection of all around, a signal poison, a lack of languor and more hurts at ease.

It doesn't take a detailed reading to make apparent the violence and anxiety of Stein's sounds as they hit the ear and of the troubling connotations and resonances that match and support those sounds as they take shape in the reader's mind. "Sugar" ends on a relaxed, affirmative note, "A nice old chain is widening, it is absent, it is laid by," which does not, however, wholly assuage the anxiety about that nice old chain articulated in the body of the piece.

In "Transatlantic Interview," Stein focuses her response to "Sugar" on those first two paragraphs, which she sees as a poetic treatment of water: "'A mind under is exact and so it is necessary to have a mouth and eyeglasses' (the fourth sentence). That impresses any person, so to speak it is part of the water and is therefore valid. It is supposed to continue the actual realism of water, of a great body of water."

Water is an important recurring motif in *Tender Buttons*, particularly in conjunction with containment and vision. References to water occur throughout; several subtitles in the *Objects* section (*Rooms* has no subtitles) concern water either explicitly or obliquely, especially in relation to containment or protection, such as "Mildred's Umbrella," "A Seltzer Bottle," "A Mounted Umbrella," "Careless Water," "Water Raining," "An Umbrella," "A Little Bit of a Tumbler." The opening section of *Objects*, and therefore of *Tender Buttons*, condenses (as it were) the motifs of water, containment, and vision: "A Carafe, That Is A Blind Glass" (the second poem of *Objects* is entitled "Glazed Glitter," continuing the "blindness," or opacity, of the opening glass carafe).

"Sugar" associates water not only with anxious sexuality and violence, as we have already seen, but also with the crucial modernist issues of leveling and annihilation. Water, (traditionally) the feminine, is the enabling medium for the new writing, which breaks and remakes the rigid form of the noun. At the same time, water is the medium that can drown, obliterate, prevent vision: "A mind under is exact and so it is necessary to have a mouth and eye glasses." This sentence connects a drowned mind, the exactness of the symbolic, its exigency ("necessary"), the pre-oedipal mouth that utters the presymbolic and attaches to the body of the mother, the "eye glasses" that protect symbolic vision from presymbolic annihilation, and that also suggest the "glasses" that *contain* water.

Water is also "a mountain," and involves "a question of sudden rises." Later, "crestfallen" is associated with "open," "mounting" with "chaining," and a "wet crossing" with "a likeness, any likeness, a likeness has blisters, it has that and teeth." At the level of "actual realism," "a great body of water" has waves: mountains, sudden rises, that can become *crest*fallen. Waves rise in contradiction to the leveling force of water ("water seeks its own level"). Like those of the other modernists, Stein's position in relation to twentieth-century democratic, egalitarian leveling was as equivocal as her position in relation to feminine self-assertion. She decried Roosevelt, distrusted "big government," and allied herself politically, if at all, with American "rugged individualism." She was a close friend in the thirties and forties of the collaborationist Bernard Faÿ, whose interventions on her behalf with the Vichy government enabled her and Alice Toklas, also Jewish, to remain miraculously unmolested in occupied France. But, on the other side, "The Winner Loses, A Picture of Occupied France" is a tribute to the Resistance, she excoriates Hitler as "Angel Harper" in *Mrs. Reynolds,* and, most importantly, she links to the egalitarian-democratic principle of "one man one vote" her notion of the "twentieth-century composition" as a composition in which there is no dominant center, in fact no center at all; each element is as important as every other element, and as important as the whole.

"Crestfallen and open," "mounting and chaining": these water-related conjunctions are perfect representations of Stein's ambivalence. "Crestfallen" has negative connotations but denotes leveling and is associated with "open," which has positive political and literary connotations; "mounting" has predominantly positive connotations but also denotes hierarchy as well as hierarchical, animalistic sex, and is associated with "chaining," which has negative connotations, invoking the constraints of the old order, again both political and literary (chains can suggest linearity). Similarly, "wet crossing and a likeness" links representation ("a likeness") with water and transgression, or at least stepping over (boundaries), going from one side to another. Concomitantly, "any likeness, a likeness has blisters, it has that and teeth, it has the staggering blindly": sucking mouths develop teeth, which enable them to speak as well as to bite; blisters come from (subversive) friction; staggering blindly, again, is the terrifying punishment for the wet crossing.

Rebellion against patriarchal poetry is a dangerous act for a woman writer in the modernist period, generally accom-

panied by rage and fear. We can admire once again how little Stein was hampered, to what a great extent she actually achieved her project of breaking the rigid form of the noun.

Susan M. Schultz (essay date 1992)

SOURCE: "Gertrude Stein's Self-Advertisement," in *Raritan,* Vol. XII, No. 2, Fall, 1992, pp. 71-87.

[*In the following essay, Schultz discusses Stein's ruminations on her writing career in "Stanzas in Meditation" and her autobiographical prose works.*]

> I often think how celebrated I am.
> It is difficult not to think how celebrated I am.
> And if I think how celebrated I am
> They know who know that I am new
> That is I knew I know how celebrated I am
> And after all it astonishes even me.
>
> All this is to be for me.

Gertrude Stein defies the attempts we make at describing her career historically; the antihistorical historian par excellence, Stein wrote two autobiographies in 1932 alone. The first purports to be history, albeit the history of another's life; *The Autobiography of Alice B. Toklas* is one of Stein's most ostensibly accessible works. The second, **"Stanzas in Meditation,"** records the process of telling rather than offering us the tale itself. But the very accessibility of the Toklas autobiography tends to obscure its central sleight of hand, as well as its left hook at literary tradition, for Stein not only writes as her own muse—Alice B. Toklas—but she has Toklas perform a service quite different from that of the traditional muse. Conventionally, the muse has been at once the power behind the text and the text's best audience. But Stein's muse does not so much inspire as advertise her work; her muse promotes the text as a literary, not a spiritual, agent. Even more radically, the work that Stein has Toklas advertise is not the work that she finds herself "writing"; instead, it is the kind of experimental work that we find in **"Stanzas in Meditation,"** work that eschews the muse. Toklas, then, invites us to forget Toklas, just as Stein invites us to become one with Stein. The central subject of the second autobiography, like the first, is the question of audience: for whom is Stein writing, herself or someone else? To what extent can she become her own audience? To what extent does the equation of the artist with her audience obviate or exacerbate the modern artist's problem with audience? She poses these questions in both works, although her strategies are more radical in **"Stanzas in Meditation."**

This doubling of concerns is only appropriate for an author as concerned with repetition and difference as Stein. Creation is for Stein tantamount to repetition since, lacking a muse apart from herself, Stein (at least figuratively) lacks a subject or an audience. Language becomes poetry, in

Stein's experimental work, not because it names the world, but precisely because it refuses to do so, over and again. Surprisingly perhaps, Stein's poetics are radical for their very formalism; the text insists on its separateness from its possible subjects, not on its union with them. But Stein's formalism is not that of the New Critics; rather it seems closer to the self-reflexive formalism of her contemporary, Laura Riding, and to the unacknowledged formalism of contemporary language poets. Both Riding and the language poets write poems whose primary subject is the material—the language—that creates them. Stein's long poem **"Stanzas in Meditation"** resists closure only insofar as it resists a muse outside of itself. Stein seeks to find something internal to poetry itself on which to authorize her text. In a poem whose title *sounds* Romantic, Stein deconstructs the Romantic landscape and moves toward a purely linguistic one, which cannot be described because it is a landscape of words, not a place.

This problem is as sexual as it is linguistic. Stein's repetitions bespeak the impossibility of ever actually saying the same thing twice—she is the Heraclitus of modern writers. But they also testify to her ambivalence about the sameness that her repetitions seem to assert. The sameness that Stein desires with her audience is metaphorically like the lesbian union she shared with Toklas. She parodies the homosexual nature of that union of like with like in her conflation of herself with Toklas in the *Autobiography*. She parodies that intimacy again in the first sentence of *Everybody's Autobiography,* published in 1937—"Alice B. Toklas did hers and now anybody will do theirs"—in which she—anybody, everybody—becomes one with all audiences, not just with Toklas. To write everybody's autobiography is both to deny the difference between writer and reader and to assert control over the reader's reception of the text.

Throughout her autobiographies Stein expresses the desire to do away with difference at the same time as she questions the worthiness of her desire to do so. Her text is a mirror in which she perceives herself. But what distinguishes her from other mirror-writers (Renaissance sonneteers such as Sidney, Spenser, and Shakespeare come to mind) is the literalism of her metaphor: Petrarch perhaps saw only himself in the mirror of Laura, but he re-represented himself as other—as a woman. Not only does Stein look for herself in her text; she is the mirror in which she looks. Thus the lesbian union that she exploits in the Toklas "autobiography" becomes a trope for a far more primary narcissism than that of Petrarch and his followers.

So, while a poet like Laura Riding was ready and willing to rid herself of an audience, Stein wanted (however ambivalently) not just to have an audience, but to be that audience, just as she is Toklas in the *Autobiography*. According to my reading, the word "audience" does not "[spell] everything that was corrupt" for Stein, as Ulla Dydo claims. Instead, the *Autobiography* is nothing if not a plea for an audience, as well as an extended complaint about the misconceptions of the as-yet-uneducated audience. Thus Stein/Toklas describes Stein's bewilderment in the face of Matisse's nonacceptance: "It bothered her

and angered her because she did not understand why because to her it was so alright, just as later she did not understand why since the writing was all so clear and natural they mocked at and were enraged by her work." Stein is more ambivalent about her audience in **"Stanzas in Meditation,"** but only because she fears that her readers will not accept her; she is every bit as anxious for control over her audience.

In *The Autobiography of Alice B. Toklas* Stein, though she speaks of herself (through Toklas) as one of the three geniuses of the century, is one artist among many. The book is something of an apology—or polemic—for modernism's central credos. Like her fellow moderns Eliot and Pound, Stein/Toklas associates herself with a new classicism that is an antidote to Romantic emotionalism. If her audience refuses to recognize the clarity of her modernism, she will adopt a classical analogy, as Stein/Toklas does in appealing to the authority of a French critic: "The sentences of which Marcel Brion, the French critic has written, by exactitude, austerity, absence of variety in light and shade, by refusal of the use of the subconscious Gertrude Stein achieves a symmetry which has a close analogy to the symmetry of the musical fugue of Bach." Or, in Toklas's "own" words:

> Gertrude Stein, in her work, has always been possessed by the intellectual passion for exactitude in the description of inner and outer reality. She has produced a simplification by this concentration, and as a result the destruction of associational emotion in poetry and prose. She knows that beauty, music, decoration, the result of emotion should never be the cause, even event should not be the cause of emotion nor should they be the material of poetry and prose. Nor should emotion itself be the cause of poetry or prose.

This is at least as elegant an expression of the modernist creed as Eliot's "Tradition and the Individual Talent"; Stein, writing in 1932, fights her own belatedness by making some rather extravagant claims for her earlier work.

> Gertrude Stein had written the story of Melanctha the negress, the second story of Three Lives which was the first definite step away from the nineteenth century and into the twentieth century in literature.

> She realizes that in English literature in her time she is the only one. She has always known it and now she says it.

> [*Tender Buttons*] as everyone knows, had an enormous influence on all young writers. . . .

And:

> It was in Saint-Remy and during this winter that she wrote the poetry that has so greatly influenced the younger generation.

Stein is, if anything, less obscure about her position in **"Stanzas,"** where she chides herself for wishing too desperately for an audience. The very circularity of the passage that follows, in which she listens to herself think about the problem of audience, insures that the work matters because it is hers, but is hers only insofar as it examines its relation to its audience. **"Stanzas"** is so long, then, because it forms a loop. From Stanza VII of Part II:

> When they were not only laden with best wishes
> But indeed not inclined for them to be careless
> Might they be often more than ever especially
> Made to be thought carelessly a vacation
> That they will like this less.
> Let me listen to me and not to them
> Can I be very well and happy
> Can I be whichever they can thrive
> Or just can they not.
> They do not think not only only
> But always with prefer
> And therefore I like what is mine
> For which not only willing but willingly
> Because which it matters.

But this is to jump ahead of things; Stein sets up several questions from the beginning of this 150-odd page poem. Richard Bridgman is right to identify the "they"'s so often referred to (twenty-four times in Stanza I alone) as a reference to Stein's audience. That Stein's particular audience is Toklas also seems evident in the passage that follows.

> They like it as well as they ever did
> But it is very often just by the time
> That they are able to separate
> In which case in effect they could
> Not only be very often present perfectly
> In each way which ever they chose.
> All of this never matters in authority
> But this which they need as they are alike
> Or in an especial case they will fulfill
> Not only what they have at their instigation
> Made for it as a decision in its entirety

Stein's particular anxiety is revealed in the line, "All of this never matters in authority"; if she, as writer, wielded authority over her audience, in other words, none of this would be a problem. That she does not in this instance do so is because "they are alike," as she and Toklas are alike in the *Autobiography*. As she writes in Stanza XIII of Part IV, "This is an autobiography in two instances." The two instances, of course, may refer to the two autobiographies she was writing at the time, or to the two people whose autobiographies she was writing as one. And the problem, it seems, has to do not so much with the audience's particular likes or dislikes, but with its attendant separation from the writer: "But it is very often just by the time / That they are able to separate."

Stein's anxiety is heightened by the threat she feels from her audience; it threatens to control her, and she has to plead with herself to ignore the audience outside her, and instead to heed the one within.

> It is always what they will out loud
> Can they like me oh can they like me.
> No one can know who can like me . . .
> Let me listen to me and not to them
> Can I be very well and happy
> Can I be whichever they can thrive
> Or just can they not.
> They do not think not only only
> But always with prefer
> And therefore I like what is mine
> For which not only willing but willingly
> Because which it matters.

The last line ends her thought ambiguously; whether she likes her work because it matters, or whether it matters because she likes it, is not clear. The making of "material" is obviously important to Stein—an enormously prolific writer—as a sign that matter matters. And, by extension, her material will insure that she, the mother of the text, will also matter.

> It is for this that they come there and stay.
> Should it be well done or should it be well done
> Or can they be very likely or not at all
> Not only known but well known.
> I often think I would like this for that
> Or not as likely
> Not only this they do
> But for which not for which for which
> This they do.
> Should it be mine as pause it is mine
> That should be satisfying

The concluding "should" clause seems to confirm Stein's inability to find her work satisfying on its own terms; work "well done" ought to insure the result of its being "well known." One final example (and there are dozens more) should complete the picture of a writer who cared so desperately not to care what her audience thought of her.

> I have been worried I will be worried again
> And if again is again is it
> Not to be interested in how they think
> Oh yes not to be interested in how they think
> Oh oh yes not to be interested in how they think.

The only means which Stein finds to persuade her audience is to incorporate or to absorb it into herself, as she claims to do in Stanza XIV of Part II, playing on an ambiguity in the word *absorb*:

> It is not only early that they make no mistake
> A nightingale and a robin.
> Or rather that which can which
> Can which he which they can choose which
> They know or not like that
> They make this be once or not alike
> Not by this time only when they like
> To have been very much absorbed.
> And so they find it so
> And so they are
> There

There which is not only here but here as well as
  there.
They like whatever I like.

The obsessive use of "they" gives way arbitrarily to a use of "it" in Stanza II of Part I, separated only by enjambment from the first stanza. The problem unraveled in this stanza is that the separation between writer and audience—one not permitted in *The Autobiography of Alice B. Toklas*—causes strife. They (here, most likely, Toklas herself) do not always like what they read, or worse yet, they are not always interested in it.

> They could have pleasure as they change
> Or leave it all for it as they can be
> Not only left to them as restless
> For which it is not only left and left alone
> They will stop it as they like
> Because they call it further mutinously

Stein snipes further at her audience: Toklas passes on her work, she more than implies, because it is named after her. As I have already suggested, the intimate connection between Stein and her muse has sexual overtones. The "they"s seem first to be Stein and Toklas, who are "always alike," and then to be the audience beyond them: "For which they will not like what there is." Probably Stein's conflation of inside and outside here (including the phrase "mind do they come," which suggests both a mental and a sexual process) reflects on her own ambivalence about a coupling—and a writing—that she knows is considered "strange." The word "like," then, is rife with meaning; it signifies "likeness," as in a simile, and also denotes affection: one likes what one is like. "Or however not a difference between like and liked." Sexuality redeems what has been unlike, and unlikeable, in what preceded this passage:

> As they will willingly pass when they are restless
> Just as they like it called for them
> All who have been left in their sense
> All should boisterous make it an attachment
> For which they will not like what there is
> More than enough and they can be thought
> Always alike and mind do they come
> Or should they care which it would be strange.

Yet Stein must force this likeness, too, as she does in Part IV, where she talks most explicitly about the dual autobiography she is embarked upon, and conflates herself with Toklas more overtly than she does in *The Autobiography of Alice B. Toklas* (with the exception of that book's remarkable last paragraph). Stein first parrots the Toklas of the *Autobiography* in her assertions that Stein is a genius:

> She knew that she could know
> That a genius was a genius
> Because just so she could know
> She did know three or so
> So she says and what she says
> No one can deny or try
> What if she says.

This simply rephrases Toklas's claim in the first chapter of the *Autobiography* that "I may say that only three times in my life have I met a genius and each time a bell within me rang and I was not mistaken, and I may say in each case it was before there was any general recognition of the quality of genius in them." In the poem, Stein blithely adds that no one will know which autobiography of the two this is. Then farther into the stanza she baldly announces her absorption of Toklas into herself: "She will be me when this you see." And, even more strongly:

> I would have liked to be the only one
> One is one.
> If I am would I have liked to be the only one.
> Yes just this.
> If I am one I would have liked to be the only one
> Which I am.

The author so uncomfortable with mere "likeness" for the gaps that it leaves between lovers, or between the writer and her audience, closes that gap by declaring oneness with her muse. Her assertion is not without its violence; to declare that "all this is to be for me," as she does at the end of the stanza, is to deny the reader the liberty of interpretation. Interpretation, of course, depends upon just those gaps and holes in the text that Stein proclaims nonexistent, filled. She requires opacity precisely so that she can possess her text. That she also wished to "possess" Toklas is clear in her description of her as a "prostitute" in many journal entries early in their relationship.

Stein's discussion of authority has everything to do with the names that are given objects in the world, objects that are seen through the names we give to them; later in the poem, she will claim to "look" without describing, to regard the landscape without giving it the old names. In other words, she means to have her own authority, unlike those persons described in Stanza X of Part I who "call a pail a pail and make a mountain cover / Not only their clouds but their own authority." In this stanza she parodies Keats, an old authority.

> It might be very well that lilies of the valley have a
>   fragrance
> And that they ripen soon
> And that they are gathered in great abundance
> And that they will not be refreshing but only
> Very lovely with green leaves
> Or managed just the same when payed or offered
> Even if they do.

The last two lines sound a discordant note; surely even bad gardeners don't usually think of paying off their flowers. But in conflating a Romantic-sounding description of flowers with a reference to payment, Stein ushers in a difference between what she terms "god" and "mammon" in her lecture "What is English Literature," published in 1935. In that piece, she distinguishes between writing that sounds like old writing and writing that does not.

> If you write the way it has already been written the
> way writing has already been written then you are

serving mammon, because you are living by something someone has already been earning or earned. If you write as you are to be writing then you are serving as a writer god because you are not earning anything. . . . But really there is no choice.

There is humor in her assertion that "writer gods" don't earn anything. But Stein is not only criticizing the Keatsian rhetoric she imitates; she is also criticizing the way in which it describes the world mimetically. "They" are the ones who describe the world in old and familiar language. From Stanza XV of Part I:

When they find the clouds white and the sky blue
The hills green and different in shape too
And the next to what followed when the other bird
  flew
And what he did when he dug out what he was told
  to
And which way they will differ if they tell him too
They do it by hand and they carry it all too
Up the way they did still have it to do
And so they think well of well-wishers.
I have my well-wishers thank you.

This kind of repetition of small talk—one imagines that she is describing a party of some sort—is deflated by her final, defensive, statement that she too has well-wishers. What she dislikes here about small talk (and what she so revels in in *The Autobiography of Alice B. Toklas*) is its mimetic representation of the world outside language. But mimesis requires a muse, whereas the kind of literature that Stein so obviously has in mind in **"Stanzas in Meditation"** refuses the muse entrance. She has moved beyond the "Portraits" she had written earlier in her career, portraits sometimes identified only by their titles, but portraits of others nonetheless. In her "self-portrait," Stein curiously reduces herself to the movement of language itself, and to the vacillation between a language that communicates and a language that is purely private. What Stein does for herself in **"Stanzas"** is to try to become self-sufficient; her necessary failure is spelled out in her abiding need to address—or to redress—an audience. Even if that audience is only herself, it signifies her failure to be one with herself. To be one with herself would mean doing away with language, something that Stein cannot do, as long as she writes.

Thus it seems unsurprising in this context that in "What is English Literature" Stein insists on the separation of life and art, because art can be a mirror of the self, but not coeval with it. Art, according to Stein, is essentially other than life. "And now," she asks there, "why does the representation of things that being painted do not look at all like the things look to me from which they are painted why does such a representation give me pleasure and hold my attention." Having asked herself this question, she answers as follows: "it has achieved an existence in and for itself, it exists on as being an oil painting on a flat surface and it has its own life and like it or not there it is and I can look at it and it does hold my attention." That is why, she remarks later on, that "one comes to any oil

painting through any other oil painting." Art has its own language, which one appreciates after one has learned it separately from the language of the real. In *Everybody's Autobiography,* Stein recounts a conversation with an Egyptian man in which he describes the difference between spoken language and the language of art in Arabic; she tells him that this separation will soon be true for English.

That is very interesting I said, now the English language I said has gone just the other way, they always tried to write like anybody talked and it is only comparatively lately that it is true that the written language knows that that is of no interest and cannot be done that is to write as anybody talks because what anybody talks because everybody talks as the newspapers and movies and radios tell them to talk the spoken language is no longer interesting and so gradually the written language says something and says it differently than the spoken language.

Part of what drew Stein to art was its stasis. Her feeling on looking at a painting of Waterloo was that art was deathly: "I remember standing on the little platform in the center and almost consciously knowing that there was no air. There was no air, there was no feeling of air. . . . It the oil painting showed it as an oil painting. That is what an oil painting is." In fact, good paintings stop movement, though the painter's first desire is to make the painting move.

If the language of art was to separate itself from the language of life, how was the language of literature to change? The answer comes in Stein's shift from particularity to abstraction, from the language of resemblance or likeness to that of unlikeness. Thus Stein comes to distinguish between the descriptiveness that appeals to an audience and the abstraction that loses it. As if to counter Stevens's "Description without Place," Stein asserts, "I can look at a landscape without describing it." The task of renouncing a Romantic relationship between the self and the landscape, Stein avers, is not an easy one:

It is not easy to turn away from delight in moon-
  light.
Nor indeed to deny that some heat comes
But only now they know that in each way
Not whether better or either to like
Or plan whichever whether they will plan to share
Theirs which indeed which can they care
Or rather whether well and whether.
Can it not be after all their share.
This which is why they will be better than before
Makes it most readily more than readily mine.

Stein's language turns rapidly from particular reference, which in the first instance ("moon-light") is also a symbolic, Romantic trope, to a language emptied of direct reference ("they," "theirs," "this," "which"), which is *hers* and yet also impersonal.

Stein's renunciation of landscape description had come earlier than her expression of the difficulty of renouncing Romantic images, however. In Stanza II of Part III, she explicitly denudes the landscape of content before turning her attention back to the stanzas themselves.

> It is not only that I have not described
> A lake in trees only there are not trees
> Just not there where they do not like not having
>   these
> Trees.
> It is a lake so and so or oh
> Which if it is could it does it for it
> Not make any do or do or it
> By this it is a chance inclined.
> They did not come from there to stay they were
>   hired
> They will originally will do
> It is not only mine but also
> They will three often do it.
> Not now.
> Do I mind
> Went one.
> I wish to remain to remember that stanzas go on

Stein questions her own presence in the stanza's last line; if the landscape is denuded of everything, including description, then where is the author?

Her language steadily loses mimetic value as the poem continues; in Stanza LXVI of Part V, she deliberately conflates a "plain" with plainness. It is here that language becomes the landscape rather than a means of describing it. (I am reminded of Beckett's conflation of the self with the landscape on which his speaker rests in "Lessness.")

> Once in a while as they did not go again
> They felt that it would be plain
> A plain would be a plain
> And in between
> There would be that would be plain
> And in between
> There would be that would be plain
> That there would be as plain
> It would be as it would be plain
> Plain it is and it is a plain
> And addition to as plain
> Plainly not only not a plain
> But well a plain.
> A plain is a mountain not made round
> And so a plain is a plain as found

And yet, at the end of this poem about a poet's renunciation of audience, Stein ushers her muse back in, and her language once again becomes instrumental; one cannot but think that her invitation to the muse, and to an audience, comes too late.

> No what I wish to say is this.
> Fifty percent of the roses should be cut
> The rest should bloom upon their branch . . .
> Because because there is very little wind here
> Enough of rain sometimes too much
> But even so it is a pleasure that whether
> Will they remain or will they go even so.

And, apparently to Toklas: "I can I wish I do love none but you." The final stanza is worthy of the inconclusive conclusion to Whitman's "Song of Myself" and announces Stein's presence in the poetic world, much as his "Preface" to *Leaves of Grass* had some seventy years previously.

> I call carelessly that the door is open
> Which if they can refuse to open
> No one can rush to close.
> Let them be mine therefor.
> Everybody knows that I chose.
> Therefor if therefor before I close.
> I will therefore offer therefor I offer this.
> Which if I refuse to miss can be miss is mine.
> I will be well welcome when I come.
> Because I am coming.
> Certainly I come having come.
>   These stanzas are done.

Stein's final choice seems a conservative one; she writes, finally, for a muse, and in so doing her poetry becomes more lyrical, more Romantic—especially in its obvious bow to Whitman. Yet this conclusion seems less earned than imposed, as if in the turning of Stein's mind toward and then away from her audience, she merely happened upon these conciliatory lines.

Stein's final bow to the audience raises the question of the troubled relation between her desire to find an audience and the obscurity that would seem to deny her such an audience. I would suggest that Stein *uses* such obscurity as an important card in her long career of self-advertisement. The self-effacement of **"Stanzas"** covers up what is actually the opposite impulse (just as Stein becomes at once everybody and nobody in *Everybody's Autobiography*). The writer who proclaims over and again that she is "the only one," and that she is one of the three great geniuses of the century, displays that genius in works so obscure that even devoted readers of *The Autobiography of Alice B. Toklas* or *Everybody's Autobiography* might turn away from them. The unreadable text is less a text, in the usual sense, than an icon—less an act of communication than of bravado. A work such as **"Stanzas in Meditation"** becomes a commodity through which Stein can buy the label of genius, and become famous less for what she writes than for the fact that she writes so obscurely. That she recognized the sometimes humorous connection between autobiography and publicity is clear from a passage in *Everybody's Autobiography:* "But now well now how can you dream about a personality when it is always being created for you by a publicity, how can you believe what you make up when publicity makes them up to be so much realer than you can dream. And so autobiography is written which is in a way a way to say that publicity is right, they are as the public see them. Well yes."

"Stanzas in Meditation" forces us to reconsider Stein's use of the word "autobiography," as well as our own. For how can a writer who believes (at least in this poem) in the utter separation of the text from the world write an autobiography, or several autobiographies? What does it mean to tell one's story only "for oneself and strangers," to paraphrase Stein in the opening to *The Making of Americans?* Where are we to find Stein—in *The Autobiography of Alice B. Toklas,* in **"Stanzas in Meditation,"** or in *Everybody's Autobiography?* Perhaps the lesson that Stein teaches us is that the autobiographer makes and remakes herself out of her perceived relationship with her audience. Stein's triumph in **"Stanzas"**—however uneven—is to show to what extent that relationship defines the writer, even when she tries to write without either a muse or an audience.

Margaret Dickie   (essay date 1993)

SOURCE: "Women Poets and the Emergence of Modernism," in *The Columbia History of American Poetry,* edited by Jay Parini, Columbia University Press, 1993, pp. 233-59.

[*In the following excerpt, Dickie presents an overview of Stein's role in the early years of experimentation in Modernist poetry.*]

Early recognition of Stein's importance rested largely on her prose, which formed the bulk of her published work: *Three Lives* (1909), *Tender Buttons* (1914), *Geography and Plays* (1922), *The Making of Americans* (1925). Although she was writing poetry during this period (and *Tender Buttons* is itself a prose poem), most of her poetry was not published until after her death, in *Bee Time Vine and Other Pieces (1913-1927)* (1953), *Painted Lace and Other Pieces (1914-1937)* (1955), and *Stanzas in Meditation and Other Poems (1929-1933)* (1956).

However, this distinction of genre is not entirely accurate, and even here Stein is more experimental than this commentary has allowed. Her work is not easily separated into genres; she worked to overthrow the conventions of genre, to mix prose and poetry, and to question the idea of a continuous work. What is printed in the form of prose, *Tender Buttons,* for example, may have none of the narrative, grammatical, or syntactical continuity that typifies prose. Furthermore, the continuity of a long prose piece can be interrupted by an abrupt change in style, as in the case of *Tender Buttons*, where the third and final section, *Rooms*, was composed almost certainly in 1911, before the first two sections completed in 1913, and represents an earlier style of writing. Even this minor shift of chronology is important because Stein moved rapidly through changes of style, and an arbitrary rearrangement of her writing in a single volume would confuse a sense of her development. She was relentless in her experimentations, claiming that once she found it could be done, she lost interest in it. . . .

In the period when Stein wrote *Tender Buttons* she was engaged in creating an imagery of the female body, focusing on details of the female anatomy and beginning to consider her own work as a writing of the body in what has been called an uncanny anticipation of the theoretical formulations of Luce Irigaray and Julia Kristeva some fifty years later. In *Tender Buttons*, for example, she uses frequent images of the color red, suggesting menstruation and defloration as well as stains, bleedings, and secretions. Also, she makes the connection between menstrual or uterine images and her own writing in **"A Petticoat,"** where she lists, "A white light, a disgrace, an ink spot, a rosy charm," placing the "ink spot" of writing next to the rosy spot on her petticoat.

From 1914 to 1919 Stein began to write plays, using speech fragments or "voices," and working with commonplace, even banal phrases that are quite different from the "lively words" of her earlier nonreferential period. For example, **"White Wines"** begins, "Cunning very cunning and cheap, at that rate a sale is a place to use type writing. Shall we go home." Later, in **"Lifting Belly"** (1915-1917), Stein's interest in ordinary speech rhythms creates a simple conversation between two lovers. The conversation in this style has a referential meaning that much of Stein's experimental writing seems designed to deny. Its interest is in its subject, the erotic experience of two women lovers, the wit of its language (Stein was living in a town outside Belley when she wrote it, for example), and the playfulness of its tone. But, like earlier experiments, **"Lifting Belly"** is also marked by verbal excess and the play in language, indications again of an interest in the text's surface pleasure and what has come to be called *jouissance*.

In the 1920s Stein moved away from this experiment to concentrate on another aspect of the surface of the text, the melody of words, as a way of investigating the possibilities of sound itself. She claimed that she liked to set a sentence for herself as a tuning fork and metronome and write to that time and tune. In **"Sonnets That Please,"** from *Bee Time Vine*, she used the melody of the nursery rhyme: "I see the luck / And the luck sees me / I see the lucky one be lucky. / I see the love / And the loves sees me." She could also echo the rhythm and tone of more serious poetry, as in **"Stanzas in Meditation,"** part 2, stanza 1: "Full well I know that she is there / Much as she will she can be there / But which I know which I know when / Which is my way to be there then." But **"Stanzas"** retains the playfulness that characterizes much of Stein's work, opening with "I caught a bird which made a ball" and continuing through 164 stanzas to conclude in the penultimate stanza with "Thank you for hurrying through."

From her experimentation with melody and her efforts to play with the music of poetry, Stein moved in the late twenties and early thirties to reinvent for herself some of the structures of literary order she had abandoned earlier. In **"A Description of the Fifteenth of November: A Portrait of T. S. Eliot,"** she writes a parody of pompous literary language, mixing sense and nonsense: "On the fifteenth of November we have been told that she will go either here or there and in company with some one who will attempt to be of aid in any difficulty that may be pronounced as at all likely to occur." But even here, repetition, the recurring motif of the fifteenth of November, holds together this collection of entirely arbitrary material.

She appeared to be interested in this period in continuity and cumulative significance, organizing her work around successions of single words. **"Patriarchal Poetry"** (1927) keeps the title phrase as a refrain throughout the text in order to display the banality of the poetic tradition that Stein wanted to overthrow. The long poem contains variations of rhythm and purpose. Repetitive phrases constitute some lines, such as "Patriarchal poetry reasonably. / Patriarchal poetry administratedly. / Patriarchal poetry with them too." At other points she uses straightforward statement—"Patriarchal poetry makes no mistake makes no mistake in estimating the value to be placed upon the best and most arranged of considerations of this." Here, clearly, she has abandoned the play on words in order to convey quite directly her negative judgment and subversive intent.

In the late twenties and early thirties Stein wrote in a variety of styles, composing short works and the lengthy *A Novel of Thank You* and two of her most experimental works, *Four Saints in Three Acts* and *Lucy Church Amiably*. But these works belong to conventional genres of drama and prose narrative in which she worked in the thirties and forties. With the publication of *The Autobiography of Alice B. Toklas* in 1933 Stein achieved the kind of popular reputation she had sought, and, in that decade, at least, her work, became, if not less experimental, at least more willing to negotiate with the conventional. She returned later in her career to experiments in prose that anticipated the *nouveau roman*.

The immediately recognized importance of Gertrude Stein's writing in the emerging stages of Modernist poetry was her willingness to detach words from referential meaning and employ them as painters used paint or musicians used sound. Stieglitz linked her work to the analytical Cubism of her friend Picasso. Williams compared the music of her work to that of Bach, arguing for its abstract design. And Sherwood Anderson compared her to American women of the old sort, scorning factory-made foods in her "word kitchen." Like Stieglitz and Williams, Anderson too felt she would be understood better at some future time when her audience would catch up to her experiments.

In her own lifetime, of course, she did become better known, but not for her experimental writing. Until recently, she remained a writer's writer. In a late interview she reported being asked how she managed to get so much publicity. She answered that it was because she had such a small audience. She advised artists to begin with a small audience that really believes in their work because such an audience will make a big noise whereas a big audience does not make a noise at all. This perception of her position is both true and untrue. She had a small and influential audience among her contemporaries; but the publicity she attracted (and courted) came not from that audience so much as from her acquaintance with influential painters and writers and her willingness to publicize it. Still, it is the small audience interested in experimental writing that can be credited with renewed exploration of her work.

What they value in Stein's work is her willingness to attempt an extreme revolution in the use of words. For example, if she shared with Williams an interest in the abstract design of an arrangement of words, she was willing to detach those words from referentiality more fully than he was. His "so much depends / upon / / a red wheel / barrow" is not so thoroughly cut off from referentiality as her **"One or Two. I've Finished"**: "There / Why / There / Why / There / Able / Idle."

This fearlessness in experimenting with words manifests itself also in her willingness to break with narrative continuity, established genres, and the linear logic that supports them. As a result, she was free to explore new ways in which her experience might be incorporated in a text. Moreover, her prolonged search for a way of expressing her own erotic experience and her love relationships allowed for the widest range of experimental writing, from the early hermetic style that encoded her subject in *The Making of Americans* to the more open repetitive expression of **"Lifting Belly."** In this endeavor she brought into literary language a range of experience not much explored by other Modernists. Perhaps only Hart Crane among the male Modernists wrote anything approaching this kind of poetry, although, at this time H.D. was developing her own hermetic rendering of love poetry.

Stein's contribution to Modernist experimentation is deeply dependent upon everything that patriarchal categories devalue: women's erotic experience, the material of language, the play of irrational process in narrative, the surface pleasure of the text. *Tender Buttons* (1911-1913) is a discovery of an aspect of language and experience that, as one critic has argued, exposes the sacrificial enterprise of male culture and envisions a means of subversion that anticipates an important strand in later Modernism. Stein's formal experimentation started from her study with William James and her commitment to the experimentation of pragmatism. And it derived also from her questioning of authority in her private life. In breaking free both formally and thematically from the linear logic of patriarchal language, Stein was able to uncover the hidden erotic pleasure of everyday life and the language that expresses it. Her emphasis on the signifier in its play of rhythm, repetition, sound association, and intonation, marks her as a precursor of the feminist theorists writing in the late twentieth century.

Krzysztof Ziarek (essay date 1993)

SOURCE: "The Poetics of Event: Stein, the Avant-Garde, and the Aesthetic Turn of Philosophy," in *Sagetrieb*, Vol. 12, No. 3, Winter, 1993, pp. 125-48.

[*In the following excerpt, Ziarek discusses "Patriarchal Poetry" as an avant-garde work of rebellion against traditional poetic styles.*]

Apart from explicit references to pleasure and liking, Stein's writing generates a sense of enjoyment specifically through its patterns of repetition and its continuous undermining and putting in play of grammatical and logical rules. In Stein's texts, anxiety arises in the face of the impossibility of imposing the strictures of understanding and interpretation upon them. When allowed to unfold in their own idiosyncratic way, Stein's works can be more readily described, as many critics have remarked, through playfulness, irony, pleasure, perhaps even *jouissance,* which would make those texts closer to *écriture féminine* and its feminist concerns. For even though Stein subverts literary and linguistic conventions in order nearly to bring to words the unwritten or blank space from which language unfolds, its "chora," to use another one of Kristeva's terms [from Julia Kristeva, *Revolution in Poetic Language*], her texts clearly derive often ironic, almost perverse, "pleasure" from the linguistic play and freedom that they induce.

Indeed, for Stein, bringing the poetic forward, onto the page, has to do with inscribing the "chora" of language, a possibility contingent always upon undoing conventional grammar and writing new, poetic, "grammars." Stein styles herself, especially through her "distaste" for and avoidance of nouns, as a grammarian in search of a grammar and a vocabulary for a thinking that would see the world in its "intense existence" as an event, a happening, rather than a static collection of things or entities: "I am a grammarian," she explains in *How to Write*; section titles from *How to Write*, "Arthur A Grammar" and "A Grammarian," and the title of the essay "Poetry and Grammar" bear testimony to Stein's interest in playing with and undoing the grammatical by means of the poetic, a move that may remind us of Kristeva's loosening of the symbolic via the semiotic. In Stein's work, the poetic becomes synonymous with the intratextual space, so often evoked in **"Stanzas in Meditation,"** which, by withdrawing itself, both lets the text constitute itself and continuously holds open the possibility of its own reemergence and rupture of grammatical and discursive structures: "Or only once or not with not as only not once / Could they come where they were / . . . / Letting once make it spell which they do." Reminiscent also of Heidegger's understanding of thought as always already thinking the event of its occurrence, its world, Stein's "language in meditation" explores the space of writing in which the text emerges. The sense of an always already delayed grasp of the "immediacy" of the text, of the difficulty that thought has attending to and "spelling" its own presence ("Could they come where they were") is produced in Stein's work through the tension between the structures of literary language and their continually erased poetic intratext.

In **"Stanzas in Meditation"** and **"Patriarchal Poetry,"** Stein attempts to bring this interplay directly to the surface of language: "For before let it before to be before spell to be before to be before to have to be to be for before to be tell to be . . . ." After the first paragraph of **"Patriarchal Poetry"** announces Stein's desire to unfasten and "carry away" the structures of patriarchal language, poetry, and culture, the second paragraph, quoted above, begins to mark a space "before" words, before language has to spell and to be (as signification or representation), and thus to spell "to be." Trying to retain the performative character of this linguistic occurrence, Stein not only excludes nouns but also undoes grammatical strictures to give her language more of a dynamic and a

protean, ever-shifting, quality. The tireless repetition and variation of the same phrases—for, before, let it, to be—combined with the absence of punctuation marks, creates the impression of language in a melted state, free to combine and coalesce in ways unexpected, unacceptable, or even repressed by discursive practices. In order to spell what transpires "before to be before to have to be"—before language congeals into its historically and culturally authorized forms—Stein's texts engage, as it were, in their own form of cryptography, in the continuous process of transposing the space before words into the written text. As a form of intralingual or intratextual transposition, such writing aims to bring to words the erased, unknown, "language," often sought by feminist critiques of aesthetics—what DuPlessis [in her essay "For the Etruscans"] provocatively calls the "Etruscan language."

"Patriarchal Poetry" makes clear that it is in this "semiotic" state or space that language possesses its most disruptive potential, one that Stein's texts induce in order to subvert, put into question, and play with not only literary or textual practices but also the culture and society that have instituted them. *How to Write* suggests that Stein's reimagining of literary language has as its specific purpose developing a new mode of thinking that would not only transform literary inscription but overhaul traditional ways of conceiving the world in terms of representation and signification. In "Poetry and Grammar," Stein proposes to subvert literary practice, its predilection for nouns and their definitional function, by means of writing as it were apart from substantives and thus gaining access to what she terms the "intense existence" of things and the world: "I had to feel anything and everything that for me was existing so intensely that I could put it down in writing as a thing in itself without necessarily using its name" [*Lectures in America*]. For Stein, "intense existence" refers to things regarded in terms of the event—as the ever-shifting matrix of relations reconstituted into the singularity of its occurrence—rather than as objects endowed with an essence and definable by means of nouns or substantives. The intensity Stein has in mind describes the idiomatic character of each happening, the particularity of its configuration and circumstances, which are lost in the generality of linguistic naming. Existing intensely—as always singular events—things evade grammatical and semantic categories, and Stein's writing proposes to revise and adjust literary language accordingly. "Poetry and Grammar" offers then another way of formulating what in *How to Write* takes the shape of the poetics of event—focused on the unfolding of the world into language rather than on description, definition, and propositional statements—characteristic of the avant-garde's challenge to aesthetics. For Stein this difficult and elusive poetics has the task of finding what the last section of *How to Write* describes as "a vocabulary for thinking." This vocabulary comprises much more than just lexical items; it offers in fact a matrix for thinking the event that would be different from thinking in substantive forms: concepts, ideas, propositions, in short, "nouns."

Reimagining thinking away from concepts and definitions, away from its practices of nominalization/objectification, and toward its poetic form, makes Stein's work central not only to the avant-garde's revision of aesthetics but also to the critique of modernity and its cultural manifestations. The relevance of Stein's writing is less in terms of specific representations, images, or cultural practices and more with respect to the very elements—linguistic, conceptual, iconic—that make up the order of representation. Thus, in *Tender Buttons*, Stein's implicit critique of the exclusion of domesticity and ordinary language from high modernist art takes the form of undoing definitional and descriptive patterns in reference to everyday objects, utensils, meals, and living spaces. In **"Patriarchal Poetry,"** it is not the images of femininity (with the exception of the sonnet) that Stein takes apart but instead the discourse of patriarchal culture: objectification, definition, possession through cognition, erasure of difference, linear progression, propositional forms of language. Stein often identifies these features with the "poetry of nouns"—the objectifying discourse characteristic of modern rationality—which, operating exclusively in terms of the name, the proper, property, identity, and substance, obliterates the event-character of experience. Stein appears to descend in her texts to this elemental level of engagement with language in order to put her critique into play at the roots of language, as it were, where it can most disconcert and put into question language practices that other radical discourses still have to follow, even if their "content" may explicitly disavow and criticize them. Beyond this, however, the elemental linguistic energy that Stein's texts produce, her playfulness and irony, serve purposes that reach across literary practice, into its cultural and social significance and into the critical potential inherent in the social functions of art.

In **"Patriarchal Poetry,"** the declared literary, cultural, and, by extension, philosophical aim is the resistance to patriarchal culture and its dominant "poetry":

> How do you do it.
> Patriarchal Poetry might be withstood.
> Patriarchal Poetry at peace.
> Patriarchal Poetry a piece.
> Patriarchal Poetry in peace.
> Patriarchal Poetry in pieces.
> Patriarchal Poetry as peace to return to Patriarchal
>   Poetry
>   at peace.
> Patriarchal Poetry or peace to return to Patriarchal
>   Poetry
>   or pieces of Patriarchal Poetry.
> Very pretty very prettily very prettily very pretty
>   very
>   prettily.

Ironically playing "piece(s)" against "peace," Stein indicates the desire and the possibility of withstanding Patriarchal Poetry and leaving it "in pieces" rather than "in peace." Although Stein's poem makes clear that we have to "return" to Patriarchal Poetry, since there is no easy exit from patriarchal forms of culture and writing, the trajectory of this return and the shape in which Patriarchal Poetry will find itself depends above all upon what kind of writing one performs and upon the use to which one puts language.

Works like **"Patriarchal Poetry"** suggest that Stein's literary practice moves toward uncovering the link between elemental linguistic configurations and their potential to both identify and explode the "patriarchal grammar" of the world—its matrix of the relations of difference, dependence, and power. As Stein indicates in *How to Write,* grammar holds the key to the order of discourse and representation that the tradition seeks to repeat and perpetuate. The repetitiveness of grammar, its insistence on following rules, reflects for Stein the cultural order that links stability with the figure of the father and with patriarchal power—the order of sameness, repetition, and predictability that erases difference. The last line of **"Patriarchal Poetry"** is one of the most telling examples in this context: "Patriarchal poetry and twice patriarchal poetry." Stein's linking of this repetitiveness and predictability of grammar with the central role of nouns in language suggests that the everyday itself is "patriarchal"—structured and regulated by the hierarchical rules of representation that assure the dominance of the "more valuable" substantive forms of objectified knowledge.

At the same time, though, "Grammar is in our power"—it is open to revision, transformation, and rewriting, the operations that Stein's texts continuously perform on their language and inherited conventions. Identifying the phallocratic complicity of traditional grammar with the grammar of culture—"Grammar is contained in father . . ."—Stein counters the hegemony of this "patriarchal poetry" by bringing to our attention the disruptive and transformative power of language, especially of its "poetic" space. In this gesture, she points out the pertinence of the avant-garde revisions of aesthetics, even in their extreme, exploratory articulations, to the critical and transformative powers within culture; more, her writing allows us to identify the intersections of the "elementary" work that avant-garde artists undertake on the discourses of art (for example, Malevich in painting, Khlebnikov, Beckett, or Bialoszewski in literature) with the issues of power, domination, and cultural monopoly. One could argue that it is texts like **"Patriarchal Poetry"** that show us not only that literature is never, even at the apparent extreme of experimentation, purely formal or "for its own sake," but also how such elemental and seemingly confined literature in fact encodes subversive intent and practice into its very mode of writing.

Wayne Koestenbaum (essay date 1995)

SOURCE: "Stein is Nice," in *Parnassus*, Vol. XX, Nos. 1 & 2, 1995, pp. 297-319.

[*In the following excerpt, Koestenbaum describes Stein's poetry as having appealing qualities of indefiniteness and as producing a liberating effect through its lack of focus and disregard of generic restrictions.*]

1

Reading Gertrude Stein takes enormous patience. The skeptical reader might wonder: What if Stein is not worth this level of attentiveness? What if her writing doesn't reward close scrutiny?

Ask of your own life the same hard question: What if you stare fervently into your own mind and discover nothing there?

Stein insists that we enlarge our capacities—*even if the enterprise turns out to be bankrupt.* Reading Stein, we imagine a literature, a cognition, that demands inordinate latitude and longitude; we hypothesize a literature as vast and self-sufficient as she imagined hers to be. Whether or not Stein achieved it, by reading her we are postulating the existence of such a spacious poetics; we are bringing such a poetics into being, even if it only exists in the form of the ambitions we attribute to Stein, the fealty that she requires of us, the expectations that she arouses and then excuses. Reading Stein is a process of having desire excited and then forgiven: She says, *you wanted a literature as huge and undetermined as the one I am offering you. I forgive you for the hedonism and the hubris of that wish.*

Be nice to Stein; you will thereby learn to be tolerant of your own Steinian voracity—a hunger for sentences, a dissatisfaction with every extant sentence except those that you invented, an intolerance for any sentence that you are not in the midst of writing.

2

Much of Stein's work remains unread, classified as unreadable. Three recent offerings begin to change this picture: Ulla E. Dydo's masterful compilation of largely forgotten Stein pieces, *A Stein Reader,* in a handsome purple-covered paperback from Northwestern University Press, complete with detailed headnotes but, mercifully, no footnotes; Sun & Moon's pristine ivory-covered reissue of *Stanzas in Meditation*; and Dalkey Archive Press's reissue of *A Novel of Thank You,* with an illuminating introduction by critic Steven Meyer. Dydo has criticized Sun & Moon for reprinting what she calls, with reason, a "corrupt" text of the **"Stanzas"**—a revised version, in which, at the insistence of Alice B. Toklas, Stein removed and disguised the many occurrences of the word "may," which apparently were oblique references to Stein's former lover May Bookstaver. Though I look forward to an edition of the "original" **"Stanzas,"** with all the "Mays" intact, I am nonetheless grateful to have this reprint of the 1956 Yale University Press edition, which John Ashbery, among others, read, and which therefore has a certain literary-historical importance, whatever its textual inconsistencies.

The reappearance, in the last two years, of these major Stein works (more are forthcoming: Sun & Moon promises the publication of Stein's magnum opus, the thousand-page *The Making of Americans*) means that the odd Stein, not the Stein of the *Autobiography of Alice B. Toklas,* but the defiant Baby Woojums of **"Stanzas in Meditation,"** has become part of our contemporary literary landscape. And yet some of the pleasure of Stein— whether in print or out of print—consists in the difficulty of access to her texts and her meanings, and the privacy that this affords her reader. Because academics have largely left Stein uncolonized, she is still free to function, in our reading and writing lives, apart from fossilized rules of what matters and why it matters. Because Stein doesn't quite count, as a modernist or as a postmodernist; because her reputation combines the offbeat and the central (a wonderful paradox, the major minor writer, or the minor major), we are free to make of her what we wish, and to read her more obscure texts in a state of liberated remoteness from dogma, protocol, and usefulness. There have been convincing feminist and lesbian reappraisals of Stein's work, including such studies as Harriet Scott Chessman's *The Public Is Invited to Dance,* and Language poets have laid claim to the anti-referential Stein; but despite these moves to make Stein useful, she remains under-read, and therefore *neutral.* Her texts can be marshalled, coherently and legitimately, to bolster a thousand different arguments; but there will always be a Stein text— say, *A Long Gay Book*—which no one will have bothered to explain and which no one is reading, and which, therefore, if you choose to read it, you will be more or less alone with it, alone with Stein, and at liberty to use it or not use it as you see fit, without having to explain her meanings or nonmeanings to any authorities, without having to summarize or redact, without even having to remember it, after you've put it down. Because you won't ever have time to read all of Stein (there will always be more manuscripts, more letters), she will forever exceed your grasp, resist enclosure, and permit you, therefore, to reverse and foil your own grasping readerly gestures. Reading Stein is always reading in a void, reading the void, reading to avoid—to avoid plot, significance, work, pain, and the past.

Stein is not *about* anything. She will not force anything on you, except her own dreams of magnificence, and her certainty that her magnificence is your property, too; because she's void, it doesn't matter who owns her sentences. They're not worth anything; but because they evade accounting, and because they do not circulate with any regularity, it is your right to determine their worth. And it will not be a tragedy if you decide that they are worthless. Even if they're radically devalued, they won't vanish: There are too many. Even if each sentence is worth only a penny, pennies add up.

I am at liberty, reading Stein, to interpret or not interpret her as I see fit—because she occupies a nether world (the territory of the majestic has-been) where magnification and diminution occur at a startling frequency, without warning; and where the perversity and eccentricity of individual taste still hold sway.

3

Stein writes against maturity, against development. Her writing is "a rested development." She rests—naps, dreams—by enjoying the arrested state of going nowhere.

Stein's paradigm of the writer was the baby: the author as infant. Alice B. Toklas and Carl Van Vechten referred to her as Baby Woojums. But in Stein's terms, to be a baby is not to be asexual. In fact, Stein's babyishness, her immaturity, is a profoundly sexual condition. From **"Mildred's Thoughts"** (reprinted in *A Stein Reader*):

> Baby I am happily married Baby. To whom am I happily married.

> Baby I am happily married to my husband. Baby. And to whom is my husband married. Baby. My husband is married to me. Baby. And to whom is my husband happily married. Baby. My husband is happily married to me.

> Baby. When was I married.

> Baby. I was married like a queen before I was seen.

> Baby. And how was I seen.

> Baby. As a baby queen. Baby. And so I was married as a baby it would seem.

To be a baby is a condition of supreme mastery: Like Emily Dickinson, Stein constructed a literary system in which she was undisputed potentate—a Baby Queen, enjoying full sexual privileges. We need to approach Baby's throne if we want to understand the system; but Baby is too busy with her pleasures to answer our petty queries.

4

In Stein, the central amusement or beauty is often the name, the proper noun, that arrives, unexplained, uncontextualized. Jane Bowles and John Ashbery give this pleasure, too (they might have borrowed it from Stein): A character in Bowles's fragment, "Friday," announces, "My name is Agnes Leather," and we are free, as readers, to meditate on Leather and Agnes, their interpenetration, without the narrator moderating the debate. In Stein, the proper name offers respite from dry diction and nonreferentiality; the proper name seems to refer to someone— seems to bring with it a plot, a teleology (this person was born, desired, died)—but the context never appears, and the name sits solitary on our plate. In **"Stanzas"** Stein writes:

> I think very well of Susan but I do not know her
> name
> I think very well of Ellen but which is not the
> same
> I think very well of Paul I tell him not to do so
> I think very well of Francis Charles but do I do so
> I think very well of Thomas but I do not not do so
> I think very well of not very well of William

Knowledge and ignorance co-exist; I think very well of Susan but I do not know her name, even if I can say "Susan." The name is the tip of gossip's iceberg; each name implies a verdict, a titter, a possible condemnation.

Has the person behaved appropriately? Or has Susan disobeyed? Is Susan a saint? In Stein, names canonize; just to be named is to become part of a Parnassian dramatis personae.

My favorite name in all of Stein is "Kitty Buss." The name is amusing because each word—Kitty, Buss—has a secondary connotation. "Kitty" is a diminutive for "kitten"; "buss" is slang for "to kiss." This is the Agnes Leather effect: To the reader, "Agnes Leather" is a marriage of lamb and leather, not a person. Similarly, Stein writes, in **"Pink Melon Joy,"** "James Death is a nice name." The last name is death, but it is also just his name. Therefore the phrase "James Death" goes somewhere—toward meaning, toward "death"—but also sits plumply motionless on the page, just a name of someone we'll never know, James Death (inevitably I misread it as James *Dean*).

Stein understood that names are comic, accurate, and eerie. They signify our social and psychological identities but they also allegorize us—turn us into death, into kitty, into leather. The buzz of names in Stein's work, like entering a party and hearing the pleasant roar of conversations and laughter, reminds us that people are everywhere, that society (Stein's work reflects and rewrites society) is full of overdetermined relationships and kinship structures, most of which we won't be able to figure out or master. In **"Saints and Singing"** (from *The Stein Reader*), she writes, "Constance and Elisabeth have not the same name. One is Constance Street and the other is Elisabeth Elkus." Constance and Elisabeth stop at their names: *street* and *elkus* prematurely arrest the process of identification even while seeming to justify the arrest by saying, "Now we know who you are: you are street, you are elkus."

5

Constance Street is not my business. Most of human history is not my business. Despite Stein's ample desire to include everything in her work—in *The Making of Americans* she attempted a history of every kind of human being who had ever lived—she also relentlessly specialized, deciding what mattered to her, and dispensing with all dross. In *Lectures in America* she wrote, "It is awfully important to know what is and what is not your business. I know that one of the most profoundly exciting moments of my life was when at about sixteen I suddenly concluded that I would not make all knowledge my province." Desire's specialization: Stein chose language, and Alice. I choose Stein, and language: I choose Stein as a way of choosing language. Stein's private life was not our business: and so she omitted it (except as it appears in code) from her texts. To choose Stein is to refuse every other writer.

Your only business, when reading Stein, is the sentence before your eyes. Not the sentence you've just finished, or the sentence you're about to begin. Just the sentence unfolding right now. To attempt to synthesize Stein's attributes or stories is an infringement on her privacy; what Stein meant, or how the sentences fit together, is not the reader's business. The reader's business is the sentence as it stands. And to have one's responsibilities limited, in this fashion, is a tremendous relief; Stein allows one the peacefulness of staring into space—*her* space.

6

The story in a Stein text—even those, like "Miss Furr and Miss Skeene," that purport to have a sort of plot—is the way a word, or a set of words, permutates, the way a word, like a reusable train ticket, is used (or stamped, or perforated) by the various sentences and fragments it passes through. What the word means is none of your business, but it is indubitably your business where the word travels. So in "Miss Furr and Miss Skeene" your business is the travel of "quite," of "voice," of "regular," of "cultivating," of "living," of "then," of "not," of "sat," of "stayed," of "little things," and of "gay." What "gay" means will not be decided; but you can follow where "gay" goes, how "gay" moves, impatient and ambulatory, through sentences—so that "gay" begins to seem a drive or a propulsive force more than a stable attribute or personality characteristic. Similarly, reading "A Book Concluding With As A Wife Has A Cow A Love Story," your business is "cow," "wife," "as," "love story," "day," "prepare," "happening," "expect," "now," "just," "feel," "six," and "and." These are the significant players, whose movements the reader must monitor. Or simply observe their progress, lazily noting their recurrence. Be surprised by their absence and then relieved by their sudden reappearance. . . .

Stein's quest was the redefinition of beauty. Although her work seems to repudiate conventional aesthetic beauty, she subtly claimed it. In "Composition as Explanation," she observed: "If every one were not so indolent they would realise that beauty is beauty even when it is irritating and stimulating not only when it is accepted and classic." Stein's irritating surface is nonetheless beautiful, in its occasional straightforwardness as well as in its perpetual flight from directness; the beauty lies in her attention to objects, names, pleasures, commonplaces, banalities, indulgences, impieties, as well as in her unceasing campaign for the preservation of the syllable, the exact sound of one syllable landing next to another. In this attentiveness she is one of our purest poets. Amid the din of her often unmeaningful sentences, the clang of the syllable is always audible. Her words don't hide from a reader's scrutiny. And so I turn to Stein because I want intimacy with language at its most atomistic; I want truck with the grubby particles of English, and with the narcisssism of the American voice declaiming the pleasure that may be taken in speech's ordinariness. From *A Long Gay Book:* "Pale pet, red pet, pink pet, blue pet, white pet, dark pet, real pet, fresh pet . . ." It is pleasant to greet, as if for the first time, the word "pet," to hear "pet" next to "white" and "dark," to think about petting and about Stein's relation to companions (animal and human), and to consider questions of family, camaraderie, and solitude within the bracing framework of a syllable-by-syllable list, each word ringing out with brass banality—*pale pet, red pet, pink pet, blue pet, white pet, dark pet, fresh pet. . . .*

Is this poetry or prose? Thankfully one needn't decide. **"Stanzas in Meditation"** declares itself poetry, and is divided into verse lines. But much of the work collected in *A Stein Reader* also falls into lines. Do we consider the following passage from **"A Circular Play"** to be a poem, dialogue from a play, or a series of ultra-brief prose paragraphs?

> Sing circles.
>
> Can you believe that Mary Ethel has plans.
> Indeed I do and I respect her husband.
> Do you dislike her children.
> I have not always had a prejudice against twins.
> To be catholic to be african to be Eastern.
> Have you always had a prejudice against twins.
> Tomorrow we go.
> If you say so.
>
> Circular watches.
>
> Methods.
> How do you recognise hats.
> How do you marry.

Are these fragments of dialogue, each separate line to be uttered by a different character? Or are these lines of a poem, spoken by one haphazard yet subtly unified authorial voice? Or are these minute paragraphs of a prose work broken up into titled fragments ("Sing circles," "Circular watches")? One reads Stein as if it were poetry not simply because it is dense and highly patterned, but because of its arrangement on the page. Indeed, the passage quoted above is not particularly dense. Each line, interpreted separately, is an ordinary idiomatic statement, located in an implied social milieu. What makes the passage "poetic" is not only the disjunction between the separate lines, and the absence of overall narrative, but the erasure of *paragraph:* the paragraph—that prose unit which Stein said was "emotional," as opposed to sentences—has been eliminated, or converted into a poetic line. Indeed, Stein's paragraphs satisfy because they are radically abbreviated, often as short as "Methods," or "How do you marry," or "If you say so." Stack together fourteen paragraphs as short as "Tomorrow we go," and you have a sonnet.

Here, for example, is a short poem by Stein, from *Stanzas in Meditation*, notable for the directness of its praise of the landscape which she often refused to describe but always seemed to be staring at ("I can look at a landscape without describing it"):

> I could not be in doubt
> About.
> The beauty of San Remy.
> That is to say
> The hills small hills
> Beside or rather really all behind.
> Where the Roman arches stay
> One of the Roman arches
> Is not an arch
> But a monument

To which they mean
Yes I mean I mean.
Not only when but before.
I can often remember to be surprised
By what I see and saw.
It is not only wonderfully
But like before.

Stein refused to submit to the tyranny of writing referentially *about* a subject. She can say "about" because she rhymes it with "doubt" (she doubts that language can be "about" anything), and because she puts a period after the "about," interrupting the movement toward the direct object, "The beauty of San Remy," which becomes its own sentence.

I said that Stein's principal purpose was redefining beauty; what this project means, in the context of the above stanza, is that sometimes Stein lets herself be surprised by what she sees and what she saw, but usually she will seesaw, and because of her oscillation between tenses and between sight and blindness, the arch will not long remain an arch, the cited object will not long remain cited. Even within the seesawing—the process of a paragraph's or sentence's decomposition—she remains solidly a lover of beauty in Alice and beauty in landscape, beauty in exile and beauty in home. It is dizzying to watch Stein move so confidently across the prose/poetry divide, without embarrassment, and to see her end the long **"Stanzas"** with the unemphatic "These stanzas are done," as if saying, *Time to move on to other stanzas, or I told you I could write a long poem.*

Is **"Stanzas"** a poem? Is *A Novel of Thank You* a novel? Probably *A Novel of Thank You* is a poem, too. Or else it doesn't matter. Stein impersonating Toklas in the *Autobiography* says, "I always say that you cannot tell what a picture really is or what an object really is until you dust it every day and you cannot tell what a book is until you type it or proof-read it." *A Novel of Thank You* is a fake novel; **"Stanzas in Meditation"** is a fake poem. They are only novel or poem because they chose the appellation, somewhat arbitrarily. Novels are nice; poems are nice. Stein knew the novel's niceness, wanted to inhabit that niceness, and so often called her works novels. The designation "poem" must have seemed less nice, because she less frequently chose it. Even when she did opt for it, as in **"Identity A Poem,"** she dared us to *identify* her text as a poem or to distinguish a poem's quiddity. Stein's **"Stanzas"** suggest the roominess she still believed could travel under the name "poem," as her *Novel* suggests the size and permission she believed that "novel" could still, this late, afford. Each book wants to meet its genre head-on: wants to be a novel, wants to be a poem. The intensity of this wish equals our readerly desire to feel contained by genre, to believe that "novel" or "stanzas" can promise a unique brand of aesthetic sensation. The title's *Thank You* is Stein's statement of wishing the genre well ("thank you for being a novel" or "thank you, novel, for remaining alive"), as *Of Meditation* is her salute to the stanza, her sanguine promise that stanzas abet meditation rather than impede it.

Stein's method: Call it a novel, or a poem, and put in it everything you want. Everything is nice, and so use everything: In "Composition as Explanation" she described her method as "using everything." The appeal of "poem" or "novel," as genres, today, consists in their promise of having enough room to hold everything and everybody.

Christopher J. Knight (essay date 1995)

SOURCE: "Gertrude Stein and *Tender Buttons*," in *The Patient Particulars: American Modernism and the Technique of Originality*, Bucknell University Press, 1995, pp. 80-116.

[*In the following excerpt, Knight applies theories of artistic perception to Stein's poetic style in* Tender Buttons, *emphasizing Stein's desire to create subjective impressions of the world rather than to produce concrete descriptions as in more traditional poetry.*]

Like [Claude] Monet, [Stein] sets out to do the impossible: to see the things of this world with such concentration, such intensity, that she would block out everything that is not the object of attention, all backdrop, all relations, everything that is not included in the thing-itself. Her titles—**"A Shawl," "A Table," "A Book,"**—are often the only clues regarding the representational nature of her pieces. Still they, along with everything else we know about Stein's artistic intentions, are clues enough to warrant our relating the Stein of *Tender Buttons* and the early portraits with the Monet of the last canvases. If, as Shattuck argues, Monet never really broke through into the world of full-fledged abstraction, an abstraction that is nonrepresentational even while it is figurative, . . . one may also say much the same about Stein—that her work remains, more or less, grounded in an aesthetics of representation. This is not to deny the almost opaque nature of her verbal constructions; rather, it is to say that the abstractness of Stein's work follows more from an intention to offer "an exact reproduction of either an outer or an inner reality" than from an interest in abstraction itself. And it is to factor in this intention as a legitimate point of discussion.

Thus I locate Stein's work in the tradition of an innocent eye aesthetic. This tradition, as [Roger] Shattuck and E. H. Gombrich, among others, have pointed out, had many advocates during the nineteenth century. The phrase itself was coined by Ruskin:

> The perception of solid Form is entirely a matter of experience. We *see* nothing but flat colours; and it is only by a series of experiments that we find out that a stain of black or grey indicates the dark side of a solid substance, or that a faint hue indicates that the object in which it appears is far away. The whole technical power of painting depends on our recovery of what may be called the *innocence of the eye;* that is to say, of a sort of childish perception of these flat stains of colour, merely as such, without consciousness of what they signify,—as a blind man would see them if suddenly gifted with sight.

Other advocates of the "innocent eye" included Jules Laforgue, Henri Bergson, Roger Fry, T. E. Hulme, and, closer to home, William James in his *Principles of Psychology*. James's views deserve quotation, not only because they so nicely articulate both the concept of the "innocent eye" and the nineteenth-century psychological notions underlying it, but also because James (who, early on, aspired to be a painter) had an immediate influence upon Stein herself:

> The whole education of the artist consists in his learning to see the presented sign as well as the represented things. No matter what the field of visions *means,* he sees it also as it *feels*—that is, as a collection of patches of color bounded by lines—the whole forming an optional diagram whose intrinsic proportions one who is not an artist has hardly a conscious inkling. The ordinary man's attention passes *over* them to their import; the artist turns back and dwells *upon* them for their own sake. "Don't draw the thing as it *is,* but as it *looks*" is the endless advice of every teacher to his pupil; forgetting that what it "is" is what it would also "look" provided it were placed in what we have called the "normal" situation for vision. In this situation the sensation as "sign" and the sensation as "object" coalesce into one, and there is no contrast between them.

Tender Buttons (1914) is Stein's attempt "to express the rhythm of the visible world" [*The Autobiography of Alice B. Toklas*]. For a long while, she "had been interested only in the insides of people, their character and what went on inside of them." However, troubled by the nagging sense that "after all the human being essentially is not paintable," she felt it best to turn her attention to still lifes so as to get a better hold on both her world and art. She wanted to concentrate upon the simple description of things—domestic things—and "to live in looking" [*Geographical History of America*]. Accordingly, sight is the principle faculty in *Tender Buttons*, and while it has probably been so in any age, one still finds real affinities between Stein's project here and that of Michel Foucault's Classical episteme, (*The Order of Things*). (Foucault: "sight [has] an almost exclusive privilege, being the sense by which we perceive extent and establish proof, and, in consequence, the means to an analysis *partes extra partes* acceptable to everyone." Repeatedly, Stein here speaks of things as being seen. For example, in **"A Piece of Coffee,"** she writes, "The *sight* of a reason, the same *sight* slighter, the *sight* of a simpler negative answer, the same sore sounder, the intention to wishing, the same splendor, the same furniture" [*Tender Buttons*]. And in **"A Box"**: "A box is made sometimes and them *to see to see* to it neatly and to have the holes stopped up makes it necessary to use paper" [empahsis added]. As Stein herself says elsewhere, "you see I feel with my eyes."

One consequence of Stein's privileging of sight or "looking" in *Tender Buttons* is the special status now bestowed upon both appearance and color. In the first instance, the problematic of appearance might be set in the terms that Heidegger used in *Being and Time*, though Heidegger and Stein would clearly differ about the possibilities of approaching that which does not show itself. "Appearance, as the appearance of something," Heidegger writes, "does *not* mean that something shows itself; rather, it means that something makes itself known which does not show itself. It makes itself known through something that does show itself. Appearing is a *not showing itself*" [Martin Heidegger, *Being and Time*]. However, unlike Heidegger, Stein would like to think that essences, things-in-themselves, are captured and revealed in her still lifes. The names affixed to each (i.e., **"A Chair," "A Cutlet," "Water Raining,"** etc.) offer us the ostensible object of attention, the appearance, even while we wait for the more essential thing-in-itself to be evinced. Again and again we find Stein using the word favored in the Heidegger passage, "show," to suggest that a real essence is making itself known. As for example in **"A Mounted Umbrella"**:

> What was the use of not leaving it there where it would hang what was the use if there was no chance of ever seeing it come there and *show* that it was handsome and right in the way it *showed* it. The lesson is to learn that it does *show* it and that nothing, that there is nothing, that there is no more to do about it and just so much more is there plenty of reason for making an exchange. (emphasis added)

If appearances do not yield up essences in *Tender Buttons*—and I do not think they do—Stein's objects are nevertheless quite sensuously considered, particularly in terms of color. Everywhere one looks, one finds things being described not by their color but by an emotional relation which Stein discovers between the object and the spoken color. For instance, in **"A Long Dress,"** several colors are needed to simulate not the appearance of the dress but its essence, its inner "intensity of movement": "Where is the serene length, it is there and a *dark* place is not a *dark* place, only a *white* and *red* are *black,* only a *yellow* and *green* are *blue*, a *pink* is *scarlet*, a bow is every *color*." The same is true of the the unnamed substance in **"A Substance In A Cushion"**:

> A closet, a closet does not connect under the bed. The band if it is *white* and *black,* the band has a *green* string. A sight a whole sight and a little groan grinding makes a trimming such a sweet singing trimming and a *red* thing not a round thing but a *white* thing, a *red* thing and a *white* thing (emphasis added).

Stein's interest in color, like her interest in sound, related back not, she said, to her emotions (though I read her interest in colors back this way) but to her strong desire to know just what was any object's thingness. "I began to wonder," she wrote, "at about this time just what one saw when one looked at anything really looked at anything. Did one see sound, and what was the relation between color and sound, did it make itself by description by a world that meant it or did it make itself by a word in itself." For Stein, an object clearly is something solid and sensuous, to be best understood through such physical qualities as sound and color. Here, one is reminded of Wittgenstein's statement in the *Tractatus*—a text which, in its ambitions, is remarkably similar to *Tender Buttons*—that

A speck in the visual field, though it need not be red, must have some colour: it is, so to speak, surrounded by color-space. Notes must have *some* pitch, objects of the sense of touch *some* degree of hardness, and so on.

In like manner, one is also reminded again of Heidegger [in his *Basic writings*] and his elevation of the truth of *aisthesis,* "the straightforward sensuous perception of something":

> To the extent that an *aisthesis* aims at its *idia* [what is its own]—the beings genuinely accessible only *through* it and *for* it for example, *looking* at colors—perception is always true. This means that looking always discovers color, hearing always discovers tones. What is in the purest and most original sense "true"—that is, what only discovers in such a way that it can never cover up anything—is pure *noein,* straight forwardly observant apprehension of the simplest determinations of the Being of beings as such.

Stein would probably feel uncomfortable with the metaphysical cast of Heidegger's language, yet her own intentions—governed as they are by her pursuit of things-in-themselves, of essences—are also decidedly metaphysical, as she seeks, in her own way, the Heideggerean Being of beings. Still, at the same time, Stein is a firmly committed realist—"I am essentially a realist"—ever wishing to accent the solidity of things. In *Tender Buttons,* she repeatedly speaks of things not only in terms of their apparent qualities, color and sound, but also in terms of their more material qualities: number, measure, weight, difference. As for example in **"A Box"**:

> A custom which is necessary when a box is used and taken is that a *larger part* of the time there are *three* which have *different* connections. The *one* is on the table. The *two* are on the table. The *three* are on the table. The *one, one* is the same *length* as is shown by the cover being *longer.* The other is *different* there is more cover that shows it. The other is *different* and that makes the corners have the same shade the *eight* are in *singular* arrangement to make *four* necessary. (emphasis added)

Here, Stein would suggest, to borrow Wittgenstein's phrasing, that "the world divides into facts," and that these facts, while tenuously connected, are more interesting in their isolation than in their connectiveness. This is a significant departure from her early work in which Stein celebrated not difference but resemblance. The two interests, difference and resemblance, need not be contradictory. Onc can havc difference within resemblance, and resemblance within difference, and the sense is that these two alternatives operate within a single, more inclusive scheme, one that Stein herself does not reject. As she says elsewhere [in her *Picasso*], "Everything being alike everything naturally everything is different simply different naturally simply different." Yet at the same time, if Stein's categories presuppose the acceptance of a metaphysics, her movement in the direction of difference is in itself a

celebration of physics. While it really does not yet push her to "Act so that there is no use in a centre," it does eventually do so. That is, if in *Tender Buttons* Stein is writing mostly within a traditional conception of metaphysics, it appears by the end of this work, and in much of the work (say, for example, *Four Saints in Three Acts*) which postdates the text, that she moves away from a traditional metaphysics and begins to find, upon reflection, that, in Derrida's words [in his *Writing and Difference*], "there was no center, that the center could not be thought in the form of a present-being, that the center had no natural site, that it was not a fixed locus but a function, a sort of nonlocus in which an infinite number of sign-substitutes came into play." This is not to escape metaphysics per se, so much as to deflect it through a radical accentuation of difference. In any case, such inventions make themselves felt, I think, somewhat later in Stein's career.

Meanwhile, in *Tender Buttons* Stein appears more taken with an atomistic conception of things. Her whole sense both of time and of space is that of measurements ingrained with clear-cut delineations. Even as time and space are forms of objects, they contain within themselves separation, gaps between one moment in time and the next, between one point in space and another. For example, in **"Roastbeef,"** both time and space are spoken of as being divided:

> All the time that there is use there is use and any time there is a surface there is a surface, and every time there is an exception there is an exception and every time there is a division there is a dividing. Any time there is a surface there is a surface and every time there is a suggestion there is a suggestion and every time there is silence there is silence and every time that is languid there is that there then and not oftener, not always, not particular, tender and changing and external and central and surrounded and singular and simple and the same.

Stein is obsessed with questions of definition, of defining what is and what is not an object. *Tender Buttons* is nothing if it is not first an exercise in definition, Stein's ambition being to translate into one language that which is found in another. Stein might not be happy with the term "translate," thinking of herself more as a presenter of realities; still, the ubiquitousness of the verb "to be," repeatedly used here to describe one thing in terms of another, makes the term warrantable. For example, in **"A Piano"** Stein uses the verb "to be" to establish a host of relations that are quite syllogistic:

> If the speed *is* open, if the color *is* careless, if the selection of a strong scent *is* not awkward, if the button holder *is* held by all the wavering color and there *is* no color, not any color. If there *is* no dirt in a pin and there can be none scarely, if there *is* not then the place *is* the same as up standing. (emphasis added)

Consequent with definition and the use of the copula is, of course, meaning, itself being a statement of a correspondent relation. This same meaning, like definition and

copulative syntax, might further be said to be dependent upon perception, upon the interpretative act that
first recognizes things in relation. As Heidegger writes
[in *Being and Time*], "Perception is consummated when
one *addresses* oneself to something as something and
discusses it as such. This amounts to *interpretation* in
the broadest sense; and on the basis of such interpretation, perception becomes an act of *making determinate*."
And Gadamer [in *Truth and Method*]: "Perception always includes meaning." In *Tender Buttons*, certainly,
Stein "somehow manage[s] . . . to endow all phenomena with meaning"—"somehow manages" because she
is always attending to objects: to what they are and
what they mean. In *Rooms*, for example, meaning is
repeatedly spoken of and repeatedly added to: "This
means clearness it *means* a regular notion of exercise,
it *means* more than that, it *means* liking counting, it
means more than that, it does not *mean* exchanging a
line" (emphasis added). The same is true in **"A Table,"**
though here the spoken of meanings seem less additive
than synonymous:

> A table *means* does it not my dear it *means* a whole
> steadiness. Is it likely that a change.

> A table *means* more than a glass even a looking glass
> is tall. A table *means* necessary places and a revision
> a revision of a little thing it *means* it does *mean* that
> there has been a stand, a stand where it did shake.
> (emphasis added)

As things in **Tender Buttons** are solid and admit of definition and meaning, they also bespeak the classical (in
the sense of physics) qualities of change, use, and necessity. In the first instance, while it is understood that objects are solid and stable, it is also understood that they
are always caught up in a larger process of change. As
Wittgenstein writes, "Objects are what is unalterable and
subsistent; their configuration is what is changing and
unstable." Change is the law that governs all things. So it
is, in **Tender Buttons**, that the "cloud does *change* with
the movements of the moon and the narrow quite narrow
suggestion of the building"; that "[l]ight blue and the same
red with purple makes a *change*"; and that "[a] *change*, a
final *change* includes potatoes."

Meanwhile, in the second instance, everything must have
a "use" if it is to have a meaning, which is to say if it is
to be perceived and understood to exist. Stein's sensibility,
in this respect, is a pragmatic one. One measures things
by their practical effects: "What was the *use* of not leaving it [an umbrella] there where it would hang what was
the *use* if there was no chance of ever seeing it come
there and show that it was handsome and right in the way
it showed it" (emphasis added). If a thing has no practical
effect, what difference does it make whether it exists or
not? The presumption is that it does not. One of course
thinks back to James, as well as Peirce, who wrote, "Consider what effects, that might conceivably have practical
bearings, we conceive the object of our conception to have.
Then, our conception of these effects is the whole of our
conception of the object."

Not surprisingly, practical effects are to be found everywhere in **Tender Buttons**. Thus "back books are *used* to
secure tears and church [and] . . . are even *used* to exchange black slippers" (emphasis added); "[t]he *use* of [a
seltzer bottle] is manifold" (emphasis added); and "[t]he
one way to *use* custom is to *use* soap and silk for cleaning" (emphasis added). There is even "some *use*," it seems,
"in not mentioning changing and in establishing the temperature" (emphasis added).

And just as change and use have their important roles to
play in **Tender Buttons**, so too does necessity. By necessity
here is meant, in Wittgenstein's words, that "objects stand
in a determinate relation to one another." Given the logic
of experience, which exists prior to experience, things
could not stand other than as they do. "[T]he only necessity
that exists is *logical* necessity," and while this might strike
us, as it did Paul de Man [in his *Allegories of Reading*],
as "an unwarranted reversal of cause and effect," it was
for Stein a controlling metaphor, albeit not recognized as
such. Thus necessity may be discovered in every relation,
just as the language of necessity, in **Tender Buttons**, may
be discovered on virtually every page. Thus, "[a] large
box is handily made of what is *necessary* to replace any
substance" (emphasis added); "[a] mind under is exact
and so it is *necessary* to have a mouth and eye glasses"
(emphasis added); and "[a] hurt mended stick, a hurt
mended cup, a hurt mended article of exceptional relaxation and annoyance, a hurt mended, hurt and mended is so
necessary that no mistake is intended" (emphasis added).

When one understands that Stein, amidst all the playfulness, still conceives things as being both necessary and
determinate, it is easier to understand what she wants her
language to do vis-à-vis its referent—that is, to "create a
word relationship between the word and the things seen"
[From *A Primer*]. For what Stein desires most is an almost mathematical exactitude between sign and referent:
"While I was writing I didn't want, when I used one
word, to make it carry with it too many associations. I
wanted as far as possible to make it exact, as exact as
mathematics; that is to say, for example, if one and one
make two, I wanted to get words to have as much exactness as that" [*How Writing is Written*]. For this, Stein
needed to believe that sense was determinate, that the
planes of objects and of language had a commensurate
logic, guaranteeing that if she held, as she said she did in
Tender Buttons, "to the absolute refusal of never using a
word that was not an exact word," and "that the word or
words that make what [she] looked at be itself [would]
always [be the] words that . . . very exactly related themselves to that thing at which [she] was looking" [*Lectures
in America*]. This did not mean that Stein knew the exact
nature or location of this commensurate logic; it only
meant that she recognized its existence. Again, to go back
to the *Tractatus*:

> The propositions of logic describe the scaffolding of
> the world, or rather they represent it. They have no
> "subject-matter." They presuppose that names have
> meaning and elementary propositions sense; and that
> is their connexion with the world.

Yet while Stein felt that language and reality shared the same logic, she showed more frustration than did Wittgenstein concerning the consequences. That is, if Wittgenstein, conceiving such a logic as a transcendental, believed that "[o]bjects can only be *named*[,]" not *"put . . . into words,"* the Stein of *Tender Buttons* desired more than representation, even one grounded in acommensurate logic and possessing the exactitude of mathematics. She yearned to "put [things] into words," to go beyond simply naming. Stein now felt little more than indifference for names: "The name of a thing might be something in itself if it could come to be real enough but just as a name it was not enough something." The problem was that a name was something too static; it was not quick enough to capture the moment to moment quality of anything's existing:

> We that is any human being existing, has inevitably to feel the thing anything being existing, but the name of that thing of that anything is no longer anything to thrill any one except children. So as everybody has to be a poet, what was there to do. This that I have just described, the creating it without naming it . . . .

Stein began to ask herself whether "there [was] not a way of naming things that would not invent names, but mean names without naming them," if there was not a way of "looking at anything until something that was not the name of that thing but was in a way that actual thing would come to be written." Not surprisingly, Stein felt there was a way—a way first to entrap and then to unfold the noumenon of reality upon the flypaper of language. In fact, doing so did not even require a whole new language: "Of course you might say why not invent new names new languages but that cannot be done." And so, she spoke of Shakespeare and the forest of Arden as illustrative of some special sort of evocation that did not entail naming:

> Shakespeare in the forest of Arden had created a forest without mentioning the things that make a forest. You feel it all but he does not name its names.

> Now that was a thing that I too felt in me the need of making it be a thing that could be named without using its name. After all one had known its name anything's name for so long, and so the name was not new but the thing being alive was always new.

Here, Stein argued, the trick was not to focus one's attention upon the name but upon the thing-in-itself. Discovering this (the thing-in-itself), its name, its essential thisness, would soon follow. As Stein, discussing *Tender Buttons*, writes: "I began to discover the name of things, that is not to discover the names but discover the things to see the things to look at and in doing so I had of course to name them not to give them new names but to see that I could find out how to know that they were there by their names or by replacing their names." In the process, Stein found herself surprised to discover that the words used to bring the thing-in-itself forward were not those usually associated with the object, that as often as not they had "nothing whatever to do with what words would do that described that thing."

It would appear, then, that much of the difficulty of Stein's language and of *Tender Buttons* in particular follows from this ambition to name things as they are found in their singular states of existing. That is, if we accept Stein's description, the difficulty follows not from a deficiency of exactitude but from its overabundance. "Every word" may well have "the same passionate exactness of meaning that it is supposed to have," yet now it is put to a wholly different purpose: to transcribe the ever fluid conditions of things, something which words, traditionally conceived, simply do not express. What Stein argues is that things are actions, that their unchangingness is merely apparent, not actual. The problem though is how to present things in flux when the available language allies itself with the stable and the abstract.

There is no easy answer to such a problem, and Stein's solutions are not always the happiest. In *Tender Buttons*, more and more anxious to realize the essence of a "thing's being existing," Stein turns away from the cinematic model of *The Making of Americans* and the early portraits and toward a concentrated attention encapsulated in phrases that are at once less attentuated and more enigmatical. All along, she aims to pass through the obstacle of a thing's name so as to know and feel the thing in its immediacy:

> As I say a noun is a name of a thing, and therefore slowly if you feel what is inside that thing you do not call it by the name by which it is known. Everybody knows that by the way they do when they are in love and a writer should always have that intensity of emotion about whatever is the object about which he writes.

Here, knowing and feeling are not the same, for the first is both subordinated to and embodied in the second. That is, to feel something is to know it, to know it in the best and most immediate way possible. Knowledge, Stein felt, always presented the problems of memory and resemblance. Feeling, in contrast, did not. As such, particularly in *Tender Buttons*, it became Stein's aim to push language as close to the object-in-itself as possible. Later, in the *Tractatus,* Wittgenstein himself wrote that "a picture is attached to reality; it reaches out to it"; and that within its relations there were to be found correlations with things, correlations that act as the picture's "feelers, . . . with which the picture touches reality." Yet even this formulation, had it been available, would not have suited Stein, so serious was she about trying to "completely replace . . . the noun by the thing in itself."

Maybe it would be better to say that the formulation would *not entirely* suit Stein, for while she is dedicated to writing the sign and referent, she still clearly holds by the dualism. One sees evidence of this both in practice and in theory. At the same time, Stein is beginning to conceive of language in a different way, not in the way of correspondence within which the planes of language and things stand parallel, but rather, in the way of language as an enveloping net faithfully contouring the ever various and lumpish matter of reality. Language, unbuttressed, is allowed to collapse in upon the object, even as the latter remains in motion.

By way of illustration, let us examine the still life **"A Little Bit Of A Tumbler,"** from the section *Objects*:

> A shining indication of yellow consists in their having been more of the same color than could have been expected when all four were bought. This was the hope which made the six and seven have no use for any more places and this necessarily spread into nothing. Spread into nothing.

Here, Stein takes an object, a tumbler, and avoiding all mention of its name (title excepted) tries to duplicate it in a word picture, a picture that is all along dictated by the need to see the object in its moment to moment existing, or, as Stein herself writes, to see it in "a space that is filled with moving, a space of time that is filled always filled with moving." To allow description here to stop with the name "tumbler," Stein thinks not enough. The name is too static; it does not begin to suggest just how alive with movement the object actually is. Better and more realistic than this kind of naming is to describe the object "by suggestion the way a painter" does, mindful at each moment of the need "to get the picture of it clear and separate in . . . [the] mind and create a word relationship between the word and the things seen." Explicating her own still life, Stein writes [in *A Primer*]:

> "A shining indication of yellow . . ." suggests a tumbler and something in it. ". . . when all four of them were bought" suggests there were four of them. I try to call to the eye the way it appears by suggestion the way a painter can do it. This is difficult and takes a lot of work and concentration to do it. I want to indicate it without calling in other things. "This was the hope which made the six and seven have no use for any more places . . ." Places bring up a reality. ". . . and this necessarily spread into nothing," which does broken tumbler which is the end of the story.

Stein's own explication tells us what we perhaps already knew: that she really does not do what she set out to, which is to make the word be the thing; that she, while hesitant to admit it, is much more engaged in the making of metaphors, of substitutions, than she is in the making of non-linguistic things. "To write," Derrida says [in *Writing and Difference*], "is to have the passion of the origin," and Stein more than any other writer has this passion. Yet even this will not produce the thing-in-itself, will not produce an imitation that stops being an imitation, that is something other than what is imitated. Again, as Derrida writes [in *Dissemination*], "Imitation does not correspond to its essence, is not what it is—imitation—unless it is in some way at fault or rather in default. It is bad by nature. It is only good insofar as it is bad. Since (de)fault is inscribed within it, it has no nature; nothing is properly its own."

Stein offers in **Tender Buttons** a technique of originality which, despite the self-promotion, remains but a technique—a simulation of the thing-in-itself. The technique is clever and imaginative and to be valued for these reasons. But one makes a mistake, as Stein's close friend Mabel Dodge made a mistake, to claim too much for these still lifes, to claim, as Dodge herself did in a letter to Stein, that they represent the "'noumenon' captured": "There are things hammered out of consciousness into black & white that have never been expressed before—so far as I know. States of being put into words the 'noumenon' captured—as few have done it." Dodge's claim seems more wishful than true. And when she argues (in the same letter) that Stein's efforts "help us get at Truth instead of away from it as 'literature' so sadly does," what we find is one more attempt to circumvent the rhetorical dimension of the *trivium* (logic, grammar, rhetoric), an attempt which, while characteristic of this generation's authors, nevertheless always fails. As Derrida reminds us, "the thing itself is a sign."

Meanwhile, claims such as Dodge's are telling; they remind us of just how slanted the contemporary aesthetic was toward epistemology, and they also particularly remind us of the force which the "innocent eye" still carried. Again, what one finds here is a tradition which, paralleling the growth of classical science, stressed the absolute thereness of reality and the possibility, given enough concentration, of knowing it. Stein is both a major and a culminating figure in this tradition. Few others take the assumptions of the innocent eye, both in practice and theory, to the point that she does. They take her to a place quite different from where she began. Her latter work is so non-referential and playful that it seems almost to have no connection to the classical aesthetic of correspondence upon which so much of the significant work (i.e., *Three Lives, The Making of Americans, Tender Buttons*, etc.) is, surprisingly, predicated. However, even later, in the theoretical work, Stein never really does reject the classical aesthetic of the innocent eye. . . .

Of course, all this looking, all this attention to things existing, had a celebratory quality about it. It spoke of art not only as something epistemological but also as something—and this was not really intended—spiritual. That is, to think of things-in-themselves as possessing their own inherent worth is, in effect, to think of them as holy, as requiring respect and attention. And this, conjoined with the faith that language and world are necessarily linked, makes for a suggestion that the cosmos does bespeak a transcendent unity, or godhead. Thus does the art of presentation become synonymous, in one sense, with a species of ontological argument, though again, Stein would be quick to deny this. She may write, "Blessed are the patient particulars," yet her intention appears less holy than secular.

Still, Stein celebrates things, believing them somehow graced with prior importance, even if this importance should only be attested to by their singularity, by their strangeness. In **"A Box,"** she suggests the need to acknowledge "the strange*ness* in the strangeness"—that is, the fact that things exist at all, that there is something rather than nothing: "[I]t is so rudimentary to be analysed and see a fine substance strangely, it is so earnest to have a green point not to red but to point again" (11). And in **"Sausages,"** she tells us, "any extra leaf is so strange and singular a red breast."

The result is that feelings of wonder and joy are frequent in *Tender Buttons*. Words and phrases such as "astonishment," "cheerfulness," "enthusiastic," "pleasure," "splendor," "spectacle," "violent kind of delightfulness," etc. describe Stein's own delight in "being living," her own affection for the "stouter symmetry":

> Lovely snipe and tender turn, excellent vapor and slender butter, all the splinter and the trunk, all the poisonous darkening drunk, all the joy in weak success, all the joyful tenderness, all the section and the tea, all the stouter symmetry.

Meanwhile, that Stein should not only explore the genre of the still life but also work to see its domestic things as pleasurable in themselves suggest purposes that relate not only to epistemology but also to gender. My examination has concentrated upon the former, for this is the problematic which most interests me. Yet most problems admit of a multitude of solutions, and Stein's *Tender Buttons* appears not to be the exception. And here, rather than recapitulate the interesting argument which sees Stein's writing as exemplifying an *écriture féminine*, I should like briefly to refer to Norman Bryson's equally interesting observations about the gendered history of the still life. The genre itself, as Bryson explains, has always been looked at somewhat askance by the art community, for the reason that it was less abstract (and hence "masculine") than descriptive (and hence "feminine"). If it were commonly believed (as it seems to have been) that, in Joshua Reynolds's words, "[t]he value and rank of every art is in proportion to the mental labour employed in it, or the mental pleasure produced by it," and that all great art aspires to the level of "general ideas," then it should not surprise that the still life, so generally rhopographic in its values, was not more highly esteemed as a genre. Or that when it was, it was for the reasons that the values of the table were converted into "higher" values, allying the canvas with the megalographic: "And for as long as painting's mode of vision would be constructed by men, the space in which women were obliged to lead their lives would be taken from them and imagined through values of the 'greater' existence from which they were excluded."

In *Tender Buttons*, meanwhile, Stein's handling of the domestic scene appears radically rhopographic, so resistant does she seem to the "higher" values. She might celebrate the holiness of things, yet she does so from a most secular and materialistic point of view, which either refuses to locate or despairs of locating meaning outside of human experience. Certainly, despair is the note struck in the line from *Food*, "Why is there so much useless suffering." Stein herself does not know the answer; and though she is ever engaged in creating meanings in *Tender Buttons*, Stein seems to place little faith in their permanency. This sense of things is perhaps only implicit here; however, it is made more explicit elsewhere. For example, on the point of transcendental meaning, Stein, believing that the world does "not mean much," writes that "[t]he meaningless of why makes all the nothingness so real." And on the point of heaven, Stein, affirming its demise, writes: "Certainly it lasted heaven a very little time all things considered that is considered as long as anything is."

The ideas of heaven and the soul might once have been "interesting," yet they are no longer. The earth and the body now prove the more fascinating realities. As Stein writes, respecting the latter, "Why interest one's self in the souls of people when the faces, the head, the body can tell everything." Why interest oneself in the spiritual when everything can be understood in terms of the physical? Similarly, why feel any anxiety about eternity (cf. Pascal: "The eternal silence of these infinite spaces frightens me.") when it either exists here and now or it does not exist at all. "[E]ternity is not all troubling any one because every one knows that here on this earth are the only men and everybody knows all there is on this earth and everybody knows that there is all there is to it" [This and the following quotations are from *Everybody's Autobiography*]. And if this were not the case, Stein wonders, would it make any difference? Would the spiritual not simply be another variation upon the physical?

> I never did take on spirits either then or later they had nothing to do with the problems of everlasting not for me, because anybody can know that the earth is covered all over with people and if the air is too what is the difference to any one there are an awful lot of them anyway and in a way I really am only interested in what a genius can say the rest is just there anyway.

As witnessed here, Stein's interest in people and things was not unflagging. It just seemed that way, given the enormous engagement that such texts as *The Making of Americans, Tender Buttons*, and the portraits demanded. Yet Stein could tire of people ("there are an awful lot of them") and things; and while her work almost presents itself as a constant effort to redeem people and things from the hell of oblivion, there is no extraordinary importance apparently attributed to them. "Human beings have no meaning," and left "alone to live and die," they appear fragile and small before the universe's immensity, no different from any other animal: "[T]here are men only upon this earth and anything like anybody does it what is the difference between eternity and anything."

Stein confesses that at first she found the idea of our insignificance frightening: "It was frightening when the first comet I saw made it real that the stars were worlds and the earth only one of them." And unreal: "There is no realism now, life is not real it is earnest, it is strange." Still, she grew accepting of the idea, to the point where she could turn around and take pleasure in her world: "we are on the earth and we have to live on it and there is beyond all there it is and here we are, and we are always here and we are always there and any little while it is a pleasure, and a pleasure is a pleasure as yes it is a pleasure as a treasure." Which, in a sense, is what *Tender Buttons* and all of Stein's work amounts to: a pleasure in the "being living," in the moment to moment feel of experience.

FURTHER READING

Bibliographies

White, Ray Lewis. *Gertrude Stein and Alice B. Toklas: A Reference Guide.* Boston: G. K. Hall, 1984, 282 p.
  An annotated bibliography of writings on Stein.

Wilson, Robert A. *Gertrude Stein: A Bibliography.* New York: Phoenix Bookshop, 1974, 227 p.
  Descriptive bibliography includes translations, recordings, and biographical materials.

Biographies

Gallup, Donald, ed. *The Flowers of Friendship: Letters Written to Gertrude Stein.* New York: Alfred A. Knopf, 1953, 417 p.
  Reprints letters from William James, Leo Stein, Picasso, Mabel Dodge, Carl Van Vechten, Hemingway, and many others in an attempt "to indicate some of the influences which made Gertrude Stein into the woman and the writer she became."

Hobhouse, Janet. *Everybody Who Was Anybody: A Biography of Gertrude Stein.* New York: G. P. Putnam's Sons, 1975, 244 p.
  Biography featuring many photographs and reproductions of art works associated with Stein.

Mellow, James R. *Charmed Circle: Gertrude Stein and Company.* New York: Praeger, 1974, 528 p.
  Biography focusing on Stein as a literary celebrity, including many anecdotes about her friendships with Hemingway, F. Scott Fitzgerald, Picasso, and others.

Sprigge, Elizabeth. *Gertrude Stein: Her Life and Work.* New York: Harper and Brothers, 1957, 277 p.
  First full-length biography of Stein.

Stendhal, Renate. *Gertrude Stein in Words and Pictures.* London: Thames and Hudson, 1995, 286 p.
  Photobiography.

Toklas, Alice B. *What is Remembered.* New York: Holt, Rinehart, and Winston, 1963, 186 p.
  Memoir focusing on Toklas's years with Stein.

Wagner-Martin, Linda. *Favored Strangers: Gertrude Stein and Her Family.* New Brunswick, N.J.: Rutgers University Press, 1995, 346 p.
  Focus on Stein's relationship with her family and involvement with the art world of Paris.

Wineapple, Brenda. *Sister Brother: Gertrude and Leo Stein.* London: Bloomsbury, 1996, 514 p.
  Thorough study of the relationship between Stein and her brother and its influence on her career.

Criticism

Aldington, Richard. "The Disciples of Gertrude Stein." *Poetry* XVII, No. 1 (October 1920): 35-40.
  Asserts that many modern French poets, including Guillaume Appollinaire, Jean Cocteau, and the Dadaists, were influenced by Stein.

Bloom, Harold, ed. *Gertrude Stein.* New York: Chelsea House, 1956, 215 p.
  Contains essays by fifteen critics, including Sherwood Anderson, Allegra Stewart, Richard Bridgman, Donald Sutherland, Thornton Wilder, and William H. Gass.

Bowers, Jane Palatini. *Gertrude Stein.* New York: St. Martin's Press, 1993, 174 p.
  Discusses Stein's creative consciousness, including her interest in generic constraints.

Bridgman, Richard. *Gertrude Stein in Pieces.* London: Oxford University Press, 1970, 411 p.
  Highly regarded critical study of Stein's prose and poetry.

Chessman, Harriet. *The Public is Invited to Dance: Representation, the Body, and Dialogue in Gertrude Stein.* Stanford: Stanford University Press, 1989, 247 p.
  Examines the intimacy of Stein's poems and places them in the context of Stein's reactions to Romanticism.

DeKoven, Marianne. *A Different Language: Gertrude Stein's Experimental Writing.* Madison: University of Wisconsin Press, 1983, 175 p.
  Feminist analysis of Stein's experimental writings; proposes that Stein developed new modes of expression as an alternative to patriarchal literary traditions.

Dubnick, Randa. *The Structure of Obscurity: Gertrude Stein, Language, and Cubism.* Urbana: University of Illinois Press, 1983, 161 p.
  Structuralist study of the evolution of Stein's abstract style comparing the stages of her literary development to the developmental phases of Cubism.

Dydo, Ulla E. "To Have the Winning Language: Texts and Contexts of Gertrude Stein." In *Coming to Light: American Women Poets in the Twentieth Century,* edited by Diane Wood Middlebrook and Marilyn Yalom. Ann Arbor: University of Michigan Press, 1975, 270 p.
  Reveals autobiographical basis for much of Stein's poetry.

Fifer, Elizabeth. "Is Flesh Advisable? The Interior Theater of Gertrude Stein." In *Rescued Readings,* pp. 46-58. Detroit: Wayne State University Press, 1992.
  Identifies allusions to Stein's erotic life in her early poetry.

Gass, William H. "Gertrude Stein and the Geography of the Sentence." In *The World Within the Word,* pp. 63-123. New York: Alfred A. Knopf, 1978.
  Interprets and evaluates Stein's literary innovation, particularly the hermetic approach to language she introduced in *Tender Buttons.*

Hoffman, Michael J., ed. *The Development of Abstractionism in the Writings of Gertrude Stein.* Philadelphia: University of Pennsylvania Press, 1965, 229 p.

Contains essays by thirty-eight critics, including Kenneth Burke, Edmund Wilson, B. F. Skinner, and Thornton Wilder.

Kaufmann, Michael. "Gertrude Stein's Re-Vision of Print and Language in *Tender Buttons*." In *Textual Bodies: Modernism, Postmodernism, and Print,* pp. 52-67. Lewisburg: Bucknell University Press, 1994.

Semantic explication of *Tender Buttons.*

Perloff, Marjorie. "Poetry as Word-System: The Art of Gertrude Stein." *American Poetry Review* 8, No. 5 (September-October 1979): 33-43.

Detailed analysis of Stein's use of language.

Schmitz, Neil. "Gertrude Stein as Post-Modernist: The Rhetoric of *Tender Buttons*." *Journal of Modern Literature* 3, No. 5 (July 1974): 1203-18.

Examines *Tender Buttons* in the context of Postmodernist narrative style.

Skinner, B. F. "Has Gertrude Stein a Secret?" *The Atlantic Monthly* 153, No. 1 (January, 1934): 50-7.

Dismisses *Tender Buttons* as an experiment in automatic writing.

Stewart, Allegra. *Gertrude Stein and the Present*. Cambridge, Mass.: Harvard University Press, 1967, 223 p.

Discusses Stein's connections to early modern philosophy.

Additional coverage of Stein's life and career is contained in the following sources published by Gale Research: *Twentieth-Century Literary Criticism,* Vols. 1, 6, 28, 48; *DISCovering Authors*; *Contemporary Authors,* Vol. 104, 132; *Concise Dictionary of AmericanLiterary Biography 1917-1929*; *Dictionary of Literary Biography,* Vols. 4, 54, 86; *Major Twentieth-Century Writers*; and *World Literature Criticism, 1500 to Present.*

Wang Wei
699?-761?

(Also called Wang Mo-ch'i). Chinese poet.

INTRODUCTION

The poet-painter Wang Wei is ranked among the most illustrious men of arts and letters from the T'ang dynasty, one of the great golden ages of Chinese cultural history. Traditionally viewed as the father of monochrome landscape painting (the Southern School), Wang is also recognized as one of the few poets, along with the highly revered T'ang poets Li Po and Tu Fu, to master the art of "lyric poetry" (*shih*). Wang's poems, chiefly characterized by their meditative symbolism and graceful simplicity, exemplified his belief that poetry and painting were mirrors of one another, each medium was meant to emulate and reflect the beauty of the other. Although a distinguished court poet, Wang is most widely regarded for his nature poems, a body of verse that explores the edifying beauty of the natural world.

Biographical Information

Wang was born to a powerful noble family in Ch'i-hsien, located in Shansi Province. His family had a tradition of government service, and he counted thirteen prime ministers among his ancestors. Wang was well educated as befitted a future courtier, and he excelled in poetry, music, and art. Indeed, his remarkable poetic abilities were apparent as early as the age of nine. Wang easily passed the government examinations and, at the age of 21, received the prestigious *chin-shih* ("advanced scholar") degree in the imperial civil-service examination system. This "doctoral" degree was principally based on his musical skill. After passing the examination, Wang was appointed Assistant Director of the Imperial Directorate of Music. This was the first of what was to be many government appointments. Wang pursued an unremarkable career in the service of the imperial government, serving in various official capacities and suffering professional setbacks due to political upheaval. During the An Lu-shan Rebellion, Wang was captured and forced to serve the rebel administration. The intercession of his high-ranking brother Wang Chin, together with the contents of a poem Wang composed while imprisoned by the rebel forces, helped save him from charges of collaboration with the enemy when imperial forces recaptured the capital at Ch'ang-an. Wang's later years were overshadowed by disillusionment and sadness following the deaths of his wife and his mother. He died while serving in the Department of State in his early sixties.

Wang Wei's undistinguished official career was frequently interspersed with periods of seclusion in the grounds of his private villa at Wan Ch'uan (Wang River), where he sought respite from the intrigue, corruption, and uncertainty of court life. The poems he composed while studying Buddhism and meditating in the quiet of nature reveal his love for landscape and country living together with his longing for peace and seclusion. The outward simplicity of his poems' imagery belies the profoundly metaphysical nature of the underlying concepts, that of man's place in nature and the pursuit of enlightenment through denial and retreat from the world. It has been argued that much of the conflict in Wang Wei's life and poetry springs from the contrary inclinations resulting from the dual influence of Confucianism, which urges political ambition, and Taoism, which teaches quiet meditation and a passive attitude regarding events in the physical world.

Major Works

Of the 420 poems in Wang Wei's canon, there are approximately 370 poems that can be genuinely attributed to him. The style of the poems is simple and uncomplicated, and the underlying feelings are those of tranquility and detachment. The poems fall into three general categories: court poems that capture a vignette of life in the Imperial court, Buddhist themes and images, and nature scenes stripped of all ornament. The poems in this last category are his most famous, and include the *Wang-ch'uan chi* (Felly River Collection), a twenty-quatrain poem describing his country villa. Other well-known poems include "Answering Magistrate Chang," an example of a court poem, and Wang's "Deer Park," one of the most-often-anthologized Chinese poems, frequently cited as an archetypal nature poem. Wang's poetry is considered in the same league as Tu Fu and Li Po, the great T'ang lyric poets. While it lacks exuberance of Li Po or the controlled intellectuality of Tu Fu, Wang's poetry fuses literature and art with nature in the most simple and placid language.

Critical Reception

Despite Wang Wei's popularity in China and the West, he has been the subject of very few critical studies in any language. Some critics speculate that the primary reason for this neglect is that the apparent simplicity of much of Wang's poetry obscures the disconcertingly elusive philosophical premises from which Wang draws his inspiration, and the complexity of these ideas discourages penetrating analysis of his poetry. Despite the paucity of critical analysis concerning his poetry, Wang Wei remains one of the most translatable and widely translated of

Chinese poets. Indeed, Wang Wei's poetry can be found in nearly every anthology of Chinese poetry available.

PRINCIPAL TRANSLATED WORKS

Hiding the Universe: Poems by Wang Wei (poetry) [translated by Wai-lim Yip] 1972

Poems of Wang Wei (poetry) [translated by G. W. Robinson] 1973

The Poetry of Wang Wei (poetry) [translated Pauline Yu] 1980

Laughing Lost in the Mountains: Poems of Wang Wei (poetry) [translated by Tony Barnstone, Willis Barnstone, and Xu Haixin] 1992

CRITICISM

Fe Obaña (essay date 1970)

SOURCE: "Discovering Chinese Poetry (an insight into three poems by Wang Wei)," in *The Diliman Review*, Vol. XVIII, No. 1, January, 1970, pp. 91-6.

[*In the following essay, the critic examines the function of imagery in Chinese nature poems.*]

"My Hermitage in the Bamboo Grove"

Deep in the bamboo grove, sitting alone,
I thrum my lute as I whistle a tune.
No one knows I am in this thicket
Save the bright moon looking down on me.

"With Official Lu Hsiang, Passing Hermit Ts'ui Hsin-Chung's Bower"

Green forests cover the four directions with dense
    deep shade.
Every day untrodden mosses cushion the courtyard
    more thickly in bluish gray.
Under tall pines the hermit sprawls, leg
    outstretched,
Turning upon the vulgar crowd only the whites of
    his eyes.

"Light Verse on a Rock"

I pity the inert rock by a flowing stream
And the willows trailing fingers into my wine-cup . . .
But who can say the spring wind is not aware of
    the sound in my heart?
Why else should it blow these frail falling petals
    about me?

This paper makes no pretension towards an adequate critical evaluation of Wang Wei. Rather it is a personal appreciation of a poet who must suffer a reading in translation. And since the problem of translation belongs to Linguistics proper, it will suffice to note that this paper describes a personal insight into Chinese poetry.

The delicate balance maintained between a picturesque description of Nature and the feeling or sentiments evoked by this poetic landscape is the primary characteristic that my readings have made me conscious of. Basically, this delicate balance relies heavily on the disciplined control of the imagery, the pivotal vessel gathering the formal construction and the affective translation of the formal construction into poetry. Viewed in the light of the Chinese language and grammar—each character representing an idea and with an absence of grammatical connectives—my attention was arrested by the sequence of images that a Chinese poem contained, their possible symbolic range or associations (within my limited frame of reference not extending towards the realm of Chinese scholarship), their contextual allusions and derivations (as illuminated upon by textual footnoting). [Liv James, *The Art of Chinese Poetry*, 1962.] A comprehensive insight into the functional relations of the imagery and its effective attributes consequently gives the theme.

The first two poems, **"My Hermitage in the Bamboo Grove"** and **"With Official Lu Hsiang, Passing Hermit Ts'ui Hsiu-Chung's Bower"** have for their subject matter the Buddhic hermit, or the learned sage. To the Chinese he is the highest expression of the ideal man. The first poem is simple enough having for the first two lines a description of his condition as a recluse "deep in the bamboo grove . . . thrum(ing a) lute as (he) whistle a tune". The last two lines however emphasize the aspect of solitude in his life. "No one knows I am in this thicket/ Save the bright moon looking down on me." "The bright moon" becomes the sympathetic companion of his contemplative days.

The second poem although bearing for its subject matter the solitary hermit, too, uses imagery that describes more sharply the life of a hermit "under tall pines . . . sprawls, legs outstretched" and defines his superiority over the "vulgar crowd (with) the whites of his eyes". The "Bamboo grove" has been replaced by a more impenetrable locale "green forests" which "cover the four directions" leading towards the center which is the hermit's abode. The idea of being in the crossroads of man's life is contradicted by the "untrodden mosses cushion the courtyard more thickly in bluish gray (everyday)". Perhaps if we refer back to the title (without historically identifying the two personages mentioned), we find that one is a public official and one a hermit and, of course, Wang Wei himself. Did the visit create for the poet an impression that they were intruding upon the serenity of the hermit's life, that their visit was a matter of inconsequence to his existence? Still, "green forests cover the four directions with dense deep shade" leaves this way of life open to all who would trod its depths.

"Light Verse on a Rock" is a deceptive title for a quietly sorrowful poem. And because of this I will include three stages by which the poem opened itself to my eyes.

"The spring wind" and "the frail falling petals" fix the time just before summer when the last flowers of spring are withering away. I would rather consider "the inert rock" and "the willows" as expressive of the "I's" refusal to indulge in outright self-pity and therefore the author made use of these images to substitute for "I's" consciousness. While "the flowing stream" and "wine-cup" suggest strongly the process of growing old and life slipping away, these images are juxtaposed along side the temporal images. "But who can say the spring wind is not aware of the sound in my heart?" And "the sound of (his) heart" resounds frighteningly as "the inert rock by the flowing stream/And the willows trailing fingers into my wine-cup" giving rise to the thought of a death of the heart—a great sorrow over a lost love perhaps or a disenchantment over life's vicissitudes. "The inert rock" conjures a hardened feeling and "the willows trailing fingers into my wine-cup" suggests a line of sorrows. And yet, taking the last two lines "But who can say the spring wind is not aware of the sound in my heart?/Why else should it blow these frail falling petals about me?", the preceding interpretation seems to be an overreading when I explain it thus as Nature's oneness with the poet's reshaping of her according to his emotional state (an affective fallacy).

James Liu writes "Nature is not viewed from a personal angle at a particular time, but as it always is. The presence of the poet is withdrawn or unobtrusively submerged in the total picture." And with further explanations, James Liu warns the reader of an existing difference between the Western idea of Nature and the Chinese idea of nature. It seems that an absorption with the self in conflict and the associative participation of Nature as the primum mobile is a Western-oriented viewpoint. Taken in this manner, **"Light Verse on a Rock"** must be seen not as an egotistical outpouring but rather as a tragic recognition of the transience of time, and correspondingly of life, as expressed by the allusion on "the spring wind" and the image of "the frail falling petals." Aside from these, "my wine-cup" and "the flowing stream" remain as symbolic of the life process while "the inert rock" and "the willow trailing fingers" become the unchanging, cyclical "abiding features of Nature as contrasted over the brevity of life." The third line, therefore, actually does not mean its syntactical meaning "But who can say the spring wind is not aware of the sound in my heart?" Rather it meant its reverse order of meaning-the heart is aware of the spring wind . . ."Why else should it (the wind) blow these frail falling petals about me?" Two interrogative lines ending a four-line verse silently requires the reader's recognition of the "eternal renewal of Nature." What happened to the connotative image of "the willows" as symbolic of sorrow?

Still the poem remains a puzzle. An essential core is not touched. First of all, looking at its formal construction, the poem seems to be divided into two by the presence of three dots between the first two lines and the last two lines. Taking this division we discover that it is the sep-

arating pause between two voices or two consciousness sharing the same feeling. The first two lines expresses the "I" pitying "the inert rock" making it symbolic of someone (the author perhaps?) beside the changes of "the flowing stream" and being so suffers certain sorrows as the image of "the willows" suggests. "The willows trailing fingers into my wine-cup . . ." is really a puzzle or problem because if there is any sorrowing done then "my wine-cup" reverts back to "I" who pities "the inert rock." "The inert rock" must be a substitute image for the "I", avoiding sentimental self-indulgment. The last two lines show "the spring wind . . . aware of the sound in my heart?/Why else should it blow these frail falling petals about me?" (How does one define "the sound in my heart".) We at once see that "the spring wind" does the same thing as the "I" does: "I pity the inert rock" and "the spring wind is aware of the sound in my heart." There is an identity of consciousness here; both acting out the same impulse. "The inert rock" then symbolizes not someone but the heart that is sorrowing and which can not forget the reasons for this sorrowing beside "the flowing stream" or the general flow of life. The theme of sorrow has been translated first into the author's detached recognition and second into the season's sympathetic concordance. In this poem, what rises to the fore is not so much the imagery; this becomes secondary to the harmonic correspondence between the two consciousness: I and Nature.

I have attempted to show the process by which I have begun to understand the mechanics of Chinese poetry using Wang Wei as a representative poet having been born during the Tang Dynasty—China's Golden Age of Chinese Poetry. Discovering the range of meaning each image contains establishes the relational fabric of the thoughts and feelings of the poem's lines.

> While Chinese poetry may fail to compare with Western poetry for magnitude of conception and intensity of emotion, it often surpasses the latter in sensitivity of perception, delicacy of feeling, and subtlety of expression. It is not exaggeration to claim that Chinese poetry is one of the chief glories of Chinese culture and one of the highest achievements of the Chinese mind. [Liv James, *The Art of Chinese Poetry*.]

Wai-lim Yip (essay date 1971-72)

SOURCE: "Wang Wei and the Aesthetic of Pure Experience," in *Tamkang Review*, Vol. 2, No. 2, October 1971-April 1972, pp. 199-208.

[*In the following essay, the critic asserts that Wang Wei's nature poetry is not simply about nature but that it actually becomes nature through the Taoist emphasis on pure experience.*]

1

The best introduction to Wang Wei's poetry is a poem of *Ars Poetica* by Ssu-k'ung T'u (837-908):

Bend down—and there it is:
No need to wrest it from others.
With the Way, in complete consort—
The mere touch of a hand is spring:
The way we come upon blooming flowers,
The way we see the year renew itself.
What comes this way will stay;
What is gotten by force will drain away.
A secluded man in an empty mountain,
As rain drops, picks some blades of duckweeds.
Freely to feel the flash of dawn:
Leisurely, with the celestial balance.

To let criticism take wings requires the defeat of poetry. We are giving the readers an anatomized bird, a conceptualized Nature.

Wang Wei is Nature or Phenomenon as it is: no trace of conceptualization. Compare, for instance, the following two poems:

   "Bird-Singing Stream"   Wang Wei

Man at leisure. Cassia flowers fall.
Quiet night. Spring mountain is empty.
Moon rises. Startles—a mountain bird.
It sings at times in the spring stream.

   "Of Mere Being" (1955)   Wallace Stevens

The palm at the end of the mind,
Beyond the last thought, rises
In the bronze distance,
A gold-feathered bird
Sings in the palm, without human meaning,
Without human feeling, a foreign song.

You know then that it is not the reason
That makes us happy or unhappy.
The bird sings. Its feathers shine.

The palm stands on the edge of space.
The wind moves slowly into the branches.
The bird's fire-fangled feathers dangle down.

In Wang Wei, the scenery *speaks* and *acts*. The poet has become, even before the act of composition, Phenomenon itself and hence can allow the thing in it to emerge *as they are* without being contaminated by intellectuality. The poet does not step in; he views things as things view themselves. Stevens has always wanted to achieve this same mode of presentation by striving to become the objects themselves.

   One must have a mind of winter
   To regard frost and boughs . . .
                   "The Snow Man"

But he often ends up writing *about the process of becoming the objects* with much analysis in between the reader and the objects. "Of Mere Being" could be written this way:

The palm rises
In the bronze distance.
A gold-feathered bird
Sings in the palm a song.
The bird sings. Its feathers shine.
The palm stands on the edge of space.
The wind moves slowly in the branches.
The bird's fire-fangled feathers dangle down.

With the analytical elements eliminated, this poem would come closer to Stevens' own ideal: Not Ideas About the Thing but the Thing Itself [title of one of his poems], closer to pure actions and states of being.

Wang Wei is Phenomenon itself: no trace of conceptualization.

2

The process of conceptualization seems to have dominated much of English poetry. A diptych by Gary Snyder demonstrates this fact to us beautifully:

            the text

Sourdough mountain called a fire in:
Up Thunder Creek, high on a ridge.
Hiked eighteen hours, finally found
A snag and a hundred feet around on fire:
All afternoon and into night
Digging the fire line
Falling the burning snag
It fanned sparks down like shooting stars
Over the dry woods, starting spot-fires
Flaring in the wind up Skagit valley
From the Sound.
Toward morning it rained.
We slept in mud and ashes,
Woke at dawn, the fire was out,
The sky was clear, we saw
The last glimmer of the morning star.

            the myth

Fire up Thunder Creek and the mountain—troy's
   burning!
The cloud mutters
The mountains are your mind.
The woods bristle there,
Dogs barking and children shrieking
Rise from below.

Rains falls for centuries
Soaking the loose rocks in space
Sweet rain, the fire's out
The black snag glistens in the rain
& the last wisp of smoke floats up
Into the absolute cold
Into the spiral whorls of fire

The storms of the Milky Way
"Buddha incense in an empty world"

Black pit cold and light-year
Flame tongue of the dragon
Licks the sun

The sun is but a morning star

The first panel is the approximation of the cuts and turns of Phenomenon as it comes to the poet; the second panel is the projection into the objects in Phenomenon historical, cyclical and human meanings. The "myth" section operates on a metaphoric or symbolic level: the objects presented are vehicles for an aura of meanings. The "text" section is non-metaphoric, non-symbolic: the objects presented are nothing more than the objects themselves; the poet catches the rhythm of Nature, the "true measure of things" as the final aesthetic meaning of the poem. As such, the "text" section comes closest to Wang Wei.

Wang Wei does not rely on metaphoric or symbolic function, although such a function is central in English (and perhaps in all European) poetry. Only recent poetry begins to depart from this central function: Canto 49 of Ezra Pound (which is constructed out of a series of Chinese poems written by a Japanese), early Williams and a great deal of Snyder's poetry.

Ezra Pound advocates a poetry of concrete details without commentary as early as 1911. But Pound is not totally free from conceptualizations. As he puts it, his poetry remains the permanent basis of psychology and metaphysics. To be exact, except a few imagist poems and the above-mentioned Canto, his poetry offers a concrete surface (which in itself is an important break from traditional poetry) which darts into a subjective reality. But early Williams took Pound's dictum seriously and has given us a poetry of pure perception—a poetry in which there is no attempt to project objects in concrete existence through metaphoric or symbolic devices into conceptions canonized by some human-imposed abstract systems, i.e., there is no translation of concrete data into abstract concepts. "No symbolism is acceptable," says Williams, for he realizes, as his most recent apologist J. Hillis Miller has rightly put it, "Romantic and symbolist poetry is usually an art of willed transformation. In this it is, like science and technology, an example of that changing of things into artifacts which assimilates them into the human world. Williams' poetry, on the other hand, is content to let things be. A good poet, [Williams] says, 'doesn't *select* his material. What is there to select? It is.'" Witness this example:

NANTUCKET

Flowers through the window
lavender and yellow

changed by white curtains—
Smell of cleanliness—

Sunshine of late afternoon—
On the glass tray

A glass pitcher, the tumbler
turned down, by which

a key is lying—and the
immaculate white bed.

Here, there is no translation of things into concepts; none of the objects in the poem function symbolically. They are what they are, caught by the poet's eye in a unique moment of light and color. In it, the unity is not the unity that reaches back to a noumenal realm of "meanings" (Platonic or otherwise) for sanction and confirmation. The unity here is a unity of pure spatial relations as existing physically, not metaphysically, promoted and heightened for us by the poet's manipulation of spotlighting visuality. Williams, without too much fanfare, has become the priest and performer of T. E. Hulme's aesthetic ideal: "Make you continuously see a physical thing." This effect is achieved by a radical rejection of the abstract process of conceptualization that has enslaved the English poets since Plato. But our eighth-century poet Wang Wei, sanctioned by more than ten centuries of aesthetic agreement, has no such bondage to undo and has given us the same effect with much finesse.

3

Wang Wei's poetry is doubtlessly bound up with the Taoist (in particular, Chuang Tzu's) emphasis on pure experience—experience in which we have no interference of intellectual knowledge. Intellectual knowledge, often involving linguistic means of rationalization, tends to force the materials at hand into an abstraction or abstractions rather than to yield to the concreteness of things. Pure experience means to receive the immediate presentation of things; intellectual interference necessarily distorts the concrete data in Phenomenon. A poet of pure experience takes it for granted that every form of existence in Phenomenon is right in its place—none is superior to the other—and needs no human justification (such as naming, imparting meaning and ordering) for its being such. The poet seeks to identify himself with Phenomenon, which, in the Taoist view, is the totality of the spontaneity of all forms of existence, by merging with it. To paraphrase the words of Chuang Tzu: not to hide a boat in a ravine (which is only one segment of Phenomenon in which one tends to see it as a causally determined unit) but to hide Phenomenon in Phenomenon (in which no causal relation needs to be established). It is no accident that a Taoist should stress the fast of the mind or sitting-in-forgetfulness, for it is only by emptying out all traces of intellectual interference that one can fully respond, as does a mirror or still water, to the things in their concreteness, particularly to their spontaneously and simultaneously harmonious presences. This state of mind no doubt most resembles the trancelike consciousness, although, unlike the case of most mystical experience, this consciousness does not work up to a leap into the noumenal world; to the Taoist, the phenomenal is the noumenal.

This trancelike consciousness is dominant in Wang Wei's poetry:

Empty mountain: no man
But voices of men are heard.
"Deer Enclosure"

Falling flowers are still, still, cries a mountain bird.
"Composed on the Cold Food Day"

Man at leisure. Cassia flowers fall.
Quiet night. Spring mountain is empty.
Moon rises. Startles—a mountain bird.
It sings at times in the spring stream.

In this consciousness, as I once said, the poet has "another hearing, another vision. He hears voices we normally do not hear. He sees activities we are not normally aware of." This is precisely what Lu Chi (261-303) meant when he said (to use a more emphatic translation of his line):

In the zero of silence, to search of sound

It is also what Ssu-k'ung T'u meant when he said:

wait in silence—
It is here the scheme is seen

. . . . .

Harken the music among bamboos
Such beauty: full-load homeward bend.

The state of stillness, emptiness, silence or quiescence is ubiquitous in all Wang Wei's poems. He is the quietest poet in Chinese and perhaps in all literary history. The "voices" one hears in his poetry are those one hears in absolute silence. This is true in all above examples. Or witness these:

High on the tree-tips, the hibiscus
Sets forth red calyces in the mountain.
A stream hut, quiet. No one around.
It blooms and falls, blooms and falls.
"Hsin-i Village"

Latter part of the sacrificial month: tuneful and free were sunlight and air. Mountains I could have crossed. You were reviewing the *Classics*. To disturb you would be immoral, so I went into the mountains, rested at Kan-p'ei Temple and ate with monks before heading home. North to wade Yüan-pa. Clear moon shone all over. Night deepened. I mounted the Hua-tzu Hill. The Wang River whirled in ripples, up and down with the moon. Cold mountains: distant lights flickered beyond the forests. Deep lanes: dogs barked like leopards. Hamlets and villages: pounding of grains alternated with intermittent ringing of bells. This minute, sitting alone, page-boys all muted, I think of days of old: Hand in hand. Compose poems. Down twisting sidepaths toward limpid streams. . . .

"From the mountains: a letter to P'ei Ti"

To turn from these examples to a poem by Rilke:

Blumenmuskel, die Anemone
Wiesenmorgen nach und nach erschliesst,
bis in ihren Schooss das polyphone
Licht der lauten Himmel sich ergiesst,

in den stillen Blütenstern gespannter
Muskel des unendlichen Empfangs,
manchmal so von Fülle übermannter,
dass der Ruhewink des Untergangs

kaum vermag die weitzurüchgeschnellten
Blätterränger dir zurückzugeben:
du, Entschluss und Kraft von wieviel Welten!
Wir Gewaltsamen, wir währen länger,
Aber wann, in welchem aller Leben,
sind wir endlich offen und Empfänger?

We may say this is also a "quiet" poem in which, through a trancelike consciousness, we seem to be seeing the movement of the saphead hearing the silent music of the spheres (like Mallarmé) and the perceiver has almost become the sap and the music itself, yet we find the poet caught in a kind of metaphysical unrest from which Wang Wei is entirely free.

In a mode of consciousness in which there is no disturbance of intellectual impositions, no hurry-scurry to establish causal relations, each object or moment is given the fullest chance to emerge in spotlighting distinctiveness very much the way everything appears keenly fresh in the orbit of a child's vision. Wang Wei's poetry is particularly noted for its visual immediacy and authenticity: visual perspicuity in each phase of perception (in this case, we may say reception) and different gradations of color and light in the natural makeup of the scenery. The visual order of his images (or moments) in the poem (i.e. the linguistic artifact) follows naturally the cuts and turns of our experiencing the fluctuations of Phenomenon.

The river flows beyond the sky and earth.
The mountain's color, between seen and unseen.
"Floating on the River of Han"

White clouds—looking back—close up.
Green mists—entering—become nothing.
"Mount Chungnan"

Tall bamboos reflect sky's arc.
Flashes of blue wash ripples.
Darkly into the Road of Shang-Hill—
Even woodcutters do not know.
"Frost-Bamboo Ranges"

Vast desert: a lone smoke, straight.
Long river: the setting sun, round.
"As Envoy to the Barbarian Pass"

Boating on a wide river:
Confluent water reaches sky's end.
Sky-waves suddenly open up:
Towns: millions of houses.
Farther on: cities are visible.
Instantly, mulberries and hemps.
Back view of native country:
Teeming water merges with cloud-mist.
"Crossing River to Ch'ing-ho"

Like the making of each shot in the movies in which its position, distance, tone and thickness of light and color, direction of its movement and tempo (smoothness and abruptness included) of its movement are all attended to, Wang Wei's images achieve similar cinematic distinctiveness suggesting all the other elements that have gone into the makeup of a shot. It is my belief that the Southern Sung landscape painters, notably Ma Yüan (fl. c. 1190-1230) and Hsia Kuei (fl. c. 1190-1230) and quite a few Ch'an painters such as Yü-chien, were more inspired by Wang Wei's handling of different tones and gradations of color and light in his poetry than by his paintings. The visual order (strictly speaking, it should be called visual rhythm) being of such importance in the whole scheme of color and light, we will find that any violation of this order in translation will deface Wang Wei's unique mode of presentation as one example will show.

> Empty mountain: no man (is visible)

becomes, in Witter Bynner's hand,

> There seems to be no one on the empty mountain . . .

The analytical or explanatory "There seems to be no one . . ." has destroyed completely the dramatic presentation of the two phases of perception and putting "no one" ahead of "empty mountain" violates the stance or consciousness of the poet in that unique moment: we need the *emptiness,* the *openness* first before we have incident or action (i.e. in this case).

4

While the emptying out of intellectual interference allows the things in Phenomenon to emerge in their cinematic concreteness, it also enables the reader (the poet having become Phenomenon itself) to see all sides of a moment of experience simultaneously, in fact, of many moments simultaneously, because the presentation deriving from the aesthetics of pure experience (as we have explained above) is free from concerns of linear development and causal relation which are a product of the intellect. A clear-cut example is **"Mount Chungnan"**:

> The Chungnan ranges verge on the Capital,
> [viewer on level ground looking from afar—
> Moment 1]
> Mountain upon mountain to sea's brim.
> White clouds—looking back—close up.
> [viewer coming out—Moment 2]
> Green mists—entering—become nothing,
> [viewer entering—Moment 3]
> Terrestrial divisions change at the middle peak.
> [viewer atop peak looking down—Moment 4]
> Shade and light differ with every valley.
> [viewer on both sides of Mount simultaneously—
> Moment 5]
> To stay over in some stranger's house—
> Across the water, call to ask a woodcutter.
> [viewer down on level ground—Moment 6]

Like in most Chinese landscape paintings, this poem assumes a bird's-eye view which is the only possible way to see many different moments simultaneously. This is again, to repeat Chuang Tzu's words, not to hide the boat in the ravine (specific time and locale) but to hide Phenomenon in Phenomenon (in which case time and space becomes indistinguishable, in which case we are only aware of blocks of experience moving in and out of Phenomenon, blocks of experience interdefining one another). Wang Wei has provided us with an artifice whose visual immediacy and authenticity brings the reader right into the fluctuations of Phenomenon, an artifice, at the same time, that enlarges infinitely the reader's psychological horizon (morphologically through visual horizon) by lifting the reader off the ground, making it possible for him to view the entire Phenomenon itself.

Such is the art of Wang Wei.

Such is his value—if we had to make value judgements against the will of Wang Wei.

Marsha L. Wagner   (review date 1973)

SOURCE: A review of *Poems of Wang Wei*, in *Literature East & West*, Vol. XVII, No. 2, 3, 4, June, September, and December, 1973, pp. 421-23.

[*In this review, Wagner comments favorably on G. W. Robinson's translations of Wang Wei's poems and praises his poetic judgment.*]

. . . G. W. Robinson's graceful translations of over 120 of Wang Wei's poems constitute the most successful English version to date.

Robinson's selection generally overlaps previous translations, emphasizing Wang Wei's most popular and personal poetry while avoiding more heavily allusive court poems and Buddhist poems. It is regrettable that Robinson did not include more poems which have not been anthologized in the past; not all of Wang Wei's occasional poetry is as devoid of feeling and interest as Robinson suggests. His criterion was to choose poems which did not require extensive annotation, and the relatively few explanatory notes which Robinson does give, although brief, are clear and adequate for the general reader.

The introductory comments offer a summary of Wang Wei's life and of T'ang poetic forms, intended for the lay reader. In spite of its brevity, the introduction confronts the significant issue underlying Wang Wei's complicated stance in his poetry: the "unresolved conflict . . . between the worldly and the mystical sides of his nature". The two helpful appendices present Wang Wei's famous **"Letter to P'ei Ti from the hills"** (which, Robinson claims, represents his true interests) and T'ao Yüan-ming's "The Story of the Peach Blossom Spring" as an illuminating comparison with Wang Wei's poetic version of the story, translated within the text. However, in the appendix Robinson omits the poem which is actually part of T'ao Yüan-ming's tale, and since this omitted verse section is more metaphorical and philosophical than the introductory prose account, Robinson's contrast betweenT'ao's "matter-of-fact" and Wang's "symbolic" treatments is somewhat over-simplified.

The volume begins with the twenty quatrains of the **"Wang River Sequence,"** but the arrangement is basically arbitrary thereafter. There are some tenuous groupings by content—for example, nine poems which mention "white clouds" are clustered together; Robinson suggests that this image consistently has non-literal connotations for Wang Wei. The lack of consistent ordering by topic, style, line length, or chronology (dubious at best) makes a book of refreshing variety for casual reading, but is frustrating when one is looking for a particular poem or the treatment of a specific theme.

Wang Wei's poetry is notably difficult to translate. His style is apparently plain, and many of his images are characteristically generalized or even archetypal. Yet this very simplicity and abstraction open up the poetry to several levels of interpretation. Wang Wei exploits ambiguity, both in syntax and in diction, especially with the word *k'ung,* which may connote, even simultaneously, physical emptiness, worldly vanity, and the Buddhist Void or *Śūnyatū.* Thus the vague mystery of Wang Wei's landscapes suggests a subtle and complex vision. The translator's task is to retain the open-ended vagueness of the original within the more limited lexical precision and grammatical specificity of English.

Robinson modestly allows Wang Wei's poems to speak for themselves. He seeks a comfortable compromise between literal fidelity and English fluency. He tends to favor, but not rigidly, the first person singular in speaker, the plural of generalized nouns, and the present progressive verb tense. Robinson uses grammatical connectives sparingly, but adds them when necessary to clarify the meaning or to smooth out the syntax. He does not attempt to force the Chinese content into English rhyme or meter, but his translations are given recognizable form by his usual faithfulness to the Chinese lineation. He systematically breaks all seven-syllable lines into two parts at the caesura, while all five-syllable lines are rendered as single lines in English. His minimal use of punctuation—with no punctuation, except occasional dashes, at line endings until the end of the poem—is disconcerting at first, but the ultimate effect is to emphasize the semantic content and natural pauses in the Chinese meter without calling attention to the translator's style.

Robinson's graceful simplicity and unstrained fluency are apparent, for example, in his translation of the twelfth poem of the Wang River Sequence, **"Willow Waves."**

> The two rows of perfect trees
> Fall reflected in the clear ripples
> And do not copy those by the palace moat
> Where the spring wind sharpens the good-bye.

In this quatrain Robinson avoids Wai-lim Yip's over-punctuated and over-literal awkwardness, which labors for a "Chinese" flavor—by using reduplication even when it does not occur in the original, for example:

> In rows, silken trees after silken trees,
> Their shadows thrown upon limpid waves.
> Unlike those upon the palace moat—
> Spring winds: sorrow, sorrow at farewell.

On the other hand, Robinson also avoids rhapsodic embellishments, such as those by Chang and Walmsley, who strive for a Western romantic tone:

> The swaying branches of the willow row mingle
>   their silken garments in caresses.
> Reflected shadows ripple the clear water.
> Be not like those willows seeping on the
>   imperial embankment
> Which sadden people parting in the cold spring
>   wind . . .

"Willow Waves" also illustrates the liberties Robinson takes with literal accuracy. He modifies the details of the Chinese (the first line, for example, literally reads: "divided - rows - meet - silk/beautiful - trees") in the interests of English fluency and assonance. Elsewhere, Robinson occasionally employs similar poetic license, with uneven results. In at least two cases (**"Good-bye to Tsu the Third at Chichou,"** and **"In answer to Assistant Magistrate Chang,"**) he deviates not only from lexical accuracy, but he unfortunately distorts the original lineation.

But for the most part, Robinson's translations reveal his commitment to conveying syntactical sense as well as imagestic force, and he usually displays sound literary judgment. His general fidelity to the original is admirable given that his translations read with such elegant ease in English.

Stephen Owen (essay date 1981)

SOURCE: "Wang Wei: The Artifice of Simplicity," in *The Great Age of Chinese Poetry: The High T'ang,* Yale University Press, 1981, pp. 27-51.

[*In the following excerpt, Owen examines the perceived conflict between public and private life in Wang Wei's poetry.*]

> Wang Wei, your brother, was the most revered man of letters in all the world. He served throughout the former reign, and his fame was great among the treasures of the age. High he soared among Chou's Odes; deeply he reverenced the Songs of Ch'u. In all his works the humors of the cosmos were in harmony, and the rules of musicality were correct in his noble rhymes. The waterfall sent his lush imagination leaping into the sky; scattering clouds spread his innermost emotions with them.

Emperor Tai-tsung to Wang Chin in 763, on the presentation of Wang Wei's collected works to the throne.

Now, late in life, I love only stillness;
The affairs of the world touch not my heart.
I look within, there find no great plans,
Know nothing more than return to the forests of
    home.

Wang Wei, **"Answering Magistrate Chang"**

It is an important and nearly universal attribute of high civilization that those who have attained wealth and power are fascinated by the prospect of renouncing what they once coveted so greatly. In the eighth century there began in earnest a peculiarly intense relationship between the high official and the recluse or eccentric, a relationship that was to continue in many forms throughout the remaining centuries of traditional Chinese civilization.

As an individual phenomenon, the conflict between the attractions of public and private life had been a long established theme in the literary tradition. But only in the High T'ang did a fascination with rejection of public service become a pervasive theme in upper-class literary life. During the Eastern Han, Chang Heng may have written a "Return to the Fields" *fu,* but imperial recognition came for his *fu* on the capitals. Early in the T'ang, T'ai-tsung still preferred a Shang-kuan Yi to a Wang Chi. But by the mid-eighth century we find the emperor Tai-tsung extravagantly praising the poetry of Wang Wei, the greater part of which concerned the renunciation of court and the public life. Wang Wei's own life and work enacts this same contradiction between social position and personal values.

The precise dates of Wang Wei's life are the subject of much scholarly debate. He was born either in 699 or 701 and died in 759 or 761. The major biographical sources are in conflict, but the dates 699 to 761 are the most plausible. Though Wang Wei's father and grandfather were never more than middle-level officials, they were members of the powerful T'ai-yüan Wang clan, and thus it is impossible to say to what extent their rank in the central government reflected their actual local power or their national social prestige. Wang Wei's mother was a Po-ling Ts'ui, another old and prominent clan. Thus, in terms of social prestige, Wang Wei's background was the highest of the major High T'ang poets, and it should be no surprise that he found a warm welcome in the courts of the T'ang princes.

During his teens Wang went to the capital, ostensibly to take the preliminary examination, but more likely to obtain the patronage of an imperial prince. This had long been one accepted course by which a young man of good family sought advancement, and young Wang Wei could not have known that the powers of the princes and the old patterns of poetic advancement were to be irrevocably changed. After four rulers in a single decade, no one could foresee that Hsüan-tsung was to exert firm control over his imperial family and to reign for over forty years.

Wang Wei's collection contains a small number of juvenalia, datable from text notes probably written by Wang Chin or Wang Wei himself. The inclusion of juvenalia is an unusual feature in T'ang collections; in the case of Wang Wei they may have served to validate the biographical convention of literary precosity or perhaps to represent the works for which Wang achieved youthful fame in the capital. It is possible these juvenalia were revised later in Wang's life, but some few are indeed juvenile, while others represent the heptasyllabic song style popular in the early eighth century. Several of the juvenalia, however, rank among Wang Wei's best-known works. One such poem was written at age seventeen in Ch'ang-an; the occasion was the Double Ninth Festival, when it was customary to climb some high place and think on absent friends and relations.

**"On the Double Ninth: Remembering My
    Brothers East of the Mountains"**

Alone in a strange land,
    and I here, a stranger,
Each time this holiday comes
    I long doubly for my kin,
And know that brothers far away
    are climbing someplace high,
Decking themselves with dogwood twigs,
    short one person.

The word repetition in the first line and the clever play on strangenesses, doublings, and absences show a firm mastery of the court poet's rhetorical craft. But young Wang Wei already infused rhetorical play with something deeper, a psychological seriousness and speculative capability that belong firmly in the High T'ang.

Wang Wei passed the preliminary examination in 717, becoming a candidate from the capital prefecture, a position of prestige with a relative certainty of success in the *chin-shih* examination. This latter he passed in 721. During this period Wang Wei enjoyed the patronage of several imperial princes, most notably Li Fan. The surviving anecdotes concerning Wang's relations with Li Fan are all of dubious authenticity, but they do suggest that he was famous as a musician in addition to his poetic reputation. Wang Wei was also, of course, a painter, and though we know little of his musical interests after this period, his reputation as a painter grew and endured. Few critics of his poetry or painting fail to cite the [following] couplet:

I erred in this life, becoming a poet.
In some life before I'm sure I was a painter.

And though Wang admits his true vocation in this life, most of those who have written on his poetry have found something of the painter's eye in his work.

It was probably in the court of Li Fan that Wang Wei met Ts'ui Hao, a lifelong friend, and their names were paired as two of the most famous poets of the day. Together with the older poets of Li Fan's court, they celebrated the prince's outings in the old court style, and with far more grace than the emperor's poets dared summon.

"His Majesty Lends the Prince of Ch'i His Chiu-ch'eng Palace that My Prince May Escape the Heat: To My Prince's Command"

The Imperial Prince withdraws afar
    from the Gates of Rose Phoenix,
A Royal missive lends him this distant
    palace of azure mists.
Outside its windows clouds and fog
    rise from our very robes,
Roll up the curtains; its streams and hills
    enter into a mirror.
By its woodlands the sounds of water
    drown out our laughter and chatter,
From its cliffs bright colors of trees
    shade the latticework.
It's by no means certain that homes of gods
    are any finer than this,
So why did pipe-playing Wang-tzu Ch'iao
    head off to the emerald sky?

The fourth line probably refers to the reflection in a lake or pool, but it may suggest the framing space of the window. The closing comparison to the dwellings of the immortals was a virtual requirement in the old court poetic style: since joys even superior to those of the immortals can be found in this place on earth, why seek apotheosis like Wang-tzu Ch'iao?

After passing the metropolitan examination, Wang Wei received a minor position in the Music Office, perhaps because of his abilities as a musician. Soon thereafter Wang became involved in political difficulties the true origins of which are not altogether clear: he was accused of having permitted a musician to perform a dance that must have been taboo, but possibly this was no more than a pretext for dismissal. Wang's difficulties probably stemmed from his associations with the princes at a time when Hsüan-tsung had decided to curb the constant threat they presented to the throne.

Whatever the true causes, Wang Wei was demoted to a low post in Chi-chou in modern Shantung. On his journey east Wang turned to the great tradition of exile poetry and produced the first datable examples of the controlled, austere style for which he was to become famous. The relatively unornamented diction of these poems followed the exile poetry of Tu Shen-yen, Shen Ch'üan-ch'i, Sung Chih-wen, and Chang Yüeh, but Wang Wei's exile poems went far beyond mere simplicity of diction: their depth and complexity revealed the hand of a major poet.

One of the many elements that constitute the greatness of these poems is a serious interest in perception: how things are seen, how the physical world controls how things are seen, and how the forms of perception have inner significance. In the following poem from the Chi-chou journey, the poet is scarcely present at all: his function is to move

and see. But the succession of scenes and their implied viewpoints enact a pattern basic to the human experience of journeys.

"Crossing the Yellow River to Ch'ing-ho"

Drift by boat upon the Great River,
Massed waters touching the sky's very edge.
Sky and waves suddenly split apart—
The million houses of a district capital.
And further on, see walls and market,
Then clearly appears mulberry, hemp.
I look back toward my homeland—
Vast floods stretching to the clouds.

Two points in space define a journey: a starting point and a destination. Whichever point draws the traveler's eyes reveals a state of mind that need be expressed only in describing the direction of vision. Similarly, when the poet's eyes shift from destination toward home, the act defines a sudden change of heart.

But vision is not free: what the poet sees is determined by the indifferent features of topography, which here assume a dramatic and protean form in the riverscape. With its power to conceal or expose, the riverscape possesses the corollary power to create interest and longing in the human mind: it controls visual absence and loss, the necessary stimuli of desire. The riverscape creates expectant interest in what lies hidden ahead on the far bank, then dissipates that interest in revelation. His curiosity sated, the poet looks back and meets a second dramatic revelation, in this case not of a place but of a loss of place. The poem is intensely visual, but no reader could call it descriptive; the focus of interest lies not on what is seen but on the interior life of the perceiving poet. But beyond the interior concerns of the occasional lyric, there is a general interest in the relativity of perception and in the relationship between perception and human response.

As in Wang Han's poem, the simplicity of diction thwarts the average reader's interest in ornamental craft and demands that the reader look more deeply to the significance implicit in the structure of representation. Like Wang Han, Wang Wei strives for a kind of authenticity—not the authenticity of universal responses achieved through typological convention, but an authenticity of unmediated perception. By making the poem represent what is seen more than the poet in the act of seeing, the poet would have the reader's eyes repeat the experience of the poet's eyes and thus share directly his inner responses. Objective closure becomes a means to avoid the direct statement of emotion, to make the reader experience what the poet felt when he turned his head to look home and saw only vast stretches of the river.

The ornamental craft over which Wang had such perfect mastery was avoided even more intensely in his later poetry; Wang Wei's style achieved an austere simplicity that became the touchstone of his individual poetic voice. Again the poet gazes over a broad stretch of water:

"South Cottage"

A light boat goes off to south cottage;
North cottage, hard to reach over vast waters.
Look at men's houses on the other bank—
So far away we cannot recognize them.

Like other quatrains from the *Wang Stream Collection,* "South Cottage" is animated by a mask of naïvete and understatement built upon the kind of structural genius seen in the preceding poem. Wang Wei also learned to draw in unobtrusive echoes from earlier poetry: the last couple there unmistakably echoes several famous Early T'ang poems suggesting isolation and anonymity in both a positive and a negative sense. The enigmatic value of the last line shows greater poetic maturity than the easily identifiable moods of **"Crossing the Yellow River to Ch'ing-ho,"** but Wang's interest in the relativity of perception remains constant. Distance prevents the poet from recognizing men he probably knows (the cottage is on his estate) and grants him an anonymity that may be the negative value of loneliness or the positive value of reclusion.

Wang Wei returned from his Chi-chou exile sometime during the mid 720s. Little is known of his life between his return and 734, when Chang Chiu-ling became minister and promoted Wang to a responsible position in the government. Some scholars have suggested that it was during this period that Wang purchased the Wang Stream Estate, formerly owned by Sung Chih-wen. Whether Wang acquired the estate at this time or later in the 740s, he loved it dearly and celebrated its beauty in the *Wang Stream Collection,* a small series of quatrains written by Wang together with his friend P'ei Ti. For partings, banquets, and *yung-wu* series, small collections of one or more scrolls (*chüan*) were common, but the form of the *Wang Stream Collection* was something new. The two poets took turns treating a series of set topics, points of interest on the estate that together constituted a programmatic journey through the landscape. By the second half of the eighth century the collection had become an immense success and a model for many subsequent quatrain series, including one by the Mid-T'ang poet Han Yü. In aesthetic sensibility and intellectual interests, few T'ang poets were as far apart as Wang Wei and Han Yü; Han's uncharacteristically meek submission to the model of the *Wang Stream Collection* suggests something of its compelling influence.

In 734 Wang Wei petitioned the new minister, Chang Chiu-ling, for a post. Chang's circle was filled with men bearing surnames like Wang, P'ei, Ts'ui, and Wei—the great families of the capital. Wang Wei's close friends and supporters came largely from these families, and it was a group in which he could be comfortable. During this period Wang again turned his talents to the court and formal banquet poems requisite when accompanying the great court figures on their outings. But Wang was neither a courtier-poet nor a member of the court literary establishment; rather he held a political post, Comissioner of the Right.

When Chang Chiu-ling fell from power in 737 and was exiled to Ching-chou, Wang's genuine distress occasioned several poetic consolations for his patron. As a member of Chang's party, Wang Wei had reason to be concerned for his own position: a few months after Chang's fall, he was ordered away from the capital on a mission to the northwestern frontier, where he served as regional censor. Several occasional poems on frontier themes and probably several of his border *yüeh-fu* date from this period. Some of Wang's border poems, such as **"Army Song",** are among the finest of their kind, but they belong to the tradition of the mannered frontier *yüeh-fu* of the Southern Dynasties. The conservatism of Wang's literary training is apparent in the contrast between these poems and contemporary border songs by Kao Shih and others, poems that began a more spirited style that was to culminate a decade later in the work of Ts'en Shen.

"Arriving at the Frontier on a Mission"

With a single coach I'll visit the frontiers.
And of client kingdoms, pass by Chü-yen.
Voyaging tumbleweed leaves the passes of Han,
A homebound goose enters Tartar skies.
Great desert: one column of smoke stands straight;
Long river: the setting sun hangs round.
At Hsiao ramparts I met a mounted messenger—
"The Grand Marshall is now at Mount Yen-jan."

Like many famous T'ang poems, including the Wang Wan poem quoted earlier, this piece is remembered for a single couplet, the third, whose balanced geometry of forms represents one characteristic of Wang Wei's descriptive art. But surrounding the memorable couplet is a highly conservative poem. The last line closely echoes the closing of a frontier *yüeh-fu* by the Liang poet Wu Yün. For all Wang Wei's undeniable originality, his work was more deeply rooted in the Early T'ang than that of any other major High T'ang poet.

Wang Wei's stay in the Northwest was brief: General Ts'ui Hsi-yi, in whose camp Wang was stationed, died soon after Wang's arrival, and in 738 or 739 the poet returned to Ch'ang-an. A year later he was sent off to the provinces again, this time to take charge of the preliminary examinations in the South. Another of Wang's friends and sponsors, P'ei Yao-ch'ing, posted Wang back to the central government, but probably because of his associations with Chang Chiu-ling, he held a post that was low for one of his age and background. From 742 until 755, when the capital fell to the rebel army, Wang held a succession of such posts, perhaps no more than sinecures. During the 740s and early 750s the poet probably spent most of his time at his estate, enjoying the fellowship of his many friends and writing poems for them on how his gates were always closed to visitors.

Like many other officials left behind in Hsüan-tsung's unseemly flight from Ch'ang-an, Wang Wei fell captive to An Lu-shan's army and was given the undesired honor of an office in the rebel government. Wang is said to have tried desperately to avoid complicity with the rebels by taking drugs to simulate incapacitating sickness. When the capitals were retaken, he was imprisoned by T'ang forces on the charge of treason. Conveniently, Wang Wei's brother Wang Chin was then serving in the Bureau of Justice and managed to have the charges against his brother dropped: the extenuating evidence was a poem that Wang had given to P'ei Ti while imprisoned by the rebels, a poem that obliquely expressed the poet's loyalty to the T'ang house. Beyond this short expression of distress—and the motives for its fabrication after the fact are overwhelming—Wang Wei's poetic silence on the An Lu-shan Rebellion is remarkable. The fact that Wang spent most of the rebellion in An Lu-shan's prison is sufficient to explain why he never wrote vehement attacks on the rebel occupation as Tu Fu did, but his silence after his release is perhaps best explained by the proprieties of poetic topic that Wang Wei usually followed: the rebellion and its devastation simply would not come to mind in the kind of private meditation and social exchange that dominated his last poems.

Restored to good position in the central government by Su-tsung, Wang Wei held a series of high posts until his death, probably in 761. During his last years Wang is said to have become increasingly devout as a Buddhist layman, leading an austere and simple life. His last great poems have a quality all their own: even Wang's masterful descriptive powers were abandoned, and there remained a starkness of style that avoided any hint of artful craft.

"Villa on Chung-nan Mountain"

In middle age I grew truly to love the Way,
Now late, my home lies at South Mountain's edge.
When the mood comes, I always go alone,
I know all about its wonders, without motive, alone.
I'll walk to the place where the waters end
Or sit and watch times when the clouds rise.
Maybe I'll run into an old man of the woods—
We'll laugh, chat, no hour that we have to be
　　home.

A concern with time appeared powerfully in Wang Wei's later poetry. Various aspects of spontaneous action were measured against actions planned or done with fixed purpose and fixed times. Wang's interest in the organization of space, which can be seen in **"Crossing the Yellow River to Ch'ing-ho,"** became an analogous interest in the organization of time by will and hidden motives. The paradoxical "goal of spontaneity" appeared in an equally paradoxical art that sought to be artless.

Another aspect of Wang's concern with time was his interest in life changes, usually as part of a process of renunciation and growing freedom. More than most poets, Wang Wei saw his own life and those of others as processes of becoming. From his early years he foresaw the deepening wisdom, religiousness, and abandonment of worldly ties in old age, and the poet fulfilled his prophecy for himself. The opening of the preceding poem is a variation on a set opening trope that recurs through Wang's poetry:

Now, late in life, I love only stillness,
The affairs of the world touch not my heart.

In my youth understanding was shallow,
Drove myself to study to grasp profit, fame.

　　. . . . .

Now in winter's clarity I see the far mountains,
Massed snows, a frozen blue-green
And sparkling white, emerge from eastern forests,
Stirring in me desire to leave this world.

Late I learned that pure and true law,
Daily grow more distant from the crowds of men.

My youth is not worth speaking of—
I saw the Way when years were already long.

Wang had seen similar processes in the lives of others as early as his Chi-chou exile. The lament for passing youth and hair growing white had little place in Wang Wei's poetry: for him old age was a visionary state, and in his private poetry he celebrated each stage by which it drew nearer.

It is difficult to know which poets were considered the greatest contemporaries by K'ai-yüan and T'ien-pao readers. Critical and prefatory tropes such as "the most famous of the age" were applied generously to a wide range of indisputably minor poets, and even when these laudatory evaluations are not mere politeness, they involve more disturbing unknowns such as "precisely when" and "to what audience." The K'ai-yüan and T'ien-pao clearly had no stable canon of contemporary writers, but a few figures stood out, most notably Wang Wei and Wang Ch'ang-ling. Particularly in the last decade of his life and the two decades following his death, Wang Wei has a strong claim to having been considered the greatest poet of the day. His late prestige with the imperial family was surely one factor in the admiration of his younger contemporaries, but he was also the central social figure in the world of poetry; his acquaintance with other contemporary poets was broad and his influence tremendous. The capital poets of the later eighth century reused and misused the style he perfected until it became tedious. Gradually, in the last decades of the later eighth century, interest in other K'ai-yüan and T'ien-pao poets, such as Wang Ch'ang-ling and Li Po, began to challenge Wang Wei's dominance, and when the great Mid-T'ang writers reevaluated their High T'ang past, Li Po and Tu Fu were raised to the pre-eminence they have held ever since. Wang Wei came to be ranked just below Li and Tu, and though he was occasionally criticized and his position challenged, his reputation remained relatively stable, with none of the fluctuations in popularity that other High T'ang poets suffered.

Wang Wei's collected works were presented to the throne in 763 in an edition prepared by his brother Wang Chin, then minister. Wang Chin claimed that the collection represented only a small proportion of Wang Wei's entire output, the greater part of which had been lost in the rebellion. The presence of an authorized edition in the imperial library so soon after the poet's death is one factor responsible for the relative stability of the text. Textual problems do exist, but these are minimal in comparison to the collections of some other poets, like Meng Hao-jan. A few interpolations have been identified, but on the whole, Wang's collection is a secure one.

The image of Wang Wei that has endured since the T'ang has been of a meditative poet, a private poet, and a landscape poet. This image is to some degree justified, because Wang Wei saw himself in similar terms. But at the same time Wang Wei was one of the most social and urbane of T'ang poets. There is great variety both in his poetry and in the facets of of his personality. He could abandon the strong poetic identity that permeates his reclusive poetry to write the most gifted and graceful court poetry since Sung Chih-wen and Shen Ch'üan-ch'i. When he was innovative, he could work either through the traditions of his predecessors or deliberately take new departures. During his Chi-chou exile he created major poetry out of a base of Early T'ang exile poetry, but he also could boldly modify elements of the *Ch'u-tz'u* for a new kind of poetry in the exile tradition. The poet who concealed interior processes of thought and emotion beneath a descriptive surface also hid the theme of exile beneath the description of a shamanistic performance near Chichou. The model was the "Nine Songs" of the *Ch'u-tz'u:* the accepted interpretation of these poems in the T'ang was that Ch'ü Yüan had composed them as revisions of popular shamanistic performances he had seen in his exile. When Wang Wei wrote such a poem, it carried a silent literary-historical context, a tacit assumption of the role of Ch'ü Yüan in his unjust exile. The two songs are not veiled satire or metaphorical complaints; rather, they evoke exile out of the famous poetry of the past.

"Second Song for the Worship of the Goddess at Yü Mountain: 'Bidding the Goddess Farewell'"

In a swirl they come forward and bow
    there before the hall,
Eyes filled with love-longing
    toward the sacred mats like jade.
She came but did not speak,
    Her will was not made known,
And She is the evening rain,
    makes the empty mountains somber.
The pipes grieve in shrillness,
Flurried strings throb with longing,
The carriage of the goddess
    is about to turn majestically.
In a flash clouds draw back,
    the rain ceases,
And green stand the mountains
    amid water's splashing flow.

In this case, the use of *Ch'u-tz'u* meter echoes specific source texts, but Wang also followed in the footsteps of Sung Chih-wen by using *Ch'u-tz'u* meter for personal poetry. But Wang complicated the expressively emotional mode associated with the meter, forcing it to work at curious cross-purposes to the quiet surface of the poems.

"A Song on Gazing at Chung-nan Mountain: For Hsü of the Secretariat"

One evening you came out
    from the Secretariat,
Sad how affairs in this world of dust
    go so often awry.
You halted your horse
    by a two-trunked sāla tree,
Gazed on green mountains,
    did not go home.

In much of Wang Wei's poetry there is a law of repression: the universal feeling of homesickness, the literary historical context of grief in exile, or the modal associations of a meter will tell the reader that some deeper significance or intense emotion lies beneath the poem's placid surface. The song above and other seemingly simple poems are fed by the energy of that repression.

In addition to *Ch'u-tz'u* meter, Wang Wei experimented with the six-character line and achieved perhaps the greatest success of any Chinese poet in that awkward meter. On at least one occasion Wang followed T'ao Ch'ien's characteristic use of the tetrasyllabic line, for associations of simple primitive dignity.

Beyond metrical experimentation, Wang Wei possessed a wider thematic and stylistic range than any T'ang poet before him, perhaps wider than any earlier Chinese poet. He could treat border themes and the semierotic themes of palace poetry with genius. In the tradition of temple visiting poems, Wang sometimes followed his Early T'ang predecessors, but he also used the abstruse terminology of Buddhism in several poems and demonstrated a Buddhist learning far greater than any of his immediate predecessors. He could write playfully joking poems, including a semicolloquial piece that may represent an attempt at dialect poetry. In short, Wang Wei was a High T'ang poet not only in developing a truly individual poetic voice, but also in his degree of mastery over traditional poems and in his powers of innovation.

Wang Wei's most significant contribution to the development of a genre probably lay in his treatment of the quatrain. All literary forms are, to some degree, oriented toward closure; regulated verse (*lü-shih*) is a partial exception because so much of the reader's attention is directed to the aesthetics of the middle couplets. But of all genres, the quatrain had always been the most dependent on closure for success. Wang Wei could use the pointed, epigrammatic closure of the Early T'ang quatrain, though he preferred the imagistic closure that was popular in the High T'ang. But Wang also developed another form of closure that carried the quatrain even farther away from epigram: Wang's quatrains often ended in enigmatic understatement—a statement, a question, or an image that was so simple or seemed so incomplete that the reader was compelled to look beneath it for the importance expected in quatrain closure.

The success of this new form of closure depended entirely on generic expectations, and Wang Wei manipulated those expectations, teasing the reader to look for profundity beneath a mask of simplicity. The distrust of surfaces, the disjunction between appearance and reality, and the hiddenness of meaning had not been prominent features of the poetry of the preceding two and a half centuries: court poetry was a poetry of surfaces—what was said was indeed what was meant. Court poetry's metaphors permitted easy substitutions—the court for Heaven, courtiers for immortals.

The rule of repression in the realm of emotional response became a rule of hiddenness in the cognitive realm. The hiddenness of truth did have deep roots in the philosophical tradition; in contrast to the West, in the Chinese tradition truth usually lay not behind a mask of orphic complexity but rather behind a mask of guileless simplicity. To draw on this philosophical tradition was to alter entirely the way in which poetry was read: what was said was no longer necessarily all that was meant, and the surface mood might not be the real mood. Particularly in the *Wang Stream Collection,* we find poems that are visually complete but intellectually incomplete, which tease the reader to decipher some hidden truth.

"Rapids by the Luan Trees"

The moaning of wind in autumn rain,
Swift water trickling over stones.
Leaping waves strike one another—
A white egret startles up, comes down again.

Even in less enigmatic quatrains, there is often a strange uncertainty about the full significance of Wang's flat statements.

"Look Down from the High Terrace: Seeing Off Reminder Li"

I say goodbye, looking down from this high terrace
Where stream and plain stretch in endless distances.
At sunset the birds return in flight
And travelers go on and away, never ceasing.

The reader knows that the movements of men and birds constitute a ground for comparison, but there is no clue whether the travelers are like the birds, moving off to where they belong, or unlike the homing birds, moving on and on in the constant toil of human life. At the time of composition, the circumstances of occasion may have provided the clue, but the popularity of the poem in later centuries suggests that the relationship was more interesting in uncertainty. The poem signals "analogy" to the reader and then blocks the reader from defining the analogy.

Wang Wei's public poetry was not always mere graciousness, nor was it always written to command. In a poem to encourage the emperor to perform the state sacrifices on Mount Hua, Wang wrote in a style entirely different than his court poetry or his reclusive poetry. He began by praising the mountain in cosmic terms and modulated to the theme of imperial glory with a public dignity more characteristic of Tu Fu or Han Yü than the manner usu-

ally associated with Wang Wei. If Wang's inclination to private experience was a more fertile source for his poetry, his public values were also strong, and the genuine conflict between them gave real force to Wang's gestures of renunciation.

Conflict generated natural pressures on structural conventions and proprieties such as unity of response. Even in the High T'ang a shift of resolution midway through the course of a poem was unusual; it occurs in Wang Wei as the enactment of conflict between public and private values, between family obligation and the desire to withdraw.

"Offhand Composition III"

At day's evening I see the T'ai-hang Mountains.
I fall into brooding that I cannot go.
"Well, tell me then, why is that so?"
The web of the world has snared me.
My little sister grows taller each day,
My brothers have not yet married,
The family's poor, my salary low,
And our savings, not what they once were.
So often I have longed to fly away,
But I hesitated, looked back again.
The site of Sun Teng's Whistling Terrace,
Still out there somewhere among pine and bamboo.
No, I'm not all that far from it—
Old friends are already on their way.
Daily the stains of desire fade away,
Meditation's stillness grows daily more firm.
Suddenly I resolve to go!
Why wait till my years are approaching their end?

The value conflict between social obligation and private inclinations to freedom were as much a part of the intellectual interests of the age as they were a central concern of Wang Wei. But in Wang Wei's poetry this conflict is part of a much larger pattern of renunciation. It is not simply a stable state of conflict: there is a primary value, usually a social one, and the dominant movement is one of negation. This central act of negation occurs in literary terms, in intellectual terms, and in terms of the poet's self-image.

The literary gesture of negation lay in renouncing those kinds of poetry associated with public social life and the court. In the work of many other High T'ang poets the same impulse took the form of an antithetical movement, finding in eccentricity a conscious violation of poetic decorum and restraint. Li Po and a wide number of minor poets chose this path of opposition in gestures of wild spontaneity, but in Wang Wei's case, the movement was one of negation rather than antithesis. Wang's characteristic eremitic poetry is austere, written in a language stripped of ornament, a language of basic words:

The river flows out beyond Heaven and Earth,
The mountain's color, between Being and
 Nonbeing.

In contrast to poets like Li Po, Wang Wei had been deeply trained in the craft and rhetoric of court poetry. Wang was unable to oppose the feigned wonder and excitement of court poetry with a show of spontaneous wonder and excitement; instead, Wang opposed the danger of falseness of feeling by its true negation—absence of feeling. If genuine feeling is to be present, it must be hidden, only implied, spared the manipulative self-consciousness implicit in overt expression.

The restraint and stylistic control of the court poet's training appeared clearly in Wang Wei's best personal poetry, particularly in his descriptive art. But Wang used that control against the tradition it grew out of, against artifice.

"Returning to Mount Sung"

A clear stream lined by long tracts of brush,
There horse and coach go rumbling away.
The flowing waters seem to have purpose,
And birds of evening join to turn home.
Grass-grown walls look down on an ancient ford,
As setting sunlight fills the autumn mountains,
And far, far beneath the heights of Mount Sung,
I return and close my gate.

Return was one of the most compelling themes in the poetry of Wang Wei and that of his contemporaries, return to what is basic and natural. High T'ang poets knew the place they were leaving in their various "returns"— the artificial world of capital society with its dangers, frustrations, and humiliations, as well as its poetry. However, the goals of their "returns," their definitions of "the natural," were often quite different.

In Wang Wei's poetry the object of a return was usually a form of stillness and inaction: the poet chose to cut himself off from the world rather than to show his disdain for society's decorum by acting as he pleased. Wang Wei's version of freedom was a "freedom from" rather than a "freedom to." As in the preceding poem, return to stillness was often indicated in the closure of a poem by a gesture that symbolized renunciation of human society and the end of discourse—shutting a gate:

In eastern marshes, the beauty of spring's plants,
In deep sorrow I shut my wicker gate.

And he who is still—tell me why it is so
That his briar gate is closed in broad daylight?

Shutting a gate is simply one of many final gestures of renunciation in Wang Wei's poetry. It may be a refusal to go home, thereby rejecting the social structure of time; sometimes it is an explicitly Buddhist gesture towards asceticism and self-negation:

At sunset by the curve of a deserted pool
I sit in meditation, mastering
    the poison dragon of passion.

If you would learn escape from sickness and old
    age,
For you there is only the discipline of Non-Life.

The Buddhist allegory **"Climbing Pien-chüeh Temple"** illustrates the progress of the soul from the illusion of the physical world to the extinction of self in Nirvana. The beauty of the temple landscape serves only to draw the deluded soul onward along the right path: it is the "City of Illusion" of Buddhist parable, a hollow thing of outward sensual attraction that entices the weary and unenlightened soul towards enlightenment.

A bamboo path leads through the First Stage
Where the City of Illusion appears from Lotus
    Peak.
Up in its windows all Ch'u is encompassed,
Above its forests Nine Rivers lies level.
Pliant grasses accepted for sitting in meditation,
Tall pines echo with sutra chanting.
Then dwelling in void, beyond the Clouds of Law,
Observe the World, attain Non-Life.

The visually present landscape of a temple-visiting poem is superimposed on an allegorical landscape, structured to lead the passive soul to transcendence. Lured up the mountain by the illusory natural and architectural beauty, the soul attains a vantage point that disorders its habitual perspective. Grasses yield softly to the contemplative body as the soul and the eyes of the poem are drawn upward with the sounds of sutra chanting, past the pines and clouds, past the final stage of the Clouds of Law (Dharma), to transcendence. And in the notion that the beauty of temple and landscape exist only to overcome the illusion of beauty, we find an emblem for a rigorous poetic craft that exists to overcome craft.

As a progress to silence, isolation, or nothingness, the poem is an act of regression, a return. But the poem need not regress as far as these anterior states of Chinese cosmogony. A poem might return only as far as some earlier kind of poetry—regression of language—or to some primal activity such as farming. One of the most interesting of such poems moves back to both the primal activity, farming, and to the primal poetry, the ritual hymns of Chou in the *Shih-ching*. The poem echoed is *Shih* 290, which begins:

They clear away grass, clear away bushes,
In their plowing the earth is laid open,
A thousand pairs of plowmen turn up roots
In the marshes, on the path-banks.
Here the master, here the eldest,
Here the younger sons, their children,
Here strong helpers, here the servants
In multitudes eating in the fields.
The men think lovingly on their wives,
The wives rely upon their husbands.
And sharp are their ploughshares
As they set to work on the south acres.

Wang Wei uses this vision of primitive agrarian harmony in his characteristically enigmatic fashion:

"An Evening Under Newly Cleared Skies"

Under clearing skies the plains stretch broad,
No dirt in the air as far as eyes see.

A city gate looks down upon a ford,
Village trees reach to the mouth of a stream.
Silvery waters bright beyond the fields,
Green peaks emerge behind near mountains.
These are farming months—no one takes their ease,
All the family is at work on the south acres.

Wang Wei's poem begins in stillness and clarity as the eye moves over the static relationships of the landscape and out to the edge of its broadened field of vision. In this still and harmonious world emptied of movement and human presence, Wang Wei shifts abruptly in closure to mankind, which is "not at ease." Though not at ease, mankind has its own harmony, doing what is proper in the season. It is a strange poem and lists the business of humanity as yet another "item" in the tranquil landscape. The natural is identified with the primal, and mankind is put in its proper place, in the ancient and eternal labors of farming.

After renouncing the complexities of capital society and its poetry, the poet "returns" to a primal, natural state—to the stillness behind a closed door or to the religious stillness of enlightenment or to the primitive world of earlier poetry. Sometimes a poem will end in action, as in the preceding poem, or even in the eccentric version of the natural that was favored by Wang's contemporaries—but such natural action must come from a ground of stillness.

"Dwelling in Ease at Wang Stream: To P'ei Ti"

Chill mountains growing ever more azure,
Autumn waters daily rush by.
I lean on a staff outside my wicker gate,
Face to the wind, hear cicadas of evening.
At the river crossing the last of setting sun,
A lone column of smoke rises from a village.
Once again I meet old Chieh-yü drunk,
And we sing crazy songs before the five willows.

Chieh-yü was the legendary "madman of Ch'u," the representative example of the eccentric whose seeming madness concealed true wisdom. Five willows echoes the "Master of Five Willows," a fictional biography by T'ao Ch'ien describing the ideal recluse. As the preceding poem integrated human activity into the natural world, here the still and tranquil scene reduces wild madness to a gentle and decorous lunacy in the landscape.

On an intellectual level the act of negation in Wang Wei's poetry was inextricably bound up with Wang Wei's Buddhism. Many critics have pointed out Wang's obsessive use of terms like k'ung ("emptiness," "the Void," Sunyata, "in vain") that have meaning both in the secular poetic tradition and in Buddhist thought. Wang knew at least a few sutras well, drew terms from them, and alluded to them. But no matter how devout a Buddhist, Wang Wei was a poet and not a Buddhist thinker; religion played a significant role in his poetry, but the poetic tradition and the concept of poetry it presumed excluded the possibility of a truly religious or devotional poetry. Not until the

early ninth century did the scope of poetry broaden enough to admit a discursive and meditative treatment of religious values; this can be found in some of the poems of Po Chü-yi. But for a body of poetry whose primary orientation was religious, one must go outside the secular poetic tradition to the collections of Han-shan and Wang Fan-chih.

A third theme developed out of the twin themes of negation and return: this was unselfconsciousness. In one form it involved a negation of the will that projected into the future and manipulated it. Or in social terms it was a negation of motivated behavior, of treating one's fellow man in such a way as to advance or confirm one's social position.

Unselfconsciousness and its opposition to social privilege appear clearly in the closing of the following poem. The closure uses two allusions to the Taoist text *Lieh-tzu*. The first story concerns Lao-tzu's rebuke to Yang Chu for allowing himself to appear so grand that others paid him deference. Yang Chu mended his ways, and when he returned to the inn where he had been staying, the innkeeper and guests, previously respectful, now ignored him and even squabbled to take possession of the mat he was sitting on. The second story tells of a man who was fond of seagulls, and when he would visit them on the shore, they approached him without fear. His father then urged him to trap them by taking advantage of their trust, but the next time the man returned to the shore—this time with a motive—the gulls sensed it and fled.

"Written after Long Rains at My Villa by Wang Stream"

Long rains in deserted forests,
  smoking fires burn slowly,
Steaming greens, boiling millet, the men
  take their meals on the eastern acreage.
Over the mists of watery fields
  a white egret flies.
In the shade of a summer wood
  a yellow oriole warbling.
Here in the mountains practice stillness,
  watch flowers that bloom for a day,
Beneath the pines fast in purity
  and harvest dewy mallows.
An old man of wilderness long ago ceased
  squabbling for the mat,
So why should the seagulls ever
  suspect him any more?

The theme of unselfconsciousness appeared early in Wang Wei's poetry in a poem on T'ao Ch'ien's "Peach Blossom Spring," from the year 717. Wang reinterpreted the story in the retelling, emphasizing the unselfconsciousness of the fisherman when he found the utopian village. But once the fisherman was received by the villagers and had settled for the night, verbs of thinking, longing, planning, and remembering filled the poem. Once the fisherman "wanted" to go home and "wanted" to return to Peach

Blossom Spring again, of course he was unable to find the way. Wang Wei's reinterpretation of the fable was the first of a long series of poems retelling the story in later centuries.

Negation of will is related to the negation of self, a theme with both Taoist and Buddhist dimensions. In much of his descriptive poetry, the speaking poet became an eye passing over the landscape and isolating significant elements. As in any literary form, the disappearance of the poetic artificer was an unattainable goal: Wang Wei's powerful organizing consciousness mediated between the world seen and the representation. But that manipulative consciousness tried to negate its presence by hiding from the surface of the poem, and by creating enigma to thwart the reader's impulse to find simple meaning. The conventions of poetic structure demanded personal response in the closure: Wang Wei would often give his "response" in a gesture of renunciation, a response that denied further response, further acts, or further emotions.

Such quintessentially negative gestures may not be true for the greater part of Wang Wei's poetry, but they do appear in most of the poems for which Wang was later admired, poems that embodied his poetic identity. Often Wang described a world of objects in static relationships or harmonious movement and then, at the end, positioned himself in that world:

A fire on shore, a lone boat spending the night,
Fishermen's houses, there evening birds return.
Vast and empty, heaven and earth grow dark—
The heart is as calm as the broad stream.

These lines work through traditional poetic associations: the single fire of the boatmen suggests loneliness; the return of the birds calls to mind personal return and homesickness; the sunset evokes melacholy. In **"Crossing the Yellow River to Ch'ing-ho,"** the poet structured the visual scenes dramatically to create an interior narrative. In this poem, written also on the journey to Chi-chou, the poet tried to overcome the interiority of the scene by the objective eye that reduced these fragments of the world and its own conciousness (*hsin* "heart" "mind") to a series of "items" in the calm scene. The consciousness moves through the world with the steadiness of the river, passing things and not fixing on them.

Wang Wei's independence and originality did not preclude a base of Early T'ang convention in much of his work. How close he stands to seventh-century compositional technique can be appreciated only by contrast to a later T'ang treatment. To cite one telling example, after a poem in praise of the capital region, Wang closed with a shift to the figure of Ssuma Hsiang-ju, the Han *fu* writer, excluded from the delights of capital society and sick in Mao-ling, near the capital.

"Sightseeing on a Winter Day"

I walked forth from the city's eastern gate
And let my gaze sweep a thousand miles.

Green mountains stretched behind azure forests,
The crimson sun was a ball on the level land.
North of the Wei, sight sped to Han-tan,
And to East of the Passes, out of Han-ku.
A thousand directions converge on the land of
　　Ch'in,
Satraps of the Nine Regions come to court.
As the cock crows in Hsien-yang City,
Caps and awnings go on in succession.
The minister visits the nobility,
Lords banquet the royal chamberlain.
Now Hsiang-ju is old and sick
And returns alone to Mao-ling for night.

The poem is a High T'ang transformation of the seventh-century song on the capital, best represented by Lu Chao-lin's "Ch'ang-an: *ku-yi*" and by Lo Pin-wang's "The Imperial Capital." The closing shift from the glory of the capital region to the figure of the suffering outsider was an irresistible instinct of Early T'ang poetic convention. Lu Chao-lin's poem had closed with Yang Hsiung, the Han intellectual who had become the medieval exemplary recluse; Lo Pin-wang's poem closed with Chia Yi, the Han political writer whose talents were unappreciated. The structural convention was compelling; Wang Wei asserted his identity through the conventions of closure, through his choice of Ssu-ma Hsiang-ju as the outsider and emblem for himself. Hsiang-ju was the Han figure who would most strongly represent the true poet.

About a century later Li Shang-yin echoed the closing of the poem above (and of another poem by Wang) in a quatrain in which he, like Wang Wei, assumed the role of Ssu-ma Hsiang-ju.

"To Secretary Ling-hu"

From Mount Sung's clouds, from the trees of Ch'in,
　　long have I dwelt apart.
A carp-form letter-case came from afar,
　　in it a single letter.
Oh, ask no more of those who once were
　　guests in the garden of Liang—
At Mao-ling in the autumn rain,
　　sick Hsiang-ju.

The pathos in the figure of the outsider was achieved in the Early T'ang poems by an abrupt closing shift away from a lengthy praise of the capital's delights. Wang Wei may have abbreviated the rhetorical praise of the capital, but the technique was essentially the same. Li Shang-yin was able to concentrate on the figure in isolation and to represent the intense pathos of his condition without a long rhetorical contrast. The conventional antithesis of joyful communality survives only as an echo, as Ssu-ma Hsiang-ju's former happiness as a "guest in the Garden of Liang." Indeed, the antithetical joy survives only as something "not to be spoken of," and that negative imperative points to the isolated poet for whom memory is pain. The structural convention of Early T'ang poetry had not disappeared entirely, but it had been transformed almost beyond recognition.

Among the major High T'ang poets, only Tu Fu surpassed Wang Wei in the seriousness of his use of the literary past. Wang's use of early poetry has already been seen in the closure of his poems on renunciation and return. Despite his conscious primitivism in echoing the *Shih-ching* and *Ch'ut z'u,* Wang generally avoided the ethical *fu-ku* associations of those early poems. From the tradition of the pentasyllabic *shih,* Wang often borrowed elements from the poetry of Ts'ao Chih, Pao Chao, Hsieh Ling-yün, Hsieh T'iao, and Yü Hsin. But no poet or group of poems exerted as powerful an appeal for Wang as the poetry of T'ao Ch'ien.

During the centuries that followed his death, T'ao Ch'ien's influence was slight. Poets echoed lines and phrases from his work, but he was not considered a major poet. The *Chin History* classified him as an exemplary recluse rather than as a man of letters, while Chung Jung's *Shih-p'in* ranked his work only in the second level of excellence. But T'ao's poetry was particularly well represented in the *Wen-hsüan,* which may have been one factor in his increasing popularity during the eighth century. The major exception to sixth-century and seventh-century indifference to T'ao was the Early T'ang poet Wang Chi: few poets were as exclusively devoted to a single predecessor as Wang Chi was to T'ao Ch'ien, but even in that case T'ao served primarily as a model of personality rather than as a true literary model. The T'ao Ch'ien revival that took place in the 720s and 730s established T'ao's pre-eminence in Six Dynasties poetry, a position never challenged in later dynasties. The T'ao Ch'ien revival began in the works of a few poets and soon spread to the wider circle of capital poets. In part this phenomenon reflects Tao's genuine appeal to the new High T'ang taste, but in part it also seems that the T'ao Ch'ien persona was merely fashionable. If the note dating Wang Wei's **"Peach Blossom Spring"** to 717 is correct, then that poem was one of the earliest monuments to the new interest in T'ao Ch'ien. Wang Wei and Ch'u Kuang-hsi were the poets most strongly under T'ao's spell, and it was probably from them that interest spread to other members of their circle.

At times Wang Wei simply imitated T'ao Ch'ien's style, as in one of his **"Offhand Compositions",** written specifically in T'ao's praise. However, the more serious use of T'ao's poetry lay in integrating T'ao's casual simplicity with the sophistication and craft of the eighth-century capital poet. This Wang Wei accomplished to perfection, and the two antithetical voices seem to merge as one.

"To P'ei Ti"

The scenery is lovely in the evening of the day,
As here with you I write new poems
And, calm, gaze into the distant sky,
Our chins resting on our *ju-yi* staffs.
The spring wind stirs all the plants,
Orchid and iris grow by my hedge.
Through a haze the sun warms the bed chamber
And a farmer comes to bring me word:

Joyously spring returns to the marshes,
Waters rise, full and churning, by the banks.
And though peach and plum haven't blossomed,
Buds and leaflings fill their branches.
Sir, get your walking stick ready to go home—
I tell you, it's time for farming soon.

Some of the echoes of T'ao's poetry here are identifiable textual references, while others are simply turns of phrase. Wang Wei's fascination with T'ao's manner did not lead to subordination to the older poet: T'ao's characteristic celebration of the free and joyful self must be tied to the order of the natural world, the scene at hand that was the central concern of court poet's descriptive art. T'ao might describe an agrarian scene, but the primary emphasis lay on the poet. The High T'ang poet cannot resist halting the movement of the poem now and again to focus on some picturesque, static scene. The thematic development is also Wang Wei's own—from poetry to contemplative stillness to natural action.

Wang Wei's first line would remind every educated reader of the seventh line of T'ao's "Drinking Wine: V": "Mountain air is lovely in the evening of the day." Later, when Wang Wei speaks of his hedge, the reader must think back to T'ao Ch'ien's famous hedge in the fifth line of the same poem. Wang has orchid and iris growing by his hedge, while T'ao "picks chrysanthemums" by his. But T'ao does not lack orchid and iris: in poem XVII of the "Drinking Wine" series, they grow in his front yard. To ensure that his readers hear T'ao Ch'ien's famous hedge echoing behind his own, Wang uses the personal pronoun *wo,* "my." During the age of court poetry, personal pronouns had been gradually driven from poetic diction, but T'ao used them often. In the hands of a T'ang poet, an informal pronoun like *wo* suggested "natural language" and a certain archaic directness. The second line of Wang's poem echoes the second poem of T'ao's "Moving House" series:

In spring and autumn are many lovely days,
I climb a high place and write new poems.

One could continue to extract fragments of T'ao Ch'ien's work from the remainder of Wang Wei's poem, but our primary concern is with the significance of these echoes. Wang Wei's poem is a fine work with its own integrity and not simply a pastiche of phrases from T'ao Ch'ien. Their function is essentially modal: as the *ku-feng* carried with it implicit messages of political concern and moral rectitude, so the style of T'ao Ch'ien possessed an aura of honest simplicity and basic agrarian values. On the one hand, Wang Wei is not making allusion to the full contexts of specific poems by T'ao; on the other hand, he is not simply repeating the T'ao Ch'ien manner as Wang Chi did. Rather, Wang Wei is using the T'ao Ch'ien mode to give an added dimension to a poem that also carries his own personal voice.

Of those now considered major High T'ang poets, Wang Wei was not only the most prominent in his own time, he was also the earliest to attain prominence. Meng Hao-jan was an older poet, and a few of his better works antedate the early 720s when Wang Wei began to produce major poetry. But Wang Wei early became an influential figure in capital poetry, while Meng Hao-jan was at best considered an interesting provincial with a moderate gift for poetry. When Meng Hao-jan met Wang Wei in the capital in approximately 734, Wang Wei was the established poet. Meng's chronological priority has tempted at least one critic to see the influence of Meng upon Wang Wei's work, but if there was much interchange, the influence would probably have gone in the other direction. Wang Wei was socially superior and better known; writing to Wang, Meng paid him the most telling gesture of deference: he wrote in Wang Wei's distinctive poetic voice and not his own.

Other hints in the two collections tend to confirm Wang's poetic, if not chronological, priority; for instance, on his journey to Chi-chou in the early 720s, Wang wrote:

> In a strange land, cut off from companions,
> A lone wanderer grows closer to his servant boy.

It is highly unlikely that Wang would have known Meng Hao-jan's poetry at this stage. In an undatable poem by Meng, but a poem presumed to be from his later years, we read:

> Gradually I grow farther from flesh and blood
> And become ever closer to my servant boy.

One line is clearly borrowed from the other, and we can be reasonably certain that it was Meng who borrowed from Wang. Meng Hao-jan is the greatest of Wang's early contemporaries, but the scope of Wang's work is broader, his style more clearly individual, his intellectual concerns more serious, and the quality of his work consistently greater than that of Meng Hao-jan.

High T'ang writers usually thought of contemporary poetry in terms of couplets rather than whole poems. Wang Wei was a master of the parallel couplet. The distinctive aspects of his couplet art were imitated: geometrical balance of forms, plain words for grand scenes, an unmatched clarity and restraint. Even when his couplets are in the general style of his lesser contemporaries, he was the superior craftsman. When he wrote of Wang Wei's art, Tu Fu spoke of his couplets:

> Most known, those fine couplets that fill the entire
> world.

The individual aspects of his couplet style were one of Wang's major contributions to T'ang poetry: he replaced the dense, ingenious couplets of Early T'ang poetry with a purity and simplicity of style that was extremely compelling. He stripped away the visual complexities of what he called "the realm of vision" (*yen-chieh*), leaving a world of simple forms and elements in meaningful relationships. But the purity and simplicity of his style was not the spontaneous "natural language" that other poets sought:

though it opposed the artifice of poetic craft, it was itself a highly sophisticated manifestation of that same craft. In this we have the emblem of the paradox that echoes in every aspect of Wang Wei's poetry—the craft that tries to overcome craft, the artifice of simplicity. Later critics saw only the simplicity, the poet of nature and reclusion; but in his own time he was, in the words of a friend, "of this age, the master craftsman of poetry."

Chou Shan (essay date 1982)

SOURCE: "Beginning with Images in the Nature Poetry of Wang Wei," *Harvard Journal of Asiatic Studies,* Vol. 42, No. 1, June, 1982, pp. 117-36.

[*In the following essay, the critic argues that the nature poems contain "the essence of Wang Wei's achievement" and that they describe the relationship of landscape to poetry.*]

Wang Wei (701-61) is a poet whose reputation primarily rests on his nature poems. Although in the poems which have survived other themes are well represented—elaborate and perfect poems about the emperor's court, sentimental sketches of bucolic life, poems expressing friendship—it is with the nature poems that his name is universally identified. The prominence given a handful of nature poems reflects both the judgment that they contain the essence of Wang Wei's achievement and an acknowledgment of the position they occupy in the evolution of nature poetry. The sense displayed in these poems of a life lived in harmony with nature marks an important development in the appeal of landscape and nature to the poetic sensibility.

The world of Wang Wei's nature poems is a narrow one of simple and recurring scenes—a brief wind lifts his sash, a slight chill hangs in the air, light fills the mountainside, a bell sounds once. These are small moments intensified, during which nothing much happens. In general, Wang Wei does not draw any conclusions from scenes so presented—and this is the problem. A small area of experience has been sharply delimited, but within this area the reader is not guided to an interpretation. The clarity of the moment distilled seems to bespeak openness, yet the reader who feels that a meaning beyond that moment has been intended finds it concealed and the poems lacking in internal clues. In this Wang Wei reminds me of Imagist poets, in which the sharpness of the observed details contrasts with the vagueness of the interpretation which has been implied. That a meaning beyond that captured moment has been intended seems a reasonable expectation. Indeed, given Wang Wei's enduring reputation, it seems a necessary one; for it is hardly possible that any nature poetry can continue to hold our attention that does not project a certain amount of significance onto the landscape presented.

The problem of significance—what is there besides descriptions of nature?—has been recognized for a long time.

A major response has been concerned with identifying the Buddhist meaning of Wang Wei's poetry. This attempt seems justified in view of the whole of Wang Wei's poetry and also the known facts of his life. Wang Wei began the serious study of Buddhism about the age of thirty, adopted the *tzu* of Mo-chieh (which together with his *ming* Wei formed the Chinese transliteration of the name of the sage Vimalakīrti), and began to move in Buddhist circles. In his poetry, his Buddhist interests are reflected in the many poems written to monks, in his appreciative descriptions of their lives, and in the frequent references to Buddhist practices and goals in his own life. These visible effects on his poetry are not disputed, but the most interesting claim of influence is made in a strong form. This is that the Buddhist influence is present in exactly those of the nature poems which show no overt signs of Buddhism, that is, those of Wang Wei's nature poems which I have described as simple and yet elusive.

The poems meant are such as these:

> In Ching Brook white stones just out,
> The sky is cold, red leaves thinning.
> On the mountain path, there had been no rain,
> The cloudless blue, clothes are dampened.
> **"In the mountains"**

> All at rest, the cassia flowers fall.
> The night is quiet, the spring mountains empty.
> The moon appears, startling mountain birds,
> Which from time to time cry out from the spring ravine.
> **"Birdcries Stream"**

Of the first poem the Sung-dynasty monk Hui-hung (1071-1128) reports the opinion that it is full of *t'ien-ch'ü* "the essence of nature." Of the second the Ming-dynasty critic Hu Ying-lin (1551-1602) declares that Wang Wei had entered into the ranks of Ch'an Buddhists. The Ch'ing anthologist Shen Te-Ch'ien (1673-1769) says that Wang Wei's poetry does not use Ch'an vocabulary but often attains Ch'an meaning. Such views of the poems are widespread and usually expressed in similarly general terms.

Some modern scholars have therefore recently added various qualifying suggestions to the equation of Wang Wei's nature poems with Buddhist influences. Iritani Sensuke discusses the "Wang-ch'uan chi" in terms of its *Ch'u tz'u* elements, its realism, and its mysticism, but does not bring in Buddhism. Fujiyoshi Masumi emphasizes the limited influence of Buddhism on the T'ang nobility in general and the importance of Taoism in its mediating role between Confucian ideals of service and Buddhist withdrawal. Pauline Yu is at pains to show that Wang Wei's attitude towards retirement from public life was not uncomplicated. None of them denies the pervasiveness of Buddhism in Wang Wei's life and in his works taken as a whole.

I think that ultimately we will have to refer to Buddhism at least in order to appreciate the full context out of which Wang Wei wrote and possibly in order to appreciate the full meaning of the nature poems. However there are aspects of the poems which we can consider before this final appeal that do not deny the possibility of Buddhist influence and yet may make easier the problem of defining this influence. This consideration begins by recognizing the nature of the problems posed by the poems.

I think of the problems as of two kinds. The first is that the literary qualities of the poems are hard to define; hence the persistent fascination with Buddhism as a key to them. Literarily the poems are elusive because they seem to defy further analysis, so simple is the setting, so precise the imagery and unhurried the tone. The stillness and tranquillity seem impossible to explicate further. Discussion would merely intrude paraphrase onto these spare scenes. The poems resist any response other than acceptance; they appear to be the simplest statements about themselves.

The second is that in those poems where Wang Wei does not use Buddhist terms—and these constitute the majority of what I have called nature poems—the Buddhist themes prove elusive to specify. I suggest that we deal with this problem by secularizing it, by looking first to see whether any philosophical viewpoint, rather than a specifically Buddhist one, is expressed in the poems. Then we may ask whether this philosophy can be identified with some aspect of Buddhism. This approach brings us to the more familiar uncertainty that the true meaning or intent of poems might always remain to some degree unverifiable, and especially so in poems, like these and like the Imagist poems, where the reader finds few guides to an interpretation. Differing literary analyses would then stress different themes, not all of which would have Buddhist analogs, but each of which may nonetheless be literarily acceptable.

I propose in this essay to begin with an analysis of some literary qualities of Wang Wei's nature poems and from this analysis to make a suggestion about the problem of meaning in these poems.

The spareness of a Wang Wei scene is not a reflection of nature but the consequence of careful selection. The images which make up each poem are simple; the elements which make up the images are few. I suggest that it is the physical spacing displayed in the images which provides a key to the remoteness and the uncanny stillness which are their chief impression on the reader.

A central image in the nature poems is the physical isolation of the poet. Not only does he live away from man, but he chooses to live in the mountains, which encircle him on all sides. Furthermore he is often stationed inside an enclosure of some kind:

> I sit alone in a secluded bamboo thicket.
> The bright moon shines among the pines.
> The bright moon shines on me.
> The mountain moon shines on a zither played.

The moon by creating a well of light around the poet emphasizes his placement in a clearing.

Further, the poet is not only isolated, but his existence is not even suspected by others:

> Deep in the forest, no one knows [of me].

He suggests the same isolation for a friend:

> On the wide waters, no one will know [of you].

Again, of monasteries Wang Wei likes to emphasize that to the unsuspecting they do not exist:

> From the city, seen afar, a deserted cloud-capped
>   mountain.
> From the city walls, looking out,
> One would see only white clouds.

The poet lives alone in harmony with nature, but he has not dissolved into nature. As a personality he is self-effacing: there is generally no emotion reaching out to the landscape, no emotion aroused in turn by the landscape. Rather, the continued existence of his ego is expressed by the insistence on an active separation between himself and others. Again, this separation often takes the form of exclusion. One aspect of an experience that he savors is the exclusion of others from it. In poems by Meng Hao-jan (691-740) which describe scenes similar to Wang Wei's, it only gradually becomes apparent to the reader that the poet is alone, for the fact is not stated. Wang Wei, on the other hand, tells us many times and in so many words that no one is around. *Wu jen* ("there is no one") and *pu chien jen* ("I see no one") are used repeatedly. *K'ung* ("empty") is often used of a forest or a mountain to mean that no one is about, save for the poet. This absence of people gives to his solitude a delicious edge:

> The house by the stream is quiet, unpeopled.
> In profusion, [magnolias] blossom and fall.

Where once there had been people living, there is now no one, and the scene is the more piquant. The same sense of specialness can be seen in the poet's being privy to the secrets of the landscape:

> Beautiful spots which only I know of.

Where he walks, no one else seems to have walked:

> Beneath ancient trees, an unused path.

Another type of isolation is often established by the first two characters (the first phrase) of short poems:

> All at rest, the cassia flowers fall.
> The night is still, all movements cease.
> In the empty mountains, after the new rain.

(The second example is twice used as a first line.) Inside the bell jar of quietude defined by the first two characters, the remainder of the poem takes place. Within a poem Wang Wei will often define a space by the silence which pervades it. This silence is then broken by a sound which also emphasizes the space defined:

> The mountains are still, the spring even noisier.
> The valley is still, the spring even noisier.
> The valley is still, the autumn spring noisy.
> The valley is still, only the pines whisper.

Or the sound occurs first, then the space is defined:

> The travellers echo through the empty forest.

The image of isolation explains other types of images that occur, in particular Wang Wei's preference for sound over sight. Again, he can be very insistent, both that he sees nothing, and that he hears only sounds:

> Empty mountains, I see no one,
> But hear the echoes of people's voices.
> The bamboos ring with the returning washerwomen.

The effect is that of a one-way mirror. Through sound images, the poet knows about other people's existence without their guessing his.

Sound has the additional advantage that what the poet hears need not be close by, but can be transmitted over an intervening distance. This distance then acts as an invisible barrier that expresses his isolation:

> From the valley mouth, the sound of a distant bell.
> The fisherman's song enters deep into this tributary.
> Deep in the mountains—from where?—a bell.

The last is a refinement, a sound whose source is unknown. The barrier is sometimes made explicit by the use of *ko* ("separated by"):

> At times I hear dogs on the far side of the grove.
> Across the river I ask the woodcutter.
> On the far shore I see homes.

We can compare these examples with a characteristic pose found in Meng Hao-jan's poetry. The figure of Meng's poet is often on a river bank, or by a jetty, from which he can also see the people making the noise. The Meng Hao-jan line "From the mountain temple a bell sounds, day is already dusk" contains elements familiar in Wang Wei too—the temple, the bell, dusk—but in Meng Hao-jan is followed by the cheerful noise of people actually seen "By the fish dam, at the ferry, the clamor of everyone wanting to cross". For Wang Wei, on the other hand, the consciousness of humans a distance away and dwindling further makes his solitude the more sweet. It is a solitude that perseveres on the edges of other people's activities and is the consequence not only of the circumstances of composition but of a certain control by imagery of the physical spacing.

It is not hard to find in the work of other poets, especially Meng Hao-jan, lines which are similar to some cited here. The world created in the poem as a whole, however, is almost always different. One much praised line by Wang Wei, for example, in its crucial part can be found in Sung Chih-wen:

> Returning rays enter the cliffs and valley. ["Sent to Yang Chiung while confined to bed at Hot Springs Villa,"in *Tō dai no Shihen*]

In Wang Wei:

> Returning rays enter the deep forest.

The returning rays are the afternoon light, which shines in the opposite direction from earlier in the day. In Sung Chih-wen, the line is one of twenty in a poem confiding the poet's hopes and fears during his recovery from an illness. In Wang Wei, it forms part of a pattern of solitude:

> Empty mountains, I see no one,
> But hear the echoes of people's voices.
> Returning rays enter the deep forest,
> Shining once more upon green moss.

The arrangement of sights and sounds, seemingly so artlessly noted as they impinge upon the poet's consciousness, constitute the whole of Wang Wei's world. The exclusion of other concerns is what is meant I think by the common description of Wang Wei's nature poems as the first ones to have been "pure." The subsequent unity of the poet with this world is then effortless, so pared is this world. The poet is able to transcend the world through immersion in nature in part because his natural world already transcends our natural world.

The spacing controlled by the images is physical and literal. I would like to suggest that the same control of spacing has a metaphorical and sometimes symbolic existence on the level of the whole poem. It is possible to interpret the themes of some poems in terms of distance and barriers, and also to offer such an interpretation for other poems which seem to be solely description.

The control of space, for instance, is implicit in one common theme we find, the theme that on the other side of an intervening distance exists a desirable state which I think we may call truth. In one of the ways in which this pattern is worked out, the truth is attained by bridging the distance. This distance is usually bridged only unknowingly: a journey is made which is not deliberately undertaken. At least the goal is not deliberately sought. This is the pattern found in the poem **"Visiting Hsiang-chi Monastery"**:

> I had not known of Hsiang-chi Monastery
> When I was several *li* into the cloudy peak.
> Beneath ancient tress, an unused path,
> Deep in the mountains—from where?—a bell.
> Noise from a spring burbles over sharp rocks,
> The sun's light chills the dark pines.
> At dusk, by the empty curve of the pond,
> Meditation to subdue the poisonous dragon.

The poem begins with the poet isolating himself from men by asserting a limited ordinary knowledge of his world, in this case the existence of Hsiang-chi Monastery. Without saying what he has in mind (for the first couplet constitutes only a denial of a purpose), the poet moves towards and, in the last couplet, reaches the hidden monastery. At this point, in the last line, the image of isolation is repeated at a higher level: the figure in the last line, either a monk or the poet himself, withdraws from his world and from us into meditation.

Real journeys of course often imply a journey of another kind, and not always as subtly as in this poem. In the poems **"Green Stream"** and **"The Shih-men Monastery in the Lan-t'ien Mountains,"** Wang Wei is explicit about the truth reached at journey's end. In the first, the traveller rounds a bend in the river and sees a spot ideal for living in retirement. In the second, the traveller happens upon five or six hermit monks, living peacefully unbothered by any knowledge of the world outside. It is of course a second Peach Blossom Spring. In both endings, the identification of man and nature is achieved by the fact of his finding an ideal natural end to his journey. Although the moral is obvious, the pattern of the journey is the same as the Hsiang-chi Monastery one. The journeys are made without a purpose, the discoveries are serendipitous, and the distances deceptive. It is just that in these poems Wang Wei depends rather on the charm of such qualities than on the profundity of the meaning. Two couplets from each poem illustrate this:

> To reach Yellow Flowers River,
> One must always follow the waters of Green Stream.
> Hugging the mountains, it makes ten thousand turns,
> The true distance no more than a hundred *li*.
>
> From afar I had admired the beauty of trees in clouds.
> At first I thought we were on a different course.
> How was I to know the clear stream wound around
> And led to the mountain before us?

Although in the journey poems, the distance is bridged and the truth temporarily seen, in other poems, the stronger theme, and I think the more profound one, is expressed that though the truth lies on the other side of an intervening distance, only across this distance is it knowable. This variant is less obvious than the journey theme and not directly stated. Therefore the tracing of this theme through imagery poses a problem of interpretation. A certain image might be more than an element in the scenery, it might contribute to the poem's meaning, but how much significance we are meant to find in that image is not specified by Wang Wei. Instead we have to bring together hints scattered through many poems to lend some weight to the reading of a single occurrence which might otherwise be a case of over-reading. There is no certainty, however, that in each case the same truth is being so delicately hinted at. These uncertainties do not exist in every poem; Wang Wei can be disconcertingly flat about his meaning. However, where the uncertainties do exist, in Wang Wei it is not enough to consider each occurrence of the image on its own.

The function of the image of white clouds, an image which occurs in about twenty poems, illustrates this problem of interpretation. In many of the poems, the reader feels that the white clouds must be a significant image, but what it is and what is implied in each case is not always specified. I would like to go into this in a little detail.

An example of the unfixed significance of white clouds occurs in the following poem:

> Playing on flutes, we cross to the far shore.
> At day's end, I see off my friends.
> On the lake, I turn back once—
> Around the hill's green are wreathed white clouds.

The poem is the eleventh of the set of twenty quatrains, the **"Wang-ch'uan Garland,"** which Wang Wei wrote about various scenic points on his country estate. This one is entitled **"Lake Yi."** Is it as simple as it appears to be? The first two lines are purely narration. Are the last two lines more significant? Is it significant that the white clouds are placed last? I will return to this poem later.

In several other poems, the white clouds lie in the unspecified distance, and mark a place towards which some are headed and to which others long to go. It seems to be the ultimate and natural resolution of the scenes of nature described, the home of one's true self. Accordingly, the verb *kuei* ("to go home") is often used of going there. Examples are:

> I am returning to the foot of the Southern
>   Mountains
>
>   . . . . .
>
> Where white clouds will never fail.
> My heart has always been in the green hills,
> As though to keep company with the massed white
>   clouds.
> Saddled for going home, beyond the white clouds.

These white clouds exist only in the mind, clearly a symbol for a longed-for place, though, unlike the Peach Blossom Spring, not a readily describable ideal place.

In general, no one is shown as having reached that place, although no difficulties are placed in the way of going. The white clouds are far away, but there is no implication that they are unreachable, or that one needs special qualifications—wisdom, unworldliness, etc.—to make the journey. It is simply that they are described from a distance. People do live among the white clouds. For example, in lines quoted earlier, monasteries are located within the clouds. But those clouds exist only for the viewer looking upon them from a distance. In poems where one is actually at the monastery, it is only an inhabited monastery and white clouds are not mentioned. There is no line such as "In the midst of white clouds." In a poem about the majestic Chung-shan Mountain, when the poet "turns to look, the white clouds have closed up", but when he "enters it, in the blue mist I see nothing". The image is beautifully apt, for clouds do dissolve into mist when one is in them, so when the poet has covered the distance, he enters to see "nothing."

This double view of the same place depending upon the poet's location and emphasizing the inaccessibility of the place is seen very clearly in the poem **"Lament for Yin Yao"**:

> We escorted your return for burial on Shih-lou
>   Mountain.
> Dark and green, the pines, the cypresses, as the
>   guests turned home.
> Your bones are buried under white clouds, for all
>   time.
> Only the flowing stream reaches the human world.

The poet has accompanied his friend's coffin to Shih-lou Mountain and seen his burial. After his return, he visualizes it as the place of the white clouds, remote, its only communication with the world a stream.

The white clouds are most within reach when they can be gazed upon. The two together, the viewer and the clouds, define the boundaries of an ideal world. The poet's content is to sit and gaze:

> I walk to where the waters end
> And sit and watch the clouds begin.
>
> In the past we stopped on our excursions
> When we had come to where the clouds end.

Wang Wei admires a friend's study:

> I envy your refuge here:
> A distant view of white clouds.

Now let us return to the poem **"Lake Yi"**:

> Playing on flutes, we cross to the far shore.
> At day's end, I see off my friends.
> On the lake, I turn back once—
> Around the hill's green are wreathed white clouds.

The poet has made a pleasant excursion out of seeing off his friends, and in line 3 he recrosses the lake to return home. When part way on this crossing he turns to look back, he is looking towards the place, and the day, he has just left: the green hills and white clouds show an untroubled serenity. What is the meaning of this sight? The recrossing of the lake has placed a distance between that day's gaieties and the quiet now. The white clouds confirm that distance; they reveal nothing of what had passed that day and hint at the finality of its pastness. Their presence—their passivity almost—is a comment on the pleasures of the day. That the image can bear the weight of such a firm closural function with some confidence is due not to the poem alone but also to the occurrences of the image in other poems.

It is interesting to see a later evolution in the white clouds image in a poem by Yuan Mei (1716-98). In this poem, "white clouds" has lost its faint capacity to hint at some meaning. The last couplet of a 32-line poem, the clouds nicely end the poet's visit to an unsophisticated village. Naturally the Peach Blossom Spring story is also referred to. I give the first and last couplets:

> I saw in the distance peach orchards in leaf,
> But did not know what village it was.
>
> . . . . .
>
> My one regret is that I must leave it;
> I turn my head; there are only white clouds.

The white clouds, the distance, peach blossoms, and rustic utopia have all blended together in Yuan Mei's easy geniality.

As an image acquires more significance, its vividness in nature begins to fade. The reader begins to discount the literalness of some of the recurring images: the white clouds in a sense had to be there across Lake Yi. The immediacy of the scene gives way before the philosophical meaning that is implied in the recurrence of the images. This is true of the sound of the bell, of the white clouds, and of other images such as the empty mountains or the woodcutters. As the literalness of the images loses force, the questions of the reader about the philosophical meanings grow stronger. As in the case of the white clouds, one could consider all the occurrences together in order to return to an understanding of one poem. Knowing how much to draw upon Buddhist thought as an extra-poetical context would help in these circumstances. We may learn for instance the weight of *pu chih* ("do not know") when it occurs without an object, and of *k'ung* ("empty"), so central a concept in Buddhism. In this paper I have suggested mainly literal readings because I want to emphasize that these words first have a literal function in the poem. The pattern of images I have suggested I hope will prove to hold on several levels and to remain an identifying mark for Wang Wei on the simplest level of the visualizable world he created.

Can poems be explained at a less elaborate length by referring directly to Buddhism? I think that itis a step which follows literary analysis. At this point, for example, we may ask whether the gazing upon clouds can be considered a secular form of contemplation. The unstriving movement towards knowledge I described as a theme is certainly familiar from Buddhism, as is the distance between humans and an enlightened state. I suggest that by fully tracing out a theme, one then knows what kinds of correspondences to seek in Buddhist philosophies. In other words the literary analysis precedes the philosophical one. The theme is after all expressed in literary terms. To say that **"Visiting Hsiang-chi Monastery"** is Buddhistic because it is a monastery the poet visited rather than because of other qualities in the poem eliminates its literary existence. The problem, however, with this approach—literary analysis preceding philosophical analysis—is that the answers tend to be restricted to a kind of perception

of Buddhist influence that is probably too diffuse to satisfy those readers who feel vividly the Buddhist nature of the poems. These answers tend to boil down to the conclusion that certain themes thread through the poems because the consciousness that brought them before us was imbued with Buddhism. Only the themes perceived (and the examples selected) might vary with the analysis. What this approach cannot provide is an answer which states that these poems in their details specifically contain certain Buddhist views of phenomena and truth.

What if we began from the other direction, by considering the possible Buddhist meaning before the literary detail? Of the critics who do give examples of what they mean by the Ch'an nature of Wang Wei's poetry, few also explain how to read the poems that way. Tu Sung-po is one who does, and so I give his reading of the first two poems translated in this essay as an illustration of the direct philosophical approach:

> In Ching Brook white stones jut out,
> The sky is cold, red leaves thinning.
> On the mountain path, there had been no rain,
> The cloudless blue, clothes are dampened.
>
> **"In the mountains"**

> All at rest, the cassia flowers fall.
> The night is quiet, the spring mountains empty.
> The moon appears, startling mountain birds,
> Which from time to time cry out from the spring ravine.
>
> **"Birdcries Stream"**

Of **"In the mountains"** Tu Sung-po writes:

> Concealed are principles of Ch'an. The first two lines show that when the visible is exhausted the *tao* manifests itself and that the essential is revealed through its function. The second couplet shows that the *tao* has no physical form, but can be responded to and known. If one does not bring to the poem this kind of empathy, then he will see only the technical skill of the polished lines and completely miss what may be called the *t'ien-ch'ü* of the lines.

And of **"Birdcries Stream"**:

> When a person is at rest, all reaches its quietest. He becomes aware of the falling of the cassia flowers. His mind and his setting are as one and thus he becomes aware of the emptiness of the spring mountains. Into this quietness enters a sudden stimulus: the moon comes out and the birds cry in alarm. Thus is illustrated the sphere of stimulus.

One great difference is that this type of interpretation can only be couched in Buddhist terms . . . . Is it possible to arrive at the same explanation of the poems through literary analysis? Yes and no. In the poem **"In the mountains,"** the second couplet has a certain mysteriousness about it (why are his clothes damp? is there a mist? why an empty sky rather than cloudless [for cloudless is my paraphrase]?. . . . One naturally asks whether the mystery spills over into the other lines and imparts a deeper meaning to the whole poem. For the literary critic, the question is raised by the poem itself in the unexpectedness of the description. I have no explanation for the poem myself, but Tu Sung-po does. Comparing his with the poem, I can see that the mysteriously wet clothes can be accounted for as an image of the nonphysical *tao,* but why involve the first couplet? Literarily the couplets are quite different, but the philosophies Tu attaches to them are of equal weight. If symbolism can be read into the landscape of the first couplet, why not into every landscape described? What are the limits?

The interpretation of **"Birdcries Stream"** is problematical in a different way. There is no mystery in the poem, and one could give the same description of the poem's development from silence to sudden sound without bringing up Buddhist terminology. The assignment of a technical term, stimulus, to the moon's appearance is the chief addition. What a Buddhist reading misses is that, because of the name of the stream and the title of the poem, the birds' being startled into cries turns the poem on one level into an etymological poem. The literary critic would raise a question about the poem's meaning only because otherwise it seems an inconsequential, though very nice, poem.

Tu Sung-po may well be right in both poems about Wang Wei's intent. There is no way directly to verify it. The Chinese tradition seems to allow an interpretation that parallels the poem without being anchored in it at any point. The oddest example is the way in which love poems from the *Shih ching* were used, according to the *Tso chuan,* in interstate diplomacy with perfect understanding on all sides. (The *Shih ching* poem sung by the envoy substitutes for speech and the poem's scenario is supposed to parallel the situation between the two states.) This is interesting because it is a well-documented instance of the complete confidence and total agreement with which certain poems were at one time understood—and yet from an external source, the discipline of folklore and mythology, we can say with some sureness that theirs was a misunderstanding about the nature of the poems. The question in Wang Wei's case is whether he intended his nature poems to carry a parallel philosophical life as some of the *Shih ching* poems did a political life. Short of external proof, the question is complicated to resolve. The position of the literary critic is conservative in not assuming any intention on the poet's part that cannot be discovered within the poem. Perhaps by this method, however, not enough meaning can be recovered from the poems to do them full justice.

There is overlap and empathy between poetry and Ch'an Buddhism, especially in rhetorical devices. Thus all critics assume that it is Ch'an which permeates Wang Wei's poems, though in fact which sect or sects he held to is not known. In choosing to write poetry, however, Wang Wei displayed no consciousness that language might be unable to express truths, as the Ch'an sect taught. Moreover, although there is empathy between poetry and Ch'an, between poetry and true Buddhist (or Ch'an) poems there

is a great difference. In Buddhist poems written to convey a teaching or to voice a truth seen at the moment of enlightenment, the intent of the author is unmistakable: everything in such a poem stands for something else and the whole illustrates a lesson. The appeal is in the beauty of thought. In poetry, there is no such certainty about the creator's intent, and the appeal is in the beauty of language. There is no evidence that, devout as Wang Wei was, he ever attained enlightenment, though such themes hover around his poems.

However much these poems are Buddhistic in premise or inspiration, the level in the poetry that can be paraphrased by reference to Buddhist philosophies is probably not unique to Wang Wei. Poetry, unlike religion, values the language in which a truth is conveyed as much as the truth itself; the paraphrased truth of a poem deprived of the language of which it is composed may be no more than cliché, whereas the truth of religion is absolute, unqualifiable by clumsiness of expression. It is by using the secular tools of language that Wang Wei has preserved for us so much of the beauty of his temporal world and of its eternal principles.

A. C. Ang (essay date 1989)

SOURCE: "Taoist-Buddhist Elements in Wang Wei's Poetry," in *Chinese Culture,* Vol. XXX, No. 1, March, 1989, pp. 79-89.

[In this essay, Ang examines the role language plays in Wang Wei's poetry and assesses its effect on mood and theme.]

> My heart has always been serene:
> The clear river is equally at peace.

Wang Wei's (701-761) poetry is often characterized by its harmonious and integrated tone. As a poet-painter and devout Buddhist, Wang Wei's poetry presents a concrete natural world not only pictorially but also transcendentally or metaphysically. In other words, he expresses his poems aesthetically and philosophically. These characteristics are particularly apparent in his so-called Buddhist poems as well as in his nature poems. Most of the poems in these two categories are permeated by a sense of Buddhist quietism or Taoist ideal. Thus, in his poetry, he presents not only a strong sense of solitude and emptiness, but also things in their natural state. In addition, Wang Wei is capable of attaining a state of selfless contemplation and allows his consciousness to dissolve in order to merge with nature. The following poem is a good example:

"Bird Call Valley"

> Man at leisure, cassia flowers fall.
> The night still, spring mountain empty.
> The moon emerges, startling mountain birds:
> At times they call within the spring valley.

This poem presents not only the spirit of a tranquil spring night in the mountain but also the feeling of serenity. *"Ching"* (quiet) and *"xian"* (leisure) are the main themes of this poem. Because it is a quiet night, it seems that even the emerging of the moon can startle mountain birds, and the cry of these birds, too, becomes more distinct. This effect is similar to a line of the poem entitled "Stone Gate Monastery on Mt. Lantian": "During night meditation, mountains are even stiller." According to James Liu, [*The Art of Chinese Poetry,* University of Chicago Press, (1983).] the idea of leisure (*xian*) "carries no derogatory implications." Instead, it implies more "a state of mind free from worldly cares and desires and at peace with itself and with Nature." Indeed, *xian* is one of the key words in Wang Wei's poetry, as illustrated in the following lines:

> The autumn plain, away from man, is at rest.
> *qiu yuan ren wai xian*
>
> Life in retreat: each day is pure and tranquil.
> *xian ju ri qing jing*
>
> Green beauty, tranquil and at leisure.
> *lu yan xian qie jing*
>
> My heart and the broad river are at peace.
> *xin yu guang chuan xian*
>
> The clear moon is white and serene.
> *qing ye hao fang xian*

In the lines above, we notice that *xian* (leisure) is always followed by *ching* (tranquil or quiet). It is precisely because the poet's "heart has always been serene"and can even be at peace with "the broad river" that the objects he perceives are all in a state of serenity. By "practicing peace" the poet is able to state that he has "already realized solitude is a joy" and his "life is more than serene". Wang Wei also claims that "In late years I care for tranquility-/ A myriad affairs do not concern my heart". It is because of this absence of worldly affairs in the poet's mind that the colors within the pines ("And colors are tranquil deep within the pines"), and voices in the creeks ("Tranquil words are deep within the creeks") also appear tranquil.

In many Chinese poems, the flowing of water and the falling of petals often suggest a sense of sadness; however, Wang Wei's poetry is an exception. He sees the fallen petals as part of nature or nature's cycle. For example, the line "Man at leisure, cassia flowers fall" (**"Bird Call Valley"**), presents a sense of naturalness very similar to a line in his poem, **"Farewell to Spring"**: "Year after year Spring returns." in the same poem, the poet remarks: "No need to regret that flowers fall and scatter." This concept of nature probably stems from the Taoist's or Buddhist's perception of life, especially the latter, because the belief in 'reincarnation' very much resembles the cycle of nature. Wang Wei's world of nature can further be seen in the following poems:

> 1) At the tips of the branches, lotuslike flowers,
>   In the mountains, putting forth red calyxes;

> The hut in the gorge is quiet, without people:
> In profusion, they bloom and then fall.

> 2) The bright moon among the pines is shining;
>   The clear stream on the rocks is flowing.

> 3) Far, far over the watery paddies, flying white
>   egrets;
>   Dense, dense in the summer trees, warbling
>   yellow orioles.

In the above poems, all things pursue their own course without interfering with each other. The flowers bloom and fall according to natural order. In the hemistiche-structure of poem No. 2, the bright moon performs its natural cycle, whereas the clear spring follows its own course. In poem No. 3, the white egrets and the yellow orioles are in harmony with their respective living environments: the far and boundless paddyfield and the dense, shady summer trees. From the above poems, we may say that the poet "seeks to identify himself with Phenomenon, which, in the Taoist view, is the totality of the spontaneity of all forms of existence, by merging with it." [Wai-lim Yip, "Wang Wei and Pure Experience," in Introduction to *Hiding the Universe,* 1972.].

Seeking solitude is a common practice for the Chinese poets, especially those with Taoist or Buddhist perceptions. Wang Wei is a typical example. In his poetry, there is a strong sense of solitude which can be seen in the following poem:

"Bamboo Lodge"

> Alone I sit amid the dark bamboo,
> Play the zither and whistle loud again.
> In the deep wood men do not know
> The bright moon comes to shine on me.

The first line alludes to a poem from **"The Mountain Spirit"** (*Shan gui*). This line establishes the same mood as the line from *Shan gui* but is immediately countered by the second line, in which human activities are involved: the actions of playing the zither and of whistling. Both actions further confirm the poet's participation in nature. Hence, even though the word "alone" (*du*) clearly expresses the poet's solitude, still the readers are convinced that this solitude is being deliberately sought. There is no feeling of loneliness nor that of longing for the presence of humans. The words "dark" (*yu*) and "deep" (*shen*) imply that the location is a mysterious place; no one knows where it is—thus it is an ideal place for the poet to play the zither and whistle aloud. In the final line "The bright moon comes to shine on me" (*min yueh lai xiang zhao*), the word *xiang* implies "a sense of mutual participation." By using this word, Wang Wei skillfully and subtly projects a human dimension onto a natural object which thereby elevates the poem to a transcendental state. In other words, the poem demonstrates the poet's withdrawal from human society and his free access to nature, so as "to get close to the Way."

The sense of emptiness is another recurring theme in Wang Wei's poetry, and it can be seen in the following poem, one of his best known pieces:

"Deer Enclosure"

Empty mountain: no man,
But voices of men are heard.
Sun's reflection reaches into the woods
And shines upon the green moss.

The word "empty" is a direct translation from the Sanskrit of the term *sunyata* (meaning "emptiness" or "the Void") in *Heart Sutra*. This is one of Wang Wei's favorite words, and it is usually combined with others, such as "forest" or "mountain"; the term "empty mountain" for example, occurs frequently. This image of the "empty mountain" not only connotes the isolation and purity of the remote retreat but also "suggests a transcendent vision of the illusory material world." This is, of course, a spiritual world which allows the poet to free himself from mundane affairs. The first line explicitly indicates that the mountain is empty and no one is to be seen, yet the following line says, "But voices of men are heard." One may wonder where the "voices" come from, but according to Wai-lim Yip, the poet has "another hearing . . . He hears voices we normally do not hear." The "voices" of the unseen men resemble the sound of the bell from the unseen temple in **"Visiting the Temple of Gathered Fragrance"**: "Deep in the mountains, where is the bell?" That the source of the "voices," like that of the bell, is unknown denotes a mysterious setting. In the last two lines, the poet's sharp perception enables him to perceive the sun's reflection which reaches into the wood and shines upon the green moss. Yip suggests of these lines that here the poet is expressing "another vision . . . he sees activities that we are not normally aware of." This is also what Sikong Tu (837-908) means in his poem *Chungdan* (Placidity): "By nature it dwells,/Its mysterious essence so subtle." In other words, nature itself embodies mysteriousness. From the poem **"Deer Enclosure,"** we therefore see that the poet identifies himself with nature and completely dissolves himself in a selfless contemplative world, or in, to use Wang Guowei's term, a "'World' without a self". In fact, Wang Wei's poetry is in great contrast to another devout Buddhist, the poet Xie Lingyun (385-433). The world of Xie's poetry is a "'World' with a self". In other words, his poetry is bound to human society and often ends with a tone of frustration. For instance, the poem, "On Making a Trip to the Southern Pavilion" displays this sentiment:

Who is there that can tell what I am saying?
Only my good friends understand my heart.

Another poem, *"On Climbing the Highest Peak of Stone Gate"* also shows Xie's despondency:

I only regret that there is no kindred soul,
To climb with me this ladder to the clouds in the
    blue.

When he follows the Jinzhu Torrent, he writes:

The sensitive heart will find beauty everywhere—
But with whom can I discuss such subtleties now?

When he sets out from Guilai and looks at Twin Streams, he laments:

. . . it is not wind and rain that give me cause for
    regret,
But having no friend to whom I can pour out my
    heart.

In all these lines, the delight of nature does not make the poet, feel happier; it only reminds him of his need for human company. But in Wang Wei's poetry, especially his nature poems, we see that there is no desire for human companionship nor is there a negative sense of isolation in his mountain excursions. What is manifested in his poems is the purity of his life in retreat, free from the bounds of human society.

Wang Wei approaches all forms of nature in their native purity. This perhaps is "an existential practice of his Taoist concept of nature, *tzu-jan* [*ziran*] or self-so-ness, as well as his Buddhist belief of *ju-lai* [*rulai*] or suchness." Thus, Wang Wei's nature poetry, or rather, landscape poetry, is an appreciation of nature itself. He never projects his emotion onto the scene nor does he display violent emotion in response to natural scenery. The **"Deer Enclosure"** mentioned earlier and the following lines from **"In the Mountain"** are two exemplary poems that view nature in its pristine state:

In the Bramble Stream, white stones stick out.
Cold weather: red leaves are sparse.
No rain along the mountain path.
Skyward greenery wets one's clothes.

Besides the colourful autumn images, the objects are presented here in their natural form; there is no artificiality in them, nor are they colored by the poet's emotion.

Wang Wei also depicts majestic mountain scenery with the same kind of aesthetic distance, giving it a perspective of calmness and serenity. An example of this can be seen in the following couplets:

1)White clouds, when I look back, close behind me.
    Green mists, when I enter, become nothing.

2)The river flows beyond the sky and earth.
    The mountain's color, between seen and unseen.

3)In clear winter I see the distant mountains,
    The gathered snow, the frozen azure green.

4)On the lake with one turn of the head:
    Mountain green rolls into white clouds.

The reader is neither disturbed nor overjoyed by the grandeur of the scenes described in these couplets; rather he shares Wang Wei's peaceful contemplation looking at these pleasing sights. These couplets also demonstrate Wang Wei's pictorial composition through poetic imagery, or his artistic manipulation of light and color. He harmonizes and constrasts color and textures in each of the couplets: the "white clouds" and "green mists" which become invisible when viewed from a distance; the mountain's color which is "between seen and unseen"; the "gathered snow" and the "azure green" which gives an attractive picture in a clear winter day; the "white clouds" embracing the green mountain in an instant. All these images present both a delightful visual feature of the natural scene as well as a mysterious, transcendental experience. The image of "white clouds" especially connotes "an important non-literal significance," which also represents "some incorporeal, ideally pure country of the spirit." The association of "white clouds" with a country retreat is a conventional, poetic tradition in Wang Wei's time. As a devout Buddhist and as a recluse, Wang Wei is no exception. The image of "white clouds," which occurs eight times in his Buddhist and nature poems, not only denotes his fondness for the term but also suggests a Buddhist spirituality or the purity of his life in retreat.

Wang Wei's yearning for nature is basically a Taoist ideal, but his approach tends to be that of a Buddhist's. This characteristic is manifested in the following poem:

"Climbing to the Monastery of Perception"

A bamboo path leads up from the lowland -
On lotus peaks emerges the Conjured City.
From within a window all three Chu states;
Above the forests the nine level rivers.
On soft grass monks sit cross-legged.
Tall pines echo the chanting sounds.
Emptily dwelling beyond the Dharma cloud,
They contemplate the world, attaining nonrebirth.

The entire poem has Buddhist connotations; it is a "Buddhist allegory," in which the beautiful temple landscape only serves as a means to draw "the soul from the illusion of the physical world to the extinction of self in Nirvana." The forgetting of the self is made more obvious by the use of Buddhist terms. "Conjured city" (*huacheng*) alludes to a short, simple parable about morality in the seventh chapter of the *Lotus Sutra*. This story is used to illustrate the Buddhist's "expedient means" or "skill-in-means" (*upaya*) and his power of devising ways to help people overcome obstacles to achieve enlightenment. Here, "Conjured city" implies the path that leads to Buddhahood. To "sit cross-legged" (*fuzuo*) is to sit in a Buddhist posture. "Dharma cloud" (*fayun*) or in Sanskrit, *dharmamegha,* is the tenth stage of the bodhisattva's progression toward enlightenment. "Nonrebirth" (*wusheng*) is the Sanskrit term, *anutpada,* which denotes the path to eternity, the liberation from the cycle of rebirth. Here, the term "nonrebirth" connotes the annihilation of self. Wang Wei's belief in and commitment to Buddhism are so strong that the term "nonrebirth" appears several times in his poetry, for example:

1) I vow to stay until their pure chants end,
   Sitting correctly to study *nonrebirth*. (italics mine)

2) Singlemindedly within the demands of the Dharma,
   I wish to accept the rewards of *nonrebirth*.

3) If you wish to know how to shed the illness of age—
   There is only the study of *nonrebirth*.

Sutra-chanting and meditation are other important items in Wang Wei's poems, and are evident in the following lines:

1) When birds arrive he speaks of Dharma again;
   When guests depart he *meditates* in peace once more. (italics mine)

2) At morning *chants* the forest has not yet dawned;
   During night *meditation,* mountains are even stiller.

3) Toward dusk by the curve of an empty pond,
   Peaceful *meditation* controls poison dragons.

4) In the mountains many companions in the Dharma
   Meditate and *chant,* forming a group of their own.

In Wang Wei's poems, there are several sedentary images; besides *fuzuo* (to sit cross-legged or to sit in a Buddhist posture) as mentioned above, there are others, such as *chanzuo* (sitting in peace or meditation), *yezuo* (to sit at night), *duanzuo* (sitting correctly), *duzuo* (sitting alone) and *zuokan* (sit and watch). These sitting postures not only imply Wang Wei's strong affinity for Buddhism but also indicate his mind is in a peaceful state, and that he yearns for peaceful life. Probably because of this attitude towards life, Wang Wei has been seen as "the quietest poet in Chinese and perhaps in all literary history."

Though Wang Wei's poetry appears simple, it embodies a deep layer of artistic complexity. Many of Wang Wei's nature poems are subtly colored by Buddhist or Taoist overtones, and perhaps because of these elements they contain his fullest artistic expression and greatest intellectual wisdom. This great achievement is evident in the poet's keen perception and profound philosophical thought, that for which Wang Wei has been admired throughout the ages.

Haili Kong (essay date 1993)

SOURCE: "The Point of View—The Narrative Quality in Wang Wei's Poems," in *Tamkang Review,* Vol. 24, No. 2, Winter, 1993, pp. 2-18.

[*In the following essay, the critic explores how Wang Wei's "'painter's eye' influenced his poetic narration."*]

There are paintings in the poems of Wang Wei, and there are poems in his paintings.

　　　　　　　　　　　　　　　　—Su Shih
　　　　　　　　　　　(*Ch'üan T'ang shih* 125. 1234)

Wang Wei occupies a special position among the most famous T'ang poets for many reasons. One of the reasons for this, I think, is the narrative quality in his poems, especially his way of handling point of view. Wang Wei was mainly a poet, but also a painter and musician. Naturally, when he writes poems with the brush-pen, Wang Wei may consciously or unconsciously write with a painter's eye and musician's ears which would enable him to add and cultivate some unique dimensions to his poetry. In the following discussion, I will explore the use of "point of view" in some of his most representative poems and his unique artistic features. According to Stanzel, [Stanzel, Franz Karl, *A Theory of Narrative,* 1989.] "Point of view is a precise term." The general meaning of it is "viewpoint," "attitude toward a question." The special meaning of it is "standpoint from which a story is narrated or from which an event is perceived by a character in the narrative." Concretely speaking, the special meaning of "point of view" contains two functions: one is to narrate, "to transmit something in words"; the other is "to experience, to perceive, to know as a character what is happening in the fictional space." The term "point of view" I am discussing here is confined in its special meaning. My main concern is to see how these two functional aspects of "point of view" work separately or overlappingly in Wang Wei's poems.

Visual Pleasure

In his *The Great Age of Chinese Poetry the High T'ang,* [Yale University Press, 1981.] Owen says that "most of those who have written on his [Wang Wei] poetry have found something of the painter's eye in his work." However, it would still be interesting to see how to define "the painter's eye" and how it affects Wang Wei's poetry. "The painter's eye" could be considered as a creative subjectivity in the process of creation, or as an aesthetic object set in the poem and perceptible to the sensitive reader. Here, I want to isolate the artistic work by ignoring the would-be poet's subjective activity in the process of his writing, and focus on the possible objective interpretation from a reader's appreciative perspective. For me, the so called "painter's eye" here mainly refers to a special visual quality in the written discourse. Concretely speaking, the reader in his/her reading may feel that he sees the described objects through an imaginary eye (implied author's eye), and observes the well-organized perspective layers by an adjustable zoomlens, and finally gets the wholeness of a picture in the mind. Of course, the imaginary picture we may get from Wang Wei will have nothing to do with abstract, fragmentary modern or post-modern paintings. Instead, we should expect a classical Chinese brush-pen painting. It's flat rather than three-dimensional, impressionistic rather than detailed and realistic. When Lessing talks about the difference between painting (including sculpture) and poetry in his famous *Laocoön,* [trans, R. Philimore, in *Critical Theory Since Plato,* Hazard Adams

ed., 1971.] he points out that painting employs "figures and colors in space," and poetry "articulate[s] sounds in time." The objects and signs in painting are "coexistent" and those in poetry are "successive." That is to say, painting "can only avail itself of one moment of action." In this sense, what I try to do here is to find out how Wang Wei grasps a most significant moment, "the most pregnant" "by which what has gone before and what is to follow will be most intelligible." Of course this fixed moment here appears in a written form, in a special Chinese poetic form, either the ancient-style (including *yüeh-fu*) or the modern style poetry. The poet cannot show the described objects in a moment to the audience all at once, like a real painting which allows the audience to choose where to start their seeing. The poet has to show it in successive sequence. But Wang Wei uses highly condensed language and limited lines to describe sometimes a special moment in his poems that may be called "narrating pictures." This kind of almost "frozen" moment is confined and framed in a nice quatrain with a painting quality. The audience is led line-by-line to grasp the whole picture in the poem. This line-by-line successive process may represent the movement of the painter's eye, only through which one can perceive the picture part by part, and then draw a whole picture in one's mind by the inspired imagination. The twenty poems in Wang Wei's **Wang Ch'uan Collection** are probably the most representative in terms of this painting or "painterly" quality. Each poem describes one famous scene of the Wang ch'uan estate. Let us first look at **"Deer Walled,"** one among the twenty poems.

"Deer Walled"

> In the empty mountain no one is seen,
> Only heard are the echoes of someone's talking.
> Returning sunlight penetrates the deep woods,
> Once again illuminates the top of green moss.

Obviously these two couplets focus on describing one scene, but from two different standings. In the first couplet, the key word is "empty," which is both descriptive and allusive. The mountain is empty, not because of lack of trees, plants and animals, but for lack of human beings. In this sense, we may interpret the meaning of "emptiness" as getting away or being remote from the human society, the worldly land. Further, "emptiness" could refer to the Buddhist term *sunyata* that "connotes a sense of fullness in the 'emptiness,' a void which is pregnant with implied meanings" [Wagner, Marshall L., *Wang Wei,* 1981.] So, this is a paradoxical term which can be perceived only by someone holding a somehow transcendental standing. The second line of the first couplet actually reveals the paradoxical "emptiness" by telling us that the echoes of someone's talking can be heard. That is to say there are some people on the mountain. The seeming subversive second line at least conveys two messages: a) the viewer/implied poet must stand in a remote and distant spot to look and hear; b) a very few people are around the Deer Walled on this mountain. In other words, this first couplet tells us of the viewer's position, the emptiness on the mountain and the invisible but audible people. What a vague and blank picture. Suddenly the second couplet brings the colors and physical images into our imagined picture. The penetration of the sunlight into the deep woods brings lightness and warmth to the shadowy and cold spot, and to the green moss. Surprisingly the destination of the sunlight, or that of discourse is such a trivial moss in the deep woods. In other words, the viewer's/reader's eye is led from distant mountain to the close-up, from an abstract and vague impression to a concrete and clear perception, from generality to particularity. All the objects in the poem are still and quiet except the movement of the echoes and the sunlight that won't affect the stillness of the whole scene. It's almost a momentary catch. On the other hand, the viewer's eye has to move. In a sense, the movement of the viewer's eye follows the poet's eye, and builds up the appreciative process and therefore gains the visual pleasure. The balanced parallelism in the poem also enforces this pleasure, such as seeing and hearing, warmth (sunlight) and coldness (green moss). The words "returning" and "once again" may indicate the time. But it is still ambiguous, because we are not sure whether it refers to the rising sun or the setting sun. All those concrete and visible images may contain implicit and suggestive meanings at a metaphysical level that definitely help make the audience more interested in speculating about the ambiguity and the philosophy of the poem.

If you say **"Deer Walled"** is dealing with a vision of both a visible and invisible realm, then the following poem seems simpler in a sense.

"The Bird Chirping Ravine"

While man is at leisure, cassia blossoms fall,
While night is serene, spring mountains are empty.
The appearance of the moon startles the mountain
  birds,
Now and then they chirp within the spring ravine.

This is another modern-style (*chin-t'i*) landscape poem. It seems that the images here are clearer. "Man is at leisure," "night," "the moon" and the twice-appearing word "spring" convince us of the time: a moon-lit night in spring. In this moment, the poet nicely grasps two opposing audio-elements—the soundless "serenity" and the sound "chirping," which naturally lead to a visible scene. Because of the quietness, the falling of those tiny cassia blossoms can be heard; because the falling of those tiny cassia blossoms can be heard, the quietness is justified. This mutually supporting compound of cause and effect provides us a very quiet picture. But we don't know how far we can see. We may only hear the falling sound and sense the fragrant smell of "cassia blossoms." The sudden appearance of the moon not only startles the birds and breaks the quietness, but also brings light and the visibility to the world, and to the viewer. Then we may hear the echoes of the birds' chirping in the ravine and see the ravine under the moon shine and probably birds as well. This is exclusively a nature picture, because the poet puts the human being aside from the very beginning. Here again appears the ambiguous "emptiness," otherwise the poem should have been easier to interpret. The "empty" mountain

could refer to the darkness of the night, the quietness of nature, the hollowness of a ravine and the absence of human being. Like the "empty mountain" in **"Deer Walled,"** its surface layer is denied immediately, because of the existence of birds and the ravine that under the moon comes to light. But the "emptiness" doesn't mean physically nothing, but nothing in the "nothingness" in the Buddhist sense, or in the epistemological sense. Just this "emptiness" adds some philosophical taste to the poem, like most of Wang Wei's landscape poems. Different from **"Deer Walled,"** the viewer here seems to stand at the same spot to gaze at the spring ravine under the moon by hearing the birds' chirping and smelling the cassia blossoms. The viewer keeps his distance to observe this natural scene without moving. This is the second mode for the viewer or the readers to enjoy the visual pleasure in Wang Wei's poems.

"Visiting the Temple of Accumulated Fragrance"

I don't know where the Temple of Accumulated
  Fragrance is,
After several *li* entering the clouded peaks.
In the ancient woods is a path without people,
Deep in the mountains where is the bell?
The gurgling of a spring is swallowed by the
  dangerous rocks,
The color of the setting sun cools the green pines.
In the light dusk by the bend of an empty pond,
Peaceful meditation overpowers the poisonous
  dragon.

In this poem, we may clearly see the shifting viewpoint. Here we can see several pictures rather than one. The narrating voice comes from the visitor, who may be a purposeful pilgrim or an accidental traveller. And the voice and the eye are identical except in the last couplet. Reading this poem is like following the progressive movement of a cinematic camera, the "eye," to the destination—the Temple of Accumulated Fragrance. We can see "the clouded peaks" from a certain distance, then are close enough to see the inside of the ancient woods, the path without people, and when we get deep enough in the mountain and hear the bell sound, we can see the "spring" and the "dangerous rocks," the "color of the setting sun" and "the green pine." The last scene is the temple that we cannot see but imagine, based on some suggestions, such as the "empty pond" that should be close by the temple and big enough to accommodate the allusive "poisonous dragon." The problem here is that we are likely to lose the original point of view. The previous viewer's (visitor's) eyes suddenly become ambiguous. We are not sure whether the viewer thinks of the allusion of overpowering "the poisonous dragon" by seeing the "empty pond" or watches a monk sitting there and meditating, or the viewer himself sits there and meditates. If it is the meditation of the viewer, then we, the audience, see the viewer's meditation by the other viewer's eye. This shifting point of view may stimulate the audience's contemplative pleasure, and fit the ambiguity and vagueness of the couplet. In his **"Recalling my Brothers in the East of Hua Mountain during the Double Nine Festival,"** Wang Wei uses a similar method in the last couplet: "From the distance I know that you, my brothers, must climb to the heights. / All are wearing dogwood but find one person is missing." After the description of his nostalgic and home-sick sentiments from the viewer's/poet's point of view, the last line suddenly shifts the viewing angle and makes the "brothers" find the absence of the viewer/poet. This reversed subject and object also creates the other viewer by whose eyes the audience continues his imaginary picture.

After the discussion of the three modes of using the point of view in Wang Wei's poems (changing the viewing distance; unchanged viewing stand; and shifting the viewers from one to the other), we can probably find out that we may develop a visual pleasure in reading Wang Wei's landscape poems, especially when we consider such a reading process as a viewing process and the narrator's "point of view" as perceiving.

Audio Effect

When talking about the audio-effect in Wang Wei's poems, I shall focus on the narrating voice rather than on other sounds such as a bird's chirping or a spring's gurgling.

In the poems analyzed above, we may notice that the reader's appreciative channel goes mainly through the "eyes" of the first person narrator "I." In other words, the narrator "I," whether visible or hidden, is an "experiencing self" who functions as protagonist and witness, besides narrating the poem. We may imagine that the "I" stands there and gazes at the empty spring ravine, or climbs the mountain to the Temple. However, in those landscape poems, the voice or the "I" is usually fading away and transformed into a visualized picture.

Now I want to explore the narrating voice by analyzing the following poems.

"Farewell"

I dismount and invite you, Sir, to drink wine,
Asking where you are going.
You say "I didn't accomplish my wishes,
And am returning to live at the foot of Southern
  Mountain.
Only go ahead and don't ask again,
White clouds don't have ending time.

"Farewell" is a popular topic for poets in general. Wang Wei's parting poem has its own strength. He is admirably able to treat the very complex emotional attachment of the friendship in a seemingly simple, even plain and detached way. In **"Farewell,"** an ancient-style poem, the first line gives us two images, "horse" and "wine" that are commonly associated with parting and friendship. That the narrator "I" dismounts indicates that he comes all the way riding a horse to see his friend off. Then the "I" not only invites the second person "you" to drink wine but also talks with him. Therefore the single voice narrating turns to a typical dialogue: one questions and the other answers. It seems that the "I" doesn't know where the "you" goes. In other words, because the "you" couldn't

accomplish the wishes and might be forced to leave, the "you" didn't tell friends about the leaving. Then the "I" found out and then hurried by horse to see the "you" off. A friend in need is a friend indeed. This simple dialogue reveals their would-be profound emotional tie. We can see the worries, concerns and attitude without snobbery of the "I" toward the "you" through the dialogue. Especially the last two lines express the warm concern and encouragement in a more explicit way. "White clouds" is the last metaphorical image in the poem. "White" is usually associated with purity and innocence, and "clouds" contains a floating and transcendental quality. The last line may be interpreted like this: you, like the white clouds, stand innocent and high, float away or keep distance from this world. There will be no limit or boundary for you in terms of time and space. According to Pauling Yü [*The Poetry of Wang Wei*, 1980.] "the impossibility of identifying the interlocutors has led many Western critics to conclude that '**Farewell**' is actually a kind of soliloquy or internal monologue." It is possible that the narrator "I" is talking with the other "I" of his divided self, consulting the other "I" if the "I" should retreat from court life. It is also possible that Wang Wei had such a modern sense to talk with his other self in the poem. However, it is still an uncertain hypothesis. It seems to me that there is an interlocutor anyway, whether it is the other self or a friend. So the dialogic form is certain and the two voices exist. We have to admit that such a dialogic and dramatic scene produces an audio-effect and a special appreciative angle. In another poem, **"Unclassified Poem,"** by Wang Wei, we can see a simple questioning form.

You, my lord, come from my home town,
And should know the things there.
The day you left, in the front of the silk window,
Were the plum trees still in blossom?

Here, we seem to be able to hear one voice questioning. The absent interlocutor and unanswered question may evoke many echoes in the reader's mind, and show the eagerness and homesickness of the questioner/addresser. Such a special and sensitive question about "the plum tree" would be hard to answer even for someone from his home town. It seems to me this is more like an expressive monologue in a questioning form which does not necessarily expect an accurate answer, although there is a "you," a supposed questionee. In **"Farewell in the Mountains,"** there is another type monologue in its second couplet.

"Farewell in the Mountains"

In the mountains a parting is over,
In the sunset I shut the brushwood gate.
The spring grass next year will turn green,
Will the prince return or not?

Right after the first very descriptive couplet, a monologue is again in a questioning form. But this question is obviously asking the self of the addresser about the absent other. This monotonous voice not only expresses his concern for the friend ("Will the prince return or not?") but also creates an imaginary scene ("The spring grass next year will turn green"). In other words, the reader may see two scenes: one is current and "real," the other in the future and visionary. The real scene is narrated by the addresser to the reader, the visionary one by the same addresser but to himself. We as readers can sense the friendship and the relationship between the addresser and his absent friend.

"Sitting alone on an Autumn Night"

Sitting alone I feel sad about the hair on my two
    temples,
In the empty reception hall nearly at the time of the
    second watch.
In the rain mountain fruits fall,
Under the lamp grass insects chirp.
White hair is finally hard to change back,
Yellow gold is impossible to be produced.
If one wants to know how to get rid of sickness or
    age,
The only way is to learn nonrebirth.

This poem is in a monologue style too. But it is different. This is actually a kind of self-anatomical meditation. The first two couplets tell us the setting: a quiet and raining night, the empty hall; the mood: solitude and sadness; the sound: the falling rain and mountain fruit and the insects' chirping. The second couplet turns to the narrator's philosophical recognition of the self and life. This personal reawareness is narrated in a persuasive and didactic way. Another similar instance can be found in the couple lines from **"Visiting Monk Hsüan"**:

My early years are not worth talking about,
When I recognized the Way I was old in age.
How could I regret the things in the past?
The rest of my life can be luckily nurtured.

The narrator's denial of the past and his joyful new recognition of the truth, either "nonrebirth" or the "Way," lend a strong religious color to those meditative monologues. Still we can see the sadness and fear of the narrator for sickness and age as the undertone pervading the poem.

"Six Casually Written Poems"

When old age comes, I am too lazy to write poems,
Only old age follows me as companion.
In this my life I am mistakenly a poet,
In my previous life I must have been a painter.
I am unable to give up lingering habits,
And am accidentally known by the people of this
    world.
My given name and byname are just all showing
    this,
But this heart is still not understood.

This casually written poem has a strong confessional quality. The sadness and fear are still haunting here. The narrator "I" seems more critical with himself and his relation with others. The repetition of *"chih,"* "knowing" or "understanding," sets up the tone for this confessional monologue. Here "understanding" is not the narrator's

"understanding" of some truth ("nonrebirth" etc.) or the "self," but the other's "understanding" about him. In other words, the narrator is willing to open himself up to the other due to the existence of some misunderstanding about him. People know him as a poet and painter, but may not understand his heart. The narrator would like the people to take his given name (Wei) and byname (Mo-chieh) as his symbolic identity and a clue to read his mind because the combination of his given name and byname indicates his Buddhist belief which he considers as the foundation of his thoughts, even more important than his being as a poet or a painter. In general, those self-anatomical or confessional monologues in Wang Wei's poems can also be taken as "solitary conversation with oneself." Bakhtin says that "this is a new relationship to one's self, to one's own particular 'I'—with no witness, without any concessions to the voice of the a 'third person,' whoever it might be" [Bakhtin, M. M. *The Dialogic Imagination,* trans. Emerson and Holquist, 1981]. This "self" as the implied addressee is a more rational and spiritual "self" who only listens and never answers or argues. It may be the religious consciousness that makes Wang Wei write those soliloquies down. The voice in those poems is always intimate and private, and strongly invites the reader to enter the heart of the narrator/implied author.

The audio-effect of the narrating voice plays an important role in Wang Wei's poems. Whether in the dialogue or in the monologue, the first person voice, sometimes with a second voice involved, produces a special dramatic effect in this lyric form. Here, obviously the use of "point of view" functions as narrating and experiencing as well.

Narrator as Storyteller

When the narrator "I" hides himself behind the curtain, when the second person "you" disappears from the stage, the narrator becomes a third person "he," a storyteller. In other words, the narrator is talking about the other's stories rather than the story of his/self. Wang Wei's short quatrain **"Lady Hsi"** has this story-telling quality.

"Lady Hsi"

Don't let the favor of today
Allow her to forget the affection of the past.
Looking at the flowers, tears fill her eyes,
She doesn't speak to the king of Ch'u.

This poem is based on a historical story from the *Tso-chuan.* Of course it is almost impossible to have a complete story plot within these four lines. The poet only catches a most touching moment: "Looking at the flowers, tears fill her eyes," to describe the deep but unspeakable pain in the heart of Lady Hsi. The flowers become or symbolize the mirror image of the self of Lady Hsi, pretty but venerable like a doll in the other's hands. The first two lines tell us the reason of the sadness of the lady, the last line the result of it. Besides those, the poet makes the reader imagine all the rest of the story. This is not even a rhapsody, but has what Ching-hsing Wang calls "a quasi narrative quality." If we consider **"Lady Hsi"** a small portrait, then **"Song of Li Ling"** is more like a story.

"Song of Li Ling"

In the Han dynasty there was general Li,
Offspring of three generations of generals.
With knotted hair he already had wonderful
    strategies,
In youth he turned out a strong warrior.
Making a long drive pushing the enemies to the
    border,
He entered deep into the Shan *yü's* rampart.
Banners were lined up facing each other,
Pipes and drums were mournful beyond description.
The sun dusked at the edge of the desert,
The battle sounds amid smoke and dust.
In order to cause the fall and demise of the
    barbarians,
How could he only demand the capture of the
    famous
    prince.
Since having lost the support of the strong army,
Then he was stuck in the yurts with shame.
In his younger years he received imperial favor
    from
    Han,
How could he bear sitting there, thinking of this?
Deep in his heart he wished to repay,
He devoted his body but was unable to die.
He stretched the neck and looked for Tzu ch'ing,
"Except you, who will care for me?"

Portraying a historical figure in this poem, the narrator gives us a series of narrative displays, chronologically from Li Ling's family background, his glorious youth to his tragic climax (detained by the enemy and abandoned by the court). After narrating briefly the biographical facts of Li Ling, again the narrator creates a dramatic scene, like that in **"Lady Hsi,"** of Li Ling's painful thinking of himself in the yurt. Even we can hear Li Ling's internal monologue that demonstrates and intensifies Li Ling's desperation for help and sympathy. This psychological description not only makes this character portrayal more vivid and profound, but also reflects implicitly the narrator's understanding and compassion. Based on these two historical figure-portrayal poems of Wang Wei, we are probably able to sum up two features: one is that the most touching and typical scene[s] is always created for a dramatic effect and deep exploration of the figure's psyche. The other is that the third person narrator is hidden in the narrating process. The narrative point of view here seems like purely detached narrating. Only in the special couplet—the emotional climax, the implied narrator's tendency may be discernible.

Some of Wang Wei's frontier poems may be considered "travelogues," where the narrating point of view is like a camera-eye following and picturing the most exciting events on the trip.

"Marching Song"

Blowing horns push the marching men,
The clamor of the marching men arises.

The reed instruments sound sad and horses' neigh
    confused,
Struggling to ferry across the Gold River's waters.
The sun dusks at the edge of the desert,
The battle sounds amid smoke and dust.
Making efforts to tie up the neck of the famous
    prince,
Return and present him to the son of Heaven.

Except the last couplet here that expresses the purpose and the confident promise of this military expedition, the **"Marching Song,"** a poem in *yüeh-fu* style, provides us a series of picturesque scenes about this marching in a chronological order. The first scene shows how the marching starts: the sound of blowing horns, the clamor of the marching soldiers. The second scene is the troop crossing the Gold River. The third one is the battlefield. The movement of the changing scenes and time displays the process of the marching. The narrator's voice seems from the third person, who closely followed the marching but at the same time keeps a certain distance. In other words, the narrator is paradoxically a detached observer as well as an engaged participant in the marching. There is no personal pronoun in the poem, but the hidden narrator should be the witness or the observer, besides his main role as speaker of the travelogue. The last couplet reveals the narrator's tendency by showing a joyful mood about the coming victory for this marching. In other words, the narrator is not a neutral but tendentious observer and speaker. We, as reader, hear the narrator's voice and imagine the scenes which are based on his words and selected by his choice. We seem to follow the marching army along as we follow the narrator's voice or his camera-eye. This kind of travelogue quality can be found in many other of Wang Wei's poems, such as **"Carrying Mission to the Frontier," "Hunting Watch,"** and **"Song of the Peach Fountainhead"** etc.

We may see clearly from the discussion above that, when Wang Wei tells of historical stories, events or trips in his poems, he most likely employs a third-person narrator who is omniscient and tells the stories of historical figures or events in an external perspective, or who is a witness or observer and depicts a trip or an event in a retrospective way. This third person narrator may be called a storyteller in terms of narrative quality, although those "stories" are actually only fragmentary episodes, or a series of picturesque descriptions, or lack of detailed plots.

In sum, narrativity plays a fairly important role in Wang Wei's poetic creation. In some of his ancient-style and *yüeh-fu* style poems, even some modern-style poems like **"Lady Hsi,"** we can see the narrative quality by way of analyzing the narrating or experiencing narrator's point of view. Wang Wei amazingly changes his narrator's position quite often, such as from the first person narrator to the second, or to the third person, then the point of view changes correspondingly. These changes usually indicate or determine the distance between the narrator/signifier and the narrated/signified. Schorer considered "the uses of point of view not only as a mode of dramatic delimitation, but, more particular, of thematic definition". Just as Stanzel pointed out, "Form is the relativizing externalization of the content," the analysis of the use of "point of view" is actually an alternative approach to decoding the content of any literary discourse. My attention to the fairly complicated use of "point of view" in Wang Wei's seemingly simple poems intends to pave a smoother avenue toward a better understanding of Wang Wei.

Sam Hamill (essay date 1993)

SOURCE: "Wang Wei and Saigyo: Two Buddhist Mountain Poets," in *American Poetry Review,* Vol. 22, No. 2, March/April, 1993, pp. 45-8.

[*In the following excerpt, Hamill explores the Buddhist influences on Wang Wei's poetry and empahsizes the impact classical T'ang dynasy poetry has had on modern American poetry.*]

Perhaps no aspect of classical Chinese poetry in translation has touched contemporary American verse more deeply than the "nature poery" of the T'ang dynasty. From the three hundred-odd poems of Cold Mountain (Han Shan), poems that often fall into a kind of Buddhist doggerel, to the almost selfless poems of Wang Wei, the western poet has been drawn to the evocative and descriptive powers of the ancient Chinese poet writing alone in his hermitage deep in the mountains.

While the translations by Gary Snyder, Burton Watson, and Red Pine have brought a large audience to Han Shan, Wang Wei has generally fared less well. Several accurate translations have been available in recent years, but none have sparkled like any of the above. That may be in part because Wang Wei is a better poet, a more subtle stylist, and far less ecstatic or declamatory.

While Wang Wei and Han Shan may represent two prominent branches of what I shall call Buddhist Mountain Poetry, both are indebted to the grandfather of all Chinese recluse-poets, T'ao Ch'ien (also called T'ao Yuan-ming) who lived (365-427 C.E.) during the turmoil of the Six Dynasties period when northern China was rulled by non-Chinese "barbarians," and southern China, where T'ao Ch'ien lived, was ruled by successive tyrants. The poets of the high T'ang added a more sophisticated Buddhist element—T'ao Ch'ien was in many ways a model of Confucian integrity and likely knew Buddhism slightly, as a new philosophy introduced to him by friends on Mount Lu, before the blossoming of *chan* (zen). His plain, simple, and direct style of writing inspired many a poet through the centuries, as did his many homages to the wine cup.

In his wise introduction to **Hiding the Universe: Poems by Wang Wei** (1972), Wai-lim Yip compares Wang's **"Bird-Singing Stream"** with Wallace Stevens's "Of Mere Being," noting that in Wang's poems things tend to "emerge *as they are* without being contaminated by intel-

lectuality." In Stevens, "A gold-feathered bird/Sings in the palm, without human meaning,/Without human feeling, a foreign song." And Stevens "often ends up writing *about the process of becoming the objects* with much analysis between himself and the objects," whereas Wang presents phenomena as it is:

"Bird-Singing Stream"

Man at leisure. Cassia flowers fall.
Quiet night. Spring mountain is empty.
Moon rises. Startles—a mountain bird.
It sings at times in the spring stream.

Yip's translation conveys something of the density of the original, but only at some expense to the poem's American English dress: it sounds fragmented, and Wang Wei is in no way a poet of shards and fragments—on the contrary, he is a poet of totality. Yip is quite literal, taking no great interpretive liberties with his text. But Wang, among the most contemplative of poets, wrote in a style that might best be described as effortless and selfless, and Yip's English misses that tone. Nonetheless, he does evoke much of the classic four-line, five-character-per-line form of the original.

A devout Buddhist, Wang Wei did not "view nature" from an outside perspective; rather, he was himself a part of nature. His treatment of the natural world was neither objective nor analytical. But his poems are loaded with associative and evocative power. The "white clouds" that frequently appear in his poems may be considered real, literal clouds. In other Buddhist poets, "white clouds" often represent "barriers" between the novitiate and "highest perfect enlightenment." In Wang's nature poem, there is only "nature."

In G.W. Robinson's translation, *Poems of Wang Wei,* this poem becomes:

"Birds Calling in the Valley"

Men at rest, cassia flowers falling
Night still, spring hills empty
The moon rises, rouses birds in the hills
And sometimes they cry in the spring valley.

While the movement of the whole is a bit less fragmented, the on-again, off-again punctuation with the weight of heaped-up phrases at the beginning of the poem make it move with more awkwardness than it should. The "hills" in the third line is redundant. This translation is adequate but slack, exhibiting none of the clean, direct, imagistic style of T'ao Ch'ien and his literary descendents.

Pauline Lu, in *The Poetry of Wang Wei* sounds a lot like Wai-lim Yip:

"Bird Call Valley"

Man at leisure, cassia flowers fall.
The night still, spring mountain empty.

The moon emerges, startling mountain birds:
At times they call within the spring valley.

Her translation carries a better sense of movement than either of the former, each line turning on a kind of axis as it does in the original, creating a lucid, literal equivalent. But the poem still leaves me dissatisfied in its English garb. The language lacks a poet's touch, it doesn't carry what a good ear could contribute. "Man at leisure"? Too indefinite in English. "At times they call" also is too slack to convey the tension of the original.

While each of these versions is in some way "good enough" for study or commentary, none really rises to the occasion like this new version from the collaborative team of Tony Barnstone, Willis Barnstone, and Xu Haixin, from *Laughing Lost in the Mountains: Poems of Wang Wei* (1992):

"Birds Sing in the Ravine"

Few people see the acacia blossoms fall,
night is quiet, the spring mountain empty.
The sudden moon alarms mountain birds.
Long moment of song in the spring ravine.

While the "person at leisure" magically becomes "few people," I don't feel the spirit of the poem has been violated. I would also remove the "is" in line two. Line and syntax work harmoniously. The "sudden" moon lends a little tension, and the "alarm" grants permission as it were for the closing sentence fragment, a fragment that opens out *into* nature like birdsong itself. If this translation fails to note the spaces *between* bird cry and bird cry, it nonetheless compresses the experience of the poem. And the wonderful lilt of song of the closing line! I think Mr. Wang would be pleased.

Wang Wei was the eldest of five brothers raised in a literary family in Shansi province. He was a precocious poet, musician, and landscape painter who passed his advanced examinations at the age of twenty-two. He served in various official posts, reportedly attempted suicide when he was imprisoned during the An Lu-shan Rebellion, and only a poem written to his friend Pei Di from Bodhi Temple saved him from being charged as a collaborator during the aftermath of the rebellion. He was returned to office, and died while serving in the Department of State in his early sixties.

But he is most revered for his nature poems. Far less exuberant or reckless than Li T'ai-po, and far simpler and less cerebral than the incomparable, passionate Tu Fu, Wang made elegant simplicity his greatest asset. As a devout Buddhist with a notable Taoist influence, he was perhaps a perfect counterpart to Tu Fu's Confucianism and Li Po's Taoism. Whereas Tu Fu's nature poems are a record of exile and a sweeping social conscience, Wang's represent a great spiritual vision.

All Chinese "country poets" are in one way or another descendents of T'ao Ch'ien. Wang draws directly on his straight-forwardness, his uncluttered syntax, and his intimate knowledge of place and season. But Wang Wei shares little of the former's deep ambiguity of emotion: where T'ao Ch'ien sings the beauties of solitary wildness, he also finds melancholy, frustration, and fear (as does Tu Fu); Wang, on the other hand, finds the deep spiritual aloneness of Mahayana Buddhism, a teaching that declares equality among all living things and thus a reverence for wildness resulting in calm affirmation. The ordinary rural and sub-rural landscape inspired Wang Wei *because* it was mundane, and *because* it represented the junction of human and non-human life.

The introduction to the Barnstone translation draws an interesting comparison between Wang and the modern Spanish poet Antonio Machado:

> Wang an official, Machado a teacher in a rural *instituto*, both poets find their eyes in nature. They were not scribes of the imagination, like Dante, but of their daily and nightly vision. They tended to dream—but not nocturnal dreams associated with sleep and fantasy. Theirs was a reverie of ordinary landscapes, which their minds transposed as they gazed at them with eyes wide open. In nature Wang—and later Machado—found a literal script for his vision.

Not only a reverie of ordinary landscapes, but certainly in Wang's case, a *reverence* for ordinary landscapes. The translators stress the Taoist influence especially, quoting Chuang Tzu's advocacy of stillness, emptiness, of not-having, and underscoring the point by noting Wang's frequent use of "empty mountain" in poems like **"Deer Park"** and **"Living in the Mountain on an Autumn Night."** They also note that the character used for "empty" is *kong,* the Chinese word for the Sanskrit *Sunyata,* the Buddhist concept of emptiness that is altogether different from our customary use of the word "empty." And indeed, his poems are also loaded with empty forests and empty nights, Buddhist-inspired images that ring with clarity and numinous detail. Zen was in many ways a Chinese adaptation of Indian Buddhism, bringing to its fundamental teaching a profoundly Taoist interpretation: "In China," the Chinese say, "everything becomes Chinese."

"You Asked About My Life. I Send You, Pei Di, These Lines"

A wide icy river floats to far uncertainty.
The autumn rain is eternal in the mist.
You ask me about Deep South Mountain.
My heart knows it is beyond white clouds.

The poet combines definite images with signifying abstraction—icy river connected to uncertainty; "eternal" rain to mist. Are the "white clouds" Buddhist barriers between the poet and Nirvana, or are they literal white clouds passing between the poet and his beloved home in the mountains? Perhaps both. Longing for one's home is a kind of desire, and as a poet and Buddhist Wang aimed to transcend desire. In this poem, implied desire figures prominently, carrying the emotional center. The transcendent vision remains virtually unspoken, buried in the evocation of the natural world. Rain, mist, and white clouds are standard Buddhist symbolism, but in Wang's hands take on added significance.

The Barnstones quote Burton Watson's classic *Chinese Lyricism* (Columbia University Press, 1971) on a type of Buddhist poetry "in which the philosophical meaning lies [far] below the surface. The imagery functions on both the descriptive and the symbolic levels at once, and it is not often possible to pin down the exact symbolic content of an image." This kind of poetry is not forthrightly didactic—it delivers no direct sermon and cites no sutra. It represents Buddhist philosophy in a practice so refined as to transcend formal Buddhist liturgy.

Years ago, I translated Wang's **"Return to Wang River"**:

> In the gorge where bells resound
> there are few fishermen or woodsmen.
>
> Before I know it, dusk closes the mountains down.
> Alone, I return again to white clouds
>
> and trembling water chestnuts
> where the willow catkins easily take flight.
>
> Spring grass colors the eastern landscape.
> Snared in a web of grief, I close my wooden door.

In the Barnstone translation, the poem reads:

> Bells stir in the mouth of the gorge.
> Few fishermen or woodcutters are left.
> Far off in the mountains is twilight.
> Alone I come back to white clouds.
> Weak water chestnut stems can't hold still.
> Willow catkins are light and blow about.
> To the east is a rice paddy, color of spring grass.
> I close the thorn gate, seized by grief.

It is a poem others have tackled with varying degrees of success. Robinson leaves out all punctuation and gets quite wordy: "And I am going alone towards the white clouds home/ Water-chestnut flowers so delicate so hardly still . . ." closing, "Colours of spring on the banks of the marsh to the east/ And I am melancholy as I shut my door." Ugh.

In one of the stranger crimes against the Chinese, David Young translated this poem in his *Four T'ang Poets* (1980), turning each line into a triad, even changing the title to "Returning to My Cottage." It's a good example of how *not* to translate a poem. His closure is, well, pathetic: "it's and/ to walk in the house/ and shut the door." This is not "elegant simplicity," but what Willis Hawley called "dumbing it down."

I admire the uncluttered completeness of the Barnstone translation, the *ease* of the poem as a whole. No artificial language, but enough ear at work to let the line—each line—convey its own sense of unity. I do not like "Far off in the mountain is twilight" because of the inversion and

its tinny ring, and because it fails to convey the poet's sense of discovery of twilight. The use of "twilight" where I had used "dusk" however is a good stroke, carrying the added weight of implication by plurisignation—is it the poet's own twilight? The choice of "twilight" over "dusk" also demonstrates the translator's need to interpret. The Barnstone translation also gets the rice shoot/ grass comparison I "dumbed out."

All poetry offers variable possibilities in translation. Often, small, subtle matters of interpretation make all the difference. Robinson, while "getting the meaning" all right, completely misses the right tone for Wang Wei in American English; in London, all those piled up prepositional phrases may please the ear, sounding remarkably simple, direct, and uncluttered like the original—in contemporary American English, it sounds mundane, flabby, prosy. Young tries to turn Wang Wei into William Carlos Williams-style imagism, but succeeds only in creating *Amygism*.

To the Chinese, Wang is *the* great poet of impersonality. His poetry is a record of a lifelong struggle to be free of desire, free even of the desire to be free of desire, a nonstruggle to attain non-attainment. Often severely self-critical, he begins **"Written in the Mountains in Early Autumn"** by saying, "I'm talentless and dare not inflict myself on this bright reign./ Perhaps I'll go to the East River and mend my old fence." Humility before his task is a signature of Wang Wei. Autumn "abruptly falls," and he listens to crickets and cicadas. "Alone in the empty forest, I have an appointment with white clouds." He completely disappears into "nature" without losing *presence*.

At a conference on "the power of animals" years ago, Gary Snyder pointed out that we are most deeply into our "animal intelligence" when we are alone. The aloneness of a Zen mountain poet like Wang Wei is not the portentous melancholy Robinson's translation might suggest, nor is it the pathetic sadness of Young's version. The poem is *not* about sadness at all, but grief and aloneness—an entirely different emotional complex that must be seen in a Buddhist context. It is the aloneness of completion, the aloneness that is not-alone, the aloneness of transcendental animal consciousness, of mere beingness without self-consciousness. At the close of his poem, the poet discovers his own sense of aloneness. He becomes a part of his white clouds, the clouds become a symbol of transcendent grace, the speaker and the listener and the images blending into a single note of eternal resolution. It is spring, new rice-shoots growing brilliantly green. Spring, a time of birth; but twilight simultaneously. The poet is caught—snared—between the two which are not two, but one: springtime-twilight-whitecloud-poet. Closing the poem on a note of self-awareness indicates the poet has yet to attain "highest perfect enlightenment" and therefore remains caught in the realm of *samsara,* the cycle of birth and death. He grieves over the transience of things, including himself.

Wang's poetry arises out of the complex simplicity of his language, but can't be found in a dictionary. Capturing his tone, his grace-note, is the translator's greatest challenge. Eliot Weinberger's wonderful essay, *Nineteen Ways of Looking at Wang Wei* (1987), examines nineteen versions of a poem of one quatrain, **"Deer Park,"** with wonderful insight. The final line of the poem, in literal trot:

Return (again) shine green moss above

Of all the versions under Weinberger's discussion, only Gary Snyder notes that the light is shining through the moss *overhead*—apparently only Snyder recognizing that moss grows in trees. The noted Sinologist James J. Y. Liu even goes so far as to supply "ground" for the moss. In the Barnstone translation it reads:

"Deer Park"

Nobody in sight on the empty mountain
but human voices are heard far off.
Low sun slips deep in the forest
and lights the green hanging moss.

To make translations work at their best in English, the translator must aspire to the poet's powerful evocation. The language is very simple; the vision is very complex. The slant rhyme of "off" and "moss" is just right. The *l* and *s* sounds in the closing couplet also convey some sense of the musicality of the original. My only quarrel with this version is that I believe the light is shining *through* the green moss overhead. This translation at least gets the moss in the right place.

In **"Autumn Meditation,"** the moon sails "Heavenly River," the Milky Way, and in four lines reveals a world:

The balcony's icy wind stirs my clothing.
Night. The drum endures. The jade waterclock
    slows.
The moon sails the Heavenly River, soaking its
    light.
A magpie breaks from an autumn tree. Many leaves
    fall.

The human element vanishes in falling leaves. The poet transcends the "world of illusion" by achieving pure consciousness through attentive meditation. The world is as it is: transient. In the hands of most modern poets, the magpie would become personified or the imagery would carry added abstract philosophical argument. Here, the poet and the world are one.

Laughing Lost in the Mountains is the best translation of a substantial number of Wang Wei's poems to appear in English. In addition to breathtaking poems of nature and hermitage, there are many wonderful formal court poems, letter poems, and portraits, all in suitable American English dress. This should become the standard Wang Wei for a generation of readers.

Four hundred years after the birth of Wang Wei, the most famous medieval Buddhist nature poet of Japan was born to a minor branch of the powerful Fujiwara clan in the old capital city of Heian, present day Kyoto. Saigyo (1118-1190) spent twenty-three years in and around court life in Heian-kyo, Peace-and-Tranquility Capital, becoming a captain in the elite guard of the imperial familybefore taking Buddhist vows and removing himself to a hermitage. His biography is clouded in legend and folklore. Scholars agree that he lived at times near Mt. Koya and Mt. Yoshino, and his poems record many long journeys.

FURTHER READING

Criticism

Bynner, Witter. "At the Foot of This Mountain." *Poetry*. Vol. XCVI, No. 5 (August 1960): 309-13.
> Assesses the influence of Taoism on Wang's poetry.

Pollack, David. "Wang Wei in Kamakura: A Consideration of the Structural Poetics of Mishima's *Spring Snow*." *Harvard Journal of Asiatic Studies*. Vol. 48, No. 2 (December 1988): 383-402.
> Examines Wang's influence on Mishima Yukio's novel *Spring Snow*.

Robinson, G. W. "Introduction." in *Poems of Wang Wei*, pp. 13-25. Harmondsworth: Penguin Books Ltd., 1973.
> Provides biographical and historical background for Wang Wei.

Wai-lim Yip. "Wang Wei and Pure Experience." in *Hiding the Universe*, pp. V-XV. New York: Grossman Publishers, 1972.
> A condensed version of the essay titled "Wang Wei and the Aesthetics of Pure Experience" in *Tamkang Review* that assesses the Taoist influence on his poetry.

Zhaoming Qian. "Ezra Pound's Encounter with Wang Wei: Toward the Ideogrammic Method of the Cantos." *Twentieth Century Literature*. Vol. 39, No. 3 (Fall 1993): 266-82.
> Examines Wang Wei's influence on Pound's *Cantos*. Explores Pound's assertion of Wang's moderity and resemblance to the French Symybolist movement.

Zuoya Cao. "Poetry and Zen: A Comparison of Wang Wei and Basho." *Tamkang Review*. Vol. 24, No. 2 (Winter 1993): 23-41.
> Compares Wang to Basho, a seventeenth-century Japanese poet, and argues that each poet emphasized different aspects of Zen.

Poetry Criticism
INDEXES

Literary Criticism Series
Cumulative Author Index

Cumulative Nationality Index

Cumulative Title Index

How to Use This Index

The main references

Calvino, Italo
1923-1985.....CLC 5, 8, 11, 22, 33, 39,
73; SSC 3

list all author entries in the following Gale Literary Criticism series:

BLC = *Black Literature Criticism*
CLC = *Contemporary Literary Criticism*
CLR = *Children's Literature Review*
CMLC = *Classical and Medieval Literature Criticism*
DA = *DISCovering Authors*
DAB = *DISCovering Authors: British*
DAC = *DISCovering Authors: Canadian*
DC = *Drama Criticism*
HLC = *Hispanic Literature Criticism*
LC = *Literature Criticism from 1400 to 1800*
NCLC = *Nineteenth-Century Literature Criticism*
PC = *Poetry Criticism*
SSC = *Short Story Criticism*
TCLC = *Twentieth-Century Literary Criticism*
WLC = *World Literature Criticism, 1500 to the Present*

The cross-references

See also CANR 23; CA 85-88;
obituary CA 116

list all author entries in the following Gale biographical and literary sources:

AAYA = *Authors & Artists for Young Adults*
AITN = *Authors in the News*
BEST = *Bestsellers*
BW = *Black Writers*
CA = *Contemporary Authors*
CAAS = *Contemporary Authors Autobiography Series*
CABS = *Contemporary Authors Bibliographical Series*
CANR = *Contemporary Authors New Revision Series*
CAP = *Contemporary Authors Permanent Series*
CDALB = *Concise Dictionary of American Literary Biography*
CDBLB = *Concise Dictionary of British Literary Biography*
DAM = *DISCovering Authors: Modules*
  DRAM: Dramatists Module; MST: Most-Studied Authors Module;
  MULT: Multicultural Authors Module; NOV: Novelists Module;
  POET: Poets Module; POP: Popular Fiction and Genre Authors Module
DLB = *Dictionary of Literary Biography*
DLBD = *Dictionary of Literary Biography Documentary Series*
DLBY = *Dictionary of Literary Biography Yearbook*
HW = *Hispanic Writers*
JRDA = *Junior DISCovering Authors*
MAICYA = *Major Authors and Illustrators for Children and Young Adults*
MTCW = *Major 20th-Century Writers*
NNAL = *Native North American Literature*
SAAS = *Something about the Author Autobiography Series*
SATA = *Something about the Author*
YABC = *Yesterday's Authors of Books for Children*

Literary Criticism Series
Cumulative Author Index

Arundel, Honor (Morfydd)
1919-1973 . . . . CLC 17
See also CA 21-22; 41-44R; CAP 2;
CLR 35; SATA 4; SATA-Obit 24

Arzner, Dorothy 1897-1979 . . . . CLC 98

Asch, Sholem 1880-1957 . . . . TCLC 3
See also CA 105

Ash, Shalom
See Asch, Sholem

Ashbery, John (Lawrence)
1927- . . . . . . CLC 2, 3, 4, 6, 9, 13, 15, 25,
41, 77; DAM POET
See also CA 5-8R; CANR 9, 37; DLB 5,
165; DLBY 81; INT CANR-9; MTCW

Ashdown, Clifford
See Freeman, R(ichard) Austin

Ashe, Gordon
See Creasey, John

Ashton-Warner, Sylvia (Constance)
1908-1984 . . . . CLC 19
See also CA 69-72; 112; CANR 29; MTCW

Asimov, Isaac
1920-1992 . . . . . . CLC 1, 3, 9, 19, 26, 76,
92; DAM POP
See also AAYA 13; BEST 90:2; CA 1-4R;
137; CANR 2, 19, 36; CLR 12; DLB 8;
DLBY 92; INT CANR-19; JRDA;
MAICYA; MTCW; SATA 1, 26, 74

Assis, Joaquim Maria Machado de
See Machado de Assis, Joaquim Maria

Astley, Thea (Beatrice May)
1925- . . . . CLC 41
See also CA 65-68; CANR 11, 43

Aston, James
See White, T(erence) H(anbury)

Asturias, Miguel Angel
1899-1974 . . . . CLC 3, 8, 13;
DAM MULT, NOV; HLC
See also CA 25-28; 49-52; CANR 32;
CAP 2; DLB 113; HW; MTCW

Atares, Carlos Saura
See Saura (Atares), Carlos

Atheling, William
See Pound, Ezra (Weston Loomis)

Atheling, William, Jr.
See Blish, James (Benjamin)

Atherton, Gertrude (Franklin Horn)
1857-1948 . . . . TCLC 2
See also CA 104; 155; DLB 9, 78

Atherton, Lucius
See Masters, Edgar Lee

Atkins, Jack
See Harris, Mark

Atkinson, Kate. . . . . CLC 99

Attaway, William (Alexander)
1911-1986 . . . . CLC 92; BLC;
DAM MULT
See also BW 2; CA 143; DLB 76

Atticus
See Fleming, Ian (Lancaster)

Atwood, Margaret (Eleanor)
1939- . . . . . CLC 2, 3, 4, 8, 13, 15, 25, 44,
84; DA; DAB; DAC; DAM MST, NOV,
POET; PC 8; SSC 2; WLC
See also AAYA 12; BEST 89:2; CA 49-52;
CANR 3, 24, 33; DLB 53;
INT CANR-24; MTCW; SATA 50

Aubigny, Pierre d'
See Mencken, H(enry) L(ouis)

Aubin, Penelope 1685-1731(?) . . . . LC 9
See also DLB 39

Auchincloss, Louis (Stanton)
1917- . . . . CLC 4, 6, 9, 18, 45;
DAM NOV; SSC 22
See also CA 1-4R; CANR 6, 29, 55; DLB 2;
DLBY 80; INT CANR-29; MTCW

Auden, W(ystan) H(ugh)
1907-1973 . . . . . CLC 1, 2, 3, 4, 6, 9, 11,
14, 43; DA; DAB; DAC; DAM DRAM,
MST, POET; PC 1; WLC
See also AAYA 18; CA 9-12R; 45-48;
CANR 5; CDBLB 1914-1945; DLB 10,
20; MTCW

Audiberti, Jacques
1900-1965 . . . . . . CLC 38; DAM DRAM
See also CA 25-28R

Audubon, John James
1785-1851 . . . . NCLC 47

Auel, Jean M(arie)
1936- . . . . CLC 31; DAM POP
See also AAYA 7; BEST 90:4; CA 103;
CANR 21; INT CANR-21; SATA 91

Auerbach, Erich 1892-1957 . . . . TCLC 43
See also CA 118; 155

Augier, Emile 1820-1889 . . . . NCLC 31

August, John
See De Voto, Bernard (Augustine)

Augustine, St. 354-430 . . . . . . CMLC 6; DAB

Aurelius
See Bourne, Randolph S(illiman)

Aurobindo, Sri 1872-1950 . . . . TCLC 63

Austen, Jane
1775-1817 . . . . . NCLC 1, 13, 19, 33, 51;
DA; DAB; DAC; DAM MST, NOV;
WLC
See also AAYA 19; CDBLB 1789-1832;
DLB 116

Auster, Paul 1947- . . . . CLC 47
See also CA 69-72; CANR 23, 52

Austin, Frank
See Faust, Frederick (Schiller)

Austin, Mary (Hunter)
1868-1934 . . . . TCLC 25
See also CA 109; DLB 9, 78

Autran Dourado, Waldomiro
See Dourado, (Waldomiro Freitas) Autran

Averroes 1126-1198 . . . . CMLC 7
See also DLB 115

Avicenna 980-1037 . . . . CMLC 16
See also DLB 115

Avison, Margaret
1918- . . . . CLC 2, 4, 97; DAC;
DAM POET
See also CA 17-20R; DLB 53; MTCW

Axton, David
See Koontz, Dean R(ay)

Ayckbourn, Alan
1939- . . . . . . CLC 5, 8, 18, 33, 74; DAB;
DAM DRAM
See also CA 21-24R; CANR 31; DLB 13;
MTCW

Aydy, Catherine
See Tennant, Emma (Christina)

Ayme, Marcel (Andre) 1902-1967 . . . CLC 11
See also CA 89-92; CLR 25; DLB 72;
SATA 91

Ayrton, Michael 1921-1975 . . . . CLC 7
See also CA 5-8R; 61-64; CANR 9, 21

Azorin. . . . . CLC 11
See also Martinez Ruiz, Jose

Azuela, Mariano
1873-1952 . . . . . TCLC 3; DAM MULT;
HLC
See also CA 104; 131; HW; MTCW

Baastad, Babbis Friis
See Friis-Baastad, Babbis Ellinor

Bab
See Gilbert, W(illiam) S(chwenck)

Babbis, Eleanor
See Friis-Baastad, Babbis Ellinor

Babel, Isaac
See Babel, Isaak (Emmanuilovich)

Babel, Isaak (Emmanuilovich)
1894-1941(?) . . . . . . TCLC 2, 13; SSC 16
See also CA 104; 155

Babits, Mihaly 1883-1941 . . . . TCLC 14
See also CA 114

Babur 1483-1530. . . . . LC 18

Bacchelli, Riccardo 1891-1985 . . . . . CLC 19
See also CA 29-32R; 117

Bach, Richard (David)
1936- . . . . . . CLC 14; DAM NOV, POP
See also AITN 1; BEST 89:2; CA 9-12R;
CANR 18; MTCW; SATA 13

Bachman, Richard
See King, Stephen (Edwin)

Bachmann, Ingeborg 1926-1973. . . . . CLC 69
See also CA 93-96; 45-48; DLB 85

Bacon, Francis 1561-1626 . . . . LC 18, 32
See also CDBLB Before 1660; DLB 151

Bacon, Roger 1214(?)-1292 . . . . . . CMLC 14
See also DLB 115

Bacovia, George. . . . . TCLC 24
See also Vasiliu, Gheorghe

Badanes, Jerome 1937-. . . . . CLC 59

Bagehot, Walter 1826-1877 . . . . . . NCLC 10
See also DLB 55

Bagnold, Enid
1889-1981 . . . . . . CLC 25; DAM DRAM
See also CA 5-8R; 103; CANR 5, 40;
DLB 13, 160; MAICYA; SATA 1, 25

Bagritsky, Eduard 1895-1934 . . . . . TCLC 60

Bagrjana, Elisaveta
See Belcheva, Elisaveta

Bagryana, Elisaveta. . . . . CLC 10
See also Belcheva, Elisaveta
See also DLB 147

Author Index

Barthelme, Donald
1931-1989 ...... CLC 1, 2, 3, 5, 6, 8, 13,
23, 46, 59; DAM NOV; SSC 2
See also CA 21-24R; 129; CANR 20;
DLB 2; DLBY 80, 89; MTCW; SATA 7;
SATA-Obit 62

Barthelme, Frederick 1943- .... CLC 36
See also CA 114; 122; DLBY 85; INT 122

Barthes, Roland (Gerard)
1915-1980 .... CLC 24, 83
See also CA 130; 97-100; MTCW

Barzun, Jacques (Martin) 1907- .... CLC 51
See also CA 61-64; CANR 22

Bashevis, Isaac
See Singer, Isaac Bashevis

Bashkirtseff, Marie 1859-1884 ... NCLC 27

Basho
See Matsuo Basho

Bass, Kingsley B., Jr.
See Bullins, Ed

Bass, Rick 1958- .... CLC 79
See also CA 126; CANR 53

Bassani, Giorgio 1916- .... CLC 9
See also CA 65-68; CANR 33; DLB 128,
177; MTCW

Bastos, Augusto (Antonio) Roa
See Roa Bastos, Augusto (Antonio)

Bataille, Georges 1897-1962 .... CLC 29
See also CA 101; 89-92

Bates, H(erbert) E(rnest)
1905-1974 .... CLC 46; DAB;
DAM POP; SSC 10
See also CA 93-96; 45-48; CANR 34;
DLB 162; MTCW

Bauchart
See Camus, Albert

Baudelaire, Charles
1821-1867 .... NCLC 6, 29, 55; DA;
DAB; DAC; DAM MST, POET; PC 1;
SSC 18; WLC

Baudrillard, Jean 1929- .... CLC 60

Baum, L(yman) Frank 1856-1919 ... TCLC 7
See also CA 108; 133; CLR 15; DLB 22;
JRDA; MAICYA; MTCW; SATA 18

Baum, Louis F.
See Baum, L(yman) Frank

Baumbach, Jonathan 1933- ...... CLC 6, 23
See also CA 13-16R; CAAS 5; CANR 12;
DLBY 80; INT CANR-12; MTCW

Bausch, Richard (Carl) 1945- ...... CLC 51
See also CA 101; CAAS 14; CANR 43;
DLB 130

Baxter, Charles
1947- .... CLC 45, 78; DAM POP
See also CA 57-60; CANR 40; DLB 130

Baxter, George Owen
See Faust, Frederick (Schiller)

Baxter, James K(eir) 1926-1972 .... CLC 14
See also CA 77-80

Baxter, John
See Hunt, E(verette) Howard, (Jr.)

Bayer, Sylvia
See Glassco, John

Baynton, Barbara 1857-1929 ...... TCLC 57

Beagle, Peter S(oyer) 1939-........ CLC 7
See also CA 9-12R; CANR 4, 51;
DLBY 80; INT CANR-4; SATA 60

Bean, Normal
See Burroughs, Edgar Rice

Beard, Charles A(ustin)
1874-1948 .... TCLC 15
See also CA 115; DLB 17; SATA 18

Beardsley, Aubrey 1872-1898 ..... NCLC 6

Beattie, Ann
1947- .... CLC 8, 13, 18, 40, 63;
DAM NOV, POP; SSC 11
See also BEST 90:2; CA 81-84; CANR 53;
DLBY 82; MTCW

Beattie, James 1735-1803 .... NCLC 25
See also DLB 109

Beauchamp, Kathleen Mansfield 1888-1923
See Mansfield, Katherine
See also CA 104; 134; DA; DAC;
DAM MST

Beaumarchais, Pierre-Augustin Caron de
1732-1799 .... DC 4
See also DAM DRAM

Beaumont, Francis
1584(?)-1616 .... LC 33; DC 6
See also CDBLB Before 1660; DLB 58, 121

Beauvoir, Simone (Lucie Ernestine Marie
Bertrand) de
1908-1986 .... CLC 1, 2, 4, 8, 14, 31, 44,
50, 71; DA; DAB; DAC; DAM MST,
NOV; WLC
See also CA 9-12R; 118; CANR 28;
DLB 72; DLBY 86; MTCW

Becker, Carl 1873-1945 .... TCLC 63:
See also DLB 17

Becker, Jurek 1937-............ CLC 7, 19
See also CA 85-88; DLB 75

Becker, Walter 1950-............... CLC 26

Beckett, Samuel (Barclay)
1906-1989 ...... CLC 1, 2, 3, 4, 6, 9, 10,
11, 14, 18, 29, 57, 59, 83; DA; DAB;
DAC; DAM DRAM, MST, NOV;
SSC 16; WLC
See also CA 5-8R; 130; CANR 33;
CDBLB 1945-1960; DLB 13, 15;
DLBY 90; MTCW

Beckford, William 1760-1844 .... NCLC 16
See also DLB 39

Beckman, Gunnel 1910-........... CLC 26
See also CA 33-36R; CANR 15; CLR 25;
MAICYA; SAAS 9; SATA 6

Becque, Henri 1837-1899........ NCLC 3

Beddoes, Thomas Lovell
1803-1849 .... NCLC 3
See also DLB 96

Bede c. 673-735............... CMLC 20
See also DLB 146

Bedford, Donald F.
See Fearing, Kenneth (Flexner)

Beecher, Catharine Esther
1800-1878 .... NCLC 30
See also DLB 1

Beecher, John 1904-1980.......... CLC 6
See also AITN 1; CA 5-8R; 105; CANR 8

Beer, Johann 1655-1700............ LC 5
See also DLB 168

Beer, Patricia 1924-.............. CLC 58
See also CA 61-64; CANR 13, 46; DLB 40

Beerbohm, Max
See Beerbohm, (Henry) Max(imilian)

Beerbohm, (Henry) Max(imilian)
1872-1956 ....TCLC 1, 24
See also CA 104; 154; DLB 34, 100

Beer-Hofmann, Richard
1866-1945 .... TCLC 60
See also DLB 81

Begiebing, Robert J(ohn) 1946-..... CLC 70
See also CA 122; CANR 40

Behan, Brendan
1923-1964 .... CLC 1, 8, 11, 15, 79;
DAM DRAM
See also CA 73-76; CANR 33;
CDBLB 1945-1960; DLB 13; MTCW

Behn, Aphra
1640(?)-1689 ...... LC 1, 30; DA; DAB;
DAC; DAM DRAM, MST, NOV,
POET; DC 4; PC 13; WLC
See also DLB 39, 80, 131

Behrman, S(amuel) N(athaniel)
1893-1973 .... CLC 40
See also CA 13-16; 45-48; CAP 1; DLB 7,
44

Belasco, David 1853-1931 .... TCLC 3
See also CA 104; DLB 7

Belcheva, Elisaveta 1893- .... CLC 10
See also Bagryana, Elisaveta

Beldone, Phil "Cheech"
See Ellison, Harlan (Jay)

Beleno
See Azuela, Mariano

Belinski, Vissarion Grigoryevich
1811-1848 .... NCLC 5

Belitt, Ben 1911-.................. CLC 22
See also CA 13-16R; CAAS 4; CANR 7;
DLB 5

Bell, Gertrude 1868-1926........ TCLC 67
See also DLB 174

Bell, James Madison
1826-1902 .... TCLC 43; BLC;
DAM MULT
See also BW 1; CA 122; 124; DLB 50

Bell, Madison Smartt 1957-........ CLC 41
See also CA 111; CANR 28, 54

Bell, Marvin (Hartley)
1937- .... CLC 8, 31; DAM POET
See also CA 21-24R; CAAS 14; DLB 5;
MTCW

Bell, W. L. D.
See Mencken, H(enry) L(ouis)

Bellamy, Atwood C.
See Mencken, H(enry) L(ouis)

Bellamy, Edward 1850-1898 ...... NCLC 4
See also DLB 12

Bellin, Edward J.
See Kuttner, Henry

Belloc, (Joseph) Hilaire (Pierre Sebastien
    Rene Swanton)
    1870-1953 . . . **TCLC 7, 18; DAM POET**
    See also CA 106; 152; DLB 19, 100, 141,
    174; YABC 1

Belloc, Joseph Peter Rene Hilaire
    See Belloc, (Joseph) Hilaire (Pierre Sebastien
    Rene Swanton)

Belloc, Joseph Pierre Hilaire
    See Belloc, (Joseph) Hilaire (Pierre Sebastien
    Rene Swanton)

Belloc, M. A.
    See Lowndes, Marie Adelaide (Belloc)

Bellow, Saul
    1915- . . . . . . **CLC 1, 2, 3, 6, 8, 10, 13, 15,
    25, 33, 34, 63, 79; DA; DAB; DAC;
    DAM MST, NOV, POP; SSC 14; WLC**
    See also AITN 2; BEST 89:3; CA 5-8R;
    CABS 1; CANR 29, 53;
    CDALB 1941-1968; DLB 2, 28; DLBD 3;
    DLBY 82; MTCW

Belser, Reimond Karel Maria de   1929-
    See Ruyslinck, Ward
    See also CA 152

Bely, Andrey . . . . **TCLC 7; PC 11**
    See also Bugayev, Boris Nikolayevich

Benary, Margot
    See Benary-Isbert, Margot

Benary-Isbert, Margot   1889-1979 . . . **CLC 12**
    See also CA 5-8R; 89-92; CANR 4;
    CLR 12; MAICYA; SATA 2;
    SATA-Obit 21

Benavente (y Martinez), Jacinto
    1866-1954 . . . . . **TCLC 3; DAM DRAM,
    MULT**
    See also CA 106; 131; HW; MTCW

Benchley, Peter (Bradford)
    1940- . . . . . **CLC 4, 8; DAM NOV, POP**
    See also AAYA 14; AITN 2; CA 17-20R;
    CANR 12, 35; MTCW; SATA 3, 89

Benchley, Robert (Charles)
    1889-1945 . . . . **TCLC 1, 55**
    See also CA 105; 153; DLB 11

Benda, Julien   1867-1956 . . . . **TCLC 60**
    See also CA 120; 154

Benedict, Ruth   1887-1948 . . . . **TCLC 60**

Benedikt, Michael   1935- . . . . **CLC 4, 14**
    See also CA 13-16R; CANR 7; DLB 5

Benet, Juan   1927- . . . . **CLC 28**
    See also CA 143

Benet, Stephen Vincent
    1898-1943 . . . . . . **TCLC 7; DAM POET;
    SSC 10**
    See also CA 104; 152; DLB 4, 48, 102;
    YABC 1

Benet, William Rose
    1886-1950 . . . . . . **TCLC 28; DAM POET**
    See also CA 118; 152; DLB 45

Benford, Gregory (Albert)   1941- . . . . **CLC 52**
    See also CA 69-72; CANR 12, 24, 49;
    DLBY 82

Bengtsson, Frans (Gunnar)
    1894-1954 . . . . **TCLC 48**

Benjamin, David
    See Slavitt, David R(ytman)

Benjamin, Lois
    See Gould, Lois

Benjamin, Walter   1892-1940 . . . . . **TCLC 39**

Benn, Gottfried   1886-1956 . . . . **TCLC 3**
    See also CA 106; 153; DLB 56

Bennett, Alan
    1934- . . . **CLC 45, 77; DAB; DAM MST**
    See also CA 103; CANR 35, 55; MTCW

Bennett, (Enoch) Arnold
    1867-1931 . . . . **TCLC 5, 20**
    See also CA 106; 155; CDBLB 1890-1914;
    DLB 10, 34, 98, 135

Bennett, Elizabeth
    See Mitchell, Margaret (Munnerlyn)

Bennett, George Harold   1930-
    See Bennett, Hal
    See also BW 1; CA 97-100

Bennett, Hal . . . . **CLC 5**
    See also Bennett, George Harold
    See also DLB 33

Bennett, Jay   1912- . . . . **CLC 35**
    See also AAYA 10; CA 69-72; CANR 11,
    42; JRDA; SAAS 4; SATA 41, 87;
    SATA-Brief 27

Bennett, Louise (Simone)
    1919- . . . . . **CLC 28; BLC; DAM MULT**
    See also BW 2; CA 151; DLB 117

Benson, E(dward) F(rederic)
    1867-1940 . . . . **TCLC 27**
    See also CA 114; DLB 135, 153

Benson, Jackson J.   1930- . . . . **CLC 34**
    See also CA 25-28R; DLB 111

Benson, Sally   1900-1972 . . . . **CLC 17**
    See also CA 19-20; 37-40R; CAP 1;
    SATA 1, 35; SATA-Obit 27

Benson, Stella   1892-1933 . . . . **TCLC 17**
    See also CA 117; 155; DLB 36, 162

Bentham, Jeremy   1748-1832 . . . . . **NCLC 38**
    See also DLB 107, 158

Bentley, E(dmund) C(lerihew)
    1875-1956 . . . . **TCLC 12**
    See also CA 108; DLB 70

Bentley, Eric (Russell)   1916- . . . . **CLC 24**
    See also CA 5-8R; CANR 6; INT CANR-6

Beranger, Pierre Jean de
    1780-1857 . . . . **NCLC 34**

Berdyaev, Nicolas
    See Berdyaev, Nikolai (Aleksandrovich)

Berdyaev, Nikolai (Aleksandrovich)
    1874-1948 . . . . **TCLC 67**
    See also CA 120

Berendt, John (Lawrence)   1939- . . . . **CLC 86**
    See also CA 146

Berger, Colonel
    See Malraux, (Georges-)Andre

Berger, John (Peter)   1926- . . . . . . **CLC 2, 19**
    See also CA 81-84; CANR 51; DLB 14

Berger, Melvin H.   1927- . . . . **CLC 12**
    See also CA 5-8R; CANR 4; CLR 32;
    SAAS 2; SATA 5, 88

Berger, Thomas (Louis)
    1924- . . . . **CLC 3, 5, 8, 11, 18, 38;
    DAM NOV**
    See also CA 1-4R; CANR 5, 28, 51; DLB 2;
    DLBY 80; INT CANR-28; MTCW

Bergman, (Ernst) Ingmar
    1918- . . . . **CLC 16, 72**
    See also CA 81-84; CANR 33

Bergson, Henri   1859-1941 . . . . **TCLC 32**

Bergstein, Eleanor   1938- . . . . **CLC 4**
    See also CA 53-56; CANR 5

Berkoff, Steven   1937- . . . . **CLC 56**
    See also CA 104

Bermant, Chaim (Icyk)   1929- . . . . . . **CLC 40**
    See also CA 57-60; CANR 6, 31, 57

Bern, Victoria
    See Fisher, M(ary) F(rances) K(ennedy)

Bernanos, (Paul Louis) Georges
    1888-1948 . . . . **TCLC 3**
    See also CA 104; 130; DLB 72

Bernard, April   1956- . . . . **CLC 59**
    See also CA 131

Berne, Victoria
    See Fisher, M(ary) F(rances) K(ennedy)

Bernhard, Thomas
    1931-1989 . . . . **CLC 3, 32, 61**
    See also CA 85-88; 127; CANR 32, 57;
    DLB 85, 124; MTCW

Berriault, Gina   1926- . . . . **CLC 54**
    See also CA 116; 129; DLB 130

Berrigan, Daniel   1921- . . . . **CLC 4**
    See also CA 33-36R; CAAS 1; CANR 11,
    43; DLB 5

Berrigan, Edmund Joseph Michael, Jr.
    1934-1983
    See Berrigan, Ted
    See also CA 61-64; 110; CANR 14

Berrigan, Ted . . . . **CLC 37**
    See also Berrigan, Edmund Joseph Michael,
    Jr.
    See also DLB 5, 169

Berry, Charles Edward Anderson   1931-
    See Berry, Chuck
    See also CA 115

Berry, Chuck . . . . **CLC 17**
    See also Berry, Charles Edward Anderson

Berry, Jonas
    See Ashbery, John (Lawrence)

Berry, Wendell (Erdman)
    1934- . . . . **CLC 4, 6, 8, 27, 46;
    DAM POET**
    See also AITN 1; CA 73-76; CANR 50;
    DLB 5, 6

Berryman, John
    1914-1972 . . . . . . **CLC 1, 2, 3, 4, 6, 8, 10,
    13, 25, 62; DAM POET**
    See also CA 13-16; 33-36R; CABS 2;
    CANR 35; CAP 1; CDALB 1941-1968;
    DLB 48; MTCW

Bertolucci, Bernardo   1940- . . . . **CLC 16**
    See also CA 106

Bertrand, Aloysius   1807-1841 . . . . **NCLC 31**

Bertran de Born   c. 1140-1215 . . . . . **CMLC 5**

Besant, Annie (Wood)   1847-1933 . . . **TCLC 9**
    See also CA 105

Bragg, Melvyn 1939- . . . . **CLC 10**
See also BEST 89:3; CA 57-60; CANR 10,
48; DLB 14

Braine, John (Gerard)
1922-1986 . . . . **CLC 1, 3, 41**
See also CA 1-4R; 120; CANR 1, 33;
CDBLB 1945-1960; DLB 15; DLBY 86;
MTCW

Brammer, William 1930(?)-1978 . . . . **CLC 31**
See also CA 77-80

Brancati, Vitaliano 1907-1954 . . . . . **TCLC 12**
See also CA 109

Brancato, Robin F(idler) 1936- . . . . . **CLC 35**
See also AAYA 9; CA 69-72; CANR 11,
45; CLR 32; JRDA; SAAS 9; SATA 23

Brand, Max
See Faust, Frederick (Schiller)

Brand, Millen 1906-1980 . . . . **CLC 7**
See also CA 21-24R; 97-100

Branden, Barbara . . . . **CLC 44**
See also CA 148

Brandes, Georg (Morris Cohen)
1842-1927 . . . . **TCLC 10**
See also CA 105

Brandys, Kazimierz 1916- . . . . **CLC 62**

Branley, Franklyn M(ansfield)
1915- . . . . **CLC 21**
See also CA 33-36R; CANR 14, 39;
CLR 13; MAICYA; SAAS 16; SATA 4,
68

Brathwaite, Edward Kamau
1930- . . . . **CLC 11; DAM POET**
See also BW 2; CA 25-28R; CANR 11, 26,
47; DLB 125

Brautigan, Richard (Gary)
1935-1984 . . . . **CLC 1, 3, 5, 9, 12, 34, 42;**
DAM NOV
See also CA 53-56; 113; CANR 34; DLB 2,
5; DLBY 80, 84; MTCW; SATA 56

Brave Bird, Mary 1953-
See Crow Dog, Mary (Ellen)
See also NNAL

Braverman, Kate 1950- . . . . **CLC 67**
See also CA 89-92

Brecht, Bertolt
1898-1956 . . . . . . **TCLC 1, 6, 13, 35; DA;**
DAB; DAC; DAM DRAM, MST; DC 3;
WLC
See also CA 104; 133; DLB 56, 124; MTCW

Brecht, Eugen Berthold Friedrich
See Brecht, Bertolt

Bremer, Fredrika 1801-1865 . . . . . **NCLC 11**

Brennan, Christopher John
1870-1932 . . . . **TCLC 17**
See also CA 117

Brennan, Maeve 1917- . . . . **CLC 5**
See also CA 81-84

Brentano, Clemens (Maria)
1778-1842 . . . . **NCLC 1**
See also DLB 90

Brent of Bin Bin
See Franklin, (Stella Maraia Sarah) Miles

Brenton, Howard 1942- . . . . **CLC 31**
See also CA 69-72; CANR 33; DLB 13;
MTCW

Breslin, James 1930-
See Breslin, Jimmy
See also CA 73-76; CANR 31; DAM NOV;
MTCW

Breslin, Jimmy . . . . **CLC 4, 43**
See also Breslin, James
See also AITN 1

Bresson, Robert 1901- . . . . **CLC 16**
See also CA 110; CANR 49

Breton, Andre
1896-1966 . . . . . **CLC 2, 9, 15, 54; PC 15**
See also CA 19-20; 25-28R; CANR 40;
CAP 2; DLB 65; MTCW

Breytenbach, Breyten
1939(?)- . . . . . . **CLC 23, 37; DAM POET**
See also CA 113; 129

Bridgers, Sue Ellen 1942- . . . . **CLC 26**
See also AAYA 8; CA 65-68; CANR 11,
36; CLR 18; DLB 52; JRDA; MAICYA;
SAAS 1; SATA 22, 90

Bridges, Robert (Seymour)
1844-1930 . . . . **TCLC 1; DAM POET**
See also CA 104; 152; CDBLB 1890-1914;
DLB 19, 98

Bridie, James . . . . **TCLC 3**
See also Mavor, Osborne Henry
See also DLB 10

Brin, David 1950- . . . . **CLC 34**
See also AAYA 21; CA 102; CANR 24;
INT CANR-24; SATA 65

Brink, Andre (Philippus)
1935- . . . . **CLC 18, 36**
See also CA 104; CANR 39; INT 103;
MTCW

Brinsmead, H(esba) F(ay) 1922- . . . . **CLC 21**
See also CA 21-24R; CANR 10; MAICYA;
SAAS 5; SATA 18, 78

Brittain, Vera (Mary)
1893(?)-1970 . . . . **CLC 23**
See also CA 13-16; 25-28R; CAP 1; MTCW

Broch, Hermann 1886-1951 . . . . **TCLC 20**
See also CA 117; DLB 85, 124

Brock, Rose
See Hansen, Joseph

Brodkey, Harold (Roy) 1930-1996 . . **CLC 56**
See also CA 111; 151; DLB 130

Brodsky, Iosif Alexandrovich 1940-1996
See Brodsky, Joseph
See also AITN 1; CA 41-44R; 151;
CANR 37; DAM POET; MTCW

Brodsky, Joseph
1940-1996 . . **CLC 4, 6, 13, 36, 100; PC 9**
See also Brodsky, Iosif Alexandrovich

Brodsky, Michael Mark 1948- . . . . . **CLC 19**
See also CA 102; CANR 18, 41

Bromell, Henry 1947- . . . . **CLC 5**
See also CA 53-56; CANR 9

Bromfield, Louis (Brucker)
1896-1956 . . . . **TCLC 11**
See also CA 107; 155; DLB 4, 9, 86

Broner, E(sther) M(asserman)
1930- . . . . **CLC 19**
See also CA 17-20R; CANR 8, 25; DLB 28

Bronk, William 1918- . . . . **CLC 10**
See also CA 89-92; CANR 23; DLB 165

Bronstein, Lev Davidovich
See Trotsky, Leon

Bronte, Anne 1820-1849 . . . . **NCLC 4**
See also DLB 21

Bronte, Charlotte
1816-1855 . . . . . **NCLC 3, 8, 33, 58; DA;**
DAB; DAC; DAM MST, NOV; WLC
See also AAYA 17; CDBLB 1832-1890;
DLB 21, 159

Bronte, Emily (Jane)
1818-1848 . . . . **NCLC 16, 35; DA; DAB;**
DAC; DAM MST, NOV, POET; PC 8;
WLC
See also AAYA 17; CDBLB 1832-1890;
DLB 21, 32

Brooke, Frances 1724-1789 . . . . **LC 6**
See also DLB 39, 99

Brooke, Henry 1703(?)-1783 . . . . **LC 1**
See also DLB 39

Brooke, Rupert (Chawner)
1887-1915 . . . . **TCLC 2, 7; DA; DAB;**
DAC; DAM MST, POET; WLC
See also CA 104; 132; CDBLB 1914-1945;
DLB 19; MTCW

Brooke-Haven, P.
See Wodehouse, P(elham) G(renville)

Brooke-Rose, Christine 1926- . . . . . . **CLC 40**
See also CA 13-16R; DLB 14

Brookner, Anita
1928- . . . . **CLC 32, 34, 51; DAB;**
DAM POP
See also CA 114; 120; CANR 37, 56;
DLBY 87; MTCW

Brooks, Cleanth 1906-1994 . . . . . **CLC 24, 86**
See also CA 17-20R; 145; CANR 33, 35;
DLB 63; DLBY 94; INT CANR-35;
MTCW

Brooks, George
See Baum, L(yman) Frank

Brooks, Gwendolyn
1917- . . . . . . **CLC 1, 2, 4, 5, 15, 49; BLC;**
DA; DAC; DAM MST, MULT, POET;
PC 7; WLC
See also AAYA 20; AITN 1; BW 2;
CA 1-4R; CANR 1, 27, 52;
CDALB 1941-1968; CLR 27; DLB 5, 76,
165; MTCW; SATA 6

Brooks, Mel . . . . **CLC 12**
See also Kaminsky, Melvin
See also AAYA 13; DLB 26

Brooks, Peter 1938- . . . . **CLC 34**
See also CA 45-48; CANR 1

Brooks, Van Wyck 1886-1963 . . . . . . **CLC 29**
See also CA 1-4R; CANR 6; DLB 45, 63,
103

Brophy, Brigid (Antonia)
1929-1995 . . . . **CLC 6, 11, 29**
See also CA 5-8R; 149; CAAS 4; CANR 25,
53; DLB 14; MTCW

Brosman, Catharine Savage 1934- . . . . **CLC 9**
See also CA 61-64; CANR 21, 46

Brother Antoninus
See Everson, William (Oliver)

Broughton, T(homas) Alan 1936- . . . **CLC 19**
See also CA 45-48; CANR 2, 23, 48

Broumas, Olga 1949- . . . . CLC 10, 73
See also CA 85-88; CANR 20

Brown, Alan 1951- . . . . CLC 99

Brown, Charles Brockden
1771-1810 . . . . NCLC 22
See also CDALB 1640-1865; DLB 37, 59, 73

Brown, Christy 1932-1981 . . . . CLC 63
See also CA 105; 104; DLB 14

Brown, Claude
1937- . . . . . CLC 30; BLC; DAM MULT
See also AAYA 7; BW 1; CA 73-76

Brown, Dee (Alexander)
1908- . . . . CLC 18, 47; DAM POP
See also CA 13-16R; CAAS 6; CANR 11, 45; DLBY 80; MTCW; SATA 5

Brown, George
See Wertmueller, Lina

Brown, George Douglas
1869-1902 . . . . TCLC 28

Brown, George Mackay
1921-1996 . . . . CLC 5, 48, 100
See also CA 21-24R; 151; CAAS 6;
CANR 12, 37; DLB 14, 27, 139; MTCW;
SATA 35

Brown, (William) Larry 1951- . . . . . . CLC 73
See also CA 130; 134; INT 133

Brown, Moses
See Barrett, William (Christopher)

Brown, Rita Mae
1944- . . . . . CLC 18, 43, 79; DAM NOV,
POP
See also CA 45-48; CANR 2, 11, 35;
INT CANR-11; MTCW

Brown, Roderick (Langmere) Haig-
See Haig-Brown, Roderick (Langmere)

Brown, Rosellen 1939- . . . . CLC 32
See also CA 77-80; CAAS 10; CANR 14, 44

Brown, Sterling Allen
1901-1989 . . . . CLC 1, 23, 59; BLC;
DAM MULT, POET
See also BW 1; CA 85-88; 127; CANR 26;
DLB 48, 51, 63; MTCW

Brown, Will
See Ainsworth, William Harrison

Brown, William Wells
1813-1884 . . . . NCLC 2; BLC;
DAM MULT; DC 1
See also DLB 3, 50

Browne, (Clyde) Jackson 1948(?)- . . . CLC 21
See also CA 120

Browning, Elizabeth Barrett
1806-1861 . . . . NCLC 1, 16, 61; DA;
DAB; DAC; DAM MST, POET; PC 6;
WLC
See also CDBLB 1832-1890; DLB 32

Browning, Robert
1812-1889 . . . . NCLC 19; DA; DAB;
DAC; DAM MST, POET; PC 2
See also CDBLB 1832-1890; DLB 32, 163;
YABC 1

Browning, Tod 1882-1962 . . . . CLC 16
See also CA 141; 117

Brownson, Orestes (Augustus)
1803-1876 . . . . NCLC 50

Bruccoli, Matthew J(oseph) 1931- . . CLC 34
See also CA 9-12R; CANR 7; DLB 103

Bruce, Lenny . . . . CLC 21
See also Schneider, Leonard Alfred

Bruin, John
See Brutus, Dennis

Brulard, Henri
See Stendhal

Brulls, Christian
See Simenon, Georges (Jacques Christian)

Brunner, John (Kilian Houston)
1934-1995 . . . . . . CLC 8, 10; DAM POP
See also CA 1-4R; 149; CAAS 8; CANR 2, 37; MTCW

Bruno, Giordano 1548-1600 . . . . LC 27

Brutus, Dennis
1924- . . . . . CLC 43; BLC; DAM MULT,
POET
See also BW 2; CA 49-52; CAAS 14;
CANR 2, 27, 42; DLB 117

Bryan, C(ourtlandt) D(ixon) B(arnes)
1936- . . . . CLC 29
See also CA 73-76; CANR 13;
INT CANR-13

Bryan, Michael
See Moore, Brian

Bryant, William Cullen
1794-1878 . . . . . NCLC 6, 46; DA; DAB;
DAC; DAM MST, POET
See also CDALB 1640-1865; DLB 3, 43, 59

Bryusov, Valery Yakovlevich
1873-1924 . . . . TCLC 10
See also CA 107; 155

Buchan, John
1875-1940 . . . . TCLC 41; DAB;
DAM POP
See also CA 108; 145; DLB 34, 70, 156;
YABC 2

Buchanan, George 1506-1582 . . . . LC 4

Buchheim, Lothar-Guenther 1918- . . . CLC 6
See also CA 85-88

Buchner, (Karl) Georg
1813-1837 . . . . NCLC 26

Buchwald, Art(hur) 1925- . . . . CLC 33
See also AITN 1; CA 5-8R; CANR 21;
MTCW; SATA 10

Buck, Pearl S(ydenstricker)
1892-1973 . . . . CLC 7, 11, 18; DA; DAB;
DAC; DAM MST, NOV
See also AITN 1; CA 1-4R; 41-44R;
CANR 1, 34; DLB 9, 102; MTCW;
SATA 1, 25

Buckler, Ernest
1908-1984 . . CLC 13; DAC; DAM MST
See also CA 11-12; 114; CAP 1; DLB 68;
SATA 47

Buckley, Vincent (Thomas)
1925-1988 . . . . CLC 57
See also CA 101

Buckley, William F(rank), Jr.
1925- . . . . CLC 7, 18, 37; DAM POP
See also AITN 1; CA 1-4R; CANR 1, 24,
53; DLB 137; DLBY 80; INT CANR-24;
MTCW

Buechner, (Carl) Frederick
1926- . . . . . . CLC 2, 4, 6, 9; DAM NOV
See also CA 13-16R; CANR 11, 39;
DLBY 80; INT CANR-11; MTCW

Buell, John (Edward) 1927- . . . . CLC 10
See also CA 1-4R; DLB 53

Buero Vallejo, Antonio 1916- . . . CLC 15, 46
See also CA 106; CANR 24, 49; HW;
MTCW

Bufalino, Gesualdo 1920(?)- . . . . CLC 74

Bugayev, Boris Nikolayevich 1880-1934
See Bely, Andrey
See also CA 104

Bukowski, Charles
1920-1994 . . . . CLC 2, 5, 9, 41, 82;
DAM NOV, POET
See also CA 17-20R; 144; CANR 40;
DLB 5, 130, 169; MTCW

Bulgakov, Mikhail (Afanas'evich)
1891-1940 . . . . TCLC 2, 16;
DAM DRAM, NOV; SSC 18
See also CA 105; 152

Bulgya, Alexander Alexandrovich
1901-1956 . . . . TCLC 53
See also Fadeyev, Alexander
See also CA 117

Bullins, Ed
1935- . . . . CLC 1, 5, 7; BLC;
DAM DRAM, MULT; DC 6
See also BW 2; CA 49-52; CAAS 16;
CANR 24, 46; DLB 7, 38; MTCW

Bulwer-Lytton, Edward (George Earle Lytton)
1803-1873 . . . . NCLC 1, 45
See also DLB 21

Bunin, Ivan Alexeyevich
1870-1953 . . . . TCLC 6; SSC 5
See also CA 104

Bunting, Basil
1900-1985 . . . . CLC 10, 39, 47;
DAM POET
See also CA 53-56; 115; CANR 7; DLB 20

Bunuel, Luis
1900-1983 . . . . CLC 16, 80;
DAM MULT; HLC
See also CA 101; 110; CANR 32; HW

Bunyan, John
1628-1688 . . . . . . LC 4; DA; DAB; DAC;
DAM MST; WLC
See also CDBLB 1660-1789; DLB 39

Burckhardt, Jacob (Christoph)
1818-1897 . . . . NCLC 49

Burford, Eleanor
See Hibbert, Eleanor Alice Burford

Burgess, Anthony
. CLC 1, 2, 4, 5, 8, 10, 13, 15, 22, 40, 62,
81, 94; DAB
See also Wilson, John (Anthony) Burgess
See also AITN 1; CDBLB 1960 to Present;
DLB 14

Burke, Edmund
1729(?)-1797 . . . . . . LC 7, 36; DA; DAB;
DAC; DAM MST; WLC
See also DLB 104

Campos, Alvaro de
See Pessoa, Fernando (Antonio Nogueira)

Camus, Albert
1913-1960 .... CLC 1, 2, 4, 9, 11, 14, 32,
63, 69; DA; DAB; DAC; DAM DRAM,
MST, NOV; DC 2; SSC 9; WLC
See also CA 89-92; DLB 72; MTCW

Canby, Vincent 1924-............ CLC 13
See also CA 81-84

Cancale
See Desnos, Robert

Canetti, Elias
1905-1994 .... CLC 3, 14, 25, 75, 86
See also CA 21-24R; 146; CANR 23;
DLB 85, 124; MTCW

Canin, Ethan 1960-............... CLC 55
See also CA 131; 135

Cannon, Curt
See Hunter, Evan

Cape, Judith
See Page, P(atricia) K(athleen)

Capek, Karel
1890-1938 ...... TCLC 6, 37; DA; DAB;
DAC; DAM DRAM, MST, NOV; DC 1;
WLC
See also CA 104; 140

Capote, Truman
1924-1984 ...... CLC 1, 3, 8, 13, 19, 34,
38, 58; DA; DAB; DAC; DAM MST,
NOV, POP; SSC 2; WLC
See also CA 5-8R; 113; CANR 18;
CDALB 1941-1968; DLB 2; DLBY 80,
84; MTCW; SATA 91

Capra, Frank 1897-1991........... CLC 16
See also CA 61-64; 135

Caputo, Philip 1941-.............. CLC 32
See also CA 73-76; CANR 40

Card, Orson Scott
1951- ...... CLC 44, 47, 50; DAM POP
See also AAYA 11; CA 102; CANR 27, 47;
INT CANR-27; MTCW; SATA 83

Cardenal, Ernesto
1925- .... CLC 31; DAM MULT,
POET; HLC
See also CA 49-52; CANR 2, 32; HW;
MTCW

Cardozo, Benjamin N(athan)
1870-1938 .... TCLC 65
See also CA 117

Carducci, Giosue 1835-1907....... TCLC 32

Carew, Thomas 1595(?)-1640........ LC 13
See also DLB 126

Carey, Ernestine Gilbreth 1908-.... CLC 17
See also CA 5-8R; SATA 2

Carey, Peter 1943-......... CLC 40, 55, 96
See also CA 123; 127; CANR 53; INT 127;
MTCW

Carleton, William 1794-1869...... NCLC 3
See also DLB 159

Carlisle, Henry (Coffin) 1926-...... CLC 33
See also CA 13-16R; CANR 15

Carlsen, Chris
See Holdstock, Robert P.

Carlson, Ron(ald F.) 1947-........ CLC 54
See also CA 105; CANR 27

Carlyle, Thomas
1795-1881 ...... NCLC 22; DA; DAB;
DAC; DAM MST
See also CDBLB 1789-1832; DLB 55; 144

Carman, (William) Bliss
1861-1929 .... TCLC 7; DAC
See also CA 104; 152; DLB 92

Carnegie, Dale 1888-1955 .... TCLC 53

Carossa, Hans 1878-1956........ TCLC 48
See also DLB 66

Carpenter, Don(ald Richard)
1931-1995 .... CLC 41
See also CA 45-48; 149; CANR 1

Carpentier (y Valmont), Alejo
1904-1980 .... CLC 8, 11, 38;
DAM MULT; HLC
See also CA 65-68; 97-100; CANR 11;
DLB 113; HW

Carr, Caleb 1955(?)-.............. CLC 86
See also CA 147

Carr, Emily 1871-1945........... TCLC 32
See also DLB 68

Carr, John Dickson 1906-1977 ...... CLC 3
See also CA 49-52; 69-72; CANR 3, 33;
MTCW

Carr, Philippa
See Hibbert, Eleanor Alice Burford

Carr, Virginia Spencer 1929-....... CLC 34
See also CA 61-64; DLB 111

Carrere, Emmanuel 1957- .... CLC 89

Carrier, Roch
1937- ... CLC 13, 78; DAC; DAM MST
See also CA 130; DLB 53

Carroll, James P. 1943(?)-......... CLC 38
See also CA 81-84

Carroll, Jim 1951- .... CLC 35
See also AAYA 17; CA 45-48; CANR 42

Carroll, Lewis .... NCLC 2, 53; WLC
See also Dodgson, Charles Lutwidge
See also CDBLB 1832-1890; CLR 2, 18;
DLB 18, 163; JRDA

Carroll, Paul Vincent 1900-1968.... CLC 10
See also CA 9-12R; 25-28R; DLB 10

Carruth, Hayden
1921- ...... CLC 4, 7, 10, 18, 84; PC 10
See also CA 9-12R; CANR 4, 38; DLB 5,
165; INT CANR-4; MTCW; SATA 47

Carson, Rachel Louise
1907-1964 .... CLC 71; DAM POP
See also CA 77-80; CANR 35; MTCW;
SATA 23

Carter, Angela (Olive)
1940-1992 ...... CLC 5, 41, 76; SSC 13
See also CA 53-56; 136; CANR 12, 36;
DLB 14; MTCW; SATA 66;
SATA-Obit 70

Carter, Nick
See Smith, Martin Cruz

Carver, Raymond
1938-1988 .... CLC 22, 36, 53, 55;
DAM NOV; SSC 8
See also CA 33-36R; 126; CANR 17, 34;
DLB 130; DLBY 84, 88; MTCW

Cary, Elizabeth, Lady Falkland
1585-1639 .... LC 30

Cary, (Arthur) Joyce (Lunel)
1888-1957 .... TCLC 1, 29
See also CA 104; CDBLB 1914-1945;
DLB 15, 100

Casanova de Seingalt, Giovanni Jacopo
1725-1798 .... LC 13

Casares, Adolfo Bioy
See Bioy Casares, Adolfo

Casely-Hayford, J(oseph) E(phraim)
1866-1930 .... TCLC 24; BLC;
DAM MULT
See also BW 2; CA 123; 152

Casey, John (Dudley) 1939-........ CLC 59
See also BEST 90:2; CA 69-72; CANR 23

Casey, Michael 1947-.............. CLC 2
See also CA 65-68; DLB 5

Casey, Patrick
See Thurman, Wallace (Henry)

Casey, Warren (Peter) 1935-1988 ... CLC 12
See also CA 101; 127; INT 101

Casona, Alejandro.................. CLC 49
See also Alvarez, Alejandro Rodriguez

Cassavetes, John 1929-1989........ CLC 20
See also CA 85-88; 127

Cassian, Nina 1924- .... PC 17

Cassill, R(onald) V(erlin) 1919-... CLC 4, 23
See also CA 9-12R; CAAS 1; CANR 7, 45;
DLB 6

Cassirer, Ernst 1874-1945 .... TCLC 61

Cassity, (Allen) Turner 1929- .... CLC 6, 42
See also CA 17-20R; CAAS 8; CANR 11;
DLB 105

Castaneda, Carlos 1931(?)-......... CLC 12
See also CA 25-28R; CANR 32; HW;
MTCW

Castedo, Elena 1937- .... CLC 65
See also CA 132

Castedo-Ellerman, Elena
See Castedo, Elena

Castellanos, Rosario
1925-1974 ...... CLC 66; DAM MULT;
HLC
See also CA 131; 53-56; DLB 113; HW

Castelvetro, Lodovico 1505-1571..... LC 12

Castiglione, Baldassare 1478-1529 ... LC 12

Castle, Robert
See Hamilton, Edmond

Castro, Guillen de 1569-1631........ LC 19

Castro, Rosalia de
1837-1885 ...... NCLC 3; DAM MULT

Cather, Willa
See Cather, Willa Sibert

Cather, Willa Sibert
1873-1947 .... TCLC 1, 11, 31; DA;
DAB; DAC; DAM MST, NOV; SSC 2;
WLC
See also CA 104; 128; CDALB 1865-1917;
DLB 9, 54, 78; DLBD 1; MTCW;
SATA 30

Cato, Marcus Porcius
234B.C.-149B.C............. CMLC 21

Catton, (Charles) Bruce
1899-1978 . . . . CLC 35
See also AITN 1; CA 5-8R; 81-84;
CANR 7; DLB 17; SATA 2;
SATA-Obit 24

Catullus c. 84B.C.-c. 54B.C. . . . . . CMLC 18

Cauldwell, Frank
See King, Francis (Henry)

Caunitz, William J. 1933-1996 . . . . . CLC 34
See also BEST 89:3; CA 125; 130; 152;
INT 130

Causley, Charles (Stanley) 1917- . . . . . CLC 7
See also CA 9-12R; CANR 5, 35; CLR 30;
DLB 27; MTCW; SATA 3, 66

Caute, David 1936- . . . . CLC 29; DAM NOV
See also CA 1-4R; CAAS 4; CANR 1, 33;
DLB 14

Cavafy, C(onstantine) P(eter)
1863-1933 . . . . TCLC 2, 7; DAM POET
See also Kavafis, Konstantinos Petrou
See also CA 148

Cavallo, Evelyn
See Spark, Muriel (Sarah)

Cavanna, Betty . . . . CLC 12
See also Harrison, Elizabeth Cavanna
See also JRDA; MAICYA; SAAS 4;
SATA 1, 30

Cavendish, Margaret Lucas
1623-1673 . . . . LC 30
See also DLB 131

Caxton, William 1421(?)-1491(?) . . . . . LC 17
See also DLB 170

Cayrol, Jean 1911- . . . . CLC 11
See also CA 89-92; DLB 83

Cela, Camilo Jose
1916- . . . . . CLC 4, 13, 59; DAM MULT;
HLC
See also BEST 90:2; CA 21-24R; CAAS 10;
CANR 21, 32; DLBY 89; HW; MTCW

Celan, Paul . . . . . . CLC 10, 19, 53, 82; PC 10
See also Antschel, Paul
See also DLB 69

Celine, Louis-Ferdinand
. . . . CLC 1, 3, 4, 7, 9, 15, 47
See also Destouches, Louis-Ferdinand
See also DLB 72

Cellini, Benvenuto 1500-1571 . . . . LC 7

Cendrars, Blaise . . . . CLC 18
See also Sauser-Hall, Frederic

Cernuda (y Bidon), Luis
1902-1963 . . . . CLC 54; DAM POET
See also CA 131; 89-92; DLB 134; HW

Cervantes (Saavedra), Miguel de
1547-1616 . . . . LC 6, 23; DA; DAB;
DAC; DAM MST, NOV; SSC 12; WLC

Cesaire, Aime (Fernand)
1913- . . . . CLC 19, 32; BLC;
DAM MULT, POET
See also BW 2; CA 65-68; CANR 24, 43;
MTCW

Chabon, Michael 1963- . . . . CLC 55
See also CA 139; CANR 57

Chabrol, Claude 1930- . . . . CLC 16
See also CA 110

Challans, Mary 1905-1983
See Renault, Mary
See also CA 81-84; 111; SATA 23;
SATA-Obit 36

Challis, George
See Faust, Frederick (Schiller)

Chambers, Aidan 1934- . . . . CLC 35
See also CA 25-28R; CANR 12, 31; JRDA;
MAICYA; SAAS 12; SATA 1, 69

Chambers, James 1948-
See Cliff, Jimmy
See also CA 124

Chambers, Jessie
See Lawrence, D(avid) H(erbert Richards)

Chambers, Robert W. 1865-1933 . . . TCLC 41

Chandler, Raymond (Thornton)
1888-1959 . . . . TCLC 1, 7; SSC 23
See also CA 104; 129; CDALB 1929-1941;
DLBD 6; MTCW

Chang, Jung 1952- . . . . CLC 71
See also CA 142

Channing, William Ellery
1780-1842 . . . . NCLC 17
See also DLB 1, 59

Chaplin, Charles Spencer
1889-1977 . . . . CLC 16
See also Chaplin, Charlie
See also CA 81-84; 73-76

Chaplin, Charlie
See Chaplin, Charles Spencer
See also DLB 44

Chapman, George
1559(?)-1634 . . . . . LC 22; DAM DRAM
See also DLB 62, 121

Chapman, Graham 1941-1989 . . . . . . CLC 21
See also Monty Python
See also CA 116; 129; CANR 35

Chapman, John Jay 1862-1933 . . . . . TCLC 7
See also CA 104

Chapman, Lee
See Bradley, Marion Zimmer

Chapman, Walker
See Silverberg, Robert

Chappell, Fred (Davis) 1936- . . . . CLC 40, 78
See also CA 5-8R; CAAS 4; CANR 8, 33;
DLB 6, 105

Char, Rene(-Emile)
1907-1988 . . . . CLC 9, 11, 14, 55;
DAM POET
See also CA 13-16R; 124; CANR 32;
MTCW

Charby, Jay
See Ellison, Harlan (Jay)

Chardin, Pierre Teilhard de
See Teilhard de Chardin, (Marie Joseph)
Pierre

Charles I 1600-1649 . . . . LC 13

Charyn, Jerome 1937- . . . . CLC 5, 8, 18
See also CA 5-8R; CAAS 1; CANR 7;
DLBY 83; MTCW

Chase, Mary (Coyle) 1907-1981 . . . . . . DC 1
See also CA 77-80; 105; SATA 17;
SATA-Obit 29

Chase, Mary Ellen 1887-1973 . . . . CLC 2
See also CA 13-16; 41-44R; CAP 1;
SATA 10

Chase, Nicholas
See Hyde, Anthony

Chateaubriand, Francois Rene de
1768-1848 . . . . NCLC 3
See also DLB 119

Chatterje, Sarat Chandra 1876-1936(?)
See Chatterji, Saratchandra
See also CA 109

Chatterji, Bankim Chandra
1838-1894 . . . . NCLC 19

Chatterji, Saratchandra . . . . TCLC 13
See also Chatterje, Sarat Chandra

Chatterton, Thomas
1752-1770 . . . . LC 3; DAM POET
See also DLB 109

Chatwin, (Charles) Bruce
1940-1989 . . CLC 28, 57, 59; DAM POP
See also AAYA 4; BEST 90:1; CA 85-88;
127

Chaucer, Daniel
See Ford, Ford Madox

Chaucer, Geoffrey
1340(?)-1400 . . . . LC 17; DA; DAB;
DAC; DAM MST, POET
See also CDBLB Before 1660; DLB 146

Chaviaras, Strates 1935-
See Haviaras, Stratis
See also CA 105

Chayefsky, Paddy . . . . CLC 23
See also Chayefsky, Sidney
See also DLB 7, 44; DLBY 81

Chayefsky, Sidney 1923-1981
See Chayefsky, Paddy
See also CA 9-12R; 104; CANR 18;
DAM DRAM

Chedid, Andree 1920- . . . . CLC 47
See also CA 145

Cheever, John
1912-1982 . . . . . . CLC 3, 7, 8, 11, 15, 25,
64; DA; DAB; DAC; DAM MST, NOV,
POP; SSC 1; WLC
See also CA 5-8R; 106; CABS 1; CANR 5,
27; CDALB 1941-1968; DLB 2, 102;
DLBY 80, 82; INT CANR-5; MTCW

Cheever, Susan 1943- . . . . CLC 18, 48
See also CA 103; CANR 27, 51; DLBY 82;
INT CANR-27

Chekhonte, Antosha
See Chekhov, Anton (Pavlovich)

Chekhov, Anton (Pavlovich)
1860-1904 . . . . . TCLC 3, 10, 31, 55; DA;
DAB; DAC; DAM DRAM, MST; SSC 2;
WLC
See also CA 104; 124; SATA 90

Chernyshevsky, Nikolay Gavrilovich
1828-1889 . . . . NCLC 1

Cherry, Carolyn Janice 1942-
See Cherryh, C. J.
See also CA 65-68; CANR 10

Cherryh, C. J. . . . . CLC 35
See also Cherry, Carolyn Janice
See also DLBY 80

Cook, Roy
See Silverberg, Robert

Cooke, Elizabeth 1948- . . . . **CLC 55**
See also CA 129

Cooke, John Esten 1830-1886 . . . . . **NCLC 5**
See also DLB 3

Cooke, John Estes
See Baum, L(yman) Frank

Cooke, M. E.
See Creasey, John

Cooke, Margaret
See Creasey, John

Cook-Lynn, Elizabeth
1930- . . . . **CLC 93; DAM MULT**
See also CA 133; DLB 175; NNAL

Cooney, Ray . . . . **CLC 62**

Cooper, Douglas 1960- . . . . **CLC 86**

Cooper, Henry St. John
See Creasey, John

Cooper, J(oan) California
. . . . **CLC 56; DAM MULT**
See also AAYA 12; BW 1; CA 125;
CANR 55

Cooper, James Fenimore
1789-1851 . . . . **NCLC 1, 27, 54**
See also CDALB 1640-1865; DLB 3;
SATA 19

Coover, Robert (Lowell)
1932- . . . . **CLC 3, 7, 15, 32, 46, 87;
DAM NOV; SSC 15**
See also CA 45-48; CANR 3, 37; DLB 2;
DLBY 81; MTCW

Copeland, Stewart (Armstrong)
1952- . . . . **CLC 26**

Coppard, A(lfred) E(dgar)
1878-1957 . . . . **TCLC 5; SSC 21**
See also CA 114; DLB 162; YABC 1

Coppee, Francois 1842-1908 . . . . . . **TCLC 25**

Coppola, Francis Ford 1939- . . . . **CLC 16**
See also CA 77-80; CANR 40; DLB 44

Corbiere, Tristan 1845-1875 . . . . . **NCLC 43**

Corcoran, Barbara 1911- . . . . **CLC 17**
See also AAYA 14; CA 21-24R; CAAS 2;
CANR 11, 28, 48; DLB 52; JRDA;
SAAS 20; SATA 3, 77

Cordelier, Maurice
See Giraudoux, (Hippolyte) Jean

Corelli, Marie 1855-1924 . . . . **TCLC 51**
See also Mackay, Mary
See also DLB 34, 156

Corman, Cid . . . . **CLC 9**
See also Corman, Sidney
See also CAAS 2; DLB 5

Corman, Sidney 1924-
See Corman, Cid
See also CA 85-88; CANR 44; DAM POET

Cormier, Robert (Edmund)
1925- . . . . **CLC 12, 30; DA; DAB; DAC;
DAM MST, NOV**
See also AAYA 3, 19; CA 1-4R; CANR 5,
23; CDALB 1968-1988; CLR 12; DLB 52;
INT CANR-23; JRDA; MAICYA;
MTCW; SATA 10, 45, 83

Corn, Alfred (DeWitt III) 1943- . . . . **CLC 33**
See also CA 104; CAAS 25; CANR 44;
DLB 120; DLBY 80

Corneille, Pierre
1606-1684 . . . . **LC 28; DAB; DAM MST**

Cornwell, David (John Moore)
1931- . . . . **CLC 9, 15; DAM POP**
See also le Carre, John
See also CA 5-8R; CANR 13, 33; MTCW

Corso, (Nunzio) Gregory 1930- . . . **CLC 1, 11**
See also CA 5-8R; CANR 41; DLB 5, 16;
MTCW

Cortazar, Julio
1914-1984 . . . . . . **CLC 2, 3, 5, 10, 13, 15,
33, 34, 92; DAM MULT, NOV; HLC;
SSC 7**
See also CA 21-24R; CANR 12, 32;
DLB 113; HW; MTCW

CORTES, HERNAN 1484-1547 . . . . . **LC 31**

Corwin, Cecil
See Kornbluth, C(yril) M.

Cosic, Dobrica 1921- . . . . **CLC 14**
See also CA 122; 138

Costain, Thomas B(ertram)
1885-1965 . . . . **CLC 30**
See also CA 5-8R; 25-28R; DLB 9

Costantini, Humberto
1924(?)-1987 . . . . **CLC 49**
See also CA 131; 122; HW

Costello, Elvis 1955- . . . . **CLC 21**

Cotter, Joseph Seamon Sr.
1861-1949 . . . . **TCLC 28; BLC;
DAM MULT**
See also BW 1; CA 124; DLB 50

Couch, Arthur Thomas Quiller
See Quiller-Couch, Arthur Thomas

Coulton, James
See Hansen, Joseph

Couperus, Louis (Marie Anne)
1863-1923 . . . . **TCLC 15**
See also CA 115

Coupland, Douglas
1961- . . . . **CLC 85; DAC; DAM POP**
See also CA 142; CANR 57

Court, Wesli
See Turco, Lewis (Putnam)

Courtenay, Bryce 1933- . . . . **CLC 59**
See also CA 138

Courtney, Robert
See Ellison, Harlan (Jay)

Cousteau, Jacques-Yves 1910- . . . . . . **CLC 30**
See also CA 65-68; CANR 15; MTCW;
SATA 38

Coward, Noel (Peirce)
1899-1973 . . . . **CLC 1, 9, 29, 51;
DAM DRAM**
See also AITN 1; CA 17-18; 41-44R;
CANR 35; CAP 2; CDBLB 1914-1945;
DLB 10; MTCW

Cowley, Malcolm 1898-1989 . . . . **CLC 39**
See also CA 5-8R; 128; CANR 3, 55;
DLB 4, 48; DLBY 81, 89; MTCW

Cowper, William
1731-1800 . . . . . . **NCLC 8; DAM POET**
See also DLB 104, 109

Cox, William Trevor
1928- . . . . **CLC 9, 14, 71; DAM NOV**
See also Trevor, William
See also CA 9-12R; CANR 4, 37, 55;
DLB 14; INT CANR-37; MTCW

Coyne, P. J.
See Masters, Hilary

Cozzens, James Gould
1903-1978 . . . . **CLC 1, 4, 11, 92**
See also CA 9-12R; 81-84; CANR 19;
CDALB 1941-1968; DLB 9; DLBD 2;
DLBY 84; MTCW

Crabbe, George 1754-1832 . . . . **NCLC 26**
See also DLB 93

Craddock, Charles Egbert
See Murfree, Mary Noailles

Craig, A. A.
See Anderson, Poul (William)

Craik, Dinah Maria (Mulock)
1826-1887 . . . . **NCLC 38**
See also DLB 35, 163; MAICYA; SATA 34

Cram, Ralph Adams 1863-1942 . . . . **TCLC 45**

Crane, (Harold) Hart
1899-1932 . . . . **TCLC 2, 5; DA; DAB;
DAC; DAM MST, POET; PC 3; WLC**
See also CA 104; 127; CDALB 1917-1929;
DLB 4, 48; MTCW

Crane, R(onald) S(almon)
1886-1967 . . . . **CLC 27**
See also CA 85-88; DLB 63

Crane, Stephen (Townley)
1871-1900 . . . . **TCLC 11, 17, 32; DA;
DAB; DAC; DAM MST, NOV, POET;
SSC 7; WLC**
See also AAYA 21; CA 109; 140;
CDALB 1865-1917; DLB 12, 54, 78;
YABC 2

Crase, Douglas 1944- . . . . **CLC 58**
See also CA 106

Crashaw, Richard 1612(?)-1649 . . . . . . **LC 24**
See also DLB 126

Craven, Margaret
1901-1980 . . . . **CLC 17; DAC**
See also CA 103

Crawford, F(rancis) Marion
1854-1909 . . . . **TCLC 10**
See also CA 107; DLB 71

Crawford, Isabella Valancy
1850-1887 . . . . **NCLC 12**
See also DLB 92

Crayon, Geoffrey
See Irving, Washington

Creasey, John 1908-1973 . . . . **CLC 11**
See also CA 5-8R; 41-44R; CANR 8;
DLB 77; MTCW

Crebillon, Claude Prosper Jolyot de (fils)
1707-1777 . . . . **LC 28**

Credo
See Creasey, John

Creeley, Robert (White)
1926- . . . . . **CLC 1, 2, 4, 8, 11, 15, 36, 78;
DAM POET**
See also CA 1-4R; CAAS 10; CANR 23, 43;
DLB 5, 16, 169; MTCW

Daudet, (Louis Marie) Alphonse
1840-1897 . . . . NCLC 1
See also DLB 123

Daumal, Rene 1908-1944 . . . . TCLC 14
See also CA 114

Davenport, Guy (Mattison, Jr.)
1927- . . . . CLC 6, 14, 38; SSC 16
See also CA 33-36R; CANR 23; DLB 130

Davidson, Avram 1923-
See Queen, Ellery
See also CA 101; CANR 26; DLB 8

Davidson, Donald (Grady)
1893-1968 . . . . CLC 2, 13, 19
See also CA 5-8R; 25-28R; CANR 4;
DLB 45

Davidson, Hugh
See Hamilton, Edmond

Davidson, John 1857-1909 . . . . TCLC 24
See also CA 118; DLB 19

Davidson, Sara 1943- . . . . CLC 9
See also CA 81-84; CANR 44

Davie, Donald (Alfred)
1922-1995 . . . . CLC 5, 8, 10, 31
See also CA 1-4R; 149; CAAS 3; CANR 1,
44; DLB 27; MTCW

Davies, Ray(mond Douglas) 1944- . . CLC 21
See also CA 116; 146

Davies, Rhys 1903-1978 . . . . CLC 23
See also CA 9-12R; 81-84; CANR 4;
DLB 139

Davies, (William) Robertson
1913-1995 . . . . . CLC 2, 7, 13, 25, 42, 75,
91; DA; DAB; DAC; DAM MST, NOV,
POP; WLC
See also BEST 89:2; CA 33-36R; 150;
CANR 17, 42; DLB 68; INT CANR-17;
MTCW

Davies, W(illiam) H(enry)
1871-1940 . . . . TCLC 5
See also CA 104; DLB 19, 174

Davies, Walter C.
See Kornbluth, C(yril) M.

Davis, Angela (Yvonne)
1944- . . . . CLC 77; DAM MULT
See also BW 2; CA 57-60; CANR 10

Davis, B. Lynch
See Bioy Casares, Adolfo; Borges, Jorge
Luis

Davis, Gordon
See Hunt, E(verette) Howard, (Jr.)

Davis, Harold Lenoir 1896-1960 . . . . CLC 49
See also CA 89-92; DLB 9

Davis, Rebecca (Blaine) Harding
1831-1910 . . . . TCLC 6
See also CA 104; DLB 74

Davis, Richard Harding
1864-1916 . . . . TCLC 24
See also CA 114; DLB 12, 23, 78, 79;
DLBD 13

Davison, Frank Dalby 1893-1970 . . . CLC 15
See also CA 116

Davison, Lawrence H.
See Lawrence, D(avid) H(erbert Richards)

Davison, Peter (Hubert) 1928- . . . . . CLC 28
See also CA 9-12R; CAAS 4; CANR 3, 43;
DLB 5

Davys, Mary 1674-1732 . . . . LC 1
See also DLB 39

Dawson, Fielding 1930- . . . . CLC 6
See also CA 85-88; DLB 130

Dawson, Peter
See Faust, Frederick (Schiller)

Day, Clarence (Shepard, Jr.)
1874-1935 . . . . TCLC 25
See also CA 108; DLB 11

Day, Thomas 1748-1789 . . . . LC 1
See also DLB 39; YABC 1

Day Lewis, C(ecil)
1904-1972 . . . . CLC 1, 6, 10;
DAM POET; PC 11
See also Blake, Nicholas
See also CA 13-16; 33-36R; CANR 34;
CAP 1; DLB 15, 20; MTCW

Dazai, Osamu . . . . TCLC 11
See also Tsushima, Shuji

de Andrade, Carlos Drummond
See Drummond de Andrade, Carlos

Deane, Norman
See Creasey, John

**de Beauvoir, Simone (Lucie Ernestine Marie
Bertrand)**
See Beauvoir, Simone (Lucie Ernestine
Marie Bertrand) de

de Brissac, Malcolm
See Dickinson, Peter (Malcolm)

de Chardin, Pierre Teilhard
See Teilhard de Chardin, (Marie Joseph)
Pierre

Dee, John 1527-1608 . . . . LC 20

Deer, Sandra 1940- . . . . CLC 45

De Ferrari, Gabriella 1941- . . . . CLC 65
See also CA 146

Defoe, Daniel
1660(?)-1731 . . . . LC 1; DA; DAB; DAC;
DAM MST, NOV; WLC
See also CDBLB 1660-1789; DLB 39, 95,
101; JRDA; MAICYA; SATA 22

de Gourmont, Remy(-Marie-Charles)
See Gourmont, Remy (-Marie-Charles) de

de Hartog, Jan 1914- . . . . CLC 19
See also CA 1-4R; CANR 1

de Hostos, E. M.
See Hostos (y Bonilla), Eugenio Maria de

de Hostos, Eugenio M.
See Hostos (y Bonilla), Eugenio Maria de

Deighton, Len . . . . CLC 4, 7, 22, 46
See also Deighton, Leonard Cyril
See also AAYA 6; BEST 89:2;
CDBLB 1960 to Present; DLB 87

Deighton, Leonard Cyril 1929-
See Deighton, Len
See also CA 9-12R; CANR 19, 33;
DAM NOV, POP; MTCW

Dekker, Thomas
1572(?)-1632 . . . . . LC 22; DAM DRAM
See also CDBLB Before 1660; DLB 62, 172

Delafield, E. M. 1890-1943 . . . . . . TCLC 61
See also Dashwood, Edmee Elizabeth
Monica de la Pasture
See also DLB 34

de la Mare, Walter (John)
1873-1956 . . . . TCLC 4, 53; DAB; DAC;
DAM MST, POET; SSC 14; WLC
See also CDBLB 1914-1945; CLR 23;
DLB 162; SATA 16

Delaney, Franey
See O'Hara, John (Henry)

Delaney, Shelagh
1939- . . . . CLC 29; DAM DRAM
See also CA 17-20R; CANR 30;
CDBLB 1960 to Present; DLB 13;
MTCW

Delany, Mary (Granville Pendarves)
1700-1788 . . . . LC 12

Delany, Samuel R(ay, Jr.)
1942- . . . . CLC 8, 14, 38; BLC;
DAM MULT
See also BW 2; CA 81-84; CANR 27, 43;
DLB 8, 33; MTCW

De La Ramee, (Marie) Louise 1839-1908
See Ouida
See also SATA 20

de la Roche, Mazo 1879-1961 . . . . . . CLC 14
See also CA 85-88; CANR 30; DLB 68;
SATA 64

Delbanco, Nicholas (Franklin)
1942- . . . . CLC 6, 13
See also CA 17-20R; CAAS 2; CANR 29,
55; DLB 6

del Castillo, Michel 1933- . . . . CLC 38
See also CA 109

Deledda, Grazia (Cosima)
1875(?)-1936 . . . . TCLC 23
See also CA 123

Delibes, Miguel . . . . CLC 8, 18
See also Delibes Setien, Miguel

Delibes Setien, Miguel 1920-
See Delibes, Miguel
See also CA 45-48; CANR 1, 32; HW;
MTCW

DeLillo, Don
1936- . . . . . CLC 8, 10, 13, 27, 39, 54, 76;
DAM NOV, POP
See also BEST 89:1; CA 81-84; CANR 21;
DLB 6, 173; MTCW

de Lisser, H. G.
See De Lisser, H(erbert) G(eorge)
See also DLB 117

De Lisser, H(erbert) G(eorge)
1878-1944 . . . . TCLC 12
See also de Lisser, H. G.
See also BW 2; CA 109; 152

Deloria, Vine (Victor), Jr.
1933- . . . . CLC 21; DAM MULT
See also CA 53-56; CANR 5, 20, 48;
DLB 175; MTCW; NNAL; SATA 21

Del Vecchio, John M(ichael)
1947- . . . . CLC 29
See also CA 110; DLBD 9

de Man, Paul (Adolph Michel)
1919-1983 . . . . CLC 55
See also CA 128; 111; DLB 67; MTCW

De Marinis, Rick 1934-.......... **CLC 54**
See also CA 57-60; CAAS 24; CANR 9, 25, 50

Dembry, R. Emmet
See Murfree, Mary Noailles

Demby, William
1922- ..... **CLC 53; BLC; DAM MULT**
See also BW 1; CA 81-84; DLB 33

de Menton, Francisco
See Chin, Frank (Chew, Jr.)

Demijohn, Thom
See Disch, Thomas M(ichael)

de Montherlant, Henry (Milon)
See Montherlant, Henry (Milon) de

Demosthenes 384B.C.-322B.C. ... **CMLC 13**
See also DLB 176

de Natale, Francine
See Malzberg, Barry N(athaniel)

Denby, Edwin (Orr) 1903-1983..... **CLC 48**
See also CA 138; 110

Denis, Julio
See Cortazar, Julio

Denmark, Harrison
See Zelazny, Roger (Joseph)

Dennis, John 1658-1734........... **LC 11**
See also DLB 101

Dennis, Nigel (Forbes) 1912-1989.... **CLC 8**
See also CA 25-28R; 129; DLB 13, 15; MTCW

De Palma, Brian (Russell) 1940-.... **CLC 20**
See also CA 109

De Quincey, Thomas 1785-1859 ... **NCLC 4**
See also CDBLB 1789-1832; DLB 110; 144

Deren, Eleanora 1908(?)-1961
See Deren, Maya
See also CA 111

Deren, Maya .... **CLC 16**
See also Deren, Eleanora

Derleth, August (William)
1909-1971 .... **CLC 31**
See also CA 1-4R; 29-32R; CANR 4; DLB 9; SATA 5

Der Nister 1884-1950........... **TCLC 56**

de Routisie, Albert
See Aragon, Louis

Derrida, Jacques 1930-........ **CLC 24, 87**
See also CA 124; 127

Derry Down Derry
See Lear, Edward

Dersonnes, Jacques
See Simenon, Georges (Jacques Christian)

Desai, Anita
1937- .... **CLC 19, 37, 97; DAB; DAM NOV**
See also CA 81-84; CANR 33, 53; MTCW; SATA 63

de Saint-Luc, Jean
See Glassco, John

de Saint Roman, Arnaud
See Aragon, Louis

Descartes, Rene 1596-1650 ...... **LC 20, 35**

De Sica, Vittorio 1901(?)-1974 ..... **CLC 20**
See also CA 117

Desnos, Robert 1900-1945....... **TCLC 22**
See also CA 121; 151

Destouches, Louis-Ferdinand
1894-1961 .... **CLC 9, 15**
See also Celine, Louis-Ferdinand
See also CA 85-88; CANR 28; MTCW

de Tolignac, Gaston
See Griffith, D(avid Lewelyn) W(ark)

Deutsch, Babette 1895-1982 .... **CLC 18**
See also CA 1-4R; 108; CANR 4; DLB 45; SATA 1; SATA-Obit 33

Devenant, William 1606-1649 ...... **LC 13**

Devkota, Laxmiprasad
1909-1959 .... **TCLC 23**
See also CA 123

De Voto, Bernard (Augustine)
1897-1955 .... **TCLC 29**
See also CA 113; DLB 9

De Vries, Peter
1910-1993 .... **CLC 1, 2, 3, 7, 10, 28, 46; DAM NOV**
See also CA 17-20R; 142; CANR 41; DLB 6; DLBY 82; MTCW

Dexter, John
See Bradley, Marion Zimmer

Dexter, Martin
See Faust, Frederick (Schiller)

Dexter, Pete
1943- .... **CLC 34, 55; DAM POP**
See also BEST 89:2; CA 127; 131; INT 131; MTCW

Diamano, Silmang
See Senghor, Leopold Sedar

Diamond, Neil 1941- .... **CLC 30**
See also CA 108

Diaz del Castillo, Bernal 1496-1584 .. **LC 31**

di Bassetto, Corno
See Shaw, George Bernard

Dick, Philip K(indred)
1928-1982 .... **CLC 10, 30, 72; DAM NOV, POP**
See also CA 49-52; 106; CANR 2, 16; DLB 8; MTCW

Dickens, Charles (John Huffam)
1812-1870 ...... **NCLC 3, 8, 18, 26, 37, 50; DA; DAB; DAC; DAM MST, NOV; SSC 17; WLC**
See also CDBLB 1832-1890; DLB 21, 55, 70, 159, 166; JRDA; MAICYA; SATA 15

Dickey, James (Lafayette)
1923-1997 .... **CLC 1, 2, 4, 7, 10, 15, 47; DAM NOV, POET, POP**
See also AITN 1, 2; CA 9-12R; 156; CABS 2; CANR 10, 48; CDALB 1968-1988; DLB 5; DLBD 7; DLBY 82, 93; INT CANR-10; MTCW

Dickey, William 1928-1994 ..... **CLC 3, 28**
See also CA 9-12R; 145; CANR 24; DLB 5

Dickinson, Charles 1951-.......... **CLC 49**
See also CA 128

Dickinson, Emily (Elizabeth)
1830-1886 .... **NCLC 21; DA; DAB; DAC; DAM MST, POET; PC 1; WLC**
See also CDALB 1865-1917; DLB 1; SATA 29

Dickinson, Peter (Malcolm)
1927-.................... **CLC 12, 35**
See also AAYA 9; CA 41-44R; CANR 31; CLR 29; DLB 87, 161; JRDA; MAICYA; SATA 5, 62

Dickson, Carr
See Carr, John Dickson

Dickson, Carter
See Carr, John Dickson

Diderot, Denis 1713-1784 .... **LC 26**

Didion, Joan
1934- .. **CLC 1, 3, 8, 14, 32; DAM NOV**
See also AITN 1; CA 5-8R; CANR 14, 52; CDALB 1968-1988; DLB 2, 173; DLBY 81, 86; MTCW

Dietrich, Robert
See Hunt, E(verette) Howard, (Jr.)

Dillard, Annie
1945- .... **CLC 9, 60; DAM NOV**
See also AAYA 6; CA 49-52; CANR 3, 43; DLBY 80; MTCW; SATA 10

Dillard, R(ichard) H(enry) W(ilde)
1937-....................... **CLC 5**
See also CA 21-24R; CAAS 7; CANR 10; DLB 5

Dillon, Eilis 1920-1994........... **CLC 17**
See also CA 9-12R; 147; CAAS 3; CANR 4, 38; CLR 26; MAICYA; SATA 2, 74; SATA-Obit 83

Dimont, Penelope
See Mortimer, Penelope (Ruth)

Dinesen, Isak........ **CLC 10, 29, 95; SSC 7**
See also Blixen, Karen (Christentze Dinesen)

Ding Ling...................... **CLC 68**
See also Chiang Pin-chin

Disch, Thomas M(ichael) 1940-... **CLC 7, 36**
See also AAYA 17; CA 21-24R; CAAS 4; CANR 17, 36, 54; CLR 18; DLB 8; MAICYA; MTCW; SAAS 15; SATA 92

Disch, Tom
See Disch, Thomas M(ichael)

d'Isly, Georges
See Simenon, Georges (Jacques Christian)

Disraeli, Benjamin 1804-1881 .. **NCLC 2, 39**
See also DLB 21, 55

Ditcum, Steve
See Crumb, R(obert)

Dixon, Paige
See Corcoran, Barbara

Dixon, Stephen 1936-..... **CLC 52; SSC 16**
See also CA 89-92; CANR 17, 40, 54; DLB 130

Dobell, Sydney Thompson
1824-1874 .... **NCLC 43**
See also DLB 32

Doblin, Alfred .... **TCLC 13**
See also Doeblin, Alfred

Dobrolyubov, Nikolai Alexandrovich
1836-1861 .... **NCLC 5**

Dobyns, Stephen 1941-........... **CLC 37**
See also CA 45-48; CANR 2, 18

Doctorow, E(dgar) L(aurence)
1931- . . . . . **CLC 6, 11, 15, 18, 37, 44, 65;**
DAM NOV, POP
See also AITN 2; BEST 89:3; CA 45-48;
CANR 2, 33, 51; CDALB 1968-1988;
DLB 2, 28, 173; DLBY 80; MTCW

Dodgson, Charles Lutwidge 1832-1898
See Carroll, Lewis
See also CLR 2; DA; DAB; DAC;
DAM MST, NOV, POET; MAICYA;
YABC 2

Dodson, Owen (Vincent)
1914-1983 . . . . **CLC 79; BLC;**
DAM MULT
See also BW 1; CA 65-68; 110; CANR 24;
DLB 76

Doeblin, Alfred 1878-1957 . . . . **TCLC 13**
See also Doblin, Alfred
See also CA 110; 141; DLB 66

Doerr, Harriet 1910- . . . . **CLC 34**
See also CA 117; 122; CANR 47; INT 122

Domecq, H(onorio) Bustos
See Bioy Casares, Adolfo; Borges, Jorge
Luis

Domini, Rey
See Lorde, Audre (Geraldine)

Dominique
See Proust, (Valentin-Louis-George-Eugene-)
Marcel

Don, A
See Stephen, Leslie

Donaldson, Stephen R.
1947- . . . . **CLC 46; DAM POP**
See also CA 89-92; CANR 13, 55;
INT CANR-13

Donleavy, J(ames) P(atrick)
1926- . . . . **CLC 1, 4, 6, 10, 45**
See also AITN 2; CA 9-12R; CANR 24, 49;
DLB 6, 173; INT CANR-24; MTCW

Donne, John
1572-1631 . . . . **LC 10, 24; DA; DAB;**
DAC; DAM MST, POET; PC 1
See also CDBLB Before 1660; DLB 121,
151

Donnell, David 1939(?)- . . . . **CLC 34**

Donoghue, P. S.
See Hunt, E(verette) Howard, (Jr.)

Donoso (Yanez), Jose
1924-1996 . . . . **CLC 4, 8, 11, 32, 99;**
DAM MULT; HLC
See also CA 81-84; 155; CANR 32;
DLB 113; HW; MTCW

Donovan, John 1928-1992 . . . . **CLC 35**
See also AAYA 20; CA 97-100; 137;
CLR 3; MAICYA; SATA 72;
SATA-Brief 29

Don Roberto
See Cunninghame Graham, R(obert)
B(ontine)

Doolittle, Hilda
1886-1961 . . . . . **CLC 3, 8, 14, 31, 34, 73;**
DA; DAC; DAM MST, POET; PC 5;
WLC
See also H. D.
See also CA 97-100; CANR 35; DLB 4, 45;
MTCW

Dorfman, Ariel
1942- . . . . **CLC 48, 77; DAM MULT;**
HLC
See also CA 124; 130; HW; INT 130

Dorn, Edward (Merton) 1929- . . . **CLC 10, 18**
See also CA 93-96; CANR 42; DLB 5;
INT 93-96

Dorsan, Luc
See Simenon, Georges (Jacques Christian)

Dorsange, Jean
See Simenon, Georges (Jacques Christian)

Dos Passos, John (Roderigo)
1896-1970 . . . . . . **CLC 1, 4, 8, 11, 15, 25,**
34, 82; DA; DAB; DAC; DAM MST,
NOV; WLC
See also CA 1-4R; 29-32R; CANR 3;
CDALB 1929-1941; DLB 4, 9; DLBD 1;
MTCW

Dossage, Jean
See Simenon, Georges (Jacques Christian)

Dostoevsky, Fedor Mikhailovich
1821-1881 . . . . . . **NCLC 2, 7, 21, 33, 43;**
DA; DAB; DAC; DAM MST, NOV;
SSC 2; WLC

Doughty, Charles M(ontagu)
1843-1926 . . . . **TCLC 27**
See also CA 115; DLB 19, 57, 174

Douglas, Ellen . . . . **CLC 73**
See also Haxton, Josephine Ayres;
Williamson, Ellen Douglas

Douglas, Gavin 1475(?)-1522 . . . . **LC 20**

Douglas, Keith 1920-1944 . . . . **TCLC 40**
See also DLB 27

Douglas, Leonard
See Bradbury, Ray (Douglas)

Douglas, Michael
See Crichton, (John) Michael

Douglas, Norman 1868-1952 . . . . . . **TCLC 68**

Douglass, Frederick
1817(?)-1895 . . . . **NCLC 7, 55; BLC; DA;**
DAC; DAM MST, MULT; WLC
See also CDALB 1640-1865; DLB 1, 43, 50,
79; SATA 29

Dourado, (Waldomiro Freitas) Autran
1926- . . . . **CLC 23, 60**
See also CA 25-28R; CANR 34

Dourado, Waldomiro Autran
See Dourado, (Waldomiro Freitas) Autran

Dove, Rita (Frances)
1952- . . . . **CLC 50, 81; DAM MULT,**
POET; PC 6
See also BW 2; CA 109; CAAS 19;
CANR 27, 42; DLB 120

Dowell, Coleman 1925-1985 . . . . **CLC 60**
See also CA 25-28R; 117; CANR 10;
DLB 130

Dowson, Ernest (Christopher)
1867-1900 . . . . **TCLC 4**
See also CA 105; 150; DLB 19, 135

Doyle, A. Conan
See Doyle, Arthur Conan

Doyle, Arthur Conan
1859-1930 . . . . **TCLC 7; DA; DAB;**
DAC; DAM MST, NOV; SSC 12; WLC
See also AAYA 14; CA 104; 122;
CDBLB 1890-1914; DLB 18, 70, 156;
MTCW; SATA 24

Doyle, Conan
See Doyle, Arthur Conan

Doyle, John
See Graves, Robert (von Ranke)

Doyle, Roddy 1958(?)- . . . . **CLC 81**
See also AAYA 14; CA 143

Doyle, Sir A. Conan
See Doyle, Arthur Conan

Doyle, Sir Arthur Conan
See Doyle, Arthur Conan

Dr. A
See Asimov, Isaac; Silverstein, Alvin

Drabble, Margaret
1939- . . . . **CLC 2, 3, 5, 8, 10, 22, 53;**
DAB; DAC; DAM MST, NOV, POP
See also CA 13-16R; CANR 18, 35;
CDBLB 1960 to Present; DLB 14, 155;
MTCW; SATA 48

Drapier, M. B.
See Swift, Jonathan

Drayham, James
See Mencken, H(enry) L(ouis)

Drayton, Michael 1563-1631 . . . . **LC 8**

Dreadstone, Carl
See Campbell, (John) Ramsey

Dreiser, Theodore (Herman Albert)
1871-1945 . . . . **TCLC 10, 18, 35; DA;**
DAC; DAM MST, NOV; WLC
See also CA 106; 132; CDALB 1865-1917;
DLB 9, 12, 102, 137; DLBD 1; MTCW

Drexler, Rosalyn 1926- . . . . **CLC 2, 6**
See also CA 81-84

Dreyer, Carl Theodor 1889-1968 . . . . **CLC 16**
See also CA 116

Drieu la Rochelle, Pierre(-Eugene)
1893-1945 . . . . **TCLC 21**
See also CA 117; DLB 72

Drinkwater, John 1882-1937 . . . . . . **TCLC 57**
See also CA 109; 149; DLB 10, 19, 149

Drop Shot
See Cable, George Washington

Droste-Hulshoff, Annette Freiin von
1797-1848 . . . . **NCLC 3**
See also DLB 133

Drummond, Walter
See Silverberg, Robert

Drummond, William Henry
1854-1907 . . . . **TCLC 25**
See also DLB 92

Drummond de Andrade, Carlos
1902-1987 . . . . **CLC 18**
See also Andrade, Carlos Drummond de
See also CA 132; 123

Drury, Allen (Stuart) 1918- . . . . **CLC 37**
See also CA 57-60; CANR 18, 52;
INT CANR-18

Dryden, John
  1631-1700 . . . . LC 3, 21; DA; DAB;
    DAC; DAM DRAM, MST, POET;
    DC 3; WLC
  See also CDBLB 1660-1789; DLB 80, 101,
    131

Duberman, Martin   1930- . . . . CLC 8
  See also CA 1-4R; CANR 2

Dubie, Norman (Evans)   1945- . . . . . . CLC 36
  See also CA 69-72; CANR 12; DLB 120

Du Bois, W(illiam) E(dward) B(urghardt)
  1868-1963 . . . . CLC 1, 2, 13, 64, 96;
    BLC; DA; DAC; DAM MST, MULT,
    NOV; WLC
  See also BW 1; CA 85-88; CANR 34;
    CDALB 1865-1917; DLB 47, 50, 91;
    MTCW; SATA 42

Dubus, Andre
  1936- . . . . CLC 13, 36, 97; SSC 15
  See also CA 21-24R; CANR 17; DLB 130;
    INT CANR-17

Duca Minimo
  See D'Annunzio, Gabriele

Ducharme, Rejean   1941- . . . . CLC 74
  See also DLB 60

Duclos, Charles Pinot   1704-1772 . . . . . LC 1

Dudek, Louis   1918- . . . . CLC 11, 19
  See also CA 45-48; CAAS 14; CANR 1;
    DLB 88

Duerrenmatt, Friedrich
  1921-1990 . . . . . . CLC 1, 4, 8, 11, 15, 43;
    DAM DRAM
  See also CA 17-20R; CANR 33; DLB 69,
    124; MTCW

Duffy, Bruce   (?)- . . . . CLC 50

Duffy, Maureen   1933- . . . . CLC 37
  See also CA 25-28R; CANR 33; DLB 14;
    MTCW

Dugan, Alan   1923- . . . . CLC 2, 6
  See also CA 81-84; DLB 5

du Gard, Roger Martin
  See Martin du Gard, Roger

Duhamel, Georges   1884-1966 . . . . CLC 8
  See also CA 81-84; 25-28R; CANR 35;
    DLB 65; MTCW

Dujardin, Edouard (Emile Louis)
  1861-1949 . . . . TCLC 13
  See also CA 109; DLB 123

Dumas, Alexandre (Davy de la Pailleterie)
  1802-1870 . . . . NCLC 11; DA; DAB;
    DAC; DAM MST, NOV; WLC
  See also DLB 119; SATA 18

Dumas, Alexandre
  1824-1895 . . . . NCLC 9; DC 1

Dumas, Claudine
  See Malzberg, Barry N(athaniel)

Dumas, Henry L.   1934-1968 . . . . . CLC 6, 62
  See also BW 1; CA 85-88; DLB 41

du Maurier, Daphne
  1907-1989 . . . . CLC 6, 11, 59; DAB;
    DAC; DAM MST, POP; SSC 18
  See also CA 5-8R; 128; CANR 6, 55;
    MTCW; SATA 27; SATA-Obit 60

Dunbar, Paul Laurence
  1872-1906 . . . . . . TCLC 2, 12; BLC; DA;
    DAC; DAM MST, MULT, POET; PC 5;
    SSC 8; WLC
  See also BW 1; CA 104; 124;
    CDALB 1865-1917; DLB 50, 54, 78;
    SATA 34

Dunbar, William   1460(?)-1530(?) . . . . LC 20
  See also DLB 132, 146

Duncan, Dora Angela
  See Duncan, Isadora

Duncan, Isadora   1877(?)-1927 . . . . . TCLC 68
  See also CA 118; 149

Duncan, Lois   1934- . . . . CLC 26
  See also AAYA 4; CA 1-4R; CANR 2, 23,
    36; CLR 29; JRDA; MAICYA; SAAS 2;
    SATA 1, 36, 75

Duncan, Robert (Edward)
  1919-1988 . . . . CLC 1, 2, 4, 7, 15, 41, 55;
    DAM POET; PC 2
  See also CA 9-12R; 124; CANR 28; DLB 5,
    16; MTCW

Duncan, Sara Jeannette
  1861-1922 . . . . TCLC 60
  See also DLB 92

Dunlap, William   1766-1839 . . . . NCLC 2
  See also DLB 30, 37, 59

Dunn, Douglas (Eaglesham)
  1942- . . . . CLC 6, 40
  See also CA 45-48; CANR 2, 33; DLB 40;
    MTCW

Dunn, Katherine (Karen)   1945- . . . . . CLC 71
  See also CA 33-36R

Dunn, Stephen   1939- . . . . CLC 36
  See also CA 33-36R; CANR 12, 48, 53;
    DLB 105

Dunne, Finley Peter   1867-1936 . . . . TCLC 28
  See also CA 108; DLB 11, 23

Dunne, John Gregory   1932- . . . . CLC 28
  See also CA 25-28R; CANR 14, 50;
    DLBY 80

Dunsany, Edward John Moreton Drax
    Plunkett   1878-1957
  See Dunsany, Lord
  See also CA 104; 148; DLB 10

Dunsany, Lord . . . . TCLC 2, 59
  See also Dunsany, Edward John Moreton
    Drax Plunkett
  See also DLB 77, 153, 156

du Perry, Jean
  See Simenon, Georges (Jacques Christian)

Durang, Christopher (Ferdinand)
  1949- . . . . CLC 27, 38
  See also CA 105; CANR 50

Duras, Marguerite
  1914-1996 . . . . . CLC 3, 6, 11, 20, 34, 40,
    68, 100
  See also CA 25-28R; 151; CANR 50;
    DLB 83; MTCW

Durban, (Rosa) Pam   1947- . . . . CLC 39
  See also CA 123

Durcan, Paul
  1944- . . . . CLC 43, 70; DAM POET
  See also CA 134

Durkheim, Emile   1858-1917 . . . . . . TCLC 55

Durrell, Lawrence (George)
  1912-1990 . . . . CLC 1, 4, 6, 8, 13, 27, 41;
    DAM NOV
  See also CA 9-12R; 132; CANR 40;
    CDBLB 1945-1960; DLB 15, 27;
    DLBY 90; MTCW

Durrenmatt, Friedrich
  See Duerrenmatt, Friedrich

Dutt, Toru   1856-1877 . . . . NCLC 29

Dwight, Timothy   1752-1817 . . . . . . NCLC 13
  See also DLB 37

Dworkin, Andrea   1946- . . . . CLC 43
  See also CA 77-80; CAAS 21; CANR 16,
    39; INT CANR-16; MTCW

Dwyer, Deanna
  See Koontz, Dean R(ay)

Dwyer, K. R.
  See Koontz, Dean R(ay)

Dylan, Bob   1941- . . . . . . CLC 3, 4, 6, 12, 77
  See also CA 41-44R; DLB 16

Eagleton, Terence (Francis)   1943-
  See Eagleton, Terry
  See also CA 57-60; CANR 7, 23; MTCW

Eagleton, Terry . . . . CLC 63
  See also Eagleton, Terence (Francis)

Early, Jack
  See Scoppettone, Sandra

East, Michael
  See West, Morris L(anglo)

Eastaway, Edward
  See Thomas, (Philip) Edward

Eastlake, William (Derry)   1917- . . . . . CLC 8
  See also CA 5-8R; CAAS 1; CANR 5;
    DLB 6; INT CANR-5

Eastman, Charles A(lexander)
  1858-1939 . . . . . TCLC 55; DAM MULT
  See also DLB 175; NNAL; YABC 1

Eberhart, Richard (Ghormley)
  1904- . . CLC 3, 11, 19, 56; DAM POET
  See also CA 1-4R; CANR 2;
    CDALB 1941-1968; DLB 48; MTCW

Eberstadt, Fernanda   1960- . . . . CLC 39
  See also CA 136

Echegaray (y Eizaguirre), Jose (Maria Waldo)
  1832-1916 . . . . TCLC 4
  See also CA 104; CANR 32; HW; MTCW

Echeverria, (Jose) Esteban (Antonino)
  1805-1851 . . . . NCLC 18

Echo
  See Proust, (Valentin-Louis-George-Eugene-)
    Marcel

Eckert, Allan W.   1931- . . . . CLC 17
  See also AAYA 18; CA 13-16R; CANR 14,
    45; INT CANR-14; SAAS 21; SATA 29,
    91; SATA-Brief 27

Eckhart, Meister   1260(?)-1328(?) . . CMLC 9
  See also DLB 115

Eckmar, F. R.
  See de Hartog, Jan

Eco, Umberto
  1932- . . . CLC 28, 60; DAM NOV, POP
  See also BEST 90:1; CA 77-80; CANR 12,
    33, 55; MTCW

Eddison, E(ric) R(ucker)
1882-1945 . . . . TCLC 15
See also CA 109; 156

Edel, (Joseph) Leon 1907- . . . . . . CLC 29, 34
See also CA 1-4R; CANR 1, 22; DLB 103;
INT CANR-22

Eden, Emily 1797-1869 . . . . NCLC 10

Edgar, David
1948- . . . . CLC 42; DAM DRAM
See also CA 57-60; CANR 12; DLB 13;
MTCW

Edgerton, Clyde (Carlyle) 1944- . . . . CLC 39
See also AAYA 17; CA 118; 134; INT 134

Edgeworth, Maria 1768-1849. . . NCLC 1, 51
See also DLB 116, 159, 163; SATA 21

Edmonds, Paul
See Kuttner, Henry

Edmonds, Walter D(umaux) 1903- . . CLC 35
See also CA 5-8R; CANR 2; DLB 9;
MAICYA; SAAS 4; SATA 1, 27

Edmondson, Wallace
See Ellison, Harlan (Jay)

Edson, Russell . . . . CLC 13
See also CA 33-36R

Edwards, Bronwen Elizabeth
See Rose, Wendy

Edwards, G(erald) B(asil)
1899-1976 . . . . CLC 25
See also CA 110

Edwards, Gus 1939- . . . . CLC 43
See also CA 108; INT 108

Edwards, Jonathan
1703-1758 . . . . LC 7; DA; DAC;
DAM MST
See also DLB 24

Efron, Marina Ivanovna Tsvetaeva
See Tsvetaeva (Efron), Marina (Ivanovna)

Ehle, John (Marsden, Jr.) 1925- . . . . CLC 27
See also CA 9-12R

Ehrenbourg, Ilya (Grigoryevich)
See Ehrenburg, Ilya (Grigoryevich)

Ehrenburg, Ilya (Grigoryevich)
1891-1967 . . . . CLC 18, 34, 62
See also CA 102; 25-28R

Ehrenburg, Ilyo (Grigoryevich)
See Ehrenburg, Ilya (Grigoryevich)

Eich, Guenter 1907-1972 . . . . CLC 15
See also CA 111; 93-96; DLB 69, 124

Eichendorff, Joseph Freiherr von
1788-1857 . . . . NCLC 8
See also DLB 90

Eigner, Larry . . . . CLC 9
See also Eigner, Laurence (Joel)
See also CAAS 23; DLB 5

Eigner, Laurence (Joel) 1927-1996
See Eigner, Larry
See also CA 9-12R; 151; CANR 6

Einstein, Albert 1879-1955 . . . . TCLC 65
See also CA 121; 133; MTCW

Eiseley, Loren Corey 1907-1977 . . . . . CLC 7
See also AAYA 5; CA 1-4R; 73-76;
CANR 6

Eisenstadt, Jill 1963- . . . . CLC 50
See also CA 140

Eisenstein, Sergei (Mikhailovich)
1898-1948 . . . . TCLC 57
See also CA 114; 149

Eisner, Simon
See Kornbluth, C(yril) M.

Ekeloef, (Bengt) Gunnar
1907-1968 . . . . CLC 27; DAM POET
See also CA 123; 25-28R

Ekelof, (Bengt) Gunnar
See Ekeloef, (Bengt) Gunnar

Ekwensi, C. O. D.
See Ekwensi, Cyprian (Odiatu Duaka)

Ekwensi, Cyprian (Odiatu Duaka)
1921- . . . . . . CLC 4; BLC; DAM MULT
See also BW 2; CA 29-32R; CANR 18, 42;
DLB 117; MTCW; SATA 66

Elaine . . . . TCLC 18
See also Leverson, Ada

El Crummo
See Crumb, R(obert)

Elia
See Lamb, Charles

Eliade, Mircea 1907-1986 . . . . CLC 19
See also CA 65-68; 119; CANR 30; MTCW

Eliot, A. D.
See Jewett, (Theodora) Sarah Orne

Eliot, Alice
See Jewett, (Theodora) Sarah Orne

Eliot, Dan
See Silverberg, Robert

Eliot, George
1819-1880 . . . . . NCLC 4, 13, 23, 41, 49;
DA; DAB; DAC; DAM MST, NOV;
WLC
See also CDBLB 1832-1890; DLB 21, 35, 55

Eliot, John 1604-1690 . . . . LC 5
See also DLB 24

Eliot, T(homas) S(tearns)
1888-1965 . . . . . CLC 1, 2, 3, 6, 9, 10, 13,
15, 24, 34, 41, 55, 57; DA; DAB; DAC;
DAM DRAM, MST, POET; PC 5;
WLC 2
See also CA 5-8R; 25-28R; CANR 41;
CDALB 1929-1941; DLB 7, 10, 45, 63;
DLBY 88; MTCW

Elizabeth 1866-1941 . . . . TCLC 41

Elkin, Stanley L(awrence)
1930-1995 . . . . . . CLC 4, 6, 9, 14, 27, 51,
91; DAM NOV, POP; SSC 12
See also CA 9-12R; 148; CANR 8, 46;
DLB 2, 28; DLBY 80; INT CANR-8;
MTCW

Elledge, Scott . . . . CLC 34

Elliot, Don
See Silverberg, Robert

Elliott, Don
See Silverberg, Robert

Elliott, George P(aul) 1918-1980 . . . . . CLC 2
See also CA 1-4R; 97-100; CANR 2

Elliott, Janice 1931- . . . . CLC 47
See also CA 13-16R; CANR 8, 29; DLB 14

Elliott, Sumner Locke 1917-1991 . . . CLC 38
See also CA 5-8R; 134; CANR 2, 21

Elliott, William
See Bradbury, Ray (Douglas)

Ellis, A. E. . . . . CLC 7

Ellis, Alice Thomas . . . . CLC 40
See also Haycraft, Anna

Ellis, Bret Easton
1964- . . . . CLC 39, 71; DAM POP
See also AAYA 2; CA 118; 123; CANR 51;
INT 123

Ellis, (Henry) Havelock
1859-1939 . . . . TCLC 14
See also CA 109

Ellis, Landon
See Ellison, Harlan (Jay)

Ellis, Trey 1962- . . . . CLC 55
See also CA 146

Ellison, Harlan (Jay)
1934- . . . . . . CLC 1, 13, 42; DAM POP;
SSC 14
See also CA 5-8R; CANR 5, 46; DLB 8;
INT CANR-5; MTCW

Ellison, Ralph (Waldo)
1914-1994 . . . . CLC 1, 3, 11, 54, 86;
BLC; DA; DAB; DAC; DAM MST,
MULT, NOV; WLC
See also AAYA 19; BW 1; CA 9-12R; 145;
CANR 24, 53; CDALB 1941-1968;
DLB 2, 76; DLBY 94; MTCW

Ellmann, Lucy (Elizabeth) 1956- . . . . CLC 61
See also CA 128

Ellmann, Richard (David)
1918-1987 . . . . CLC 50
See also BEST 89:2; CA 1-4R; 122;
CANR 2, 28; DLB 103; DLBY 87;
MTCW

Elman, Richard 1934- . . . . CLC 19
See also CA 17-20R; CAAS 3; CANR 47

Elron
See Hubbard, L(afayette) Ron(ald)

Eluard, Paul . . . . TCLC 7, 41
See also Grindel, Eugene

Elyot, Sir Thomas 1490(?)-1546 . . . . . LC 11

Elytis, Odysseus
1911-1996 . . . . CLC 15, 49, 100;
DAM POET
See also CA 102; 151; MTCW

Emecheta, (Florence Onye) Buchi
1944- . . CLC 14, 48; BLC; DAM MULT
See also BW 2; CA 81-84; CANR 27;
DLB 117; MTCW; SATA 66

Emerson, Ralph Waldo
1803-1882 . . . . . NCLC 1, 38; DA; DAB;
DAC; DAM MST, POET; WLC
See also CDALB 1640-1865; DLB 1, 59, 73

Eminescu, Mihail 1850-1889 . . . . . NCLC 33

Empson, William
1906-1984 . . . . CLC 3, 8, 19, 33, 34
See also CA 17-20R; 112; CANR 31;
DLB 20; MTCW

Enchi Fumiko (Ueda) 1905-1986 . . . . CLC 31
See also CA 129; 121

Ende, Michael (Andreas Helmuth)
1929-1995 . . . . CLC 31
See also CA 118; 124; 149; CANR 36;
CLR 14; DLB 75; MAICYA; SATA 61;
SATA-Brief 42; SATA-Obit 86

Endo, Shusaku
1923-1996 . . . . . . CLC 7, 14, 19, 54, 99;
DAM NOV
See also CA 29-32R; 153; CANR 21, 54;
MTCW

Engel, Marian 1933-1985 . . . . CLC 36
See also CA 25-28R; CANR 12; DLB 53;
INT CANR-12

Engelhardt, Frederick
See Hubbard, L(afayette) Ron(ald)

Enright, D(ennis) J(oseph)
1920- . . . . CLC 4, 8, 31
See also CA 1-4R; CANR 1, 42; DLB 27;
SATA 25

Enzensberger, Hans Magnus
1929- . . . . CLC 43
See also CA 116; 119

Ephron, Nora 1941- . . . . CLC 17, 31
See also AITN 2; CA 65-68; CANR 12, 39

Epicurus 341B.C.-270B.C. . . . . CMLC 21
See also DLB 176

Epsilon
See Betjeman, John

Epstein, Daniel Mark 1948- . . . . CLC 7
See also CA 49-52; CANR 2, 53

Epstein, Jacob 1956- . . . . CLC 19
See also CA 114

Epstein, Joseph 1937- . . . . CLC 39
See also CA 112; 119; CANR 50

Epstein, Leslie 1938- . . . . CLC 27
See also CA 73-76; CAAS 12; CANR 23

Equiano, Olaudah
1745(?)-1797 . . . . LC 16; BLC;
DAM MULT
See also DLB 37, 50

Erasmus, Desiderius 1469(?)-1536. . . . LC 16

Erdman, Paul E(mil) 1932- . . . . CLC 25
See also AITN 1; CA 61-64; CANR 13, 43

Erdrich, Louise
1954- . . . . CLC 39, 54; DAM MULT,
NOV, POP
See also AAYA 10; BEST 89:1; CA 114;
CANR 41; DLB 152, 175; MTCW;
NNAL

Erenburg, Ilya (Grigoryevich)
See Ehrenburg, Ilya (Grigoryevich)

Erickson, Stephen Michael 1950-
See Erickson, Steve
See also CA 129

Erickson, Steve . . . . CLC 64
See also Erickson, Stephen Michael

Ericson, Walter
See Fast, Howard (Melvin)

Eriksson, Buntel
See Bergman, (Ernst) Ingmar

Ernaux, Annie 1940- . . . . CLC 88
See also CA 147

Eschenbach, Wolfram von
See Wolfram von Eschenbach

Eseki, Bruno
See Mphahlele, Ezekiel

Esenin, Sergei (Alexandrovich)
1895-1925 . . . . TCLC 4
See also CA 104

Eshleman, Clayton 1935- . . . . CLC 7
See also CA 33-36R; CAAS 6; DLB 5

Espriella, Don Manuel Alvarez
See Southey, Robert

Espriu, Salvador 1913-1985 . . . . CLC 9
See also CA 154; 115; DLB 134

Espronceda, Jose de 1808-1842 . . . NCLC 39

Esse, James
See Stephens, James

Esterbrook, Tom
See Hubbard, L(afayette) Ron(ald)

Estleman, Loren D.
1952- . . . . . . CLC 48; DAM NOV, POP
See also CA 85-88; CANR 27;
INT CANR-27; MTCW

Eugenides, Jeffrey 1960(?)- . . . . CLC 81
See also CA 144

Euripides c. 485B.C.-406B.C. . . . . DC 4
See also DA; DAB; DAC; DAM DRAM,
MST; DLB 176

Evan, Evin
See Faust, Frederick (Schiller)

Evans, Evan
See Faust, Frederick (Schiller)

Evans, Marian
See Eliot, George

Evans, Mary Ann
See Eliot, George

Evarts, Esther
See Benson, Sally

Everett, Percival L. 1956- . . . . CLC 57
See also BW 2; CA 129

Everson, R(onald) G(ilmour)
1903- . . . . CLC 27
See also CA 17-20R; DLB 88

Everson, William (Oliver)
1912-1994 . . . . CLC 1, 5, 14
See also CA 9-12R; 145; CANR 20; DLB 5,
16; MTCW

Evtushenko, Evgenii Aleksandrovich
See Yevtushenko, Yevgeny (Alexandrovich)

Ewart, Gavin (Buchanan)
1916-1995 . . . . CLC 13, 46
See also CA 89-92; 150; CANR 17, 46;
DLB 40; MTCW

Ewers, Hanns Heinz 1871-1943 . . . TCLC 12
See also CA 109; 149

Ewing, Frederick R.
See Sturgeon, Theodore (Hamilton)

Exley, Frederick (Earl)
1929-1992 . . . . CLC 6, 11
See also AITN 2; CA 81-84; 138; DLB 143;
DLBY 81

Eynhardt, Guillermo
See Quiroga, Horacio (Sylvestre)

Ezekiel, Nissim 1924- . . . . CLC 61
See also CA 61-64

Ezekiel, Tish O'Dowd 1943- . . . . CLC 34
See also CA 129

Fadeyev, A.
See Bulgya, Alexander Alexandrovich

Fadeyev, Alexander . . . . TCLC 53
See also Bulgya, Alexander Alexandrovich

Fagen, Donald 1948- . . . . CLC 26

Fainzilberg, Ilya Arnoldovich 1897-1937
See Ilf, Ilya
See also CA 120

Fair, Ronald L. 1932- . . . . CLC 18
See also BW 1; CA 69-72; CANR 25;
DLB 33

Fairbairns, Zoe (Ann) 1948- . . . . CLC 32
See also CA 103; CANR 21

Falco, Gian
See Papini, Giovanni

Falconer, James
See Kirkup, James

Falconer, Kenneth
See Kornbluth, C(yril) M.

Falkland, Samuel
See Heijermans, Herman

Fallaci, Oriana 1930- . . . . CLC 11
See also CA 77-80; CANR 15; MTCW

Faludy, George 1913- . . . . CLC 42
See also CA 21-24R

Faludy, Gyoergy
See Faludy, George

Fanon, Frantz
1925-1961 . . . . CLC 74; BLC;
DAM MULT
See also BW 1; CA 116; 89-92

Fanshawe, Ann 1625-1680 . . . . LC 11

Fante, John (Thomas) 1911-1983 . . . CLC 60
See also CA 69-72; 109; CANR 23;
DLB 130; DLBY 83

Farah, Nuruddin
1945- . . . . . . CLC 53; BLC; DAM MULT
See also BW 2; CA 106; DLB 125

Fargue, Leon-Paul 1876(?)-1947 . . . TCLC 11
See also CA 109

Farigoule, Louis
See Romains, Jules

Farina, Richard 1936(?)-1966 . . . . CLC 9
See also CA 81-84; 25-28R

Farley, Walter (Lorimer)
1915-1989 . . . . CLC 17
See also CA 17-20R; CANR 8, 29; DLB 22;
JRDA; MAICYA; SATA 2, 43

Farmer, Philip Jose 1918- . . . . CLC 1, 19
See also CA 1-4R; CANR 4, 35; DLB 8;
MTCW

Farquhar, George
1677-1707 . . . . LC 21; DAM DRAM
See also DLB 84

Farrell, J(ames) G(ordon)
1935-1979 . . . . CLC 6
See also CA 73-76; 89-92; CANR 36;
DLB 14; MTCW

Farrell, James T(homas)
1904-1979 . . . . CLC 1, 4, 8, 11, 66
See also CA 5-8R; 89-92; CANR 9; DLB 4,
9, 86; DLBD 2; MTCW

Farren, Richard J.
See Betjeman, John

Flecker, (Herman) James Elroy
1884-1915 . . . . **TCLC 43**
See also CA 109; 150; DLB 10, 19

Fleming, Ian (Lancaster)
1908-1964 . . . . . . **CLC 3, 30; DAM POP**
See also CA 5-8R; CDBLB 1945-1960;
DLB 87; MTCW; SATA 9

Fleming, Thomas (James) 1927- . . . . **CLC 37**
See also CA 5-8R; CANR 10;
INT CANR-10; SATA 8

Fletcher, John 1579-1625 . . . . . **LC 33; DC 6**
See also CDBLB Before 1660; DLB 58

Fletcher, John Gould 1886-1950 . . . **TCLC 35**
See also CA 107; DLB 4, 45

Fleur, Paul
See Pohl, Frederik

Flooglebuckle, Al
See Spiegelman, Art

Flying Officer X
See Bates, H(erbert) E(rnest)

Fo, Dario 1926- . . . . . **CLC 32; DAM DRAM**
See also CA 116; 128; MTCW

Fogarty, Jonathan Titulescu Esq.
See Farrell, James T(homas)

Folke, Will
See Bloch, Robert (Albert)

Follett, Ken(neth Martin)
1949- . . . . . . **CLC 18; DAM NOV, POP**
See also AAYA 6; BEST 89:4; CA 81-84;
CANR 13, 33, 54; DLB 87; DLBY 81;
INT CANR-33; MTCW

Fontane, Theodor 1819-1898 . . . . . **NCLC 26**
See also DLB 129

Foote, Horton
1916- . . . . **CLC 51, 91; DAM DRAM**
See also CA 73-76; CANR 34, 51; DLB 26;
INT CANR-34

Foote, Shelby
1916- . . . . . . **CLC 75; DAM NOV, POP**
See also CA 5-8R; CANR 3, 45; DLB 2, 17

Forbes, Esther 1891-1967 . . . . **CLC 12**
See also AAYA 17; CA 13-14; 25-28R;
CAP 1; CLR 27; DLB 22; JRDA;
MAICYA; SATA 2

Forche, Carolyn (Louise)
1950- . . . . **CLC 25, 83, 86; DAM POET;
PC 10**
See also CA 109; 117; CANR 50; DLB 5;
INT 117

Ford, Elbur
See Hibbert, Eleanor Alice Burford

Ford, Ford Madox
1873-1939 . . . . **TCLC 1, 15, 39, 57;
DAM NOV**
See also CA 104; 132; CDBLB 1914-1945;
DLB 162; MTCW

Ford, John 1895-1973 . . . . **CLC 16**
See also CA 45-48

Ford, Richard . . . . **CLC 99**

Ford, Richard 1944- . . . . **CLC 46**
See also CA 69-72; CANR 11, 47

Ford, Webster
See Masters, Edgar Lee

Foreman, Richard 1937- . . . . **CLC 50**
See also CA 65-68; CANR 32

Forester, C(ecil) S(cott)
1899-1966 . . . . **CLC 35**
See also CA 73-76; 25-28R; SATA 13

Forez
See Mauriac, Francois (Charles)

Forman, James Douglas 1932- . . . . . . **CLC 21**
See also AAYA 17; CA 9-12R; CANR 4,
19, 42; JRDA; MAICYA; SATA 8, 70

Fornes, Maria Irene 1930- . . . . . . **CLC 39, 61**
See also CA 25-28R; CANR 28; DLB 7;
HW; INT CANR-28; MTCW

Forrest, Leon 1937- . . . . **CLC 4**
See also BW 2; CA 89-92; CAAS 7;
CANR 25, 52; DLB 33

Forster, E(dward) M(organ)
1879-1970 . . . . . **CLC 1, 2, 3, 4, 9, 10, 13,
15, 22, 45, 77; DA; DAB; DAC;
DAM MST, NOV; WLC**
See also AAYA 2; CA 13-14; 25-28R;
CANR 45; CAP 1; CDBLB 1914-1945;
DLB 34, 98, 162; DLBD 10; MTCW;
SATA 57

Forster, John 1812-1876 . . . . **NCLC 11**
See also DLB 144

Forsyth, Frederick
1938- . . **CLC 2, 5, 36; DAM NOV, POP**
See also BEST 89:4; CA 85-88; CANR 38;
DLB 87; MTCW

Forten, Charlotte L. . . . . **TCLC 16; BLC**
See also Grimke, Charlotte L(ottie) Forten
See also DLB 50

Foscolo, Ugo 1778-1827 . . . . **NCLC 8**

Fosse, Bob . . . . **CLC 20**
See also Fosse, Robert Louis

Fosse, Robert Louis 1927-1987
See Fosse, Bob
See also CA 110; 123

Foster, Stephen Collins
1826-1864 . . . . **NCLC 26**

Foucault, Michel
1926-1984 . . . . **CLC 31, 34, 69**
See also CA 105; 113; CANR 34; MTCW

Fouque, Friedrich (Heinrich Karl) de la Motte
1777-1843 . . . . **NCLC 2**
See also DLB 90

Fourier, Charles 1772-1837 . . . . . . **NCLC 51**

Fournier, Henri Alban 1886-1914
See Alain-Fournier
See also CA 104

Fournier, Pierre 1916- . . . . **CLC 11**
See also Gascar, Pierre
See also CA 89-92; CANR 16, 40

Fowles, John
1926- . . . . . . **CLC 1, 2, 3, 4, 6, 9, 10, 15,
33, 87; DAB; DAC; DAM MST**
See also CA 5-8R; CANR 25; CDBLB 1960
to Present; DLB 14, 139; MTCW;
SATA 22

Fox, Paula 1923- . . . . **CLC 2, 8**
See also AAYA 3; CA 73-76; CANR 20,
36; CLR 1, 44; DLB 52; JRDA;
MAICYA; MTCW; SATA 17, 60

Fox, William Price (Jr.) 1926- . . . . . **CLC 22**
See also CA 17-20R; CAAS 19; CANR 11;
DLB 2; DLBY 81

Foxe, John 1516(?)-1587 . . . . **LC 14**

Frame, Janet
1924- . . . . **CLC 2, 3, 6, 22, 66, 96**
See also Clutha, Janet Paterson Frame

France, Anatole . . . . **TCLC 9**
See also Thibault, Jacques Anatole Francois
See also DLB 123

Francis, Claude 19(?)- . . . . **CLC 50**

Francis, Dick
1920- . . . . **CLC 2, 22, 42; DAM POP**
See also AAYA 5, 21; BEST 89:3; CA 5-8R;
CANR 9, 42; CDBLB 1960 to Present;
DLB 87; INT CANR-9; MTCW

Francis, Robert (Churchill)
1901-1987 . . . . **CLC 15**
See also CA 1-4R; 123; CANR 1

Frank, Anne(lies Marie)
1929-1945 . . . . **TCLC 17; DA; DAB;
DAC; DAM MST; WLC**
See also AAYA 12; CA 113; 133; MTCW;
SATA 87; SATA-Brief 42

Frank, Elizabeth 1945- . . . . **CLC 39**
See also CA 121; 126; INT 126

Frankl, Viktor E(mil) 1905- . . . . **CLC 93**
See also CA 65-68

Franklin, Benjamin
See Hasek, Jaroslav (Matej Frantisek)

Franklin, Benjamin
1706-1790 . . . . . **LC 25; DA; DAB; DAC;
DAM MST**
See also CDALB 1640-1865; DLB 24, 43,
73

Franklin, (Stella Maraia Sarah) Miles
1879-1954 . . . . **TCLC 7**
See also CA 104

Fraser, (Lady) Antonia (Pakenham)
1932- . . . . **CLC 32**
See also CA 85-88; CANR 44; MTCW;
SATA-Brief 32

Fraser, George MacDonald 1925- . . . . **CLC 7**
See also CA 45-48; CANR 2, 48

Fraser, Sylvia 1935- . . . . **CLC 64**
See also CA 45-48; CANR 1, 16

Frayn, Michael
1933- . . . . **CLC 3, 7, 31, 47;
DAM DRAM, NOV**
See also CA 5-8R; CANR 30; DLB 13, 14;
MTCW

Fraze, Candida (Merrill) 1945- . . . . . **CLC 50**
See also CA 126

Frazer, J(ames) G(eorge)
1854-1941 . . . . **TCLC 32**
See also CA 118

Frazer, Robert Caine
See Creasey, John

Frazer, Sir James George
See Frazer, J(ames) G(eorge)

Frazier, Ian 1951- . . . . **CLC 46**
See also CA 130; CANR 54

Frederic, Harold 1856-1898 . . . . . . **NCLC 10**
See also DLB 12, 23; DLBD 13

Frederick, John
See Faust, Frederick (Schiller)

Frederick the Great 1712-1786 . . . . . . **LC 14**

Fredro, Aleksander 1793-1876..... NCLC 8

Freeling, Nicolas 1927- .... CLC 38
See also CA 49-52; CAAS 12; CANR 1, 17,
50; DLB 87

Freeman, Douglas Southall
1886-1953 .... TCLC 11
See also CA 109; DLB 17

Freeman, Judith 1946-............ CLC 55
See also CA 148

Freeman, Mary Eleanor Wilkins
1852-1930 .... TCLC 9; SSC 1
See also CA 106; DLB 12, 78

Freeman, R(ichard) Austin
1862-1943 .... TCLC 21
See also CA 113; DLB 70

French, Albert 1943- .... CLC 86

French, Marilyn
1929- .... CLC 10, 18, 60;
DAM DRAM, NOV, POP
See also CA 69-72; CANR 3, 31;
INT CANR-31; MTCW

French, Paul
See Asimov, Isaac

Freneau, Philip Morin 1752-1832.. NCLC 1
See also DLB 37, 43

Freud, Sigmund 1856-1939 .... TCLC 52
See also CA 115; 133; MTCW

Friedan, Betty (Naomi) 1921-...... CLC 74
See also CA 65-68; CANR 18, 45; MTCW

Friedlander, Saul 1932-........... CLC 90
See also CA 117; 130

Friedman, B(ernard) H(arper)
1926-........................ CLC 7
See also CA 1-4R; CANR 3, 48

Friedman, Bruce Jay 1930-.... CLC 3, 5, 56
See also CA 9-12R; CANR 25, 52; DLB 2,
28; INT CANR-25

Friel, Brian 1929-........... CLC 5, 42, 59
See also CA 21-24R; CANR 33; DLB 13;
MTCW

Friis-Baastad, Babbis Ellinor
1921-1970 .... CLC 12
See also CA 17-20R; 134; SATA 7

Frisch, Max (Rudolf)
1911-1991 ..... CLC 3, 9, 14, 18, 32, 44;
DAM DRAM, NOV
See also CA 85-88; 134; CANR 32;
DLB 69, 124; MTCW

Fromentin, Eugene (Samuel Auguste)
1820-1876 .... NCLC 10
See also DLB 123

Frost, Frederick
See Faust, Frederick (Schiller)

Frost, Robert (Lee)
1874-1963 .... CLC 1, 3, 4, 9, 10, 13, 15,
26, 34, 44; DA; DAB; DAC; DAM MST,
POET; PC 1; WLC
See also AAYA 21; CA 89-92; CANR 33;
CDALB 1917-1929; DLB 54; DLBD 7;
MTCW; SATA 14

Froude, James Anthony
1818-1894 .... NCLC 43
See also DLB 18, 57, 144

Froy, Herald
See Waterhouse, Keith (Spencer)

Fry, Christopher
1907- ..... CLC 2, 10, 14; DAM DRAM
See also CA 17-20R; CAAS 23; CANR 9,
30; DLB 13; MTCW; SATA 66

Frye, (Herman) Northrop
1912-1991 .... CLC 24, 70
See also CA 5-8R; 133; CANR 8, 37;
DLB 67, 68; MTCW

Fuchs, Daniel 1909-1993 .... CLC 8, 22
See also CA 81-84; 142; CAAS 5;
CANR 40; DLB 9, 26, 28; DLBY 93

Fuchs, Daniel 1934- .... CLC 34
See also CA 37-40R; CANR 14, 48

Fuentes, Carlos
1928- ...... CLC 3, 8, 10, 13, 22, 41, 60;
DA; DAB; DAC; DAM MST, MULT,
NOV; HLC; SSC 24; WLC
See also AAYA 4; AITN 2; CA 69-72;
CANR 10, 32; DLB 113; HW; MTCW

Fuentes, Gregorio Lopez y
See Lopez y Fuentes, Gregorio

Fugard, (Harold) Athol
1932- .... CLC 5, 9, 14, 25, 40, 80;
DAM DRAM; DC 3
See also AAYA 17; CA 85-88; CANR 32,
54; MTCW

Fugard, Sheila 1932- .... CLC 48
See also CA 125

Fuller, Charles (H., Jr.)
1939- .... CLC 25; BLC; DAM DRAM,
MULT; DC 1
See also BW 2; CA 108; 112; DLB 38;
INT 112; MTCW

Fuller, John (Leopold) 1937-....... CLC 62
See also CA 21-24R; CANR 9, 44; DLB 40

Fuller, Margaret .... NCLC 5, 50
See also Ossoli, Sarah Margaret (Fuller
marchesa d')

Fuller, Roy (Broadbent)
1912-1991 .... CLC 4, 28
See also CA 5-8R; 135; CAAS 10;
CANR 53; DLB 15, 20; SATA 87

Fulton, Alice 1952-............... CLC 52
See also CA 116; CANR 57

Furphy, Joseph 1843-1912........ TCLC 25

Fussell, Paul 1924-............... CLC 74
See also BEST 90:1; CA 17-20R; CANR 8,
21, 35; INT CANR-21; MTCW

Futabatei, Shimei 1864-1909 ..... TCLC 44

Futrelle, Jacques 1875-1912 ...... TCLC 19
See also CA 113; 155

Gaboriau, Emile 1835-1873 ...... NCLC 14

Gadda, Carlo Emilio 1893-1973 .... CLC 11
See also CA 89-92; DLB 177

Gaddis, William
1922- ..... CLC 1, 3, 6, 8, 10, 19, 43, 86
See also CA 17-20R; CANR 21, 48; DLB 2;
MTCW

Gage, Walter
See Inge, William (Motter)

Gaines, Ernest J(ames)
1933- .... CLC 3, 11, 18, 86; BLC;
DAM MULT
See also AAYA 18; AITN 1; BW 2;
CA 9-12R; CANR 6, 24, 42;
CDALB 1968-1988; DLB 2, 33, 152;
DLBY 80; MTCW; SATA 86

Gaitskill, Mary 1954-............. CLC 69
See also CA 128

Galdos, Benito Perez
See Perez Galdos, Benito

Gale, Zona
1874-1938 ...... TCLC 7; DAM DRAM
See also CA 105; 153; DLB 9, 78

Galeano, Eduardo (Hughes) 1940-... CLC 72
See also CA 29-32R; CANR 13, 32; HW

Galiano, Juan Valera y Alcala
See Valera y Alcala-Galiano, Juan

Gallagher, Tess
1943- .. CLC 18, 63; DAM POET; PC 9
See also CA 106; DLB 120

Gallant, Mavis
1922- .... CLC 7, 18, 38; DAC;
DAM MST; SSC 5
See also CA 69-72; CANR 29; DLB 53;
MTCW

Gallant, Roy A(rthur) 1924- .... CLC 17
See also CA 5-8R; CANR 4, 29, 54;
CLR 30; MAICYA; SATA 4, 68

Gallico, Paul (William) 1897-1976 ... CLC 2
See also AITN 1; CA 5-8R; 69-72;
CANR 23; DLB 9, 171; MAICYA;
SATA 13

Gallo, Max Louis 1932-........... CLC 95
See also CA 85-88

Gallois, Lucien
See Desnos, Robert

Gallup, Ralph
See Whitemore, Hugh (John)

Galsworthy, John
1867-1933 ...... TCLC 1, 45; DA; DAB;
DAC; DAM DRAM, MST, NOV;
SSC 22; WLC 2
See also CA 104; 141; CDBLB 1890-1914;
DLB 10, 34, 98, 162

Galt, John 1779-1839............ NCLC 1
See also DLB 99, 116, 159

Galvin, James 1951-.............. CLC 38
See also CA 108; CANR 26

Gamboa, Federico 1864-1939...... TCLC 36

Gandhi, M. K.
See Gandhi, Mohandas Karamchand

Gandhi, Mahatma
See Gandhi, Mohandas Karamchand

Gandhi, Mohandas Karamchand
1869-1948 ..... TCLC 59; DAM MULT
See also CA 121; 132; MTCW

Gann, Ernest Kellogg 1910-1991.... CLC 23
See also AITN 1; CA 1-4R; 136; CANR 1

Garcia, Cristina 1958- .... CLC 76
See also CA 141

Gide, Andre (Paul Guillaume)
1869-1951 .... TCLC 5, 12, 36; DA;
DAB; DAC; DAM MST, NOV; SSC 13;
WLC
See also CA 104; 124; DLB 65; MTCW

Gifford, Barry (Colby) 1946-....... CLC 34
See also CA 65-68; CANR 9, 30, 40

Gilbert, W(illiam) S(chwenck)
1836-1911 ..... TCLC 3; DAM DRAM,
POET
See also CA 104; SATA 36

Gilbreth, Frank B., Jr. 1911-....... CLC 17
See also CA 9-12R; SATA 2

Gilchrist, Ellen
1935- .... CLC 34, 48; DAM POP;
SSC 14
See also CA 113; 116; CANR 41; DLB 130;
MTCW

Giles, Molly 1942- .... CLC 39
See also CA 126

Gill, Patrick
See Creasey, John

Gilliam, Terry (Vance) 1940-....... CLC 21
See also Monty Python
See also AAYA 19; CA 108; 113;
CANR 35; INT 113

Gillian, Jerry
See Gilliam, Terry (Vance)

Gilliatt, Penelope (Ann Douglass)
1932-1993 .... CLC 2, 10, 13, 53
See also AITN 2; CA 13-16R; 141;
CANR 49; DLB 14

Gilman, Charlotte (Anna) Perkins (Stetson)
1860-1935 .... TCLC 9, 37; SSC 13
See also CA 106; 150

Gilmour, David 1949-............ CLC 35
See also CA 138, 147

Gilpin, William 1724-1804....... NCLC 30

Gilray, J. D.
See Mencken, H(enry) L(ouis)

Gilroy, Frank D(aniel) 1925-........ CLC 2
See also CA 81-84; CANR 32; DLB 7

Gilstrap, John 1957(?)-............ CLC 99

Ginsberg, Allen
1926- ...... CLC 1, 2, 3, 4, 6, 13, 36, 69;
DA; DAB; DAC; DAM MST, POET;
PC 4; WLC 3
See also AITN 1; CA 1-4R; CANR 2, 41;
CDALB 1941-1968; DLB 5, 16, 169;
MTCW

Ginzburg, Natalia
1916-1991 .... CLC 5, 11, 54, 70
See also CA 85-88; 135; CANR 33;
DLB 177; MTCW

Giono, Jean 1895-1970......... CLC 4, 11
See also CA 45-48; 29-32R; CANR 2, 35;
DLB 72; MTCW

Giovanni, Nikki
1943- ...... CLC 2, 4, 19, 64; BLC; DA;
DAB; DAC; DAM MST, MULT, POET
See also AITN 1; BW 2; CA 29-32R;
CAAS 6; CANR 18, 41; CLR 6; DLB 5,
41; INT CANR-18; MAICYA; MTCW;
SATA 24

Giovene, Andrea 1904-............. CLC 7
See also CA 85-88

Gippius, Zinaida (Nikolayevna) 1869-1945
See Hippius, Zinaida
See also CA 106

Giraudoux, (Hippolyte) Jean
1882-1944 .... TCLC 2, 7; DAM DRAM
See also CA 104; DLB 65

Gironella, Jose Maria 1917-....... CLC 11
See also CA 101

Gissing, George (Robert)
1857-1903 .... TCLC 3, 24, 47
See also CA 105; DLB 18, 135

Giurlani, Aldo
See Palazzeschi, Aldo

Gladkov, Fyodor (Vasilyevich)
1883-1958 .... TCLC 27

Glanville, Brian (Lester) 1931-...... CLC 6
See also CA 5-8R; CAAS 9; CANR 3;
DLB 15, 139; SATA 42

Glasgow, Ellen (Anderson Gholson)
1873(?)-1945 .... TCLC 2, 7
See also CA 104; DLB 9, 12

Glaspell, Susan 1882(?)-1948...... TCLC 55
See also CA 110; 154; DLB 7, 9, 78;
YABC 2

Glassco, John 1909-1981 .... CLC 9
See also CA 13-16R; 102; CANR 15;
DLB 68

Glasscock, Amnesia
See Steinbeck, John (Ernst)

Glasser, Ronald J. 1940(?)-........ CLC 37

Glassman, Joyce
See Johnson, Joyce

Glendinning, Victoria 1937-........ CLC 50
See also CA 120; 127; DLB 155

Glissant, Edouard
1928- .... CLC 10, 68; DAM MULT
See also CA 153

Gloag, Julian 1930- .... CLC 40
See also AITN 1; CA 65-68; CANR 10

Glowacki, Aleksander
See Prus, Boleslaw

Gluck, Louise (Elisabeth)
1943- .... CLC 7, 22, 44, 81;
DAM POET; PC 16
See also CA 33-36R; CANR 40; DLB 5

Gobineau, Joseph Arthur (Comte) de
1816-1882 .... NCLC 17
See also DLB 123

Godard, Jean-Luc 1930-........... CLC 20
See also CA 93-96

Godden, (Margaret) Rumer 1907-... CLC 53
See also AAYA 6; CA 5-8R; CANR 4, 27,
36, 55; CLR 20; DLB 161; MAICYA;
SAAS 12; SATA 3, 36

Godoy Alcayaga, Lucila 1889-1957
See Mistral, Gabriela
See also BW 2; CA 104; 131; DAM MULT;
HW; MTCW

Godwin, Gail (Kathleen)
1937- .... CLC 5, 8, 22, 31, 69;
DAM POP
See also CA 29-32R; CANR 15, 43; DLB 6;
INT CANR-15; MTCW

Godwin, William 1756-1836...... NCLC 14
See also CDBLB 1789-1832; DLB 39, 104,
142, 158, 163

Goebbels, Josef
See Goebbels, (Paul) Joseph

Goebbels, (Paul) Joseph
1897-1945 .... TCLC 68
See also CA 115; 148

Goebbels, Joseph Paul
See Goebbels, (Paul) Joseph

Goethe, Johann Wolfgang von
1749-1832 .... NCLC 4, 22, 34; DA;
DAB; DAC; DAM DRAM, MST,
POET; PC 5; WLC 3
See also DLB 94

Gogarty, Oliver St. John
1878-1957 .... TCLC 15
See also CA 109; 150; DLB 15, 19

Gogol, Nikolai (Vasilyevich)
1809-1852 .... NCLC 5, 15, 31; DA;
DAB; DAC; DAM DRAM, MST; DC 1;
SSC 4; WLC
See also AITN 1; BW 1; CA 124; 114;
DLB 33

Goines, Donald
1937(?)-1974 .... CLC 80; BLC;
DAM MULT, POP
See also AITN 1; BW 1; CA 124; 114;
DLB 33

Gold, Herbert 1924-....... CLC 4, 7, 14, 42
See also CA 9-12R; CANR 17, 45; DLB 2;
DLBY 81

Goldbarth, Albert 1948-......... CLC 5, 38
See also CA 53-56; CANR 6, 40; DLB 120

Goldberg, Anatol 1910-1982 .... CLC 34
See also CA 131; 117

Goldemberg, Isaac 1945-.......... CLC 52
See also CA 69-72; CAAS 12; CANR 11,
32; HW

Golding, William (Gerald)
1911-1993 .... CLC 1, 2, 3, 8, 10, 17, 27,
58, 81; DA; DAB; DAC; DAM MST,
NOV; WLC
See also AAYA 5; CA 5-8R; 141;
CANR 13, 33, 54; CDBLB 1945-1960;
DLB 15, 100; MTCW

Goldman, Emma 1869-1940...... TCLC 13
See also CA 110; 150

Goldman, Francisco 1955-......... CLC 76

Goldman, William (W.) 1931-.... CLC 1, 48
See also CA 9-12R; CANR 29; DLB 44

Goldmann, Lucien 1913-1970 ...... CLC 24
See also CA 25-28; CAP 2

Goldoni, Carlo
1707-1793 .... LC 4; DAM DRAM

Goldsberry, Steven 1949-.......... CLC 34
See also CA 131

Goldsmith, Oliver
1728-1774 ...... LC 2; DA; DAB; DAC;
DAM DRAM, MST, NOV, POET;
WLC
See also CDBLB 1660-1789; DLB 39, 89,
104, 109, 142; SATA 26

Goldsmith, Peter
See Priestley, J(ohn) B(oynton)

Green, Julian (Hartridge) 1900-
   See Green, Julien
   See also CA 21-24R; CANR 33; DLB 4, 72;
   MTCW

Green, Julien .... CLC 3, 11, 77
   See also Green, Julian (Hartridge)

Green, Paul (Eliot)
   1894-1981 ...... CLC 25; DAM DRAM
   See also AITN 1; CA 5-8R; 103; CANR 3;
   DLB 7, 9; DLBY 81

Greenberg, Ivan 1908-1973
   See Rahv, Philip
   See also CA 85-88

Greenberg, Joanne (Goldenberg)
   1932- .... CLC 7, 30
   See also AAYA 12; CA 5-8R; CANR 14,
   32; SATA 25

Greenberg, Richard 1959(?)- .... CLC 57
   See also CA 138

Greene, Bette 1934- .... CLC 30
   See also AAYA 7; CA 53-56; CANR 4;
   CLR 2; JRDA; MAICYA; SAAS 16;
   SATA 8

Greene, Gael .... CLC 8
   See also CA 13-16R; CANR 10

Greene, Graham
   1904-1991 .... CLC 1, 3, 6, 9, 14, 18, 27,
     37, 70, 72; DA; DAB; DAC; DAM MST,
     NOV; WLC
   See also AITN 2; CA 13-16R; 133;
   CANR 35; CDBLB 1945-1960; DLB 13,
   15, 77, 100, 162; DLBY 91; MTCW;
   SATA 20

Greer, Richard
   See Silverberg, Robert

Gregor, Arthur 1923- .... CLC 9
   See also CA 25-28R; CAAS 10; CANR 11;
   SATA 36

Gregor, Lee
   See Pohl, Frederik

Gregory, Isabella Augusta (Persse)
   1852-1932 .... TCLC 1
   See also CA 104; DLB 10

Gregory, J. Dennis
   See Williams, John A(lfred)

Grendon, Stephen
   See Derleth, August (William)

Grenville, Kate 1950- .... CLC 61
   See also CA 118; CANR 53

Grenville, Pelham
   See Wodehouse, P(elham) G(renville)

Greve, Felix Paul (Berthold Friedrich)
   1879-1948
   See Grove, Frederick Philip
   See also CA 104; 141; DAC; DAM MST

Grey, Zane
   1872-1939 .... TCLC 6; DAM POP
   See also CA 104; 132; DLB 9; MTCW

Grieg, (Johan) Nordahl (Brun)
   1902-1943 .... TCLC 10
   See also CA 107

Grieve, C(hristopher) M(urray)
   1892-1978 .... CLC 11, 19; DAM POET
   See also MacDiarmid, Hugh; Pteleon
   See also CA 5-8R; 85-88; CANR 33;
   MTCW

Griffin, Gerald 1803-1840 .... NCLC 7
   See also DLB 159

Griffin, John Howard 1920-1980.... CLC 68
   See also AITN 1; CA 1-4R; 101; CANR 2

Griffin, Peter 1942- .... CLC 39
   See also CA 136

Griffith, D(avid Lewelyn) W(ark)
   1875(?)-1948 .... TCLC 68
   See also CA 119; 150

Griffith, Lawrence
   See Griffith, D(avid Lewelyn) W(ark)

Griffiths, Trevor 1935- .... CLC 13, 52
   See also CA 97-100; CANR 45; DLB 13

Grigson, Geoffrey (Edward Harvey)
   1905-1985 .... CLC 7, 39
   See also CA 25-28R; 118; CANR 20, 33;
   DLB 27; MTCW

Grillparzer, Franz 1791-1872...... NCLC 1
   See also DLB 133

Grimble, Reverend Charles James
   See Eliot, T(homas) S(tearns)

Grimke, Charlotte L(ottie) Forten
   1837(?)-1914
   See Forten, Charlotte L.
   See also BW 1; CA 117; 124; DAM MULT,
   POET

Grimm, Jacob Ludwig Karl
   1785-1863 .... NCLC 3
   See also DLB 90; MAICYA; SATA 22

Grimm, Wilhelm Karl 1786-1859 .. NCLC 3
   See also DLB 90; MAICYA; SATA 22

Grimmelshausen, Johann Jakob Christoffel
   von 1621-1676 .... LC 6
   See also DLB 168

Grindel, Eugene 1895-1952
   See Eluard, Paul
   See also CA 104

Grisham, John 1955- .. CLC 84; DAM POP
   See also AAYA 14; CA 138; CANR 47

Grossman, David 1954- .... CLC 67
   See also CA 138

Grossman, Vasily (Semenovich)
   1905-1964 .... CLC 41
   See also CA 124; 130; MTCW

Grove, Frederick Philip .... TCLC 4
   See also Greve, Felix Paul (Berthold
   Friedrich)
   See also DLB 92

Grubb
   See Crumb, R(obert)

Grumbach, Doris (Isaac)
   1918- .... CLC 13, 22, 64
   See also CA 5-8R; CAAS 2; CANR 9, 42;
   INT CANR-9

Grundtvig, Nicolai Frederik Severin
   1783-1872 .... NCLC 1

Grunge
   See Crumb, R(obert)

Grunwald, Lisa 1959- .... CLC 44
   See also CA 120

Guare, John
   1938- .... CLC 8, 14, 29, 67;
     DAM DRAM
   See also CA 73-76; CANR 21; DLB 7;
   MTCW

Gudjonsson, Halldor Kiljan 1902-
   See Laxness, Halldor
   See also CA 103

Guenter, Erich
   See Eich, Guenter

Guest, Barbara 1920- .... CLC 34
   See also CA 25-28R; CANR 11, 44; DLB 5

Guest, Judith (Ann)
   1936- .... CLC 8, 30; DAM NOV, POP
   See also AAYA 7; CA 77-80; CANR 15;
   INT CANR-15; MTCW

Guevara, Che .... CLC 87; HLC
   See also Guevara (Serna), Ernesto

Guevara (Serna), Ernesto 1928-1967
   See Guevara, Che
   See also CA 127; 111; CANR 56;
   DAM MULT; HW

Guild, Nicholas M. 1944-......... CLC 33
   See also CA 93-96

Guillemin, Jacques
   See Sartre, Jean-Paul

Guillen, Jorge
   1893-1984 ...... CLC 11; DAM MULT,
     POET
   See also CA 89-92; 112; DLB 108; HW

Guillen, Nicolas (Cristobal)
   1902-1989 .... CLC 48, 79; BLC;
     DAM MST, MULT, POET; HLC
   See also BW 2; CA 116; 125; 129; HW

Guillevic, (Eugene) 1907-......... CLC 33
   See also CA 93-96

Guillois
   See Desnos, Robert

Guillois, Valentin
   See Desnos, Robert

Guiney, Louise Imogen
   1861-1920 .... TCLC 41
   See also DLB 54

Guiraldes, Ricardo (Guillermo)
   1886-1927 .... TCLC 39
   See also CA 131; HW; MTCW

Gumilev, Nikolai Stephanovich
   1886-1921 .... TCLC 60

Gunesekera, Romesh............... CLC 91

Gunn, Bill .... CLC 5
   See also Gunn, William Harrison
   See also DLB 38

Gunn, Thom(son William)
   1929- .... CLC 3, 6, 18, 32, 81;
     DAM POET
   See also CA 17-20R; CANR 9, 33;
   CDBLB 1960 to Present; DLB 27;
   INT CANR-33; MTCW

Gunn, William Harrison 1934(?)-1989
   See Gunn, Bill
   See also AITN 1; BW 1; CA 13-16R; 128;
   CANR 12, 25

Gunnars, Kristjana 1948-......... CLC 69
   See also CA 113; DLB 60

Gurganus, Allan
   1947- .... CLC 70; DAM POP
   See also BEST 90:1; CA 135

Gurney, A(lbert) R(amsdell), Jr.
   1930- .... CLC 32, 50, 54; DAM DRAM
   See also CA 77-80; CANR 32

Harling, Robert   1951(?)- .... **CLC 53**
See also CA 147

Harmon, William (Ruth)   1938- ..... **CLC 38**
See also CA 33-36R; CANR 14, 32, 35;
SATA 65

Harper, F. E. W.
See Harper, Frances Ellen Watkins

Harper, Frances E. W.
See Harper, Frances Ellen Watkins

Harper, Frances E. Watkins
See Harper, Frances Ellen Watkins

Harper, Frances Ellen
See Harper, Frances Ellen Watkins

Harper, Frances Ellen Watkins
1825-1911 .... **TCLC 14; BLC;**
DAM MULT, POET
See also BW 1; CA 111; 125; DLB 50

Harper, Michael S(teven)   1938- .. **CLC 7, 22**
See also BW 1; CA 33-36R; CANR 24;
DLB 41

Harper, Mrs. F. E. W.
See Harper, Frances Ellen Watkins

Harris, Christie (Lucy) Irwin
1907- .... **CLC 12**
See also CA 5-8R; CANR 6; DLB 88;
JRDA; MAICYA; SAAS 10; SATA 6, 74

Harris, Frank   1856-1931 .... **TCLC 24**
See also CA 109; 150; DLB 156

Harris, George Washington
1814-1869 .... **NCLC 23**
See also DLB 3, 11

Harris, Joel Chandler
1848-1908 .... **TCLC 2; SSC 19**
See also CA 104; 137; DLB 11, 23, 42, 78,
91; MAICYA; YABC 1

Harris, John (Wyndham Parkes Lucas)
Beynon   1903-1969
See Wyndham, John
See also CA 102; 89-92

Harris, MacDonald .... **CLC 9**
See also Heiney, Donald (William)

Harris, Mark   1922- .... **CLC 19**
See also CA 5-8R; CAAS 3; CANR 2, 55;
DLB 2; DLBY 80

Harris, (Theodore) Wilson   1921- .... **CLC 25**
See also BW 2; CA 65-68; CAAS 16;
CANR 11, 27; DLB 117; MTCW

Harrison, Elizabeth Cavanna   1909-
See Cavanna, Betty
See also CA 9-12R; CANR 6, 27

Harrison, Harry (Max)   1925- ...... **CLC 42**
See also CA 1-4R; CANR 5, 21; DLB 8;
SATA 4

Harrison, James (Thomas)
1937- .... **CLC 6, 14, 33, 66; SSC 19**
See also CA 13-16R; CANR 8, 51;
DLBY 82; INT CANR-8

Harrison, Jim
See Harrison, James (Thomas)

Harrison, Kathryn   1961- .... **CLC 70**
See also CA 144

Harrison, Tony   1937- .... **CLC 43**
See also CA 65-68; CANR 44; DLB 40;
MTCW

Harriss, Will(ard Irvin)   1922- ...... **CLC 34**
See also CA 111

Harson, Sley
See Ellison, Harlan (Jay)

Hart, Ellis
See Ellison, Harlan (Jay)

Hart, Josephine
1942(?)- .... **CLC 70; DAM POP**
See also CA 138

Hart, Moss
1904-1961 ...... **CLC 66; DAM DRAM**
See also CA 109; 89-92; DLB 7

Harte, (Francis) Bret(t)
1836(?)-1902 .... **TCLC 1, 25; DA; DAC;**
DAM MST; SSC 8; WLC
See also CA 104; 140; CDALB 1865-1917;
DLB 12, 64, 74, 79; SATA 26

Hartley, L(eslie) P(oles)
1895-1972 .... **CLC 2, 22**
See also CA 45-48; 37-40R; CANR 33;
DLB 15, 139; MTCW

Hartman, Geoffrey H.   1929- .... **CLC 27**
See also CA 117; 125; DLB 67

Hartmann von Aue
c. 1160-c. 1205 .... **CMLC 15**
See also DLB 138

Hartmann von Aue   1170-1210.... **CMLC 15**

Haruf, Kent   1943- .... **CLC 34**
See also CA 149

Harwood, Ronald
1934- .... **CLC 32; DAM DRAM, MST**
See also CA 1-4R; CANR 4, 55; DLB 13

Hasek, Jaroslav (Matej Frantisek)
1883-1923 .... **TCLC 4**
See also CA 104; 129; MTCW

Hass, Robert
1941- .... **CLC 18, 39, 99; PC 16**
See also CA 111; CANR 30, 50; DLB 105

Hastings, Hudson
See Kuttner, Henry

Hastings, Selina. .... **CLC 44**

Hathorne, John   1641-1717......... **LC 38**

Hatteras, Amelia
See Mencken, H(enry) L(ouis)

Hatteras, Owen .... **TCLC 18**
See also Mencken, H(enry) L(ouis); Nathan,
George Jean

Hauptmann, Gerhart (Johann Robert)
1862-1946 ...... **TCLC 4; DAM DRAM**
See also CA 104; 153; DLB 66, 118

Havel, Vaclav
1936- .... **CLC 25, 58, 65;**
DAM DRAM; DC 6
See also CA 104; CANR 36; MTCW

Haviaras, Stratis .... **CLC 33**
See also Chaviaras, Strates

Hawes, Stephen   1475(?)-1523(?) ..... **LC 17**

Hawkes, John (Clendennin Burne, Jr.)
1925- ...... **CLC 1, 2, 3, 4, 7, 9, 14, 15,**
27, 49
See also CA 1-4R; CANR 2, 47; DLB 2, 7;
DLBY 80; MTCW

Hawking, S. W.
See Hawking, Stephen W(illiam)

Hawking, Stephen W(illiam)
1942- .... **CLC 63**
See also AAYA 13; BEST 89:1; CA 126;
129; CANR 48

Hawthorne, Julian   1846-1934 ..... **TCLC 25**

Hawthorne, Nathaniel
1804-1864 .... **NCLC 39; DA; DAB;**
DAC; DAM MST, NOV; SSC 3; WLC
See also AAYA 18; CDALB 1640-1865;
DLB 1, 74; YABC 2

Haxton, Josephine Ayres   1921-
See Douglas, Ellen
See also CA 115; CANR 41

Hayaseca y Eizaguirre, Jorge
See Echegaray (y Eizaguirre), Jose (Maria
Waldo)

Hayashi Fumiko   1904-1951...... **TCLC 27**

Haycraft, Anna
See Ellis, Alice Thomas
See also CA 122

Hayden, Robert E(arl)
1913-1980 ...... **CLC 5, 9, 14, 37; BLC;**
DA; DAC; DAM MST, MULT, POET;
PC 6
See also BW 1; CA 69-72; 97-100; CABS 2;
CANR 24; CDALB 1941-1968; DLB 5,
76; MTCW; SATA 19; SATA-Obit 26

Hayford, J(oseph) E(phraim) Casely
See Casely-Hayford, J(oseph) E(phraim)

Hayman, Ronald   1932-........... **CLC 44**
See also CA 25-28R; CANR 18, 50;
DLB 155

Haywood, Eliza (Fowler)
1693(?)-1756 .... **LC 1**

Hazlitt, William   1778-1830 ...... **NCLC 29**
See also DLB 110, 158

Hazzard, Shirley   1931- .... **CLC 18**
See also CA 9-12R; CANR 4; DLBY 82;
MTCW

Head, Bessie
1937-1986 .... **CLC 25, 67; BLC;**
DAM MULT
See also BW 2; CA 29-32R; 119; CANR 25;
DLB 117; MTCW

Headon, (Nicky) Topper   1956(?)- ... **CLC 30**

Heaney, Seamus (Justin)
1939- ...... **CLC 5, 7, 14, 25, 37, 74, 91;**
DAB; DAM POET
See also CA 85-88; CANR 25, 48;
CDBLB 1960 to Present; DLB 40;
DLBY 95; MTCW

Hearn, (Patricio) Lafcadio (Tessima Carlos)
1850-1904 .... **TCLC 9**
See also CA 105; DLB 12, 78

Hearne, Vicki   1946- .... **CLC 56**
See also CA 139

Hearon, Shelby   1931-............. **CLC 63**
See also AITN 2; CA 25-28R; CANR 18,
48

Heat-Moon, William Least.......... **CLC 29**
See also Trogdon, William (Lewis)
See also AAYA 9

Hebbel, Friedrich
1813-1863 .... **NCLC 43; DAM DRAM**
See also DLB 129

Hebert, Anne
1916- .... CLC 4, 13, 29; DAC;
DAM MST, POET
See also CA 85-88; DLB 68; MTCW

Hecht, Anthony (Evan)
1923- ...... CLC 8, 13, 19; DAM POET
See also CA 9-12R; CANR 6; DLB 5, 169

Hecht, Ben 1894-1964 .... CLC 8
See also CA 85-88; DLB 7, 9, 25, 26, 28, 86

Hedayat, Sadeq 1903-1951........ TCLC 21
See also CA 120

Hegel, Georg Wilhelm Friedrich
1770-1831 .... NCLC 46
See also DLB 90

Heidegger, Martin 1889-1976 ...... CLC 24
See also CA 81-84; 65-68; CANR 34;
MTCW

Heidenstam, (Carl Gustaf) Verner von
1859-1940 .... TCLC 5
See also CA 104

Heifner, Jack 1946- .... CLC 11
See also CA 105; CANR 47

Heijermans, Herman 1864-1924 ... TCLC 24
See also CA 123

Heilbrun, Carolyn G(old) 1926-..... CLC 25
See also CA 45-48; CANR 1, 28

Heine, Heinrich 1797-1856 .... NCLC 4, 54
See also DLB 90

Heinemann, Larry (Curtiss) 1944- .. CLC 50
See also CA 110; CAAS 21; CANR 31;
DLBD 9; INT CANR-31

Heiney, Donald (William) 1921-1993
See Harris, MacDonald
See also CA 1-4R; 142; CANR 3

Heinlein, Robert A(nson)
1907-1988 ...... CLC 1, 3, 8, 14, 26, 55;
DAM POP
See also AAYA 17; CA 1-4R; 125;
CANR 1, 20, 53; DLB 8; JRDA;
MAICYA; MTCW; SATA 9, 69;
SATA-Obit 56

Helforth, John
See Doolittle, Hilda

Hellenhofferu, Vojtech Kapristian z
See Hasek, Jaroslav (Matej Frantisek)

Heller, Joseph
1923- .... CLC 1, 3, 5, 8, 11, 36, 63; DA;
DAB; DAC; DAM MST, NOV, POP;
WLC
See also AITN 1; CA 5-8R; CABS 1;
CANR 8, 42; DLB 2, 28; DLBY 80;
INT CANR-8; MTCW

Hellman, Lillian (Florence)
1906-1984 ...... CLC 2, 4, 8, 14, 18, 34,
44, 52; DAM DRAM; DC 1
See also AITN 1, 2; CA 13-16R; 112;
CANR 33; DLB 7; DLBY 84; MTCW

Helprin, Mark
1947- .... CLC 7, 10, 22, 32;
DAM NOV, POP
See also CA 81-84; CANR 47; DLBY 85;
MTCW

Helvetius, Claude-Adrien
1715-1771 .... LC 26

Helyar, Jane Penelope Josephine 1933-
See Poole, Josephine
See also CA 21-24R; CANR 10, 26;
SATA 82

Hemans, Felicia 1793-1835 ...... NCLC 29
See also DLB 96

Hemingway, Ernest (Miller)
1899-1961 .... CLC 1, 3, 6, 8, 10, 13, 19,
30, 34, 39, 41, 44, 50, 61, 80; DA; DAB;
DAC; DAM MST, NOV; SSC 25; WLC
See also AAYA 19; CA 77-80; CANR 34;
CDALB 1917-1929; DLB 4, 9, 102;
DLBD 1; DLBY 81, 87; MTCW

Hempel, Amy 1951- .... CLC 39
See also CA 118; 137

Henderson, F. C.
See Mencken, H(enry) L(ouis)

Henderson, Sylvia
See Ashton-Warner, Sylvia (Constance)

Henley, Beth .... CLC 23; DC 6
See also Henley, Elizabeth Becker
See also CABS 3; DLBY 86

Henley, Elizabeth Becker 1952-
See Henley, Beth
See also CA 107; CANR 32; DAM DRAM,
MST; MTCW

Henley, William Ernest
1849-1903 .... TCLC 8
See also CA 105; DLB 19

Hennissart, Martha
See Lathen, Emma
See also CA 85-88

Henry, O......... TCLC 1, 19; SSC 5; WLC
See also Porter, William Sydney

Henry, Patrick 1736-1799 .... LC 25

Henryson, Robert 1430(?)-1506(?).... LC 20
See also DLB 146

Henry VIII 1491-1547............. LC 10

Henschke, Alfred
See Klabund

Hentoff, Nat(han Irving) 1925- ..... CLC 26
See also AAYA 4; CA 1-4R; CAAS 6;
CANR 5, 25; CLR 1; INT CANR-25;
JRDA; MAICYA; SATA 42, 69;
SATA-Brief 27

Heppenstall, (John) Rayner
1911-1981 .... CLC 10
See also CA 1-4R; 103; CANR 29

Heraclitus
c. 540B.C.-c. 450B.C......... CMLC 22
See also DLB 176

Herbert, Frank (Patrick)
1920-1986 ...... CLC 12, 23, 35, 44, 85;
DAM POP
See also AAYA 21; CA 53-56; 118;
CANR 5, 43; DLB 8; INT CANR-5;
MTCW; SATA 9, 37; SATA-Obit 47

Herbert, George
1593-1633 .... LC 24; DAB;
DAM POET; PC 4
See also CDBLB Before 1660; DLB 126

Herbert, Zbigniew
1924- .... CLC 9, 43; DAM POET
See also CA 89-92; CANR 36; MTCW

Herbst, Josephine (Frey)
1897-1969 .... CLC 34
See also CA 5-8R; 25-28R; DLB 9

Hergesheimer, Joseph
1880-1954 .... TCLC 11
See also CA 109; DLB 102, 9

Herlihy, James Leo 1927-1993 ...... CLC 6
See also CA 1-4R; 143; CANR 2

Hermogenes fl. c. 175- .... CMLC 6

Hernandez, Jose 1834-1886...... NCLC 17

Herodotus c. 484B.C.-429B.C..... CMLC 17
See also DLB 176

Herrick, Robert
1591-1674 ..... LC 13; DA; DAB; DAC;
DAM MST, POP; PC 9
See also DLB 126

Herring, Guilles
See Somerville, Edith

Herriot, James
1916-1995 .... CLC 12; DAM POP
See also Wight, James Alfred
See also AAYA 1; CA 148; CANR 40;
SATA 86

Herrmann, Dorothy 1941-......... CLC 44
See also CA 107

Herrmann, Taffy
See Herrmann, Dorothy

Hersey, John (Richard)
1914-1993 .... CLC 1, 2, 7, 9, 40, 81, 97;
DAM POP
See also CA 17-20R; 140; CANR 33;
DLB 6; MTCW; SATA 25;
SATA-Obit 76

Herzen, Aleksandr Ivanovich
1812-1870 .... NCLC 10, 61

Herzl, Theodor 1860-1904........ TCLC 36

Herzog, Werner 1942-............ CLC 16
See also CA 89-92

Hesiod c. 8th cent. B.C.-......... CMLC 5
See also DLB 176

Hesse, Hermann
1877-1962 .... CLC 1, 2, 3, 6, 11, 17, 25,
69; DA; DAB; DAC; DAM MST, NOV;
SSC 9; WLC
See also CA 17-18; CAP 2; DLB 66;
MTCW; SATA 50

Hewes, Cady
See De Voto, Bernard (Augustine)

Heyen, William 1940- .... CLC 13, 18
See also CA 33-36R; CAAS 9; DLB 5

Heyerdahl, Thor 1914-............ CLC 26
See also CA 5-8R; CANR 5, 22; MTCW;
SATA 2, 52

Heym, Georg (Theodor Franz Arthur)
1887-1912 .... TCLC 9
See also CA 106

Heym, Stefan 1913-.............. CLC 41
See also CA 9-12R; CANR 4; DLB 69

Heyse, Paul (Johann Ludwig von)
1830-1914 .... TCLC 8
See also CA 104; DLB 129

Heyward, (Edwin) DuBose
1885-1940 .... TCLC 59
See also CA 108; DLB 7, 9, 45; SATA 21

Hibbert, Eleanor Alice Burford
    1906-1993 .... **CLC 7; DAM POP**
    See also BEST 90:4; CA 17-20R; 140;
    CANR 9, 28; SATA 2; SATA-Obit 74

Hichens, Robert S. 1864-1950 ..... **TCLC 64**
    See also DLB 153

Higgins, George V(incent)
    1939- .... **CLC 4, 7, 10, 18**
    See also CA 77-80; CAAS 5; CANR 17, 51;
    DLB 2; DLBY 81; INT CANR-17;
    MTCW

Higginson, Thomas Wentworth
    1823-1911 .... **TCLC 36**
    See also DLB 1, 64

Highet, Helen
    See MacInnes, Helen (Clark)

Highsmith, (Mary) Patricia
    1921-1995 .... **CLC 2, 4, 14, 42;**
                        DAM NOV, POP
    See also CA 1-4R; 147; CANR 1, 20, 48;
    MTCW

Highwater, Jamake (Mamake)
    1942(?)- .... **CLC 12**
    See also AAYA 7; CA 65-68; CAAS 7;
    CANR 10, 34; CLR 17; DLB 52;
    DLBY 85; JRDA; MAICYA; SATA 32,
    69; SATA-Brief 30

Highway, Tomson
    1951- ..... **CLC 92; DAC; DAM MULT**
    See also CA 151; NNAL

Higuchi, Ichiyo 1872-1896 ...... **NCLC 49**

Hijuelos, Oscar
    1951- .... **CLC 65; DAM MULT, POP;**
                        HLC
    See also BEST 90:1; CA 123; CANR 50;
    DLB 145; HW

Hikmet, Nazim 1902(?)-1963 ...... **CLC 40**
    See also CA 141; 93-96

Hildegard von Bingen
    1098-1179 .... **CMLC 20**
    See also DLB 148

Hildesheimer, Wolfgang
    1916-1991 .... **CLC 49**
    See also CA 101; 135; DLB 69, 124

Hill, Geoffrey (William)
    1932- ... **CLC 5, 8, 18, 45; DAM POET**
    See also CA 81-84; CANR 21;
    CDBLB 1960 to Present; DLB 40;
    MTCW

Hill, George Roy 1921- .... **CLC 26**
    See also CA 110; 122

Hill, John
    See Koontz, Dean R(ay)

Hill, Susan (Elizabeth)
    1942- .. **CLC 4; DAB; DAM MST, NOV**
    See also CA 33-36R; CANR 29; DLB 14,
    139; MTCW

Hillerman, Tony
    1925- .... **CLC 62; DAM POP**
    See also AAYA 6; BEST 89:1; CA 29-32R;
    CANR 21, 42; SATA 6

Hillesum, Etty 1914-1943 .... **TCLC 49**
    See also CA 137

Hilliard, Noel (Harvey) 1929- ...... **CLC 15**
    See also CA 9-12R; CANR 7

Hillis, Rick 1956- .... **CLC 66**
    See also CA 134

Hilton, James 1900-1954 .... **TCLC 21**
    See also CA 108; DLB 34, 77; SATA 34

Himes, Chester (Bomar)
    1909-1984 .... **CLC 2, 4, 7, 18, 58; BLC;**
                        DAM MULT
    See also BW 2; CA 25-28R; 114; CANR 22;
    DLB 2, 76, 143; MTCW

Hinde, Thomas .... **CLC 6, 11**
    See also Chitty, Thomas Willes

Hindin, Nathan
    See Bloch, Robert (Albert)

Hine, (William) Daryl 1936- .... **CLC 15**
    See also CA 1-4R; CAAS 15; CANR 1, 20;
    DLB 60

Hinkson, Katharine Tynan
    See Tynan, Katharine

Hinton, S(usan) E(loise)
    1950- .... **CLC 30; DA; DAB; DAC;**
                        DAM MST, NOV
    See also AAYA 2; CA 81-84; CANR 32;
    CLR 3, 23; JRDA; MAICYA; MTCW;
    SATA 19, 58

Hippius, Zinaida .... **TCLC 9**
    See also Gippius, Zinaida (Nikolayevna)

Hiraoka, Kimitake 1925-1970
    See Mishima, Yukio
    See also CA 97-100; 29-32R; DAM DRAM;
    MTCW

Hirsch, E(ric) D(onald), Jr. 1928- ... **CLC 79**
    See also CA 25-28R; CANR 27, 51;
    DLB 67; INT CANR-27; MTCW

Hirsch, Edward 1950- .... **CLC 31, 50**
    See also CA 104; CANR 20, 42; DLB 120

Hitchcock, Alfred (Joseph)
    1899-1980 .... **CLC 16**
    See also CA 97-100; SATA 27;
    SATA-Obit 24

Hitler, Adolf 1889-1945 .... **TCLC 53**
    See also CA 117; 147

Hoagland, Edward 1932- .... **CLC 28**
    See also CA 1-4R; CANR 2, 31, 57; DLB 6;
    SATA 51

Hoban, Russell (Conwell)
    1925- .... **CLC 7, 25; DAM NOV**
    See also CA 5-8R; CANR 23, 37; CLR 3;
    DLB 52; MAICYA; MTCW; SATA 1,
    40, 78

Hobbes, Thomas 1588-1679 .... **LC 36**
    See also DLB 151

Hobbs, Perry
    See Blackmur, R(ichard) P(almer)

Hobson, Laura Z(ametkin)
    1900-1986 .... **CLC 7, 25**
    See also CA 17-20R; 118; CANR 55;
    DLB 28; SATA 52

Hochhuth, Rolf
    1931- ..... **CLC 4, 11, 18; DAM DRAM**
    See also CA 5-8R; CANR 33; DLB 124;
    MTCW

Hochman, Sandra 1936- .... **CLC 3, 8**
    See also CA 5-8R; DLB 5

Hochwaelder, Fritz
    1911-1986 ...... **CLC 36; DAM DRAM**
    See also CA 29-32R; 120; CANR 42;
    MTCW

Hochwalder, Fritz
    See Hochwaelder, Fritz

Hocking, Mary (Eunice) 1921- ..... **CLC 13**
    See also CA 101; CANR 18, 40

Hodgins, Jack 1938- .... **CLC 23**
    See also CA 93-96; DLB 60

Hodgson, William Hope
    1877(?)-1918 .... **TCLC 13**
    See also CA 111; DLB 70, 153, 156

Hoeg, Peter 1957- .... **CLC 95**
    See also CA 151

Hoffman, Alice
    1952- .... **CLC 51; DAM NOV**
    See also CA 77-80; CANR 34; MTCW

Hoffman, Daniel (Gerard)
    1923- .... **CLC 6, 13, 23**
    See also CA 1-4R; CANR 4; DLB 5

Hoffman, Stanley 1944- .... **CLC 5**
    See also CA 77-80

Hoffman, William M(oses) 1939- ... **CLC 40**
    See also CA 57-60; CANR 11

Hoffmann, E(rnst) T(heodor) A(madeus)
    1776-1822 .... **NCLC 2; SSC 13**
    See also DLB 90; SATA 27

Hofmann, Gert 1931- .... **CLC 54**
    See also CA 128

Hofmannsthal, Hugo von
    1874-1929 .... **TCLC 11; DAM DRAM;**
                        DC 4
    See also CA 106; 153; DLB 81, 118

Hogan, Linda
    1947- .... **CLC 73; DAM MULT**
    See also CA 120; CANR 45; DLB 175;
    NNAL

Hogarth, Charles
    See Creasey, John

Hogarth, Emmett
    See Polonsky, Abraham (Lincoln)

Hogg, James 1770-1835 .... **NCLC 4**
    See also DLB 93, 116, 159

Holbach, Paul Henri Thiry Baron
    1723-1789 .... **LC 14**

Holberg, Ludvig 1684-1754 .... **LC 6**

Holden, Ursula 1921- .... **CLC 18**
    See also CA 101; CAAS 8; CANR 22

Holderlin, (Johann Christian) Friedrich
    1770-1843 .... **NCLC 16; PC 4**

Holdstock, Robert
    See Holdstock, Robert P.

Holdstock, Robert P. 1948- .... **CLC 39**
    See also CA 131

Holland, Isabelle 1920- .... **CLC 21**
    See also AAYA 11; CA 21-24R; CANR 10,
    25, 47; JRDA; MAICYA; SATA 8, 70

Holland, Marcus
    See Caldwell, (Janet Miriam) Taylor
    (Holland)

Hollander, John 1929- ...... **CLC 2, 5, 8, 14**
    See also CA 1-4R; CANR 1, 52; DLB 5;
    SATA 13

Hollander, Paul
See Silverberg, Robert

Holleran, Andrew 1943(?)-........ **CLC 38**
See also CA 144

Hollinghurst, Alan 1954-....... **CLC 55, 91**
See also CA 114

Hollis, Jim
See Summers, Hollis (Spurgeon, Jr.)

Holly, Buddy 1936-1959 .... **TCLC 65**

Holmes, John
See Souster, (Holmes) Raymond

Holmes, John Clellon 1926-1988.... **CLC 56**
See also CA 9-12R; 125; CANR 4; DLB 16

Holmes, Oliver Wendell
1809-1894 .... **NCLC 14**
See also CDALB 1640-1865; DLB 1;
SATA 34

Holmes, Raymond
See Souster, (Holmes) Raymond

Holt, Victoria
See Hibbert, Eleanor Alice Burford

Holub, Miroslav 1923-............. **CLC 4**
See also CA 21-24R; CANR 10

Homer
c. 8th cent. B.C.-..... **CMLC 1, 16; DA;**
DAB; DAC; DAM MST, POET
See also DLB 176

Honig, Edwin 1919-.............. **CLC 33**
See also CA 5-8R; CAAS 8; CANR 4, 45;
DLB 5

Hood, Hugh (John Blagdon)
1928-.................... **CLC 15, 28**
See also CA 49-52; CAAS 17; CANR 1, 33;
DLB 53

Hood, Thomas 1799-1845....... **NCLC 16**
See also DLB 96

Hooker, (Peter) Jeremy 1941-...... **CLC 43**
See also CA 77-80; CANR 22; DLB 40

hooks, bell .... **CLC 94**
See also Watkins, Gloria

Hope, A(lec) D(erwent) 1907-.... **CLC 3, 51**
See also CA 21-24R; CANR 33; MTCW

Hope, Brian
See Creasey, John

Hope, Christopher (David Tully)
1944-....................... **CLC 52**
See also CA 106; CANR 47; SATA 62

Hopkins, Gerard Manley
1844-1889 .... **NCLC 17; DA; DAB;**
DAC; DAM MST, POET; PC 15; WLC
See also CDBLB 1890-1914; DLB 35, 57

Hopkins, John (Richard) 1931-...... **CLC 4**
See also CA 85-88

Hopkins, Pauline Elizabeth
1859-1930 .... **TCLC 28; BLC;**
DAM MULT
See also BW 2; CA 141; DLB 50

Hopkinson, Francis 1737-1791 ...... **LC 25**
See also DLB 31

Hopley-Woolrich, Cornell George 1903-1968
See Woolrich, Cornell
See also CA 13-14; CAP 1

Horatio
See Proust, (Valentin-Louis-George-Eugene-)
Marcel

Horgan, Paul (George Vincent O'Shaughnessy)
1903-1995 ...... **CLC 9, 53; DAM NOV**
See also CA 13-16R; 147; CANR 9, 35;
DLB 102; DLBY 85; INT CANR-9;
MTCW; SATA 13; SATA-Obit 84

Horn, Peter
See Kuttner, Henry

Hornem, Horace Esq.
See Byron, George Gordon (Noel)

Hornung, E(rnest) W(illiam)
1866-1921 .... **TCLC 59**
See also CA 108; DLB 70

Horovitz, Israel (Arthur)
1939- .... **CLC 56; DAM DRAM**
See also CA 33-36R; CANR 46; DLB 7

Horvath, Odon von
See Horvath, Oedoen von
See also DLB 85, 124

Horvath, Oedoen von 1901-1938... **TCLC 45**
See also Horvath, Odon von
See also CA 118

Horwitz, Julius 1920-1986......... **CLC 14**
See also CA 9-12R; 119; CANR 12

Hospital, Janette Turner 1942-..... **CLC 42**
See also CA 108; CANR 48

Hostos, E. M. de
See Hostos (y Bonilla), Eugenio Maria de

Hostos, Eugenio M. de
See Hostos (y Bonilla), Eugenio Maria de

Hostos, Eugenio Maria
See Hostos (y Bonilla), Eugenio Maria de

Hostos (y Bonilla), Eugenio Maria de
1839-1903 .... **TCLC 24**
See also CA 123; 131; HW

Houdini
See Lovecraft, H(oward) P(hillips)

Hougan, Carolyn 1943- .... **CLC 34**
See also CA 139

Household, Geoffrey (Edward West)
1900-1988 .... **CLC 11**
See also CA 77-80; 126; DLB 87; SATA 14;
SATA-Obit 59

Housman, A(lfred) E(dward)
1859-1936 ...... **TCLC 1, 10; DA; DAB;**
DAC; DAM MST, POET; PC 2
See also CA 104; 125; DLB 19; MTCW

Housman, Laurence 1865-1959..... **TCLC 7**
See also CA 106; 155; DLB 10; SATA 25

Howard, Elizabeth Jane 1923- ... **CLC 7, 29**
See also CA 5-8R; CANR 8

Howard, Maureen 1930- ..... **CLC 5, 14, 46**
See also CA 53-56; CANR 31; DLBY 83;
INT CANR-31; MTCW

Howard, Richard 1929-...... **CLC 7, 10, 47**
See also AITN 1; CA 85-88; CANR 25;
DLB 5; INT CANR-25

Howard, Robert Ervin 1906-1936... **TCLC 8**
See also CA 105

Howard, Warren F.
See Pohl, Frederik

Howe, Fanny 1940- .... **CLC 47**
See also CA 117; SATA-Brief 52

Howe, Irving 1920-1993.......... **CLC 85**
See also CA 9-12R; 141; CANR 21, 50;
DLB 67; MTCW

Howe, Julia Ward 1819-1910 ..... **TCLC 21**
See also CA 117; DLB 1

Howe, Susan 1937-.............. **CLC 72**
See also DLB 120

Howe, Tina 1937-................ **CLC 48**
See also CA 109

Howell, James 1594(?)-1666 .... **LC 13**
See also DLB 151

Howells, W. D.
See Howells, William Dean

Howells, William D.
See Howells, William Dean

Howells, William Dean
1837-1920 .... **TCLC 7, 17, 41**
See also CA 104; 134; CDALB 1865-1917;
DLB 12, 64, 74, 79

Howes, Barbara 1914-1996 .... **CLC 15**
See also CA 9-12R; 151; CAAS 3;
CANR 53; SATA 5

Hrabal, Bohumil 1914-1997..... **CLC 13, 67**
See also CA 106; 156; CAAS 12; CANR 57

Hsun, Lu
See Lu Hsun

Hubbard, L(afayette) Ron(ald)
1911-1986 .... **CLC 43; DAM POP**
See also CA 77-80; 118; CANR 52

Huch, Ricarda (Octavia)
1864-1947 .... **TCLC 13**
See also CA 111; DLB 66

Huddle, David 1942- .... **CLC 49**
See also CA 57-60; CAAS 20; DLB 130

Hudson, Jeffrey
See Crichton, (John) Michael

Hudson, W(illiam) H(enry)
1841-1922 .... **TCLC 29**
See also CA 115; DLB 98, 153, 174;
SATA 35

Hueffer, Ford Madox
See Ford, Ford Madox

Hughart, Barry 1934-.............. **CLC 39**
See also CA 137

Hughes, Colin
See Creasey, John

Hughes, David (John) 1930- .... **CLC 48**
See also CA 116; 129; DLB 14

Hughes, Edward James
See Hughes, Ted
See also DAM MST, POET

Hughes, (James) Langston
1902-1967 ..... **CLC 1, 5, 10, 15, 35, 44;**
BLC; DA; DAB; DAC; DAM DRAM,
MST, MULT, POET; DC 3; PC 1;
SSC 6; WLC
See also AAYA 12; BW 1; CA 1-4R;
25-28R; CANR 1, 34; CDALB 1929-1941;
CLR 17; DLB 4, 7, 48, 51, 86; JRDA;
MAICYA; MTCW; SATA 4, 33

Hughes, Richard (Arthur Warren)
  1900-1976 ...... **CLC 1, 11; DAM NOV**
  See also CA 5-8R; 65-68; CANR 4;
  DLB 15, 161; MTCW; SATA 8;
  SATA-Obit 25

Hughes, Ted
  1930- .... **CLC 2, 4, 9, 14, 37; DAB;**
                                  DAC; PC 7
  See also Hughes, Edward James
  See also CA 1-4R; CANR 1, 33; CLR 3;
  DLB 40, 161; MAICYA; MTCW;
  SATA 49; SATA-Brief 27

Hugo, Richard F(ranklin)
  1923-1982 .... **CLC 6, 18, 32;**
                                      DAM POET
  See also CA 49-52; 108; CANR 3; DLB 5

Hugo, Victor (Marie)
  1802-1885 .... **NCLC 3, 10, 21; DA;**
    DAB; DAC; DAM DRAM, MST, NOV,
                            POET; PC 17; WLC
  See also DLB 119; SATA 47

Huidobro, Vicente
  See Huidobro Fernandez, Vicente Garcia

Huidobro Fernandez, Vicente Garcia
  1893-1948 .... **TCLC 31**
  See also CA 131; HW

Hulme, Keri 1947- .... **CLC 39**
  See also CA 125; INT 125

Hulme, T(homas) E(rnest)
  1883-1917 .... **TCLC 21**
  See also CA 117; DLB 19

Hume, David 1711-1776............. **LC 7**
  See also DLB 104

Humphrey, William 1924-......... **CLC 45**
  See also CA 77-80; DLB 6

Humphreys, Emyr Owen 1919-..... **CLC 47**
  See also CA 5-8R; CANR 3, 24; DLB 15

Humphreys, Josephine 1945-.... **CLC 34, 57**
  See also CA 121; 127; INT 127

Huneker, James Gibbons
  1857-1921 .... **TCLC 65**
  See also DLB 71

Hungerford, Pixie
  See Brinsmead, H(esba) F(ay)

Hunt, E(verette) Howard, (Jr.)
  1918- .... **CLC 3**
  See also AITN 1; CA 45-48; CANR 2, 47

Hunt, Kyle
  See Creasey, John

Hunt, (James Henry) Leigh
  1784-1859 ..... **NCLC 1; DAM POET**

Hunt, Marsha 1946-............. **CLC 70**
  See also BW 2; CA 143

Hunt, Violet 1866-1942 .... **TCLC 53**
  See also DLB 162

Hunter, E. Waldo
  See Sturgeon, Theodore (Hamilton)

Hunter, Evan
  1926- .... **CLC 11, 31; DAM POP**
  See also CA 5-8R; CANR 5, 38; DLBY 82;
  INT CANR-5; MTCW; SATA 25

Hunter, Kristin (Eggleston) 1931-... **CLC 35**
  See also AITN 1; BW 1; CA 13-16R;
  CANR 13; CLR 3; DLB 33;
  INT CANR-13; MAICYA; SAAS 10;
  SATA 12

Hunter, Mollie 1922-............. **CLC 21**
  See also McIlwraith, Maureen Mollie
  Hunter
  See also AAYA 13; CANR 37; CLR 25;
  DLB 161; JRDA; MAICYA; SAAS 7;
  SATA 54

Hunter, Robert (?)-1734............. **LC 7**

Hurston, Zora Neale
  1903-1960 .... **CLC 7, 30, 61; BLC; DA;**
    DAC; DAM MST, MULT, NOV; SSC 4
  See also AAYA 15; BW 1; CA 85-88;
  DLB 51, 86; MTCW

Huston, John (Marcellus)
  1906-1987 .... **CLC 20**
  See also CA 73-76; 123; CANR 34; DLB 26

Hustvedt, Siri 1955-............... **CLC 76**
  See also CA 137

Hutten, Ulrich von 1488-1523...... **LC 16**

Huxley, Aldous (Leonard)
  1894-1963 ..... **CLC 1, 3, 4, 5, 8, 11, 18,**
    35, 79; DA; DAB; DAC; DAM MST,
                                  NOV; WLC
  See also AAYA 11; CA 85-88; CANR 44;
  CDBLB 1914-1945; DLB 36, 100, 162;
  MTCW; SATA 63

Huysmans, Charles Marie Georges
  1848-1907
  See Huysmans, Joris-Karl
  See also CA 104

Huysmans, Joris-Karl........... TCLC 7, 69
  See also Huysmans, Charles Marie Georges
  See also DLB 123

Hwang, David Henry
  1957-.... **CLC 55; DAM DRAM; DC 4**
  See also CA 127; 132; INT 132

Hyde, Anthony 1946-............. **CLC 42**
  See also CA 136

Hyde, Margaret O(ldroyd) 1917-... **CLC 21**
  See also CA 1-4R; CANR 1, 36; CLR 23;
  JRDA; MAICYA; SAAS 8; SATA 1, 42,
  76

Hynes, James 1956(?)-............ **CLC 65**

Ian, Janis 1951- .... **CLC 21**
  See also CA 105

Ibanez, Vicente Blasco
  See Blasco Ibanez, Vicente

Ibarguengoitia, Jorge 1928-1983.... **CLC 37**
  See also CA 124; 113; HW

Ibsen, Henrik (Johan)
  1828-1906 .... **TCLC 2, 8, 16, 37, 52;**
    DA; DAB; DAC; DAM DRAM, MST;
                                  DC 2; WLC
  See also CA 104; 141

Ibuse Masuji 1898-1993........... **CLC 22**
  See also CA 127; 141

Ichikawa, Kon 1915-.............. **CLC 20**
  See also CA 121

Idle, Eric 1943-.................. **CLC 21**
  See also Monty Python
  See also CA 116; CANR 35

Ignatow, David 1914-...... **CLC 4, 7, 14, 40**
  See also CA 9-12R; CAAS 3; CANR 31, 57;
  DLB 5

Ihimaera, Witi 1944- .... **CLC 46**
  See also CA 77-80

Ilf, Ilya........................ TCLC 21
  See also Fainzilberg, Ilya Arnoldovich

Illyes, Gyula 1902-1983............ **PC 16**
  See also CA 114; 109

Immermann, Karl (Lebrecht)
  1796-1840 .... **NCLC 4, 49**
  See also DLB 133

Inclan, Ramon (Maria) del Valle
  See Valle-Inclan, Ramon (Maria) del

Infante, G(uillermo) Cabrera
  See Cabrera Infante, G(uillermo)

Ingalls, Rachel (Holmes) 1940-..... **CLC 42**
  See also CA 123; 127

Ingamells, Rex 1913-1955 .... **TCLC 35**

Inge, William (Motter)
  1913-1973 .. **CLC 1, 8, 19; DAM DRAM**
  See also CA 9-12R; CDALB 1941-1968;
  DLB 7; MTCW

Ingelow, Jean 1820-1897........ **NCLC 39**
  See also DLB 35, 163; SATA 33

Ingram, Willis J.
  See Harris, Mark

Innaurato, Albert (F.) 1948(?)- .. **CLC 21, 60**
  See also CA 115; 122; INT 122

Innes, Michael
  See Stewart, J(ohn) I(nnes) M(ackintosh)

Ionesco, Eugene
  1909-1994 .... **CLC 1, 4, 6, 9, 11, 15, 41,**
    86; DA; DAB; DAC; DAM DRAM,
                                  MST; WLC
  See also CA 9-12R; 144; CANR 55;
  MTCW; SATA 7; SATA-Obit 79

Iqbal, Muhammad 1873-1938 ..... **TCLC 28**

Ireland, Patrick
  See O'Doherty, Brian

Iron, Ralph
  See Schreiner, Olive (Emilie Albertina)

Irving, John (Winslow)
  1942- ..... **CLC 13, 23, 38; DAM NOV,**
                                      POP
  See also AAYA 8; BEST 89:3; CA 25-28R;
  CANR 28; DLB 6; DLBY 82; MTCW

Irving, Washington
  1783-1859 ..... **NCLC 2, 19; DA; DAB;**
                      DAM MST; SSC 2; WLC
  See also CDALB 1640-1865; DLB 3, 11, 30,
  59, 73, 74; YABC 2

Irwin, P. K.
  See Page, P(atricia) K(athleen)

Isaacs, Susan 1943- ... **CLC 32; DAM POP**
  See also BEST 89:1; CA 89-92; CANR 20,
  41; INT CANR-20; MTCW

Isherwood, Christopher (William Bradshaw)
  1904-1986 .... **CLC 1, 9, 11, 14, 44;**
                              DAM DRAM, NOV
  See also CA 13-16R; 117; CANR 35;
  DLB 15; DLBY 86; MTCW

Ishiguro, Kazuo
    1954- . . . . . . CLC 27, 56, 59; DAM NOV
    See also BEST 90:2; CA 120; CANR 49;
    MTCW

Ishikawa, Hakuhin
    See Ishikawa, Takuboku

Ishikawa, Takuboku
    1886(?)-1912 . . . . TCLC 15;
                                 DAM POET; PC 10
    See also CA 113; 153

Iskander, Fazil 1929- . . . . CLC 47
    See also CA 102

Isler, Alan (David) 1934- . . . . CLC 91
    See also CA 156

Ivan IV 1530-1584 . . . . LC 17

Ivanov, Vyacheslav Ivanovich
    1866-1949 . . . . TCLC 33
    See also CA 122

Ivask, Ivar Vidrik 1927-1992. . . . . . CLC 14
    See also CA 37-40R; 139; CANR 24

Ives, Morgan
    See Bradley, Marion Zimmer

J. R. S.
    See Gogarty, Oliver St. John

Jabran, Kahlil
    See Gibran, Kahlil

Jabran, Khalil
    See Gibran, Kahlil

Jackson, Daniel
    See Wingrove, David (John)

Jackson, Jesse 1908-1983 . . . . CLC 12
    See also BW 1; CA 25-28R; 109; CANR 27;
    CLR 28; MAICYA; SATA 2, 29;
    SATA-Obit 48

Jackson, Laura (Riding) 1901-1991
    See Riding, Laura
    See also CA 65-68; 135; CANR 28; DLB 48

Jackson, Sam
    See Trumbo, Dalton

Jackson, Sara
    See Wingrove, David (John)

Jackson, Shirley
    1919-1965 . . . . CLC 11, 60, 87; DA;
                         DAC; DAM MST; SSC 9; WLC
    See also AAYA 9; CA 1-4R; 25-28R;
    CANR 4, 52; CDALB 1941-1968; DLB 6;
    SATA 2

Jacob, (Cyprien-)Max 1876-1944 . . . TCLC 6
    See also CA 104

Jacobs, Jim 1942-. . . . . CLC 12
    See also CA 97-100; INT 97-100

Jacobs, W(illiam) W(ymark)
    1863-1943 . . . . TCLC 22
    See also CA 121; DLB 135

Jacobsen, Jens Peter 1847-1885 . . NCLC 34

Jacobsen, Josephine 1908- . . . . CLC 48
    See also CA 33-36R; CAAS 18; CANR 23,
    48

Jacobson, Dan 1929- . . . . CLC 4, 14
    See also CA 1-4R; CANR 2, 25; DLB 14;
    MTCW

Jacqueline
    See Carpentier (y Valmont), Alejo

Jagger, Mick 1944-. . . . . CLC 17

Jakes, John (William)
    1932- . . . . . . CLC 29; DAM NOV, POP
    See also BEST 89:4; CA 57-60; CANR 10,
    43; DLBY 83; INT CANR-10; MTCW;
    SATA 62

James, Andrew
    See Kirkup, James

James, C(yril) L(ionel) R(obert)
    1901-1989 . . . . CLC 33
    See also BW 2; CA 117; 125; 128; DLB 125;
    MTCW

James, Daniel (Lewis) 1911-1988
    See Santiago, Danny
    See also CA 125

James, Dynely
    See Mayne, William (James Carter)

James, Henry Sr. 1811-1882 . . . . . NCLC 53

James, Henry
    1843-1916 . . . . . . TCLC 2, 11, 24, 40, 47,
        64; DA; DAB; DAC; DAM MST, NOV;
                                      SSC 8; WLC
    See also CA 104; 132; CDALB 1865-1917;
    DLB 12, 71, 74; DLBD 13; MTCW

James, M. R.
    See James, Montague (Rhodes)
    See also DLB 156

James, Montague (Rhodes)
    1862-1936 . . . . TCLC 6; SSC 16
    See also CA 104

James, P. D. . . . . CLC 18, 46
    See also White, Phyllis Dorothy James
    See also BEST 90:2; CDBLB 1960 to
    Present; DLB 87

James, Philip
    See Moorcock, Michael (John)

James, William 1842-1910. . . . . TCLC 15, 32
    See also CA 109

James I 1394-1437 . . . . LC 20

Jameson, Anna 1794-1860 . . . . NCLC 43
    See also DLB 99, 166

Jami, Nur al-Din 'Abd al-Rahman
    1414-1492 . . . . LC 9

Jandl, Ernst 1925- . . . . CLC 34

Janowitz, Tama
    1957- . . . . CLC 43; DAM POP
    See also CA 106; CANR 52

Japrisot, Sebastien 1931-. . . . . CLC 90

Jarrell, Randall
    1914-1965 . . . . CLC 1, 2, 6, 9, 13, 49;
                                      DAM POET
    See also CA 5-8R; 25-28R; CABS 2;
    CANR 6, 34; CDALB 1941-1968; CLR 6;
    DLB 48, 52; MAICYA; MTCW; SATA 7

Jarry, Alfred
    1873-1907 . . . . TCLC 2, 14;
                                 DAM DRAM; SSC 20
    See also CA 104; 153

Jarvis, E. K.
    See Bloch, Robert (Albert); Ellison, Harlan
    (Jay); Silverberg, Robert

Jeake, Samuel, Jr.
    See Aiken, Conrad (Potter)

Jean Paul 1763-1825 . . . . NCLC 7

Jefferies, (John) Richard
    1848-1887 . . . . NCLC 47
    See also DLB 98, 141; SATA 16

Jeffers, (John) Robinson
    1887-1962 . . . . CLC 2, 3, 11, 15, 54; DA;
        DAC; DAM MST, POET; PC 17; WLC
    See also CA 85-88; CANR 35;
    CDALB 1917-1929; DLB 45; MTCW

Jefferson, Janet
    See Mencken, H(enry) L(ouis)

Jefferson, Thomas 1743-1826 . . . . NCLC 11
    See also CDALB 1640-1865; DLB 31

Jeffrey, Francis 1773-1850. . . . . . NCLC 33
    See also DLB 107

Jelakowitch, Ivan
    See Heijermans, Herman

Jellicoe, (Patricia) Ann 1927- . . . . . . CLC 27
    See also CA 85-88; DLB 13

Jen, Gish . . . . CLC 70
    See also Jen, Lillian

Jen, Lillian 1956(?)-
    See Jen, Gish
    See also CA 135

Jenkins, (John) Robin 1912- . . . . CLC 52
    See also CA 1-4R; CANR 1; DLB 14

Jennings, Elizabeth (Joan)
    1926- . . . . CLC 5, 14
    See also CA 61-64; CAAS 5; CANR 8, 39;
    DLB 27; MTCW; SATA 66

Jennings, Waylon 1937-. . . . . CLC 21

Jensen, Johannes V. 1873-1950. . . . TCLC 41

Jensen, Laura (Linnea) 1948- . . . . . . CLC 37
    See also CA 103

Jerome, Jerome K(lapka)
    1859-1927 . . . . TCLC 23
    See also CA 119; DLB 10, 34, 135

Jerrold, Douglas William
    1803-1857 . . . . NCLC 2
    See also DLB 158, 159

Jewett, (Theodora) Sarah Orne
    1849-1909 . . . . TCLC 1, 22; SSC 6
    See also CA 108; 127; DLB 12, 74;
    SATA 15

Jewsbury, Geraldine (Endsor)
    1812-1880 . . . . NCLC 22
    See also DLB 21

Jhabvala, Ruth Prawer
    1927- . . . . CLC 4, 8, 29, 94; DAB;
                                      DAM NOV
    See also CA 1-4R; CANR 2, 29, 51;
    DLB 139; INT CANR-29; MTCW

Jibran, Kahlil
    See Gibran, Kahlil

Jibran, Khalil
    See Gibran, Kahlil

Jiles, Paulette 1943-. . . . . CLC 13, 58
    See also CA 101

Jimenez (Mantecon), Juan Ramon
    1881-1958 . . . . . TCLC 4; DAM MULT,
                            POET; HLC; PC 7
    See also CA 104; 131; DLB 134; HW;
    MTCW

Jimenez, Ramon
    See Jimenez (Mantecon), Juan Ramon

Jimenez Mantecon, Juan
See Jimenez (Mantecon), Juan Ramon

Joel, Billy .... CLC 26
See also Joel, William Martin

Joel, William Martin 1949-
See Joel, Billy
See also CA 108

John of the Cross, St. 1542-1591 .... LC 18

Johnson, B(ryan) S(tanley William)
1933-1973 .... CLC 6, 9
See also CA 9-12R; 53-56; CANR 9;
DLB 14, 40

Johnson, Benj. F. of Boo
See Riley, James Whitcomb

Johnson, Benjamin F. of Boo
See Riley, James Whitcomb

Johnson, Charles (Richard)
1948- .... CLC 7, 51, 65; BLC;
DAM MULT
See also BW 2; CA 116; CAAS 18;
CANR 42; DLB 33

Johnson, Denis 1949- .... CLC 52
See also CA 117; 121; DLB 120

Johnson, Diane 1934- .... CLC 5, 13, 48
See also CA 41-44R; CANR 17, 40;
DLBY 80; INT CANR-17; MTCW

Johnson, Eyvind (Olof Verner)
1900-1976 .... CLC 14
See also CA 73-76; 69-72; CANR 34

Johnson, J. R.
See James, C(yril) L(ionel) R(obert)

Johnson, James Weldon
1871-1938 .... TCLC 3, 19; BLC;
DAM MULT, POET
See also BW 1; CA 104; 125;
CDALB 1917-1929; CLR 32; DLB 51;
MTCW; SATA 31

Johnson, Joyce 1935- .... CLC 58
See also CA 125; 129

Johnson, Lionel (Pigot)
1867-1902 .... TCLC 19
See also CA 117; DLB 19

Johnson, Mel
See Malzberg, Barry N(athaniel)

Johnson, Pamela Hansford
1912-1981 .... CLC 1, 7, 27
See also CA 1-4R; 104; CANR 2, 28;
DLB 15; MTCW

Johnson, Robert 1911(?)-1938 ..... TCLC 69

Johnson, Samuel
1709-1784 ..... LC 15; DA; DAB; DAC;
DAM MST; WLC
See also CDBLB 1660-1789; DLB 39, 95,
104, 142

Johnson, Uwe
1934-1984 .... CLC 5, 10, 15, 40
See also CA 1-4R; 112; CANR 1, 39;
DLB 75; MTCW

Johnston, George (Benson) 1913- ... CLC 51
See also CA 1-4R; CANR 5, 20; DLB 88

Johnston, Jennifer 1930- .... CLC 7
See also CA 85-88; DLB 14

Jolley, (Monica) Elizabeth
1923- .... CLC 46; SSC 19
See also CA 127; CAAS 13

Jones, Arthur Llewellyn 1863-1947
See Machen, Arthur
See also CA 104

Jones, D(ouglas) G(ordon) 1929-.... CLC 10
See also CA 29-32R; CANR 13; DLB 53

Jones, David (Michael)
1895-1974 .... CLC 2, 4, 7, 13, 42
See also CA 9-12R; 53-56; CANR 28;
CDBLB 1945-1960; DLB 20, 100; MTCW

Jones, David Robert 1947-
See Bowie, David
See also CA 103

Jones, Diana Wynne 1934- .... CLC 26
See also AAYA 12; CA 49-52; CANR 4,
26, 56; CLR 23; DLB 161; JRDA;
MAICYA; SAAS 7; SATA 9, 70

Jones, Edward P. 1950- .... CLC 76
See also BW 2; CA 142

Jones, Gayl
1949- .... CLC 6, 9; BLC; DAM MULT
See also BW 2; CA 77-80; CANR 27;
DLB 33; MTCW

Jones, James 1921-1977.... CLC 1, 3, 10, 39
See also AITN 1, 2; CA 1-4R; 69-72;
CANR 6; DLB 2, 143; MTCW

Jones, John J.
See Lovecraft, H(oward) P(hillips)

Jones, LeRoi .... CLC 1, 2, 3, 5, 10, 14
See also Baraka, Amiri

Jones, Louis B. .... CLC 65
See also CA 141

Jones, Madison (Percy, Jr.) 1925- ... CLC 4
See also CA 13-16R; CAAS 11; CANR 7,
54; DLB 152

Jones, Mervyn 1922- .... CLC 10, 52
See also CA 45-48; CAAS 5; CANR 1;
MTCW

Jones, Mick 1956(?)- .... CLC 30

Jones, Nettie (Pearl) 1941- .... CLC 34
See also BW 2; CA 137; CAAS 20

Jones, Preston 1936-1979 .... CLC 10
See also CA 73-76; 89-92; DLB 7

Jones, Robert F(rancis) 1934- .... CLC 7
See also CA 49-52; CANR 2

Jones, Rod 1953- .... CLC 50
See also CA 128

Jones, Terence Graham Parry
1942- .... CLC 21
See also Jones, Terry; Monty Python
See also CA 112; 116; CANR 35; INT 116

Jones, Terry
See Jones, Terence Graham Parry
See also SATA 67; SATA-Brief 51

Jones, Thom 1945(?)- .... CLC 81

Jong, Erica
1942- .... CLC 4, 6, 8, 18, 83;
DAM NOV, POP
See also AITN 1; BEST 90:2; CA 73-76;
CANR 26, 52; DLB 2, 5, 28, 152;
INT CANR-26; MTCW

Jonson, Ben(jamin)
1572(?)-1637 ...... LC 6, 33; DA; DAB;
DAC; DAM DRAM, MST, POET;
DC 4; PC 17; WLC
See also CDBLB Before 1660; DLB 62, 121

Jordan, June
1936- ..... CLC 5, 11, 23; DAM MULT,
POET
See also AAYA 2; BW 2; CA 33-36R;
CANR 25; CLR 10; DLB 38; MAICYA;
MTCW; SATA 4

Jordan, Pat(rick M.) 1941- .... CLC 37
See also CA 33-36R

Jorgensen, Ivar
See Ellison, Harlan (Jay)

Jorgenson, Ivar
See Silverberg, Robert

Josephus, Flavius c. 37-100 ...... CMLC 13

Josipovici, Gabriel 1940- .... CLC 6, 43
See also CA 37-40R; CAAS 8; CANR 47;
DLB 14

Joubert, Joseph 1754-1824 .... NCLC 9

Jouve, Pierre Jean 1887-1976 ...... CLC 47
See also CA 65-68

Joyce, James (Augustine Aloysius)
1882-1941 .... TCLC 3, 8, 16, 35, 52;
DA; DAB; DAC; DAM MST, NOV,
POET; SSC 3; WLC
See also CA 104; 126; CDBLB 1914-1945;
DLB 10, 19, 36, 162; MTCW

Jozsef, Attila 1905-1937......... TCLC 22
See also CA 116

Juana Ines de la Cruz 1651(?)-1695 ... LC 5

Judd, Cyril
See Kornbluth, C(yril) M.; Pohl, Frederik

Julian of Norwich 1342(?)-1416(?) .... LC 6
See also DLB 146

Juniper, Alex
See Hospital, Janette Turner

Junius
See Luxemburg, Rosa

Just, Ward (Swift) 1935- .... CLC 4, 27
See also CA 25-28R; CANR 32;
INT CANR-32

Justice, Donald (Rodney)
1925- .... CLC 6, 19; DAM POET
See also CA 5-8R; CANR 26, 54;
DLBY 83; INT CANR-26

Juvenal c. 55-c. 127 .... CMLC 8

Juvenis
See Bourne, Randolph S(illiman)

Kacew, Romain 1914-1980
See Gary, Romain
See also CA 108; 102

Kadare, Ismail 1936- .... CLC 52

Kadohata, Cynthia................. CLC 59
See also CA 140

Kafka, Franz
1883-1924 .... TCLC 2, 6, 13, 29, 47, 53;
DA; DAB; DAC; DAM MST, NOV;
SSC 5; WLC
See also CA 105; 126; DLB 81; MTCW

Kahanovitsch, Pinkhes
See Der Nister

Kahn, Roger 1927-............... CLC 30
See also CA 25-28R; CANR 44; DLB 171;
SATA 37

Kain, Saul
See Sassoon, Siegfried (Lorraine)

Kaiser, Georg   1878-1945 . . . . TCLC 9
See also CA 106; DLB 124

Kaletski, Alexander   1946- . . . . CLC 39
See also CA 118; 143

Kalidasa   fl. c. 400- . . . . CMLC 9

Kallman, Chester (Simon)
   1921-1975 . . . . CLC 2
See also CA 45-48; 53-56; CANR 3

Kaminsky, Melvin   1926-
See Brooks, Mel
See also CA 65-68; CANR 16

Kaminsky, Stuart M(elvin)   1934- . . . CLC 59
See also CA 73-76; CANR 29, 53

Kane, Francis
See Robbins, Harold

Kane, Paul
See Simon, Paul (Frederick)

Kane, Wilson
See Bloch, Robert (Albert)

Kanin, Garson   1912- . . . . CLC 22
See also AITN 1; CA 5-8R; CANR 7;
   DLB 7

Kaniuk, Yoram   1930- . . . . CLC 19
See also CA 134

Kant, Immanuel   1724-1804 . . . . . . NCLC 27
See also DLB 94

Kantor, MacKinlay   1904-1977 . . . . . . CLC 7
See also CA 61-64; 73-76; DLB 9, 102

Kaplan, David Michael   1946- . . . . . . CLC 50

Kaplan, James   1951- . . . . CLC 59
See also CA 135

Karageorge, Michael
See Anderson, Poul (William)

Karamzin, Nikolai Mikhailovich
   1766-1826 . . . . NCLC 3
See also DLB 150

Karapanou, Margarita   1946- . . . . CLC 13
See also CA 101

Karinthy, Frigyes   1887-1938 . . . . . . TCLC 47

Karl, Frederick R(obert)   1927- . . . . . CLC 34
See also CA 5-8R; CANR 3, 44

Kastel, Warren
See Silverberg, Robert

Kataev, Evgeny Petrovich   1903-1942
See Petrov, Evgeny
See also CA 120

Kataphusin
See Ruskin, John

Katz, Steve   1935- . . . . CLC 47
See also CA 25-28R; CAAS 14; CANR 12;
   DLBY 83

Kauffman, Janet   1945- . . . . CLC 42
See also CA 117; CANR 43; DLBY 86

Kaufman, Bob (Garnell)
   1925-1986 . . . . CLC 49
See also BW 1; CA 41-44R; 118; CANR 22;
   DLB 16, 41

Kaufman, George S.
   1889-1961 . . . . . . CLC 38; DAM DRAM
See also CA 108; 93-96; DLB 7; INT 108

Kaufman, Sue . . . . CLC 3, 8
See also Barondess, Sue K(aufman)

Kavafis, Konstantinos Petrou   1863-1933
See Cavafy, C(onstantine) P(eter)
See also CA 104

Kavan, Anna   1901-1968 . . . . . . CLC 5, 13, 82
See also CA 5-8R; CANR 6, 57; MTCW

Kavanagh, Dan
See Barnes, Julian (Patrick)

Kavanagh, Patrick (Joseph)
   1904-1967 . . . . CLC 22
See also CA 123; 25-28R; DLB 15, 20;
   MTCW

Kawabata, Yasunari
   1899-1972 . . . . CLC 2, 5, 9, 18;
                           DAM MULT; SSC 17
See also CA 93-96; 33-36R

Kaye, M(ary) M(argaret)   1909- . . . . . CLC 28
See also CA 89-92; CANR 24; MTCW;
   SATA 62

Kaye, Mollie
See Kaye, M(ary) M(argaret)

Kaye-Smith, Sheila   1887-1956 . . . . . TCLC 20
See also CA 118; DLB 36

Kaymor, Patrice Maguilene
See Senghor, Leopold Sedar

Kazan, Elia   1909- . . . . CLC 6, 16, 63
See also CA 21-24R; CANR 32

Kazantzakis, Nikos
   1883(?)-1957 . . . . TCLC 2, 5, 33
See also CA 105; 132; MTCW

Kazin, Alfred   1915- . . . . CLC 34, 38
See also CA 1-4R; CAAS 7; CANR 1, 45;
   DLB 67

Keane, Mary Nesta (Skrine)   1904-1996
See Keane, Molly
See also CA 108; 114; 151

Keane, Molly . . . . CLC 31
See also Keane, Mary Nesta (Skrine)
See also INT 114

Keates, Jonathan   19(?)- . . . . CLC 34

Keaton, Buster   1895-1966 . . . . CLC 20

Keats, John
   1795-1821 . . . . NCLC 8; DA; DAB;
            DAC; DAM MST, POET; PC 1; WLC
See also CDBLB 1789-1832; DLB 96, 110

Keene, Donald   1922- . . . . CLC 34
See also CA 1-4R; CANR 5

Keillor, Garrison . . . . CLC 40
See also Keillor, Gary (Edward)
See also AAYA 2; BEST 89:3; DLBY 87;
   SATA 58

Keillor, Gary (Edward)   1942-
See Keillor, Garrison
See also CA 111; 117; CANR 36;
   DAM POP; MTCW

Keith, Michael
See Hubbard, L(afayette) Ron(ald)

Keller, Gottfried   1819-1890 . . . . NCLC 2
See also DLB 129

Kellerman, Jonathan
   1949- . . . . CLC 44; DAM POP
See also BEST 90:1; CA 106; CANR 29, 51;
   INT CANR-29

Kelley, William Melvin   1937- . . . . . . CLC 22
See also BW 1; CA 77-80; CANR 27;
   DLB 33

Kellogg, Marjorie   1922- . . . . CLC 2
See also CA 81-84

Kellow, Kathleen
See Hibbert, Eleanor Alice Burford

Kelly, M(ilton) T(erry)   1947- . . . . . . CLC 55
See also CA 97-100; CAAS 22; CANR 19,
   43

Kelman, James   1946- . . . . CLC 58, 86
See also CA 148

Kemal, Yashar   1923- . . . . CLC 14, 29
See also CA 89-92; CANR 44

Kemble, Fanny   1809-1893 . . . . NCLC 18
See also DLB 32

Kemelman, Harry   1908-1996 . . . . CLC 2
See also AITN 1; CA 9-12R; 155; CANR 6;
   DLB 28

Kempe, Margery   1373(?)-1440(?) . . . . . LC 6
See also DLB 146

Kempis, Thomas a   1380-1471 . . . . . . LC 11

Kendall, Henry   1839-1882 . . . . NCLC 12

Keneally, Thomas (Michael)
   1935- . . . . . . CLC 5, 8, 10, 14, 19, 27, 43;
                                          DAM NOV
See also CA 85-88; CANR 10, 50; MTCW

Kennedy, Adrienne (Lita)
   1931- . . . . . CLC 66; BLC; DAM MULT;
                                              DC 5
See also BW 2; CA 103; CAAS 20; CABS 3;
   CANR 26, 53; DLB 38

Kennedy, John Pendleton
   1795-1870 . . . . NCLC 2
See also DLB 3

Kennedy, Joseph Charles   1929-
See Kennedy, X. J.
See also CA 1-4R; CANR 4, 30, 40;
   SATA 14, 86

Kennedy, William
   1928- . . . CLC 6, 28, 34, 53; DAM NOV
See also AAYA 1; CA 85-88; CANR 14,
   31; DLB 143; DLBY 85; INT CANR-31;
   MTCW; SATA 57

Kennedy, X. J. . . . . CLC 8, 42
See also Kennedy, Joseph Charles
See also CAAS 9; CLR 27; DLB 5;
   SAAS 22

Kenny, Maurice (Francis)
   1929- . . . . CLC 87; DAM MULT
See also CA 144; CAAS 22; DLB 175;
   NNAL

Kent, Kelvin
See Kuttner, Henry

Kenton, Maxwell
See Southern, Terry

Kenyon, Robert O.
See Kuttner, Henry

Kerouac, Jack . . . . . CLC 1, 2, 3, 5, 14, 29, 61
See also Kerouac, Jean-Louis Lebris de
See also CDALB 1941-1968; DLB 2, 16;
   DLBD 3; DLBY 95

Kerouac, Jean-Louis Lebris de   1922-1969
See Kerouac, Jack
See also AITN 1; CA 5-8R; 25-28R;
   CANR 26, 54; DA; DAB; DAC;
   DAM MST, NOV, POET, POP; MTCW;
   WLC

Kerr, Jean 1923-................. CLC **22**
See also CA 5-8R; CANR 7; INT CANR-7

Kerr, M. E. .... CLC **12, 35**
See also Meaker, Marijane (Agnes)
See also AAYA 2; CLR 29; SAAS 1

Kerr, Robert .... CLC **55**

Kerrigan, (Thomas) Anthony
1918-...................... CLC **4, 6**
See also CA 49-52; CAAS 11; CANR 4

Kerry, Lois
See Duncan, Lois

Kesey, Ken (Elton)
1935-...... CLC **1, 3, 6, 11, 46, 64; DA;**
DAB; DAC; DAM MST, NOV, POP;
WLC
See also CA 1-4R; CANR 22, 38;
CDALB 1968-1988; DLB 2, 16; MTCW;
SATA 66

Kesselring, Joseph (Otto)
1902-1967 ..... CLC **45; DAM DRAM,**
MST
See also CA 150

Kessler, Jascha (Frederick) 1929-.... CLC **4**
See also CA 17-20R; CANR 8, 48

Kettelkamp, Larry (Dale) 1933-.... CLC **12**
See also CA 29-32R; CANR 16; SAAS 3;
SATA 2

Key, Ellen 1849-1926........... TCLC **65**

Keyber, Conny
See Fielding, Henry

Keyes, Daniel
1927-............. CLC **80; DA; DAC;**
DAM MST, NOV
See also CA 17-20R; CANR 10, 26, 54;
SATA 37

Keynes, John Maynard
1883-1946 .... TCLC **64**
See also CA 114; DLBD 10

Khanshendel, Chiron
See Rose, Wendy

Khayyam, Omar
1048-1131 .... CMLC **11; DAM POET;**
PC 8

Kherdian, David 1931-........... CLC **6, 9**
See also CA 21-24R; CAAS 2; CANR 39;
CLR 24; JRDA; MAICYA; SATA 16, 74

Khlebnikov, Velimir .... TCLC **20**
See also Khlebnikov, Viktor Vladimirovich

Khlebnikov, Viktor Vladimirovich 1885-1922
See Khlebnikov, Velimir
See also CA 117

Khodasevich, Vladislav (Felitsianovich)
1886-1939 .... TCLC **15**
See also CA 115

Kielland, Alexander Lange
1849-1906 .... TCLC **5**
See also CA 104

Kiely, Benedict 1919-.......... CLC **23, 43**
See also CA 1-4R; CANR 2; DLB 15

Kienzle, William X(avier)
1928-........... CLC **25; DAM POP**
See also CA 93-96; CAAS 1; CANR 9, 31;
INT CANR-31; MTCW

Kierkegaard, Soren 1813-1855.... NCLC **34**

Killens, John Oliver 1916-1987..... CLC **10**
See also BW 2; CA 77-80; 123; CAAS 2;
CANR 26; DLB 33

Killigrew, Anne 1660-1685.......... LC **4**
See also DLB 131

Kim
See Simenon, Georges (Jacques Christian)

Kincaid, Jamaica
1949-............. CLC **43, 68; BLC;**
DAM MULT, NOV
See also AAYA 13; BW 2; CA 125;
CANR 47; DLB 157

King, Francis (Henry)
1923-........... CLC **8, 53; DAM NOV**
See also CA 1-4R; CANR 1, 33; DLB 15,
139; MTCW

King, Martin Luther, Jr.
1929-1968 .... CLC **83; BLC; DA; DAB;**
DAC; DAM MST, MULT
See also BW 2; CA 25-28; CANR 27, 44;
CAP 2; MTCW; SATA 14

King, Stephen (Edwin)
1947-............. CLC **12, 26, 37, 61;**
DAM NOV, POP; SSC 17
See also AAYA 1, 17; BEST 90:1;
CA 61-64; CANR 1, 30, 52; DLB 143;
DLBY 80; JRDA; MTCW; SATA 9, 55

King, Steve
See King, Stephen (Edwin)

King, Thomas
1943- ..... CLC **89; DAC; DAM MULT**
See also CA 144; DLB 175; NNAL

Kingman, Lee..................... CLC **17**
See also Natti, (Mary) Lee
See also SAAS 3; SATA 1, 67

Kingsley, Charles 1819-1875 ..... NCLC **35**
See also DLB 21, 32, 163; YABC 2

Kingsley, Sidney 1906-1995........ CLC **44**
See also CA 85-88; 147; DLB 7

Kingsolver, Barbara
1955-......... CLC **55, 81; DAM POP**
See also AAYA 15; CA 129; 134; INT 134

Kingston, Maxine (Ting Ting) Hong
1940- .... CLC **12, 19, 58; DAM MULT,**
NOV
See also AAYA 8; CA 69-72; CANR 13,
38; DLB 173; DLBY 80; INT CANR-13;
MTCW; SATA 53

Kinnell, Galway
1927- ...... CLC **1, 2, 3, 5, 13, 29**
See also CA 9-12R; CANR 10, 34; DLB 5;
DLBY 87; INT CANR-34; MTCW

Kinsella, Thomas 1928- .... CLC **4, 19**
See also CA 17-20R; CANR 15; DLB 27;
MTCW

Kinsella, W(illiam) P(atrick)
1935-............. CLC **27, 43; DAC;**
DAM NOV, POP
See also AAYA 7; CA 97-100; CAAS 7;
CANR 21, 35; INT CANR-21; MTCW

Kipling, (Joseph) Rudyard
1865-1936 ...... TCLC **8, 17; DA; DAB;**
DAC; DAM MST, POET; PC 3; SSC 5;
WLC
See also CA 105; 120; CANR 33;
CDBLB 1890-1914; CLR 39; DLB 19, 34,
141, 156; MAICYA; MTCW; YABC 2

Kirkup, James 1918- .... CLC **1**
See also CA 1-4R; CAAS 4; CANR 2;
DLB 27; SATA 12

Kirkwood, James 1930(?)-1989 ...... CLC **9**
See also AITN 2; CA 1-4R; 128; CANR 6,
40

Kirshner, Sidney
See Kingsley, Sidney

Kis, Danilo 1935-1989 .... CLC **57**
See also CA 109; 118; 129; MTCW

Kivi, Aleksis 1834-1872 .... NCLC **30**

Kizer, Carolyn (Ashley)
1925- ..... CLC **15, 39, 80; DAM POET**
See also CA 65-68; CAAS 5; CANR 24;
DLB 5, 169

Klabund 1890-1928.............. TCLC **44**
See also DLB 66

Klappert, Peter 1942-............. CLC **57**
See also CA 33-36R; DLB 5

Klein, A(braham) M(oses)
1909-1972 .... CLC **19; DAB; DAC;**
DAM MST
See also CA 101; 37-40R; DLB 68

Klein, Norma 1938-1989 .... CLC **30**
See also AAYA 2; CA 41-44R; 128;
CANR 15, 37; CLR 2, 19;
INT CANR-15; JRDA; MAICYA;
SAAS 1; SATA 7, 57

Klein, T(heodore) E(ibon) D(onald)
1947-...................... CLC **34**
See also CA 119; CANR 44

Kleist, Heinrich von
1777-1811 .... NCLC **2, 37;**
DAM DRAM; SSC 22
See also DLB 90

Klima, Ivan 1931-..... CLC **56; DAM NOV**
See also CA 25-28R; CANR 17, 50

Klimentov, Andrei Platonovich 1899-1951
See Platonov, Andrei
See also CA 108

Klinger, Friedrich Maximilian von
1752-1831 .... NCLC **1**
See also DLB 94

Klopstock, Friedrich Gottlieb
1724-1803 .... NCLC **11**
See also DLB 97

Knapp, Caroline 1959-............ CLC **99**
See also CA 154

Knebel, Fletcher 1911-1993........ CLC **14**
See also AITN 1; CA 1-4R; 140; CAAS 3;
CANR 1, 36; SATA 36; SATA-Obit 75

Knickerbocker, Diedrich
See Irving, Washington

Knight, Etheridge
1931-1991 .... CLC **40; BLC;**
DAM POET; PC 14
See also BW 1; CA 21-24R; 133; CANR 23;
DLB 41

Knight, Sarah Kemble 1666-1727 ..... LC **7**
See also DLB 24

Knister, Raymond 1899-1932...... TCLC **56**
See also DLB 68

Knowles, John
1926- ...... CLC 1, 4, 10, 26; DA; DAC;
DAM MST, NOV
See also AAYA 10; CA 17-20R; CANR 40;
CDALB 1968-1988; DLB 6; MTCW;
SATA 8, 89

Knox, Calvin M.
See Silverberg, Robert

Knox, John c. 1505-1572 .... LC 37
See also DLB 132

Knye, Cassandra
See Disch, Thomas M(ichael)

Koch, C(hristopher) J(ohn) 1932- ... CLC 42
See also CA 127

Koch, Christopher
See Koch, C(hristopher) J(ohn)

Koch, Kenneth
1925- ...... CLC 5, 8, 44; DAM POET
See also CA 1-4R; CANR 6, 36, 57; DLB 5;
INT CANR-36; SATA 65

Kochanowski, Jan 1530-1584........ LC 10

Kock, Charles Paul de
1794-1871 .... NCLC 16

Koda Shigeyuki 1867-1947
See Rohan, Koda
See also CA 121

Koestler, Arthur
1905-1983 .... CLC 1, 3, 6, 8, 15, 33
See also CA 1-4R; 109; CANR 1, 33;
CDBLB 1945-1960; DLBY 83; MTCW

Kogawa, Joy Nozomi
1935- ...... CLC 78; DAC; DAM MST,
MULT
See also CA 101; CANR 19

Kohout, Pavel 1928-.............. CLC 13
See also CA 45-48; CANR 3

Koizumi, Yakumo
See Hearn, (Patricio) Lafcadio (Tessima
Carlos)

Kolmar, Gertrud 1894-1943...... TCLC 40

Komunyakaa, Yusef 1947-...... CLC 86, 94
See also CA 147; DLB 120

Konrad, George
See Konrad, Gyoergy

Konrad, Gyoergy 1933- ...... CLC 4, 10, 73
See also CA 85-88

Konwicki, Tadeusz 1926-..... CLC 8, 28, 54
See also CA 101; CAAS 9; CANR 39;
MTCW

Koontz, Dean R(ay)
1945- ...... CLC 78; DAM NOV, POP
See also AAYA 9; BEST 89:3, 90:2;
CA 108; CANR 19, 36, 52; MTCW;
SATA 92

Kopit, Arthur (Lee)
1937- ..... CLC 1, 18, 33; DAM DRAM
See also AITN 1; CA 81-84; CABS 3;
DLB 7; MTCW

Kops, Bernard 1926-.............. CLC 4
See also CA 5-8R; DLB 13

Kornbluth, C(yril) M. 1923-1958.... TCLC 8
See also CA 105; DLB 8

Korolenko, V. G.
See Korolenko, Vladimir Galaktionovich

Korolenko, Vladimir
See Korolenko, Vladimir Galaktionovich

Korolenko, Vladimir G.
See Korolenko, Vladimir Galaktionovich

Korolenko, Vladimir Galaktionovich
1853-1921 .... TCLC 22
See also CA 121

Korzybski, Alfred (Habdank Skarbek)
1879-1950 .... TCLC 61
See also CA 123

Kosinski, Jerzy (Nikodem)
1933-1991 .... CLC 1, 2, 3, 6, 10, 15, 53,
70; DAM NOV
See also CA 17-20R; 134; CANR 9, 46;
DLB 2; DLBY 82; MTCW

Kostelanetz, Richard (Cory) 1940- .. CLC 28
See also CA 13-16R; CAAS 8; CANR 38

Kostrowitzki, Wilhelm Apollinaris de
1880-1918
See Apollinaire, Guillaume
See also CA 104

Kotlowitz, Robert 1924-............ CLC 4
See also CA 33-36R; CANR 36

Kotzebue, August (Friedrich Ferdinand) von
1761-1819 .... NCLC 25
See also DLB 94

Kotzwinkle, William 1938- ... CLC 5, 14, 35
See also CA 45-48; CANR 3, 44; CLR 6;
DLB 173; MAICYA; SATA 24, 70

Kowna, Stancy
See Szymborska, Wislawa

Kozol, Jonathan 1936-............ CLC 17
See also CA 61-64; CANR 16, 45

Kozoll, Michael 1940(?)- .... CLC 35

Kramer, Kathryn 19(?)- .... CLC 34

Kramer, Larry 1935- .. CLC 42; DAM POP
See also CA 124; 126

Krasicki, Ignacy 1735-1801....... NCLC 8

Krasinski, Zygmunt 1812-1859 .... NCLC 4

Kraus, Karl 1874-1936........... TCLC 5
See also CA 104; DLB 118

Kreve (Mickevicius), Vincas
1882-1954 .... TCLC 27

Kristeva, Julia 1941- .... CLC 77
See also CA 154

Kristofferson, Kris 1936-.......... CLC 26
See also CA 104

Krizanc, John 1956-............. CLC 57

Krleza, Miroslav 1893-1981........ CLC 8
See also CA 97-100; 105; CANR 50;
DLB 147

Kroetsch, Robert
1927- .... CLC 5, 23, 57; DAC;
DAM POET
See also CA 17-20R; CANR 8, 38; DLB 53;
MTCW

Kroetz, Franz
See Kroetz, Franz Xaver

Kroetz, Franz Xaver 1946- .... CLC 41
See also CA 130

Kroker, Arthur 1945-............. CLC 77

Kropotkin, Peter (Aleksieevich)
1842-1921 .... TCLC 36
See also CA 119

Krotkov, Yuri 1917-.............. CLC 19
See also CA 102

Krumb
See Crumb, R(obert)

Krumgold, Joseph (Quincy)
1908-1980 .... CLC 12
See also CA 9-12R; 101; CANR 7;
MAICYA; SATA 1, 48; SATA-Obit 23

Krumwitz
See Crumb, R(obert)

Krutch, Joseph Wood 1893-1970.... CLC 24
See also CA 1-4R; 25-28R; CANR 4;
DLB 63

Krutzch, Gus
See Eliot, T(homas) S(tearns)

Krylov, Ivan Andreevich
1768(?)-1844 .... NCLC 1
See also DLB 150

Kubin, Alfred (Leopold Isidor)
1877-1959 .... TCLC 23
See also CA 112; 149; DLB 81

Kubrick, Stanley 1928-............ CLC 16
See also CA 81-84; CANR 33; DLB 26

Kumin, Maxine (Winokur)
1925- ..... CLC 5, 13, 28; DAM POET;
PC 15
See also AITN 2; CA 1-4R; CAAS 8;
CANR 1, 21; DLB 5; MTCW; SATA 12

Kundera, Milan
1929- .... CLC 4, 9, 19, 32, 68;
DAM NOV; SSC 24
See also AAYA 2; CA 85-88; CANR 19,
52; MTCW

Kunene, Mazisi (Raymond) 1930-... CLC 85
See also BW 1; CA 125; DLB 117

Kunitz, Stanley (Jasspon)
1905- .... CLC 6, 11, 14
See also CA 41-44R; CANR 26, 57;
DLB 48; INT CANR-26; MTCW

Kunze, Reiner 1933-.............. CLC 10
See also CA 93-96; DLB 75

Kuprin, Aleksandr Ivanovich
1870-1938 .... TCLC 5
See also CA 104

Kureishi, Hanif 1954(?)-........... CLC 64
See also CA 139

Kurosawa, Akira
1910- .... CLC 16; DAM MULT
See also AAYA 11; CA 101; CANR 46

Kushner, Tony
1957(?)- .... CLC 81; DAM DRAM
See also CA 144

Kuttner, Henry 1915-1958........ TCLC 10
See also CA 107; DLB 8

Kuzma, Greg 1944-................ CLC 7
See also CA 33-36R

Kuzmin, Mikhail 1872(?)-1936 .... TCLC 40

Kyd, Thomas
1558-1594 .... LC 22; DAM DRAM;
DC 3
See also DLB 62

Lind, Jakov . . . . CLC 1, 2, 4, 27, 82
See also Landwirth, Heinz
See also CAAS 4

Lindbergh, Anne (Spencer) Morrow
1906- . . . . CLC 82; DAM NOV
See also CA 17-20R; CANR 16; MTCW;
SATA 33

Lindsay, David 1878-1945 . . . . TCLC 15
See also CA 113

Lindsay, (Nicholas) Vachel
1879-1931 . . . . TCLC 17; DA; DAC;
DAM MST, POET; WLC
See also CA 114; 135; CDALB 1865-1917;
DLB 54; SATA 40

Linke-Poot
See Doeblin, Alfred

Linney, Romulus 1930- . . . . CLC 51
See also CA 1-4R; CANR 40, 44

Linton, Eliza Lynn 1822-1898 . . . . NCLC 41
See also DLB 18

Li Po 701-763 . . . . CMLC 2

Lipsius, Justus 1547-1606 . . . . LC 16

Lipsyte, Robert (Michael)
1938- . . . . CLC 21; DA; DAC;
DAM MST, NOV
See also AAYA 7; CA 17-20R; CANR 8,
57; CLR 23; JRDA; MAICYA; SATA 5,
68

Lish, Gordon (Jay) 1934- . . CLC 45; SSC 18
See also CA 113; 117; DLB 130; INT 117

Lispector, Clarice 1925-1977 . . . . CLC 43
See also CA 139; 116; DLB 113

Littell, Robert 1935(?)- . . . . CLC 42
See also CA 109; 112

Little, Malcolm 1925-1965
See Malcolm X
See also BW 1; CA 125; 111; DA; DAB;
DAC; DAM MST, MULT; MTCW

Littlewit, Humphrey Gent.
See Lovecraft, H(oward) P(hillips)

Litwos
See Sienkiewicz, Henryk (Adam Alexander
Pius)

Liu E 1857-1909 . . . . TCLC 15
See also CA 115

Lively, Penelope (Margaret)
1933- . . . . CLC 32, 50; DAM NOV
See also CA 41-44R; CANR 29; CLR 7;
DLB 14, 161; JRDA; MAICYA; MTCW;
SATA 7, 60

Livesay, Dorothy (Kathleen)
1909- . . . . CLC 4, 15, 79; DAC;
DAM MST, POET
See also AITN 2; CA 25-28R; CAAS 8;
CANR 36; DLB 68; MTCW

Livy c. 59B.C.-c. 17 . . . . CMLC 11

Lizardi, Jose Joaquin Fernandez de
1776-1827 . . . . NCLC 30

Llewellyn, Richard
See Llewellyn Lloyd, Richard Dafydd
Vivian
See also DLB 15

Llewellyn Lloyd, Richard Dafydd Vivian
1906-1983 . . . . CLC 7, 80
See also Llewellyn, Richard
See also CA 53-56; 111; CANR 7;
SATA 11; SATA-Obit 37

Llosa, (Jorge) Mario (Pedro) Vargas
See Vargas Llosa, (Jorge) Mario (Pedro)

Lloyd Webber, Andrew 1948-
See Webber, Andrew Lloyd
See also AAYA 1; CA 116; 149;
DAM DRAM; SATA 56

Llull, Ramon c. 1235-c. 1316 . . . . . CMLC 12

Locke, Alain (Le Roy)
1886-1954 . . . . TCLC 43
See also BW 1; CA 106; 124; DLB 51

Locke, John 1632-1704 . . . . LC 7, 35
See also DLB 101

Locke-Elliott, Sumner
See Elliott, Sumner Locke

Lockhart, John Gibson
1794-1854 . . . . NCLC 6
See also DLB 110, 116, 144

Lodge, David (John)
1935- . . . . CLC 36; DAM POP
See also BEST 90:1; CA 17-20R; CANR 19,
53; DLB 14; INT CANR-19; MTCW

Loennbohm, Armas Eino Leopold 1878-1926
See Leino, Eino
See also CA 123

Loewinsohn, Ron(ald William)
1937- . . . . CLC 52
See also CA 25-28R

Logan, Jake
See Smith, Martin Cruz

Logan, John (Burton) 1923-1987 . . . . . CLC 5
See also CA 77-80; 124; CANR 45; DLB 5

Lo Kuan-chung 1330(?)-1400(?) . . . . . . LC 12

Lombard, Nap
See Johnson, Pamela Hansford

London, Jack . . TCLC 9, 15, 39; SSC 4; WLC
See also London, John Griffith
See also AAYA 13; AITN 2;
CDALB 1865-1917; DLB 8, 12, 78;
SATA 18

London, John Griffith 1876-1916
See London, Jack
See also CA 110; 119; DA; DAB; DAC;
DAM MST, NOV; JRDA; MAICYA;
MTCW

Long, Emmett
See Leonard, Elmore (John, Jr.)

Longbaugh, Harry
See Goldman, William (W.)

Longfellow, Henry Wadsworth
1807-1882 . . . . . NCLC 2, 45; DA; DAB;
DAC; DAM MST, POET
See also CDALB 1640-1865; DLB 1, 59;
SATA 19

Longley, Michael 1939- . . . . CLC 29
See also CA 102; DLB 40

Longus fl. c. 2nd cent. - . . . . CMLC 7

Longway, A. Hugh
See Lang, Andrew

Lonnrot, Elias 1802-1884 . . . . NCLC 53

Lopate, Phillip 1943- . . . . CLC 29
See also CA 97-100; DLBY 80; INT 97-100

Lopez Portillo (y Pacheco), Jose
1920- . . . . CLC 46
See also CA 129; HW

Lopez y Fuentes, Gregorio
1897(?)-1966 . . . . CLC 32
See also CA 131; HW

Lorca, Federico Garcia
See Garcia Lorca, Federico

Lord, Bette Bao 1938- . . . . CLC 23
See also BEST 90:3; CA 107; CANR 41;
INT 107; SATA 58

Lord Auch
See Bataille, Georges

Lord Byron
See Byron, George Gordon (Noel)

Lorde, Audre (Geraldine)
1934-1992 . . . . CLC 18, 71; BLC;
DAM MULT, POET; PC 12
See also BW 1; CA 25-28R; 142; CANR 16,
26, 46; DLB 41; MTCW

Lord Houghton
See Milnes, Richard Monckton

Lord Jeffrey
See Jeffrey, Francis

Lorenzini, Carlo 1826-1890
See Collodi, Carlo
See also MAICYA; SATA 29

Lorenzo, Heberto Padilla
See Padilla (Lorenzo), Heberto

Loris
See Hofmannsthal, Hugo von

Loti, Pierre . . . . TCLC 11
See also Viaud, (Louis Marie) Julien
See also DLB 123

Louie, David Wong 1954- . . . . CLC 70
See also CA 139

Louis, Father M.
See Merton, Thomas

Lovecraft, H(oward) P(hillips)
1890-1937 . . . . TCLC 4, 22; DAM POP;
SSC 3
See also AAYA 14; CA 104; 133; MTCW

Lovelace, Earl 1935- . . . . CLC 51
See also BW 2; CA 77-80; CANR 41;
DLB 125; MTCW

Lovelace, Richard 1618-1657 . . . . LC 24
See also DLB 131

Lowell, Amy
1874-1925 . . . . TCLC 1, 8; DAM POET;
PC 13
See also CA 104; 151; DLB 54, 140

Lowell, James Russell 1819-1891 . . NCLC 2
See also CDALB 1640-1865; DLB 1, 11, 64,
79

Lowell, Robert (Traill Spence, Jr.)
1917-1977 . . . CLC 1, 2, 3, 4, 5, 8, 9, 11,
15, 37; DA; DAB; DAC; DAM MST,
NOV; PC 3; WLC
See also CA 9-12R; 73-76; CABS 2;
CANR 26; DLB 5, 169; MTCW

Lowndes, Marie Adelaide (Belloc)
1868-1947 . . . . TCLC 12
See also CA 107; DLB 70

Lowry, (Clarence) Malcolm
1909-1957 . . . . **TCLC 6, 40**
See also CA 105; 131; CDBLB 1945-1960;
DLB 15; MTCW

Lowry, Mina Gertrude 1882-1966
See Loy, Mina
See also CA 113

Loxsmith, John
See Brunner, John (Kilian Houston)

Loy, Mina . . . . **CLC 28; DAM POET; PC 16**
See also Lowry, Mina Gertrude
See also DLB 4, 54

Loyson-Bridet
See Schwob, (Mayer Andre) Marcel

Lucas, Craig 1951- . . . . **CLC 64**
See also CA 137

Lucas, George 1944- . . . . **CLC 16**
See also AAYA 1; CA 77-80; CANR 30;
SATA 56

Lucas, Hans
See Godard, Jean-Luc

Lucas, Victoria
See Plath, Sylvia

Ludlam, Charles 1943-1987 . . . . . **CLC 46, 50**
See also CA 85-88; 122

Ludlum, Robert
1927- . . . **CLC 22, 43; DAM NOV, POP**
See also AAYA 10; BEST 89:1, 90:3;
CA 33-36R; CANR 25, 41; DLBY 82;
MTCW

Ludwig, Ken . . . . **CLC 60**

Ludwig, Otto 1813-1865 . . . . **NCLC 4**
See also DLB 129

Lugones, Leopoldo 1874-1938 . . . . . **TCLC 15**
See also CA 116; 131; HW

Lu Hsun 1881-1936 . . . . . . **TCLC 3; SSC 20**
See also Shu-Jen, Chou

Lukacs, George . . . . **CLC 24**
See also Lukacs, Gyorgy (Szegeny von)

Lukacs, Gyorgy (Szegeny von) 1885-1971
See Lukacs, George
See also CA 101; 29-32R

Luke, Peter (Ambrose Cyprian)
1919-1995 . . . . **CLC 38**
See also CA 81-84; 147; DLB 13

Lunar, Dennis
See Mungo, Raymond

Lurie, Alison 1926- . . . . **CLC 4, 5, 18, 39**
See also CA 1-4R; CANR 2, 17, 50; DLB 2;
MTCW; SATA 46

Lustig, Arnost 1926- . . . . **CLC 56**
See also AAYA 3; CA 69-72; CANR 47;
SATA 56

Luther, Martin 1483-1546 . . . . **LC 9, 37**

Luxemburg, Rosa 1870(?)-1919 . . . . **TCLC 63**
See also CA 118

Luzi, Mario 1914- . . . . **CLC 13**
See also CA 61-64; CANR 9; DLB 128

Lyly, John 1554(?)-1606 . . . . **DC 7**
See also DAM DRAM; DLB 62, 167

L'Ymagier
See Gourmont, Remy (-Marie-Charles) de

Lynch, B. Suarez
See Bioy Casares, Adolfo; Borges, Jorge
Luis

Lynch, David (K.) 1946- . . . . **CLC 66**
See also CA 124; 129

Lynch, James
See Andreyev, Leonid (Nikolaevich)

Lynch Davis, B.
See Bioy Casares, Adolfo; Borges, Jorge
Luis

Lyndsay, Sir David 1490-1555 . . . . . . **LC 20**

Lynn, Kenneth S(chuyler) 1923- . . . . **CLC 50**
See also CA 1-4R; CANR 3, 27

Lynx
See West, Rebecca

Lyons, Marcus
See Blish, James (Benjamin)

Lyre, Pinchbeck
See Sassoon, Siegfried (Lorraine)

Lytle, Andrew (Nelson) 1902-1995 . . **CLC 22**
See also CA 9-12R; 150; DLB 6; DLBY 95

Lyttelton, George 1709-1773 . . . . **LC 10**

Maas, Peter 1929- . . . . **CLC 29**
See also CA 93-96; INT 93-96

Macaulay, Rose 1881-1958 . . . . . **TCLC 7, 44**
See also CA 104; DLB 36

Macaulay, Thomas Babington
1800-1859 . . . . **NCLC 42**
See also CDBLB 1832-1890; DLB 32, 55

MacBeth, George (Mann)
1932-1992 . . . . **CLC 2, 5, 9**
See also CA 25-28R; 136; DLB 40; MTCW;
SATA 4; SATA-Obit 70

MacCaig, Norman (Alexander)
1910- . . . . . **CLC 36; DAB; DAM POET**
See also CA 9-12R; CANR 3, 34; DLB 27

MacCarthy, (Sir Charles Otto) Desmond
1877-1952 . . . . **TCLC 36**

MacDiarmid, Hugh
. . . . **CLC 2, 4, 11, 19, 63; PC 9**
See also Grieve, C(hristopher) M(urray)
See also CDBLB 1945-1960; DLB 20

MacDonald, Anson
See Heinlein, Robert A(nson)

Macdonald, Cynthia 1928- . . . . . . **CLC 13, 19**
See also CA 49-52; CANR 4, 44; DLB 105

MacDonald, George 1824-1905 . . . . . **TCLC 9**
See also CA 106; 137; DLB 18, 163;
MAICYA; SATA 33

Macdonald, John
See Millar, Kenneth

MacDonald, John D(ann)
1916-1986 . . . . **CLC 3, 27, 44;**
DAM NOV, POP
See also CA 1-4R; 121; CANR 1, 19;
DLB 8; DLBY 86; MTCW

Macdonald, John Ross
See Millar, Kenneth

Macdonald, Ross . . . . . **CLC 1, 2, 3, 14, 34, 41**
See also Millar, Kenneth
See also DLBD 6

MacDougal, John
See Blish, James (Benjamin)

MacEwen, Gwendolyn (Margaret)
1941-1987 . . . . **CLC 13, 55**
See also CA 9-12R; 124; CANR 7, 22;
DLB 53; SATA 50; SATA-Obit 55

Macha, Karel Hynek 1810-1846 . . **NCLC 46**

Machado (y Ruiz), Antonio
1875-1939 . . . . **TCLC 3**
See also CA 104; DLB 108

Machado de Assis, Joaquim Maria
1839-1908 . . . . . **TCLC 10; BLC; SSC 24**
See also CA 107; 153

Machen, Arthur . . . . **TCLC 4; SSC 20**
See also Jones, Arthur Llewellyn
See also DLB 36, 156

Machiavelli, Niccolo
1469-1527 . . . . **LC 8, 36; DA; DAB;**
DAC; DAM MST

MacInnes, Colin 1914-1976 . . . . . . **CLC 4, 23**
See also CA 69-72; 65-68; CANR 21;
DLB 14; MTCW

MacInnes, Helen (Clark)
1907-1985 . . . . . **CLC 27, 39; DAM POP**
See also CA 1-4R; 117; CANR 1, 28;
DLB 87; MTCW; SATA 22;
SATA-Obit 44

Mackay, Mary 1855-1924
See Corelli, Marie
See also CA 118

Mackenzie, Compton (Edward Montague)
1883-1972 . . . . **CLC 18**
See also CA 21-22; 37-40R; CAP 2;
DLB 34, 100

Mackenzie, Henry 1745-1831 . . . . **NCLC 41**
See also DLB 39

Mackintosh, Elizabeth 1896(?)-1952
See Tey, Josephine
See also CA 110

MacLaren, James
See Grieve, C(hristopher) M(urray)

Mac Laverty, Bernard 1942- . . . . **CLC 31**
See also CA 116; 118; CANR 43; INT 118

MacLean, Alistair (Stuart)
1922-1987 . . . . **CLC 3, 13, 50, 63;**
DAM POP
See also CA 57-60; 121; CANR 28; MTCW;
SATA 23; SATA-Obit 50

Maclean, Norman (Fitzroy)
1902-1990 . . . . **CLC 78; DAM POP;**
SSC 13
See also CA 102; 132; CANR 49

MacLeish, Archibald
1892-1982 . . . . **CLC 3, 8, 14, 68;**
DAM POET
See also CA 9-12R; 106; CANR 33; DLB 4,
7, 45; DLBY 82; MTCW

MacLennan, (John) Hugh
1907-1990 . . . . **CLC 2, 14, 92; DAC;**
DAM MST
See also CA 5-8R; 142; CANR 33; DLB 68;
MTCW

MacLeod, Alistair
1936- . . . . . . **CLC 56; DAC; DAM MST**
See also CA 123; DLB 60

MacNeice, (Frederick) Louis
1907-1963 ...... **CLC 1, 4, 10, 53; DAB;
DAM POET**
See also CA 85-88; DLB 10, 20; MTCW

MacNeill, Dand
See Fraser, George MacDonald

Macpherson, James   1736-1796 ...... **LC 29**
See also DLB 109

Macpherson, (Jean) Jay   1931- ...... **CLC 14**
See also CA 5-8R; DLB 53

MacShane, Frank   1927- .... **CLC 39**
See also CA 9-12R; CANR 3, 33; DLB 111

Macumber, Mari
See Sandoz, Mari(e Susette)

Madach, Imre   1823-1864 .... **NCLC 19**

Madden, (Jerry) David   1933- .... **CLC 5, 15**
See also CA 1-4R; CAAS 3; CANR 4, 45;
DLB 6; MTCW

Maddern, Al(an)
See Ellison, Harlan (Jay)

Madhubuti, Haki R.
1942- .... **CLC 6, 73; BLC;
DAM MULT, POET; PC 5**
See also Lee, Don L.
See also BW 2; CA 73-76; CANR 24, 51;
DLB 5, 41; DLBD 8

Maepenn, Hugh
See Kuttner, Henry

Maepenn, K. H.
See Kuttner, Henry

Maeterlinck, Maurice
1862-1949 ...... **TCLC 3; DAM DRAM**
See also CA 104; 136; SATA 66

Maginn, William   1794-1842 ...... **NCLC 8**
See also DLB 110, 159

Mahapatra, Jayanta
1928- .... **CLC 33; DAM MULT**
See also CA 73-76; CAAS 9; CANR 15, 33

Mahfouz, Naguib (Abdel Aziz Al-Sabilgi)
1911(?)-
See Mahfuz, Najib
See also BEST 89:2; CA 128; CANR 55;
DAM NOV; MTCW

Mahfuz, Najib .... **CLC 52, 55**
See also Mahfouz, Naguib (Abdel Aziz
Al-Sabilgi)
See also DLBY 88

Mahon, Derek   1941- .... **CLC 27**
See also CA 113; 128; DLB 40

Mailer, Norman
1923- ...... **CLC 1, 2, 3, 4, 5, 8, 11, 14,
28, 39, 74; DA; DAB; DAC; DAM MST,
NOV, POP**
See also AITN 2; CA 9-12R; CABS 1;
CANR 28; CDALB 1968-1988; DLB 2,
16, 28; DLBD 3; DLBY 80, 83; MTCW

Maillet, Antonine   1929- ...... **CLC 54; DAC**
See also CA 115; 120; CANR 46; DLB 60;
INT 120

Mais, Roger   1905-1955 .... **TCLC 8**
See also BW 1; CA 105; 124; DLB 125;
MTCW

Maistre, Joseph de   1753-1821 .... **NCLC 37**

Maitland, Frederic   1850-1906 ..... **TCLC 65**

Maitland, Sara (Louise)   1950- ...... **CLC 49**
See also CA 69-72; CANR 13

Major, Clarence
1936- .... **CLC 3, 19, 48; BLC;
DAM MULT**
See also BW 2; CA 21-24R; CAAS 6;
CANR 13, 25, 53; DLB 33

Major, Kevin (Gerald)
1949- .... **CLC 26; DAC**
See also AAYA 16; CA 97-100; CANR 21,
38; CLR 11; DLB 60; INT CANR-21;
JRDA; MAICYA; SATA 32, 82

Maki, James
See Ozu, Yasujiro

Malabaila, Damiano
See Levi, Primo

Malamud, Bernard
1914-1986 ...... **CLC 1, 2, 3, 5, 8, 9, 11,
18, 27, 44, 78, 85; DA; DAB; DAC;
DAM MST, NOV, POP; SSC 15; WLC**
See also AAYA 16; CA 5-8R; 118; CABS 1;
CANR 28; CDALB 1941-1968; DLB 2,
28, 152; DLBY 80, 86; MTCW

Malaparte, Curzio   1898-1957 ..... **TCLC 52**

Malcolm, Dan
See Silverberg, Robert

Malcolm X .... **CLC 82; BLC**
See also Little, Malcolm

Malherbe, Francois de   1555-1628 ..... **LC 5**

Mallarme, Stephane
1842-1898 .... **NCLC 4, 41;
DAM POET; PC 4**

Mallet-Joris, Francoise   1930- ...... **CLC 11**
See also CA 65-68; CANR 17; DLB 83

Malley, Ern
See McAuley, James Phillip

Mallowan, Agatha Christie
See Christie, Agatha (Mary Clarissa)

Maloff, Saul   1922- .... **CLC 5**
See also CA 33-36R

Malone, Louis
See MacNeice, (Frederick) Louis

Malone, Michael (Christopher)
1942- .... **CLC 43**
See also CA 77-80; CANR 14, 32, 57

Malory, (Sir) Thomas
1410(?)-1471(?) ...... **LC 11; DA; DAB;
DAC; DAM MST**
See also CDBLB Before 1660; DLB 146;
SATA 59; SATA-Brief 33

Malouf, (George Joseph) David
1934- .... **CLC 28, 86**
See also CA 124; CANR 50

Malraux, (Georges-)Andre
1901-1976 ...... **CLC 1, 4, 9, 13, 15, 57;
DAM NOV**
See also CA 21-22; 69-72; CANR 34;
CAP 2; DLB 72; MTCW

Malzberg, Barry N(athaniel)   1939- ... **CLC 7**
See also CA 61-64; CAAS 4; CANR 16;
DLB 8

Mamet, David (Alan)
1947- .... **CLC 9, 15, 34, 46, 91;
DAM DRAM; DC 4**
See also AAYA 3; CA 81-84; CABS 3;
CANR 15, 41; DLB 7; MTCW

Mamoulian, Rouben (Zachary)
1897-1987 .... **CLC 16**
See also CA 25-28R; 124

Mandelstam, Osip (Emilievich)
1891(?)-1938(?) ...... **TCLC 2, 6; PC 14**
See also CA 104; 150

Mander, (Mary) Jane   1877-1949 ... **TCLC 31**

Mandeville, John   fl. 1350- .... **CMLC 19**
See also DLB 146

Mandiargues, Andre Pieyre de .... **CLC 41**
See also Pieyre de Mandiargues, Andre
See also DLB 83

Mandrake, Ethel Belle
See Thurman, Wallace (Henry)

Mangan, James Clarence
1803-1849 .... **NCLC 27**

Maniere, J.-E.
See Giraudoux, (Hippolyte) Jean

Manley, (Mary) Delariviere
1672(?)-1724 .... **LC 1**
See also DLB 39, 80

Mann, Abel
See Creasey, John

Mann, Emily   1952- .... **DC 7**
See also CA 130; CANR 55

Mann, (Luiz) Heinrich   1871-1950 ... **TCLC 9**
See also CA 106; DLB 66

Mann, (Paul) Thomas
1875-1955 .... **TCLC 2, 8, 14, 21, 35, 44,
60; DA; DAB; DAC; DAM MST, NOV;
SSC 5; WLC**
See also CA 104; 128; DLB 66; MTCW

Mannheim, Karl   1893-1947 .... **TCLC 65**

Manning, David
See Faust, Frederick (Schiller)

Manning, Frederic   1887(?)-1935 ... **TCLC 25**
See also CA 124

Manning, Olivia   1915-1980 ...... **CLC 5, 19**
See also CA 5-8R; 101; CANR 29; MTCW

Mano, D. Keith   1942- .... **CLC 2, 10**
See also CA 25-28R; CAAS 6; CANR 26,
57; DLB 6

Mansfield, Katherine
.. **TCLC 2, 8, 39; DAB; SSC 9, 23; WLC**
See also Beauchamp, Kathleen Mansfield
See also DLB 162

Manso, Peter   1940- .... **CLC 39**
See also CA 29-32R; CANR 44

Mantecon, Juan Jimenez
See Jimenez (Mantecon), Juan Ramon

Manton, Peter
See Creasey, John

Man Without a Spleen, A
See Chekhov, Anton (Pavlovich)

Manzoni, Alessandro   1785-1873 .. **NCLC 29**

Mapu, Abraham (ben Jekutiel)
1808-1867 .... **NCLC 18**

Mara, Sally
See Queneau, Raymond

Marat, Jean Paul 1743-1793 . . . . **LC 10**

Marcel, Gabriel Honore
    1889-1973 . . . . **CLC 15**
    See also CA 102; 45-48; MTCW

Marchbanks, Samuel
    See Davies, (William) Robertson

Marchi, Giacomo
    See Bassani, Giorgio

Margulies, Donald . . . . **CLC 76**

Marie de France c. 12th cent. - . . . . **CMLC 8**

Marie de l'Incarnation 1599-1672 . . . . **LC 10**

Marier, Captain Victor
    See Griffith, D(avid Lewelyn) W(ark)

Mariner, Scott
    See Pohl, Frederik

Marinetti, Filippo Tommaso
    1876-1944 . . . . **TCLC 10**
    See also CA 107; DLB 114

Marivaux, Pierre Carlet de Chamblain de
    1688-1763 . . . . **LC 4; DC 7**

Markandaya, Kamala . . . . **CLC 8, 38**
    See also Taylor, Kamala (Purnaiya)

Markfield, Wallace 1926- . . . . **CLC 8**
    See also CA 69-72; CAAS 3; DLB 2, 28

Markham, Edwin 1852-1940 . . . . . **TCLC 47**
    See also DLB 54

Markham, Robert
    See Amis, Kingsley (William)

Marks, J
    See Highwater, Jamake (Mamake)

Marks-Highwater, J
    See Highwater, Jamake (Mamake)

Markson, David M(errill) 1927- . . . . **CLC 67**
    See also CA 49-52; CANR 1

Marley, Bob . . . . **CLC 17**
    See also Marley, Robert Nesta

Marley, Robert Nesta 1945-1981
    See Marley, Bob
    See also CA 107; 103

Marlowe, Christopher
    1564-1593 . . . . . **LC 22; DA; DAB; DAC;**
                DAM DRAM, MST; DC 1; WLC
    See also CDBLB Before 1660; DLB 62

Marlowe, Stephen 1928-
    See Queen, Ellery
    See also CA 13-16R; CANR 6, 55

Marmontel, Jean-Francois
    1723-1799 . . . . **LC 2**

Marquand, John P(hillips)
    1893-1960 . . . . **CLC 2, 10**
    See also CA 85-88; DLB 9, 102

Marques, Rene
    1919-1979 . . . . . . **CLC 96; DAM MULT;**
                                        HLC
    See also CA 97-100; 85-88; DLB 113; HW

Marquez, Gabriel (Jose) Garcia
    See Garcia Marquez, Gabriel (Jose)

Marquis, Don(ald Robert Perry)
    1878-1937 . . . . **TCLC 7**
    See also CA 104; DLB 11, 25

Marric, J. J.
    See Creasey, John

Marrow, Bernard
    See Moore, Brian

Marryat, Frederick 1792-1848 . . . . **NCLC 3**
    See also DLB 21, 163

Marsden, James
    See Creasey, John

Marsh, (Edith) Ngaio
    1899-1982 . . . . . . **CLC 7, 53; DAM POP**
    See also CA 9-12R; CANR 6; DLB 77;
    MTCW

Marshall, Garry 1934- . . . . **CLC 17**
    See also AAYA 3; CA 111; SATA 60

Marshall, Paule
    1929- . . . . **CLC 27, 72; BLC;**
                        DAM MULT; SSC 3
    See also BW 2; CA 77-80; CANR 25;
    DLB 157; MTCW

Marsten, Richard
    See Hunter, Evan

Marston, John
    1576-1634 . . . . **LC 33; DAM DRAM**
    See also DLB 58, 172

Martha, Henry
    See Harris, Mark

Martial c. 40-c. 104 . . . . **PC 10**

Martin, Ken
    See Hubbard, L(afayette) Ron(ald)

Martin, Richard
    See Creasey, John

Martin, Steve 1945- . . . . **CLC 30**
    See also CA 97-100; CANR 30; MTCW

Martin, Valerie 1948- . . . . **CLC 89**
    See also BEST 90:2; CA 85-88; CANR 49

Martin, Violet Florence
    1862-1915 . . . . **TCLC 51**

Martin, Webber
    See Silverberg, Robert

Martindale, Patrick Victor
    See White, Patrick (Victor Martindale)

Martin du Gard, Roger
    1881-1958 . . . . **TCLC 24**
    See also CA 118; DLB 65

Martineau, Harriet 1802-1876 . . . . **NCLC 26**
    See also DLB 21, 55, 159, 163, 166;
    YABC 2

Martines, Julia
    See O'Faolain, Julia

Martinez, Jacinto Benavente y
    See Benavente (y Martinez), Jacinto

Martinez Ruiz, Jose 1873-1967
    See Azorin; Ruiz, Jose Martinez
    See also CA 93-96; HW

Martinez Sierra, Gregorio
    1881-1947 . . . . **TCLC 6**
    See also CA 115

Martinez Sierra, Maria (de la O'LeJarraga)
    1874-1974 . . . . **TCLC 6**
    See also CA 115

Martinsen, Martin
    See Follett, Ken(neth Martin)

Martinson, Harry (Edmund)
    1904-1978 . . . . **CLC 14**
    See also CA 77-80; CANR 34

Marut, Ret
    See Traven, B.

Marut, Robert
    See Traven, B.

Marvell, Andrew
    1621-1678 . . . . . . **LC 4; DA; DAB; DAC;**
                DAM MST, POET; PC 10; WLC
    See also CDBLB 1660-1789; DLB 131

Marx, Karl (Heinrich)
    1818-1883 . . . . **NCLC 17**
    See also DLB 129

Masaoka Shiki . . . . **TCLC 18**
    See also Masaoka Tsunenori

Masaoka Tsunenori 1867-1902
    See Masaoka Shiki
    See also CA 117

Masefield, John (Edward)
    1878-1967 . . . . **CLC 11, 47; DAM POET**
    See also CA 19-20; 25-28R; CANR 33;
    CAP 2; CDBLB 1890-1914; DLB 10, 19,
    153, 160; MTCW; SATA 19

Maso, Carole 19(?)- . . . . **CLC 44**

Mason, Bobbie Ann
    1940- . . . . **CLC 28, 43, 82; SSC 4**
    See also AAYA 5; CA 53-56; CANR 11,
    31; DLB 173; DLBY 87; INT CANR-31;
    MTCW

Mason, Ernst
    See Pohl, Frederik

Mason, Lee W.
    See Malzberg, Barry N(athaniel)

Mason, Nick 1945- . . . . **CLC 35**

Mason, Tally
    See Derleth, August (William)

Mass, William
    See Gibson, William

Masters, Edgar Lee
    1868-1950 . . . . . . **TCLC 2, 25; DA; DAC;**
                        DAM MST, POET; PC 1
    See also CA 104; 133; CDALB 1865-1917;
    DLB 54; MTCW

Masters, Hilary 1928- . . . . **CLC 48**
    See also CA 25-28R; CANR 13, 47

Mastrosimone, William 19(?)- . . . . . . **CLC 36**

Mathe, Albert
    See Camus, Albert

Mather, Cotton 1663-1728 . . . . **LC 38**
    See also CDALB 1640-1865; DLB 24, 30,
    140

Mather, Increase 1639-1723 . . . . **LC 38**
    See also DLB 24

Matheson, Richard Burton 1926- . . . **CLC 37**
    See also CA 97-100; DLB 8, 44; INT 97-100

Mathews, Harry 1930- . . . . **CLC 6, 52**
    See also CA 21-24R; CAAS 6; CANR 18,
    40

Mathews, John Joseph
    1894-1979 . . . . . . **CLC 84; DAM MULT**
    See also CA 19-20; 142; CANR 45; CAP 2;
    DLB 175; NNAL

Mathias, Roland (Glyn) 1915- . . . . . . **CLC 45**
    See also CA 97-100; CANR 19, 41; DLB 27

Matsuo Basho 1644-1694 . . . . **PC 3**
    See also DAM POET

Mattheson, Rodney
See Creasey, John

Matthews, Greg 1949- . . . . **CLC 45**
See also CA 135

Matthews, William 1942- . . . . **CLC 40**
See also CA 29-32R; CAAS 18; CANR 12, 57; DLB 5

Matthias, John (Edward) 1941- . . . . . . **CLC 9**
See also CA 33-36R; CANR 56

Matthiessen, Peter
1927- . . . . **CLC 5, 7, 11, 32, 64;**
DAM NOV
See also AAYA 6; BEST 90:4; CA 9-12R; CANR 21, 50; DLB 6, 173; MTCW; SATA 27

Maturin, Charles Robert
1780(?)-1824 . . . . **NCLC 6**

Matute (Ausejo), Ana Maria
1925- . . . . **CLC 11**
See also CA 89-92; MTCW

Maugham, W. S.
See Maugham, W(illiam) Somerset

Maugham, W(illiam) Somerset
1874-1965 . . . . **CLC 1, 11, 15, 67, 93;**
DA; DAB; DAC; DAM DRAM, MST,
NOV; SSC 8; WLC
See also CA 5-8R; 25-28R; CANR 40; CDBLB 1914-1945; DLB 10, 36, 77, 100, 162; MTCW; SATA 54

Maugham, William Somerset
See Maugham, W(illiam) Somerset

Maupassant, (Henri Rene Albert) Guy de
1850-1893 . . . . . **NCLC 1, 42; DA; DAB;**
DAC; DAM MST; SSC 1; WLC
See also DLB 123

Maupin, Armistead
1944- . . . . **CLC 95; DAM POP**
See also CA 125; 130; INT 130

Maurhut, Richard
See Traven, B.

Mauriac, Claude 1914-1996 . . . . **CLC 9**
See also CA 89-92; 152; DLB 83

Mauriac, Francois (Charles)
1885-1970 . . . . **CLC 4, 9, 56; SSC 24**
See also CA 25-28; CAP 2; DLB 65; MTCW

Mavor, Osborne Henry 1888-1951
See Bridie, James
See also CA 104

Maxwell, William (Keepers, Jr.)
1908- . . . . **CLC 19**
See also CA 93-96; CANR 54; DLBY 80; INT 93-96

May, Elaine 1932- . . . . **CLC 16**
See also CA 124; 142; DLB 44

Mayakovski, Vladimir (Vladimirovich)
1893-1930 . . . . **TCLC 4, 18**
See also CA 104

Mayhew, Henry 1812-1887 . . . . . . **NCLC 31**
See also DLB 18, 55

Mayle, Peter 1939(?)- . . . . **CLC 89**
See also CA 139

Maynard, Joyce 1953- . . . . **CLC 23**
See also CA 111; 129

Mayne, William (James Carter)
1928- . . . . **CLC 12**
See also AAYA 20; CA 9-12R; CANR 37; CLR 25; JRDA; MAICYA; SAAS 11; SATA 6, 68

Mayo, Jim
See L'Amour, Louis (Dearborn)

Maysles, Albert 1926- . . . . **CLC 16**
See also CA 29-32R

Maysles, David 1932- . . . . **CLC 16**

Mazer, Norma Fox 1931- . . . . **CLC 26**
See also AAYA 5; CA 69-72; CANR 12, 32; CLR 23; JRDA; MAICYA; SAAS 1; SATA 24, 67

Mazzini, Guiseppe 1805-1872 . . . . **NCLC 34**

McAuley, James Phillip
1917-1976 . . . . **CLC 45**
See also CA 97-100

McBain, Ed
See Hunter, Evan

McBrien, William Augustine
1930- . . . . **CLC 44**
See also CA 107

McCaffrey, Anne (Inez)
1926- . . . . . . **CLC 17; DAM NOV, POP**
See also AAYA 6; AITN 2; BEST 89:2; CA 25-28R; CANR 15, 35, 55; DLB 8; JRDA; MAICYA; MTCW; SAAS 11; SATA 8, 70

McCall, Nathan 1955(?)- . . . . **CLC 86**
See also CA 146

McCann, Arthur
See Campbell, John W(ood, Jr.)

McCann, Edson
See Pohl, Frederik

McCarthy, Charles, Jr. 1933-
See McCarthy, Cormac
See also CANR 42; DAM POP

McCarthy, Cormac 1933- . . . . . **CLC 4, 57, 59**
See also McCarthy, Charles, Jr.
See also DLB 6, 143

McCarthy, Mary (Therese)
1912-1989 . . . . . . **CLC 1, 3, 5, 14, 24, 39,**
59; SSC 24
See also CA 5-8R; 129; CANR 16, 50; DLB 2; DLBY 81; INT CANR-16; MTCW

McCartney, (James) Paul
1942- . . . . **CLC 12, 35**
See also CA 146

McCauley, Stephen (D.) 1955- . . . . . **CLC 50**
See also CA 141

McClure, Michael (Thomas)
1932- . . . . **CLC 6, 10**
See also CA 21-24R; CANR 17, 46; DLB 16

McCorkle, Jill (Collins) 1958- . . . . . . **CLC 51**
See also CA 121; DLBY 87

McCourt, James 1941- . . . . **CLC 5**
See also CA 57-60

McCoy, Horace (Stanley)
1897-1955 . . . . **TCLC 28**
See also CA 108; 155; DLB 9

McCrae, John 1872-1918 . . . . **TCLC 12**
See also CA 109; DLB 92

McCreigh, James
See Pohl, Frederik

McCullers, (Lula) Carson (Smith)
1917-1967 . . . . **CLC 1, 4, 10, 12, 48, 100;**
DA; DAB; DAC; DAM MST, NOV;
SSC 9, 24; WLC
See also AAYA 21; CA 5-8R; 25-28R; CABS 1, 3; CANR 18; CDALB 1941-1968; DLB 2, 7, 173; MTCW; SATA 27

McCulloch, John Tyler
See Burroughs, Edgar Rice

McCullough, Colleen
1938(?)- . . . . **CLC 27; DAM NOV, POP**
See also CA 81-84; CANR 17, 46; MTCW

McDermott, Alice 1953- . . . . **CLC 90**
See also CA 109; CANR 40

McElroy, Joseph 1930- . . . . **CLC 5, 47**
See also CA 17-20R

McEwan, Ian (Russell)
1948- . . . . **CLC 13, 66; DAM NOV**
See also BEST 90:4; CA 61-64; CANR 14, 41; DLB 14; MTCW

McFadden, David 1940- . . . . **CLC 48**
See also CA 104; DLB 60; INT 104

McFarland, Dennis 1950- . . . . **CLC 65**

McGahern, John
1934- . . . . **CLC 5, 9, 48; SSC 17**
See also CA 17-20R; CANR 29; DLB 14; MTCW

McGinley, Patrick (Anthony)
1937- . . . . **CLC 41**
See also CA 120; 127; CANR 56; INT 127

McGinley, Phyllis 1905-1978 . . . . . . **CLC 14**
See also CA 9-12R; 77-80; CANR 19; DLB 11, 48; SATA 2, 44; SATA-Obit 24

McGinniss, Joe 1942- . . . . **CLC 32**
See also AITN 2; BEST 89:2; CA 25-28R; CANR 26; INT CANR-26

McGivern, Maureen Daly
See Daly, Maureen

McGrath, Patrick 1950- . . . . **CLC 55**
See also CA 136

McGrath, Thomas (Matthew)
1916-1990 . . . . **CLC 28, 59; DAM POET**
See also CA 9-12R; 132; CANR 6, 33; MTCW; SATA 41; SATA-Obit 66

McGuane, Thomas (Francis III)
1939- . . . . **CLC 3, 7, 18, 45**
See also AITN 2; CA 49-52; CANR 5, 24, 49; DLB 2; DLBY 80; INT CANR-24; MTCW

McGuckian, Medbh
1950- . . . . **CLC 48; DAM POET**
See also CA 143; DLB 40

McHale, Tom 1942(?)-1982 . . . . **CLC 3, 5**
See also AITN 1; CA 77-80; 106

McIlvanney, William 1936- . . . . **CLC 42**
See also CA 25-28R; DLB 14

McIlwraith, Maureen Mollie Hunter
See Hunter, Mollie
See also SATA 2

McInerney, Jay
1955- .... **CLC 34; DAM POP**
See also AAYA 18; CA 116; 123;
CANR 45; INT 123

McIntyre, Vonda N(eel) 1948- ..... **CLC 18**
See also CA 81-84; CANR 17, 34; MTCW

McKay, Claude
.... **TCLC 7, 41; BLC; DAB; PC 2**
See also McKay, Festus Claudius
See also DLB 4, 45, 51, 117

McKay, Festus Claudius 1889-1948
See McKay, Claude
See also BW 1; CA 104; 124; DA; DAC;
DAM MST, MULT, NOV, POET;
MTCW; WLC

McKuen, Rod 1933- .... **CLC 1, 3**
See also AITN 1; CA 41-44R; CANR 40

McLoughlin, R. B.
See Mencken, H(enry) L(ouis)

McLuhan, (Herbert) Marshall
1911-1980 .... **CLC 37, 83**
See also CA 9-12R; 102; CANR 12, 34;
DLB 88; INT CANR-12; MTCW

McMillan, Terry (L.)
1951- ...... **CLC 50, 61; DAM MULT,**
NOV, POP
See also AAYA 21; BW 2; CA 140

McMurtry, Larry (Jeff)
1936- .... **CLC 2, 3, 7, 11, 27, 44;**
DAM NOV, POP
See also AAYA 15; AITN 2; BEST 89:2;
CA 5-8R; CANR 19, 43;
CDALB 1968-1988; DLB 2, 143;
DLBY 80, 87; MTCW

McNally, T. M. 1961- .... **CLC 82**

McNally, Terrence
1939- .. **CLC 4, 7, 41, 91; DAM DRAM**
See also CA 45-48; CANR 2, 56; DLB 7

McNamer, Deirdre 1950- .... **CLC 70**

McNeile, Herman Cyril 1888-1937
See Sapper
See also DLB 77

McNickle, (William) D'Arcy
1904-1977 ...... **CLC 89; DAM MULT**
See also CA 9-12R; 85-88; CANR 5, 45;
DLB 175; NNAL; SATA-Obit 22

McPhee, John (Angus) 1931- ...... **CLC 36**
See also BEST 90:1; CA 65-68; CANR 20,
46; MTCW

McPherson, James Alan
1943- .... **CLC 19, 77**
See also BW 1; CA 25-28R; CAAS 17;
CANR 24; DLB 38; MTCW

McPherson, William (Alexander)
1933- .... **CLC 34**
See also CA 69-72; CANR 28;
INT CANR-28

Mead, Margaret 1901-1978 .... **CLC 37**
See also AITN 1; CA 1-4R; 81-84;
CANR 4; MTCW; SATA-Obit 20

Meaker, Marijane (Agnes) 1927-
See Kerr, M. E.
See also CA 107; CANR 37; INT 107;
JRDA; MAICYA; MTCW; SATA 20, 61

Medoff, Mark (Howard)
1940- .... **CLC 6, 23; DAM DRAM**
See also AITN 1; CA 53-56; CANR 5;
DLB 7; INT CANR-5

Medvedev, P. N.
See Bakhtin, Mikhail Mikhailovich

Meged, Aharon
See Megged, Aharon

Meged, Aron
See Megged, Aharon

Megged, Aharon 1920- .... **CLC 9**
See also CA 49-52; CAAS 13; CANR 1

Mehta, Ved (Parkash) 1934- .... **CLC 37**
See also CA 1-4R; CANR 2, 23; MTCW

Melanter
See Blackmore, R(ichard) D(oddridge)

Melikow, Loris
See Hofmannsthal, Hugo von

Melmoth, Sebastian
See Wilde, Oscar (Fingal O'Flahertie Wills)

Meltzer, Milton 1915- .... **CLC 26**
See also AAYA 8; CA 13-16R; CANR 38;
CLR 13; DLB 61; JRDA; MAICYA;
SAAS 1; SATA 1, 50, 80

Melville, Herman
1819-1891 ..... **NCLC 3, 12, 29, 45, 49;**
DA; DAB; DAC; DAM MST, NOV;
SSC 1, 17; WLC
See also CDALB 1640-1865; DLB 3, 74;
SATA 59

Menander
c. 342B.C.-c. 292B.C. .... **CMLC 9;**
DAM DRAM; DC 3
See also DLB 176

Mencken, H(enry) L(ouis)
1880-1956 .... **TCLC 13**
See also CA 105; 125; CDALB 1917-1929;
DLB 11, 29, 63, 137; MTCW

Mendelsohn, Jane 1965(?)- .... **CLC 99**
See also CA 154

Mercer, David
1928-1980 .... **CLC 5; DAM DRAM**
See also CA 9-12R; 102; CANR 23;
DLB 13; MTCW

Merchant, Paul
See Ellison, Harlan (Jay)

Meredith, George
1828-1909 .. **TCLC 17, 43; DAM POET**
See also CA 117; 153; CDBLB 1832-1890;
DLB 18, 35, 57, 159

Meredith, William (Morris)
1919- .. **CLC 4, 13, 22, 55; DAM POET**
See also CA 9-12R; CAAS 14; CANR 6, 40;
DLB 5

Merezhkovsky, Dmitry Sergeyevich
1865-1941 .... **TCLC 29**

Merimee, Prosper
1803-1870 .... **NCLC 6; SSC 7**
See also DLB 119

Merkin, Daphne 1954- .... **CLC 44**
See also CA 123

Merlin, Arthur
See Blish, James (Benjamin)

Merrill, James (Ingram)
1926-1995 .... **CLC 2, 3, 6, 8, 13, 18, 34,**
91; DAM POET
See also CA 13-16R; 147; CANR 10, 49;
DLB 5, 165; DLBY 85; INT CANR-10;
MTCW

Merriman, Alex
See Silverberg, Robert

Merritt, E. B.
See Waddington, Miriam

Merton, Thomas
1915-1968 .. **CLC 1, 3, 11, 34, 83; PC 10**
See also CA 5-8R; 25-28R; CANR 22, 53;
DLB 48; DLBY 81; MTCW

Merwin, W(illiam) S(tanley)
1927- ...... **CLC 1, 2, 3, 5, 8, 13, 18, 45,**
88; DAM POET
See also CA 13-16R; CANR 15, 51; DLB 5,
169; INT CANR-15; MTCW

Metcalf, John 1938- .... **CLC 37**
See also CA 113; DLB 60

Metcalf, Suzanne
See Baum, L(yman) Frank

Mew, Charlotte (Mary)
1870-1928 .... **TCLC 8**
See also CA 105; DLB 19, 135

Mewshaw, Michael 1943- .... **CLC 9**
See also CA 53-56; CANR 7, 47; DLBY 80

Meyer, June
See Jordan, June

Meyer, Lynn
See Slavitt, David R(ytman)

Meyer-Meyrink, Gustav 1868-1932
See Meyrink, Gustav
See also CA 117

Meyers, Jeffrey 1939- .... **CLC 39**
See also CA 73-76; CANR 54; DLB 111

Meynell, Alice (Christina Gertrude Thompson)
1847-1922 .... **TCLC 6**
See also CA 104; DLB 19, 98

Meyrink, Gustav .... **TCLC 21**
See also Meyer-Meyrink, Gustav
See also DLB 81

Michaels, Leonard
1933- .... **CLC 6, 25; SSC 16**
See also CA 61-64; CANR 21; DLB 130;
MTCW

Michaux, Henri 1899-1984 ...... **CLC 8, 19**
See also CA 85-88; 114

Michelangelo 1475-1564 .... **LC 12**

Michelet, Jules 1798-1874 .... **NCLC 31**

Michener, James A(lbert)
1907(?)- .... **CLC 1, 5, 11, 29, 60;**
DAM NOV, POP
See also AITN 1; BEST 90:1; CA 5-8R;
CANR 21, 45; DLB 6; MTCW

Mickiewicz, Adam 1798-1855 ..... **NCLC 3**

Middleton, Christopher 1926- ...... **CLC 13**
See also CA 13-16R; CANR 29, 54;
DLB 40

Middleton, Richard (Barham)
1882-1911 .... **TCLC 56**
See also DLB 156

Middleton, Stanley 1919-........ CLC 7, 38
See also CA 25-28R; CAAS 23; CANR 21,
46; DLB 14

Middleton, Thomas
1580-1627 ...... LC 33; DAM DRAM,
MST; DC 5
See also DLB 58

Migueis, Jose Rodrigues 1901-..... CLC 10

Mikszath, Kalman 1847-1910 ..... TCLC 31

Miles, Jack .... CLC 100

Miles, Josephine (Louise)
1911-1985 .... CLC 1, 2, 14, 34, 39;
DAM POET
See also CA 1-4R; 116; CANR 2, 55;
DLB 48

Militant
See Sandburg, Carl (August)

Mill, John Stuart 1806-1873 .. NCLC 11, 58
See also CDBLB 1832-1890; DLB 55

Millar, Kenneth
1915-1983 .... CLC 14; DAM POP
See also Macdonald, Ross
See also CA 9-12R; 110; CANR 16; DLB 2;
DLBD 6; DLBY 83; MTCW

Millay, E. Vincent
See Millay, Edna St. Vincent

Millay, Edna St. Vincent
1892-1950 ...... TCLC 4, 49; DA; DAB;
DAC; DAM MST, POET; PC 6
See also CA 104; 130; CDALB 1917-1929;
DLB 45; MTCW

Miller, Arthur
1915- .... CLC 1, 2, 6, 10, 15, 26, 47, 78;
DA; DAB; DAC; DAM DRAM, MST;
DC 1; WLC
See also AAYA 15; AITN 1; CA 1-4R;
CABS 3; CANR 2, 30, 54;
CDALB 1941-1968; DLB 7; MTCW

Miller, Henry (Valentine)
1891-1980 .... CLC 1, 2, 4, 9, 14, 43, 84;
DA; DAB; DAC; DAM MST, NOV;
WLC
See also CA 9-12R; 97-100; CANR 33;
CDALB 1929-1941; DLB 4, 9; DLBY 80;
MTCW

Miller, Jason 1939(?)- .... CLC 2
See also AITN 1; CA 73-76; DLB 7

Miller, Sue 1943-..... CLC 44; DAM POP
See also BEST 90:3; CA 139; DLB 143

Miller, Walter M(ichael, Jr.)
1923-..................... CLC 4, 30
See also CA 85-88; DLB 8

Millett, Kate 1934-............... CLC 67
See also AITN 1; CA 73-76; CANR 32, 53;
MTCW

Millhauser, Steven 1943-....... CLC 21, 54
See also CA 110; 111; DLB 2; INT 111

Millin, Sarah Gertrude 1889-1968 .. CLC 49
See also CA 102; 93-96

Milne, A(lan) A(lexander)
1882-1956 .... TCLC 6; DAB; DAC;
DAM MST
See also CA 104; 133; CLR 1, 26; DLB 10,
77, 100, 160; MAICYA; MTCW;
YABC 1

Milner, Ron(ald)
1938- ..... CLC 56; BLC; DAM MULT
See also AITN 1; BW 1; CA 73-76;
CANR 24; DLB 38; MTCW

Milnes, Richard Monckton
1809-1885 .... NCLC 61
See also DLB 32

Milosz, Czeslaw
1911- .... CLC 5, 11, 22, 31, 56, 82;
DAM MST, POET; PC 8
See also CA 81-84; CANR 23, 51; MTCW

Milton, John
1608-1674 ...... LC 9; DA; DAB; DAC;
DAM MST, POET; WLC
See also CDBLB 1660-1789; DLB 131, 151

Min, Anchee 1957-............... CLC 86
See also CA 146

Minehaha, Cornelius
See Wedekind, (Benjamin) Frank(lin)

Miner, Valerie 1947- .... CLC 40
See also CA 97-100

Minimo, Duca
See D'Annunzio, Gabriele

Minot, Susan 1956- .... CLC 44
See also CA 134

Minus, Ed 1938-................. CLC 39

Miranda, Javier
See Bioy Casares, Adolfo

Mirbeau, Octave 1848-1917....... TCLC 55
See also DLB 123

Miro (Ferrer), Gabriel (Francisco Victor)
1879-1930 .... TCLC 5
See also CA 104

Mishima, Yukio
.... CLC 2, 4, 6, 9, 27; DC 1; SSC 4
See also Hiraoka, Kimitake

Mistral, Frederic 1830-1914 ...... TCLC 51
See also CA 122

Mistral, Gabriela............ TCLC 2; HLC
See also Godoy Alcayaga, Lucila

Mistry, Rohinton 1952-...... CLC 71; DAC
See also CA 141

Mitchell, Clyde
See Ellison, Harlan (Jay); Silverberg, Robert

Mitchell, James Leslie 1901-1935
See Gibbon, Lewis Grassic
See also CA 104; DLB 15

Mitchell, Joni 1943-.............. CLC 12
See also CA 112

Mitchell, Joseph (Quincy)
1908-1996 .... CLC 98
See also CA 77-80; 152

Mitchell, Margaret (Munnerlyn)
1900-1949 ...... TCLC 11; DAM NOV,
POP
See also CA 109; 125; CANR 55; DLB 9;
MTCW

Mitchell, Peggy
See Mitchell, Margaret (Munnerlyn)

Mitchell, S(ilas) Weir 1829-1914 .. TCLC 36

Mitchell, W(illiam) O(rmond)
1914-...... CLC 25; DAC; DAM MST
See also CA 77-80; CANR 15, 43; DLB 88

Mitford, Mary Russell 1787-1855.. NCLC 4
See also DLB 110, 116

Mitford, Nancy 1904-1973........ CLC 44
See also CA 9-12R

Miyamoto, Yuriko 1899-1951 ..... TCLC 37

Mo, Timothy (Peter) 1950(?)-...... CLC 46
See also CA 117; MTCW

Modarressi, Taghi (M.) 1931-...... CLC 44
See also CA 121; 134; INT 134

Modiano, Patrick (Jean) 1945-..... CLC 18
See also CA 85-88; CANR 17, 40; DLB 83

Moerck, Paal
See Roelvaag, O(le) E(dvart)

Mofolo, Thomas (Mokopu)
1875(?)-1948 .... TCLC 22; BLC;
DAM MULT
See also CA 121; 153

Mohr, Nicholasa
1935- ..... CLC 12; DAM MULT; HLC
See also AAYA 8; CA 49-52; CANR 1, 32;
CLR 22; DLB 145; HW; JRDA; SAAS 8;
SATA 8

Mojtabai, A(nn) G(race)
1938-................. CLC 5, 9, 15, 29
See also CA 85-88

Moliere
1622-1673 ..... LC 28; DA; DAB; DAC;
DAM DRAM, MST; WLC

Molin, Charles
See Mayne, William (James Carter)

Molnar, Ferenc
1878-1952 ..... TCLC 20; DAM DRAM
See also CA 109; 153

Momaday, N(avarre) Scott
1934- ..... CLC 2, 19, 85, 95; DA; DAB;
DAC; DAM MST, MULT, NOV, POP
See also AAYA 11; CA 25-28R; CANR 14,
34; DLB 143, 175; INT CANR-14;
MTCW; NNAL; SATA 48;
SATA-Brief 30

Monette, Paul 1945-1995.......... CLC 82
See also CA 139; 147

Monroe, Harriet 1860-1936....... TCLC 12
See also CA 109; DLB 54, 91

Monroe, Lyle
See Heinlein, Robert A(nson)

Montagu, Elizabeth 1917- .... NCLC 7
See also CA 9-12R

Montagu, Mary (Pierrepont) Wortley
1689-1762 .... LC 9; PC 16
See also DLB 95, 101

Montagu, W. H.
See Coleridge, Samuel Taylor

Montague, John (Patrick)
1929-.................... CLC 13, 46
See also CA 9-12R; CANR 9; DLB 40;
MTCW

Montaigne, Michel (Eyquem) de
1533-1592 ...... LC 8; DA; DAB; DAC;
DAM MST; WLC

Montale, Eugenio
1896-1981 .... CLC 7, 9, 18; PC 13
See also CA 17-20R; 104; CANR 30;
DLB 114; MTCW

Montesquieu, Charles-Louis de Secondat
1689-1755 . . . . LC 7

Montgomery, (Robert) Bruce 1921-1978
See Crispin, Edmund
See also CA 104

Montgomery, L(ucy) M(aud)
1874-1942 . . . . TCLC 51; DAC;
DAM MST
See also AAYA 12; CA 108; 137; CLR 8;
DLB 92; DLBD 14; JRDA; MAICYA;
YABC 1

Montgomery, Marion H., Jr. 1925- . . CLC 7
See also AITN 1; CA 1-4R; CANR 3, 48;
DLB 6

Montgomery, Max
See Davenport, Guy (Mattison, Jr.)

Montherlant, Henry (Milon) de
1896-1972 . . . . CLC 8, 19; DAM DRAM
See also CA 85-88; 37-40R; DLB 72;
MTCW

Monty Python
See Chapman, Graham; Cleese, John
(Marwood); Gilliam, Terry (Vance); Idle,
Eric; Jones, Terence Graham Parry; Palin,
Michael (Edward)
See also AAYA 7

Moodie, Susanna (Strickland)
1803-1885 . . . . NCLC 14
See also DLB 99

Mooney, Edward 1951-
See Mooney, Ted
See also CA 130

Mooney, Ted . . . . CLC 25
See also Mooney, Edward

Moorcock, Michael (John)
1939- . . . . CLC 5, 27, 58
See also CA 45-48; CAAS 5; CANR 2, 17,
38; DLB 14; MTCW

Moore, Brian
1921- . . . . . . CLC 1, 3, 5, 7, 8, 19, 32, 90;
DAB; DAC; DAM MST
See also CA 1-4R; CANR 1, 25, 42; MTCW

Moore, Edward
See Muir, Edwin

Moore, George Augustus
1852-1933 . . . . TCLC 7; SSC 19
See also CA 104; DLB 10, 18, 57, 135

Moore, Lorrie . . . . CLC 39, 45, 68
See also Moore, Marie Lorena

Moore, Marianne (Craig)
1887-1972 . . . . CLC 1, 2, 4, 8, 10, 13, 19,
47; DA; DAB; DAC; DAM MST, POET;
PC 4
See also CA 1-4R; 33-36R; CANR 3;
CDALB 1929-1941; DLB 45; DLBD 7;
MTCW; SATA 20

Moore, Marie Lorena 1957-
See Moore, Lorrie
See also CA 116; CANR 39

Moore, Thomas 1779-1852 . . . . NCLC 6
See also DLB 96, 144

Morand, Paul 1888-1976 . . CLC 41; SSC 22
See also CA 69-72; DLB 65

Morante, Elsa 1918-1985 . . . . CLC 8, 47
See also CA 85-88; 117; CANR 35;
DLB 177; MTCW

Moravia, Alberto
1907-1990 . . . . CLC 2, 7, 11, 27, 46
See also Pincherle, Alberto
See also DLB 177

More, Hannah 1745-1833 . . . . NCLC 27
See also DLB 107, 109, 116, 158

More, Henry 1614-1687 . . . . LC 9
See also DLB 126

More, Sir Thomas 1478-1535 . . . . LC 10, 32

Moreas, Jean . . . . TCLC 18
See also Papadiamantopoulos, Johannes

Morgan, Berry 1919- . . . . CLC 6
See also CA 49-52; DLB 6

Morgan, Claire
See Highsmith, (Mary) Patricia

Morgan, Edwin (George) 1920- . . . . . CLC 31
See also CA 5-8R; CANR 3, 43; DLB 27

Morgan, (George) Frederick
1922- . . . . CLC 23
See also CA 17-20R; CANR 21

Morgan, Harriet
See Mencken, H(enry) L(ouis)

Morgan, Jane
See Cooper, James Fenimore

Morgan, Janet 1945- . . . . CLC 39
See also CA 65-68

Morgan, Lady 1776(?)-1859 . . . . . . NCLC 29
See also DLB 116, 158

Morgan, Robin 1941- . . . . CLC 2
See also CA 69-72; CANR 29; MTCW;
SATA 80

Morgan, Scott
See Kuttner, Henry

Morgan, Seth 1949(?)-1990 . . . . CLC 65
See also CA 132

Morgenstern, Christian
1871-1914 . . . . TCLC 8
See also CA 105

Morgenstern, S.
See Goldman, William (W.)

Moricz, Zsigmond 1879-1942 . . . . . TCLC 33

Morike, Eduard (Friedrich)
1804-1875 . . . . NCLC 10
See also DLB 133

Mori Ogai . . . . TCLC 14
See also Mori Rintaro

Mori Rintaro 1862-1922
See Mori Ogai
See also CA 110

Moritz, Karl Philipp 1756-1793 . . . . . . LC 2
See also DLB 94

Morland, Peter Henry
See Faust, Frederick (Schiller)

Morren, Theophil
See Hofmannsthal, Hugo von

Morris, Bill 1952- . . . . CLC 76

Morris, Julian
See West, Morris L(anglo)

Morris, Steveland Judkins 1950(?)-
See Wonder, Stevie
See also CA 111

Morris, William 1834-1896 . . . . NCLC 4
See also CDBLB 1832-1890; DLB 18, 35,
57, 156

Morris, Wright 1910-. . . CLC 1, 3, 7, 18, 37
See also CA 9-12R; CANR 21; DLB 2;
DLBY 81; MTCW

Morrison, Chloe Anthony Wofford
See Morrison, Toni

Morrison, James Douglas 1943-1971
See Morrison, Jim
See also CA 73-76; CANR 40

Morrison, Jim . . . . CLC 17
See also Morrison, James Douglas

Morrison, Toni
1931- . . . . CLC 4, 10, 22, 55, 81, 87;
BLC; DA; DAB; DAC; DAM MST,
MULT, NOV, POP
See also AAYA 1; BW 2; CA 29-32R;
CANR 27, 42; CDALB 1968-1988;
DLB 6, 33, 143; DLBY 81; MTCW;
SATA 57

Morrison, Van 1945- . . . . CLC 21
See also CA 116

Morrissy, Mary 1958- . . . . CLC 99

Mortimer, John (Clifford)
1923- . . . . . . CLC 28, 43; DAM DRAM,
POP
See also CA 13-16R; CANR 21;
CDBLB 1960 to Present; DLB 13;
INT CANR-21; MTCW

Mortimer, Penelope (Ruth) 1918- . . . . CLC 5
See also CA 57-60; CANR 45

Morton, Anthony
See Creasey, John

Mosher, Howard Frank 1943- . . . . . . CLC 62
See also CA 139

Mosley, Nicholas 1923- . . . . CLC 43, 70
See also CA 69-72; CANR 41; DLB 14

Mosley, Walter
1952- . . . . . CLC 97; DAM MULT, POP
See also AAYA 17; BW 2; CA 142;
CANR 57

Moss, Howard
1922-1987 . . . . CLC 7, 14, 45, 50;
DAM POET
See also CA 1-4R; 123; CANR 1, 44;
DLB 5

Mossgiel, Rab
See Burns, Robert

Motion, Andrew (Peter) 1952-. . . . . . CLC 47
See also CA 146; DLB 40

Motley, Willard (Francis)
1909-1965 . . . . CLC 18
See also BW 1; CA 117; 106; DLB 76, 143

Motoori, Norinaga 1730-1801 . . . . NCLC 45

Mott, Michael (Charles Alston)
1930- . . . . CLC 15, 34
See also CA 5-8R; CAAS 7; CANR 7, 29

Mountain Wolf Woman
1884-1960 . . . . CLC 92
See also CA 144; NNAL

Moure, Erin 1955- . . . . CLC 88
See also CA 113; DLB 60

Nerval, Gerard de
1808-1855 ..... NCLC 1; PC 13; SSC 18

Nervo, (Jose) Amado (Ruiz de)
1870-1919 .... TCLC 11
See also CA 109; 131; HW

Nessi, Pio Baroja y
See Baroja (y Nessi), Pio

Nestroy, Johann 1801-1862 ...... NCLC 42
See also DLB 133

Neufeld, John (Arthur) 1938- ...... CLC 17
See also AAYA 11; CA 25-28R; CANR 11,
37, 56; MAICYA; SAAS 3; SATA 6, 81

Neville, Emily Cheney 1919- .... CLC 12
See also CA 5-8R; CANR 3, 37; JRDA;
MAICYA; SAAS 2; SATA 1

Newbound, Bernard Slade 1930-
See Slade, Bernard
See also CA 81-84; CANR 49;
DAM DRAM

Newby, P(ercy) H(oward)
1918- .... CLC 2, 13; DAM NOV
See also CA 5-8R; CANR 32; DLB 15;
MTCW

Newlove, Donald 1928- .... CLC 6
See also CA 29-32R; CANR 25

Newlove, John (Herbert) 1938- ..... CLC 14
See also CA 21-24R; CANR 9, 25

Newman, Charles 1938- .... CLC 2, 8
See also CA 21-24R

Newman, Edwin (Harold) 1919- .... CLC 14
See also AITN 1; CA 69-72; CANR 5

Newman, John Henry
1801-1890 .... NCLC 38
See also DLB 18, 32, 55

Newton, Suzanne 1936- .... CLC 35
See also CA 41-44R; CANR 14; JRDA;
SATA 5, 77

Nexo, Martin Andersen
1869-1954 .... TCLC 43

Nezval, Vitezslav 1900-1958 ...... TCLC 44
See also CA 123

Ng, Fae Myenne 1957(?)- .... CLC 81
See also CA 146

Ngema, Mbongeni 1955- .... CLC 57
See also BW 2; CA 143

Ngugi, James T(hiong'o) .... CLC 3, 7, 13
See also Ngugi wa Thiong'o

Ngugi wa Thiong'o
1938- ..... CLC 36; BLC; DAM MULT,
NOV
See also Ngugi, James T(hiong'o)
See also BW 2; CA 81-84; CANR 27;
DLB 125; MTCW

Nichol, B(arrie) P(hillip)
1944-1988 .... CLC 18
See also CA 53-56; DLB 53; SATA 66

Nichols, John (Treadwell) 1940- .... CLC 38
See also CA 9-12R; CAAS 2; CANR 6;
DLBY 82

Nichols, Leigh
See Koontz, Dean R(ay)

Nichols, Peter (Richard)
1927- .... CLC 5, 36, 65
See also CA 104; CANR 33; DLB 13;
MTCW

Nicolas, F. R. E.
See Freeling, Nicolas

Niedecker, Lorine
1903-1970 .... CLC 10, 42; DAM POET
See also CA 25-28; CAP 2; DLB 48

Nietzsche, Friedrich (Wilhelm)
1844-1900 .... TCLC 10, 18, 55
See also CA 107; 121; DLB 129

Nievo, Ippolito 1831-1861 .... NCLC 22

Nightingale, Anne Redmon 1943-
See Redmon, Anne
See also CA 103

Nik. T. O.
See Annensky, Innokenty (Fyodorovich)

Nin, Anais
1903-1977 ...... CLC 1, 4, 8, 11, 14, 60;
DAM NOV, POP; SSC 10
See also AITN 2; CA 13-16R; 69-72;
CANR 22, 53; DLB 2, 4, 152; MTCW

Nishiwaki, Junzaburo 1894-1982 .... PC 15
See also CA 107

Nissenson, Hugh 1933- .... CLC 4, 9
See also CA 17-20R; CANR 27; DLB 28

Niven, Larry .... CLC 8
See also Niven, Laurence Van Cott
See also DLB 8

Niven, Laurence Van Cott 1938-
See Niven, Larry
See also CA 21-24R; CAAS 12; CANR 14,
44; DAM POP; MTCW

Nixon, Agnes Eckhardt 1927- ...... CLC 21
See also CA 110

Nizan, Paul 1905-1940 .... TCLC 40
See also DLB 72

Nkosi, Lewis
1936- ..... CLC 45; BLC; DAM MULT
See also BW 1; CA 65-68; CANR 27;
DLB 157

Nodier, (Jean) Charles (Emmanuel)
1780-1844 .... NCLC 19
See also DLB 119

Nolan, Christopher 1965- .... CLC 58
See also CA 111

Noon, Jeff 1957- .... CLC 91
See also CA 148

Norden, Charles
See Durrell, Lawrence (George)

Nordhoff, Charles (Bernard)
1887-1947 .... TCLC 23
See also CA 108; DLB 9; SATA 23

Norfolk, Lawrence 1963- .... CLC 76
See also CA 144

Norman, Marsha
1947- .... CLC 28; DAM DRAM
See also CA 105; CABS 3; CANR 41;
DLBY 84

Norris, Benjamin Franklin, Jr.
1870-1902 .... TCLC 24
See also Norris, Frank
See also CA 110

Norris, Frank
See Norris, Benjamin Franklin, Jr.
See also CDALB 1865-1917; DLB 12, 71

Norris, Leslie 1921- .... CLC 14
See also CA 11-12; CANR 14; CAP 1;
DLB 27

North, Andrew
See Norton, Andre

North, Anthony
See Koontz, Dean R(ay)

North, Captain George
See Stevenson, Robert Louis (Balfour)

North, Milou
See Erdrich, Louise

Northrup, B. A.
See Hubbard, L(afayette) Ron(ald)

North Staffs
See Hulme, T(homas) E(rnest)

Norton, Alice Mary
See Norton, Andre
See also MAICYA; SATA 1, 43

Norton, Andre 1912- .... CLC 12
See also Norton, Alice Mary
See also AAYA 14; CA 1-4R; CANR 2, 31;
DLB 8, 52; JRDA; MTCW; SATA 91

Norton, Caroline 1808-1877 ...... NCLC 47
See also DLB 21, 159

Norway, Nevil Shute 1899-1960
See Shute, Nevil
See also CA 102; 93-96

Norwid, Cyprian Kamil
1821-1883 .... NCLC 17

Nosille, Nabrah
See Ellison, Harlan (Jay)

Nossack, Hans Erich 1901-1978 ..... CLC 6
See also CA 93-96; 85-88; DLB 69

Nostradamus 1503-1566 .... LC 27

Nosu, Chuji
See Ozu, Yasujiro

Notenburg, Eleanora (Genrikhovna) von
See Guro, Elena

Nova, Craig 1945- .... CLC 7, 31
See also CA 45-48; CANR 2, 53

Novak, Joseph
See Kosinski, Jerzy (Nikodem)

Novalis 1772-1801 .... NCLC 13
See also DLB 90

Nowlan, Alden (Albert)
1933-1983 .. CLC 15; DAC; DAM MST
See also CA 9-12R; CANR 5; DLB 53

Noyes, Alfred 1880-1958 .... TCLC 7
See also CA 104; DLB 20

Nunn, Kem 19(?)- .... CLC 34

Nye, Robert
1939- .... CLC 13, 42; DAM NOV
See also CA 33-36R; CANR 29; DLB 14;
MTCW; SATA 6

Nyro, Laura 1947- .... CLC 17

Oates, Joyce Carol
1938- ...... CLC 1, 2, 3, 6, 9, 11, 15, 19,
33, 52; DA; DAB; DAC; DAM MST,
NOV, POP; SSC 6; WLC
See also AAYA 15; AITN 1; BEST 89:2;
CA 5-8R; CANR 25, 45;
CDALB 1968-1988; DLB 2, 5, 130;
DLBY 81; INT CANR-25; MTCW

O'Brien, Darcy 1939-............. CLC 11
See also CA 21-24R; CANR 8

O'Brien, E. G.
See Clarke, Arthur C(harles)

O'Brien, Edna
1936- .... CLC 3, 5, 8, 13, 36, 65;
DAM NOV; SSC 10
See also CA 1-4R; CANR 6, 41;
CDBLB 1960 to Present; DLB 14;
MTCW

O'Brien, Fitz-James 1828-1862... NCLC 21
See also DLB 74

O'Brien, Flann........ CLC 1, 4, 5, 7, 10, 47
See also O Nuallain, Brian

O'Brien, Richard 1942-........... CLC 17
See also CA 124

O'Brien, Tim
1946- .... CLC 7, 19, 40; DAM POP
See also AAYA 16; CA 85-88; CANR 40;
DLB 152; DLBD 9; DLBY 80

Obstfelder, Sigbjoern 1866-1900... TCLC 23
See also CA 123

O'Casey, Sean
1880-1964 ...... CLC 1, 5, 9, 11, 15, 88;
DAB; DAC; DAM DRAM, MST
See also CA 89-92; CDBLB 1914-1945;
DLB 10; MTCW

O'Cathasaigh, Sean
See O'Casey, Sean

Ochs, Phil 1940-1976............. CLC 17
See also CA 65-68

O'Connor, Edwin (Greene)
1918-1968 .... CLC 14
See also CA 93-96; 25-28R

O'Connor, (Mary) Flannery
1925-1964 .... CLC 1, 2, 3, 6, 10, 13, 15,
21, 66; DA; DAB; DAC; DAM MST,
NOV; SSC 1, 23; WLC
See also AAYA 7; CA 1-4R; CANR 3, 41;
CDALB 1941-1968; DLB 2, 152;
DLBD 12; DLBY 80; MTCW

O'Connor, Frank........... CLC 23; SSC 5
See also O'Donovan, Michael John
See also DLB 162

O'Dell, Scott 1898-1989........... CLC 30
See also AAYA 3; CA 61-64; 129;
CANR 12, 30; CLR 1, 16; DLB 52;
JRDA; MAICYA; SATA 12, 60

Odets, Clifford
1906-1963 .... CLC 2, 28, 98;
DAM DRAM; DC 6
See also CA 85-88; DLB 7, 26; MTCW

O'Doherty, Brian 1934-........... CLC 76
See also CA 105

O'Donnell, K. M.
See Malzberg, Barry N(athaniel)

O'Donnell, Lawrence
See Kuttner, Henry

O'Donovan, Michael John
1903-1966 .... CLC 14
See also O'Connor, Frank
See also CA 93-96

Oe, Kenzaburo
1935- ..... CLC 10, 36, 86; DAM NOV;
SSC 20
See also CA 97-100; CANR 36, 50;
DLBY 94; MTCW

O'Faolain, Julia 1932-....... CLC 6, 19, 47
See also CA 81-84; CAAS 2; CANR 12;
DLB 14; MTCW

O'Faolain, Sean
1900-1991 .... CLC 1, 7, 14, 32, 70;
SSC 13
See also CA 61-64; 134; CANR 12;
DLB 15, 162; MTCW

O'Flaherty, Liam
1896-1984 .... CLC 5, 34; SSC 6
See also CA 101; 113; CANR 35; DLB 36,
162; DLBY 84; MTCW

Ogilvy, Gavin
See Barrie, J(ames) M(atthew)

O'Grady, Standish (James)
1846-1928 .... TCLC 5
See also CA 104

O'Grady, Timothy 1951-.......... CLC 59
See also CA 138

O'Hara, Frank
1926-1966 .... CLC 2, 5, 13, 78;
DAM POET
See also CA 9-12R; 25-28R; CANR 33;
DLB 5, 16; MTCW

O'Hara, John (Henry)
1905-1970 .... CLC 1, 2, 3, 6, 11, 42;
DAM NOV; SSC 15
See also CA 5-8R; 25-28R; CANR 31;
CDALB 1929-1941; DLB 9, 86; DLBD 2;
MTCW

O Hehir, Diana 1922-............ CLC 41
See also CA 93-96

Okigbo, Christopher (Ifenayichukwu)
1932-1967 .... CLC 25, 84; BLC;
DAM MULT, POET; PC 7
See also BW 1; CA 77-80; DLB 125;
MTCW

Okri, Ben 1959-................. CLC 87
See also BW 2; CA 130; 138; DLB 157;
INT 138

Olds, Sharon
1942- ..... CLC 32, 39, 85; DAM POET
See also CA 101; CANR 18, 41; DLB 120

Oldstyle, Jonathan
See Irving, Washington

Olesha, Yuri (Karlovich)
1899-1960 .... CLC 8
See also CA 85-88

Oliphant, Laurence
1829(?)-1888 .... NCLC 47
See also DLB 18, 166

Oliphant, Margaret (Oliphant Wilson)
1828-1897 .... NCLC 11, 61; SSC 25
See also DLB 18, 159

Oliver, Mary 1935-......... CLC 19, 34, 98
See also CA 21-24R; CANR 9, 43; DLB 5

Olivier, Laurence (Kerr)
1907-1989 .... CLC 20
See also CA 111; 150; 129

Olsen, Tillie
1913- ..... CLC 4, 13; DA; DAB; DAC;
DAM MST; SSC 11
See also CA 1-4R; CANR 1, 43; DLB 28;
DLBY 80; MTCW

Olson, Charles (John)
1910-1970 ..... CLC 1, 2, 5, 6, 9, 11, 29;
DAM POET
See also CA 13-16; 25-28R; CABS 2;
CANR 35; CAP 1; DLB 5, 16; MTCW

Olson, Toby 1937-............... CLC 28
See also CA 65-68; CANR 9, 31

Olyesha, Yuri
See Olesha, Yuri (Karlovich)

Ondaatje, (Philip) Michael
1943- .... CLC 14, 29, 51, 76; DAB;
DAC; DAM MST
See also CA 77-80; CANR 42; DLB 60

Oneal, Elizabeth 1934-
See Oneal, Zibby
See also CA 106; CANR 28; MAICYA;
SATA 30, 82

Oneal, Zibby .... CLC 30
See also Oneal, Elizabeth
See also AAYA 5; CLR 13; JRDA

O'Neill, Eugene (Gladstone)
1888-1953 ...... TCLC 1, 6, 27, 49; DA;
DAB; DAC; DAM DRAM, MST; WLC
See also AITN 1; CA 110; 132;
CDALB 1929-1941; DLB 7; MTCW

Onetti, Juan Carlos
1909-1994 .... CLC 7, 10; DAM MULT,
NOV; SSC 23
See also CA 85-88; 145; CANR 32;
DLB 113; HW; MTCW

O Nuallain, Brian 1911-1966
See O'Brien, Flann
See also CA 21-22; 25-28R; CAP 2

Oppen, George 1908-1984 .... CLC 7, 13, 34
See also CA 13-16R; 113; CANR 8; DLB 5,
165

Oppenheim, E(dward) Phillips
1866-1946 .... TCLC 45
See also CA 111; DLB 70

Origen c. 185-c. 254............ CMLC 19

Orlovitz, Gil 1918-1973........... CLC 22
See also CA 77-80; 45-48; DLB 2, 5

Orris
See Ingelow, Jean

Ortega y Gasset, Jose
1883-1955 ..... TCLC 9; DAM MULT;
HLC
See also CA 106; 130; HW; MTCW

Ortese, Anna Maria 1914-......... CLC 89
See also DLB 177

Ortiz, Simon J(oseph)
1941- .... CLC 45; DAM MULT,
POET; PC 17
See also CA 134; DLB 120, 175; NNAL

Orton, Joe .... CLC 4, 13, 43; DC 3
See also Orton, John Kingsley
See also CDBLB 1960 to Present; DLB 13

Orton, John Kingsley 1933-1967
See Orton, Joe
See also CA 85-88; CANR 35;
DAM DRAM; MTCW

Paterson, Katherine (Womeldorf)
1932- .... CLC 12, 30
See also AAYA 1; CA 21-24R; CANR 28;
CLR 7; DLB 52; JRDA; MAICYA;
MTCW; SATA 13, 53, 92

Patmore, Coventry Kersey Dighton
1823-1896 .... NCLC 9
See also DLB 35, 98

Paton, Alan (Stewart)
1903-1988 ...... CLC 4, 10, 25, 55; DA;
DAB; DAC; DAM MST, NOV; WLC
See also CA 13-16; 125; CANR 22; CAP 1;
MTCW; SATA 11; SATA-Obit 56

Paton Walsh, Gillian 1937-
See Walsh, Jill Paton
See also CANR 38; JRDA; MAICYA;
SAAS 3; SATA 4, 72

Paulding, James Kirke 1778-1860.. NCLC 2
See also DLB 3, 59, 74

Paulin, Thomas Neilson 1949-
See Paulin, Tom
See also CA 123; 128

Paulin, Tom .... CLC 37
See also Paulin, Thomas Neilson
See also DLB 40

Paustovsky, Konstantin (Georgievich)
1892-1968 .... CLC 40
See also CA 93-96; 25-28R

Pavese, Cesare
1908-1950 ..... TCLC 3; PC 13; SSC 19
See also CA 104; DLB 128, 177

Pavic, Milorad 1929- .... CLC 60
See also CA 136

Payne, Alan
See Jakes, John (William)

Paz, Gil
See Lugones, Leopoldo

Paz, Octavio
1914- .... CLC 3, 4, 6, 10, 19, 51, 65;
DA; DAB; DAC; DAM MST, MULT,
POET; HLC; PC 1; WLC
See also CA 73-76; CANR 32; DLBY 90;
HW; MTCW

p'Bitek, Okot
1931-1982 .... CLC 96; BLC;
DAM MULT
See also BW 2; CA 124; 107; DLB 125;
MTCW

Peacock, Molly 1947-............. CLC 60
See also CA 103; CAAS 21; CANR 52;
DLB 120

Peacock, Thomas Love
1785-1866 .... NCLC 22
See also DLB 96, 116

Peake, Mervyn 1911-1968 ...... CLC 7, 54
See also CA 5-8R; 25-28R; CANR 3;
DLB 15, 160; MTCW; SATA 23

Pearce, Philippa .... CLC 21
See also Christie, (Ann) Philippa
See also CLR 9; DLB 161; MAICYA;
SATA 1, 67

Pearl, Eric
See Elman, Richard

Pearson, T(homas) R(eid) 1956- .... CLC 39
See also CA 120; 130; INT 130

Peck, Dale 1967- .... CLC 81
See also CA 146

Peck, John 1941- .... CLC 3
See also CA 49-52; CANR 3

Peck, Richard (Wayne) 1934-...... CLC 21
See also AAYA 1; CA 85-88; CANR 19,
38; CLR 15; INT CANR-19; JRDA;
MAICYA; SAAS 2; SATA 18, 55

Peck, Robert Newton
1928- .. CLC 17; DA; DAC; DAM MST
See also AAYA 3; CA 81-84; CANR 31;
CLR 45; JRDA; MAICYA; SAAS 1;
SATA 21, 62

Peckinpah, (David) Sam(uel)
1925-1984 .... CLC 20
See also CA 109; 114

Pedersen, Knut 1859-1952
See Hamsun, Knut
See also CA 104; 119; MTCW

Peeslake, Gaffer
See Durrell, Lawrence (George)

Peguy, Charles Pierre
1873-1914 .... TCLC 10
See also CA 107

Pena, Ramon del Valle y
See Valle-Inclan, Ramon (Maria) del

Pendennis, Arthur Esquir
See Thackeray, William Makepeace

Penn, William 1644-1718........... LC 25
See also DLB 24

Pepys, Samuel
1633-1703 ..... LC 11; DA; DAB; DAC;
DAM MST; WLC
See also CDBLB 1660-1789; DLB 101

Percy, Walker
1916-1990 .... CLC 2, 3, 6, 8, 14, 18, 47,
65; DAM NOV, POP
See also CA 1-4R; 131; CANR 1, 23;
DLB 2; DLBY 80, 90; MTCW

Perec, Georges 1936-1982 .... CLC 56
See also CA 141; DLB 83

Pereda (y Sanchez de Porrua), Jose Maria de
1833-1906 .... TCLC 16
See also CA 117

Pereda y Porrua, Jose Maria de
See Pereda (y Sanchez de Porrua), Jose
Maria de

Peregoy, George Weems
See Mencken, H(enry) L(ouis)

Perelman, S(idney) J(oseph)
1904-1979 ...... CLC 3, 5, 9, 15, 23, 44,
49; DAM DRAM
See also AITN 1, 2; CA 73-76; 89-92;
CANR 18; DLB 11, 44; MTCW

Peret, Benjamin 1899-1959 .... TCLC 20
See also CA 117

Peretz, Isaac Loeb 1851(?)-1915... TCLC 16
See also CA 109

Peretz, Yitzkhok Leibush
See Peretz, Isaac Loeb

Perez Galdos, Benito 1843-1920... TCLC 27
See also CA 125; 153; HW

Perrault, Charles 1628-1703 .... LC 2
See also MAICYA; SATA 25

Perry, Brighton
See Sherwood, Robert E(mmet)

Perse, St.-John .... CLC 4, 11, 46
See also Leger, (Marie-Rene Auguste) Alexis
Saint-Leger

Perutz, Leo 1882-1957.......... TCLC 60
See also DLB 81

Peseenz, Tulio F.
See Lopez y Fuentes, Gregorio

Pesetsky, Bette 1932-............. CLC 28
See also CA 133; DLB 130

Peshkov, Alexei Maximovich 1868-1936
See Gorky, Maxim
See also CA 105; 141; DA; DAC;
DAM DRAM, MST, NOV

Pessoa, Fernando (Antonio Nogueira)
1888-1935 .... TCLC 27; HLC
See also CA 125

Peterkin, Julia Mood 1880-1961.... CLC 31
See also CA 102; DLB 9

Peters, Joan K. 1945-............. CLC 39

Peters, Robert L(ouis) 1924-........ CLC 7
See also CA 13-16R; CAAS 8; DLB 105

Petofi, Sandor 1823-1849....... NCLC 21

Petrakis, Harry Mark 1923-........ CLC 3
See also CA 9-12R; CANR 4, 30

Petrarch
1304-1374 .... CMLC 20; DAM POET;
PC 8

Petrov, Evgeny .... TCLC 21
See also Kataev, Evgeny Petrovich

Petry, Ann (Lane) 1908- ...... CLC 1, 7, 18
See also BW 1; CA 5-8R; CAAS 6;
CANR 4, 46; CLR 12; DLB 76; JRDA;
MAICYA; MTCW; SATA 5

Petursson, Halligrimur 1614-1674 .... LC 8

Philips, Katherine 1632-1664........ LC 30
See also DLB 131

Philipson, Morris H. 1926-........ CLC 53
See also CA 1-4R; CANR 4

Phillips, Caryl
1958- .... CLC 96; DAM MULT
See also BW 2; CA 141; DLB 157

Phillips, David Graham
1867-1911 .... TCLC 44
See also CA 108; DLB 9, 12

Phillips, Jack
See Sandburg, Carl (August)

Phillips, Jayne Anne
1952- .... CLC 15, 33; SSC 16
See also CA 101; CANR 24, 50; DLBY 80;
INT CANR-24; MTCW

Phillips, Richard
See Dick, Philip K(indred)

Phillips, Robert (Schaeffer) 1938-... CLC 28
See also CA 17-20R; CAAS 13; CANR 8;
DLB 105

Phillips, Ward
See Lovecraft, H(oward) P(hillips)

Piccolo, Lucio 1901-1969......... CLC 13
See also CA 97-100; DLB 114

Pickthall, Marjorie L(owry) C(hristie)
1883-1922 .... TCLC 21
See also CA 107; DLB 92

Pico della Mirandola, Giovanni
1463-1494 . . . . **LC 15**

Piercy, Marge
1936- . . . . **CLC 3, 6, 14, 18, 27, 62**
See also CA 21-24R; CAAS 1; CANR 13,
43; DLB 120; MTCW

Piers, Robert
See Anthony, Piers

Pieyre de Mandiargues, Andre 1909-1991
See Mandiargues, Andre Pieyre de
See also CA 103; 136; CANR 22

Pilnyak, Boris . . . . **TCLC 23**
See also Vogau, Boris Andreyevich

Pincherle, Alberto
1907-1990 . . . . . **CLC 11, 18; DAM NOV**
See also Moravia, Alberto
See also CA 25-28R; 132; CANR 33;
MTCW

Pinckney, Darryl 1953- . . . . **CLC 76**
See also BW 2; CA 143

Pindar 518B.C.-446B.C. . . . . **CMLC 12**
See also DLB 176

Pineda, Cecile 1942- . . . . **CLC 39**
See also CA 118

Pinero, Arthur Wing
1855-1934 . . . . . **TCLC 32; DAM DRAM**
See also CA 110; 153; DLB 10

Pinero, Miguel (Antonio Gomez)
1946-1988 . . . . **CLC 4, 55**
See also CA 61-64; 125; CANR 29; HW

Pinget, Robert 1919- . . . . **CLC 7, 13, 37**
See also CA 85-88; DLB 83

Pink Floyd
See Barrett, (Roger) Syd; Gilmour, David;
Mason, Nick; Waters, Roger; Wright,
Rick

Pinkney, Edward 1802-1828 . . . . . **NCLC 31**

Pinkwater, Daniel Manus 1941- . . . . **CLC 35**
See also Pinkwater, Manus
See also AAYA 1; CA 29-32R; CANR 12,
38; CLR 4; JRDA; MAICYA; SAAS 3;
SATA 46, 76

Pinkwater, Manus
See Pinkwater, Daniel Manus
See also SATA 8

Pinsky, Robert
1940- . . **CLC 9, 19, 38, 94; DAM POET**
See also CA 29-32R; CAAS 4; DLBY 82

Pinta, Harold
See Pinter, Harold

Pinter, Harold
1930- . . . . . **CLC 1, 3, 6, 9, 11, 15, 27, 58,
73; DA; DAB; DAC; DAM DRAM,
MST; WLC**
See also CA 5-8R; CANR 33; CDBLB 1960
to Present; DLB 13; MTCW

Piozzi, Hester Lynch (Thrale)
1741-1821 . . . . **NCLC 57**
See also DLB 104, 142

Pirandello, Luigi
1867-1936 . . . . . . **TCLC 4, 29; DA; DAB;
DAC; DAM DRAM, MST; DC 5;
SSC 22; WLC**
See also CA 104; 153

Pirsig, Robert M(aynard)
1928- . . . . **CLC 4, 6, 73; DAM POP**
See also CA 53-56; CANR 42; MTCW;
SATA 39

Pisarev, Dmitry Ivanovich
1840-1868 . . . . **NCLC 25**

Pix, Mary (Griffith) 1666-1709 . . . . **LC 8**
See also DLB 80

Pixerecourt, Guilbert de
1773-1844 . . . . **NCLC 39**

Plaidy, Jean
See Hibbert, Eleanor Alice Burford

Planche, James Robinson
1796-1880 . . . . **NCLC 42**

Plant, Robert 1948- . . . . **CLC 12**

Plante, David (Robert)
1940- . . . . **CLC 7, 23, 38; DAM NOV**
See also CA 37-40R; CANR 12, 36;
DLBY 83; INT CANR-12; MTCW

Plath, Sylvia
1932-1963 . . . . . **CLC 1, 2, 3, 5, 9, 11, 14,
17, 50, 51, 62; DA; DAB; DAC;
DAM MST, POET; PC 1; WLC**
See also AAYA 13; CA 19-20; CANR 34;
CAP 2; CDALB 1941-1968; DLB 5, 6,
152; MTCW

Plato
428(?)B.C.-348(?)B.C. . . . . **CMLC 8; DA;
DAB; DAC; DAM MST**
See also DLB 176

Platonov, Andrei . . . . **TCLC 14**
See also Klimentov, Andrei Platonovich

Platt, Kin 1911- . . . . **CLC 26**
See also AAYA 11; CA 17-20R; CANR 11;
JRDA; SAAS 17; SATA 21, 86

Plautus c. 251B.C.-184B.C. . . . . **DC 6**

Plick et Plock
See Simenon, Georges (Jacques Christian)

Plimpton, George (Ames) 1927- . . . . . **CLC 36**
See also AITN 1; CA 21-24R; CANR 32;
MTCW; SATA 10

Plomer, William Charles Franklin
1903-1973 . . . . **CLC 4, 8**
See also CA 21-22; CANR 34; CAP 2;
DLB 20, 162; MTCW; SATA 24

Plowman, Piers
See Kavanagh, Patrick (Joseph)

Plum, J.
See Wodehouse, P(elham) G(renville)

Plumly, Stanley (Ross) 1939- . . . . **CLC 33**
See also CA 108; 110; DLB 5; INT 110

Plumpe, Friedrich Wilhelm
1888-1931 . . . . **TCLC 53**
See also CA 112

Poe, Edgar Allan
1809-1849 . . . . **NCLC 1, 16, 55; DA;
DAB; DAC; DAM MST, POET; PC 1;
SSC 1, 22; WLC**
See also AAYA 14; CDALB 1640-1865;
DLB 3, 59, 73, 74; SATA 23

Poet of Titchfield Street, The
See Pound, Ezra (Weston Loomis)

Pohl, Frederik 1919- . . . . . **CLC 18; SSC 25**
See also CA 61-64; CAAS 1; CANR 11, 37;
DLB 8; INT CANR-11; MTCW;
SATA 24

Poirier, Louis 1910-
See Gracq, Julien
See also CA 122; 126

Poitier, Sidney 1927- . . . . **CLC 26**
See also BW 1; CA 117

Polanski, Roman 1933- . . . . **CLC 16**
See also CA 77-80

Poliakoff, Stephen 1952- . . . . **CLC 38**
See also CA 106; DLB 13

Police, The
See Copeland, Stewart (Armstrong);
Summers, Andrew James; Sumner,
Gordon Matthew

Polidori, John William
1795-1821 . . . . **NCLC 51**
See also DLB 116

Pollitt, Katha 1949- . . . . **CLC 28**
See also CA 120; 122; MTCW

Pollock, (Mary) Sharon
1936- . . . . **CLC 50; DAC; DAM DRAM,
MST**
See also CA 141; DLB 60

Polo, Marco 1254-1324 . . . . **CMLC 15**

Polonsky, Abraham (Lincoln)
1910- . . . . **CLC 92**
See also CA 104; DLB 26; INT 104

Polybius c. 200B.C.-c. 118B.C. . . . . **CMLC 17**
See also DLB 176

Pomerance, Bernard
1940- . . . . **CLC 13; DAM DRAM**
See also CA 101; CANR 49

Ponge, Francis (Jean Gaston Alfred)
1899-1988 . . . . . **CLC 6, 18; DAM POET**
See also CA 85-88; 126; CANR 40

Pontoppidan, Henrik 1857-1943 . . . **TCLC 29**

Poole, Josephine . . . . **CLC 17**
See also Helyar, Jane Penelope Josephine
See also SAAS 2; SATA 5

Popa, Vasko 1922-1991 . . . . **CLC 19**
See also CA 112; 148

Pope, Alexander
1688-1744 . . . . . . **LC 3; DA; DAB; DAC;
DAM MST, POET; WLC**
See also CDBLB 1660-1789; DLB 95, 101

Porter, Connie (Rose) 1959(?)- . . . . . **CLC 70**
See also BW 2; CA 142; SATA 81

Porter, Gene(va Grace) Stratton
1863(?)-1924 . . . . **TCLC 21**
See also CA 112

Porter, Katherine Anne
1890-1980 . . . . . . **CLC 1, 3, 7, 10, 13, 15,
27; DA; DAB; DAC; DAM MST, NOV;
SSC 4**
See also AITN 2; CA 1-4R; 101; CANR 1;
DLB 4, 9, 102; DLBD 12; DLBY 80;
MTCW; SATA 39; SATA-Obit 23

Porter, Peter (Neville Frederick)
1929- . . . . **CLC 5, 13, 33**
See also CA 85-88; DLB 40

Porter, William Sydney 1862-1910
See Henry, O.
See also CA 104; 131; CDALB 1865-1917;
DA; DAB; DAC; DAM MST; DLB 12,
78, 79; MTCW; YABC 2

Portillo (y Pacheco), Jose Lopez
See Lopez Portillo (y Pacheco), Jose

Post, Melville Davisson
1869-1930 .... TCLC 39
See also CA 110

Potok, Chaim
1929- .... CLC 2, 7, 14, 26; DAM NOV
See also AAYA 15; AITN 1, 2; CA 17-20R;
CANR 19, 35; DLB 28, 152;
INT CANR-19; MTCW; SATA 33

Potter, Beatrice
See Webb, (Martha) Beatrice (Potter)
See also MAICYA

Potter, Dennis (Christopher George)
1935-1994 .... CLC 58, 86
See also CA 107; 145; CANR 33; MTCW

Pound, Ezra (Weston Loomis)
1885-1972 ...... CLC 1, 2, 3, 4, 5, 7, 10,
13, 18, 34, 48, 50; DA; DAB; DAC;
DAM MST, POET; PC 4; WLC
See also CA 5-8R; 37-40R; CANR 40;
CDALB 1917-1929; DLB 4, 45, 63;
MTCW

Povod, Reinaldo 1959-1994 .... CLC 44
See also CA 136; 146

Powell, Adam Clayton, Jr.
1908-1972 .... CLC 89; BLC;
DAM MULT
See also BW 1; CA 102; 33-36R

Powell, Anthony (Dymoke)
1905- .... CLC 1, 3, 7, 9, 10, 31
See also CA 1-4R; CANR 1, 32;
CDBLB 1945-1960; DLB 15; MTCW

Powell, Dawn 1897-1965 .... CLC 66
See also CA 5-8R

Powell, Padgett 1952-............. CLC 34
See also CA 126

Power, Susan..................... CLC 91

Powers, J(ames) F(arl)
1917- .... CLC 1, 4, 8, 57; SSC 4
See also CA 1-4R; CANR 2; DLB 130;
MTCW

Powers, John J(ames) 1945-
See Powers, John R.
See also CA 69-72

Powers, John R. .... CLC 66
See also Powers, John J(ames)

Powers, Richard (S.) 1957- .... CLC 93
See also CA 148

Pownall, David 1938-............. CLC 10
See also CA 89-92; CAAS 18; CANR 49;
DLB 14

Powys, John Cowper
1872-1963 .... CLC 7, 9, 15, 46
See also CA 85-88; DLB 15; MTCW

Powys, T(heodore) F(rancis)
1875-1953 .... TCLC 9
See also CA 106; DLB 36, 162

Prager, Emily 1952-.............. CLC 56

Pratt, E(dwin) J(ohn)
1883(?)-1964 .... CLC 19; DAC;
DAM POET
See also CA 141; 93-96; DLB 92

Premchand..................... TCLC 21
See also Srivastava, Dhanpat Rai

Preussler, Otfried 1923-.......... CLC 17
See also CA 77-80; SATA 24

Prevert, Jacques (Henri Marie)
1900-1977 .... CLC 15
See also CA 77-80; 69-72; CANR 29;
MTCW; SATA-Obit 30

Prevost, Abbe (Antoine Francois)
1697-1763 .... LC 1

Price, (Edward) Reynolds
1933- .... CLC 3, 6, 13, 43, 50, 63;
DAM NOV; SSC 22
See also CA 1-4R; CANR 1, 37, 57; DLB 2;
INT CANR-37

Price, Richard 1949- .... CLC 6, 12
See also CA 49-52; CANR 3; DLBY 81

Prichard, Katharine Susannah
1883-1969 .... CLC 46
See also CA 11-12; CANR 33; CAP 1;
MTCW; SATA 66

Priestley, J(ohn) B(oynton)
1894-1984 .... CLC 2, 5, 9, 34;
DAM DRAM, NOV
See also CA 9-12R; 113; CANR 33;
CDBLB 1914-1945; DLB 10, 34, 77, 100,
139; DLBY 84; MTCW

Prince 1958(?)- .... CLC 35

Prince, F(rank) T(empleton) 1912-... CLC 22
See also CA 101; CANR 43; DLB 20

Prince Kropotkin
See Kropotkin, Peter (Aleksieevich)

Prior, Matthew 1664-1721........... LC 4
See also DLB 95

Pritchard, William H(arrison)
1932- .... CLC 34
See also CA 65-68; CANR 23; DLB 111

Pritchett, V(ictor) S(awdon)
1900- .... CLC 5, 13, 15, 41;
DAM NOV; SSC 14
See also CA 61-64; CANR 31; DLB 15,
139; MTCW

Private 19022
See Manning, Frederic

Probst, Mark 1925- .... CLC 59
See also CA 130

Prokosch, Frederic 1908-1989.... CLC 4, 48
See also CA 73-76; 128; DLB 48

Prophet, The
See Dreiser, Theodore (Herman Albert)

Prose, Francine 1947-.............. CLC 45
See also CA 109; 112; CANR 46

Proudhon
See Cunha, Euclides (Rodrigues Pimenta) da

Proulx, E. Annie 1935- .... CLC 81

**Proust, (Valentin-Louis-George-Eugene-)
Marcel**
1871-1922 .... TCLC 7, 13, 33; DA;
DAB; DAC; DAM MST, NOV; WLC
See also CA 104; 120; DLB 65; MTCW

Prowler, Harley
See Masters, Edgar Lee

Prus, Boleslaw 1845-1912 .... TCLC 48

Pryor, Richard (Franklin Lenox Thomas)
1940- .... CLC 26
See also CA 122

Przybyszewski, Stanislaw
1868-1927 .... TCLC 36
See also DLB 66

Pteleon
See Grieve, C(hristopher) M(urray)
See also DAM POET

Puckett, Lute
See Masters, Edgar Lee

Puig, Manuel
1932-1990 .... CLC 3, 5, 10, 28, 65;
DAM MULT; HLC
See also CA 45-48; CANR 2, 32; DLB 113;
HW; MTCW

Purdy, Al(fred Wellington)
1918- .... CLC 3, 6, 14, 50; DAC;
DAM MST, POET
See also CA 81-84; CAAS 17; CANR 42;
DLB 88

Purdy, James (Amos)
1923- .... CLC 2, 4, 10, 28, 52
See also CA 33-36R; CAAS 1; CANR 19,
51; DLB 2; INT CANR-19; MTCW

Pure, Simon
See Swinnerton, Frank Arthur

Pushkin, Alexander (Sergeyevich)
1799-1837 ..... NCLC 3, 27; DA; DAB;
DAC; DAM DRAM, MST, POET;
PC 10; WLC
See also SATA 61

P'u Sung-ling 1640-1715 .... LC 3

Putnam, Arthur Lee
See Alger, Horatio, Jr.

Puzo, Mario
1920- ..... CLC 1, 2, 6, 36; DAM NOV,
POP
See also CA 65-68; CANR 4, 42; DLB 6;
MTCW

Pygge, Edward
See Barnes, Julian (Patrick)

Pym, Barbara (Mary Crampton)
1913-1980 .... CLC 13, 19, 37
See also CA 13-14; 97-100; CANR 13, 34;
CAP 1; DLB 14; DLBY 87; MTCW

Pynchon, Thomas (Ruggles, Jr.)
1937- ..... CLC 2, 3, 6, 9, 11, 18, 33, 62,
72; DA; DAB; DAC; DAM MST, NOV,
POP; SSC 14; WLC
See also BEST 90:2; CA 17-20R; CANR 22,
46; DLB 2, 173; MTCW

Pythagoras
c. 570B.C.-c. 500B.C......... CMLC 22
See also DLB 176

Qian Zhongshu
See Ch'ien Chung-shu

Qroll
See Dagerman, Stig (Halvard)

Quarrington, Paul (Lewis) 1953-.... CLC 65
See also CA 129

Quasimodo, Salvatore 1901-1968 ... **CLC 10**
See also CA 13-16; 25-28R; CAP 1;
DLB 114; MTCW

Quay, Stephen 1947- .... **CLC 95**

Quay, The Brothers
See Quay, Stephen; Quay, Timothy

Quay, Timothy 1947-............. **CLC 95**

Queen, Ellery................. **CLC 3, 11**
See also Dannay, Frederic; Davidson,
Avram; Lee, Manfred B(ennington);
Marlowe, Stephen; Sturgeon, Theodore
(Hamilton); Vance, John Holbrook

Queen, Ellery, Jr.
See Dannay, Frederic; Lee, Manfred
B(ennington)

Queneau, Raymond
1903-1976 .... **CLC 2, 5, 10, 42**
See also CA 77-80; 69-72; CANR 32;
DLB 72; MTCW

Quevedo, Francisco de 1580-1645.... **LC 23**

Quiller-Couch, Arthur Thomas
1863-1944 .... **TCLC 53**
See also CA 118; DLB 135, 153

Quin, Ann (Marie) 1936-1973...... **CLC 6**
See also CA 9-12R; 45-48; DLB 14

Quinn, Martin
See Smith, Martin Cruz

Quinn, Peter 1947-............... **CLC 91**

Quinn, Simon
See Smith, Martin Cruz

Quiroga, Horacio (Sylvestre)
1878-1937 ..... **TCLC 20; DAM MULT;**
HLC
See also CA 117; 131; HW; MTCW

Quoirez, Francoise 1935-........... **CLC 9**
See also Sagan, Francoise
See also CA 49-52; CANR 6, 39; MTCW

Raabe, Wilhelm 1831-1910 .... **TCLC 45**
See also DLB 129

Rabe, David (William)
1940- ...... **CLC 4, 8, 33; DAM DRAM**
See also CA 85-88; CABS 3; DLB 7

Rabelais, Francois
1483-1553 ...... **LC 5; DA; DAB; DAC;**
DAM MST; WLC

Rabinovitch, Sholem 1859-1916
See Aleichem, Sholom
See also CA 104

Rachilde 1860-1953 .... **TCLC 67**
See also DLB 123

Racine, Jean
1639-1699 .... **LC 28; DAB; DAM MST**

Radcliffe, Ann (Ward)
1764-1823 .... **NCLC 6, 55**
See also DLB 39

Radiguet, Raymond 1903-1923 .... **TCLC 29**
See also DLB 65

Radnoti, Miklos 1909-1944 ...... **TCLC 16**
See also CA 118

Rado, James 1939-............... **CLC 17**
See also CA 105

Radvanyi, Netty 1900-1983
See Seghers, Anna
See also CA 85-88; 110

Rae, Ben
See Griffiths, Trevor

Raeburn, John (Hay) 1941-........ **CLC 34**
See also CA 57-60

Ragni, Gerome 1942-1991 .... **CLC 17**
See also CA 105; 134

Rahv, Philip 1908-1973 .... **CLC 24**
See also Greenberg, Ivan
See also DLB 137

Raine, Craig 1944- .... **CLC 32**
See also CA 108; CANR 29, 51; DLB 40

Raine, Kathleen (Jessie) 1908- ... **CLC 7, 45**
See also CA 85-88; CANR 46; DLB 20;
MTCW

Rainis, Janis 1865-1929 .... **TCLC 29**

Rakosi, Carl...................... **CLC 47**
See also Rawley, Callman
See also CAAS 5

Raleigh, Richard
See Lovecraft, H(oward) P(hillips)

Raleigh, Sir Walter 1554(?)-1618 .... **LC 31**
See also CDBLB Before 1660; DLB 172

Rallentando, H. P.
See Sayers, Dorothy L(eigh)

Ramal, Walter
See de la Mare, Walter (John)

Ramon, Juan
See Jimenez (Mantecon), Juan Ramon

Ramos, Graciliano 1892-1953 ..... **TCLC 32**

Rampersad, Arnold 1941-......... **CLC 44**
See also BW 2; CA 127; 133; DLB 111;
INT 133

Rampling, Anne
See Rice, Anne

Ramsay, Allan 1684(?)-1758 .... **LC 29**
See also DLB 95

Ramuz, Charles-Ferdinand
1878-1947 .... **TCLC 33**

Rand, Ayn
1905-1982 ...... **CLC 3, 30, 44, 79; DA;**
DAC; DAM MST, NOV, POP; WLC
See also AAYA 10; CA 13-16R; 105;
CANR 27; MTCW

Randall, Dudley (Felker)
1914- ...... **CLC 1; BLC; DAM MULT**
See also BW 1; CA 25-28R; CANR 23;
DLB 41

Randall, Robert
See Silverberg, Robert

Ranger, Ken
See Creasey, John

Ransom, John Crowe
1888-1974 .... **CLC 2, 4, 5, 11, 24;**
DAM POET
See also CA 5-8R; 49-52; CANR 6, 34;
DLB 45, 63; MTCW

Rao, Raja 1909- ... **CLC 25, 56; DAM NOV**
See also CA 73-76; CANR 51; MTCW

Raphael, Frederic (Michael)
1931- .... **CLC 2, 14**
See also CA 1-4R; CANR 1; DLB 14

Ratcliffe, James P.
See Mencken, H(enry) L(ouis)

Rathbone, Julian 1935- .... **CLC 41**
See also CA 101; CANR 34

Rattigan, Terence (Mervyn)
1911-1977 ...... **CLC 7; DAM DRAM**
See also CA 85-88; 73-76;
CDBLB 1945-1960; DLB 13; MTCW

Ratushinskaya, Irina 1954- .... **CLC 54**
See also CA 129

Raven, Simon (Arthur Noel)
1927- .... **CLC 14**
See also CA 81-84

Rawley, Callman 1903-
See Rakosi, Carl
See also CA 21-24R; CANR 12, 32

Rawlings, Marjorie Kinnan
1896-1953 .... **TCLC 4**
See also AAYA 20; CA 104; 137; DLB 9,
22, 102; JRDA; MAICYA; YABC 1

Ray, Satyajit
1921-1992 ... **CLC 16, 76; DAM MULT**
See also CA 114; 137

Read, Herbert Edward 1893-1968.... **CLC 4**
See also CA 85-88; 25-28R; DLB 20, 149

Read, Piers Paul 1941- ...... **CLC 4, 10, 25**
See also CA 21-24R; CANR 38; DLB 14;
SATA 21

Reade, Charles 1814-1884 .... **NCLC 2**
See also DLB 21

Reade, Hamish
See Gray, Simon (James Holliday)

Reading, Peter 1946- .... **CLC 47**
See also CA 103; CANR 46; DLB 40

Reaney, James
1926- ...... **CLC 13; DAC; DAM MST**
See also CA 41-44R; CAAS 15; CANR 42;
DLB 68; SATA 43

Rebreanu, Liviu 1885-1944 ...... **TCLC 28**

Rechy, John (Francisco)
1934- .... **CLC 1, 7, 14, 18;**
DAM MULT; HLC
See also CA 5-8R; CAAS 4; CANR 6, 32;
DLB 122; DLBY 82; HW; INT CANR-6

Redcam, Tom 1870-1933 .... **TCLC 25**

Reddin, Keith.................... **CLC 67**

Redgrove, Peter (William)
1932- .... **CLC 6, 41**
See also CA 1-4R; CANR 3, 39; DLB 40

Redmon, Anne.................... **CLC 22**
See also Nightingale, Anne Redmon
See also DLBY 86

Reed, Eliot
See Ambler, Eric

Reed, Ishmael
1938- .... **CLC 2, 3, 5, 6, 13, 32, 60;**
BLC; DAM MULT
See also BW 2; CA 21-24R; CANR 25, 48;
DLB 2, 5, 33, 169; DLBD 8; MTCW

Reed, John (Silas) 1887-1920 ...... **TCLC 9**
See also CA 106

Reed, Lou........................ **CLC 21**
See also Firbank, Louis

Reeve, Clara 1729-1807 .... **NCLC 19**
See also DLB 39

Reich, Wilhelm 1897-1957........ **TCLC 57**

Reid, Christopher (John) 1949- . . . . . **CLC 33**
See also CA 140; DLB 40

Reid, Desmond
See Moorcock, Michael (John)

Reid Banks, Lynne 1929-
See Banks, Lynne Reid
See also CA 1-4R; CANR 6, 22, 38;
CLR 24; JRDA; MAICYA; SATA 22, 75

Reilly, William K.
See Creasey, John

Reiner, Max
See Caldwell, (Janet Miriam) Taylor
(Holland)

Reis, Ricardo
See Pessoa, Fernando (Antonio Nogueira)

Remarque, Erich Maria
1898-1970 . . . . **CLC 21; DA; DAB; DAC;**
DAM MST, NOV
See also CA 77-80; 29-32R; DLB 56;
MTCW

Remizov, A.
See Remizov, Aleksei (Mikhailovich)

Remizov, A. M.
See Remizov, Aleksei (Mikhailovich)

Remizov, Aleksei (Mikhailovich)
1877-1957 . . . . **TCLC 27**
See also CA 125; 133

Renan, Joseph Ernest
1823-1892 . . . . **NCLC 26**

Renard, Jules 1864-1910 . . . . **TCLC 17**
See also CA 117

Renault, Mary . . . . **CLC 3, 11, 17**
See also Challans, Mary
See also DLBY 83

Rendell, Ruth (Barbara)
1930- . . . . **CLC 28, 48; DAM POP**
See also Vine, Barbara
See also CA 109; CANR 32, 52; DLB 87;
INT CANR-32; MTCW

Renoir, Jean 1894-1979 . . . . **CLC 20**
See also CA 129; 85-88

Resnais, Alain 1922- . . . . **CLC 16**

Reverdy, Pierre 1889-1960 . . . . **CLC 53**
See also CA 97-100; 89-92

Rexroth, Kenneth
1905-1982 . . . . . . **CLC 1, 2, 6, 11, 22, 49;**
DAM POET
See also CA 5-8R; 107; CANR 14, 34;
CDALB 1941-1968; DLB 16, 48, 165;
DLBY 82; INT CANR-14; MTCW

Reyes, Alfonso 1889-1959 . . . . **TCLC 33**
See also CA 131; HW

Reyes y Basoalto, Ricardo Eliecer Neftali
See Neruda, Pablo

Reymont, Wladyslaw (Stanislaw)
1868(?)-1925 . . . . **TCLC 5**
See also CA 104

Reynolds, Jonathan 1942- . . . . **CLC 6, 38**
See also CA 65-68; CANR 28

Reynolds, Joshua 1723-1792 . . . . **LC 15**
See also DLB 104

Reynolds, Michael Shane 1937- . . . . **CLC 44**
See also CA 65-68; CANR 9

Reznikoff, Charles 1894-1976 . . . . **CLC 9**
See also CA 33-36; 61-64; CAP 2; DLB 28,
45

Rezzori (d'Arezzo), Gregor von
1914- . . . . **CLC 25**
See also CA 122; 136

Rhine, Richard
See Silverstein, Alvin

Rhodes, Eugene Manlove
1869-1934 . . . . **TCLC 53**

R'hoone
See Balzac, Honore de

Rhys, Jean
1890(?)-1979 . . . . **CLC 2, 4, 6, 14, 19, 51;**
DAM NOV; SSC 21
See also CA 25-28R; 85-88; CANR 35;
CDBLB 1945-1960; DLB 36, 117, 162;
MTCW

Ribeiro, Darcy 1922-1997 . . . . **CLC 34**
See also CA 33-36R; 156

Ribeiro, Joao Ubaldo (Osorio Pimentel)
1941- . . . . **CLC 10, 67**
See also CA 81-84

Ribman, Ronald (Burt) 1932- . . . . **CLC 7**
See also CA 21-24R; CANR 46

Ricci, Nino 1959- . . . . **CLC 70**
See also CA 137

Rice, Anne 1941- . . . . . **CLC 41; DAM POP**
See also AAYA 9; BEST 89:2; CA 65-68;
CANR 12, 36, 53

Rice, Elmer (Leopold)
1892-1967 . . . . . . **CLC 7, 49; DAM DRAM**
See also CA 21-22; 25-28R; CAP 2; DLB 4,
7; MTCW

Rice, Tim(othy Miles Bindon)
1944- . . . . **CLC 21**
See also CA 103; CANR 46

Rich, Adrienne (Cecile)
1929- . . . . **CLC 3, 6, 7, 11, 18, 36, 73, 76;**
DAM POET; PC 5
See also CA 9-12R; CANR 20, 53; DLB 5,
67; MTCW

Rich, Barbara
See Graves, Robert (von Ranke)

Rich, Robert
See Trumbo, Dalton

Richard, Keith . . . . **CLC 17**
See also Richards, Keith

Richards, David Adams
1950- . . . . **CLC 59; DAC**
See also CA 93-96; DLB 53

Richards, I(vor) A(rmstrong)
1893-1979 . . . . **CLC 14, 24**
See also CA 41-44R; 89-92; CANR 34;
DLB 27

Richards, Keith 1943-
See Richard, Keith
See also CA 107

Richardson, Anne
See Roiphe, Anne (Richardson)

Richardson, Dorothy Miller
1873-1957 . . . . **TCLC 3**
See also CA 104; DLB 36

Richardson, Ethel Florence (Lindesay)
1870-1946
See Richardson, Henry Handel
See also CA 105

Richardson, Henry Handel . . . . **TCLC 4**
See also Richardson, Ethel Florence
(Lindesay)

Richardson, John
1796-1852 . . . . **NCLC 55; DAC**
See also DLB 99

Richardson, Samuel
1689-1761 . . . . . . **LC 1; DA; DAB; DAC;**
DAM MST, NOV; WLC
See also CDBLB 1660-1789; DLB 39

Richler, Mordecai
1931- . . . . **CLC 3, 5, 9, 13, 18, 46, 70;**
DAC; DAM MST, NOV
See also AITN 1; CA 65-68; CANR 31;
CLR 17; DLB 53; MAICYA; MTCW;
SATA 44; SATA-Brief 27

Richter, Conrad (Michael)
1890-1968 . . . . **CLC 30**
See also AAYA 21; CA 5-8R; 25-28R;
CANR 23; DLB 9; MTCW; SATA 3

Ricostranza, Tom
See Ellis, Trey

Riddell, J. H. 1832-1906 . . . . **TCLC 40**

Riding, Laura . . . . **CLC 3, 7**
See also Jackson, Laura (Riding)

Riefenstahl, Berta Helene Amalia 1902-
See Riefenstahl, Leni
See also CA 108

Riefenstahl, Leni . . . . **CLC 16**
See also Riefenstahl, Berta Helene Amalia

Riffe, Ernest
See Bergman, (Ernst) Ingmar

Riggs, (Rolla) Lynn
1899-1954 . . . . . **TCLC 56; DAM MULT**
See also CA 144; DLB 175; NNAL

Riley, James Whitcomb
1849-1916 . . . . . . **TCLC 51; DAM POET**
See also CA 118; 137; MAICYA; SATA 17

Riley, Tex
See Creasey, John

Rilke, Rainer Maria
1875-1926 . . . . **TCLC 1, 6, 19;**
DAM POET; PC 2
See also CA 104; 132; DLB 81; MTCW

Rimbaud, (Jean Nicolas) Arthur
1854-1891 . . . . . **NCLC 4, 35; DA; DAB;**
DAC; DAM MST, POET; PC 3; WLC

Rinehart, Mary Roberts
1876-1958 . . . . **TCLC 52**
See also CA 108

Ringmaster, The
See Mencken, H(enry) L(ouis)

Ringwood, Gwen(dolyn Margaret) Pharis
1910-1984 . . . . **CLC 48**
See also CA 148; 112; DLB 88

Rio, Michel 19(?)- . . . . **CLC 43**

Ritsos, Giannes
See Ritsos, Yannis

Ritsos, Yannis 1909-1990 . . . . . **CLC 6, 13, 31**
See also CA 77-80; 133; CANR 39; MTCW

Ritter, Erika 1948(?)- . . . . **CLC 52**

Rossetti, Dante Gabriel
1828-1882 . . . . NCLC 4; DA; DAB;
DAC; DAM MST, POET; WLC
See also CDBLB 1832-1890; DLB 35

Rossner, Judith (Perelman)
1935- . . . . CLC 6, 9, 29
See also AITN 2; BEST 90:3; CA 17-20R;
CANR 18, 51; DLB 6; INT CANR-18;
MTCW

Rostand, Edmond (Eugene Alexis)
1868-1918 . . . . . . TCLC 6, 37; DA; DAB;
DAC; DAM DRAM, MST
See also CA 104; 126; MTCW

Roth, Henry 1906-1995 . . . . CLC 2, 6, 11
See also CA 11-12; 149; CANR 38; CAP 1;
DLB 28; MTCW

Roth, Joseph 1894-1939 . . . . TCLC 33
See also DLB 85

Roth, Philip (Milton)
1933- . . . . . . CLC 1, 2, 3, 4, 6, 9, 15, 22,
31, 47, 66, 86; DA; DAB; DAC;
DAM MST, NOV, POP; WLC
See also BEST 90:3; CA 1-4R; CANR 1, 22,
36, 55; CDALB 1968-1988; DLB 2, 28,
173; DLBY 82; MTCW

Rothenberg, Jerome 1931- . . . . CLC 6, 57
See also CA 45-48; CANR 1; DLB 5

Roumain, Jacques (Jean Baptiste)
1907-1944 . . . . TCLC 19; BLC;
DAM MULT
See also BW 1; CA 117; 125

Rourke, Constance (Mayfield)
1885-1941 . . . . TCLC 12
See also CA 107; YABC 1

Rousseau, Jean-Baptiste 1671-1741 . . . LC 9

Rousseau, Jean-Jacques
1712-1778 . . . . LC 14, 36; DA; DAB;
DAC; DAM MST; WLC

Roussel, Raymond 1877-1933 . . . . . TCLC 20
See also CA 117

Rovit, Earl (Herbert) 1927- . . . . CLC 7
See also CA 5-8R; CANR 12

Rowe, Nicholas 1674-1718 . . . . LC 8
See also DLB 84

Rowley, Ames Dorrance
See Lovecraft, H(oward) P(hillips)

Rowson, Susanna Haswell
1762(?)-1824 . . . . NCLC 5
See also DLB 37

Roy, Gabrielle
1909-1983 . . . . CLC 10, 14; DAB; DAC;
DAM MST
See also CA 53-56; 110; CANR 5; DLB 68;
MTCW

Rozewicz, Tadeusz
1921- . . . . CLC 9, 23; DAM POET
See also CA 108; CANR 36; MTCW

Ruark, Gibbons 1941- . . . . CLC 3
See also CA 33-36R; CAAS 23; CANR 14,
31, 57; DLB 120

Rubens, Bernice (Ruth) 1923- . . . CLC 19, 31
See also CA 25-28R; CANR 33; DLB 14;
MTCW

Rubin, Harold
See Robbins, Harold

Rudkin, (James) David 1936- . . . . . . CLC 14
See also CA 89-92; DLB 13

Rudnik, Raphael 1933- . . . . CLC 7
See also CA 29-32R

Ruffian, M.
See Hasek, Jaroslav (Matej Frantisek)

Ruiz, Jose Martinez . . . . CLC 11
See also Martinez Ruiz, Jose

Rukeyser, Muriel
1913-1980 . . . . CLC 6, 10, 15, 27;
DAM POET; PC 12
See also CA 5-8R; 93-96; CANR 26;
DLB 48; MTCW; SATA-Obit 22

Rule, Jane (Vance) 1931- . . . . CLC 27
See also CA 25-28R; CAAS 18; CANR 12;
DLB 60

Rulfo, Juan
1918-1986 . . . . CLC 8, 80; DAM MULT;
HLC; SSC 25
See also CA 85-88; 118; CANR 26;
DLB 113; HW; MTCW

Rumi, Jalal al-Din 1297-1373 . . . . CMLC 20

Runeberg, Johan 1804-1877 . . . . . . NCLC 41

Runyon, (Alfred) Damon
1884(?)-1946 . . . . TCLC 10
See also CA 107; DLB 11, 86, 171

Rush, Norman 1933- . . . . CLC 44
See also CA 121; 126; INT 126

Rushdie, (Ahmed) Salman
1947- . . . . CLC 23, 31, 55, 100; DAB;
DAC; DAM MST, NOV, POP
See also BEST 89:3; CA 108; 111;
CANR 33, 56; INT 111; MTCW

Rushforth, Peter (Scott) 1945- . . . . . CLC 19
See also CA 101

Ruskin, John 1819-1900 . . . . TCLC 63
See also CA 114; 129; CDBLB 1832-1890;
DLB 55, 163; SATA 24

Russ, Joanna 1937- . . . . CLC 15
See also CA 25-28R; CANR 11, 31; DLB 8;
MTCW

Russell, George William 1867-1935
See Baker, Jean H.
See also CA 104; 153; CDBLB 1890-1914;
DAM POET

Russell, (Henry) Ken(neth Alfred)
1927- . . . . CLC 16
See also CA 105

Russell, Willy 1947- . . . . CLC 60

Rutherford, Mark . . . . TCLC 25
See also White, William Hale
See also DLB 18

Ruyslinck, Ward 1929- . . . . CLC 14
See also Belser, Reimond Karel Maria de

Ryan, Cornelius (John) 1920-1974 . . . CLC 7
See also CA 69-72; 53-56; CANR 38

Ryan, Michael 1946- . . . . CLC 65
See also CA 49-52; DLBY 82

Rybakov, Anatoli (Naumovich)
1911- . . . . CLC 23, 53
See also CA 126; 135; SATA 79

Ryder, Jonathan
See Ludlum, Robert

Ryga, George
1932-1987 . . CLC 14; DAC; DAM MST
See also CA 101; 124; CANR 43; DLB 60

S. S.
See Sassoon, Siegfried (Lorraine)

Saba, Umberto 1883-1957 . . . . TCLC 33
See also CA 144; DLB 114

Sabatini, Rafael 1875-1950 . . . . TCLC 47

Sabato, Ernesto (R.)
1911- . . . . CLC 10, 23; DAM MULT;
HLC
See also CA 97-100; CANR 32; DLB 145;
HW; MTCW

Sacastru, Martin
See Bioy Casares, Adolfo

Sacher-Masoch, Leopold von
1836(?)-1895 . . . . NCLC 31

Sachs, Marilyn (Stickle) 1927- . . . . . CLC 35
See also AAYA 2; CA 17-20R; CANR 13,
47; CLR 2; JRDA; MAICYA; SAAS 2;
SATA 3, 68

Sachs, Nelly 1891-1970 . . . . CLC 14, 98
See also CA 17-18; 25-28R; CAP 2

Sackler, Howard (Oliver)
1929-1982 . . . . CLC 14
See also CA 61-64; 108; CANR 30; DLB 7

Sacks, Oliver (Wolf) 1933- . . . . CLC 67
See also CA 53-56; CANR 28, 50;
INT CANR-28; MTCW

Sade, Donatien Alphonse Francois Comte
1740-1814 . . . . NCLC 47

Sadoff, Ira 1945- . . . . CLC 9
See also CA 53-56; CANR 5, 21; DLB 120

Saetone
See Camus, Albert

Safire, William 1929- . . . . CLC 10
See also CA 17-20R; CANR 31, 54

Sagan, Carl (Edward) 1934-1996 . . . . CLC 30
See also AAYA 2; CA 25-28R; 155;
CANR 11, 36; MTCW; SATA 58

Sagan, Francoise . . . . CLC 3, 6, 9, 17, 36
See also Quoirez, Francoise
See also DLB 83

Sahgal, Nayantara (Pandit) 1927- . . . CLC 41
See also CA 9-12R; CANR 11

Saint, H(arry) F. 1941- . . . . CLC 50
See also CA 127

St. Aubin de Teran, Lisa 1953-
See Teran, Lisa St. Aubin de
See also CA 118; 126; INT 126

Sainte-Beuve, Charles Augustin
1804-1869 . . . . NCLC 5

**Saint-Exupery, Antoine (Jean Baptiste Marie
Roger) de**
1900-1944 . . . . TCLC 2, 56; DAM NOV;
WLC
See also CA 108; 132; CLR 10; DLB 72;
MAICYA; MTCW; SATA 20

St. John, David
See Hunt, E(verette) Howard, (Jr.)

Saint-John Perse
See Leger, (Marie-Rene Auguste) Alexis
Saint-Leger

Saintsbury, George (Edward Bateman)
    1845-1933 .... TCLC 31
    See also DLB 57, 149

Sait Faik .... TCLC 23
    See also Abasiyanik, Sait Faik

Saki .... TCLC 3; SSC 12
    See also Munro, H(ector) H(ugh)

Sala, George Augustus .... NCLC 46

Salama, Hannu 1936- .... CLC 18

Salamanca, J(ack) R(ichard)
    1922- .... CLC 4, 15
    See also CA 25-28R

Sale, J. Kirkpatrick
    See Sale, Kirkpatrick

Sale, Kirkpatrick 1937- .... CLC 68
    See also CA 13-16R; CANR 10

Salinas, Luis Omar
    1937- ..... CLC 90; DAM MULT; HLC
    See also CA 131; DLB 82; HW

Salinas (y Serrano), Pedro
    1891(?)-1951 .... TCLC 17
    See also CA 117; DLB 134

Salinger, J(erome) D(avid)
    1919- ...... CLC 1, 3, 8, 12, 55, 56; DA;
        DAB; DAC; DAM MST, NOV, POP;
            SSC 2; WLC
    See also AAYA 2; CA 5-8R; CANR 39;
        CDALB 1941-1968; CLR 18; DLB 2, 102,
        173; MAICYA; MTCW; SATA 67

Salisbury, John
    See Caute, David

Salter, James 1925- .... CLC 7, 52, 59
    See also CA 73-76; DLB 130

Saltus, Edgar (Everton)
    1855-1921 .... TCLC 8
    See also CA 105

Saltykov, Mikhail Evgrafovich
    1826-1889 .... NCLC 16

Samarakis, Antonis 1919- .... CLC 5
    See also CA 25-28R; CAAS 16; CANR 36

Sanchez, Florencio 1875-1910..... TCLC 37
    See also CA 153; HW

Sanchez, Luis Rafael 1936-........ CLC 23
    See also CA 128; DLB 145; HW

Sanchez, Sonia
    1934- ...... CLC 5; BLC; DAM MULT;
            PC 9
    See also BW 2; CA 33-36R; CANR 24, 49;
        CLR 18; DLB 41; DLBD 8; MAICYA;
        MTCW; SATA 22

Sand, George
    1804-1876 .... NCLC 2, 42, 57; DA;
        DAB; DAC; DAM MST, NOV; WLC
    See also DLB 119

Sandburg, Carl (August)
    1878-1967 .... CLC 1, 4, 10, 15, 35; DA;
        DAB; DAC; DAM MST, POET; PC 2;
            WLC
    See also CA 5-8R; 25-28R; CANR 35;
        CDALB 1865-1917; DLB 17, 54;
        MAICYA; MTCW; SATA 8

Sandburg, Charles
    See Sandburg, Carl (August)

Sandburg, Charles A.
    See Sandburg, Carl (August)

Sanders, (James) Ed(ward) 1939- ... CLC 53
    See also CA 13-16R; CAAS 21; CANR 13,
        44; DLB 16

Sanders, Lawrence
    1920- .... CLC 41; DAM POP
    See also BEST 89:4; CA 81-84; CANR 33;
        MTCW

Sanders, Noah
    See Blount, Roy (Alton), Jr.

Sanders, Winston P.
    See Anderson, Poul (William)

Sandoz, Mari(e Susette)
    1896-1966 .... CLC 28
    See also CA 1-4R; 25-28R; CANR 17;
        DLB 9; MTCW; SATA 5

Saner, Reg(inald Anthony) 1931- .... CLC 9
    See also CA 65-68

Sannazaro, Jacopo 1456(?)-1530...... LC 8

Sansom, William
    1912-1976 ...... CLC 2, 6; DAM NOV;
            SSC 21
    See also CA 5-8R; 65-68; CANR 42;
        DLB 139; MTCW

Santayana, George 1863-1952..... TCLC 40
    See also CA 115; DLB 54, 71; DLBD 13

Santiago, Danny .... CLC 33
    See also James, Daniel (Lewis)
    See also DLB 122

Santmyer, Helen Hoover
    1895-1986 .... CLC 33
    See also CA 1-4R; 118; CANR 15, 33;
        DLBY 84; MTCW

Santos, Bienvenido N(uqui)
    1911-1996 ...... CLC 22; DAM MULT
    See also CA 101; 151; CANR 19, 46

Sapper .... TCLC 44
    See also McNeile, Herman Cyril

Sapphire 1950- .... CLC 99

Sappho
    fl. 6th cent. B.C.- .... CMLC 3;
            DAM POET; PC 5
    See also DLB 176

Sarduy, Severo 1937-1993 .... CLC 6, 97
    See also CA 89-92; 142; DLB 113; HW

Sargeson, Frank 1903-1982 .... CLC 31
    See also CA 25-28R; 106; CANR 38

Sarmiento, Felix Ruben Garcia
    See Dario, Ruben

Saroyan, William
    1908-1981 ..... CLC 1, 8, 10, 29, 34, 56;
        DA; DAB; DAC; DAM DRAM, MST,
            NOV; SSC 21; WLC
    See also CA 5-8R; 103; CANR 30; DLB 7,
        9, 86; DLBY 81; MTCW; SATA 23;
        SATA-Obit 24

Sarraute, Nathalie
    1900- .... CLC 1, 2, 4, 8, 10, 31, 80
    See also CA 9-12R; CANR 23; DLB 83;
        MTCW

Sarton, (Eleanor) May
    1912-1995 .... CLC 4, 14, 49, 91;
            DAM POET
    See also CA 1-4R; 149; CANR 1, 34, 55;
        DLB 48; DLBY 81; INT CANR-34;
        MTCW; SATA 36; SATA-Obit 86

Sartre, Jean-Paul
    1905-1980 .... CLC 1, 4, 7, 9, 13, 18, 24,
        44, 50, 52; DA; DAB; DAC;
        DAM DRAM, MST, NOV; DC 3; WLC
    See also CA 9-12R; 97-100; CANR 21;
        DLB 72; MTCW

Sassoon, Siegfried (Lorraine)
    1886-1967 .... CLC 36; DAB;
        DAM MST, NOV, POET; PC 12
    See also CA 104; 25-28R; CANR 36;
        DLB 20; MTCW

Satterfield, Charles
    See Pohl, Frederik

Saul, John (W. III)
    1942- ...... CLC 46; DAM NOV, POP
    See also AAYA 10; BEST 90:4; CA 81-84;
        CANR 16, 40

Saunders, Caleb
    See Heinlein, Robert A(nson)

Saura (Atares), Carlos 1932-....... CLC 20
    See also CA 114; 131; HW

Sauser-Hall, Frederic 1887-1961.... CLC 18
    See also Cendrars, Blaise
    See also CA 102; 93-96; CANR 36; MTCW

Saussure, Ferdinand de
    1857-1913 .... TCLC 49

Savage, Catharine
    See Brosman, Catharine Savage

Savage, Thomas 1915- .... CLC 40
    See also CA 126; 132; CAAS 15; INT 132

Savan, Glenn 19(?)- .... CLC 50

Sayers, Dorothy L(eigh)
    1893-1957 ..... TCLC 2, 15; DAM POP
    See also CA 104; 119; CDBLB 1914-1945;
        DLB 10, 36, 77, 100; MTCW

Sayers, Valerie 1952-............. CLC 50
    See also CA 134

Sayles, John (Thomas)
    1950-.................. CLC 7, 10, 14
    See also CA 57-60; CANR 41; DLB 44

Scammell, Michael 1935-.......... CLC 34
    See also CA 156

Scannell, Vernon 1922- .... CLC 49
    See also CA 5-8R; CANR 8, 24, 57;
        DLB 27; SATA 59

Scarlett, Susan
    See Streatfeild, (Mary) Noel

Schaeffer, Susan Fromberg
    1941-.................. CLC 6, 11, 22
    See also CA 49-52; CANR 18; DLB 28;
        MTCW; SATA 22

Schary, Jill
    See Robinson, Jill

Schell, Jonathan 1943-............ CLC 35
    See also CA 73-76; CANR 12

Schelling, Friedrich Wilhelm Joseph von
    1775-1854 .... NCLC 30
    See also DLB 90

Schendel, Arthur van 1874-1946... TCLC 56

Scherer, Jean-Marie Maurice 1920-
    See Rohmer, Eric
    See also CA 110

Schevill, James (Erwin) 1920-....... CLC 7
    See also CA 5-8R; CAAS 12

Serna, Ramon Gomez de la
See Gomez de la Serna, Ramon

Serpieres
See Guillevic, (Eugene)

Service, Robert
See Service, Robert W(illiam)
See also DAB; DLB 92

Service, Robert W(illiam)
1874(?)-1958 ...... TCLC 15; DA; DAC;
DAM MST, POET; WLC
See also Service, Robert
See also CA 115; 140; SATA 20

Seth, Vikram
1952- .... CLC 43, 90; DAM MULT
See also CA 121; 127; CANR 50; DLB 120;
INT 127

Seton, Cynthia Propper
1926-1982 .... CLC 27
See also CA 5-8R; 108; CANR 7

Seton, Ernest (Evan) Thompson
1860-1946 .... TCLC 31
See also CA 109; DLB 92; DLBD 13;
JRDA; SATA 18

Seton-Thompson, Ernest
See Seton, Ernest (Evan) Thompson

Settle, Mary Lee 1918- .... CLC 19, 61
See also CA 89-92; CAAS 1; CANR 44;
DLB 6; INT 89-92

Seuphor, Michel
See Arp, Jean

Sevigne, Marie (de Rabutin-Chantal) Marquise
de 1626-1696 .... LC 11

Sewall, Samuel 1652-1730 .... LC 38
See also DLB 24

Sexton, Anne (Harvey)
1928-1974 .... CLC 2, 4, 6, 8, 10, 15, 53;
DA; DAB; DAC; DAM MST, POET;
PC 2; WLC
See also CA 1-4R; 53-56; CABS 2;
CANR 3, 36; CDALB 1941-1968; DLB 5,
169; MTCW; SATA 10

Shaara, Michael (Joseph, Jr.)
1929-1988 .... CLC 15; DAM POP
See also AITN 1; CA 102; 125; CANR 52;
DLBY 83

Shackleton, C. C.
See Aldiss, Brian W(ilson)

Shacochis, Bob .... CLC 39
See also Shacochis, Robert G.

Shacochis, Robert G. 1951-
See Shacochis, Bob
See also CA 119; 124; INT 124

Shaffer, Anthony (Joshua)
1926- .... CLC 19; DAM DRAM
See also CA 110; 116; DLB 13

Shaffer, Peter (Levin)
1926- ...... CLC 5, 14, 18, 37, 60; DAB;
DAM DRAM, MST; DC 7
See also CA 25-28R; CANR 25, 47;
CDBLB 1960 to Present; DLB 13;
MTCW

Shakey, Bernard
See Young, Neil

Shalamov, Varlam (Tikhonovich)
1907(?)-1982 .... CLC 18
See also CA 129; 105

Shamlu, Ahmad 1925- .... CLC 10

Shammas, Anton 1951-............ CLC 55

Shange, Ntozake
1948- .... CLC 8, 25, 38, 74; BLC;
DAM DRAM, MULT; DC 3
See also AAYA 9; BW 2; CA 85-88;
CABS 3; CANR 27, 48; DLB 38; MTCW

Shanley, John Patrick 1950-....... CLC 75
See also CA 128; 133

Shapcott, Thomas W(illiam) 1935-.. CLC 38
See also CA 69-72; CANR 49

Shapiro, Jane..................... CLC 76

Shapiro, Karl (Jay) 1913- .. CLC 4, 8, 15, 53
See also CA 1-4R; CAAS 6; CANR 1, 36;
DLB 48; MTCW

Sharp, William 1855-1905 .... TCLC 39
See also DLB 156

Sharpe, Thomas Ridley 1928-
See Sharpe, Tom
See also CA 114; 122; INT 122

Sharpe, Tom..................... CLC 36
See also Sharpe, Thomas Ridley
See also DLB 14

Shaw, Bernard.................... TCLC 45
See also Shaw, George Bernard
See also BW 1

Shaw, G. Bernard
See Shaw, George Bernard

Shaw, George Bernard
1856-1950 ... TCLC 3, 9, 21; DA; DAB;
DAC; DAM DRAM, MST; WLC
See also Shaw, Bernard
See also CA 104; 128; CDBLB 1914-1945;
DLB 10, 57; MTCW

Shaw, Henry Wheeler
1818-1885 .... NCLC 15
See also DLB 11

Shaw, Irwin
1913-1984 .... CLC 7, 23, 34;
DAM DRAM, POP
See also AITN 1; CA 13-16R; 112;
CANR 21; CDALB 1941-1968; DLB 6,
102; DLBY 84; MTCW

Shaw, Robert 1927-1978 .... CLC 5
See also AITN 1; CA 1-4R; 81-84;
CANR 4; DLB 13, 14

Shaw, T. E.
See Lawrence, T(homas) E(dward)

Shawn, Wallace 1943- .... CLC 41
See also CA 112

Shea, Lisa 1953-................. CLC 86
See also CA 147

Sheed, Wilfrid (John Joseph)
1930-................. CLC 2, 4, 10, 53
See also CA 65-68; CANR 30; DLB 6;
MTCW

Sheldon, Alice Hastings Bradley
1915(?)-1987
See Tiptree, James, Jr.
See also CA 108; 122; CANR 34; INT 108;
MTCW

Sheldon, John
See Bloch, Robert (Albert)

Shelley, Mary Wollstonecraft (Godwin)
1797-1851 .... NCLC 14, 59; DA; DAB;
DAC; DAM MST, NOV; WLC
See also AAYA 20; CDBLB 1789-1832;
DLB 110, 116, 159; SATA 29

Shelley, Percy Bysshe
1792-1822 .... NCLC 18; DA; DAB;
DAC; DAM MST, POET; PC 14; WLC
See also CDBLB 1789-1832; DLB 96, 110,
158

Shepard, Jim 1956-............... CLC 36
See also CA 137; SATA 90

Shepard, Lucius 1947- .... CLC 34
See also CA 128; 141

Shepard, Sam
1943- .... CLC 4, 6, 17, 34, 41, 44;
DAM DRAM; DC 5
See also AAYA 1; CA 69-72; CABS 3;
CANR 22; DLB 7; MTCW

Shepherd, Michael
See Ludlum, Robert

Sherburne, Zoa (Morin) 1912-..... CLC 30
See also AAYA 13; CA 1-4R; CANR 3, 37;
MAICYA; SAAS 18; SATA 3

Sheridan, Frances 1724-1766........ LC 7
See also DLB 39, 84

Sheridan, Richard Brinsley
1751-1816 .... NCLC 5; DA; DAB;
DAC; DAM DRAM, MST; DC 1; WLC
See also CDBLB 1660-1789; DLB 89

Sherman, Jonathan Marc.......... CLC 55

Sherman, Martin 1941(?)- .... CLC 19
See also CA 116; 123

Sherwin, Judith Johnson 1936-... CLC 7, 15
See also CA 25-28R; CANR 34

Sherwood, Frances 1940-......... CLC 81
See also CA 146

Sherwood, Robert E(mmet)
1896-1955 ...... TCLC 3; DAM DRAM
See also CA 104; 153; DLB 7, 26

Shestov, Lev 1866-1938 .... TCLC 56

Shevchenko, Taras 1814-1861 .... NCLC 54

Shiel, M(atthew) P(hipps)
1865-1947 .... TCLC 8
See also CA 106; DLB 153

Shields, Carol 1935-......... CLC 91; DAC
See also CA 81-84; CANR 51

Shields, David 1956-.............. CLC 97
See also CA 124; CANR 48

Shiga, Naoya 1883-1971... CLC 33; SSC 23
See also CA 101; 33-36R

Shilts, Randy 1951-1994 .... CLC 85
See also AAYA 19; CA 115; 127; 144;
CANR 45; INT 127

Shimazaki, Haruki 1872-1943
See Shimazaki Toson
See also CA 105; 134

Shimazaki Toson................. TCLC 5
See also Shimazaki, Haruki

Sholokhov, Mikhail (Aleksandrovich)
1905-1984 .... CLC 7, 15
See also CA 101; 112; MTCW;
SATA-Obit 36

Shone, Patric
See Hanley, James

Shreve, Susan Richards 1939- ...... **CLC 23**
See also CA 49-52; CAAS 5; CANR 5, 38;
MAICYA; SATA 46; SATA-Brief 41

Shue, Larry
1946-1985 ...... **CLC 52; DAM DRAM**
See also CA 145; 117

Shu-Jen, Chou 1881-1936
See Lu Hsun
See also CA 104

Shulman, Alix Kates 1932- ...... **CLC 2, 10**
See also CA 29-32R; CANR 43; SATA 7

Shuster, Joe 1914- .... **CLC 21**

Shute, Nevil .... **CLC 30**
See also Norway, Nevil Shute

Shuttle, Penelope (Diane) 1947- ..... **CLC 7**
See also CA 93-96; CANR 39; DLB 14, 40

Sidney, Mary 1561-1621 .... **LC 19**

Sidney, Sir Philip
1554-1586 ..... **LC 19; DA; DAB; DAC;**
DAM MST, POET
See also CDBLB Before 1660; DLB 167

Siegel, Jerome 1914-1996 .... **CLC 21**
See also CA 116; 151

Siegel, Jerry
See Siegel, Jerome

Sienkiewicz, Henryk (Adam Alexander Pius)
1846-1916 .... **TCLC 3**
See also CA 104; 134

Sierra, Gregorio Martinez
See Martinez Sierra, Gregorio

Sierra, Maria (de la O'LeJarraga) Martinez
See Martinez Sierra, Maria (de la
O'LeJarraga)

Sigal, Clancy 1926- .... **CLC 7**
See also CA 1-4R

Sigourney, Lydia Howard (Huntley)
1791-1865 .... **NCLC 21**
See also DLB 1, 42, 73

Siguenza y Gongora, Carlos de
1645-1700 .... **LC 8**

Sigurjonsson, Johann 1880-1919 ... **TCLC 27**

Sikelianos, Angelos 1884-1951 .... **TCLC 39**

Silkin, Jon 1930- .... **CLC 2, 6, 43**
See also CA 5-8R; CAAS 5; DLB 27

Silko, Leslie (Marmon)
1948- .... **CLC 23, 74; DA; DAC;**
DAM MST, MULT, POP
See also AAYA 14; CA 115; 122;
CANR 45; DLB 143, 175; NNAL

Sillanpaa, Frans Eemil 1888-1964 ... **CLC 19**
See also CA 129; 93-96; MTCW

Sillitoe, Alan
1928- .... **CLC 1, 3, 6, 10, 19, 57**
See also AITN 1; CA 9-12R; CAAS 2;
CANR 8, 26, 55; CDBLB 1960 to
Present; DLB 14, 139; MTCW; SATA 61

Silone, Ignazio 1900-1978 .... **CLC 4**
See also CA 25-28; 81-84; CANR 34;
CAP 2; MTCW

Silver, Joan Micklin 1935- .... **CLC 20**
See also CA 114; 121; INT 121

Silver, Nicholas
See Faust, Frederick (Schiller)

Silverberg, Robert
1935- .... **CLC 7; DAM POP**
See also CA 1-4R; CAAS 3; CANR 1, 20,
36; DLB 8; INT CANR-20; MAICYA;
MTCW; SATA 13, 91

Silverstein, Alvin 1933- .... **CLC 17**
See also CA 49-52; CANR 2; CLR 25;
JRDA; MAICYA; SATA 8, 69

Silverstein, Virginia B(arbara Opshelor)
1937- .... **CLC 17**
See also CA 49-52; CANR 2; CLR 25;
JRDA; MAICYA; SATA 8, 69

Sim, Georges
See Simenon, Georges (Jacques Christian)

Simak, Clifford D(onald)
1904-1988 .... **CLC 1, 55**
See also CA 1-4R; 125; CANR 1, 35;
DLB 8; MTCW; SATA-Obit 56

Simenon, Georges (Jacques Christian)
1903-1989 .... **CLC 1, 2, 3, 8, 18, 47;**
DAM POP
See also CA 85-88; 129; CANR 35;
DLB 72; DLBY 89; MTCW

Simic, Charles
1938- .... **CLC 6, 9, 22, 49, 68;**
DAM POET
See also CA 29-32R; CAAS 4; CANR 12,
33, 52; DLB 105

Simmel, Georg 1858-1918 .... **TCLC 64**

Simmons, Charles (Paul) 1924- ..... **CLC 57**
See also CA 89-92; INT 89-92

Simmons, Dan 1948- ... **CLC 44; DAM POP**
See also AAYA 16; CA 138; CANR 53

Simmons, James (Stewart Alexander)
1933- .... **CLC 43**
See also CA 105; CAAS 21; DLB 40

Simms, William Gilmore
1806-1870 .... **NCLC 3**
See also DLB 3, 30, 59, 73

Simon, Carly 1945- .... **CLC 26**
See also CA 105

Simon, Claude
1913- .... **CLC 4, 9, 15, 39; DAM NOV**
See also CA 89-92; CANR 33; DLB 83;
MTCW

Simon, (Marvin) Neil
1927- .... **CLC 6, 11, 31, 39, 70;**
DAM DRAM
See also AITN 1; CA 21-24R; CANR 26,
54; DLB 7; MTCW

Simon, Paul (Frederick) 1941(?)- ... **CLC 17**
See also CA 116; 153

Simonon, Paul 1956(?)- .... **CLC 30**

Simpson, Harriette
See Arnow, Harriette (Louisa) Simpson

Simpson, Louis (Aston Marantz)
1923- .... **CLC 4, 7, 9, 32; DAM POET**
See also CA 1-4R; CAAS 4; CANR 1;
DLB 5; MTCW

Simpson, Mona (Elizabeth) 1957- ... **CLC 44**
See also CA 122; 135

Simpson, N(orman) F(rederick)
1919- .... **CLC 29**
See also CA 13-16R; DLB 13

Sinclair, Andrew (Annandale)
1935- .... **CLC 2, 14**
See also CA 9-12R; CAAS 5; CANR 14, 38;
DLB 14; MTCW

Sinclair, Emil
See Hesse, Hermann

Sinclair, Iain 1943- .... **CLC 76**
See also CA 132

Sinclair, Iain MacGregor
See Sinclair, Iain

Sinclair, Irene
See Griffith, D(avid Lewelyn) W(ark)

Sinclair, Mary Amelia St. Clair 1865(?)-1946
See Sinclair, May
See also CA 104

Sinclair, May .... **TCLC 3, 11**
See also Sinclair, Mary Amelia St. Clair
See also DLB 36, 135

Sinclair, Roy
See Griffith, D(avid Lewelyn) W(ark)

Sinclair, Upton (Beall)
1878-1968 ...... **CLC 1, 11, 15, 63; DA;**
DAB; DAC; DAM MST, NOV; WLC
See also CA 5-8R; 25-28R; CANR 7;
CDALB 1929-1941; DLB 9;
INT CANR-7; MTCW; SATA 9

Singer, Isaac
See Singer, Isaac Bashevis

Singer, Isaac Bashevis
1904-1991 .... **CLC 1, 3, 6, 9, 11, 15, 23,**
38, 69; DA; DAB; DAC; DAM MST,
NOV; SSC 3; WLC
See also AITN 1, 2; CA 1-4R; 134;
CANR 1, 39; CDALB 1941-1968; CLR 1;
DLB 6, 28, 52; DLBY 91; JRDA;
MAICYA; MTCW; SATA 3, 27;
SATA-Obit 68

Singer, Israel Joshua 1893-1944 ... **TCLC 33**

Singh, Khushwant 1915- .... **CLC 11**
See also CA 9-12R; CAAS 9; CANR 6

Sinjohn, John
See Galsworthy, John

Sinyavsky, Andrei (Donatevich)
1925- .... **CLC 8**
See also CA 85-88

Sirin, V.
See Nabokov, Vladimir (Vladimirovich)

Sissman, L(ouis) E(dward)
1928-1976 .... **CLC 9, 18**
See also CA 21-24R; 65-68; CANR 13;
DLB 5

Sisson, C(harles) H(ubert) 1914- ..... **CLC 8**
See also CA 1-4R; CAAS 3; CANR 3, 48;
DLB 27

Sitwell, Dame Edith
1887-1964 .... **CLC 2, 9, 67;**
DAM POET; PC 3
See also CA 9-12R; CANR 35;
CDBLB 1945-1960; DLB 20; MTCW

Sjoewall, Maj 1935- .... **CLC 7**
See also CA 65-68

Sjowall, Maj
  See Sjoewall, Maj

Skelton, Robin 1925- . . . . CLC 13
  See also AITN 2; CA 5-8R; CAAS 5;
  CANR 28; DLB 27, 53

Skolimowski, Jerzy 1938- . . . . CLC 20
  See also CA 128

Skram, Amalie (Bertha)
  1847-1905 . . . . TCLC 25

Skvorecky, Josef (Vaclav)
  1924- . . . . CLC 15, 39, 69; DAC;
                                                    DAM NOV
  See also CA 61-64; CAAS 1; CANR 10, 34;
  MTCW

Slade, Bernard . . . . CLC 11, 46
  See also Newbound, Bernard Slade
  See also CAAS 9; DLB 53

Slaughter, Carolyn 1946- . . . . CLC 56
  See also CA 85-88

Slaughter, Frank G(ill) 1908- . . . . . . CLC 29
  See also AITN 2; CA 5-8R; CANR 5;
  INT CANR-5

Slavitt, David R(ytman) 1935- . . . . CLC 5, 14
  See also CA 21-24R; CAAS 3; CANR 41;
  DLB 5, 6

Slesinger, Tess 1905-1945 . . . . TCLC 10
  See also CA 107; DLB 102

Slessor, Kenneth 1901-1971 . . . . CLC 14
  See also CA 102; 89-92

Slowacki, Juliusz 1809-1849 . . . . . NCLC 15

Smart, Christopher
  1722-1771 . . . LC 3; DAM POET; PC 13
  See also DLB 109

Smart, Elizabeth 1913-1986 . . . . CLC 54
  See also CA 81-84; 118; DLB 88

Smiley, Jane (Graves)
  1949- . . . . CLC 53, 76; DAM POP
  See also CA 104; CANR 30, 50;
  INT CANR-30

Smith, A(rthur) J(ames) M(arshall)
  1902-1980 . . . . CLC 15; DAC
  See also CA 1-4R; 102; CANR 4; DLB 88

Smith, Adam 1723-1790 . . . . LC 36
  See also DLB 104

Smith, Alexander 1829-1867 . . . . . NCLC 59
  See also DLB 32, 55

Smith, Anna Deavere 1950- . . . . CLC 86
  See also CA 133

Smith, Betty (Wehner) 1896-1972 . . . CLC 19
  See also CA 5-8R; 33-36R; DLBY 82;
  SATA 6

Smith, Charlotte (Turner)
  1749-1806 . . . . NCLC 23
  See also DLB 39, 109

Smith, Clark Ashton 1893-1961 . . . . CLC 43
  See also CA 143

Smith, Dave . . . . CLC 22, 42
  See also Smith, David (Jeddie)
  See also CAAS 7; DLB 5

Smith, David (Jeddie) 1942-
  See Smith, Dave
  See also CA 49-52; CANR 1; DAM POET

Smith, Florence Margaret 1902-1971
  See Smith, Stevie
  See also CA 17-18; 29-32R; CANR 35;
  CAP 2; DAM POET; MTCW

Smith, Iain Crichton 1928- . . . . CLC 64
  See also CA 21-24R; DLB 40, 139

Smith, John 1580(?)-1631 . . . . LC 9

Smith, Johnston
  See Crane, Stephen (Townley)

Smith, Joseph, Jr. 1805-1844 . . . . NCLC 53

Smith, Lee 1944- . . . . CLC 25, 73
  See also CA 114; 119; CANR 46; DLB 143;
  DLBY 83; INT 119

Smith, Martin
  See Smith, Martin Cruz

Smith, Martin Cruz
  1942- . . . . . CLC 25; DAM MULT, POP
  See also BEST 89:4; CA 85-88; CANR 6,
  23, 43; INT CANR-23; NNAL

Smith, Mary-Ann Tirone 1944- . . . . . CLC 39
  See also CA 118; 136

Smith, Patti 1946- . . . . CLC 12
  See also CA 93-96

Smith, Pauline (Urmson)
  1882-1959 . . . . TCLC 25

Smith, Rosamond
  See Oates, Joyce Carol

Smith, Sheila Kaye
  See Kaye-Smith, Sheila

Smith, Stevie . . . . CLC 3, 8, 25, 44; PC 12
  See also Smith, Florence Margaret
  See also DLB 20

Smith, Wilbur (Addison) 1933- . . . . . CLC 33
  See also CA 13-16R; CANR 7, 46; MTCW

Smith, William Jay 1918- . . . . CLC 6
  See also CA 5-8R; CANR 44; DLB 5;
  MAICYA; SAAS 22; SATA 2, 68

Smith, Woodrow Wilson
  See Kuttner, Henry

Smolenskin, Peretz 1842-1885 . . . . NCLC 30

Smollett, Tobias (George) 1721-1771 . . LC 2
  See also CDBLB 1660-1789; DLB 39, 104

Snodgrass, W(illiam) D(e Witt)
  1926- . . . . CLC 2, 6, 10, 18, 68;
                                                    DAM POET
  See also CA 1-4R; CANR 6, 36; DLB 5;
  MTCW

Snow, C(harles) P(ercy)
  1905-1980 . . . . CLC 1, 4, 6, 9, 13, 19;
                                                    DAM NOV
  See also CA 5-8R; 101; CANR 28;
  CDBLB 1945-1960; DLB 15, 77; MTCW

Snow, Frances Compton
  See Adams, Henry (Brooks)

Snyder, Gary (Sherman)
  1930- . . CLC 1, 2, 5, 9, 32; DAM POET
  See also CA 17-20R; CANR 30; DLB 5, 16,
  165

Snyder, Zilpha Keatley 1927- . . . . . . CLC 17
  See also AAYA 15; CA 9-12R; CANR 38;
  CLR 31; JRDA; MAICYA; SAAS 2;
  SATA 1, 28, 75

Soares, Bernardo
  See Pessoa, Fernando (Antonio Nogueira)

Sobh, A.
  See Shamlu, Ahmad

Sobol, Joshua . . . . CLC 60

Soderberg, Hjalmar 1869-1941 . . . . TCLC 39

Sodergran, Edith (Irene)
  See Soedergran, Edith (Irene)

Soedergran, Edith (Irene)
  1892-1923 . . . . TCLC 31

Softly, Edgar
  See Lovecraft, H(oward) P(hillips)

Softly, Edward
  See Lovecraft, H(oward) P(hillips)

Sokolov, Raymond 1941- . . . . CLC 7
  See also CA 85-88

Solo, Jay
  See Ellison, Harlan (Jay)

Sologub, Fyodor . . . . TCLC 9
  See also Teternikov, Fyodor Kuzmich

Solomons, Ikey Esquir
  See Thackeray, William Makepeace

Solomos, Dionysios 1798-1857 . . . NCLC 15

Solwoska, Mara
  See French, Marilyn

Solzhenitsyn, Aleksandr I(sayevich)
  1918- . . . . . . CLC 1, 2, 4, 7, 9, 10, 18, 26,
             34, 78; DA; DAB; DAC; DAM MST,
                                                    NOV; WLC
  See also AITN 1; CA 69-72; CANR 40;
  MTCW

Somers, Jane
  See Lessing, Doris (May)

Somerville, Edith 1858-1949 . . . . . . TCLC 51
  See also DLB 135

Somerville & Ross
  See Martin, Violet Florence; Somerville,
  Edith

Sommer, Scott 1951- . . . . CLC 25
  See also CA 106

Sondheim, Stephen (Joshua)
  1930- . . . . CLC 30, 39; DAM DRAM
  See also AAYA 11; CA 103; CANR 47

Sontag, Susan
  1933- . . . . CLC 1, 2, 10, 13, 31;
                                                    DAM POP
  See also CA 17-20R; CANR 25, 51; DLB 2,
  67; MTCW

Sophocles
  496(?)B.C.-406(?)B.C. . . . . CMLC 2; DA;
          DAB; DAC; DAM DRAM, MST; DC 1
  See also DLB 176

Sordello 1189-1269 . . . . CMLC 15

Sorel, Julia
  See Drexler, Rosalyn

Sorrentino, Gilbert
  1929- . . . . CLC 3, 7, 14, 22, 40
  See also CA 77-80; CANR 14, 33; DLB 5,
  173; DLBY 80; INT CANR-14

Soto, Gary
  1952- . . . . CLC 32, 80; DAM MULT;
                                                    HLC
  See also AAYA 10; CA 119; 125;
  CANR 50; CLR 38; DLB 82; HW;
  INT 125; JRDA; SATA 80

Steptoe, Lydia
See Barnes, Djuna

Sterchi, Beat 1949-.............. **CLC 65**

Sterling, Brett
See Bradbury, Ray (Douglas); Hamilton, Edmond

Sterling, Bruce 1954-............ **CLC 72**
See also CA 119; CANR 44

Sterling, George 1869-1926....... **TCLC 20**
See also CA 117; DLB 54

Stern, Gerald 1925-......... **CLC 40, 100**
See also CA 81-84; CANR 28; DLB 105

Stern, Richard (Gustave) 1928-... **CLC 4, 39**
See also CA 1-4R; CANR 1, 25, 52;
DLBY 87; INT CANR-25

Sternberg, Josef von 1894-1969..... **CLC 20**
See also CA 81-84

Sterne, Laurence
1713-1768 ...... **LC 2; DA; DAB; DAC;
DAM MST, NOV; WLC**
See also CDBLB 1660-1789; DLB 39

Sternheim, (William Adolf) Carl
1878-1942 .... **TCLC 8**
See also CA 105; DLB 56, 118

Stevens, Mark 1951-............. **CLC 34**
See also CA 122

Stevens, Wallace
1879-1955 .... **TCLC 3, 12, 45; DA;
DAB; DAC; DAM MST, POET; PC 6;
WLC**
See also CA 104; 124; CDALB 1929-1941;
DLB 54; MTCW

Stevenson, Anne (Katharine)
1933-.................... **CLC 7, 33**
See also CA 17-20R; CAAS 9; CANR 9, 33;
DLB 40; MTCW

Stevenson, Robert Louis (Balfour)
1850-1894 ..... **NCLC 5, 14; DA; DAB;
DAC; DAM MST, NOV; SSC 11; WLC**
See also CDBLB 1890-1914; CLR 10, 11;
DLB 18, 57, 141, 156, 174; DLBD 13;
JRDA; MAICYA; YABC 2

Stewart, J(ohn) I(nnes) M(ackintosh)
1906-1994 .... **CLC 7, 14, 32**
See also CA 85-88; 147; CAAS 3;
CANR 47; MTCW

Stewart, Mary (Florence Elinor)
1916-.............. **CLC 7, 35; DAB**
See also CA 1-4R; CANR 1; SATA 12

Stewart, Mary Rainbow
See Stewart, Mary (Florence Elinor)

Stifle, June
See Campbell, Maria

Stifter, Adalbert 1805-1868...... **NCLC 41**
See also DLB 133

Still, James 1906-................ **CLC 49**
See also CA 65-68; CAAS 17; CANR 10,
26; DLB 9; SATA 29

Sting
See Sumner, Gordon Matthew

Stirling, Arthur
See Sinclair, Upton (Beall)

Stitt, Milan 1941-................ **CLC 29**
See also CA 69-72

Stockton, Francis Richard 1834-1902
See Stockton, Frank R.
See also CA 108; 137; MAICYA; SATA 44

Stockton, Frank R. .... **TCLC 47**
See also Stockton, Francis Richard
See also DLB 42, 74; DLBD 13;
SATA-Brief 32

Stoddard, Charles
See Kuttner, Henry

Stoker, Abraham 1847-1912
See Stoker, Bram
See also CA 105; DA; DAC; DAM MST,
NOV; SATA 29

Stoker, Bram
1847-1912 .... **TCLC 8; DAB; WLC**
See also Stoker, Abraham
See also CA 150; CDBLB 1890-1914;
DLB 36, 70

Stolz, Mary (Slattery) 1920-....... **CLC 12**
See also AAYA 8; AITN 1; CA 5-8R;
CANR 13, 41; JRDA; MAICYA;
SAAS 3; SATA 10, 71

Stone, Irving
1903-1989 .... **CLC 7; DAM POP**
See also AITN 1; CA 1-4R; 129; CAAS 3;
CANR 1, 23; INT CANR-23; MTCW;
SATA 3; SATA-Obit 64

Stone, Oliver (William) 1946-...... **CLC 73**
See also AAYA 15; CA 110; CANR 55

Stone, Robert (Anthony)
1937-.................. **CLC 5, 23, 42**
See also CA 85-88; CANR 23; DLB 152;
INT CANR-23; MTCW

Stone, Zachary
See Follett, Ken(neth Martin)

Stoppard, Tom
1937-...... **CLC 1, 3, 4, 5, 8, 15, 29, 34,
63, 91; DA; DAB; DAC; DAM DRAM,
MST; DC 6; WLC**
See also CA 81-84; CANR 39;
CDBLB 1960 to Present; DLB 13;
DLBY 85; MTCW

Storey, David (Malcolm)
1933-..... **CLC 2, 4, 5, 8; DAM DRAM**
See also CA 81-84; CANR 36; DLB 13, 14;
MTCW

Storm, Hyemeyohsts
1935-............. **CLC 3; DAM MULT**
See also CA 81-84; CANR 45; NNAL

Storm, (Hans) Theodor (Woldsen)
1817-1888 .... **NCLC 1**

Storni, Alfonsina
1892-1938 ..... **TCLC 5; DAM MULT;
HLC**
See also CA 104; 131; HW

Stoughton, William 1631-1701....... **LC 38**
See also DLB 24

Stout, Rex (Todhunter) 1886-1975 ... **CLC 3**
See also AITN 2; CA 61-64

Stow, (Julian) Randolph 1935-.. **CLC 23, 48**
See also CA 13-16R; CANR 33; MTCW

Stowe, Harriet (Elizabeth) Beecher
1811-1896 ..... **NCLC 3, 50; DA; DAB;
DAC; DAM MST, NOV; WLC**
See also CDALB 1865-1917; DLB 1, 12, 42,
74; JRDA; MAICYA; YABC 1

Strachey, (Giles) Lytton
1880-1932 .... **TCLC 12**
See also CA 110; DLB 149; DLBD 10

Strand, Mark
1934- .. **CLC 6, 18, 41, 71; DAM POET**
See also CA 21-24R; CANR 40; DLB 5;
SATA 41

Straub, Peter (Francis)
1943-............ **CLC 28; DAM POP**
See also BEST 89:1; CA 85-88; CANR 28;
DLBY 84; MTCW

Strauss, Botho 1944-............. **CLC 22**
See also DLB 124

Streatfeild, (Mary) Noel
1895(?)-1986 .... **CLC 21**
See also CA 81-84; 120; CANR 31;
CLR 17; DLB 160; MAICYA; SATA 20;
SATA-Obit 48

Stribling, T(homas) S(igismund)
1881-1965 .... **CLC 23**
See also CA 107; DLB 9

Strindberg, (Johan) August
1849-1912 ...... **TCLC 1, 8, 21, 47; DA;
DAB; DAC; DAM DRAM, MST; WLC**
See also CA 104; 135

Stringer, Arthur 1874-1950 .... **TCLC 37**
See also DLB 92

Stringer, David
See Roberts, Keith (John Kingston)

Strugatskii, Arkadii (Natanovich)
1925-1991 .... **CLC 27**
See also CA 106; 135

Strugatskii, Boris (Natanovich)
1933-..................... **CLC 27**
See also CA 106

Strummer, Joe 1953(?)-........... **CLC 30**

Stuart, Don A.
See Campbell, John W(ood, Jr.)

Stuart, Ian
See MacLean, Alistair (Stuart)

Stuart, Jesse (Hilton)
1906-1984 .... **CLC 1, 8, 11, 14, 34**
See also CA 5-8R; 112; CANR 31; DLB 9,
48, 102; DLBY 84; SATA 2;
SATA-Obit 36

Sturgeon, Theodore (Hamilton)
1918-1985 .... **CLC 22, 39**
See also Queen, Ellery
See also CA 81-84; 116; CANR 32; DLB 8;
DLBY 85; MTCW

Sturges, Preston 1898-1959....... **TCLC 48**
See also CA 114; 149; DLB 26

Styron, William
1925-.......... **CLC 1, 3, 5, 11, 15, 60;
DAM NOV, POP; SSC 25**
See also BEST 90:4; CA 5-8R; CANR 6, 33;
CDALB 1968-1988; DLB 2, 143;
DLBY 80; INT CANR-6; MTCW

Suarez Lynch, B.
See Bioy Casares, Adolfo; Borges, Jorge
Luis

Su Chien 1884-1918
See Su Man-shu
See also CA 123

Suckow, Ruth 1892-1960.......... **SSC 18**
See also CA 113; DLB 9, 102

Sudermann, Hermann 1857-1928 .. **TCLC 15**
See also CA 107; DLB 118

Sue, Eugene 1804-1857 .... **NCLC 1**
See also DLB 119

Sueskind, Patrick 1949-.......... **CLC 44**
See also Suskind, Patrick

Sukenick, Ronald 1932-..... **CLC 3, 4, 6, 48**
See also CA 25-28R; CAAS 8; CANR 32;
DLB 173; DLBY 81

Suknaski, Andrew 1942- .... **CLC 19**
See also CA 101; DLB 53

Sullivan, Vernon
See Vian, Boris

Sully Prudhomme 1839-1907...... **TCLC 31**

Su Man-shu.................... **TCLC 24**
See also Su Chien

Summerforest, Ivy B.
See Kirkup, James

Summers, Andrew James 1942-..... **CLC 26**

Summers, Andy
See Summers, Andrew James

Summers, Hollis (Spurgeon, Jr.)
1916- .... **CLC 10**
See also CA 5-8R; CANR 3; DLB 6

Summers, (Alphonsus Joseph-Mary Augustus)
Montague 1880-1948........ **TCLC 16**
See also CA 118

Sumner, Gordon Matthew 1951-.... **CLC 26**

Surtees, Robert Smith
1803-1864 .... **NCLC 14**
See also DLB 21

Susann, Jacqueline 1921-1974....... **CLC 3**
See also AITN 1; CA 65-68; 53-56; MTCW

Su Shih 1036-1101 .... **CMLC 15**

Suskind, Patrick
See Sueskind, Patrick
See also CA 145

Sutcliff, Rosemary
1920-1992 .... **CLC 26; DAB; DAC;**
DAM MST, POP
See also AAYA 10; CA 5-8R; 139;
CANR 37; CLR 1, 37; JRDA; MAICYA;
SATA 6, 44, 78; SATA-Obit 73

Sutro, Alfred 1863-1933........... **TCLC 6**
See also CA 105; DLB 10

Sutton, Henry
See Slavitt, David R(ytman)

Svevo, Italo
1861-1928 .... **TCLC 2, 35; SSC 25**
See also Schmitz, Aron Hector

Swados, Elizabeth (A.) 1951-....... **CLC 12**
See also CA 97-100; CANR 49; INT 97-100

Swados, Harvey 1920-1972 .... **CLC 5**
See also CA 5-8R; 37-40R; CANR 6;
DLB 2

Swan, Gladys 1934- .... **CLC 69**
See also CA 101; CANR 17, 39

Swarthout, Glendon (Fred)
1918-1992 .... **CLC 35**
See also CA 1-4R; 139; CANR 1, 47;
SATA 26

Sweet, Sarah C.
See Jewett, (Theodora) Sarah Orne

Swenson, May
1919-1989 .... **CLC 4, 14, 61; DA; DAB;**
DAC; DAM MST, POET; PC 14
See also CA 5-8R; 130; CANR 36; DLB 5;
MTCW; SATA 15

Swift, Augustus
See Lovecraft, H(oward) P(hillips)

Swift, Graham (Colin) 1949-.... **CLC 41, 88**
See also CA 117; 122; CANR 46

Swift, Jonathan
1667-1745 ...... **LC 1; DA; DAB; DAC;**
DAM MST, NOV, POET; PC 9; WLC
See also CDBLB 1660-1789; DLB 39, 95,
101; SATA 19

Swinburne, Algernon Charles
1837-1909 ...... **TCLC 8, 36; DA; DAB;**
DAC; DAM MST, POET; WLC
See also CA 105; 140; CDBLB 1832-1890;
DLB 35, 57

Swinfen, Ann...................... **CLC 34**

Swinnerton, Frank Arthur
1884-1982 .... **CLC 31**
See also CA 108; DLB 34

Swithen, John
See King, Stephen (Edwin)

Sylvia
See Ashton-Warner, Sylvia (Constance)

Symmes, Robert Edward
See Duncan, Robert (Edward)

Symonds, John Addington
1840-1893 .... **NCLC 34**
See also DLB 57, 144

Symons, Arthur 1865-1945 .... **TCLC 11**
See also CA 107; DLB 19, 57, 149

Symons, Julian (Gustave)
1912-1994 .... **CLC 2, 14, 32**
See also CA 49-52; 147; CAAS 3; CANR 3,
33; DLB 87, 155; DLBY 92; MTCW

Synge, (Edmund) J(ohn) M(illington)
1871-1909 .... **TCLC 6, 37;**
DAM DRAM; DC 2
See also CA 104; 141; CDBLB 1890-1914;
DLB 10, 19

Syruc, J.
See Milosz, Czeslaw

Szirtes, George 1948-............. **CLC 46**
See also CA 109; CANR 27

Szymborska, Wislawa 1923- .... **CLC 99**
See also CA 154

T. O., Nik
See Annensky, Innokenty (Fyodorovich)

Tabori, George 1914-............. **CLC 19**
See also CA 49-52; CANR 4

Tagore, Rabindranath
1861-1941 .... **TCLC 3, 53;**
DAM DRAM, POET; PC 8
See also CA 104; 120; MTCW

Taine, Hippolyte Adolphe
1828-1893 .... **NCLC 15**

Talese, Gay 1932-................ **CLC 37**
See also AITN 1; CA 1-4R; CANR 9;
INT CANR-9; MTCW

Tallent, Elizabeth (Ann) 1954- ..... **CLC 45**
See also CA 117; DLB 130

Tally, Ted 1952-................. **CLC 42**
See also CA 120; 124; INT 124

Tamayo y Baus, Manuel
1829-1898 .... **NCLC 1**

Tammsaare, A(nton) H(ansen)
1878-1940 .... **TCLC 27**

Tan, Amy (Ruth)
1952- .... **CLC 59; DAM MULT, NOV,**
POP
See also AAYA 9; BEST 89:3; CA 136;
CANR 54; DLB 173; SATA 75

Tandem, Felix
See Spitteler, Carl (Friedrich Georg)

Tanizaki, Jun'ichiro
1886-1965 ...... **CLC 8, 14, 28; SSC 21**
See also CA 93-96; 25-28R

Tanner, William
See Amis, Kingsley (William)

Tao Lao
See Storni, Alfonsina

Tarassoff, Lev
See Troyat, Henri

Tarbell, Ida M(inerva)
1857-1944 .... **TCLC 40**
See also CA 122; DLB 47

Tarkington, (Newton) Booth
1869-1946 .... **TCLC 9**
See also CA 110; 143; DLB 9, 102;
SATA 17

Tarkovsky, Andrei (Arsenyevich)
1932-1986 .... **CLC 75**
See also CA 127

Tartt, Donna 1964(?)-............ **CLC 76**
See also CA 142

Tasso, Torquato 1544-1595 .... **LC 5**

Tate, (John Orley) Allen
1899-1979 .... **CLC 2, 4, 6, 9, 11, 14, 24**
See also CA 5-8R; 85-88; CANR 32;
DLB 4, 45, 63; MTCW

Tate, Ellalice
See Hibbert, Eleanor Alice Burford

Tate, James (Vincent) 1943- .. **CLC 2, 6, 25**
See also CA 21-24R; CANR 29, 57; DLB 5,
169

Tavel, Ronald 1940-............... **CLC 6**
See also CA 21-24R; CANR 33

Taylor, C(ecil) P(hilip) 1929-1981... **CLC 27**
See also CA 25-28R; 105; CANR 47

Taylor, Edward
1642(?)-1729 .... **LC 11; DA; DAB;**
DAC; DAM MST, POET
See also DLB 24

Taylor, Eleanor Ross 1920-......... **CLC 5**
See also CA 81-84

Taylor, Elizabeth 1912-1975 ... **CLC 2, 4, 29**
See also CA 13-16R; CANR 9; DLB 139;
MTCW; SATA 13

Taylor, Henry (Splawn) 1942-...... **CLC 44**
See also CA 33-36R; CAAS 7; CANR 31;
DLB 5

Taylor, Kamala (Purnaiya) 1924-
See Markandaya, Kamala
See also CA 77-80

Taylor, Mildred D. . . . . CLC 21
See also AAYA 10; BW 1; CA 85-88;
CANR 25; CLR 9; DLB 52; JRDA;
MAICYA; SAAS 5; SATA 15, 70

Taylor, Peter (Hillsman)
1917-1994 . . . . . CLC 1, 4, 18, 37, 44, 50,
71; SSC 10
See also CA 13-16R; 147; CANR 9, 50;
DLBY 81, 94; INT CANR-9; MTCW

Taylor, Robert Lewis 1912-. . . . . CLC 14
See also CA 1-4R; CANR 3; SATA 10

Tchekhov, Anton
See Chekhov, Anton (Pavlovich)

Teasdale, Sara 1884-1933. . . . . TCLC 4
See also CA 104; DLB 45; SATA 32

Tegner, Esaias 1782-1846. . . . . NCLC 2

Teilhard de Chardin, (Marie Joseph) Pierre
1881-1955 . . . . TCLC 9
See also CA 105

Temple, Ann
See Mortimer, Penelope (Ruth)

Tennant, Emma (Christina)
1937- . . . . CLC 13, 52
See also CA 65-68; CAAS 9; CANR 10, 38;
DLB 14

Tenneshaw, S. M.
See Silverberg, Robert

Tennyson, Alfred
1809-1892 . . . . NCLC 30; DA; DAB;
DAC; DAM MST, POET; PC 6; WLC
See also CDBLB 1832-1890; DLB 32

Teran, Lisa St. Aubin de . . . . CLC 36
See also St. Aubin de Teran, Lisa

Terence
195(?)B.C.-159B.C. . . . . . CMLC 14; DC 7

Teresa de Jesus, St. 1515-1582 . . . . . . LC 18

Terkel, Louis 1912-
See Terkel, Studs
See also CA 57-60; CANR 18, 45; MTCW

Terkel, Studs . . . . CLC 38
See also Terkel, Louis
See also AITN 1

Terry, C. V.
See Slaughter, Frank G(ill)

Terry, Megan 1932- . . . . CLC 19
See also CA 77-80; CABS 3; CANR 43;
DLB 7

Tertz, Abram
See Sinyavsky, Andrei (Donatevich)

Tesich, Steve 1943(?)-1996. . . . . . CLC 40, 69
See also CA 105; 152; DLBY 83

Teternikov, Fyodor Kuzmich 1863-1927
See Sologub, Fyodor
See also CA 104

Tevis, Walter 1928-1984 . . . . CLC 42
See also CA 113

Tey, Josephine. . . . . TCLC 14
See also Mackintosh, Elizabeth
See also DLB 77

Thackeray, William Makepeace
1811-1863 . . . . NCLC 5, 14, 22, 43; DA;
DAB; DAC; DAM MST, NOV; WLC
See also CDBLB 1832-1890; DLB 21, 55,
159, 163; SATA 23

Thakura, Ravindranatha
See Tagore, Rabindranath

Tharoor, Shashi 1956- . . . . CLC 70
See also CA 141

Thelwell, Michael Miles 1939- . . . . . CLC 22
See also BW 2; CA 101

Theobald, Lewis, Jr.
See Lovecraft, H(oward) P(hillips)

Theodorescu, Ion N. 1880-1967
See Arghezi, Tudor
See also CA 116

Theriault, Yves
1915-1983 . . CLC 79; DAC; DAM MST
See also CA 102; DLB 88

Theroux, Alexander (Louis)
1939- . . . . CLC 2, 25
See also CA 85-88; CANR 20

Theroux, Paul (Edward)
1941- . . . . CLC 5, 8, 11, 15, 28, 46;
DAM POP
See also BEST 89:4; CA 33-36R; CANR 20,
45; DLB 2; MTCW; SATA 44

Thesen, Sharon 1946-. . . . . CLC 56

Thevenin, Denis
See Duhamel, Georges

Thibault, Jacques Anatole Francois
1844-1924
See France, Anatole
See also CA 106; 127; DAM NOV; MTCW

Thiele, Colin (Milton) 1920- . . . . CLC 17
See also CA 29-32R; CANR 12, 28, 53;
CLR 27; MAICYA; SAAS 2; SATA 14,
72

Thomas, Audrey (Callahan)
1935- . . . . CLC 7, 13, 37; SSC 20
See also AITN 2; CA 21-24R; CAAS 19;
CANR 36; DLB 60; MTCW

Thomas, D(onald) M(ichael)
1935- . . . . CLC 13, 22, 31
See also CA 61-64; CAAS 11; CANR 17,
45; CDBLB 1960 to Present; DLB 40;
INT CANR-17; MTCW

Thomas, Dylan (Marlais)
1914-1953 . . . TCLC 1, 8, 45; DA; DAB;
DAC; DAM DRAM, MST, POET;
PC 2; SSC 3; WLC
See also CA 104; 120; CDBLB 1945-1960;
DLB 13, 20, 139; MTCW; SATA 60

Thomas, (Philip) Edward
1878-1917 . . . . . . TCLC 10; DAM POET
See also CA 106; 153; DLB 19

Thomas, Joyce Carol 1938- . . . . CLC 35
See also AAYA 12; BW 2; CA 113; 116;
CANR 48; CLR 19; DLB 33; INT 116;
JRDA; MAICYA; MTCW; SAAS 7;
SATA 40, 78

Thomas, Lewis 1913-1993 . . . . CLC 35
See also CA 85-88; 143; CANR 38; MTCW

Thomas, Paul
See Mann, (Paul) Thomas

Thomas, Piri 1928-. . . . . CLC 17
See also CA 73-76; HW

Thomas, R(onald) S(tuart)
1913- . . . . CLC 6, 13, 48; DAB;
DAM POET
See also CA 89-92; CAAS 4; CANR 30;
CDBLB 1960 to Present; DLB 27;
MTCW

Thomas, Ross (Elmore) 1926-1995 . . CLC 39
See also CA 33-36R; 150; CANR 22

Thompson, Francis Clegg
See Mencken, H(enry) L(ouis)

Thompson, Francis Joseph
1859-1907 . . . . TCLC 4
See also CA 104; CDBLB 1890-1914;
DLB 19

Thompson, Hunter S(tockton)
1939- . . . . CLC 9, 17, 40; DAM POP
See also BEST 89:1; CA 17-20R; CANR 23,
46; MTCW

Thompson, James Myers
See Thompson, Jim (Myers)

Thompson, Jim (Myers)
1906-1977(?) . . . . CLC 69
See also CA 140

Thompson, Judith . . . . CLC 39

Thomson, James
1700-1748 . . . . . LC 16, 29; DAM POET
See also DLB 95

Thomson, James
1834-1882 . . . . . NCLC 18; DAM POET
See also DLB 35

Thoreau, Henry David
1817-1862 . . . . NCLC 7, 21, 61; DA;
DAB; DAC; DAM MST; WLC
See also CDALB 1640-1865; DLB 1

Thornton, Hall
See Silverberg, Robert

Thucydides c. 455B.C.-399B.C. . . . . CMLC 17
See also DLB 176

Thurber, James (Grover)
1894-1961 . . . . CLC 5, 11, 25; DA; DAB;
DAC; DAM DRAM, MST, NOV; SSC 1
See also CA 73-76; CANR 17, 39;
CDALB 1929-1941; DLB 4, 11, 22, 102;
MAICYA; MTCW; SATA 13

Thurman, Wallace (Henry)
1902-1934 . . . . TCLC 6; BLC;
DAM MULT
See also BW 1; CA 104; 124; DLB 51

Ticheburn, Cheviot
See Ainsworth, William Harrison

Tieck, (Johann) Ludwig
1773-1853 . . . . NCLC 5, 46
See also DLB 90

Tiger, Derry
See Ellison, Harlan (Jay)

Tilghman, Christopher 1948(?)-. . . . . CLC 65

Tillinghast, Richard (Williford)
1940- . . . . CLC 29
See also CA 29-32R; CAAS 23; CANR 26,
51

Timrod, Henry 1828-1867 . . . . NCLC 25
See also DLB 3

Tindall, Gillian 1938-. . . . . CLC 7
See also CA 21-24R; CANR 11

Tuohy, Frank................... CLC 37
   See also Tuohy, John Francis
   See also DLB 14, 139

Tuohy, John Francis 1925-
   See Tuohy, Frank
   See also CA 5-8R; CANR 3, 47

Turco, Lewis (Putnam) 1934- ... CLC 11, 63
   See also CA 13-16R; CAAS 22; CANR 24,
   51; DLBY 84

Turgenev, Ivan
   1818-1883 .... NCLC 21; DA; DAB;
     DAC; DAM MST, NOV; DC 7; SSC 7;
     WLC

Turgot, Anne-Robert-Jacques
   1727-1781 .... LC 26

Turner, Frederick 1943-.......... CLC 48
   See also CA 73-76; CAAS 10; CANR 12,
   30, 56; DLB 40

Tutu, Desmond M(pilo)
   1931- ..... CLC 80; BLC; DAM MULT
   See also BW 1; CA 125

Tutuola, Amos
   1920- .... CLC 5, 14, 29; BLC;
     DAM MULT
   See also BW 2; CA 9-12R; CANR 27;
   DLB 125; MTCW

Twain, Mark
   ..... TCLC 6, 12, 19, 36, 48, 59; SSC 6;
     WLC
   See also Clemens, Samuel Langhorne
   See also AAYA 20; DLB 11, 12, 23, 64, 74

Tyler, Anne
   1941- .... CLC 7, 11, 18, 28, 44, 59;
     DAM NOV, POP
   See also AAYA 18; BEST 89:1; CA 9-12R;
   CANR 11, 33, 53; DLB 6, 143; DLBY 82;
   MTCW; SATA 7, 90

Tyler, Royall 1757-1826.......... NCLC 3
   See also DLB 37

Tynan, Katharine 1861-1931 .... TCLC 3
   See also CA 104; DLB 153

Tyutchev, Fyodor 1803-1873 ..... NCLC 34

Tzara, Tristan
   1896-1963 .... CLC 47; DAM POET
   See also Rosenfeld, Samuel; Rosenstock,
   Sami; Rosenstock, Samuel
   See also CA 153

Uhry, Alfred
   1936- ..... CLC 55; DAM DRAM, POP
   See also CA 127; 133; INT 133

Ulf, Haerved
   See Strindberg, (Johan) August

Ulf, Harved
   See Strindberg, (Johan) August

Ulibarri, Sabine R(eyes)
   1919- .... CLC 83; DAM MULT
   See also CA 131; DLB 82; HW

Unamuno (y Jugo), Miguel de
   1864-1936 ... TCLC 2, 9; DAM MULT,
     NOV; HLC; SSC 11
   See also CA 104; 131; DLB 108; HW;
   MTCW

Undercliffe, Errol
   See Campbell, (John) Ramsey

Underwood, Miles
   See Glassco, John

Undset, Sigrid
   1882-1949 .... TCLC 3; DA; DAB;
     DAC; DAM MST, NOV; WLC
   See also CA 104; 129; MTCW

Ungaretti, Giuseppe
   1888-1970 .... CLC 7, 11, 15
   See also CA 19-20; 25-28R; CAP 2;
   DLB 114

Unger, Douglas 1952-............. CLC 34
   See also CA 130

Unsworth, Barry (Forster) 1930-.... CLC 76
   See also CA 25-28R; CANR 30, 54

Updike, John (Hoyer)
   1932- ...... CLC 1, 2, 3, 5, 7, 9, 13, 15,
     23, 34, 43, 70; DA; DAB; DAC;
     DAM MST, NOV, POET, POP;
     SSC 13; WLC
   See also CA 1-4R; CABS 1; CANR 4, 33,
   51; CDALB 1968-1988; DLB 2, 5, 143;
   DLBD 3; DLBY 80, 82; MTCW

Upshaw, Margaret Mitchell
   See Mitchell, Margaret (Munnerlyn)

Upton, Mark
   See Sanders, Lawrence

Urdang, Constance (Henriette)
   1922- .... CLC 47
   See also CA 21-24R; CANR 9, 24

Uriel, Henry
   See Faust, Frederick (Schiller)

Uris, Leon (Marcus)
   1924- .... CLC 7, 32; DAM NOV, POP
   See also AITN 1, 2; BEST 89:2; CA 1-4R;
   CANR 1, 40; MTCW; SATA 49

Urmuz
   See Codrescu, Andrei

Urquhart, Jane 1949-........ CLC 90; DAC
   See also CA 113; CANR 32

Ustinov, Peter (Alexander) 1921-.... CLC 1
   See also AITN 1; CA 13-16R; CANR 25,
   51; DLB 13

Vaculik, Ludvik 1926-............. CLC 7
   See also CA 53-56

Valdez, Luis (Miguel)
   1940- ..... CLC 84; DAM MULT; HLC
   See also CA 101; CANR 32; DLB 122; HW

Valenzuela, Luisa
   1938- ... CLC 31; DAM MULT; SSC 14
   See also CA 101; CANR 32; DLB 113; HW

Valera y Alcala-Galiano, Juan
   1824-1905 .... TCLC 10
   See also CA 106

Valery, (Ambroise) Paul (Toussaint Jules)
   1871-1945 .... TCLC 4, 15;
     DAM POET; PC 9
   See also CA 104; 122; MTCW

Valle-Inclan, Ramon (Maria) del
   1866-1936 ..... TCLC 5; DAM MULT;
     HLC
   See also CA 106; 153; DLB 134

Vallejo, Antonio Buero
   See Buero Vallejo, Antonio

Vallejo, Cesar (Abraham)
   1892-1938 .... TCLC 3, 56;
     DAM MULT; HLC
   See also CA 105; 153; HW

Vallette, Marguerite Eymery
   See Rachilde

Valle Y Pena, Ramon del
   See Valle-Inclan, Ramon (Maria) del

Van Ash, Cay 1918-.............. CLC 34

Vanbrugh, Sir John
   1664-1726 ...... LC 21; DAM DRAM
   See also DLB 80

Van Campen, Karl
   See Campbell, John W(ood, Jr.)

Vance, Gerald
   See Silverberg, Robert

Vance, Jack........................ CLC 35
   See also Vance, John Holbrook
   See also DLB 8

Vance, John Holbrook 1916-
   See Queen, Ellery; Vance, Jack
   See also CA 29-32R; CANR 17; MTCW

Van Den Bogarde, Derek Jules Gaspard Ulric
   Niven 1921-
   See Bogarde, Dirk
   See also CA 77-80

Vandenburgh, Jane .... CLC 59

Vanderhaeghe, Guy 1951- .... CLC 41
   See also CA 113

van der Post, Laurens (Jan)
   1906-1996 .... CLC 5
   See also CA 5-8R; 155; CANR 35

van de Wetering, Janwillem 1931- .. CLC 47
   See also CA 49-52; CANR 4

Van Dine, S. S.................... TCLC 23
   See also Wright, Willard Huntington

Van Doren, Carl (Clinton)
   1885-1950 .... TCLC 18
   See also CA 111

Van Doren, Mark 1894-1972..... CLC 6, 10
   See also CA 1-4R; 37-40R; CANR 3;
   DLB 45; MTCW

Van Druten, John (William)
   1901-1957 .... TCLC 2
   See also CA 104; DLB 10

Van Duyn, Mona (Jane)
   1921- .... CLC 3, 7, 63; DAM POET
   See also CA 9-12R; CANR 7, 38; DLB 5

Van Dyne, Edith
   See Baum, L(yman) Frank

van Itallie, Jean-Claude 1936-....... CLC 3
   See also CA 45-48; CAAS 2; CANR 1, 48;
   DLB 7

van Ostaijen, Paul 1896-1928 ..... TCLC 33

Van Peebles, Melvin
   1932- .... CLC 2, 20; DAM MULT
   See also BW 2; CA 85-88; CANR 27

Vansittart, Peter 1920-............ CLC 42
   See also CA 1-4R; CANR 3, 49

Van Vechten, Carl 1880-1964 ...... CLC 33
   See also CA 89-92; DLB 4, 9, 51

Van Vogt, A(lfred) E(lton) 1912-..... CLC 1
   See also CA 21-24R; CANR 28; DLB 8;
   SATA 14

Varda, Agnes 1928- .... CLC 16
   See also CA 116; 122

Vargas Llosa, (Jorge) Mario (Pedro)
1936- . . . . CLC 3, 6, 9, 10, 15, 31, 42, 85;
DA; DAB; DAC; DAM MST, MULT,
NOV; HLC
See also CA 73-76; CANR 18, 32, 42;
DLB 145; HW; MTCW

Vasiliu, Gheorghe 1881-1957
See Bacovia, George
See also CA 123

Vassa, Gustavus
See Equiano, Olaudah

Vassilikos, Vassilis 1933- . . . . CLC 4, 8
See also CA 81-84

Vaughan, Henry 1621-1695 . . . . LC 27
See also DLB 131

Vaughn, Stephanie . . . . CLC 62

Vazov, Ivan (Minchov)
1850-1921 . . . . TCLC 25
See also CA 121; DLB 147

Veblen, Thorstein (Bunde)
1857-1929 . . . . TCLC 31
See also CA 115

Vega, Lope de 1562-1635 . . . . LC 23

Venison, Alfred
See Pound, Ezra (Weston Loomis)

Verdi, Marie de
See Mencken, H(enry) L(ouis)

Verdu, Matilde
See Cela, Camilo Jose

Verga, Giovanni (Carmelo)
1840-1922 . . . . TCLC 3; SSC 21
See also CA 104; 123

Vergil
70B.C.-19B.C. . . . . . CMLC 9; DA; DAB;
DAC; DAM MST, POET; PC 12

Verhaeren, Emile (Adolphe Gustave)
1855-1916 . . . . TCLC 12
See also CA 109

Verlaine, Paul (Marie)
1844-1896 . . . . NCLC 2, 51;
DAM POET; PC 2

Verne, Jules (Gabriel)
1828-1905 . . . . TCLC 6, 52
See also AAYA 16; CA 110; 131; DLB 123;
JRDA; MAICYA; SATA 21

Very, Jones 1813-1880 . . . . NCLC 9
See also DLB 1

Vesaas, Tarjei 1897-1970 . . . . CLC 48
See also CA 29-32R

Vialis, Gaston
See Simenon, Georges (Jacques Christian)

Vian, Boris 1920-1959 . . . . TCLC 9
See also CA 106; DLB 72

Viaud, (Louis Marie) Julien 1850-1923
See Loti, Pierre
See also CA 107

Vicar, Henry
See Felsen, Henry Gregor

Vicker, Angus
See Felsen, Henry Gregor

Vidal, Gore
1925- . . . . . CLC 2, 4, 6, 8, 10, 22, 33, 72;
DAM NOV, POP
See also AITN 1; BEST 90:2; CA 5-8R;
CANR 13, 45; DLB 6, 152;
INT CANR-13; MTCW

Viereck, Peter (Robert Edwin)
1916- . . . . CLC 4
See also CA 1-4R; CANR 1, 47; DLB 5

Vigny, Alfred (Victor) de
1797-1863 . . . . . NCLC 7; DAM POET
See also DLB 119

Vilakazi, Benedict Wallet
1906-1947 . . . . TCLC 37

**Villiers de l'Isle Adam, Jean Marie Mathias
Philippe Auguste Comte**
1838-1889 . . . . NCLC 3; SSC 14
See also DLB 123

Villon, Francois 1431-1463(?) . . . . PC 13

Vinci, Leonardo da 1452-1519 . . . . LC 12

Vine, Barbara . . . . CLC 50
See also Rendell, Ruth (Barbara)
See also BEST 90:4

Vinge, Joan D(ennison)
1948- . . . . CLC 30; SSC 24
See also CA 93-96; SATA 36

Violis, G.
See Simenon, Georges (Jacques Christian)

Visconti, Luchino 1906-1976 . . . . CLC 16
See also CA 81-84; 65-68; CANR 39

Vittorini, Elio 1908-1966 . . . . . . CLC 6, 9, 14
See also CA 133; 25-28R

Vizinczey, Stephen 1933- . . . . CLC 40
See also CA 128; INT 128

Vliet, R(ussell) G(ordon)
1929-1984 . . . . CLC 22
See also CA 37-40R; 112; CANR 18

Vogau, Boris Andreyevich 1894-1937(?)
See Pilnyak, Boris
See also CA 123

Vogel, Paula A(nne) 1951- . . . . CLC 76
See also CA 108

Voight, Ellen Bryant 1943- . . . . CLC 54
See also CA 69-72; CANR 11, 29, 55;
DLB 120

Voigt, Cynthia 1942- . . . . CLC 30
See also AAYA 3; CA 106; CANR 18, 37,
40; CLR 13; INT CANR-18; JRDA;
MAICYA; SATA 48, 79; SATA-Brief 33

Voinovich, Vladimir (Nikolaevich)
1932- . . . . CLC 10, 49
See also CA 81-84; CAAS 12; CANR 33;
MTCW

Vollmann, William T.
1959- . . . . . . CLC 89; DAM NOV, POP
See also CA 134

Voloshinov, V. N.
See Bakhtin, Mikhail Mikhailovich

Voltaire
1694-1778 . . . . . LC 14; DA; DAB; DAC;
DAM DRAM, MST; SSC 12; WLC

von Daeniken, Erich 1935- . . . . CLC 30
See also AITN 1; CA 37-40R; CANR 17,
44

von Daniken, Erich
See von Daeniken, Erich

von Heidenstam, (Carl Gustaf) Verner
See Heidenstam, (Carl Gustaf) Verner von

von Heyse, Paul (Johann Ludwig)
See Heyse, Paul (Johann Ludwig von)

von Hofmannsthal, Hugo
See Hofmannsthal, Hugo von

von Horvath, Odon
See Horvath, Oedoen von

von Horvath, Oedoen
See Horvath, Oedoen von

von Liliencron, (Friedrich Adolf Axel) Detlev
See Liliencron, (Friedrich Adolf Axel)
Detlev von

Vonnegut, Kurt, Jr.
1922- . . . . . . CLC 1, 2, 3, 4, 5, 8, 12, 22,
40, 60; DA; DAB; DAC; DAM MST,
NOV, POP; SSC 8; WLC
See also AAYA 6; AITN 1; BEST 90:4;
CA 1-4R; CANR 1, 25, 49;
CDALB 1968-1988; DLB 2, 8, 152;
DLBD 3; DLBY 80; MTCW

Von Rachen, Kurt
See Hubbard, L(afayette) Ron(ald)

von Rezzori (d'Arezzo), Gregor
See Rezzori (d'Arezzo), Gregor von

von Sternberg, Josef
See Sternberg, Josef von

Vorster, Gordon 1924- . . . . CLC 34
See also CA 133

Vosce, Trudie
See Ozick, Cynthia

Voznesensky, Andrei (Andreievich)
1933- . . . . . . CLC 1, 15, 57; DAM POET
See also CA 89-92; CANR 37; MTCW

Waddington, Miriam 1917- . . . . CLC 28
See also CA 21-24R; CANR 12, 30;
DLB 68

Wagman, Fredrica 1937- . . . . CLC 7
See also CA 97-100; INT 97-100

Wagner, Richard 1813-1883 . . . . NCLC 9
See also DLB 129

Wagner-Martin, Linda 1936- . . . . CLC 50

Wagoner, David (Russell)
1926- . . . . CLC 3, 5, 15
See also CA 1-4R; CAAS 3; CANR 2;
DLB 5; SATA 14

Wah, Fred(erick James) 1939- . . . . . . CLC 44
See also CA 107; 141; DLB 60

Wahloo, Per 1926-1975 . . . . CLC 7
See also CA 61-64

Wahloo, Peter
See Wahloo, Per

Wain, John (Barrington)
1925-1994 . . . . CLC 2, 11, 15, 46
See also CA 5-8R; 145; CAAS 4; CANR 23,
54; CDBLB 1960 to Present; DLB 15, 27,
139, 155; MTCW

Wajda, Andrzej 1926- . . . . CLC 16
See also CA 102

Wakefield, Dan 1932- . . . . CLC 7
See also CA 21-24R; CAAS 7

Wakoski, Diane
1937- . . . . CLC **2, 4, 7, 9, 11, 40;**
DAM POET; PC 15
See also CA 13-16R; CAAS 1; CANR 9;
DLB 5; INT CANR-9

Wakoski-Sherbell, Diane
See Wakoski, Diane

Walcott, Derek (Alton)
1930- . . . . CLC **2, 4, 9, 14, 25, 42, 67, 76;**
BLC; DAB; DAC; DAM MST, MULT,
POET; DC 7
See also BW 2; CA 89-92; CANR 26, 47;
DLB 117; DLBY 81; MTCW

Waldman, Anne 1945- . . . . CLC **7**
See also CA 37-40R; CAAS 17; CANR 34;
DLB 16

Waldo, E. Hunter
See Sturgeon, Theodore (Hamilton)

Waldo, Edward Hamilton
See Sturgeon, Theodore (Hamilton)

Walker, Alice (Malsenior)
1944- . . . . CLC **5, 6, 9, 19, 27, 46, 58;**
BLC; DA; DAB; DAC; DAM MST,
MULT, NOV, POET, POP; SSC 5
See also AAYA 3; BEST 89:4; BW 2;
CA 37-40R; CANR 9, 27, 49;
CDALB 1968-1988; DLB 6, 33, 143;
INT CANR-27; MTCW; SATA 31

Walker, David Harry 1911-1992. . . . CLC **14**
See also CA 1-4R; 137; CANR 1; SATA 8;
SATA-Obit 71

Walker, Edward Joseph 1934-
See Walker, Ted
See also CA 21-24R; CANR 12, 28, 53

Walker, George F.
1947- . . . . CLC **44, 61; DAB; DAC;**
DAM MST
See also CA 103; CANR 21, 43; DLB 60

Walker, Joseph A.
1935- . . . . CLC **19; DAM DRAM, MST**
See also BW 1; CA 89-92; CANR 26;
DLB 38

Walker, Margaret (Abigail)
1915- . . . . CLC **1, 6; BLC; DAM MULT**
See also BW 2; CA 73-76; CANR 26, 54;
DLB 76, 152; MTCW

Walker, Ted. . . . . CLC **13**
See also Walker, Edward Joseph
See also DLB 40

Wallace, David Foster 1962- . . . . CLC **50**
See also CA 132

Wallace, Dexter
See Masters, Edgar Lee

Wallace, (Richard Horatio) Edgar
1875-1932 . . . . TCLC **57**
See also CA 115; DLB 70

Wallace, Irving
1916-1990 . . . . . CLC **7, 13; DAM NOV,**
POP
See also AITN 1; CA 1-4R; 132; CAAS 1;
CANR 1, 27; INT CANR-27; MTCW

Wallant, Edward Lewis
1926-1962 . . . . CLC **5, 10**
See also CA 1-4R; CANR 22; DLB 2, 28,
143; MTCW

Walley, Byron
See Card, Orson Scott

Walpole, Horace 1717-1797. . . . . LC **2**
See also DLB 39, 104

Walpole, Hugh (Seymour)
1884-1941 . . . . TCLC **5**
See also CA 104; DLB 34

Walser, Martin 1927- . . . . CLC **27**
See also CA 57-60; CANR 8, 46; DLB 75,
124

Walser, Robert
1878-1956 . . . . TCLC **18; SSC 20**
See also CA 118; DLB 66

Walsh, Jill Paton. . . . . CLC **35**
See also Paton Walsh, Gillian
See also AAYA 11; CLR 2; DLB 161;
SAAS 3

Walter, Villiam Christian
See Andersen, Hans Christian

Wambaugh, Joseph (Aloysius, Jr.)
1937- . . . . CLC **3, 18; DAM NOV, POP**
See also AITN 1; BEST 89:3; CA 33-36R;
CANR 42; DLB 6; DLBY 83; MTCW

Ward, Arthur Henry Sarsfield 1883-1959
See Rohmer, Sax
See also CA 108

Ward, Douglas Turner 1930- . . . . CLC **19**
See also BW 1; CA 81-84; CANR 27;
DLB 7, 38

Ward, Mary Augusta
See Ward, Mrs. Humphry

Ward, Mrs. Humphry
1851-1920 . . . . TCLC **55**
See also DLB 18

Ward, Peter
See Faust, Frederick (Schiller)

Warhol, Andy 1928(?)-1987. . . . . CLC **20**
See also AAYA 12; BEST 89:4; CA 89-92;
121; CANR 34

Warner, Francis (Robert le Plastrier)
1937- . . . . CLC **14**
See also CA 53-56; CANR 11

Warner, Marina 1946- . . . . CLC **59**
See also CA 65-68; CANR 21, 55

Warner, Rex (Ernest) 1905-1986. . . . CLC **45**
See also CA 89-92; 119; DLB 15

Warner, Susan (Bogert)
1819-1885 . . . . NCLC **31**
See also DLB 3, 42

Warner, Sylvia (Constance) Ashton
See Ashton-Warner, Sylvia (Constance)

Warner, Sylvia Townsend
1893-1978 . . . . CLC **7, 19; SSC 23**
See also CA 61-64; 77-80; CANR 16;
DLB 34, 139; MTCW

Warren, Mercy Otis 1728-1814. . . NCLC **13**
See also DLB 31

Warren, Robert Penn
1905-1989 . . . . CLC **1, 4, 6, 8, 10, 13, 18,**
39, 53, 59; DA; DAB; DAC; DAM MST,
NOV, POET; SSC 4; WLC
See also AITN 1; CA 13-16R; 129;
CANR 10, 47; CDALB 1968-1988;
DLB 2, 48, 152; DLBY 80, 89;
INT CANR-10; MTCW; SATA 46;
SATA-Obit 63

Warshofsky, Isaac
See Singer, Isaac Bashevis

Warton, Thomas
1728-1790 . . . . LC **15; DAM POET**
See also DLB 104, 109

Waruk, Kona
See Harris, (Theodore) Wilson

Warung, Price 1855-1911. . . . . TCLC **45**

Warwick, Jarvis
See Garner, Hugh

Washington, Alex
See Harris, Mark

Washington, Booker T(aliaferro)
1856-1915 . . . . TCLC **10; BLC;**
DAM MULT
See also BW 1; CA 114; 125; SATA 28

Washington, George 1732-1799. . . . . LC **25**
See also DLB 31

Wassermann, (Karl) Jakob
1873-1934 . . . . TCLC **6**
See also CA 104; DLB 66

Wasserstein, Wendy
1950- . . . . CLC **32, 59, 90;**
DAM DRAM; DC 4
See also CA 121; 129; CABS 3; CANR 53;
INT 129

Waterhouse, Keith (Spencer)
1929- . . . . CLC **47**
See also CA 5-8R; CANR 38; DLB 13, 15;
MTCW

Waters, Frank (Joseph)
1902-1995 . . . . CLC **88**
See also CA 5-8R; 149; CAAS 13; CANR 3,
18; DLBY 86

Waters, Roger 1944-. . . . . CLC **35**

Watkins, Frances Ellen
See Harper, Frances Ellen Watkins

Watkins, Gerrold
See Malzberg, Barry N(athaniel)

Watkins, Gloria 1955(?)-
See hooks, bell
See also BW 2; CA 143

Watkins, Paul 1964-. . . . . CLC **55**
See also CA 132

Watkins, Vernon Phillips
1906-1967 . . . . CLC **43**
See also CA 9-10; 25-28R; CAP 1; DLB 20

Watson, Irving S.
See Mencken, H(enry) L(ouis)

Watson, John H.
See Farmer, Philip Jose

Watson, Richard F.
See Silverberg, Robert

Waugh, Auberon (Alexander) 1939- . . CLC **7**
See also CA 45-48; CANR 6, 22; DLB 14

Waugh, Evelyn (Arthur St. John)
1903-1966 ..... CLC 1, 3, 8, 13, 19, 27,
44; DA; DAB; DAC; DAM MST, NOV,
POP; WLC
See also CA 85-88; 25-28R; CANR 22;
CDBLB 1914-1945; DLB 15, 162; MTCW

Waugh, Harriet 1944- .... CLC 6
See also CA 85-88; CANR 22

Ways, C. R.
See Blount, Roy (Alton), Jr.

Waystaff, Simon
See Swift, Jonathan

Webb, (Martha) Beatrice (Potter)
1858-1943 .... TCLC 22
See also Potter, Beatrice
See also CA 117

Webb, Charles (Richard) 1939-...... CLC 7
See also CA 25-28R

Webb, James H(enry), Jr. 1946-.... CLC 22
See also CA 81-84

Webb, Mary (Gladys Meredith)
1881-1927 .... TCLC 24
See also CA 123; DLB 34

Webb, Mrs. Sidney
See Webb, (Martha) Beatrice (Potter)

Webb, Phyllis 1927-.............. CLC 18
See also CA 104; CANR 23; DLB 53

Webb, Sidney (James)
1859-1947 .... TCLC 22
See also CA 117

Webber, Andrew Lloyd............. CLC 21
See also Lloyd Webber, Andrew

Weber, Lenora Mattingly
1895-1971 .... CLC 12
See also CA 19-20; 29-32R; CAP 1;
SATA 2; SATA-Obit 26

Weber, Max 1864-1920 .... TCLC 69
See also CA 109

Webster, John
1579(?)-1634(?) ...... LC 33; DA; DAB;
DAC; DAM DRAM, MST; DC 2; WLC
See also CDBLB Before 1660; DLB 58

Webster, Noah 1758-1843 .... NCLC 30

Wedekind, (Benjamin) Frank(lin)
1864-1918 ...... TCLC 7; DAM DRAM
See also CA 104; 153; DLB 118

Weidman, Jerome 1913-............ CLC 7
See also AITN 2; CA 1-4R; CANR 1;
DLB 28

Weil, Simone (Adolphine)
1909-1943 .... TCLC 23
See also CA 117

Weinstein, Nathan
See West, Nathanael

Weinstein, Nathan von Wallenstein
See West, Nathanael

Weir, Peter (Lindsay) 1944- .... CLC 20
See also CA 113; 123

Weiss, Peter (Ulrich)
1916-1982 .... CLC 3, 15, 51;
DAM DRAM
See also CA 45-48; 106; CANR 3; DLB 69,
124

Weiss, Theodore (Russell)
1916- .... CLC 3, 8, 14
See also CA 9-12R; CAAS 2; CANR 46;
DLB 5

Welch, (Maurice) Denton
1915-1948 .... TCLC 22
See also CA 121; 148

Welch, James
1940- ..... CLC 6, 14, 52; DAM MULT,
POP
See also CA 85-88; CANR 42; DLB 175;
NNAL

Weldon, Fay
1933- .... CLC 6, 9, 11, 19, 36, 59;
DAM POP
See also CA 21-24R; CANR 16, 46;
CDBLB 1960 to Present; DLB 14;
INT CANR-16; MTCW

Wellek, Rene 1903-1995........... CLC 28
See also CA 5-8R; 150; CAAS 7; CANR 8;
DLB 63; INT CANR-8

Weller, Michael 1942- .... CLC 10, 53
See also CA 85-88

Weller, Paul 1958- .... CLC 26

Wellershoff, Dieter 1925-.......... CLC 46
See also CA 89-92; CANR 16, 37

Welles, (George) Orson
1915-1985 .... CLC 20, 80
See also CA 93-96; 117

Wellman, Mac 1945- .... CLC 65

Wellman, Manly Wade 1903-1986 .. CLC 49
See also CA 1-4R; 118; CANR 6, 16, 44;
SATA 6; SATA-Obit 47

Wells, Carolyn 1869(?)-1942 ...... TCLC 35
See also CA 113; DLB 11

Wells, H(erbert) G(eorge)
1866-1946 .... TCLC 6, 12, 19; DA;
DAB; DAC; DAM MST, NOV; SSC 6;
WLC
See also AAYA 18; CA 110; 121;
CDBLB 1914-1945; DLB 34, 70, 156;
MTCW; SATA 20

Wells, Rosemary 1943-............ CLC 12
See also AAYA 13; CA 85-88; CANR 48;
CLR 16; MAICYA; SAAS 1; SATA 18,
69

Welty, Eudora
1909- ...... CLC 1, 2, 5, 14, 22, 33; DA;
DAB; DAC; DAM MST, NOV; SSC 1;
WLC
See also CA 9-12R; CABS 1; CANR 32;
CDALB 1941-1968; DLB 2, 102, 143;
DLBD 12; DLBY 87; MTCW

Wen I-to 1899-1946 .... TCLC 28

Wentworth, Robert
See Hamilton, Edmond

Werfel, Franz (V.) 1890-1945 ...... TCLC 8
See also CA 104; DLB 81, 124

Wergeland, Henrik Arnold
1808-1845 .... NCLC 5

Wersba, Barbara 1932-............ CLC 30
See also AAYA 2; CA 29-32R; CANR 16,
38; CLR 3; DLB 52; JRDA; MAICYA;
SAAS 2; SATA 1, 58

Wertmueller, Lina 1928- .... CLC 16
See also CA 97-100; CANR 39

Wescott, Glenway 1901-1987....... CLC 13
See also CA 13-16R; 121; CANR 23;
DLB 4, 9, 102

Wesker, Arnold
1932- .... CLC 3, 5, 42; DAB;
DAM DRAM
See also CA 1-4R; CAAS 7; CANR 1, 33;
CDBLB 1960 to Present; DLB 13;
MTCW

Wesley, Richard (Errol) 1945-....... CLC 7
See also BW 1; CA 57-60; CANR 27;
DLB 38

Wessel, Johan Herman 1742-1785 .... LC 7

West, Anthony (Panther)
1914-1987 .... CLC 50
See also CA 45-48; 124; CANR 3, 19;
DLB 15

West, C. P.
See Wodehouse, P(elham) G(renville)

West, (Mary) Jessamyn
1902-1984 .... CLC 7, 17
See also CA 9-12R; 112; CANR 27; DLB 6;
DLBY 84; MTCW; SATA-Obit 37

West, Morris L(anglo) 1916-..... CLC 6, 33
See also CA 5-8R; CANR 24, 49; MTCW

West, Nathanael
1903-1940 ..... TCLC 1, 14, 44; SSC 16
See also CA 104; 125; CDALB 1929-1941;
DLB 4, 9, 28; MTCW

West, Owen
See Koontz, Dean R(ay)

West, Paul 1930- .... CLC 7, 14, 96
See also CA 13-16R; CAAS 7; CANR 22,
53; DLB 14; INT CANR-22

West, Rebecca 1892-1983 .. CLC 7, 9, 31, 50
See also CA 5-8R; 109; CANR 19; DLB 36;
DLBY 83; MTCW

Westall, Robert (Atkinson)
1929-1993 .... CLC 17
See also AAYA 12; CA 69-72; 141;
CANR 18; CLR 13; JRDA; MAICYA;
SAAS 2; SATA 23, 69; SATA-Obit 75

Westlake, Donald E(dwin)
1933- .... CLC 7, 33; DAM POP
See also CA 17-20R; CAAS 13; CANR 16,
44; INT CANR-16

Westmacott, Mary
See Christie, Agatha (Mary Clarissa)

Weston, Allen
See Norton, Andre

Wetcheek, J. L.
See Feuchtwanger, Lion

Wetering, Janwillem van de
See van de Wetering, Janwillem

Wetherell, Elizabeth
See Warner, Susan (Bogert)

Whale, James 1889-1957 .... TCLC 63

Whalen, Philip 1923- .... CLC 6, 29
See also CA 9-12R; CANR 5, 39; DLB 16

Wharton, Edith (Newbold Jones)
1862-1937 ...... TCLC 3, 9, 27, 53; DA;
DAB; DAC; DAM MST, NOV; SSC 6;
WLC
See also CA 104; 132; CDALB 1865-1917;
DLB 4, 9, 12, 78; DLBD 13; MTCW

Wharton, James
See Mencken, H(enry) L(ouis)

Wharton, William (a pseudonym)
.... CLC **18, 37**
See also CA 93-96; DLBY 80; INT 93-96

Wheatley (Peters), Phillis
1754(?)-1784 .... LC **3**; BLC; DA; DAC;
DAM MST, MULT, POET; PC **3**; WLC
See also CDALB 1640-1865; DLB 31, 50

Wheelock, John Hall 1886-1978 .... CLC **14**
See also CA 13-16R; 77-80; CANR 14;
DLB 45

White, E(lwyn) B(rooks)
1899-1985 .. CLC **10, 34, 39**; DAM POP
See also AITN 2; CA 13-16R; 116;
CANR 16, 37; CLR 1, 21; DLB 11, 22;
MAICYA; MTCW; SATA 2, 29;
SATA-Obit 44

White, Edmund (Valentine III)
1940- .... CLC **27**; DAM POP
See also AAYA 7; CA 45-48; CANR 3, 19,
36; MTCW

White, Patrick (Victor Martindale)
1912-1990 .. CLC **3, 4, 5, 7, 9, 18, 65, 69**
See also CA 81-84; 132; CANR 43; MTCW

White, Phyllis Dorothy James 1920-
See James, P. D.
See also CA 21-24R; CANR 17, 43;
DAM POP; MTCW

White, T(erence) H(anbury)
1906-1964 .... CLC **30**
See also CA 73-76; CANR 37; DLB 160;
JRDA; MAICYA; SATA 12

White, Terence de Vere
1912-1994 .... CLC **49**
See also CA 49-52; 145; CANR 3

White, Walter F(rancis)
1893-1955 .... TCLC **15**
See also White, Walter
See also BW 1; CA 115; 124; DLB 51

White, William Hale 1831-1913
See Rutherford, Mark
See also CA 121

Whitehead, E(dward) A(nthony)
1933- .... CLC **5**
See also CA 65-68

Whitemore, Hugh (John) 1936- ..... CLC **37**
See also CA 132; INT 132

Whitman, Sarah Helen (Power)
1803-1878 .... NCLC **19**
See also DLB 1

Whitman, Walt(er)
1819-1892 ..... NCLC **4, 31**; DA; DAB;
DAC; DAM MST, POET; PC **3**; WLC
See also CDALB 1640-1865; DLB 3, 64;
SATA 20

Whitney, Phyllis A(yame)
1903- .... CLC **42**; DAM POP
See also AITN 2; BEST 90:3; CA 1-4R;
CANR 3, 25, 38; JRDA; MAICYA;
SATA 1, 30

Whittemore, (Edward) Reed (Jr.)
1919- .... CLC **4**
See also CA 9-12R; CAAS 8; CANR 4;
DLB 5

Whittier, John Greenleaf
1807-1892 .... NCLC **8, 59**
See also DLB 1

Whittlebot, Hernia
See Coward, Noel (Peirce)

Wicker, Thomas Grey 1926-
See Wicker, Tom
See also CA 65-68; CANR 21, 46

Wicker, Tom .... CLC **7**
See also Wicker, Thomas Grey

Wideman, John Edgar
1941- .... CLC **5, 34, 36, 67**; BLC;
DAM MULT
See also BW 2; CA 85-88; CANR 14, 42;
DLB 33, 143

Wiebe, Rudy (Henry)
1934- .... CLC **6, 11, 14**; DAC;
DAM MST
See also CA 37-40R; CANR 42; DLB 60

Wieland, Christoph Martin
1733-1813 .... NCLC **17**
See also DLB 97

Wiene, Robert 1881-1938 .... TCLC **56**

Wieners, John 1934- .... CLC **7**
See also CA 13-16R; DLB 16

Wiesel, Elie(zer)
1928- ...... CLC **3, 5, 11, 37**; DA; DAB;
DAC; DAM MST, NOV
See also AAYA 7; AITN 1; CA 5-8R;
CAAS 4; CANR 8, 40; DLB 83;
DLBY 87; INT CANR-8; MTCW;
SATA 56

Wiggins, Marianne 1947- .... CLC **57**
See also BEST 89:3; CA 130

Wight, James Alfred 1916-
See Herriot, James
See also CA 77-80; SATA 55;
SATA-Brief 44

Wilbur, Richard (Purdy)
1921- ... CLC **3, 6, 9, 14, 53**; DA; DAB;
DAC; DAM MST, POET
See also CA 1-4R; CABS 2; CANR 2, 29;
DLB 5, 169; INT CANR-29; MTCW;
SATA 9

Wild, Peter 1940- .... CLC **14**
See also CA 37-40R; DLB 5

Wilde, Oscar (Fingal O'Flahertie Wills)
1854(?)-1900 .... TCLC **1, 8, 23, 41**; DA;
DAB; DAC; DAM DRAM, MST, NOV;
SSC **11**; WLC
See also CA 104; 119; CDBLB 1890-1914;
DLB 10, 19, 34, 57, 141, 156; SATA 24

Wilder, Billy .... CLC **20**
See also Wilder, Samuel
See also DLB 26

Wilder, Samuel 1906-
See Wilder, Billy
See also CA 89-92

Wilder, Thornton (Niven)
1897-1975 ...... CLC **1, 5, 6, 10, 15, 35,
82**; DA; DAB; DAC; DAM DRAM,
MST, NOV; DC **1**; WLC
See also AITN 2; CA 13-16R; 61-64;
CANR 40; DLB 4, 7, 9; MTCW

Wilding, Michael 1942- .... CLC **73**
See also CA 104; CANR 24, 49

Wiley, Richard 1944- .... CLC **44**
See also CA 121; 129

Wilhelm, Kate .... CLC **7**
See also Wilhelm, Katie Gertrude
See also AAYA 20; CAAS 5; DLB 8;
INT CANR-17

Wilhelm, Katie Gertrude 1928-
See Wilhelm, Kate
See also CA 37-40R; CANR 17, 36; MTCW

Wilkins, Mary
See Freeman, Mary Eleanor Wilkins

Willard, Nancy 1936- .... CLC **7, 37**
See also CA 89-92; CANR 10, 39; CLR 5;
DLB 5, 52; MAICYA; MTCW;
SATA 37, 71; SATA-Brief 30

Williams, C(harles) K(enneth)
1936- .... CLC **33, 56**; DAM POET
See also CA 37-40R; CAAS 26; CANR 57;
DLB 5

Williams, Charles
See Collier, James L(incoln)

Williams, Charles (Walter Stansby)
1886-1945 .... TCLC **1, 11**
See also CA 104; DLB 100, 153

Williams, (George) Emlyn
1905-1987 ...... CLC **15**; DAM DRAM
See also CA 104; 123; CANR 36; DLB 10,
77; MTCW

Williams, Hugo 1942- .... CLC **42**
See also CA 17-20R; CANR 45; DLB 40

Williams, J. Walker
See Wodehouse, P(elham) G(renville)

Williams, John A(lfred)
1925- ... CLC **5, 13**; BLC; DAM MULT
See also BW 2; CA 53-56; CAAS 3;
CANR 6, 26, 51; DLB 2, 33;
INT CANR-6

Williams, Jonathan (Chamberlain)
1929- .... CLC **13**
See also CA 9-12R; CAAS 12; CANR 8;
DLB 5

Williams, Joy 1944- .... CLC **31**
See also CA 41-44R; CANR 22, 48

Williams, Norman 1952- .... CLC **39**
See also CA 118

Williams, Sherley Anne
1944- ..... CLC **89**; BLC; DAM MULT,
POET
See also BW 2; CA 73-76; CANR 25;
DLB 41; INT CANR-25; SATA 78

Williams, Shirley
See Williams, Sherley Anne

Williams, Tennessee
1911-1983 ..... CLC **1, 2, 5, 7, 8, 11, 15,
19, 30, 39, 45, 71**; DA; DAB; DAC;
DAM DRAM, MST; DC **4**; WLC
See also AITN 1, 2; CA 5-8R; 108;
CABS 3; CANR 31; CDALB 1941-1968;
DLB 7; DLBD 4; DLBY 83; MTCW

Williams, Thomas (Alonzo)
1926-1990 .... CLC **14**
See also CA 1-4R; 132; CANR 2

Williams, William C.
See Williams, William Carlos

Williams, William Carlos
1883-1963 .... **CLC 1, 2, 5, 9, 13, 22, 42, 67; DA; DAB; DAC; DAM MST, POET; PC 7**
See also CA 89-92; CANR 34; CDALB 1917-1929; DLB 4, 16, 54, 86; MTCW

Williamson, David (Keith) 1942- .... **CLC 56**
See also CA 103; CANR 41

Williamson, Ellen Douglas 1905-1984
See Douglas, Ellen
See also CA 17-20R; 114; CANR 39

Williamson, Jack .... **CLC 29**
See also Williamson, John Stewart
See also CAAS 8; DLB 8

Williamson, John Stewart 1908-
See Williamson, Jack
See also CA 17-20R; CANR 23

Willie, Frederick
See Lovecraft, H(oward) P(hillips)

Willingham, Calder (Baynard, Jr.)
1922-1995 .... **CLC 5, 51**
See also CA 5-8R; 147; CANR 3; DLB 2, 44; MTCW

Willis, Charles
See Clarke, Arthur C(harles)

Willy
See Colette, (Sidonie-Gabrielle)

Willy, Colette
See Colette, (Sidonie-Gabrielle)

Wilson, A(ndrew) N(orman) 1950- .. **CLC 33**
See also CA 112; 122; DLB 14, 155

Wilson, Angus (Frank Johnstone)
1913-1991 .. **CLC 2, 3, 5, 25, 34; SSC 21**
See also CA 5-8R; 134; CANR 21; DLB 15, 139, 155; MTCW

Wilson, August
1945- .... **CLC 39, 50, 63; BLC; DA; DAB; DAC; DAM DRAM, MST, MULT; DC 2**
See also AAYA 16; BW 2; CA 115; 122; CANR 42, 54; MTCW

Wilson, Brian 1942- .... **CLC 12**

Wilson, Colin 1931- .... **CLC 3, 14**
See also CA 1-4R; CAAS 5; CANR 1, 22, 33; DLB 14; MTCW

Wilson, Dirk
See Pohl, Frederik

Wilson, Edmund
1895-1972 .... **CLC 1, 2, 3, 8, 24**
See also CA 1-4R; 37-40R; CANR 1, 46; DLB 63; MTCW

Wilson, Ethel Davis (Bryant)
1888(?)-1980 .... **CLC 13; DAC; DAM POET**
See also CA 102; DLB 68; MTCW

Wilson, John 1785-1854 .... **NCLC 5**

Wilson, John (Anthony) Burgess 1917-1993
See Burgess, Anthony
See also CA 1-4R; 143; CANR 2, 46; DAC; DAM NOV; MTCW

Wilson, Lanford
1937- ..... **CLC 7, 14, 36; DAM DRAM**
See also CA 17-20R; CABS 3; CANR 45; DLB 7

Wilson, Robert M. 1944- .... **CLC 7, 9**
See also CA 49-52; CANR 2, 41; MTCW

Wilson, Robert McLiam 1964- ..... **CLC 59**
See also CA 132

Wilson, Sloan 1920- .... **CLC 32**
See also CA 1-4R; CANR 1, 44

Wilson, Snoo 1948- .... **CLC 33**
See also CA 69-72

Wilson, William S(mith) 1932- ..... **CLC 49**
See also CA 81-84

Winchilsea, Anne (Kingsmill) Finch Counte
1661-1720 .... **LC 3**

Windham, Basil
See Wodehouse, P(elham) G(renville)

Wingrove, David (John) 1954- ...... **CLC 68**
See also CA 133

Winters, Janet Lewis .... **CLC 41**
See also Lewis, Janet
See also DLBY 87

Winters, (Arthur) Yvor
1900-1968 .... **CLC 4, 8, 32**
See also CA 11-12; 25-28R; CAP 1; DLB 48; MTCW

Winterson, Jeanette
1959- .... **CLC 64; DAM POP**
See also CA 136

Winthrop, John 1588-1649 .... **LC 31**
See also DLB 24, 30

Wiseman, Frederick 1930- .... **CLC 20**

Wister, Owen 1860-1938 .... **TCLC 21**
See also CA 108; DLB 9, 78; SATA 62

Witkacy
See Witkiewicz, Stanislaw Ignacy

Witkiewicz, Stanislaw Ignacy
1885-1939 .... **TCLC 8**
See also CA 105

Wittgenstein, Ludwig (Josef Johann)
1889-1951 .... **TCLC 59**
See also CA 113

Wittig, Monique 1935(?)- .... **CLC 22**
See also CA 116; 135; DLB 83

Wittlin, Jozef 1896-1976 .... **CLC 25**
See also CA 49-52; 65-68; CANR 3

Wodehouse, P(elham) G(renville)
1881-1975 ... **CLC 1, 2, 5, 10, 22; DAB; DAC; DAM NOV; SSC 2**
See also AITN 2; CA 45-48; 57-60; CANR 3, 33; CDBLB 1914-1945; DLB 34, 162; MTCW; SATA 22

Woiwode, L.
See Woiwode, Larry (Alfred)

Woiwode, Larry (Alfred) 1941- ... **CLC 6, 10**
See also CA 73-76; CANR 16; DLB 6; INT CANR-16

Wojciechowska, Maia (Teresa)
1927- .... **CLC 26**
See also AAYA 8; CA 9-12R; CANR 4, 41; CLR 1; JRDA; MAICYA; SAAS 1; SATA 1, 28, 83

Wolf, Christa 1929- .... **CLC 14, 29, 58**
See also CA 85-88; CANR 45; DLB 75; MTCW

Wolfe, Gene (Rodman)
1931- .... **CLC 25; DAM POP**
See also CA 57-60; CAAS 9; CANR 6, 32; DLB 8

Wolfe, George C. 1954- .... **CLC 49**
See also CA 149

Wolfe, Thomas (Clayton)
1900-1938 ..... **TCLC 4, 13, 29, 61; DA; DAB; DAC; DAM MST, NOV; WLC**
See also CA 104; 132; CDALB 1929-1941; DLB 9, 102; DLBD 2; DLBY 85; MTCW

Wolfe, Thomas Kennerly, Jr. 1931-
See Wolfe, Tom
See also CA 13-16R; CANR 9, 33; DAM POP; INT CANR-9; MTCW

Wolfe, Tom .... **CLC 1, 2, 9, 15, 35, 51**
See also Wolfe, Thomas Kennerly, Jr.
See also AAYA 8; AITN 2; BEST 89:1; DLB 152

Wolff, Geoffrey (Ansell) 1937- ..... **CLC 41**
See also CA 29-32R; CANR 29, 43

Wolff, Sonia
See Levitin, Sonia (Wolff)

Wolff, Tobias (Jonathan Ansell)
1945- .... **CLC 39, 64**
See also AAYA 16; BEST 90:2; CA 114; 117; CAAS 22; CANR 54; DLB 130; INT 117

Wolfram von Eschenbach
c. 1170-c. 1220 .... **CMLC 5**
See also DLB 138

Wolitzer, Hilma 1930- .... **CLC 17**
See also CA 65-68; CANR 18, 40; INT CANR-18; SATA 31

Wollstonecraft, Mary 1759-1797 ...... **LC 5**
See also CDBLB 1789-1832; DLB 39, 104, 158

Wonder, Stevie .... **CLC 12**
See also Morris, Steveland Judkins

Wong, Jade Snow 1922- .... **CLC 17**
See also CA 109

Woodcott, Keith
See Brunner, John (Kilian Houston)

Woodruff, Robert W.
See Mencken, H(enry) L(ouis)

Woolf, (Adeline) Virginia
1882-1941 .... **TCLC 1, 5, 20, 43, 56; DA; DAB; DAC; DAM MST, NOV; SSC 7; WLC**
See also CA 104; 130; CDBLB 1914-1945; DLB 36, 100, 162; DLBD 10; MTCW

Woollcott, Alexander (Humphreys)
1887-1943 .... **TCLC 5**
See also CA 105; DLB 29

Woolrich, Cornell 1903-1968 .... **CLC 77**
See also Hopley-Woolrich, Cornell George

Wordsworth, Dorothy
1771-1855 .... **NCLC 25**
See also DLB 107

Wordsworth, William
1770-1850 .... **NCLC 12, 38; DA; DAB; DAC; DAM MST, POET; PC 4; WLC**
See also CDBLB 1789-1832; DLB 93, 107

Wouk, Herman
    1915- .. CLC 1, 9, 38; DAM NOV, POP
    See also CA 5-8R; CANR 6, 33; DLBY 82;
    INT CANR-6; MTCW

Wright, Charles (Penzel, Jr.)
    1935- . . . . CLC 6, 13, 28
    See also CA 29-32R; CAAS 7; CANR 23,
    36; DLB 165; DLBY 82; MTCW

Wright, Charles Stevenson
    1932- . . . . CLC 49; BLC 3;
                        DAM MULT, POET
    See also BW 1; CA 9-12R; CANR 26;
    DLB 33

Wright, Jack R.
    See Harris, Mark

Wright, James (Arlington)
    1927-1980 . . . . CLC 3, 5, 10, 28;
                        DAM POET
    See also AITN 2; CA 49-52; 97-100;
    CANR 4, 34; DLB 5, 169; MTCW

Wright, Judith (Arandell)
    1915- . . . . CLC 11, 53; PC 14
    See also CA 13-16R; CANR 31; MTCW;
    SATA 14

Wright, L(aurali) R. 1939- . . . . CLC 44
    See also CA 138

Wright, Richard (Nathaniel)
    1908-1960 . . . . CLC 1, 3, 4, 9, 14, 21, 48,
    74; BLC; DA; DAB; DAC; DAM MST,
                    MULT, NOV; SSC 2; WLC
    See also AAYA 5; BW 1; CA 108;
    CDALB 1929-1941; DLB 76, 102;
    DLBD 2; MTCW

Wright, Richard B(ruce) 1937- . . . . . . CLC 6
    See also CA 85-88; DLB 53

Wright, Rick 1945- . . . . CLC 35

Wright, Rowland
    See Wells, Carolyn

Wright, Stephen Caldwell 1946- . . . . CLC 33
    See also BW 2

Wright, Willard Huntington 1888-1939
    See Van Dine, S. S.
    See also CA 115

Wright, William 1930- . . . . CLC 44
    See also CA 53-56; CANR 7, 23

Wroth, LadyMary 1587-1653(?) . . . . . LC 30
    See also DLB 121

Wu Ch'eng-en 1500(?)-1582(?). . . . . . . LC 7

Wu Ching-tzu 1701-1754 . . . . LC 2

Wurlitzer, Rudolph 1938(?)- . . . CLC 2, 4, 15
    See also CA 85-88; DLB 173

Wycherley, William
    1641-1715 . . . . . LC 8, 21; DAM DRAM
    See also CDBLB 1660-1789; DLB 80

Wylie, Elinor (Morton Hoyt)
    1885-1928 . . . . TCLC 8
    See also CA 105; DLB 9, 45

Wylie, Philip (Gordon) 1902-1971. . . CLC 43
    See also CA 21-22; 33-36R; CAP 2; DLB 9

Wyndham, John. . . . . CLC 19
    See also Harris, John (Wyndham Parkes
    Lucas) Beynon

Wyss, Johann David Von
    1743-1818 . . . . NCLC 10
    See also JRDA; MAICYA; SATA 29;
    SATA-Brief 27

Xenophon
    c. 430B.C.-c. 354B.C. . . . . CMLC 17
    See also DLB 176

Yakumo Koizumi
    See Hearn, (Patricio) Lafcadio (Tessima
    Carlos)

Yanez, Jose Donoso
    See Donoso (Yanez), Jose

Yanovsky, Basile S.
    See Yanovsky, V(assily) S(emenovich)

Yanovsky, V(assily) S(emenovich)
    1906-1989 . . . . CLC 2, 18
    See also CA 97-100; 129

Yates, Richard 1926-1992 . . . . . CLC 7, 8, 23
    See also CA 5-8R; 139; CANR 10, 43;
    DLB 2; DLBY 81, 92; INT CANR-10

Yeats, W. B.
    See Yeats, William Butler

Yeats, William Butler
    1865-1939 . . . . . TCLC 1, 11, 18, 31; DA;
        DAB; DAC; DAM DRAM, MST,
                        POET; WLC
    See also CA 104; 127; CANR 45;
    CDBLB 1890-1914; DLB 10, 19, 98, 156;
    MTCW

Yehoshua, A(braham) B.
    1936- . . . . CLC 13, 31
    See also CA 33-36R; CANR 43

Yep, Laurence Michael 1948- . . . . . . CLC 35
    See also AAYA 5; CA 49-52; CANR 1, 46;
    CLR 3, 17; DLB 52; JRDA; MAICYA;
    SATA 7, 69

Yerby, Frank G(arvin)
    1916-1991 . . . . CLC 1, 7, 22; BLC;
                        DAM MULT
    See also BW 1; CA 9-12R; 136; CANR 16,
    52; DLB 76; INT CANR-16; MTCW

Yesenin, Sergei Alexandrovich
    See Esenin, Sergei (Alexandrovich)

Yevtushenko, Yevgeny (Alexandrovich)
    1933- . . . . CLC 1, 3, 13, 26, 51;
                        DAM POET
    See also CA 81-84; CANR 33, 54; MTCW

Yezierska, Anzia 1885(?)-1970 . . . . . CLC 46
    See also CA 126; 89-92; DLB 28; MTCW

Yglesias, Helen 1915-. . . . . CLC 7, 22
    See also CA 37-40R; CAAS 20; CANR 15;
    INT CANR-15; MTCW

Yokomitsu Riichi 1898-1947 . . . . . . TCLC 47

Yonge, Charlotte (Mary)
    1823-1901 . . . . TCLC 48
    See also CA 109; DLB 18, 163; SATA 17

York, Jeremy
    See Creasey, John

York, Simon
    See Heinlein, Robert A(nson)

Yorke, Henry Vincent 1905-1974 . . . CLC 13
    See also Green, Henry
    See also CA 85-88; 49-52

Yosano Akiko 1878-1942 . . TCLC 59; PC 11

Yoshimoto, Banana . . . . CLC 84
    See also Yoshimoto, Mahoko

Yoshimoto, Mahoko 1964-
    See Yoshimoto, Banana
    See also CA 144

Young, Al(bert James)
    1939- . . . . . CLC 19; BLC; DAM MULT
    See also BW 2; CA 29-32R; CANR 26;
    DLB 33

Young, Andrew (John) 1885-1971. . . . CLC 5
    See also CA 5-8R; CANR 7, 29

Young, Collier
    See Bloch, Robert (Albert)

Young, Edward 1683-1765. . . . . LC 3
    See also DLB 95

Young, Marguerite (Vivian)
    1909-1995 . . . . CLC 82
    See also CA 13-16; 150; CAP 1

Young, Neil 1945-. . . . . CLC 17
    See also CA 110

Young Bear, Ray A.
    1950- . . . . CLC 94; DAM MULT
    See also CA 146; DLB 175; NNAL

Yourcenar, Marguerite
    1903-1987 . . . . CLC 19, 38, 50, 87;
                        DAM NOV
    See also CA 69-72; CANR 23; DLB 72;
    DLBY 88; MTCW

Yurick, Sol 1925-. . . . . CLC 6
    See also CA 13-16R; CANR 25

Zabolotskii, Nikolai Alekseevich
    1903-1958 . . . . TCLC 52
    See also CA 116

Zamiatin, Yevgenii
    See Zamyatin, Evgeny Ivanovich

Zamora, Bernice (B. Ortiz)
    1938- . . . . . CLC 89; DAM MULT; HLC
    See also CA 151; DLB 82; HW

Zamyatin, Evgeny Ivanovich
    1884-1937 . . . . TCLC 8, 37
    See also CA 105

Zangwill, Israel 1864-1926. . . . . . . TCLC 16
    See also CA 109; DLB 10, 135

Zappa, Francis Vincent, Jr. 1940-1993
    See Zappa, Frank
    See also CA 108; 143; CANR 57

Zappa, Frank. . . . . CLC 17
    See also Zappa, Francis Vincent, Jr.

Zaturenska, Marya 1902-1982. . . . CLC 6, 11
    See also CA 13-16R; 105; CANR 22

Zeami 1363-1443. . . . . DC 7

Zelazny, Roger (Joseph)
    1937-1995 . . . . CLC 21
    See also AAYA 7; CA 21-24R; 148;
    CANR 26; DLB 8; MTCW; SATA 57;
    SATA-Brief 39

Zhdanov, Andrei A(lexandrovich)
    1896-1948 . . . . TCLC 18
    See also CA 117

Zhukovsky, Vasily 1783-1852 . . . . NCLC 35

Ziegenhagen, Eric . . . . CLC 55

Zimmer, Jill Schary
    See Robinson, Jill

Zimmerman, Robert
See Dylan, Bob

Zindel, Paul
      1936- ..... **CLC 6, 26; DA; DAB; DAC;**
          DAM DRAM, MST, NOV; DC 5
  See also AAYA 2; CA 73-76; CANR 31;
    CLR 3, 45; DLB 7, 52; JRDA; MAICYA;
    MTCW; SATA 16, 58

Zinov'Ev, A. A.
See Zinoviev, Alexander (Aleksandrovich)

Zinoviev, Alexander (Aleksandrovich)
      1922- .... **CLC 19**
  See also CA 116; 133; CAAS 10

Zoilus
See Lovecraft, H(oward) P(hillips)

Zola, Emile (Edouard Charles Antoine)
      1840-1902 ...... **TCLC 1, 6, 21, 41; DA;**
          DAB; DAC; DAM MST, NOV; WLC
  See also CA 104; 138; DLB 123

Zoline, Pamela 1941- .... **CLC 62**

Zorrilla y Moral, Jose 1817-1893.. **NCLC 6**

Zoshchenko, Mikhail (Mikhailovich)
      1895-1958 .... **TCLC 15; SSC 15**
  See also CA 115

Zuckmayer, Carl 1896-1977........ **CLC 18**
  See also CA 69-72; DLB 56, 124

Zuk, Georges
See Skelton, Robin

Zukofsky, Louis
      1904-1978 .... **CLC 1, 2, 4, 7, 11, 18;**
            DAM POET; PC 11
  See also CA 9-12R; 77-80; CANR 39;
    DLB 5, 165; MTCW

Zweig, Paul 1935-1984......... **CLC 34, 42**
  See also CA 85-88; 113

Zweig, Stefan 1881-1942 .... **TCLC 17**
  See also CA 112; DLB 81, 118

Zwingli, Huldreich 1484-1531....... **LC 37**

Cumulative Nationality Index

PC Cumulative Title Index

Title Index

Title Index

ISBN 0-7876-0958-7

90000

9 780787 609580